THE CHARLTON STANDARD CATALOGUE OF CANADIAN BANK NOTES

4TH EDITION

W.K. CROSS

PUBLISHER

R. J. GRAHAM

EDITOR

The Charlton Press

Toronto, Ontario • Palm Harbor, Florida

National Library of Canada Cataloguing in Publication Data

Main entry under title:

The Charlton standard catalogue of Canadian bank notes

4th ed.
Includes bibliographical references and index
ISBN 0-88968-230-5 (perfect bound : 4th edition).-
ISBN 0-88968-205-4 (case bound : 4th edition)

1. Bank notes--Canada--Catalogs. I. Graham, R. J. II Title: Canadian bank notes

HG657.C45 2002 769.5'5971 C2001-903634-5

Printed in Canada
in the Province of Ontario

The Charlton Press

Editorial Office
P.O. Box 820, Station Willowdale B, North York, Ontario. M2K 2R1
Telephone: (416) 488-1418 Fax: (416) 488-4656
Telephone: (800) 442-6042 Fax: (800) 442.1542
www.charltonpress.com; e-mail: chpress@charltonpress.com

ACKNOWLEDGEMENT

The Charlton Press wish to thank all those who have helped and assisted in the third and previous editions of the *Charlton Standard Catalogue of Canadian Bank Notes*. They helped build the foundation for the fourth.

EDITORIAL

Editor	Robert J. Graham
Editorial Assistant	Davina Rowan

CONTRIBUTORS TO THE 4TH EDITION

Special thanks are extended to Don Olmstead and Charles Moore, who were frequently consulted for their expertise and responded generously.

Walter Allen	Harold Don Allen	Dick Becker
Geoff Bell	Jay Bellove	Paul Berry
Harold Brown	Jim Charlton	Lionel Conn
Graham Esler	Ronald A. Greene	James A. Haxby
Wendy Hoare	Serge Laramee	D. E. Leitch
Chris Ryan	Paul Wallis	

PRICING PANEL

Ted Bailey	Harry M. Eisenhauer	Michael Findlay
Nick Gerbinski	Ronald A. Greene	Iain Laing
Andrew McKaig	Charles D. Moore	Don Olmstead
Lub Wojtiw		

INSTITUTIONS

American Bank Note Company	British American Bank Note Company
Bank of Canada, National Currency Collection	Canadian Bankers Association
Canadian Imperial Bank of Commerce	Bank of Montreal
Bank of Nova Scotia	Royal Bank of Canada
Toronto Dominion Bank	

CORRECTIONS

The publisher welcomes information, for future editions, from interested collectors and dealers concerning any aspect of the listings in this book.

Visit the Charlton Press Web Site at
WWW.CHARLTONPRESS.COM

FOREWARD TO THE FOURTH EDITION

A number of new features appear in this edition. Please read these brief explanatory notes in order to obtain the maximum benefit from your catalogue.

PROOF AND SPECIMEN NOTES

An effort has been made to list all proof and specimen notes which are likely to be involved in transactions. Others certainly exist which were not recorded in time for this edition, but most will be quite rare and unavailable. Values for proof and specimen notes follow the pricing tables for the issued notes.

In past editions, proof and specimen notes were listed only where the corresponding issued note was unknown. Recent releases by bank note companies and others of this type of material onto the collector market have increased the need for a more comprehensive listing.

Proof and specimen notes are priced in uncirculated condition only. Adjustments will need to be made for pricing damaged or creased examples. Circular punched holes are normal on specimen notes, and sometimes on proofs, and should not result in any price reduction.

Back proofs are often available. These are typically valued at about one-quarter of the value of the corresponding face proof where the back design consists only of the bank name, lathework and counters. Back proofs with one or more vignettes would be worth about one-third as much as the corresponding face.

GRADING

All valuations are assigned for notes graded by **Canadian standards.** These may be more rigorous than the benchmarks used in some other countries, and the reader is referred to the grading guide on page (ix) in this catalogue.

Prices are for "original" notes, which have not been pressed or washed in an effort to give them the appearance of a higher grade.

Notes are priced in grades up to the highest thought to be available to private collectors. If the finest recorded note outside of institutions has a split grade, pricing continues to the higher grade. For very rare notes, prices may not be provided for certain intermediate grades thought not to exist.

A column has been added for notes in Good (G) condition in this edition in cases where they are commonly involved in transactions or are scare in better grades.

LISTINGS

The notation "institutional collection only" indicates that the designated note is not available to private collectors. The state of knowledge of existing notes and their locations, while greatly improved in recent years, is still imperfect. Some notes will undoubtedly turn up which are now believed to exist only in museum or archive conditions. Conversely, there will be a great many more which will prove in time to be limited to institutions and unavailable to the collecting public.

The practive of assigning separate cataloge numbers to otherwise identicle notes with various manuscript year dates has been discontinued in cases where these notes are quite rare and collecting in such detail would be extremely challenging. The different dates are still reported, and anyone wishing to collect by date will in no way be inconvenienced. Where numbers of notes extant support popular collecting by manuscript date, their separate cataloguing is continued.

R. J. GRAHAM

TABLE OF CONTENTS

TABLE OF CONTENTS (cont.)

INTRODUCTION

Paper money in Canada has a much longer and interesting history than many would suspect. During the early days of French regime, North Americas first paper money was made on the backs of ordinary playing cards or parts of them. This famous playing card money even preceded the notes of the American colonies to the south.

In those long distant days paper money was a new idea and it was only a representative of coined money. A note was a promise to pay real money (coins) if the note holder so desired.

In the last 50 years, however, it has assumed a greater place in our everyday lives. It has supplanted coins to a large extent and reduced coins to a change-making and machine slug function. The traditional will pay (coins) to the bearer on demand has been replaced by this note is legal tender.

Collectors of Canadian paper money have much to chose from. The earliest banks, whether chartered or private, issued their own notes. Many merchants did as well. In addition to the private issues were government notes on the municipal, provincial, and federal levels. This tradition of government vs. private issues has persisted to some degree right up to the present day.

Canadas bank notes begin with the short-lived Canadian Banking Company in Montreal in the 1790s and continued with the early issues of the Montreal Bank, the Quebec Bank and the Bank of Upper Canada after the War of 1812. Over the years many banks came and went. Gradually, by the twentieth century, the number of banks was reduced through absorptions and mergers, leaving the familiar banks where we do our business today.

Bank notes not only reflect the fascinating history of our reputable financial institutions but of a number of fraudulent ones as well. Consequently, some notes have survived to be enjoyed by collectors because the bank that issued them ultimately failed, leaving them unredeemable, or because they were issued by a sham bank and were never redeemable at any time.Such losses to holders of notes of charter banks ended with the 1890 Bank Act revision, which provided for a fund to guarantee the redemption of notes of failed banks. Subsequently, notes of the few banks which failed after 1890 were sometimes redeemable at even more than their face value, because they gathered interest from the time of the bank suspension of their redemption until redemption through the fund which was provided for.

Merchants notes remain generally less appreciated and collected compared to the other types of Canadian notes. This situation will undoubtedly change with time as the other series become increasingly expensive to collect. The scrip issue by merchants is a large and important series. It includes crude notes issued prior to 1800, a large group of notes issued in Upper and Lower Canada in the late 1830s, fur trade issues by the Hudsons Bay Co. and modern pieces like Canadian Tire money. This field not only offers great collecting opportunities but it also offers an area where much research remains to be done.

Unquestionably the most popular Canadian notes are those issued by the various provincial governments and by the Federal governments after Confederation. The provincial issues begin with the French regime notes in the 1680s to the 1750s, followed by British colonial issues from the 1790s up to Confederation. The notes of the Province of Canada, dated 1866, are particularly popular with collectors. Their denominations range from $1 to $500 although notes above the $2 are practically never available.

Notes of the Dominion government, called Dominion notes, cover an even broader range of denominations, including the 25c note (shinplaster), the $4 note and the very rare $1000 note. Dominion notes were first issued in 1870 and remained in general circulation until about 1940.

Most of the paper money now in circulation is issued by our central bank, the Bank of Canada. In 1935, with the opening of the Bank of Canada, the withdrawal of Dominion notes was ordered and the chartered banks were required to gradually reduce the circulation of their own notes. It was the governments intention to essentially replace both types of notes with Bank of Canada notes by 1950. The latest date to appear on a chartered bank note is 1943 (the Royal Bank of Canada $5). In 1950 the chartered banks paid over to the Bank of Canada $13,302,046.60, the face value of their outstanding notes, and since that time the Bank of Canada has been responsible for their redemption. As the chartered bank notes are redeemed, the Bank of Canada credits the amounts of the banks that originally issued the notes.

The opportunities for specialization within the Canadian paper money series are numerous. In the chartered series some collectors attempt to assemble a collection of all notes issued by a particular bank or a currently existing bank and all the banks that it absorbed along the way.

Others save a single note from each bank. Still others collect notes payable in a particular section of the country, that is, they collect on a regional basis. Since the government series is smaller than the chartered series, collectors of government notes tend to save varieties as well as basic types of notes.They concentrate on signature differences, seal colour varieties and even series letters and plate number combinations. Clearly, the study and collecting of Canadian paper money offers a great number of challenges and something for all tastes.

It is interesting that only in the past forty years has the collecting of Canadian paper money enjoyed its deservedly widespread appeal. Just as the establishment of the Canadian Numismatic Association in 1950 responded to and stimulated the interest in Canadian coins, tokens and medals, so the founding of the Canadian Paper Money Society in 1964 signalled the coming of age of age of Canadian paper money collecting. A major stimulus for this hobby came with the inclusion of paper money in a number of general and specialized catalogues in the sixties and early seventies. This book represents the new and growing interest in Canadian paper currency.

HOW TO USE THIS CATALOGUE

1. GENERAL

Generally speaking this catalogue has been arranged in the same format as the paper money sections of the previous Charlton Standard Catalogues. Due to the enormous expansion which has occurred, a complete index has been provided for easy access to the information compiled. It is strongly suggested that the index be utilized as, for instance, banks quite often overlapped different designs of notes within the same time period. The index is found on page 417.

II. CANADIAN BANKS SECTIONS

A. Alphabetical Listings of Banks

As in previous editions the issuing banks are in alphabetical order with the words THE, BANK and OF (orLA, BANQUE and DE) ignored. Thus, Molsons Bank is listed before The Bank of Montreal. Each note is assigned a set of numbers. The first set designates the individual bank. The following sets (up to three designates further aspects of each note and provide a comprehensive, expandable, Bank Note Numbering System.

B. Introductory Information

At the beginning of the listing for each bank the period of operation and the location of the head office are stated. Below this the redeemability status of the notes and a brief historical sketch are given where such information is available.

C. Order of the Note Listings Within Each Bank

Generally speaking, a bank puts out its notes in issues or groups. An issue usually consists of a design set and thus several denominations linked through either a vignette (an engraved picture) or a common style. The present catalogue departs from previous editions in listing the bank notes first by design set (issue). Issues or design set are denoted by two numbers for each design set section. An attempt has been made to indicate features common to each design set in the title, eg., Randolph Portrait Issue, Blue Protector Issue. Major alterations within the design set are denoted by a third set of two (55-10-02) numbers. By using this system, it is much easier for the reader to appreciate the note issuing patterns of each bank and for the first time to construct a checklist of the basic design for each bank. Although all notes with the same design are generally listed under a single issue number, in a few cases where an old design reappears after a long absence, a new issue number is used. Such cases are indicated in the issues titles.

D. Subsidiary Information

1. Designs and colours: The main vignettes appearing on each note are described in the same order as they occur on the notes, with oblique lines separating descriptions, eg., beaver/ship/cattle. Where there is no vignette illustrated on a particular portion of the note, a slash (-) appears in place of the description. Where there are two main vignettes appearing on one portion of the note, they are described from top to bottom with a semi-colon (;) separating the descriptions, eg., beaver; ship; arm and

hammer; cattle. Special knowledge is not required to understand the descriptions of most vignettes, however, the allegorical figures and human figures used to represent or personify abstract concepts, need some explanation. In the descriptions the following figures are usually described as they appear below rather than giving the details of what the woman is holding, what she is wearing, and so on.

The exact details of these figures can vary slightly, but the following are the most commonly encountered:

Justice: blindfolded woman, with balance in one hand and sword in the other.

Commerce: woman holding a caduceus; usually seated amid bales, casks and/or goods.

Agricultural: woman with sickle, sheaf and produce or cornucopeia

Britannia: helmeted woman, with trident or spear and often a shield.

Mercury: man wearing winged helmet, usually holding caduceus.

Neptune: bearded man holding trident, usually in or around the sea.

Quotation marks are also used in describing the vignettes;

A. From the name of the painting or other source from which the engraving was derived.

B. From the actual name found on the engravings as originally done by the engraving companies.

2. Imprint: The banknote company imprint is given for each note or issue. The imprint indicates the company that engraved the plates and/or printed notes from them. The dual imprint, eg. ABNC and BABIN, indicates plates originally engraved by the American Bank Note Company that were later used by the British American Bank Note Company for printing notes.

3. Signature: For each issue, all of the printed and some of the manuscript (mss.) (handwritten with pen and ink) signatures are given. There are two kinds of printed signatures: engraved (engr.) and typographed (typed).

Engraved signatures are engraved into the face plate and are printed at the same time as the face design. For notes printed from the same part of a plate the positions of the engraved signatures relative to the frame do not vary.

Typed signatures, however, are added after the rest of the note has been printed. Consequently, the signatures may be found to be in slightly different positions when the notes are compared. Typed signatures usually have flat, broad strokes in contrast to the thin strokes of the engraved signatures.

4. Issue Dating: Unlike the previous catalogue, dates are now listed, in most cases, almost exactly as they appear on the notes. Most manuscript dates are shown as written, but in a few cases where the same date appears in more than one manner, eg. Jan. 2, 2 Jan., only one has been shown.

5. Protectors: Protectors are coloured overprints which give the denomination of the note and serve as an anticounterfeiting device. They can occur either as a word (ONE) or numeral (1 1) type and usually appear on the face of the note, reading normally, as well as on the back, often in mirror image.

Sometimes protectors are found printed on only the face or the back.

6. Overprints and Stamps: Overprints, extra details added by a printing press after the notes have otherwise been completed, are listed for each issue. Stamps differ from overprints in being added by hand, with a rubber or wooden implement. If an overprint appears on separate lines on the note, this is indicated by an oblique(/), eg. PAYABLE AT/LONDON.

7. General Treatment of Varieties: Most engraved differences are given separate listings. Where branch names are engraved in the plates, subheadings are always formed. However, when a branch name has been added as an overprint, it is given a separate treatment only in special cases like DAWSON, YUKON and Winnipeg. Usually, overprints are simply listed at the beginning of each issue.

8. Remainders®, Essays(E), Proofs(P) and Specimens(S): Whenever possible, fully completed notes (those signed, numbered and dated) are listed. In cases where fully completed notes are not known or when other forms are much more common, remainders, proofs or specimens are listed.

A remainder is a regular note which has not has all of the blanks filled in. Remainders are sometimes encountered with spurious signatures, dates, etc.; this does not change their status.

Failing the availability of completed or remainder notes either specimens or proofs are listed.

A specimen is not intended for circulation, but is used to acquaint bank empoyees and others with the characteristics of the genuine notes. It is normally printed on banknote paper with face and back designs the same as the issued note; however, it usually has serial numbers consisting of all Os and is overprinted or stamped SPECIMEN, often in the signature areas.

Proofs are trial or sample impressions taken from the printing plates usually on very thin paper backed with card, but some are printed directly on card. They often have no serial numbers and may or may not be stamped with the word SPECIMEN. FACE PROOF is indicated when the face impression only is printed (usually the case).

Essays are trial printings made to introduce new designs or test new manufacturing concepts. Essays might also test new papers and/or the construction of new bank notes such as, the addition of foil or heliograms to the note. Essays are produced to gain approval or acceptance of new features before a note is officially authorized. Essays are extremely rare.

Models are paste ups, using lathework, counters and engravings or photographs, to illustrate a proposed note showing a design concept. It is an example and often the artists or engravers working stage before an essay.

9. Sheets of Notes: Notes were usually printed in sheets of four, which could be all the same denomination or a mixture of two or more denominations. The form for the listings is $1, 1, 3, 5, which for this example refers to a sheet consisting, from top to bottom, of a $1, a $1, a $3 and a $5 note.

III. THE CHARLTON CATALOGUE NUMBERING SYSTEM

Each note is assigned a set of numbers. The first set designates the individual Bank. The following sets (up to three) designate further aspects of each note and provide a comprehensive, expandable, Bank Note Numbering System. A banknote is identified by a number in the following form:

55-10-02-02

The first set of numerals represent the bank number. The banks are numbered beginning with 5 for the Bank of Acadia and jump-numbered by five thereafter allowing for future expansion.

The second series of numerals represents the design concept or issue. This series consists of two numbers for the issue number, starting at 10 and jump-numbered by two, again to allow for expansion. Thus, for example shown above, the note would be from the first issue or design set.

The third set of two numbers represent any major alteration that might occur within the design set. The numbers are again, jump-numbered to allow for expansion. This set of numbers may be omitted if no major alterations occur.

The fourth set records all the varieties that are found. Following these numbers can ba a series of upper or lower case letters indicating further information about the note.

The following table will help the collector in understanding the numbering system.

BANK NUMBER - 5, 10, 15, etc.

DESIGN CONCEPT 10, 12, 14, etc.	A series of notes bound together by a common design concept, etc. printer, denomination, theme, date or domicile. Examples: vignettes, small bank crest, Issue of 1860, overall green tint, Kingston Jamaica, pounds issue.
MAJOR ALTERATION 02,04,06, etc.	When the design concept has been altered by; colour change addition or alteration of a back design domicile, etc. Example: Addition of a agency branch bane or any significant change to the original design concept.
VARIETY 02,04,06, etc.	Denominations, signatures and different type faces; manuscript, typographed, issue dates, major overprints, protectors; size and colour denomination altered.
TYPE OF NOTE Upper case letters (as required)	R-Remainder, S-Specimen, P-Proof, E-Essay, A-Altered. Issued notes will not have upper case letters.

MINOR VARIETY Lower case letters a,b,c, etc. (as required)	Imprints, Minor overprints, Stamps, Minor Design changes. Example: change in size or style of type face of General Manager or President

The major alteration number is dropped when not required.
Bank numbers are generally jump-numbered by fives.
Design concepts, major alterations and minor varieties are jump-numbered by a minimum of one.

IV. GRADING

Methodology

When grading a note it is essential to first determine if the note may be safely removed from its holder without causing any damage due to brittleness, unseen tears, glue remnants, etc. Then carefully remove the note and holding it lightly, consider the general appearance, amount of wear, the hue and intensity of the colour of both the face and the back. Determine a preliminary grade. If the note is fine or better it should be held obliquely in line with a good light source. Move it around at various angles, such that the light will reflect off the note highlighting any ripples, counting creases, tears, pinholes, cancellations, repairs or fading. Mastery of this technique is mandatory for successful grading of paper money. When these aspects have been carefully considered,decide if they are "normal" for the preliminary grade which was determined. If not, the grade may have to be reduced depending on the number and severity of the defects, or the defects will have to be listed in addition to the overall grade, followed by any unusual defects that would downgrade the note. Careful inspection to determine the correct grade will lead to greater trust and confidence between buyers and sellers of notes.

Grade Descriptions

Uncurculated — Unc: A perfect note. Crisp and clean as issued and without any folds, creases, blemishes or discolouration. Colours have original hue and brightness. Some issues may have ripples (as made). Mention must be made if the design is not perfectly centered with usual width of margins.

About Circulated — AU: Similar to Uncirculated, but with the allowance of a light fold (usually a vertical centre fold) or two or three very light counting folds, but not both. Counting creases resulting in broken paper fibres, or any other creases, reduce the grade depending on their number and severity. The practice of using "almost" and "about" to designate a slightly lower grade, or a plus in the case of lower grades to designate in-between grades is common, e.g. "Almost AU" or "EF plus". Notes not perfectly centered with usual width of margins must be so described.

Extremely Fine — EF: Similar to Almost Uncirculated but the centre fold, vertical or horizontal, may be a crease, i.e. paper fibres are broken, or there may be up to three heavy counting folds (not creases) or two light creases, but no combination of the above. There should be almost no evidence of wear, soiling or blemishes. The centering and margins if not perfect must be noted.

Very Fine — VF: A fairly crisp and clean note. It may have several major and minor creases and folds, and some evidence of wear especially along the edges or at the corners. There may be some slight decrease in hue and intensity of the colours. The design in the creases should not be worn off.

Fine — F: A note with considerable evidence of circulation. Numerous creases and folds, but a small degree of firmness remaining. Usually fairly soiled and the hue and intensity of the colour are slightly reduced. There may be a slight amount of the design worn off along the major creases.

Very Good — VG: A heavily circulated note but with all the major design still visible. Usually limp with no crispness or firmness, quite soiled, hue and intensity of the colour will be faded or altered. A moderate amount of the design may be worn off along the major creases or in the "counting crease" areas. Numerous other defects may apply (see list below).

Good — G: Soft and very limp, often with tears and small pieces missing. Usually some of the major design is worn off. Note may be quite dark in appearance. Manuscript signatures, dates and sheet numbers may be faint or unreadable. Usually has numerous other defects.

Fair — FR: Similar to Good, but larger pieces missing. Manuscript signatures, dates and sheet numbers may be worn off or entirely faded out. Often has numerous tears and other defects.

Poor — P: As a Fair note, but with a major portion of the note torn off or the design obliterated. Often numerous tape repairs. Generally collectable only because of rarity.

In addition, to accurately grade a note it is necessary to consider any additional impairments. These should include:

1. Minor counting creases or edge defects, especially for EF and AU grades.
2. Tears, pinholes or signature perforations.
3. Stains, smudges, crayon marks or writing.
4. Missing corners, cut and punch cancellations or edge defects.
5. Rubber stamp impressions.
6. Any repairs, such as with sticky tape, scotch tape, stamp hinges, etc.
7. Chemical damage, paste or glue from attachment to a page.
8. Poorly centered or badly trimmed edges.

A note with portions missing should be graded as if it were a whole note, the the amount missing should be fully described.

Proof, specimen and essay notes are commonly accepted as being in uncirculated condition. Otherwise, they should be described as impaired, with the type and degree of impairment stated.

This grading has been endorsed by the Canadian Paper Money Society.

V. USEFUL TERMINOLOGY AND INFORMATION

A. Kinds of Banks.

1. Private Bank: A bank which operated without a charter, usually as a private partnership.

2. Chartered Bank: A bank that was incorporated by an act of parliament and sold stock to the general public.

3. Spurious or Phantom Bank: A bank which has no legal existence, whose name is found on notes intended to deceive the unwary. Such spurious notes were often made in vague imitation of some legitimate banks notes, using the colloquial name of such an institution, eg., The Kingston Bank or The Gore Bank of Hamilton.

4. Wildcat Bank: A bank with a legal existence, but whose main purpose was to push its notes on the public, with no intention of redeeming most of them, eg. The Bank of Clifton or The International Bank of Canada.

B. Kinds of Fraudulent Notes

1. Counterfeit: A facsimile copy of a note of a legitimate bank.

2. Spurious: A note that is of a design that does not correspond to any notes issued by a legitimate bank. Spurious notes can purport to be redeemable at a legitimate or a phantom bank.

3. Altered: In the Canadian context, a genuine note on which the name of the bank has been fraudulently changed to that of another bank.

4. Raised: A note which has been fraudulently modified so as to appear to be of a higher denomination.

C. Parts of Notes

1. Face: The front of the note, sometimes incorrectly referred to as the obverse.

2. Back: The subordinate side of the note, sometimes incorrectly called the reverse. Many notes were printed with blank or plain backs.

3. Vignette: An engraved picture (Portrait or scene) on a bank note.

4. Counter: A word, letter or number indicating the denomination of a note.

5. Payee: The person or organization to whom a note is made payable. The payee on many modern notes is simply referred to as the bearer.

6. Domicile: The specific city or town where the note was made payable.

7. Tint: The background coloured design found on notes. The tint is printed before the face or back plate, as opposed to a protector, which is an overprint. In the 19th century tints were usually printed by the engraved plate method. Gradually, beginning in the late 19th century, bank note companies switched over to printing tints by lithography.

D. Printing methods

1. Letterpress (or Typography): IN this process the design is the highest part of the printing plate and is flat. When the plate is inked only the design receives the ink by virtue of its location. Letterpress results in a fairly thick and flat layer of ink on the note. Sheet numbers, protectors and most overprints were added by this method of printing.

2. Engraved Plate (or Intaglio): The design is cut into a flat sheet of metal, and in contrast to letterpress, the design is below the flat upper surface of the plate. The plate is inked and the flat surface wiped clean, leaving ink only in the recessed (engraved) areas which is then transferred to the paper during printing. The resulting image has a 3-dimensional character. Most notes were printed by this means since it made possible the highest resolution of fine lines and the most life-like portraits. This method also provided the best security against counterfeiting.

3. Lithography: In the latter part of the 19th century lithography was used to print the coloured background (tint) on some notes. As it was practised then, lithography involved the photography of a design and its transfer via a negative to the surface of a special stone coated with a layer of a photosensitive material. After treatment, only the image on the stone would pick up the ink. This type of printing resulted in the transfer of a thin flat layer of ink.

E. Printers

Printers names, abbreviations or monograms will usually appear as part of the frame design or below it on the face and/or back. In some instances the engravers name may also appear in a similar location of a note. The following abbreviations identify printers for many of the notes listed in this volume.

F. How Notes Were Numbered

1. Sheet Number: As a general rule, 19th century bank notes were printed in sheets. Within each sheet all of the notes were given the same number - the sheet number. Notes were generally given black or blue numbers. Occasionally when the first numbers reached their limit, a new number series would start in a different colour.

2. Check Letter: Since more than one note in a sheet could bear the same number, each note was provided with a distinguishing letter - a check letter.

3. Series Letter: For a particularly large issue of notes, where all the available sheet numbers had been used, the same numbers would be started over again, preceded or followed by a series letter. A new series letter would be used for each successive cycle of sheet numbers. Commonly, the first series would have no series letter and the second would have an A, the third a B, and so on.

4. Serial Number: From the above it should be clear that the serial number, the designation that uniquely defines a note, must include not only the sheet number but also the check letter and series letter if they are present.

ABBREVIATIONS FOR BANK NOTE PRINTERS IMPRINTS

ABBREV.	IMPRINT
ABN	American Bank Note Company
BABN	British American Bank Note Co. Ltd.
Br Am BN	British American Bank Note Company
Britton & Co.	Lith. Britton & Co. S.F.
BFL	Barclay & Fry Ltd. (England)
BG	Burton and Gurley, New York
BGE	Burton, Gurley, Edmonds, New York
BWC	Bradbury, Wilkinson & Co. (England)
Canada BN	Canada Bank Note Company
CBC	Columbian Banknote Co.
CBN	Canadian Bank Note Company
CDB & E	Casilear, Durand, Burton & Edmonds, New York
Con BN	Continental Bank Note Company
CS & E	Charles Skipper & East (England)
CWT	C.W. Torbett
DS & H	Danforth, Spencer & Huffy, New York
DTL	Draper, Toppan, Longacre & Co.
DU	Danforth, Underwood & Co. N.Y.
DW	Co. Danforth, Wright & Co., N.Y. & Phila.
EAW	E.A. Wright
FDU	Fairman, Draper & Underwood, N.Y.
FLBN	Franklin-Lee Bank Note Company
Graphic	Graphic
HLBNC	Homer Lee Bank Note Co.
HS	Harris & Sealey, Engravers, New York
HW	Hay & Whiting New York
IBNC	International Bank Note Company
JBNC	Jeffries Bank Note Company
Jones	Jones

ABBREV.	IMPRINT
JDW	Jocelyn, Draper, Welsh & Co.
K. McKenzie	Kenneth McKenzie, Printer, London
LR	Leney & Rollinfon
L Perrault	Louis Perrault, Montreal
NBNC	National Bank Note Company
NEBN	New England Bank Note Company, Boston
NYBC	New York Bank Note Company
PBC	Perkins, Bacon & Co. (England)
PB & P	Perkins, Bacon & Petch (England)
PH	Perkins, Heath
Reed, A	Reed
RS	Reed, Stiles & Co.
RWH	Rawdon, Wright, Hatch and Company
RWHE	Rawdon, Wright, Hatch & Edson
SBNC	Security Banknote Company
SH & D	Spencer, Hufty & Danforth, Phila.
SJHS	St. John & Halifax Steam Lith. Company
Starke & Co.	Starke & Co. Printers, Montreal
Star Office	Star Office
T dL R	Thomas de La Rue (England)
TP	Terry Pelton & Co., Boston and Prov.
TC	Toppan Carpenter & Company
UBS & H	Underwood, Bald, Spencer & Hufty, Phila.
Union BN	Union Bank Note Company
USBNC	United States Banknote Corp.
W & S	Waterlow & Sons Ltd. (England)
WBN	The Western Bank Note Company, Chicago
WH & W	Wellstood, Hay & Whiting, New York
Western	Western Printing & Lithographing Co. Ltd., Calgary
WWS	W.W. Sprague & Co. Ltd. (England)

FRATERNAL ORGANIZATIONS

Listed below are a number of organizations dedicated to the preservation, study and enjoyment of paper currency. All will be delighted to hear from collectors interested in any aspect of paper

THE CANADIAN PAPER MONEY SOCIETY

Established in 1964 and incorporated in 1972, the Society is a non-profit, historical and educational organization interested in Canadian bank notes, banking and other Canadian paper money. It publishes the The Canadian Paper Money Journal quarterly and has library and other facilities available. The Society is sustained by regular members contributions of $25.00 per year or $300.00 Life Membership donation to the Income Trust Fund, the official address of the Society is P.O. Box 465, West Hill Post Office, West Hill, Ontario M1E 2P0.

THE CANADIAN NUMISMATIC ASSOCIATION

The CNA was founded in 1950 and incorporated in 1962. It is a non-profit educatinal association which has members in every province in Canada, every state in the U.S. and many other countries. Its objective is to encourage and promote the science of numismatics by acquirement and study of coins, paper money, medals, tokens and all other numismatic items with special emphisis on material pertaining to Canada. Membership includes use of the associations library material as wel as a subscription to *The Canadian Numismatic Journal*, a monthly magazine devoted to Canadian numismatics. Annual membership fees are $25.00 for those over 21 years of age, $12.50 for those under the age of 21, $35.00 for a family membership and $25.00 for a club, society, library or other non-profit organization. Life membership id $400.00. the current executive secretary is Mr. Jenneth B. Prophet and he may be reached at P.O. Box 226, Barrie, Ontario, Canada L4M 4T2.

THE INTERNATIONAL BANK NOTE SOCIETY

The IBNS was founded in 1961 and now has a membership of over 1,500 with representation from over 60 countries. The currant annual dues are as follows: regular membership $17.50, Family Membership $22.50, and Junior Membership $9.00. Life Memberships are also available for $300.00 U.S. The Society publishes the IBNS Journal quarterly which is distributed free of charge (by Surface Mail) to its members. The current general secretary is Mr. Milan Alusic, P.O. Box 1222, Racine, Wisconsin, 53405, U.S.A.

SOCIETY OF PAPER MONEY COLLECTORS

In June 1964 the Society was incorporated as a non-profit organization under the laws of the district of Columbia. Membership now numbers approximately 2,300 the majority of which reside in Canada and the U.S. But there is representation throughout the world. The SPMC publishes Paper Money bimonthly in the odd months and sends it to its members. Annual dues are $24.00 (U.S.A.), $29.00 (Canada and Mexico) and $34.00 (Foreign), in U.S. Funds. Make remittance payable to SPMC and send application and cheque to: Frank Clark, SPMC Membership Director, P.O. Box 117060, Carrollton, TX 75011, U.S.A.

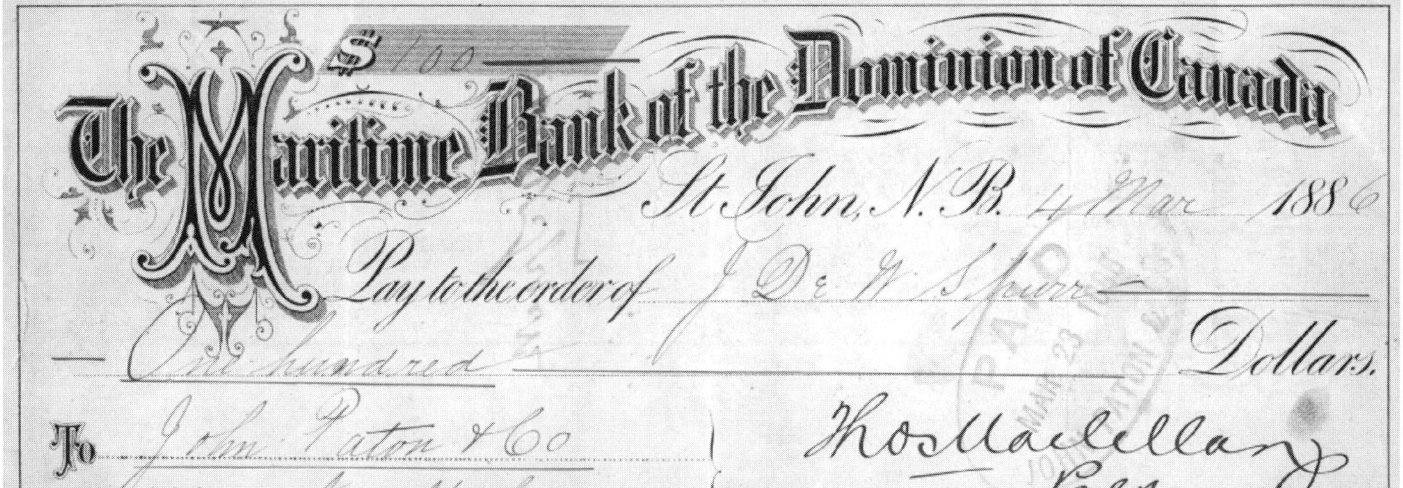

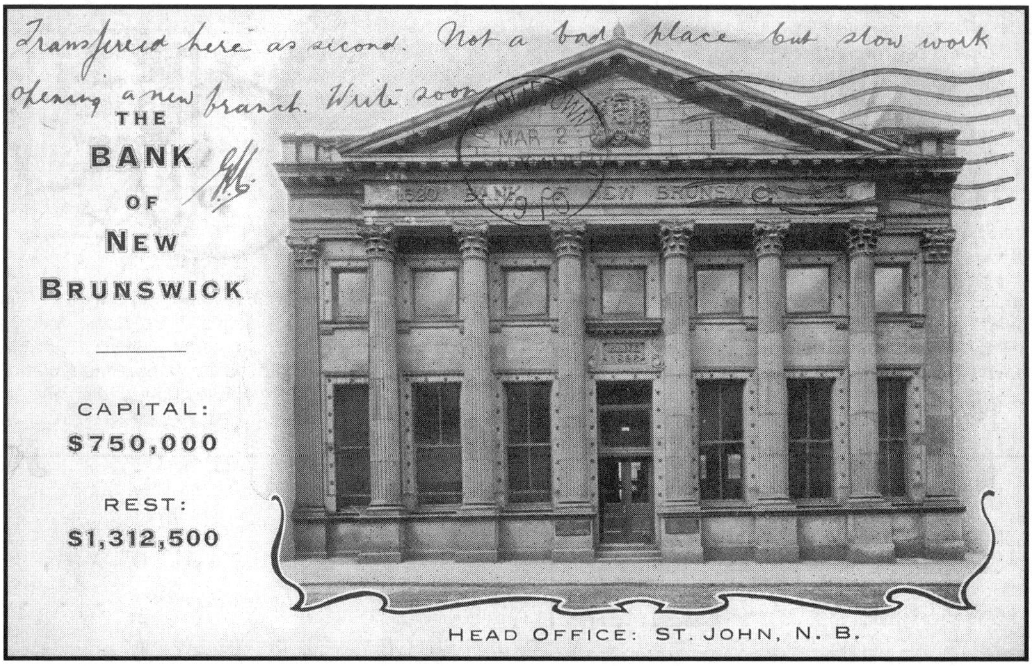
Transferred here as second. Not a bad place but slow work opening a new branch. Write soon
THE
BANK
OF
NEW
BRUNSWICK
CAPITAL:
$750,000
REST:
$1,312,500
MAR 2
HEAD OFFICE: ST. JOHN, N. B.

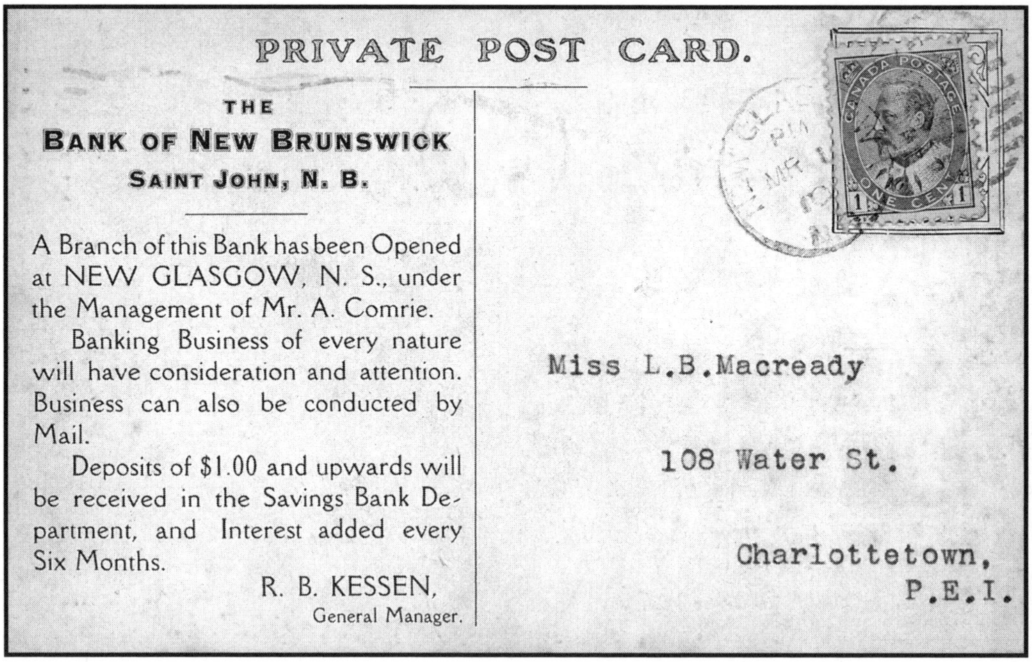

PRIVATE POST CARD.

THE
BANK OF NEW BRUNSWICK
SAINT JOHN, N. B.

A Branch of this Bank has been Opened at NEW GLASGOW, N. S., under the Management of Mr. A. Comrie.

Banking Business of every nature will have consideration and attention. Business can also be conducted by Mail.

Deposits of $1.00 and upwards will be received in the Savings Bank Department, and Interest added every Six Months.

R. B. KESSEN,
General Manager.

Miss L.B.Macready

108 Water St.

Charlottetown,
P.E.I.

THE BANK OF ACADIA

1872-1873

LIVERPOOL, NOVA SCOTIA

BANK NUMBER 5 ***NONREDEEMABLE***

Established in 1872 in Liverpool, Nova Scotia, The Bank of Acadia was in existence for only three months and twenty-six days, making it the shortest-lived bank in Canadian history. It re-opened for a few days after its failure to redeem some of its notes, but with the exception of the government, note holders not reimbursed at this time received nothing. The government held notes worth several thousand dollars but received only 25 cents on the dollar.

5-10. ISSUE OF 1872

DESIGNS AND COLOURS

5-10-02
$4 Face Design: —/cherubs and ornate 4/—
Colour: Black with green tint

Back Design: Lathework, counters and bank name
Colour: Green

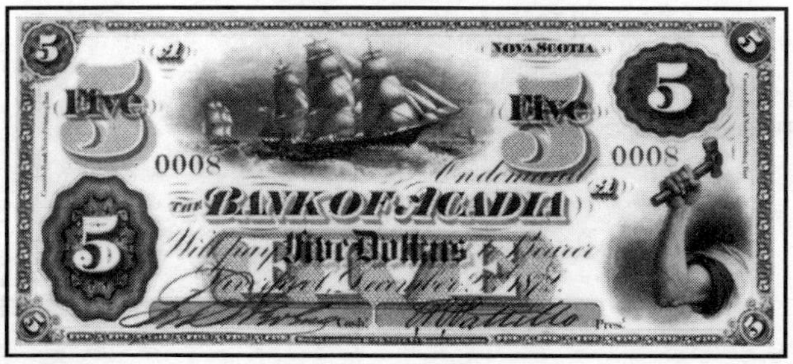

5-10-04
$5 Face Design: —/ships "Clipper"/arm and hammer "muscle"
Colour: Black with green tint

Back Design: Lathework, counters and bank name
Colour: Green

5-10-06
$10 Face Design: —/cherubs and ornate X/—
Colour: Black with green tint

Back Design: Lathework, counters and bank name
Colour: Green

5-10-08
$20 Face Design: Sailing ship/"Steamboat Canada"
Colour: Black with green tint

Back Design: Lathework, counters; Bank of Acadia
Colour: Green

IMPRINT
British American Bank Note Co. Montreal & Ottawa

SIGNATURES

left	right
mss. G.E. Stevens	mss. T.R. Pattillo

ISSUE DATING
Engraved
2nd Dec. 1872

Cat.No.	Denom.	Date	G	VG	F	VF	EF	AU
10-02	$4	1872	200.	400.	700.	1,500.	2,500.	—
10-04	$5	1872	750.	1,500.	2,500.	4,000.	—	—
10-06	$10	1872	500.	1,000.	2,000.	3,500.	—	—
10-08	$20	1872	2,500.	3,500.	4,500.	6,000.	—	—

THE ACCOMMODATION BANK

1836-1837

KINGSTON, UPPER CANADA

BANK NUMBER 10 ***NONREDEEMABLE***

This bank appears to have been established in either Kingston or Bath in 1836 despite opposition by the local people. The British Whig of September 30, 1836, discusses its establishment in Kingston, however, both the Kingston Chronicle and the British Whig of January 7, 1837 report an Accommodation Bank established at Bath. This bank appears to be a spurious bank.

10-10. ISSUE OF 1837

IMPRINT
Rawdon, Wright, Hatch New-York

SIGNATURES

left	right
mss. J. Everitt	mss. J. Miller

ISSUE DATING
Partially Engraved__18__:
1837: Jany 26

Notes read "will pay to bearer twenty shillings twelve months after date."

2. No ________ above vignette

DESIGNS AND COLOURS

10-10-02-02R
$4 (20s) Face Design: —/seated Justice figure with lion at right/—
Colour: Black with no tint

Back Design: Plain

Cat.No.	Denom.	Date	Variety	G	VG	F	VF	EF	AU
10-02-02R	$4(20s)	18__	Design 02*	75.	150.	200.	275.	475.	—

* Remainder - unsigned, undated and unnumbered.

4. Redeemable at the UPPER CANADA BANK at Kingston... engraved above vignette.

DESIGNS AND COLOURS

10-10-04-02R

$4 (20s) Face Design: —/seated Justice figure with lion at right/—
Colour: Black with no tint

Back Design: Plain

Cat. No.	Denom	Date	Variety	G	VG	F	VF	EF	AU
10-04-02R	$4(20s)	18__	Design 04**	75.	150.	200.	275.	475.	—
10-04-02	$4(20s)	1837	Design 04***	300.	600.	900.	1,200.	2,000.	—

** Remainder - signed but undated and unnumbered.
*** Completed note.

THE AGRICULTURAL BANK

1837

MONTREAL, LOWER CANADA

BANK NUMBER 15 ***NONREDEEMABLE***

Probably trading on the name of The Agricultural Bank in Toronto, The Agricultural Bank in Montreal was a phantom bank. In all probability, these notes were never issued by the "bank". Signatures and dates are likely spurious.

15-10. **BURTON & GURLEY. NEW YORK PRINTINGS**

DESIGNS AND COLOURS

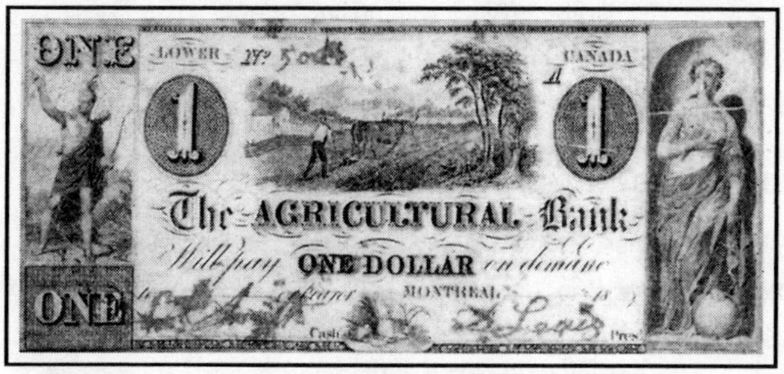

15-10-02

$1 Face Design: Indian/farmer ploughing with oxen; farm implements and sheaves below/ allegorical female
Colour: Black with no tint

Back Design: Plain

15-10-04

$2 Face Design: Farmer with grain under tree/seated "Agriculture" figure, sheaves and cattle; bear beside tree below/helmeted female
Colour: Black with no tint

Back Design: Plain

15-10-06

$3 Face Design: Women with rakes/seated "Agriculture" figure, tools, shield with "3"; crown below/ farmer ploughing with oxen

Colour: Black with no tint

Back Design: Plain

IMPRINT

Burton & Gurley. New -York

SIGNATURES

left	right
mss. various	mss. various

Note: Spurious signatures usually in blue or brown ink.

ISSUE DATING

Partially engraved__18__:
Incomplete or various dates in the 1840s
June 4, 1841
Apr 10th, 1842
May 3rd, 1842
May 3rd, 1843
June 4th, 1837
June 7th, 1843
Aug 2, 1846
Feb. 1, 1847

Note: Issues of this bank were used as sources for altered United States obsolete notes.

Cat.No.	Denom.	Date	G	VG	F	VF	EF	AU
10-02	$1	18__	125.	250.	350.	500.	—	—
10-04	$2	18__	125.	250.	350.	500.	—	—
10-06	$3	18__	200.	400.	550.	800.	—	—

THE AGRICULTURAL BANK

1834-1837

TORONTO, UPPER CANADA

BANK NUMBER 20 ***NONREDEEMABLE***

The first bank in Canada to pay interest on deposits, The Agricultural Bank was established in 1834 in Toronto as the private bank of Truscott, Green & Company, a joint-stock firm. Liquidated in November of 1837, a substantial portion of its notes and other liabilities were unprovided for, the partners having left the country. The bank's policy of paying interest was criticized in the beginning by other banks but became general practice soon afterwards.

The Agricultural Bank also began personal savings accounts on which cheques could be written, making it one of the first banks in Canada to do so.

There is a $1 note dated "1 April 1833". The date is presumably an error, either a clerical error in writing out the date which accidentally antedated the note, or the last 3 is a misinterpreted 5.

20-10. RAWDON, WRIGHT, HATCH & Co. PRINTINGS PAYABLE AT TORONTO

DESIGNS AND COLOURS

20-10-04

$1 (5s) Face Design: —/horse; beaver below/woman holding wheat

Colour: Black with no tint

Back Design: Plain

20-10-08

$2 (10s) Face Design: Men with livestock/beehive, cornucopia, sheaf, spinning wheel; beaver below/ men with livestock

Colour: Black with no tint

Back Design: Plain

20-10-14

$4 (20s) Face Design: Plough in oval (sideways)/woman and Indian, Crest; beaver below/sheaf in oval
Colour: Black with no tint

Back Design: Plain

20-10-18

$5 (25s) Face Design: Beaver/seated woman, sheaf and cattle/men with livestock
Colour: Black with no tint

Back Design: Plain

20-10-20

$10 (50s) Face Design: —/farmers cutting grain with cradles; beaver below/King William IV
Colour: Black with no tint

Back Design: Plain

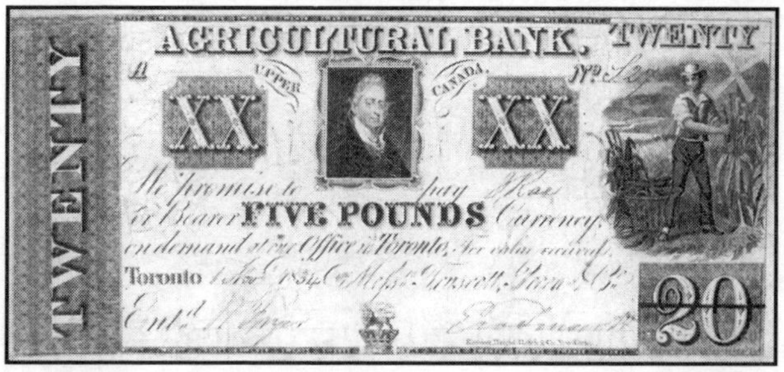

20-10-24

$20 (£5) Face Design: —/King William IV; lion on crown below/farmer picking corn
Colour: Black with no tint

Back Design: Plain

IMPRINT

Rawdon, Wright, Hatch & Co. New York

SIGNATURES

	left	right
1834-1835:	mss. W. Fryer	mss. Geo Truscott
	mss. W. Fryer	mss. J.C. Green
	mss. F. Franklin	mss. J.C. Green
	mss. H.J.Hensleigh	mss. Geo. Truscott
1837:	mss. F. Franklin	mss. Geo. Truscott
1837:	mss. H.J.Hensleigh	mss. Geo. Truscott

ISSUE DATING

Partially Engraved__18__:

$1 (5s) 1834: 1 April, Aug. 8, Oct. 1, Oct. 20, Nov. 1, Dec. 1
1835: Feb. 2, July 1
$2 (10s) 1834: Aug. 8, Aug. 18, Sept. 1, 1 Oct,16th Oct, Nov. 1, Dec. 1
1835: Feb. 1, Feb. 2, May 1, July 1
1837: Sept. 21, mss. "One year after date"; Oct. 5
$4 (20s) 1833: 1st Apr.
1834: 30th Aug, 1 Sept, 1 Oct.
1837: 1 Mar., mss. "One year after date"
$5 (25s) 1834: Aug. 8 , 30 Aug., 1 Sept., Oct., 16 Oct., Nov. 1, 1 Dec.
1837: 1 Mar.
$10 (50s) 1834: Jan. 1, Feb. 1, 1 Sept.
1835: Jan. 1
$20 (£5) 1834: Sept. 1, 1 Nov.

OVERPRINTS

A,C,D,E,F,G,H,O,R,SS,U,V in black. Some notes have a purple stamp on the back "Harveys of Bristol" mirror image in a circle

Cat.No.	Denom.	Date	G	VG	F	VF	EF	AU
10-02	$1(5s)	1834	50.	100.	150.	225.	375.	—
10-04	$1(5s)	1835	50.	100.	150.	225.	375.	—
10-06	$2(10s)	1834	50.	100.	150.	225.	375.	—
10-08	$2(10s)	1835	50.	100.	150.	225.	375.	—
10-09	$2(10s)	1837	50.	100.	150.	225.	375.	—
10-10	$2(10s)	1837*	100.	200.	300.	450.	750.	—
10-12	$4(20s)	1833	85.	175.	250.	375.	575.	—
10-14	$4(20s)	1834	85.	175.	250.	375.	575.	—
10-15	$4(20s)	1835	85.	175.	250.	375.	575.	—
10-16	$4(20s)	1837*	150.	300.	450.	600.	—	—
10-18	$5(25s)	1834	70.	140.	200.	275.	475.	—
10-19	$5(25s)	1837	70.	140.	200.	275.	—	—
10-20	$10(50s)	1834	475.	900.	1,200.	1,800.	—	—
10-22	$10(50s)	1835	475.	900.	1,200.	1,800.	—	—
10-24	$20(£5)	1834	850.	1,650.	2,500.	3,000.	4,500.	—

* "One year after date".

20-12. NEW ENGLAND BANK NOTE CO. PRINTING PAYABLE IN MONTREAL

DESIGNS AND COLOURS

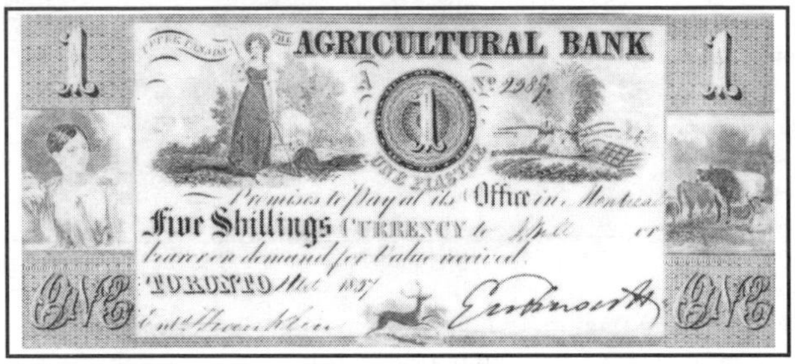

20-12-04-02
$1(5s) Face Design: Portrait of girl/woman raking hay/deer below/ sheaf and plough/cattle
Colour: Black with no tint

Back Design: Plain

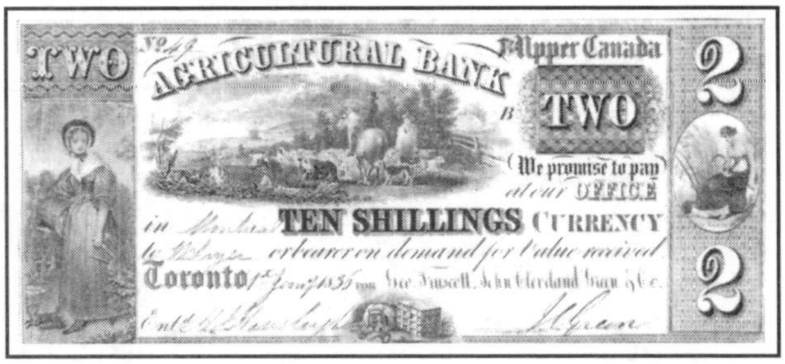

20-12-02-06
$2(10s) Face Design: Milkmaid/pastoral scene; dog with key beside strongbox below/seated female with sickle, grain in oval
Colour: Black with no tint

Back Design: Plain

20-12-02-10
$4(20s) Face Design: Boy with rake/cherubs/milkmaid; farm produce below/cherubs/smithy shoeing horse
Colour: Black with no tint

Back Design: Plain

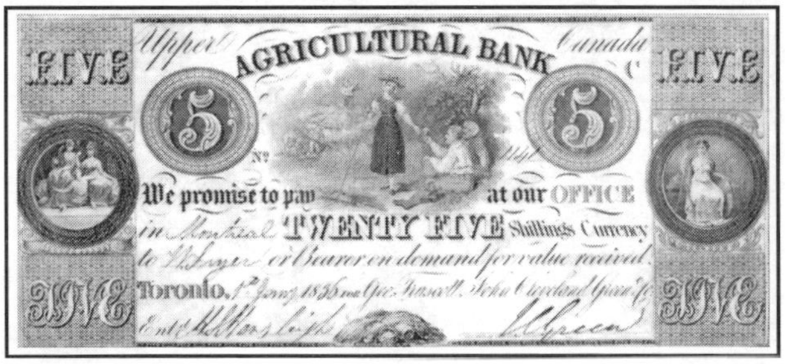

20-12-02-14
$5(25s) Face Design: Female group/haying scene; farm produce below/seated Britannia
Colour: Black with no tint

Back Design: Plain

IMPRINT
New England Bank Note Co. Boston

SIGNATURES

	left	right
1835:	mss. F.Franklin	mss. Geo. Truscott
	mss. H.J. Hensleigh	mss. J.C. Green
1836:	mss. H.J. Hensleigh	mss. J.C. Green
1837:	mss. F.Franklin	mss. Geo. Truscott

2. FOR GEO. TRUSCOTT...ENGRAVED AT BOTTOM 1835-1836

ISSUE DATING
Partially Engraved__18__:
$1 (5s) 1835: Oct. 1, 1 Nov., 1 Dec.
1836: Jan. 1
$2 (10s) 1835: Jan. 1, Oct. 1, 1 Nov., 1 Dec.
1836: Jan. 1
$4 (20s) 1835: Oct. 1, 1st Nov, Dec. 1
1836: 1 Jany
$5 (25s) 1835: Oct. 1, Nov. 1, 1 Dec.
1836: 1 Jan., October 1st

OVERPRINTS STAMP
"B" in black, "C" in red
"B" in black
"H" in black
"C" in red
"A. Colton/BOOKSELLER BRANTFORD" at right end in black
"4 4" written over cherubs at both sides.

Cat.No.	Denom.	Date	VG	F	VF	EF	AU	Unc
12-02-02	$1(5s)	1835	40.	50.	80.	150.	200.	250.
12-02-04	$1(5s)	1836	40.	50.	80.	150.	200.	250.
12-02-06	$2(10s)	1835	40.	50.	80.	150.	200.	250.
12-02-08	$2(10s)	1836	40.	50.	80.	150.	200.	250.
12-02-10	$4(20s)	1835	60.	80.	125.	200.	250.	300.
12-02-12	$4(20s)	1836	60.	80.	125.	200.	250.	300.
12-02-14	$5(25s)	1835	40.	50.	80.	150.	200.	250.
12-02-16	$5(25s)	1836	40.	50.	80.	150.	200.	250.

4. "FOR GEO. TRUSCOTT..." OMITTED, AND "THE" ADDED TO BANK NAME 1837

ISSUE DATING
Partially Engraved__18__:
1837: 1 Oct.

Cat.No.	Denom.	Date	VG	F	VF	EF	AU	Unc
12-04-02	$1(5s)	1837	30.	40.	70.	120.	160.	200.
12-04-04	$2(10s)	1837	30.	40.	70.	120.	160.	200.
12-04-06	$4(20s)	1837	50.	70.	100.	150.	200.	250.
12-04-08	$5(25s)	1837	30.	40.	70.	120.	160.	200.

ARMAN'S BANK

1837

MONTREAL (LOWER CANADA)

BANK NUMBER 25 ***NONREDEEMABLE***

There is no evidence that a bank by this name ever existed. The notes themselves, as well as their denominations, are strongly suggestive of merchant's scrip. Only the name of the issuer provides any linkage, however tenuous, to a real or pretended bank.

25-10. ISSUE OF 1837

DESIGNS AND COLOURS

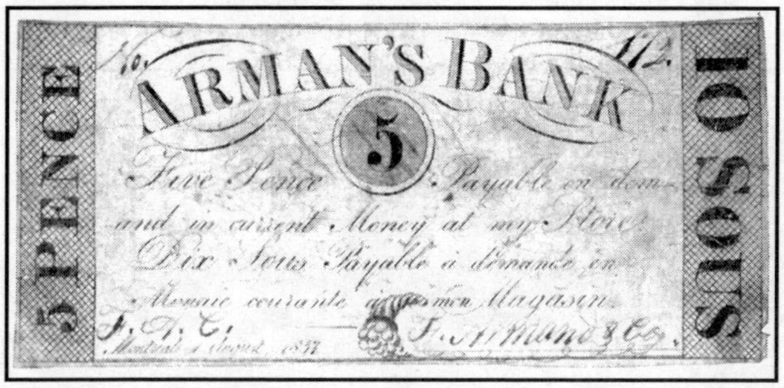

25-10-02

5d (10 sous) Face Design: —/numeral inside shaded circle; cornucopia/—
Colour: Black with no tint
Back Design: Plain

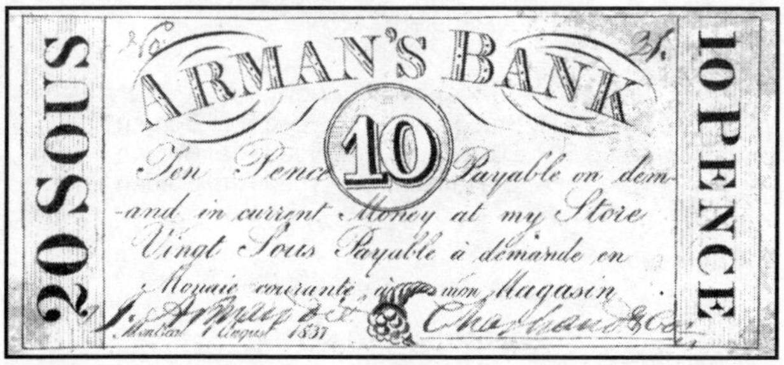

25-10-04

10d (20 sous) Face Design: —/numeral inside shaded circle; cornucopia/—
Colour: Black with no tint
Back Design: Plain

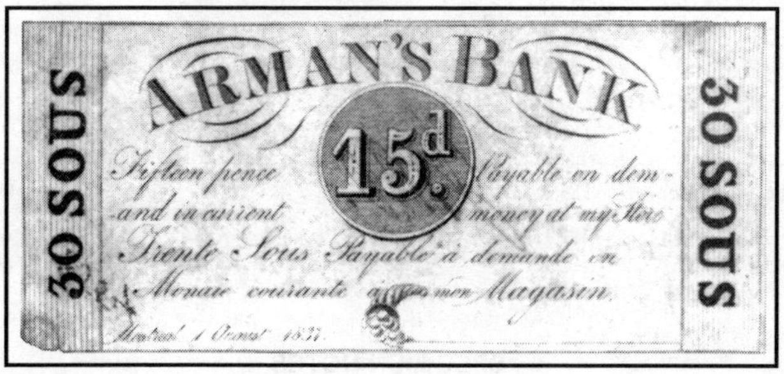

25-10-06

15d (30 sous) Face Design: —/numeral inside shaded circle; cornucopia/—
Colour: Black with no tint
Back Design: Plain

IMPRINT

None

SIGNATURES

left	**right**
mss. various	mss. various

ISSUE DATING
Engraved

1 August 1837

Cat.No.	Denom.	Date	G	VG	F	VF	EF	Unc
10-02	5d(10 sous)	1837	125.	250.	350.	—	—	—
10-04	10d(20 sous)	1837	125.	250.	350.	—	—	—
10-06	15d(30 sous)	1837	125.	250.	350.	—	—	—

BARCLAYS BANK (CANADA)

1929-1956

MONTREAL, QUEBEC

BANK NUMBER 30 ***REDEEMABLE***

An important event in Canadian banking history occurred in 1929 with the entry of one of the leading British banks, Barclays Bank, Limited. It became a new chartered bank, Barclays Bank (Canada) with its head office in Montreal. Although the bank had a Canadian Board of Directors, its operations remained under the control of the parent institution in England. The Canadian bank's first president was Sir Robert Borden. A statement issued by the management noted that the object of the bank in Canada was, "to establish another link in the chain of their affiliations with a view of fostering trade with the Empire". Branches were established in Toronto and Vancouver and paid-up capital reached $3 million by 1950. By this time deposits exceeded $30 million and in 1956 amalgamated with The Imperial Bank of Canada.

30-10. ISSUE OF 1929 LARGE SIZE NOTES

DESIGNS AND COLOURS

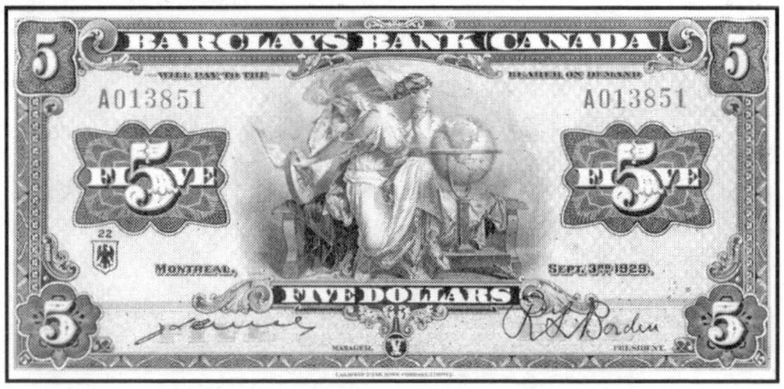

30-10-02

$5 Face Design: —/seated female with globe/—
Colour: Black with blue-green tint

Back Design: Lathework, counters, bank name and bank building
Colour: Green

30-10-04

$10 Face Design: —/seated female with globe/—
Colour: Black with orange tint

Back Design: Lathework, counters, bank name and bank building
Colour: Orange

30-10-06

$20 Face Design: —/seated female with globe/—
Colour: Black with blue tint

Back Design: Lathework, counters, bank name and bank building
Colour: Blue

IMPRINT

Canadian Bank Note Company, Limited

SIGNATURES

left	right
typed J.R. Bruce	typed R.L. Borden
typed F.H. Dickenson	typed R.L. Borden
typed H.A. Stevenson	typed R.L. Borden

ISSUE DATING

Engraved

Sept. 3rd 1929

CIRCULATING NOTES

Cat.No.	Denom.	Date	Variety	VG	F	VF	EF	AU	Unc
10-02	$5	1929	Bruce, I	500.	650.	950.	1,600.	2,400.	3,200.
10-02a	$5	1929	Dickenson, I	—	—	1,100.	1,800.	—	—
10-02b	$5	1929	Stevenson, I	—	700.	1,000.	1,675.	2,500.	—
10-04	$10	1929	Bruce, I	—	—	1.150.	1,900	—	—
10-04a	$10	1929	Dickenson, I	500.	650.	950.	1,600	2,400.	—
10-04b	$10	1929	Stevenson, I	650.	850.	—		—	—
10-06	$20	1929	Bruce, I	500.	650.	950.	1,600	2,400.	—
10-06b	$20	1929	Stevenson, I	550.	700.	1,000.	1,700	2,550.	—

PROOF NOTES

Cat. No.	Denom.	Date		Unc
10-02P	$5	1929	FACE PROOF	400.
10-04P	$10	1929	FACE PROOF	400.
10-06P	$20	1929	FACE PROOF	400.

SPECIMEN NOTES

Cat. No.	Denom.	Date		Unc
10-02S	$5	1929	SPECIMEN	1,000.
10-04S	$10	1929	SPECIMEN	1,000.
10-06S	$20	1929	SPECIMEN	1,000.

30.12. **ISSUE OF 1935**
SMALL SIZE NOTES

DESIGNS AND COLOURS

30-12-02

$5 Face Design: —/seated female with globe/—
Colour: Black with blue-green tint

Back Design: Lathework, counters, bank name and bank building

30-12-06

$10 Face Design: —/seated female with globe/—
Colour: Black with orange tint

Back Design: Lathework, counters, bank name and bank building
Colour: Orange

IMPRINT

Canadian Bank Note Company, Limited

SIGNATURES

left	**right**
typed H.A. Stevenson	typed R.L. Borden
typed H.A. Stevenson	typed A.A. Magee

ISSUE DATING

Engraved

Jany 2nd, 1935

CIRCULATING NOTES

Cat.No.	Denom.	Date	Variety	VG	F	VF	EF	AU	Unc
12-02	$5	1935	Borden, r.	100.	140.	200.	400.	700.	1,000.
12-06	$10	1935	Borden, r.	80.	115.	175.	350.	575.	800.
12-08	$10	1935	Magee, r.	80.	115.	175.	350.	575.	800.

PROOF NOTES

Cat. No.	Denom.	Date	Variety		Unc
12-02P	$5	1935		FACE PROOF	400.
12-06P	$10	1935		FACE PROOF	400.

SPECIMEN NOTES

Cat. No.	Denom.	Date	Variety		Unc
12-02S	$5	1935	Borden, r.	SPECIMEN	750.
12-04S	$5	1935	Magee, r.	SPECIMEN	1,000.
12-06S	$10	1935	Borden, r.	SPECIMEN	750.
12-08S	$10	1935	Magee, r.	SPECIMEN	750.

LA BANQUE DE BOUCHERVILLE

1830s

BOUCHERVILLE, BAS CANADA

BANK NUMBER 35 ***NONREDEEMABLE***

La Banque de Boucherville was established in 1836 or 1837 in Lower Canada on a “joint stock” basis. It did not flourish.

35-10. **BOURNE PRINTING**

DESIGNS AND COLOURS

35-10-02

$1 Face Design: No vignette, French text.
Colour: Black with no tint

Black Design: Plain

IMPRINT

Bourne Sc.

SIGNATURES

left	**right**
none	none
A. Duquette	H. Haineault

ISSUE DATING

Partially Engraved__18__

1837: 23 Juin

Cat.No.	Denom.	Date	Variety	VG	F	VF	EF	Unc
10-02R	$1	18__	Remainder*	—	—	—	100.	200.
10-02	$1	1837		30.	60.	85.	140.	250.

* Unsigned, undated and unnumbered.

THE BANK OF BRANTFORD

1857-1860's

BRANTFORD, CANADA WEST

BANK NUMBER 40 ***NONREDEEMABLE***

Established in Brantford, Canada West in 1857, The Bank of Brantford, during its relatively short period of operation, managed to circulate a considerable number of notes. Most of their notes were released in the United States. In Ontario they were considered suspicious and not readily accepted.

40-10. PAYABLE AT BRANTFORD, OVERALL GREEN TINT

DESIGNS AND COLOURS

40-10-02-02a

$1 Face Design: St. George slaying dragon/ girl with calves/cattle scene
Colour: Black with overall green tint

Back Design: Plain

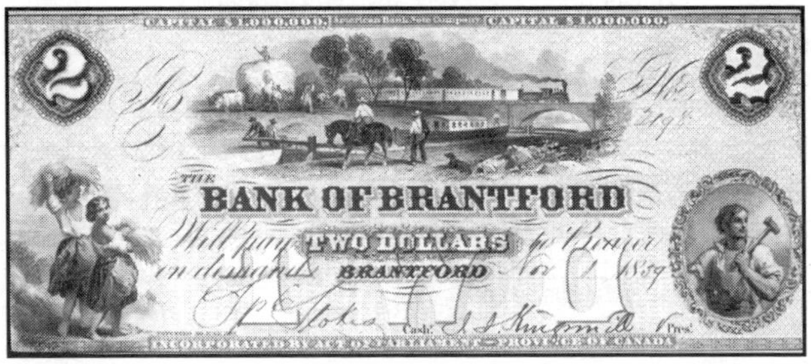

40-10-02-04

$2 Face Design: Girl with sheaves/boat in locks, train/ man with hammer
Colour: Black with overall green tint
Back Design: Plain

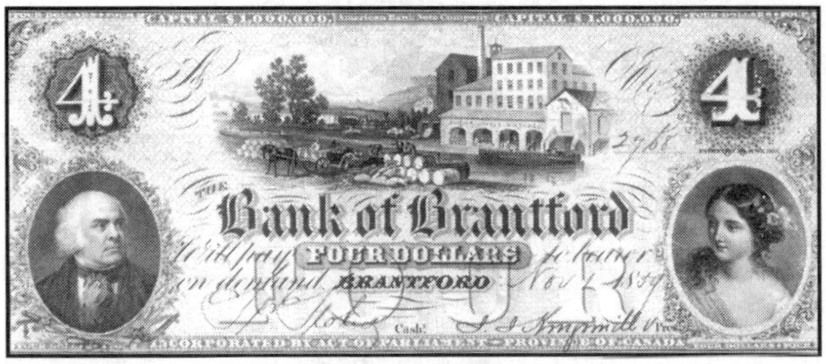

40-10-02-06

$4 Face Design: Portrait of Lord Elgin/ unloading wagon at canal, mill in back-ground/young girl
Colour: Black with overall green tint

Back Design: Plain

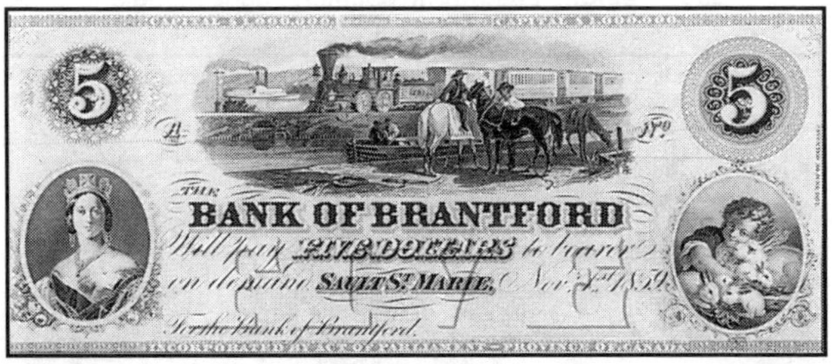

40-10-04-08

$5 Face Design: Queen Victoria (Winterhalter portrait) train, boats and horses/Solomon Carvalho's "Child with rabbits"
Colour: Black with overall green tint

Back Design: Plain

40-10-02

Purple overprint on Back: "Fred Westbrook 10 mile champion of Canada Hotel Belmont, Brantford, Ontario" Man on bicycle design, all in purple
Colour: Purple

40-10-04

Green overprint on back: "Fred Westbrook 10 mile champion of Canada Hotel Belmont, Brantford, Ontario" Man on bicycle design, all in green

Colour: Green

IMPRINT

American Bank Note Company

2. PARTIALLY ENGRAVED DATE

SIGNATURES

left	right
mss. S.P. Stokes	mss. J.J. Kingsmill
mss. S.P. Stokes	mss. Peter Carroll

ISSUE DATING

Partially Engraved__18__:

1859: Nov. 1

OVERPRINT

Face:"ISSUED AND PAYABLE AT THE AGENCY IN/ HONITON, 1st May, 1862." in blue

Cat.No.	Den.	Date	Variety	VG	F	VF	EF	AU	Unc
10-02-02	$1	1859	No o/p	75.	100.	150.	325.	400.	500.
10-02-02a	$1	1859	Kingsmill, Blue o/p	100.	125.	190.	350.	—	—
10-02-02b	$1	1859	Carrole, Blue o/p	100.	125.	190.	350.	—	—
10-02-04	$2	1859		60.	75.	110.	200.	275.	350.
10-02-04a	$2	1859	Westbrook, Purple o/p	80.	100.	150.	300.	375.	450.
10-02-06	$4	1859		70.	85.	125.	225.	300.	375.
10-02-06a	$4	1859	Westbrook, Purple o/p	90.	110.	165.	325.	400.	500.
10-02-08	$5	1859		60.	75.	110.	200.	275.	350.
10-02-08a	$5	1859	Westbrook, Purple o/p	80.	100.	150.	300.	375.	450.

4. ENGRAVED DATE

SIGNATURES

left	right
mss. S.P. Stokes	mss. Peter Carroll

ISSUE DATING

Engraved

Novr. 1st, 1859

OVERPRINT

Face: ISSUED AND PAYABLE AT THE AGENCY IN/HONITON 1st May, 1862. in blue

Cat.No.	Den.	Date	Variety	VG	F	VF	EF	AU	Unc
10-04-02	$1	1859	No o/p	75.	100.	150.	325.	400.	500.
10-04-02a	$1	1859	Blue o/p	100.	125.	190.	350.	—	—
10-04-04	$2	1859	No o/p	70.	85.	125.	225.	300.	375.
10-04-04a	$2	1859	Blue o/p	100.	125.	190.	350.	—	—
10-04-04b	$2	1859	Westbrook, green o/p	110.	140.	220.	—	—	—
10-04-06	$4	1859		70.	85.	125.	225.	300.	375.
10-04-06a	$4	1859	Westbrook, green o/p	110.	140.	220.	—	—	—
10-04-08	$5	1859		60.	75.	110.	200.	275.	350.
10-04-08a	$5	1859	Westbrook, purple o/p	80.	100.	150.	300.	375.	450.

40-12. PAYABLE AT SAULT ST. MARIE, OVERALL RED TINT

DESIGNS AND COLOURS

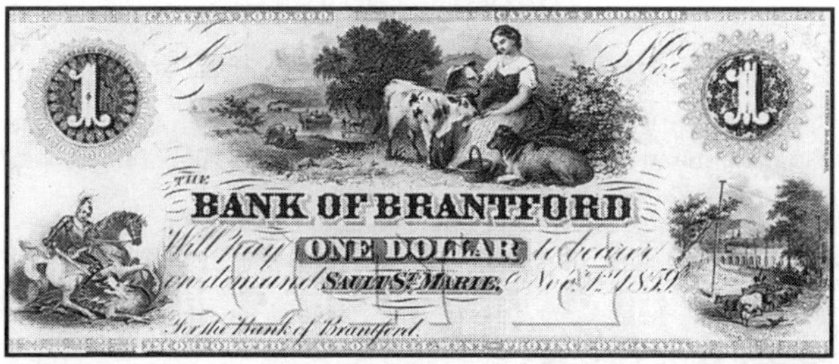

40-12-02R

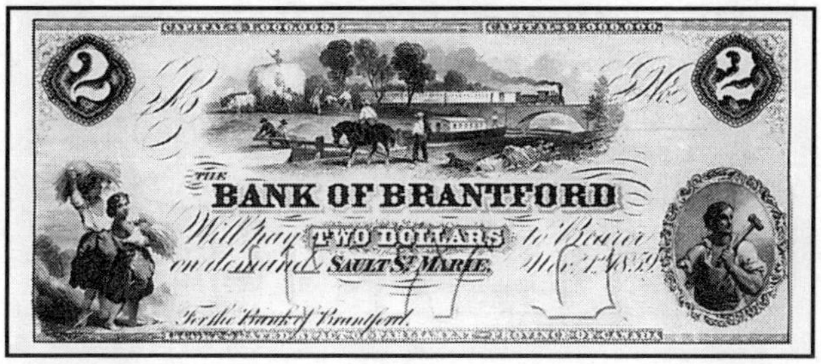

40-12-04R

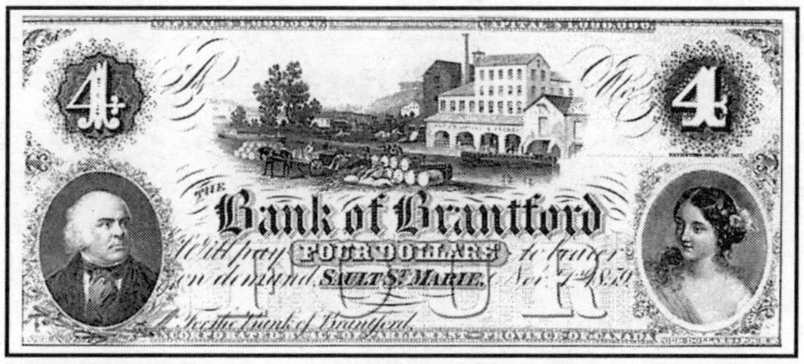

40-12-06R

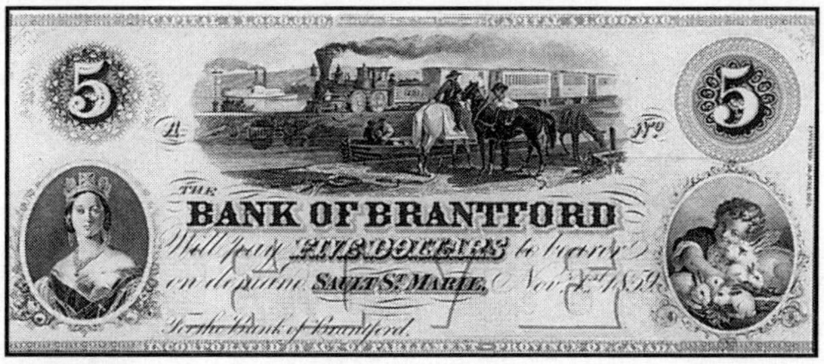

40-12-08R

SIGNATURES

left	right
none	none

ISSUE DATING

Engraved

Novr 1st 1859

Cat.No.	Denom.	Date	Variety	VG	F	VF	EF	AU	Unc
12-02R	$1	1859	Remainder*	—	—	—	150.	175.	225.
12-04R	$2	1859	Remainder*	—	—	—	150.	175.	225.
12-06R	$4	1859	Remainder*	—	—	—	175.	200.	250.
12-08R	$5	1859	Remainder*	—	—	—	150.	175.	225.

*Unsigned and unnumbered.

THE BRITISH CANADIAN BANK

1883-1884

TORONTO, ONTARIO

BANK NUMBER 45 ***NONREDEEMABLE***

Established in Winnipeg, Manitoba in 1882, The British Canadian Bank changed its name from the North Western Bank in 1883, but its charter was never used.

45-10. **BABN PRINTINGS 1884**

DESIGNS AND COLOURS

45-10-02P

$5 Face Design: Train and ships at wharf/—/—
Colour: Black with green tint

Back Design: Lathework, counters and bank name
Colour: Green

45-10-04P

$10 Face Design: Youthful bust of Queen Victoria/—/ 10 with seated Britannia, native child and lion
Colour: Black with green tint

Back Design: Lathework, counters and bank name
Colour: Green

IMPRINT

British American Bank Note Company, Montreal

SIGNATURES

left	**right**
none	none

ISSUE DATING

Engraved

September 15th, 1884
Sept. 15th 1884

PROOF NOTES

Cat.No.	Denom.	Date		Unc
10-02P	$5	1884	FACE PROOF	900.
10-04P	$10	1884	FACE PROOF	900.

THE BANK OF BRITISH COLUMBIA

1862-1901

VICTORIA, VANCOUVER ISLAND

BANK NUMBER 50 ***REDEEMABLE***

The Royal charter incorporating The Bank of British Columbia was granted on May 31, 1862 and ran for twenty years. In its prospectus, its preliminary advertising and the watermark of its earliest notes, the name of the institution appeared as The Chartered Bank of British Columbia and Vancouver Island. On July, 1862, the directors changed the name to correspond with the chartered name. The bank opened for business in Victoria within a few days of the change.

On May 11, 1883, the charter was renewed for one year, and in 1894 the ten year extension of the bank's charter obtained May 27, 1884 expired and was renewed under the same terms for another seven years. This charter was to expire July 1, 1901, with the understanding that it would not likely be renewed again, although the bank still had the option of a Dominion charter.

At a general meeting in July of 1900, The Canadian Bank of Commerce submitted a proposal of amalgamation to the shareholders and at a special meeting in December of that year, the shareholders of The Bank of British Columbia agreed to accept the offer and its shares were purchased by The Canadian Bank of Commerce on January 2, 1901.

There is no relation between this bank and the one more recently chartered under the name of the Bank of British Columbia.

50-10. "VICTORIA COIN" ISSUE 1862-1863 LARGE SIZE NOTES (20.8 x 12.3 cm.)

Notes of this issue were printed on paper watermarked "The Chartered Bank of British Columbia and Vancouver's Island" on first issues and later "Bank of British Columbia".

DESIGNS AND COLOURS

Notes of this issue have Queen Victoria facing left, as on the obverse of the British Indian rupee coin, at the left end of the note.

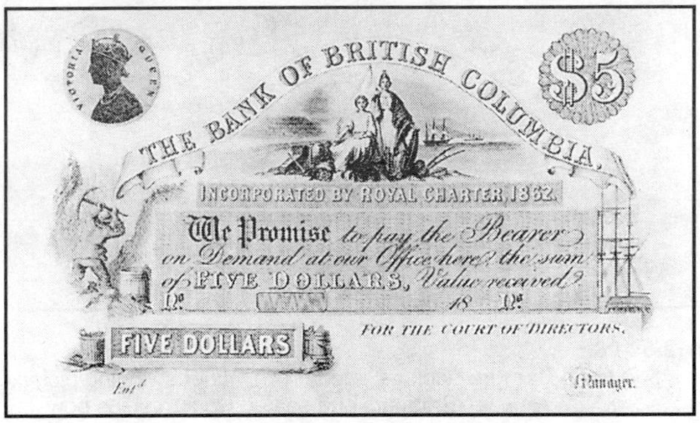

50-10-04

$5 Face Design: Victoria coin; miner swinging pickaxe/ Britannia and seated woman/ships stern
Colour: Black with blue tint
Back Design: Plain

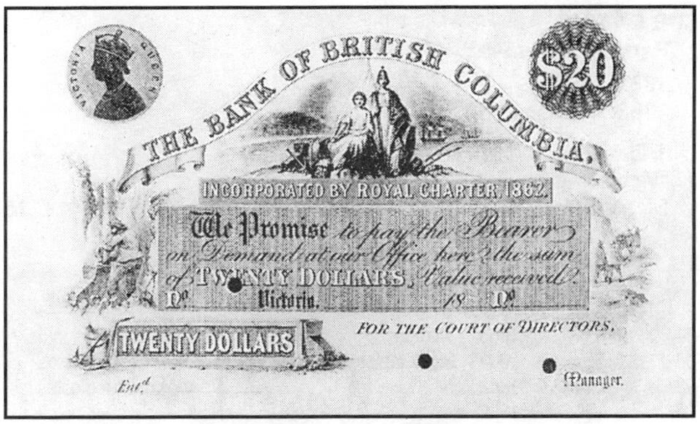

50-10-08

$20 Face Design: Victoria coin; miner pouring ore/ Britannia and seated woman/ miners walking
Colour: Black with blue tint
Back Design: Plain

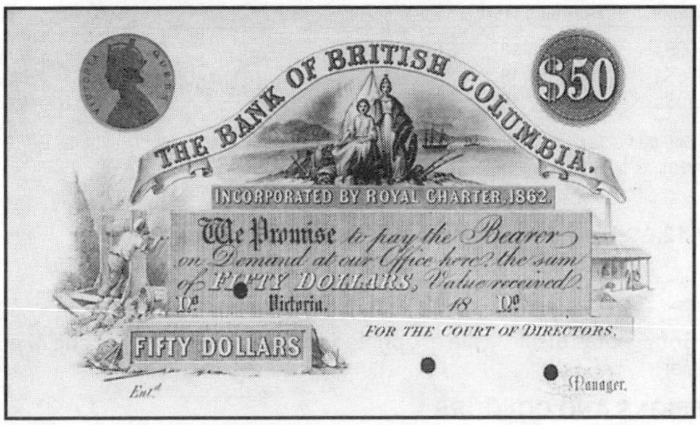

50-10-10

$50 Face Design: Victoria coin; miner at crank/ Britannia and seated woman/ships stern
Colour: Black with blue tint
Back Design: Plain

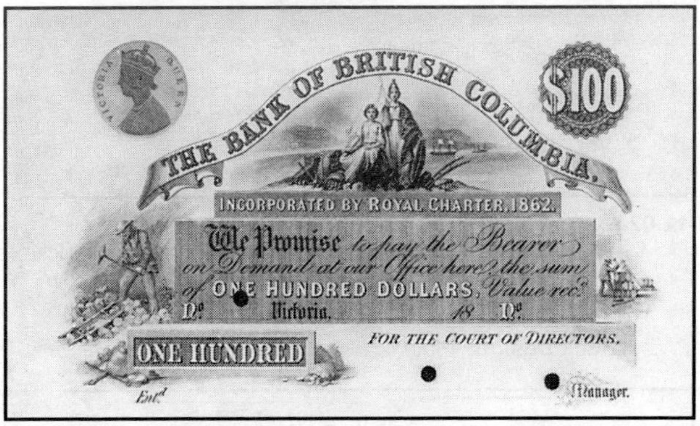

50-10-12

$100 Face Design: Victoria coin; miner holding pickaxe/ Britannia and seated woman/man working
Colour: Black with blue tint
Back Design: Plain

IMPRINT

Rixon & Arnold

SIGNATURES

left	right
mss. various	mss. various

ISSUE DATING

Partially Engraved__18__:

1862: Nov. 28
1863: 6th Jany

VARIETIES

"Victoria" following left note number space
Blank tablet following left note number space

CIRCULATING NOTES

Cat.No.	Denom.	Date	Variety	VG	F	VF	EF	Unc
10-04	$5	1863	Victoria	Institutional collection only				
10-06	$5	1863	Blank tablet	No known issued notes				
10-08	$20	1862		No known issued notes				
10-10	$50	1862		No known issued notes				
10-12	$100	1863		All redeemed				

SPECIMEN NOTES

Cat. No.	Denom.	Date			Unc
10-08S	$20	18__	SPECIMEN	Institutional collection only	
10-10S	$50	18__	SPECIMEN	Institutional collection only	
10-12S	$100	18__	SPECIMEN	Institutional collection only	

Cat. No.	Denom.	Date			Unc
10-06Sa	$5*	18__	SPECIMEN	RARE - est.	6,000.
10-08Sa	$20*	18__	SPECIMEN	RARE - est.	6,000.
10-10Sa	$50*	18__	SPECIMEN	RARE - est.	6,000.

*Unsigned notes cancelled for use as specimens for the customs department of the BC Government.

50-12. "VICTORIA MEDALLION" ISSUE 1863-1875 SMALL SIZE NOTES

Some notes of this issue are printed on watermarked white, buff or pink paper.

DESIGNS AND COLOURS

Notes of this issue have a gothic portrait of Queen Victoria facing right, on a medallion without legend, at the left end of the notes.

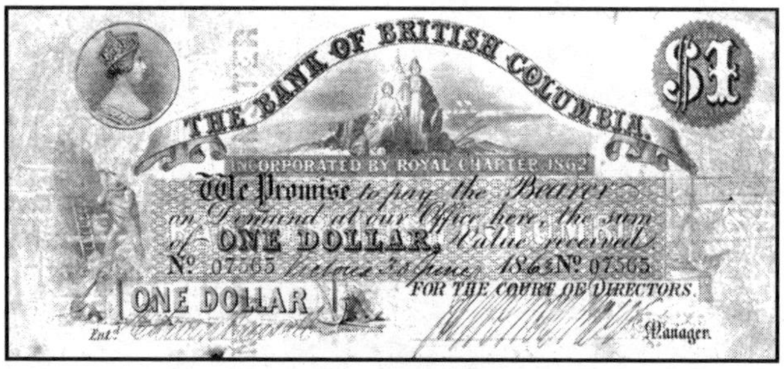

50-12-02a

$1 Face Design: Victoria "medallion"; miner swinging pickaxe/ Britannia and seated woman/ships bow
Colour: Black with blue tint
Back Design: Plain

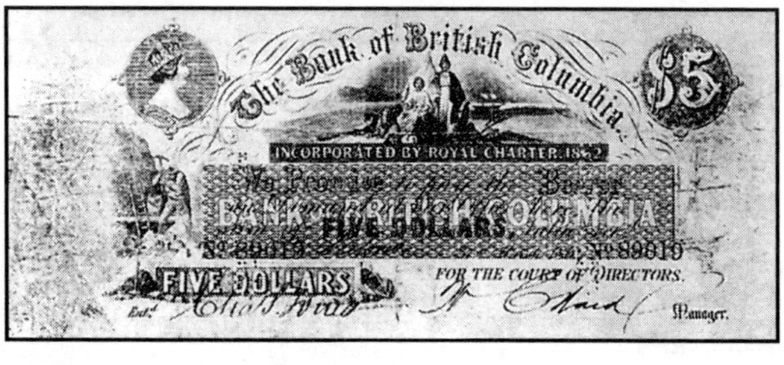

50-12-04-02

$5 Face Design: Victoria "medallion"; miner swinging pickaxe/ Britannia and seated woman/ships bow
Colour: Black with blue tint
Back Design: Plain

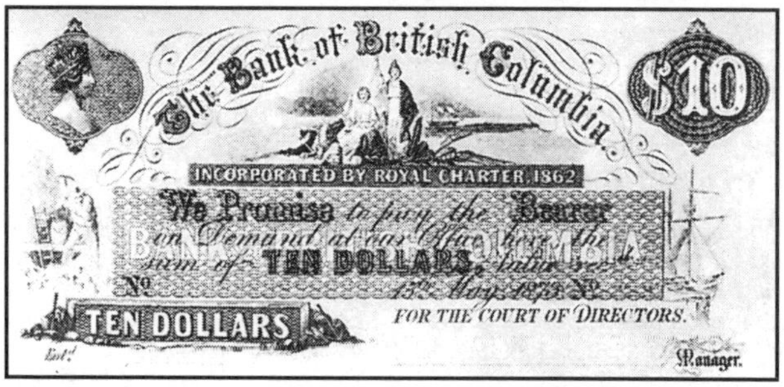

50-12-04-04R

$10 Face Design: Victoria "medallion"; miner swinging pickaxe/ Britannia and seated woman/ships bow
Colour: Black with blue tint
Back Design: Plain

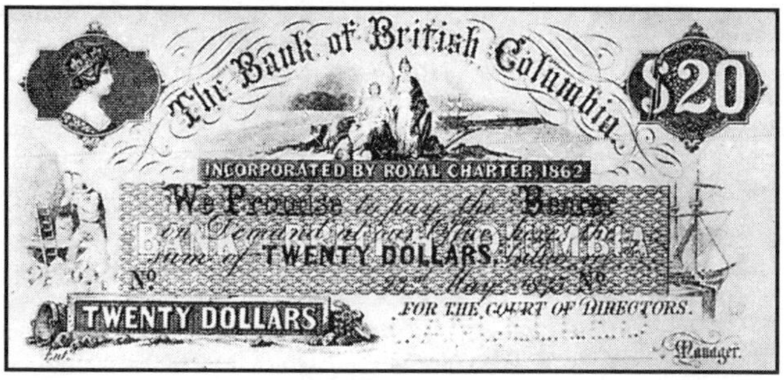

50-12-04-06R

$20 Face Design: Victoria "medallion"; miner swinging pickaxe/ Britannia and seated woman/ships bow
Colour: Black with blue tint
Back Design: Plain

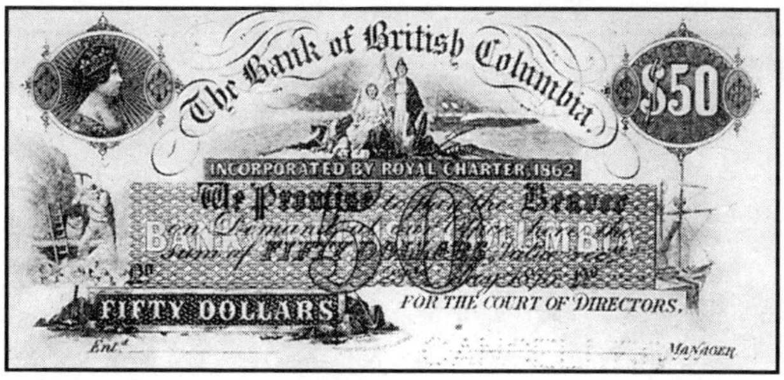

50-12-04-08R

$50 Face Design: Victoria "medallion"; miner swinging pickaxe/ Britannia and seated woman/ships bow
Colour: Black with blue tint
Back Design: Plain

IMPRINT

Wm. Brown & Co. Sc. London

SIGNATURES

left	right
mss. various	mss. various

2. PARTIALLY ENGRAVED DATE 1863

ISSUE DATING

Partially Engraved __18__:

1863: 24 June, 30 June

STAMP

NEW WESTMINSTER in blue vertically at left end

CIRCULATING NOTES

Cat.No.	Denom.	Date	Variety	G	VG	F	VF	EF	AU
12-02	$1	1863				RARE - est.			6,000.
12-02a	$1	1863	o/p NEW WESTMINSTER			RARE - est.			6,000.

SPECIMEN NOTES

Cat. No.	Denom.	Date			Unc
12-02-Sa	$1*	18__	SPECIMEN	RARE - est.	6,000.

* Unsigned notes cancelled for use as specimens for the customs department of the BC government.

4. FULLY ENGRAVED DATE 1864 - 1875

ISSUE DATING

Engraved

March 31st 1864
15th May 1873
23rd May 1875

Cat.No.	Denom.	Date	Variety	Unc
12-04-02	$5	1864		Institutional collection only
12-04-04R	$10	1873	Remainder	Institutional collection only
12-04-06R	$20	1875	Remainder	Institutional collection only
12-04-08R	$50	1875	Remainder	Institutional collection only

50-14. ISSUE OF 1879

DESIGNS AND COLOURS

50-14-02-02

$5 Face Design: Sailing ship/Queen Victoria/mine
Colour: Black with no tint
Back Design: Lathework and counters with "PAYABLE AT VICTORIA"
Colour: Green

50-14-02-04S

$10 Face Design: Sailing ship/Queen Victoria/mine
Colour: Black with no tint
Back Design: Lathework and counters with "PAYABLE AT VICTORIA"
Colour: Green

50-14-02-06

$20 Face Design: Sailing ship/Queen Victoria/mine
Colour: Black with no tint
Back Design: Lathework and counters with "PAYABLE AT VICTORIA"
Colour Green

50-14-02-08

$50 Face Design: Sailing ship/Queen Victoria/mine
Colour: Black with no tint
Back Design: Lathework and counters
See subheadings
Colour: Green

50-14-02-10

$100 Face Design: Sailing ship/Queen Victoria/mine
Colour: Black with no tint
Back Design: Lathework and counters
See subheadings
Colour: Green

IMPRINT

Wm. Brown & Co. 40 & 41 Old Broad St. London

SIGNATURES

left	right
mss. various	mss. various

ISSUE DATING

Engraved

1st June 1879

PROTECTOR

Green "word" on face only

2. RED SERIAL NUMBER ON FACE ONLY

Cat.No.	Denom.	Date	VG	F	VF	EF	Unc
14-02-02	$5	1879			Institutional collection only		
14-02-04	$10	1879			Institutional collection only		
14-02-06	$20	1879			No known issued notes		
14-02-08	$50	1879			Institutional collection only		
14-02-10	$100	1879			Institutional collection only		

4. BLACK SERIAL NUMBER ON FACE, REPEATED ON BACK

CIRCULATING NOTES

Cat.No.	Denom.	Date	VG	F	VF	EF	Unc
14-04-02	$5	1879			Institutional collection only		
14-04-04	$10	1879			Institutional collection only		
14-04-06	$20	1879			RARE - VG est.		6,000.
14-04-08	$50	1879			Institutional collection only		
14-04-10	$100	1879			Institutional collection only		

SPECIMEN NOTES

Cat. No.	Denom.	Date	Variety	Unc
14-04-02S	$5	1879	perforated WBCo Specimen	Institutional collection only
14-04-04S	$10	1879	perforated WBCo Specimen	Institutional collection only
14-04-06S	$20	1879	perforated WBCo Specimen	Institutional collection only
14-04-10S	$100	1879	perforated WBCo Specimen	Institutional collection only

50-16. ISSUE OF 1894

DESIGNS AND COLOURS

50-16-02

$5 Face Design: —/Britannia and seated woman, mountains in background/—
Colour: Black with pale yellow and green tint

Back Design: Latherwork, counters and bank name
Colour: Green

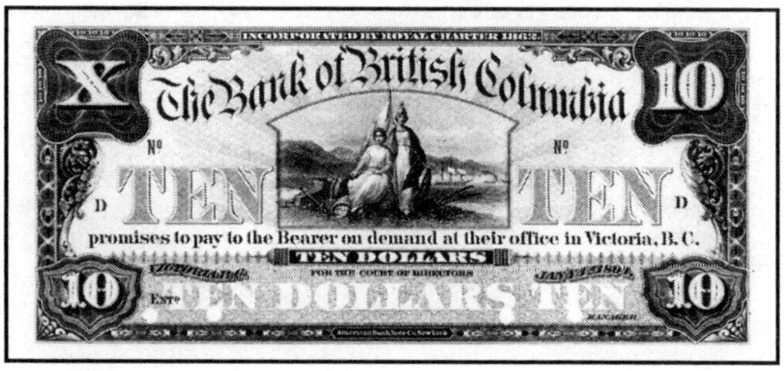

50-16-04

$10 Face Design: —/Britannia and seated woman, mountains in background/—
Colour: Black with yellow and blue tint

Back Design: Lathework, counters and bank name
Colour: Blue

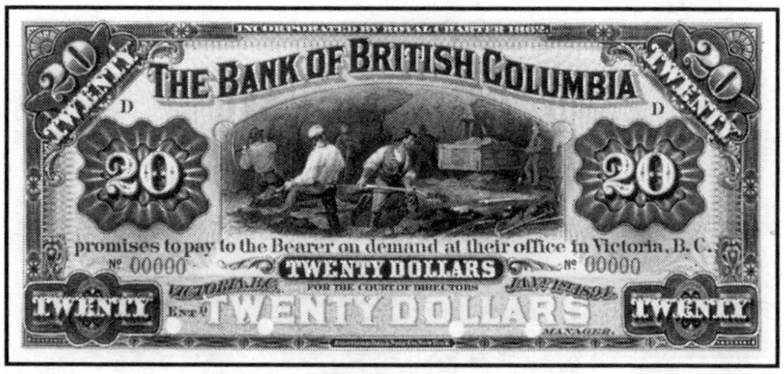

50-16-06

$20 Face Design: —/miners/—
Colour: Black with yellow and red-brown tint

Back Design: Lathework, counters and bank name
Colour: Dark brown

50-16-08

$50 Face Design: —/Royal Crest/—
Colour: Black with pale yellow and deep orange tint

Back Design: Lathework, counters and bank name
Colour: Red-orange

IMPRINT

$5: American Bank Note Co. N.Y.
$10, 20, 50: American Bank Note Co. New York

SIGNATURES

left	right
mss. various	mss. various

ISSUE DATING

Engraved

Jany 1st 1894

CIRCULATING NOTES

Cat.No.	Denom.	Date	G	VG	F	VF	EF	Unc
16-02	$5	1894		RARE - VG - est.				6,000.
16-04	$10	1894		Institutional collection only				
16-06	$20	1894		Institutional collection only				
16-08	$50	1894		Institutional collection only				

PROOF NOTES

Cat. No.	Denom.	Date		Unc
16-02P	$5	1894	FACE PROOF	700.
16-04P	$10	1894	FACE PROOF	700.
16-06P	$20	1894	FACE PROOF	700.
16-08P	$50	1894	FACE PROOF	700.

SPECIMEN NOTES

Cat. No.	Denom.	Date		Unc
16-02S	$5	1894	SPECIMEN	2,000.
16-04S	$10	1894	SPECIMEN	2,000.
16-06S	$20	1894	SPECIMEN	2,000.
16-08S	$50	1894	SPECIMEN	2,000.

THE BANK OF BRITISH NORTH AMERICA

1836-1918

BANK NUMBER 55 ***REDEEMABLE***

The Bank of British North America was formed in England in 1836 as a private institution to conduct business through branches in the various North American provinces. Each branch obtained a Provincial Charter. The bank began business with capital of £1 million without double liability to shareholders. In 1840 the promoters of the bank secured a Royal Charter, which stipulated that no notes smaller than £1 could be issued. Only The Bank of British North America, of all the chartered banks, made use of the Free Banking Act of 1850 to enable it to again extend its issue to $1 and $2 notes, which it did until 1870. The expansion of this bank in Canada influenced the Canadian banking system through the infusion of large numbers of young British bankers who had received their early training in British banks. Once in Canada, these young bankers gradually joined other Canadian institutions and at one time no less than eleven Canadian banks were under the general management of former employees of The Bank of British North America.

In London the directors of the bank found it increasingly difficult to conduct operations in Canada during World War I. Although the bank was well managed and sound, the war had imposed restrictions on travel and communications, making it difficult for the directors to keep in touch with Canadian conditions. They concluded that a merger would be advantageous, and in April of 1918 the bank was absorbed by The Bank of Montreal. At the time of merger, the bank had a paid-up capital of nearly $5 million, a reserve fund of about $3 million, total assets of $78 million, and was represented by 92 branches.

55-10. EARLY "BANK CREST" ISSUES 1837 - 1847

DESIGNS AND COLOURS

Face Design: various with "Bank Crest"
Colour: Black with no tint

Back Design: Plain

IMPRINT

Perkins, Bacon & Petch, London

2. "HALIFAX NOVA SCOTIA BRANCH" ISSUE

55-10-02-02P

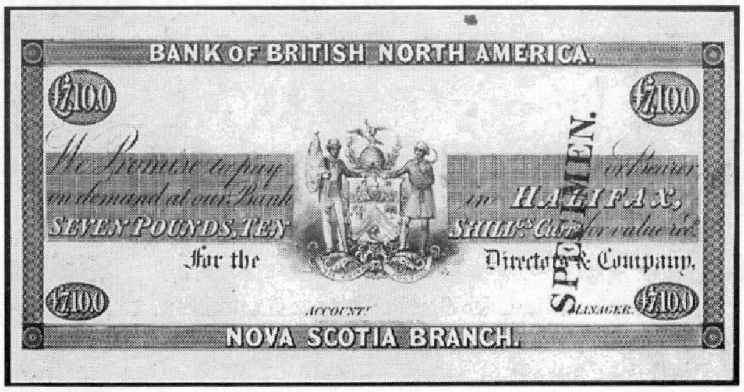

55-10-02-04P

ISSUE DATING

Entire date added letterpress with serial numbers

PROOF NOTES

Cat.No.	Denom.	Date	Unc
10-02-02P	£5	no date	650.
10-02-04P	£7.10	no date	800.

4. "MONTREAL LOWER CANADA" ISSUE

55-10-04-08P

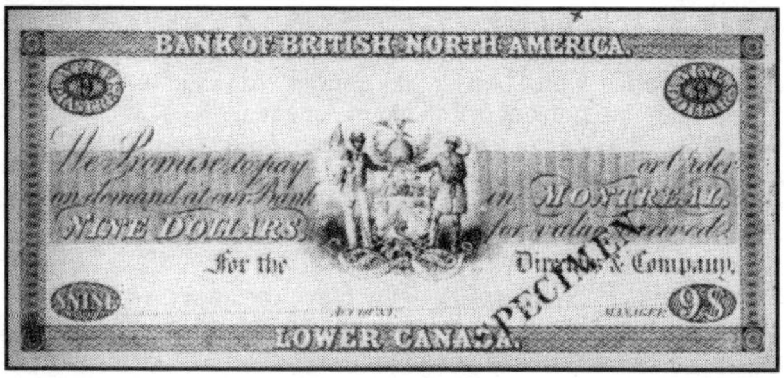

55-10-04-10P

Photograph not available
at press time

55-10-04-12

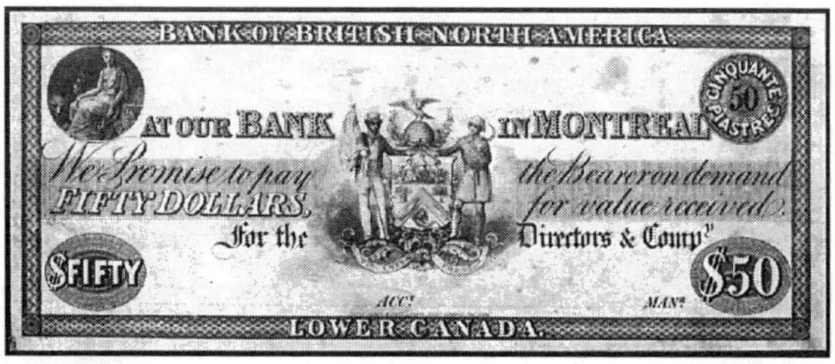

55-10-04-20P

SIGNATURES

Left	Right
mss. various	mss. various

ISSUE DATING

Entire date added letterpress with serial numbers:

$1: Septr. 1 1838

Partially Engraved__18__:

CIRCULATING NOTES

Cat.No.	Denom.	Date	G	VG	F	VF	EF
10-04-02	$1	1838	400.	800.	1,000.	1,500.	—
10-04-02R	$1	1838 remainder	200.	400.	500.	600.	750.
10-04-08	$7	no date		No known issued notes			
10-04-10	$9	no date		No known issued notes			
10-04-12	$10	18__		No known issued notes			
10-04-20	$50	no date		No known issued notes			

PROOF NOTES

Cat. No.	Denom.	Date		Unc
10-04-08P	$7	no date	PROOF	1,500.
10-04-10P	$9	no date	PROOF	1,500.
10-04-12P	$10	18__	PROOF	650.
10-04-20P	$50	no date	PROOF	650.

5. MONTREAL BRANCH ISSUE

55-10-05-20P

ISSUE DATING

Partially Engraved ___ 18___:

PROOF NOTES

Cat.No.	Denom	Date		Unc
10-05-12P	$10		Surviving proofs not confirmed	
10-05-20P	$50	18__	PROOF	750.

6. "QUEBEC LOWER CANADA" ISSUE

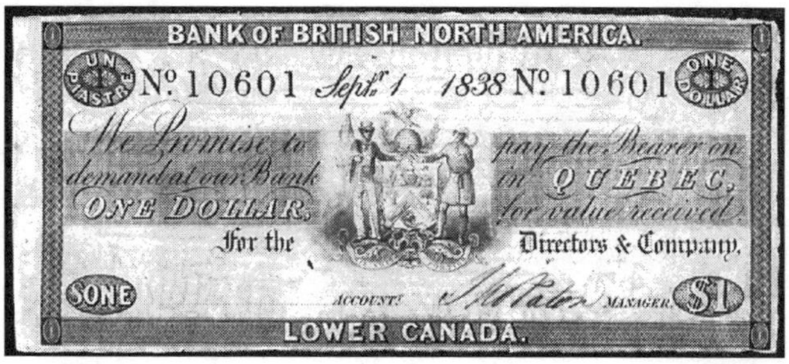

55-10-06-02

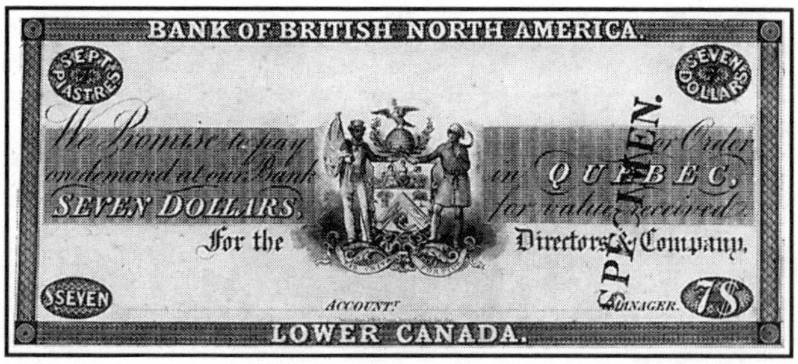

55-10-06-10P

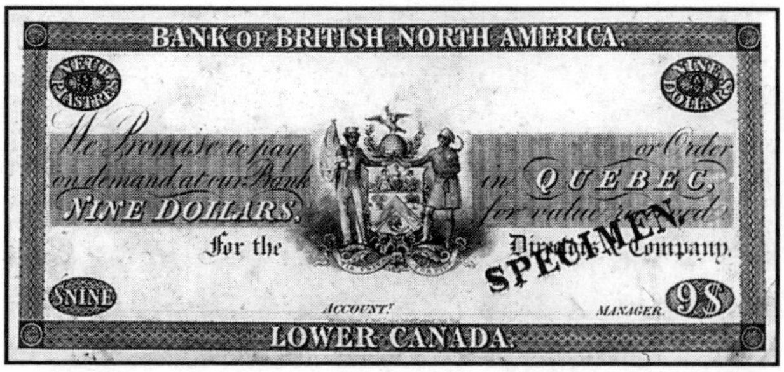

55-10-06-12P

ISSUE DATING

Entire date added letterpress with serial numbers:
Sept. 1 1838

CIRCULATING NOTES

Cat.No.	Denom.	Date	G	VG	F	VF	EF
10-06-02	$1	1838	400.	800.	1,000.	1,500	—
10-06-10	$7	no date	No known issued notes				
10-06-12	$9	no date	No known issued notes				

PROOF NOTES

Cat. No.	Denom.	Date		Unc
10-06-10P	$7	no date	PROOF	1,600.
10-06-12P	$9	no date	PROOF	1,600.

7. QUEBEC BRANCH ISSUE

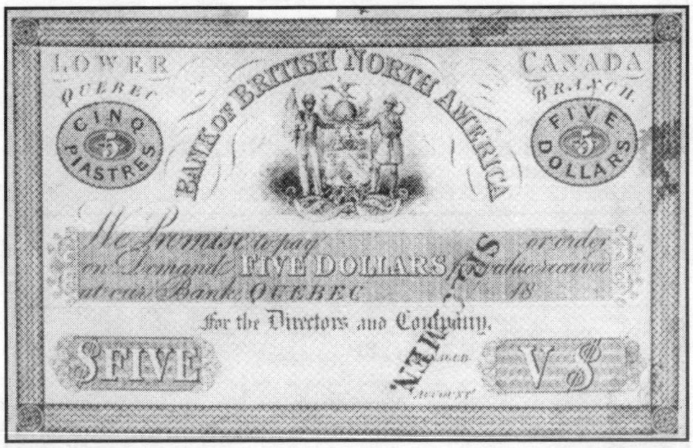

55-10-07-08P

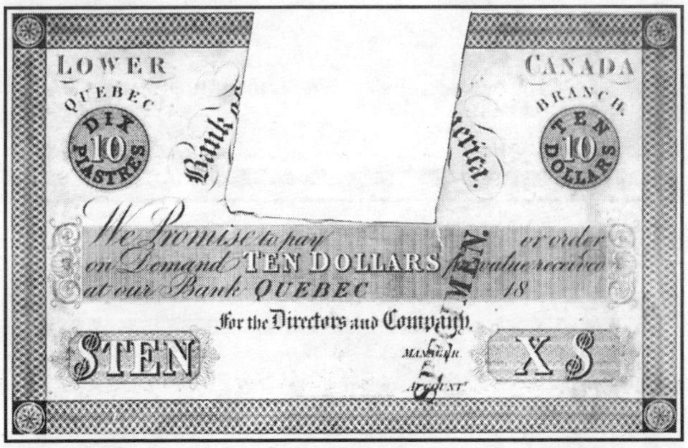

55-10-07-14P

55-10-07-30P

ISSUE DATING

Partially Engraved ___ 18 ___:

PROOF NOTES

Cat.No.	Denom	Date		Unc
10-07-08P	$5	18__	PROOF	500.
10-07-14P	$10	18__	PROOF	500.
10-07-30P	$50	18__	PROOF	650.

8. "ST. JOHN, NEW BRUNSWICK" ISSUE

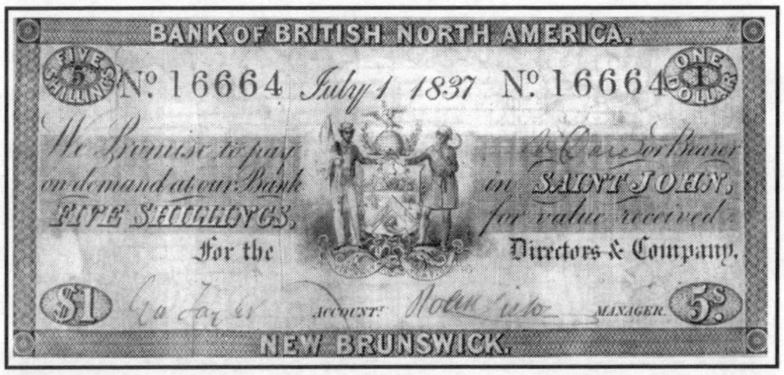

55-10-08-02

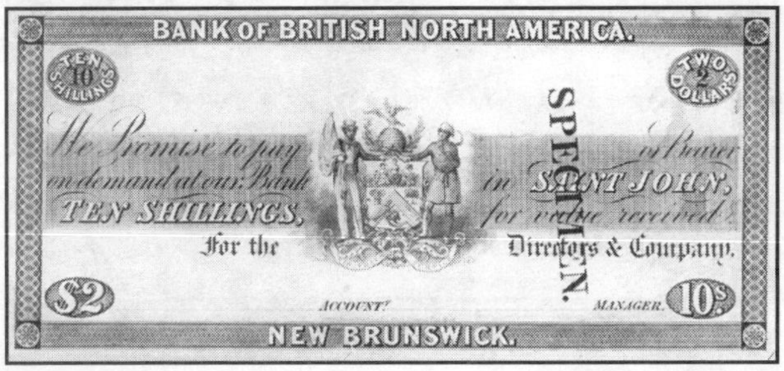

55-10-08-04P

ISSUE DATING

Entire date added letterpress with serial numbers:
July 1 1837

CIRCULATING NOTES

Cat.No.	Denom.	Date	G	VG	F	VF	EF
10-08-02	$1(5s)	1837	500.	1,000.	1,250.	1,750.	—
10-08-04	$2(10s)	no date	No known issued notes				
10-08-06	$4 (20s)	no date	No known issued notes				
10-08-08	$5 (25s)	no date	No known issued notes				
10-08-14	$10 (50s)	no date	No known issued notes				
10-08-20	$50 (£12.10)	no date	No known issued notes				

PROOF NOTES

Cat. No.	Denom.	Date		Unc
10-08-04P	$2 (10s)	no date	PROOF	850.
10-08-06P	$4 (20s)	no date	PROOF	850.
10-08-08P	$5 (25s)	no date	PROOF	850.
10-08-14P	$10 (50s)	no date	PROOF	850.
10-08-20P	$50 (£12.10)	no date	PROOF	850.

10. "ST. JOHN'S, NEWFOUNDLAND" ISSUE LARGE SIZE NOTES (21.5 x 14 cm.)

55-10-10-01P

55-10-10-02P

55-10-10-04P

ISSUE DATING

Partially Engraved__18__:

1837: Mar. 20

Engraved

1st of July. 1847

CIRCULATING NOTES

Cat.No.	Denom.	Date	G	VG	F	VF	EF
10-10-01	10s	18__			No known issued notes		
10-10-02	£1	1837	1,000.	2,000.	2,600.	—	—
10-10-04	£5	1847			No known issued notes		
10-10-08	£20	18__			No known issued notes		

PROOF NOTES

Cat. No.	Denom.	Date		Unc
10-10-01P	10s	18__	PROOF	800.
10-10-02P	£1	18__	PROOF	800.
10-10-04P	£5	1847	PROOF	800.
10-10-08P	£20	18__	PROOF	800.

12. "TORONTO, UPPER CANADA BRANCH" ISSUE

55-10-12-02P

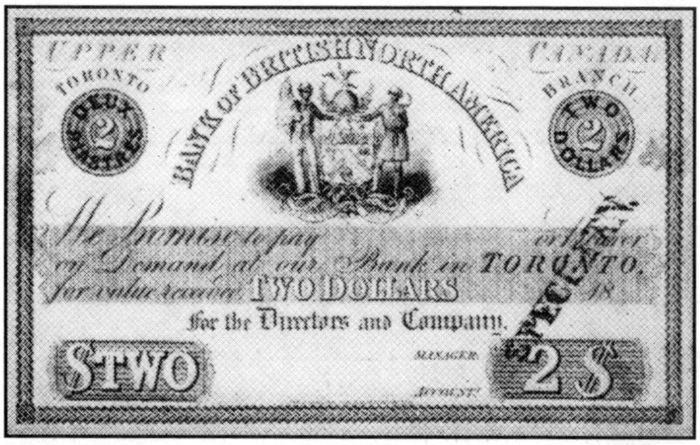

55-10-12-04P

55-10-12-08P

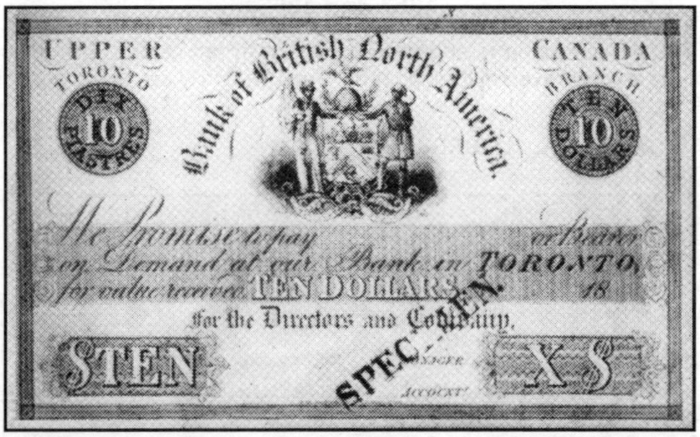

55-10-12-14P

ISSUE DATING

Partially Engraved__18__:

PROOF NOTES

Cat.No.	Denom.	Date		Unc
10-12-02P	$1	18__	PROOF	800.
10-12-04P	$2	18__	PROOF	800.
10-12-08P	$5	18__	PROOF	800.
10-12-14P	$10	18__	PROOF	800.

55-12. "MINIATURE ROYAL CREST" ISSUES 1841-1872

Notes of these issues have a miniature Royal Crest at the bottom centre and a complete frame.

2. "BRANTFORD" ISSUE

The branch name is engraved at the lower left centre and vertically inside the right and left vignettes.

DESIGNS AND COLOURS

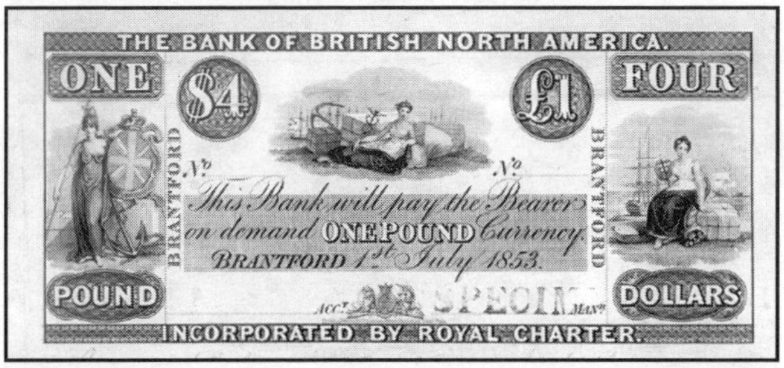

55-12-02-02P

$4 (£1) Face Design: Britannia/reclining "Commerce" figure/ Seated "Commerce" figure

Colour: Black with no tint

Back Design: Plain

55-12-02-04

$5(£1.5) Face Design: Bank Crest/beehive/sheep, plough in foreground

Colour: Black with no tint

Back Design: Plain

IMPRINT

Perkins, Bacon & Petch, London

ISSUE DATING

Engraved

5th July 1852

1st July 1853

PROTECTOR

$5: (£1.5) Green word and numeral on face and back

CIRCULATING NOTES

Cat.No.	Denom.	Date	G	VG	F	VF	EF
12-02-02	$4(£1)	1853	No known issued notes				
12-02-04	$5(£1.5)	1852	400.	800.	1,000.	1.500.	—

PROOF NOTES

Cat. No.	Denom.	Date		Unc
12-02-02P	$4 (£1)	1853	PROOF	400.

4. "FREDERICTON NEW BRUNSWICK" ISSUE

The branch name is engraved at the lower left centre and vertically inside the right and left vignettes.

DESIGNS AND COLOURS

55-12-04-02P

£1 Face Design: Britannia/beehive/seated "Commerce" figure

Colour: Black with no tint

Back Design: Plain

IMPRINT

Perkins, Bacon & Petch, London

ISSUE DATING

Engraved

1st Septr 1847

PROOF NOTES

Cat.No.	Denom.	Date		Unc
12-04-02P	£1	1847	PROOF	500.

5. "HALIFAX" ISSUE

The branch name is engraved at the lower left of centre and vertically at the ends.

DESIGNS AND COLOURS

55-12-05-04P

£5 Face Design: Seated Indian/ships/Britannia
Colour: Black with no tint

Back Design: Plain

IMPRINT

Perkins, Bacon & Co., London

ISSUE DATING

Partially Engraved__18__:

PROOF NOTES

Cat.No.	Denom.	Date		Unc
12-05-04P	£5	18__	PROOF	500.

6. HAMILTON "BRANTFORD" AGENCY ISSUE

DESIGNS AND COLOURS

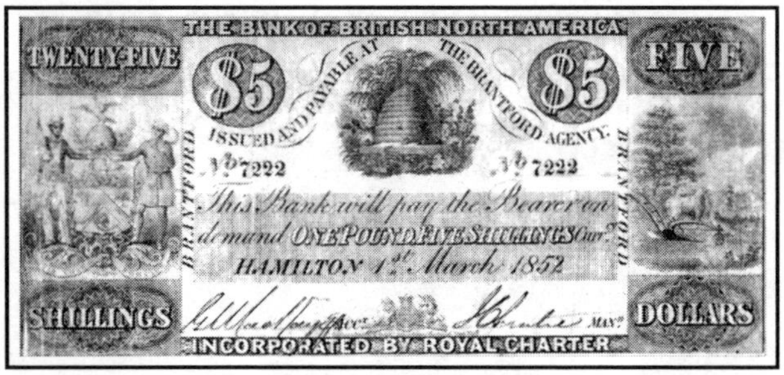

55-12-06-02

$5(25s) Face Design: Bank Crest/beehive/ sheep, plough in foreground
Colour: Black with no tint

Back Design: Plain

IMPRINT

Perkins, Bacon & Co. London

ISSUE DATING

Engraved

1st March 1852

Cat.No.	Denom.	Date	G	VG	F	VF	EF	Unc
12-06-02	$5(25s)	1852	400.	800.	1,000.	1,500.	—	—

8. HAMILTON "DUNDAS" AGENCY ISSUES 1853 and 1856

The branch name is engraved at the lower left centre. The agency names are engraved at the upper right and vertically inside the right and left vignettes.

DESIGNS AND COLOURS

55-12-08-04P

$4 (£1) Face Design: Standing female with beehive and ship/ Two allegorical females/Bank Crest
Colour: Black with no tint

Back Design: Plain

55-12-08-06P

$5 (£1.5) Face Design: Brittania/ships/seated "Commerce" figure in floral frame
Colour: Black with no tint

Back Design: Plain

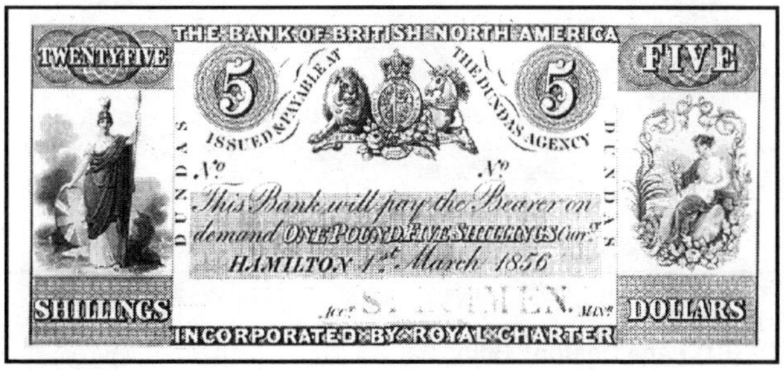

55-12-08-08P

$5 (£1.5) Face Design: Brittania/Royal Crest/seated "Commerce" figure in floral frame
Colour: Black with no tint

Back Design: Plain

55-12-08-10P

$10 (£2.10) Face Design: Sheep, plough in foreground/cherubs/Indian camp

Colour: Black with no tint

Back Design: Plain

IMPRINT

Perkins, Bacon & Co. London

ISSUE DATING

Engraved

1st March 1852
2nd Feby 1853
1st March 1856

PROOF NOTES

Cat.No.	Denom.	Date		Unc
12-08-04P	$4(£1)	18__	PROOF	400.
12-08-06P	$5(£1.5)	1852	PROOF	400.
12-08-08P	$5(£1.5)	1856	PROOF	400.
12-08-10P	$10(£2.10)	1853	PROOF	400.

10. HAMILTON "SIMCOE" AGENCY ISSUE

The branch name is engraved at the lower left centre. The agency names are engraved at the upper right and vertically inside the right and left vignettes.

DESIGNS AND COLOURS

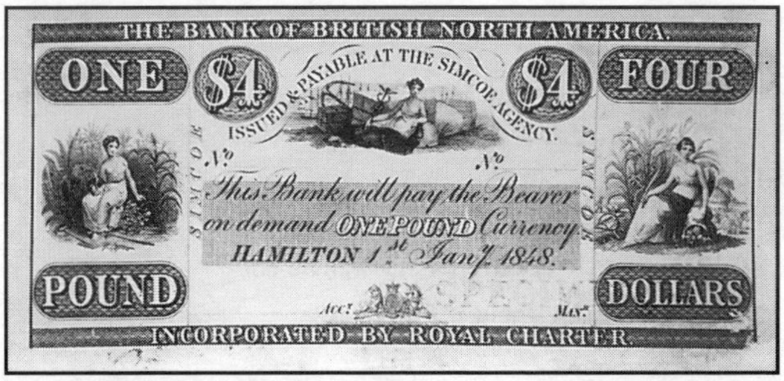

55-12-10-04P

$4 (£1) Face Design: Seated "Agriculture" figure/reclining "Commerce" figure/seated "Agriculture" figure

Colour: Black with no tint

Back Design: Plain

Photo Not Available

55-12-10-06P

$5 (£1.5) Face Design: Unknown

Colour: Black with no tint

Back Design: Plain

IMPRINT

Perkins, Bacon & Co. London

ISSUE DATING

Engraved

Jan.1, 1845
1st Jany 1848

CIRCULATING NOTES

Cat.No.	Denom.	Date	G	VG	F	VF	EF
12-10-02	$4(£1)	1845	400.	800.	1,000.	1,500.	—
12-10-04	$4(£1)	1848	No known issued notes				
12-10-06	$5(£1.5)	1848	No known issued notes				

PROOF NOTES

Cat. No.	Denom.	Date		Inc
12-10-04P	$4 (£1)	1848	PROOF	400.
12-10-06P	$5 (£1.5)	1848	PROOF	400.

12. "HAMILTON" BRANCH ISSUE

DEIGNS AND COLOURS

The branch name is engraved at the lower left centre and vertically at the ends.

55-12-12-04

$4 (£1) Face Design: Reclining allegorical female/three seated allegorical women/seated Indian

Colour: Black with no tint

Back Design: Plain

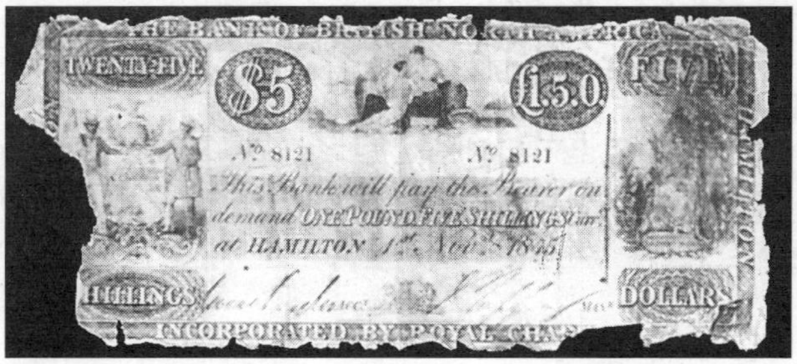

55-12-12-08

$5 (£1.5.0) Face Design: Bank Crest/seated allegorical female with one arm on beehive and the other around "Commerce" figure/Queen Victoria on throne

Colour: Black with no tint

Back Design: Plain

55-12-12-12

$10 (£2.10) Face Design: "Agriculture" figure in circle/sheep, plough in foreground/beehive/ commerce figures
Colour: Black with no tint
Back Design: Plain

Photo Not Available

55-12-12-14P

$50 (£12.10) Face Design: Seated "Justice" figure, fasces/Royal Arms/"Commerce" figure with lute
Colour: Black with no tint

Back Design: Plain

IMPRINT

Perkins, Bacon & Co., London

ISSUE DATING

Engraved

1st Novr 1845
1st Novr 1852
May 1, 1853
May 1, 1855
1st March 1856

PROTECTOR

Issued Notes of the 1850s: Blue "word" across mock coins on the face only
$4 (£1) 1852: Green "word" on face and back

OVERPRINT

$4 (£1) 1855: PARIS in blue

CIRCULATING NOTES

Cat.No.	Denom.	Date	G	VG	F	VF	EF
12-12-02	$4(£1)	1845	400.	800.	1,000.	1,500.	—
12-12-04	$4(£1)	1852	400.	800.	1,000.	1,500.	—
12-12-06	$4(£1)	1855	400.	800.	1,000.	1,500.	—
12-12-08	$5(£1.5)	1845	400.	800.	1,000.	1,500.	—
12-12-10	$5(£1.5)	1855	400.	800.	1,000.	1,500.	—
12-12-12	$10(£2.10)	1853	400.	800.	1,000.	1,500.	—
12-12-14	$50 (£12.10)	1856		No known issued notes			

PROOF NOTES

Cat. No.	Denom.	Date		Unc
12-12-14P	$50(£12.10)	1856	PROOF	400.

14. "KINGSTON" ISSUE

The Branch name is engraved at the lower left centre and vertically inside the right and left vignettes.

DESIGNS AND COLOURS

55-12-14-08

$4 Face Design: Seated Indian/reclining "Commerce" figure/ seated woman with cornucopia, corn and cattle in background
Colour: Black with no tint

Back Design: Plain

55-12-14-12

$5 Face Design: Queen Victoria on throne/two seated allegorical women holding hands/ seated Indian
Colour: Black, with no tint

Back Design: Plain

Photo Not Available

55-12-14-14P

$10 Face Design: View of city and harbour/two seated allegorical women/Bank Crest
Colour: Back with no tint

Back Design: Plain

55-12-14-16P

$20 Face Design: Britannia/small seated "Commerce" figure/ view of city and harbour
Colour: Black with no tint

Back Design: Plain

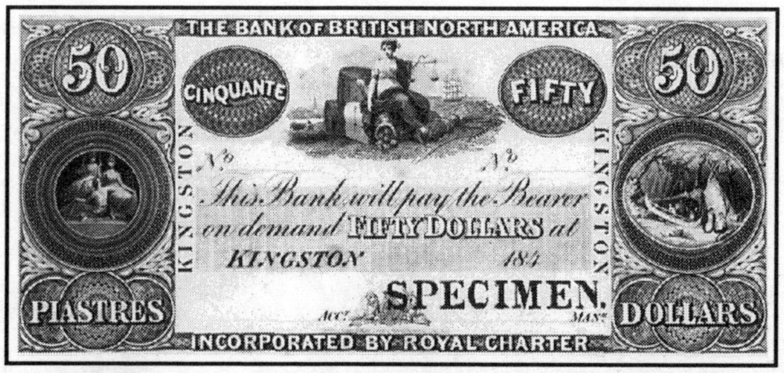

55-12-14-18P

$50 Face Design: Small "Commerce", Britannia and Agriculture figures in circle/seated allegorical woman with cornucopia and balance/Indians, canoe, teepee

Colour: Black with no tint

Back Design: Plain

IMPRINT

Perkins, Bacon & Co. London
Perkins, Bacon & Petch, London

ISSUE DATING

Partially Engraved:__18__:

Remainder of date added letterpress with serial numbers: __18__: Feb 1, 1852

Entire date added letterpress with serial numbers: ________________: July 1, 1853

Engraved

$4: 1st July 1853
$5: Aug. 4, 1852

PROTECTOR

Some Notes of the 1850's: Green "word" on face and back

CIRCULATING NOTES

Cat.No.	Denom.	Date		G	VG	F	VF	EF
12-14-02	$4	1852		400.	800.	1,000.	1,500.	—
12-14-06R	$4	1853	no ptr*	—	—	—	—	800.
12-14-08	$4	1853	Green ptr.	400.	800.	1,000.	1,500.	—
12-14-12	$5	1852		400.	800.	1,000.	1,500.	—
12-14-14	$10	184_			No known issued notes			
12-14-16	$20	184_			No known issued notes			
12-14-18	$50	184_			No known issued notes			

* Remainder - unsigned, dated and numbered.

PROOF NOTES

Cat. No.	Denom.	Date		Unc
12-14-02P	$4	184_	PROOF	400.
12-14-10P	$5	184_	PROOF	400.
12-14-14P	$10	184_	PROOF	400.
12-14-16P	$20	184_	PROOF	400.
12-14-18P	$50	184_	PROOF	400.

16. "LONDON" ISSUE

The branch name is engraved at the lower left and vertically inside the right and left end vignettes.

DESIGNS AND COLOURS

55-12-16-02P

$4 (£1) Face Design: Seated Britannia with lion and anchor/ Bank Crest/seated "Justice" figure, fasces

Colour: Black with no tint

Back Design: Plain

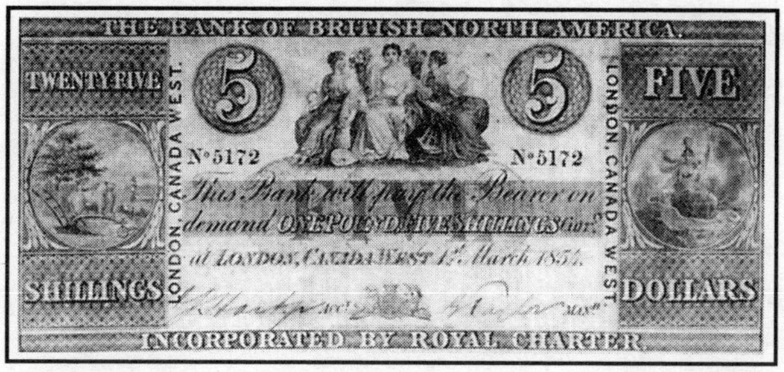

55-12-16-06

$5 (25s) Face Design: Sheep, plough in foreground/three seated allegorical women/small Britannia seated on shell in water

Colour: Black with no tint

Back Design: Plain

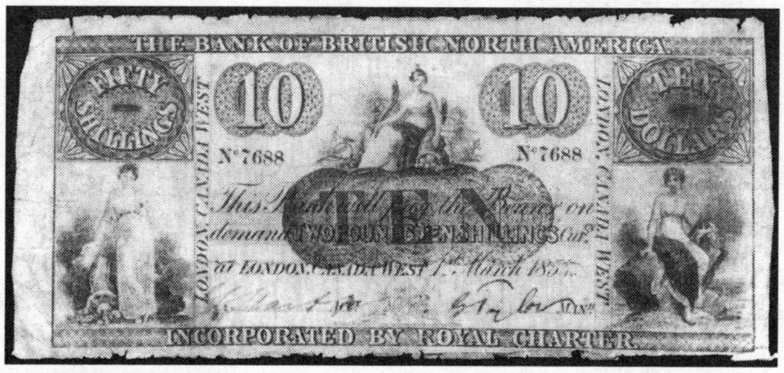

55-12-16-08

$10 (50s) Face Design: "Agriculture" figure with cornucopia/seated "Agriculture" figure with cornucopia/woman seated with hand on harp

Colour: Black with no tint

Back Design: Plain

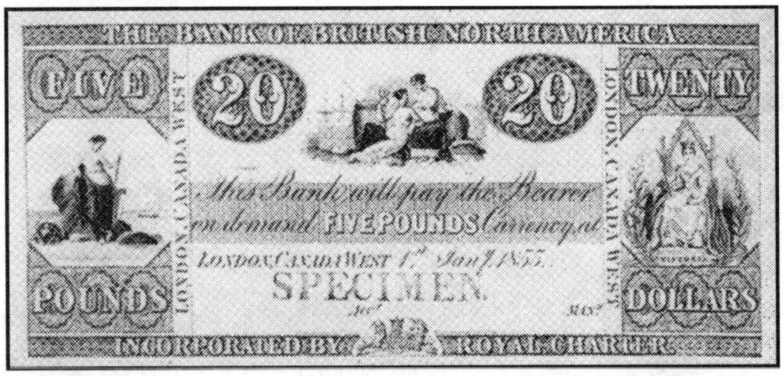

55-12-16-10P

$20 Face Design: Commerce figure and ship/commerce allegory/Victoria on throne
Colour: Black with no tint

Back Design: Plain

55-12-16-12P

$50 Face Design: Agricultural figure/harvest figure/ commerce figure
Colour: Black with no tint

Back Design: Plain

IMPRINT

Perkins, Bacon & Co London.

ISSUE DATING

Engraved

1st March 1854
1st Jany 1855
1st Jan 1856

PROTECTOR

Issued Notes: Blue "word" on mock coins on face only

OVERPRINT

1856: "NAPANEE" in red

CIRCULATING NOTES

Cat.No.	Denom.	Date	G	VG	F	VF	EF
12-16-02	$4(£1)	1854	No known issued notes				
12-16-04	$4(£1)	1856	400.	800.	1,000.	1,500.	—
12-16-06	$5(25s)	1854	400.	800.	1,000.	1,500.	—
12-16-08	$10(50s)	1854	400.	800.	1,000.	1,500.	—
12-16-10	$20(£5)	1855	No known issued notes				
12-16-12	$50(£12.10)	1855	No known issued notes				

PROOF NOTES

Cat. No.	Denom.	Date		Unc
12-16-02P	$4 (£1)	1854	PROOF	400.
12-16-10P	$20 (£5)	1855	PROOF	400.
12-16-12P	$50 (£12.10)	1855	PROOF	400.

17. MONTREAL "BYTOWN" AGENCY ISSUE

The branch name is engraved at the lower left centre. The agency name is engraved at the upper centre and vertically inside the left and right vignettes.

DESIGN AND COLOURS

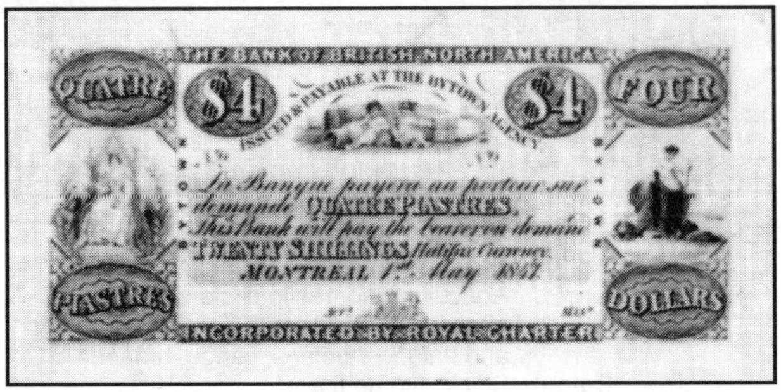

55-12-17-06P

$4 (20s) Face Design: Queen Victoria on throne/cherubs/agriculture figure, cornucopia
Colour: Black with no tint

Back Design: Plain

IMPRINT

Perkins, Bacon & Co., London

ISSUE DATING

Engraved

1st May 1847

PROOF NOTES

Cat.No.	Denom.	Date		Unc
12-17-06P	$4(20s)	1847	PROOF	400.

18. "MONTREAL" ISSUE

The branch name is engraved at the lower left and vertically inside the right and left end vignettes.

DESIGN AND COLOURS

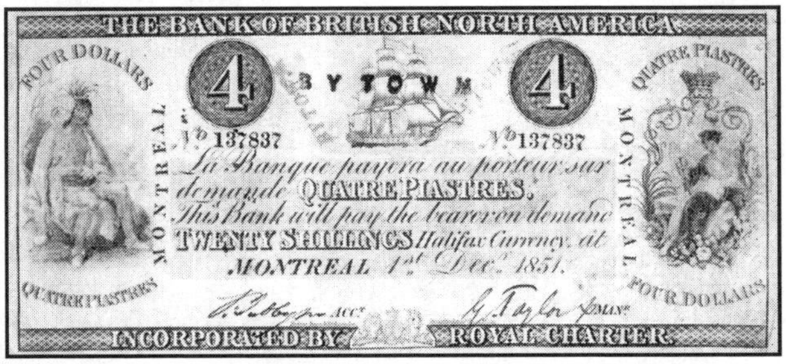

55-12-18-22

$4 (20s) Face Design: Seated Indian/sailing ship/ seated "Commerce" figure in crowned frame
Colour: Black with no tint

Back Design: Plain

55-12-18-52
$5 (£1.5) Face Design: Brocks monument/sailing ship/Queen Victoria on throne
Colour: Black with no tint
Back Design: Plain

55-12-18-62P
$10 (£2.10) Face Design: Indian camp/seated "Commerce" figure/view of harbour entrance
Colour: Black with no tint
Back Design: Plain

55-12-18-72P
$20 (£5) Face Design: View of Montreal buildings/three allegorical women/monument, houses
Colour: Black with no tint
Back Design: Plain

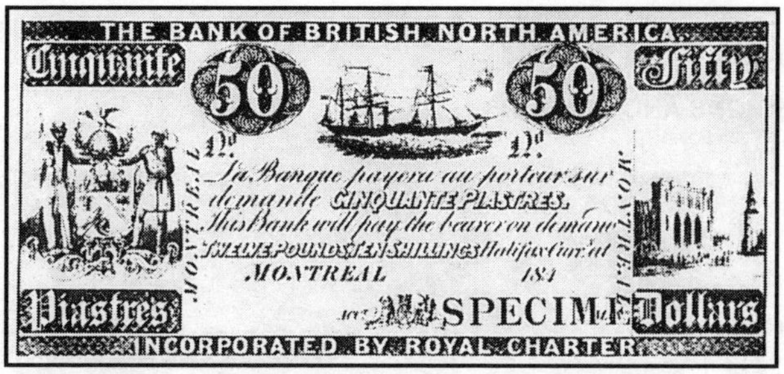

55-12-18-82P
$50 (£12.10) Face Design: Bank Crest/steamship/view of Montreal buildings
Colour: Back with no tint
Back Design: Plain

IMPRINT
Perkins, Bacon & Petch, London

ISSUE DATING
Partially Engraved__18__:
$4 (20s) 1841: Jan. 1
1847: Jan. 1
Partially Engraved __184__:
$4 (20s) & $5 (£1.5) 1841: Jan. 1
$20 (£5) 1847: Jan 1
Engraved
1st Decr 1851
1st Decr 1852
1st Jany 1854

PROTECTOR
1852 & 1854 Green "word" on face and back
Green "word" on mock coins, face only

OVERPRINT
$4 (20s): "BYTOWN" in black and red
$4 (20s): "PARIS" in black and red
$20 (£5): "PAYABLE IN OTTAWA" in red

CIRCULATING NOTES

Cat.No.	Denom.	Date	G	VG	F	VF	EF
12-18-02	$4(20s)	1841	400.	800.	1,000.	1,500	—
12-18-12	$4(20s)	1847	400.	800.	1,000.	1,500	—
12-18-22	$4(20s)	1851	400.	800.	1,000.	1,500	—
12-18-32	$4(20s)	1852	400.	800.	1,000.	1,500	—
12-18-42	$5(£1.5)	1841	400.	800.	1,000.	1,500	—
12-18-52	$5(£1.5)	1854	400.	800.	1,000.	1,500	—
12-18-62	$10(£2.10)	184-	No known issued notes				
12-18-72	$20(£5)	1847	400.	800.	1,000.	1,500.	—
12-18-82	$50(£12.10)	184-	No known issued notes				

PROOF NOTES

Cat. No.	Denom.	Date		Unc
12-18-22P	$4 (20s)	1851	PROOF	400.
12-18-62P	$10 (£2.10)	184_	PROOF	400.
12-18-72P	$20 (£5)	184_	PROOF	400.
12-18-82P	$50 (£12.10)	184_	PROOF	400.

20. "QUEBEC" ISSUE

The branch name is engraved at the lower left and vertically at the ends.

DESIGNS AND COLOURS

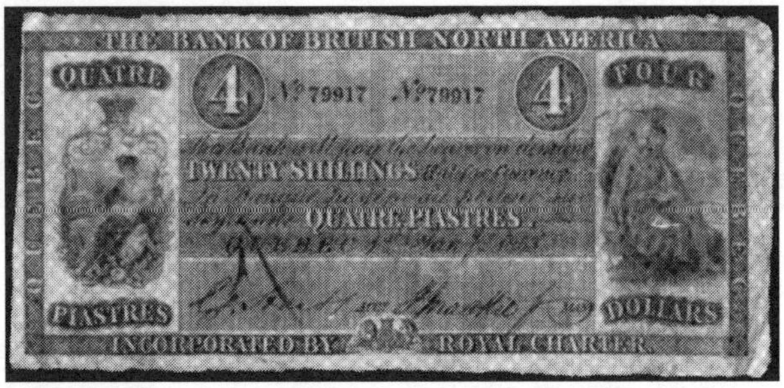

55-12-20-04P
$4 (20s) Face Design: Seated "Commerce" figure in crowned frame/—/seated Indian
Colour: Black with no tint

Back Design: Plain

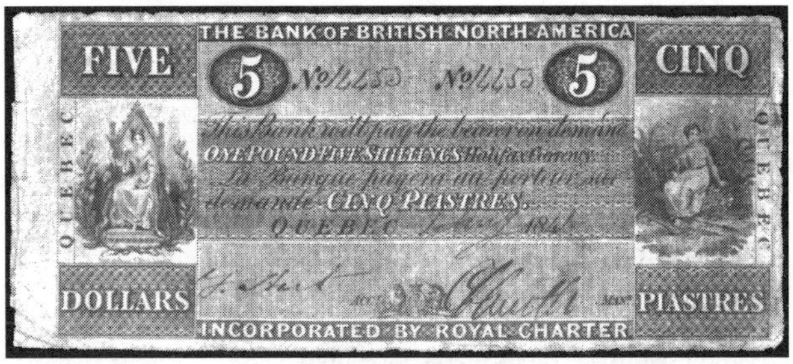

55-12-20-06
$5 (£1.5) Face Design: Queen Victoria on throne/—/seated "Commerce" figure with sickle, field in background
Colour: Black with no tint

Back Design: Plain

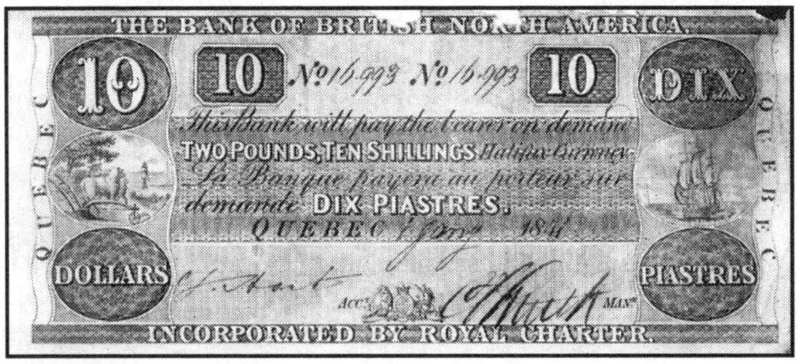

55-12-20-08
$10 (£2.10) Face Design: Sheep and plough/—/sailing ship
Colour: Black with no tint

Back Design: Plain

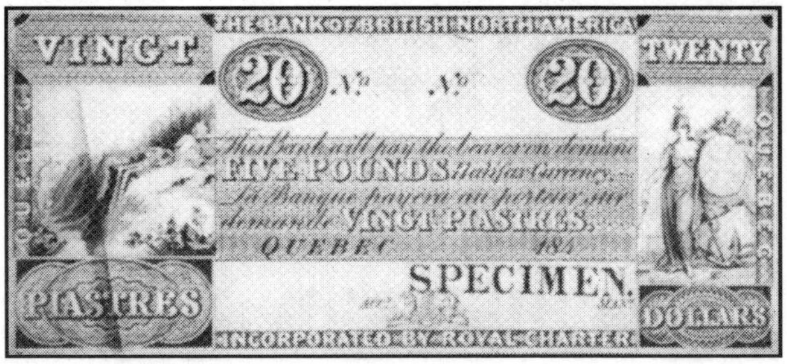

55-12-20-10P
£5 Face Design: Falls/—/Britannia
Colour: Black with no tint

Back Design: Plain

IMPRINT
Perkins, Bacon, Petch, London

ISSUE DATING
Partially Engraved ___18___:
$4:
$5 & $10 1841: 1 Jany
Partially Engraved ___184__:
Engraved
1 Jany, 1853

CIRCULATING NOTES

Cat.No.	Denom.	Date	G	VG	F	VF	EF
12-20-04	$4(20s)	1853	400.	800.	1,000.	1,500.	—
12-20-06	$5(£1.5)	1841	400.	800.	1,000.	1,500.	—
12-20-08	$10(£2.10)	1841	400.	800.	1,000.	1,500.	—
12-20-10	$20(£5)	184_	No known issued notes				

PROOF NOTES

Cat. No.	Denom.	Date		Unc
12-20-04P	$4 (20s)	18__	PROOF	400.
12-20-10P	$20 (£5)	184_	PROOF	400.

22. "ST. JOHN, NEW BRUNSWICK" ISSUE

The branch name is engraved at the lower left and vertically inside the right and left end vignettes.

DESIGNS AND COLOURS

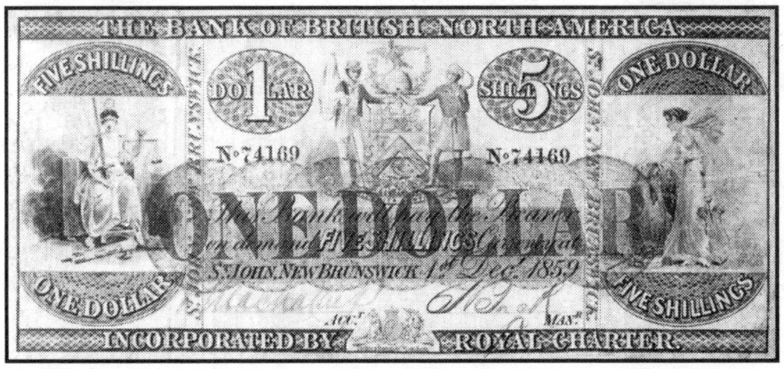

55-12-22-02
$1 (5s) Face Design: Seated "Justice" figure, fasces/ "Bank Crest/Commerce" figure with lute "1" over Dollar" in oval left, "5" over "Shillings" in oval right
Colour: Black with no tint

Back Design: Plain

55-12-22-04
$1 (5s) Face Design: Seated "Justice" figure, fasces/ Bank Crest/"Commerce" figure with lute
Colour: Black with no tint

Back Design: Plain

55-12-22-06
$2 (10s) Face Design: Small Britannia seated on shell in water/ small seated "Commerce" figure/small "Commerce", Britannia and "Agriculture" figures in circle
Colour: Black with no tint

Back Design: Plain

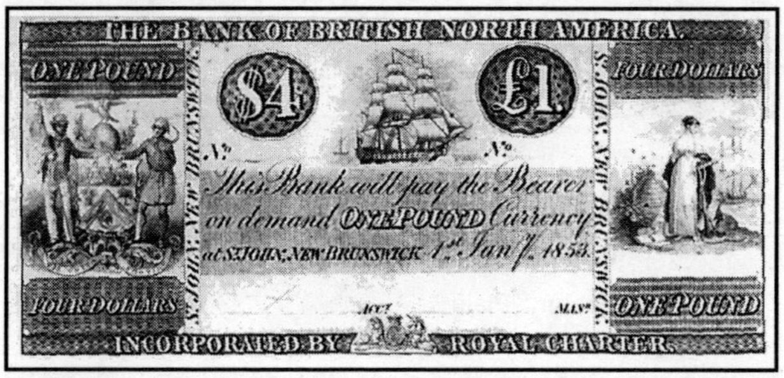

55-12-22-08P
$4 (£1) Face Design: Bank Crest/ship/woman with anchor and beehive
Colour: Black with no tint

Back Design: Plain

55-12-22-12
$5 (£1.5) Face Design: Bank Crest/ship/woman with anchor and beehive
Colour: Black with no tint

Back Design: Plain

Photo Not Available

55-12-22-14P
$20 (£5) Face Design: Queen Victoria (Chalon portrait)/two allegorical women/reclining women with ship in the distance
Colour: Black with no tint

Back Design: Plain

Photo Not Available

55-12-22-16P
$40 (£10) Face Design: Queen Victoria (Chalon portrait)/Bank Crest/—
Colour: Black with no tint

Back Design: Plain

IMPRINT

Perkins, Bacon & Co. London

ISSUE DATING

Engraved

1st Jany. 1853
2nd Jany. 1854
1st Decr. 1859
1st Decr. 1862
1st Sept. 1869
2nd Jany. 1871

PROTECTOR

Issued Notes: Green "word" on mock coins on face only

OVERPRINT

$5: "V V" in red

CIRCULATING NOTES

Cat.No.	Denom.	Date	G	VG	F	VF	EF
12-22-01	$1(5s)	1854	No known issued notes				
12-22-02	$1(5s)	1859	375.	750.	925.	1,400.	—
12-22-04	$1(5s)	1862	375.	750.	925.	1,400.	—
12-22-06	$2(10s)	1854	375.	750.	925.	1,400.	—
12-22-08	$4(£1)	1853	No known issued notes				
12-22-10	$4(£1)	1871	No known issued notes				
12-22-12	$5(£1.5)	1862	375.	750.	925.	1,400.	—
12-22-13	$5(£1.5)	1869	No known issued notes				
12-22-14	$20(£5)	18__	No known issued notes				
12-22-16	$40(£10)	18__	No known issued notes				

PROOF NOTES

Cat. No.	Denom.	Date		Unc
12-22-01P	$1 (5s)	1854	PROOF	400.
12-22-08P	$4 (£1)	1853	PROOF	500.
12-22-10P	$4 (£1)	1871	PROOF	500.
12-22-13P	$5 (£1.5)	1869	PROOF	400.
12-22-14P	$20 (£5)	18__	PROOF	500.
12-22-16P	$40 (£10)	18__	PROOF	800.

24. "ST. STEPHEN NEW BRUNSWICK" ISSUE

The branch name is engraved at the lower left and vertically inside the right and left end vignettes.

DESIGNS AND COLOURS

55-12-24-02P
$4 (£1) Face Design: Bank Crest/ship/woman with anchor and beehive
Colour: Black with no tint
Back Design: Plain

IMPRINT
Perkins, Bacon & Petch, London

ISSUE DATING
Engraved
12th Augt 1872

PROOF NOTES

Cat.No.	Denom.	Date		Unc
12-24-02P	$4(£1)	1872	PROOF	500.

26. "TORONTO" DOLLAR ISSUE

The branch name is engraved at the centre left and vertically at the ends.

DESIGNS AND COLOURS

Photo Not Available

55-12-26-02P
$4 Face Design: Unknown
Colour: Black with no tint
Back Design: Plain

55-12-26-04P
$5 Face Design: River, cliffs & tower/—/seated "Commerce" figure in crowned frame
Colour: Black with no tint
Back Design: Plain

55-12-26-06P
$10 Face Design: Canadian Niagara Falls/—/Queen Victoria on throne
Colour: Black with no tint
Back Design: Plain

55-12-26-08P
$20 Face Design: Bank Crest/—/Canadian Niagara Falls
Colour: Black with no tint
Back Design: Plain

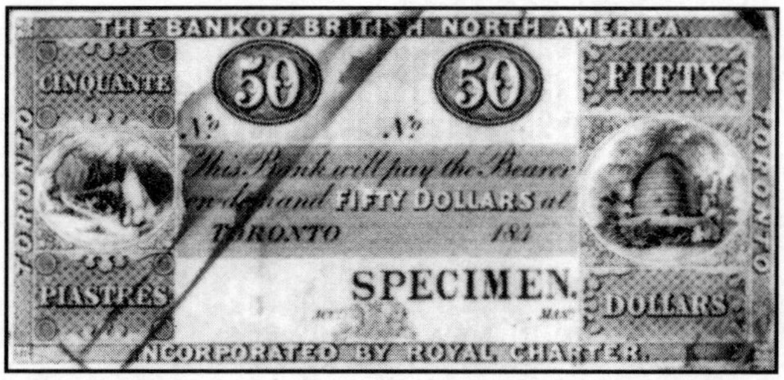

55-12-26-10P

$50 Face Design: Indian camp/—/Beehive with flowers
Colour: Black with no tint

Back Design: Plain

IMPRINT

Perkins, Bacon & Petch, London.

ISSUE DATING

Partially Engraved__184__:

PROOF NOTES

Cat.No.	Denom.	Date		Unc
12-26-02P	$4	184-	PROOF	600.
12-26-04P	$5	184-	PROOF	600.
12-26-06P	$10	184-	PROOF	600.
12-26-08P	$20	184-	PROOF	600.
12-26-10P	$50	184-	PROOF	600.

28. "TORONTO" DOLLAR/ POUNDS AND SHILLINGS ISSUE

The branch name is engraved at the centre left and verticaly at the ends.

DESIGNS AND COLOURS

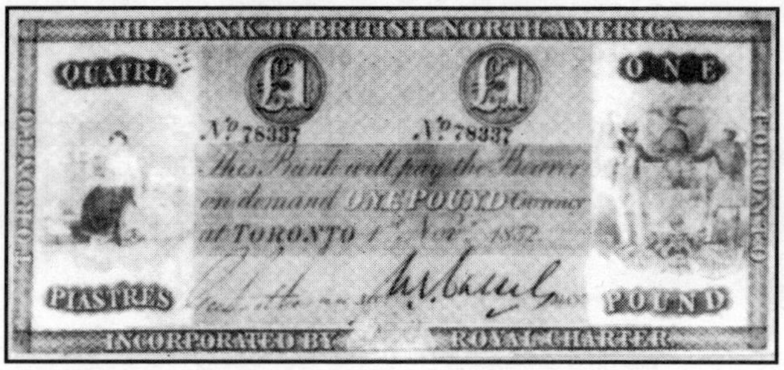

55-12-28-04

$4 (£1) Face Design: Seated 'Commerce" figure/—/Bank crest
Colour: Black with no tint

Back Design: Plain

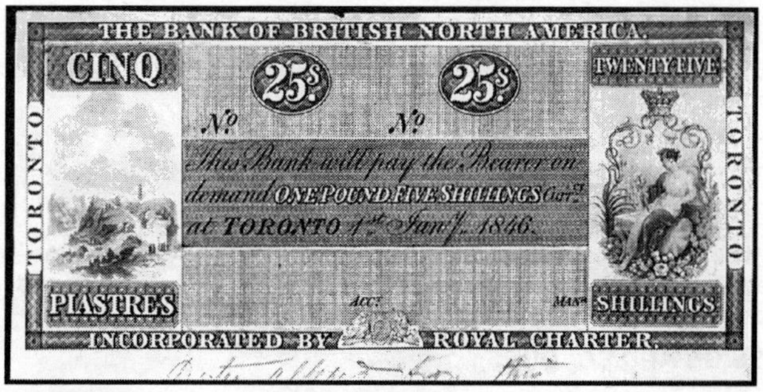

55-12-28-06P

$5 (25s) Face Design: River, cliffs & tower/—/ seated "Commerce" figure in crowded frame
Colour: Black with no tint

Back Design: Plain

Photo Not Available

55-12-28-08P

$5 (25s) Face Design: Seated "Commerce" figure/—/Bank Crest
Colour: Black with no tint

Back Design: Plain

Photo Not Available

55-12-28-10

$10 (50s) Face Design: Canadian Niagara Falls/—/Queen Victoria on throne
Colour: Black with no tint

Back Design: Plain

ISSUE DATING

Engraved

1st Jany 1846
1st Novr 1852
Unknown, 1864
Jan 4, 1865

CIRCULATING NOTES

Cat.No.	Denom.	Date	G	VG	F	VF	EF
12-28-02	$4(£1)	1846			No known issued notes		
12-28-04	$4(£1)	1852	375.	750.	925.	1,400.	—
12-28-06	$5(£1.5s)(25s)	1846			No known issued notes		
12-28-08	$5(25s)	1865			No known issued notes		
12-28-10	$10(50s)	1864	375.	750.	925	1,400.	—

PROOF NOTES

Cat. No.	Denom.	Date		Unc
12-28-02P	$4 (£1)	1846	PROOF	400.
12-28-06P	$5 (£1.5) (25s)	1846	PROOF	400.
12-28-08P	$5 (25s)	1865	PROOF	400.

55-13 LARGE ROYAL CREST ISSUE 1856

Notes of these issues have a large royal crest at the top centre and a complete frame.

10. HAMILTON "DUNDAS" AGENCY ISSUE 1856

The branch name is engraved at lower left of centre. The agency names are engraved at upper right and vertically inside the right and left vignettes.

DESIGN AND COLOURS

55-13-10-06P
$5 (£1.5) Face Design: Britannia/Royal Crest/ seated "Commerce" figure in crowned frame
Colour: Back with no tint

Back Design: Plain

IMPRINT
Perkins, Bacon & Co., London

ISSUE DATING
Engraved
1st March 1856

PROOF NOTES

Cat.No.	Denom.	Date		Unc
13-10-06P	$5(£1.5)	1856	PROOF	400.

14. "HAMILTON" ISSUE

The branch name is engraved at lower left of centre and vertically inside the right and left vignettes.

DESIGNS AND COLOURS

55-13-14-20P
$50 (£12.10) Face Design: Seated "Justice" figure, fasces/Royal Crest/"Commerce" figure with lute
Colour: Black with no tint

Back Design: Plain

IMPRINT
Perkins, Bacon & Co., London

ISSUE DATING
Engraved
1st March 1856

PROOF NOTES

Cat.No.	Denom.	Date		Unc
13-14-20P	$50(£12.10)	1856	PROOF	500.

26. "ST. JOHN, NEW BRUNSWICK" ISSUE

The branch name is engraved at the lower left of centre and vertically inside the right and left vignettes.

DESIGNS AND COLOURS

55-13-26-20P
$50 Face Design: Woman standing, cornucopia/Royal Crest/ seated female "Commerce" figure with cask and bale, buildings
Colour: Black with no tint

Back Design: Plain

IMPRINT
Perkins, Bacon & Co. London

ISSUE DATING
Engraved
1st September 1866
1st January 1870

PROOF NOTES

Cat.No.	Denom.	Date		Unc
13-26-20P	$50	1866	PROOF	500.
13-26-24P	$50	1870	PROOF	500.

55-14. "NO FRAME" $1 and $2 ISSUES 1852 - 1868

There are different designs for each place of issue. Notes of these issues lack a frame.

IMPRINT
Perkins, Bacon & Co. London.

ISSUE DATING
Engraved
1st December 1852
1st Decr, 1852
1st January 1856
1st Jany, 1856

2. "BRANTFORD" ISSUE

DESIGNS AND COLOURS

$1: The branch names are located at the upper right and lower left.

$2: The branch names are located at the lower left and one or two ovals at the top.

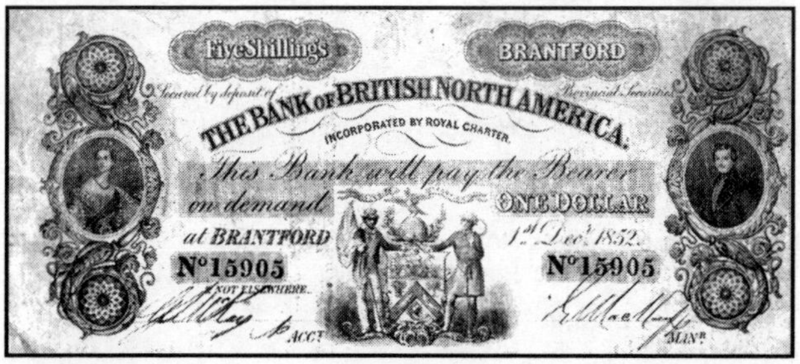

55-14-02-02

$1 (5s) Face Design: Queen Victoria/Bank Crest/Prince Albert
Colour: Black with no tint

Back Design: Plain

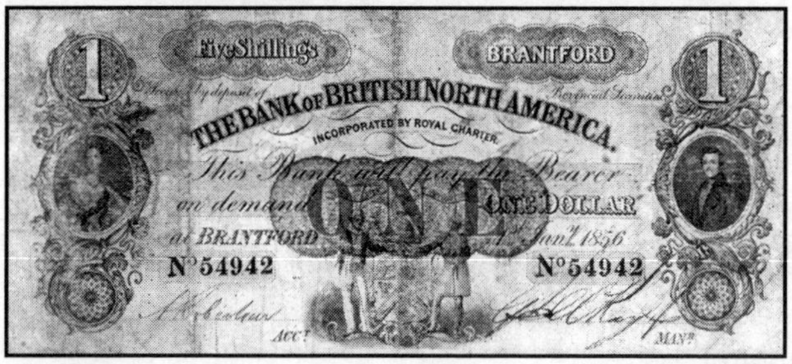

55-14-02-04

$1 (5s) Face Design: Similar to Toronto Issue, see 55-14-16.

Photo Not Available

55-14-02-08

$2 (10s) Face Design: Queen Victoria/ Bank Crest/Prince Albert
Colour: Black with no tint

Back Design: Plain

PROTECTOR

1852: Red numeral on the face only on some notes.
1856: Blue word on mock coins on the face only.

CIRCULATING NOTES

Cat.No.	Denom.	Date	G	VG	F	VF	EF	AU
14-02-02	$1(5s)	1852	400.	800.	1,000.	1,500.	—	—
14-02-04	$1(5s)	1856	400.	800.	1,000.	1,500.	—	—
14-02-06	$2(10s)	1852		No known issued notes				
14-02-08	$2(10s)	1856	400.	800.	1,000.	1,500.	—	—

PROOF NOTES

Cat. No.	Denom.	Date		Unc
14-02-06P	$2(10s)	1852	PROOF	500.

4. "HAMILTON" ISSUE

DESIGNS AND COLOURS

Similar to Brantford Issue, see 55-14-02.

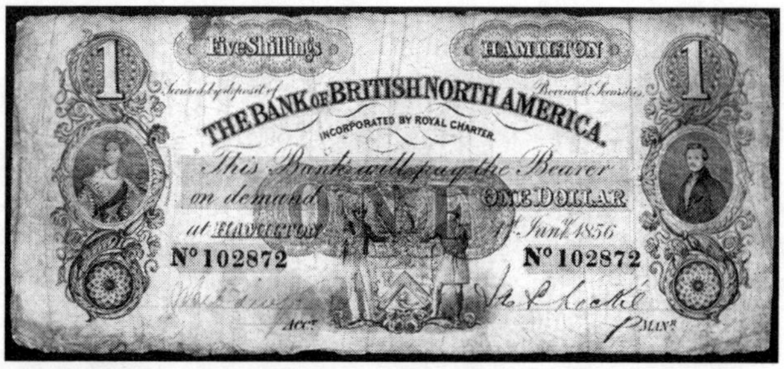

55-14-04-06

PROTECTOR

1852: Blue "numeral" on the face only
1852: Blue "word" on mock coins on the face only
1856: Blue "word" on mock coins on the face only

Cat.No.	Denom.	Date	Variety	G	VG	F	VF	EF	Unc
14-04-02	$1(5s)	1852	Blue "1 1"	400.	800.	1,000.	1,500.	—	—
14-04-04	$1(5s)	1852	Blue "ONE"	400.	800.	1,000.	1,500.	—	—
14-04-06	$1(5s)	1856		400.	800.	1,000.	1,500.	—	—
14-04-10	$2(10s)	1856	Blue "TWO"	400.	800.	1,000.	1,500.	—	—

6. "KINGSTON" ISSUE

DESIGNS AND COLOURS

Similar to Brantford Issue, see 55-14-02.

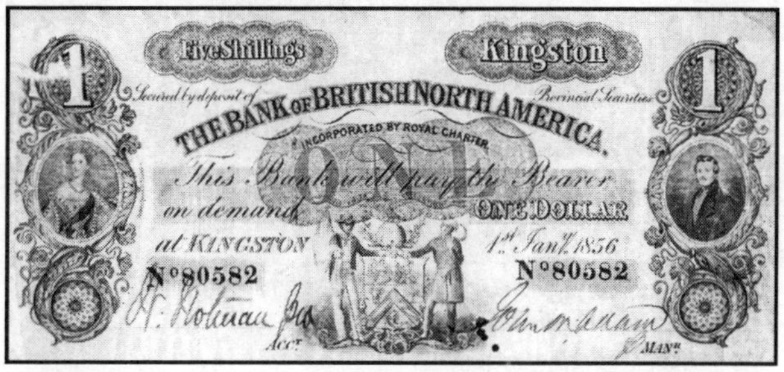

55-14-06-04

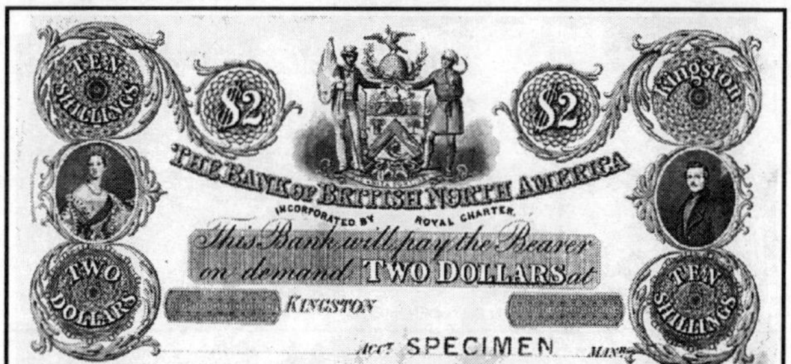

55-14-06-06P

PROTECTOR

Blue "word" on mock coins on the face only

CIRCULATING NOTES

Cat.No.	Denom.	Date	G	VG	F	VF	EF
14-06-04	$1(5s)	1856	375.	750.	925.	1,400.	—
14-06-08	$2(10s)	1856	375.	750.	925.	1,400.	—

PROOF NOTES

Cat. No.	Denom.	Date		Unc
14-06-06P	$2 (10s)	no date	PROOF	400.

8. "LONDON" ISSUE

DESIGN AND COLOURS

Similar to Brantford Issue, see 55-14-02.

Photo Not Available

PROTECTOR

Blue "word" on mock coins on the face only

CIRCULATING NOTES

Cat.No.	Denom.	Date	G	VG	F	VF	EF
14-08-04	$1(5s)	1856	375.	750.	925.	1,400.	—
14-08-08	$2 (10s)	1856			No known issued notes		

PROOF NOTES

Cat. No.	Denom.	Date		Unc
14-08-08P	$2(10s)	no date	PROOF	400.

10. "MONTREAL" ISSUES

DESIGNS AND COLOURS

1852: The branch names are located at the upper right and lower left.

1856: The branch names are located at the top centre and lower left.

DESIGNS AND COLOURS

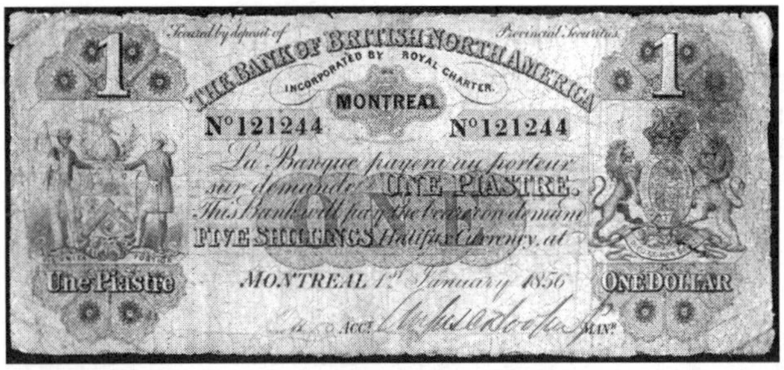

55-14-10-04

$1 (5s) Face Design: Bank Crest/—/Royal Arms

Colours: Black with no tint

Back Design: Plain

55-14-10-04a

$1 (5s) Face Design: Bank Crest/—/Royal Arms

Colour: Black with no tint

Back Design: Plain

55-14-10-06

$2 (10s) Face Design: Royal Arms/—/Bank Crest

Colour: Black with no tint

Back Design: Plain

55-14-10-08

$2 (10s) Face Design: Royal Arms/—/Bank Crest

Colour: Black with no tint

Back Design: Plain

IMPRINT

Perkins, Bacon & Co. London.

ISSUE DATING

Engraved

1st December 1852

1st January 1856

PROTECTOR

1852: Red "numeral" on the face only

1856: Blue "word" on mock coins face only

OVERPRINT

$2 1852: "BYTOWN" in black in the centre and at the end

$1 1856: "OTTAWA" in blue in the centre and vertically inside right and left vignettes.

$2 1856: "OTTAWA" in blue in the centre and vertically inside right and left vignettes. PAYABLE IN OTTAWA in red

Cat.No.	Denom.	Date	Variety	G	VG	F	VF	EF
14-10-02	$1(5s)	1852		375.	750.	925.	1,400.	—
14-10-04	$1(5s)	1856		375.	750.	925.	1,400.	—
14-10-04a	$1(5s)	1856	o/p Ottawa	400.	800.	1,000.	1,600.	—
14-10-06	$2(10s)	1852		375.	750.	925.	1,400.	—
14-10-08	$2(10s)	1856		375.	750.	925.	1,400.	—
14-10-08a	$2(10s)	1856	o/p Ottawa	400.	800.	1,000.	1,600.	—

12. "QUEBEC ISSUE"

DESIGN AND COLOURS

Similar to Montreal Issue, see 55-14-10.

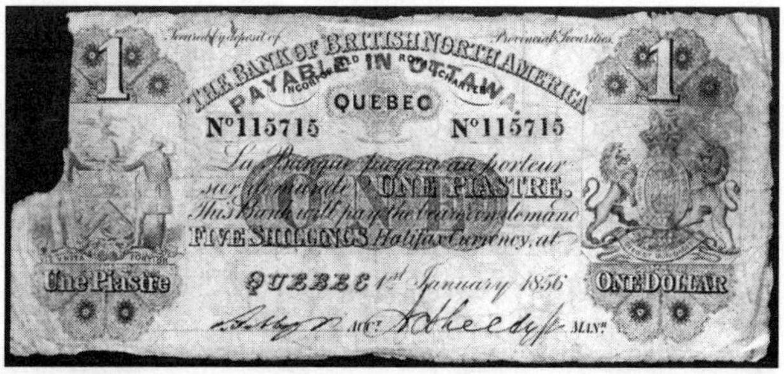

55-14-12-04

55-14-12-05P

55-14-12-08

ISSUE DATING

Engraved

1st December 1852
1st January 1856

PROTECTOR

1852: Red "numeral" on the face only
1856: Blue "word" on mock coins on the face only

OVERPRINT

$1: "PAYABLE IN OTTAWA" in red

CIRCULATING NOTES

Cat.No.	Denom.	Date	G	VG	F	VF	EF
14-12-02	$1(5s)	1852	375.	750.	925.	1,400.	—
14-12-04	$1(5s)	1856	375.	750.	925.	1,400.	—
14-12-06	$2(10s)	1852	375.	750.	925.	1,400.	—
14-12-08	$2(10s)	1856	375.	750.	925.	1,400.	—

PROOF NOTES

Cat.No.	Denom.	Date	Unc
14-12-05P	$2(10s)	no date	400.

14. "ST. JOHN, NEW BRUNSWICK" ISSUE

DESIGNS AND COLOURS

$1: The branch names are engraved at the upper right and lower left.

$2: The branch names are engraved at the lower left and twice at the top.

ISSUE DATING

Engraved

31 August 1866
15 July 1868
1 December 1868

55-14-14-02

1868 $1 Face Design: Queen Victoria (Chalon portrait)/ Bank Crest/Prince Consort
Colour: Black with no tint
Back Design: Plain

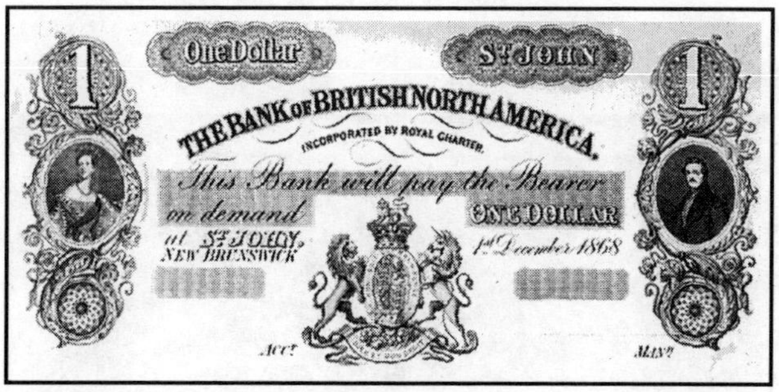

55-14-14-04P

1868 $1 Face Design: Queen Victoria (Chalon portrait)/ Royal Arms/Prince Consort
Colour: Black with no tint
Back Design: Plain

55-14-14-08

$2 Face Design: Seated Indian/small Royal Arms/ Lion, Britannia, 2 in shield over anchor
Colour: Black with no tint

CIRCULATING NOTES

Cat.No.	Denom.	Date	G	VG	F	VF	EF
14-14-02	$1	1866	400.	800.	1,000.	1,500.	—
14-14-04	$1	1868	400.	800.	1,000.	1,500.	—
14-14-08	$2	1868	400.	800.	1,000.	1,500.	—

PROOF NOTES

Cat. No.	Denom.	Date		Unc
14-14-02P	$1	1866	PROOF	500.
14-14-04P	$1	1868	PROOF	500.

16. "TORONTO" ISSUE

DESIGNS AND COLOURS

55-14-16-04

$1 (5s) Face Design: Queen Victoria (Chalon portrait) in oval/ Bank Arms/Prince Consort in oval

Colour: Black with no tint

Back Design: Plain

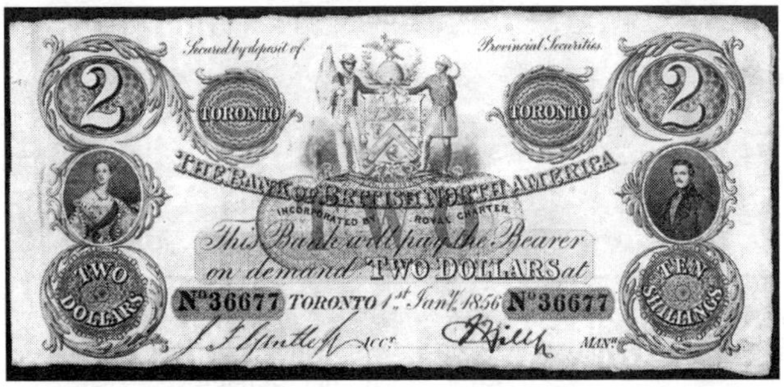

55-14-16-08

$2 (10S) Face Design: Queen Victoria (Chalon portrait) in oval/ Bank Arms/Prince Consort in oval

Colour: Black with no tint

Back Design: Plain

ISSUE DATING

Engraved

1st Jany 1856

PROTECTOR

1852: Red "numeral" on face only

1856: Blue "word" on mock coins on face only

OVERPRINT

$1 1856: "PAYABLE IN LONDON" on dark blue across centre of note.

Cat.No.	Denom.	Date	G	VG	F	VF	EF
14-16-02	$1(5s)	1852	375.	750.	925.	1,400.	—
14-16-04	$1(5s)	1856	375.	750.	925.	1,400.	—
14-16-04a	$1(5s)	1856 o/p LONDON	600.	1,200.	—	—	—
14-16-08	$2(10s)	1856	375.	750.	925.	1,400.	—

18. "VICTORIA VANCOUVER'S ISLAND" ISSUE

The branch names are engraved at the lower left and twice at the top.

DESIGNS AND COLOURS

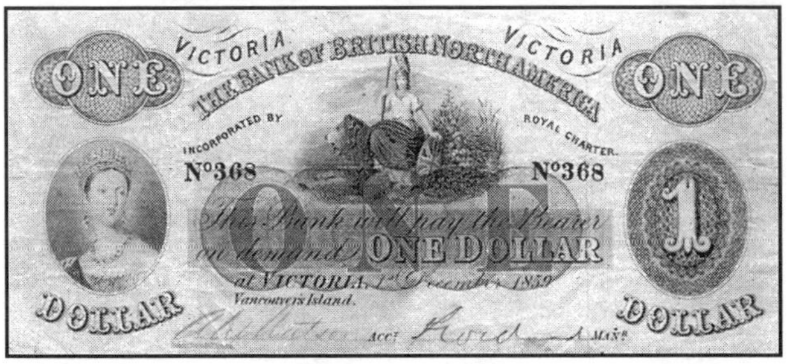

55-14-18-04

$1 Face Design: Queen Victoria (Chalon portrait) in oval/ seated Britannia with lion at left//counter

Colour: Black with no tint

Back Design: Plain

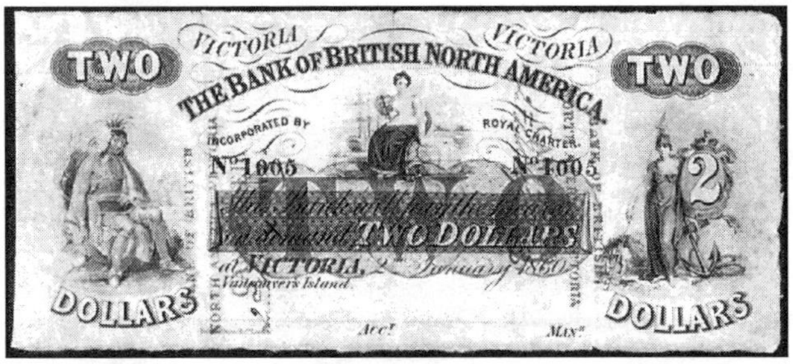

55-14-18-14Sa

$2 Face Design: Seated Indian/seated Commerce figure/ Britannia, counter

Colour: Black with no tint

Back Design: Plain

IMPRINT

Perkins, Bacon & Co. London

ISSUE DATING

Partially Engraved:__18__:

Engraved

1st December 1859
2nd January 1860
Dec. 2 1867

PROTECTOR

Issued and Specimen Notes: Green "word" on mock coins on face and back

CIRCULATING NOTES

Cat.No.	Denom.	Date	G	VG	F	VF	EF
14-18-02	$1	18__			No known issued notes		
14-18-04	$1	1859	2,500.	4,000.	—	—	—
14-18-10	$1	1867			No known issued notes		
14-18-12	$2	18__			No known issued notes		
14-18-14	$2	1860			No known issued notes		

PROOF NOTES

Cat. No.	Denom.	Date		Unc
14-18-02P	$1	18__	PROOF	700.
14-18-04P	$1	1859	PROOF	700.
14-18-10P	$1	1867	PROOF	700.
14-18-12P	$2	18__	PROOF	700.
14-18-14P	$2	1860	PROOF	700.

SPECIMEN NOTES

Cat. No.	Denom.	Date		Unc
14-18-04Sa	$1	1859*	SPECIMEN	3,500.
14-18-14Sa	$2	1859*	SPECIMEN	3,500.

*Unsigned notes stamped for use as specimens for the customs department of the BC government.

55-16. COMMON DENOMINATION DESIGN PAYABLE AT SEPARATE BRANCHES 1859 - 1875

DESIGNS AND COLOURS

$4 Face Design: Seated "Justice" figure/Royal Crest/ seated woman with sheaf and sickle
Colour: Black with no tint

Back Design: Plain

$5 Face Design: Seated Britannia, lion/Royal Crest/ Queen Victoria on throne
Colour: Black with no tint

Back Design: Plain

$10 Face Design: —/Royal Crest/—
Colour: Black with no tint

Back Design: Plain

$20 Face Design: Sheep, beehive and tools
Colour: Black with no tint

Back Design: Plain

$20 Face Design: —/radiant Royal Crest/—
Colour: Black with no tint

Back Design: Plain

$50 Face Design: Seated woman with lute/Royal Crest/ seated "Commerce" figure
Colour: Black with no tint

Back Design: Plain

2. "BRANTFORD" ISSUE

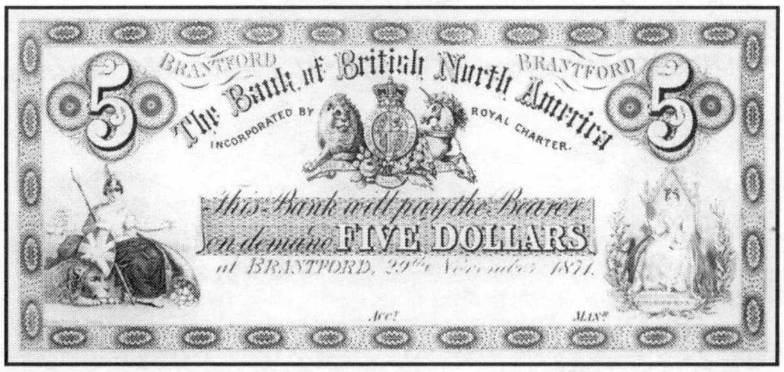

55-16-02-02

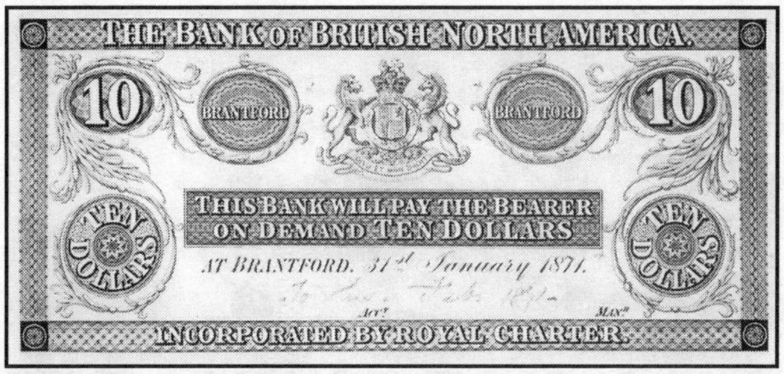

55-16-02-04P

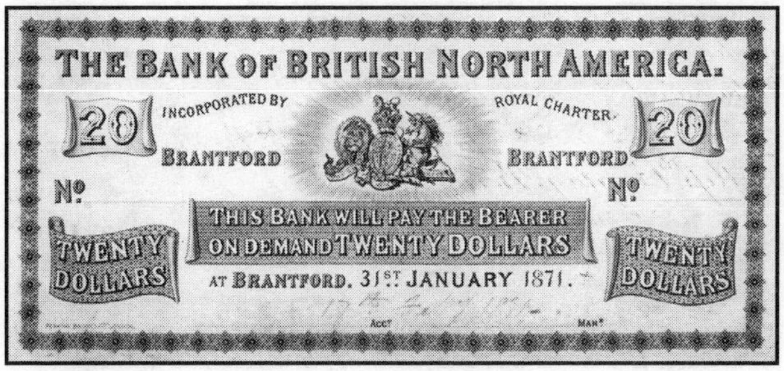

55-16-02-06P

ISSUE DATING

Engraved

$5: 31st January 1871
29th November 1871
$5, $10 & $20: 31st January 1871

CIRCULATING NOTES

Cat.No.	Denom.	Date	G	VG	F	VF	EF
16-02-02	$5	1871	250.	500.	650.	1,000.	—
16-02-04	$10	1871			No known issued notes		
16-02-06	$20*	1871			No known issued notes		

PROOF NOTES

Cat. No.	Denom.	Date		Unc
16-02-02P	$5	1871	PROOF	400.
16-02-04P	$10	1871	PROOF	400.
16-02-06P	$20*	1871	PROOF	500.

*Radiant Royal Crest design.

4. "HALIFAX, NOVA SCOTIA" ISSUE

55-16-04-14P

55-16-04-31

55-16-04-32P

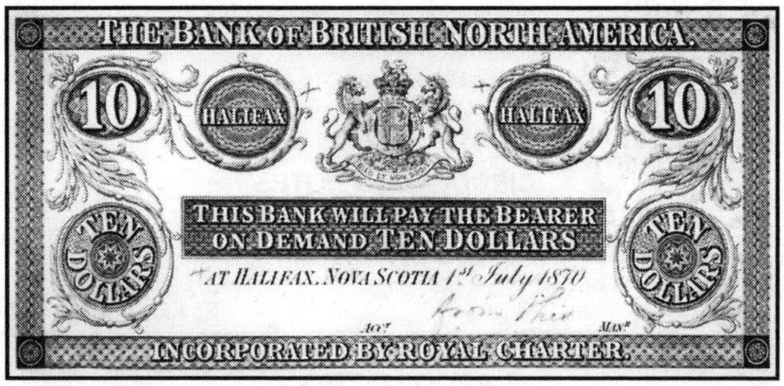

55-16-04-46P

55-16-04-62P

IMPRINT

Perkins, Bacon & Co. London.

ISSUE DATING

Engraved

$4: 31 January 1871
1st January 1872
Dec. 1, 1874

$5: 1st July 1870
2nd Jany 1871
1st July 1871
1st Novr 1871
1st Decr 1874
Dec. 1, 1874

$10: 1st July 1870
1st July 1871
July 1, 1871
Dec. 1, 1874

$20: 24th May 1865
1st July 1871
1 Novr 1871
1 Decr 1874

PROTECTOR

Issued Notes: Green "word" on mock coins face only

OVERPRINT

$5 1st July, 1871: "HALIFAX" at the ends and "PAYABLE IN DOMINION CURRENCY" across the top, both in red

$5 1st Novr. 1871: "Canada Currency" at both ends in red

CIRCULATING NOTES

Cat.No.	Denom.	Date	Variety	G	VG	F	VF	EF
16-04-14	$4	1872				No known issued notes		
16-04-18	$4	1874				No known issued notes		
16-04-26	$5	1870				No known issued notes		
16-04-30	$5	1871	(2nd Jan)			No known issued notes		
16-04-31	$5	1871	(1st July)	475.	950.	1,200.	1,600.	—
16-04-32	$5	1871	(1st Novr)			No known issued notes		
16-04-38	$5	1874				No known issued notes		
16-04-46	$10	1870				No known issued notes		
16-04-50	$10	1871				No known issued notes		
16-04-58	$10	1874				No known issued notes		
16-04-62	$20	1865				No known issued notes		
16-04-70	$20	1871	Canadian Currency o/p			No known issued notes		

PROOF NOTES

Cat. No.	Denom.	Date	Variety		Unc
16-04-14P	$4	1872		PROOF	500.
16-04-18P	$4	1874		PROOF	500.
16-04-26P	$5	1870		PROOF	400.
16-04-30P	$5	1871	(2nd Jan)	PROOF	400.
16-04-32P	$5	1871	(1st Novr)	PROOF	400.
16-04-38P	$5	1874		PROOF	400.
16-04-46P	$10	1870		PROOF	400.
16-04-50P	$10	1871		PROOF	400.
16-04-58P	$10	1874		PROOF	400.
16-04-62P	$20*	1865		PROOF	450.
16-04-70P	$20	1871	Canada Currency o/p	PROOF	450.

* Royal Crest design.

6. "HAMILTON" ISSUE

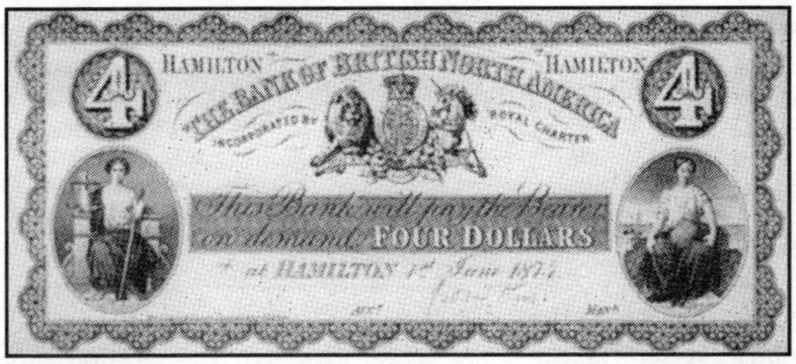

55-16-06-01P

55-16-06-02P

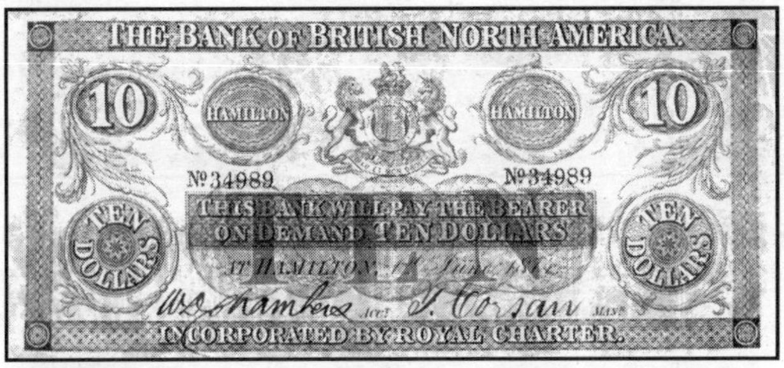

55-16-06-06

ISSUE DATING

Engraved

$4: 1st June 1874
$5: 1st June 1874
May 1, 1875
$10: 1st June 1874

CIRCULATING NOTES

Cat.No.	Denom.	Date	G	VG	F	VF	EF
16-06-01	$4	1874			No known issued notes		
16-06-02	$5	1874			No known issued notes		
16-06-04	$5	1875			No known issued notes		
16-06-06	$10	1874	375.	750.	925.	1,400.	—

PROOF NOTES

Cat. No.	Denom.	Date		Unc
16-06-01P	$4	1874	PROOF	300.
16-06-02P	$5	1874	PROOF	300.
16-06-04P	$5	1875	PROOF	300.

8. "KINGSTON" ISSUE

55-16-08-02

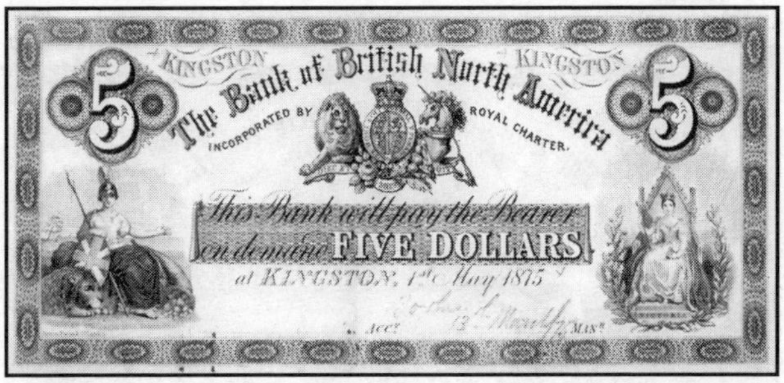

55-16-08-08P

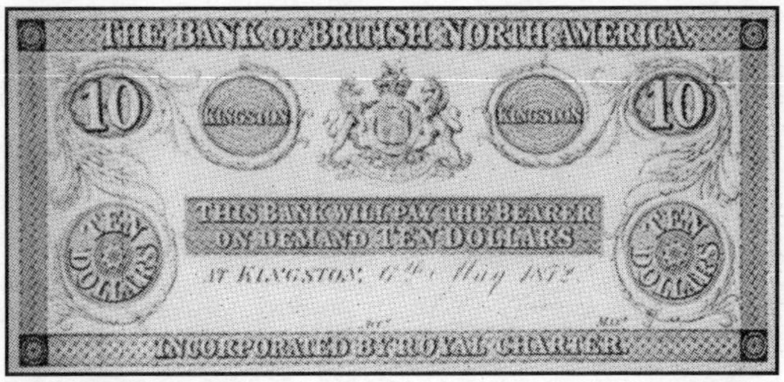

55-16-08-10P

ISSUE DATING

Engraved

$4: May 4, 1872, 1st May 1875
$5: 1st May 1875
$10: 6th May, 1872, 1 May 1875

CIRCULATING NOTES

Cat.No.	Denom.	Date	G	VG	F	VF	EF
16-08-02	$4	1872	375.	750.	925.	1,400.	—
16-08-04	$4	1875			No known issued notes		
16-08-08	$5	1875			No known issued notes		
16-08-10	$10	1872			No known issued notes		
16-08-12	$10	1875			No known issued notes		

PROOF NOTES

Cat. No.	Denom.	Date		Unc
16-08-04P	$4	1875	PROOF	300.
16-08-08P	$5	1875	PROOF	300.
16-08-10P	$10	1872	PROOF	300.
16-08-12P	$10	1875	PROOF	300.

10. "LONDON, CANADA WEST; LONDON ONTARIO" ISSUE

55-16-10-06P

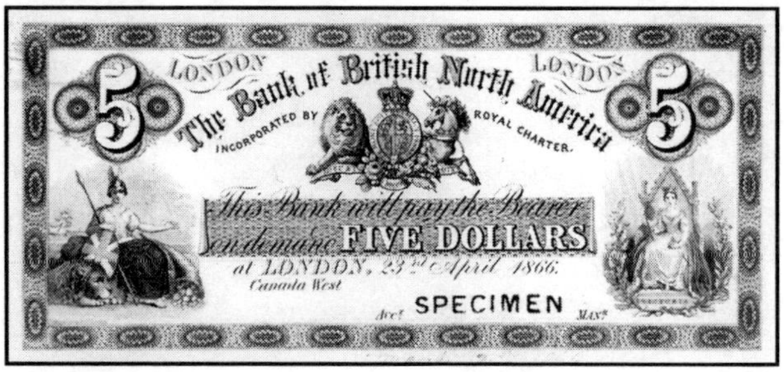

55-16-10-10P

55-16-10-20P

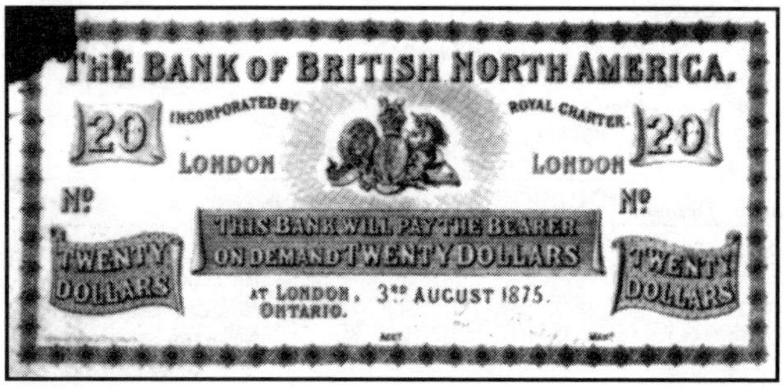

55-16-10-30P

ISSUE DATING

Engraved

$4: 3rd August 1875
$5: 23rd April 1866
1st August 1872
3rd August 1875
$10: 24th May, 1866
$20: 3rd August, 1875

CIRCULATING NOTES

Cat.No.	Denom.	Date	G	VG	F	VF	EF
16-10-06	$4	1875			No known issued notes		
16-10-10	$5	1866			No known issued notes		
16-10-12	$5	1872			No known issued notes		
16-10-14	$5	1875	375.	750.	925.	1,400	—
16-10-20	$10	1866			No known issued notes		
16-10-30	$20	1875			No known issued notes		

PROOF NOTES

Cat. No.	Denom.	Date		Unc
16-10-06P	$4	1875	PROOF	400.
16-10-10P	$5	1866	PROOF	300.
16-10-12P	$5	1872	PROOF	300.
16-10-20P	$10	1866	PROOF	350.
16-10-30P	$20	1875	PROOF	450.

12. "MONTREAL" ISSUE

Photo Not Available

55-16-12-08

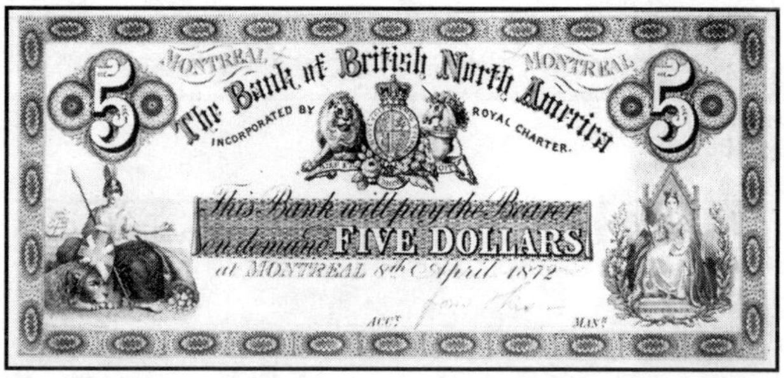

55-16-12-16P

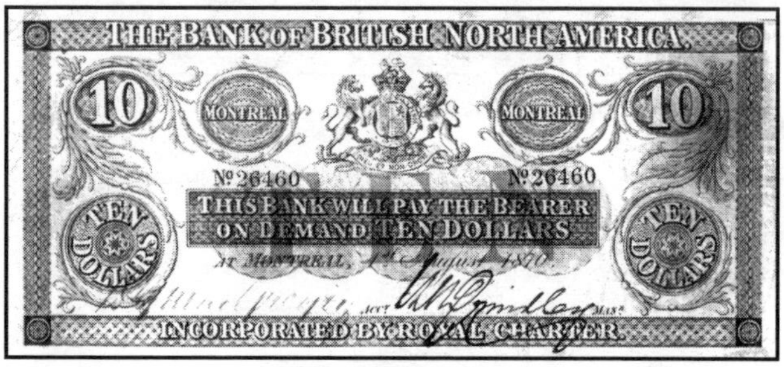

55-16-12-22

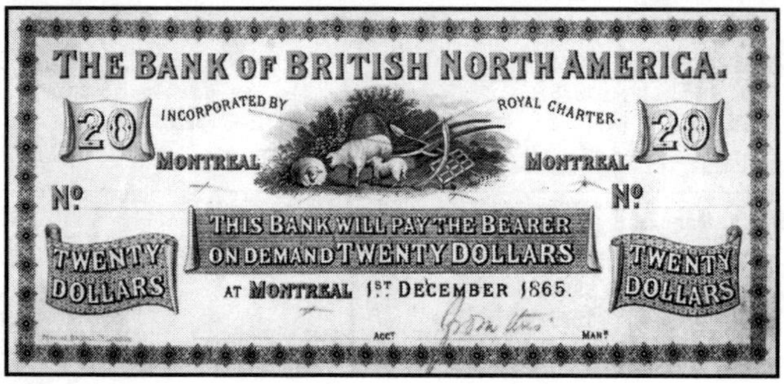

55-16-12-30P

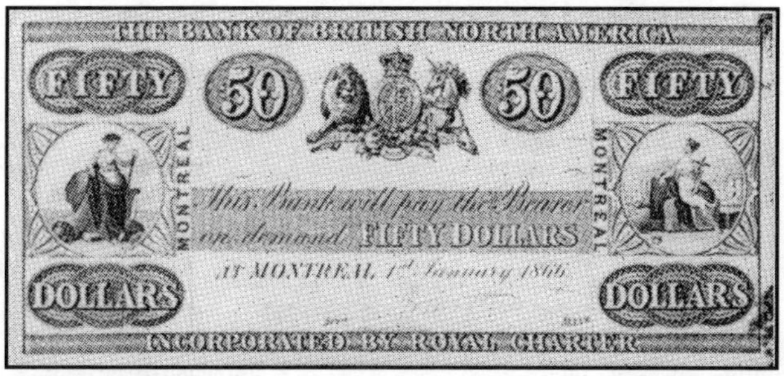

55-16-12-40P

ISSUE DATING

Engraved

$4: Dec. 1, 1873
$5: 1st August 1870
8th April 1872
$10: 30th November 1865
1 August 1870
$20: 1st December 1865
$50: 1st January 1866

CIRCULATING NOTES

Cat.No.	Denom.	Date	G	VG	F	VF	EF
16-12-08	$4	1873	375.	750.	925.	1,400.	—
16-12-14	$5	1870			No known issued notes		
16-12-16	$5	1872			No known issued notes		
16-12-20	$10	1865			No known issued notes		
16-12-22	$10	1870	375.	750.	925.	1,400.	—
16-12-30	$20*	1865			No known issued notes		
16-12-40	$50	1866			No known issued notes		

PROOF NOTES

Cat. No.	Denom.	Date		Unc
16-12-14P	$5	1870	PROOF	300.
16-12-16P	$5	1872	PROOF	300.
16-12-20P	$10	1865	PROOF	350.
16-12-30P	$20*	1865	PROOF	450.
16-12-40P	$50	1866	PROOF	650.

* Sheep, beehive and tools design.

13. "NAPANEE" ISSUE

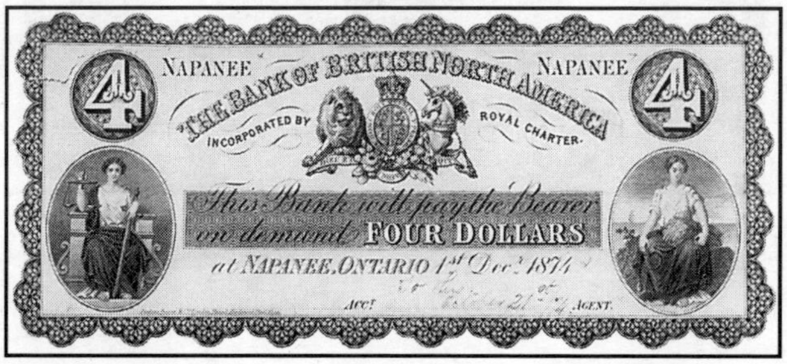

55-16-13-10P

ISSUE DATING

Engraved

$4: 1st Decr 1874

PROOF NOTES

Cat.No.	Denom	Date		Unc
16-13-10	$4	1874	PROOF	400.

14. "OTTAWA" ISSUE

55-16-14-08P

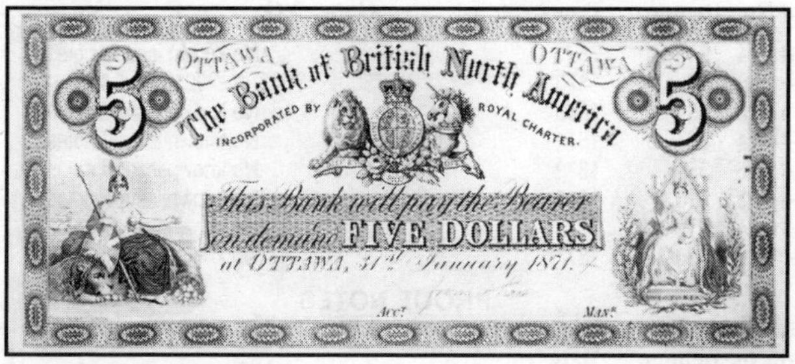

55-16-14-14P

55-16-14-24P

55-16-14-34P

ISSUE DATING
Engraved

$4: 1st Decr 1871
1st Decr 1873

$5: 10th August 1865
31st January 1871
May 1, 1872

$10: 1st September 1865
31st January 1871

$20: 23rd April 1867
31st January 1871

OVERPRINT
1873: "ARNPRIOR" in blue at the ends

CIRCULATING NOTES

Cat.No.	Denom.	Date	G	VG	F	VF	EF
16-14-04	$4	1871			No known issued notes		
16-14-08	$4	1873	375.	750.	925.	1,400.	—
16-14-12	$5	1865			No known issued notes		
16-14-14	$5	1871			No known issued notes		
16-14-16	$5	1872			No known issued notes		
16-14-22	$10	1865			No known issued notes		
16-14-24	$10	1871			No known issued notes		
16-14-34	$20*	1871			No known issued notes		

PROOF NOTES

Cat. No.	Denom.	Date		Unc
16-14-04P	$4	1871	PROOF	400.
16-14-12P	$5	1865	PROOF	300.
16-14-14P	$5	1871	PROOF	300.
16-14-16P	$5	1872	PROOF	350.
16-14-22P	$10	1865	PROOF	350.
16-14-24P	$10	1871	PROOF	350.
16-14-34P	$20*	1871	PROOF	450.

* Royal Crest design.

16. "QUEBEC" ISSUE

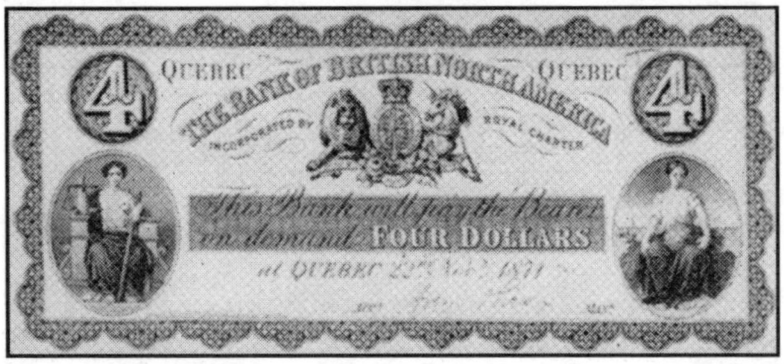

55-16-16-08P

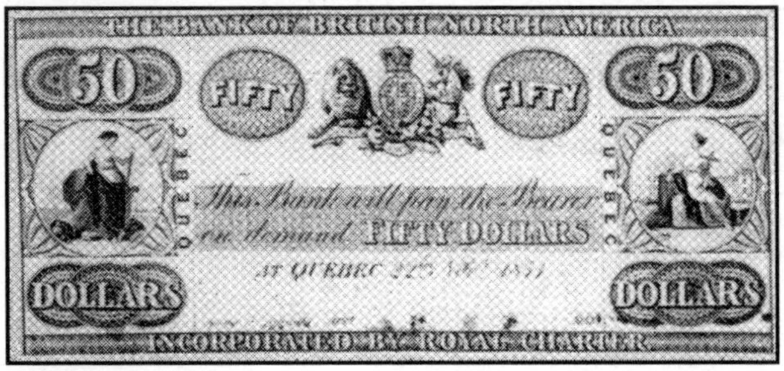

55-16-16-24P

ISSUE DATING
Engraved

$4: 22 Novr 1871
$5: 22nd Novr 1871
$10: 22nd Novr 1871
$20: 22nd Novr 1871
$50: 22nd Novr 1871

CIRCULATING NOTES

Cat.No.	Denom.	Date	G	VG	F	VF	EF
16-16-08	$4	1871	375.	750.	925.	1,400.	—
16-16-12	$5	1871			No known issued notes		
16-16-16	$10	1871			No known issued notes		
16-16-20	$20	1871			No known issued notes		
16-16-24	$50	1871			No known issued notes		

PROOF NOTES

Cat. No.	Denom.	Date		Unc
16-16-08P	$4	1871	PROOF	300.
16-16-12P	$5	1871	PROOF	300.
16-16-16P	$10	1871	PROOF	350.
16-16-20P	$20	1871	PROOF	450.
16-16-24P	$50	1871	PROOF	650.

18. "ST. JOHN, NEW BRUNSWICK" ISSUE

55-16-18-08

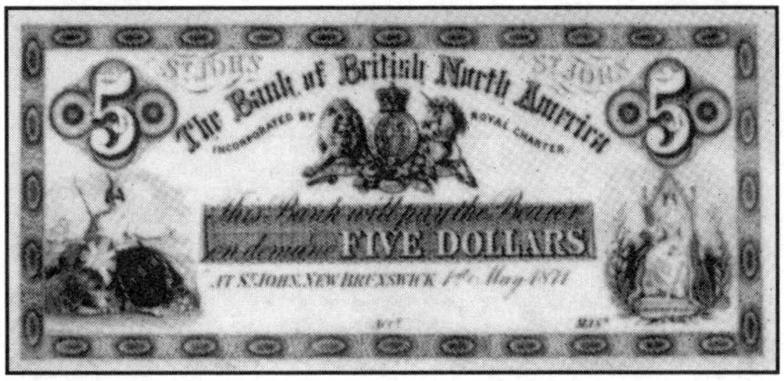

55-16-18-14P

Photograph Not Available

55-16-18-20P

55-16-18-28P

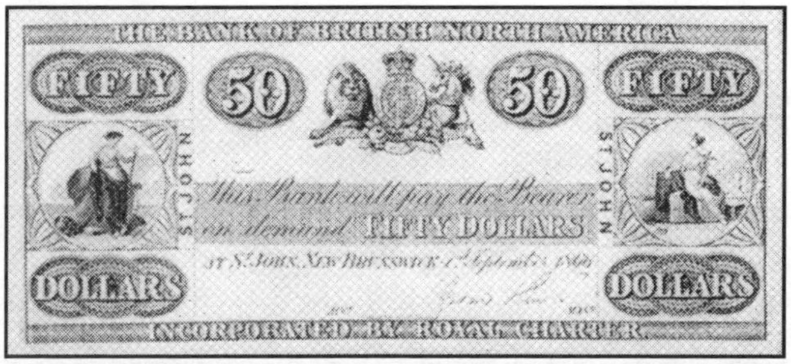

55-16-18-34P

55-16-18-40P

ISSUE DATING

Engraved

$4: 31 May, 1871
31st May 1872

$5: 1st May 1871
1st May 1872
1 Octr 1873

$10: 1 Janr, 1870
18th June, 1872

$20: 1 Septr 1869
29th April, 1871
29th April, 1872

$50: 1st Septr, 1866
1st Janr, 1870
18th June 1872

PROTECTOR

Green "word" on mock coins face only

OVERPRINT

$4 1872: "FREDERICTON" in blue at the ends
$4 1872: "MONCTON" in blue across the centre

CIRCULATING NOTES

Cat.No.	Denom.	Date	G	VG	F	VF	EF
16-18-06	$4	1871	No known issued notes				
16-18-08	$4	1872	550.	1,100.	1,500.	2,000.	—
16-18-14	$5	1871	No known issued notes				
16-18-16	$5	1872	No known issued notes				
16-18-17	$5	1873	No known issued notes				
16-18-20	$10	1870	No known issued notes				
16-18-24	$10	1872	No known issued notes				
16-18-28	$20	1869	No known issued notes				
16-18-30	$20	1871	No known issued notes				
16-18-32	$20	1872	No known issued notes				
16-18-34	$50	1866	No known issued notes				
16-18-36	$50	1870	No known issued notes				
16-18-40	$50	1872	No known issued notes				

PROOF NOTES

Cat. No.	Denom.	Date		Unc
16-18-06P	$4	1871	PROOF	500.
16-18-14P	$5	1871	PROOF	350.
16-18-16P	$5	1872	PROOF	400.
16-18-17P	$5	1873	PROOF	400.
16-18-20P	$10	1870	PROOF	400.
16-18-24P	$10	1872	PROOF	450.
16-18-28P	$20	1869	PROOF	450.
16-18-30P	$20*	1871	PROOF	450.
16-18-32P	$20*	1872	PROOF	450.
16-18-34P	$50	1866	PROOF	650.
16-18-36P	$50	1870	PROOF	650.
16-18-40P	$50	1872	PROOF	650.

20. "TORONTO" ISSUE

55-16-20-08P

55-16-20-14P

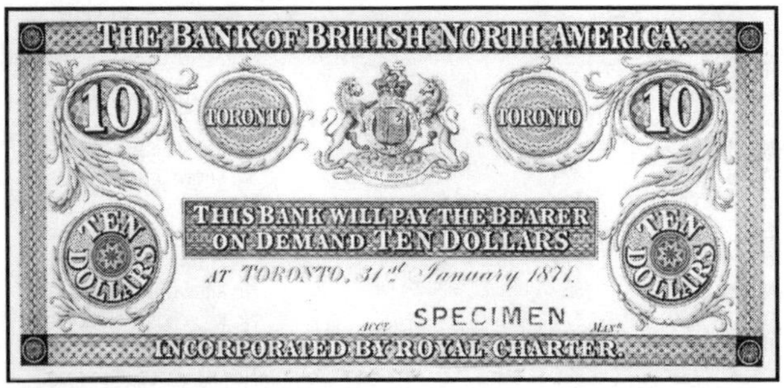

55-16-20-22P

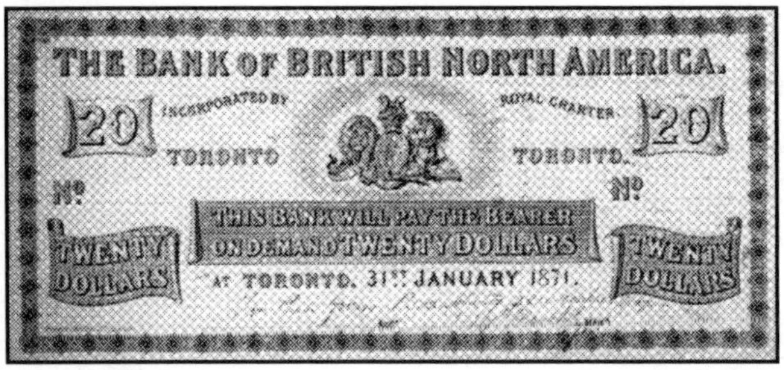

55-16-20-40P

ISSUE DATING

Engraved

$4: 8th Decr. 1871

$5: 4th January 1865
1st January 1871
31st January 1871

$10: 23rd April, 1864
31st January 1871

$20: 31st January 1871

OVERPRINT

$5 1865: "DUNNVILLE" in red vertically near ends.

CIRCULATING NOTES

Cat.No.	Denom.	Date	G	VG	F	VF	EF
16-20-08	$4	1871			No known issued notes		
16-20-14	$5	1865	275.	550.	750.	1,150.	—
16-20-18	$5	1871			No known issued notes		
16-20-22	$10	1864	375.	750.	925.	1,400.	—
16-20-28	$10	1871			No known issued notes		
16-20-40	$20	1871			No known issued notes		

PROOF NOTES

Cat. No.	Denom.	Date		Unc
16-20-08P	$4	1871	PROOF	400.
16-20-18P	$5	1871	PROOF	300.
16-20-28P	$10	1871	PROOF	350.
16-20-40P	$20	1871	PROOF	400.

22. "VICTORIA, VANCOUVER'S ISLAND" ISSUE

55-16-22-04Sa

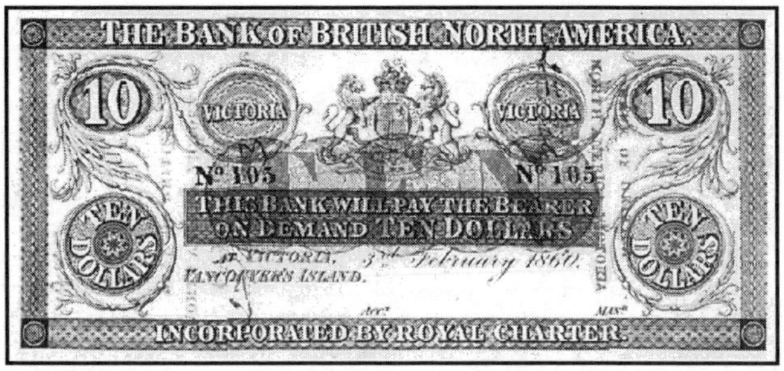

55-16-22-16Sa

55-16-22-36Sa

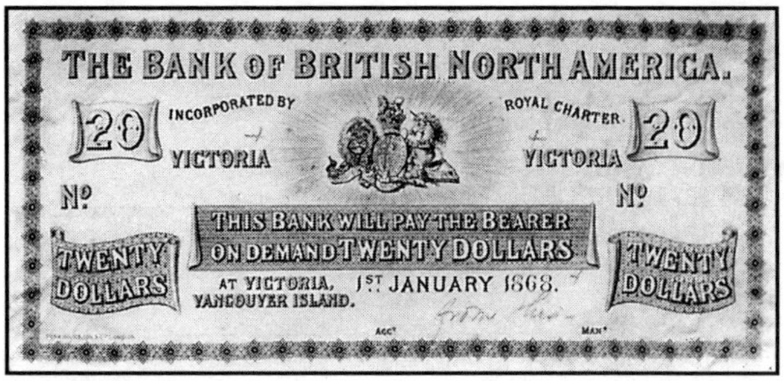

55-16-22-42P

Both varieties of the $20 face design are shown, but the individual branches used only one in their note issue.

ISSUE DATING

Remainder of date added letterpress:

$5__18__: 27th Septr. 1859

Engraved

$5: 23rd April 1867

$10: 3rd February 1860
9th November 1867
16 October 1873

$20: 5th March 1860
1st January, 1868
16 October 1873

PROOF NOTES

Cat.No.	Denom.	Date		Unc
16-22-06P	$5	18__	PROOF	700.
16-22-08P	$5	1867	PROOF	700.
16-22-16P	$10	1860	PROOF	700.
16-22-20P	$10	1867	PROOF	700.
16-22-32P	$10	1873	PROOF	700.
16-22-36P	$20*	1860	PROOF	600.
16-22-38P	$20*	1873	PROOF	700.
16-22-42P	$20**	1868	PROOF	700.
16-22-48	$20**	1873	PROOF	700.

* Sheep, beehive and tools design.
** Royal Crest design.

SPECIMEN NOTES

Cat. No.	Denom.	Date		VF	EF	Unc
16-22-04Sa	$5*	1859	SPECIMEN	—	4,000.	—
16-22-16Sa	$10*	1860	SPECIMEN	—	4,000.	—
16-22-36Sa	$20* **	1860	SPECIMEN	—	4,000.	—

* Unsigned notes stamped for use as specimens for the customs department of the BC government.
** Sheep, behive and tools design.

24. BRANCH NAME TO BE FILLED IN MANUSCRIPT 1861 - 1872

DESIGNS AND COLOURS

55-16-24-02P

$100 Face Design: Cherubs/Royal Crest/cherubs
Colour: Black with no tint

Back Design: Plain

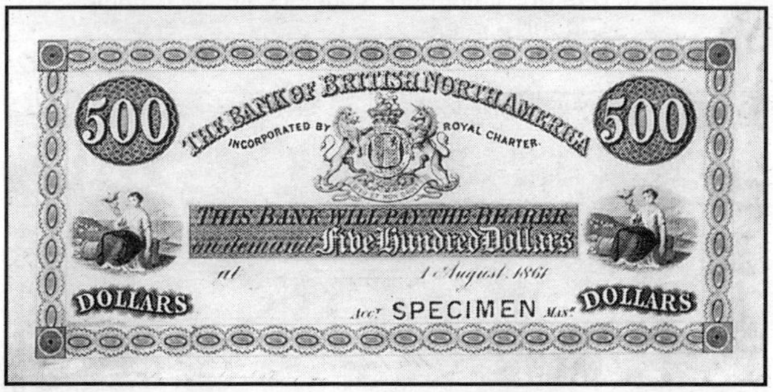

55-16-24-08P

$500 Face Design: Seated "Commerce" figure/Royal Crest/seated "Commerce" figure
Colour: Black with no tint

Back Design: Plain

55-16-24-10P

$1000 Face Design: Seated "Commerce" figures, cask, bale and ship/Royal Crest/Seated "Commerce" figures, cask, bale and ship
Colour: Black with no tint

Back Design: Plain

ISSUE DATING

Engraved

1 August 1861
15 August 1861
5 September 1861
15 August 1865
22 November, 1866
22 November 1871
Apr. 15, 1872
1 March 1875

PROTECTOR

Green "word" on face

PROOF NOTES

Cat.No.	Denom.	Date		Unc
16-24-02P	$100	1861	PROOF	500.
16-24-03P	$100	1865	PROOF	500.
16-24-04P	$100	1866	PROOF	500.
16-24-05P	$100	1871	PROOF	500.
16-24-06P	$100	1872	PROOF	500.
16-24-07P	$100	1875	PROOF	500.
16-24-08P	$500	1861	PROOF	2,000.
16-24-10P	$1,000	1861	PROOF	2,500.

55-18. GENERAL ISSUES PAYABLE AT ALL BRANCHES 1876 - 1877

DESIGNS AND COLOURS

55-18-02

$4 Face Design: Seated Britannia, lion/Royal Crest Queen Victoria on throne
Colour: Black with green tint

Back Design: Lathework, counters and The Bank of British North America
Colour: Green

55-18-04
$5 Face Design: Seated Britannia and lion "Britannia No. 2"/ Royal Crest/Queen Victoria on throne
Colour: Black with green tint

Back Design: Lathework, counters; The Bank of British North America
Colour: Green

55-18-10
$10 Face Design: Seated Britannia, lion/Royal Crest/ Queen Victoria on throne
Colour: See varieties

Back Design: Lathework, counters and bank name
Colour: Green

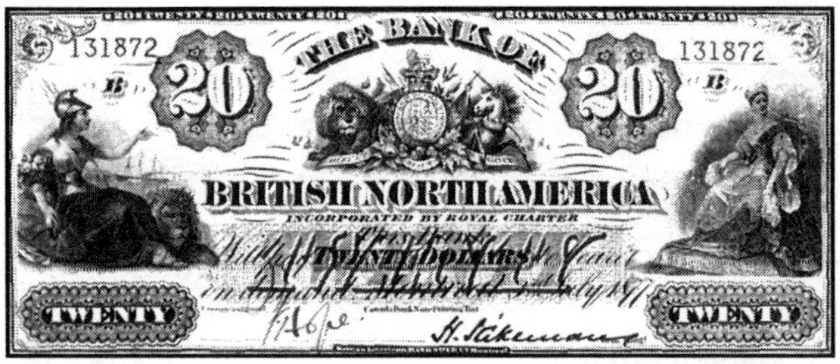

55-18-14
$20 Face Design: Seated Britannia, lion/Royal Crest/ Queen Victoria on throne
Colour: Black with green tint

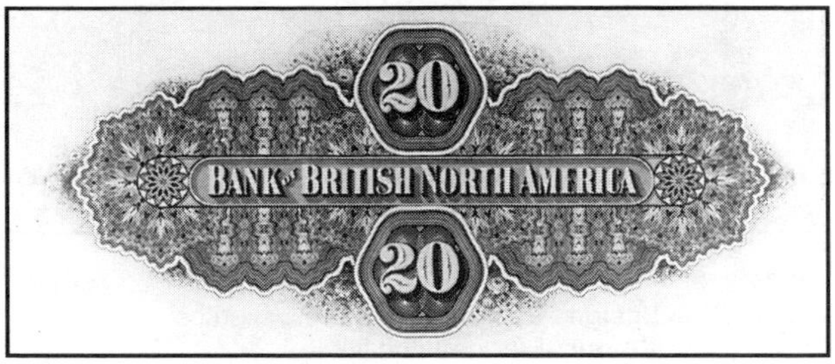

Back Design: Lathework, counters and bank name
Colour: Green

55-18-18
$50 Face Design: Seated Britannia, lion/Royal Crest/ Queen Victoria on throne
Colour: Black with green tint

Back Design: Lathework, counters and bank name

55-18-22

$100 Face Design: Seated Britannia, lion/Royal Crest/ Queen Victoria on throne
Colour: Black with green tint

Back Design: Lathework, counters and bank name

IMPRINT

British American Bank Note Co. Montreal

SIGNATURES

	left	right
All denominations:	mss. various	mss. various
Some $20 - $100:	mss. various	engr. R.R. Grindley
	mss. various	engr. H. Stikeman

ISSUE DATING

Engraved

1st July, 1876
1 st July 1877
3rd July, 1877

VARIETIES

$10 Face Colour: Black with green tint
$10 Face Colour: Blue with red-brown tint

CIRCULATING NOTES

Cat.No.	Denom.	Date	Variety	G	VG	F	VF	EF
18-02	$4	1877		600.	1,200.	1,500.	2,500.	—
18-04	$5*	1877		300.	600.	800.	1,200.	—
18-04C	$5	1877	Counterfeit	60.	125.	175.	—	—
18-06	$10	1876	Green tint	No known issued notes				
18-08	$10	1877	Green tint	500.	1,000.	1,500.	2,000.	—
18-10	$10	1877	Red Brown tint	625.	1,250.	1,750.	2,250.	—
18-12	$20	1877	Grindley,r.	500.	1,000.	1,500.	2,000.	—
18-14	$20	1877	Stikeman,r.	500.	1,000.	1,500.	2,000.	—
18-16	$50	1877	Grindley,r.	1,000.	2,000.	2,600.	3,500.	—
18-18	$50	1877	Stikeman, r.	1,000.	2,000.	2,600.	3,500.	—
18-20	$100	1877	Grindley,r.	1,200.	2,400.	3,000.	4,000.	—
18-22	$100	1877	Stikeman, r.	1,200.	2,400.	3,000.	4,000.	—

* Beware of counterfeits.

PROOF NOTES

Cat. No.	Denom.	Date		Unc
18-06P	$10	1876 Green tint	PROOF	500.

Proofs exist for 1877-dates notes. UNC $300 - $500.

55-20. $5 ISSUE OF 1884

DESIGNS AND COLOURS

55-20-02

$5 Face Design: —/Queen Victoria/—
Colour: Blue with orange tint (Five on mock coins)

55-20-04P

Back Design: Lathework, counters and bank name
Colour: Black with orange tint

IMPRINT
Perkins, Bacon & Co. London. on face and back

SIGNATURES

left	right
mss. C. Deacon	mss. W. Collier

ISSUE DATING
Engraved
1st May 1884

CIRCULATING NOTES

Cat.No.	Denom.	Date		G	VG	F	VF	EF
20-02	$5	1884	Montreal	750.	1,500.	2,000.	3,000.	—
20-04	$5	1884	Victoria			No known issued notes		

PROOF NOTES

Cat. No.	Denom.	Date		Unc
20-02P	$5	1884	Montreal	350.
20-04P	$5	1884	Victoria	650.

55-22. ISSUE OF 1886 AND 1889

DESIGNS AND COLOURS

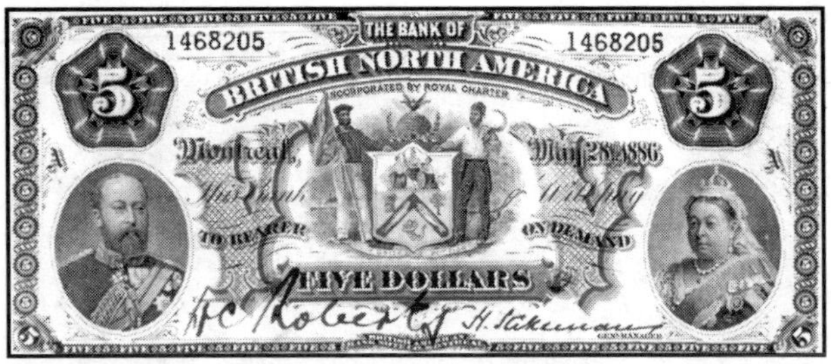

55-22-04
$5 Face Design: Prince of Wales/Bank Crest/Queen Victoria
Colour: Black with green tint

Back Design: Lathework, counters and bank name
Colour: Green

55-22-06
$10 Face Design: St. George slaying dragon/ Queen Victoria/Bank Crest
Colour: Black with green tint

Back Design: Lathework, counters, bank name and bank crest
Colour: Green

IMPRINT
British American Bank Note Co. Ottawa
British American Bank Note Co. Montreal

SIGNATURES

left	right
mss. various	mss. various
mss. various	engr. H. Stikeman

ISSUE DATING
Engraved
May 28th, 1886
3rd July, 1889

CIRCULATING NOTES

Cat.No.	Den.	Date	Variety	G	VG	F	VF	EF	Unc
22-02	$5	1886	Mss. Signature,r.	110.	225.	300.	500.	800.	—
22-04	$5	1886	Stikeman,r.	100.	200.	275.	450.	700.	950.
22-06	$10	1889	Mss. signature,r.	120.	240.	325.	525.	850.	—
22-08	$10	1889	Stikeman,r.	105.	210.	290.	475.	750.	—

SPECIMEN NOTES

Cat. No.	Den.	Date	Variety	Unc
Specimens exist for this issue				650.

55-24. ISSUE OF 1911

DESIGNS AND COLOURS

55-24-04
$5 Face Design: Small Royal Crest/King George V/ small Canadian Crest
Colour: Back with green tint

Back Design: Lathework, counters, bank name and bank crest
Colour: Green

55-24-07
$10 Face Design: Small Royal Crest/Queen Mary/ small bank crest
Colour: Black with blue-green tint

Back Design: Lathework, counters, bank name and bank crest
Colour: Blue

55-24-10
$20 Face Design: Small Royal crest/King Edward VII/ small Canadian crest
Colour: Black with red-orange tint

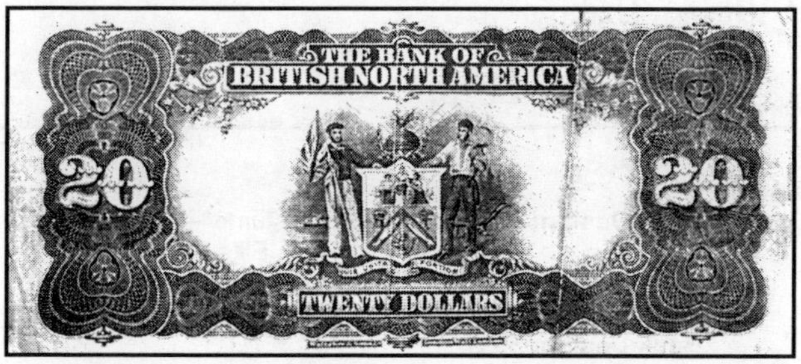

Back Design: Lathework, counters; The Bank of British North American and Bank Crest
Colour: Brown

55-24-14S
$50 Face Design: /Queen Alexandra/
Colour: Black with lilac tint

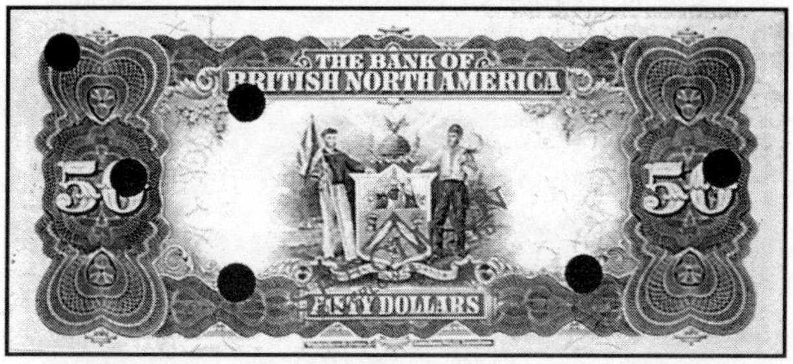

Back Design: Lathework, counters, bank name and bank crest
Colour: Purple

55-24-16S
$100 Face Design: Small Royal crest/Queen Victoria/ small bank crest
Colour: Orange

Back Design: Lathework, counters, bank name and bank crest
Colour: Brown

IMPRINT

Waterlow & Sons Ld. London
Waterlow & Sons Ld. London Wall, London
Waterlow & Sons Limited, London Wall, London EC

SIGNATURES

left	**right**
mss. various	engr. H. Stikeman
mss. various	engr. H.B. Mackenzie

ISSUE DATING

Engraved

July 3rd, 1911

CIRCULATING NOTES

Cat.No.	Den.	Date	Variety	VG	F	VF	EF	AU	Unc
24-02	$5	1911	Stikeman,r.	300.	500.	700.	1,000.	1,500.	2,000.
24-04	$5	1911	Mackenzie,r.	300.	500.	700.	1,000.	1,500.	2,000.
24-06	$10	1911	Stikeman,r.	450.	750.	1,000.	—	—	—
24-07	$10	1911	Mackenzie,r.	300.	500.	700.	1,000.	1,500.	—
24-10	$20	1911	Mackenzie,r.	2,000.	3,000.	4,000.	—	—	—
24-14	$50	1911	Mackenzie,r.	2,000.	3,000.	4,000.	—	—	—
24-16	$100	1911	Mackenzie,r.	2,500.	4,000.	5,500.	—	—	—

SPECIMEN NOTES

Cat. No.	Den.	Date	Variety		Unc
24-02S	$5	1911	Stikeman, r.	SPECIMEN	650.
24-04S	$5	1911	Mackenzie. R.	SPECIMEN	650.
24-06S	$10	1911	Stikeman, r.	SPECIMEN	650.
24-07S	$10	1911	Mackenzie, r.	SPECIMEN	650.
24-08S	$20	1911	Stikeman, r.	SPECIMEN	750.
24-10S	$20	1911	Mackenzie, r.	SPECIMEN	750.
24-12S	$50	1911	Stikeman, r.	SPECIMEN	750.
24-14S	$50	1911	Mackenzie, r.	SPECIMEN	750.
24-16S	$100	1911	Mackenzie, r.	SPECIMEN	750.

CANADA BANK

1792

MONTREAL, LOWER CANADA

BANK NUMBER 60 ***NONREDEEMABLE***

The Canada Bank may have been established in 1792 in Montreal as a private company. It is possible that it was established because of fur trade rivalry.

60-10. ISSUE OF 1792

This issue comes in notes of two sizes: — shillings 11.2 x 8.2 cm and — pounds 20 x 12 cm. Both sizes were printed on watermarked paper.

DESIGNS AND COLOURS

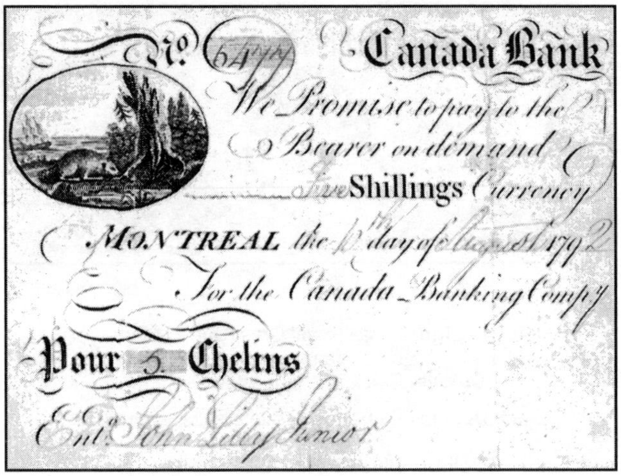

60-10-04

Shillings Face Design: Beaver gnawing at stump/—/ Engraved "For the Canada Banking Comp.y"

Colour: Black with no tint

Back Design: Plain

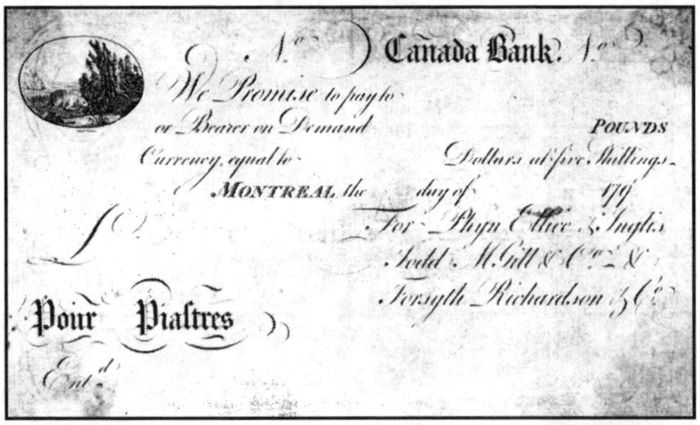

60-10-06R

Pounds Face Design: Beaver gnawing at stump/—/ Engraved "For Phyn Ellis & Inglis"/Todd McGill & Co. &/"Forsyth, Richardson & Co."

Colour: Black with no tint

Back Design: Plain

IMPRINT
Albby Sc., London

SIGNATURES
left only
mss. John Lilly Junior

ISSUE DATING
Partially Engraved__179_:
The 10th day of August, 1792

Notes 10-04 and 10-06 are remainders, * unsigned, undated and unnumbered.

Cat.No.	Denom.	Date	Variety	VG	F	VF	EF	Unc
10-02R	— shillings	179_	Remainder*	400.	600.	800.	1,500.	—
10-04	5 shillings	1792		600.	900.	1,350.	2,000.	—
10-06R	— pounds	179_	Remainder*	900.	1,300.	2,000.	3,500.	—

THE CANADA BANK

1855

TORONTO, CANADA WEST

BANK NUMBER 65 ***NONREDEEMABLE***

This bank intended to operate under The Free Banking Act, but never opened for business under the name of The Canada Bank. It is the Bank of Canada in the Province of Canada, chartered in 1858, and which later operated as The Canadian Bank of Commerce. See "History of the Canadian Bank of Commerce" Vol. 2, Victor Ross, Pages 9 & 18.

65-10. DANFORTH, WRIGHT & CO. PRINTINGS 1855

DESIGNS AND COLOURS

Photo Not Available

65-10-01P
$1 Face Design: Queen Victoria/Niagara Falls/Prince Albert
Colour: Black with no tint

Back Design: Plain

65-10-02P
$1 (5s) Face Design: Queen Victoria (Chalon portrait)/ Roebling Suspension Bridge/ Prince /Albert
Colour: Black with no tint

Back Design: Plain

65-10-04P
$2 (10s) Face Design: Woman with sickle and grain sprigs/ Royal Crest/
Colour: Black with no tint

Back Design: Plain

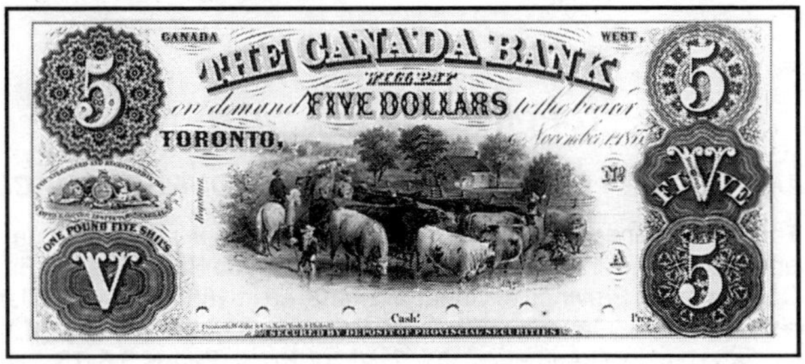

65-10-06P
$5 (£1.5) Face Design: —/cattle standing in pond drinking/—
Colour: Black with no tint

Back Design: Plain

IMPRINT
Danforthm Wright & Co. New York and Philad'a

SIGNATURES

Left	**right**
None	none

ISSUE DATING
Engraved

November 1st, 1855

PROOF NOTES

Cat. No.	Denom.	Date	Variety		Unc
10-01P	$1 (5s)	1855	Falls	FACE PROOF	750.
10-02P	$1 (5s)	1855	Bridge	FACE PROOF	750.
10-04P	$2 (10s)	1855		FACE PROOF	750.
10-06P	$5 (£1.5)	1855		FACE PROOF	750.
Full sheet $1.1.2.5					4,000.

THE BANK OF CANADA

1818 - 1831

MONTREAL, LOWER CANADA

BANK NUMBER 70 ***NONREDEEMABLE***

The Bank of Canada began business in 1818 as a private corporation. It submitted its first petition to incorporate in December of 1820, and obtained a charter in 1822. By 1825 a rapid decline had taken place in its business and the problems of the institution were compounded by the depression of 1826. By 1831 all business by the bank was discontinued and it was to be absorbed by The Bank of Montreal upon the lapse of its charter. There is no relation between this bank and the present Bank of Canada.

70-10 **FIRST ISSUE 1818 - 1822**

DESIGNS AND COLOURS

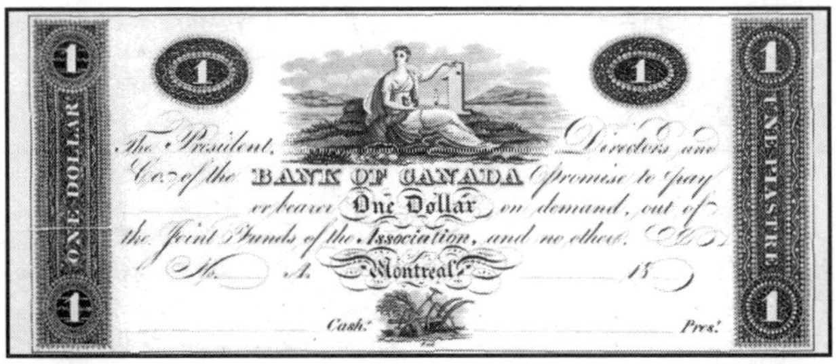

70-10-02P
$1 Face Design: —/seated woman with cornucopia and left hand on 1, agricultural tools and sheaves below/—
Colour: Black with no tint

Back Design: Plain

70-10-04P
$2 Face Design: Seated woman with sword and right hand on 2, small ship below/—Inscribed "AT THE MECHANICS' BANK IN THE CITY OF N. YORK." and 2's in top counters
Colour: Black with no tint

Back Design: Plain

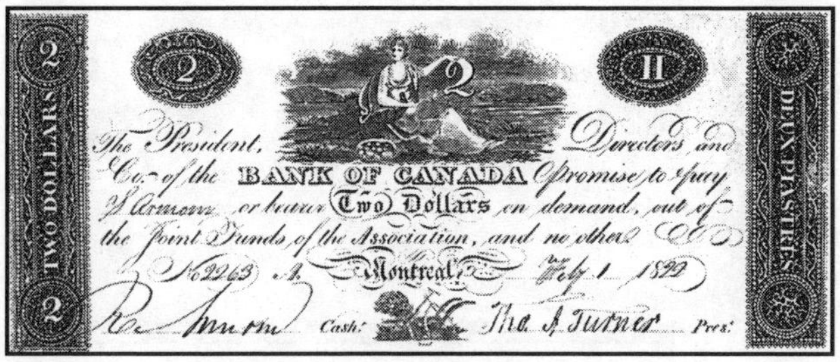

70-10-06
$2 Face Design: Seated woman with cornucopia and left hand on 2; agriculture tools and sheaves below/—and "2" "II" in counters at top
Colour: Black with no tint
Back Design: Plain

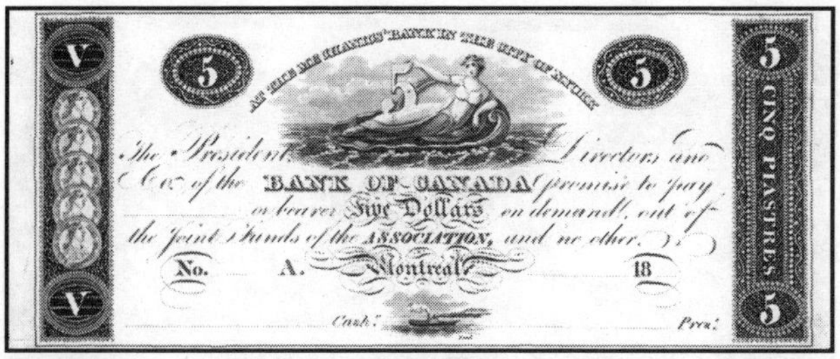

70-10-08P
$5 Face Design: Five Spanish dollars/woman afloat with right hand on 5, paddlewheeler below/"Inscribed" AT THE MECHANICS' BANK IN THE CITY OF N.YORK."
Colour: Black with no tint
Back Design: Plain

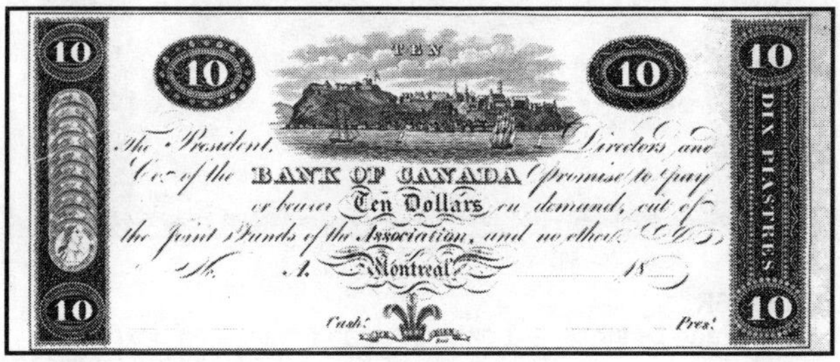

70-10-10P
$10 Face Design: Ten Spanish dollars/town and citadel on hill, Prince of Wales crest below/—
Colour: Black with no tint
Back Design: Plain

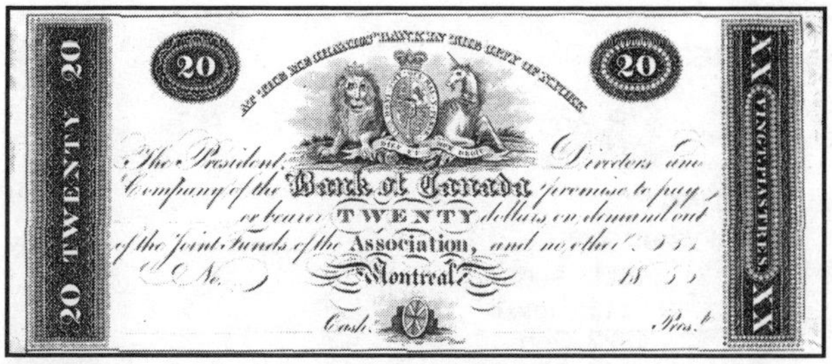

70-10-12P
$20 Face Design: —/Royal Crest, shield against bales below/—Inscribed "AT THE MECHANICS' BANK IN THE CITY OF N. YORK"
Colour: Black with no tint
Back Design: Plain

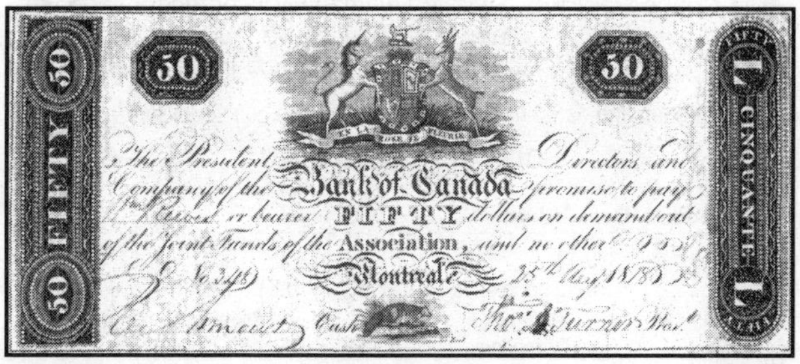

70-10-14
$50 Face Design: —/Crest, beaver below/—
Colour: Black with no tint
Back Design: Plain

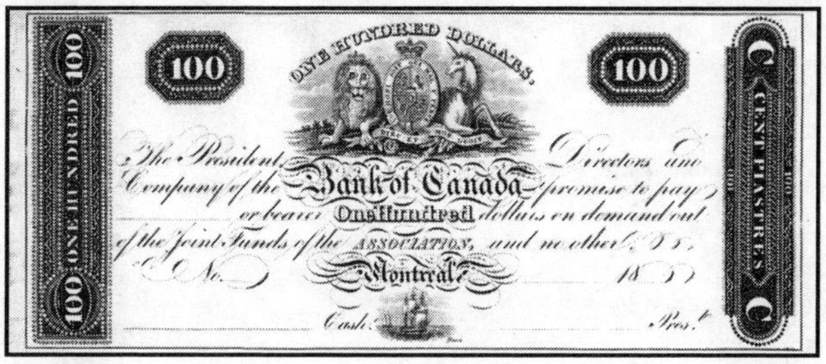

70-10-16P
$100 Face Design: —/Royal Crest, ships below/—
Colour: Black with no tint
Back Design: Plain

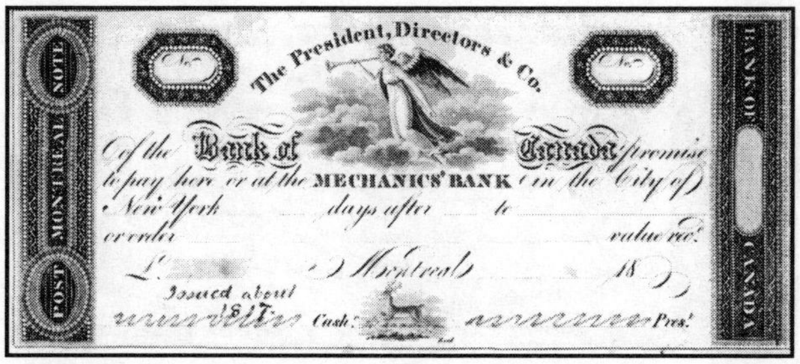

70-10-18P
Post Note Face Design: Angel in clouds blowing trumpet, running deer at bottom
Colour: Black with no tint
Back Design: Plain

IMPRINT

Reed

SIGNATURES

left	right
mss. R. Armour	mss. Tho. A. Turner
mss. R. Armour	mss. H. MacKenzie

ISSUE DATING

Partially Engraved: __18__:

$1 **1818:** Aug. 1
1819: Nov. 6
$2 **1822:** Feb. 1
$50 **1818:** 25th Augt

POST NOTE: **1818:** 17 Sept.
1822: 17 Augt

VARIETIES

$2 Face Design: —/seated woman with sword and right hand on 2, small ship below/— Inscribed "AT THE MECHANICS' BANK IN THE CITY OF N. YORK." and 2's in top counters

$2 Face Design: —/seated woman with cornucopia and left hand on 2, agriculture tools and sheaves below/-and "2" "II" in counters at top

Note: Most signed and dated notes of the first issue are counterfeits.

CIRCULATING NOTES

Cat.No.	Denom.	Date	Variety	G	VG	F	VF	EF	Unc
10-02	$1	1818-19		125.	250.	400.	700.	1,000.	—
10-02C	$1	1818-19	counterfeit	50.	100.	125.	175.	250.	—
10-04	$2	18__	Sword vign		No known issued notes				
10-06C	$2	1822	Cornucopia vign*	50.	100.	125.	175.	250.	—
10-08	$5	18__			No known issued notes				
10-10	$10	18__			No known issued notes				
10-12	$20	18__			No known issued notes				
10-14	$50	1818		350.	600.	—	—	—	—
10-14C	$50	1818	Counterfeit	90.	140.	—	—	—	—
10-16	$100	18__			No known issued notes				
10-17	$500	18__			No known issued notes				
10-18a	Post Note	1818		250.	400.	—	—	—	—
10-18b	Post Note	1822		250.	400.	—	—	—	—

*(Counterfeit)

PROOF NOTES

Cat. No.	Denom.	Date	Variety		Unc
10-02P	$1	18__		PROOF	500.
10-04P	$2	18__	Sword vign.	PROOF	500.
10-08P	$5	18__		PROOF	500.
10-10P	$10	18__		PROOF	500.
10-12P	$20	18__		PROOF	500.
10-14P	$50	18__		PROOF	500.
10-16P	$100	18__		PROOF	500.
10-17P	$500	18__		PROOF	750.
10-18P	Post Note	18__		PROOF	400.

70-12. SECOND ISSUE 1818 - 1823

DESIGN AND COLOURS

70-12-02-01R

$1 Face Design: —/Horse pulling couple in sleigh; coin below/—Payee engraved "J. Dewitt"
Colour: Black with no tint

Back Design: Plain

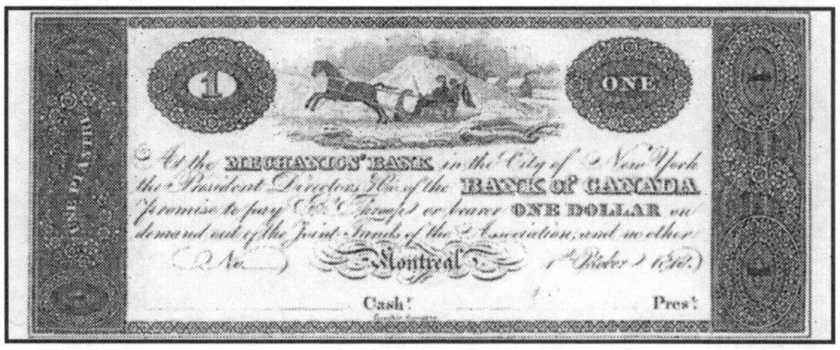

70-12-02-02R

$1 Face Design: —/Horse pulling couple in sleigh/— Inscribed "AT THE MECHANICS' BANK in the city of New York", and 1, ONE in top counters; Payee engraved "B. Throop"
Colour: Black with no tint

Back Design: Plain

70-12-02-03

$2 Face Design: —/seated woman with sickle, two coins below/—Payee engraved "T. Fisher"
Colour: Black with no tint

Back Design: Plain

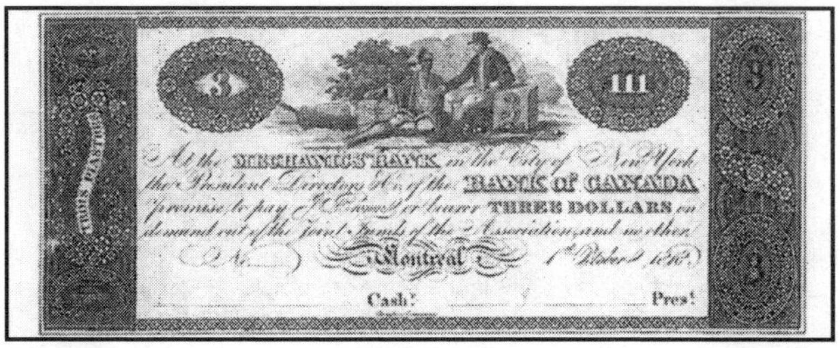

70-12-02-06R

$3 Face Design: —/boat, native and man, 3 on box/— Inscribed "AT THE MECHANICS' BANK in the city of New York", and 3, 111 in top counters. Payee engraved "J. Brown"
Colour: Black with no tint

Back Design: Plain

70-12-02-07R

$5 Face Design: —/boat, seated native with lion, five coins below/—Payee engraved "S. S. Keyes"
Colour: Black with no tint

Back Design: Plain

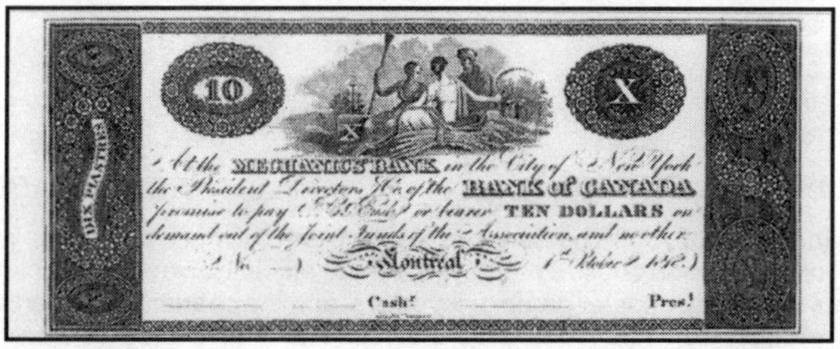

70-12-02-10

$10 Face Design: —/Ship, X on box, three people, sheaves etc./—Inscribed "AT THE MECHANICS' BANK in the City if New York." Payee engraved "T.C. Bush"

Colour: Black with no tint

Back Design: Plain

IMPRINT

Graphic Company

SIGNATURES

left	right
mss. R. Armour	mss. Tho. A. Turner
mss. R. Armour	mss. H. Mackenzie

2. ENGRAVED DATE, ENGRAVED PAYEE'S NAME

ISSUE DATING

Engraved

1st October 1818

Cat.No.	Den.	Date	Variety	G	VG	F	VF	EF	Unc
12-02-01R	$1	1818		—	—	—	—	750.	—
12-02-02R	$1	1818	Mechanics Bank	—	—	—	—	750.	—
12-02-03	$2	1818		110.	225.	300.	425.	750.	—
12-02-04	$2	1818	Mechanics Bank		Note not confirmed				
12-02-05	$3	1818			Note not confirmed				
12-02-06R	$3	1818	Mechanics Bank	—	—	—	—	750.	—
12-02-07	$5	1818		110.	225.	300.	425.	750.	—
12-02-08	$5	1818	Mechanics Bank		Note not confirmed				
12-02-09	$10	1818			Note not confirmed				
12-02-10R	$10	1818	Mechanics Bank	—	—	—	—	750.	—

4. PARTIALLY ENGRAVED DATE, PAYEE'S NAME NOT ENGRAVED

70-12-04-02

$5 Face Design: —/seated Indian with lion and 5, five coins below/—

Colour: Black with no tint

Back Design: Plain

ISSUE DATING

Partially Engraved__18__:

1819: June 4
1820: 6th January
1823: June 4th

Cat.No.	Denom.	Date	G	VG	F	VF	EF	Unc
12-04-02	$5	1819-23	100.	200.	300.	400.	750.	—

70-13 REED AND STILES ISSUE

DESIGNS AND COLOURS

70-13-30C

$5 Face Design: —/Ship building, woman,FIVE/—; five coins below

Colour: Black with no tint

Back Design: Plain

IMPRINT

Reed and Stiles

SIGNATURES

left	right
mss. R. Armour	mss. H. MacKenzie

ISSUE DATING

Partially Engraved: ___18 ___:

$5 1823: 1 June

Cat.No.	Denom.	Date	Variety	G	VG	F	VF	EF	AU
13-30C	$5	1823	Counterfeit	40.	80.	100.	135.	175.	200.

Note: These notes are probably all counterfeit. Design is similar to Montreal Bank 550-14-08

70-14. **GRAPHIC ISSUE OF 1822**

DESIGNS AND COLOURS

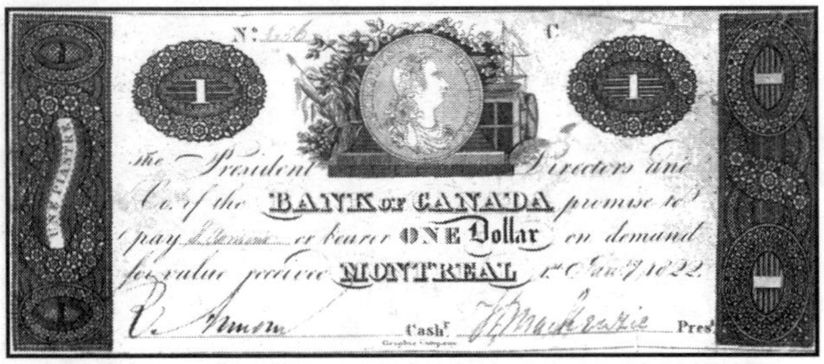

70-14-02

$1 Face Design: —/"coin" of George IV superimposed over produce/—
Colour: Black with no tint

Back Design: Plain

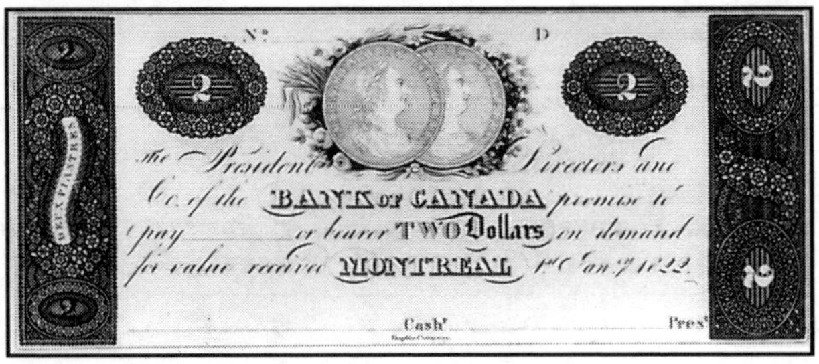

70-14-04

$2 Face Design: —/two "coins" of George IV superimposed over flowers/—
Colour: Black with no tint

Back Design: Plain

IMPRINT

Graphic Company

SIGNATURES

left	**right**
mss. R.Armour	mss. Tho. A.Turner
mss. R.Armour	mss. H. Mackenzie

ISSUE DATING

Engraved

1st Janry, 1822

Note: Beware of counterfeits.

Cat.No.	Denom.	Date	G	VG	F	VF	EF	AU
14-02	$1	1822	100.	200.	300.	400.	750.	—
14-04	$2	1822	100.	200.	300.	400.	750.	—

THE CANADIAN BANK OF COMMERCE

1867 - 1961

TORONTO, ONTARIO

BANK NUMBER 75 ***REDEEMABLE***

In August of 1858 The Bank of Canada in the Province of Canada was incorporated and chose Toronto as its head office. However, this charter was bought by another group of investors, and the charter was amended by August 15, 1866, changing the name to The Canadian Bank of Commerce. On May 15, 1867, the bank opened for business in Toronto with an authorized capital of $1,000,000.

The bank showed rapid progress and by 1871 had 18 branches in Ontario and 1 in Montreal. In 1870 it absorbed The Gore Bank, an institution which at one time had shared a leading position with The Bank of Upper Canada and The Commercial Bank. Further expansion occurred following amalgamations with The Bank of British Columbia in 1901, The Halifax Banking Company in 1903, The Merchants Bank of P.E.I. in 1906 and The Eastern Townships Bank in 1912. Total assets of the bank had grown from $3 million in 1868 to $70 million in 1901, $113 million in 1906 and $246 Million in 1912.

Continuing to expand during World War I, the bank's assets reached $440 million by 1918, ranking it as the third largest bank in Canada. Like other banks, it gave considerable assistance to the government, and despite wartime operating conditions it continued to expand its business. In 1961 it amalgamated with The Imperial Bank of Canada to form the Canadian Imperial Bank of Commerce.

75-10. **ISSUES OF 1867 - 1871**

DESIGNS AND COLOURS

75-10-02b

$1 Face Design: Woman on shell pulled by dolphins/ small female head below/Indian maiden
Colour: Black with green tint

Back Design: Lathework, counters and bank name
Colour: Green

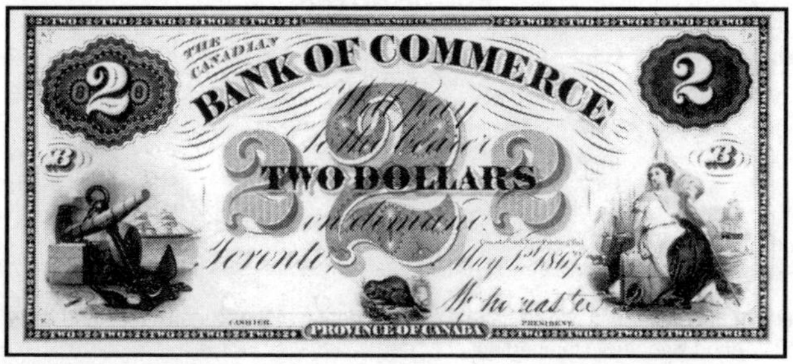

75-10-04P

$2 Face Design: Anchor, box and barrel “Exports”/ small beaver below/seated woman at wharf
Colour: Black with green tint

Back Design: Lathework, counters and bank name
Colour: Green

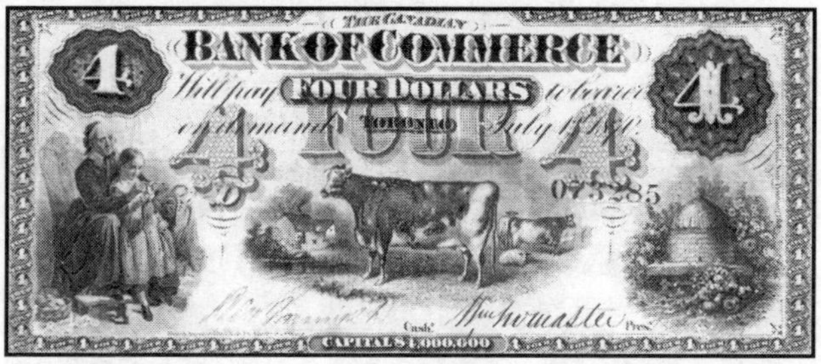

75-10-06

$4 Face Design: Old woman teaching girl to knit, “The first lesson”/cattle/beehive
Colour: Black with green tint

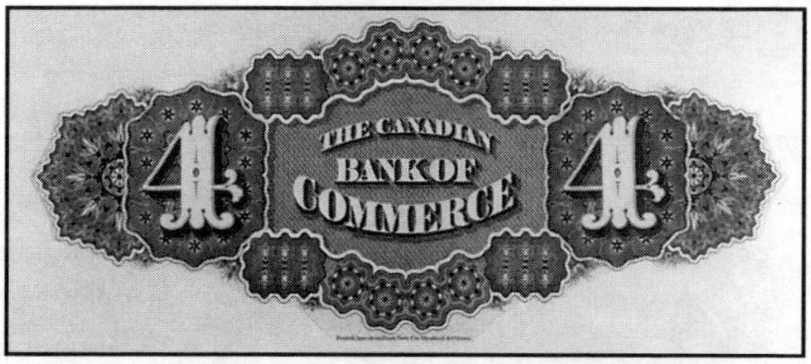

Back Design: Lathework, counters and bank name
Colour: Green

75-10-08

$5 Face Design: —/Queen Victoria in “Window’s weeds”/— See varieties
Colour: Black with green tint

Back Design: Lathework, counters and bank name
Colour: Green

75-10-18P

$10 Face Design: —/Royal Crest/— See varieties
Colour: Black with green tint

Back Design: Lathework, counters and bank name
Colour: Green

75-10-22

$50 Face Design: Seated allegorical female "Intelligence" /—/seated allegorical female holding torch, child "Science" See varieties

Colour: Black with green tint

Back Design: Lathework, counters and bank name

Colour: Green

IMPRINT

British American Bank Note Co. Montreal & Ottawa

SIGNATURES

left	**right or below**
mss. various	engr. Wm. McMaster

ISSUE DATING

Engraved

May 1st, 1867
July 1st, 1870
May 1st, 1871

OVERPRINT

Some notes of 1867:
"GUELPH" in blue
"HAMILTON" in blue
"LONDON" in blue
"ST. CATHARINES" in blue
"G" in red and "ST. CATHARINES" in blue

VARIETIES

Face Design: "CAPITAL $4,000.000" printed at bottom
Face Design: "CAPITAL $6,000.000" printed at bottom

CIRCULATING NOTES

Cat.No.	Denom.	Date	Variety	G	VG	F	VF	EF
10-02	$1	1867	no o/p	500.	1,000.	1,500.	2,000.	—
10-02a	$1	1867	LONDON o/p	550.	1,100.	1,600.	2,200.	—
10-02b	$1	1867	other o/p	700.	1,400.	2,000.	2,750.	—
10-04	$2	1867	no o/p	750.	1,500.	2,500.	—	—
10-04a	$2	1867	with o/p	800.	1,600.	2,750.	—	—
10-06	$4	1870		400.	800.	1,200.	2,000.	—
10-08	$5	1867	no o/p	1,000.	2,000.	3,500.	—	—
10-08a	$5	1867	with o/p	1,100.	2,200.	3,750.	—	—
10-10	$5	1871*	"CAPITAL $4,000.000"	1,250.	2,500.	4,250.	—	—
10-12	$5	1871*	"CAPITAL $6,000.000"	1,250.	2,500.	4,250.	—	—
10-12C	$5	1871	Counterfeit	75.	150.	200.	—	—
10-14	$10	1867		Institutional collections only				
10-16	$10	1871**	"CAPITAL $4,000.000"	Institutional collections only				
10-18	$10	1871**	"CAPITAL $6,000,000"	Institutional collections only				
10-18C	$10	1871	Counterfeit	50.	100.	140.	—	—
10-20	$50	1870	"CAPITAL $4,000.000"	Institutional collections only				
10-22	$50	1870	"CAPITAL $6,000.000"	Institutional collections only				

PROOF NOTES

Cat. No.	Denom.	Date		Unc
10-02P	$1	1867	FACE PROOF	500.
10-04P	$2	1867	FACE PROOF	500.
10-06P	$4	1870	FACE PROOF	500.
10-08P	$5	1867	FACE PROOF	500.
10-14P	$10	1867	FACE PROOF	500.
10-16P	$10	1871	FACE PROOF	600.
10-20P	$50	1870	FACE PROOF	750.

*Beware of counterfeits, which have a poor rendering of the Queen's face and have the left-hand signature stamped on.

**Beware of well done counterfeits.

75-12. ISSUES OF 1879 and 1887

DESIGNS AND COLOURS

75-12-02P

$5 Face Design: —/Hon. Wm. McMaster/— See varieties

Colour: Black with green tint

Back Design: Lathework, counters and bank name

Colour: Green

75-12-04

$5 Face Design: —/Hon. Wm. McMaster/— See varieties

Colour: Black with green tint

Back Design: Lathework, counters, bank name and Coat of Arms

Colour: Green

75-12-06P

$10 Face Design: —/Hon. Wm. McMaster/ship/ Henry W. Darling
Colour: Black with green tint

Back Design: Lathework, counters and bank name
Colour: Green

IMPRINT

British American Bank Note Co. Montreal

SIGNATURES

left	**right**
$5: engr. Wm. McMaster	mss. various
$10: mss. various	engr. Henry W. Darling

ISSUE DATING

Engraved

1st Jan. 1879
3rd Jan, 1887

VARIETIES

$5 Face Design: Rectangular frame around portrait
$5 Face Design: Oval frame around portrait

CIRCULATING NOTES

Cat.No.	Denom.	Date	Variety	G	VG	F	VF	EF
12-02	$5	1879	Rectangular	—	2,000.	3,000.	6,000.	—
12-04	$5	1879	Oval	1,500.	2,500.	3,500.	7,000.	—
12-06	$10	1887	No known issued notes					

PROOF NOTES

Cat. No.	Denom.	Date	Variety		Unc
12-02P	$5	1879	Rectangular	FACE PROOF	600.
12-06P	$10	1887		FACE PROOF	Rare

75-14. ISSUES OF 1888 - 1912

DESIGNS AND COLOURS

$5, $10 & 100: Amounts of capital printed under the bank seal.
$20 & $50: Amount of capital printed at top of note.

75-14-04c

$5 Face Design: Woman with books, lamp/—/ Bank Seal
Colour: Black with orange and yellow-brown tint

Back Design: Lathework, counters, bank name and bank building
Colour: Brown

75-14-18

$10 Face Design: Bank Seal/helmeted woman's head and cherubs/child painting
Colour: Black with yellow and rose tint

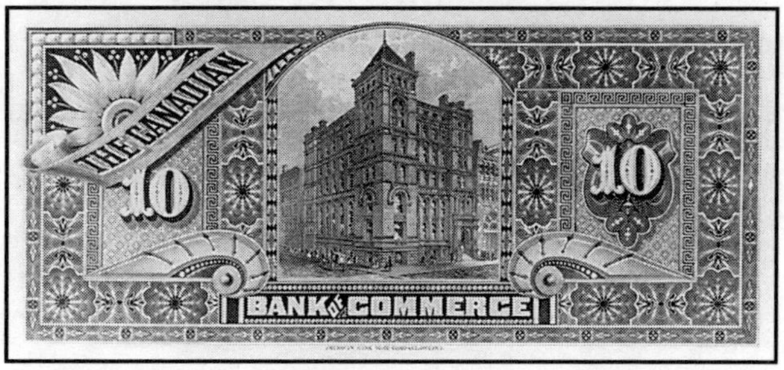

Back Design: Lathework, counters, bank name and bank building
Colour: Blue

75-14-42

$20 Face Design: Ships, child and dolphin/Bank Seal/ seated woman with globe and urn
Colour: Black with orange and green tint

Back Design: Lathework, counters, bank name and bank building
Colour: Orange

75-14-50

$50 Face Design: —/seated woman with urn, lyre/—
Colour: Black with yellow and brown tint

Back Design: Lathework, counters, bank name and bank building
Colour: Brown

75-14-62S

$100 Face Design: —/seated woman with books, globe/—
Colour: Black with orange and blue tint

Back Design: Lathework, counters, bank name, bank building and griffens
Colour: Green

IMPRINT

American Bank Note Co. New York
American Bank Note Company, Ottawa

SIGNATURES

	Left	right	Capital
1888:	engr. Henry W. Darling	mss. various	$ 6,000,000
1892:	engr. Geo. A. Cox	mss. various	$ 6,000,000
1893:	engr. Geo. A. Cox	mss. various	$ 6,000,000
1901:	engr. Geo. A. Cox	mss. various	$ 8,000,000
1906:	engr. Geo. A. Cox	mss. various	$10,000,000
1907:	typed B.E. Walker	mss. various	$10,000,000
1912:	typed B.E. Walker	mss. various	$15,000,000
	typed B.E. Walker	typed A.H. Ireland	$15,000,000
	typed B.E. Walker	typed John Aird	$15,000,000
	typed B.E. Walker	typed Alex Laird	$15,000,000

ISSUE DATING

Engraved

2nd January 1888	2nd January 1906
2nd January 1892	8th January 1907
3rd July 1893	1st May 1912
2nd January 1901	

VARIETIES

$5 1892 Face Design: Imprint American Bank Note Co. New York, vertically at right
$5 1892 Face Design: Imprint American Bank Note Company, Ottawa, horizontally at bottom
$5 1912 Face Design: Black face check letter A, B, C or D (plain series)
$5 1912 Face Design: White face check letter A, B, C or D ("A" series - prefix A precedes sheet number)

OVERPRINT

A. "D D" or "SS" in red
B. "YUKON" twice in blue, green or purple
C. "DAWSON" twice in red
D. "DAWSON" twice in red or green
E. "E E" or "H H" in red
F. "YUKON" twice in red, green or orange
G. "YUKON" Twice in brown

CIRCULATING NOTES

Cat.No.	Denom.	Date	Variety	G	VG	F	VF	EF
14-02	$5	1888		1,100.	1,800.	—	—	—
14-04	$5	1892	imprint at right	100.	200.	300.	550.	—
14-04a	$5	1892	imprint at bottom	100.	200.	300.	550.	—
14-04b	$5	1892	D D or S S o/p (A)	250.	500.	700	—	—
14-04c	$5	1892	YUKON o/p (B)	3,750.	7,500.	10,000.	12,000.	—
14-06	$5	1901		85.	175.	250	450.	700.
14-06a	$5	1901	"DAWSON" o/p (C)	—	—	10,000.	—	—
14-08	$5	1906		125.	250.	500.	—	—
14-08a	$5	1906	"E E" o/p	200.	400.	700.	—	—
14-08b	$5	1906	"H H" o/p	175.	350.	600.	—	—
14-10	$5	1907		70.	140.	200.	375.	600.
14-12	$5	1912	Mss. signature, r.	100.	200.	300.	500.	—
14-14	$5	1912	Ireland, r. black face check letter	55.	110.	160.	325.	525.
14-14a	$5	1912	Ireland, r. white face check letter	55.	110.	160.	325.	525.
14-16	$10	1888		300.	600.	1,000.	—	—
14-18	$10	1892		125.	250.	425.	700	—
14-18a	$10	1892	"YUKON" o/p (B)	—	—	13,000.	—	—
14-20	$10	1901		135.	275.	475.	750.	1,000.
14-20a	$10	1901	"DAWSON" o/p (C)	Institutional collection only				
14-22	$10	1906		125.	250.	400.	550.	900.
14-24	$10	1907		100.	200.	350.	500.	800.
14-26	$10	1912	Mss. signature, r.	100.	200.	300.	500.	—
14-28	$10	1912	Ireland, r.	70.	140.	200.	400.	600.
14-30	$20	1888		1,200.	2,000.	—	—	—
14-32	$20	1892		No known issued notes				
14-32a	$20	1892	"YUKON" o/p (F)	No known issued notes				
14-34	$20	1901		No known issued notes				
14-34a	$20	1901	"YUKON" o/p (G)	No known issued notes				
14-34b	$20	1901	"DAWSON" o/p (C)	No known issued notes				
14-36	$20	1906		600.	1,200.	—	—	—
14-38	$20	1907		600.	1,200.	—	—	—
14-40	$20	1912	Mss. signature, r.	150.	300.	—	—	—
14-42	$20	1912	Aird, r.	90.	180.	300.	500.	800.
14-44	$50	1893		No known issued notes				
14-44a	$50	1893	"YUKON" o/p (F)	No known issued notes				
14-46	$50	1901		No known issued notes				
14-46a	$50	1901	"DAWSON" o/p (D)	No known issued notes				
14-48	$50	1906		1,000.	2,000.	—	—	—
14-50	$50	1907		800.	1,600.	—	—	—
14-52	$50	1912	Mss. signature, r.	No known issued notes				
14-54	$50	1912	Laird or Aird,r.	600.	1,200.	—	—	—
14-56	$100	1888		Institutional collection only				
14-57	$100	1898		No known issued notes				
14-58	$100	1901		No known issued notes				
14-60	$100	1906		No known issued notes				
14-61	$100	1907		No known issued notes				
14-62	$100	1912	Mss. signature, r.	Institutional collection only				
14-64	$100	1912	Laird or Aird,r.	600.	1,200.	—	—	—

PROOF NOTES

Proofs exist for many issues. General pricing guidelines for UNC face proofs are:

$5, $10	$300.
$20	$450.
$50	$550.
$100	$700.

SPECIMEN NOTES

Specimens exist of nearly all issues, 1888 to 1912. General pricing guidlines for UNC specimens are:

$5, $10, $20	$600.
$5, $10, $20 YUKON o/p	$4,500.
$50	$750.
$50 YUKON o/p	$6,000.
$100	$1,000.
$100 YUKON o/p	$6,000.

Uncut specimen sheets (4) sell for a premium of 20 to 25% over the value of the individual notes.

75-16. **ISSUE OF 1917**

DESIGNS AND COLOURS

75-16-02-02

$5 Face Design: Allegorical group: Mercury with "Architecture" at left and "Inventor" to the right

Back Design: Mercury/British Crown over Bank Seal/Ceres

75-16-04-12a

$10 Face Design: Pastoral landscape: Juno with bull, Ceres, goat herd

Back Design: Mercury/British Crown over Bank Seal/Ceres

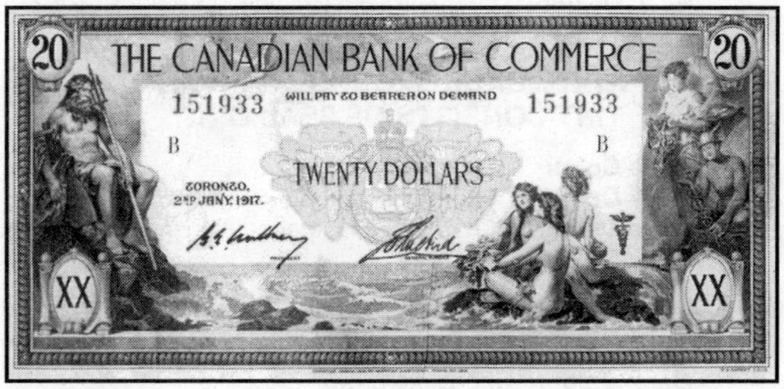

75-16-02-08

$20 Face Design: Seascape: Neptune, sea-maidens, Mercury and maiden

Back Design: Mercury/British Crown over Bank Seal/Ceres

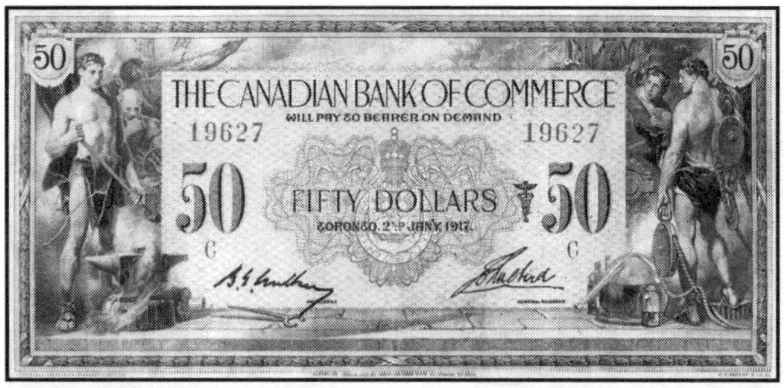

75-16-04-22

$50 Face Design: Industry: vulcan, herculean youths surrounded by symbols of science and industry

Back Design: Mercury/British Crown over Bank Seal/Ceres

75-16-02-12

$100 Face Design: Rocky wastes, mountains and forests, with Mercury and Manufacturing at left, three goddesses at centre left and a sturdy pioneer and explorer at the right

Back Design: Mercury/British Crown over Bank Seal/Ceres

2. WHITE BACKGROUND ON FACE, TINT CONSISTS OF SEAL ONLY

$5 Face Colour: See varieties
Back Colour: Olive green
$10 Face Colour: Black with blue, green, lilac and orange tint
Back Colour: Blue
$20 Face Colour: Black with blue, green, lilac and orange tint
Back Colour: Orange
$50 Face Colour: Black with blue, green, ochre and red tint
Back Colour: Chocolate brown
$100 Face Colour: Black with blue, olive, orange and brown tint
Back Colour: Purple

IMPRINT

American Bank Note Co, Ottawa
Canada Bank Note Company Limited, Ottawa

SIGNATURES

	left	right
$5-$50	typed B.E. Walker	typed John Aird
$100	typed John Aird	typed S.H. Logan

ISSUE DATING

Engraved

2nd Jany. 1917

VARIETIES

$5 Face Colour: Black with green and red tint
(02-02) (numbers up to 505500)
$5 Face Colour: Black with blue, lilac, green and red tint
(02-04) (numbers over 505500)

CIRCULATING NOTES

Cat.No.	Den.	Date	Variety	VG	F	VF	EF	AU	Unc
16-02-02	$5	1917	Green and red seal*	100.	150.	300.	500.	750.	—
16-02-04	$5	1917	Multicoloured seal*	150.	225.	450.	750.	1,100.	—
16-02-06	$10	1917	White backgr.	80.	125.	200.	400.	600.	800.
16-02-08	$20	1917	White backgr.	125.	200.	300.	600.	900.	—
16-02-10	$50	1917	White backgr.	2,500.	3,500.	—	—	—	—
16-02-12	$100	1917	White backgr.	200.	250.	300.	500.	750.	1,000.

Note: These prices apply to notes with **white backgrounds only**. For notes with overall face tints, please refer to the next section.

PROOF NOTES

Proofs of the 1917 issue are common. Face Proofs, UNC $200 - $300

4. OVERALL FACE TINTS WITH SEAL

DESIGNS AND COLOURS

$5. Face Colour: Black with overall green and blue, lilac, green and red tint
Back Colour: Olive green
$10 Face Colour: Black with overall orange and blue, lilac, green and red tint
Back Colour: Olive green
$10 Face Colour: Black with overall orange and blue, green, lilac and orange tint
Back Colour: Blue

Note: A few $10 notes with a cream coloured background have been seen, but are due to a chemical change of the orange tint, and do not constitute a separate variety.

$20 Face Colour: Black with overall yellow and blue, green, lilac and rose tint
Back Colour: Orange
$50 Face Colour: Black with overall olive green and blue, green, ochre and red tint
Back Colour: Brown

IMPRINT

American Bank Note Co. Ottawa
Canadian Bank Note Company Limited, Ottawa

SIGNATURES

	left	right
$5:	typed B.E. Walker	typed John Aird
	typed John Aird	typed F.M. Gibson
	typed John Aird	typed S.H. Logan
$10:	typed B.E. Walker	typed John Aird
	typed John Aird	typed C.W. Rowley
	typed John Aird	typed S.H. Logan
$20:	typed B.E. Walker	typed John Aird
	typed John Aird	typed A.St.L. Trigge
	typed John Aird	typed S.H. Logan
$50:	typed B.E. Walker	typed John Aird
	typed B.E. Walker	typed S.H. Logan
	typed John Aird	typed S.H. Logan

ISSUE DATING

Engraved

Jan. 2, 1917

VARIETIES

$5, $10, $20 Logan, R.: General Manager in lower case, typed GENERAL MANAGER in small capitals, engraved

$5, $10 Walker,l.: Overall face tint, no CBN imprint bottom left margin
Overall face tint, CBN imprint bottom left margin

$5, $10, $20, Logan r.: Small Logan
Large Logan
Decorative Logan

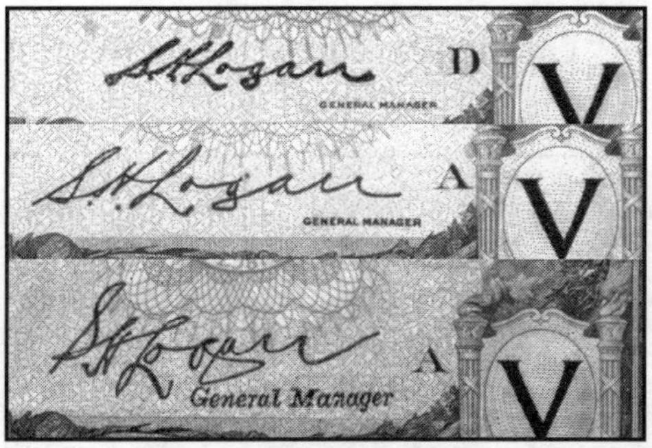

WALKER-AIRD SIGNATURES

Cat.No.	Den.	Date	Variety	VG	F	VF	EF	AU	Unc
16-04-02	$5	1917	Green tint, with CBN	75.	110.	175.	300.	—	—
16-04-02a	$5	1917	Green tint, no CBN	90.	130.	200.	350.	—	—
16-04-08	$10	1917	Orange tint, no CBN	75.	110.	175.	300.	—	—
16-04-08a	$10	1917	Orange tint, with CBN	80.	120.	190.	325.	—	—
16-04-16	$20	1917	Yellow tint	175.	300.	500.	800.	1,200.	—
16-04-22	$50	1917	Olive tint	200.	275.	350.	750.	1,125.	—
16-04-22a	$50	1917	Walker-Logan Signatures	Institutional collection only					

TRANSITIONAL SIGNATURES AND AIRD-LOGAN SIGNATURES

GENERAL MANAGER IN SMALL CAPITALS BELOW LOWER RIGHT SIGNATURE

Cat. No.	Den.	Date	Variety	VG	F	VF	EF	AU	Unc
16-04-04	$5	1917	Gibson, r.	125.	200.	350.	600.	—	—
16-04-06a	$5	1917	Small Logan, r.	50.	75.	100.	175.	275.	400.
16-04-06b	$5	1917	Large Logan, r.	60.	90.	120.	200.	300.	450.
16-04-06d	$5	1917	Decor. Logan, r.	90.	130.	200.	350.	—	—
16-04-10a	$10	1917	Rowley, r.	175.	300.	500.	800.	—	—
16-04-12a	$10	1917	Small Logan, r.	50.	75.	100.	175.	275.	400.
16-04-12b	$10	1917	Large Logan. r.	60.	90.	120.	200.	300.	450.
16-04-12d	$10	1917	Decor. Logan, r.	90.	130.	200.	350.	—	—
16-04-20a	$20	1917	Small Logan, r.	100.	125.	175.	300.	450.	—
16-04-20b	$20	1917	Large Logan, r.	160.	250.	350.	—	—	—
16-04-24	$50	1917	Small Logan, r.	200.	275.	400.	900.	—	—

General Manager IN LOWER CASE ITALICS BELOW LOWER RIGHT SIGNATURE

Cat. No.	Den.	Date	Variety	VG	F	VF	EF	AU	Unc
16-04-06	$5	1917	Small Logan, r.	90.	130.	200.	350.	—	—
16-04-06c	$5	1917	Decor. Logan, r.	90.	130.	200.	350.	—	—
16-04-10	$10	1917	Rowley, r.	115.	180.	325.	550.	—	—
16-04-12	$10	1917	Small Logan, r.	90.	130.	200.	350.	—	—
16-04-12c	$10	1917	Decor. Logan, r	90.	130.	200.	350.	—	—
16-04-18	$20	1917	Trigge r.	1,000.	2,000.	3,000.	4,000.	—	—
16-04-20	$20	1917	Small Logan, r.	200.	350.	600.	—	—	—
16-04-20c	$20	1917	Decor. Logan, r	200.	350.	600.	—	—	—

Proofs of the 1917 series are common. Face Proof Unc $200.00 - $300.00.

75-18. ISSUE OF 1935 SMALL SIZE NOTES

DESIGNS AND COLOURS

75-18-02

$5 Face Design: Allegorical group: Mercury with "Architecture" at left and "Invention" to the right
Colour: Black with overall green and blue, green, lilac and red tint
Back Design: Mercury/British Crown over Bank Seal/Ceres
Colour: Olive Green

75-18-06

$10 Face Design: Pastoral landscape: Juno with bull, Ceres, goat herd
Colour: Black with overall orange and blue, green, lilac and orange tint
Back Design: Mercury/British Crown over Bank Seal/Ceres
Colour: Blue

75-18-10

$20 Face Design: Seascape: Neptune, sea-maidens, Mercury and maiden
Colour: Black with overall yellow and blue, green, lilac and rose tint
Back Design: Mercury/British Crown over Bank Seal/Ceres
Colour: Orange

IMPRINT

Canadian Bank Note Company Limited

SIGNATURES

left	right
typed John Aird	typed S.H. Logan
typed S.H. Logan	typed S.M. Wedd
typed S.H. Logan	typed A.E. Arscott

ISSUE DATING

Engraved

2nd Jany. 1935

CIRCULATING NOTES

Cat.No.	Den.	Date	Variety	VG	F	VF	EF	AU	Unc
18-02	$5	1935	Logan, r.	35.	55.	85.	175.	275.	400.
18-04	$5	1935	Arscott, r.	40.	60.	95.	190.	300.	450.
18-05	$5	1935	Wedd, r*	—	—	—	—	2,200.	3,000.
18-06	$10	1935	Logan, r.	35.	55.	85.	175.	275.	400.
18-08	$10	1935	Arscott, r	40.	60.	95.	190.	300.	450.
18-10	$20	1935	Logan, r.	60.	90.	140.	275.	400.	550.

Two sheets (4) of $5 notes signed Logan-Wedd are known. One of these has been cut into individual notes.

PROOF NOTES

Cat. No.	Den.	Date	Variety		Unc
18-02P	$5	1935	B & W	FACE PROOF	200.
18-02Pa	$5	1935	Coloured	FACE PROOF	300.
18-06P	$10	1935	B & W	FACE PROOF	200.
18-06Pa	$10	1935	Coloured	FACE PROOF	300.
18-10P	$20	1935	B & W	FACE PROOF	200.
18-10Pa	$20	1935	Coloured	FACE PROOF	300.

SPECIMEN NOTES

Cat. No.	Den.	Date	Variety		Unc
18-02S	$5	1935		SPECIMEN	600.
18-06S	$10	1935		SPECIMEN	600.
18-10S	$20	1935		SPECIMEN	600.

BRITISH WEST INDIES ISSUES

Trade relations between the province of Nova Scotia and the West Indies had always been active, as far back as the early days of The Halifax Banking Company, the business of which was acquired by The Canadian Bank of Commerce in 1903. The latter opened branches in Havana, Cuba, and Kingston, Jamaica, in 1920, followed by others in Barbados and Trinidad. After the opening of these branches, application was made to local authorities for note issuing privileges similar to those enjoyed by other banks doing business in these colonies. These privileges were granted, and specially designed notes were prepared for use in Jamaica, Trinidad and Barbados. The Jamaica issues appeared in £1 and £5 denominations and the Trinidad and Barbados issues appeared in local denominations of $5, $20 and $100.

75-20. BRIDGETOWN, BARBADOS ISSUES OF 1922 and 1940 LARGE SIZE NOTES

DESIGNS AND COLOURS

75-20-04

$5 Face Design: —/seated woman with lyre and spilling water jug/—

Colour: Black with green and red-orange tint

Back Design: Counters, lathework and Bank Crest

Colour: Orange

75-20-06S

$20 Face Design: —/seated woman with globe, book and looking glass/—

Colour: Black with red-brown and green tint

Back Design: Counters, lathework and Bank Crest

Colour: Green

75-20-10

$100 Face Design: Seated woman with book and lamp/—/—
Colour: Black with blue and olive tint

Back Design: Counters, lathework and Bank Crest
Colour: Chocolate brown

IMPRINT

American Bank Note Company, Ottawa or
Canadian Bank Note Company, Limited

SIGNATURES

	left	right
1922:	typed B.E. Walker	mss. various
	typed John Aird	mss. various
1940:	typed S.H. Logan	mss. various

ISSUE DATING

Engraved

2nd January, 1922.
1st July 1940.

CIRCULATING NOTES

Cat.No.	Denom.	Date	Variety	VG	F	VF	EF	Unc
20-02	$5	1922	Walker, I.	900.	1,200.	—	—	—
20-04	$5	1922	Aird, I.	700.	900.	1,750.	—	—
20-06	$20	1922		Institutional collection only				
20-08	$20	1940		No known issued notes				
20-10	$100	1922		2,000.	—	—	—	—

PROOF NOTES

Cat. No.	Denom.	Date		Unc
20-02P	$5	1922	FACE PROOF	400.
20-06P	$20	1922	FACE PROOF	500.
20-08P	$20	1940	FACE PROOF	500.
20-10P	$100	1922	FACE PROOF	600.

SPECIMEN NOTES

Cat. No.	Denom.	Date		Unc
20-02S	$5	1922	SPECIMEN	600.
20-06S	$20	1922	SPECIMEN	750.
20-08S	$20	1940	SPECIMEN	750.
20-10S	$100	1922	SPECIMEN	1,000.

75-22. BRIDGETOWN, BARBADOS ISSUE OF 1940 SMALL SIZE NOTES

DESIGNS AND COLOURS

75-22-02S

$5 Face Design: Allegorical group: "Architecture", Mercury, "Invention"
Colour: Black with green and red-orange tint

Back Design: Lathework, counters, bank name and Mercury/British crown over Bank seal/Ceres
Colour: Orange

IMPRINT

Canadian Bank Note Company Limited

SIGNATURES

left	right
typed S.H. Logan	typed A.E. Arscott

ISSUE DATING

Engraved

July 1, 1940

CIRCULATING NOTES

Cat.No.	Denom.	Date	VG	F	VF	EF	AU
22-02	$5	1940	550.	700.	900.	1,500.	—

PROOF NOTES

Cat. No.	Denom.	Date		Unc
22-02P	$5	1940	FACE PROOF	700.

SPECIMEN NOTES

Cat. No.	Denom.	Date		Unc
22-02S	$5	1940	SPECIMEN	1,000.

75-24. KINGSTON, JAMAICA ISSUES OF 1921 and 1938 LARGE SIZE NOTES

DESIGNS AND COLOURS

75-24-02

£1 Face Design: Allegorical group: "Architecture", Mercury, "Invention"
Colour: Black with orange tint

Back Design: Lathework, counters, bank name and Mercury/British crown over Bank seal/Ceres
Colour: Brown

75-24-04

£5 Face Design: —/seated woman holding fruit/—
Colour: Black with green and red tint

Back Design: Lathework, counters, bank name and Mercury/British crown over Bank seal/Ceres
Colour: Green

75-24-06P

£5 Face Design: —/seated woman holding fruit/—
Colour: Black with green and red tint
Back Design: Lathework, counters, bank name and Mercury/British crown over Bank seal/Ceres
Colour: Green

IMPRINT

American Bank Note Company, Ottawa or
Canadian Bank Note Company, Limited

SIGNATURES

	left	right
1921:	typed B.E. Walker	mss. various
1938:	typed S.H. Logan	typed A.E. Arscott

ISSUE DATING

Engraved

1st March 1921
1st June 1938

CIRCULATING NOTES

Cat.No.	Denom.	Date	VG	F	VF	EF	AU
24-02	£1	1921	1,250.	1,750.	2,500.	3,500.	—
24-04	£5	1921	800.	1,200.	1,900.	2,800.	3,500.
24-06	£5	1938			No known issued notes		

PROOF NOTES

Cat. No.	Denom.	Date	Variety		Unc
24-02P	£1	1921	B & W	FACE PROOF	300.
24-02Pa	£1	1921	Coloured	FACE PROOF	500.
24-04P	£5	1921	B & W	FACE PROOF	250.
24-04Pa	£5	1921	Coloured	FACE PROOF	400.
24-06P	£5	1938	B & W	FACE PROOF	350.
24-06Pa	£5	1938	Coloured	FACE PROOF	600.

SPECIMEN NOTES

Cat. No.	Denom.	Date		Unc
24-02S	£5	1921	SPECIMEN	800.
24-04S	£5	1921	SPECIMEN	750.
24-06S	£5	1938	SPECIMEN	900.

75-26. KINGSTON, JAMAICA
ISSUE OF 1938
SMALL SIZE NOTES

DESIGNS AND COLOURS

75-26-02

£1 Face Design: Allegorical group: “Architecture”, Mercury, “Invention”
Colour: Black with orange tint

Back Design: Lathework, counters, bank name and Mercury/British crown over Bank seal/Ceres
Colour: Brown

IMPRINT

Canadian Bank Note Company, Ottawa

SIGNATURES

left	right
typed S.H. Logan	typed A.E. Arscott

ISSUE DATE

Engraved

1st June 1938

CIRCULATING NOTES

Cat.No.	Denom	Date	VG	F	VF	EF	AU
26-02	£1	1938	550.	700.	900.	1,500.	—

PROOF NOTES

Cat. No.	Denom.	Date		Unc
26-02P	£1	1938	FACE PROOF	600.

75-28. **PORT OF SPAIN, TRINIDAD**

ISSUES OF 1921
LARGE SIZE NOTES

DESIGNS AND COLOURS

75-28-02

$5 Face Design: —/seated woman with lyre and spilling water jug/—
Colour: Black with green and ochre tint

Back Design: Lathework, counters, bank name and Mercury/British crown over Bank seal/Ceres
Colour: Green

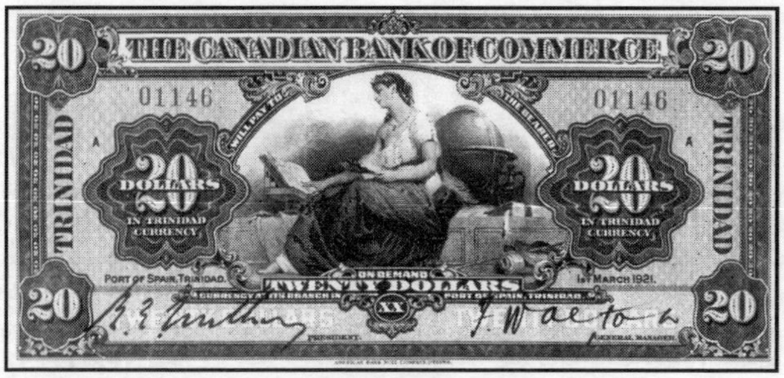

75-28-04

$20 Face Design: —/seated woman with globe, book and looking glass/—
Colour: Black with green and red tint

Back Design: Lathework, counters, bank name and Mercury/British crown over Bank seal/Ceres
Colour: Blue

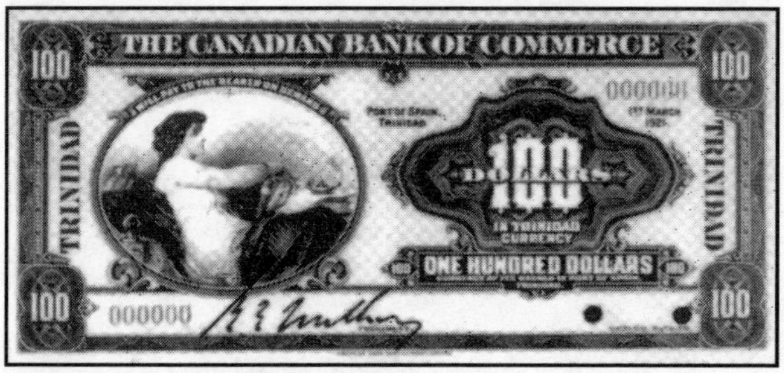

75-28-06S

$100 Face Design: Seated woman with book and lamp/—/—
Colour: Black with olive and red tint

Back Design: Lathework, counters, bank name and Mercury/British crown over Bank seal/Ceres
Colour: Red

IMPRINT

American Bank Note Company, Ottawa

SIGNATURES

left	right
typed B.E. Walker	mss. various

ISSUE DATING

Engraved

1st March 1921

CIRCULATING NOTES

Cat.No.	Denom.	Date	VG	F	VF	EF	AU
28-02	$5	1921	1,000.	1,500.	2,000.	—	—
28-04	$20	1921	1,500.	2,000.	3,000.	—	—
28-06	$100	1921	Institutional collection only				

PROOF NOTES

Cat. No.	Denom.	Date	Variety		Unc
28-02P	$5	1921	B & W	FACE PROOF	350.
28-02Pa	$5	1921	Coloured	FACE PROOF	500.
28-04P	$20	1921	B & W	FACE PROOF	350.
28-04Pa	$20	1921	Coloured	FACE PROOF	500.
28-06P	$100	1921	B & W	FACE PROOF	350.
28-06Pa	$100	1921	Coloured	FACE PROOF	500.

SPECIMEN NOTES

Cat. No.	Denom.	Date		Unc
28-02S	$5	1921	SPECIMEN	750.
28-04S	$20	1921	SPECIMEN	750.
28-06S	$100	1921	SPECIMEN	750.

75-30. PORT OF SPAIN, TRINIDAD
ISSUES OF 1939
SMALL SIZE NOTES

DESIGNS AND COLOURS

75-30-02

$5 Face Design: Allegorical group: "Architecture", Mercury, "Invention"

Colour: Black with ochre and green tint

Back Design: Lathework, counters, the Canadian Bank of Commerce, Mercury/British crown over Bank seal/Ceres

Colour: Green

75-30-04

$20 Face Design: Seascape: Neptune, sea-maidens, Mercury and maiden

Colour: Black with red-orange tint

Back Design: Lathework, counters, the Canadian Bank of Commerce, Mercury/British crown over Bank seal/Ceres

Colour: Blue

IMPRINT

Canadian Bank Note Company Limited

SIGNATURES

left	**right**
typed S.H. Logan	typed A.E. Arscott

ISSUE DATING

Engraved

1st July 1939

CIRCULATING NOTES

Cat.No.	Denom.	Date	VG	F	VF	EF	AU	Unc
30-02	$5	1939	350.	450.	650.	1,100.	—	—
30-04	$20	1939	350.	450.	650.	1,100.	1,650.	2,200.

PROOF NOTES

Cat. No.	Denom.	Date		Unc
30-02P	$5	1939	FACE PROOF	700.
30-04P	$20	1939	FACE PROOF	700.

BANQUE CANADIENNE

1836 - 1838

ST. HYACINTHE, LOWER CANADA

BANK NUMBER 80 ***NONREDEEMABLE***

Established in 1836 as a private corporation at St. Hyacinthe, Lower Canada, this bank failed in 1838 following the panic of 1837 and the suspension of specie payment, despite a measure of relief from the Legislature of Lower Canada.

80-10. DRAFT ISSUE OF 1836

Engraved: "Mssrs Archambault, Pacaud, De La Bruere"

DESIGNS AND COLOURS

80-10-02

$1 Face Design: Men and livestock/cornucopia, sheaf and spinning wheel, beaver below/ man ploughing with horses
Colour: Black with no tint

Back Design: Lathework/habitant/lathework
Colour: Blue-green

80-10-04

$2 Face Design: Britannia, anchor/seated allegorical female, cattle and sheaves, beaver below/—
Colour: Black with no tint

Back Design: Lathework/habitant/lathework
Colour: Blue-green

IMPRINT

Rawdon, Wright and Hatch, New York

SIGNATURES

left	right
none	mss. C.A. Pacaud
none	mss. A.A. Delphos

ISSUE DATING

Partially Engraved __18__:
1836: 23 Augt

Cat.No.	Denom.	Date	G	VG	F	VF	EF	Unc
10-02	$1	1836	85.	175.	250.	375.	—	—
10-04	$2	1836	100.	200.	300.	450.	—	—

80-12. NOTE ISSUE OF 1836

DESIGNS AND COLOURS

80-12-02

$5 Face Design: Indian shooting arrow/sailing ship, deer below/train (sideways)
Colour: Black with no tint

Back Design: Lathework/habitant/lathework
Colour: Green

80-12-04

$10 Face Design: Louis-Joseph Papineau/train, produce and waterfall; man in canoe below/beehive
Colour: Black with no tint

Back Design: Lathework/habitant/lathework
Colour: Green

IMPRINT

Rawdon, Wright and Hatch, New York

SIGNATURES

left	right
mss. L. Archambault	mss. Arch. Plu. De La Bruere & Cie.

ISSUE DATING

Partially Engraved __18__:
1836: Aug. 23

Cat.No.	Denom.	Date	G	VG	F	VF	EF	Unc
12-02	$5	1836	150.	300.	400.	650.	—	—
12-04	$10	1836	150.	300.	400.	650.	—	—

BANQUE CANADIENNE NATIONALE

1924 - 1979

MONTREAL, QUEBEC

BANK NUMBER 85 ***REDEEMABLE***

La Banque Nationale, chartered in Quebec City, Canada East, in 1859 and Banque d'Hochelaga, established in Montreal, Quebec, in 1873, merged in 1924 to become the Banque Canadienne Nationale, although Banque d'Hochelaga did not change its name until Feb. 1, 1925.

The key event which set the stage for the merger of the two banks actually took place in Ontario in 1923. The Home Bank of Canada had failed, and in the same year, La Banque Nationale found itself in a difficult position. An attempt was made to merge the three major Francophone banks, the Nationale, Hochelaga and La Banque Provinciale du Canada. The latter declined, so the directors of the other two banks asked the Quebec Government for assistance. The government made the merger possible by the unusual step of conveying to Banque d'Hochelaga, in full ownership, its bonds for $15 million bearing interest at 5% and maturing in 40 years. Increasing its clientele as a result of the merger, the Banque d'Hochelaga became a much larger institution. The merger greatly increased the number of branches to be operated by the Banque Canadienne Nationale. The Banque d'Hochelaga had 197 branches, the new bank a total of 263. The new bank made such progress that, despite the depression of the 1930's, it was able to reimburse the Quebec Government within 20 years, instead of the stipulated 40.

The war years of 1939 - 1945 produced only token profits for the bank, while expenses and work loads were much greater. From 1945 onwards, the bank's business volume had continued to grow at about the same pace as the national economy. It was the sixth largest bank in Canada with large operations abroad when, on Nov. 1, 1979, it merged with La Banque Provinciale du Canada to form the National Bank of Canada.

85-10. ISSUE OF 1925

DESIGNS AND COLOURS

85-10-02
$5 Face Design: J.A. Vaillancourt/monument/Beaudry Leman
Colour: Black with green tint

Back Design: Bank name, counters and Provincial Crests
Colour: Green

85-10-04
$10 Face Design: J.A. Vaillancourt/monument/Beaudry Leman
Colour: Black with brown tint

Back Design: Bank name, counters and Provincial Crests
Colour: Brown

85-10-06
$20 Face Design: J.A. Vaillancourt/monument/Beaudry Leman
Colour: Black with blue tint

Back Design: Bank name, counters and Provincial Crests
Colour: Blue

85-10-08
$50 Face Design: J.A. Vaillancourt/Maisonneuve monument/Beaudry Leman
Colour: Black with olive tint

Back Design: Bank name, counters and Provincial Crests
Colour: Olive

85-10-10
$100 Face Design: J.A. Vaillancourt/—/Beaudry Leman
Colour: Black with purple tint

Back Design: Bank name, counters and Provincial Crests
Colour: Purple

IMPRINT

Canadian Bank Note Company Limited

SIGNATURES

left	right
typed J.A. Vaillancourt	typed Beaudry Leman

ISSUE DATING

Engraved

Le 1er Fev. 1925

CIRCULATING NOTES

Cat.No.	Denom.	Date	VG	F	VF	EF	AU	Unc
10-02	$5	1925	60.	80.	125.	250.	375.	500.
10-04	$10	1925	65.	90.	150	300.	450.	600.
10-06	$20	1925	175.	250.	350.	600.	—	—
10-08	$50	1925	400.	500.	750.	1,200.	—	—
10-10	$100	1925	550.	750.	1,000.	1,700.	—	—

PROOF NOTES

Cat. No.	Denom.	Date		Unc
10-02P	$5	1925	FACE PROOF	300.
10-04P	$10	1925	FACE PROOF	300.
10-06P	$20	1925	FACE PROOF	350.
10-08P	$50	1925	FACE PROOF	400.
10-10P	$100	1925	FACE PROOF	450.

SPECIMEN NOTES

Cat. No.	Denom.	Date		Unc
10-02S	$5	1925	SPECIMEN	500.
10-04S	$10	1925	SPECIMEN	500.
10-06S	$20	1925	SPECIMEN	550.
10-08S	$50	1925	SPECIMEN	600.
10-10S	$100	1925	SPECIMEN	700.

85-12 **ISSUE OF 1929**

LARGE SIZE NOTES

DESIGNS AND COLOURS

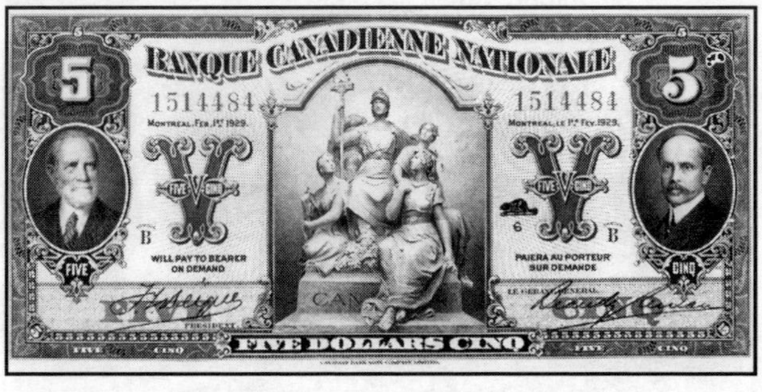

85-12-02

$5 Face Design: F.L. Beique/monument/Beaudry Leman
Colour: Black with green tint

Back Design: Bank name, counters and Provincial Crests
Colour: Green

85-12-04

$10 Face Design: F.L. Beique/monument/Beaudry Leman
Colour: Black with brown tint

Back Design: Bank name, counters and Provincial Crests
Colour: Brown

85-12-06

$20 Face Design: F.L. Beique/monument/Beaudry Leman
Colour: Black with blue tint

Back Design: Bank name, counters and Provincial Crests
Colour: Blue

85-12-08

$50 Face Design: F.L. Beique/Maisonneuve monument/ Beaudry Leman
Colour: Black with orange tint

Back Design: Bank name, counters and Provincial Crests
Colour: Orange

85-12-10S

$100 Face Design: F.L. Beique/—/Beaudry Leman
Colour: Black with purple tint

Back Design: Bank name, counters and Provincial Crests
Colour: Purple

IMPRINT

Canadian Bank Note Company Limited

SIGNATURES

left	right
typed F.L. Beique	typed Beaudry Leman

ISSUE DATING

Engraved

Le 1er Fev. 1929

CIRCULATING NOTES

Cat.No.	Denom.	Date	VG	F	VF	EF	AU	Unc
12-02	$5	1929	60.	80.	125.	250.	375.	500.
12-04	$10	1929	65.	90.	150.	300.	450.	600.
12-06	$20	1929	175.	250.	350.	600.	900.	—
12-08	$50	1929	600.	800.	—	—	—	—
12-10	$100	1929	No known issued notes					

PROOF NOTES

Cat. No.	Denom.	Date		Unc
12-02P	$5	1929	FACE PROOF	300.
12-04P	$10	1929	FACE PROOF	300.
12-06P	$20	1929	FACE PROOF	350.
12-08P	$50	1929	FACE PROOF	400.
12-12P	$100	1929	FACE PROOF	500.

85-14. **ISSUE OF 1935 SMALL SIZE NOTES**

DESIGNS AND COLOURS

85-14-02

$5 Face Design: Hon. J.M. Wilson/monument/Beaudry Leman Esq.
Colour: Black with green tint

Back Design: Lathework, counters, bank name and Provincial Crests
Colour: Green

85-14-04

$10 Face Design: Hon. J.M. Wilson/monument/Beaudry Leman Esq.
Colour: Black with brown tint

Back Design: Lathework, counters, bank name and Provincial Crests
Colour: Brown

IMPRINT
Canadian Bank Note Company Limited

SIGNATURES

left	right
typed J.M. Wilson	typed Beaudry Leman

ISSUE DATING
Engraved
Le 2 Jan. 1935

CIRCULATING NOTES

Cat.No.	Denom.	Date	VG	F	VF	EF	AU	Unc
14-02	$5	1935	50.	70.	110.	225.	350.	475.
14-04	$10	1935	50.	70.	110.	225.	350.	475.

PROOF NOTES

Cat. No.	Denom.	Date		Unc
14-02P	$5	1935	FACE PROOF	250.
14-04P	$10	1935	FACE PROOF	250.

SPECIMEN NOTES

Cat. No.	Denom.	Date		Unc
14-02S	$5	1935	SPECIMEN	500.
14-04S	$10	1935	SPECIMEN	500.

CATARACT BANK

1855 - 1858

NIAGARA CITY

PROVINCE OF CANADA

BANK NUMBER 88 ***NONREDEEMABLE***

Orders for bank-notes were placed with Danforth, Wright and Co. on June 6th 1855 and Aug. 25th, 1858. Whether any notes were actually printed or are still in existence is not known.

THE CENTRAL BANK OF CANADA

1883 - 1887

TORONTO, ONTARIO

BANK NUMBER 90 ***NONREDEEMABLE***

This bank, incorporated in 1883 with its head office in Toronto, should not be confused with the Central Bank of Canada incorporated in 1873 in Montreal. The latter bank never used its charter or issued notes, and the history of the former is one of discreditable practice, scandalous mismanagement and dishonest diversion of its resources. Its note holders were paid in full and other creditors received about 99% of their investment when the bank finally failed in 1887.

90-10. ISSUES OF 1884 and 1887

DESIGNS AND COLOURS

90-10-02
$5 Face Design: D. Blain/—/allegorical female, V and cherubs
Colour: Black with green tint

Back Design: Lathework, counters, bank name and Horses at trough
Colour: Green

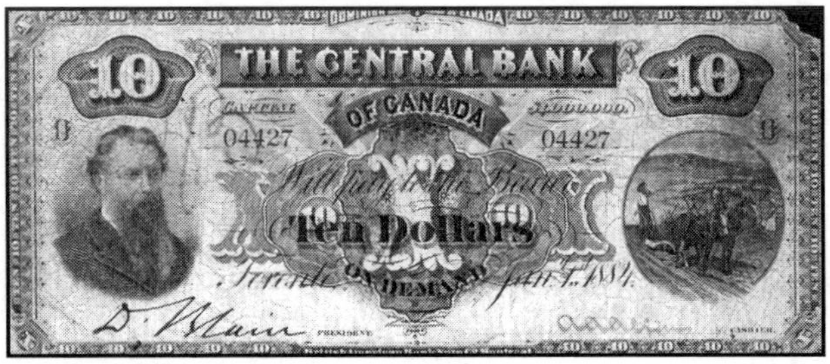

90-10-04
$10 Face Design: D. Blain/man ploughing with horses
Colour: Black with green tint

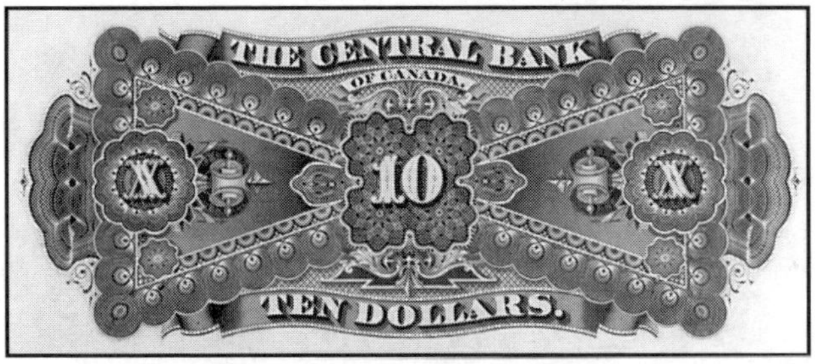

Back Design: Lathework, counters and bank name
Colour: Green

90-10-06P
$50 Face Design: D. Blain/—/A.A. Allen
Colour: Black with green tint

Back Design: Lathework, counters and bank name
Colour: Green

IMPRINT

British American Bank Note Co. Montreal

SIGNATURES

left	right
engr. D. Blain	mss. various

ISSUE DATING

Engraved

Jany. 1st, 1884
3rd Jan. 1887

CIRCULATING NOTES

Cat.No.	Denom.	Date	G	VG	F	VF	EF	AU
10-02	$5	1884	375.	750.	1,100.	—	—	—
10-04	$10	1884	450.	900.	1,300.	—	—	—
10-06	$50	1887	No known issued notes					

PROOF NOTES

Cat. No.	Denom.	Date		Unc
10-02P	$5	1884	FACE PROOF	500.
10-04P	$10	1884	FACE PROOF	500.
10-06P	$50	1887	FACE PROOF	750.

Note: A $5 back proof exists with blue tint.

CENTRAL BANK OF NEW BRUNSWICK

1834 - 1866

FREDERICTON, NEW BRUNSWICK

BANK NUMBER 95 ***NONREDEEMABLE***

This bank was established in Fredericton, New Brunswick in 1834. Its charter contained, for the first time in complete form in Canada, one of the most important requirements in that the shareholders should be liable for double the amount of their shares. The bank operated successfully for more than twenty years.

However, the business conditions in the province, affected adversely by those in Upper Canada following the collapse of the land boom, resulted in the failure of the bank in 1866. All creditors were paid in full and approximately 1% of its capital was available to divide among the shareholders.

95-10. ISSUE OF 1847 - 1857 POUNDS SHILLINGS DOLLARS

DESIGNS AND COLOURS

95-10-06-02

$1 (5s) Face Design: Blacksmith at anvil/seated "Justice" figure, lion; cargo and ships below/—
Colour: See subheadings
Back Designs: See subheadings
Colour: See subheadings

95-10-10-04

£1 Face Design: Seated Indian with rifle/Royal Crest; paddlewheeler below/—
Colour: See subheadings
Back Design: See subheadings
Colour: See subheadings

95-10-04-06

£5 Face Design: King William IV/St. George slaying dragon; lion crown below/—
Colour: See subheadings
Back Design: See subheadings
Colour: See subheadings

IMPRINT

Rawdon, Wright, Hatch & Co. New York
Rawdon, Wright, Hatch & Edson, New York

SIGNATURES

left	right
mss. Samuel W. Babbitt	mss. Wm. J. Bedell
mss. Samuel W. Babbitt	mss. G. Botsford

2. BLACK FACE AND BLUE LATHEWORK BACK 1847

ISSUE DATING

Partially Engraved: __18__:
1847: May 1

Cat.No.	Denom.	Date	G	VG	F	VF	EF	AU
10-02-02	5s	1847	Institutional collection only					
10-02-04	£1	1847	750.	1,500.	2,000.	—	—	—
10-02-06	£5	1847	No known issued notes					

4. BLUE FACE AND BROWN* LATHEWORK BACK 1847 - 1853

* Back colour varies from brown to gray-green depending on the condition of the note.

ISSUE DATING

Partially Engraved: __18__:
$1(5s) 1847: Nov.1
1853: 1 April
£1 1847: Oct. 1, Dec. 1
£5 1851: Feb. 1

Cat.No.	Denom.	Date	G	VG	F	VF	EF	AU
10-04-02	$1 (5s)	1847 - 1853	750.	1,500.	2,000.	—	—	—
10-04-04	£1	1847	750.	1,500.	2,000.	—	—	—
10-04-06	£5	1851	Institutional collection only					

6. BLUE FACE AND ORANGE LATHEWORK BACK 1844 - 1853

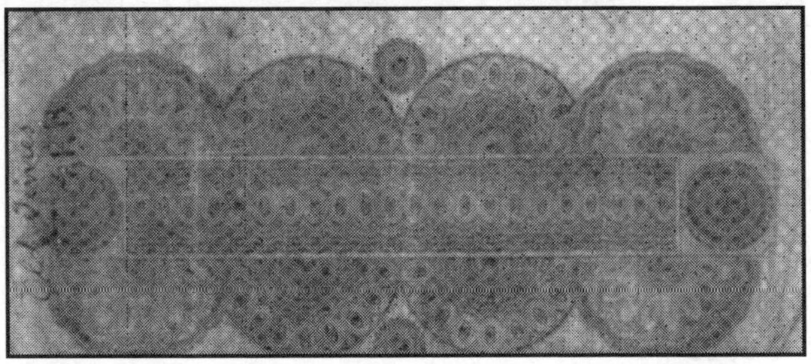

ISSUE DATING

Partially Engraved: __18__:

1844: 1 January
1846: 1 Mar
1847: 1 January
1853: 1 May
1854: 1 Oct

Cat.No.	Denom.	Date	G	VG	F	VF	EF	AU
10-06-02	$1(5s)	1852 - 1854	750.	1,500.	2,000.	—	—	—
10-06-06	£1	1844 - 1853	750.	1,500.	2,000.	—	—	—
10-06-08	£5	1853	Institutional collection only					

10. BLACK FACE AND PLAIN BACK 1856 - 1857

ISSUE DATING

Partially Engraved: __18__:

1856: 1 June, 1 Sept
1857: 1 Augt, 1 Oct.

Plain back notes are designated payable "to Chatham or bearer" (Chatham mss.). They have letter prefixes.

CIRCULATING NOTES

Cat.No.	Denom.	Date	G	VG	F	VF	EF	AU
10-10-02	$1(5s)	1856 - 1857	750.	1,500.	2,000.	—	—	—
10-10-04	£1	1856 - 1857	750.	1,500.	2,000.	—	—	—
10-10-06	£5	18__	No known issued notes					

PROOF NOTES

Cat. No.	Denom.	Date		Unc
10-10-06P	£5	18__	PROOF	900.

95-12. ISSUE OF 1860

DESIGNS AND COLOURS

95-12-02

$1 Face Design: Henry George Clopper/lion and shield/ Queen Victoria (Winterhalter portrait) in oval
Colour: Black with green tint
Back Design: Plain

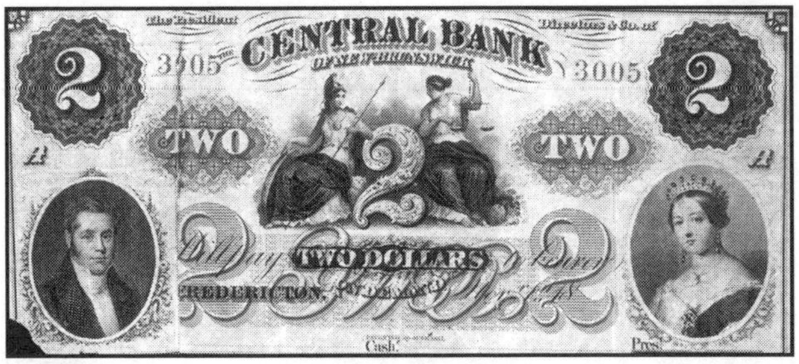

95-12-04

$2 Face Design: Henry George Clopper/seated allegorical women and ornate 2/Queen Victoria in oval
Colour: Black with green tint
Back Design: Plain

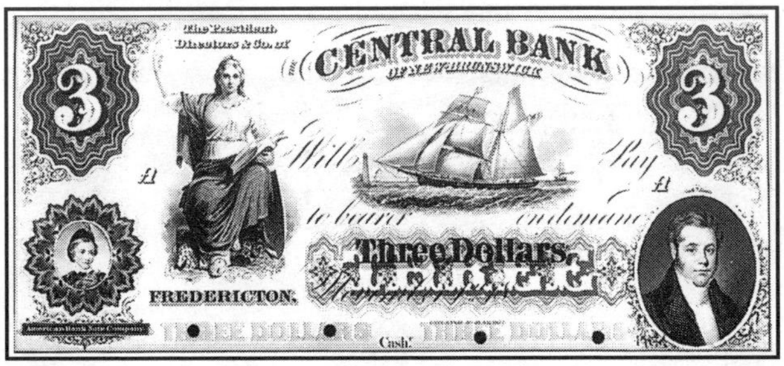

95-12-06P

$3 Face Design: Prince of Wales/allegorical female/ sailing ship/Henry George Clopper
Colour: Black with green tint
Back Design: Plain

95-12-08P

$5 Face Design: Henry George Clopper/Royal Crest/sailboat
Colour: Black with green tint

Back Design: Plain

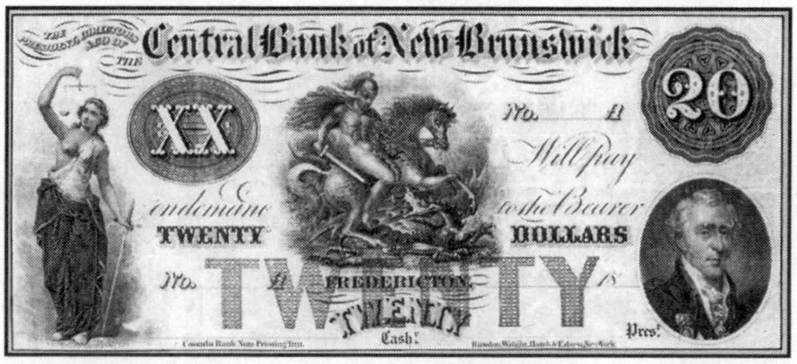

95-12-10R

$20 Face Design: "Justice" figure/St. George slaying the dragon/Wellington in oval
Colour: Black with green TWENTY

Back Design: Lathework
Colour: Green

95-12-12P

$20 Face Design: "Justice" figure/St. George slaying the dragon/Wellington in oval
Colour: Black with overall green tint

Back Design: Lathework
Colour: Green

95-12-14P

$50 Face Design: Queen Victoria (Chalon portrait) in oval/ female, ships and cornucopia/ cattle, train on bridge "The Drove"
Colour: Black with overall green tint

Back Design: Green

IMPRINT

Rawdon, Wright, Hatch & Edson, New York
or American Bank Note Company

SIGNATURES

left	right
mss. Samuel W. Babbitt	mss. G. Botsford
none	none

ISSUE DATING

Partially Engraved: __18__:

Novr 1st 18__

Engraved

November 1st 1860

VARIETIES

$20: Green "Twenty" protector
$20: "Twenty" outlined by overall green face tint

CIRCULATING NOTES

Cat.No.	Denom.	Date	Variety	G	VG	F	VF	EF	AU
12-02	$1	1860		800.	1,600.	2,200.	—	—	—
12-04R	$2*	18__		Institutional collection only					
12-06	$3	1860		Institutional collection only					
12-08	$5	1860		No known issued notes					
12-10R	$20*	18__	*Green TWENTY	1,500.	—	—	—	—	—
12-14R	$50	18__		—	—	2,500.	—	—	—

*Remainder: unsigned, undated. $20 exists with spurious signatures and date. Only the $2 is numbered.

PROOF NOTES

Cat. No.	Denom.	Date	Variety	Unc
12-06P	$3	18__	FACE PROOF	1,000.
12-08P	$5	18__	Institutional collection only FACE PROOF	
12-12P	$20	18__	Green tint FACE PROOF	900.
12-14P	$50	18__	FACE PROOF	900.

CHARLOTTE COUNTY BANK

1825 - 1865

ST. ANDREWS, NEW BRUNSWICK

BANK NUMBER 100 ***NONREDEEMABLE***

The Charlotte County Bank was established in 1825 at St. Andrew's, New Brunswick with a capital of £15,000. Its charter was for twenty years and its total liabilities were restricted to twice the paid-up capital. Although the bank ceased operations some time prior to 1865, during that year a final winding up was authorized by the government. All claims on the bank were paid but the shareholders lost their entire capital.

100-10. PERKINS AND HEATH PRINTINGS

1852 - 1859

DESIGNS AND COLOURS

100-10-02

5s Face Design: Britannia/seated allegorical female at seaside;
seated allegorical female at seaside/—
Colour: Black with no tint

Back Design: Lathework, female portraits in corners and small vignettes top and bottom
Colour: Red-brown or plain

100-10-08

£1 Face Design: Britannia/seated allegorical female at seaside;
allegorical female at seaside/—
Colour: Black with no tint

Back Design: Lathework, female portraits in corners and small vignettes top and bottom
Colour: Red-brown

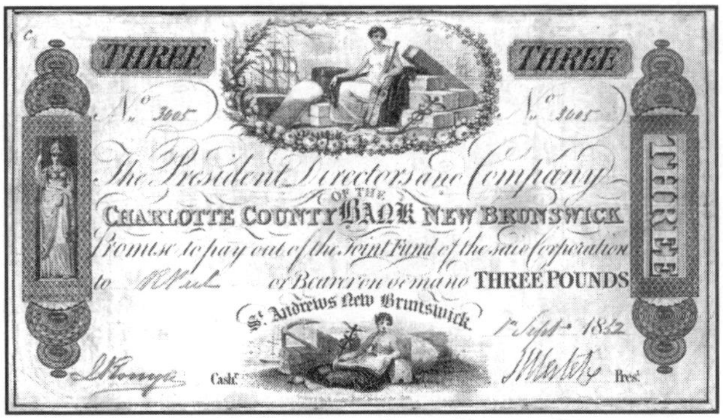

100-10-10

£3 Face Design: Britannia/seated allegorical female at seaside;
seated allegorical female at seaside/—
Colour: Black with no tint

Back Design: Lathework, female portraits in corners and small vignettes top and bottom
Colour: Red-brown

Photo Not Available

100-10-12P

£5 Face Design: Britannia/seated allegorical female at seaside;
seated allegorical female at seaside/-
Colour: Black with no tint

Back Design: Lathework, female portraits in corners and small vignettes top and bottom
Colour: Red-brown

Photo Not Available

100-10-14P

£10 Face Design: Britannia/seated allegorical female at seaside;
seated allegorical female at seaside/—
Colour: Black with no tint

Back Design: Lathework, female portraits in corners and small vignettes top and bottom
Colour: Red-brown

IMPRINT

Perkins and Heath, London

SIGNATURES

	left	right
1852:	mss. illegible	mss. H. Hatch
1853-1854:	mss. C.W. Wardlaw	mss. H. Hatch
1856:	mss. C.W. Wardlaw	mss. Geo. D. Stuart
1859:	mss. illegible	mss. H. Hatch

ISSUE DATING

Partially Engraved: __18__:

1852: 1 Sept.
1853: 12 Sept.
1854: 22 Augt.
1856: 26 Augt.
1859: Nov. 8

CIRCULATING NOTES

Cat.No.	Denom.	Date	G	VG	F	VF	EF	AU
10-02	5s	1852 - 1856	1,000.	2,000.	3,000.	—	—	—
10-07	£1	1852 - 1859	1,200.	2,400.	3,500.	—	—	—
10-10	£3	1852	—	3,000.	4,000.	—	—	—
10-12	£5	18__			No known issued notes			
10-14	£10	18__			No known issued notes			

Note: These notes are extremely rare in grades over VG

PROOF NOTES

Cat. No.	Denom.	Date		Unc
10-12P	£5	18__	FACE PROOF	700.
10-14P	£10	18__	FACE PROOF	700.

BANK OF CHARLOTTETOWN

1852

CHARLOTTETOWN, PRINCE EDWARD ISLAND

BANK NUMBER 105 ***NONREDEEMABLE***

Established in 1852, the Bank of Charlottetown was a spurious bank. The notes and drafts were the concoctions of A. Sleigh, and circulation was attempted in New York. Sleigh's lifetime was devoted to fraud and swindling.

105-10. POUNDS, SHILLINGS & PENCE NOTE ISSUE

DESIGNS AND COLOURS

These notes carry three currencies, the first P.E.I., the second Canada, N.B. Halifax and NFLD. currency and the third U.S.

105-10-02P

£5 (£4; 16 US)
Face Design: Roses, shamrock and thistle/ Royal Crest/two ships and counter "Payable at/S. Draper's New York"
Colour: Black with no tint
Back Design: Plain

105-10-04P

£5 (£4.3.4; 16.66 U.S.)
Face Design: Roses, shamrock and thistle/Royal Crest/ two ships and counter "Redeemed at/S. Draper's, New York"/and at/Wm. Elliott & COS./British Consulate/Boston
Colour: Black with no tint
Back Design: Plain

IMPRINT

Rawdon, Wright, Hatch & Edson, New York
Rawdon, Wright, Hatch & Edson, New York and New England Bank Note co. Boston

SIGNATURES

left	right
none	mss. A.Sleigh

ISSUE DATING

Partially Engraved __18__

PROOF NOTES

Cat.No.	Denom.	Date		Unc
10-02P	£5 (£4; 16 US)	18__	PROOF	900.
10-04P	£5 (£4.3.4; 16.66 US)	18__	PROOF	900.

105-12. DOLLAR DRAFT ISSUE 1852

Engraved: "To Simeon Draper, New York"

DESIGNS AND COLOURS

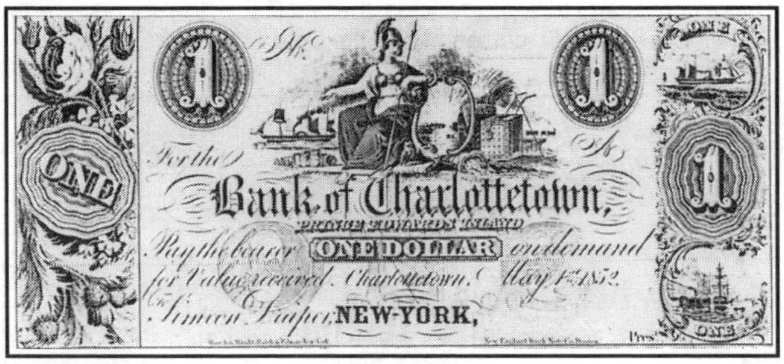

105-12-02P

Face Design: Floral panel/seated Britannia, with symbols of commerce/two small sailing ships.
Colour: black with no tint

Back Design: Plain

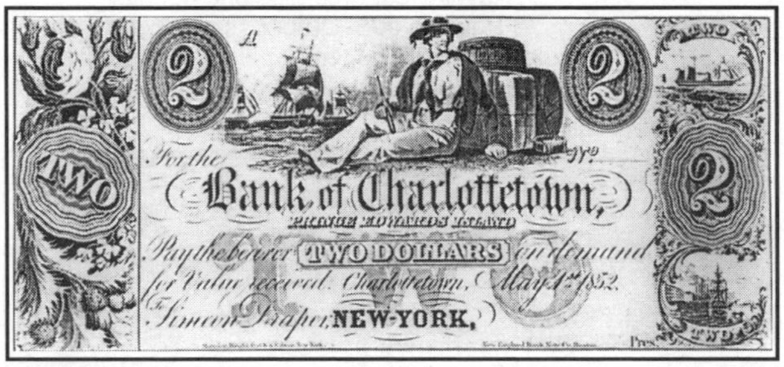

105-12-04P

$2 Face Design: Roses, shamrocks and thistles/ seated sailor/two small ships
Colour: Black with no tint

Back Design: Plain

105-12-06P

$3 Face Design: Floral panel/seated female with farm produce/ships
Colour: Black with no tint

Back Design: Plain

IMPRINT

Rawdon, Wright, Hatch & Edson New York and New England Bank Note Co. Boston

SIGNATURES

left	right
none	mss. A. Sleigh

ISSUE DATING

Engraved

May 1st, 1852

CIRCULATING NOTES

Cat.No.	Denom.	Date	G	VG	F	VF	EF	AU
12-02	$1	1852	No known issued notes					
12-04	$2	1852	Institutional collection only					
12-06	$3	1852	Institutional collection only					

PROOF NOTES

Cat. No.	Denom.	Date		Unc
12-02P	$1	1852	PROOF	900.
12-04P	$2	1852	PROOF	900.

THE CITY BANK

1833 - 1876

MONTREAL, LOWER CANADA

BANK NUMBER 110 ***NONREDEEMABLE***

On its second attempt, The City Bank received its charter and opened for business on October 14, 1833. The charter remained in effect until June 1, 1837, when it was again renewed.

By 1841 it was the fifth largest bank in terms of discounts and the fourth largest in terms of circulation.

However, in 1870, The City Bank was involved in an intricate court case regarding gold speculation which cost it $140,000. It was a severe blow in a period of impending depression. Public confidence was lost and in 1873 Sir Francis Hincks was asked to become president. A merger with The Royal Canadian Bank was completed in 1876 to form The Consolidated Bank of Canada.

110.10. BILINGUAL ISSUE 1833 - 1840's PAYABLE AT MONTREAL DENOMINATIONS IN DOLLARS ONLY

DESIGNS AND COLOURS

110-10-02a

$1 Face Design: King William IV/Indian shooting arrow/ Indian paddling canoe below/—

Colour: Black with no tint

Back Design: "Steel" over standing woman in panel/ "CITY BANK / MONTREAL"/"plate" over standing woman in panel, and overall lathework

Colour: Red

110-10-04P

$2 Face Design: —/Indian in canoe; beaver below/King William IV

Colour: Black with no tint

Back Design: Unknown

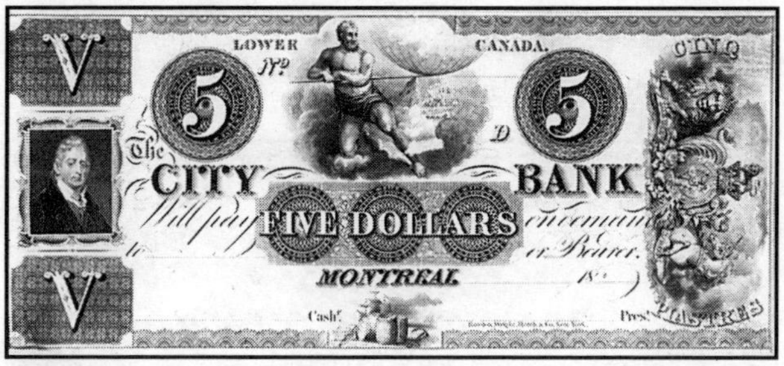

110-10-06P

$5 Face Design: King William IV/Archimedes moving the earth/ Arms (sideways)

Colour: Black with no tint

Back Design: Unknown

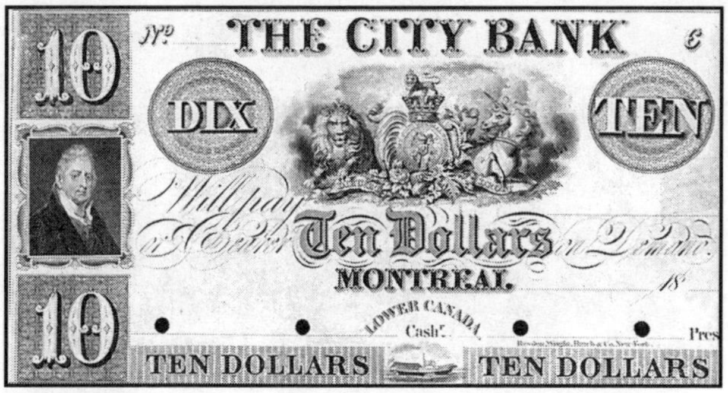

110-10-08P

$10 Face Design: King William IV/Royal Crest; ship below/ woman with sheaf of wheat

Colour: Black with no tint

Back Design: Unknown

110-10-10C

Note: Beware of counterfeit $10 notes of 1836 which have "PARLIMENT" at the left under the portrait.

$10 Face Design: King William IV/Royal Crest; ship below/woman with sheaf of wheat, has misspelled word "Parliment" at left under portrait
Colour: Black with no tint

Back Design: Unknown

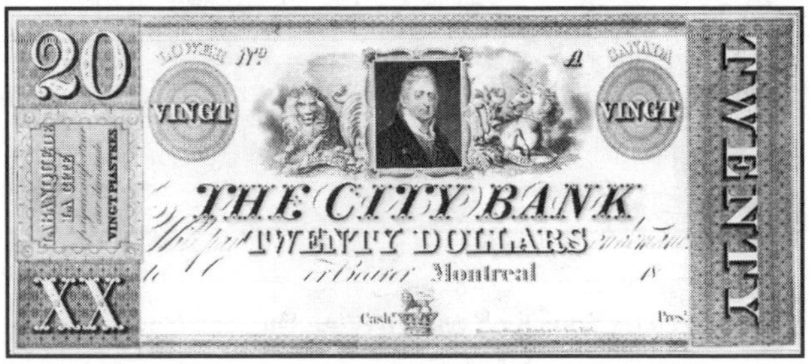

110-10-12P
$20 Face Design: —/King William IV on Royal Crest; lion on crown below/—
Colour: Black with no tint

Back Design: Unknown

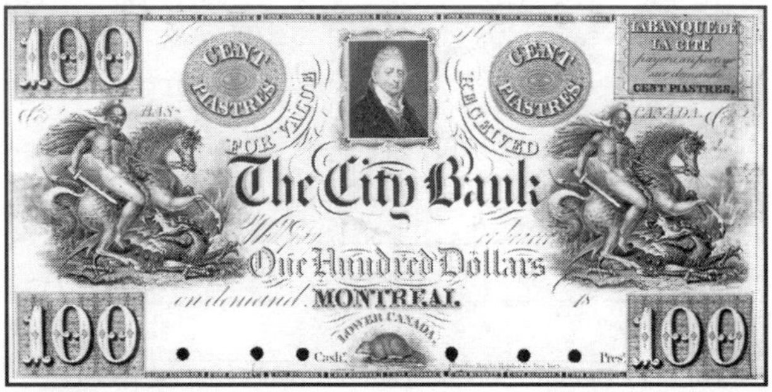

110-10-14P
$100 Face Design: St. George slaying dragon/King William IV; beaver below/St. George slaying dragon
Colour: Black with no tint

Back Design: Unknown

IMPRINT
Rawdon, Wright, Hatch & Co. New York

SIGNATURES

left	right
mss. Chs. H. Castle	mss. J. Frothingham

ISSUE DATING
Partially Engraved __18__:
1833: 10 Oct.
1834: 1 Augt

OVERPRINT
"EASTERN TOWNSHIPS" in large red letters across the face.

CIRCULATING NOTES

Cat.No.	Denom.	Date	Variety	G	VG	F	VF
10-02	$1	1833		400.	800.	1,200.	—
10-02a	$1	1833	Eastern Townships o/p	500.	1,000.	1,500.	—
10-04	$2	18__		No known issued notes			
10-06	$5	18__		No known issued notes			
10-08	$10	18__		No known issued notes			
10-10C	$10*	various	Counterfeit	50.	100.	150.	225.
10-12	$20	18__		No known issued notes			
10-14	$100	18__		No known issued notes			

PROOF NOTES

Cat. N0.	Denom.	Date		Unc
10-02P	$1	18__	PROOF	400.
10-04P	$2	18__	PROOF	400.
10-06P	$5	18__	PROOF	400.
10-08P	$10	18__	PROOF	400.
10-12P	$20	18__	PROOF	500.
10-14P	$100	18__	PROOF	500.

110-12. SEPARATE BRANCH ISSUES 1850 - 1865 DOLLARS/POUNDS & SHILLINGS

2. MONTREAL ISSUE 1851 - 1853

Branch name engraved at bottom.

DESIGNS AND COLOURS

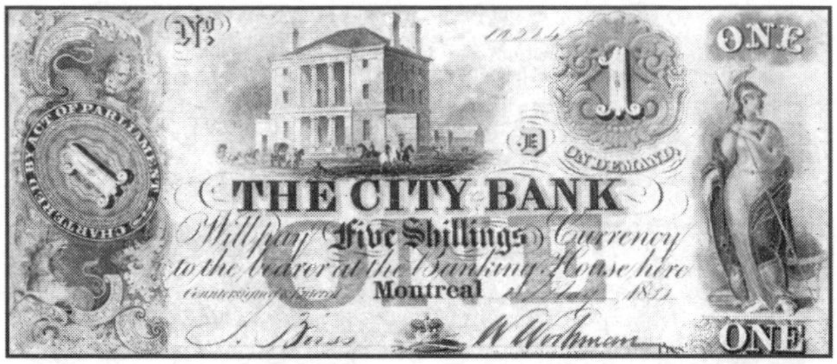

110-12-02-02
$1 (5s) Face Design: Counter with lion and unicorn/bank building; crown on swords below/Britannia
Colour: Black with no tint

Back Design: Plain

Photo Not Available

110-12-02-04P
$2 (10s) Face Design: —/bank building/man and woman
Colour: Black with no tint

Back Design: Plain

110-12-02-06

$4 (£1) Face Design: Queen Victoria (Chalon portrait)/ bank building; ship below/—
Colour: Black with no tint
Back Design: Plain

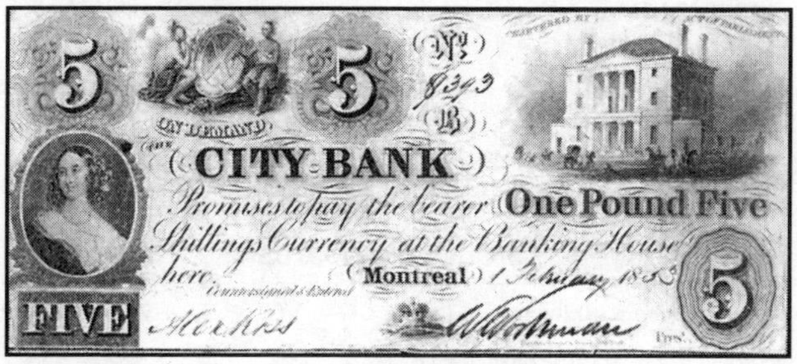

110-12-02-08

$5 (£1.5) Face Design: Portrait of young woman/Indians and shield (like Bank of Montreal Crest); crown on swords below /bank building
Colour: Black with no tint
Back Design Plain

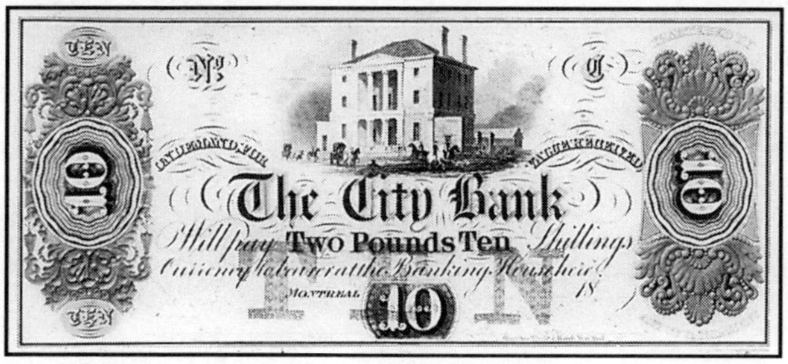

110-12-02-10P

$10 (£2.10) Face Design: —/bank building/—
Colour: Black with no tint
Back Design: Plain

Photo Not Available

110-12-02-12P

$20 (£5) Face Design: Woman/bank building/—
Colour: Black with no tint
Back Design: Plain

Photo Not Available

110-12-02-14P

$50 (£12.10) Face Design: —/bank building/—
Colour: Black with no tint
Back Design: Plain

Photo Not Available

110-12-02-16P

$100 (£25) Face Design: Prince Albert/bank building/ Queen Victoria (Chalon portrait)
Colour: Black with no tint
Back Design: Plain

IMPRINT

Rawdon, Wright, Hatch, New York
Rawdon, Wright, Hatch & Edson, New York

SIGNATURES

	left	right
1851:	mss. various	mss. W. Workman
1853:	mss. various	mss. W. Macdonald
	mss. Alex Ross	mss. W. Workman

ISSUE DATING

Partially Engraved __18__:

1851: 1 May, May 2
1853: 1 February, 1 Feby.

PROTECTOR

1851 & Proofs: Red "word" on face and back

CIRCULATING NOTES

Cat.No.	Denom.	Date	G	VG	F	VF	EF
12-02-02	$1(5s)	1851	350.	700.	1,100.	—	—
12-02-04	$2(10s)	18__	No known issued notes				
12-02-06	$4(£1)	1853	400.	800.	1,200.	—	—
12-02-08	$5(£1.5)	1853	400.	800.	1,200.	—	—
12-02-10	$10(£2.10)	18__	No known issued notes				
12-02-12	$20(£5)	18__	No known issued notes				
12-02-14	$50(£12.10)	18__	No known issued notes				
12-02-16	$100(£25)	18__	No known issued notes				

PROOF NOTES

Cat. No.	Denom.	Date		Unc
12-02-02P	$1 (5s)	18__	PROOF	400.
12-02-04P	$2 (10s)	18__	PROOF	400.
12-02-06P	$4 (£1)	18__	PROOF	400.
12-02-08P	$5 (£1.5)	18__	PROOF	400.
12-02-10P	$10 (£2.10)	18__	PROOF	400.
12-02-12P	$20 (£5)	18__	PROOF	500.
12-02-14P	$50 (£12.10)	18__	PROOF	550.
12-02-16P	$100 (£25)	18__	PROOF	600.

TORONTO ISSUE 1850 - 1865

$1 & $2: Branch name engraved at bottom centre.
$5 - $20: Branch name engraved at bottom centre and on lower right.

DESIGNS AND COLOURS

110-12-04-02

$1 Face Design: —/seated woman looking left, shield/ Queen Victoria (Chalon portrait)
Colour: Black with no tint
Back Design: Plain

110-12-04-16

$2 Face Design: —/seated woman looking right, shield/ Queen Victoria (Chalon portrait)
Colour: Black with no tint

Back Design: Plain

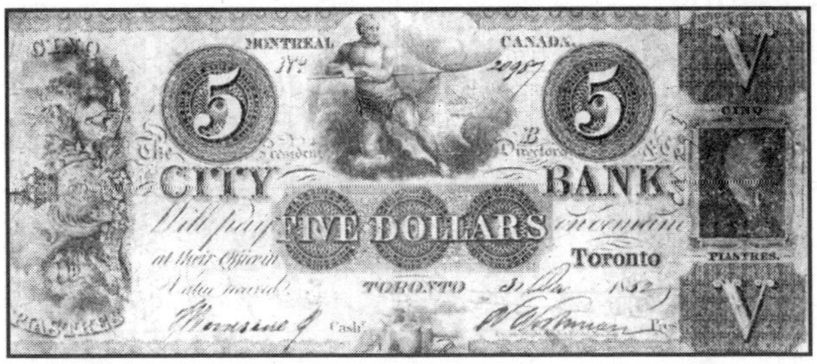

110-12-04-26

$5 Face Design: Royal Crest (sideways)/Archimedes moving the earth; cask, bales and ship below/King William IV
Colour: Black with no tint

Back Design: Plain

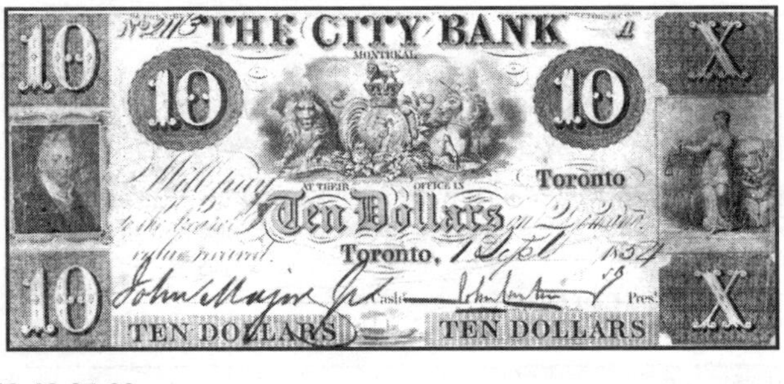

110-12-04-30

$10 Face Design: King William IV/Royal Crest; ship below/"Justice" figure
Colour: Black with no tint

Back Design: Plain

Photo Not Available

110-12-04-40P

$20 Face Design: Allegorical woman/King William IV/—
Colour: Black with no tint

Back Design: Plain

IMPRINT

$1 & $2: Rawdon, Wright, Hatch, New York

$5 & $10: Rawdon, Wright, Hatch & Edson, New York

SIGNATURES

	left	right
$1 1850:	mss. Thos. Connoly (p.)	mss. W. Workman
	mss. Walter Ross (per)	mss. John Carter (p.)
$2 1850:	mss. Thos. Connoly (p.)	mss. W. Workman
	mss. Walter Ross (per)	mss. W. MacDonald (p.)
1852:	mss. F. Woodside (p.)	mss. W. Workman
$2 1854:	mss. F. Woodside (p.)	mss. W. MacDonald
$5 1852:	mss. F. Woodside (p)	mss. W. Workman
$5 1856:	mss. F. Woodside (p.)	mss. John Carter (v.)
$10 1854:	mss. John Major (p.)	mss. John Carter (v.)
$10 1856:	mss F. Woodside (p)	mss. W. Macdonald (p)
1861:	mss. J. Moat (per)	mss. W. Macdonald (p.)

ISSUE DATING

Partially Engraved __18__:

1850: 1 Oct., 1 October
1852: 31 Dec.
1854: 1 Sept.
1856: 1st, Augt, Jany 4
1861: Aug. 1
1865: Oct. 2

PROTECTOR

1861 & 1865: Green "word" on face and back

CIRCULATING NOTES

Cat.No.	Denom.	Date	G	VG	F	VF	EF	AU
12-04-02	$1	1850-1865	250.	500.	700.	—	—	—
12-04-16	$2	1852-1856	400.	800.	1,200.	—	—	—
12-04-26	$5	1856	400.	800.	1,200.	—	—	—
12-04-30	$10	1854-1861	400.	800.	1,200.	—	—	—
12-04-40	$20	18__		No known issued notes				

PROOF NOTES

Cat. Np.	Denom.	Date	Unc
12-04-40P	$20	18__	PROOF 400.

6. QUEBEC ISSUE

Branch name engraved at bottom centre

DESIGNS AND COLOURS

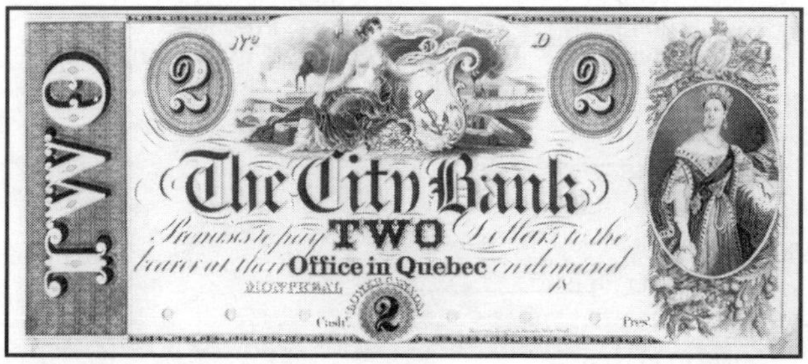

110-12-06-02P

$2 Face Design: —/seated woman looking right, shield/ Queen Victoria (Chalon portrait)

Colour: Black with no tint

Back Design: Plain

110-12-06-04P

$4 (£1) Face Design: Queen Victoria (Chalon portrait) bank building; ship below/—

Colour: Black with no tint

Back Design: Plain

IMPRINT

Rawdon, Wright & Hatch New York

SIGNATURES

left	right
none	none

ISSUE DATING

Partially Engraved __18__:

PROTECTOR

$4 (£1): Red "word" on face only

PROOF NOTES

Cat.No.	Denom.	Date		Unc
12-06-02P	$2	18__	PROOF	400.
12-06-04P	$4(£1)	18__	PROOF	500.

110-14. COMMON BRANCH ISSUE OF 1857 PROVINCE OF CANADA

DESIGNS AND COLOURS

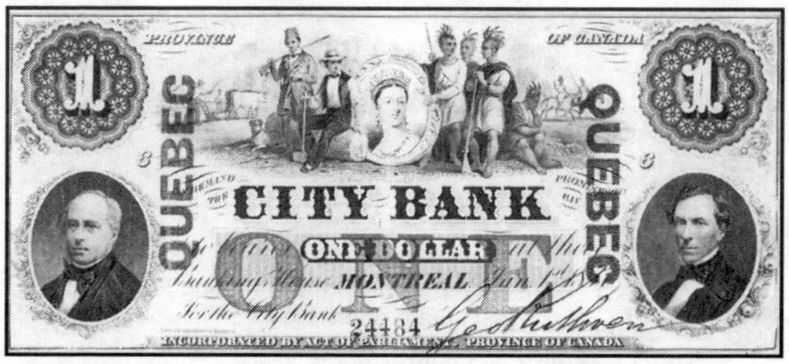

110-14-04-02a

$1 Face Design: Male portrait/Queen Victoria (Chalon portrait) on Crest/male portrait

Back Design: See subheadings

110-14-02-04

$2 Face Design: Male portrait/paddlewheel steamship and boats, city in background/male portrait

Back Design: See subheadings

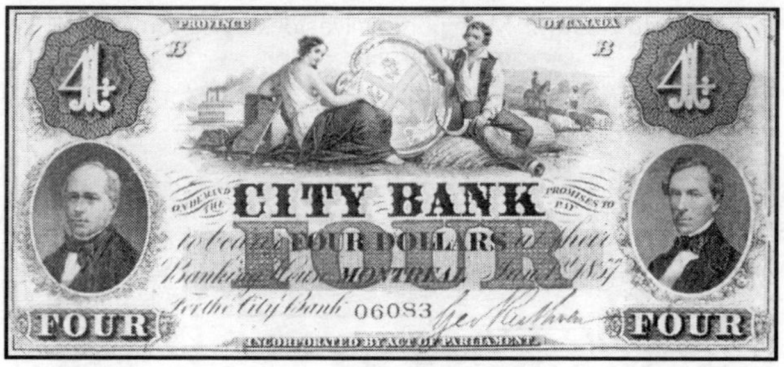

110-14-02-06

$4 Face Design: Male portrait/crest with woman and farmer/ male portrait

Back Design: See subheading

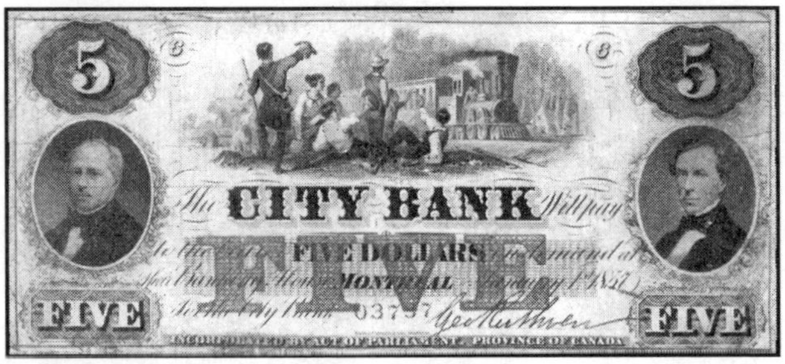

110-14-02-08

$5 Face Design: Male portrait/farmers waving to passing train/male portrait

Back Design: See subheadings

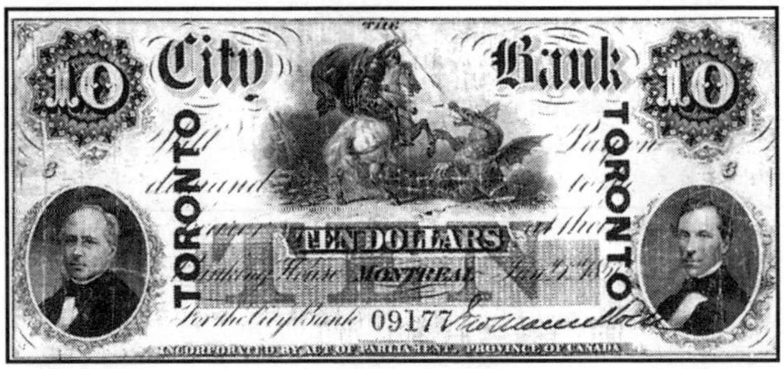

110-14-02-10a

$10 Face Design: Male portrait/St. George slaying dragon/ male portrait

Back Design: See subheadings

Photo Not Available

110-14-02-12

$20 Face Design: Male portrait/livestock by stream/ male portrait

Back Design: See subheadings

2. ORANGE BACK

DESIGNS AND COLOURS

Face Colour: Black with no tint

Back Design: Scrollwork with "CITY BANK/MONTREAL"
Colour: Orange

IMPRINT

Toppan, Carpenter & Co., Montreal

SIGNATURES

left	right
none	mss. Geo. Ruthven
none	mss. Fred MacCulloch
none	mss. Wm. G. Benson

ISSUE DATING

Engraved

Jany, 1st, 1857
January 1st, 1857

OVERPRINT

"TORONTO" in blue

STAMP

"MINES" in blue

PROTECTOR

Green "word" on face and in mirror image on the back of some notes.

CIRCULATING NOTES

Cat.No.	Denom.	Date	Variety	G	VG	F	VF	EF
14-02-02	$1	1857	no o/p	125.	250.	350.	—	—
14-02-02a	$1	1857	Toronto o/p	175.	350.	500.	—	—
14-02-04	$2	1857	no o/p	150.	300.	400.	750.	—
14-02-04a	$2	1857	Toronto o/p	200.	400.	600.	—	—
14-02-06	$4	1857	no o/p	250.	500.	800.	—	—
14-02-06a	$4	1857	Toronto o/p	300.	600.	1,000.	—	—
14-02-08	$5	1857	no o/p	200.	400.	650.	—	—
14-02-08a	$5	1857	Toronto o/p	250.	500.	850.	—	—
14-02-10	$10	1857	no o/p	400.	800.	1,100.	—	—
14-02-10a	$10	1857	Toronto o/p	450.	900.	1,350.	—	—
14-02-12	$20	1857		450.	900.	1.350.	—	—

PROOF NOTES

Cat. No.	Denom	Date		Unc
14-02-02P	$1	1857	FACE PROOF	400.

4. PLAIN BACK

DESIGNS AND COLOURS

Face Colour: Black with no tint
Back Design: Plain

IMPRINT

Toppan, Carpenter & Co., Montreal

SIGNATURES

left	right
none	mss. Geo. Ruthven
none	mss. Fred MacCulloch
none	mss. Wm. Benson

ISSUE DATING

Engraved

Jan 1st, 1857
January 1st 1857

OVERPRINT

"QUEBEC" in blue
"TORONTO" in blue

PROTECTOR

Green "word" on face, $1 and $2 mirror image on back.

Cat.No.	Denom.	Date	Variety	G	VG	F	VF	EF
14-04-02	$1	1857	no o/p	100.	200.	300.	450.	—
14-04-02a	$1	1857	town o/p	150.	300.	450.	—	—
14-04-04	$2	1857	no o/p	125.	250.	400.	600.	—
14-04-04a	$2	1857	town o/p	175.	350.	550.	—	—
14-04-06	$4	1857	no o/p	175.	350.	500.	—	—
14-04-06a	$4	1857	town o/p	225.	450.	700.	—	—
14-04-08	$5	1857	no o/p	175.	350.	500.	—	—
14-04-08a	$5	1857	town o/p	225.	450.	700.	—	—
14-04-10	$10	1857	no o/p	225.	450.	650.	—	—
14-04-10a	$10	1857	town o/p	275.	550.	850.	—	—

6. GREEN BACK

DESIGNS AND COLOURS

Face Colours: Black with green V V and panel with FIVE tint
Back Design: Scrollwork with "CITY BANK" centre and "MONTREAL" above and below
Colour: Green

IMPRINT

Toppan, Carpenter & Co., Montreal

SIGNATURES

left	right
none	mss. Geo. Ruthven
none	mss. Fred MacCulloch
none	mss. Wm.G. Benson

ISSUE DATING

Engraved

January 1st, 1857

OVERPRINT

"ST. CATHARINES" in red

Cat.No.	Denom.	Date	Variety	G	VG	F	VF	EF
14-06-02	$5	1857	no o/p	375.	750.	1,000.	—	—
14-06-02a	$5	1857	St. Catharines o/p	425.	850.	1,250.	—	—

110-16. SPURIOUS NOTE ISSUE

Fraudulent notes with design different from genuine issues of the bank.

DESIGNS AND COLOURS

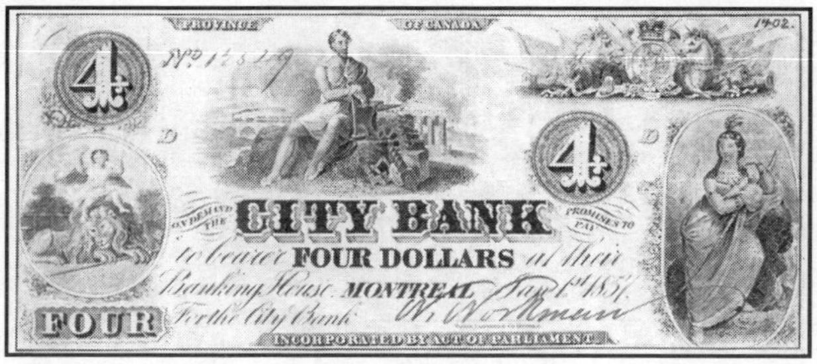

110-16-02

$4 Face Design: Cherub and lion/seated man with sledge hammer
Royal Crest; Indian Princess
Colour: Black with no tint

Back Design: Plain

IMPRINT

Toppan Carpenter & Co. Montreal

SIGNATURES

left	right
mss. various	mss. W. Workman

ISSUE DATING

Engraved

Jan. 1st, 1857

Cat.No.	Denom.	Date	G	VG	F	VF	EF
16-02	$4	1857	60.	120.	160.	240.	—

CITY BANK

1836 - 1839

ST. JOHN, NEW BRUNSWICK

BANK NUMBER 115 ***REDEEMABLE***

With a capital of £100,000, the City Bank was established in Saint John, New Brunswick in 1836. The bank merged with The Bank of New Brunswick in 1839. Its charter provided for the first time that no shareholder should own more than 20% of the capital stock.

115-10. NEW ENGLAND BANK NOTE CO. PRINTINGS 1836 - 1838

DESIGNS AND COLOURS

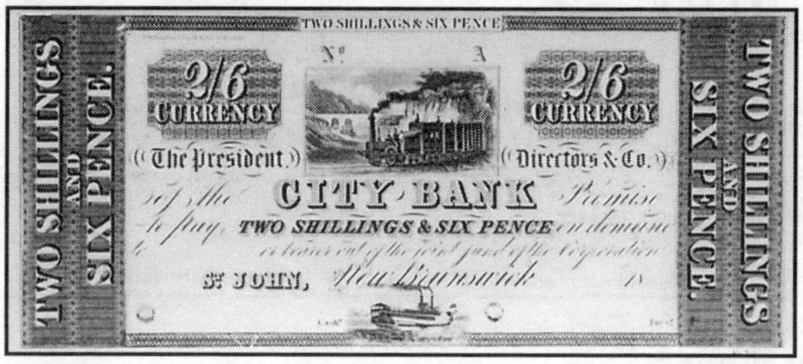

115-10-02P

2s 6d Face Design: —/early train; steamboat below/—
Colour: Black with no tint

Back Design: Plain

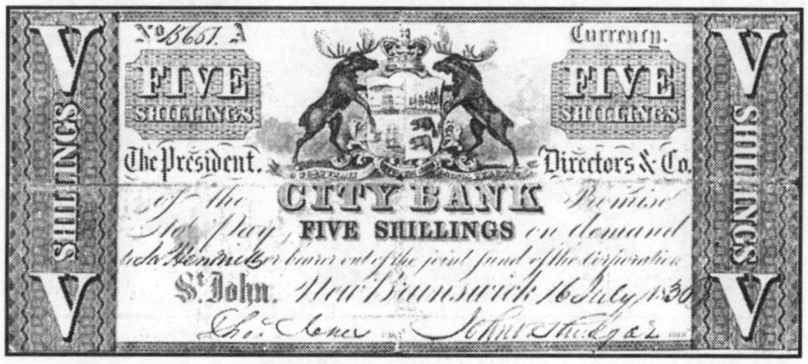

115-10-04

5s Face Design: —/two moose flanking Crest/—
Colour: Black with no tint

Back Design: Lathework
Colour: Black

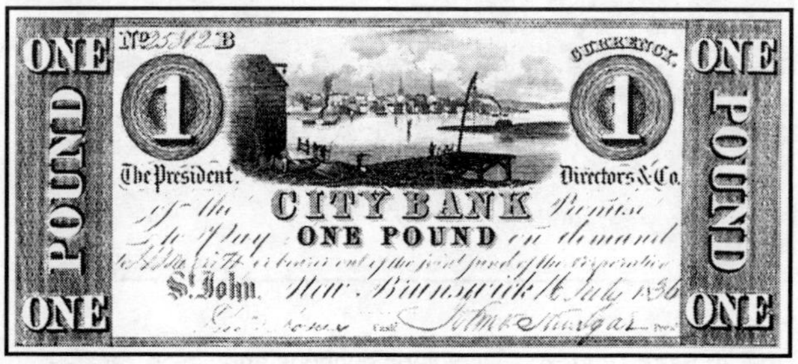

115-10-06

£1 Face Design: —/waterfront scene/—
Colour: Black with no tint

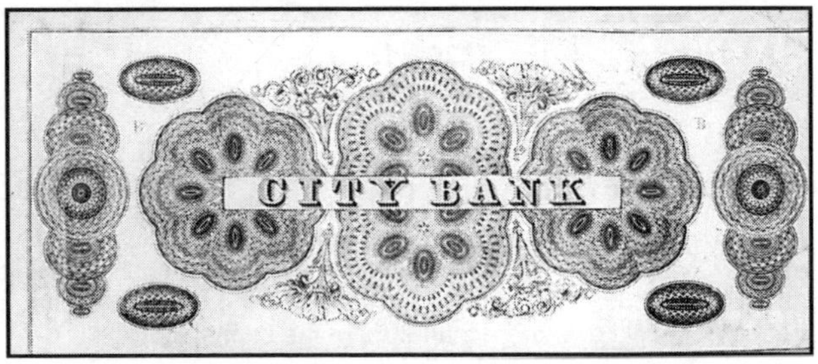

Back Design: Lathework
Colour: Black

115-10-08P
£5 Face Design: —/town, fence and cattle in foreground/—
Colour: Black with no tint

Back Design: Plain

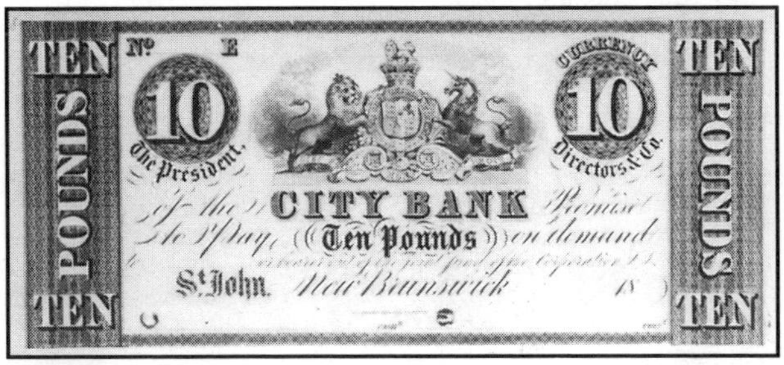

115-10-10P
£10 Face Design: —/Royal Crest/—
Colour: Black with no tint

Back Design: Plain

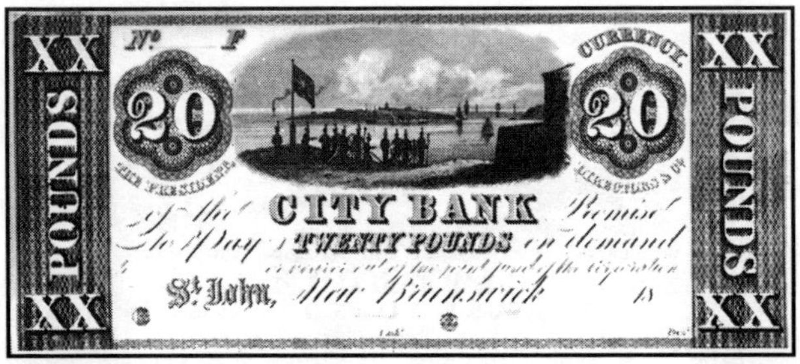

115-10-12P
£20 Face Design: —/soldiers, cannons and Union Jack/—
Colour: Black with no tint

Back Design: Plain

IMPRINT
New England Bank Note Co. Boston

SIGNATURES

left	right
mss. Thos. Jones	mss. illegible
mss. Thos. Jones	mss. John V. Thurgar

ISSUE DATING
Partially Engraved __18__:
16 July, 1836
1 Jany, 1838

CIRCULATING NOTES

Cat.No.	Denom.	Date	G	VG	F	VF	EF	AU
10-02	2s6d	1838	1,500.	2,500.	3,500.	—	—	—
10-04	5s	1836	1,500.	2,500.	3,500.	—	—	—
10-06	£1	1836	1,500.	2,500.	3,500.	—	—	—
10-08	£5	18__	No known issued notes					
10-10	£10	18__	No known issued notes					
10-12	£20	18__	No known issued notes					

PROOF NOTES

Cat. No.	Denom.	Date		Unc
10-02P	2s6d	18__	PROOF	750.
10-04P	5s	18__	PROOF	750.
10-06P	£1	18__	PROOF	750.
10-08P	£5	18__	PROOF	900.
10-10P	£10	18__	PROOF	900.
10-12P	£20	18__	PROOF	900.

THE CITY BANK OF MONTREAL

18__

TORONTO (CANADA WEST)

BANK NUMBER 120 ***NONREDEEMABLE***

No such bank is known; the note is altered from the Colonial Bank of Canada.

120-10. **ISSUE OF 18(59)**

DESIGNS AND COLOURS

120-10-02

$5 Face Design: Farm family under tree/—/ Cornelia Jocelyn

Colour: Orange-brown tint

Back Design: Plain

IMRPINT

Jocelyn, Draper, Welsh & Co.
American Bank Note Company, New York

SIGNATURES

right only
F. MaCulloch
F. Workman

ISSUE DATING

Partially Engraved: __18__

Febr. 9, 1861

Cat.No.	Denom.	Date	Variety	G	VG	F	VF	EF	Unc
10-02	$5	1861	two signatures	100.	200.	350.	—	—	—

THE BANK OF CLIFTON

1859 - 1863

CLIFTON, PROVINCE OF CANADA

BANK NUMBER 125 ***NONREDEEMABLE***

On May 31, 1858, a petition was submitted by The Zimmerman Bank asking the Legislative Assembly for amendments to their charter, one of which was a change of name. On June 2nd, an act was passed granting the petition and the corporate name was changed to The Bank of Clifton. The bank, in reality, was the old Zimmerman Bank, the officers and shareholders remaining nearly the same. In 1859 the stock was transferred to Hubbard & Co. of Chicago with control then going to Callaway and Reed. Reed was the major shareholder in The International Bank of Canada at the time of its collapse. The notes issued under the new owners were never meant to be redeemed.

The charter was withdrawn by an act of the Legislature on August 31, 1863, with Royal assent given on October 15, 1863.

125-10. **ISSUE OF 1859**

DESIGNS AND COLOURS

125-10-02-02

$1 Face Design: Clifton House Hotel/Roebling Suspension Bridge/seated allegorical female

Colour: Black with no tint

Back Design: Plain

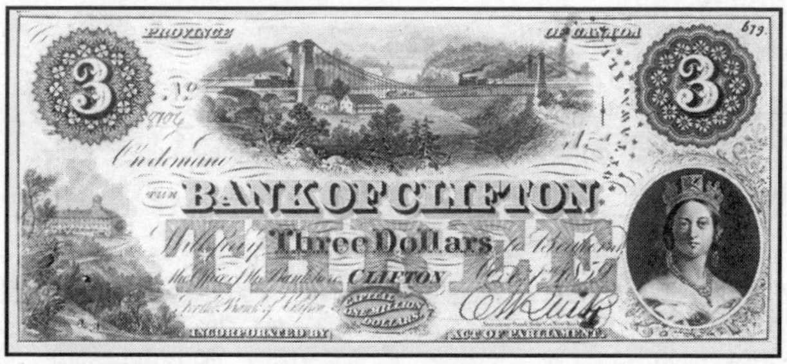

125-10-04-04

$3 Face Design: Clifton House Hotel /Roebling Suspension Bridge/ Queen Victoria (Winterhalter portrait) in oval

Colour: Black with no tint

Back Design: Plain

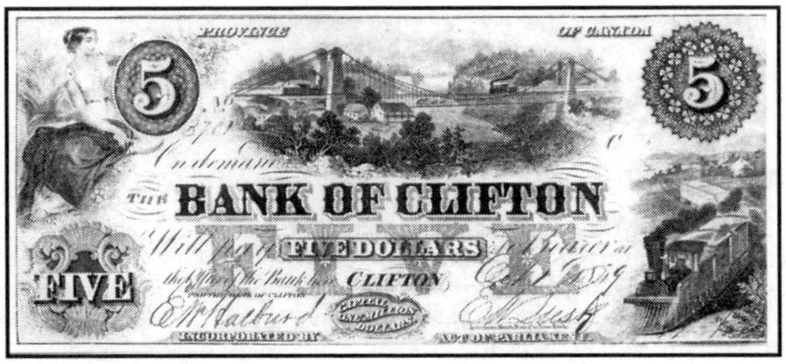

125-10-02-06
$5 Face Design: Seated female with sickle/ Roebling Suspension Bridge/train
Colour: Black with no tint
Back Design: Plain

Note: Photo above shows a Citizens Bank Delaware note altered from a $5 Bank of Clifton note.

IMPRINT
American Bank Note Co. New York

2. PARTIALLY ENGRAVED DATE TWO SIGNATURES

SIGNATURES

left	right
mss. E.W. Hulburd	mss. E.W. Lusk

ISSUE DATING
Partially Engraved ___185_:
1859: Oct. 1, Nov. 1

PROTECTOR
Red "word" on face and in mirror image on the back.

OVERPRINT
"OTTAWA, ILL." and 13 - 15 stars in black

Cat.No.	Denom.	Date	VG	F	VF	EF	AU	Unc
10-02-02	$1	1859	50.	75.	100.	210.	240.	300.
10-02-04	$3	1859	65.	125.	180.	315.	360.	450.
10-02-06	$5	1859	35.	60.	80.	175.	200.	250.

4. FULLY ENGRAVED DATE ONE SIGNATURE

SIGNATURES
right only
mss. E.W. Lusk or Evert W. Lusk

ISSUE DATING
Engraved
Octr. 1st, 1859

PROTECTOR
Red "word" on face and in mirror image on the back

OVERPRINT
"OTTAWA, ILL." and 13 - 14 stars in black

Cat.No.	Denom.	Date	VG	F	VF	EF	AU	Unc
10-04-02	$1	1859	35.	45.	65.	150.	175.	225.
10-04-04	$3	1859	60.	100.	150.	225.	260.	325.
10-04-06	$5	1859	35.	45.	65.	150.	175.	225.

125-12. ISSUE OF 1860 - 1861

DESIGNS AND COLOURS

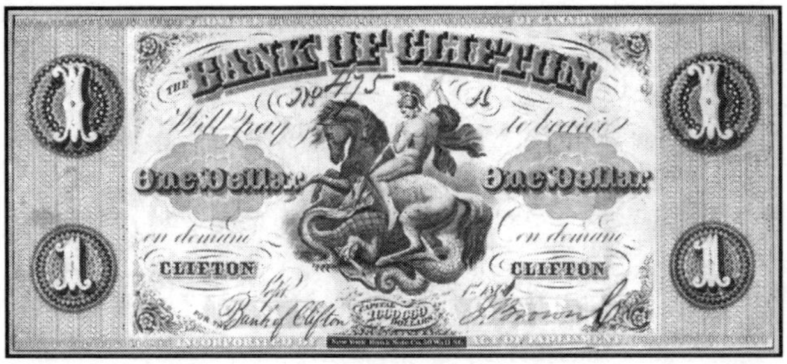

125-12-04
$1 Face Design: —/St. George slaying dragon/—
Colour: Black with red tint
Back Design: Plain

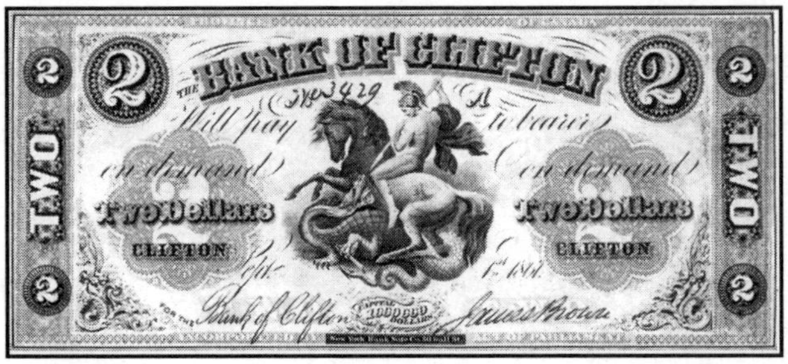

125-12-12
$2 Face Design: —/St. George slaying dragon/—
Colour: Black with red tint
Back Design: Plain

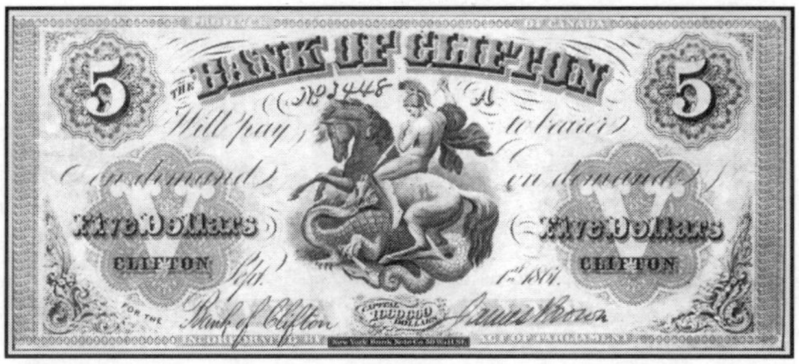

125-12-18

$5 Face Design: —/St. George slaying dragon/—
Colour: Black with red tint

Back Design: Plain

IMPRINT

New York Bank Note Co. 50 Wall St.

SIGNATURES

right only
mss. J. Brown or James Brown

ISSUE DATING

Engraved

Sept. 1, 1860
Sept. 1, 1861

OVERPRINTS

"Sassenberg & Co, Buenos Ayres" in an oval in blue
"Reedemed by Frederick Lau & Co. Bankers, 162 Fulton St. N.Y. at 3/4 per cent" in an oval in black
"Redeemable in Chicago at the office of Chadwick & Co." in red
"Redeemed in bankable funds at the office of Chadwick & Co. 5 Clark Street under the __house Chicago, Ill." in green
"Redeemed in bankable funds, by Chadwick & company banker. 54 Clark St., Chicago, Ils." in black

STAMPS

3 in blue

VARIETY

1861 Issue Date: Mss. 1 over the engraved 0 in 1860
1861 Issue Date: Engraved second 1 in 1861

Cat.No.	Denom.	Date	Variety	VG	F	VF	EF	AU	Unc
12-02	$1	1860		35.	50.	75.	175.	200.	250.
12-04	$1	1861	Mss. 1 in date	30.	40.	65.	155.	180.	225.
12-06	$1	1861	Engr. 1 in date	30.	40.	65.	155.	180.	225.
12-08	$2	1860		35.	50.	75.	175.	200.	250.
12-10	$2	1861	Mss. 1 in date	30.	40.	65.	155.	180.	225.
12-12	$2	1861	Engr. 1 in date	30.	40.	65.	155.	180.	225.
12-14	$5	1860		35.	50.	75.	175.	200.	250.
12-16	$5	1861	Mss. 1 in date	30.	40.	65.	155.	180.	225.
12-18	$5	1861	Engr. 1 in date	30.	40.	65.	155.	180.	225.

Note: A $2 note (12-12) has been seen with the colour a rusty red-brown probably the result of oxidation.

The 1859 issues were used as sources for altered United States obsolete notes, i.e. Connecticut, Delaware and Massachusetts notes.

THE COLONIAL BANK OF CANADA

1856 - 1863

TORONTO, CANADA WEST

BANK NUMBER 130 ***NONREDEEMABLE***

The Colonial Bank of Canada received its charter from a petition read to the Legislature on April 23, 1856, with Royal assent given on July 1, 1856. After several amendments to the bank's charter in 1857 and 1858, the original shareholders sold their interests.

In 1859 the new owners finally opened for business with notes put into circulation. The bank lasted only six months before its failure as a result of a run on it precipitated by the failure of The International Bank. An advertisement in the October 28, 1859 issue of the Toronto Globe stated that the bank had suspended operation. The bank's charter was repealed on August 31, 1863.

130-10. **ISSUE OF 1859**

DESIGNS AND COLOURS

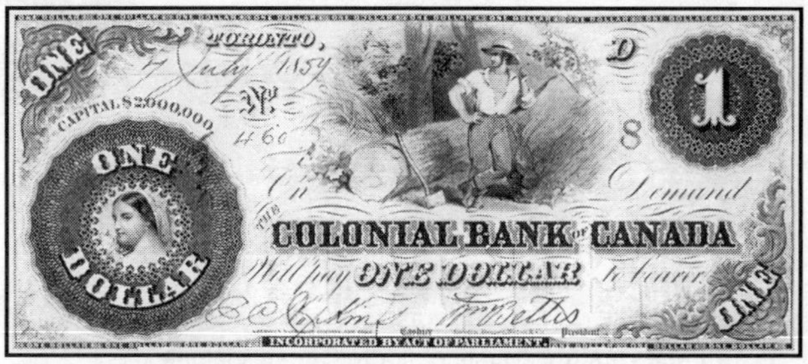

130-10-02-02

$1 Face Design: Bust of young woman/woodsman/—
Colour: See subheadings

Back Design: Plain

130-10-02-04

$2 Face Design: Indians on bluff/—/bust of young woman
Colour: See subheadings

Back Design: Plain

130-10-02-06

$3 Face Design: St. George slaying dragon/three allegorical women/Cornelia Jocelyn
Colour: See subheadings

Back Design: Plain

130-10-02-08

$4 Face Design: "Justice" figure/Queen Victoria (Winterhalter portrait)/—
Colour: See subheadings

Back Design: Plain

130-10-02-10

$5 Face Design: Farm family under tree/—/Cornelia Jocelyn
Colour: See subheadings

Back Design: Plain

130-10-02-12

$10 Face Design: Train at station/—/Indian maiden
Colour: See subheadings

Beck Design: Plain

130-10-02-14R

$20 Face Design: St. George slaying dragon/ loading hay/Cornelia Jocelyn
Colour: See subheadings

Back Design: Plain

130-10-02-16

$50 Face Design: St. George slaying dragon/ sailing ship/Cornelia Jocelyn
Colour: See subheadings

Back Design: Plain

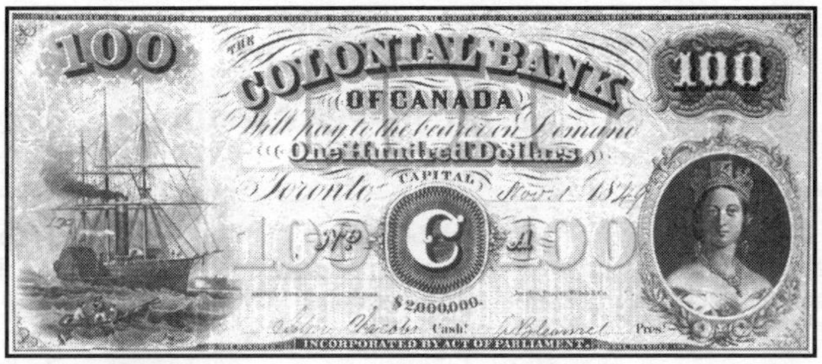

130-10-02-18R

$100 Face Design: Steamship/—/Queen Victoria (Winterhalter portrait)
Colour: See subheadings

Back Design: Plain

2. TWO SIGNATURE NOTES, ORANGE-BROWN TINT

IMPRINT

Jocelyn, Draper, Welch & Co.
American Bank Note Company, New York

SIGNATURES

left	right
mss. E.C. Hopkins	mss. Wm. Bettes
mss. E.C. Hopkins	mss. G.G. Moss (p.)
mss. T. Hough (rare)	mss. Geo. G. Moss (p.)
mss. T. Hough (rare)	mss. Wm. Bettes

ISSUE DATING

Partially Engraved__18__:

$1 1859: April 4,26,27,28,29; May 4,8; May, July 7,8,12
$2 1859: April 4,26,27,29; May 4,7,8,9,16,17,24,25; July 4,8,12,13,14
$3 1859: April 4,6; May 3,4,8,31; June 2,28; July 6
$4 1859: April 4; June 4,6,8,9,18,24
$5 1859: April 4,29; May 4,7,18; June 14,24,28,29; July 1,4
$10 1859: April 4; May 1st
$20 1859: May 2,21; Aug. 4
$50 1859: May 2,21; Aug. 4
$100 1859: May 2; Aug. 4

STAMP

Notes occur with various letters, numbers, etc. stamped on the face and back: Blue Y, X, 8; Black X, ZT

Cat.No.	Den.	Date	Variety	VG	F	VF	EF	AU	Unc
10-02-02	$1	1859	Two signatures	40	55.	80.	175.	200.	250.
10-02-02R	$1	18__	Remainder	—	—	70.	150.	175	225.
10-02-04	$2	1859	Two signatures	45.	60.	90.	185.	220.	275.
10-02-04R	$2	18__	Remainder	—	—	70.	150.	175.	225.
10-02-06	$3	1859	Two signatures	85	125.	175.	325.	400.	500.
10-02-06R	$3	18__	Remainder	—	—	100.	160.	200.	250.
10-02-08	$4	1859	Two signatures	70.	110.	150.	300.	375.	450.
10-02-08R	$4	18__	Remainder	—	—	100.	160.	200.	250.
10-02-10	$5	1859	Two signatures	45.	60.	90.	185.	220.	275.
10-02-10R	$5	18__	Remainder	—	—	70	150.	175.	225.
10-02-12	$10	1859	Two signatures	100.	135.	200.	425.	475.	600.
10-02-14	$20	1859	Completed note	1,000.	1,300.	2,000.	—	—	—
10-02-14R	$20	18__	Remainder*	400.	600.	900.	—	—	—
10-02-16	$50	1859	Completed note	600.	800.	1,200.	—	—	—
10-02-16R	$50	18__	Remainder*	175.	250.	375.	500.	—	—
10-02-18	$100	1859	Completed note	600.	800.	1,200.	—	—	—
10-02-18R	$100	18__	Remainder*	175.	250.	375.	500.	—	—

*Incomplete or spurious dates and signatures - authentically completed notes are dated May 2, May 21 or Aug. 4, 1859.

Uncut sheets exist of $1 (4 notes), $2 (4 notes), $3 (4 notes), $4 (four notes) $10 (4 notes). Value, $2,000 each sheet
Uncut sheet $20.20.50.100 notes value, $3,000.

Note: See "BANK OF TORONTO", "BANK OF UPPER CANADA" and "CITY BANK OF MONTREAL" for altered Colonial Bank notes.

4. ONE SIGNATURE NOTES, PINK TINT

DESIGNS AND COLOURS

See previous two signature issue.

130-10-04-02

130-10-04-04

130-10-04-06

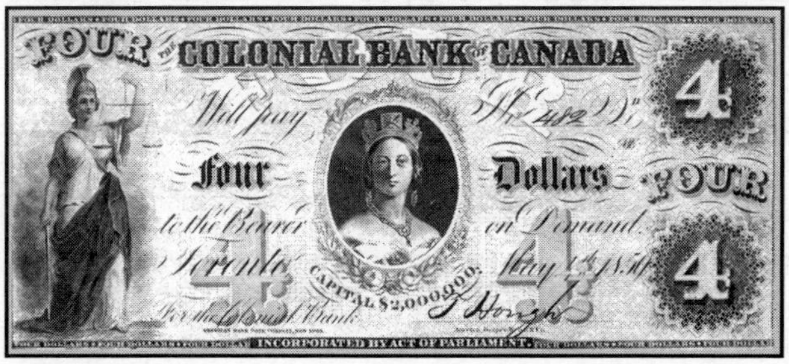

130-10-04-08

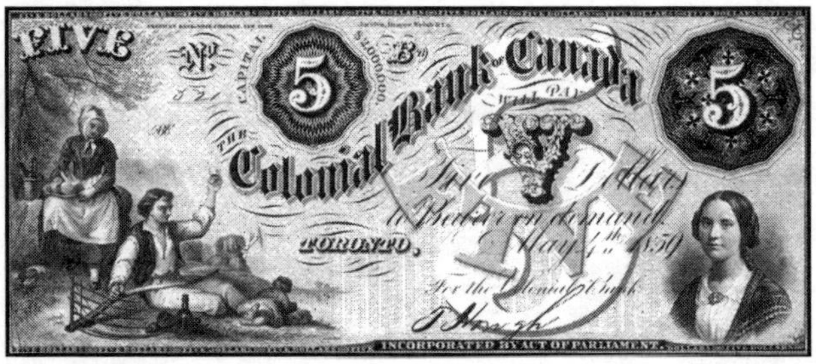

130-10-04-10

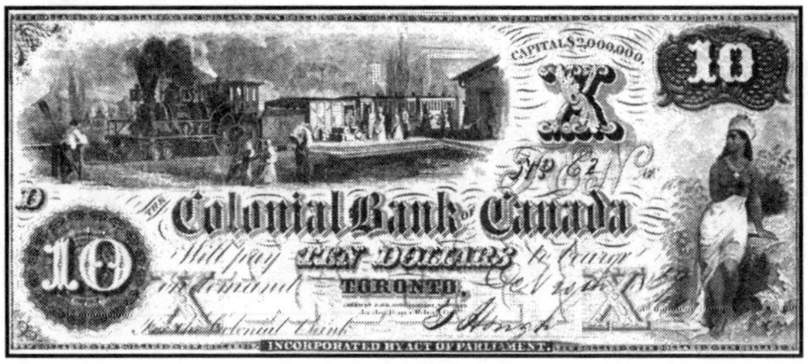

130-10-04-12

IMPRINT

Jocelyn Draper, Welch & Co.
American Bank Note Company, New York
ABNCo (monogram)

SIGNATURES

right only
mss. T. Hough
mss. G.G. Moss (rare)

ISSUE DATING

Engraved

$1 - $5: May 4th 1859

Partially Engraved __18__:

$10 1859: Oct. 20

STAMP

Notes occur with various letters, numbers, etc. stamped on the face and back. For more information see CPMS Journal April 1978.

Cat.No.	Denom.	Date		VG	F	VF	EF	AU	Unc
10-04-02	$1	1859	One signature	35.	50.	75.	150.	175.	225.
10-04-04	$2	1859	One signature	125.	175.	275.	550.	675.	—
10-04-06	$3	1859	One signature	65.	100.	135.	275.	320.	400.
10-04-08	$4	1859	One signature	65.	100.	135.	275.	320.	400.
10-04-10	$5	1859	One signature	40.	60.	85.	160.	200.	250.
10-04-12	$10	1859	One signature	110.	150.	225.	450.	500.	650.

Note: The orange-brown tint and the pink tint notes were used as altered sources for United States obsolete notes, i.e. Pennsylvania.

THE COLONIAL BANK OF CHATHAM

1837 - 1839

CHATHAM, U. C.(UPPER CANADA)

BANK NUMBER 135 ***NONREDEEMABLE***

This "spurious bank" was established in 1837 in Chatham, Upper Canada, by a group of individuals, principally from Buffalo, for the purpose of circulating its "notes" in the Buffalo area.

135-10. **ISSUE OF 1837**

DESIGNS AND COLOURS

Photo Not Available

135-10-02

$1 (5s) Face Design: Unknown
Colour: Black with no tint

Back Design: Plain

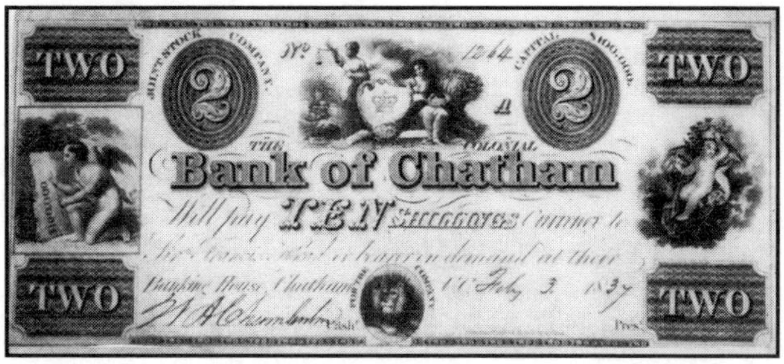

135-10-04R

$2 (10s) Face Design: Winged male figure/standing "Justice" figure, ornate shield, seated "Agriculture" figure/winged child in clouds. Engraved "Will pay - to Sir Francis Head"
Colour: Black with no tint

Back Design: Plain

135-10-06

$3 (15s) Face Design: —/seated "Justice" figure, lion; lion below/Indian with headdress Engraved "Will pay - to Sir Francis Head"
Colour: Black with no tint

Back Design: Plain

135-10-08

$5 (25s) Face Design: —/Royal Crest; lion below/King William IV
Engraved "Will pay - to Sir Francis Head"

Colour: Black with no tint

Back Design: Plain

135-10-10

$10 (50s) Face Design: —/Britannia in chariot drawn by lions; lion below/female with grain
Engraved "Payable - to Sir Francis Head"

Colour: Black with no tint

Back Design: Plain

IMPRINT

Rawdon, Wright & Hatch New York

SIGNATURES

	left	right
$1 (5s):	mss. Unknown	mss. Unknown
$2 (10s):	mss. W.A. Chamberlin	mss. Unknown
$3 (15s):	mss. W.A. Chamberlin	mss. John Clifford
$5 (25s):	mss. W.A. Chamberlin	mss. A.J. Douglas (v.)
$5 (25s):	mss. W.A. Chamberlin	mss. John Clifford
$10 (50s):	mss. W.A. Chamberlin	mss. John Clifford

ISSUE DATING

Partially Engraved __18__:

$1 (5s) 1837: Unknown
$2 (10s) 1837: Feby. 3
$3 (15s) 1837: Feby. 3, Feb. 15
$5 (25s) 1837: Jany 4, Feby. 3
$10 (50s) 1837: January 4

Cat.No.	Denom.	Date	G	VG	F	VF	EF	Unc
10-02	$1(5s)	1837				NOTE NOT CONFIRMED		
10-04R	$2(10s)	1837*	800.	1,600.	2,400.	—	—	—
10-06	$3(15s)	1837	800.	1,600.	2,400.	—	—	—
10-08	$5(25s)	1837	800.	1,600.	2,400.	—	—	—
10-10	$10(50s)	1837	800.	1,600.	2,400.	—	—	—

*Remainder: left signature only

COMMERCIAL BANK

1837

BROCKVILLE, UPPER CANADA

BANK NUMBER 140 ***NONREDEEMABLE***

The Commercial Bank at Brockville was a "spurious bank" whose fictitious notes were circulated by swindlers. The public was alerted by the watchful press in January of 1837 when the worthless notes first appeared. Despite this, the notes circulated in Upper Canada, Ohio, and Michigan.

140-10. DRAFT ISSUE OF 1834 - 1836

Engraved: "For Messrs Sims, Colburn and Co."

DESIGNS AND COLOURS

140-10-02

$5 (25s) Face Design: Sailing ship/seated allegorical figure with lute, urn (water god); cask, bales and ship below/sailing ship; Engraved "For Mess'rs Sims, Colburn & Co"

Colour: Black with no tint

Back Design: Plain

140-10-04

$10 (50s) Face Design: Allegorical female/King William IV; crown below/seated woman with grain, cattle; Engraved "For Mess'rs Sims, Colburn & Co"

Colour: Black with no tint

Back Design: Plain

IMPRINT

Burton, & Edmonds, N. York

SIGNATURES

left	right
mss. Luther R. Sims	mss. W. Colburn

ISSUE DATING

Partially Engraved __18__:

1834: Sept. 2
1836: Nov. 3

Cat.No.	Denom.	Date	G	VG	F	VF	EF	AU
10-02	$5(25s)	1836	600.	1,200.	—	—	—	—
10-04	$10(50s)	1834	600.	1,200.	—	—	—	—

COMMERCIAL BANK

1837

KINGSTON, UPPER CANADA

BANK NUMBER 145 ***NONREDEEMABLE***

This bank appears to be a "spurious bank", trading on the name of The Commercial Bank of the Midland District established in 1831 in Kingston, Upper Canada.

145-10. DRAFT ISSUE

$1: Engraved: "For the FOREIGN and DOMESTIC Exchange Company"
$2 (10s): Engraved: "For the FOREIGN and DOMESTIC EXCHANGE COMPANY"
$3 (15s): Engraved: "for the Foreign & Domestic Exchange Company"

DESIGNS AND COLOURS

145-10-02-02
$1 Face Design: Portrait of Washington/seated Mercury, ship in background; Indian paddling canoe below/portrait of Franklin
See subheadings
Colour: Black with no tint

Back Design: Plain

145-10-02-04
$2 (10s) Face Design: Sheaves/woman with grain
See subheadings
Colour: Black with no tint

Back Design: Plain

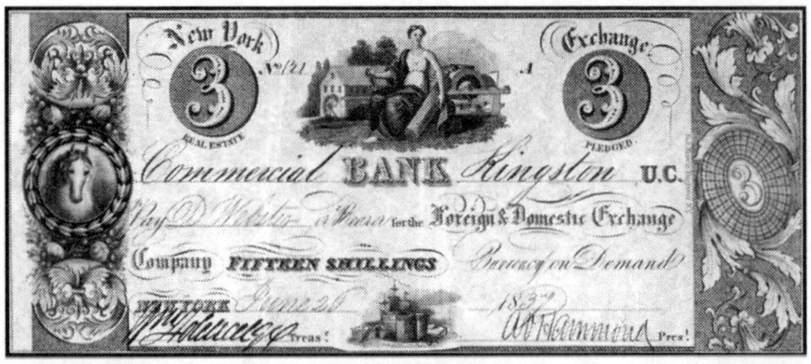

145-10-02-06
$3 (15s) Face Design: Horse's head/seated female, mill in background; casks, bales and ship below/-
See subheadings
Colour: Black with no tint

Back Design: Plain

IMPRINT
Jas. Harris, Engravr N.Y.
Jas. Harris, Engraver, N.Y.

SIGNATURES

left	**right**
mss. Wm. Holdridge	mss. A.V. Hammond

2. MANUSCRIPT "Commercial" IN BANK NAME

ISSUE DATING
Partially Engraved __18__:
$1 1837: July 18
$2 (10s) 1837: Jany 14, Jany 31, June 14, June 21, June 26, July 30
$3 (15s) 1837: Jany 14, June 17, June 21, June 26

Cat.No.	Denom.	Date	VG	F	VF	EF	AU	Unc
10-02-02	$1	1837	500.	750.	—	—	—	—
10-02-04	$2(10s)	1837	150.	175.	250.	350.	400.	500.
10-02-06	$3(15s)	1837	175.	200.	300.	400.	475.	600.
10-02-08	$5	1837	600.	900.	—	—	—	—
10-02-10	$10	1837	600.	900.	—	—	—	—

4. ENGRAVED "COMMERCIAL" IN BANK NAME

145-10-04-02
$1 Face Design: Portrait of Washington/seated Mercury, ship in background; Indian paddling canoe below/portrait of Franklin
See subheadings
Colour: Black with no tint

Back Design: Plain

ISSUE DATING
Partially Engraved ___18___:
1837: July 25

Cat.No.	Denom.	Date	G	VG	F	VF	EF	Unc
10-04-02	$1	1837	250.	500.	750.	—	—	—

THE COMMERCIAL BANK

1837

MONTREAL, LOWER CANADA

BANK NUMBER 150 ***NONREDEMABLE***

The Commercial Bank in Montreal appears to be another spurious bank of the period. Its notes were produced from the same plate as those of the Mechanics Bank in Montreal and have the same signatures.

150-10. **ISSUE OF 1837**

DESIGNS AND COLOURS

Photo Not Available

150-10-02

$3 Face Design: Dock scene/blacksmith and two women (Industry, agriculture and commerce); arm and hammer in shield below/woman with wheat leaning on pillar

Colour: Black with no tint

Back Design: Plain

Photo Not Available

150-10-04

$5 Face Design: Seated youth with mechanics' tools/seated woman resting on cogwheel: arm and hammer in shield below/blacksmith "Industry"

Colour: Black with no tint

Back Design: Plain

150-10-06

$10 Face Design: Seated woman with rake, leaning on shield/ blacksmith and two women; crouching lion in oval below/kneeling cherub inscribing rock.

Colour: Black with no tint

Back Design: Plain

IMPRINT

Rawdon, Wright & Hatch New-York

SIGNATURES

left	**right**
mss: F.E. Whiting	mss: W. Morris

ISSUE DATING

Partially Engraved __18__:

$10: June 1 1837

Cat.No.	Denom.	Date	G	VG	F	VF	EF	AU
10-02	$3	1837			Not confirmed			
10-04	$5	1837			Not confirmed			
10-06	$10	1837	50.	100.	150.	200.	300.	—

THE COMMERCIAL BANK OF CANADA

1856 - 1868

KINGSTON, PROVINCE OF CANADA

BANK NUMBER 155 ***REDEEMABLE***

Originally incorporated as The Commercial Bank of the Midland District in 1831, in Kingston, Canada West, this bank operated until 1868. Its name was changed to The Commercial Bank of Canada in 1856. It suspended specie payment in October, 1867 and in the following year was taken over by The Merchants' Bank of Canada without loss to creditors. The shareholders received about one third of the par value of the paid-up capital. The main reasons for this bank's failure were its involvement in speculation and its large extension of credit to the Detroit and Milwaukee Railway.

155-10. **"YELLOW" ISSUE**
CANADA WEST BRANCHES
1857

DESIGNS AND COLOURS

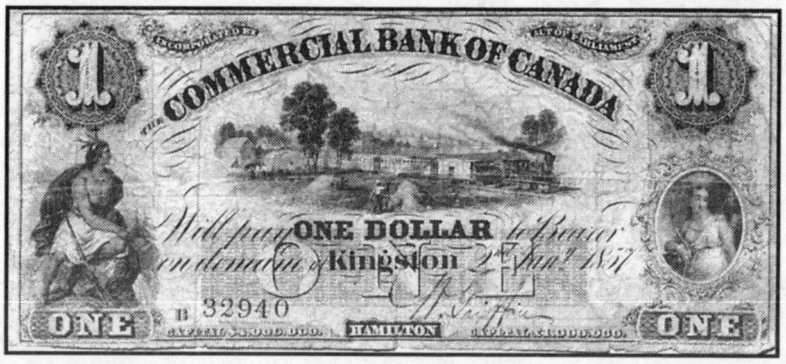

155-10-06-02

$1 Face Design: Seated Indian with rifle/train and hay field/Indian maiden in oval

Colour: Black with overall yellow tint

Back Design: Plain

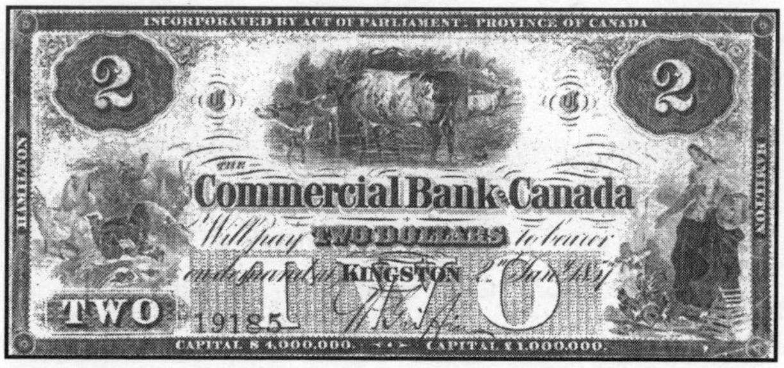

155-10-06-04

$2 Face Design: Chickens/cow and calf in stream woman feeding chickens

Colour: Black with overall yellow tint

Back Design: Plain

155-10-10-02

$5 Face Design: Surveyors/train/man with pick and shovel
Colour: Black with overall yellow tint
Back Design: See Varieties
Colour: See varieties

155-10-04-02

$10 Face Design: Queen Victoria (Winterhalter portrait) men on dock by anchor/Princess Eugenie
Colour: Black with overall yellow tint
Back Design: Lathework and bank name
Colour: Brown

IMPRINT

Toppan, Carpenter & Co. Montreal

SIGNATURES

right only
mss. W. Griffin

ISSUE DATING

Engraved

2nd Jan'y 1857

2. BROCKVILLE ISSUE

Engraved "BROCKVILLE" in frame at bottom of notes

Cat.No.	Denom.	Date	G	VG	F	VF	EF	AU
10-02-02	$1	1857	450.	900.	1,350.	—	—	—

4. GALT ISSUE

Engraved "GALT" in frame at ends of notes.

Cat.No.	Denom.	Date	G	VG	F	VF	EF	AU
10-04-02	$10	1857	Institutional collection only					

6. HAMILTON ISSUE

$1: Engraved "HAMILTON" in frame at bottom of notes.
$2: Engraved "HAMILTON" in frame at ends of notes.

Cat.No.	Denom.	Date	G	VG	F	VF	EF	AU
10-06-02	$1	1857	450.	900.	1,350.	—	—	—
10-06-04	$2	1857	450.	900.	1.350.	—	—	—

10. KINGSTON ISSUE BROWN BACK

Engraved "KINGSTON" in frame at ends of notes.

OVERPRINT

"LONDON" in red and H in black

DESIGNS AND COLOURS

$5 Back Design: Lathework and bank name
Colour: Brown

Cat.No.	Denom.	Date	G	VG	F	VF	EF	AU
10-10-02	$5	1857	Institutional collection only					

12. LONDON ISSUE PLAIN BACK

$1: Engraved: "LONDON" in frame at bottom of notes.
$2: Engraved: "LONDON" in frame at ends of notes.

STAMP

$1: "C" in back; "W" in black
$2: "S" in black

Cat.No.	Denom.	Date	Variety	G	VG	F	VF	EF	AU
10-12-02	$1	1857	no ptr	450.	900.	1,350.	—	—	—
10-12-03	$1	1857	green ONE ptr	Institutional collection only					
10-12-04	$2	1857	no ptr	450.	900.	1,350.	—	—	—

14. LONDON ISSUE BROWN BACK

DESIGNS AND COLOURS

$5: Engraved "LONDON" in frame at ends of notes.

155-10-14-04

$5 Back Design: Lathework and bank name
Colour: Brown

OVERPRINT

"S", "CL" in black

Cat.No.	Denom.	Date	G	VG	F	VF	EF	Unc
10-14-04	$5	1857	500.	1,000.	1,500.	—	—	—

16. TORONTO ISSUE

Engraved "TORONTO" in frame at bottom of notes

PROTECTOR:
$1: Red ONE on face

OVERPRINT:
$2: OWEN SOUND

STAMP
$1: OWEN SOUND in blue (with red protector)

Cat.No.	Denom.	Date		G	VG	F	VF	EF	Unc
10-16-02	$1	1857	no ptr	450.	900.	1,350.	—	—	—
10-16-03	$1	1857	red ptr	500.	—	—	—	—	—
10-16-04	$2	1857	OWEN SOUND o/p	Institutional collection only					

155-12. "GREEN" ISSUE CANADA WEST BRANCHES 1860 - 1861

DESIGNS AND COLOURS

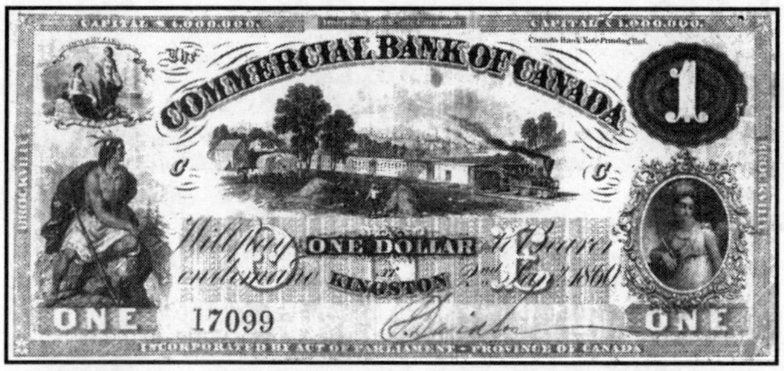

155-12-04-02
$1 Face Design: Bank Crest; seated Indian with rifle/ train and hay field/Indian maiden in oval
Colour: Black with green tint
Back Design: Plain

155-12-02-04
$2 Face Design: Bank Crest; chickens/cow and calf in stream/ woman feeding chickens
Colour: Black with green tint
Back Design: Plain

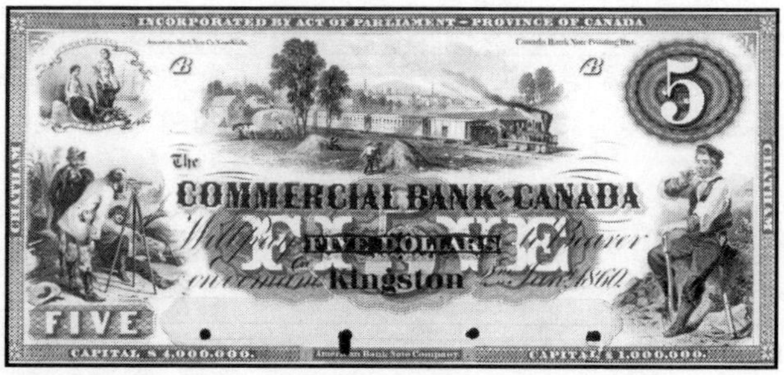

155-12-06-02P
$5 Face Design: Bank Crest; surveyors/train and hay field/ man with pick and shovel
Colour: Black with green tint
Back Design: Plain

IMPRINT
American Bank Note Co. New York
American Bank Note Company

SIGNATURES

left	right
none	mss. J.Davidson

ISSUE DATING
Engraved
2nd Jany. 1860
Jan. 2, 1861

PROTECTOR
Green outlined "word" on face and back
Green "numeral" on face and back

2. BELLEVILLE ISSUE

Engraved "BELLEVILLE" in frame at ends of notes.

Cat.No.	Denom.	Date	G	VG	F	VF	EF	AU
12-02-02	$1	1860	325.	650.	900.	—	—	—
12-02-04	$2	1860	325.	650.	900.	—	—	—

3. BERLIN ISSUE

Engraved "BERLIN" in frame at end of notes.

Cat. No.	Denom.	Date	G	VG	F	VF	EF	AU
12-03-02	$1	1860	Institutional collection only					

4. BROCKVILLE ISSUE

Engraved "BROCKVILLE" in frame at ends of notes.

STAMP
"K" in black

Cat.No.	Denom.	Date	G	VG	F	VF	EF	AU
12-04-02	$1	1860	325.	650.	900.	—	—	—

6. CHATHAM ISSUE

Engraved "CHATHAM" in frame at ends of notes.

PROOF NOTES

Cat.No.	Denom.	Date		Unc
12-06-02P	$5	1860	PROOF	450.

8. HAMILTON ISSUE

Engraved "HAMILTON" in frame at ends of notes.

Cat.No.	Denom.	Date	G	VG	F	VF	EF	AU
12-08-04	$2	1860	325.	650.	900.	—	—	—

10. INGERSOLL ISSUE

Engraved "Ingersoll" in frame at ends of notes.

Cat.No.	Denom.	Date	G	VG	F	VF	EF	AU
12-10-02	$1	1860	325.	650.	900.	—	—	—

12. KINGSTON ISSUE

Engraved "KINGSTON" in frame at ends of notes.

CIRCULATING NOTES

Cat.No.	Denom.	Date	G	VG	F	VF	EF	AU
12-12-02	$1	1860	325.	650.	900.	—	—	—
12-12-04	$1	1861	No known issued notes					
12-12-06	$2	1860	325.	650.	900.	—	—	—
12-12-08	$5	1860	No known issued notes					

PROOF NOTES

Cat. No.	Denom.	Date		Unc
12-12-02P	$1	1860	PROOF	450.
12-12-04P	$1	1861	PROOF	450.
12-12-06P	$2	1860	PROOF	450.
12-12-06P	$5	1860	PROOF	450.

14. LONDON ISSUE

Engraved "LONDON" in frame at ends of notes.

Cat.No.	Denom.	Date	G	VG	F	VF	EF	AU
12-14-02	$1	1860	325.	650.	900.	—	—	—
12-14-04	$2	1860	325.	650.	900.	—	—	—

16. PERTH ISSUE

Engraved "PERTH" in frame at ends of notes.

Cat.No.	Denom.	Date	G	VG	F	VF	EF	AU
12-16-02	$1	1860	325.	650.	900.	—	—	—

18. PORT HOPE ISSUE

Engraved "PORT HOPE" in frame at ends of notes.

PROOF NOTES

Cat.No.	Denom.	Date		Unc
12-18-04P	$2	1860	PROOF	450.

SPECIMEN NOTES

Cat. No.	Denom.	Date		Unc
12-18-04S	$2	1860	SPECIMEN	600.

An uncut sheet of $2.2.2.2. Specimens is known.

20. PRESCOTT ISSUE

Engraved "PRESCOTT" in frame at ends of notes.

PROOF NOTES

Cat.No.	Denom.	Date	Unc
12-20-02P	$2	1860	450.

22. TORONTO ISSUE

Engraved "TORONTO" in frame at ends of notes.

Cat.No.	Denom.	Date	G	VG	F	VF	EF	AU
12-22-02	$1	1860	325.	650.	900.	—	—	—

24. WINDSOR ISSUE

Engraved "WINDSOR" in frame at ends of notes.

Cat.No.	Denom.	Date	G	VG	F	VF	EF	AU
12-24-02	$1	1860	325.	650.	900.	—	—	—
12-24-04	$2	1860	325.	650.	900.	—	—	—

155-14. "YELLOW" ISSUE MONTREAL BRANCH 1857

$1, $10 & $100: Engraved "MONTREAL" at bottom centre.
$2 & $5: Engraved "MONTREAL" in the frame at ends.
$1000: Engraved "MONTREAL" at right centre.

DESIGNS AND COLOURS

155-14-02

$1 Face Design: Indian/seated farmer with scythe/ woman with sheaf over shoulder
Colour: Black with overall yellow tint

Back Design: Plain

Photo Not Available

155-14-04P

$2 Face Design: Seated Indian maiden with shield cattle and sheep near water/—
Colour: Black with overall yellow tint

Back Design: Plain

Photo Not Available

155-14-06P

$5 Face Design: Portrait of Columbus/ships in harbour/ sailor with sextant
Colour: black with overall yellow tint

Back Design: Lathework and bank name
Colour: Brown

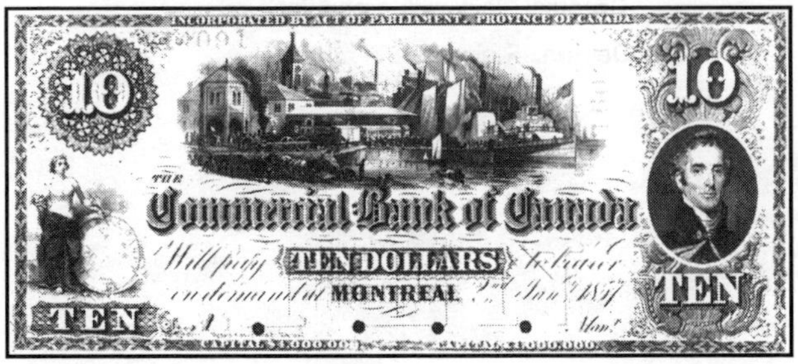

155-14-08P

$10 Face Design: Woman and Arms of Montreal/ busy harbour scene/bust of Wellington
Colour: Black with overall yellow tint

Back Design: Lathework and bank name
Colour: Brown

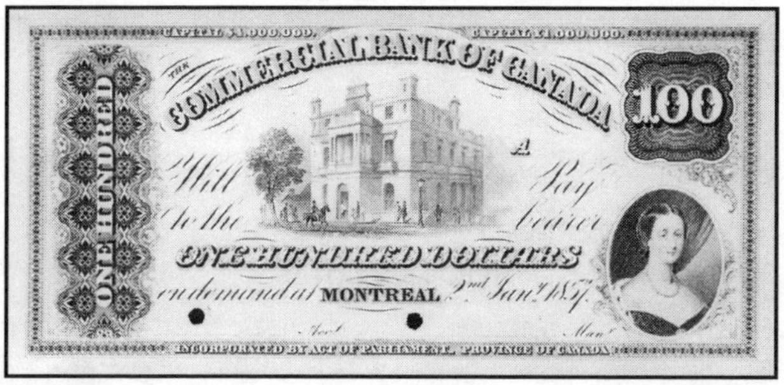

155-14-10P

$100 Face Design: —/bank building/Princess Eugenie
Colour: Black with overall yellow tint

Back Design: Lathework and bank name
Colour: Brown

155-14-12P

$1000: (£250)
Face Design: —/Princess Eugenie/—
Colour: Black with overall yellow tint

Back Design: Lathework and bank name
Colour: Brown

IMPRINT

Toppan, Carpenter & Co., Montreal

SIGNATURES

right only
mss. Tho. Kirby

ISSUE DATING

Engraved

2nd Jan'y 1857

CIRCULATING NOTES

Cat.No.	Denom.	Date	G	VG	F	VF	EF	AU
14-02	$1	1857	500.	1,000.	1,500.	—	—	—
14-04	$2	1857	No known issued notes					
14-06	$5	1857	No known issued notes					
14-08	$10	1857	500.	1,000.	1,500.	—	—	—
14-10	$100	1857	No known issued notes					
14-12	$1000(£250)	1857	No known issued notes					

PROOF NOTES

Cat. No.	Denom.	Date		Unc
14-02P	$1	1857	PROOF	500.
14-04P	$2	1857	PROOF	500.
14-06P	$5	1857	FACE PROOF	500.
14-08P	$10	1857	FACE PROOF	500.
14-10P	$100	1857	FACE PROOF	750.
14-12p	$1000 (£250.)	1857	FACE PROOF	1,500.

155-16. "GREEN" ISSUE MONTREAL BRANCH 1860 - 1862

$1 - $100: Engraved "MONTREAL" at bottom centre.
$1000: Engraved "MONTREAL" at right centre.

DESIGNS AND COLOURS

Counters at the upper left of notes in the 1857 issue were replaced by vignettes.

155-16-02P

$1 Face Design: Indian/seated farmer with scythe/ small bank crest and counter
Colour: Black with overall green tint

Back Design: Plain

155-16-04P

$2 Face Design: Seated Indian maiden with shield/ cattle and sheep near water/ small bank crest and counter
Colour: Black with overall green tint

Back Design: Plain

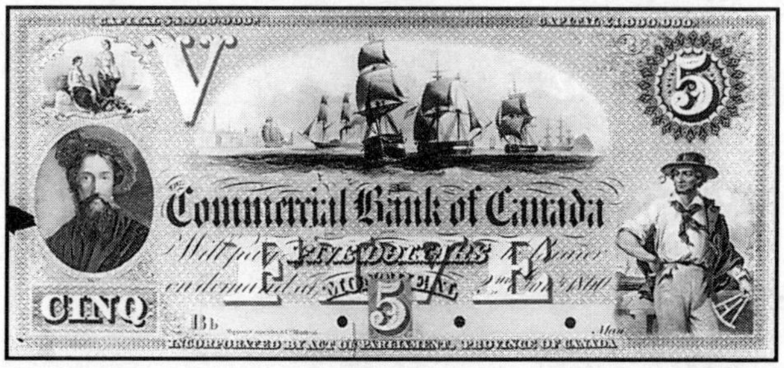

155-16-06P

$5 Face Design: Small bank crest; portrait of Columbus/ ships in harbour/sailor with sextant
Colour: Black with overall green tint

Back Design: Plain

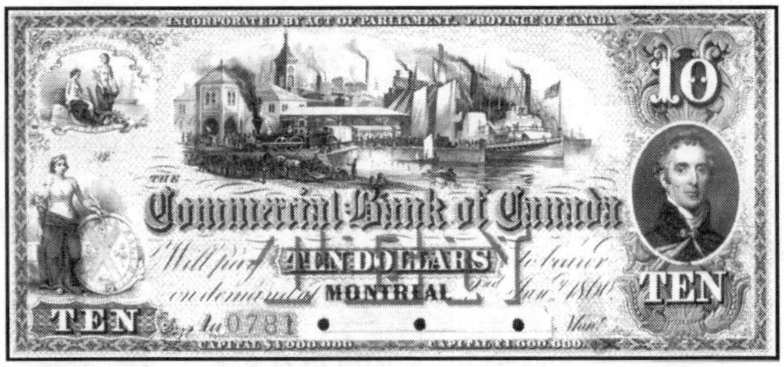

155-16-10P

$10 Face Design: Bank Crest; woman and Arms of Montreal/ busy harbour scene/bust of Wellington in oval
Colour: Black with overall green tint

Back Design: Plain

Photo Not Available

155-16-12P

$100 Face Design: —/bank building/portrait of young woman wearing hat
Colour: Black with overall green tint

Back Design: Plain

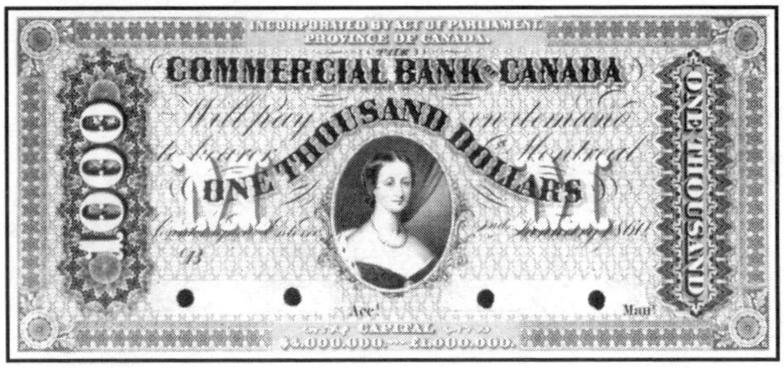

155-16-14P

$1000 Face Design: /Princess Eugenie/
Colour: Black with overall green tint

Back Design: Plain

IMPRINT

$1-$5: Toppan, Carpenter & Co. Montreal
$10: Toppan, Carpenter & Co. and American Bank Note Co. (monogram)
$100: American Bank Note Company
$1000: None

SIGNATURES

right only
mss. W. Griffin

DATING

Engraved

2nd January 1860
2nd Jany 1860
Jan. 2, 1862

PROOF NOTES

Cat.No.	Denom.	Date		Unc
16-02P	$1	1860	PROOF	500.
16-04P	$2	1860	PROOF	500.
16-06P	$5	1860	PROOF	500.
16-10P	$10	1860	PROOF	600.
16-12P	$100	1862	PROOF	750.
16-14P	$1000 (£250)	1860	PROOF	1,500.

SPECIMEN NOTES

Cat. No.	Denom.	Date		Unc
16-02S	$1	1860	SPECIMEN	600.
16-04S	$2	1860	SPECIMEN	600.
16-06S	$5	1860	SPECIMEN	600.
16-10S	$10	1860	SPECIMEN	700.
16-12S	$100	1862	SPECIMEN	1,000.
16-14S	$1000 (£250)	1860	SPECIMEN	2,000.

THE COMMERCIAL BANK OF FORT ERIE

1836 - 1839

FORT ERIE, UPPER CANADA

BANK NUMBER 160 ***NONREDEEMABLE***

Probably another of the many spurious banks whose worthless notes appeared during the winter and spring of 1837. The swindlers preyed with some success on the unwary, mainly in the border states.

160-10. **ISSUE OF 1836 - 1837**

DESIGNS AND COLOURS

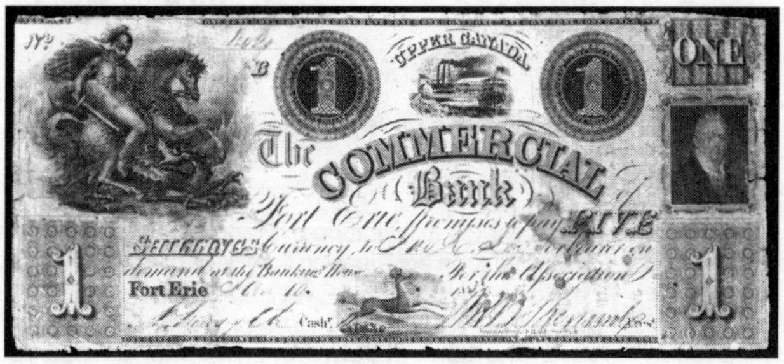

160-10-02

$1 (5s) Face Design: St. George slaying dragon/steamboat with U.S. flag; running deer below/ King William IV

Colour: Black with no tint

Back Design: Plain

160-10-04

$2 (10s) Face Design: St. George slaying dragon/Royal Crest; early train below/

Colour: Black with no tint

Back Design: Plain

160-10-06

$3 (15s) Face Design: Britannia and anchor/planting scene; paddlewheeler below/St. George slaying dragon

Colour: Black with no tint

Back Design: Plain

160-10-08

$4 (20s) Face Design: /Royal Crest; paddlewheeler below/ men cutting and women carring sheaves

Colour: Black with no tint

Back Design: Plain

160-10-10

$5 (25s) Face Design: /King William IV; beaver below/ St. George slaying dragon

Colour: Black with no tint

Back Design: Plain

160-10-18R

$10 Face Design: /Royal Crest; dogs head Fidelity below/cherub in clouds

Colour: Black with no tint

Back Design: Plain

160-10-20R

$20 Face Design: /ships and seated allegorical women, with shield and produce; dogs head Fidelity below/ Royal Crest (sideways)

Colour: Black with no tint

Back Design: Plain

IMPRINT

Rawdon, Wright & Hatch New York

SIGNATURES

left	right
mss. V. Forsyth	mss. M.B. Sherwood

ISSUE DATING

Partially Engraved __18__:

$1 1837: Jan. 10
$2 1837: Jan. 10, Jan. 4
$3 1837: Jan. 10
$4 1836: July 20
1837: Jany. 20
$5 1836: July 20
1837: Jany 20
1837: Aug. 20

Cat.No.	Den.	Date	Variety	G	VG	F	VF	EF	AU
10-02	$1	1837		85.	175.	225.	—	—	—
10-02R	$1	1837**	Spurious	70.	140.	180.	—	—	—
10-04	$2	1837		85.	175.	225.	—	—	—
10-04R	$2	1837**	Spurious	70.	140.	180.	250.	—	—
10-06	$3	1837		125.	250.	325.	—	—	—
10-06R	$3	1837**	Spurious	100.	200.	275.	—	—	—
10-08	$4	1836-1837		60.	120.	160.	225.	—	—
10-08R	$4	18__*	Remainder	50.	100.	140.	200.	—	—
10-10	$5	1836-1837		60.	120.	160.	225.	—	—
10-10R	$5	18__*	Remainder	50.	100.	140.	200.	—	—
10-12R	$10	18__*	Remainder	175.	350.	500.	—	—	—
10-14R	$20	18__**	Spurious	200.	400.	550.	—	—	—

*unsigned, undated and unnumbered.
**spurious signatures and dates.

THE COMMERCIAL BANK OF LAKE ONTARIO

1837

NIAGARA FALLS, UPPER CANADA

BANK NUMBER 165 ***NONREDEEMABLE***

Bank notes were ordered in February of 1837; however, there is no record of any notes or proofs having survived.

THE COMMERCIAL BANK OF MANITOBA

1885 - 1893

WINNIPEG, MANITOBA

BANK NUMBER 170 ***REDEEMABLE***

This bank was established in Winnipeg, Manitoba, in 1885, as an outgrowth of the private banking and finance business of McArthur, Boyle and Campbell. Its lending policies were very liberal. After the severe winter of 1892-1893, anxiety developed among the depositors which culminated in a run on the bank in July and payments were stopped. Creditors were paid in full but shareholders lost their entire equity.

170-10. **ISSUE OF 1885**

DESIGNS AND COLOURS

170-10-02P

$5 Face Design: Female figure Ceres/Indian camp (F.O.C. Darley design) Queen Victoria in oval

Colour: Black with green tint

Back Design: Flowers, Lathework, counters and bank name, flowers

Colour: Brown

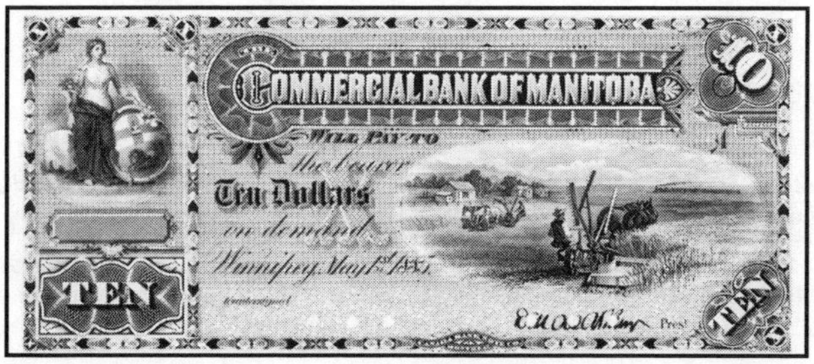

170-10-04P

$10 Face Design: Female figure Ceres//farmers reaping grain
Colour: Black with ochre tint

Back Design: Lathework, counters and bank name
Colour: Green

IMPRINT

Canada Bank Note Co. Montreal

SIGNATURES

left	right
mss. A.A. Jackson	engr. D. MacArthur

ISSUE DATING

Engraved

May 1, 1885

CIRCULATING NOTES

Cat.No.	Denom.	Date	VG	F	VF	EF	AU
10-02	$5	1885	—	9,000.	—	—	—
10-04	$10	1885	Institutional collection only				

PROOF NOTES

Cat. No.	Denom.	Date		Unc
10-02P	$5	1885	FACE PROOF	1,500.
10-04P	$10	1885	FACE PROOF	1,500.

SPECIMEN NOTES

Cat. No.	Denom.	Date		Unc
10-02S	$5	1885	SPECIMEN	2,000.
10-04S	$10	1885	SPECIMEN	2,000.

170-12. ISSUE OF 1891

DESIGNS AND COLOURS

170-12-02

$5 Face Design: Head office/Binder and horses /D. MacArthur
Colour: Black with green tint

Back Design: Lathework, counters, bank name and train at prairie station
Colour: Green

170-12-04

$10 Face Design: Head office/ploughing with team of horses/D. MacArthur
Colour: Black with green tint

Back Design: lathework, counters, bank name and Crest
Colour: Green

IMPRINT

British American Bank Note Co. Ottawa

SIGNATURES

left	right
mss. various	engr. D. MacArthur

ISSUE DATING

Engraved

2nd Jan 1891

CIRCULATING NOTES

Cat.No.	Denom.	Date	VG	F	VF	EF	Unc
12-02	$5	1891	Institutional collection only				
12-04	$10	1891	Institutional collection only				

PROOF NOTES

Cat. No.	Denom.	Date		Unc
12-02P	$5	1891	FACE PROOF	1,500.
12-04P	$10	1891	FACE PROOF	1,500.

* Proofs exist with unissued colours.

$5: face proof: orange tint, back proof: green

$10: face proof: orange tint, back proof: blue

COMMERCIAL BANK OF MONTREAL

1835 - 1837

MONTREAL, LOWER CANADA

BANK NUMBER 175 ***NONREDEEMABLE***

Established as a private company in Montreal, the Commercial Bank of Montreal operated for only a short period of time until 1837. Little is known of its operation. An 1841 counterfeit detector listed the notes as genuine, noting it was John E. Mills Bank and that all others were frauds.

175-10. DRAFT ISSUE OF 1835

Engraved: for John E. Mills & Co. at bottom

DESIGNS AND COLOURS

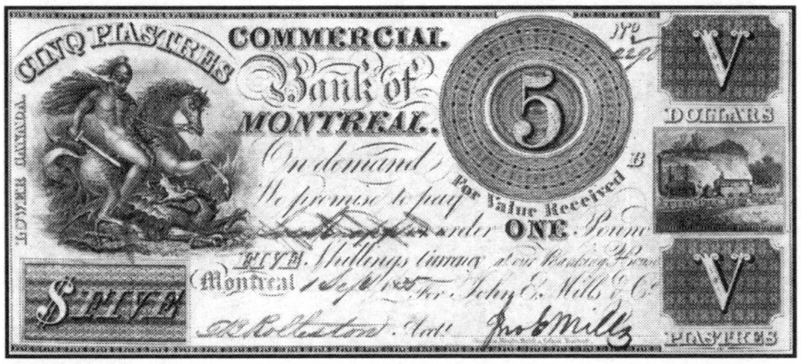

175-10-02

$5 (£1.5) Face Design: St. George slaying dragon// early train

Colour: Black with no tint

Back Design: Plain

175-10-04

$10 (£2.10) Face Design: Indian maiden//train

Colour: Black with no tint

Back Design: Plain

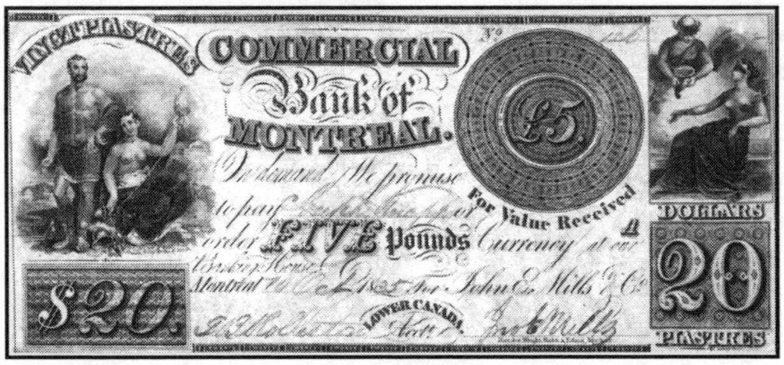

175-10-06

$20 (£5) Face Design: Allegorical "Vulcan" and Industry /allegorical Plenty and Commerce

Colour: Black with no tint

Back Design: Plain

175-10-08

$50 (£12.10) Face Design: Allegorical scene: nude woman and cupid in clouds, sea, horses below/—/—

Colour: Black with no tint

Back Design: Plain

IMPRINT

Rawdon, Wright, Hatch & Edson, New York

SIGNATURES

left	right
mss. G.B. Rolleston	mss. Jno. E. Mills

ISSUE DATING

Partially Engraved __18__:

$5 (£1.5): 1835: 1 Sep., 21 Aug.

$10 (£2.10): 1835: 1 Sep.

$20 (£5) & $50 (£12.10): 1835: 10 Oct.

Cat.No.	Denom.	Date	G	VG	F	VF	EF	AU
10-02	$5(£1.5)	1835	300.	600.	800.	1,000.	—	—
10-04	$10(£2.10)	1835	300.	600.	800.	1,000.	—	—
10-06	$20(£5)	1835	350.	700.	900.	1,200.	—	—
10-08	$50(£12.10)	1835	350.	700.	900.	1,200.	—	—

175-12 DRAFT ISSUE OF 1836

Engraved: Accepted for John E. Mills & Co. at the bottom and To John E. Mills & Co. or To John E. Mills & Company across top of the face.

DESIGNS AND COLOURS

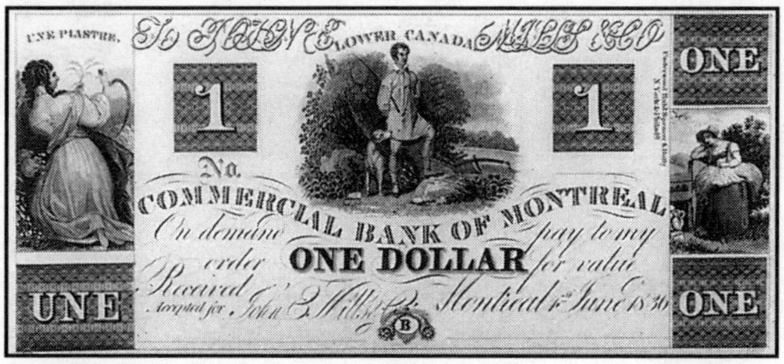

175-12-02R

$1 Face Design: Woman with sickle/man with whip and dog/farm girl leaning on fence

Colour: Black with no tint

Back Design: Plain

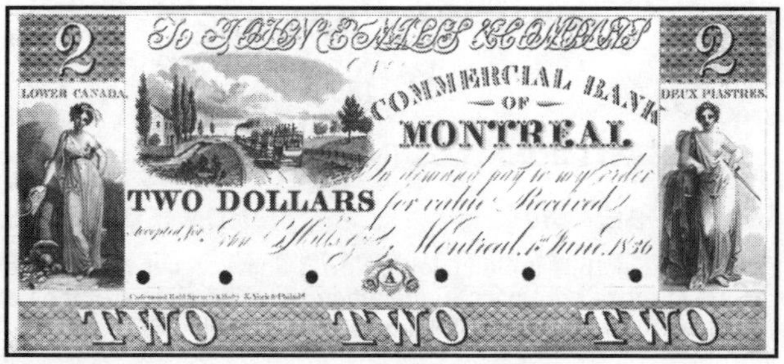

175-12-04P

$2 Face Design: Woman with sickle, cornucopia/ early train passing house/ Justice figure

Colour: Black with no tint

Back Design: Plain

IMPRINT

Underwood, Bald, Spencer & Hufty, N. York & Philada.

SIGNATURES

left	right
mss. G.B. Rolleston	mss. Jno E. Mills

ISSUE DATING

Engraved

1st June 1836

CIRCULATING NOTES

Cat.No.	Denom.	Date		G	VG	F	VF	EF	AU
12-02R	$1	1836	Remainder*	250.	500.	700.	900.	—	—
12-04	$2	1836		300.	600.	800.	1,000.	—	—

* lacks right-hand signature.

PROOF NOTES

Cat. No.	Denom.	Date		Unc
12-02P	$1	1836	PROOF	500.
12-04P	$2	1836	PROOF	500.

THE COMMERCIAL BANK OF NEW BRUNSWICK

1834 - 1868

SAINT JOHN, N.B. (NEW BRUNSWICK)

BANK NUMBER 180 ***NONREDEEMABLE***

Established in 1834 in Saint John, New Brunswick, this bank failed in 1868 due to gross corruption in management. All creditors of the bank were paid in full, but its shareholders losses amount to $495,000.

180-10. FREDERICTON BRANCH ISSUE POUNDS & SHILLINGS

Engraved: BRANCH BANK IN FREDERICTON across centre and FREDERICTON engraved at lower centre.

DESIGNS AND COLOURS

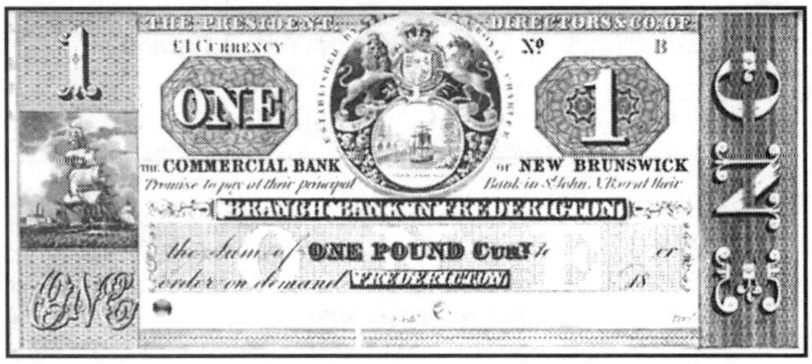

180-10-02P
£1 Face Design: Ships/Crest/
Colour: Black with no tint

Back Design: Unknown
Colour: Green

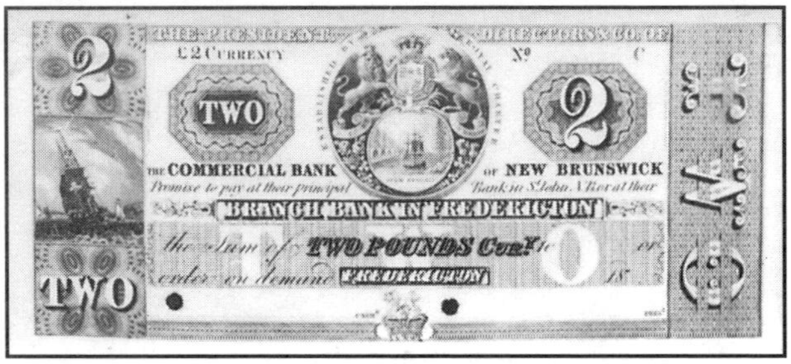

180-10-04P
£2 Face Design: Ships/Crest, lion on crown below/
Colour: Black with no tint

Back Design: Unknown
Colour: Green

180-10-06P
£5 Face Design: Britannia/Crest; lion on crown below/
Colour: Black with no tint

Back Design: Unknown
Colour: Green

IMPRINT
New England Bank Note Company

SIGNATURES

left	right
none	none

ISSUE DATING
Partially Engraved __18__:

PROOF NOTES

Cat.No.	Denom.	Date		Unc
10-02P	£1	18__	FACE PROOF	650.
10-04P	£2	18__	FACE PROOF	650.
10-06P	£5	18__	FACE PROOF	650.

180-12. MIRAMICHI BRANCH ISSUE POUNDS, SHILLINGS & PENCE

Branch name engraved at lower left. Engraved CHECK at right.

DESIGNS AND COLOURS

180-12-02P
5s Face Design: Allegorical female/Crest/-
Colour: Black with no tint

Back Design: Lathework with ships at ends
Colour: Green

180-12-04P
7s6d Face Design: Allegorical woman with lyre and cornucopia/Crest/-
Colour: Black with no tint

Back Design: Lathework with ships at ends
Colour: Green

IMPRINT
New England Bank Note Co. Boston

SIGNATURES

left	right
none	mss. Thomas C. Allan

ISSUE DATING

Partially Engraved __18__:

1837: 4 December

CIRCULATING NOTES

Cat.No.	Denom.	Date	G	VG	F	VF	EF	AU
12-02	5s	1837	600.	1,200.	1,800.	2,500.	—	—
12-04	7s6d	1837	750.	1,500.	—	—	—	—

PROOF NOTES

Cat. No.	Denom.	Date		Unc
12-02P	5s	1837	FACE PROOF	600.
12-04P	7s6d	1837	FACE PROOF	600.

180-14. ST. JOHN ISSUE POUNDS & SHILLINGS

Branch name enraved at bottom centre.

DESIGNS AND COLOURS

180-14-02P

5s Face Design: Ships, lighthouse/Crest; lion on crown below/ two men harvesting grain
Colour: Black with no tint

Back Design: Lathework with ships at ends
Colour: Green

180-14-04

£1 Face Design: Ship, cargo, fasces and scroll/Crest; lion on crown below/
Colour: Black with no tint

Back Design: Lathework and Commercial Bank
Colour: Green

180-14-10P

£2 Face Design: Ships/Crest; lion on crown below/
Colour: Black with no tint

Back Design: Unknown
Colour: Green

180-14-12

£5 Face Design: Seated Britannia/Crest; lion on crown below/
Colour: Black with no tint
Back Design: Lathework and bank name
Colour: Green

180-14-14P

£10 Face Design: Ship in oval/Crest; lion on crown below/
Colour: Black with no tint

Back Design: Unknown
Colour: Green

180-14-16P

£25 Face Design: Two ships in oval/Crest; lion on crown below/
Colour: Black with no tint

Back Design: Unknown
Colour: Green

IMPRINT

New England Bank Note Co. Boston

SIGNATURES

left	right
Mss. G.P. Sancton	mss. C. W. Ward
mss. G.P. Sancton	mss. D.J. McLaughlin
mss. G.P. Sancton	mss. Gilbert

ISSUE DATING

Partially Engraved __18__:

£1 **1847:** 30 June
1850: 1 June
1852: 1 July
1853: 1 June, 1 Novr
1857: 1 May

£5 **1853:** June 1
1857: 29 April

$10 **1838:** 10 June

CIRCULATING NOTES

Cat.No.	Denom.	Date	G	VG	F	VF	EF	Unc
14-02	5s	18__	No known issued notes					
14-04	£1	1847-1857	600.	1,200.	1,800.	—	—	—
14-10	£2	18__	No known issued notes					
14-12	£5	1853-1857	800.	1,600.	2,400.	—	—	—
14-14	£10	1838	3,000.	—	—	—	—	—
14-16	£25	18__	No known issued notes					

PROOF NOTES

Cat. No.	Denom.	Date		Unc
14-02P	5s	18__	FACE PROOF	600.
14-04P	£1	18__	FACE PROOF	600.
14-10P	$2	18__	FACE PROOF	600.
14-12P	$5	18__	FACE PROOF	600.
14-14P	$10	18__	FACE PROOF	750.
14-16P	$25	18__	FACE PROOF	1,000.

180-16. DOLLAR/POUNDS & SHILLINGS ISSUE 1860

DESIGNS AND COLOURS

180-16-02

$1 (5s) Face Design: Ships/Crest; lion on crown below/
Colour: Black with green tint

Back Design: Lathework, bank name with ships vertically at ends
Colour: Green

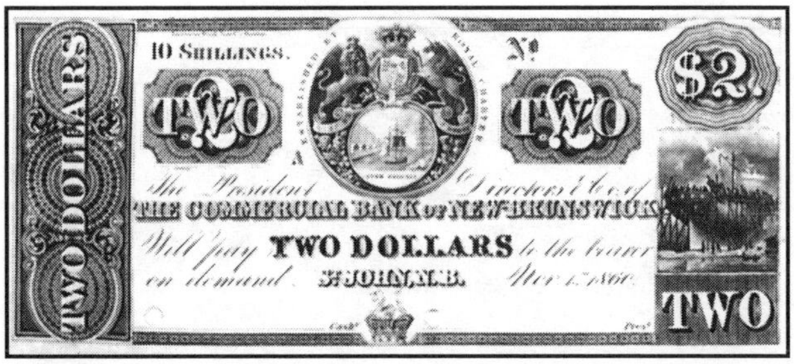

180-16-04P

$2 (10s) Face Design /Crest; lion on crown below/ shipbuilding scene
Colour: Black with green tint

Back Design: Lathework, bank name with ships vertically at ends
Colour: Green

180-16-06

$4 (£1) Face Design: Ship, cargo, fasces, and scroll/ Crest; lion on crown below/

Colour: Black with green tint

Back Design: Lathework, bank name with ships vertically at ends

Colour: Green

180-16-08P

$8 (£2) Face Design: /Crest; lion on crown below/ young girl with flower basket

Colour: Black with green tint

Back Design: Lathework, counters and bank name

Colour: Green

180-16-10P

$20 (£5) Face Design: Ship/Crest; lion on crown below/ sailor at ships wheel

Colour: Black with green tint

Back Design: Lathework, counters and bank name

Colour: Green

180-16-12P

$50 (£12.10) Face Design: /Crest; lion on crown below/ seated allegorical woman

Colour: Black with green tint

Back Design: Lathework, counters and bank name

Colour: Green

180-16-14P

$100 (£25) Face Design: /Crest; lion on crown below/ fishermen on schooner in rough sea

Colour: Black with green tint

Back Design: Lathework, counters and bank name

Colour: Green

IMPRINT

American Bank Note Co. Boston

SIGNATURES

left	right
mss. G.P. Sancton	mss. D.J. McLaughlin
mss. G.P. Sancton	mss. W.M. Parks
mss. G.P. Sancton	mss. A.M.L. Seely

ISSUE DATING

Engraved

Nov. 1st 1860

CIRCULATING NOTES

Cat.No.	Denom.	Date	G	VG	F	VF	EF	Unc
16-02	$1(5s)	1860	350.	700.	1,000.	1,500.	—	—
16-04	$2(10s)	1860	600.	1,200.	1,700.	2,500.	—	—
16-06	$4(£1)	1860	450.	900.	1,250.	1,800.	—	—
16-08	$8(£2)	1860	No known issued notes					
16-10	$20(£5)	1860	No known issued notes					
16-12	$50(£12.10)	1860	No known issued notes					
16-14	$100(£25)	1860	No known issued notes					

PROOF NOTES

Cat. No.	Denom.	Date		Unc
16-02P	$1 (5s)	1860	FACE PROOF	600.
16-04P	$2 (10s)	1860	FACE PROOF	600.
16-06P	$4 (£1)	1860	FACE PROOF	600.
16-08P	$8 (£2)	1860	FACE PROOF	2,000.
16-10P	$20 (£5)	1860	FACE PROOF	600.
16-12P	$50 (£12.10)	1860	FACE PROOF	700.
16-14P	$100 (£25)	1860	FACE PROOF	1,000.

COMMERCIAL BANK OF NEWFOUNDLAND

1857 - 1894

SAINT JOHNS, (NEWFOUNDLAND)

BANK NUMBER 185 ***REDEEMABLE***

Established in 1857, this bank, and the Union Bank of Newfoundland, failed in December of 1894 due to mismanagement and poor economic conditions. Almost the entire currency then in use in Newfoundland consisted of notes issued by these two banks. Upon their failure, business was at a stand-still and the people in a state of panic until the Canadian banks opened their first branches in Newfoundland. The Newfoundland government assumed the responsibility for the redemption of the failed banks notes, and the notes of the Commercial Bank continued to be redeemable for 20 cents on the dollar.

185-10. **ISSUE OF 1857 - 1858**
POUND ISSUE LARGE SIZE NOTES
(19.5 x 10.5 cm.)

DESIGNS AND COLOURS

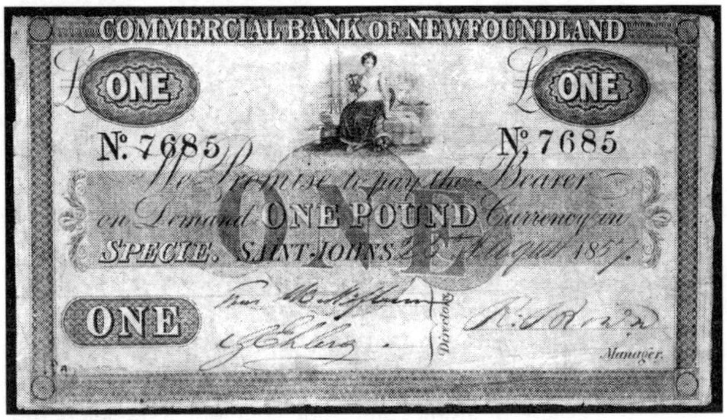

185-10-02
£1 Face Design: /seated Commerce figure with cask, bales, cornucopia and ships/
Colour: Black with no tint

Back Design: Plain

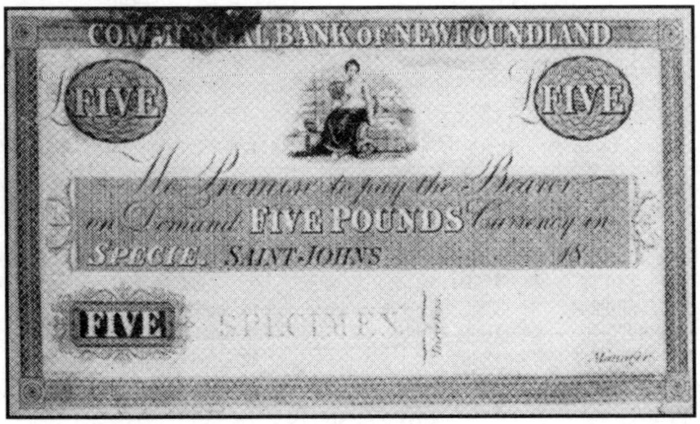

185-10-12P
£5 Face Design: /seated Commerce figure with cask, bales, cornucopia and ships/
Colour: Black with no tint

Back Design: Plain

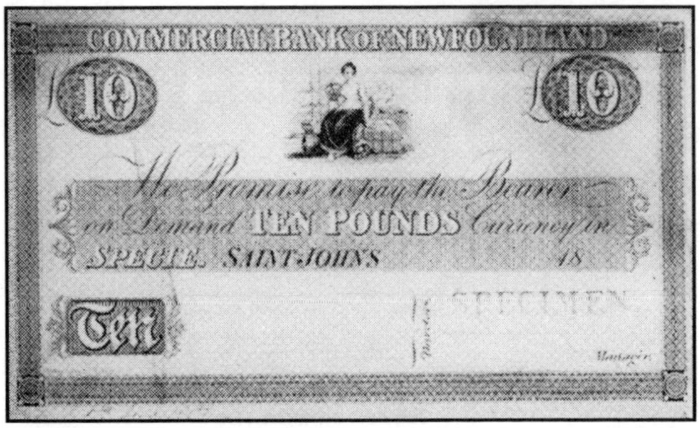

185-10-18P
£10 Face Design: /seated Commerce figure with cask, bales, cornucopia and ships/
Colour: Black with no tint

Back Design: Plain

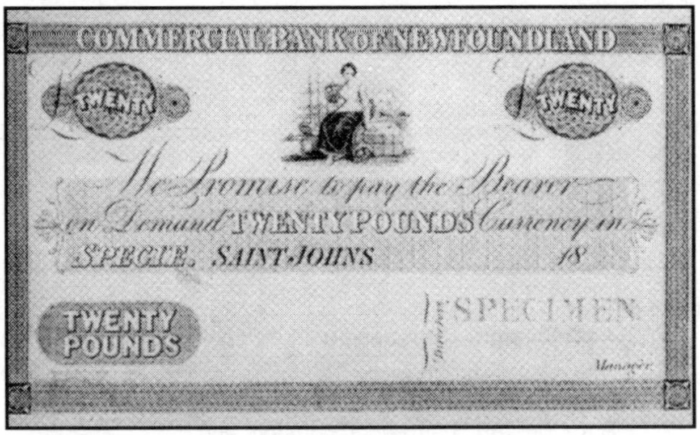

185-10-24P
£20 Face Design: /seated Commerce figure with cask, bales, cornucopia and ships/
Colour: Black with no tint

Back Design: Plain

IMPRINT
Perkins, Bacon & Co. London

SIGNATURES

left	right
mss. Francis Hepburn	mss. R. Brown
mss. G. Ehlers	

ISSUE DATING
Partially Engraved __18__:
1857: 25 August
1858: 20 Oct
1859: 5th Oct.

PROTECTOR
Red mock coins on face only

CIRCULATING NOTES

Cat.No.	Denom.	Date	G	VG	F	VF	EF	AU
10-02	£1	1857 - 1859	2,500.	4,000.	6,000.	—	—	—
10-12	£5	18__	No known issued notes					
10-18	£10	18__	No known issued notes					
10-24	£20	18__	No known issued notes					

PROOF NOTES

Cat. No.	Denom.	Date		Unc
10-02P	£1	18__	PROOF	750.
10-12P	£5	18__	PROOF	800.
10-18P	£10	18__	PROOF	800.
10-24P	£20	18__	PROOF	800.

185-12. ISSUE OF 1865 - 1867
TWO SIGNATURE SPACES AT LEFT
POUNDS DOLLAR ISSUE
SMALL SIZE NOTES
(17.5 x 8.5 cm.)

DESIGNS AND COLOURS

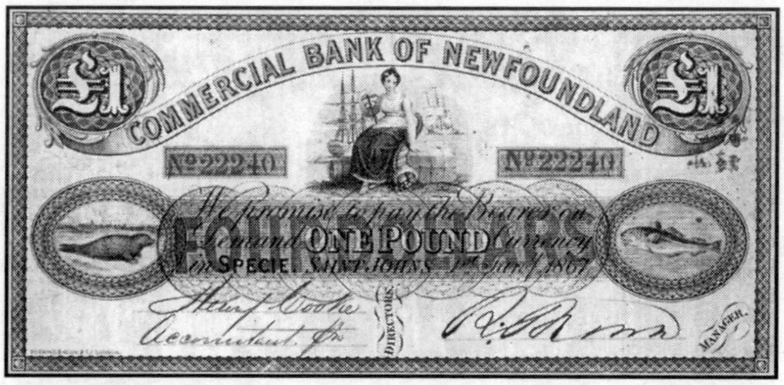

185-12-02

£1 ($4) Face Design: Seal in oval/seated Commerce figure/ codfish in oval
Colour: Black with no tint

Back Design: Plain

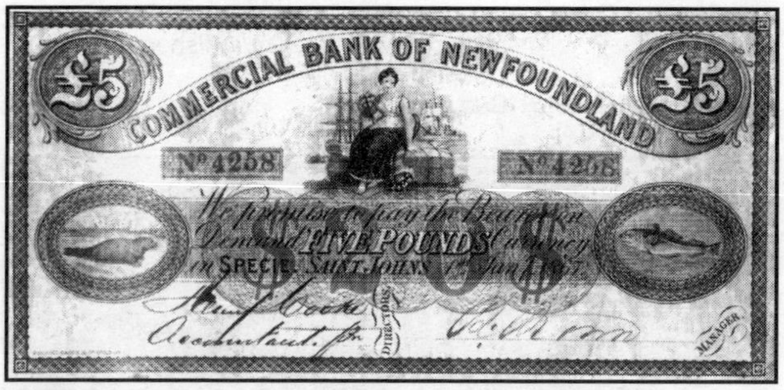

185-12-04

£5 ($20) Face Design: Seal in oval/seated Commerce figure codfish in oval
Colour: Black with no tint

Back Design: Plain

185-12-08

£10 ($40) Face Design: Seal in oval/seated Commerce figure codfish in oval
Colour: Black with no tint

Back Design: Plain

IMPRINT

Perkins, Bacon & Co. London

SIGNATURES

left	right
mss. Henry Cooke	mss. R. Brown
mss. various	

ISSUE DATING

Engraved

Unknown, 1865
1st Jany, 1867

PROTECTOR

£1: Blue FOUR DOLLARS on mock coins on face only
£5: Red-brown 20 on mock coins on face only
£10: Green 40 on mock coins on face only

Cat.No.	Denom.	Date	G	VG	F	VF	EF	AU
12-02	£1 ($4)	1867	1,000.	1,800.	2,500.	—	—	—
12-04	£5 ($20)	1867	1,000.	1,800.	2,500.	—	—	—
12-06	£10 ($40)	1865	Institutional collection only					
12-08	£10 ($40)	1867	Institutional collection only					

185-14. ISSUE OF 1874-1885
ONE SIGNATURE SPACE AT LEFT

DESIGNS AND COLOURS

See previous issue.

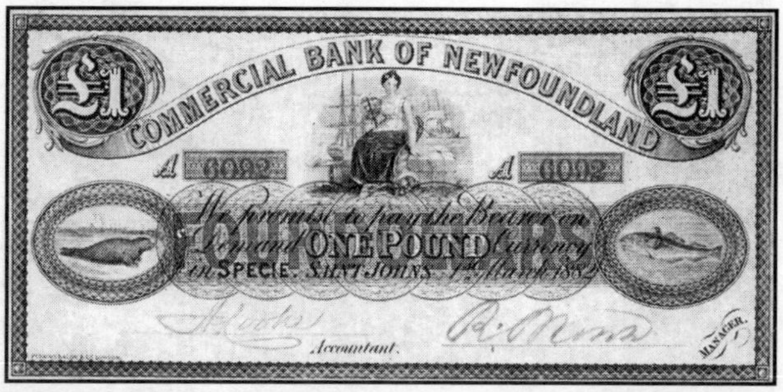

185-14-04

185-14-08

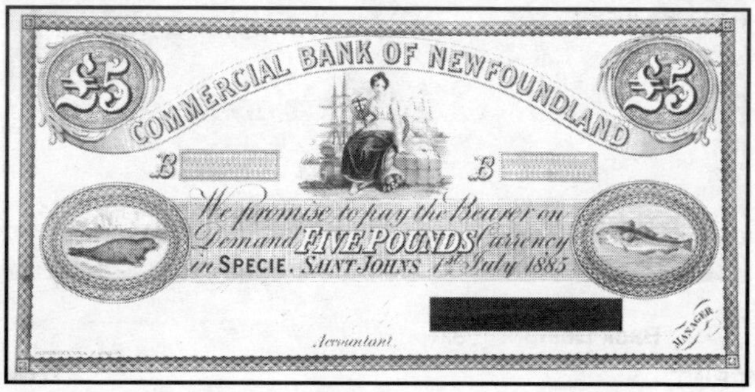

185-14-10P

SIGNATURES

left	right
mss. Henry Cooke or H Cooke	mss. R. Brown
mss. H.D. Carter	mss. Henry Cooke

ISSUE DATING

Engraved

1st Jany 1874
1st March 1882
1st July 1884
1st July 1885

PROTECTOR

£1: Blue FOUR DOLLARS on mock coins on face only
£5: Red-brown TWENTY DOLLARS on mock coins on face only

CIRCULATING NOTES

Cat.No.	Denom.	Date	G	VG	F	VF	EF	AU
14-02	£1 ($4)	1874	1,000.	1,800.	2,500.	—	—	—
14-04	£1 ($4)	1882	900.	1,600.	2,250.	—	—	—
14-06	£1 ($4)	1884	1,200.	2,100.	—	—	—	—
14-08	£5 ($20)	1874	900.	1,600.	2,250.	—	—	—
14-10	£5 ($20)	1885	No known issued notes					

PROOF NOTES

Cat. No.	Denom.	Date		Unc
14-10P	£5 ($20)	1885	PROOF	600.

185-16. $2 ISSUE OF 1881 - 1884 SMALL SIZE NOTES

DESIGNS AND COLOURS

185-16-06

$2 Face Design: Seal in oval//codfish in oval
Colour: Black with no tint

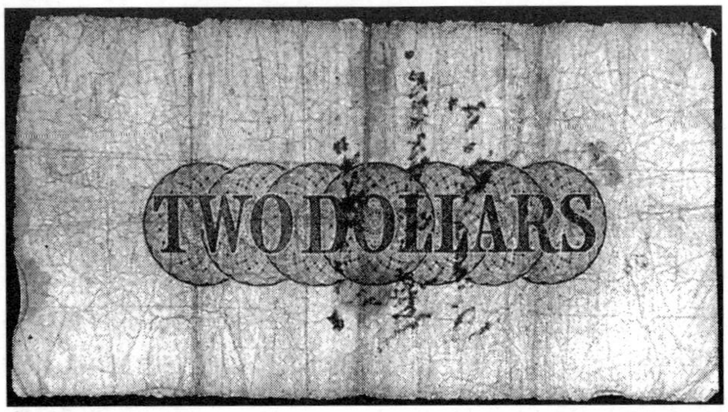

Back Design: Plain

IMPRINT

Perkins, Bacon & Co. London

SIGNATURES

	left	right
1881-1882:	mss. Henry Cooke	mss. R. Brown
1884:	mss. H.D. Carter	mss. Henry Cooke

ISSUE DATING

Engraved

1st Jan., 1881
Unknown, 1882
1st July 1884

PROTECTOR

Blue mock coins and TWO DOLLARS on back only

Cat.No.	Denom.	Date	G	VG	F	VF	EF	AU
16-02	$2	1881	600.	1,200.	—	—	—	—
16-04	$2	1882	750.	1,500.	2,000.	—	—	—
16-06	$2	1884	500.	1,000.	1,400.	2,000.	—	—

185-18. ISSUE OF 1888 DOLLAR ISSUE LARGE SIZE NOTES

DESIGNS AND COLOURS

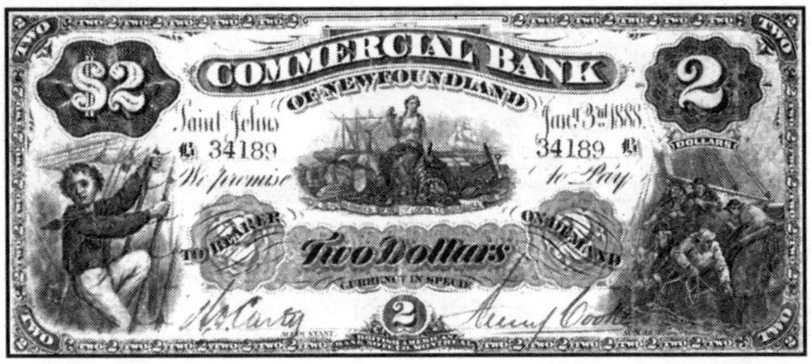

185-18-04

$2 Face Design: Young sailor climbing rigging Going aloft/ seated Commerce figure/fishermen Cod fishing
Colour: See varieties

Back Design: Lathework, counters, bank name and classical motif
Colour: Green

185-18-06

$5 Face Design: Portrait of sailor young Tar/seated Commerce figure/seals in oval
Colour: Black with green tint

Back Design: Lathework, counters and bank name
Colour: Green

185-18-08
$10 Face Design: Portrait of Queen Victoria HBM/ seated Commerce figure/ sailor standing by capstan Charlies Sailor
Colour: Black with green tint

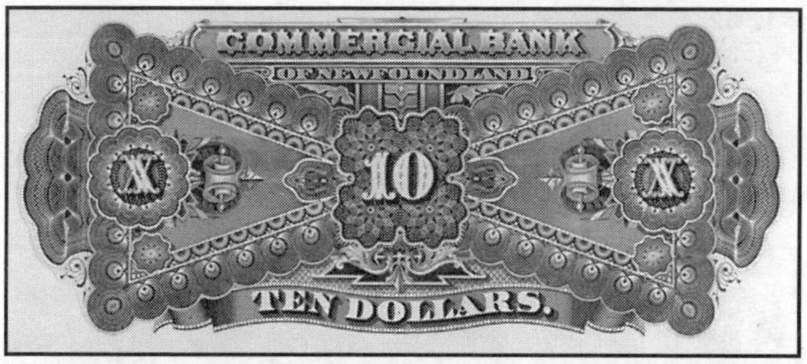

Back Design: Lathework, counters and bank name
Colour: Green

185-18-10
$20 Face Design: Fisherman with wife, baby and telescope Old Salt/seated Commerce figure/ Newfoundland dogs head My dog (Landseer)
Colour: Black with green tint

Back Design: Lathework, counters and bank name
Colour: Green

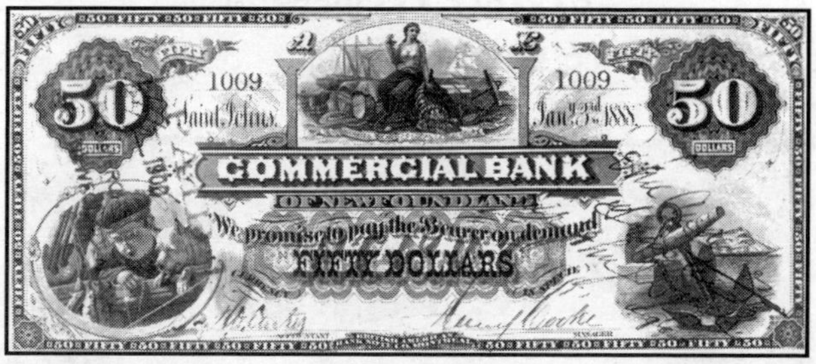

185-18-12
$50 Face Design: Boy and dog on ship Young Fisher/ seated Commerce figure/anchor, box, barrels and ship Anchor
Colour: Black with green tint

Back Design: Lathework, counters and bank name
Colour: Green

IMPRINT
British American Bank Note Co. Montreal

SIGNATURES

left	right
mss. H.D. Carter	mss. Henry Cooke

ISSUE DATING
Engraved
Jany 3rd 1888

VARIETIES
$2 Face Colour: Black with green tint
$2 Face Colour: Black with orange tint

Cat.No.	Denom.	Date		G	VG	F	VF	EF	Unc
18-02	$2	1888	Green tint	250.	500.	800.	—	—	—
18-04	$2	1888	Orange tint	100.	200.	300.	600.	—	—
18-06	$5	1888		100.	200.	300.	600.	1,000.	—
18-08	$10	1888		250.	500.	750.	1,400.	—	—
18-10	$20	1888		1,750.	3,500.	4,800.	—	—	—
18-12	$50	1888		2,000.	4,000.	5,500.	7,000.	—	—

Note: Notes which have been stamped with the guarantee of the Newfoundland Government, revaluing them at 20% of their former face values, should be considered desirable and unimpaired. Although all known examples have additional cancellation markings, they may command a premium of about 10% above the listed prices. However, notes which have been marked "Paid" or otherwise cancelled and lack the guarantee stamp will trade at a reduction of about 10% below listed prices.

THE COMMERCIAL BANK OF THE MIDLAND DISTRICT

1831 - 1856

KINGSTON, UPPER CANADA

BANK NUMBER 190 ***REDEEMABLE***

After repeated attempts, this bank finally obtained its charter in 1831 with an authorized capital of £100,000. It opened for business in the summer of 1832. In 1856, the bank changed its name to The Commercial Bank of Canada.

190-10. ISSUE OF 1832 - 1835 PAYABLE AT KINGSTON

DESIGNS AND COLOURS

190-10-04
$1 (5s) Face Design: /paddlewheel steam-boat, coin below/ two smiling cherubs faces
Colour: Black with no tint

Back Design: Plain

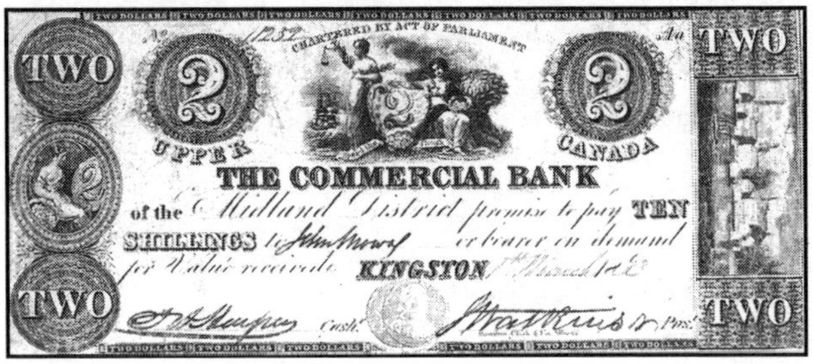

190-10-06
$2 (10s) Face Design: Seated woman in oval, figure 2/two women and shield with figure 2: Speed the Plough under shield; two coins below/view of town from harbour (sideways)
Colour: Black with no tint

Back Design: Plain

IMPRINT
Rawdon, Clark & Co. Albany

SIGNATURES

left	right
mss. F.A. Harper	mss. John S. Cartwright
mss. F.A. Harper	mss. J. Watkins (v.)
mss. F.A. Harper	mss. illegible

ISSUE DATING
Partially Engraved __18__:
$1 1832: Aug. 2
1833: 1 Novr.
$2 1833: 1st March
1835: 1 Jany.

CIRCULATING NOTES

Cat.No.	Denom.	Date	G	VG	F	VF	EF	AU
10-02	$1 (5s)	1832 - 1833	500.	1,000.	1,500.	—	—	—
10-06	$2 (10s)	1833 - 1835	600.	1,200.	1,800.	—	—	—

PROOF NOTES

Cat. No.	Denom.	Date		Unc
10-02P	$1 (5s)	18__	PROOF	500.
10-06P	$2 (10s)	18__	PROOF	500.

190.12. ISSUE OF 1836 PAYABLE AT KINGSTON

DESIGNS AND COLOURS

190-12-02
$1 (5s) Face Design: Seated Indian/maid churning butter/ woman with grain
Engraved payee: Alex McNabb
Colour: Black with no tint

Back Design: Plain

190-12-04
$2 (10s) Face Design: Harbour scene/allegorical man, urn/ allegorical man and woman
Engraved payee: Alex McNabb
Colour: Black with no tint

Back Design: Plain

190-12-06

$5 (25s) Face Design: —/bank building; leaping deer below/Mercury in clouds with cornucopia filled with coins, seated woman with caduceus below

Colour: Black with no tint

Back Design: Plain

IMPRINT

Rawdon, Wright, Hatch & Edson, New-York.

SIGNATURES

left	right
mss. F.A. Harper	mss. W. Logie (v.)
mss. F.A. Harper	mss. M. McCauley (v.)
mss. F.A. Harper	mss. J. Hamilton
mss. F.A. Harper	mss. J.S. Cartwright

ISSUE DATING

Engraved

March 1st 1836

Cat.No.	Denom.	Date	G	VG	F	VF	EF	AU
12-02	$1 (5s)	1836	500.	1,000.	1,500.	—	—	—
12-04	$2 (10s)	1836	600.	1,200.	1,800.	—	—	—
12-06	$5 (25s)	1836	Institutional collection only					

190-14. ISSUE OF 1843 PAYABLE AT MONTREAL

DESIGNS AND COLOURS

All notes have a miniature Royal Crest with the lion and unicorn on all fours at the bottom centre.

190-14-02

$1 (5s) Face Design: Prince Consort in oval, cherub in ornate I/ semi-nude Indian woman stepping out of canoe/cherub in ornate I; Queen Victoria (Chalon portrait) in oval

Colour: Black with no tint

Back Design: Plain

190-14-04

$2 (10s) Face Design: Prince Consort/allegorical women, Commerce and Agriculture/Queen Victoria (Chalon portrait)

Colour: Black with no tint

Back Design: Plain

190-14-06

$5 (25s) Face Design: Prince Consort/cherubs in ornate 5/woman and cherubs with ornate 5/cherubs in ornate 5/Queen Victoria (Chalon Portrait)

Colour: Black with no tint

Back Design: Plain

Photo Not Available

190-14-08P

$10 (50s) Face Design: Queen Victoria (Chalon Portrait//

Colour: Black with no tint

Back Design: Plain

IMPRINT

Rawdon, Wright & Hatch, New-York

Rawdon, Wright, Hatch and Edson, New-York

SIGNATURES

left	right
mss. Jno. V. Noel	mss. A.H. Campbell

ISSUE DATING

Engraved

1st July 1843

CIRCULATING NOTES

Cat.No.	Denom.	Date	G	VG	F	VF	EF	AU
14-02	$1 (5s)	1843	500.	1,000.	1,500.	—	—	—
14-04	$2 (10s)	1843	600.	1,200.	1,800.	—	—	—
14-06	$5 (25s)	1843	600.	1,200.	1,800.	—	—	—
14-08	$10 (50s)	1843	No known issued notes					

PROOF NOTES

Cat. No.	Denom.	Date		Unc
14-02P	$1 (5s)	1843	PROOF	500.
14-04P	$2 (10s)	1843	PROOF	500.
14-06P	$5 (25s)	1843	PROOF	500.
14-08P	$10 (50s)	1843	PROOF	500.

190-15 ISSUE OF 1843 PAYABLE AT KINGSTON RED PROTECTOR, BLUE BACK

190-15-06
$5 (25s) Face Design: Similar to 190-14-06 but red protector
Colour: Black with no tint

Back Design: Lathework and denomination spelled out
Colour: Blue

IMPRINT
Rawdon, Wright & Hatch, New-York

SIGNATURES

Left	**right**
mss. C.S. Campbell	mss. C.A. Ross

ISSUE DATING
Engraved
1st July 1843

PROTECTOR
Red "word" on face

Cat. No.	Denom.	Date	G	VG	F	VF	EF	AU
15-06	$5 (25s)	1843	Institutional collection only					

190-16. ISSUE OF 1846 - 1854 PAYABLE AT KINGSTON

DESIGNS AND COLOURS

190-16-02
$1 (5s) Face Design: Man with sickle and sheaves/ reclining woman and ornate 1/ sailor with telescope
Colour: Black with no tint

Back Design: Plain

Photo Not Available

190-16-12
$2 (10s) Face Design: Justice and Liberty figures/ two seated allegorical women with cornucopia/"Agricultural" and Commerce figures
Colour: Black with no tint

Back Design: Plain

190-16-14P
$5 (£1.5) Face Design: Queen Victoria (Chalon portrait)/ woman on large 5 supported by four cherubs/Prince Consort
Colour: Black with no tint

Back Design: Plain

190-16-16P
$10 (£2.10) Face Design: Queen Victoria (Chalon portrait)/ seated woman with ornate 10/ Prince consort
Colour: Black with no tint

Back Design: Plain

Photo Not Available

190-16-18P
$20 (£5) Face Design: Queen Victoria (Chalon portrait)/ seated woman with ornate 20/ Prince Consort
Colour: Black with no tint

Back Design: Plain

Photo Not Available

190-16-20P
$50 (£12.10) Face Design: Queen Victoria (Chalon portrait) on Royal Crest//
Colour: Black with no tint

Back Design: Plain

Photo Not Available

190-16-22P
$100 (£25) Face Design: /allegorical woman/Royal Crest
Colour: Black with no tint

Back Design: Plain

IMPRINT

Rawdon, Wright & Hatch, New York
Rawdon, Wright, Hatch & Edson, New York

SIGNATURES

left	right
mss. J. Rourke	mss. J.E. Pearce
mss. J. Rourke	mss. Jno. V. Noel
mss. Wm. J. Yarker	mss. C.W. Hamilton

ISSUE DATING

Partially Engraved July 18__:

1846: 1 July
1847: 1 July
1848: 1 July
1853: 1 July
1854: 1 July

OVERPRINTS

TORONTO in red
BELLEVILLE in red
BROCKVILLE in red

CIRCULATING NOTES

Cat.No.	Denom.	Date	Variety	G	VG	F	VF	EF	AU
16-02	$1(5s)	1846-1854	no o/p	500.	1,000.	1,500.	—	—	—
16-02a	$1(5s)	1846-1854	Red town o/p	750.	1,500.	2,250.	—	—	—
16-12	$2(10s)	18__			No known issued notes				
16-14	$5(£1.5)	18__			No known issued notes				
16-16	$10 (£2.10)	18__			No known issued notes				
16-18	$20 (£5)	18__			No known issued notes				
16-20	$50 (£12.10)	18__			No known issued notes				
16-22	$100 (£25)	18__			No known issued notes				

PROOF NOTES

Cat.No.	Denom.	Date		Unc
16-02P	$1 (5s)	18__	PROOF	400.
16-12P	$2 (10s)	18__	PROOF	500.
16-14P	$5 (£1.5)	18__	PROOF	500.
16-16P	$10 (£2.10)	18__	PROOF	500.
16-18P	$20 (£5)	18__	PROOF	600.
16-20P	$50 (£12.10)	18__	PROOF	600.
16-22P	$100 (£25)	18__	PROOF	700.

190.-18. ISSUE OF 185? - 1854 PAYABLE AT KINGSTON

DESIGN AND COLOURS

Photo Not Available

190-18-02P

$5 Face Design: /seated Mercury with lion/ portrait of woman
Colour: Black with no tint

Back Design: Plain

190-18-04C

$10 Face Design: Floral panel/flying allegorical male dropping coins from cornucopia/ships
Colour: Black with no tint

Back Design: Plain

IMPRINT

Rawdon, Wright & Hatch, New York

SIGNATURES

left	right
mss. J.G. Harper	mss. Jno. Hamilton

ISSUE DATING

Partially Engraved __18__:

1854: 2 Jany.

CIRCULATING NOTES

Cat.No.	Denom.	Date	Variety	G	VG	F	VF	EF	AU
18-02	$5	18__			No known issued notes				
18-04C	$10*	1854	Counterfeit	50.	100.	150.	—	—	—

*all known surviving notes are counterfeit.

PROOF NOTES

Cat. No.	Denom.	Date	Unc
18-02P	$5	18__	600.

190-20. TOPPAN CARPENTER CASILEAR $4 ISSUES OF 1854 PAYABLE AT VARIOUS BRANCHES

The branch names are engraved in vertical panels flanking the central vignette.

DESIGNS AND COLOURS

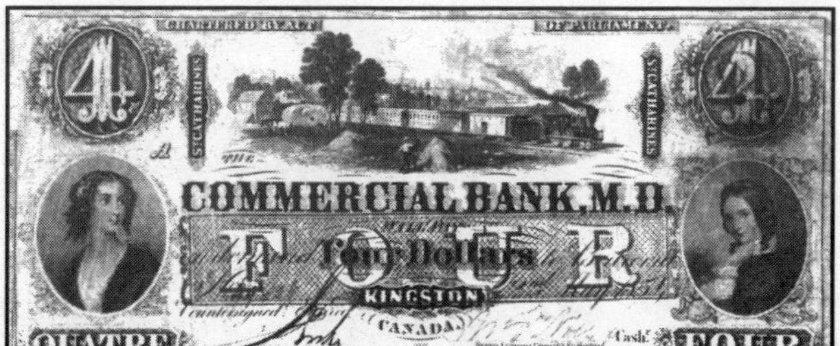

190-20-10-02

$4 Face Design: Portrait of young woman/train and farming scene/portrait of young woman
Colour: Black with no tint

Back Design: Plain

IMPRINT

Toppan, Carpenter, Casilear & Co. Montreal

SIGNATURES

left	right
mss. J. Rourke	mss. Jno. V. Noel

ISSUE DATING
Partially Engraved __185_:
Engraved
2nd May, 185_

PROTECTOR
Green panel with outlined word on the face and back

2. BROCKVILLE ISSUE

Cat.No.	Denom.	Date	G	VG	F	VF	EF	AU
20-02-02	$4	1854	400.	800.	1,100.	1,700.	—	—

4. HAMILTON ISSUE

Cat.No.	Denom.	Date	G	VG	F	VF	EF	AU
20-04-02	$4	1854	400.	800.	1,100.	1,700.	—	—

6. LONDON ISSUE

Cat.No.	Denom.	Date	G	VG	F	VF	EF	AU
20-06-02	$4	1854	Institutional collection only					

10. ST. CATHARINES ISSUE

Cat.No.	Denom.	Date	G	VG	F	VF	EF	AU
20-10-02	$4	1854	400.	800.	1,100.	1,700.	—	—

12. TORONTO ISSUE

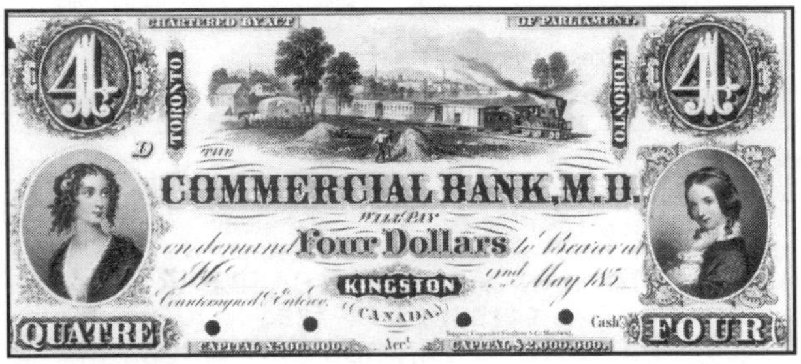

190-20-12-02P

PROOF NOTES

Cat.No.	Denom.	Date	Unc
20-12-02P	$4	185_	500.

190-22 TOPPAN, CARPENTER CASILEAR $4 ISSUE OF 185(4) ENGRAVED "MONTREAL" AT LOWER CENTRE

2. BROCKVILLE ISSUE

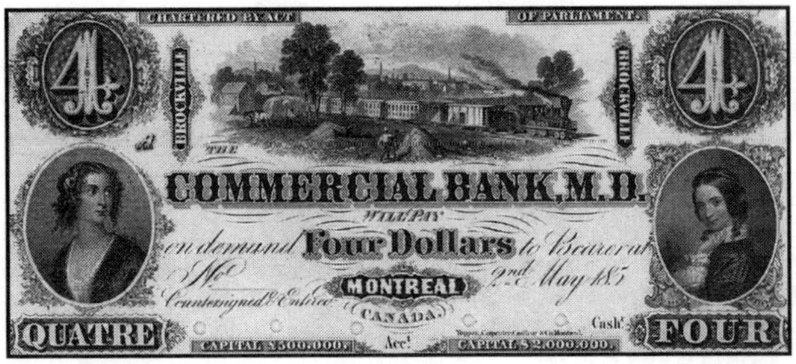

PROOF NOTES

Cat. No.	Denom.	Date	G	VG	F	VF	EF	AU
22-02-02P	$4	185_	Institutional collection only					

190-24 SPURIOUS $5 ISSUE

This fraudulent issue was the subject of frequent entries in counterfeit detectors of the 1850s and 1860s. It is crudely produced, and inferior in every respect.

DESIGNS AND COLOURS

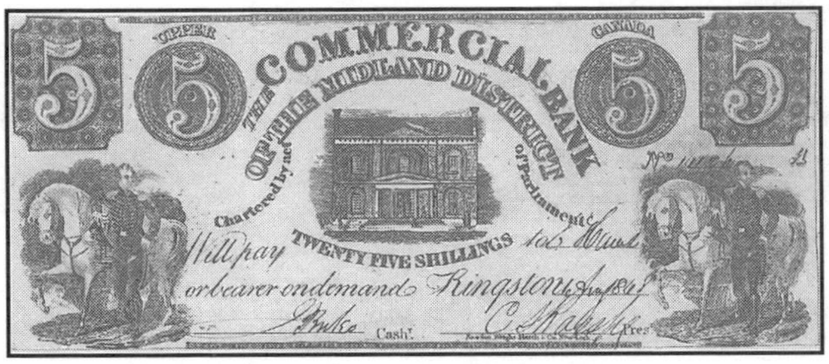

190-24-02

$5 Face Design: Military man standing beside horse/building/ military man standing beside horse
Colour: Black with no tint
Back: Plain

IMPRINT
Rawdon, Wright, Hatch & Co. New-York.

SIGNATURES

Left	**right**
Mss. J. Rules	mss. C. S. Rash

ISSUE DATING
Manuscript
1848: 1 Aug.

Cat. No.	Denom.	Date	G	VG	F	VF	EF	AU
24-02	$5	1848	75.	150.	200.	300.	400.	—

THE COMMERCIAL BANK OF WINDSOR

1864 - 1902

WINDSOR, NOVA SCOTIA

BANK NUMBER 195 ***REDEEMABLE***

Established in 1865 in Windsor, Nova Scotia, this bank was a small institution with assets totalling $1,688,000 and seven branches in operation. It was taken over by The Union Bank of Halifax in 1902 without any loss to creditors.

195-10. **ISSUE OF THE 1860's**

DESIGNS AND COLOURS

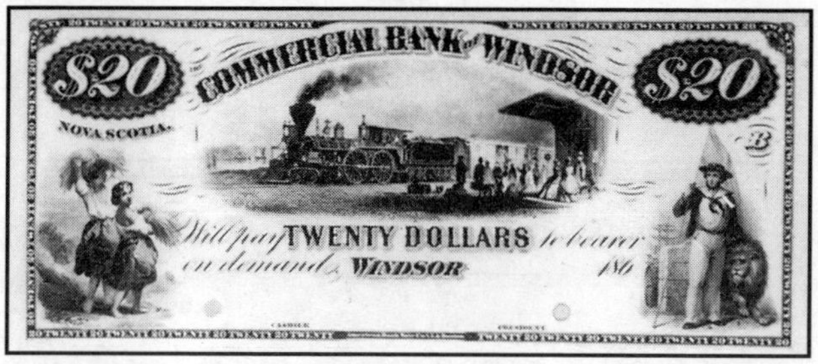

195-10-02P

$20 Face Design: Two children holding sheaves train sitting in station/sailor holding flag, bales and lion
Colour: Black with green tint

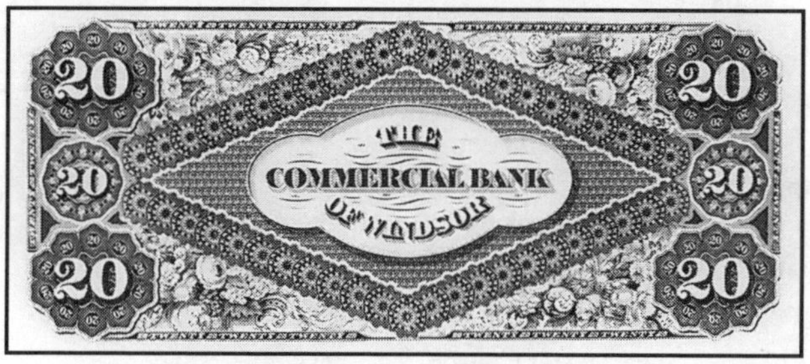

Back Design: Lathework, counters, bank name and floral designs
Colour: Green

IMPRINT

American Bank Note Co. N.Y. and Boston

SIGNATURES

left	**right**
none	none

ISSUE DATING

Partially Engraved __186__:

PROOF NOTES

Cat.No.	Denom.	Date		Unc
10-02P	$20	186_	FACE PROOF	1,500.

SPECIMEN NOTES

Cat. No.	Denom.	Date		Unc
10-02S	$20	186_	SPECIMEN	2,500.

An uncut sheet of four $20 specimens exists.

195-12. **ISSUE OF 1870**

DESIGNS AND COLOURS

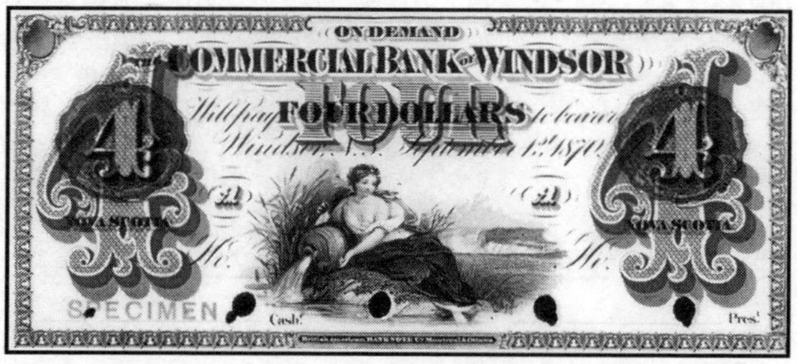

195-12-02P

$4 Face Design: —/reclining woman and water jar, Niagara Falls/—
Colour: Black with green tint

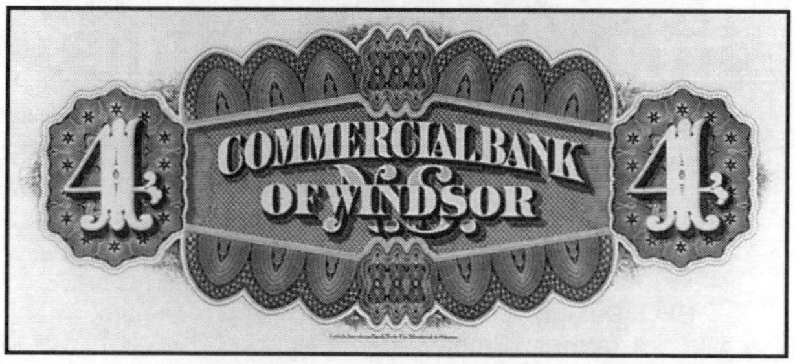

Back Design: Latheworks, counters and bank name
Colour: Green

195-12-04P

$5 Face Design: Seated woman on wharf in oval "EXPORTS"/ Royal Crest/anchor, box, barrel and ships in oval
Colour: Black with green tint

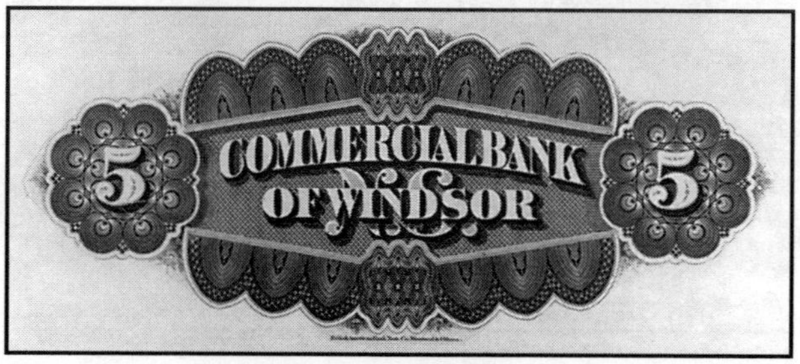

Back Design: Lathework, counters and bank name
Colour: Green

195-12-06P

$10 Face Design: —/train coming out of tunnel/—
Colour: Black with green tint

Back Design: Lathework, counters and bank name
Colour: Green

IMPRINT

British American Bank Note Co. Montreal & Ottawa

SIGNATURES

left	right
none	none

ISSUE DATING

Engraved

September 1st 1870
Sept. 1st 1870

PROOF NOTES

Cat.No.	Denom.	Date		Unc
12-02P	$4	1870	FACE PROOF	1,200.
12-04P	$5	1870	FACE PROOF	1,200.
12-06P	$10	1870	FACE PROOF	1,200.

195-14. ISSUES OF 1871 and 1898

DESIGNS AND COLOURS

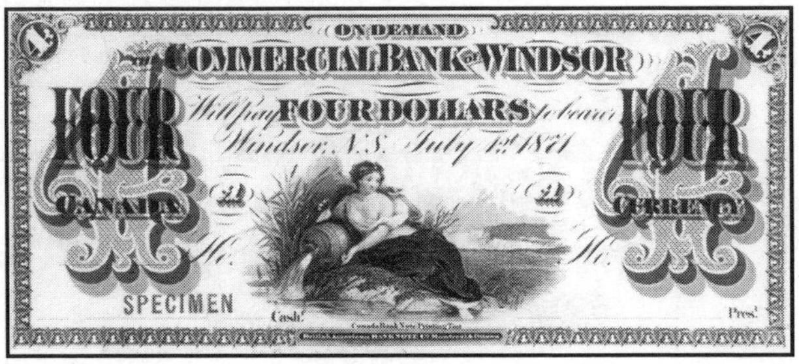

195-14-02P

$4 Face Design: —/reclining woman and water jar, Niagara Falls/—
Colour: Black with green tint

Back Design: Lathework, counters and bank name
Colour: Green

195-14-04P

$5 Face Design: Seated woman on wharf in oval "exports"/ Royal Crest/anchor, box, barrel and ships in oval
Colour: Black with green tint
Back Design: Lathework, counters and bank name
Colour: Green

195-14-08

$10 Face Design: —/train coming out of tunnel/—
Colour: Black with green tint

Back Design: Lathework, counters and bank name
Colour: Green

IMPRINT

British American Bank Note Co. Montreal & Ottawa

SIGNATURES

left	right
mss. Walter Lawson	mss. G.P. Payzant
mss. Walter Lawson	mss. A.P. Shand

ISSUE DATING

Engraved

July 1st 1871
July 1st 1898

CIRCULATING NOTES

Cat.No.	Denom.	Date	G	VG	F	VF	EF	AU
14-02	$4	1871	Institutional collection only					
14-04	$5	1871	No known issued notes					
14-06	$5	1898	No known issued notes					
14-08	$10	1871	Institutional collection only					
14-10	$10	1898	No known issued notes					

PROOF NOTES

Cat.No.	Demon.	Date		Unc
14-02P	$4	1871	FACE PROOF	1,200.
14-04P	$5	1871	FACE PROOF	1,200.
14-06P	$5	1898	FACE PROOF	1,200.
14-08P	$10	1871	FACE PROOF	1,200.
14-10P	$10	1898	FACE PROOF	1,200.

COMMERCIAL BRANCH BANK OF CANADA

1861 - 1862

COLLINGWOOD, PROVINCE OF CANADA

BANK NUMBER 200 ***NONREDEEMABLE***

There is no record of a charter being granted to the Commercial Branch Bank of Canada by the Legislature and the institution is considered a phantom bank. From the design of its "notes" they were meant to trade on the credibility of The Commercial Bank of Canada and the supposed credibility of the Bank of Western Canada.

200-10. ISSUE OF 1861 - 1862

DESIGNS AND COLOURS

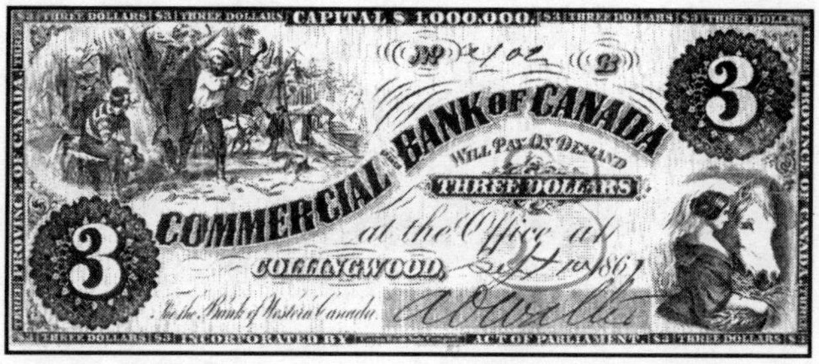

200-10-02

$3 Face Design: Woodsmen clearing forest/-/woman feeding horse. Inscribed "For the Bank of Western Canada"
Colour: Black with overall green tint

Back Design: Plain

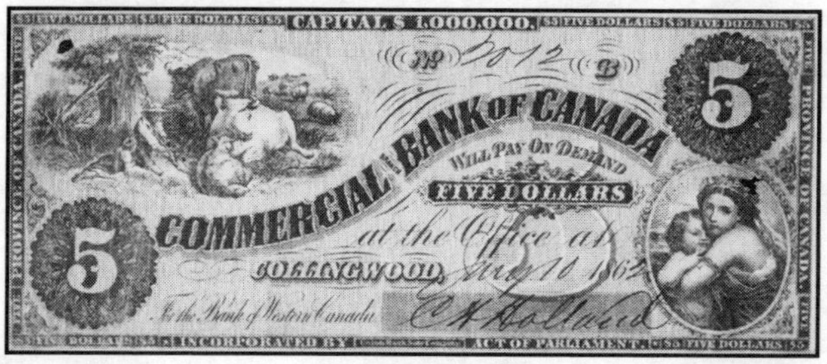

200-10-04

$5 Face Design: Farmer and child resting under tree, cattle/—/ woman holding child. Inscribed "For the Bank of Western Canada"
Colour: Black with overall green tint

Back Design: Plain

IMPRINT

Union Bank Note Company

SIGNATURES

left	right
none	mss. C.H. Holland
none	mss. A.O. Walter

ISSUE DATING

Partially Engraved ____186__:

1861: Sept. 10
1862: July 10

Cat.No.	Denom.	Date	G	VG	F	VF	EF	AU
10-02	$3	1861	300.	600.	800.	1,250.	1,800.	—
10-04	$5	1861-1862	350.	700.	900.	1,400.	—	—

THE CONSOLIDATED BANK OF CANADA

1876 - 1879

MONTREAL, QUEBEC

BANK NUMBER 205 ***NONREDEEMABLE***

The Consolidated Bank of Canada was created out of the merger of the City Bank, Montreal, and The Royal Canadian Bank, Toronto, on April 12, 1876. It was an amalgamation of two very weak institutions, and Sir Francis Hincks had taken on the impossible task of trying to make the new bank work.

Within two years the true state of affairs was beginning to show. The losses reported not only wiped out the profits for the year but reserve and contingent funds as well. There was, in fact, a deficit of approximately $450,000. It was decided to carry on but the bank's credit was so impaired that it had lost all credibility with the public.

On August 1, 1879, the bank suspended and in March, 1880, a bill was introduced in Parliament to provide for the winding up of The Consolidated Bank of Canada. All depositors were paid in full and the shareholders recovered 23 cents on the dollar.

205-10. ISSUE OF 1876

DESIGNS AND COLOURS

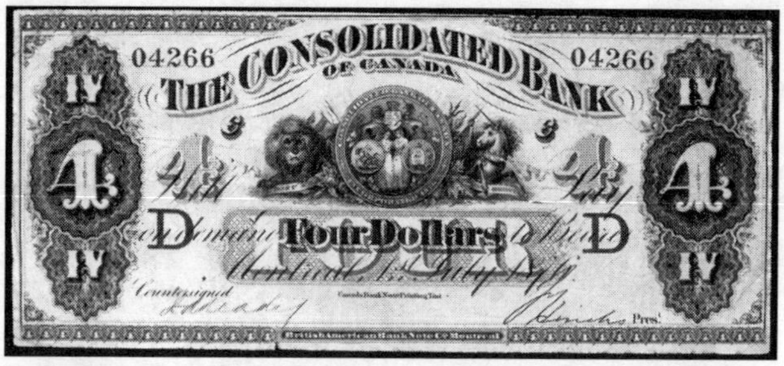

205-10-02a

$4 Face Design: —/Bank Seal in modified Royal Crest/—
Colour: Black with green tint

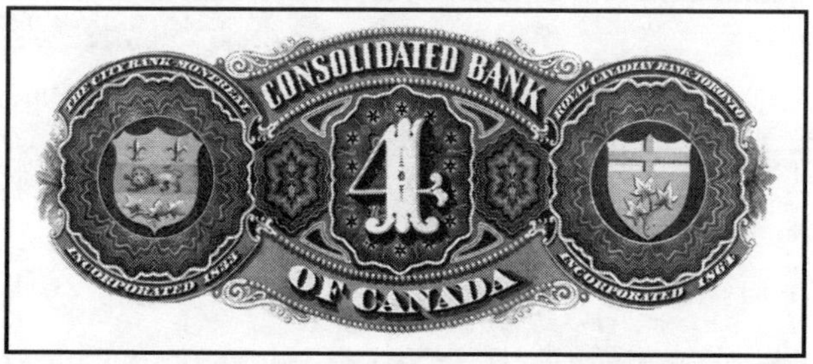

Back Design: Lathework, counters, seals and bank name
Colour: Green

205-10-04a

$5 Face Design: —/Bank Seal in modified Royal Crest/—
Colour: Black with green tint

Back Design: Lathework, counters, seals and bank name
Colour: Green

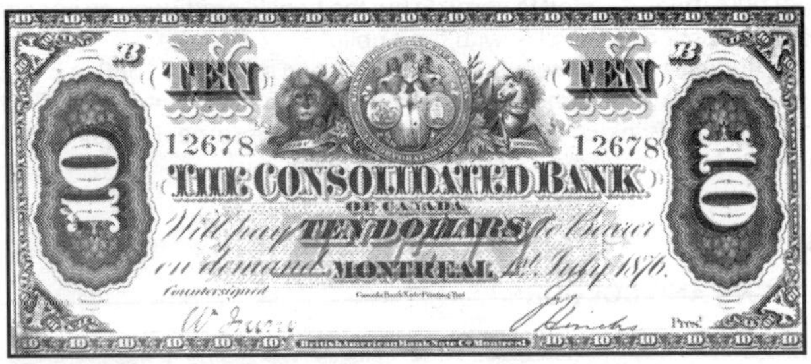

205-10-06
$10 Face Design: —/Bank Seal in modified Royal Crest/—
Colour: Black with green tint

Back Design: Lathework, counters, seals and bank name
Colour: Green

205-10-08P
$20 Face Design: —/Bank Seal in modified Royal Crest/—
Colour: Black with green tint

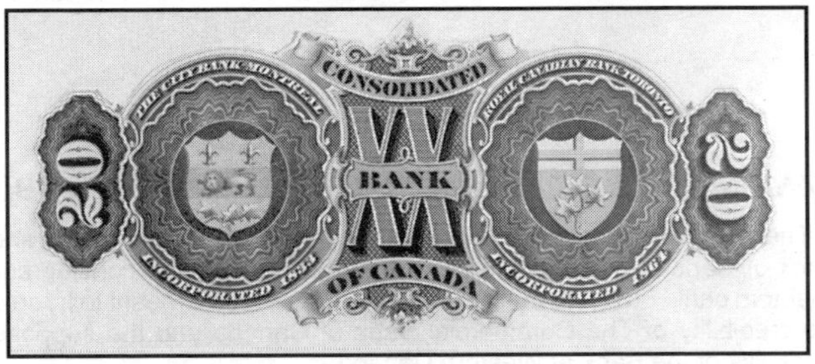

Back Design: Lathework, counters, seals and bank name
Colour: Green

205-10-10P
$50 Face Design: —/Bank Seal in modified Royal Crest/—
Colour: Black with green tint

Back Design: Lathework, counters, seals and bank name
Colour: Green

205-10-12
$100 Face Design: —/Bank Seal in modified Royal Crest/—
Colour: Black with green tint

Back Design: Lathework, counters, seals and bank name
Colour: Green

IMPRINT
British American Bank Note Co. Montreal

SIGNATURES

left	right
mss. various	engr. F. Hincks

ISSUE DATING
Engraved
1s July, 1876

OVERPRINT
"B" in blue
"NH" in blue
"BELLEVILLE" in blue
"ST. CATHARINES" in blue
"C" in blue
"SEAFORTH" in blue
"D" in blue
"SHERBROOKE" in blue
"GALT" in blue
"TORONTO" in blue
"HAMILTON" in blue
"WOODSTOCK" in blue
"N" in blue

CIRCULATING NOTES

Cat.No.	Denom.	Date	Variety	G	VG	F	VF	EF	AU
10-02	$4	1876		200.	400.	700.	1,100.	—	—
10-02a	$4	1876	blue letter o/p	250.	500.	800.	1,200.	—	—
10-02b	$4	1876	blue town o/p	300.	600.	1,000.	1,500.	—	—
10-04	$5	1876		150.	300.	450.	700.	—	—
10-04a	$5	1876	blue letter o/p	175.	350.	500.	800.	—	—
10-04b	$5	1876	blue town o/p	225.	450.	750.	1,150.	—	—
10-06	$10	1876		75.	150.	200.	300.	500.	—
10-08	$20	1876	Institutional collection only						
10-10	$50	1876	No known issued notes						
10-12	$100	1876	Institutional collection only						

PROOF NOTES

Cat. No.	Denom.	Date		Unc
10-02P	$4	1876	FACE PROOF	500.
10-04P	$5	1876	FACE PROOF	500.
10-06P	$10	1876	FACE PROOF	500.
10-08P	$20	1876	FACE PROOF	600.
10-10P	$50	1876	FACE PROOF	600.
10-12P	$100	1876	FACE PROOF	600.

Note I: $10 notes having sheet numbers 12,001 - 13,000, with check letters A, B, C and D, were stolen from the bank before any were issued. To foil thieves, the bank never circulated any of its $10 notes.

Note II: Back design has at left, "THE CITY BANK - MONTREAL, INCORPORATED 1833." around City Bank Seal and at the right "Royal Canadian Bank - Toronto, incorporated 1864" around Royal Canadian Bank Seal.

THE BANK OF THE COUNTY OF ELGIN

1855 - 1862

ST. THOMAS, PROVINCE OF CANADA

BANK NUMBER 210 ***NONREDEEMABLE***

This bank was one of the five banks organized under The Free Banking Act and it operated during the period of 1855-1862 in St. Thomas, Canada West. It started business with $100,000 deposited for Provincial securities, against which it had drew a like amount in registered notes, but never gained any great strength. The bank struggled against the competition and prestige of the chartered banks and then retired its note issue and wound up.

210.10. **ISSUE OF 1856 - 1857**

DESIGNS AND COLOURS

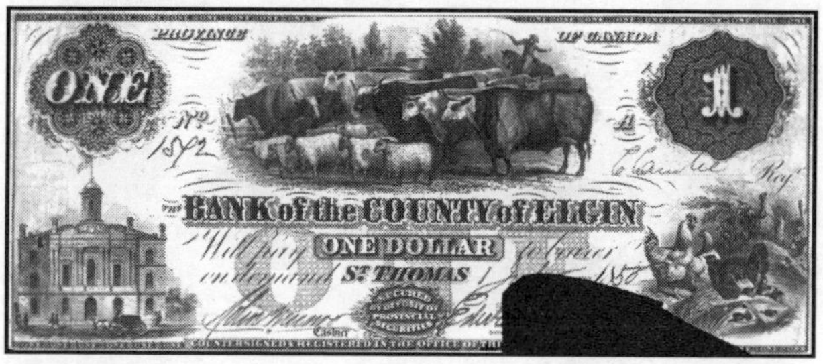

210-10-02a
$1 Face Design: Building/farmer driving livestock hens and chickens
Colour: Black with no tint

Back Design: Plain

210-10-04
$2 Face Design: Edward Ermatinger/town, bridge and train/building
Colour: Black with no tint

Back Design: Plain

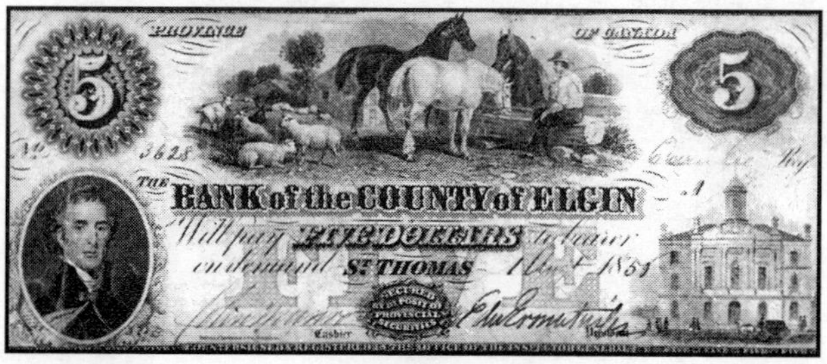

210-10-08
$5 Face Design: Duke of Wellington in oval/farmer with livestock/building
Colour: Black with no tint

Back Design: Plain

210-10-10a

$10 Face Design: Edward Ermatinger/farm family waving to passing train/building

Colour: Black with no tint

Back Design: Plain

IMPRINT

Toppan, Carpenter & Co. Montreal

SIGNATURES

left	right
mss. Colin Munro	mss. Edw. Ermatinger
mss. Colin Munro	mss. Jas. Pollock
mss. Jas. Pollock	mss. Edw. Ermatinger

ISSUE DATING

Partially Engraved __18__:

$1 1856: 25 June, 1 July, 1 Augt, 1 Sept, 1 Decr.
$2 1856: 1 Augt., 1 Dec'r.
1857: 31st Jany
$5 1856: 25 June, 1 Augt.
$10 1856: — Feb, 1 July, 1 Augt.

PROTECTOR

Red "word" on face and in mirror image on the back

Cat.No.	Den.	Date	Variety	G	VG	F	VF	EF	AU
10-02	$1	1856		450.	900.	1,500.	—	—	—
10-02a	$1	1856	Cancelled	275.	550.	900.	—	—	—
10-04	$2	1856-1857		500.	1,000.	1,750.	—	—	—
10-04a	$2	1856-1857	Cancelled	300.	600.	1,050.	—	—	—
10-08	$5	1856		525.	1,050.	1,800.	—	—	—
10-08a	$5	1856	Cancelled	325.	675.	1,100.	—	—	—
10-10	$10	1856		700.	1,400.	2,000.	—	—	—
10-10a	$10	1856	Cancelled	425.	850.	1,200.	—	—	—

Note: Notes of this bank are usually encountered cancelled, having the right signature area removed.

THE CROWN BANK OF CANADA

1904 - 1908

TORONTO, (ONTARIO)

BANK NUMBER 215 ***REDEEMABLE***

Established in Toronto in 1904, this bank amalgamated with The Northern Bank in July of 1908 to become The Northern Crown Bank which was, in turn, absorbed by The Royal Bank of Canada in July of 1918.

215-10. ISSUE OF 1904

DESIGNS AND COLOURS

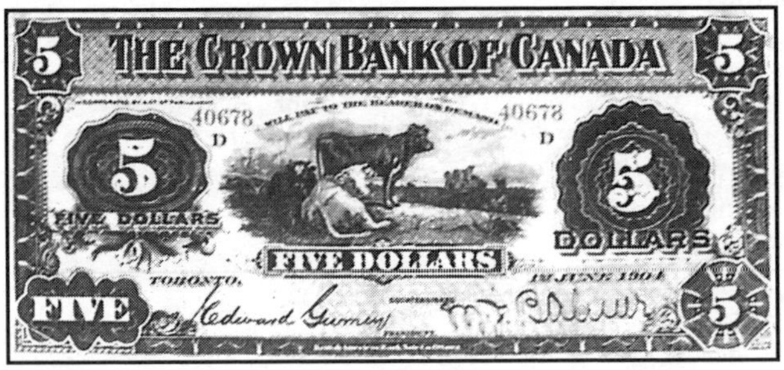

215-10-02

$5 Face Design: —/cattle in pasture/—

Colour: Black with orange and yellow tint

Back Design: Bank name, crown and floral symbols, lathework

Colour: Brown

215-10-04P

$10 Face Design: Lion on mountain/—/—

Colour: Black with brown and yellow and green tint

Back Design: Bank name, crown and floral symbols, lathework

Colour: Blue

15-10-06P

$20 Face Design: Allegorical male, child and females "UNITY"/—/—

Colour: Black with rose and blue tint

Back Design: Bank name, crown and floral symbols, lathework

Colour: Orange

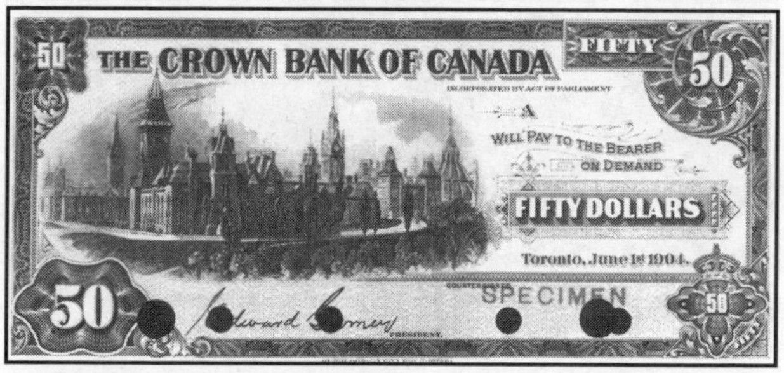

215-10-08P

$50 Face Design: Parliament buildings/—/—

Colour: Black with red and yellow tint

Back Design: Bank name, crown and floral symbols, lathework

Colour: Red-brown

IMPRINT

British American Bank Note Co. Ottawa

SIGNATURES

left	**right**
engr. Edward Gurney	mss. various

ISSUE DATING

Engraved

June 1st 1904

1st June 1904

CIRCULATING NOTES

Cat.No.	Denom.	Date	G	VG	F	VF	EF	AU
10-02	$5	1904	2,400.	4,000.	5,500.	7,500.	—	—
10-04	$10	1904	No known issued notes					
10-06	$20	1904	No known issued notes					
10-08	$50	1904	No known issued notes					

PROOF NOTES

Cat. No.	Denom.	Date		Unc
10-02P	$5	1904	FACE PROOF	900.
10-04P	$10	1904	FACE PROOF	1,000.
10-06P	$20	1904	FACE PROOF	1,000.
10-08P	$50	1904	FACE PROOF	1,200.

Note: Proofs are known for faces and backs with colours other than those listed here.

THE DOMINION BANK

1869 - 1955

TORONTO, ONTARIO

BANK NUMBER 220 ***REDEEMABLE***

This bank was established in Toronto in 1869 and amalgamated in 1955 with The Bank of Toronto to form The Toronto-Dominion Bank, now active as one of the largest banks in Canada. Its charter was obtained without difficulty, but its founders were unable to open the bank's doors to the public until February 1, 1871. In its first year of operation, the bank opened five branches. For the first time in Canadian banking history, the bank decided to open a city branch in Toronto in addition to the head office. This policy was soon followed by other banks. The bank paid dividends in its first year of operation, and by April of 1872, its assets reached the $2.5 million mark with notes in circulation of $540,508. In the years of depression following the financial crisis of 1873, the bank remained sound through good management. With the return of prosperity in 1880 and the beginning of the activities of the Canadian Pacific Railway, the bank shared in the growth in the banking business and expanded rapidly. Throughout the financial upheavals and legislative changes later, the bank had continued "with monotonous, but very comforting regularity to pay substantial dividends." It had never taken over or merged with another bank. At the time of its amalgamation with The Bank of Toronto, the bank had total assets of $538 million and 194 branches. In approving the amalgamation agreement, the Minister of Finance stated that each of the banks was in a strong financial position, but that the amalgamated institution, through a more nation-wide expansion of branch facilities should be able to offer greater competition and more efficient service to its Canadian customers. The shareholders were also informed that the new bank would start with an authorized capital of $30 million with $15 million paid-up, a reserve fund of $30 million, total assets in excess of $1 billion and 450 branches, including offices in New York and London, England. Of the 1,500,000 shares issued by the new bank, The Toronto-Dominion Bank, shareholders of The Bank of Toronto received 800,000 - 4 for each 3 of that bank - and those of The Dominion Bank received share for share, in accordance with the shareholders' equity in the two banks.

220-10. ISSUES OF 1871 and 1873

DESIGNS AND COLOURS

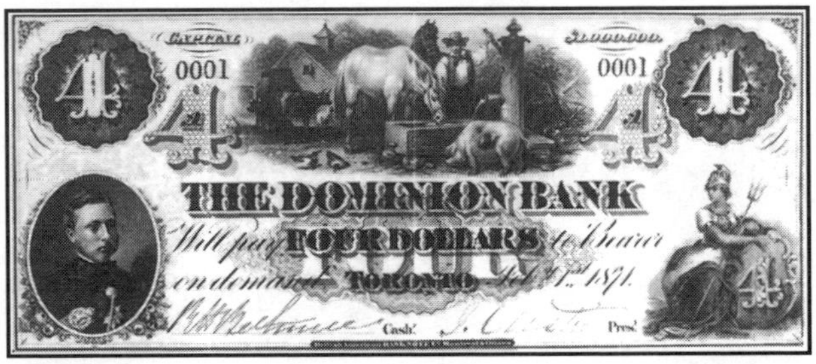

220-10-02
$4 Face Design: Prince Arthur/farmer pumping water for livestock/seated Britannia
Colour: Black with green tint

Back Design: Lathework, counters and bank name
Colour: Green

220-10-04
$5 Face Design: —/Queen Victoria in "widow's weeds" superimposed on Royal Crest/—
Colour: Black with green tint

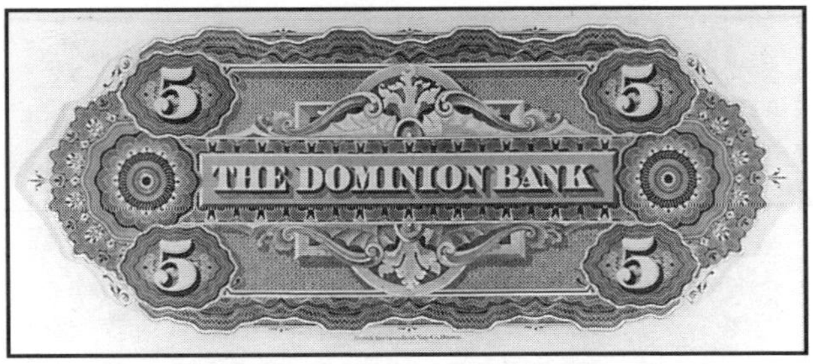

Back Design: Lathework, counters and bank name
Colour: Green

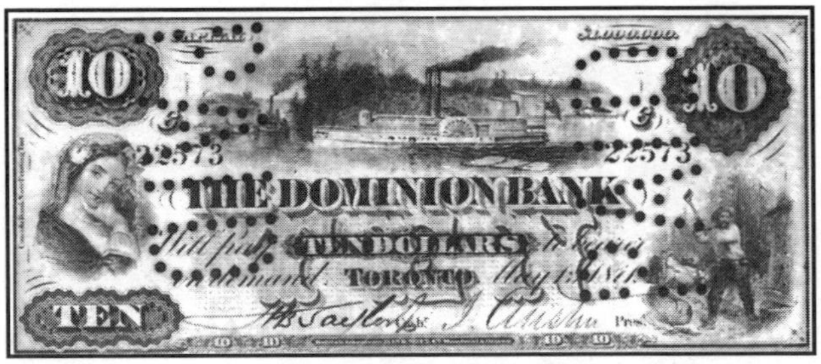

220-10-06
$10 Face Design: Girl/paddlewheel steamer "Inland commerce"/woodcutter
Colour: Black with green tint

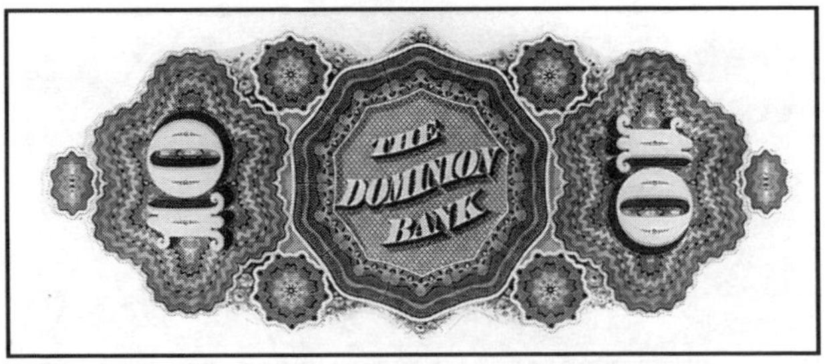

Back Design: Lathework, counters and bank name
Colour: Green

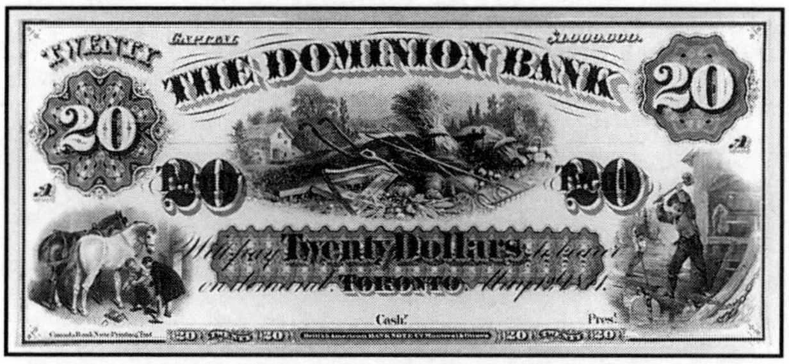

220-10-08P

$20 Face Design: Shoeing horses/"Implements of agriculture"/logger

Colour: Black with green tint

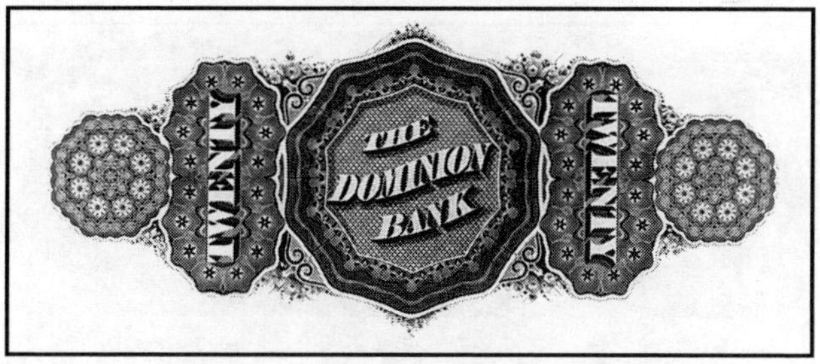

Back Design: Lathework, counters and bank name

Colour: Green

Photo Not Available

220-10-10P

$50 Face Design: Unknown

Colour: Black with green tint

Back Design: Lathework, counters and bank name

Colour: Green

220-10-12

$100 Face Design: —/woman with water jug/—

Colour: Black with green tint

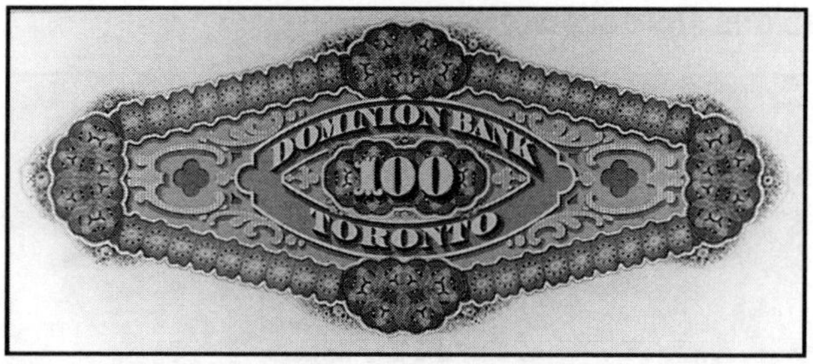

Back Design: Lathework, counters and bank name

Colour: Green

IMPRINT

British American Bank Note Co. Montreal & Ottawa

SIGNATURES

	left	**right**
	$4, $5 & $100:	
	mss. various	engr. J. Austin

ISSUE DATING

$4 & $5: Feb. 1st, 1871
$10, $20 & $50: May 1st, 1871
$100: 1st October, 1873

CIRCULATING NOTES

Cat.No.	Denom.	Date	Variety	G	VG	F	VF	EF	AU
10-02*	$4	1871		1,000.	2,000.	2,700.	4,000.	—	—
10-02C	$4	1871	Counterfeit	60.	125.	175.	225.	—	—
10-04	$5	1871		875.	1,750.	2,350.	3,500.	—	—
10-06	$10	1871		1,100.	2,200.	2,900.	4,300.	—	—
10-08	$20	1871		Institutional collection only					
10-12	$100	1873		Institutional collection only					

* Beware of counterfeits of this note

PROOF NOTES

Cat. No.	Denom.	Date	Variety		Unc
10-02P	$4	1871		FACE PROOF	750.
10-04P	$5	1871		FACE PROOF	750.
10-06P	$10	1871		FACE PROOF	750.
10-08P	$20	1871		FACE PROOF	800.
10-10P	$50	1871		FACE PROOF	850.
10-12P	$100	1873	B & W	FACE PROOF	500.
10-12Pa	$100	1873	Green tint	FACE PROOF	900.

220-12. **ISSUE OF 1876 - 1888**

DESIGNS AND COLOURS

220-12-02

$4 Face Design: Laureate woman's head/ seated woman with children/ woman's head "The Bride"
Colour: Black with green and red-brown tint

Back Design: Lathework and large 4 counter
Colour: Brown

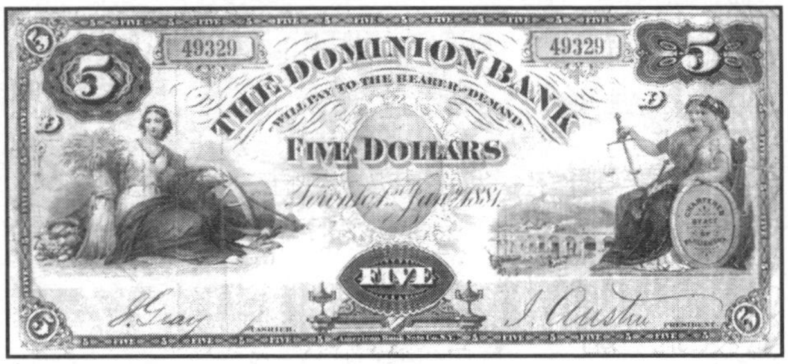

220-12-04

$5 Face Design: Seated woman with sheaf of wheat "Girl with sheaf", tools/—/two seated allegorical women
Colour: Black with blue tint

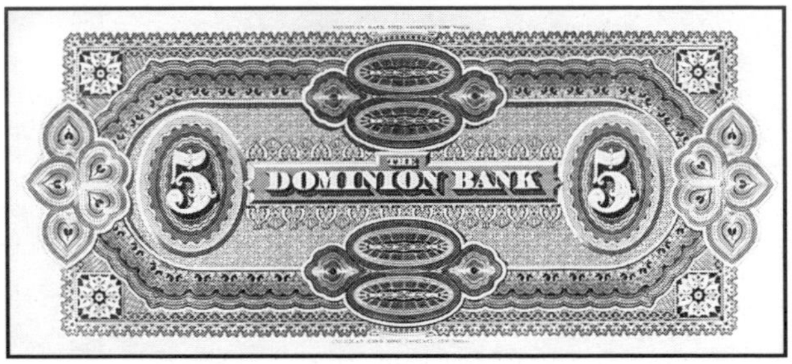

Back Design: Lathework, counters and bank name
Colour: Blue

220-12-06S

$10 Face Design: Allegorical female holding fasces/ seated allegorical female with wheat, sickle, behive
Colour: Black with ochre and green tint

Back Design: Lathework, counters, bank name and flowers/reclining Indian/—
Colour: Brown

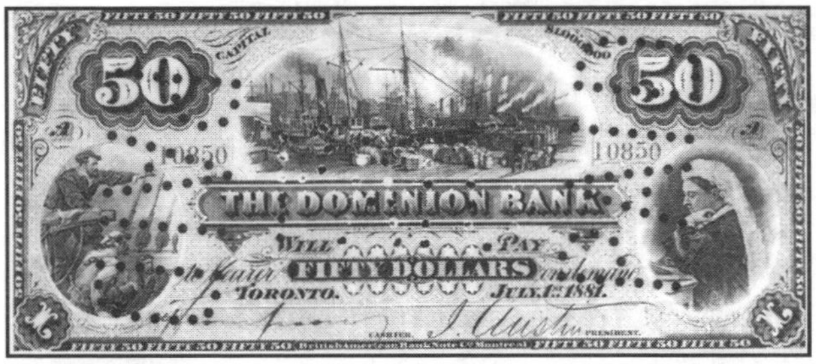

220-12-08

$50 Face Design: Cartier approaching land "Quebec"/ ships at dock/ Queen Victoria in "widow's weeds"
Colour: Black with green tint

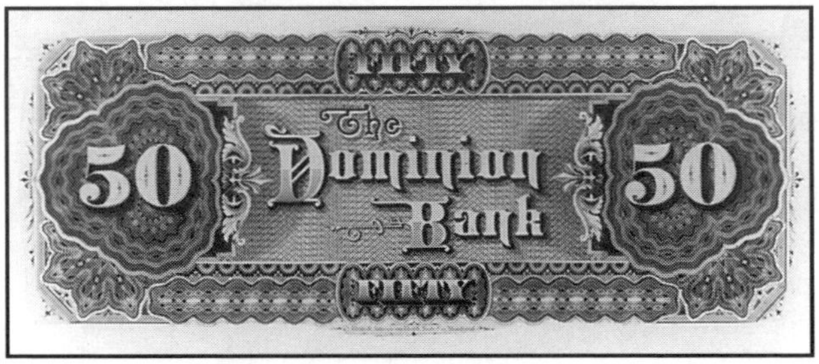

Back Design: Lathework, counters and bank name
Colour: Green

IMPRINT

$4, $5 & $10: American Bank Note Co, New York
American Bank Note Co. N.Y.
$50: British American Bank Note Co. Montreal

SIGNATURES

left	**right**
mss. various	engr. J. Austin

ISSUE DATING

Engraved

$4: 1st Jany.1876
$5: 1st Jany 1881
$10: 2nd. January, 1888
$50: July 1st, 1881

CIRCULATING NOTES

Cat.No.	Denom.	Date	Variety	G	VG	F	VF	EF	AU
12-02	$4	1876		1,000.	2,000.	2,700.	4,000.	—	—
12-04	$5	1881		875.	1,750.	2,350.	3,500.	—	—
12-06	$10	1888		1,200.	2,400.	3,200.	4,700.	—	—
12-08	$50	1881	Institutional collection only						

PROOF NOTES

Cat.No.	Denom.	Date	Variety		Unc
12-02P	$4	1876		FACE PROOF	400.
12-04P	$5	1881		FACE PROOF	500.
12-06P	$10	1888		FACE PROOF	600.
12-08P	$50	1881	B & W	FACE PROOF	500.
12-08Pa	$50	1881	Green tint	FACE PROOF	800.

SPECIMEN NOTES

Cat.No.	Denom.	Date	Variety		Unc
12-02S	$4	1876		SPECIMEN	900.
12-04S	$5	1881		SPECIMEN	900.
12-06S	$10	1888		SPECIMEN	900.

Note: $10 back proof known in green and $10 specimen with all green face tint.

220-14. ISSUE OF 1891 and 1898

DESIGNS AND COLOURS

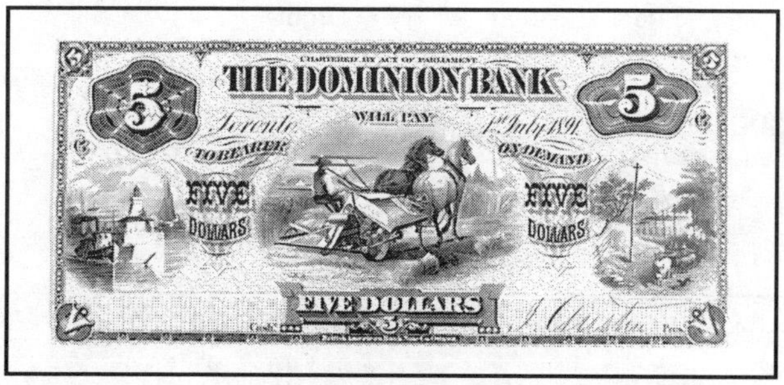

220-14-02P

$5 Face Design: "Lighthouse" and boats/binder and horses/power lines and cattle "The drove"
Colour: Black with green tint

Back Design: Lathework, counters and bank name
Colour: Green

220-14-04

$10 Face Design: Frank Smith/cattle in pasture/—
Colour: Black with overall green tint

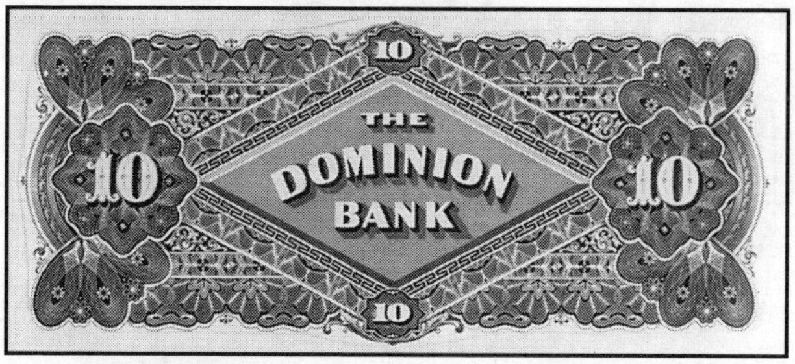

Back Design: Lathework, counters and bank name
Colour: Green

IMPRINT

British American Bank Note Co. Ottawa

SIGNATURES

	left	right
$5:	mss. various	engr. J. Austin
$10:	mss. various	engr. Frank Smith

ISSUE DATING

Engraved

1st July, 1891
July 1st, 1898

CIRCULATING NOTES

Cat.No.	Denom.	Date	G	VG	F	VF	EF	AU
14-02	$5	1891	700.	1,400.	1,800.	2,600.	—	—
14-04	$10	1898	750.	1,500.	1,900.	3,000.	—	—

PROOF NOTES

Cat. No.	Denom.	Date		Unc
14-02P	$5	1891	FACE PROOF	800.
14-04P	$10	1898	FACE PROOF	800.

Note: $10 face proof exists with yellow tint.

220-16. $5 ISSUES OF 1896 - 1925

DESIGNS AND COLOURS

220-16-02S

$5 Face Design: Woman kneeling beside anvil/—/ woman seated beside produce. Top counters with fancy scrollwork.
Colour: Black with green tint

Back Design: Unknown
Colour: Unknown

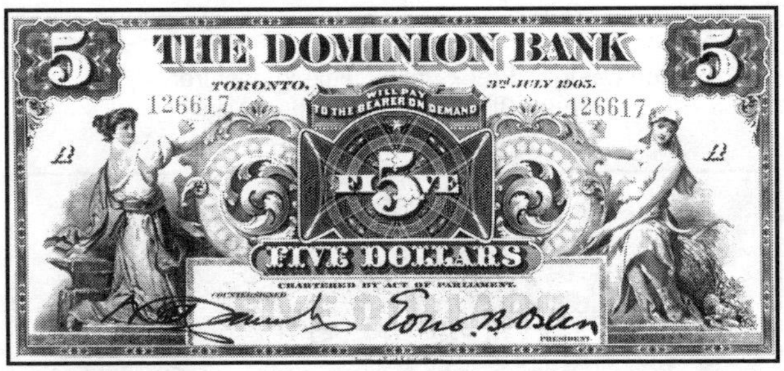

220-16-08

$5 Face Design: Kneeling woman with anvil/—/ seated woman with agricultural produce, top counters plain
Colour: Black with green tint

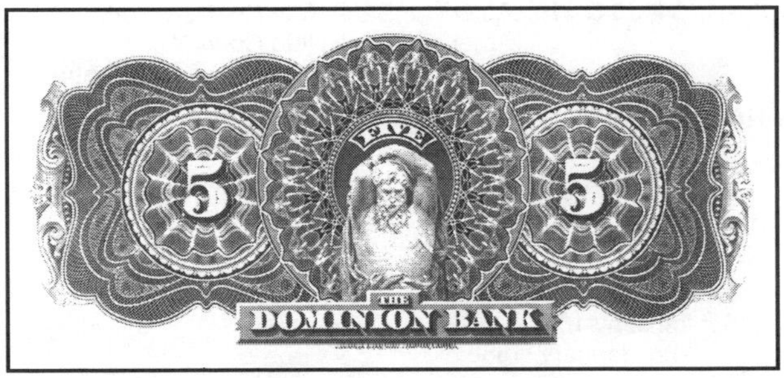

220-16-14

Back Design: Lathework, counters, bank name and Greek god,
Colour: Green

IMPRINT

American Bank Note Co. Ottawa
Canadian Bank Note Company Limited

SIGNATURES

	left	right
1896:	mss. various	engr. J. Austin
1898:	mss. various	engr. Frank Smith
1900:	mss. various	engr. Frank Smith
1905:	mss. various	typed E.B. Osler
	typed C.A. Bogert	typed E.B. Osler
1925:	typed C.A. Bogert	typed A. Nanton
	typed C.A. Bogert	typed A.W. Austin

ISSUE DATING

Engraved

1st January, 1896
Jan. 1, 1898
2nd January 1900
3rd July 1905
2nd Jany. 1925

CIRCULATING NOTES

Cat.No.	Denom.	Date	Variety	G	VG	F	VF	EF	AU
16-02	$5	1896		650.	1,300.	1,700.	3,000.	—	—
16-04	$5	1898		650.	1,300.	1,700.	3,000.	—	—
16-06	$5	1900		600.	1,200.	1,550.	2,600.	—	—
16-08	$5	1905	mss.signat,l.	95.	190.	275.	450.	800.	1,500.
16-10	$5	1905	Bogert,l.	95.	190.	275.	450.	800.	—
16-12	$5	1925	Nanton, r.	85.	175.	250.	400.	750.	—
16-14	$5	1925	Austin, r.	70.	140.	200.	325.	625.	950.

SPECIMEN NOTES

Cat. No.	Denom.	Date		Unc
16-02S	$5	1896	SPECIMEN	1,000.
16-08S	$5	1905	SPECIMEN	900.

220-18. $10 ISSUES OF 1900 - 1925

DESIGNS AND COLOURS

220-18-02

$10 Face Design: —/seated Britannia, lion/—
1900-1910 Face Colour: Black with yellow-green and green tint
Back Colour: Maroon, yellow-green and green
1925 Face Colour: Black with yellow and green tint
Back Colour: Yellow and green

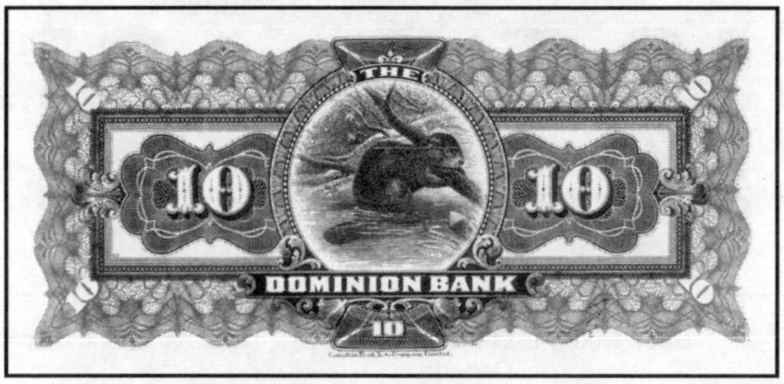

Back Design: Lathework, counters, bank name and beaver

IMPRINT

American Bank Note Company, Ottawa
Canadian Bank Note Company Limited

SIGNATURES

	left	right
1900:	mss. various	engr. Frank Smith
1910:	mss. various	typed E.B. Osler
	typed C.A. Bogert	typed E.B. Osler
1925:	typed C.A. Bogert	typed A. Nanton
	typed C.A. Bogert	typed A.W. Austin

Note: 18-04 - Engraved "Countersigned" at left. 18-06 - Engraved "General Manager" at left.

ISSUE DATING

Engraved

Jany. 2nd 1900
Jany 3rd 1910
2nd Jany. 1925

CIRCULATING NOTES

Cat.No.	Denom.	Date	Variety	G	VG	F	VF	EF	Unc
18-02	$10	1900		185.	375.	500.	800.	1,500.	—
18-04	$10	1910	Mss.signature l.	70.	140.	200.	325.	625.	1,300.
18-06	$10	1910	Bogert, l.	70.	140.	200.	325.	625.	1,300.
18-08	$10	1925	Nanton, r.	70.	140.	200.	325.	625.	—
18-10	$10	1925	Austin, r.	50.	100.	110.	225.	450.	950.

SPECIMEN NOTES

Cat. No.	Denom.	Date		Unc
18-04S	$10	1910	SPECIMEN	900.

220-20 $20 ISSUES OF 1897 - 1925

DESIGNS AND COLOURS

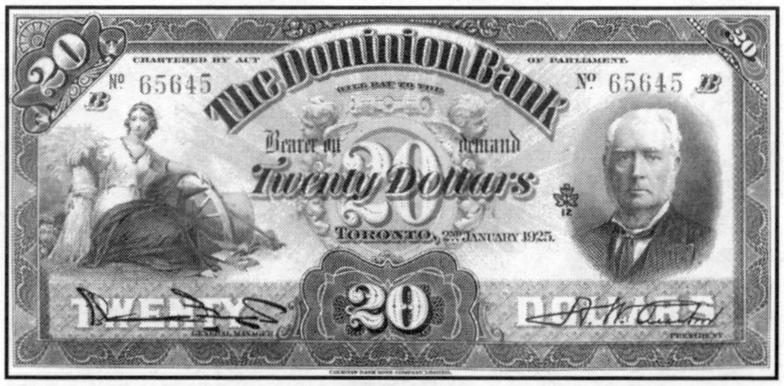

220-20-08

$20 Face Design: Seated woman with sheaf and tools "Girl with sheaf"/two statue-like cherubs surrounding 20/Frank Smith
Colour: Black with blue and yellow-green tint

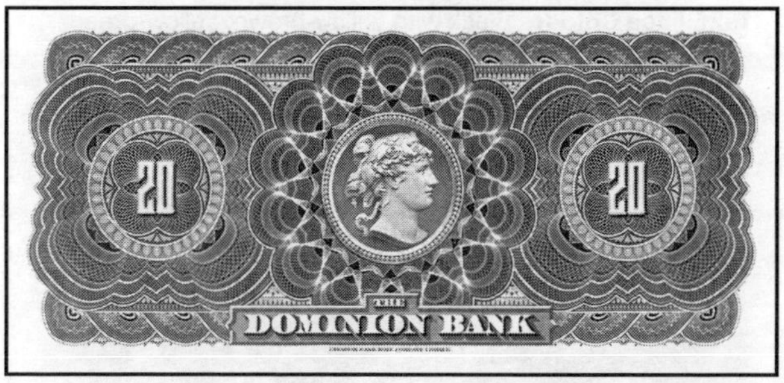

Back Design: Lathework, counters, bank name and bust of Greek goddess
Colour: Olive-green

IMPRINT

American Bank Note Company, Ottawa
Canadian Bank Note Company, Limited

SIGNATURES

	Left	right
1897:	mss. various	engr. Frank Smith
1909:	mss. various	typed E.B. Osler
	typed various	typed E.B. Osler
1925:	typed C.A. Bogert	typed A.W. Austin

Note: 20-04 - Engraved "countersigned" at left. 20-06 - Engraved "general manager" at left.

ISSUE DATE

Engraved

1st October 1897
1st October 1909
2nd January 1925

CIRCULATING NOTES

Cat.No.	Denom	Date	Variety	G	VG	F	VF	EF	AU
20-02	$20	1897		550.	1,100.	1,750.	2,600.	—	—
20-04	$20	1909	Mss. signat,l.	100.	200.	275.	450.	800.	1,500.
20-06	$20	1909	Typed signat,l.	100.	200.	275.	450.	800.	1,500.
20-08	$20	1925		85.	175.	240.	350.	700.	1,250.

SPECIMEN NOTES

Cat. No.	Denom.	Date		Unc
20-04S	$20	1909	SPECIMEN	1,000.

220-22. $50 ISSUES OF 1901 and 1925

DESIGNS AND COLOURS

220-22-04S

$50 Face Design: Beehives/—/livestock at stable door
1901 Face Colour: Black with yellow-brown, brown, yellow-green, green and purple tint
Back Colour: Brown, blue, yellow-brown, yellow-green and green
1925 Face Colour: Black with yellow-brown, yellow-green, blue and olive tint
Back Colour: Yellow-brown, yellow-green, blue and olive

Back Design: Lathework, counters, bank name and beaver

IMPRINT

American Bank Note Co. Ottawa
Canadian Bank Note Company, Limited

SIGNATURES

	left	right
1901:	mss. various	typed E.B. Osler
1901:	typed C.A. Bogert	typed E.B. Osler
1925:	typed C.A. Bogert	typed A.W. Austin

ISSUE DATING

Engraved

July 2nd 1901
2nd Jany, 1925

CIRCULATING NOTES

Cat.No.	Denom.	Date	Variety	G	VG	F	VF	EF	AU
22-02	$50	1901	mss. Signat. 1.	250.	500.	675.	1,050.	2,100.	—
22-03	$50	1902	Bogert, 1.	300.	600.	800.	—	—	—
22-04	$50	1925		175.	350.	500.	650.	1,350.	—

SPECIMEN NOTES

Cat. No.	Denom.	Date	Unc
22-02S	$50	1901	SPECIMEN 1,000.
22-04S	$50	1925	SPECIMEN 1,000.

220-24. ISSUE OF 1931

DESIGNS AND COLOURS

220-24-02

$5 Face Design: A.W. Austin/—/C.A. Bogert
Colour: Black with blue and orange tint

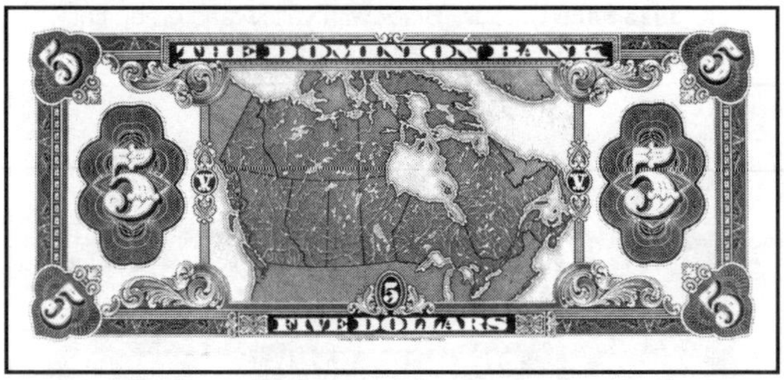

Back Design: Lathework, counters, bank name and map of Canada
Colour: Green

220-24-08

$10 Face Design: A.W. Austin/—/C.A. Bogert
Colour: Black with blue and orange tint

Back Design: Lathework, counters, bank name and map of Canada
Colour: Blue

220-24-10

$20 Face Design: A.W. Austin/two statue-like cherubs surrounding 20/C.A. Bogert
Colour: Black with purple and orange tint

Back Design: Lathework, counters, bank name and map of Canada
Colour: Purple

220-24-12S

$50 Face Design: A.W. Austin/—/C.A. Bogert
Colour: Black with yellow, pink and orange tint

Back Design: Lathework, counters, bank name and map of Canada
Colour: Orange

220-24-14

$100 Face Design: A.W. Austin/—/C.A. Bogert
Colour: Black with olive-green and orange tint

Back Design: Lathework, counters, bank name and map of Canada
Colour: Red-brown

IMPRINT

Canadian Bank Note Company, Limited

SIGNATURES

left	right
typed A.W. Austin	typed C.A. Bogert
typed C.H. Carlisle	typed Dudley Dawson

ISSUE DATING

Engraved

1st Feb'y 1931

CIRCULATING NOTES

Cat.No.	Denom.	Date	Variety	VG	F	VF	EF	AU	Unc
24-02	$5	1931	Bogert,r.	80.	110.	150.	300.	450.	600.
24-04	$5	1931	Dawson,r.	75.	100.	140.	275.	400.	550.
24-06	$10	1931	Bogert,r.	105.	150.	215.	425.	650.	850.
24-08	$10	1931	Dawson,r.	100.	140.	200.	400.	600.	800.
24-10	$20	1931		150.	200.	275.	550.	800.	—
24-12	$50	1931			No known issued notes				
24-14	$100	1931		500.	750.	1,200.	2,250.	—	—

PROOF NOTES

Cat. No.	Denom	Date		Unc
24-02P	$5	1931	FACE PROOF	250.
24-06P	$10	1931	FACE PROOF	250.
24-10P	$20	1931	FACE PROOF	250.
24-12P	$50	1931	FACE PROOF	350.
24-14P	$100	1931	FACE PROOF	350.

SPECIMEN NOTES

Cat. No.	Denom.	Date		Unc
24-10S	$20	1931	SPECIMEN	600.
24-12S	$50	1931	SPECIMEN	800.

220-26. ISSUE OF 1935 SMALL SIZE NOTES

DESIGNS AND COLOURS

220-26-02

$5 Face Design: Dudley Dawson/—/Clifton H. Carlisle
Colour: Black with green and orange tint

Back Design: Lathework, counters, bank name and map of Canada
Colour: Orange

220-26-04

$10 Face Design: Dudley Dawson/—Clifton H. Carlisle
Colour: Black with yellow, pink and orange tint

Back Design: Lathework, counters, bank name and map of Canada
Colour: Orange

IMPRINT

Canadian Bank Note Company, Limited

SIGNATURES

left	right
typed Dudley Dawson	typed C.H. Carlisle

ISSUE DATING

Engraved

2nd Jan. 1935

CIRCULATING NOTES

Cat.No.	Denom.	Date	VG	F	VF	EF	AU	Unc
26-02	$5	1935	45.	65.	100.	210.	325.	450.
26-04	$10	1935	50.	70.	110.	225.	350.	475.

PROOF NOTES

Cat.No.	Denom.	Date		Unc
26-02P	$5	1935	FACE PROOF	250.
26-04P	$10	1935	FACE PROOF	250.

220-28. ISSUE OF 1938 SMALL SIZE NOTES

DESIGNS AND COLOURS

220-28-02

$5 Face Design: Clifton H. Carlisle/—/Robert Rae
Colour: Black with orange and brown tint

Back Design: Lathework, counters, bank name and map of Canada
Colour: Brown

220-28-04

$10 Face Design: Clifton H. Carlisle/—/Robert Rae
Colour: Black with blue and yellow tint

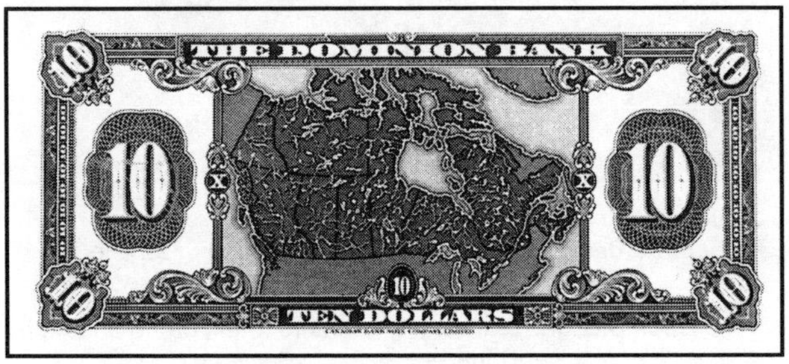

Back Design: Lathework, counters, bank name and map of Canada
Colour: Olive-green

IMPRINT

Canadian Bank Note Company, Limited

SIGNATURES

left	right
typed C.H. Carlisle	typed R. Rae

ISSUE DATING

Engraved

3rd Jan. 1938

CIRCULATING NOTES

Cat.No.	Denom.	Date	VG	F	VF	EF	AU	Unc
28-02	$5	1938	50.	70.	110.	225.	350.	475.
28-04	$10	1938	50.	70.	110.	225.	350.	475.

PROOF NOTES

Cat.No.	Denom.	Date		Unc
28-02P	$5	1938	FACE PROOF	250.
28-04P	$10	1938	FACE PROOF	250.

EASTERN BANK OF CANADA

1928 - 1934

ST. JOHN, NEW BRUNSWICK

BANK NUMBER 225 ***NONREDEEMABLE***

The Eastern Bank of Canada was incorporated in 1928 with its head office in Saint John, New Brunswick. Its stock was offered to the public in January of 1927 at $200 per share. Sufficient capital was raised to qualify for certificate to start operations, but the stock market crash in the fall of 1929, lack of public interest in the bank, and the inability of its founders to find a competent general manager resulted in the non-use of the charter. In July of 1932 the Treasury Board approved the return of the bank's note deposits and the charter lapsed through nonrenewal in the Bank Act amendment of 1934.

225-10. DESIGNS OF 1929

Notes were printed, but all were later destroyed unissued, with only proofs having survived.

DESIGNS AND COLOURS

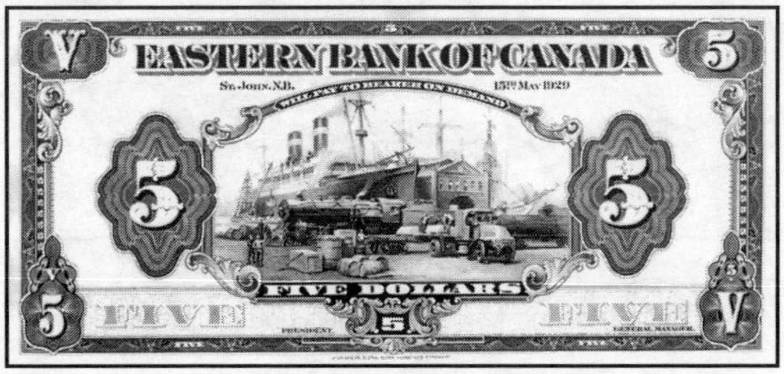

225-10-02P

$5 Face Design: —/wharf scene with truck, train and steamship/—

Colour: Black with green tint

Back Design: Lathework, counters, bank name and bank seal

Colour: Orange

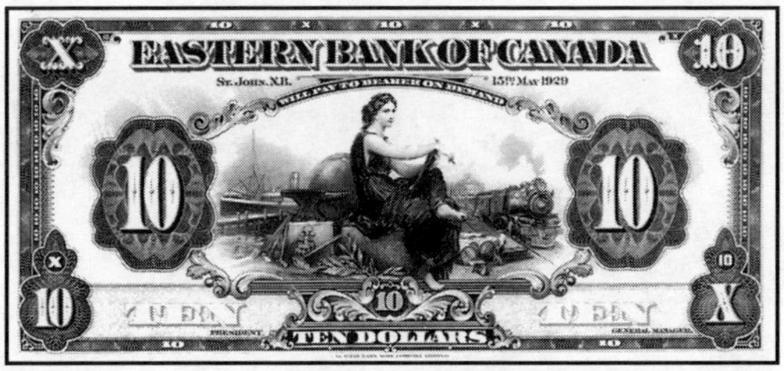

225-10-04P

$10 Face Design: —/ship, seated allegorical female, train/—

Colour: Black with brown tint

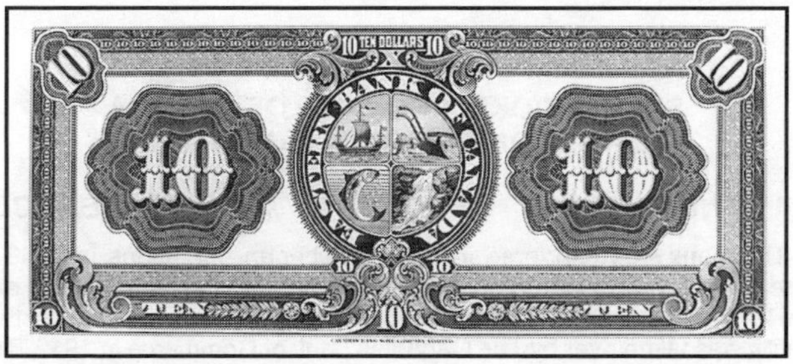

Back Design: Lathework, counters, bank name and bank seal

Colour: Blue

IMPRINT

Canadian Bank Note Company, Limited

SIGNATURES

left	right
none	none

ISSUE DATING

Engraved

15th May 1929

PROOF NOTES

Cat.No.	Denom.	Date		Unc
10-02P	$5	1929	FACE PROOF	850.
10-04P	$10	1929	FACE PROOF	850.

THE EASTERN TOWNSHIPS BANK

1855 - 1912

SHERBROOKE, PROVINCE OF CANADA
SHERBROOKE, PROVINCE OF QUEBEC

BANK NUMBER 230 ***REDEEMABLE***

This bank was chartered in 1855 and began operations in 1859 in Sherbrooke, P.Q. Its shareholders were mainly residents of the U.S. and the Eastern Township region of Quebec. The bank operated successfully until it was taken over by The Canadian Bank of Commerce in 1912. The latter acquired about 100 branches and a large number of shareholders abroad as a result of this merger.

230-10. "GREEN" ISSUE OF 1859 AND 1861

DESIGNS AND COLOURS

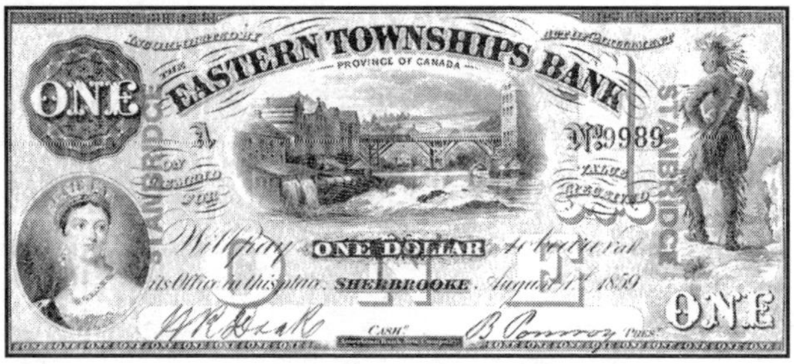

230-10-04-04a
$1 Face Design: Queen Victoria (Chalon portrait)/Magog River Falls (Sherbrooke Mills)/Indian on bluff
Colour: Black with overall green tint

Back Design: Plain

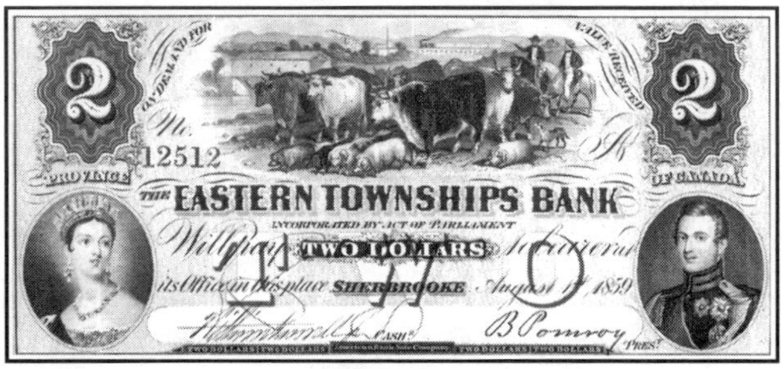

230-10-04-08
$2 Face Design: Queen Victoria (Chalon portrait)/men on horseback with livestock/Prince Consort
Colour: Black with overall green tint

Back Design: Plain

230-10-02-06P
$4 Face Design: Prince of Wales/Magog River Falls (Sherbrooke Mills)/Benjamin Pomroy
Colour: Black with overall green tint

Back Design: Plain

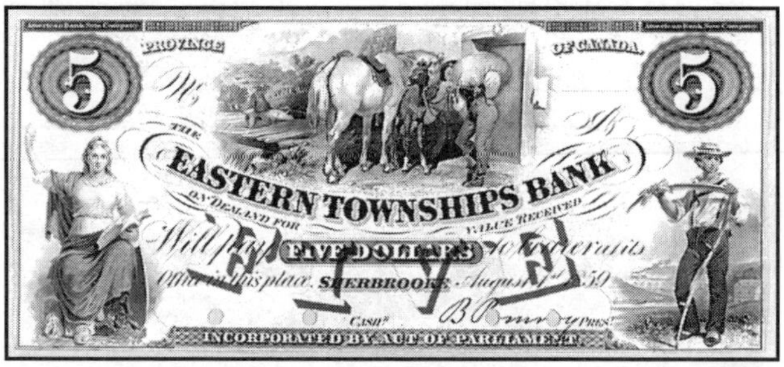

230-10-04-16P
$5 Face Design: Allegorical female/horse and colt, farmer carrying sack of grain/farmer with scythe
Colour: Black with overall green tint

Back Design: Plain

230-10-04-20P
$10 Face Design: Hunter and dog at campfire/ reclining shepherd boy/train
Colour: Black with overall green tint

Back Design: Plain

230-10-04-24P

$20 Face Design: Allegorical female, machinery/ ploughing with team of horses/ Britannia, shield: XX on shield
Colour: Black with overall green tint

Back Design: Plain

IMPRINT
American Bank Note Company

2. PARTIALLY ENGRAVED DATE 1859

SIGNATURES

left	right
mss. Wm. S. Foster	mss. B. Pomroy

ISSUE DATING
Partially Engraved__18__:
1859: Aug. 1

PROTECTOR
Red "word" on back only

OVERPRINT
"WATERLOO" twice in red

CIRCULATING NOTES

Cat.No.	Den.	Date	Variety	G	VG	F	VF	EF	AU
10-02-02	$1	1859		1,050.	2,100.	2,900.	—	—	—
10-02-02a	$1	1859	o/p WATERLOO	1,150.	2,300.	3,250.	—	—	—
10-02-04	$2	1859		1,500.	—	—	—	—	—
10-02-08	$5	1859		No known issued notes					
10-02-10	$10	1859		No known issued notes					
10-02-12	$20	1859		No known issued notes					

PROOF NOTES

Cat. No.	Den.	Date		Unc
10-02-02P	$1	18__	PROOF	900.
10-02-04P	$2	18__	PROOF	900.
10-02-06P	$4	18__	PROOF	900.
10-02-08P	$5	18__	PROOF	900.
10-02-10P	$10	18__	PROOF	900.
10-02-12P	$20	18__	PROOF	900.

4. ENGRAVED DATE 1859 AND 1861

SIGNATURES

left	right
mss. W. R. Doak	mss. B. Pomroy
mss. William Farwell Jr.	engr. B. Pomroy

ISSUE DATING
Engraved
August 1st 1859
1st February 1861

PROTECTOR
Red word on back only.

OVERPRINT
"STANBRIDGE" in red
"STANSTEAD" in red
"WATERLOO" in red

CIRCULATING NOTES

Cat.No.	Denom.	Date	Variety	G	VG	F	VF
10-04-02	$1	1859	Mss. Pomroy, r	1,050.	2,100.	—	—
10-04-02a	$1	1859	Mss Pomroy, r; town o/p	1,150.	2,300.	—	—
10-04-04	$1	1859	Engr. Pomroy, r	1,050.	2,100.	—	—
10-04-04a	$1	1859	Engr. Pomroy, r; town o/p	1,150.	2,300.	—	—
10-04-06	$2	1859	Mss. Pomroy, r	1,500.	—	—	—
10-04-06a	$2	1859	Mss Pomroy, r. Town o/p	Institutional collection only			
10-04-08	$2	1859	Engr. Pomroy, r	Institutional collection only			
10-04-08a	$2	1859	Engr. Pomroy, r; town o/p	No known issued notes			
10-04-10	$4	1861	Mss. Pomroy, r	Institutional collection only			
10-04-12	$4	1861	Engr. Pomroy, r	1,300.	2,600.	—	—
10-04-14	$5	1859	Mss. Pomroy, r	No known issued notes			
10-04-16	$5	1859	Engr. Pomroy, r	Institutional collection only			
10-04-18	$10	1859	Mss Pomroy, r	No known issued notes			
10-04-20	$10	1859	Engr. Pomroy, r	No known issued notes			
10-04-22	$20	1859	Mss Pomroy, r	No known issued notes			
10-04-24	$20	1859	Engr. Pomroy, r	Institutional collection only			

PROOF NOTES

Cat. No.	Denom.	Date	Variety		Unc
10-04-02P	$1	1859		PROOF	900.
10-04-04P	$1	1859	Engr. Pomroy, r	PROOF	900.
10-04-06P	$2	1859		PROOF	900.
10-04-08P	$2	1859	Engr. Pomroy, r	PROOF	900.
10-04-10P	$4	1861		PROOF	900.
10-04-12P	$4	1861	Engr. Pomroy, r	PROOF	900.
10-04-14P	$5	1859		Surviving proofs not confirmed	
10-04-16P	$5	1859	Engr. Pomroy, r	PROOF	900.
10-04-18P	$10	1859		Surviving proofs not confirmed	
10-04-20P	$10	1859	Engr. Pomroy, r	PROOF	900.
10-04-22P	$20	1859		Surviving proofs not confirmed	
10-04-24P	$20	1859	Engr. Pomroy, r	PROOF	900.

230-12. ISSUES OF 1873 AND 1974

DESIGNS AND COLOURS

230-12-02P

$4 Face Design: Farm animals in barn "Stable Door" Magog River Falls (Sherbrooke Mills)/ Benjamin Pomroy
Colour: Black with green tint

Back Design: Smithy shoeing white horse in stable; Lathework, counters, bank name and Sherbrooke, P.Q.
Colour: Green

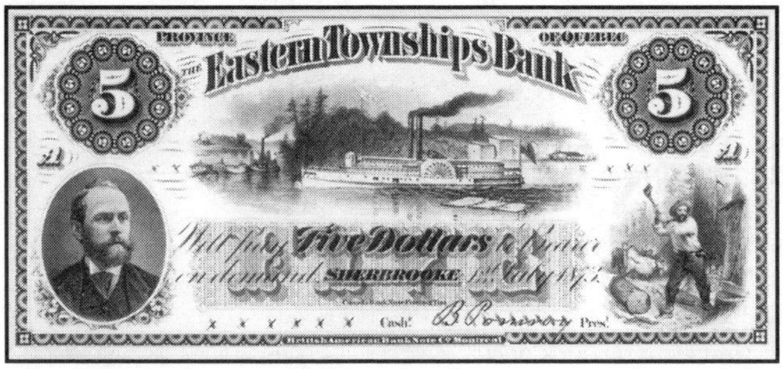

230-12-04P

$5 Face Design: Wm. Farwell/paddlewheel steamer/ wood cutter
Colour: Black with green tint

Back Design: Smithy shoeing white horse in stable; Lathework, counters, bank name and Sherbrooke, P.Q.
Colour: Green

230-12-06P

$10 Face Design: Wm. Farwell/farmer pumping water for livestock/Benjamin Pomroy
Colour: Black with green tint

Back Design: Smithy shoeing white horse in stable; Lathework, counters, bank name and Sherbrooke, P.Q.
Colour: Green

230-12-10

$50 Face Design: Train emerging from tunnel/ Wm. Farwell/Benjamin Pomroy
Colour: Black with green tint

Back Design: Smithy shoeing white horse in stable; Lathework, counters, bank name and Sherbrooke, P.Q.
Colour: Green

230-12-14

$100 Face Design: Wm. Farwell/Magog River Falls (Sherbrooke Mills) Benjamin Pomroy
Colour: Black with green tint

Back Design: Smithy shoeing white horse in stable; Lathework, counters, bank name and Sherbrooke, P.Q.
Colour: Green

IMPRINT

British American Bank Note Co. Montreal

SIGNATURES

left	right
mss. Neil Dinning	engr. B. Pomroy
mss. illegible	engr. B. Pomroy

ISSUE DATING

Engraved

1st July, 1873
1st July, 1874

CIRCULATING NOTES

Cat.No.	Denom.	Date	G	VG	F	VF	EF	AU
12-02	$4	1873	Institutional collection only					
12-04	$5	1873	No known issued notes					
12-06	$10	1873	No known issued notes					
12-08	$50	1873	Institutional collection only					
12-10	$50	1874	Institutional collection only					
12-12	$100	1873	No known issued notes					
12-14	$100	1874	Institutional collection only					

PROOF NOTES

Cat. No.	Denom.	Date		Unc
12-02P	$4	1873	FACE PROOF	900.
12-04P	$5	1873	FACE PROOF	900.
12-06P	$10	1873	FACE PROOF	900.
12-08P	$50	1873	FACE PROOF	900.
12-12P	$100	1873	FACE PROOF	900.

230-14. ISSUES OF 1879 - 1902

DESIGNS AND COLOURS

230-14-02

$4 Face Design: Farm animals in barn/Magog River Falls (Sherbrooke Mills)/R.W. Heneker
Colour: Black with green tint

Back Design: Smithy shoeing white horse in stable; lathework, counters, bank name and Sherbrooke, P.Q.
Colour: Green

230-14-06

$5 Face Design: Wm. Farwell/paddlewheel steamer "Inland Commerce"/wood cutter
Colour: Black with green tint

Back Design: Smithy shoeing white horse in stable; Lathework, counters, bank name and Sherbrooke, P.Q.
Colour: Green

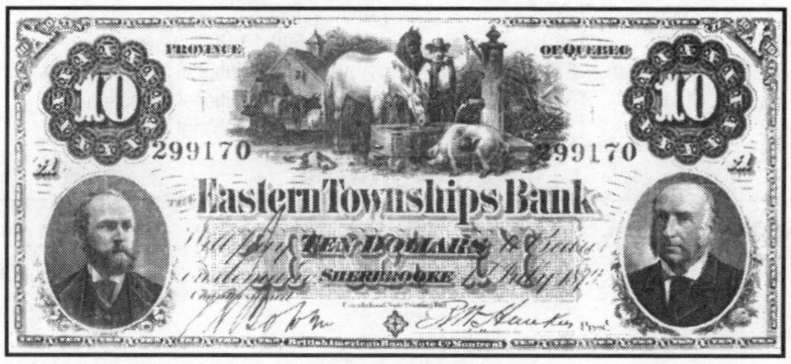

230-14-08

$10 Face Design: Wm. Farwell/farmer pumping water for livestock/R.W. Heneker
Colour: Black with green tint

Back Design: Smithy shoeing white horse in stable; Lathework, counters, bank name and Sherbrooke, P.Q.
Colour: Green

230-14-12P

$20 Face Design: Steers (From E. Landseer's painting of the "Wild cattle of Chillingham place")/—/R.W. Heneker
Colour: Black with green tint

Back Design: Lathework, counters, bank name and bull's head
Colour: Green

IMPRINT

British American Bank Note Co. Montreal

SIGNATURES

left	right
mss. Neil Dinning	engr. R.W. Heneker
mss. illegible	engr. R.W. Heneker
mss. Neil Dinning	engr. Wm. Farwell
mss. illegible	engr. Wm. Farwell

ISSUE DATING

Engraved

1st July 1879
2nd Jan. 1893
2nd July 1902

CIRCULATING NOTES

Cat.No.	Denom.	Date	G	VG	F	VF	EF	AU
14-02	$4	1879	1,100.	2,200.	3,000.	—	—	—
14-04	$5	1879	1,050.	2,100.	—	—	—	—
14-06	$5	1902	750.	1,500.	1,900.	—	—	—
14-08	$10	1879	Institutional collection only					
14-10	$10	1893	Institutional collection only					
14-12	$20	1893	Institutional collection only					

PROOF NOTES

Cat. No.	Denom.	Date		Unc.
14-08P	$10	1879	FACE PROOF	1,500.
14-12P	$20	1893	FACE PROOF	2,000.

230-16. ISSUE OF 1906

DESIGNS AND COLOURS

230-16-02

$5 Face Design: James Mackinnon/train passing hay field/-
Colour: Black with ochre and yellow tint

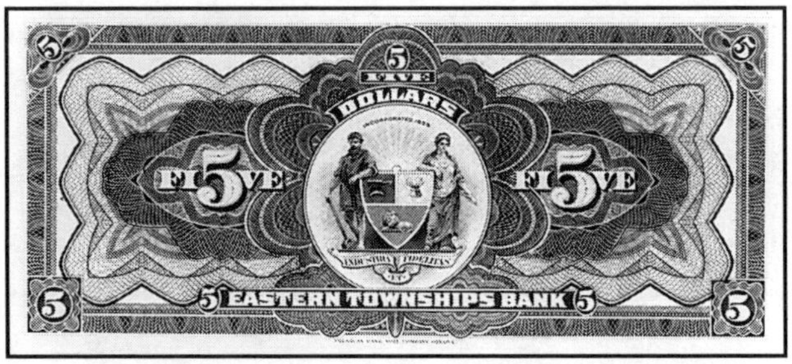

Back Design: Lathework, counters, bank name and bank crest
Colour: olive green with red, violet and pale yellow tint

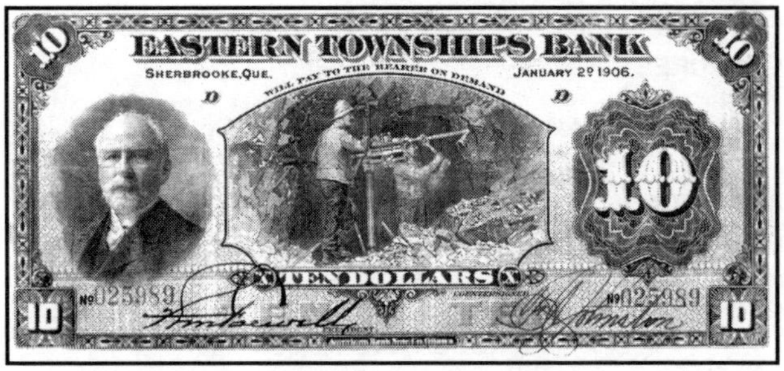

230-16-04

$10 Face Design: Wm. Farwell/mining scene
Colour: Black with red and green tint

Back Design: Lathework, counters, bank name and bank crest
Colour: Green with red, violet and pale yellow tint

IMPRINT

American Bank Note Co. Ottawa

SIGNATURES

left	right
typed Wm. Farwell	mss. various

ISSUE DATING

Engraved

January 2d, 1906
January 2nd, 1906

CIRCULATING NOTES

Cat.No.	Denom.	Date	G	VG	F	VF	EF	AU
16-02	$5	1906	450.	900.	1,400.	2,200.	3,500.	—
16-04	$10	1906	500.	1,000.	1,500.	2,500.	—	—

PROOF NOTES

Cat. No.	Denom.	Date		Unc
16-02P	$5	1906	FACE PROOF	800.
16-04P	$10	1906	FACE PROOF	800.

THE EXCHANGE BANK

1840's

QUEBEC, LOWER CANADA

BANK NUMBER 235 ***NONREDEEMABLE***

This is probably a spurious bank. A very similar note from The Exchange Bank, Providence, Rhode Island (1840s, printed by Rawdon, Wright and Hatch) is known to be spurious (Haxby RI-290-S5). Both appear to have originated from modifications of the same plate.

235-10. **ISSUE OF 1839-44**

DESIGNS AND COLOURS

235-10-04

$1 Face Design: —/seated allegorical female; small steamboat below/—

Colour: Black with no tint

Back Design: Plain

IMPRINT

None

SIGNATURES

left	**right**
mss. J. Williams	mss. S. Davis
mss. J. Weeks	mss. D. Purfes

ISSUE DATING

Partially Engraved __18__:

1839: September 29
1844: May 21st

Cat.No.	Denom.	Date	G	VG	F	VF	EF	AU
10-02	$1	1839-1844	Institutional collection only					

THE EXCHANGE BANK COMPANY OF CHIPPEWA

1837

CHIPPEWA, UPPER CANADA

BANK NUMBER 240 ***NONREDEEMABLE***

Notes purporting to be the issues of this "spurious bank" circulated in the Buffalo area in the early months of 1837. The fraud was promptly reported by the press which limited the success of this particular venture by the swindlers.

240-10. **ISSUE OF 1837**

DESIGNS AND COLOURS

240-10-02

$5 Face Design: —/produce and implements; beaver below/ seated Indian with gun

Colour: Black with no tint

Back Design: Plain

240-10-04R

$10 Face Design: —/cattle, pigs; small steamboat below/ seated "Commerce" figure leaning on shield depicting anchor

Colour: Black with no tint

Back Design: Plain

IMPRINT

Rawdon, Wright, Hatch, New-York

SIGNATURES

left	**right**
mss. buffalo (spurious)	mss. buffalo (spurious)
mss. Howard Waring	mss. Wilson Robinson

ISSUE DATING

Partially Engraved __18__:

1837: Jan. 2

Cat.No.	Denom.	Date	Variety	G	VG	F	VF	EF	AU
10-02	$5	1837		Institutional collection only					
10-02R	$5	18__	Remainder*	Institutional collection only					
10-04R	$10	18__	Remainder*	Institutional collection only					

*undated and unnumbered.

THE EXCHANGE BANK OF CANADA

1871 - 1883

MONTREAL, QUEBEC

BANK NUMBER 245 ***NONREDEEMABLE***

Established in Montreal in 1872, this bank first suspended payment in 1879 but later resumed business. The bank finally failed in 1883. It was badly managed and was accused of being a political bank. The managing director and some of his colleagues on the Board of Directors used funds to manipulate shares and obscure liabilities of the bank. Its notes were paid in full. Double liability was imposed on some of its shareholders and 66 & 1/2% was paid to the creditors.

245-10. ISSUE OF 1872 AND 1873

DESIGNS AND COLOURS

245-10-02b

$4 Face Design: T. Caverhill/seated "Justice" figure/M.H. Gault
Colour: Black with green tint

Back Design: Lathework, counters, bank name and beehive and flowers
Colour: Green

245-10-04b

$5 Face Design: T. Caverhill/allegorical female, machinery and train/M.H. Gault
Colour: Black with green tint

Back Design: Lathework, counters, bank name and beehive and flowers
Colour: Green

245-10-06P

$6 Face Design: T. Caverhill/paddlewheel steamship "Inland Commerce"/M.H. Gault
Colour: Black with green tint

Back Design: Lathework, counters, bank name, beehive and flowers
Colour: Green

245-10-08b

$10 Face Design: T. Caverhill/—/M.H. Gault
Colour: Black with green tint

Back Design: Lathework, counters, bank name, beehive and flowers
Colour: Green

245-10-10P
$25 Face Design: T. Caverhill/allegory of trade and transportation/M.H. Gault
Colour: Black with green tint

Back Design: Lathework, counters, bank name, beehive and flowers
Colour: Green

245-10-12P
$50 Face Design: T. Caverhill/M.H. Gault
Colour: Black with green tint

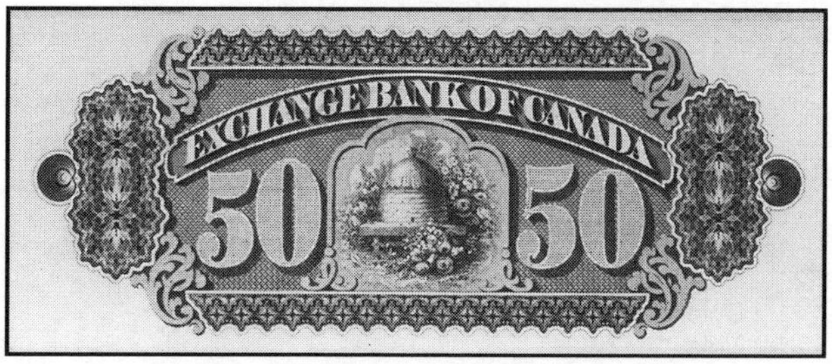

Back Design: Lathework, counters, bank name, beehive and flowers
Colour: Green

245-10-14P
$100 Face Design: T. Caverhill/woman with water jar, Niagara Falls/M.H. Gault
Colour: Black with green tint

Back Design: Lathework, counters, bank name, beehive and flowers
Colour: Green

IMPRINT

British American Bank Note Co. Montreal & Ottawa

SIGNATURES

left	**right**
mss. various	engr. M.H. Gault

ISSUE DATING

Engraved

1st Oct. 1872 — 1st November 1872
1st October 1872 — 2nd Jan. 1873
1st Novr. 1872

OVERPRINT

"A A" in blue — "HAMILTON" in blue
"AYLMER" in blue — "L" in blue
"BEDFORD" in blue — "M M" in blue (sideways)
"BRUSSELS" in blue — "PARKHILL" in blue
"C" in circle in purple — "VALLEYFIELD" in blue
"E E" in blue — "X" over "BRUSSELS" in blue
"EXETER" in blue

CIRCULATING NOTES

Cat.No.	Denom.	Date	Variety	G	VG	F	VF	EF	AU
10-02	$4	1872		375.	750.	1,200.	—	—	—
10-02a	$4	1872	letter o/p	435.	875.	1,375.	—	—	—
10-02b	$4	1872	town o/p	500.	1,000.	1,550.	—	—	—
10-04	$5	1872		375.	750.	1,200.	—	—	—
10-04a	$5	1872	letter o/p	435.	875.	1,375.	—	—	—
10-04b	$5	1872	town o/p	500.	1,000.	1,550.	—	—	—
10-06b	$6	1872	town o/p	4,000.	7,000.	—	—	—	—
10-08	$10	1872		825.	1,650.	2,200.	—	—	—
10-08a	$10	1872	letter o/p	850.	1,700.	2,300.	—	—	—
10-08b	$10	1872	town o/p	875.	1,750.	2,400.	—	—	—
10-10	$25	1872		No known issued notes					
10-12	$50	1873		No known issued notes					
10-14	$100	1873		No known issued notes					

PROOF NOTES

Cat. No.	Denom.	Date		Unc
10-02P	$4	1872	FACE PROOF	500.
10-04P	$5	1872	FACE PROOF	500.
10-06P	$6	1872	FACE PROOF	2,000.
10-08P	$10	1872	FACE PROOF	500.
10-10P	$25	1872	FACE PROOF	2,000.
10-12P	$50	1872	FACE PROOF	800.
10-14P	$100	1872	FACE PROOF	800.

THE EXCHANGE BANK OF CANADA

1860's

WINDSOR, ONTARIO

BANK NUMBER 250 — ***NONREDEEMABLE***

This "bank" never had a legal existence. The quality of printing of the notes is very low, with no engraving. Whatever purpose they may have served is not clear, since they are too poorly printed to have been successfully used to defraud.

250-10. ISSUE OF 1864

DESIGNS AND COLOURS

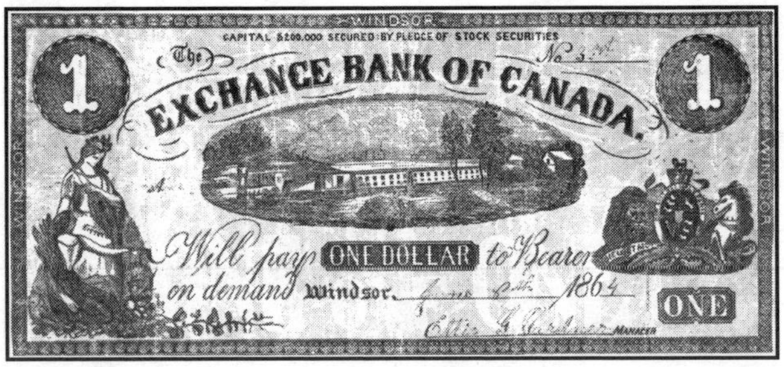

250-10-02

$1 Face Design: Britannia/early train/Arms
Colour: Black with green tint

Back Design: Plain

IMPRINT

none

SIGNATURES

right only
mss. Ettie G. Gardner

ISSUE DATING

Partially Engraved __18__:

1864: June 8th

Cat.No.	Denom.	Date	VG	F	VF	EF	Unc
10-02	$1	1864	500.	750.	—	—	—

THE EXCHANGE BANK OF TORONTO

1855 - ca.1857

TORONTO, UPPER CANADA

BANK NUMBER 255 ***NONREDEEMABLE***

Recent research by Christopher D. Ryan, unpublished at the time this catalogue went to press, shows that The Exchange Bank of Toronto commenced operations in December of 1855 as a private bank under the title of "The Banking House of R. H. Brett". In January 1856 Brett renamed his business "The Exchange Bank of Toronto", operating under the Free Banking Act, and advised that notes were to be issued shortly. However, Brett's notes were rejected by the government as not meeting the requirements of the Act. As far as is known, none of these notes entered circulation. It appears that the Bank wound-up some time in 1857 or early 1858.

255-10. DESIGNS OF 1855

DESIGNS AND COLOURS

255-10-02R

$1 Face Design: Crest/seated Indian, deer and counter/ farmer with sheaf and sickle
Colour: Black with no tint

Back Design: Plain

255-10-04R

$2 Face Design: Crest/men with cradles, cutting wheat/ ship sailing toward viewer
Colour: Black with no tint

Back Design: Plain

255-10-06R

$5 Face Design: Crest/sailing ship/woman standing with large anchor
Colour: Black with no tint

Back Design: Plain

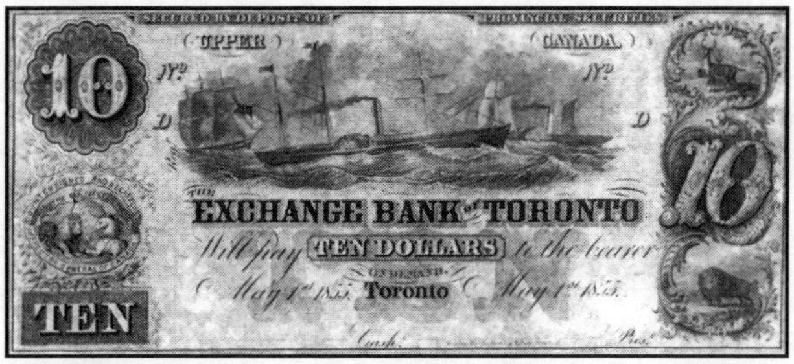

255-10-08R

$10 Face Design: Crest/steamers and sailing ships/ deer, 10 and bison
Colour: Black with no tint

Back Design: Plain

IMPRINT

Rawdon, Wright, Hatch & Edson, New-York

SIGNATURES

left	right
none	none

ISSUE DATING

Engraved

May 1st 1855

Cat.No.	Denom.	Date	Variety	VG	F	VF	EF	AU	Unc
10-02R	$1	1855	Remainder*	45.	65.	90.	150.	200.	250.
10-04R	$2	1855	Remainder*	45.	65.	90.	150.	200.	250.
10-06R	$5	1855	Remainder*	45.	65.	90.	150.	200.	250.
10-08R	$10	1855	Remainder*	45.	65.	90.	150.	200.	250.
Full Sheet	$1,2,5,10	1855	Remainder*	—	—	350.	700.	900.	—

*unsigned and unnumbered.

Note: Some $2 notes have spurious numbers and signatures, some $2 and $5 notes are numbered.

THE EXCHANGE BANK OF YARMOUTH

1867 - 1903

YARMOUTH, NOVA SCOTIA

BANK NUMBER 260 ***REDEEMABLE***

Established in 1867 in Yarmouth, Nova Scotia, this bank operated successfully but found competition with larger banks difficult. The Bank of Montreal expanded its operations in the Atlantic provinces in 1903 by absorbing The Exchange Bank of Yarmouth which had assets of $680,303.

260-10. ISSUES OF 1869 - 1902

DESIGNS AND COLOURS

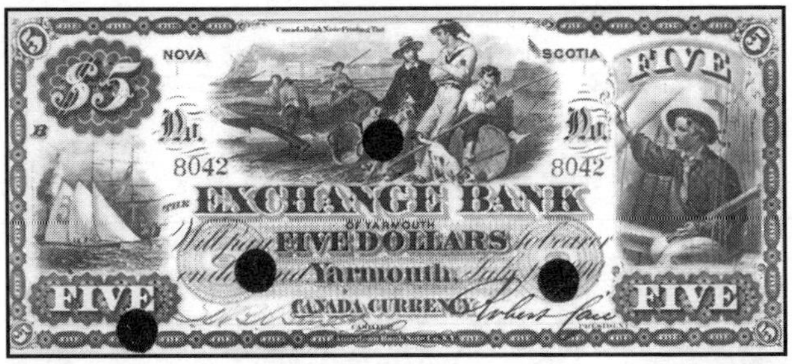

260-10-08

$5 Face Design: Sailing ships/sailor talking to man and child on shore, anchor, fisherman and small boat/ young sailor seated on ship's rail "On the look out"

Back Design: Lathework, counters and bank name

260-10-16

$10 Face Design: "Justice and commerce" figure on seashore /wharf scene, bales in foreground/shipwright chopping timbers "The ship carpenter"

Back Design: Lathework, counters and bank name

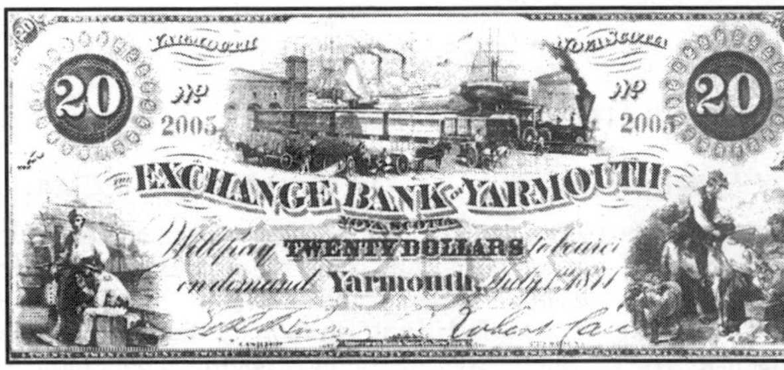

260-10-20

$20 Face Design: Two sailors on wharf "Mech's & Commerce"/ wharf scene with trains and wagons in foreground/farmer on horse drinking from trough, sheep

Back Design: Lathework, counters and bank name

1869 Face Colour: Black with orange-red tint

Back Colour: Green

1870 Face Colour: Black with green tint

Back Colour: Green

1871 Face Colour: Black with green tint

Back Colour: Green

1890 Face Colour: Black with green tint

Back Colour: Green

1900 Face Colour: Black with orange-red tint

Back Colour: Green

1902 Face Colour: Black with orange-red tint

Back Colour: Green

Orange-red tint was unstable and susceptible to fading. May appear in various shades.

IMPRINT

American Bank Note Co. N.Y.
American Bank Note Co. New York

SIGNATURES

left	right
Mss. A.S. Murray	mss. A.C. Robbins
mss. T.V.B. Bingay	mss. Robert Caie

ISSUE DATING

Engraved

Aug. 1st 1869	July 1st 1890
Aug. 1st 1870	July 1st 1900
July 1st 1871	July 1st 1902

OVERPRINT

1871: "S" in red
"CANADIAN CURRENCY" in red

1890-1902: "S" in red

CIRCULATING NOTES

Cat.No.	Denom.	Date	VG	F	VF	EF	AU
10-02	$5	1870	No known issued notes				
10-04	$5	1871	Institutional collection only				
10-06	$5	1890	Institutional collection only				
10-08	$5	1900	Institutional collection only				
10-10	$10	1870	No known issued notss				
10-12	$10	1871	No known issued notes				
10-14	$10	1890	Institutional collection only				
10-16	$10	1900	Institutional collection only				
10-18	$20	1869	No known issued notes				
10-20	$20	1871	Institutional collection only				
10-22	$20	1902	Institutional collection only				

PROOF NOTES

Cat. No.	Denom.	Date		Unc
10-18P	$20	1869	FACE PROOF	2,000.

Note: A colour trial exists with face colour: black with blue tint; back colour: blue

THE FARMER'S BANK

1840's

TORONTO, UPPER CANADA

BANK NUMBER 265 ***NONREDEEMABLE***

This bank traded on the colloquial name of the Farmers' Joint Stock Banking Company. Like the Commercial Bank (Kingston) notes, these are inscribed "For the Foreign & Domestic Exchange Company," and like those "notes", they were a fraud.

265-10. DRAFT ISSUE OF 1843

Engraved: "New York Exchange" at top

DESIGNS AND COLOURS

265-10-02

$5 (£1.5) Face Design: Plough in oval (sideways)/kneeling cherub writing on stone/woman with bow

Colour: Black with no tint

Back Design: Plain

IMPRINT

SC .N.Y. - under centre vignette

SIGNATURES

left	right
mss. illegible	mss. illegible

ISSUE DATING

Partially Engraved __18__:

1843: Aug. 3

Cat.No.	Denom.	Date	VG	F	VF	EF	Unc
10-02	$5(£1.5)	1843	Institutional collection only - one known				

THE FARMERS BANK OF CANADA

1906 - 1910

TORONTO, (ONTARIO)

BANK NUMBER 270 ***REDEEMABLE***

The Farmers Bank of Canada was established in Toronto in 1906 and failed in 1910 after suspending payments with total liabilities of about $2 million of which over $400,000 consisted of note circulation. Dishonest and incompetent management resulted in the entire loss of the paid-up capital and the deposits.

270-10. ISSUES OF 1907 and 1908

DESIGNS AND COLOURS

270-10-04

$5 Face Design: Farmer pumping water for livestock/—/—

Colour: Black with green tint

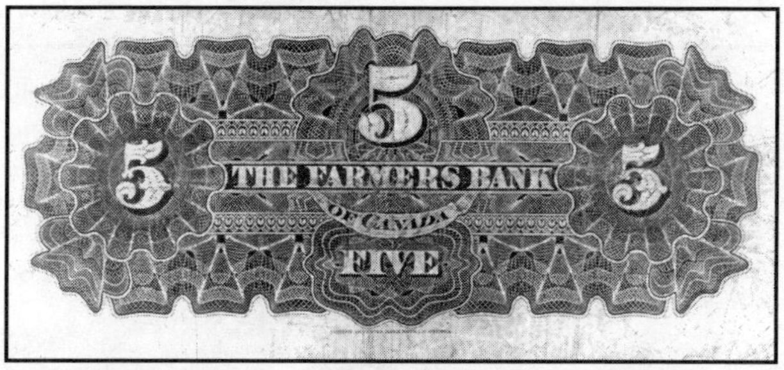

Back Design: Lathework, counters and bank name

Colour: Green

270-10-06

$10 Face Design: —/sheep grazing/—

Colour: Black with orange tint

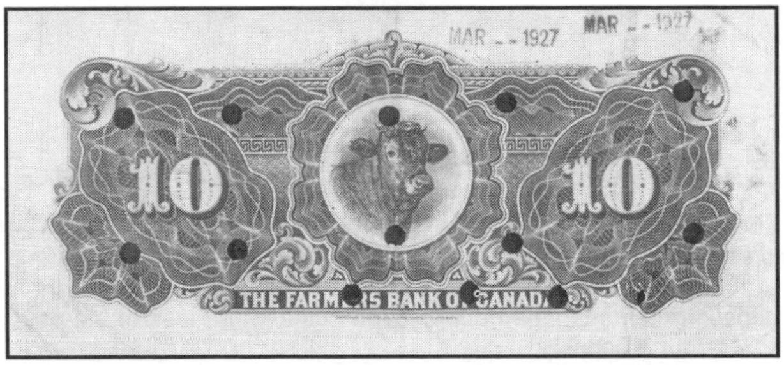

Back Design: Counter's, lathework, bank name and bull's head
Colour: Green

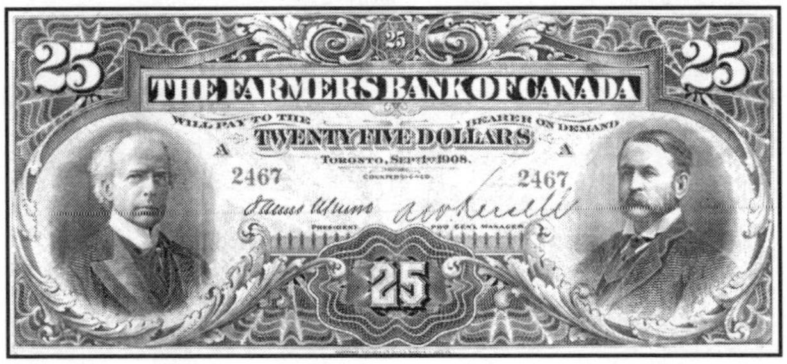

270-10-10
$25 Face Design: Sir Wilfrid Laurier/—/Premier James P. Whitney
Colour: Black with gold tint

Back Design: Lathework, counters and bank name
Colour: Gold

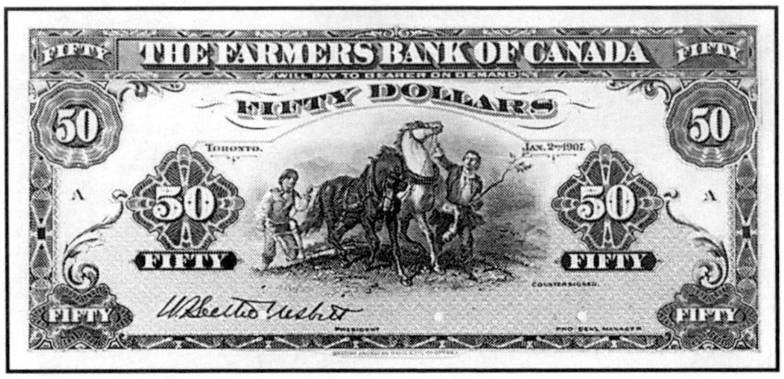

270-10-12P
$50 Face Design: —/ploughing with horses/—
Colour: Black with olive tint

Back Design: lathework, counters, bank name and woman with sickle in field
Colour: Green

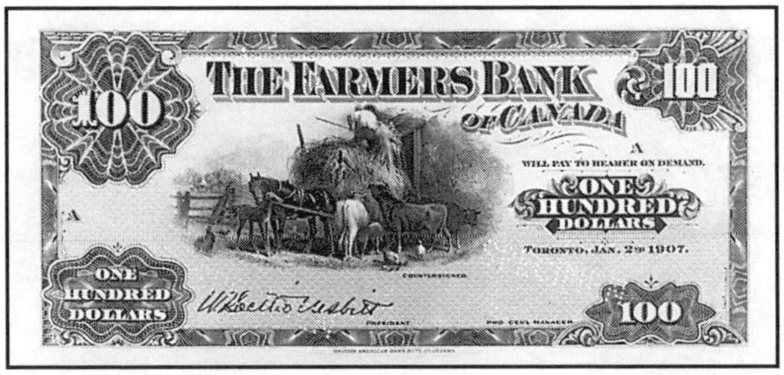

270-10-14P
$100 Face Design: —/farmer unloading hay into barn/—
Colour Black with red tint

Back Design: Lathework, counters, bank name and man and boy working at grindstone
Colour: 1. Green
: 2. Brown

IMPRINT

British American Bank Note Co. Ottawa

SIGNATURES

	left	right
1907:	engr. W. B. Nesbitt	mss. A.W. Kersell
1908:	engr. James Munro	mss. A.W. Kersell
	engr. James Munro	mss. T.H. Weir
	engr. James Munro	mss. H.A. Rinshaw

ISSUE DATING

Engraved

Jan. 2nd 1907
Sept. 1st 1908

CIRCULATING NOTES

Cat.No.	Denom.	Date	G	VG	F	VF	EF	AU
10-02	$5	1907	Institutional collection only					
10-04	$5	1908	1,250.	2,500.	3,500.	—	—	—
10-06	$10	1907	Institutional collection only					
10-08	$25	1907	No known issued notes					
10-10	$25	1908	Institutional collection only					
10-12	$50	1907	No known issued notes					
10-14	$100	1907	No known issued notes					

PROOF NOTES

Cat. No.	Denom.	Date		Unc
10-02P	$5	1907	FACE PROOF	600.
10-06P	$10	1907	FACE PROOF	600.
10-08P	$25	1907	FACE PROOF	1,500.
10-12P	$50	1907	FACE PROOF	900.
10-14P	$100	1907	FACE PROOF	1,000.

THE FARMERS' BANK OF MALDEN

1840's

MALDEN, UPPER CANADA

BANK NUMBER 275 ***NONREDEEMABLE***

275-10. **DRAPER, TOPPAN LONGACRE PRINTINGS**

DESIGNS AND COLOURS

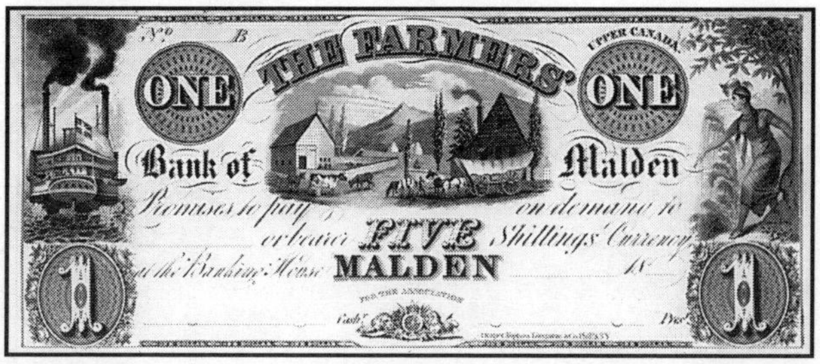

275-10-02P

$1 (5s) Face Design: Steamboat/Pioneer scene; arms below/Indian maiden
Colour: Black with no tint

Back Design: Plain

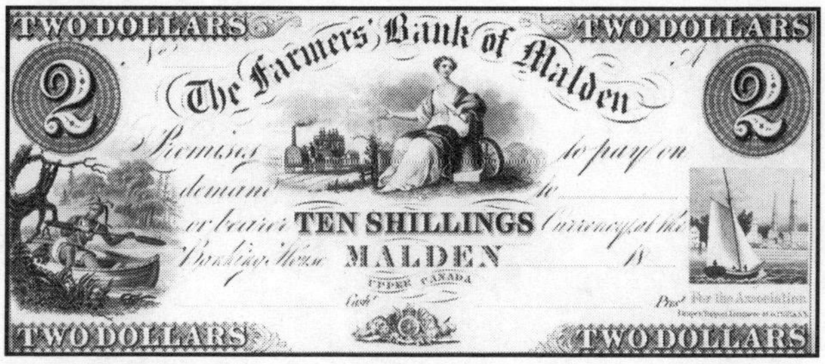

275-10-04P

$2 (10s) Face Design: Indian in canoe/seated woman and early train; small coat of arms below/sailboat and view of city (see vignette of $1 note Bank of The People, Toronto)
Colour: Black with no tint

Back Design: Plain

275-10-06P

$3 (15s) Face Design: Seated man with flag/"Commerce" figure, livestock; arms below "Commerce" figure /woman with sickle and sheaf "Agriculture"
Colour: Black with no tint

Back Design: Plain

IMPRINT
Draper, Toppan, Longacre & Co. Phila & N.Y.

SIGNATURES

	left	right
	none	none

ISSUE DATING
Partially Engraved __18__:

PROOF NOTES

Cat.No.	Denom.	Date		Unc
10-02P	$1(5s)	18__	PROOF	1,200.
10-04P	$2(10s)	18__	PROOF	1,200.
10-06P	$3(15s)	18__	PROOF	1,200.

THE FARMER'S JOINT STOCK BANKING CO.

1835 - CIRCA 1854

TORONTO, UPPER CANADA

BANK NUMBER 280 ***NONREDEEMABLE***

Established in Toronto in 1835 as a private company, it issued its own notes, even after the passage of a legislation in 1837 prohibiting note issue without legislative authority. This bank was one of the four private banks authorized to issue notes without legislative authority on an exception basis. Early in the 1840's it quietly wound up, conducting little business apart from the redemption of its circulation. In 1849 the stock was sold to unscrupulous operators who turned the business into a wildcat bank, pushing as many of its notes as possible, particularly in the United States. The notes soon fell into disrepute in Toronto and Buffalo, but the bank continued a few years more, issuing notes payable at Green Bay, Wisconsin, before finally collapsing.

280-10. ISSUE OF 1835 - 1840's

DESIGNS AND COLOURS

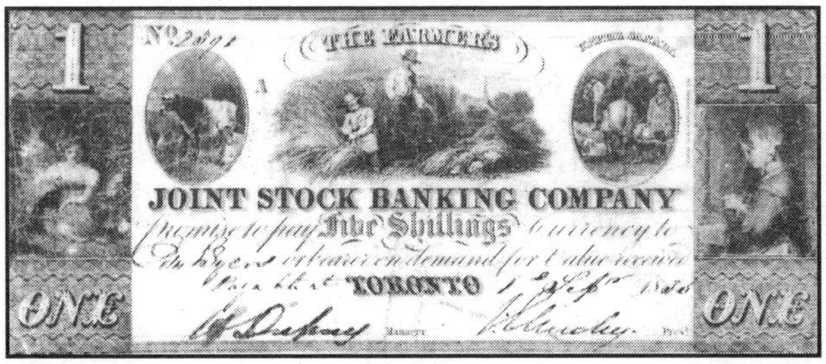

280-10-02
$1 (5s) Face Design: Seated girl in bushes/cattle/two men gathering sheaves/men and dog herding sheep/woman at window
Colour: Black with no tint
Back Design: Plain

280-10-04
$2 (10s) Face Design: Ship, cargo, fasces in oval/seated woman, haying in background/Britannia
Colour: Black with no tint
Back Design: Plain

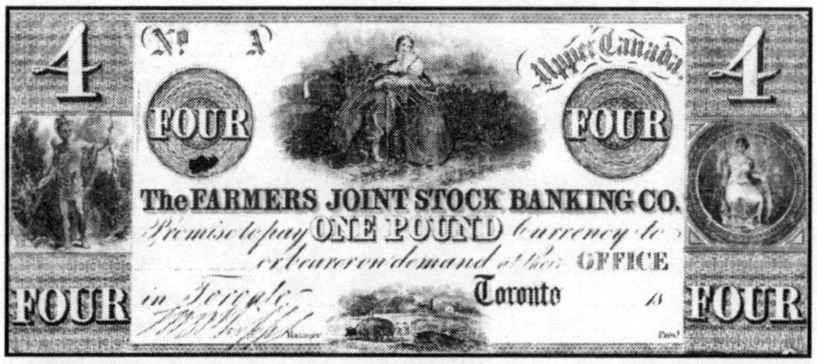

280-10-06R

$4 (£) Face Design: Indian with bow/woman with grain stalks resting with a dog; haying scene below/seated Britannia in oval
Colour: Black with no tint
Back Design: Plain

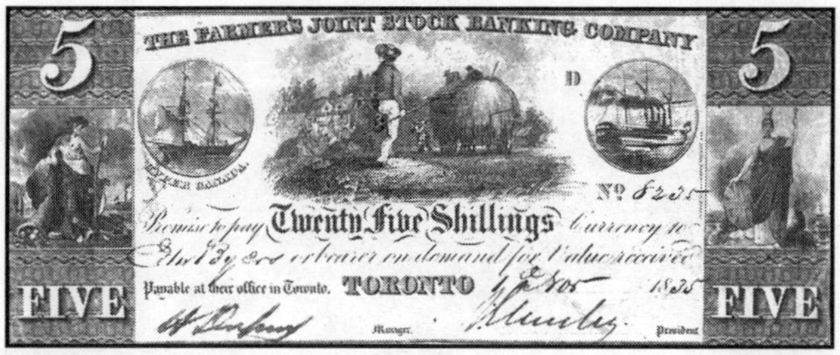

280-10-08

$5 (25s) Face Design: Allegorical female/sailing ship/haying scene steamship/Britannia
Colour: Black with no tint
Back Design: Plain

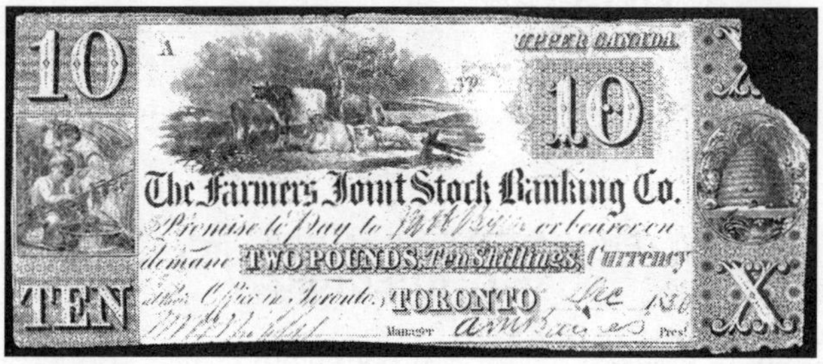

280-10-10R

$10 (£2.10) Face Design: Cherubs with grapes, grain/cattle and sheep on hilltop/beehive in oval
Colour: Black with no tint
Back Design: Plain

Photo Not Available

280-10-12P

$50 (£12.10) Face Design: Woman with flowers planting scene/man sowing/milk-maids and cows in oval/sheaf and plough
Colour: Black with no tint
Back Design: Plain

IMPRINT

New England Bank Note Co. Boston

SIGNATURES

left	right
mss. H. Dupuy	mss. J. Elmsley
mss. W. Rose	mss. J. Elmsley

ISSUE DATING

Partially Engraved __18__:

$1 1835: 1 Sep'r
$2 1837: 11th Sept.
$4 1836: 1 Feb
$5 1835: 1 Nov.
$10 1830: Dec. (spurious)

Cat.No.	Denom.	Date	G	VG	F	VF	EF	AU
10-02	$1 (5s)	1835	250.	500.	700.	—	—	—
10-04	$2 (10s)	1837	300.	600.	800.	—	—	—
10-06	$4 (£1)	1836	250.	500.	700.	—	—	—
10-06R	$4 (£1)	18__	100.	200.	250.	—	—	—
10-08	$5 (25s)	1835	300.	600.	800.	—	—	—
10-10R	$10 (£2.10)	18__	250.	500.	700.	—	—	—
10-12R	$50 (£12.10)	18__	—	—	—	—	—	500.

Note: Some notes have manuscript inscriptions "one year after date". Beware of modern reprints. A $4.4.10.50 plate was discovered in Toronto, and a few impressions were made.

280-12. ISSUE OF 1849 DENOMINATIONS IN DOLLARS AND SHILLINGS, NO PROTECTORS

DESIGNS AND COLOURS

280-12-02

$1 (5s) Face Design: Britannia/Royal Crest, griffin with key below/allegorical female
Colour: Black with no tint
Back Design: Plain

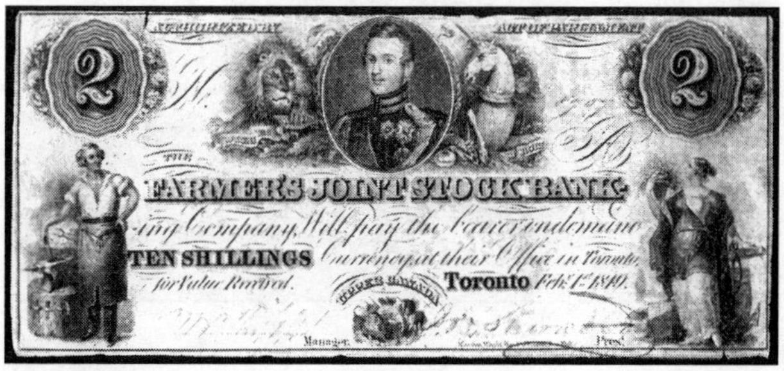

280-12-04

$2 (10s) Face Design: Blacksmith at anvil/Prince Consort on Royal Crest; lion, shield and unicorn below/woman with flowers and anchor
Colour: Black with no tint
Back Design: Plain

280-12-06

$5 (25s) Face Design: Britannia and "Justice" figure/Queen Victoria (Chalon portrait) on Royal Crest; crown and swords on cushion below/allegorical women, coins and 5

Colour: Back with no tint

Back Design: Plain

IMPRINT

Rawdon, Wright, Hatch & Edson, New York

SIGNATURES

left	**right**
mss. Wm. Phipps	mss. J.W. Sherwood

ISSUE DATING

Engraved

Feb'y 1st 1849

STAMP

"KINGSTON" in red

various letters and numbers: C, RY, Z, 7, 8.

Cat.No.	Denom.	Date	Variety	VG	F	VF	EF	AU	Unc
12-02	$1 (5s)	1849		40.	60.	90.	150.	180.	225.
12-04	$2 (10s)	1849		40.	60.	90.	150.	180.	225.
12-06	$5 (25s)	1849		35.	50.	70.	140.	160.	200.
12-06a	$5 (25s)	1849	stp KINGSTON	200.	300.	400.	500.	—	—

280-14. DENOMINATIONS IN DOLLARS ONLY

2. ENGRAVED "THE BRANCH OF" & "... Office in Green Bay Wisconsin"; NO PROTECTORS

DESIGNS AND COLOURS

280-14-02-02

$1 Face Design: Britannia/Royal Crest: griffin with key below/ allegorical female

Colour: Black with no tint

Back Design: Plain

280-14-02-04

$2 (10s) Face Design: Blacksmith at anvil/Prince Consort on Royal Crest; lion, shield and unicorn below/ woman with flowers and anchor

Colour: Black with no tint

Back Design: Plain

280-14-02-06

$5 (25s) Face Design: Britannia and "Justice" figure/Queen Victoria (Chalon portrait) on Royal Crest; crown on swords below/allegorical women, coins and 5

Colour: Black with no tint

Back Design: Plain

Cat.No.	Denom.	Date	VG	F	VF	EF	AU	Unc
14-02-02	$1	1849	250.	350.	525.	650.	800.	—
14-02-04	$2	1849	250.	350.	525.	650.	800.	—
14-02-06	$5	1849	250.	350.	525.	650.	800.	—

4. ENGRAVED "at their Office in"; RED PROTECTORS

DESIGNS AND COLOURS

See previous listing. 280-14-04-02

280-14-04-02

280-14-04-04

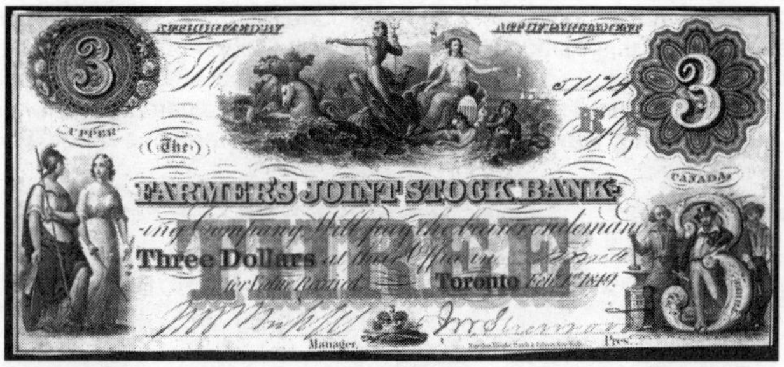

280-14-04-06

$3 (15s) Face Design: Britannia and “Justice” figure/ Neptune group, crown on swords below/three men and ornate 3

Colour: Black with no tint

Back Design: Plain

280-14-04-08

$5 (25s) Face Design: Britannia and “Justice” figure/Queen Victoria (Chalon portrait) on Royal Crest; crown and swords on cushion below/allegorical women, coins and 5

Colour: Black with no tint

Back Design: Plain

PROTECTOR

Red “word” on face and in mirror image on back.

STAMP

Various letters and numbers: C,J,RY, X, 0.

Cat.No.	Denom.	Date	Variety	VG	F	VF	EF	AU	Unc
14-04-02	$1	1849	Toronto, red ptr.	30.	40.	70.	140.	160.	200.
14-04-04	$2	1849	Toronto, red ptr.	30.	40.	70.	140.	160.	200.
14-04-06	$3	1849	Toronto, red ptr.	60.	90.	125.	190.	220.	275.
14-04-08	$5	1849	Toronto, red ptr.	30.	40.	70.	140.	160.	200.

THE FARMERS J.S. BANKING CO.

1830's

TORONTO, UPPER CANADA

BANK NUMBER 285 ***NONREDEEMABLE***

The Farmers J.S. Banking Co., a "spurious bank", evidently traded on the name of The Farmer's Joint Stock Banking Co.

285-10. CASILEAR, DURAND, BURTON & EDMONDS DESIGN

DESIGNS AND COLOURS

285-10-02R

$10 Face Design: Charles James Fox/seated female and plaque depicting lion; crown below/farm girl with wheat

Colour: Black with no tint

Back Design: Plain

IMPRINT

Casilear, Durand, Burton & Edmonds, N. York

SIGNATURES

left	**right**
none	none
Wm. Phipps (forged)	J.W. Sherwood (forged)

ISSUE DATING

Partially Engraved __18__:

$10 1849: Feb 1

Note: Denomination also written in French and German.
For the possible origin of the design for this note, see $10 note of the Peoples Bank of Toronto.

Cat.No.	Denom.	Date	Variety	VG	F	VF	EF	AU	Unc
10-02R	$10	18__	Remainder*	—	—	—	120.	140.	175.
10-02	$10	1849					Institutional collection only		

*unsigned, undated and unnumbered.

THE FARMERS BANK OF RUSTICO

1862 - 1894

RUSTICO, PROVINCE OF PRINCE EDWARD ISLAND

BANK NUMBER 290 ***NONREDEEMABLE***

This bank was established in 1862 and was chartered by the Colonial Legislature of P.E.I. in 1863. It was by far the smallest bank, measured by share capital, ever to operate in Canada. By The Bank Act of 1871, Canada made a decision to do away with small, local branchless banks and adopt a policy of nationwide banking. Some banks were forced to sell out, but the Federal government found it difficult to put The Farmers Bank of Rustico out of business. It survived on frugality and devotion. After extreme pressures and delay, the bank managed to renew its charter in 1883 and almost unbelievably, again on June 24, 1891. But the pressure was on to put this bank out of existence. The terms of this last charter were so harsh and unrealistic that they rendered effective liquidation almost impossible. The bank was authorized to amalgamate with or sell its property to any loan company but wound up its operations about 1894.

290-10. DENOMINATIONS IN DOLLARS/STERLING 1864

DESIGNS AND COLOURS

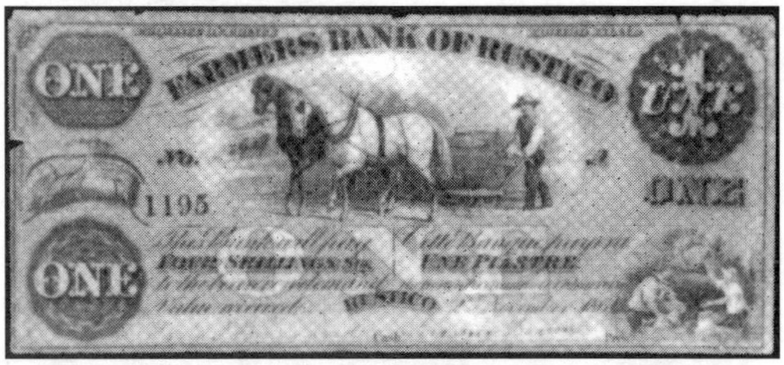

290-12-02

$1 (4s) Face Design: Sheaf of wheat, scythes/ploughing with team of horses/men shearing sheep

Colour: Black with overall green tint

Back Design: Plain

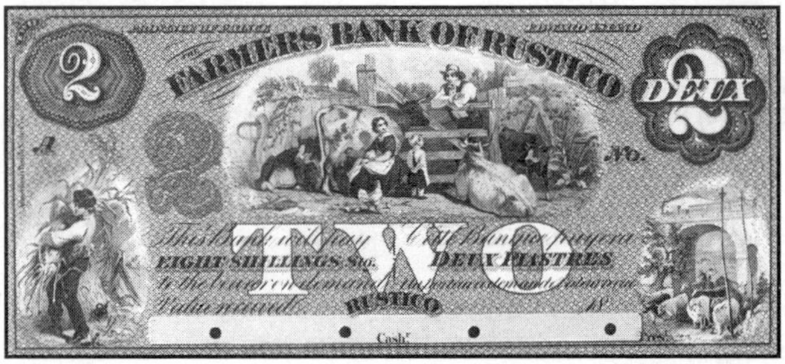

290-10-04P

$2 (8s) Face Design: Boy carrying corn stocks "Corn cob Jr."/ pastoral scene: people and animals beside fence/cattle being driven under a bridge "The Drove"

Colour: Black with overall green tint

Back Design Plain

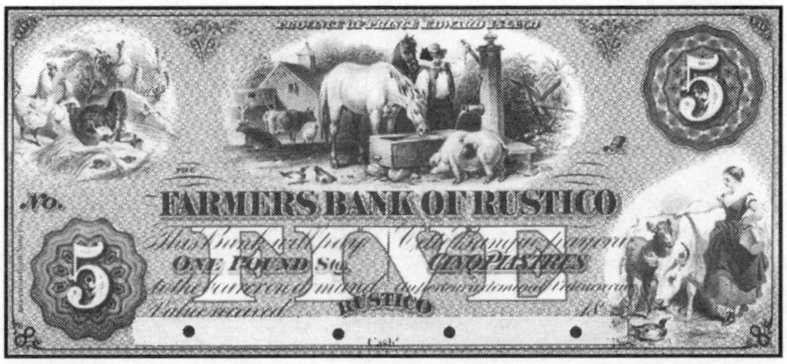

290-10-06P

$5 (£1) Face Design: Hens and chickens/farmer pumping water for livestock/milkmaid, cow, calf and duck

Colour: Black with overall green tint

Back Design: Plain

IMPRINT

American Bank Note Co.

SIGNATURES

left	right
mss. Marin J. Blanchard	mss. Jerome Doiron

ISSUE DATING

Engraved

2nd November 1864

CIRCULATING NOTES

Cat.No.	Denom.	Date	G	VG	F	VF	EF	AU
10-02	$1 (4s)	1864	Institutional collection only					
10-04	$2 (8s)	18__	No known issued notes					
10-06	$5 (£1)	18__	No known issued notes					

PROOF NOTES

Cat. No.	Denom.	Date		Unc
10-02P	$1 (4s)	18__	PROOF	1,200.
10-04P	$2 (8s)	18__	PROOF	1,200.
10-06P	$5 (£1)	18__	PROOF	1,200.

290-12. DENOMINATIONS IN DOLLARS ONLY 1872

DESIGNS AND COLOURS

See previous listings.

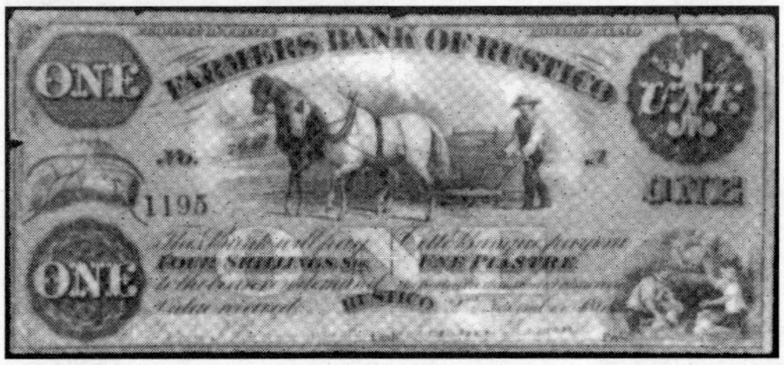

290-12-02

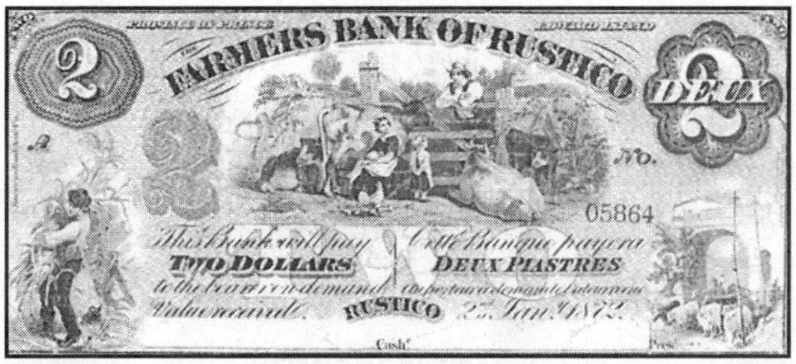

290-12-04

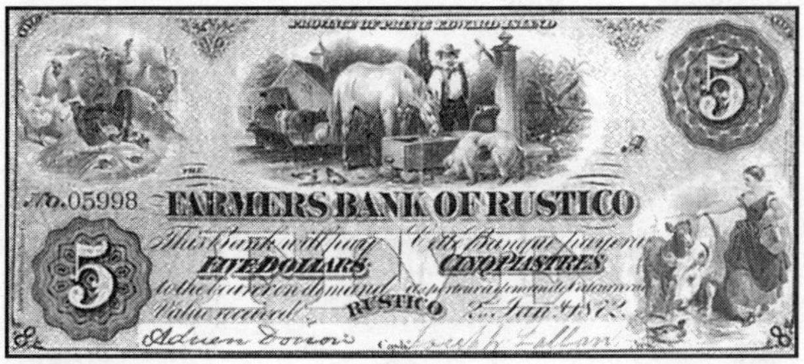

290-12-06

IMPRINT

American Bank Note Co.

British American Bank Note Co. Montreal & Ottawa

SIGNATURES

left	right
mss. Marin J. Blanchard	mss. Jerome Doiron
mss. Adrien Doiron	mss. Joseph Gallant

ISSUE DATING

Engraved

2nd Jany 1872

Notes are issued with blue or red (rare) sheet numbers.

Cat.No.	Denom.	Date	Variety	G	VG	F	VF	EF	AU
12-01	$1	1872	red sheet #	1,150.	2,300.	—	—	—	—
12-02	$1	1872	blue sheet #	1,000.	2,000.	2,500.	3,500.	—	—
12-03	$2	1872	red sheet #	—	3,100.	—	—	—	—
12-04	$2	1872	blue sheet #	1,350.	2,700.	3,300.	4,500.	—	—
12-06	$5	1872	blue sheet #	2,000.	4,000.	7,000.	10,000.	—	—
12-06R	$5	1872*	blue sheet #	—	—	4,500.	—	—	—

* Unsigned remainder

THE FARMERS BANK OF ST. JOHNS

1837 - 1838

ST. JOHNS, LOWER CANADA

BANK NUMBER 295 ***NONREDEEMABLE***

This appears to be yet another "phantom bank" which attempted to take advantage of the ecenomic and political chaos of 1837 - 1839 in order to circulate its notes, with no intention of redeeming them.

295-10. DRAFT ISSUE 1837

Engraved: "To Messrs Brooks, Gridley & Co."

DESIGNS AND COLOURS

295-10-02

$1 Face Design: Britannia/train; farm tools below/ sheaf of wheat in oval
Colour: Black with no tint

Back Design: Plain

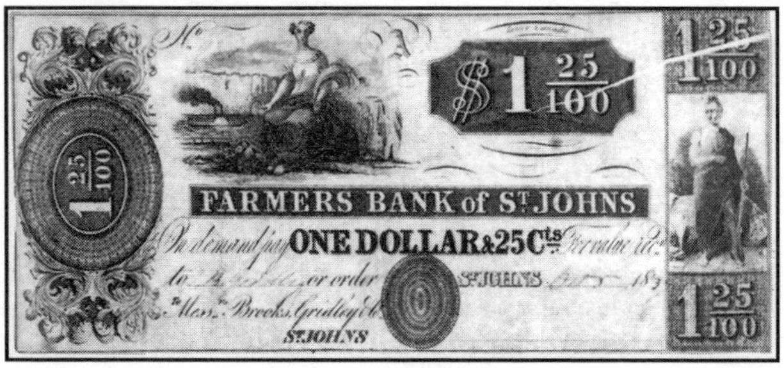

295-10-04

$1.25 Face Design: —/seated "Agriculture" figure, steamboat in background/standing Indian with rifle
Colour: Black with no tint

Back Design: Plain

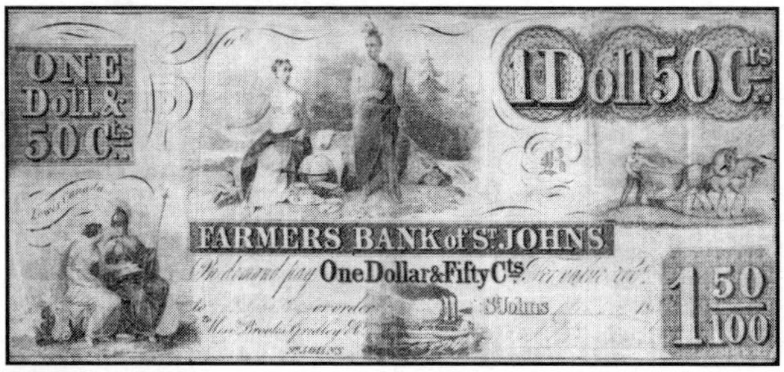

295-10-06

$1.50 Face Design: Two seated allegorical figures/seated women with globe, standing Indian; paddlewheel steamboat below/farmer ploughing with horses
Colour: Black with no tint

Back Design: Plain

295-10-08

$2 Face Design: Mercury and sailing ship/cherubs sculpting; dog below/Phoenix bird
Colour: Black with no tint

Back Design: Plain

IMPRINT

None

SIGNATURES

left	right
none	mss. J.B. Gridley
none	mss. Cossins

ISSUE DATING

Engraved

$1: Dec. 4, 1837; Dec. 5, 1837
$1.25: Dec. 5, 1837
$1.50: Dec. 5, 1837
$2: Dec. 4, 1837

Cat.No.	Denom.	Date	G	VG	F	VF	EF	AU
10-02	$1	1837	250.	500.	650.	900.	—	—
10-04	$1.25	1837	500.	1,000.	1,300.	1,800.	—	—
10-06	$1.50	1837	500.	1,000.	1,300.	1,800.	2,400.	—
10-08	$2	1837	250.	500.	650.	900.	—	—

295-12. NOTE ISSUE 1837 - 1838

DESIGNS AND COLOURS

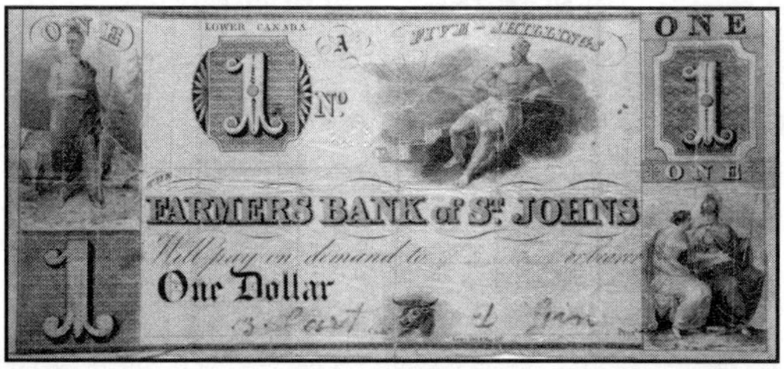

295-12-01R

$1 Face Design: Native standing with rifle/Archimedes lifting the world, bulls head below/seated Commerce and Britannia figures
Colour: Black with no tint

Back design: Plain

295-12-02R

$3 Face Design: Indian woman standing with bow & arrow/ male seated, with papers; building in background/Indian seated with plaque
Colour: Black with no tint

Back Design: Plain

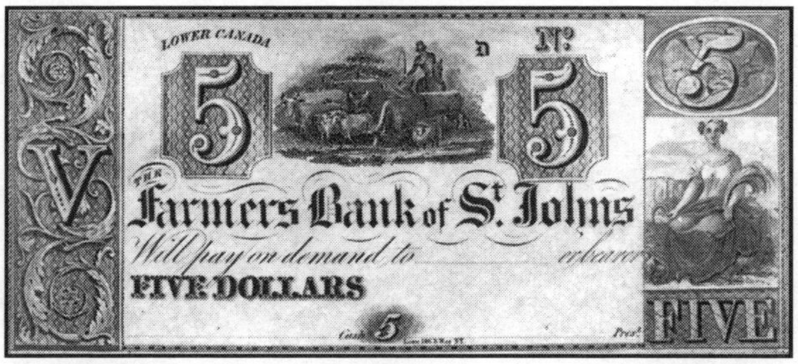

295-12-04R

$5 Face Design: —/farmer with cattle and sheep/ seated "Agriculture" figure

Colour: Black with no tint

Back Design: Plain

295-12-06R

$10 Face Design: —/farmer ploughing with horses/ seated allegorical male

Colour: Black with no tint

Back Design: Plain

IMPRINT

Lowe 146 B. Way N.Y.

SIGNATURES

left	right
John T. Rice	J. B. Chapman
John B. Gridley	G. W. Collins

ISSUE DATING

No portion of the date is engraved

$3: October 15, 1837
$5: May 21, 1838
$10: December 1st, 1837

CIRCULATING NOTES

Cat.No.	Denom.	Date	Variety	G	VG	F	VF	EF	AU
12-01R	$1	18__	Remainder	100.	200.	250.	350.	600.	—
12-02	$3	1837		Institutional collection only					
12-02R	$3	18__	Remainder*	100.	200.	250.	350.	600.	—
12-04	$5	1838		250.	500.	—	—	—	—
12-04R	$5	18__	Remainder*	100.	200.	250.	350.	600.	—
12-06	$10	1837		Institutional collection only					
12-06R	$10	18__	Remainder*	100.	200.	250.	350.	600.	—

*unsigned, undated and unnumbered, some notes with spurious signatures.

PROOF NOTES

Cat. No.	Denom.	Date		Unc
12-04P	$5	18__	PROOF	500.

THE FEDERAL BANK OF CANADA

1874 - 1888

TORONTO, PROVINCE OF ONTARIO

BANK NUMBER 300 ***NONREDEEMABLE***

This bank was originally chartered in 1872 as The Superior Bank, but it did not operate under this name. It was chartered again in 1874 under The Federal Bank of Canada with an ambitious and enterprising management. The bank's business went well until 1884 when it suffered losses in lumber deals and other weak transactions. Other banks came to its aid but to no avail. In 1885, by an Act of Parliament, its capital was reduced and $1 million was wiped out. In 1887 the bank suffered serious deposit withdrawals and note redemptions. To avoid panic, other banks again came to the rescue and advanced $2.7 million out of which all liabilities were paid off including its outstanding circulation. Assets were sufficient to wind up operations without loss.

300-10. **ISSUES OF 1874 - 1882**

DESIGNS AND COLOURS

300-10-02P

$4 Face Design: H.S. Strathy/cherubs and ornate 4/ S. Nordheimer

Colour: Black with green tint

Back Design: Lathework, counters and bank name

Colour: Green

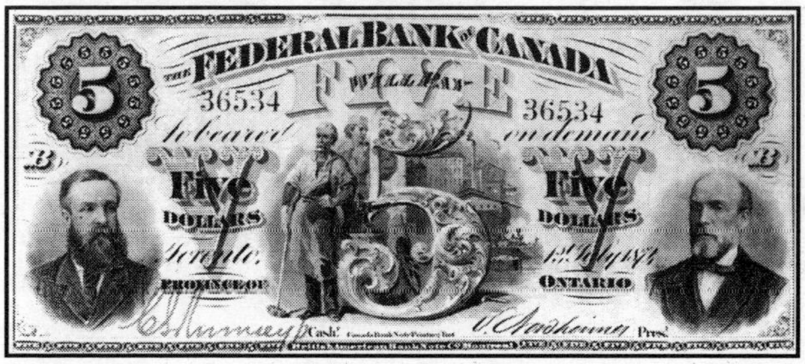

300-10-04

$5 Face Design: H.S. Strathy/workmen, ornate 5 and factories/S. Nordheimer

Colour: Black with green tint

Back Design: Lathework, counters and bank name
Colour: Green

300-10-06
$10 Face Design: H.S. Strathy/two allegorical women and ornate X/S. Nordheimer
Colour: Black with green tint

Back Design: Lathework, counters and bank name
Colour: Green

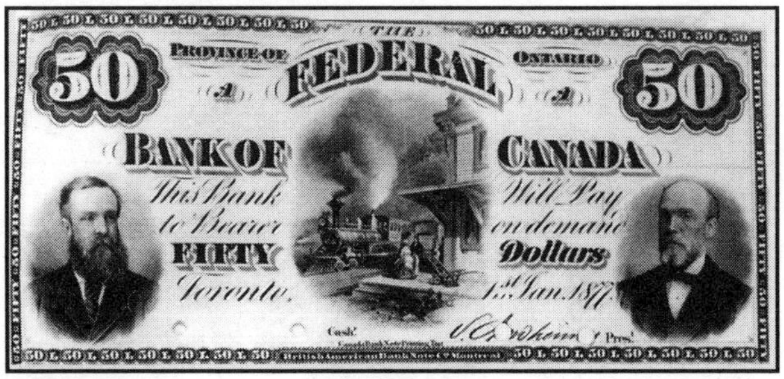

300-10-10P
$50 Face Design: H.S. Strathy/train at station/S. Nordheimer
Colour: Black with green tint

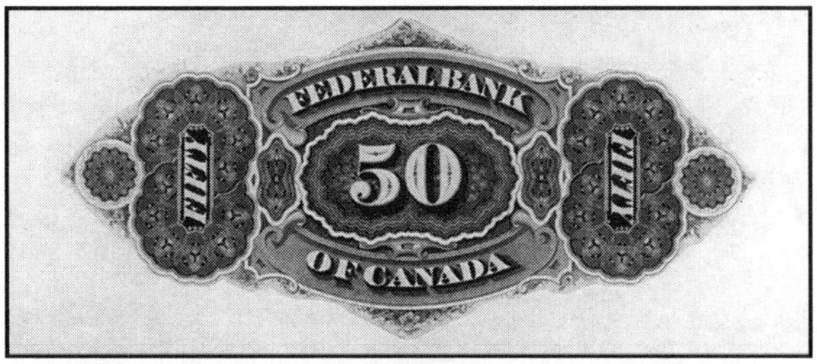

Back Design: Lathework, counters and bank name
Colour: Green

300-10-12P
$100 Face Design: H.S. Strathy/Canadian Coat of Arms/S. Nordheimer
Colour: Black with green tint

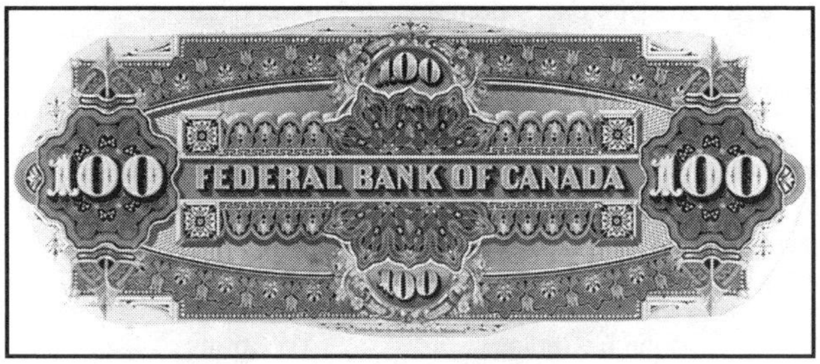

Back Design: Lathework, counters and bank name
Colour: Green

IMPRINT

British American Bank Note Co. Montreal

SIGNATURES

left	right
mss. various	engr. S. Nordheimer

ISSUE DATING

Engraved

1st July, 1874
1st Jan. 1877
Septr 1st, 1882

CIRCULATING NOTES

Cat.No.	Denom.	Date	G	VG	F	VF	EF	AU
10-02	$4	1874	250.	500.	750.	—	—	—
10-04	$5	1874	150.	300.	450.	750.	1,000.	—
10-06	$10	1874	450.	900.	1,250.	—	—	—
10-08	$10	1877	Institutional collection only					
10-10	$50	1877	No known issued notes					
10-12	$100	1882	No known issued notes					

PROOF NOTES

Cat. No.	Denom.	Date		Unc
10-02P	$4	1874	FACE PROOF	400.
10-04P	$5	1874	FACE PROOF	400.
10-10P	$50	1877	FACE PROOF	700.
10-12P	$100	1882	FACE PROOF	800.

300-12. ISSUE OF 1884

DESIGNS AND COLOURS

300-12-02P

$5 Face Design: H. S. Strathy/workmen, ornate 5 and factories/S. Nordheimer
Colour: Black with green tint

Back Design: Lathework, counters and bank name
Colour: Green

300-12-04P

$10 Face Design: H. S. Strathy/two allegorical women and ornate X/S. Nordheimer
Colour: Black with green tint

Back Design: Lathework, counters and bank name
Colour: Green

IMPRINT

British American Bank Note Co. Montreal

SIGNATURES

left	**right**
mss. various	engr. S. Nordheimer

ISSUE DATING

Engraved

1st Jan. 1884

PROOF NOTES

Cat.No.	Denom.	Date		Unc
12-02P	$5	1884	FACE PROOF	700.
12-04P	$10	1884	FACE PROOF	700.

THE BANK OF FREDERICTON

1836 - 1839

FREDERICTON, NEW BRUNSWICK

BANK NUMBER 305 ***NONREDEEMABLE***

On September 19, 1836, at a meeting of interested citizens, several resolutions were passed founding The Bank of Fredericton. In 1837 a charter was applied for through the Provincial Legislature, but it was never granted. On January 22, 1839 the shareholders of the bank voted to merge with The Commercial Bank of New Brunswick

305-10. NEW ENGLAND BANK NOTE CO. PRINTINGS 1837 - 1838

DESIGNS AND COLOURS

305-10-02

1837 5s Face Design: Girl seated on ground/steamboat and sailboats/seated Indian
Colour: Black with no tint

Back Design: Lathework and bank name
Colour: Blue

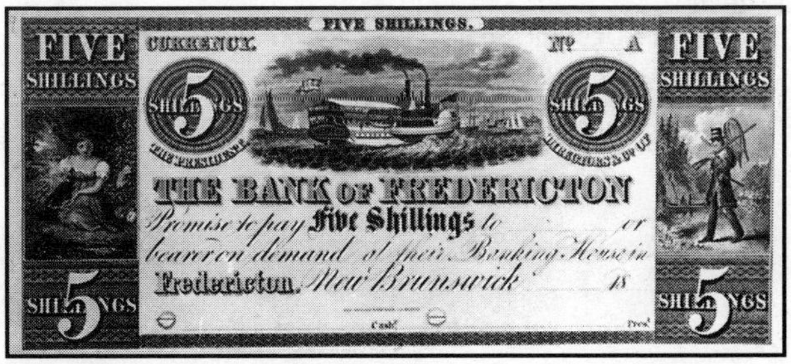

305-10-04P

1838 5s Face Design: Girl seated on ground/ steamboat and sailboats/standing hunter
Colour: Black with no tint

Back Design: Lathework and bank name
Colour: Blue

305-10-06P

10s Face Design: Man with hammer/ships at sea lion and shield in oval

Colour: Black with no tint

Back Design: Plain

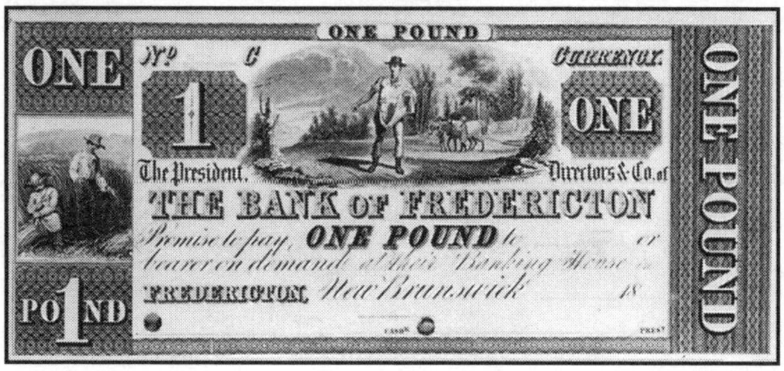

305-10-08P

£1 Face Design: Two men harvesting grain/man sowing seeds, team of horses in background/—

Colour: Black with no tint

Back Design: Plain

305-10-10P

£5 Face Design: Seated "Justice" figure/farmer, man on horseback, livestock/—

Colour: Black with no tint

Back Design: Plain

IMPRINT

left	right
mss. illegible	mss. Asa Coy

ISSUE DATING

Partially Engraved __18__:

1837: 8th May
1838: 6th March

CIRCULATING NOTES

Cat.No.	Denom.	Date	Variety	G	VG	F	VF	EF	AU
10-02	5s	1837	Indian r.	4,000.	6,000.	—	—	—	—
10-04	5s	1838	Hunter r.	4,000.	6,000.	—	—	—	—
10-06	10s	18__		No known issued notes					
10-08	£1	18__		No known issued notes					
10-10	£5	18__		No known issued notes					

PROOF NOTES

Cat. No.	Denom.	Date	Variety		Unc
10-02P	5s	18__	Indian r.	PROOF	900.
10-04P	5s	18__	Hunter r.	PROOF	900.
10-06P	10s	18__		PROOF	900.
10-08P	£1	18__		PROOF	900.
10-10P	£5	18__		PROOF	900.

THE FREE HOLDERS BANK OF THE MIDLAND DISTRICT

1837

BATH, UPPER CANADA

BANK NUMBER 310 ***NONREDEEMABLE***

This joint stock banking company was started shortly before the financial panic of 1837. Less than a month after starting up, the Legislature of Upper Canada passed a law prohibiting the formation of any further banks of this type. Therefore, before it could open for business, the firm was forced to wind up its affairs.

310-10. RAWDON, WRIGHT & HATCH PRINTINGS

DESIGNS AND COLOURS

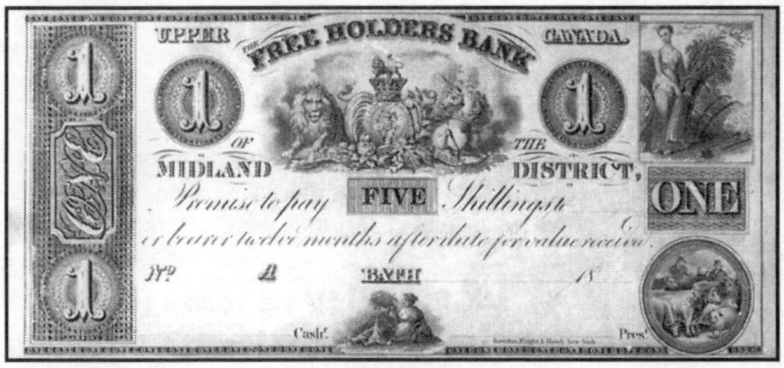

310-10-02R

$1 (5s) Face Design: —/Royal Crest; reclining “agriculture” figure below/female with sheaf; farmers and livestock

Colour: Black with no tint

Back Design: Plain

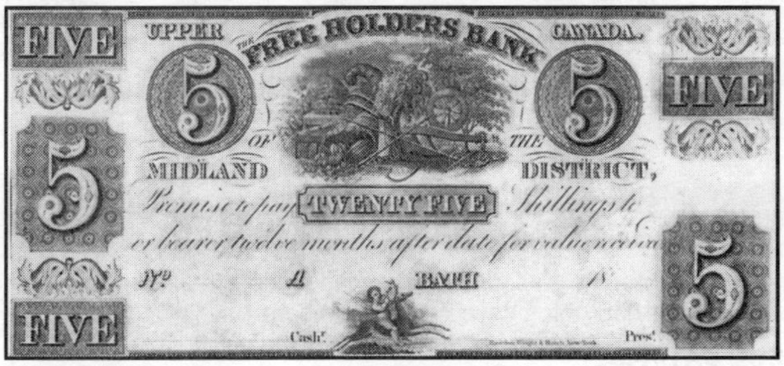

310-10-04R

$5 (25s) Face Design: —/beehive, cornucopia, sheaf, spinning wheel; child riding deer below/—

Colour: Black with no tint

Back Design: Plain

IMPRINT

Rawdon, Wright & Hatch New-York

SIGNATURES

left	right
none	none

ISSUE DATING

Partially Engraved __18__:

Cat.No.	Denom.	Date	Variety	VG	F	VF	EF	AU	Unc
10-02R	$1 (5s)	18__	Remainder*	500.	600.	800.	1,000.	1,200.	—
10-04R	$5 (25s)	18__	Remainder*	500.	600.	800.	1,000.	1,200.	—

Note I: *Unsigned, undated and unnumbered.

2: Notes were payable “Twelve months after date”.

GODERICH BANK

1834

GODERICH, UPPER CANADA

BANK NUMBER 315 ***NONREDEEMABLE***

The status of this bank has never been authoritatively established. It has been contended the bank was a legitimate private bank.

315-10. ISSUE OF 1834

DESIGNS AND COLOURS

Photo Not Available

315-10-02

$1 (5s) Face Design: Unknown

Colour: Black with no tint

Back Design: Plain

315-10-04

$2 (10s) Face Design: Lion/seated Mercury, ships in background/—

Colour: Black with no tint

Back Design: Plain

IMPRINT

C.P. Harrison Sct N. York

SIGNATURES

left	right
none	mss. Edw. C. Taylor

ISSUE DATING

Partially Engraved __18__:

1834: 12 Sept.

Cat.No.	Denom.	Date	G	VG	F	VF	EF	AU
10-02	$1(5s)	1834	600.	1,200.	1,600.	—	—	—
10-04	$2(10s)	1834	600.	1,200.	1,600.	—	—	—

THE GORE BANK

1835 - 1870

HAMILTON, U.C. (UPPER CANADA)

BANK NUMBER 320 ***REDEEMABLE***

Established in Hamilton, Upper Canada in 1835, this bank's charter, unlike any of those passed in Upper or Lower Canada, prohibited any incorporated company from holding shares of the bank and imposed double liability on its shareholders. The bank operated successfully, but tied up its funds unwisely in real estate and was hard-hit by withdrawals of deposits when its larger rivals failed. Following the collapse of the land boom in the late 1850's and the subsequent depression, the bank was absorbed by The Canadian Bank of Commerce in 1870, at about 57% on its nominal capital, after its shareholders had already effected a 40% reduction in the value of their shares.

320-10. NEW ENGLAND BANK NOTE CO. PRINTINGS 1836 - 1856

DESIGNS AND COLOURS

320-10-04-06

$1 Face Design: —/Wentworth County Court House/—
Colour: Black with no tint

Back Design: Plain

320-10-04-10

$2 Face Design: —/lion, two seated women, unicorn/—
Colour: Black with no tint

Back Design: Plain

320-10-02-06

$4 Face Design: —/Royal Crest/—
Colour: Black with no tint

Back Design: Plain

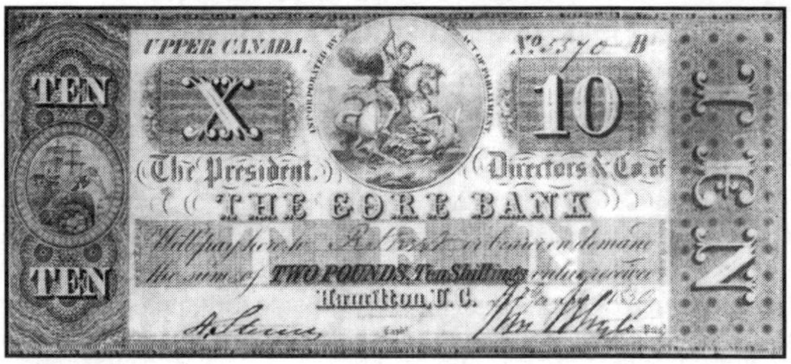

320-10-02-08

$10 Face Design: Ship, fasces and produce in oval /St. George slaying the dragon/—
Colour: Black with no tint

Back Design: Plain

IMPRINT

New England Bank Note Co. Boston

SIGNATURES

left	right
mss. A. Steven	mss. J. M. Whyte
mss. A. Steven	mss. Colin C. Ferrie
mss. Wm. G. Crawford	mss. A. Steven
mss. W. G. Cassels	mss. Robt. Park p.

2. PARTIALLY ENGRAVED DATE 1836 - 1850 PAYEE'S NAME IS MANUSCRIPT

ISSUE DATING

Partially Engraved __18__:

$1 1840: 6 Feb. **$4 1836:** Nov. 7
1849: 1 Nov. **1839:** July
1850: 1 Mar. **1850:** 1 Mar.
$2 1845: Dec. 9 **$10 1836:** Nov. 16
1839: Jan. 3

Cat.No.	Denom.	Date	G	VG	F	VF	EF	AU
10-02-02	$1	1840 - 1850	500.	900.	1,400.	—	—	—
10-02-04	$2	1845	700.	1,100.	1,700.	—	—	—
10-02-06	$4	1836 - 1850	600.	1,000.	1,600.	—	—	—
10-02-08	$10	1836 - 1839	800.	1,250.	2,000.	—	—	—

4. FULLY ENGRAVED DATE 1850 - 1856 PAYEE'S NAME IS ENGRAVED

All 1850 and some 1852 notes have manuscript sheet numbers; some 1852 and all 1856 notes have printed numbers.

ISSUE DATING

Engraved

2nd Sept. 1850
2nd Septr. 1852
2nd June, 1856

Almost all $4 notes of 1852 are extremely deceptive counterfeits. They can be identified by a doubling of the letter I in QUI in the Royal Crest and by the 52 of date 1852 being slightly higher than the 18. All counterfeits have check letter A.

Cat.No.	Denom.	Date		G	VG	F	VF	EF	AU
10-04-02	$1	1850		300.	600.	1,000.	1,300.	—	—
10-04-06	$1	1856		300.	600.	1,000.	1,300.	—	—
10-04-08	$2	1850		400.	800.	1,200.	1,600.	—	—
10-04-10	$2	1852		400.	800.	1,200.	1,600.	—	—
10-04-12	$2	1856		400.	800.	1,200.	1,600.	—	—
10-04-16	$4	1852		400.	800.	1,200.	1,600.	—	—
10-04-16C	$4	1852	Counterfeit	40.	80.	125.	175.	—	—
10-04-22	$10	1852		500.	1,000.	1,600.	2,200.	—	—

THE GORE BANK OF HAMILTON

ca. 1837

HAMILTON, UPPER CANADA

BANK NUMBER 325 ***NONREDEEMABLE***

This is a "spurious bank", evidently intended to trade on the name of The Gore Bank. The notes are crudely engraved, and printed on low quality paper. The parties behind this particular project appear to have been unsuccessful in circulating their productions, as only remainder notes are generally encountered. The $10 note is similar to the equally spurious Farmers' J.S. Banking Co. $10 note, and it is believed that all of the notes of these two "banks" were printed from the same plate.

325-10. CASILEAR, DURAND, BURTON AND EDMONDS PRINTINGS

DESIGNS AND COLOURS

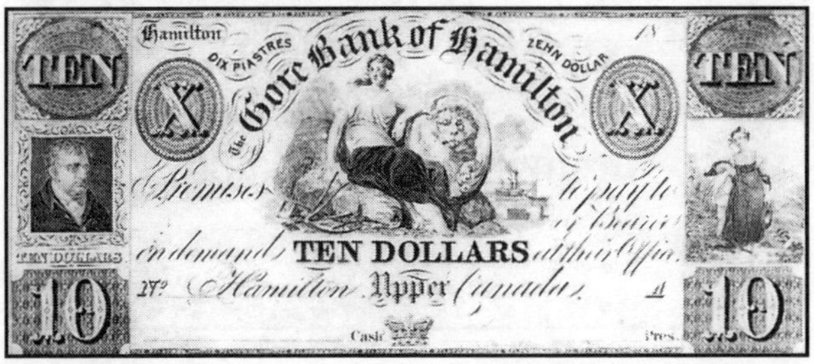

325-10-02R

$10 Face Design: James Fox/seated female with plaque depicting lion; crown below/farm girl with wheat

Colour: Black with no tint

Back Design: Plain

325-10-04R

$20 Face Design: Female with spear/King William IV farm implements below/cattle

Colour: Black with no tint

Back Design: Plain

325-10-06R

$50 Face Design: Allegorical female/King William IV on Royal Arms; head of a deer below/allegorical female

Colour: Black with no tint

Back Design: Plain

IMPRINT

Casilear, Durand, Burton and Edmonds, N. York

SIGNATURES

left	**right**
none	none

ISSUE DATING

Partially Engraved __18__:

Cat.No.	Denom.	Date	Variety	VG	F	VF	EF	AU	Unc
10-02R	$10	18__	Remainder*	—	60.	85.	150.	175.	—
10-04R	$20	18__	Remainder*	—	60.	85.	150.	175.	—
10-06R	$50	18__	Remainder*	—	60.	85.	150.	175.	—

*unsigned, undated and unnumbered.

Note: Denominations are also printed in French and German.
Some notes with spurious dates, sheet numbers and signatures.

THE GRENVILLE COUNTY BANK

1856

PRESCOTT, CANADA WEST

BANK NUMBER 330 ***NONREDEEMABLE***

Bank notes were ordered by W.D. Dickinson and S. Stanton of Prescott on Nov. 4, 1856. The plate has survived, and the $1 portion was used in the production of the Interpam Souvenir Sheet (1981). It was intended that the bank issue notes under the Free Banking Act, secured by the deposit of provincial securities. A remainder sheet, possibly sent to the bank organizers as a sample, was recently discovered, and cut into individual notes. All four notes have some discolouration at the centre.

330.10. WELLSTOOD, HAY & WHITING PRINTINGS

DESIGNS AND COLOURS

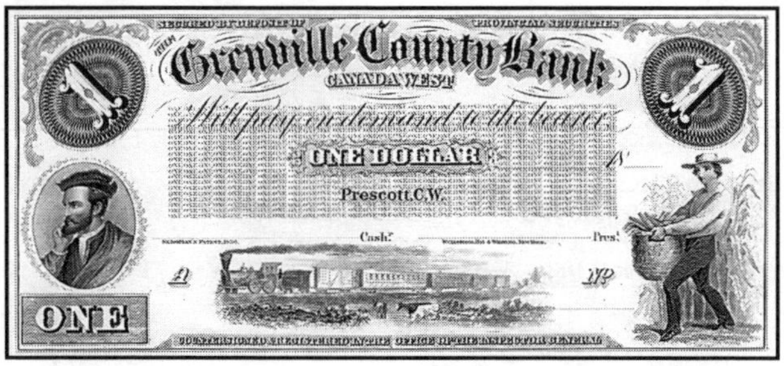

330-10-02

$1 Face Design: Jacques Cartier/train/farmer with basket of corn
Colour: Black with seropyan tint (straw yellow)

Back Design: Plain

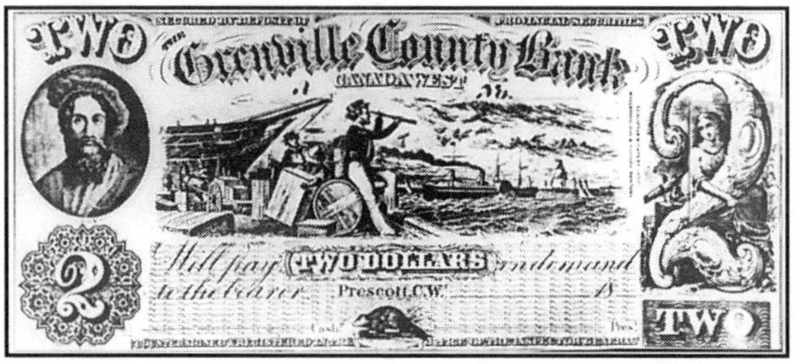

330-10-04

$2 Face Design: Christopher Columbus/dock scene; beaver below/woman and ornate 2
Colour: Black with seropyan tint (straw yellow)

Back Design: Plain

330-10-06

$5 Face Design: Prince Consort/steamship; small train below/ waterfall, train on bridge and large 5
Colour: Black with seropyan tint (straw yellow)

Back Design: Plain

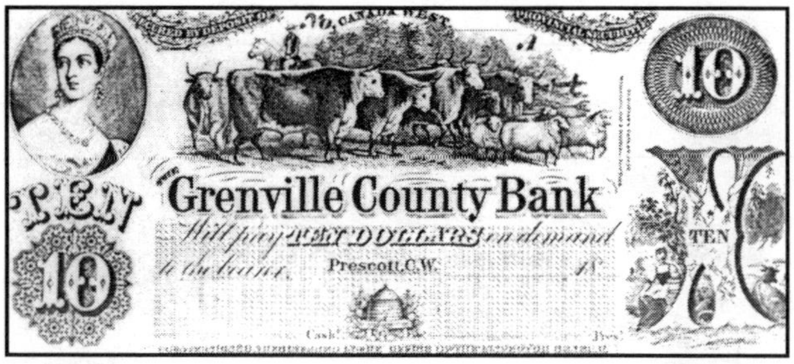

330-10-08

$10 Face Design: Queen Victoria (Chalon portrait) farmer on horseback, cattle and sheep; beehive and flowers below/seated woman and ornate X, cow
Colour: Black with seropyan tint (straw yellow)

Back Design: Plain

IMPRINT

Wellstood, Hay & Whiting, New York

SIGNATURES

left	right
none	none

ISSUE DATING

Partially Engraved __18__:

Cat.No.	Den.	Date	Variety	VG	F	VF	EF	AU	Unc
10-02R	$1*	18__	June 2001 Torex Sale	—	—	3,410.	—	—	—
10-02a	$1	18__	Interpam reprint, 1981	—	—	—	—	—	12.
10-04R	$2*	18__	June 2001 Torex Sale	—	—	1,760.	—	—	—
10-06R	$5*	18__	June 2001 Torex Sale	—	—	2,310.	—	—	—
10-08R	$10*	18__	June 2001 Torex Sale	—	—	2,750.	—	—	—

* Remainder, unsigned, undated and unnumbered.

THE HALIFAX BANKING COMPANY

1825 - 1903

HALIFAX, NOVA SCOTIA

BANK NUMBER 335 ***REDEEMABLE***

This institution commenced business as a private bank in Halifax in 1825. It was the first to give a regular banking service in Nova Scotia and its wealthy owners tried to keep the banking business to themselves. This institution continued to operate as a private company until 1872, and then as a chartered bank until 1903 when it merged with The Canadian Bank of Commerce. The bank enjoyed continuous prosperity, but its growth was hampered by lack of representation in larger financial centres.

335-10. MAVERICK PRINTINGS 1825 - ca. 1832

DESIGNS AND COLOURS

335-10-02

£1.10 Face Design: Rose, thistle and shamrock/—/fish, ox and ship

Colour: Black with no tint

Back Design: Plain

IMPRINT

Maverick

SIGNATURES

left	**right**
mss. P.C. Hill	mss. H.H. Cogswell

ISSUE DATING

Partially Engraved __18__:

1825: 1st September
1826: Sept. 1

Cat.No.	Denom.	Date	G	VG	F	VF	EF	AU
10-02	£1.10	1825-1826	Institutional collection only					

335-12. NEW ENGLAND BANK NOTE CO. PRINTINGS - ca. 1833 - 1850's

DESIGNS AND COLOURS

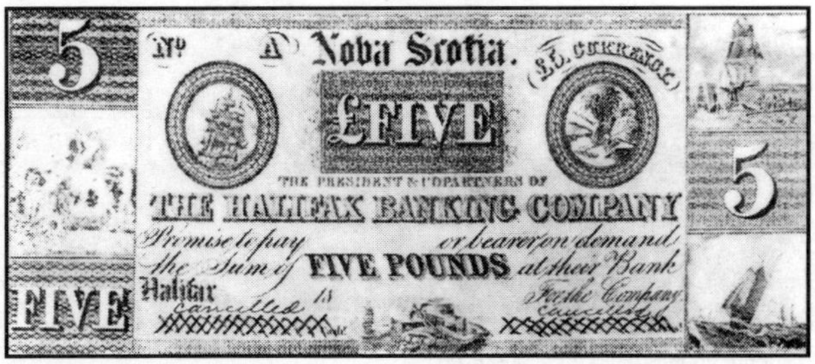

335-12-02R

£5 Face Design: Cattle/ship/cask, bales and cornucopia below/farm implements and sheaf/whaling scene; ships

Colour: Black with blue tint

Back Design: Plain

335-12-04R

£6.0.0 Face Design: Ship; whaling scene/Britannia; farm tools/harvesting scene

Colour: Black with blue tint

Back Design: Plain

335-12-06R

£6.10.0 Face Design: Ship with men fishing/beehive; farm tools below/whaling scene; cattle; whaling scene

Colour: Black with blue tint

Back Design: Plain

335-12-08R

£7.10.0 Face Design: Allegorical female/ships; casks and ship below/cattle

Colour: Black with blue tint

Back Design: Plain

IMPRINT
New England Bank Note Company, Boston

SIGNATURES

left	right
none	none

ISSUE DATING
Partially Engraved__18__:

Cat.No.	Denom.	Date	Variety	VG	F	VF	EF	Unc
12-02R	£5	18__	Remainder*	—	—	—	—	1,600.
12-04R	£6	18__	Remainder*	—	—	—	—	1,600.
12-06R	£6.10	18__	Remainder*	—	—	—	—	1,600.
12-08R	£7.10	18__	Remainder*	—	—	—	—	1,600.
Full Sheet 5,6,6.10,7.10		18__	Remainder*	—	—	—	—	7,000.

* unsigned, undated and unnumbered.

335-14. ABN
$20 ISSUE OF 1863 AND 1871

DESIGNS AND COLOURS

335-14-02-02a
$20 Face Design: —/ships in Halifax harbour/—
See subheadings
Colour: Black with green tint

Back Design: Lathework, counters and bank name
Colour: Green

IMPRINT
American Bank Note Co. New York

SIGNATURES

left	right
mss. various	mss. Wm. Pryor
mss. W. L. Pitcaithly	mss. T. Bayne (pro)

2. PLAIN COUNTERS 1863 AND 1871

ISSUE DATING
Partially Engraved __18__:
1863: 9th Decr.
Proof dated 14th Septr. (18)71
Overprinted:
1871 (July 1)

OVERPRINT
"July 1, 1871" and "CANADA CURRENCY" in red

CIRCULATING NOTES

Cat.No.	Denom.	Date	Variety	G	VG	F	VF	EF	AU
14-02-02	$20	1863	Mss. sheet #'s	Institutional collection only					
14-02-02a	$20	1863	Printed sheet #'s	—	5,000.	—	—	—	—
14-02-04	$20	1871	Date as red o/p	Institutional collection only					

PROOF NOTES

Cat. No	Denom.	Date		Unc
14-02-02P	$20	1863	FACE PROOF	900.

4. "CANADA CURRENCY" ENGRAVED IN COUNTERS 1871

335-14-04-02

ISSUE DATING
Engraved
Septr. 14th, 1871

Cat.No.	Denom.	Date	Variety	G	VG	F	VF	EF	AU
14-04-02	$20	1871	Engr. Date	Institutional collection only					

ISSUES OF 1872 AND 1880

DESIGNS AND COLOURS

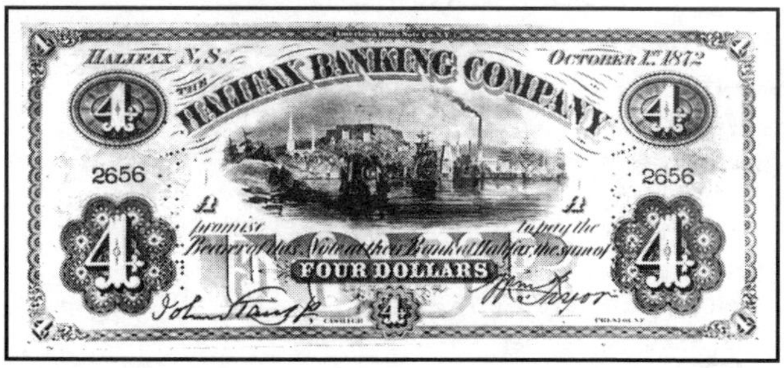

335-16-02
$4 Face Design: —/ships in Halifax harbour/—
Colour: Black with green tint

Back Design: Lathework, counters and bank name
Colour: Green

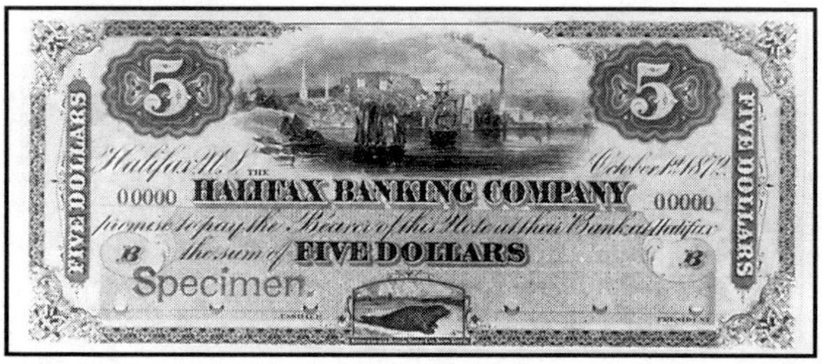

335-16-06S
$5 Face Design: —/Ships in Halifax harbour/—top 5 counters differ from 1880 note
Colour: Black with green tint. (larger than on 1880 notes)

Back Design: lathework, counters and bank name
Colour: Green

335-16-08
$5 Face Design: —/ships in Halifax harbour/—
Colour: Black with green tint

Back Design: Lathework, counters and bank name
Colour: Green

335-16-12
$10 Face Design: —/ships in Halifax harbour/—
Colour: Black with green tint

Back Design: Lathework, counters and bank name
Colour: Green

335-16. ABN PRINTINGS 1872 and 1880

IMPRINT
American Bank Note Co. New York
American Bank Note Co. N.Y.

SIGNATURES

left	right
mss. various	mss. Wm. Pryor

ISSUE DATING
Engraved
October 1st, 1872
October 1st, 1880

CIRCULATING NOTES

Cat.No.	Denom.	Date	G	VG	F	VF	EF	AU
16-02	$4	1872	Institutional collection only					
16-04	$4	1880	No known issued notes					
16-06	$5	1872	Institutional collection only					
16-08	$5	1880	—	—	6,000.	—	—	—
16-10	$10	1872	No known issued notes					
16-12	$10	1880	Institutional collection only					

PROOF NOTES

Cat. No.	Denom.	Date	Unc
16-04P	$4	1880	One proof $4.5.5.10 sheet known
16-08P	$5	1880	
16-12P	$10	1880	

SPECIMEN NOTES

Cat. No.	Denom.	Date	Unc
16-04S	$4	1880	One specimen $4.5.5.10 sheet known
16-06S	$5	1872	SPECIMEN 1,000.
16-08S	$5*	1880	
16-12S	$10	1880	

* The face tint of the $5 differs from that of the illustrated issued note.
A $4 back proof in orange (unissued colour), and a $5 back proof in green are known.

335-18. CANADA BN CO. AND ABN PRINTINGS 1880

DESIGNS AND COLOURS

Photo Not Available

335-18-02
$10 Face Design: —/ships in Halifax harbour/—
Colour: Black with green tint

Back Design: Lathework, counters and bank name
Colour: Green

Photo Not Available

335-18-04
$20 Face Design: —/ships in Halifax harbour/—
Colour: Black with green tint

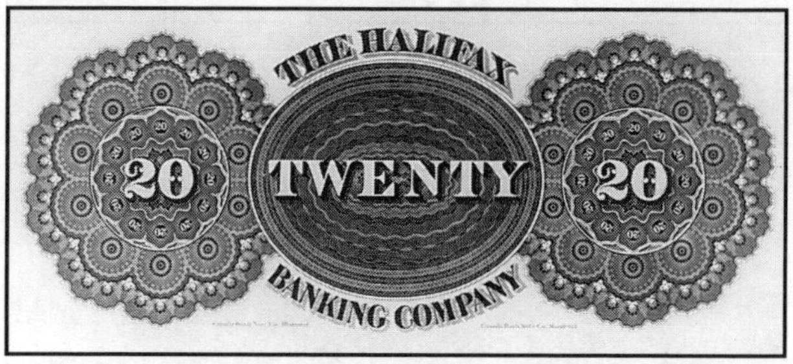

Back Design: Lathework, counters and bank name
Colour: Green

IMPRINT
American Bank Note Company
and Canada Bank Note Company

SIGNATURES

left	right
mss. various	mss. R. Uniacke

ISSUE DATING
Engraved
Oct. 1, 1880

CIRCULATING NOTES

Cat.No.	Denom.	Date	Variety	G	VG	F	VF	EF	AU
18-02	$10	1880	Canada BN Co.	Institutional collection only					
18-04	$20	1880		No known issued notes					

PROOF NOTES

Cat. No.	Denom.	Date	Variety	Unc
18-02P	$10	1880	Canada BN Co.	Institutional collection only
18-03P	$20	1871	Canada BN Co. and ABN	One each 4/on face, tint, back B/W sheets known
18-04P	$20	1880		Institutional collection only

335-20. BABN AND ABN PRINTINGS 1880

DESIGNS AND COLOURS

Photo Not Available

335-20-01

$4 Face Design: —/ships in Halifax harbour/—
Colour: Black with green tint

Back Design: lathework, counters and bank name
Colour: Green

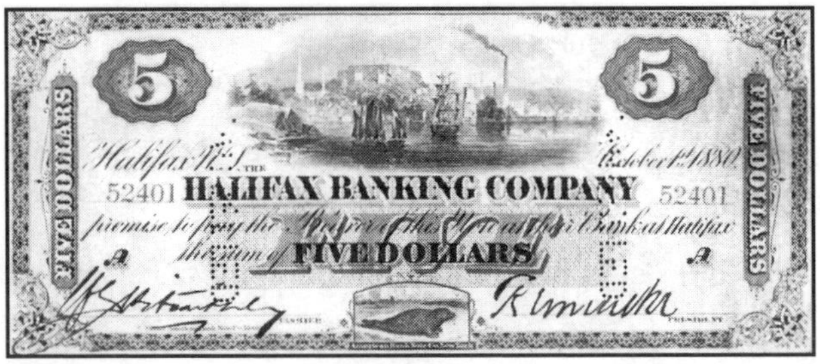

335-20-02

$5 Face Design: —/ships in Halifax harbour/—
Colour: Black with green tint

Back Design: Lathework, counters and bank name
Colour: Green

The tint has been modified and the upper counters have been reduced in size and the panel changed from plain FIVE to FIVE with a background of V5V5V5 etc.

IMPRINT

British American Bank Note Co. Montreal
American Bank Note Co. New York

SIGNATURES

left	right
mss. various	mss. R. Uniacke
mss. W.L. Pitcaithly	mss. R. Uniacke

ISSUE DATING

Engraved

October 1st, 1880

CIRCULATING NOTES

Cat.No.	Denom.	Date	Variety	G	VG	F	VF	EF	AU
20-01	$4	1880	BABN	No known issued notes					
20-02	$5	1880	ABN	—	5,000.	6,500.	—	—	—

PROOF NOTES

Cat. No.	Denom.	Date	Variety		Unc
20-01P	$4	1880	BABN	FACE PROOF	750.
20-02P	$5	1880	BABN	FACE PROOF	750.

$4.5.5.10 face, tint and back B/W proof sheets, one of each, exist(ABN Archives Sale, 1990), comprising 20-10P, 20-02P (2), and 18-02P. Imprint combinations are BABN and ABN or Canada BN Co.

335-22. CANADA BN CO. AND BABN PRINTINGS OF 1887 - 1894

DESIGNS AND COLOURS

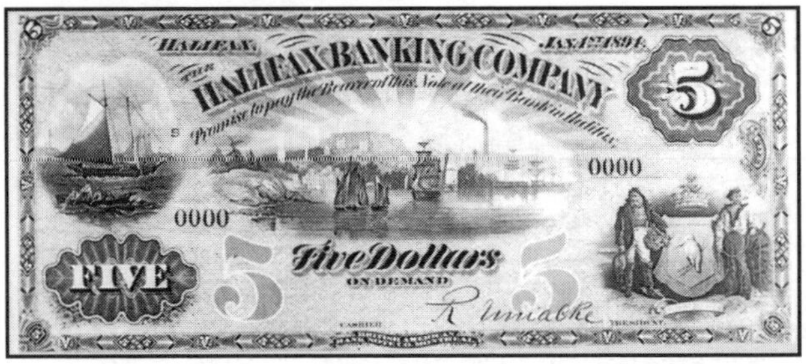

335-22-04-02S

$5 Face Design: Fishermen and sailing ships "Fishing"/ships in Halifax harbour/Crest of Halifax

Back Design: Lathework, counters and bank name

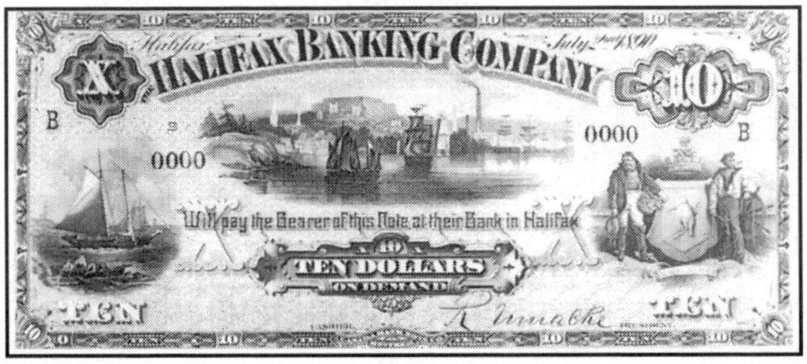

335-22-02-06

$10 Face Design: Fishermen and sailing ships "Fishing"/ships in Halifax harbour/Crest of Halifax

Back Design: Lathework, counters, bank name, crest and two griffins

335-22-02-08

$20 Face Design: Fishermen and sailing ships "Fishing"/ships in Halifax harbour/Crest of Halifax

Back Design: Lathework, counters, bank name, crest and two winged sphinxes

2. CANADA BN CO. PRINTINGS 1887 and 1890

$5 Face Colour: See varieties
Back Colour: See varieties
$10 Face Colour: Black with green tint
Back Colour: Green
$20 Face Colour: Black with green tint
Back Colour: Green

IMPRINT

Canada Bank Note Co. Montreal
Canada Bank Note Co. Ltd. Montreal

SIGNATURES

left	**right**
mss. various	engr. R. Uniacke

ISSUE DATING

Engraved

Jan. 1st 1887
July 2nd 1890

VARIETIES

$5 Face colour: Blue
Back Colour: Brown
$5 Face Colour: Black with green tint
Back Colour: Green
$5 Face Colour: Black with red tint
Back Colour: Brown

CIRCULATING NOTES

Cat.No.	Denom.	Date	Variety	G	VG	F	VF	EF	AU
22-02-02	$5	1887	Green tint	3,000.	5,000.	—	—	—	—
22-02-03	$5	1887	Blue tint	No known issued notes					
22-02-04	$5	1887	Red tint	3,000.	5,000.	—	—	—	—
22-02-06	$10	1890		Institutional collection only					
22-02-08	$20	1890		Institutional collection only					

PROOF NOTES

Cat. No.	Denom.	Date	Variety		Unc
22-02-02P	$5	1887	Green tint	FACE PROOF	750.
22-02-03P	$5	1887	Blue tint	FACE PROOF	750.
22-02-04P	$5	1887	Red tint	FACE PROOF	750.

SPECIMEN NOTES

Cat. No.	Denom.	Date		Unc
22-02-06S	$10	1890	SPECIMEN	1,000.
22-02-08S	$20	1890	SPECIMEN	1,000.

4. BABN PRINTINGS 1894

DESIGNS AND COLOURS

Same designs as 1887 issue.

$5 Face Colour: Black with blue tint
Back Colour: Blue

IMPRINT

British American Bank Note Co. Ottawa

SIGNATURES

left	**right**
mss. various	engr. R. Uniacke

ISSUE DATING

Engraved

Jan. 1st 1894

Cat.No.	Denom.	Date	G	VG	F	VF	EF	AU
22-04-02	$5	1894	3,000.	5,000.	—	—	—	—

335-24. "UNIACKE PORTRAIT" ISSUES 1896 and 1898

DESIGNS AND COLOURS

335-24-01

$5 Face Design: H.N. Wallace/ships in Halifax harbour/ R. Uniacke
Colour: Black with green tint

Back Design: Lathework, counters, bank name and Halifax Coat of Arms

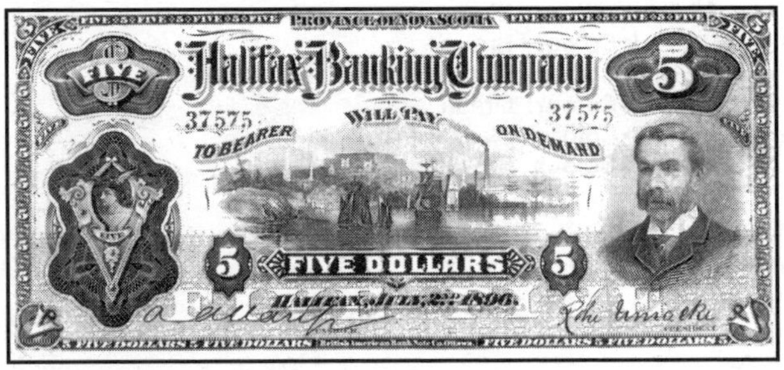

335-24-02

$5 Face Design: Ornate lathework with V & head of Mercury/ ships in Halifax harbour/R. Uniacke

Colour: Black with green tint

Back Design: Lathework, counters and bank name, Halifax coat of Arms

Colour: Green

335-24-04

$10 Face Design: Ships and pilot boats/—R. Uniacke

Colour: Black with green tint

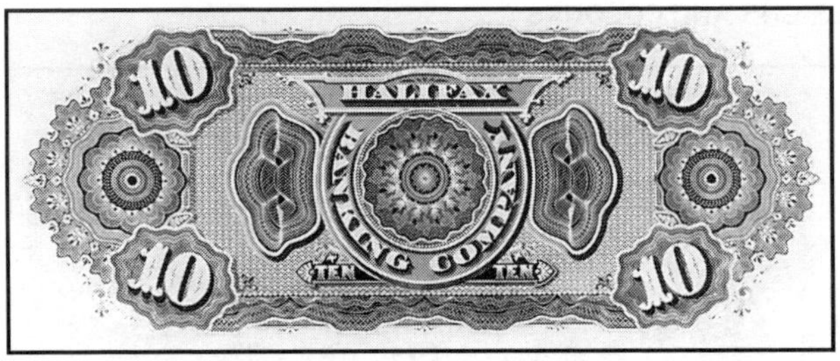

Back Design: Lathework, counters and bank name

Colour: Green

335-24-06

$20 Face Design: Crest of Halifax/—/R. Uniacke

Colour: Black with ochre tint

Back Design: Lathework, counters and bank name

Colour: Green

IMPRINT

British American Bank Note Co. Ottawa

SIGNATURES

left	right
mss. various	engr. Robie Uniacke

ISSUE DATING

Engraved

July, 2nd 1896
July 1st 1898

CIRCULATING NOTES

Cat.No.	Denom.	Date	Variety	G	VG	F	VF	EF	AU
24-01	$5	1896	Portrait I	No known issued notes					
24-02	$5	1896	Ornate V I	3,000.	5,000.	—	—	—	—
24-04	$10	1898		Institutional collection only					
24-06	$20	1898		Institutional collection only					

PROOF NOTES

Cat. No.	Denom.	Date	Variety		Unc
24-01P	$5	1896	Portrait 1.	FACE PROOF	750.
24-02P	$5	1896	Ornate V I.	FACE PROOF	750.
24-04P	$10	1898		FACE PROOF	750.
24-06P	$20	1898		FACE PROOF	750.

Note: $10 proof with orange face, brown back

THE HAMILTON BANK

1835

HAMILTON, LOWER CANADA

BANK NUMBER 340 ***NONREDEEMABLE***

Bank notes were ordered in November of 1835; however, there is no record of any notes or proofs having survived.

THE BANK OF HAMILTON

1872 - 1923

HAMILTON, (ONTARIO) DOMINION OF CANADA

BANK NUMBER 345 ***REDEEMABLE***

The bill chartering The Bank of Hamilton received Royal assent on June 14, 1872 and the bank opened its doors for business in Hamilton, Ontario the following September, a capital stock of $1 million having been subscribed. At its first Annual Meeting, June 17, 1873, a profit of $23,951.27 was declared for the preceding nine months. During the later part of 1873 the bank opened its first two agencies in Ontario, at Listowel and Port Elgin, the former being located on the Wellington, Grey and Bruce Railway, now the C.N.R. By the spring of 1877 money was becoming more plentiful and rates of discount were reduced. In spite of several setbacks that year, including the failure of some long standing banks, the bank managed to show a profit. After 30 years of operation, assets had reached almost 20 million dollars. The bank continued to grow until 1912 when the recession that affected most other financial institutions began to make its presence known. With the signing of the Armistice, however, the bank joined the rush of chartered banks to open more branches. At its 50th anniversary in 1922, amidst post-war depression, it was represented in 157 locations. With the burden of high taxation and increasing competition, The Bank of Hamilton amalgamated with The Canadian Bank of Commerce in 1923.

345-10. ISSUES OF 1872 AND 1873

DESIGNS AND COLOURS

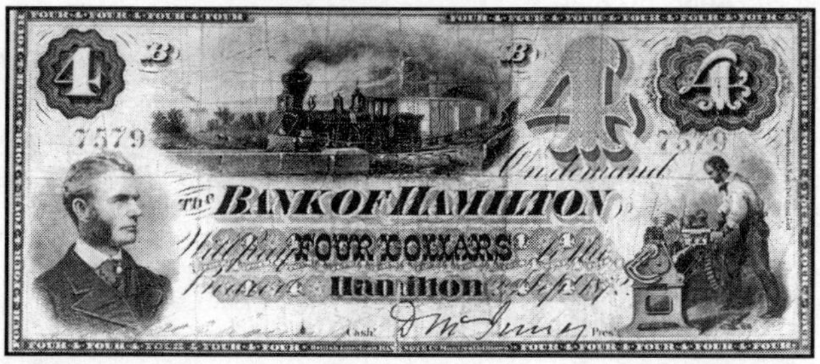

345-10-02

$4 Face Designs: D. McInnes/train/machinist at lathe
Colour: Black with green tint

Back Design: Lathework, counters, bank name and crest
Colour: Green

345-10-04P

$5 Face Design: D. McInnes/factories, blacksmith, women, workers and ornate 5
Colour: Black with green tint

Back Design: Lathework, counters, bank name and crest
Colour: Green

345-10-06

$10 Face Design: Ornate X and two seated allegorical women/ D. McInnes/—
Colour: Black with green tint

Back Design: Lathework, counters, bank name and crest
Colour: Green

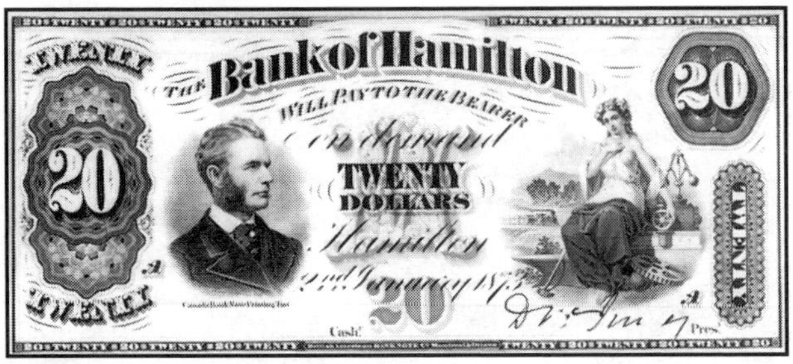

345-10-08P
$20 Face Design: D.McInnes/seated allegorical female with symbols of commerce and industry
Colour: Black with green tint

Back Design: Lathework, counters, bank name and crest
Colour: Green

345-10-10P
$50 Face Design: D.McInnes/—/farm scene
Colour: Black with green tint

Back Design: Lathework, counters, bank name and crest
Colour: Green

345-10-12P
$100 Face Design: —/D.McInnes/—
Colour: Black with green tint

Back Design: —/Crest of Hamilton/—
Colour: Green

IMPRINT

British American Bank Note Co. Montreal & Ottawa

SIGNATURES

left	**right**
mss. various	engr. D McInnes

ISSUE DATING

Engraved

1st Sept. 1872
2nd Sept. 1872
2nd January 1873

CIRCULATING NOTES

Cat.No.	Denom.	Date	G	VG	F	VF	EF	AU
10-02	$4	1872	900.	1,800.	3,000.	—	—	—
10-04	$5	1872	1,100.	2,200.	—	—	—	—
10-06	$10	1872	Institutional collection only					
10-08	$20	1873	No known issued notes					
10-10	$50	1873	No known issued notes					
10-12	$100	1873	No known issued notes					

PROOF NOTES

Cat. No.	Denom.	Date		Unc
10-02P	$4	1872	FACE PROOF	600.
10-04P	$5	1872	FACE PROOF	600.
10-06P	$10	1872	FACE PROOF	700.
10-08P	$20	1873	FACE PROOF	750.
10-10P	$50	1873	FACE PROOF	900.
10-12P	$100	1873	FACE PROOF	1,100.

345-12. **ISSUE OF MARCH 1, 1887**

DESIGNS AND COLOURS

345-12-02P

$5 Face Design: John Stuart/—/factories, workers and ornate 5
Colour: Black with green tint

Back Design: —/Crest of Hamilton/—
Colour: Green

IMPRINT

British American Bank Note Company, Montreal and Ottawa

SIGNATURE

left	**right**
none	engr. John Stuart

ISSUE DATING

Engraved

1st March, 1887

CIRCULATING NOTES

Cat.No.	Denom.	Date	G	VG	F	VF	EF	AU
12-02	$5	1887	No known issued notes					

PROOF NOTES

Cat. No.	Denom.	Date		Unc
12-02P	$5	1887	FACE PROOF	900.

345-14. **ISSUE OF DECEMBER 1, 1887**

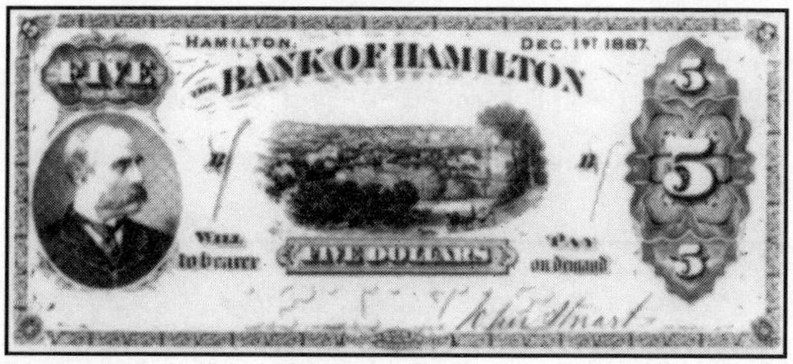

345-14-02

$5 Face Design: John Stuart/view of Hamilton from the mountain/—
Colour: Black with ochre tint

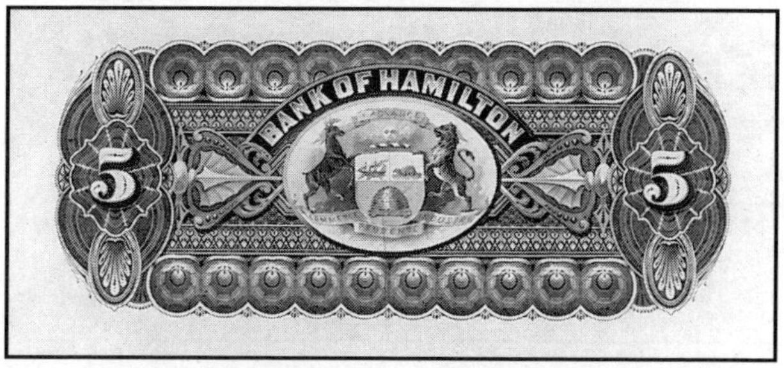

Back Design: —/Crest of Hamilton/—
Colour: Green

IMPRINT

Canada Bank Note Co. Montreal

SIGNATURE

left	**right**
mss. various	engr. John Stuart

ISSUE DATING

Engraved

Dec. 1st 1887

CIRCULATING NOTES

Cat.No.	Denom	Date	G	VG	F	VF	EF	AU
14-02	$5	1887	900.	1,800.	3,000.	—	—	—

PROOF NOTES

Cat. No.	Denom.	Date	Variety		Unc
14-04P	$5	1887	Blue face tint	FACE PROOF	700.
14-06P	$5	1887	Green face tint	FACE PROOF	700.

345-16. **ISSUE OF 1892**

DESIGNS AND COLOURS

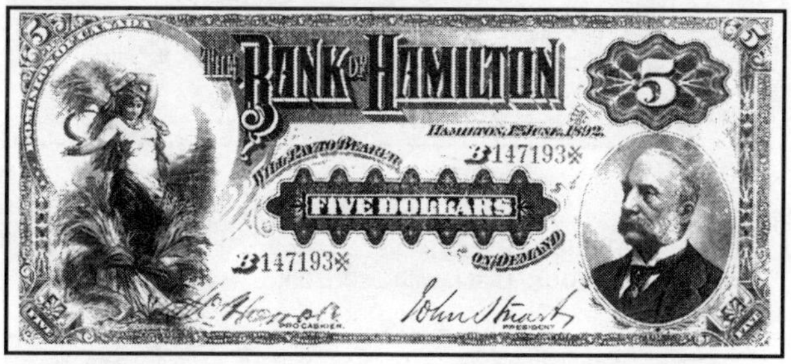

345-16-02a

$5 Face Design: "Agriculture" figure/—/John Stuart
Colour: Black with green tint

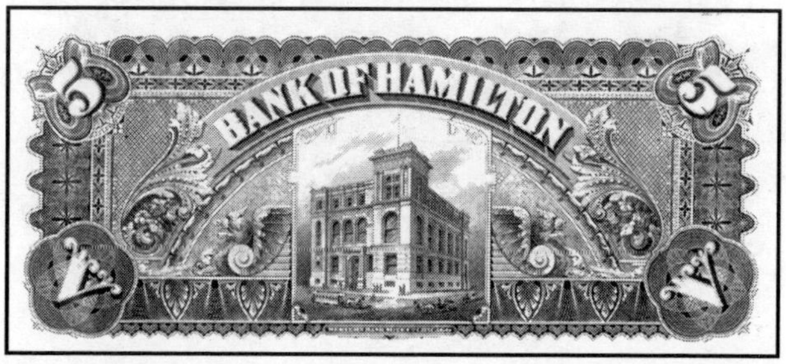

Back Design: Lathework, counters, bank name, griffins and head office
Colour: Green

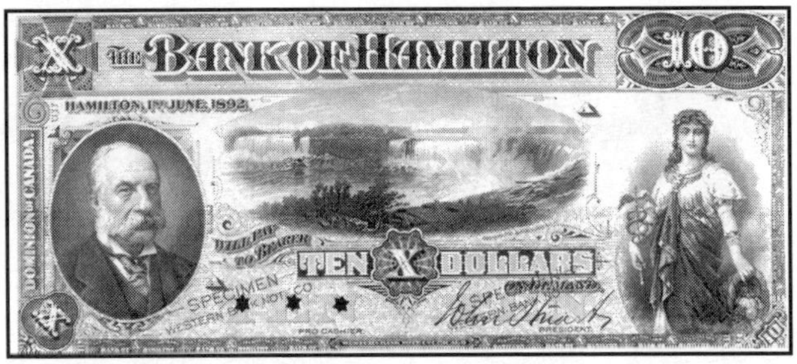

345-16-04S

$10 Face Design: John Stuart/Niagara Falls/"Commerce" figure
Colour: Black with pink tint

Back Design: Lathework, counters, bank name and head office
Colour: Red-brown

345-16-06S

$20 Face Design: Ploughing scene/John Stuart/—
Colour: Black with ochre tint

Back Design: Lathework, counters, bank name and stag's head
Colour: Brown

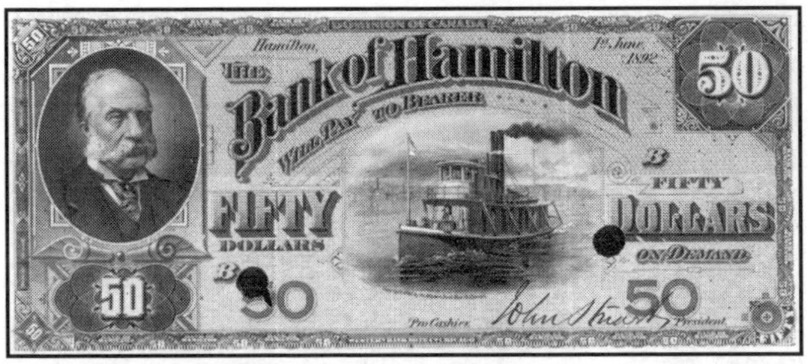

345-16-08S

$50 Face Design: John Stuart/tugboat/—
Colour: Black with olive green tint

Back Design: Lathework, counters, bank name and Indians hunting buffalo, train crossing prairie
Colour: Olive green

345-16-10S

$100 Face Design: Train "Pullman Vestibule Train/—/ John Stuart
Colour: Black with red-brown tint

Back Design: Lathework, counters and bank name
Colour: Dull red

IMPRINT

Western Bank Note Co. Chicago

SIGNATURES

left	**right**
mss. various	engr. John Stuart

ISSUE DATING

Engraved

1st June, 1892

VARIETIES

$5 1892, Face Design: engraved "Cashier" below left signature space

$5 1892, Face Design: engraved "pro Cashier" below left signature space

CIRCULATING NOTES

Cat.No.	Denom.	Date	Variety	G	VG	F	VF	EF	AU
16-02	$5	1892	engr Cashier l.	200.	400.	600.	—	—	—
16-02a	$5	1892	engr pro Cashier l.	175.	350.	525.	1,000.	—	—
16-04	$10	1892		750.	1,500.	2,500.	—	—	—
16-06	$20	1892			No known issued notes				
16-08	$50	1892			No known issued notes				
16-10	$100	1892			No known issued notes				

PROOF NOTES

Cat. No.	Denom.	Date		Unc
16-06P	$20	1892	FACE PROOF	400.

SPECIMEN NOTES

Cat. No.	Denom.	Date	Variety		Unc
16-02S	$5	1892	engr Cashier, l.	SPECIMEN	600.
16-02aS	$5	1892	engr pro Cashier, l.	SPECIMEN	600.
16-04S	$10	1892		SPECIMEN	600.
16-06S	$20	1892		SPECIMEN	700.
16-08S	$50	1892		SPECIMEN	750.
16-10S	$100	1892		SPECIMEN	800.

345-18. ISSUE OF 1904

DESIGNS AND COLOURS

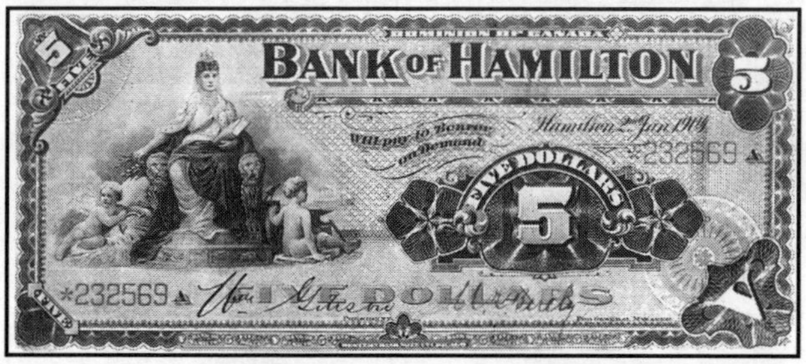

345-18-02

$5 Face Design: Queen Alexandra seated on throne/—/—

Colour: Black with green tint

Back Design: Lathework, counters and bank name

Colour: Green

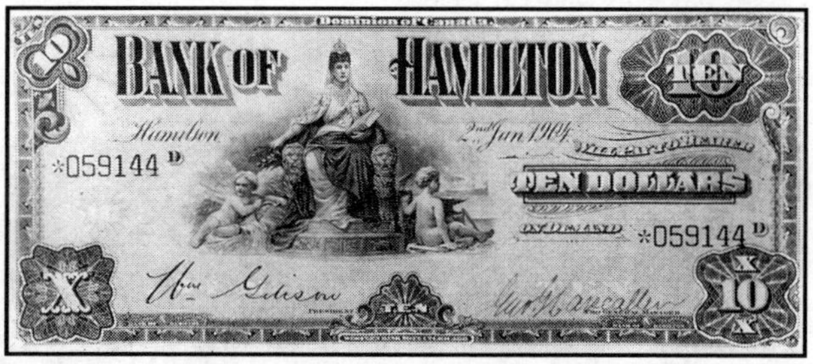

345-18-04

$10 Face Design: —/Queen Alexandra seated on throne/—

Colour: Black with orange tint

Back Design: Lathework, counters and bank name

Colour: Orange

345-18-06

$20 Face Design: —/King Edward VII/—

Colour: Black with olive green tint

Back Design: Lathework, counters and bank name

Colour: Brown

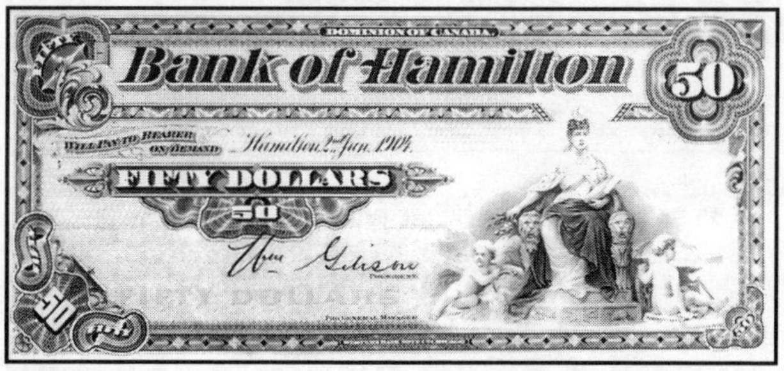

345-18-08

$50 Face Design: —/—Queen Alexandra seated on throne

Colour: Black with blue tint

Back Design: Lathework, counters and bank name

Colour: Blue

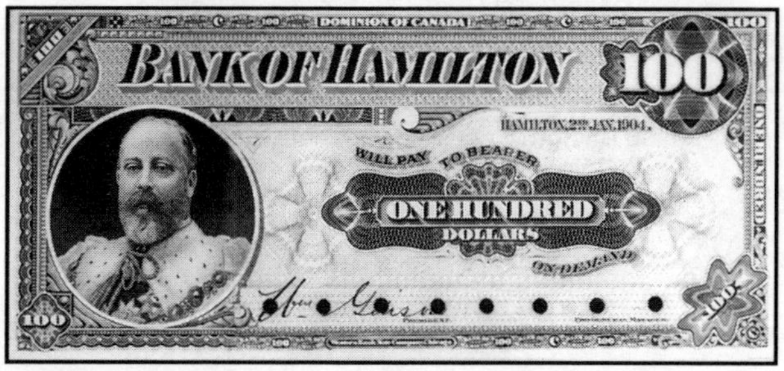

345-18-10

$100 Face Design: King Edward VII/—/—

Colour: Brown

Back Design: Lathework, counters and bank name

Colour: Brown

IMPRINT

Western Bank Note Co. Chicago
Western Bank Note Company, Chicago

SIGNATURES

left	right
engr. William Gibson	mss. various

ISSUE DATING

Engraved

2nd Jan. 1904

CIRCULATING NOTES

Cat.No.	Denom.	Date	G	VG	F	VF	EF	AU
18-02	$5	1904	300.	600.	1,000.	1,500.	—	—
18-04	$10	1904	600.	1,200.	2,000.	3,000.	—	—
18-06	$20	1904	2,000.	3,500.	—	—	—	—
18-08	$50	1904	Institutional collection only					
18-10	$100	1904	Institutional collection only					

SPECIMEN NOTES

Cat. No.	Denom.	Date		Unc
18-02S	$5	1904	SPECIMEN	800.
18-04S	$10	1904	SPECIMEN	800.
18-06S	$20	1904	SPECIMEN	800.
18-08S	$50	1904	SPECIMEN	900.
18-10S	$100	1904	SPECIMEN	1,000.

345-20. ISSUES OF 1909 AND 1914

DESIGNS AND COLOURS

345-20-02

$5 Face Design: —/seated Britannia, Agriculture and Industry allegory in background/—
Colour: Black with green tint

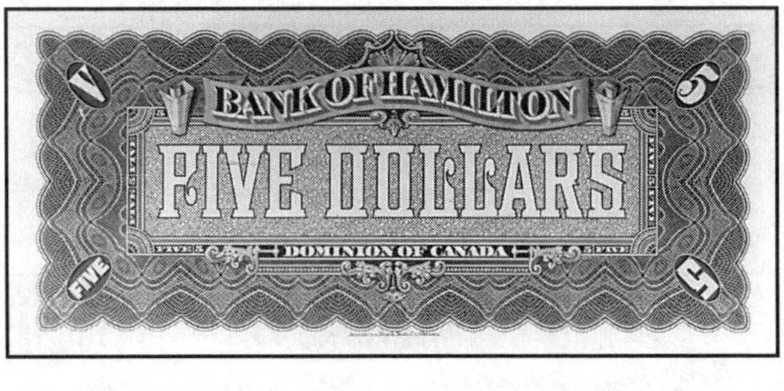

Back Design: Lathework, counters and bank name
Colour: Green

345-20-10

$10 Face Design: Seated allegorical female, Agriculture and Commerce allegory in background/—/—
Colour: Black with brown and yellow tint

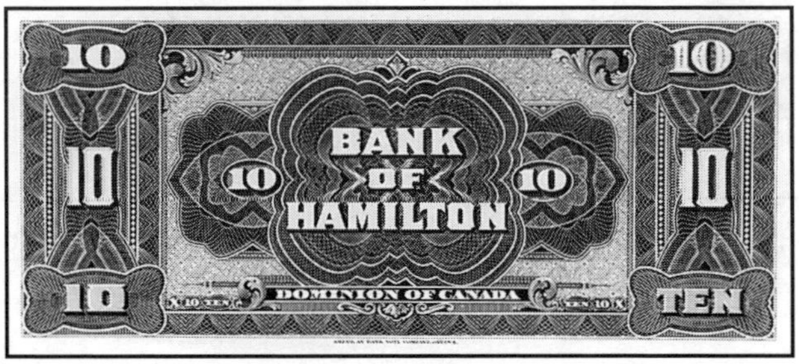

Back Design: Lathework, counters and bank name
Colour: Red-brown

345-20-16

$20 Face Design: —/—/seated Britannia, Agriculture and Industry allegory in background
Colour: Black with blue tint

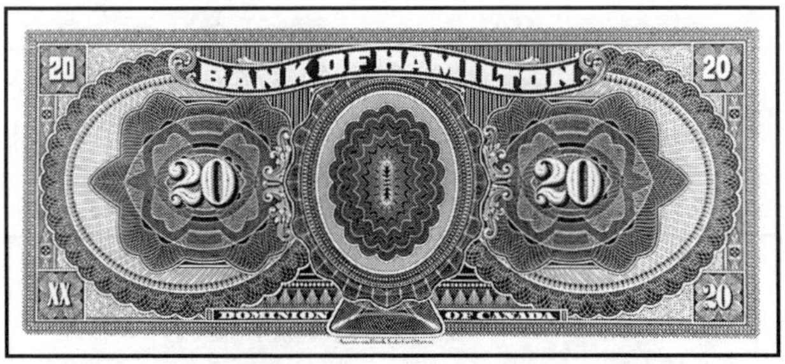

Back Design: Lathework, counters and bank name
Colour: Slate

345-20-24

$50 Face Design: —/seated allegorical female, Agriculture and Commerce allegory in background
Colour: Black with red tint

Back Design: Lathework, counters and bank name, woman's head in ornate frame
Colour: Red-orange

345-20-26

$100 Face Design: Seated Britannia, Agriculture and Commerce allegory in background/—/—
Colour: Black with green tint

Back Design: Lathework, counters and bank name
Colour: Olive green

IMPRINT

American Bank Note Co. Ottawa

SIGNATURES

	left	right
1909:	typed William Gibson	mss. various
	typed John S. Hendrie	mss. various
1914:	typed John S. Hendrie	mss. various
	typed John S. Hendrie	typed J.P. Bell

ISSUE DATING

Engraved

1st June 1909
1st June 1914

OVERPRINT

1909: "E" twice in red
"S" twice in red
1914: "C" twice in red
"E" twice in red

VARIETIES

1914: "Pro general manager" with mss. signatures
"General Manager" with Bell signature

CIRCULATING NOTES

Cat.No.	Denom.	Date	Variety	G	VG	F	VF	EF	AU
20-02	$5	1909		85.	175.	250.	400.	900.	—
20-04	$5	1914	Mss.signature,r.	70.	140.	200.	300.	700.	—
20-06	$5	1914	Bell,r.	70.	140.	200.	300.	700.	—
20-08	$10	1909		100.	200.	300.	500.	—	—
20-10	$10	1914	Mss.signature,r.	85.	175.	250.	350.	800.	—
20-12	$10	1914	Bell,r.	85.	175.	250.	350.	800.	—
20-14	$20	1909		1,600.	3,200.	—	—	—	—
20-16	$20	1914	Mss.signature,r.	175.	350.	500.	800.	—	—
20-18	$20	1914	Bell,r.	175.	350.	500.	800.	—	—
20-20	$50	1909		No known issued notes					
20-22	$50	1914	Mss.signature,r.	400.	800.	1,200.	1,600.	—	—
20-24	$50	1914	Bell,r.	400.	800.	1,200.	1,600.	—	—
20-26	$100	1909		750.	1,500.	2,500.	4,000.	—	—
20-28	$100	1914	Mss.signature,r.	750.	1,500.	2,500.	4,000.	—	—
20-30	$100	1914	Bell,r.	750.	1,500.	2,500.	4,000.	—	—

PROOF NOTES

Cat. No.	Denom.	Date		Unc
20-02P	$5	1909	FACE PROOF	500.
20-04P	$5	1914	FACE PROOF	500.
20-08P	$10	1909	FACE PROOF	500.
20-10P	$10	1914	FACE PROOF	500.
20-14P	$20	1909	FACE PROOF	500.
20-16P	$20	1914	FACE PROOF	500.
20-20P	$50	1909	FACE PROOF	500.
20-22P	$50	1914	FACE PROOF	500.
20-26P	$100	1909	FACE PROOF	500.
20-28P	$100	1914	FACE PROOF	500.

SPECIMEN NOTES

Cat. No.	Denom.	Date		Unc
20-02S	$5	1909	SPECIMEN	900.
20-04S	$5	1914	SPECIMEN	900.
20-08S	$10	1909	SPECIMEN	900.
20-10S	$10	1914	SPECIMEN	900.
20-14S	$20	1909	SPECIMEN	900.
20-16S	$20	1914	SPECIMEN	900.
20-20S	$50	1909	SPECIMEN	900.
20-22S	$50	1914	SPECIMEN	900.
20-26S	$100	1909	SPECIMEN	900.
20-28S	$100	1914	SPECIMEN	900.

345-22. "JUBILEE" ISSUE 1922

Issued for the 50th anniversary of the founding of the bank.

DESIGNS AND COLOURS

345-22-02

$5 Face Design: —/seated Britannia, Agriculture and Commerce allegory in background/—
Colour: Black with green tint

Back Design: Lathework, counters and bank name
Colour: Green

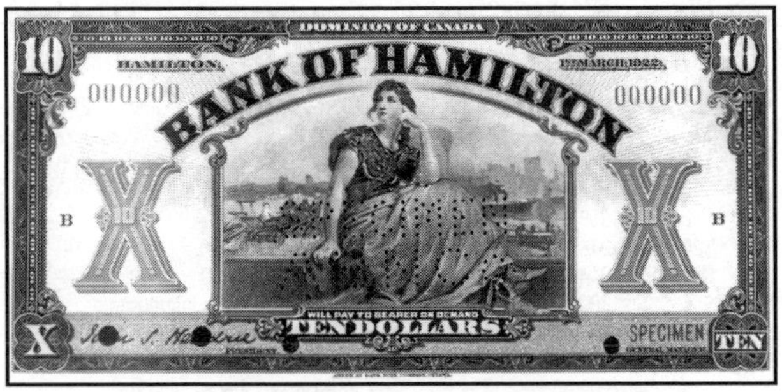

345-22-04S

$10 Face Design: —/seated allegorical female, Agriculture and Commerce allegory in background/—
Colour: Black with orange tint

Back Design: Lathework, counters and bank name
Colour: Orange

345-22-06S

$25 Face Design: Two allegorical women/—/—
Colour: Black with green, pink and purple tint

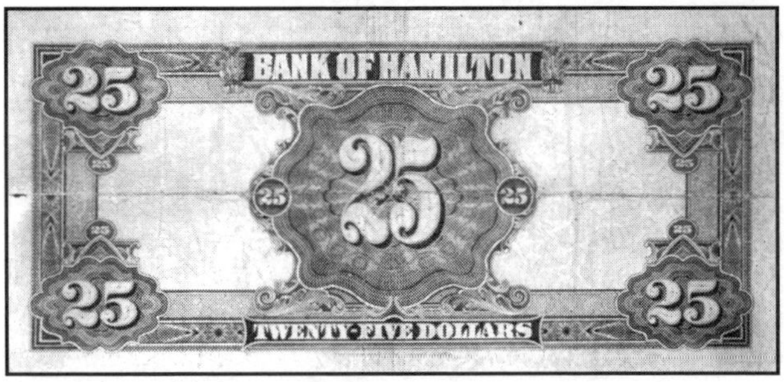

Back Design: Lathework, counters and bank name
Colour: Purple

IMPRINT

American Bank Note Company, Ottawa

SIGNATURES

left	right
typed John S. Hendrie	typed J.P. Bell

ISSUE DATING

Engraved

1st March 1922

CIRCULATING NOTES

Cat.No.	Denom.	Date	G	VG	F	VF	EF	AU
22-02	$5	1922	425.	850.	1,250.	2,000.	4,000.	—
22-04	$10	1922	500.	1,000.	1,500.	2,500.	4,800.	—
22-06	$25	1922	3,000.	5,000.	7,500.	—	—	—

PROOF NOTES

Cat. No.	Denom.	Date	Unc
22-06P	$25	1922	FACE PROOF 1,000.

SPECIMEN NOTES

Cat. No.	Denom.	Date	Unc
22-02S	$5	1922	SPECIMEN 750.
22-04S	$10	1922	SPECIMEN 750.
22-06S	$25	1922	SPECIMEN 1,500.

HART'S BANK

1835 - 1847

THREE RIVERS, L. (LOWER) CANADA

BANK NUMBER 350 ***NONREDEEMABLE***

Moses Hart, a respected member of society in Three Rivers, was one of the first bankers in Lower Canada. His application for a charter was turned down but he opened a private bank in 1835. Notes issued by private banks, consisting mostly of wealthy merchants, circulated mainly among French Canadians and were accepted more readily than those of The Bank of Montreal, since the owners of the private institution, including Moses Hart, were known and trusted members of the community. The bank finished its dealings after Hart's death in 1847.

350-10. **SCRIP ISSUE 1837**
SMALL SIZE NOTES

DESIGNS AND COLOURS

350-10-02R
5d (10 sous) Face Design: No vignettes
Colour: Black with no tint
Back Design: Plain

Photo Not Available

350-10-04R
10d (20 sous) Face Design: No vignettes
Colour: Black with no tint
Back Design: Plain

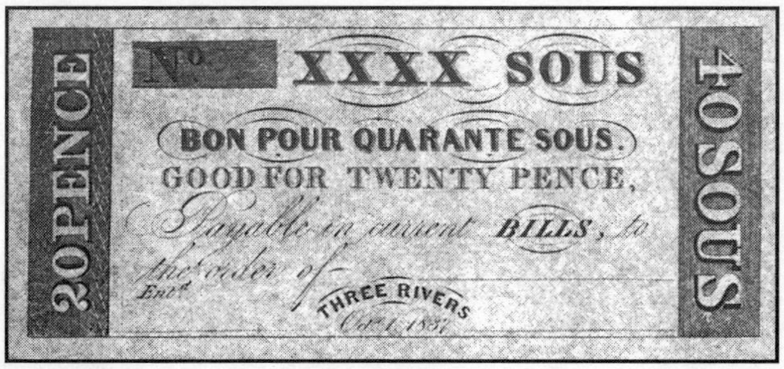

350-10-06R
20d (40 sous) Face Design: No vignettes
Colour: Black with no tint
Back Design: Plain

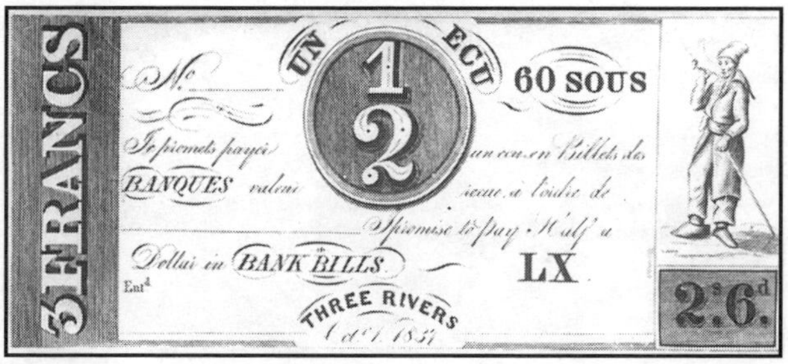

350-10-08R
3 Francs Face Design:($1/2)
(60 sous) —/—habitant smoking pipe
Colour: Black with no tint
Back Design: Plain

IMPRINT
Bourne

SIGNATURES

left	**right**
none	none

ISSUE DATING
Engraved
Oct. 1, 1837

Cat.No.	Denom.	Date/Variety	G	VF	F	VF	EF	Unc
10-02R	5d(10 sous)	1837Remainder*	—	—	—	60.	100.	200.
10-04R	10d(20 sous)	1837Remainder*	—	—	—	60.	100.	200.
10-06R	20d(40 sous)	1837Remainder*	—	—	—	60.	100.	200.
10-08R	$1/2(60 sous)	1837Remainder*	—	—	—	60.	100.	200.

*unsigned and unnumbered.

350-12. **DOLLAR ISSUE 1838**
LARGE SIZE NOTES

Reprints of this issue were produced from the original face plate in the early 20th century. (See subheads.)

ORIGINAL PRINTINGS - ORANGE BACK, NORMAL PAPER 1838

DESIGNS AND COLOURS

350-12-02
$1 Face Design: Steamboat in oval (sideways)/habitants in horse-drawn sleigh; small steamboat below/seated Indian maiden
Colour: Black with no tint

Back Design: Lathework surrounding two male portraits (sideways)
Colour: Orange

350-12-04
$3 Face Design: Seated Indian maiden/habitants in horse-drawn sleigh; ship, casks etc. below/steamboat in oval (sideways)
Colour: Black with no tint

Back Design: Lathework surrounding two male portraits (sideways)
Colour: See subheadings

350-12-06a
$5 Face Design: Seated Indian maiden/habitants in horse-drawn sleigh; ship, casks etc. below/steamboat in oval (sideways)
Colour: Black with no tint

Back Design: Lathework surrounding two male portraits (sideways)
Colour: See subheadings

REPRINTS - PLAIN BACK, THIN PAPER

DESIGNS AND COLOURS

Face Design: See original printings
Back Design: Plain

350-12-04a

IMPRINT
Bourne

SIGNATURES

Originals

left	**right**
mss. A.T. Hart	mss. M. Hart

REPRINTS

left	**right**
none	none

ISSUE DATING
Originals
Partially Engraved __18__:
$1 1838: 28 July
$3 1838: Aug' 20th

REPRINTS
Partially Engraved __18__:

Cat.No.	Denom.	Date	Variety	G	VG	F	VF	EF	Unc
12-02	$1	1838		200.	400.	600.	—	—	—
12-02a	$1	18__	Reprints*	—	—	—	—	50.	75.
12-04	$3	1838		225.	450.	700.	—	—	—
12-04a	$3	18__	Reprints*	—	—	—	—	90.	135.
12-06	$5	1838		No known issued notes					
12-06a	$5	18__	Reprints*	—	—	—	—	60.	90.

*unsigned, undated and unnumbered.

THE HATLEY BANK

1837

HATLEY, LOWER CANADA

BANK NUMBER 355 ***REDEEMABLE***

This bank is presumably a phantom bank with notes, produced to circulate in the New England area. No Bank of North America existed with similar notes in this period. The imprint has not been known for other bank notes. The note has typical United States of America obsolete vignettes.

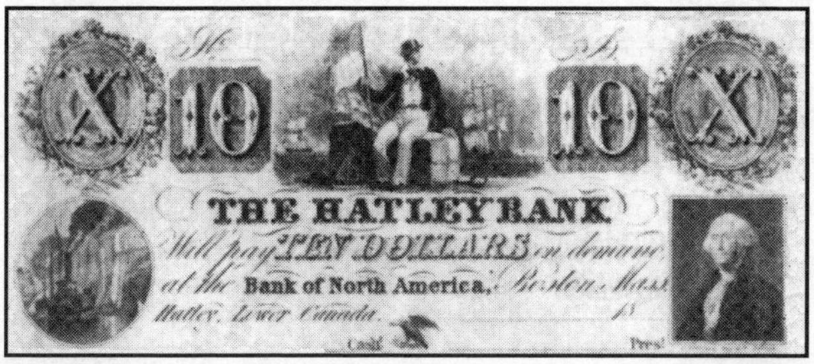

355-10-10

$10 Face Design: Ships/ sailor seated on bales, flag and ships/ Washington

Back Design: Plain

IMPRINT

W. W. Wilson. Engr. and Pr. Boston

SIGNATURES

Left	Right
Unknown	Unknown

ISSUE DATING

Partially Engraved __18__:

Cat.No.	Denom	Date	Variety	G	VG	F	VF	EF	Unc
10-10	$10	18__	Remainder	Only one known. Est. VF $3,500.					

HENRY'S BANK

1837

LA PRAIRIE and MONTREAL, LOWER CANADA

BANK NUMBER 357 ***NONREDEEMABLE***

This bank, established as a private bank in 1837 in Montreal, operated for only a short period of time. It went into liquidation as a result of an embezzlement by its cashier.

357-10. **SCRIP ISSUE OF 1837**

DESIGNS AND COLOURS

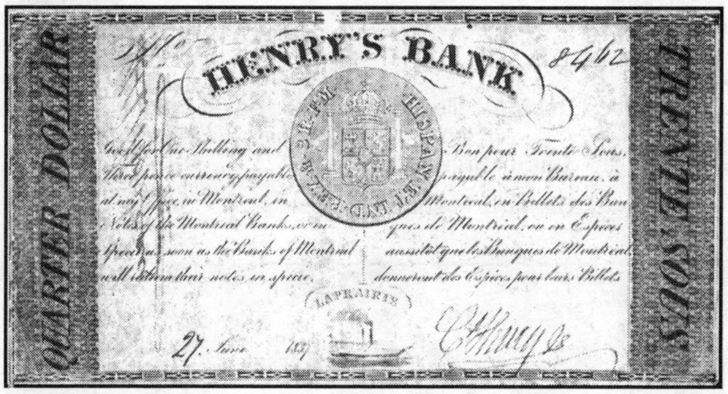

357-10-02

$1/4 (1s.3d.; 30 Sous)

Face Design: —/reverse of Mexican 2 Reales; steamboat below/—

Colour: Black with no tint

Back Design: Plain

357-10-04

$1/2(2s.6d.; 1 Ecu)

Face Design: —/obverse of Spanish coin; sheaf and agricultural tools below/—

Colour: Black with no tint

Back Design: Plain

IMPRINT

None

SIGNATURES

left	right
none	mss. C. Henry

ISSUE DATING

Partially Engraved ___18___:

Juin 1837

27 Juin 1837

Cat.No.	Denom.	Date	Variety	G	VG	F	VF	EF	Unc
10-02	$1/4	1837		25.	50.	70.	100.	150.	250.
10-02a	$1/4	1837	Reprint	—	—	—	—	—	40.
10-04	$1/2	1837		25.	50.	70.	100.	150.	250.
10-04a	$1/2	1837	Reprint	—	—	—	—	—	40.
Sheet of reprints $1/4, $1/4, $1/2								125.	

357-12. DRAFT ISSUE OF 1837

Engraved: "To Edmund Henry" at upper left.

DESIGNS AND COLOURS

357-12-02

$1 Face Design: Allegorical female/seated allegorical male; small steamboat below/allegorical female

Colour: Black with no tint

Back Design: Plain

357-12-04

$2 Face Design: Female with wheat/seated female, sheaves and cattle; small shield with 2 below/ cow and sheep

Colour: Black with no tint

Back Design: Plain

IMPRINT

Burton, Gurley & Edmunds, N. York & Bourne Agent Montreal.

SIGNATURES

left	right
mss. C. Henry & Cie	mss. L.A. Moreau

ISSUE DATING

Partially Engraved ___18___:

1837: 19 Juin, 27 Juin

Cat.No.	Denom.	Date	G	VG	F	VF	EF	AU
12-02	$1	1837	40.	80.	100.	150.	250.	—
12-04	$2	1837	40.	80.	100.	150.	250.	—

357-14. NOTE ISSUE OF 1837

DESIGNS AND COLOURS

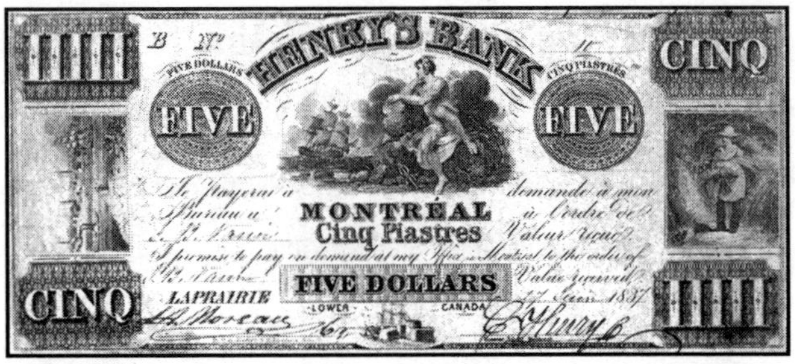

357-14-02

$5 Face Design: Ships, town in background (sideways) seated Mercury, ship in background, bales, cask and ship below/farmer standing under tree

Colour: Black with no tint

Back Design: Plain

357-14-04

$10 Face Design: —/allegorical female and eagle, small shield with X below/ornate design with TEN sideways

Colour: Black with no tint

Back Design: Plain

IMPRINT

Burton, Gurley & Edmunds, N.Y. and Bourne, Agent Montreal

SIGNATURES

left	right
mss. L.A. Moreau (Cr.)	mss. C. Henry & Cie

ISSUE DATING

Partially Engraved __18__:

27 Juin 1837

Cat.No.	Denom.	Date	G	VG	F	VF	EF	AU
14-02	$5	1837	85.	175.	225.	300.	—	—
14-04	$10	1837	100.	200.	275.	400.	—	—

BANQUE D'HOCHELAGA

1873 - 1925

BANK NUMBER 360 ***REDEEMABLE***

On May 3, 1873, Parliament passed a law incorporating the Banque d'Hochelaga and the institution opened for business in 1874 in the Place d'Arms in Montreal, the same year the Montreal Stock Exchange opened. During its first year of operations the bank began establishing branches and associating itself with other financial institutions which acted as agents in areas where the bank was not directly represented. After a modest start and slow early progress due to the short-term financial crisis between 1875 and 1896, the bank increased steadily in strength.

The decade from 1910 to 1920 was a booming one for the Banque d'Hochelaga, as it was for most Canadian banks. By the end of 1924 it had 197 branches, the largest number of banks established and administered by Francophone bankers in Quebec. In 1924, the bank merged with La Banque Nationale, having sufficient assets to assume most obligations for losses incurred by La Banque Nationale during an unsuccessful wartime financing scheme. The Quebec government made the merger possible by the unusual step of conveying to the Banque d'Hochelaga, in full ownership, its bonds for $15 million bearing interest at 5% and maturing in 40 years. On February 1, 1925 the Banque d'Hochelaga had its name changed to Banque Canadienne Nationale. Although its branch network remained largely in Quebec, it had operations across Canada and in other countries. Some of the note issues are completely in French, while others are bilingual.

360-10. ISSUES OF 1874 - 1877

DESIGNS AND COLOURS

360-10-02

$4 Face Design: Tree horses heads/milking scene "Dairy Maid"/L. Tourville
Colour: Black with green tint

Back Design: Lathework, counters and bank name
Colour: Green

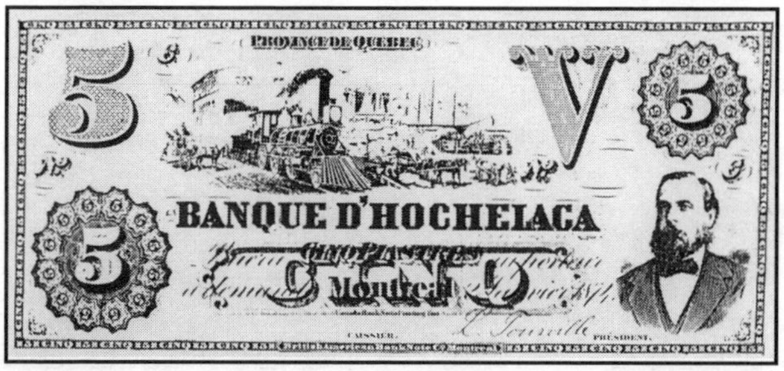

360-10-06P

$5 Face Design: —/train, ships at dockside/— L.Tourville
Colour: Black with green tint

Back Design: Lathework, counters and bank name
Colour: Green

360-10-08P

$10 Face Design: Shepherd by/Cartier approaching land/ L. Tourville
Colour: Black with green tint

Back Design: Lathework, counters and bank name
Colour: Green

360-10-10P

$20 Face Design: Dog on strongbox/female operating telegraph/L. Tourville
Colour: Black with green tint

Back Design: Lathework, counters and bank name
Colour: Green

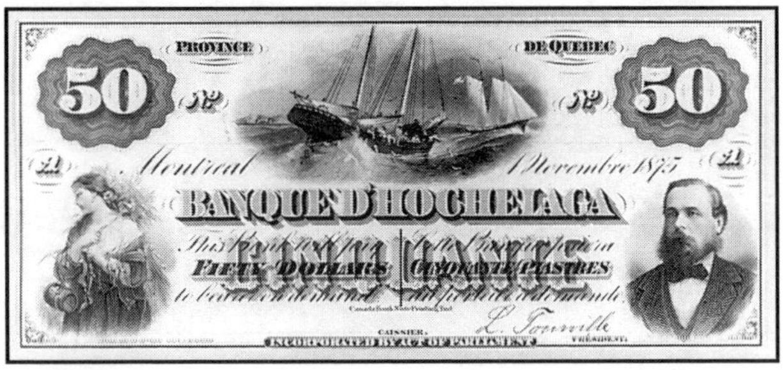

360-10-12P

$50 Face Design: Female with sheaf/fisherman and ships/ L. Tourville
Colour: Black with green tint

Back Design: Lathework, counters and bank name
Colour: Green

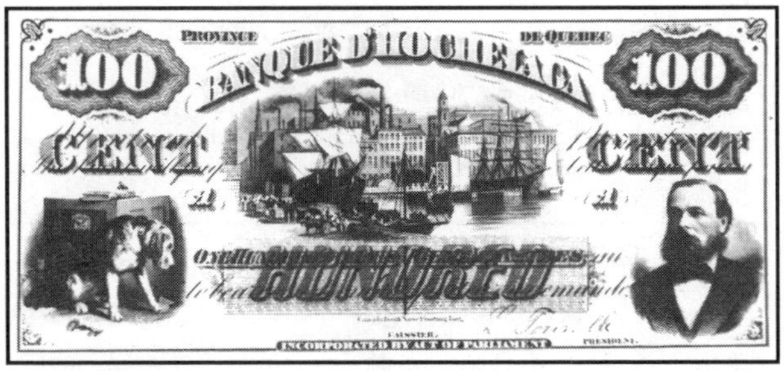

360-10-14P

$100 Face Design: Dog beside safe/ships at dockside, factories/ L. Tourville
Colour: Black with green tint

Back Design: Lathework, counters and bank name
Colour: Green

IMPRINT
British American Bank Note Co. Montreal

SIGNATURES

left	right
mss. various	engr. L. Tourville

ISSUE DATING
Engraved
2 Janvier 1874
1 Novembre 1875
2 Juillet 1877

OVERPRINT
$4 1877: "TROIS-RIVIERES" in blue

CIRCULATING NOTES

Cat.No.	Den.	Date	Variety	G	VG	F	VF	EF	AU
10-02	$4	1874		850.	1,700.	2,400.	3,300.	—	—
10-04	$4	1877		750.	1,500.	2,000.	2,800.	—	—
10-04a	$4	1877	o/p TROIS RIVIERES	900.	1,800.	2,500.	—	—	—
10-06P	$5	1874			No known issued notes				
10-08P	$10	1874			No known issued notes				
10-10P	$20	1875			No known issued notes				
10-12P	$50	1875			No known issued notes				
10-14P	$100	1875			No known issued notes				

PROOF NOTES

Cat. No.	Den.	Date		Unc
10-02P	$4	1874	FACE PROOF	500.
10-04P	$4	1877	FACE PROOF	500.
10-06P	$5	1874	FACE PROOF	500.
10-08P	$10	1874	FACE PROOF	500.
10-10P	$20	1875	FACE PROOF	500.
10-12P	$50	1875	FACE PROOF	600.
10-14P	$100	1875	FACE PROOF	600.

360-12. ISSUE OF 1880

DESIGNS AND COLOURS

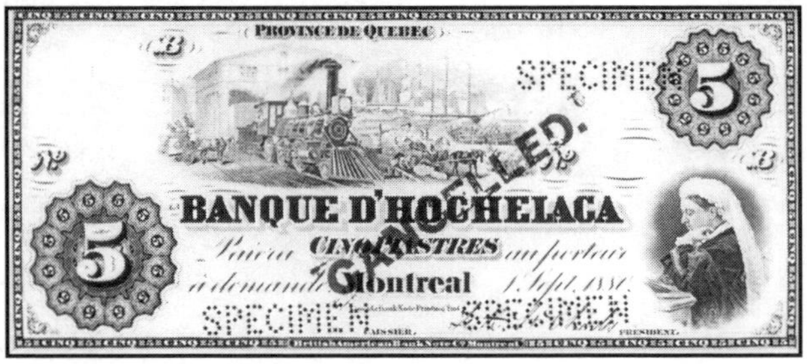

360-12-02P

$5 Face Design: —/train, ships at dockside/ Queen Victoria in "widow's weeds"
Colour: Black with green tint

Back Design: Lathework, counters and bank name
Colour: Green

360-12-04P

$10 Face Design: Shepherd boy/Cartier approaching land/ Queen Victoria in "widow's weeds"
Colour: Black with green tint

Back Design: Lathework, counters and bank name
Colour: Green

360-12-06P
$20 Face Design: Dog on strongbox/female operating telegraph/ Queen Victoria in "widow's weeds"
Colour: Black with green tint

Back Design: Lathework, counters and bank name
Colour: Green

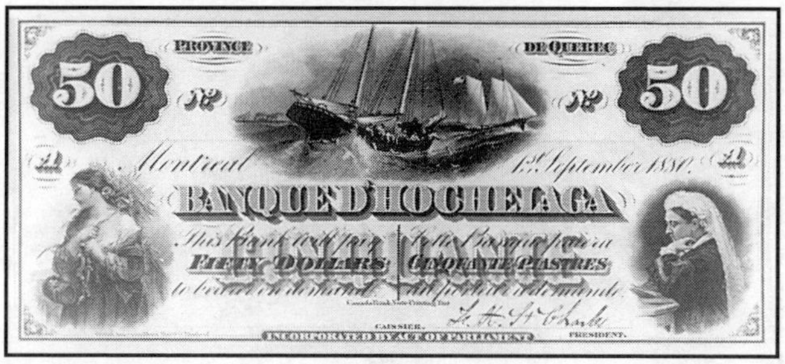

360-12-08P
$50 Face Design: Female with sheaf/fisherman and ships/Queen Victoria in "widow's weeds"
Colour: Black with green tint

Back Design: Lathework, counters and bank name
Colour: Green

360-12-10P
$100 Face Design: Dog beside safe/ships at dockside, factories/ Queen Victoria in "widow's weeds"
Colour: Black with green tint

Back Design: Lathework, counters and bank name
Colour: Green

IMPRINT
British American Bank Note Co. Montreal

SIGNATURES

left	right
mss. various	engr. F.X. St. Charles

ISSUE DATING
Engraved
1 Sept. 1880
1st September 1880

PROOF NOTES

Cat.No.	Denom.	Date		Unc
12-02P	$5	1880	FACE PROOF	500.
12-04P	$10	1880	FACE PROOF	500.
12-06P	$20	1880	FACE PROOF	500.
12-08P	$50	1880	FACE PROOF	600.
12-10P	$100	1880	FACE PROOF	600.

360-14. "MULTICOLOUR" ISSUE OF 1889

DESIGNS AND COLOURS

360-14-02Pa
$5 Face Design: Steamship and sailing ships/—/—
Colour: Black with ochre, blue and orange tint

Back Design: —/Lathework, counters and Provincial Crest/—
Colour: Blue

360-14-04P
$10 Face Design: Farmers ploughing with horses/ Samuel de Champlain
Colour: Black with blue, orange and gold tint

Back Design: —/Lathework, counters and Provincial Crest/—
Colour: Orange or blue

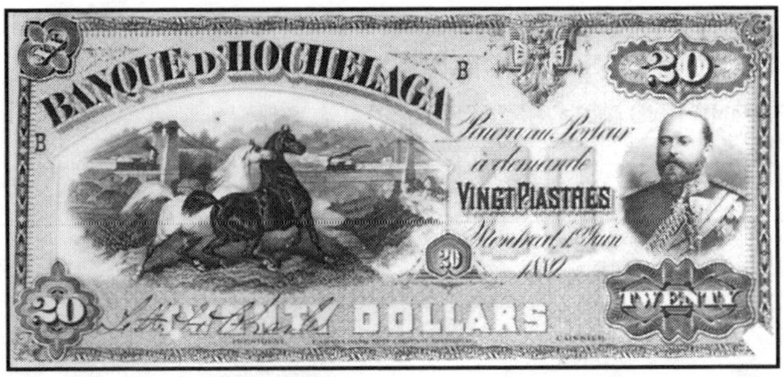

360-14-06P
$20 Face Design: Black and white horses in front of Roebling suspension bridge/—/Prince of Wales
Colour: Black with blue, red and gold tint

Back Design: —/Lathework, counters and Provincial Crest/—
Colour: Green or orange

360-14-08P
$50 Face Design: Prince of Wales/—/family on house raft
Colour: Black with blue, red and mustard yellow tint

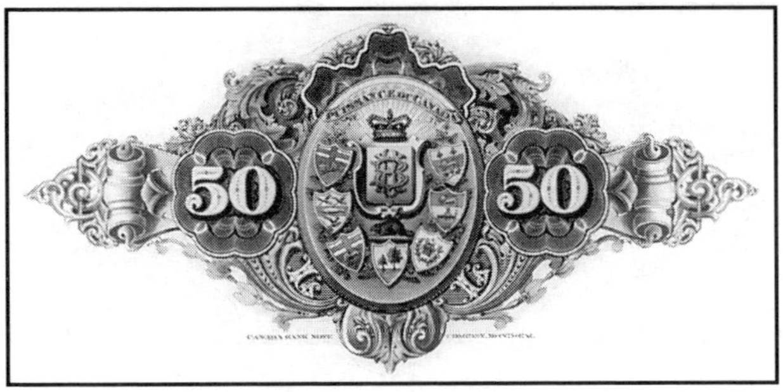

Back Design: —/Lathework, counters and Provincial Crest/—
Colour: Green

360-14-10P
$100 Face Design: Samuel de Champlain/—/Indians on bluff "Past and Present"
Colour: Black with blue, red and yellow-brown tint

Back Design: —/Lathework, counters and Provincial Crest/—
Colour: Green

IMPRINT
Canada Bank Note Co. Montreal

SIGNATURES

left	right
engr. F.X. St. Charles	mss. various

ISSUE DATING
Engraved
1889, 1er Juin

CIRCULATING NOTES

Cat. No.	Denom.	Date	Variety	G	VG	F	VF	EF	AU
14-02	$5	1889		1,000.	2,000.	2,500.	3,500.	—	—
14-04	$10	1889		No known issued notes					
14-06	$20	1889		No known issued notes					
14-08	$50	1889		No known issued notes					
14-10	$100	1889		No known issued notes					

PROOF NOTES

Cat.No.	Denom.	Date	Variety		Unc
14-02P	$5	1889	B & W	FACE PROOF	300.
14-02Pa	$5	1889	Coloured	FACE PROOF	600.
14-04P	$10	1889	B & W	FACE PROOF	300.
14-04Pa	$10	1889	Coloured	FACE PROOF	600.
14-06P	$20	1889	Coloured	FACE PROOF	600.
14-08P	$50	1889	Coloured	FACE PROOF	600.
14-10P	$100	1889	Coloured	FACE PROOF	600.

SPECIMEN NOTES

Cat. No	Denom.	Date		Unc
14-02S	$5	1889	SPECIMEN	1,000.
14-04S	$10	1889	SPECIMEN	1,000.
14-06S	$20	1889	SPECIMEN	1,000.
14-08S	$50	1889	SPECIMEN	1,000.
14-10S	$100	1889	SPECIMEN	1,000.

360-16. ISSUES OF 1894

DESIGNS AND COLOURS

360-16-02P
$5 Face Design: M.J.A. Pendergast/Montreal harbour/F.X. St. Charles
Colour: Black with green tint
Back Design: Lathework, counters and provincial crest
Colour: Green

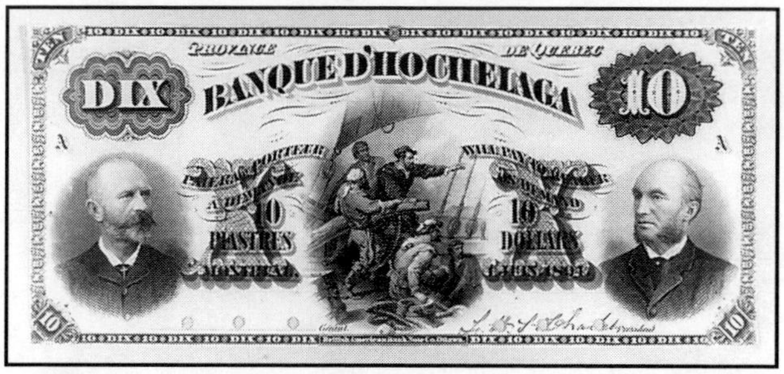

360-16-04P
$10 Face Design: M.J.A. Pendergast/Cartier approaching land/F.X. St. Charles
Colour: Black with green tint

Back Design: Lathework, counters and provincial crest
Colour: Green

IMPRINT
British American Bank Note Co. Ottawa

SIGNATURES

left	right
mss. various	engr. F.X. St. Charles

ISSUE DATING
Engraved
1 Juin, 1894

PROOF NOTES

Cat.No.	Denom.	Date		Unc
16-02P	$5	1894*	FACE PROOF	500.
16-04P	$10	1894*	FACE PROOF	500.

*Known face proofs have no tint.

360-18. ISSUES OF 1898 and 1907

DESIGNS AND COLOURS

360-18-02
$5 Face Design: M.J.A. Pendergast/steamship/F.X. St. Charles
Colour: Black with olive green tint
Back Design: Lathework, counters, bank name and Provincial Arms
Colour: Green

360-18-06
$10 Face Design: Maissoneuve monument/F.X. St. Charles/—
Colour: Black with olive tint

Back Design: Lathework, counters, bank name and Provincial Arms
Colour: Carmine

360-18-10S
$20 Face Design: Loading hay/—/F.X. St. Charles
Colour: Black with olive tint

Back Design: lathework, counters, bank name; Coat of arms/Maissoneuve monument/—
Colour: Blue

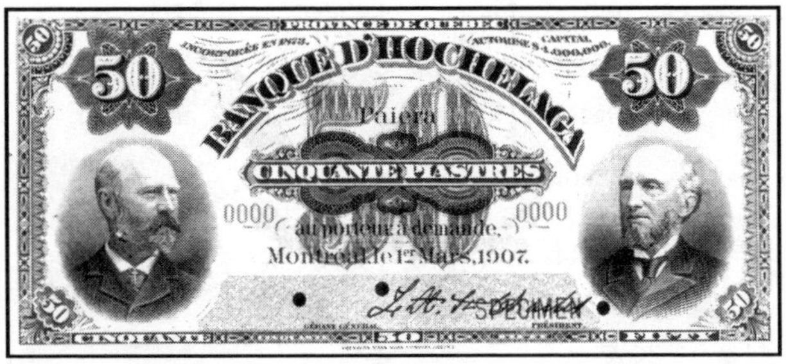

360-18-16P
$50 Face Design: M.J.A. Pendergast/—/F.X. St. Charles
Colour: Black with green and olive green tint

Back Design: Lathework, counters, bank name; Coat of Arms/Maissoneuve monument/—
Colour: Olive

360-18-20S
$100 Face Design: Dock scene/-/F.X. St. Charles
Colour: Black with olive tint

Back Design: Lathework, counters, bank name; Coat of Arms/Maissoneuve monument/—
Colour: Green

IMPRINT

American Bank Note Company. Ottawa

SIGNATURES

left	right
mss. various	typed F.X. St. Charles

ISSUE DATING

Engraved

Le 1er Mai, 1898
Le 2 Mai, 1898
Le 1er Mars, 1907

CIRCULATING NOTES

Cat.No.	Denom.	Date	G	VG	F	VF	EF	AU
18-02	$5	1898	800.	1,600.	2,400.	—	—	—
18-04	$5	1907	700.	1,400.	1,800.	—	—	—
18-06	$10	1898	800.	1,600.	2,400.	3,300.	—	—
18-08	$10	1907	No known issued notes					
18-10	$20	1898	No known issued notes					
18-12	$20	1907	No known issued notes					
18-14	$50	1898	No known issued notes					
18-16	$50	1907	No known issued notes					
18-18	$100	1898	No known issued notes					
18-20	$100	1907	No known issued notes					

PROOF NOTES

Cat. No.	Denom.	Date	Variety		Unc
18-02P	$5	1898	B & W	FACE PROOF	200.
18-02Pa	$5	1898	Coloured*	FACE PROOF	400.
18-04P	$5	1907	B & W	FACE PROOF	200.
18-04Pa	$5	1907	Coloured*	FACE PROOF	400.
18-06P	$10	1898	B & W	FACE PROOF	200.
18-06Pa	$10	1898	Coloured*	FACE PROOF	400.
18-08P	$10	1907	B & W	FACE PROOF	200.
18-08Pa	$10	1907	Coloured*	FACE PROOF	400.
18-10P	$20	1898	B & W	FACE PROOF	200.
18-10Pa	$20	1898	Coloured*	FACE PROOF	400.
18-12P	$20	1907	B & W	FACE PROOF	200.
18-14Pa	$50	1898	Coloured*	FACE PROOF	400.
18-16P	$50	1907	B & W	FACE PROOF	200.
18-16Pa	$50	1907	Coloured*	FACE PROOF	400.
18-18Pa	$100	1898	Coloured*	FACE PROOF	400.
18-20P	$100	1907	B & W	FACE PROOF	200.
18-20Pa	$100	1907	Coloured*	FACE PROOF	400.

* Black with an olive or green tint.

SPECIMEN NOTES

Cat. No.	Denom.	Date		Unc
18-08S	$10	1907	SPECIMEN	500.
18-10S	$20	1898	SPECIMEN	500.
18-12S	$20	1907	SPECIMEN	500.
18-14S	$50	1898	SPECIMEN	500.
18-16S	$50	1907	SPECIMEN	500.
18-18S	$100	1898	SPECIMEN	600.
18-20S	$100	1907	SPECIMEN	600.

360-20. ISSUE OF 1911

DESIGNS AND COLOURS

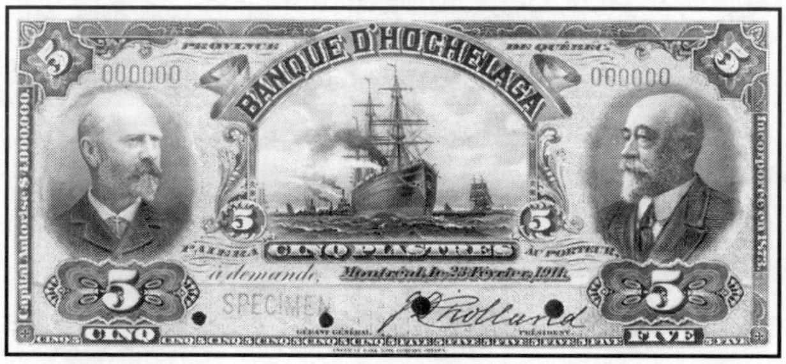

360-20-02S

$5 Face Design: J.A. Pendergast/steamship/ J.D. Rolland
Colour: Black with olive green tint

Back Design: Lathework, counters and Provincial Arms
Colour: Green

360-20-04

$10 Face Design: Maissoneuve monument/J.D. Rolland/—
Colour: Black with olive tint

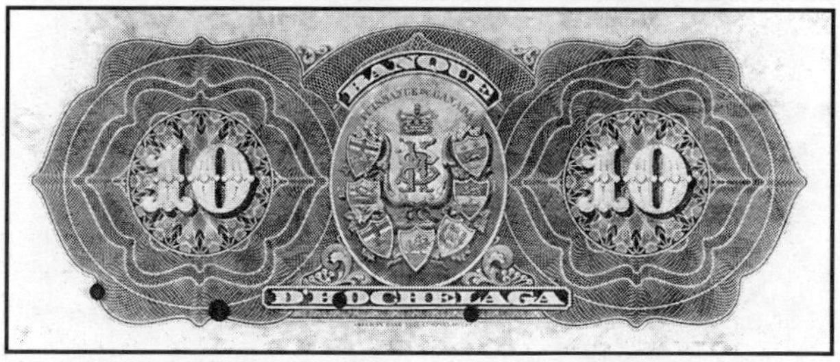

Back Design: Lathework, counters and Provincial Arms
Colour: Carmine

360-20-06P

$20 Face Design: Loading hay/—/J.D. Rolland
Colour: Black with olive tint

Back Design: Lathework, counters and Provincial Arms
Colour: Blue

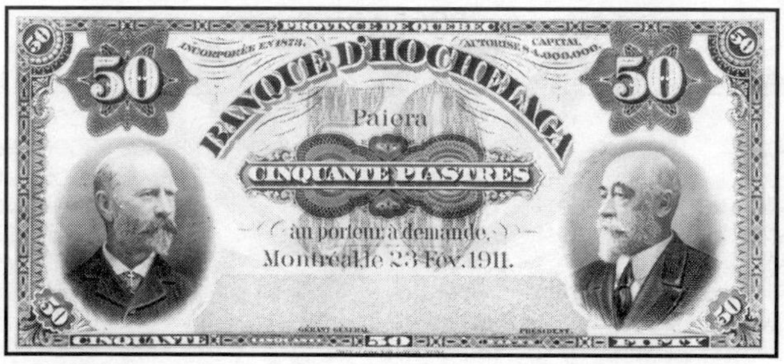

360-20-08P

$50 Face Design: J.A. Pendergast/—/J.D. Rolland
Colour: Black with green and olive green tint

Back Design: Lathework, counters, bank name, Coat of Arms/Maissoneuve monument/—
Colour: Olive

360-20-10P

$100 Face Design: Dock scene/—/J.D. Rolland
Colour: Black with olive tint

Back Design: Lathework, counters, bank name, Coat of Arms/Maissoneuve monument/—
Colour: Green

IMPRINT

American Bank Note Company, Ottawa

SIGNATURES

left	right
mss. various	typed J.D. Rolland

ISSUE DATING

Engraved

Le 23 Fevrier, 1911
Le 23 Fev. 1911

CIRCULATING NOTES

Cat.No.	Denom.	Date	G	VG	F	VF	EF	AU
20-02	$5	1911	800.	1,600.	—	—	—	—
20-04	$10	1911	800.	1,600.	2,500.	3,500.	—	—
20-06	$20	1911	No known issued notes					
20-08	$50	1911	No known issued notes					
20-10	$100	1911	No known issued notes					

PROOF NOTES

Cat. No.	Denom.	Date	Variety		Unc
20-02P	$5	1911	B & W	FACE PROOF	200.
20-02Pa	$5	1911	Coloured*	FACE PROOF	300.
20-04P	$10	1911	B & W	FACE PROOF	200.
20-04Pa	$10	1911	Coloured*	FACE PROOF	300.
20-06P	$20	1911	B & W	FACE PROOF	250.
20-06Pa	$20	1911	Coloured*	FACE PROOF	450.
20-08P	$50	1911	B & W	FACE PROOF	250.
20-08Pa	$50	1911	Coloured*	FACE PROOF	450.
20-10P	$100	1911	B & W	FACE PROOF	300.
20-10Pa	$100	1911	Coloured*	FACE PROOF	500.

*black with an olive or green tint

SPECIMEN NOTES

Cat. No.	Denom.	Date		Unc
20-02S	$5	1911	SPECIMEN	650.
20-04S	$10	1911	SPECIMEN	650.

360-22. ISSUE OF 1914

DESIGNS AND COLOURS

360-22-02

$5 Face Design: J.A. Vaillancourt/Place d'Arms/ Maissoneuve monument
Colour: Black with light blue tint

Back Design: Lathwork, counters, bank name and Provincial Arms
Colour: Blue-green

360-22-04

$10 Face Design: J.A. Vaillancourt/Quebec City/ Champlain monument
Colour: Black with yellow-orange tint

Back Design: Lathework, counters, bank name and Provincial Arms
Colour: Red-brown

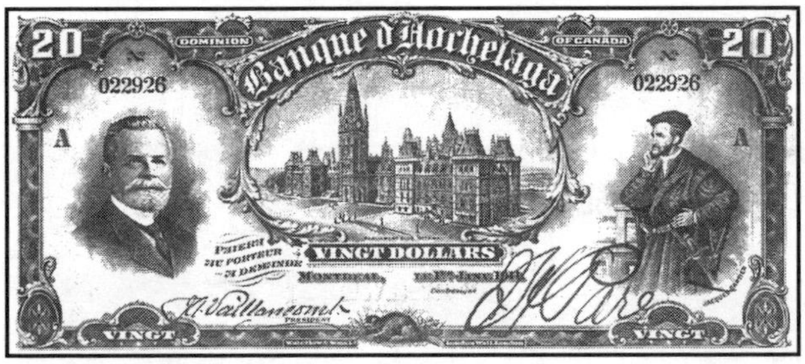

360-22-06

$20 Face Design: J.A. Vaillancourt/Parliament Buildings, Ottawa/Jacques Cartier
Colour: Black with blue green tint

Back Design: Lathework, counters, bank name and Provincial Arms
Colour: Green

360-22-08

$50 Face Design: J.A. Vaillancourt/horse-drawn combine in wheat field/farmer sowing seeds
Colour Black with salmon tint

Back Design: Lathework, counters, bank name and Provincial Arms
Colour: Brown

360-22-10

$100 Face Design: J.A. Vaillancourt/Moraine Lake/ De La Verendrye monument
Colour: Black with lilac tint

Back Design: Lathework, counters, bank name and Provincial Arms
Colour: Slate

IMPRINT

Waterlow & Sons, Ltd London
Waterlow & Sons Ltd. London Wall, London

SIGNATURES

left	**right**
engr. J.A. Vaillancourt	mss. various

ISSUE DATING

Engraved

Le 1er Janvier, 1914

CIRCULATING NOTES

Cat.No.	Denom.	Date	G	VG	F	VF	EF	Unc
22-02	$5	1914	60.	125.	175.	250.	450.	900.
22-04	$10	1914	75.	150.	225.	325.	600.	—
22-06	$20	1914	500.	1,000.	1,500.	—	—	—
22-08	$50	1914	Institutional collection only					
22-10	$100	1914	—	1,100.	1,700.	2,500.	—	—

SPECIMEN NOTES

Cat. No.	Denom.	Date		Unc
22-02S	$5	1914	SPECIMEN	500.
22-04S	$10	1914	SPECIMEN	500.
22-06S	$20	1914	SPECIMEN	600.
22-08S	$50	1914	SPECIMEN	750.
22-10S	$100	1914	SPECIMEN	750.

NOTE: Some specimen and proof notes of 1914 issue have different tints from issued notes

$5: Green Face, Green Back
$10: Blue Face, Blue Back
$10: Lilac Face, Brown Back
$20: Rose Face, Green Back
$50: Red Face, Red Back
$100: Orange Face, Brown Back

360-24. ISSUE OF 1917 AND 1920

DESIGNS AND COLOURS

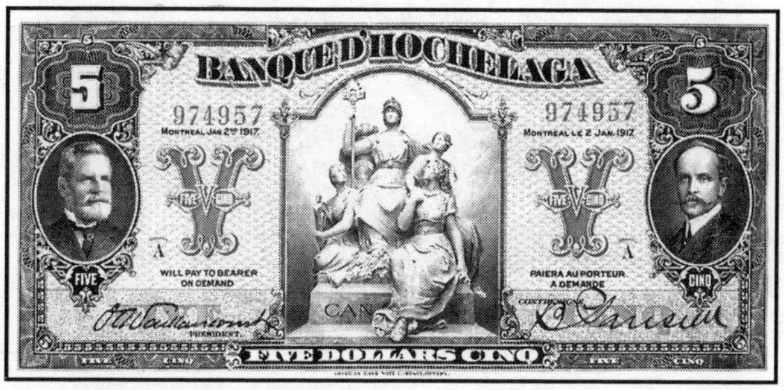

360-24-04

$5 Face Design: J.A. Vaillancourt/statue with four figures/ Beaudry Leman
Colour: Black with olive tint

Back Design: Lathework, counters, bank name and Provincial Arms
Colour: Olive

360-24-08

$10 Face Design: J.A. Vaillancourt/statue with four figures/ Beaudry Leman
Colour: Black with brown tint

Back Design: Lathework, counters, bank name and Provincial Arms
Colour: Brown

360-24-18S

$20 Face Design: J.A. Vaillancourt/statue with seated allegorical female, Arms of Canada and flag/Beaudry Leman
Colour: Black with blue tint

Back Design: Lathework, counters, bank name and Provincial Arms
Colour: Blue

360-24-24S
$50 Face Design: J.A. Vaillancourt/Maissoneuve statue/ Beaudry Leman
Colour: Black with red tint
Back Design: Lathework, counters, bank name and Provincial Arms
Colour: Orange-red

360-24-30
$100 Face Design: J.A. Vaillancourt/—/Beaudry Leman
Colour: Black with purple tint

Back Design: Lathework, counters, bank name and Provincial Arms
Colour: Purple

IMPRINT

American Bank Note Company, Ottawa

SIGNATURES

left	right
typed J.A. Vaillancourt	mss. various
typed J.A. Vaillancourt	typed Beaudry Leman

ISSUE DATING

Engraved

Jan. 2nd, 1917/le 2 Jan 1917
Jan. 2nd, 1920/le 2 Jan 1920

CIRCULATING NOTES

Cat.No.	Den.	Date	Variety	G	VG	F	VF	EF	AU
24-02	$5	1917	mss. sign,r*	75.	150.	200.	250.	600.	—
24-04	$5	1917	Leman typed,r	100.	200.	300.	400.	750.	—
24-08	$10	1917	mss. sign,r	75.	150.	200.	250.	600.	—
24-10	$10	1917	Leman typed,r	100.	200.	300.	400.	750.	—
24-18	$20	1917		250.	500.	750.	1.250.	2,000.	—
24-24	$50	1920		Institutional collection only					
24-30	$100	1920		—	—	1,200.	2,000.	2,800.	4,000.

*This variety comes with red or blue sheet numbers.

PROOF NOTES

Cat. No.	Denom.	Date			Unc
24-02P	$5	1917	B & W	FACE PROOF	200.
24-02Pa	$5	1917	Coloured	FACE PROOF	350.
24-08P	$10	1917	B & W	FACE PROOF	200.
24-08Pa	$10	1917	Coloured	FACE PROOF	350.
24-18P	$20	1917	B & W	FACE PROOF	225.
24-18Pa	$29	1917	Coloured	FACE PROOF	400.
24-24P	$50	1920	B & W	FACE PROOF	250.
24-24Pa	$50	1920	Coloured	FACE PROOF	450.
24-30P	$100	1920	B & W	FACE PROOF	300.
24-30Pa	$100	1920	Coloured	FACE PROOF	500.

SPECIMEN NOTES

Cat. No.	Denom.	Date		Unc
24-18S	$20	1917	SPECIMEN	600.
24-24S	$50	1920	SPECIMEN	750.

THE HOME BANK OF CANADA

1903 - 1923

TORONTO (ONTARIO)

BANK NUMBER 365 ***REDEEMABLE***

Originally a loan and building company, The Home Bank of Canada operated under a charter from 1905, with its head office in Toronto. Its failure in 1923 caused the largest loss to shareholders and creditors recorded up to that time in Canada. The Government of Canada, pursuant to an investigation by a Royal Commission into the responsibilities for and causes of the failure, granted relief to the extent of 35% of the claims of those individuals with claims less than $500. In addition, those with larger claims who were found upon inquiry to be in special need as a result of the failure, were also granted relief at 35%. This assistance involved a total outlay of about $3,460,000.

365-10. ISSUES OF 1904 - 1920

DESIGNS AND COLOURS

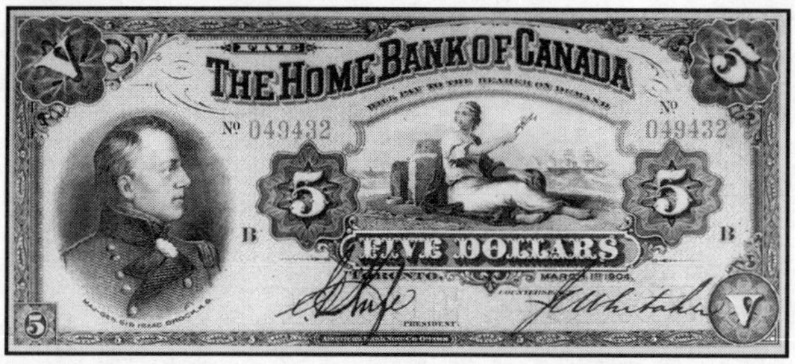

365-10-02

$5 Face Design: Maj. Gen Sir Isaac Brock K.B./seated allegorical "commerce" female, ships in background/—
Colour: Black with red tint

Back Design: Lathework, counters, bank name and three students "Mutual improvement"
Colour: Black with red, green and brown tint

365-10-14

$10 Face Design: The Ridgeway monument (1866)(Fenian Raid) woman with horse, poultry/—
Colour: Black with green tint

Back Design: Lathework, counters, bank name and three students "Mutual Improvement"
Colour: Black with red, green and brown tint

365-10-18S

$20 Face Design: Riel Rebellion monument (1885) haying scene, barge and train in background/—
Colour: Black with brown tint

Back Design Lathework, counters, bank name and three students "Mutual Improvement"
Colour: Black with red, green and brown tint

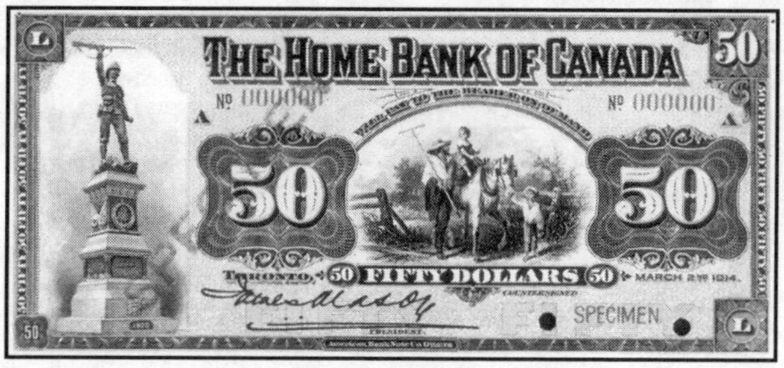

365-10-26S

$50 Face Design: Boer War monument (1900)/ farmer with horse and children/—
Colour: Black with blue tint

Back Design: Lathework, counters, bank name and three students "Mutual Improvement"
Colour: Black with red, green and brown tint

365-10-36

$100 Face Design: Champlain monument/ helmeted female in oval frame/—
Colour: Black with olive green tint

Back Design: Lathework, counters, bank name and three students "Mutual Improvement"
Colour: Black with red, green and brown tint

IMPRINT
American Bank Note Co. Ottawa

SIGNATURES

	left	right
1904:	typed E. O'Keefe	mss. various
1914:	typed James Mason	mss. various
1917:	typed M.J. Haney	mss. various
$5 & $10:		
1917:	typed M.J. Hanley	mss. various
	typed H.J. Daley	typed J. Cooper-Mason
1920:	typed S. Young	typed J. Cooper-Mason
$20 1920:	typed S. Young	mss. various

ISSUE DATING
Engraved
March 1st 1904
March 2nd 1914
March 1st 1917
March 1st 1920

OVERPRINT
$5 1904: "S S" in blue
$10 1904: "S S" in red

CIRCULATING NOTES

Cat.No.	Denom	Date	Variety	G	VG	F	VF	EF	AU
10-02	$5	1904		750.	1,500.	2,000.	3,400.	4,500.	6,000.
10-04	$5	1914		850.	1,700.	2,200.	3,700.	—	—
10-06	$5	1917	mss sig. r.	800.	1,600.	2,100.	3,550.	—	—
10-06a	$5	1917	typed sig r.	850.	1,700.	2,200.	3,700.	—	—
10-08	$5	1920		950.	1,900.	2,700.	4,250.	—	—
10-10	$10	1904		900.	1,800.	2,300.	—	—	—
10-12	$10	1914		900.	1,800.	2,300.	3,800.	—	—
10-14	$10	1917		850.	1,700.	2,200.	—	—	—
10-16	$10	1920		950.	1,900.	2,600.	4,100.	—	—
10-18	$20	1904		No known issued notes					
10-20	$20	1914		No known issued notes					
10-24	$20	1920		1,500.	2,600.	3,400.	—	—	—
10-26	$50	1904		No known issued notes					
10-28	$50	1914		No known issued notes					
10-32	$100	1904		No known issued notes					
10-34	$100	1914		No known issued notes					
10-36	$100	1917		—	3,000.	4,000.	5,500.	—	—

PROOF NOTES

Cat. No.	Denom.	Date		Unc
10-02P	$5	1904	FACE PROOF	600.
10-10P	$10	1904	FACE PROOF	600.
10-18P	$20	1904	FACE PROOF	700.
10-26P	$50	1904	FACE PROOF	800.
10-32P	$100	1904	FACE PROOF	800.
10-34P	$100	1914	FACE PROOF	800.

SPECIMEN NOTES

Cat. No.	Denom.	Date		Unc
10-02S	$5	1904	SPECIMEN	1,000.
10-10S	$10	1904	SPECIMEN	1,000.
10-18S	$20	1904	SPECIMEN	1,100.
10-20S	$20	1914	SPECIMEN	1,100.
10-26S	$50	1904	SPECIMEN	1,200.
10-28S	$50	1914	SPECIMEN	1,200.
10-32S	$100	1904	SPECIMEN	1,300.

THE BANK OF HULL

1837

HULL, LOWER CANADA

BANK NUMBER 370 ***NONREDEEMABLE***

Orders for bank-notes were placed with Rawdon, Wright, Hatch and Edson on Sept. 28th, 1837. A sheet of Proof notes is in the municipal offices of the city of Hull, Quebec. The denominations are - 30 sous or quarter dollar, 3 francs or half dollar, $1.00 or 5 shillings, $2.00 or 10 shillings, $3.00 or 15 shillings, $5.00 or 25 shillings and $10.00 or 50 shillings.

No notes are known.

THE IMPERIAL BANK OF CANADA

1873 - 1961

TORONTO (ONTARIO)

BANK NUMBER 375 ***REDEEMABLE***

Established in 1873 in Toronto by a group of businessmen, The Imperial Bank of Canada was one of the 28 banks established in the seven years following Confederation. By December of 1874, the Provisional Board was formed to raise the required capital. Of the 432 shareholders, only 160 resided in Toronto. The first office opened for business in Toronto in March of 1875. With the absorption of The Niagara District Bank the same year, branches were acquired elsewhere in Ontario.

The new branches were opened very cautiously. After 10 years the bank had 10 branches, including two in the West. In 1886 a branch was established in Calgary and in 1891 another opened in Edmonton. For some years the Alberta branch was the most northerly bank in Canada. By 1895 there were 12 branches in the West and 20 in the East. In 1899, attracted by lumbering and mining activity, the bank opened its first branch in northern Ontario. The Imperial Bank of Canada absorbed The Wyeburg Security Bank in 1931 extending its operations into Saskatchewan, and in 1956 it absorbed Barclay's Bank (Canada).

In February of 1961, the government announced it had approved an amalgamation agreement between The Canadian Bank of Commerce and the Imperial Bank of Canada, the new institution to be known as the Canadian Imperial Bank of Commerce. In due course the agreement received the required approval of the shareholders of both banks and the merger took effect in June of 1961. At this time, the two banks had 1,242 branches and total assets in excess of $4 billion. Under the agreement, shareholders of The Canadian Bank of Commerce received one share in the new bank for each share already in possession and those of The Imperial Bank of Canada received seven shares in the new bank for each six shares held in The Imperial Bank of Canada.

375-10. BABN PRINTINGS 1875 - 1906

DESIGNS AND COLOURS

75-10-02
$4 Face Design: Hon. W.H. Merritt/ornate 4 overRoyal Crest/ H.S. Howland
Colour: Black with green tint

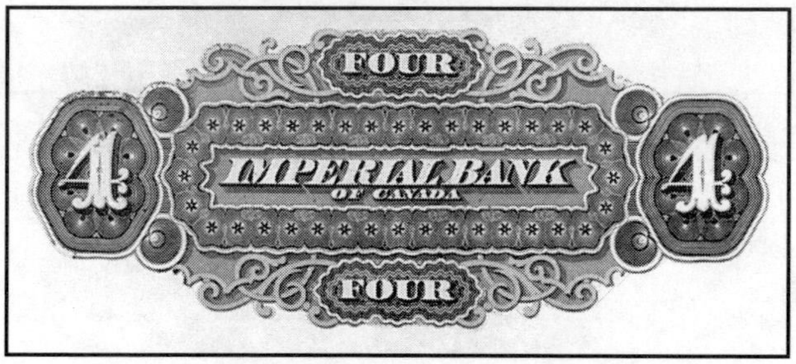

Back Design: Lathework, counters and bank name
Colour: Green

375-10-06
$5 Face Design: Hon. W.H. Merritt/ploughing scene/H.S. Howland. Bank name above central vignette
Colour: Black with green tint

Back Design: Lathework, counters and bank name
Colour: Green

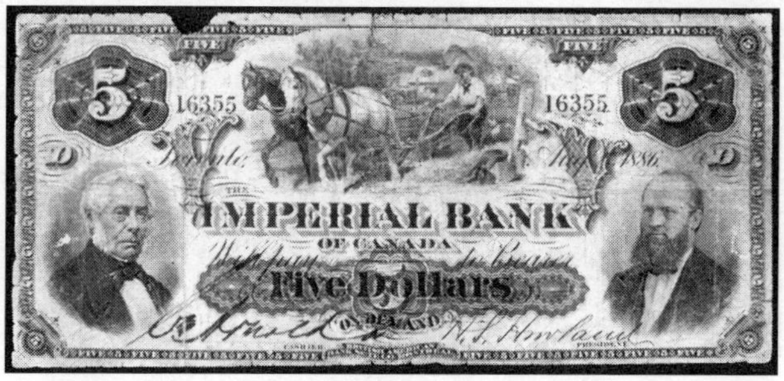

375-10-12
$5 Face Design: Hon. W.H. Merritt/ploughing scene/H.S. Howland. Bank name below central vignette
Colour: Black with green tint

Back Design: Lathework, counters and bank name
Colour: Green

375-10-18
$5 Face Design: Hon. W.H. Merritt/Royal Crest with ornate 5/ H.S. Howland
Colour 1890: Black with green tint
1895-96: Black with ochre tint

Back Design: Lathework, counters and bank name
Colour: Orange

375-10-22
$10 Face Design: Hon. W.H. Merritt/Bank Crest flanked by lion and Indian/H.S. Howland
Colour: Black with green tint

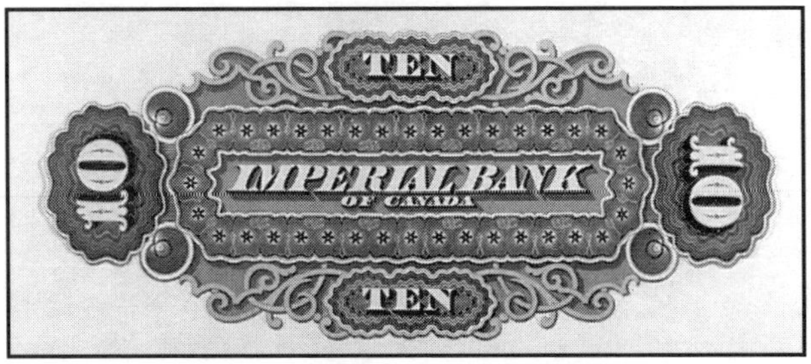

Back Design: Lathework, counters and bank name
Colour: Green

375-10-24
$20 Face Design: Farmer with horse-drawn mower/—/H.S. Howland
Colour: Black with green tint

Back Design: Lathework, counters and bank name
Colour: Green

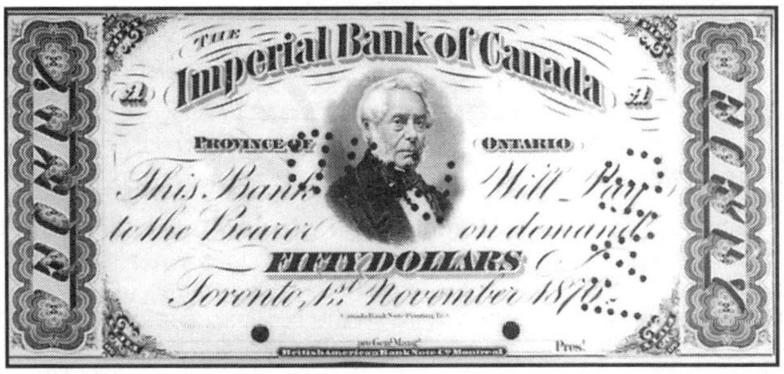

375-10-28P
$50 Face Design: —/Hon. W.H. Merritt/—
Colour: Black with green tint

Back Design: Lathework, counters and bank name
Colour: Green

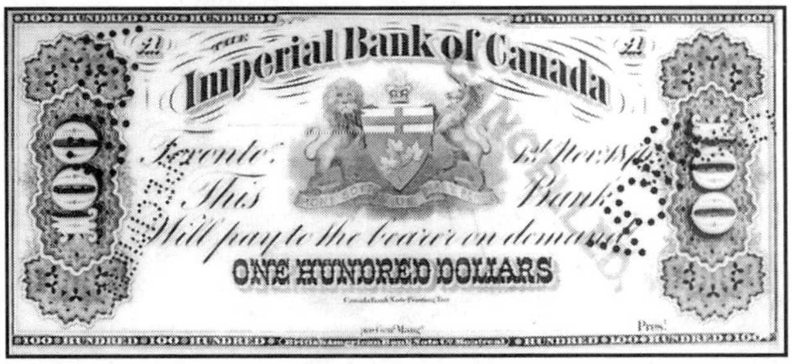

375-10-30P
$100 Face Design: —/Canadian Crest/—
Colour: Black with green tint

Back Design: Lathework, counters and bank name
Colour: Green

IMPRINT

British American Bank Note Co. Montreal
British American Bank Note Co. Ottawa

SIGNATURES

	left	right
1875:	mss. various	mss. various
1875:	mss. various	mss. H.S. Howland
1875-1896:	mss. various	engr. H.S. Howland
1906:	mss. various	engr. D.R. Wilkie

ISSUE DATING

Engraved

March 1st 1875
1st March 1875
1st November 1876
1st Nov 1876
Aug. 2nd 1886
Aug. 2nd 1890
Oct. 1, 1895
Oct. 1st 1896
1st May 1906

OVERPRINT

1875: "Z Z" in blue

CIRCULATING NOTES

Cat.No.	Denom.	Date	Variety	G	VG	F	VF	EF	AU
10-02	$4	1875	mss. r.	600.	1,200.	1,600.	2,400.	—	—
10-04	$4	1875	Engr. Howland,r.	600.	1,200.	1,600.	2,400.	—	—
10-08	$5	1875	mss. Howland,r.	600.	1,200.	1,600.	—	—	—
10-08	$5	1875	Engr. Howland,r.	600.	1,200.	1,600.	—	—	—
10-10	$5	1876			No known issued notes				
10-12	$5	1886			Institutional collection only				
10-14	$5	1890	Green tint	400.	800.	1,000.	1,500.	—	—
10-16	$5	1895	Ochre tint	450.	900.	1,200.	2,000.	—	—
10-18	$5	1896	Ochre tint	400.	800.	1,000.	1,500.	—	—
10-20	$10	1875	mss.Howland,r.	400.	800.	—	—	—	—
10-22	$10	1875	Engr.Howland,r.	400.	800.	—	—	—	—
10-24	$20	1876			Institutional collection only				
10-26	$20	1906			Institutional collection only				
10-28	$50	1876			No known issued notes				
10-30	$100	1876			No known issued notes				

PROOF NOTES

Cat. No.	Denom.	Date		Unc
10-04P	$4	1875	FACE PROOF	400.
10-08P	$5	1875	FACE PROOF	400.
10-10P	$5	1876	FACE PROOF	400.
10-12P	$5	1886	FACE PROOF	400.
10-14P	$5	1890	FACE PROOF	400.
10-22P	$10	1875	FACE PROOF	400.
10-28P	$50	1876	FACE PROOF	600.
10-30P	$100	1876	FACE PROOF	700.

375-12. **WATERLOW PRINTINGS**

1902 - 1910

Some notes of 1902 and 1907 are of extra large size.

DESIGNS AND COLOURS

375-12-06

$5 Face Design: Woman counting bags in chest/ Edward VIII as a boy/Canadian Crest
Colour: Black with ochre tint

Back Design: seated woman with tablet
Colour: Green

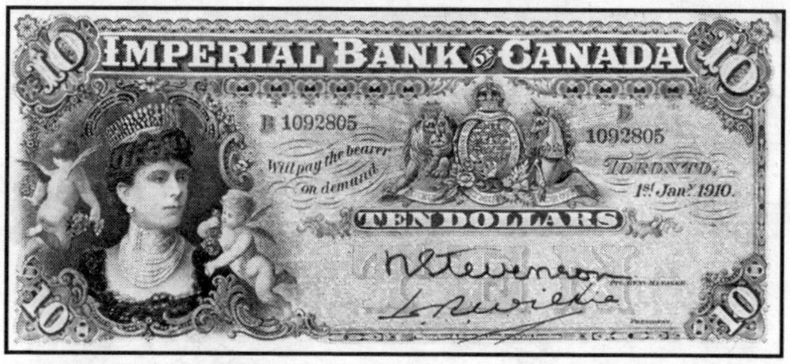

375-12-10

$10 Face Design: Queen Alexandra and cherubs/ Royal Crest/—
Colour: Black with blue tint

Back Design: —/seated woman with cherub/—
Colour: Yellow-brown

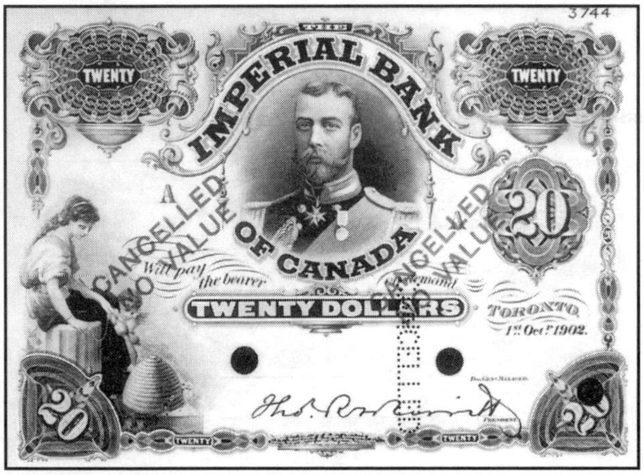

375-12-12
$20 Face Design: Seated woman and child/George V as Duke of York/—
Colour: Blue with gold, orange and violet tint

Back Design: —/woman with fruit basket/—
Colour: Green

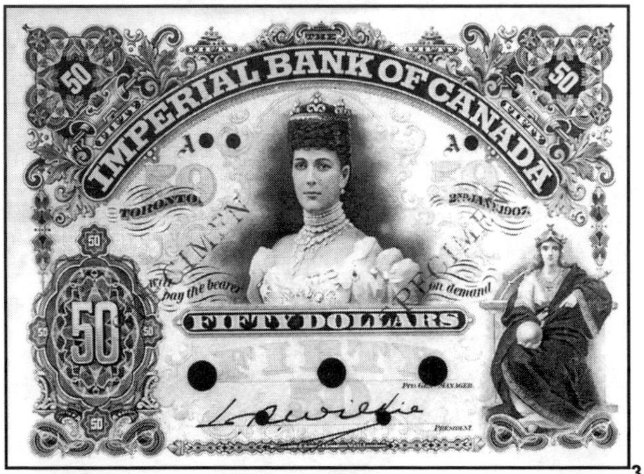

3
75-12-16
$50 Face Design: —/Queen Alexandra/seated allegorical female
Colour: Black with gold and green tint

Back Design: —/standing "Commerce" figure/—
Colour: Carmine

375-12-18S
$100 Face Design: King Edward VII, train/ornate 100 and Royal Crest/Thomas R. Merritt, ship
1902 Colour: Blue with yellow, brown and lilac tint
1907 Colour: Black with red and gold tint

Back Design: —/bank building/—
1902 Colour: Ochre
1907 Colour: Blue

Note: Some specimen notes have different tint from issued notes. $10 ochre face, green back.

IMPRINT

Waterlow & Sons Ltd., London Wall, London

SIGNATURES

	left	right
1902:	mss. various	engr. Thos. R.Merritt
1906-1910:	mss. various	engr. D.R. Wilkie

ISSUE DATING

Engraved

1st Octr 1902
1st May 1906
Jan. 2, 1907
1st Jan 1910

Note: Counterfeits of 12-10 exist

CIRCULATING NOTES

Cat.No.	Denom.	Date	Variety	G	VG	F	VF	EF	AU
12-02	$5	1902		250.	500.	750.	1,100.	—	—
12-04	$5	1906		250.	500.	750.	1,100.	—	—
12-06	$5	1910		175.	350.	500.	850.	—	—
12-08	$10	1902		No known issued notes					
12-09	$10	1907		1,750.	3,500.	—	—	—	—
12-10	$10	1910		175.	350.	500.	800.	—	—
12-10C	$10	1910	Counterfeit	60.	125.	150.	200.	—	—
12-12	$20	1902	Extra large size	Institutional collection only					
12-14	$50	1902	Extra large size	No known issued notes					
12-16	$50	1907	Extra large size	Institutional collection only					
12-18	$100	1902	Extra large size	No known issued notes					
12-20	$100	1907	Extra large size	No known issued notes					

SPECIMEN NOTES

Cat. No.	Denom.	Date	Variety		Unc
12-02S	$5	1902		SPECIMEN	700.
12-04S	$5	1906		SPECIMEN	700.
12-06S	$5	1910		SPECIMEN	700.
12-08S	$10	1902		SPECIMEN	1,000.
12-10S	$10	1910		SPECIMEN	800.
12-12S	$20	1902	Extra large size	SPECIMEN	5,000.
12-14S	$50	1902	Extra large size	SPECIMEN	5,000.
12-16S	$50	1907	Extra large size	SPECIMEN	5,000.
12-18S	$100	1902	Extra large size	SPECIMEN	5,000.
12-20S	$100	1907	Extra large size	SPECIMEN	5,000.

375-14. WATERLOW ESSAYS OF 1914

The following notes are essay and models. They are housed in an institutional collection. The $20 and $50 notes are dated 1st January, 1914.

DESIGNS AND COLOURS

375-14-02E

$5 Face Design: Woman counting bags in chest/Edward VIII as young man/Canadian crest
Colour: Black with ochre tint

Back Design: Unknown
Colour: Unknown

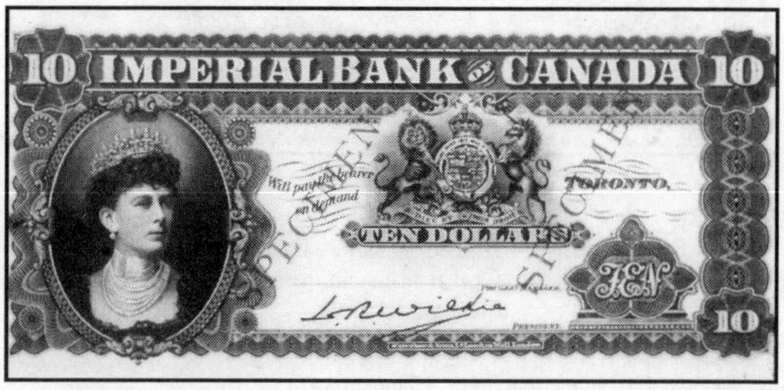

375-14-04E

$10 Face Design: Queen Alexandra in large ornate frame/ Royal Crest
Colour: Black (no tint)

Back Design: Unknown
Colour: Unknown

375-14-06E

$20 Face Design: George V as Duke of York/beaver in ornate 20, forest, factory/crest
Colour: Blue with brown and ochre tint

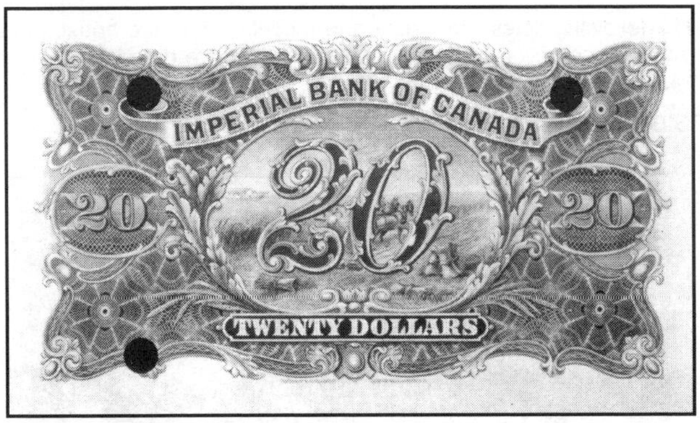

Back Design: 20/Bank name, ornate 20 over farm scene/20
Colour: Olive Green

375-14-08E
$50 Face Design: Seated Britannia figure, standing "Commerce" figure at dockside/ three warships/—
Colour: Brown with blue and orange tint

Note: $20 and $50 notes are dated 1st January, 1914.

Cat.No.	Denom	Date	Unc
14-02E	$5	none	in institutional collection SPECIMEN
14-04E	$10	none	in institutional collection PROOF
14-06E	$20	1914	in institutional collection SPECIMEN
14-08E	$50	1914	in institutional collection MODEL

375-16. OLD BABN PRINTINGS RESUMED 1915 - 1920

DESIGNS AND COLOURS

375-16-04
$5 Face Design: Hon. W.M. Merritt/Royal Crest with ornate 5/ H.S. Howland
1915 Colour: Black with yellow, green and orange tint
1916-20 Colour: Black with green tint

Back Design: Lathework, counters and bank name
Colour: Green

375-16-10
$10 Face Design: Hon. W.H. Merritt/Bank/Arms/H.S. Howland
Colour: Black with green tint

Back Design: Lathework, counters and bank name
Colour: Green

375-16-18
$20 Face Design: Farmer with horse-drawn mower/—/ H.S. Howland
Colour: Black with green tint

Back Design: Lathework, counters and bank name
Colour: Green

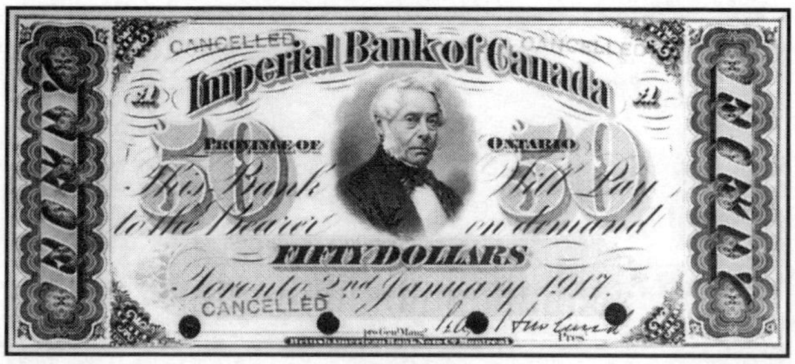

375-16-22

$50 Face Design: —/Hon. W.H. Merritt/—
Colour: Black with green tint

Back Design: Lathework, counters and bank name
Colour: Green

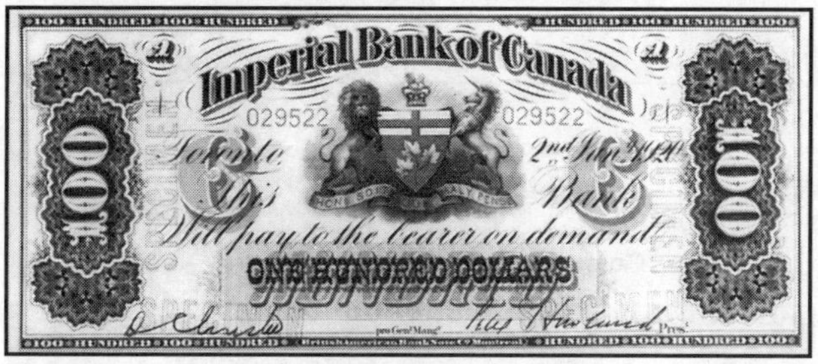

375-16-26

$100 Face Design: —/Canadian Crest/—
Colour: Black with green tint

Back Design: Lathework, counters and bank name
Colour: Green

IMPRINT

British American Bank Note Co. Montreal
British American Bank Note Co. Ottawa

SIGNATURES

left	right
mss. various	engr. Peleg Howland
Typed A.E. Phipps	engr. Peleg Howland

ISSUE DATING

Engraved

1st Oct. 1915
October 1st 1915
Oct 1st 1915
3rd Jan. 1916
2nd January 1917
2nd Jany 1917
2nd Jan. 1920

Note: Beware of counterfeits of 16-24.

CIRCULATING NOTES

Cat.No.	Denom.	Date	Variety	G	VG	F	VF	EF	AU
16-02	$5	1915		200.	400.	550.	—	—	—
16-04	$5	1916		70.	140.	200.	325.	600.	—
16-06	$5	1920		70.	140.	200.	325.	600.	—
16-10	$10	1915		70.	140.	200.	325.	600.	—
16-12	$10	1920	mss.l.	60.	120.	175.	275.	500.	—
16-14	$10	1920	Phipps,l.	150.	225.	350.	650.	—	—
16-16	$20	1915		—	400.	550.	800.	1,400.	—
16-18	$20	1920		125.	250.	350.	600.	1,100.	—
16-22	$50	1917		—	2,000.	2,750.	—	—	—
16-24	$100	1917		700.	1,400.	2,000.	3,000.	—	—
16-24c	$100	1917	Counterfeit	—	50.	75.	100.	140.	—
16-26	$100	1920		—	1,400.	2,000.	3,000.	—	—

PROOF NOTES

Cat. No	Denom.	Date	Variety		Unc
16-02P	$5	1915		FACE PROOF	400.
16-16P	$20	1915	B & W	FACE PROOF	250.
16-18P	$20	1920	B & W	FACE PROOF	250.

375-18. ISSUE OF 1923

DESIGNS AND COLOURS

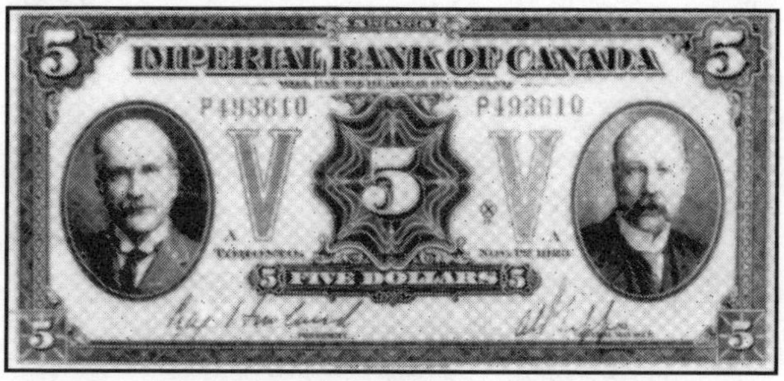

375-18-02

$5 Face Design: Peleg Howland/—/A.E. Phipps
Colour: Black with green tint

Back Design: Lathework, counters, bank name and lion over crown
Colour: Green

375-18-06

$10 Face Design: Peleg Howland/—/A.E. Phipps
Colour: Black with blue tint

Back Design: Lathework, counters, bank name and lion over crown
Colour: Blue

375-18-10

$20 Face Design: —/Peleg Howland/—
Colour: Black with brown tint

Back Design: Lathework, counters, bank name and lion over crown
Colour: Brown

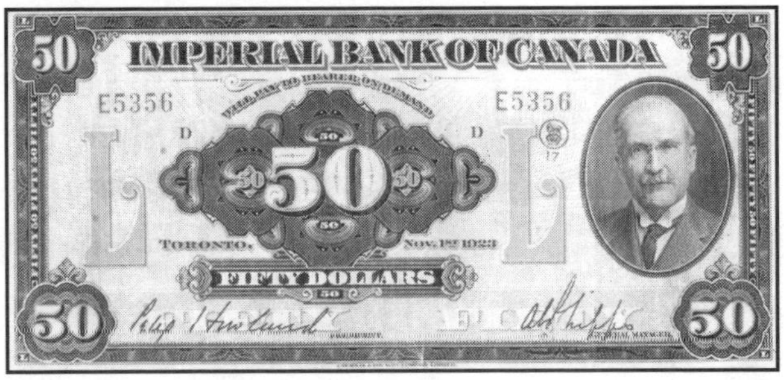

375-18-14

$50 Face Design: —/—/Peleg Howland
Colour: Black with orange tint

Back Design: Lathework, counters, bank name and lion over crown
Colour: Orange

375-18-18S

$100 Face Design: Peleg Howland/—/—
Colour: Black with olive tint

Back Design: Lathework, counters, bank name and lion over crown
Colour: Olive

IMPRINT

Canadian Bank Note Company Limited

SIGNATURES

left	right
engr. Peleg Howland	typed A.E. Phipps
typed F.A. Rolph	typed A.E. Phipps

ISSUE DATING

Engraved

Nov. 1st 1923

CIRCULATING NOTES

Cat.No.	Denom.	Date	Variety	VG	F	VF	EF	AU	Unc
18-02	$5	1923	Howland,l.	75.	100.	175.	275.	450.	600.
18-04	$5	1923	Rolph,l.	75.	100.	175.	275.	450.	600.
18-06	$10	1923	Howland,l.	75.	100.	175.	275.	450.	600.
18-08	$10	1923	Rolph,l.	75.	100.	175.	275.	450.	600.
18-10	$20	1923	Howland,l.	85.	120.	200.	300.	525.	750.
18-12	$20	1923	Rolph,l.	No known issued notes					
18-14	$50	1923	Howland,l.	300.	425.	600.	900.	1,200.	1,500.
18-16	$50	1923	Rolph,l.	325.	475.	675.	1,000.	—	—
18-18	$100	1923	Howland,l.	No known issued notes					

PROOF NOTES

Cat No.	Denom.	Date	Variety		Unc
18-02P	$5	1923		FACE PROOF	300.
18-06P	$10	1923		FACE PROOF	300.
18-10P	$20	1923		FACE PROOF	300.
18-14P	$50	1923		FACE PROOF	300.
18-18P	$100	1923	Olive tint	FACE PROOF	400.
18-18Pa	$100	1923	Red tint	FACE PROOF	400.

SPECIMEN NOTES

Cat No.	Denom.	Date		Unc
18-18S	$100	1923	SPECIMEN	1,000.

375-20. ISSUE OF 1933

DESIGNS AND COLOURS

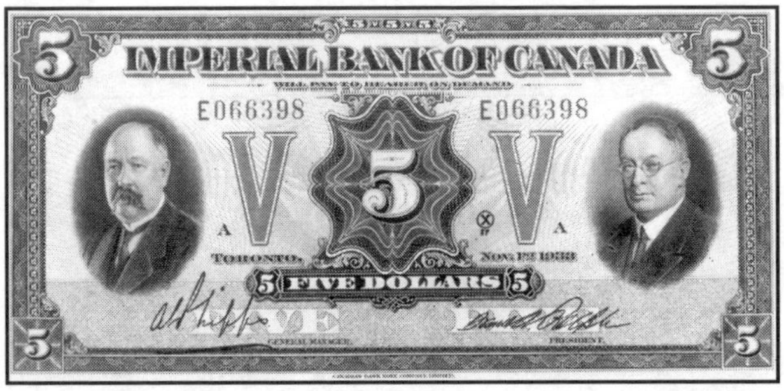

375-20-02

$5 Face Design: A.E. Phipps/—/F.A. Rolph
Colour: Black with green tint

Back Design: —/lion over crown/—
Colour: Green

375-20-04

$10 Face Design: A.E. Phipps/—/F.A. Rolph
Colour: Black with blue tint

Back Design: —/lion over crown/
Colour: Blue

375-20-06S

$20 Face Design: F.A. Rolph
Colour: Black with brown tint

Back Design: —/lion over crown/—
Colour: Brown

IMPRINT

Canad ian Bank Note Company, Limited

SIGNATURES

left	right
engr. A.E. Phipps	typed F.A. Rolph

ISSUE DATING

Engraved

Nov. 1st 1933

CIRCULATING NOTES

Cat.No.	Denom.	Date	VG	F	VF	EF	AU	Unc
20-02	$5	1933	90.	125.	200.	300.	450.	600.
20-04	$10	1933	130.	175.	300.	500.	750.	1,000.
20-06	$20	1933	No known issued notes					

PROOF NOTES

Cat. No.	Denom.	Date	Variety		Unc
20-02P	$5	1922	B & W	FACE PROOF	250.
20-02Pa	$5	1933	Green tint	FACE PROOF	350.
20-04P	$10	1933	B & W	FACE PROOF	250.
20-04Pa	$10	1933	Blue tint	FACE PROOF	350.
20-06P	$20	1933	B & W	FACE PROOF	275.
20-06Pa	$20	1933	Brown tint	FACE PROOF	400.

SPECIMEN NOTES

Cat. No.	Denom.	Date		Unc
20-06S	$20	1933	SPECIMEN	600.

375-22.

ISSUE OF 1934
SMALL SIZE NOTES

DESIGNS AND COLOURS

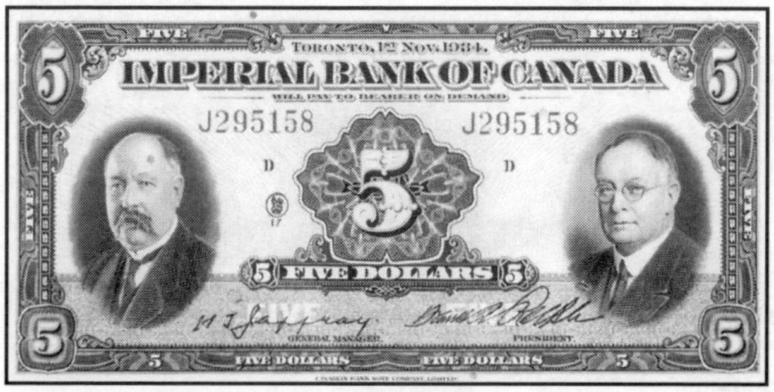

375-22-04

$5 Face Design: A.E. Phipps/—/Frank A. Rolph
Colour: Black with green tint

Back Design: —/lion over crown/—
Colour: Green

375-22-06

$10 Face Design: A.E. Phipps/—/Frank A. Rolph
Colour: Black with blue tint

Back Design: —/lion over crown/—
Colour: Blue

IMPRINT

Canadian Bank Note Company, Limited

SIGNATURES

left	right
signed A.E. Phipps	signed F.A. Rolph
signed H.T. Jaffray	signed F.A. Rolph

ISSUE DATING

Engraved

1st Nov. 1934

CIRCULATING NOTES

Cat.No.	Denom.	Date	Variety	VG	F	VF	EF	AU	Unc
22-02	$5	1934	Phipps,l.	40.	60.	95.	180.	275.	375.
22-04	$5	1934	Jaffray,l.	40.	60.	95.	180.	275.	375.
22-06	$10	1934	Phipps,l.	40.	60.	95.	190.	300.	400.
22-08	$10	1934	Jaffray,l.	40.	60.	95.	190.	300.	400.

PROOF NOTES

Cat. No.	Denom.	Date		Unc
22-02P	$5	1934	FACE PROOF	300.
22-06P	$10	1934	FACE PROOF	300.

375-24. ISSUE OF 1939

DESIGNS AND COLOURS

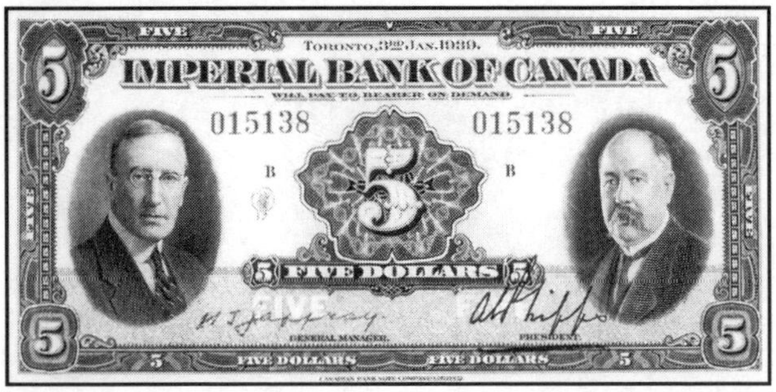

375-24-02

$5 Face Design: H.T. Jaffray/—/A.E. Phipps
Colour: Black with green tint

Back Design: —/lion over crown/—
Colour: Green

375-24-04

$10 Face Design: H.T. Jaffray/—/A.E. Phipps
Colour: Black with blue tint

Back Design: —/lion over crown/—
Colour: Blue

IMPRINT

Canadian Bank Note Company, Limited

SIGNATURES

left	right
typed H.T. Jaffray	typed A.E. Phipps

ISSUE DATING

Engraved

3rd Jan. 1939

CIRCULATING NOTES

Cat.No.	Denom.	Date	VG	F	VF	EF	AU	Unc
24-02	$5	1939	50.	70.	110.	225.	350.	475.
24-04	$10	1939	45.	65.	100.	210.	325.	450.

PROOF NOTES

Cat. No.	Denom.	Date		Unc
24-02P	$5	1939	FACE PROOF	300.
24-04P	$10	1939	FACE PROOF	300.

THE INTERNATIONAL BANK OF CANADA

1858 - 1859

TORONTO, CANADA WEST

BANK NUMBER 380 ***NONREDEEMABLE***

Originally chartered in 1857 to provide banking services in Cayuga, Ontario, amendments to the charter in 1858 permitted the bank to open in Toronto, where it operated as a "wildcat bank" for about a year before failing in October of 1859. All of the shares were owned by a Mr. Reed when it failed. A man of disreputable character, Reed was also connected with The Bank of Clifton.

The International Bank of Canada was a small local bank and records of September of 1859 indicate notes in circulation of about $119,000. Although it failed in 1859, its charter wasn't repealed until 1863.

380-10. ISSUE OF 1858

DESIGNS AND COLOURS

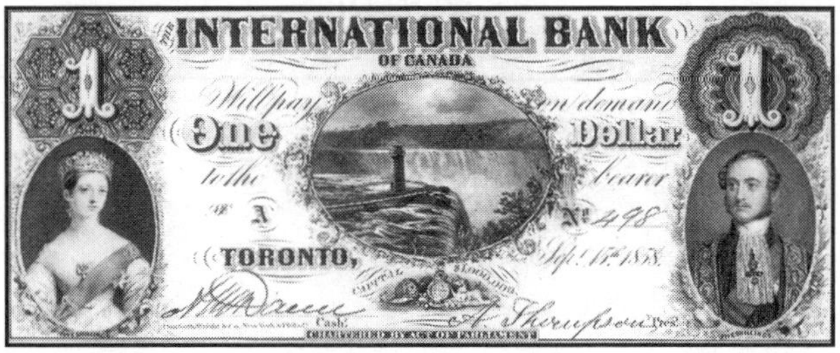

380-10-02-02

$1 Face Design: Queen Victoria (Chalon portrait)
Niagara Falls/Prince Consort
Colour: Black with no tint

Back Design: Plain

380-10-02-04

$1 Face Design: Queen Victoria (Chalon portrait)
Roebling Suspension Bridge/Prince Consort
Colour: Black with no tint

Back Design: Plain

380-10-02-06

$2 Face Design: Allegorical female/Royal Crest/—
Colour: Black with no tint

Back Design: Plain

380-10-02-08

$5 Face Design: Cattle drinking at river/—
Colour: Black with no tint

Back Design: Plain

IMPRINT

Danforth, Wright & Co., New York & Philada
ABN Co. Logo

ISSUE DATING

Engraved

September 15th, 1858

2. TWO SIGNATURES, NO PROTECTORS

SIGNATURES

left	right
mss. A.W. Dunn	engr. A. Thompson

SHEET NUMBERS

Mss. 1-2000

Cat.No.	Denom.	Date	Variety	G	VG	F	VF	EF	Unc
10-02-02	$1 Falls	1858		60.	120.	150.	225.	350.	—
10-02-02R	$1 Falls	1858	Remainder	—	—	—	—	200.	375.
10-02-04	$1 Bridge	1858		75.	150.	200.	300.	450.	—
10-02-04R	$1 Bridge	1858	Remainder	—	—	—	—	200.	375.
10-02-06	$2	1858		100.	200.	250.	400.	600.	—
10-02-06R	$2	1858	Remainder	—	—	—	—	240.	425.
10-02-08	$5	1858		100.	200.	250.	400.	600.	—
10-02-08R	$5	1858	Remainder	—	—	—	—	240.	425.

4. TWO SIGNATURES, RED PROTECTORS

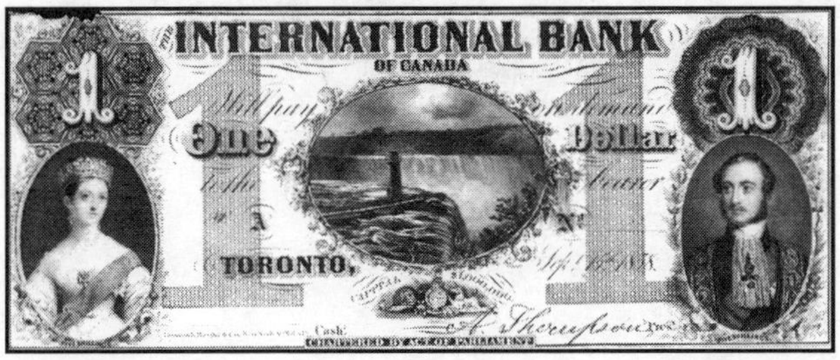

380-10-04-02R

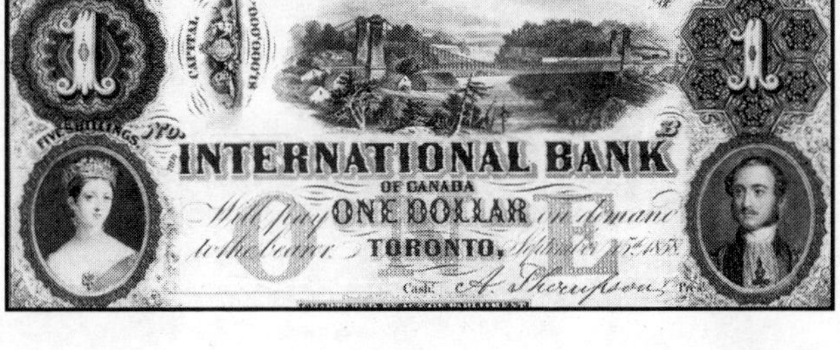

380-10-04-04R

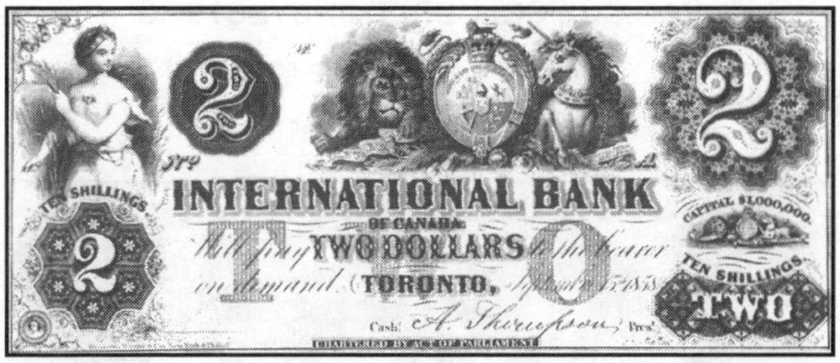

380-10-04-06R

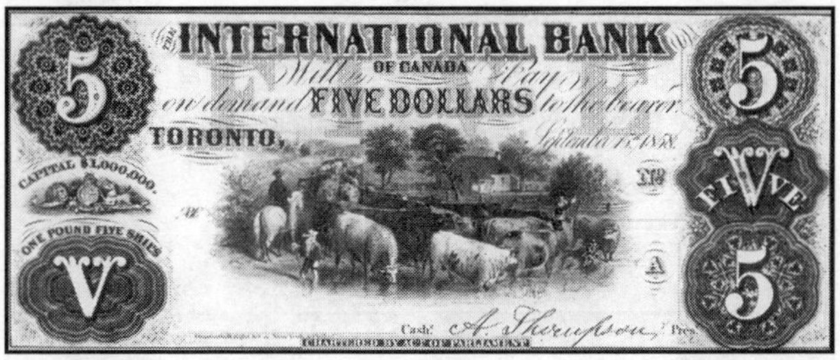

380-10-04-08R

SIGNATURES

left	right
mss. A.W. Dunn	engr. A.Thompson

PROTECTOR

$1 Falls: Red "numeral" on face and back
$1 Bridge, $2 & $5: Red "word" on face and back

SHEET NUMBERS

Mss. 1-2000

Note: Do not confuse with the commoner one signature notes of type 10-10.

Cat.No.	Denom.	Date	Variety	G	VG	F	VF	EF	Unc
10-04-02	$1 Falls	1858		75.	150.	200.	300.	450.	900.
10-04-02R	$1 Falls	1858	Remainder	—	—	—	—	250.	500.
10-04-04	$1 Bridge	1858		75.	150.	200.	300.	450.	900.
10-04-04R	$1 Bridge	1858	Remainder	—	—	—	—	250.	500.
10-04-06	$2	1858		75.	150.	200.	300.	450.	900.
10-04-06R	$2	1858	Remainder	—	—	—	—	250.	500.
10-04-08	$5	1858		75.	150.	200.	300.	450.	900.
10-04-08R	$5	1858	Remainder	—	—	—	—	250.	500.
Full sheet	$1.1.2.5	1858		—	—	—	—	—	4,000.

ONE SIGNATURE, VARIOUS COLOURED PROTECTORS

One signature space at right. "For the International Bank" in left signature space.

380-10-08-04

$1 Face Design: Queen Victoria (Chalon portrait)/ Niagara Falls/Prince Consort
Colour: Black with no tint

Back Design: Plain

380-10-14-06

$1 Face Design: Queen Victoria (Chalon portrait)/ Roebling Suspension Bridge/Prince Consort
Colour: Black with no tint

Back Design: Plain

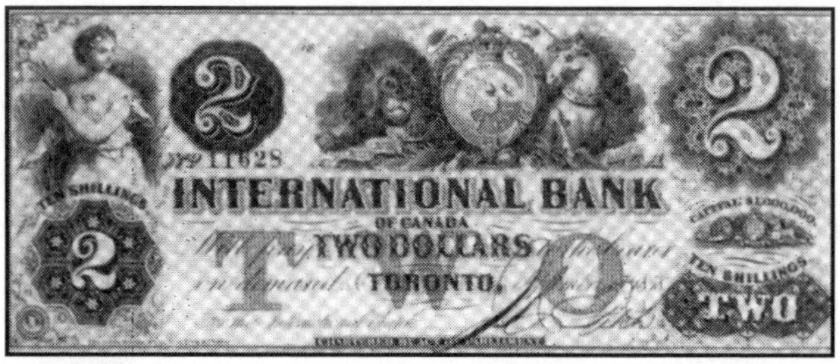

380-10-10-12

$2 Face Design: Allegorical female/Royal Crest/—
Colour: Black with no tint

Back Design: Plain

380-10-10-16

$5 Face Design: —/cattle drinking at river/—
Colour: Black with no tint

Back Design: Plain

STAMPS:

Numerous letters and numbers can be found on types 06 through 14. eg: 1,2,3,5,9,10,13,20.21.80,a,s,t,w.

6. ONE SIGNATURE, GREEN PROTECTORS

SIGNATURES

right only
mss. J.H. Markell
mss. J.R. Fitch

SHEET NUMBERS

Markell - Small blue: 1 - 1000
Fitch - Small red: 9001 - 10000, 14001 - 15000

Cat.No.	Denom.	Date	Variety	G	VG	F	VF	EF	Unc
10-06-02	$1 Falls	1858	Markell-blue #s	40.	80.	100.	150.	250.	—
10-06-04	$1 Falls	1858	Fitch-red #s	15.	35.	45.	65.	175.	250.
10-06-06	$1 Bridge	1858	Markell-blue #s	45.	90.	110.	165.	270.	—
10-06-08	$1 Bridge	1858	Fitch-red #s	15.	35.	50.	75.	200.	300.
10-06-10	$2	1858	Markell-blue #s	40.	80.	100.	150.	250.	—
10-06-12	$2	1858	Fitch-red #s	15.	35.	50.	70.	190.	275.
10-06-14	$5	1858	Markell-blue #s	40.	80.	100.	150.	250.	—
10-06-16	$5	1858	Fitch-red #s	15.	35.	45.	65.	180.	260.

8. ONE SIGNATURE, BROWN PROTECTORS

SIGNATURES

right only
mss. J.H. Markell
mss. J.R. Fitch

SHEET NUMBERS

Markell - small blue: 1001-2000
Markell - small red: 7001-8000
Fitch - Small red: 7001-8000, 15001-16000

Note: There is an overlapping or duplication of Markell and Fitch red sheet numbers in 7001-8000 range

Cat.No.	Denom.	Date	Variety	G	VG	F	VF	EF	Unc
10-08-02	$1 Falls	1858	Markell-blue #s	40.	80.	100.	150.	250.	—
10-08-02a	$1 Falls	1858	Markell-red #s	40.	80.	100.	150.	250.	—
10-08-04	$1 Falls	1858	Fitch-red #s	15.	30.	40.	55.	150.	225.
10-08-06	$1 Bridge	1858	Markell-blue #s	45.	90.	110.	165.	275.	—
10-08-06a	$1 Bridge	1858	Markell-red #s	45.	90.	110.	165.	275.	—
10-08-08	$1 Bridge	1858	Fitch-red #s	15.	35.	45.	70.	190.	275.
10-08-10	$2	1858	Markell-blue #s	40.	80.	100.	150.	260.	—
10-08-10a	$2	1858	Markell-red #s	40.	80.	100.	150.	260.	—
10-08-12	$2	1858	Fitch-red #s	15.	35.	45.	65.	180.	260.
10-08-14	$5	1858	Markell-blue #s	40.	80.	100.	150.	260.	—
10-08-14a	$5	1858	Markell-red #s	40.	80.	100.	150.	260.	—
10-08-16	$5	1858	Fitch-red #s	15.	30.	40.	60.	160.	235.

10. ONE SIGNATURE, RED PROTECTORS

SIGNATURES

right only
mss. J.H. Markell
mss. J.R. Fitch

SHEET NUMBERS

Markell small blue 2001-3000
Markell small blue 5001-6000
Fitch small blue 5001-6000, 11001-14000
Fitch large blue 16001-18000

Note: There is an overlapping or duplication of Markell and Fitch blue sheet numbers in the 5001-6000 range.

Cat.No.	Denom.	Date	Variety	G	VG	F	VF	EF	Unc
10-10-02	$1 Falls	1858	Markell-sm.blue	30.	60.	80.	120.	210.	—
10-10-04	$1 Falls	1858	Fitch-sm.blue	15.	30.	40.	60.	160.	235.
10-10-04a	$1 Falls	1858	Fitch-lg.blue	15.	30.	40.	55.	150.	225.
10-10-06	$1 Bridge	1858	Markell-sm.blue	35.	75.	100.	150.	250.	—
10-10-08	$1 Bridge	1858	Fitch-sm.blue	15.	35.	50.	70.	190.	275.
10-10-08a	$1 Bridge	1858	Fitch-lg.blue	15.	35.	45.	65.	180.	260.
10-10-10	$2	1858	Markell-sm.blue	35.	70.	95.	145.	240.	—
10-10-12	$2	1858	Fitch-sm.blue	15.	35.	50.	70.	190.	275.
10-10-12a	$2	1858	Fitch-lg.blue	15.	35.	45.	65.	180.	260.
10-10-14	$5	1858	Markell-sm.blue	30.	60.	80.	120.	210.	—
10-10-16	$5	1858	Fitch-sm.blue	15.	30.	40.	60.	160.	235.
10-10-16a	$5	1858	Fitch-lg.blue	15.	30.	40.	55.	150.	225.

12. ONE SIGNATURE, OCHRE PROTECTORS

SIGNATURES

right only
mss. J.H. Markell
mss. J.R. Fitch

SHEET NUMBERS

Markell small red 3001-4000
Fitch small red 6001-7000
Fitch small blue 10001-11000
Fitch large blue 18001-

Cat.No.	Denom.	Date	Variety	G	VG	F	VF	EF	Unc
10-12-02	$1 Falls	1858	Markell-sm.red	40.	80.	100.	150.	260.	—
10-12-04	$1 Falls	1858	Fitch-sm.red	40.	80.	100.	150.	260.	—
10-12-04a	$1 Falls	1858	Fitch-sm.blue	30.	65.	90.	135.	275.	400.
10-12-04b	$1 Falls	1858	Fitch-lg.blue	50.	100.	125.	190.	350.	500.
10-12-06	$1 Bridge	1858	Markell-sm.red	40.	80.	100.	150.	260.	—
10-12-08	$1 Bridge	1858	Fitch-sm.red	40.	80.	100.	150.	260.	—
10-12-08a	$1 Bridge	1858	Fitch-sm.blue	30.	60.	80.	120.	250.	360.
10-12-08b	$1 Bridge	1858	Fitch-lg.blue	50.	100.	125.	190.	350.	500.
10-12-10	$2	1858	Markell-sm.red	40.	80.	100.	150.	260.	—
10-12-12	$2	1858	Fitch-sm.red	40.	80.	100.	150.	260.	—
10-12-12a	$2	1858	Fitch-sm.blue	30.	60.	80.	120.	250.	360.
10-12-12b	$2	1858	Fitch-lg.blue	50.	100.	125.	190.	350.	500.
10-12-14	$5	1858	Markell-sm.red	40.	80.	100.	150.	260.	—
10-12-16	$5	1858	Fitch-sm.red	40.	80.	100.	150.	260.	—
10-12-16a	$5	1858	Fitch-sm.blue	30.	60.	75.	110.	235.	340.
10-12-16b	$5	1858	Fitch-lg.blue	50.	100.	125.	190.	350.	500.

14. ONE SIGNATURE, BLUE PROTECTORS

SIGNATURES

right only
mss. J.H. Markell
mss. J.R. Fitch

SHEET NUMBERS

Markell small red 4001-5000
Fitch small red 4001-5000, 8001-9000

STAMPS:

Numerous letters and numbers can be found on types 06 through 14. eg: 1,2,3,5,9,10,13,20,21,80,a,s,t,w.

Note: There is an overlapping or duplication of Markell and Fitch blue sheet numbers in the 4001-5000 range.

Cat.No.	Denom.	Date	Variety	G	VG	F	VF	EF	Unc
10-14-02	$1 Falls	1858	Markell-sm.red	40.	80.	100.	150.	260.	—
10-14-04	$1 Falls	1858	Fitch-sm.red	25.	50.	65.	100.	225.	325.
10-14-06	$1 Bridge	1858	Markell-sm.red	45.	90.	110.	165.	275.	—
10-14-08	$1 Bridge	1858	Fitch-sm.red	25.	50.	65.	100.	225.	325.
10-14-10	$2	1858	Markell-sm.red	40.	80.	100.	150.	260.	—
10-14-12	$2	1858	Fitch-sm.red	25.	50.	65.	100.	225.	325.
10-14-14	$5	1858	Markell-sm.red	40.	80.	100.	150.	260.	—
10-14-16	$5	1858	Fitch-sm.red	25.	50.	65.	100.	225.	325.

380-12. ISSUE OF 1859

DESIGNS AND COLOURS

The backs of this issue are green letterpress printed on thin paper.

380-12-02

$10 Face Design: Crests, book, crown/town and dock ship/ Queen Victoria (after Winterhalter portrait)
Colour: Black with no tint

Back Design: Lathework and counters
Colour: Green

380-12-04

$20 Face Design: Beavers/paddlewheel steam-ship/ Albert Edward (Prince of Wales) as a five year old child in a sailor suit
Colour: Black with no tint

Back Design: Lathework and counters
Colour: Green

380-12-06

$50 Face Design: Woman looking out to sea/ buffalo hunting/ seated Britannia with Arms of Upper Canada
Colour: Black with no tint

Back Design: Lathework and counters
Colour: Green

IMPRINT

American Bank Note Company

SIGNATURES

left	right
none	mss. J.R. Fitch

ISSUE DATING

Engraved

June 1st 1859

PROTECTOR

Green "word and numeral" on back only

SHEET NUMBERS

All have blue sheet numbers under 1000.
$10 notes have check letters A & B,
$20 & $50 have check letters A.

Cat.No.	Denom.	Date	G	VG	F	VF	EF	Unc
12-02	$10	1859	55.	115.	140.	235.	475.	675.
12-04	$20	1859	375.	750.	1,000.	1,600.	2,500.	—
12-06	$50	1859	60.	120.	150.	250.	500.	725.

BANQUE INTERNATIONALE DU CANADA

1911 - 1913

MONTREAL, (QUEBEC) DOMINION OF CANADA

BANK NUMBER 385 ***REDEEMABLE***

Established in 1911 in Montreal, the Banque Internationale du Canada was absorbed by The Home Bank of Canada on April 15, 1913. Although short-lived, it had a successful existance which enabled The Home Bank of Canada to expand in Montreal, the then financial centre of Canada.

385-10 **ISSUE OF 191**

DESIGNS AND COLOURS

385-10-02P

$5 Face Design: —/R. Forget/—
Colour: Black with greeen and yellow tint

Back Design: —/globe/—
Colour: Green

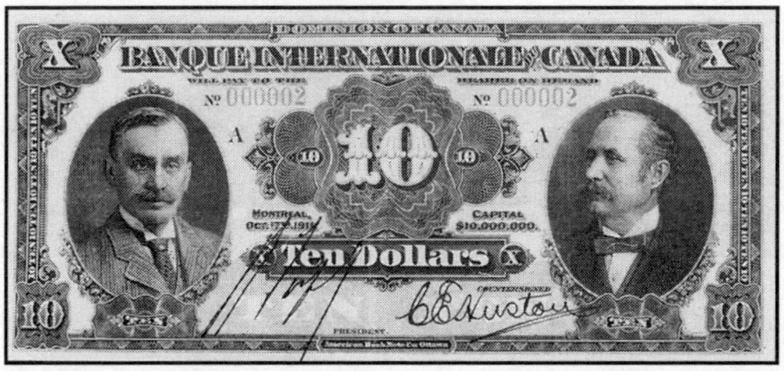

385-10-04

$10 Face Design: R. Forget/—/R. Bickerdike
Colour: Black with orange and yellow tint

Back Design: —/globe/—
Colour: Brown

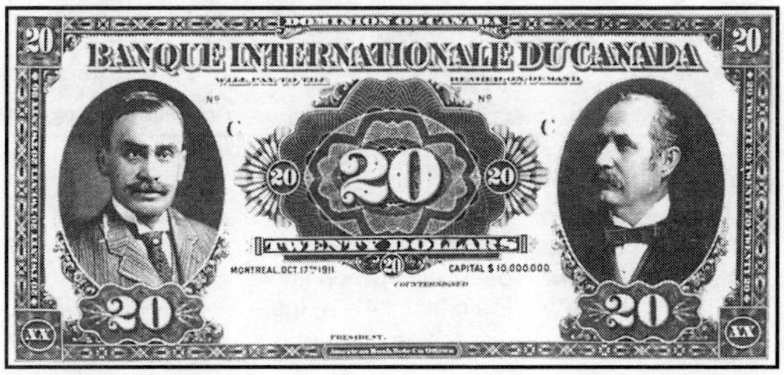

385-10-06P

Face Design: R. Forget/—/R. Bickerdike
Color: Black with olive green and yellow tint

Back Design: lathework and counters, Bank name surrounding globe
Colour: Peru brown

IMPRINT

American Bank Note Company, Ottawa
American Bank Note Co. Ottawa

SIGNATURES

left	**right**
typed R. Forget	mss. various

ISSUE DATING

Engraved

$5: Oct. 2nd, 1911
$10 & $20: Oct. 17th, 1911

OVERPRINT

"M M" in red
"QUEBEC" twice in blue

CIRCULATING NOTES

Cat. No.	Denom.	Date	Variety	VG	F	VF	EF	AU
10-02	$5	1911		—	—	—	6,000.	8,000.
10-04	$10	1911		—	4,000.	5,000.	—	—
10-04a	$10	1911	QUEBEC o/p	—	4,000.	5,000.	—	—
10-06	$20	1911		No known issued notes				

PROOF NOTES

Cat. No.	Denom.	Date	Variety		Unc
10-02P	$5	1911	B & W	FACE PROOF	600.
10-02Pa	$5	1911	Coloured	FACE PROOF	1,000.
10-04P	$10	1911		FACE PROOF	1,000.
10-06P	$20	1911		FACE PROOF	1,000.

SPECIMEN NOTES

Cat. No.	Denom.	Date	Variety		Unc
10-02S	$5	1911		SPECIMEN	2,000.
10-04S	$10	1911	no o/p	SPECIMEN	2,000.
10-04Sa	$10	1911	red o/p	SPECIMEN	2,000.
10-06S	$20	1911		SPECIMEN	2,000.

Note: A $10 back proof exists in red-brown (unissued colour)

LA BANQUE JACQUES CARTIER

1861 - 1900

MONTREAL, PROVINCE OF CANADA

BANK NUMBER 390 ***REDEEMABLE***

Established in 1861 in Montreal, this bank failed in 1899 with heavy losses, but reorganized in 1900 to become La Banque Provinciale du Canada.

390-10 ISSUE OF 1862

DESIGN AND COLOURS

390-10-02

$1 Face Design: Queen Victoria (Winterhalter portrait)/ J. Cartier/Louis H. La Fontaine
Colour: Black with green tint

Back Design: Lathework and counters
Colour: Green

390-10-04

$2 Face Design: Princess Eugenie/J. Cartier/Prince of Wales
Colour: Black with green tint

Back Design: Lathework and counters
Colours: Green

Photo Not Available

390-10-06

$5 Face Design: Louis H. LaFontaine/J. Cartier/ Jean-Louis Beaudry
Colour: Black with green tint

Back Design: Lathework and counters
Colour: Green

Photo Not Available

390-10-08

$10 Face Design: Jean-Louis Beaudry/J. Cartier/ Prince of Wales
Colour: Black with green tint

Back Design: Lathework and counters
Colour: Green

IMPRINT

American Bank Note Co. New York

SIGNATURES

left	right
mss. H Cotte	mss. J.L. Beaudry

ISSUE DATING

Engraved

2 Janvier 1862

CIRCULATING NOTES

Cat. No.	Denom.	Date	G	VG	F	VF	EF	AU
10-02	$1	1862	1,800.	3,200.	4,500.	—	—	—
10-04	$2	1892	1,800.	3,200.	4,500.	—	—	—
10-06	$5	1862	No known issued notes					
10-08	$10	1862	No known issued notes					

PROOF NOTES

Cat. No.	Denom.	Date		Unc
10-02P	$1	1862	FACE PROOF	600.
10-04P	$2	1862	FACE PROOF	600.
10-06P	$5	1862	FACE PROOF	1,000.
10-08P	$10	1862	FACE PROOF	1,000.

390-12. ISSUES OF 1870 AND 1880

DESIGNS AND COLOURS

390-12-02

$4 Face Design: Ships and seated female "Exports"/ J.Cartier/beaver
Colour: Black with green tint
Variety: Plain black 4's at top

Back Design: Queen Victoria/Bank name over quatre/ Prince Albert
Colour: Green

390-12-04
$4 Face Design: Ships and seated female "Exports"/ J. Cartier/beaver
Variety: Four's in green lathework at top
Colour: Black with green tint

Back Design: Queen Victoria/Bank name over quatre/ Prince Albert
Colour: Green

390-12-08
$5 Face Design: R. Trudeau/J. Cartier/A. Desjardins
Colour: Black with green tint

Back Design: Lathework, counters and bank name
Colour: Green

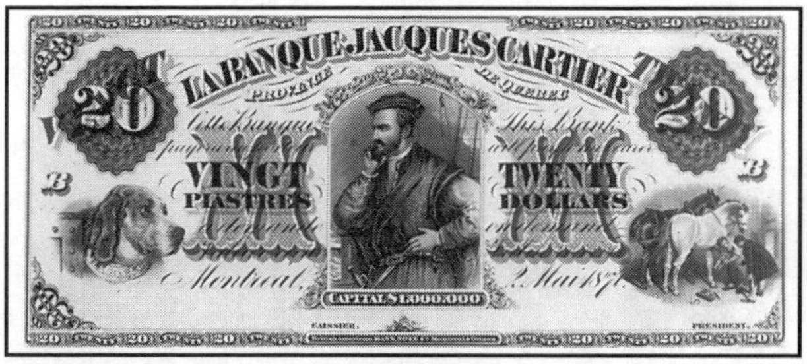

390-12-10P
$20 Face Design: Dog's head (after landseer)/J. Cartier/ blacksmith and horses
Colour: Black with green tint

Back Design: Lathework, counters and bank name
Colour: Green

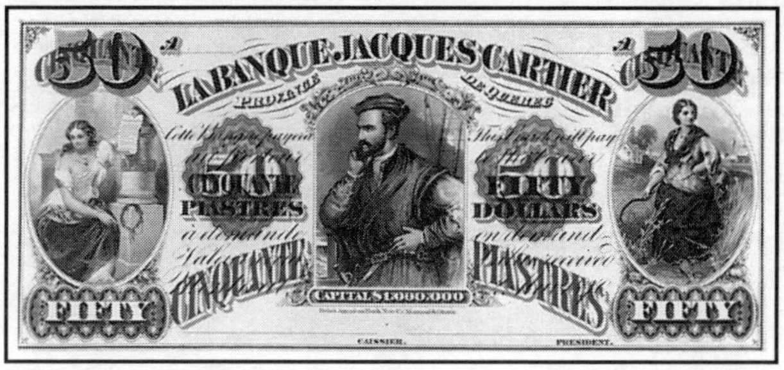

390-12-14P
$50 Face Design: Female with parchment/ J.Cartier/ female reaping grain
Colour: Black with green tint

Back Design: Lathework, counters and bank name
Colour: Green

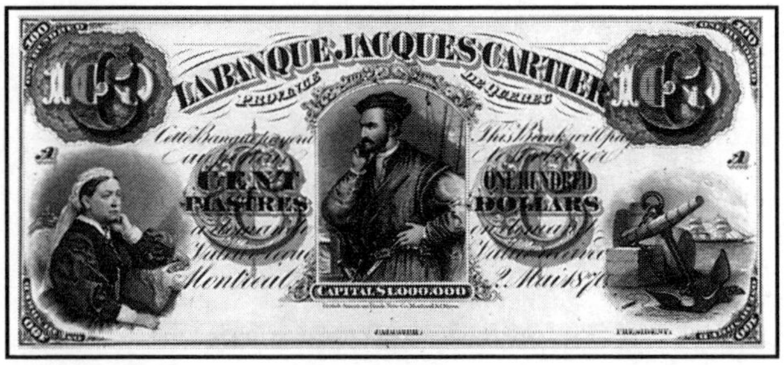

390-12-18P

$100 Face Design: Queen Victoria in "widow's weeds"/ J. Cartier/anchor barrel and bales
Colour: Black with green tint

Back Design: Lathework, counters and bank name
Colour: Green

IMPRINT

British American Bank Note Co. Montreal and Ottawa

SIGNATURES

	left	right
1870:	mss. A. Manseau	engr. R. Turdeau
	mss. A. Manseau	mss. R. Trudeau
1880:	mss. A. Manseau	engr. A. Desjardins

ISSUE DATING

Engraved

2 Mai 1870
2 Mai 1871
1st June 1880

OVERPRINT

$5 1880: "VICTORIAVILLE" twice in blue

VARIETIES

$4: Plain black 4's at top
$4: FOUR's in green lathework over black 4's at top

CIRCULATING NOTES

Cat. No.	Denom.	Date	Variety	G	VG	F	VF	EF	AU
12-02	$4	1870	Plain 4's	2,750.	4,500.	—	—	—	—
12-04	$4	1870	Green 4's	2,750.	4,500.	—	—	—	—
12-06	$5	1870		2,600.	4,200.	—	—	—	—
12-08	$5	1880		2,600.	4,200.	—	—	—	—
12-10	$20	1870			No known issued notes				
12-12	$20	1871			No known issued notes				
12-14	$50	1870			No known issued notes				
12-18	$100	1870			No known issued notes				

PROOF NOTES

Cat. No.	Denom.	Date		Unc
12-10P	$20	1870	FACE PROOF	600.
12-12P	$20	1871	FACE PROOF	600.
12-14P	$50	1870	FACE PROOF	800.
12-18P	$100	1870	FACE PROOF	800.

390-14 ISSUES OF 1886 AND 1889

DESIGNS AND COLOURS

390-14-02P

$5 Face Design: J. Cartier/farm family and animals by trough "The Old Well"/bank building

Back Design: Lathework, counters and bank name

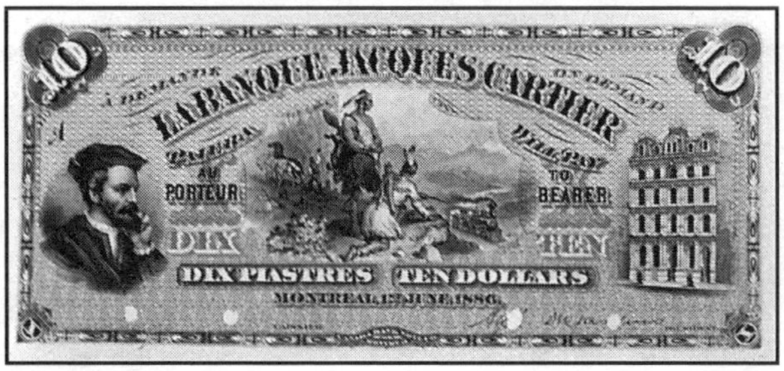

390-14-06P

$10 Face Design: J. Cartier/Indians on bluff "Past and Present"/bank building

Back Design: Lathework, counters and bank name

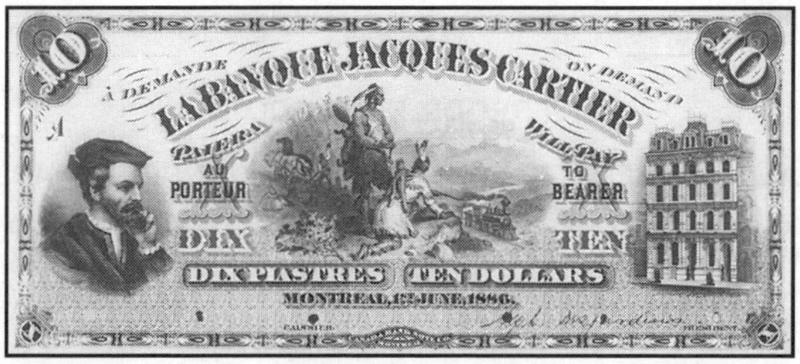

390-14-08P

1886: Face Colour: Black with green tint or black with orange and blue tint
Back Colour: Green, brown or blue
1889: Face Colour: Black with green tint ot black with orange and blue tint
Back Colour: Green, brown or blue

IMPRINT

Canada Bank Note Co. Montreal

SIGNATURES

left	right
none	engr. Alph. Desjardins

ISSUE DATING

Engraved

1st June 1886
1er Juin 1889

OVERPRINT

St. Simon in blue

CIRCULATING NOTES

Cat. No.	Denom.	Date	Variety	G	VG	F	VF	EF	AU
14-02	$5	1886				No known issued notes			
14-04	$5	1889				No known issued notes			
14-06	$10	1886	Orange tint	2,750.	4,000.	—	—	—	—
14-08	$10	1886	Green tint			No known issued notes			
14-10	$10	1889	Orange tint			Only one known to exist			
14-12	$10	1889	Green tint	—	—	—	8,000.	—	—

PROOF NOTES

Cat. No.	Denom.	Date	Variety		Unc
14-02P	$5	1886		FACE PROOF	600.
14-04P	$5	1889		FACE PROOF	600.
14-06P	$10	1886	Orange tint	FACE PROOF	600.
14-08P	$10	1886	Green tint	FACE PROOF	600.
14-12P	$10	1889	Green tint	FACE PROOF	600.

390-16. ISSUE OF 1895

DESIGNS AND COLOURS

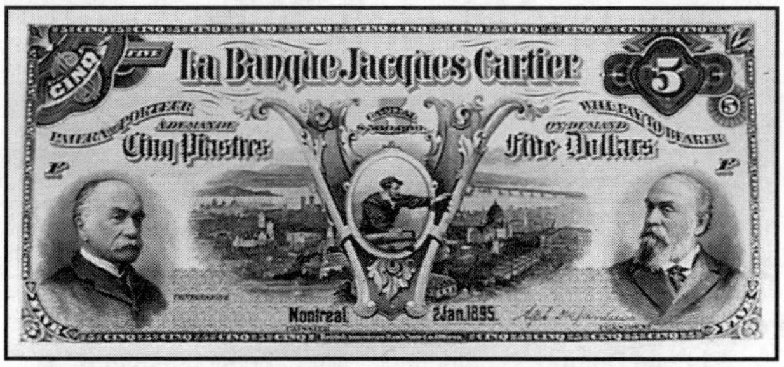

390-16-02P

$5 Face Design: A.L. De Martigny/ornate V and J. Cartier superimposed over view of Montreal from mountain/A. Desjardins
Colour: Black with green tint

Back Design: Lathework, counters and Indians on bluff
Colour: Green

390-16-04P

$10 Face Design: A.L. De Martigny/ornate X superimposed over J. Cartier aboard ship/A. Desjardins
Colour: Black with green tint

Back Design: Lathework, counters and Indians on bluff
Colour: Green

IMPRINT

British American Bank Note Co. Ottawa

SIGNATURES

left	right
none	engr. Alph. Desjardins

ISSUE DATING

Engraved

2 Jan. 1895

PROOF NOTES

Cat. No.	Denom.	Date		Unc
16-02P	$5	1895	FACE PROOF	500.
16-04P	$10	1895	FACE PROOF	500.

THE KINGSTON BANK

1837

KINGSTON, LOWER CANADA

BANK NUMBER 395 ***NONREDEEMABLE***

Possibly a phantom bank trading on the colloquial name of The Commercial Bank of the Midland District. With the addition of "New York Safety Fund" these notes were also used as supposed notes of the Kingston Bank in New York.

395-10 ISSUE OF 1837

These notes occur unsigned or with blue signatures. Rawdon, Wright, Hatch, New York imprint is obviously forged. The printing and engraving are inferior, thus clearly spurious.

DESIGNS AND COLOURS

395-10-02

$5 Face Design: Seated allegorical female/cattle, plough and train; cask, bale, cornucopia and ship below/-
Colour: Black with no tint

Back Design: Plain

IMPRINT

Rawdon, Wright, Hatch, New York (obviously spurious)

SIGNATURES

left	right
mss. W.W. Roy	mss. H.L. Moor
none	none
mss. J. Smith	mss. C. Lounsbery

ISSUE DATING

Partialy Engraved_18_:
1837: date incomplete
1841: Oct. 12
1843: Aug. 3

Note: Remainders are unsigned or signed in blue ink, incomplete date and unnumbered.

Cat. No.	Denom.	Date	Variety	G	VG	F	VF	EF	AU
10-02	$5	1837	Fully signed	65.	135.	185.	300.	—	—
10-02R	$5	1837	Remainder	55.	110.	150.	250.	—	—

THE BANK OF LIVERPOOL

1871-1879

LIVERPOOL, NOVA SCOTIA

BANK NUMBER 400 ***NONREDEEMABLE***

Established in Liverpool, Nova Scotia in 1871, The Bank of Liverpool first failed in April of 1873 but was revived in 1878 with an increase in capital. It managed to survive until the autumn of 1879. Its note issue was small and appears to have been redeemed by The Bank of Nova Scotia, its principal creditor. The Bank of Nova Scotia bought the bank's assets and paid off its note issue, which amounted to $4000.

400-10. ISSUE OF 1871

DESIGNS AND COLOURS

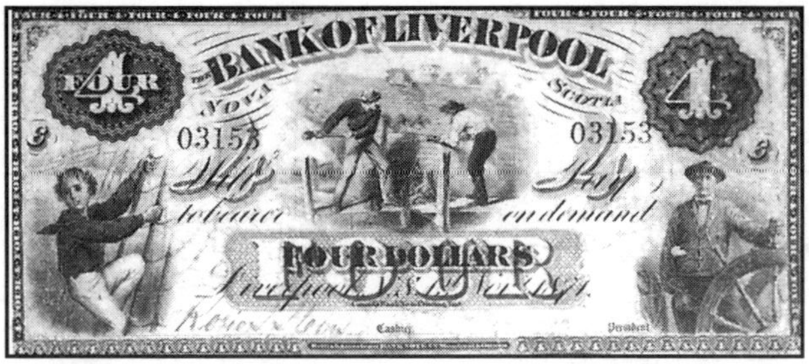

400-10-02

$4 Face Design: Boy climbing rigging "Going aloft"/ shipbuilders at work/pilot at wheel "Lachine Pilot"
Colour: Black with green tint

Back Design: Lathework, counters and bank name
Colour: Green

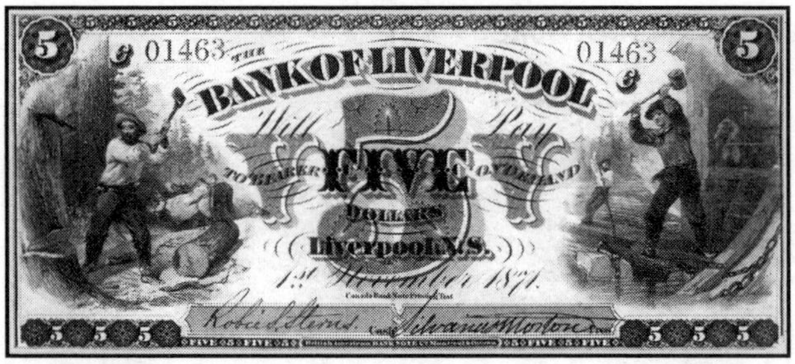

400-10-04

$5 Face Design: Lumberjack felling tree/-/loggers at work
Colour: Black with green tint

Back Design: Lathework, counters and bank name
Colour: Green

400-10-06

$10 Face Design: "Agriculture" figure/fishermen and sailing ships "On the Banks"/sailor aboard ship "Charlies Sailor"
Colour: Black with green tint

Back Design: Lathework, counters and bank name
Colour: Green

400-10-08

$20 Face Design: Bull's head/sailors on shore by mast/ three horses' head
Colour: Black with green tint

Back Design: Lathework, counters and bank name
Colour: Green

IMPRINT

British American Bank Note Co., Montreal & Ottawa

SIGNATURES

left	right
mss. Robie S. Stern	mss. Sylvanus Morton
mss. John A. Leslie, Mgr.	mss. J.F. Forbes
mss. John A. Leslie, Mgr.	mss. Thomas Rees (Vice)
mss. Robie S Stern	mss. Thomas Rees (Vice)

ISSUE DATING

Engraved

1st November 1871
1st Nov. 1871

Cat. No.	Denom	Date	G	VG	F	VF	EF	AU
10-02	$4	1871	900.	1,500.	2,000.	—	—	—
10-04	$5	1871	900.	1,500.	2,000.	3,000.	5,000.	—
10-06	$10	1871	1,800.	3,000.	—	—	—	—
10-08	$20	1871	Institutional collection only					

THE BANK OF LONDON IN CANADA

1883-1888

LONDON, DOMINION OF CANADA (ONTARIO)

BANK NUMBER 405 ***NONREDEEMABLE***

On February 21, 1883 a petition of "William Woodruff, MD. and others" received its third reading in the House of Commons for an act of incorporation in the name of The Bank of London in Canada. The bill was passed by the Commons on April 2, 1883 and received Royal assent on May 25th, 1883.The capital stock was to be $1 million divided into 10,000 shares of $100.00 each. However, the paid-up capital of the bank amounted to $140,000, with a reserve fund of $50,000 of its $1 million subscribed capital.

The bank opened its main office in 1884 with Henry Taylor as president. In 1887, the financial position of the bank appeared so sound that The Bank of Toronto, looking towards expansion, entered into negotiations with The Bank of London in Canada to take over its holdings in south-western Ontario. The deal was practically complete when The Bank of London closed down its operations on August 19, 1887 leaving a note on the door saying "The Bank of London has suspended payment." Two days earlier, Mr. Taylor left the country for the U.S., and it was reported that he had withdrawn $20,000 to take with him. Under these circumstances, The Bank of Toronto refused to proceed with negotiations

The financial statements for June and July of 1887 were quite favourable and with the election of a new president, Thomas Kent, The Bank of Toronto offered to assume the business of The Bank of London at par. In October of 1887, the directors of the bank decided to commence the payment of depositors and other creditors. The payment of London depositors was to be made by The Bank of London. The ingersoll, Watford and Brantford depositors were to be paid by The Traders Bank of Canada. Payment of others was carried out by The Bank of Toronto.

The Bank of Toronto opened its doors in London on November 9, 1887 on the same premises as The Bank of London in Canada. The share-holders voted to wind up its affairs of The Bank of London; assent was finally given to the Act on May 22, 1888 and the bank officially wound up.

405-10 **ISSUE OF 1883**

DESIGNS AND COLOURS

405-10-02R
$5 Face Design: "Implements of Agriculture"/ Henry Taylor/ dog on strongbox (after Landseer)
Colour: Black with green tint

Back Design: Lathework, counters, bank name and the City of London Crest
Colour: Green

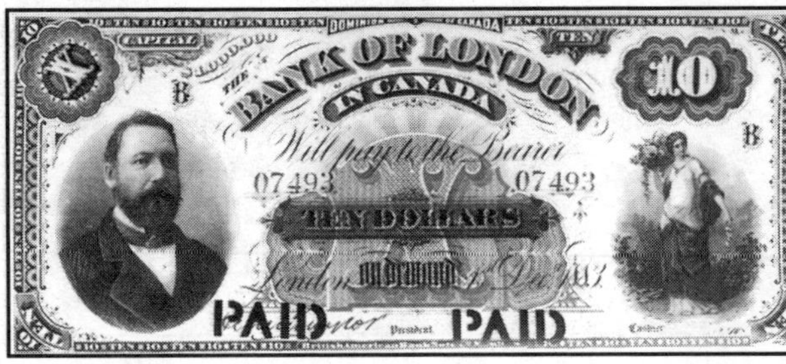

405-10-04R
$10 Face Design: Henry Taylor/—/allegorical female with flowers
Colour: Black with green tint

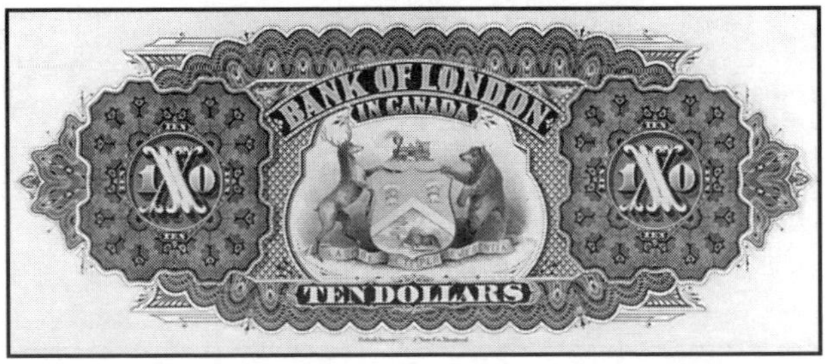

Back Design: Lathework, counters, bank name and the City of London Crest
Colour: Green

405-10-06R
$20 Face Design: Allergorical female with "stalks of wheat"/Henry Taylor/—
Colour: Black with green tint

Back Design: Lathework, counters and bank name
Colour: Green

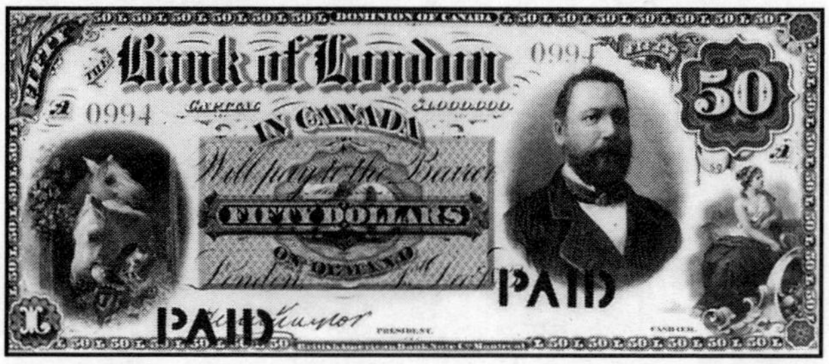

405-10-08R
$50 Face Design: Horses and pigeons at stable door (after J.F. Herring)/Henry Taylor/ seated allegorical female
Colour: Black with green tint

Back Design: Lathework, counters and bank name
Colour: Green

405-10-10R
$100 Face Design: Two cows in oval/Henry Taylor/ female operating telegraph in oval
Colour: Black with green tint

Back Design: Lathework, counters and bank name
Colour: Green

IMPRINT
British American Bank Note Co., Montreal

SIGNATURES

left	right
engr. Henry Taylor	none
engr. Henry Taylor	mss. A.M. Smart

ISSUE DATING
Engraved
1st Decr.1883

Cat No.	Demon	Date	Variety	G	VG	F	VF	EF	Unc
10-02	$5	1883	Issued	2,500.	4,000.	5,000.	—	—	—
10-02R	$5	1883	Remainder*	—	—	—	—	3,500.	—
10-04	$10	1883	Issued	Institutional collection only					
10-04R	$10	1883	Remainder*	—	—	—	—	3,500.	—
10-06R	$20	1883	Remainder*	—	—	—	—	3,500.	—
10-08R	$50	1883	Remainder*	—	—	—	—	3,500.	—
10-10R	$100	1883	Remainder*	—	—	—	—	3,500.	—

* unsigned at right.

THE BANK OF LOWER CANADA

1830s

QUEBEC, LOWER CANADA

BANK NUMBER 410 *NONREDEEMABLE*

410-10. HARRIS & SEALEY PRINTINGS

DESIGNS AND COLOURS

410-10-04R

$2 Face Design: Beehive and farm implements/ royal crest, Indian in canoe below/Britannia See varieties
Colour: Black with no tint

Back Design: Plain

410-10-06R

$2 Face Design: Beehive and farm implements/ Royal Crest, Indian in canoe below/Britannia
Colour: Black with no tint

Back Design: Plain

410-10-08R

$3 Face Design: Royal crest/allegorical figures, Indian in canoe below/Britannia
Colour: Black with no tint

Back Design: Plain

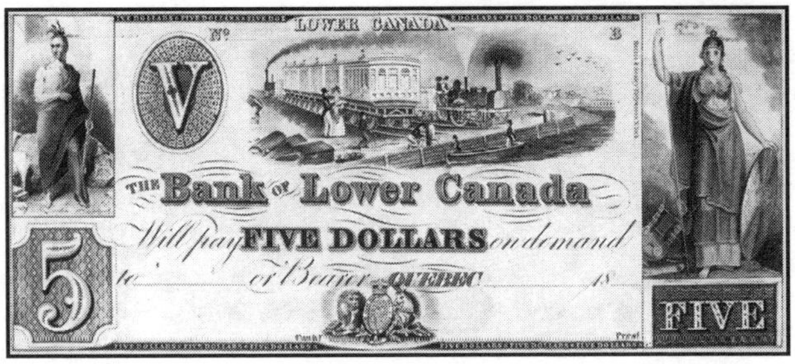

410-10-10R

$5 Face Design: Standing Indian with rifle/two trains at dock, Royal Crest below/Britannia
Colour: Black with no tint

Back Design: Plain

410-10-12

$10 Face Design: —/Sailboat and "Commerce" figure, small Royal Crest below/Britannia
Colour: Black with no tint

Back Design: Plain

IMPRINT

Harris & Sealey Engravers N. York
Harris & Sealey Engravers N.Y.

SIGNATURES

Various

ISSUE DATING

Partially engraved ____ 18 ____:

Mss. Various dates have been seen between 1839 and 1851
1840: April 4, May 4
1841: 8 Nov

VARIETIES

$1 Face Design: Engraved "A Messrs. D. Birdsey & Cie" at lower left
$1 Face Design: "D. Birdsey" omitted

Note: Notes of this bank were altered and issued in various U.S. states. See Haxby CT99-A55.

CIRCULATING NOTES

Cat. No.	Denom.	Date	Variety	G	VG	F	VF	EF	Unc
10-02	$1	18_	Engr. Birdsey		No known issued notes				
10-04R	$1	18_	Birdsey omitted	60.	125.	175.	250.	400.	750.
10-06R	$2	18_	Remainder	100.	200.	300.	425.	—	—
10-08R	$3	18_	Remainder	75.	150.	200.	275.	500.	—
10-10	$5	1840's	Fully issued	85.	175.	225.	300.	400.	750.
10-10R	$5	18__	Remainder	75.	150.	200.	275.	—	—
10-12	$10	1840's	Fully issued	85.	175.	225.	300.	400.	750.
10-12R	$10	18__	Remainder	75.	150.	200.	275.	—	—

PROOF NOTES

Cat. No.	Denom	Date	Variety	Unc
10-02P	$1	18__	Engr. Birdsey	Institutional collection only

LOWER CANADA BANK

1837

MONTREAL, LOWER CANADA

BANK NUMBER 415 ***NONREDEEMABLE***

Apparently this was a "phantom bank." Its function was presumably intended to take advantage of American citizens.

415-10 DRAFT ISSUE OF 1837

Engraved: "To Messrs. D. McDonald & Co. Montreal"

DESIGNS AND COLOURS

415-10-02

$1 Face Design: Ornate design with 1 and sea creatures/ Hercules wrestling lion; clasped hands below/ woman carrying sheaves

Colour: Black with no tint

Back Design: Plain

415-10-04

$2 Face Design: Ornate design with 2 and sea creatures/ men fighting dragons; clasped hand below/ "Commerce" figures

Colour: Black with no tint

Back Design: Plain

415-10-06P

$3 Face Design: Ornate design with 3 and sea creatures/ seated Greek philosopher "Homer"; clasped hands below/cherub with fruit basket in oval

Colour: Black with no tint

Back Design: Plain

IMPRINT

Rawdon, Wright & Hatch New-York

SIGNATURES

left	right
none	mss. G.D. White

ISSUE DATING

Partially Engraved __18__:

1837: Nov. 4

CIRCULATING NOTES

Cat.No.	Denom	Date	G	VG	F	VF	EF	AU
10-02	$1	18__	No known issued notes					
10-04	$2	1837	225.	450.	600.	—	—	—
10-06	$3	18__	No known issued notes					

PROOF NOTES

Cat. No.	Denom.	Date		Unc
10-02P	$1	18__	PROOF	400.
10-04P	$2	18__	PROOF	400.
10-06P	$3	18__	PROOF	400.

MACDONALD & CO.

1859-1866

VICTORIA, VANCOUVER ISLAND

BANK NUMBER 420 ***NONREDEEMABLE***

A private bank founded in 1859 in Victoria, British Columbia, Macdonald & Co. was the first bank west of the Great Lakes. It enjoyed prosperity in its initial years of operation, but with small resources it was increasingly difficult to compete with larger banks. After a serious robbery at its Victoria office, the bank closed its doors in 1864, with substantial losses to note holders and depositors.

ISSUE OF 1863

420-10 INDIAN AT RIGHT, ARM UPRAISED, INDIAN MAIDEN LOOKING LEFT

DESIGN AND COLOURS

420-10-02

$1 Face Design: Indian maiden/Royal Arms/bust of Indian
See subheadings
Colour: Black with no tint

Back Design: Plain

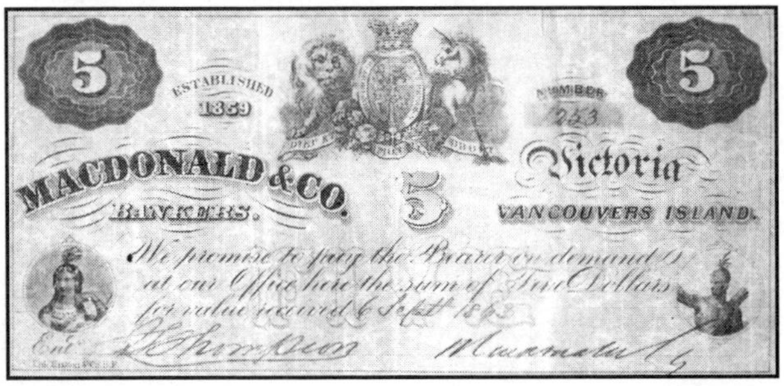

420-10-04

$5 Face Design: Indian maiden/Royal Arms/bust of Indian
Colour: Black with no tint

Back Design: Plain

420-10-06

$10 Face Design: Indian maiden/Royal Arms/bust of Indian
See subheadings
Colour: Black with no tint

Back Design: Plain

IMPRINT

Lith. Britton & Co., S.F.; all notes printed by lithography

SIGNATURES

left	right
mss. J.S. Thompson	mss. Macdonald Cy.
mss. Wm. Cocker	mss. Macdonald Cy.
mss. Robt. T. Smith	mss. Macdonald Cy

ISSUE DATING

Manuscript:

6 Sept. 1863

Cat. No.	Denom.	Date	G	VG	F	VF	EF	AU
10-02	$1	1863	45.	90.	120.	200.	—	—
10-04	$5	1863	60.	120.	160.	250.	—	—
10-06	$10	1863	80.	160.	210.	335.	—	—

420-12 INDIAN AT RIGHT, ARM DOWN, INDIAN MAIDEN LOOKING RIGHT

DESIGNS AND COLOURS

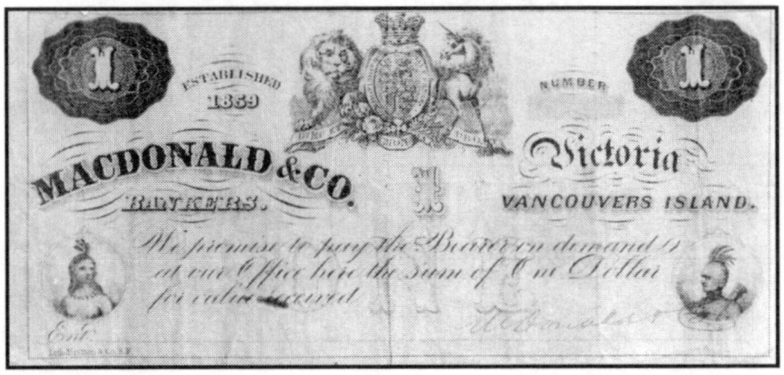

420-12-02

$1 Face Design: Indian maiden looking left/Royal Arms/
bust of Indian with arm down
Colour: Black with no tint

Back Design: Plain

420-12-04

$5 Face Design: Indian maiden looking left/Royal Arms/ bust of Indian with arm down
Colour: Black with no tint

Back Design: Plain

Cat. No.	Denom.	Date	Variety	G	VG	F	VF	EF	AU
12-02R	$1	1863	Remainder*	135.	275.	350.	550.	—	—
12-04	$5	1863		125.	250.	325.	500.	—	—
12-06	$10	1863				Notes not confirmed			

*Remainders only

THE MARITIME BANK OF THE DOMINION OF CANADA

1872-1887

ST. JOHN, NEW BRUNSWICK

BANK NUMBER 425 ***NONREDEEMABLE***

A bill to incorporated the bank was introduced on May 7, 1872, and on June 14 the act was given royal assent.

There are two different versions of the bank's early years and difficulties. It has been suggested that the bank was never fully capitalized, and its operations were hindered by lack of funds. By investing in various maritime-based industries, setbacks in the timber industry and the adverse economic conditions of the 1876 depression, the bank found itself in financial difficulty. In an attempt to improve its position, the bank sought to acquire additional capital by making further demands on its shareholders. At this point the Bank of Montreal acquired 15 percent of the shares of the Maritime Bank, which meant that Montreal-based banks now owned 25 percent of the shares.

On June 4, 1880, at the annual meeting, an injunction prevented the Bank of Montreal from voting, since an amendment to the Banking Act prohibited one bank from holding stock in another. At a special general meeting on August 10, 1880, it was resolved to remove the president, vice-president and directors and to set up a new board to wind up the bank's business. A policy of realizing assets was undertaken, but a major task remained in trying to untangle the true financial situation.

It has also been suggested that the course of events leading up to the situation of 1880 resulted from the policy of James Domville, an industrialist from St. John who controlled the bank. Allegedly, he used the bank to finance his own interests. When major losses were suffered in the late 1870s, a number of lockups resulted, all of which were at firms either owned by or associated with Domville's interests, and this precipitated the banking crisis.

The new board of directors marked a change in operational philosophy. The new managers followed traditional policies, but still found the burden of reorganizing the bank too great. Nonetheless, the desire to recoup losses led the stockholders to allow the bank to continue until its final, more costly demise in 1887. While the bank was in the process of regrouping, it found a new source of capital in Freeman's National Bank of Boston. In less than two years, this American bank supplied more than $270,000 on the collateral of notes deposited as security for loans granted to local businessmen. When the Maritime Bank of the Dominion of Canada finally closed its doors, note holders were obliged to redeem their notes through the Boston bank.

425-10 ISSUES OF 1873 AND 1875

DESIGNS AND COLOURS

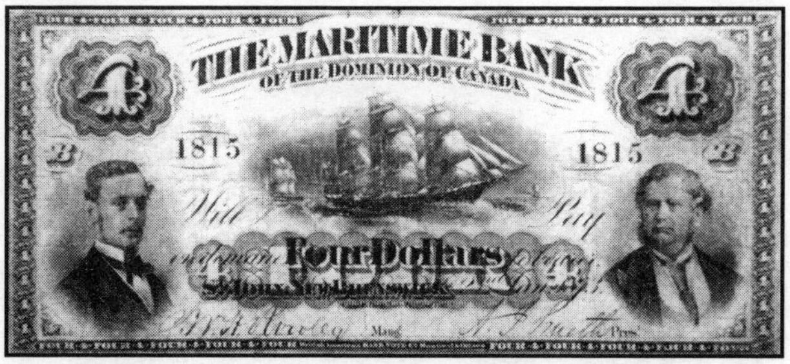

425-10-02

$4 Face Design: James Domville/sailing ships, "Clipper"/Hon. A.J. Smith
Colour: Black with green tint

Back Design: Lathework, counters, bank name, anchor, barrels and bale
Colour: Green

425-10-06P
$5 Face Design: James Domville/sailing steam ship/ Hon. A.J. Smith
Colour Black with green tint

Back Design: Lathework, counters, bank name, anchor barrels and bale

425-10-10P
$10 Face Design: Sailing ship/J. Robertson/boy climbing rigging "Going aloft"
Colour: Black with green tint

Back Design: Lathework, counters, bank name, anchor, barrels and bale

425-10-12P
$50 Face Design: Maj. Gen. J.W. Domville/Great Seal of Canada over Royal Crest/James Domville
Colour: Black with green tint

Back Design: Lathework, counters and bank name

IMPRINT

British American Bank Note Co. Montreal & Ottawa

SIGNATURES

left	**right**
mss. various	engr. A.J. Smith
mss. various	engr. James Domville

ISSUE DATING

Engraved

2nd. Jan. 1873
1st June 1875

CIRCULATING NOTES

Cat. No.	Denom.	Date	Variety	G	VG	F	VF	EF	AU
10-02	$4	1873	Smith, r.	—	5,000.	—	—	—	—
10-04	$4	1873	Domville, r.	Institutional collection only					
10-06P	$5	1873	Smith, r.	No known issued notes					
10-08P	$5	1873	Domville, r.	No known issued notes					
10-10P	$10	1873	Smith, r.	No known issued notes					
10-12P	$50	1875	Domville, r.	No known issued notes					

PROOF NOTES

Cat. No.	Denom.	Date	Variety		Unc
10-02P	$4	1873	Smith, r.	FACE PROOF	800.
10-04P	$4	1873	Domville, r.	FACE PROOF	800.
10-06P	$5	1873	Smith, r.	FACE PROOF	800.
10-08P	$5	1873	Domville, r.	FACE PROOF	800.
10-10P	$10	1873	Smith, r.	FACE PROOF	800.
10-12P	$50	1873	Domville, r.	FACE PROOF	800.

425-12 ISSUES OF 1881 AND 1882

DESIGNS AND COLOURS

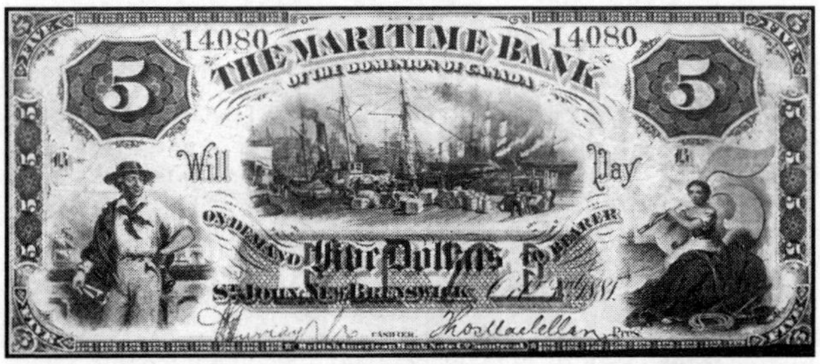

425-12-02

$5 Face Design: Sailor/dock scene/woman with telescope and 5
Colour: Black with green tint
Back Design: Counters, bank name, anchor, barrels and bale

425-12-04

$10 Face Design: Sailing ship/Queen Victoria in widow's weeds/
boy climbing rigging "Going aloft"
Colour: Black with green tint
Back Design: Counters, bank name, anchor, barrels and bale

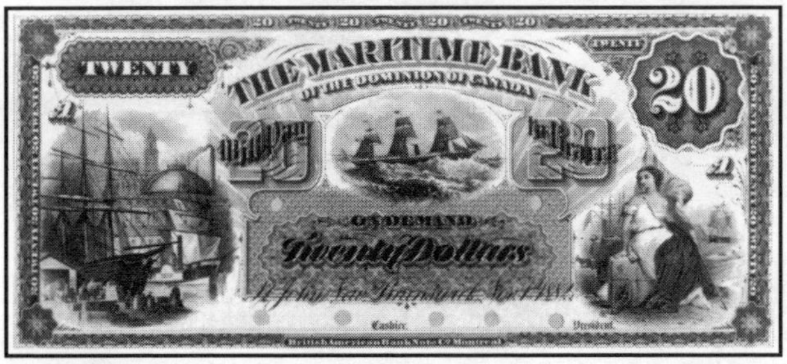

425-12-06P

$20 Face Design: Dock scene/steamship/allegorical woman with flag and bale
Colour: Black with green tint

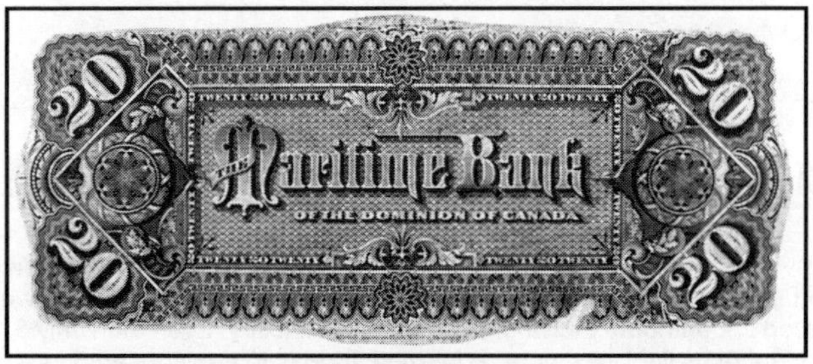

Back Design: Lathework, counters and bank name

IMPRINT
British American Bank Note Co. Montreal

SIGNATURES

left	**right**
mss. various	engr. Thos. Maclellan

ISSUE DATING
Engraved
Octr. 3rd 1881
Nov. 1st 1882

OVERPRINT
$5: "V" in red

Note: $5 and $10 come with red or blue sheet numbers.

CIRCULATING NOTES

Cat. No.	Denom.	Date	Variety	G	VG	F	VF	EF	AU
12-02	$5	1881	No o/p	1,250.	2,000.	2,500.	3,500.	—	—
12-02a	$5	1881	Red o/p	1,500.	—	—	—	—	—
12-04	$10	1881		2,000.	3,600.	—	—	—	—
12-06P	$20	1882			Institutional collection only				

PROOF NOTES

Cat. No.	Denom.	Date		Unc
12-02P	$5	1881	FACE PROOF	800.
12-04P	$10	1881	FACE PROOF	800.
12-06P	$20	1882	FACE PROOF	800.

THE MECHANICS BANK

1865-1879

MONTREAL, CANADA EAST

BANK NUMBER 430 ***NONREDEEMABLE***

Established in Montreal in 1865, this bank was managed by corrupt individuals and continued in its later years to be maintained by artificial and improper methods. After its failure in 1879, the shareholders were forced to contribute the whole of the double liability. Even then only 57.5 percent of its liabilities were redeemed. Its loss to creditors amounted to $180,000. The bank went to dangerous extremes to circulate as many of its notes as it could. After suspension, the notes were redeemed at only 57.5 cents on the dollar.

430-10 **ISSUE OF 1872**

DESIGNS AND COLOURS

430-10-04b

$4 Face Design: Two men shoeing horses/men working in carpenter's shop "Carpenters at Work" mechanic at lathe "The Lathe"

Colour: Black with green tint

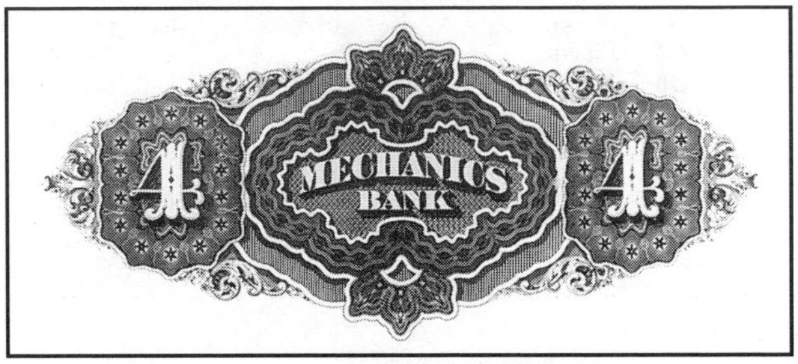

Back Design: Lathework, counters and bank name

Colour: Blue-green

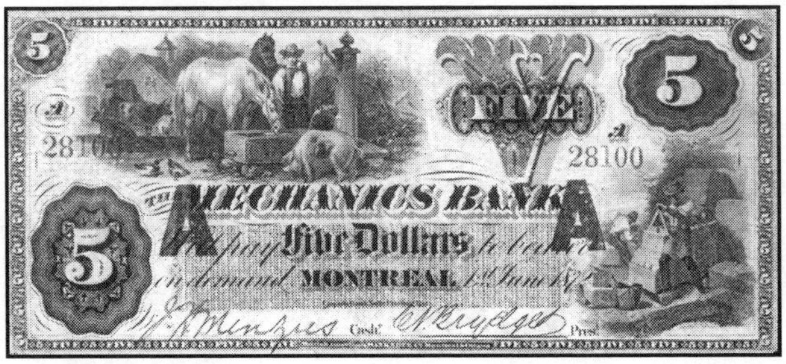

430-10-08a

$5 Face Design: Farmer pumping water for livestock/—/ stone cutters

Colour: Black with green tint

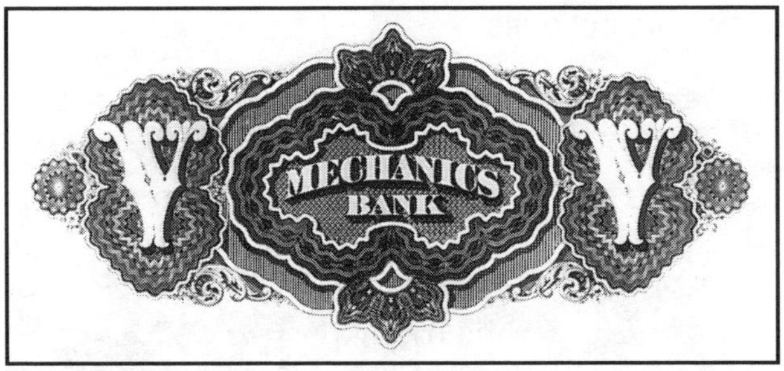

Back Design: Lathework, counters and bank name

Colour: Blue-green

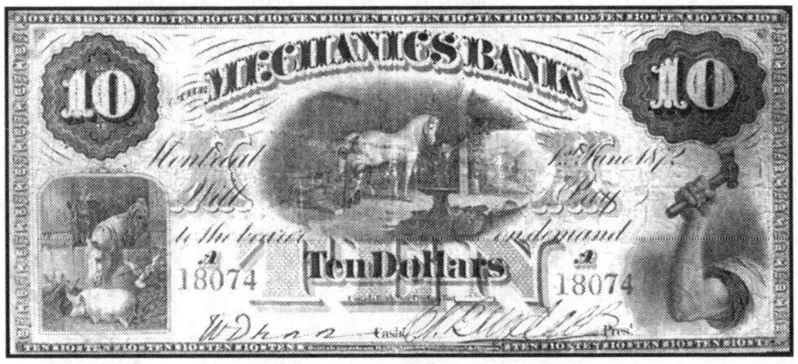

430-10-10

$10 Face Design: Farm animals at stable door "Stable Door"/ blacksmith shoeing a horse "Horse Shoeing"/ arm and hammer "muscle"

Colour: Black with green tint

Back Design: Lathework, counters and bank name

Colour: Blue-green

IMPRINT

British American Bank Note Co. Montreal & Ottawa

SIGNATURES

	left	right
$4 and $5:	mss. W. Dunn	mss. C.J. Brydges
	mss. W. Dunn	mss. W. Shanly
	mss. J.H. Menzies	engr. C.J. Brydges
$10:	mss. W. Dunn	mss. C.J. Brydges
	mss. W. Dunn	mss. Walter Shanly
	mss. J.H. Menzies	engr. C.J. Brydges

ISSUE DATING

Engraved

1st June, 1872

OVERPRINT

Engraved signature notes:

"A A" in blue
"B B" in blue
"L L" in blue
"ALEXANDRIA" twice vertically in blue
"BEAUHARNOIS" twice vertically in blue

STAMP

"A" in circle twice in purple

Cat. No.	Den.	Date	Variety	G	VG	F	VF
10-02	$4	1872	Mss. signat., r.; no o/p	100.	200.	—	—
10-02a	$4	1872	Mss. signat., r.; letter o/p	110.	225.	—	—
10-04	$4	1872	Engr. Brydges, r.; no o/p	75.	150.	250.	350.
10-04a	$4	1872	Engr. Brydges, r.; letter o/p	80.	160.	275.	375.
10-04b	$4	1872	Engr. Brydges r.; ALEXANDRIA o/p	100.	200.	325.	—
10-04c	$4	1873	Engr. Brydges, r.; BEAUHARNOIS o/p	80.	160.	275.	375.
10-06	$5	1872	Mss. signat., r.; no o/p	85.	175.	—	—
10-06a	$5	1872	Mss. signat. r.; letter o/p	90.	185.	300.	—
10-08	$5	1872	Engr. Brydges, r.; no o/p	60.	120.	175.	275.
10-08a	$5	1872	Engr. Brydges r.; letter o/p	65.	130.	200.	300.
10-08b	$5	1872	Engr. Brydges r.; ALEXANDRIA o/p	90.	185.	300.	—
10-08c	$5	1872	Engr. Brydges r.; BEAUHARNOIS o/p	65.	130.	200.	300.
10-10	$10	1872	Mss. signat., r.	500.	1,000.	1,400.	—
10-12	$10	1872	Engr. Brydges, r	500.	1,000.	1,400.	—

THE MECHANICS BANK

1837

MONTREAL, LOWER CANADA

BANK NUMBER 435 ***NONREDEEMABLE***

The notes of this "spurious bank" appeared briefly during the summer of 1837, centering circulation in Buffalo, but not in Montreal. The true nature of the "bank" was soon exposed by the press and the police.

435-10 **ISSUE OF 1837**

DESIGNS AND COLOURS

435-10-02

$3 Face Design: Dock scene/blacksmith and two women (Industry, Agriculture, Commerce); arm and hammer in shield below/woman with wheat leaning on pillar

Colour: Black with no tint

Back Design: Plain

435-10-04

$5 Face Design: Seated youth with mechanic's tools/seated woman resting on cogwheel; arm and hammer in shield below/blacksmith "Industry"

Colour: Black with no tint

Back Design: Plain

435-10-06

$10 Face Design: Seated woman with rake, leaning on shield/ blacksmith and two allegorical women (Industry, Agriculture, Commerce); crouching lion in oval below/kneeling cherub inscribing rock

Colour: Black with no tint

Back Design: Plain

IMPRINT

Rawdon, Wright & Hatch, New-York

SIGNATURES

left	right
mss. F.E. Whiting	mss. W. Morris
mss. T.T. Copley	mss. Thos. H. Sprague

ISSUE DATING

Partially engraved ___ 18___:

$5 and $10 1837: May 1

$3, $5 and $10 1837: June 1

Cat. No.	Denom.	Date	VG	F	VF	EF	AU
10-02	$3	1837	125.	175.	250.	400.	—
10-04	$5	1837	80.	100.	150.	225.	325.
10-06	$10	1837	100.	125.	200.	300.	—

THE MECHANICS BANK OF ST. JOHN'S

1837

ST. JOHN'S, LOWER CANADA

BANK NUMBER 440 ***NONREDEEMABLE***

The notes of this "spurious bank" appeared briefly during the summer of 1837, entering circulation in Buffalo, but not in St. John's. The true nature of the "bank" was quickly exposed by the press and the police.

440-10 NOTE ISSUE 1837

DESIGNS AND COLOURS

440-10-02R

$5 Face Design: Man ploughing; steamboat with American flag below/allegorical female female and two men (Agriculture, Commerce, Industry)

Colour: Black with no tint

Back Design: Plain

440-10-04

$10 Face Design: Seated woman leaning on cogwheel/train with river and town in background; arm and hammer in shield below/sailing ships (one with American flag), lighthouse

Colour Black with no tint

Back Design: Plain

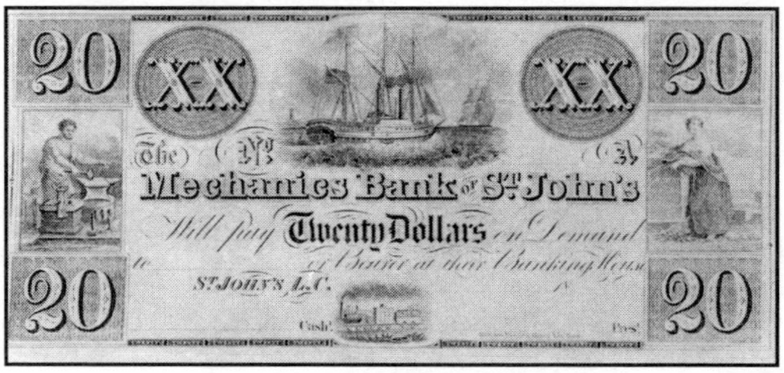

440-10-06R

$20 Face Design: Blacksmith at anvil/paddlewheel steamship with American flag, lighthouse; old train below/allegorical female

Colour Black with no tint

Back Design: Plain

IMPRINT

Rawdon, Wright & Hatch, New-York

SIGNATURES

left	right
mss. G. Hosmer	mss. H.N. Warren

ISSUE DATING

Partially engraved ___ 18___:

1837: May 20, May 21

Note: 10-02R are remainders with spurious dates and signatures 10-06R and full sheet are remainders unsigned, undated and unnumbered.

Cat. No.	Denom.	Date	G	VG	F	VF	EF	AU
10-02R	$5	18_*	100.	200.	250.	375.	600.	—
10-04	$10	1837	110.	225.	300.	450.	750.	—
10-04R	$10	18__	100.	200.	250.	375.	600.	—
10-06R	$20	18_**	135.	275.	400.	575.	—	—
Full Sheet	$5.5.10.20	18_**	—	—	—	2,400.	—	—

440-12 **DRAFT ISSUE, 1837**

DESIGNS AND COLOURS

440-12-02-02R

$1 Face Design: Seated woman leaning on cogwheel/ train, river and town in background; arm and hammer in shield below/seated youth with mechanic's tools
See subheadings

Colour: Black with no tint

Back Design: Plain

440-12-02-04

$2 Face Design: Woman with wheat resting on pillar/ blacksmith and two women (Industry, Agriculture, Commerce); steamboat with American flag below/man with scythe in wheat field. See subheadings

Colour: Black with no tint

Back Design: Plain

440-12-04-06

$3 Face Design: —/steamship, one with American flag, lighthouse; old train below/blacksmith and woman (Industry and Agriculture)
See subheadings

Colour: Black with no tint

Back Design: Plain

IMPRINT

Rawdon, Wright & Hatch New-York

2. **ENGRAVED**

"A Messrs H.N. Warren & Cie a St. John's" AT LOWER LEFT
Mss. "H.N. Warren & Cie" endorsed vertically across centre

SIGNATURES

left	right
none	mss. G. Hosmer

ISSUE DATING

Partially engraved ___ 18___:

1837: July 1, Novr 29

Cat. No.	Denom.	Date	Variety	G	VG	F	VF	EF	AU
12-02-02R	$1	18_	Remainder*	50.	100.	135.	—	—	—
12-02-04	$2	1837		60.	125.	175.	—	—	—
12-02-04R	$2	18_	Remainder*	50.	100.	135.	—	—	—
12-02-06R	$3	18_	Remainder*	75.	150.	200.	—	—	—

*spurious dates

4. **ENGRAVED**

"A Messrs T.H. Perry & Cie a St. John's" AT LOWER LEFT
Mss. "T.H. Perry & Cie" endorsed vertically across centre

SIGNATURES

left	right
none	mss. Thos. W. Frink

ISSUE DATING

Partially engraved ___ 18___:

1837: Nov. 29

Cat. No.	Denom.	Date	Variety	G	VG	F	VF	EF	AU
12-04-02	$1	1837		60.	125.	175.	—	—	—
12-04-04	$2	1837		60.	125.	175.	—	—	—
12-04-04R	$2	18_	Remainder*	50.	100.	135.	—	—	—
12-04-06	$3	1837		85.	175.	240.	—	—	—

*unsigned, undated and unnumbered

THE MERCANTILE BANKING CORPORATION

1878

HALIFAX, NOVA SCOTIA

BANK NUMBER 445 ***NONREDEEMABLE***

445-10 CHAS. SKIPPER & EAST PRINTING OF 1878 LARGE SIZE NOTES

DESIGNS AND COLOURS

445-10-02P

$10 Face Design —/sailing ships/—
Colour: Black with no tint

Back Design: Unknown

IMPRINT
Charles Skipper & East, London

SIGNATURES

left	right
none	none

ISSUE DATING
Engraved
Jany. 1st 1878

PROOF NOTES

Cat. No.	Denom.	Date		Unc
10-02P	$10	1878	FACE PROOF	800.

THE MERCHANTS BANK

1830s

MONTREAL (LOWER CANADA)

BANK NUMBER 448 ***NONREDEEMABLE***

No information concerning this bank is available. A plate is in existence in the American Bank Note Co. archives.

448-10 RWH PRINTINGS

DESIGNS AND COLOURS

$5 Face Design: Seated female "Commerce" figure; anchor in shield and ship; child riding deer below/ seated commerce figure
Colour: Black with no tint
Back Design: Plain

$10 Face Design: Ship and seated male "Commerce" figure; reclining woman below/woman in waves
Colour: Black with no tint
Back Design: Plain

$20 Face Design: Ship and seated male "Commerce" figure; strongbox and dog with key below/dock scene and ships
Colour: Black with no tint
Back Design: Plain

IMPRINT

Rawdon, Wright & Hatch, New York

SIGNATURES

left	right
none	none
Brooks	Brennan

ISSUE DATING

Partially engraved ___ 18___:

$5 1837: Apr 6

Cat. No.	Denom.	Date	G	VG	F	VF	EF	AU
10-02	$5	18_	150.	300.	450.	—	—	—
10-04	$10	18_	SURVIVING NOTES NOT CONFIRMED					
10-06	$20	18_	SURVIVING NOTES NOT CONFIRMED					

THE MERCHANTS BANK

1836-1837

TORONTO, UPPER CANADA

BANK NUMBER 450 ***NONREDEEMABLE***

The Merchants Bank was a spurious bank that pushed fictitious notes into public circulation for a limited period in 1836 and 1837.

450-10 ISSUE OF 1836-1837

DESIGNS AND COLOURS

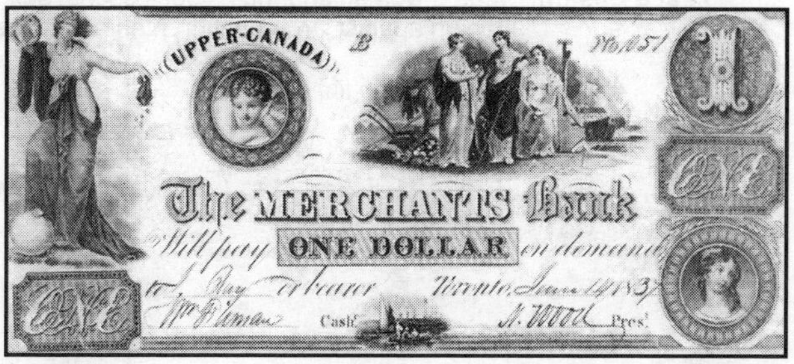

450-10-04

$1 Face Design: Woman with foot on globe, dropping coins/cherub in ornate oval/three allegorical women, produce and ship; sailing ships and small boat below/portrait of young woman in ornate oval

Colour: Black with no tint

Back Design: Plain

450-10-06

$2 Face Design: Sailing ship and tug/two allegorical women; spread eagle below/portrait of young woman in ornate oval

Colour: Black with no tint

Back Design: Plain

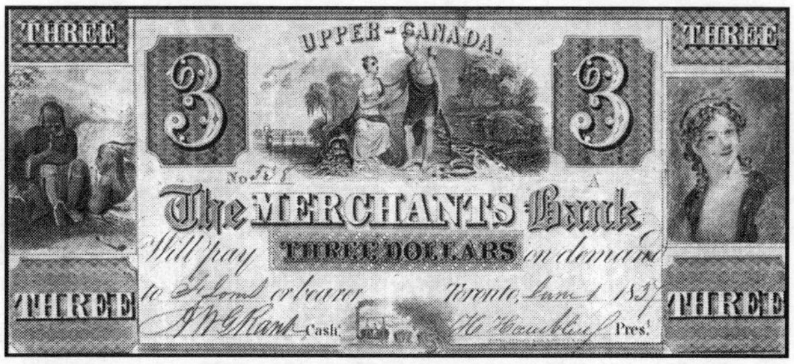

450-10-08

$3 Face Design: Two Indians and falls/seated women and Indian; trees and old train below/portrait of young woman

Colour: Black with no tint

Back Design: Plain

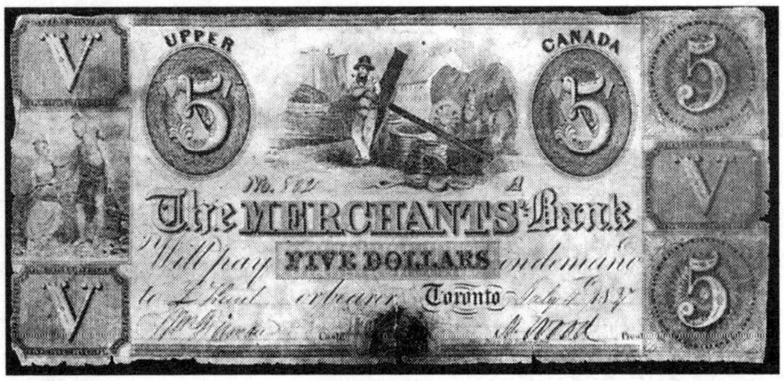

450-10-10

$5 Face Design: Seated woman and Indian/dock scene, sailor leaning against large anchor; men and ships below/-
Colour: Black with no tint

Back Design: Plain

The spurious $5 note, above, from Pennsylvania is obviously printed from the same plate, with slight modifications, as the $5 Upper Canada note. The plates for these notes have been used as the sources for printing altered, obsolete notes in Connecticut and Pennsylvania.

IMPRINT

Terry, Pelton and Co. Boston & Prov.

SIGNATURES

left	right
mss. Wm. Firman	mss. N. Wood
mss. J.G. Hunt	mss. H.Hamblin
mss. Wm. Firman	mss. Geo. R. Wait
mss. A.W.G. Rank	mss. N. Wood
mss. A.W.G. Rank	mss. H. Hamblin
mss. J.G. Hunt	mss. Geo. R. Wait

ISSUE DATING

Partially engraved _ 18_:

$1 1836: Dec 5
$1 1837: May 4, June 1, June 14
$2 1837: May 4, June 1, July 4
$3 1837: June 1
$5 1837: June 1, July 4
Full Sheet 1837: May 4

Note: 10-04 R, 10-06R and 10-08R are undated, unsigned and unnumbered. The full sheet is signed and dated, but unnumbered.

Cat. No.	Denom.	Date	Variety	G	VG	F	VF	EF	Unc
10-02	$1	1836-1837		75.	150.	200.	300.	425.	600.
10-02R	$1	1837	Remainder	—	—	—	—	250.	400.
10-06	$2	1837		75.	150.	200.	300.	425.	600.
10-06R	$2	1837	Remainder	—	—	—	—	250.	400.
10-08	$3	1837		100.	200.	250.	375.	500.	—
10-08R	$3	1837	Remainder	—	—	—	200.	300.	450.
10-10	$5	1837		250.	500.	700.	—	—	—
Full Sheet	$1.1.2.3	1837**		—	—	—	—	—	2,500.
Part Sheet	$1.2.3	1837		—	—	750.	1,000.	—	—

** Signed and dated
Remainder - no date, signatures or sheet numbers

THE MERCHANTS BANK

1864-1868

MONTREAL, (CANADA EAST)

BANK NUMBER 455 ***REDEEMABLE***

Established in Montreal in 1864, this bank changed its name to the Merchants Bank of Canada in 1868, upon absorbing the Commercial Bank of Canada. The president, Sir Hugh Allan, was destined to become a key figure in the CPR scandal of 1873.

455-10 **ISSUE OF 1864**

DESIGNS AND COLOURS

455-10-02P

$1 Face Design: Sailors at dock/wharf scene with train and wagons/Hugh Allan
Colour: Black with green tint

Back Design: Lathework and bank name
Colour: Green

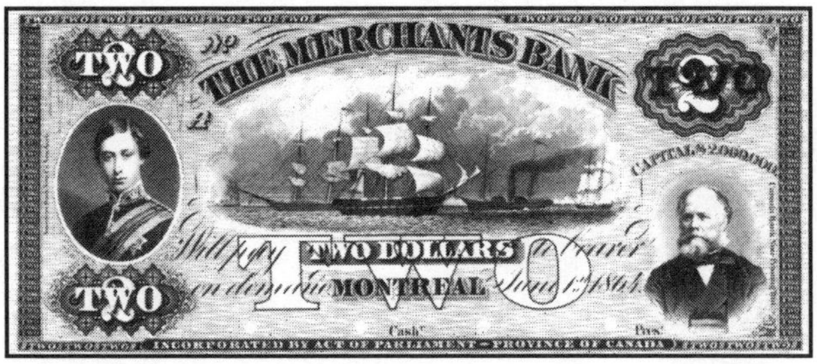

455-10-04P

$2 Face Design: Prince of Wales/steamships and sailing ships/Hugh Allan
Colour: Black with green tint

Back Design: Lathework and bank name
Colour: Green

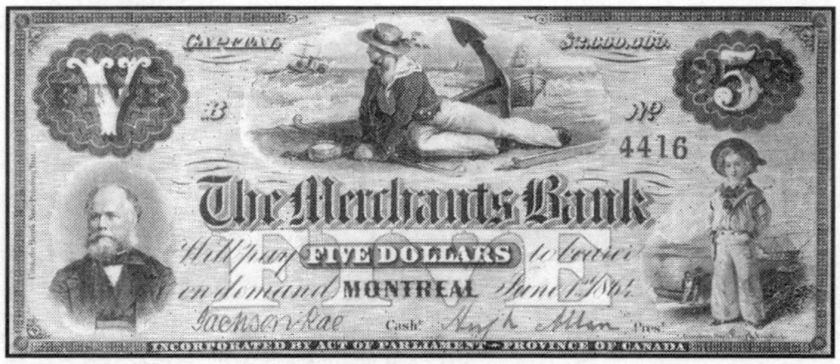

455-10-06

$5 Face Design: Hugh Allan/sailor lying on seashore, anchor/ Albert Edward, (Prince of Wales,) as a small boy in sailor suit
Colour: Back with green tint

Back Design: Lathework and bank name
Colour: Green

455-10-08P

$10 Face Design: Hugh Allan/train, men and cattle/sailor with telescope "On the look out"
Colour: Black with green tint

Back Design: Lathework and bank name
Colour: Green

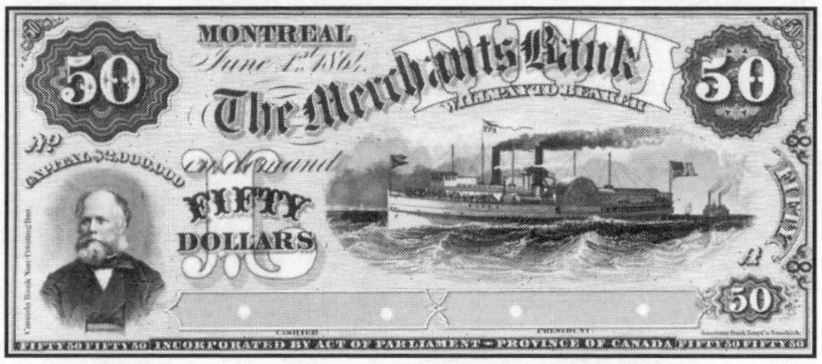

455-10-10P

$50 Face Design: Hugh Allan/paddlewheel steamer "Coast Steamer"/—
Colour: Black with green tint

Back Design: Lathework and bank name
Colour: Green

455-10-12P

$100 Face Design: Hugh Allan/paddlewheel steamer/ dog seated by strongbox
Colour: Black with green tint

Back Design: Lathework and bank name
Colour: Green

IMPRINT

American Bank Note Co., New York

SIGNATURES

left	right
mss. various	mss. Hugh Allan
mss. various	mss. A. Cameron (p.)

ISSUE DATING

Engraved

June 1st, 1864

CIRCULATING NOTES

Cat. No.	Denom.	Date	G	VG	F	VF	EF	AU
10-02	$1	1864	550.	1,100.	1,600.	—	—	—
10-04	$2	1864	600.	1,200.	1,750.	—	—	—
10-06	$5	1864	700.	1,400.	1,950.	—	—	—
10-08	$10	1864	900.	1,800.	2,500.	—	—	—
10-10	$50	1864	No known issued notes					
10-12	$100	1864	No known issued notes					

PROOF NOTES

Cat. No.	Denom.	Date		Unc
10-02P	$1	1864	FACE PROOF	500.
10-04P	$2	1864	FACE PROOF	500.
10-06P	$5	1864	FACE PROOF	600.
10-08P	$10	1864	FACE PROOF	700.
10-10P	$50	1864	FACE PROOF	900.
10-12P	$100	1864	FACE PROOF	900.

THE MERCHANTS BANK OF CANADA

1868-1923

MONTREAL, QUEBEC

BANK NUMBER 460 ***REDEEMABLE***

Established in 1864 in Montreal as the Merchants Bank, the name of the Merchants Bank of Canada was adopted in 1868. The bank lost millions during the depression of the 1870s, and George Hague, the former general manager of the Bank of Toronto, was asked to assume the management. Hague accepted and succeeded in restoring the fortunes of the bank. The bank eventually had about 400 branches and sub-agencies in Canada, as well as offices in London, England, and in New York. The bank suffered large losses through bad managerial decisions where unjustified credit was extended.

At the meeting of its shareholders that approved the sale to the Bank of Montreal in 1922, the president stated that the directors had not been aware of the position of the more important accounts in which losses were sustained, and that the general manager and the manager of the Montreal office were responsible. In 1922 the president and the general manager were charged with submitting false returns under the Bank Act, but were acquitted.

460-10 HUGH ALLAN PORTRAIT ISSUES

1868-1873

DESIGNS AND COLOURS

460-10-02a

$1 Face Design: Two sailors on wharf “Mech’s & Commerce”/ train at dockside/Hugh Allan
Colour: Black with overall green tint

Back Design: Lathework, counters and bank name
Colour: Green

460-10-04

$2 Face Design: Prince of Wales/sailing ships and steamship/ Hugh Allan
Colour: Black with overall green tint

Back Design: Lathework, counters and bank name
Colour: Green

460-10-06

$4 Face Design: Prince of Wales/cow, cottage and sheep in background/Hugh Allan
Colour: Black with overall green tint

Back Design: Lathework, counters and bank name
Colour: Green

460-10-10

$5 Face Design: Hugh Allan/sailor on shore with anchor/ Albert Edward, (Prince of Wales,) as a child in a sailor suit (after Winterhalter)
Colour: Black with overall green tint

Back Design: Lathework, counters and bank name
Colour: Green

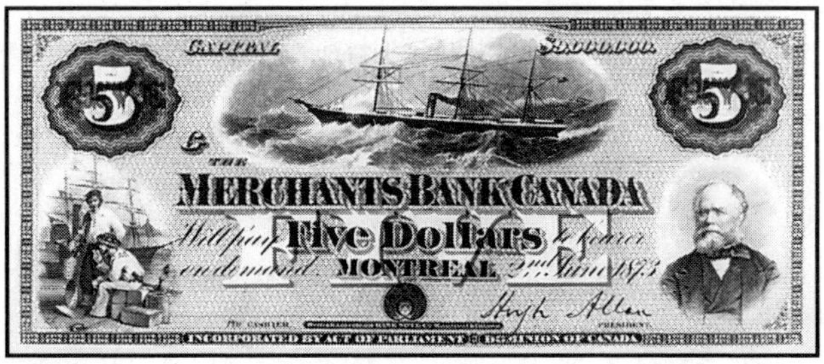

460-10-12P

$5 Face Design: Two sailors on wharf/steamship/Hugh Allan
Colour: Black with overall green tint

Back Design: Lathework, counters and bank name
Colour: Green

460-10-14

$10 Face Design: River pilot at wheel "Lachine pilot"/ head office/Hugh Allan
Colour: Black with green tint

Back Design: Lathework, counters and bank name
Colour: Green

460-10-16P

$20 Face Design: Earl of Dufferin/train/Hugh Allan
Colour: Black with green tint

Back Design: Lathework, counters and bank name
Colour: Green

IMPRINT

American Bank Note Co. New York on 1868 issues
British American Bank Note Co. Montreal & Ottawa

SIGNATURES

left	right
mss. various	engr. Hugh Allan

ISSUE DATING

Engraved

Mar. 2nd 1868
May 2nd 1870
1st Aug. 1871
$4 and $5: 2nd June 1873
$5 and $20: 1st Aug. 1873

OVERPRINT

1868: "TORONTO" in blue
1868: "PERTH" in blue

CIRCULATING NOTES

Cat. No.	Denom.	Date		G	VG	F	VF	EF	AU
10-02	$1	1868		350.	700.	1,000.	—	—	—
10-02a	$1	1868	town o/p	375.	750.	1,075.	—	—	—
10-04	$2	1868		450.	900.	1,200.	—	—	—
10-04a	$2	1868	town o/p	475.	950.	1,275.	—	—	—
10-06	$4	1870		300.	600.	900.	—	—	—
10-08	$4	1873		300.	600.	900.	—	—	—
10-10	$5	1868		350.	700.	1,000.	1,500.	—	—
10-10a	$5	1868	town o/p	375.	750.	1,075.	1,600.	—	—
10-12	$5	1873		No known issued notes					
10-14	$10	1871		600.	1,200.	1,700.	—	—	—
10-16	$20	1873		No known issued notes					

PROOF NOTES

Cat. No.	Denom.	Date		Unc
10-12P	$5	1873	FACE PROOF	600.
10-16P	$20	1873	FACE PROOF	700.

460-12 ANDREW ALLAN PORTRAIT ISSUE, 1886

DESIGNS AND COLOURS

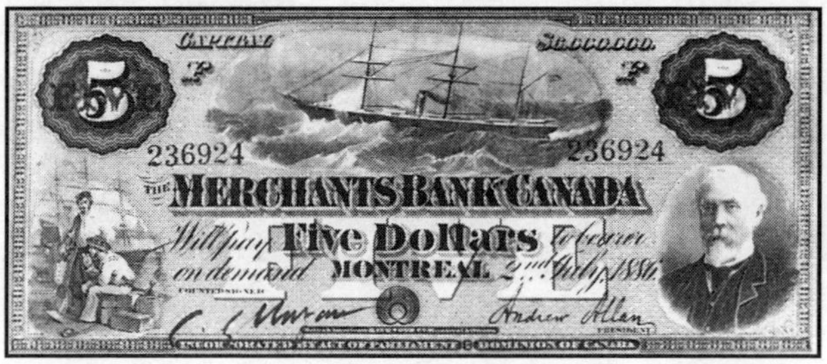

460-12-02

$5 Face Design: Sailors at dock "Mech's & Commerce"/ steamship/Andrew Allan
Colour: Black with overall green tint

Back Design: Lathework, counters and bank name
Colour: Green

460-12-04

$10 Face Design: River pilot at wheel "Lachine Pilot"/ head office/Andrew Allan
Colour: Black with overall green tint

Back Design: Lathework, counters and bank name
Colour: Green

460-12-06P

$50 Face Design: Lord Dufferin/the paddlewheel steamer "QUEBEC"/Andrew Allan
Colour: Black with overall green tint

Back Design: Lathework, counters and bank name
Colour: Green

460-12-08P

$100 Face Design: Queen Victoria in widow's weeds/ ship sailing toward viewer/Andrew Allan
Colour: Black with overall green tint

Back Design: Lathework, counters and bank name
Colour Green

IMPRINT

British American Bank Note Co. Montreal & Ottawa

SIGNATURES

left	**right**
mss. various	engr. Andrew Allan

ISSUE DATING

Engraved

2nd July, 1886

CIRCULATING NOTES

Cat. No.	Denom.	Date	G	VG	F	VF	EF	AU
12-02	$5	1886	200.	400.	500.	800.	1,250.	—
12-04	$10	1886	250.	500.	650.	1,000.	1,600.	—
12-06	$50	1886	No known issued notes					
12-08	$100	1886	No known issued notes					

PROOF NOTES

Cat. No.	Denom.	Date		Unc
12-06P	$50	1886	FACE PROOF	700.
12-08P	$100	1886	FACE PROOF	900.

460-14 MULTICOLOURED TINT ISSUES 1900 AND 1903

DESIGNS AND COLOURS

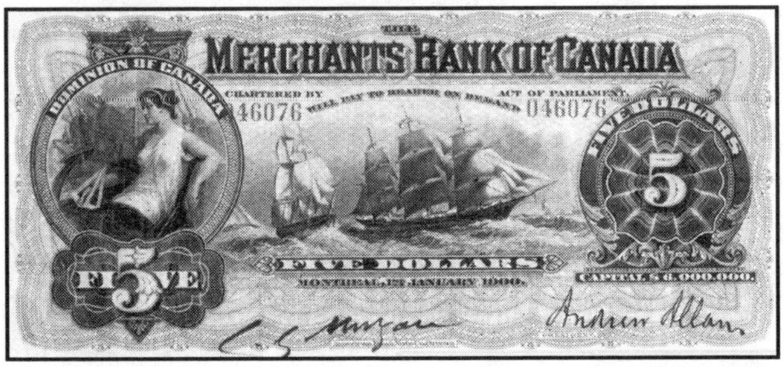

460-14-02

$5 Face Design: Woman holding sextant "Navigator"/sailing ships "The Clipper"/—
Colour: Black with blue, yellow-brown, yellow-green and lilac tint

Back Design: Lathework, counters, bank name and gypsy woman
Colour: Black with yellow-brown, yellow-green and lilac tint

460-14-08S

$10 Face Design: —/two seated allegorical women, factories and train/—
Colour: Black with red-brown, yellow-brown, blue and lilac tint

Back Design: Lathework, counters, bank name and "Justice" figure flanked by allegorical male and female
Colour: Black with red, red-brown, yellow-green and lilac tint

460-14-10S
$20 Face Design: "Steer's head" (after Landseer)/—/—
Colour: Black with green and orange tint

Back Design: Lathework, counters, bank name and Bank Crest
Colour: Black with green, red and yellow-green tint

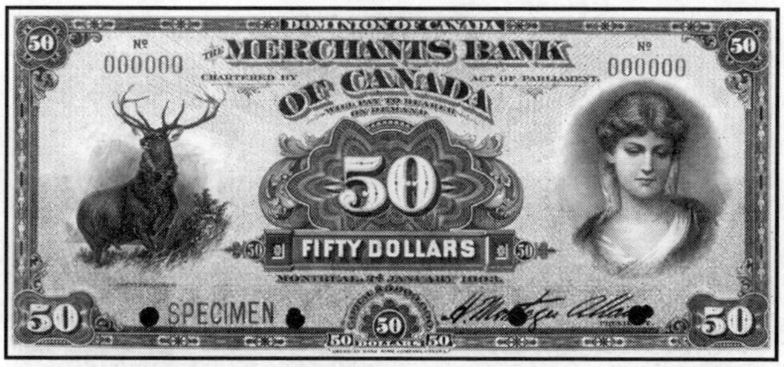

460-14-12S
$50 Face Design: Stag "Monarch of the Glen" Landseer/—/ young woman "Reverie"
Colour: Black with red and olive green tint

Back Design: Lathework, counters, bank name and Bank Crest
Colour Black with olive, yellow-brown, yellow-green and blue tint

IMPRINT

American Bank Note Co. Ottawa
American Bank Note Company, Ottawa

SIGNATURES

left	right
mss. various	engr. Andrew Allan
mss. various	engr. H. Montagu Allan

ISSUE DATING

Engraved

1st January 1900
2d January 1903

CIRCULATING NOTES

Cat. No.	Den.	Date	Variety	G	VG	F	VF	EF	AU
14-02	$5	1900	Andrew Allan, r.	300.	600.	800.	1,200.	2,000.	—
14-04	$5	1900	H. Montagu Allan, r.	275.	550.	750.	1,100.	—	—
14-06	$10	1900	Andrew Allan, r.	No known issued notes					
14-08	$10	1900	H. Montagu Allan, r.	750.	1,500.	2,000.	2,750.	—	—
14-10	$20	1903		No known issued notes					
14-12	$50	1903		No known issued notes					

PROOF NOTES

Cat. No.	Den.	Date	Variety		Unc
14-02P	$5	1900	Andrew Allan, r.	FACE PROOF	350.
14-06P	$10	1900	Andrew Allan, r.	FACE PROOF	350.
14-10P	$20	1903		FACE PROOF	450.

SPECIMEN NOTES

Cat. No.	Den.	Date	Variety		Unc
14-02S	$5	1900	Andrew Allan, r.	SPECIMEN	600.
14-04S	$5	1900	H. Montague Allan, r.	SPECIMEN	600.
14-06S	$10	1900	Andrew Allan, r.	SPECIMEN	600.
14-08S	$10	1900	H. Montague Allan, r.	SPECIMEN	600.
14-10S	$20	1903		SPECIMEN	700.
14-12S	$50	1903		SPECIMEN	800.

460-16 **ISSUES OF 1906 AND 1907**

DESIGNS AND COLOURS

460-16-02
$5 Face Design: River pilot at wheel "Lachine Pilot"/ modern steamship/H. Montagu Allan
Colour: Black with overall green tint

Back Design: Lathework, counters, bank name and two beavers
Colour: Green

460-16-04
$10 Face Design: Indian on horse "Indian Hunter"/ horse-drawn reaper/H. Montagu Allan
Colour: Black with overall green tint

Back Design: Lathework, counters, bank name and sailor with telescope
Colour: Green

460-16-06
$20 Face Design: "Steer's Head" (after Landseer)/—/—
Colour: Black with overall green tint

Back Design: Lathework, counters, bank name and sheep at pond
Colour: Green

460-16-08
$50 Face Design: Stag "Monarch of the Glen" Landseer/—/ Bank Crest
Colour: Black with overall green tint

Type I: Tint surrounds stag and beehive and crest
Type II: Tint leaves white areas around stag and beehive

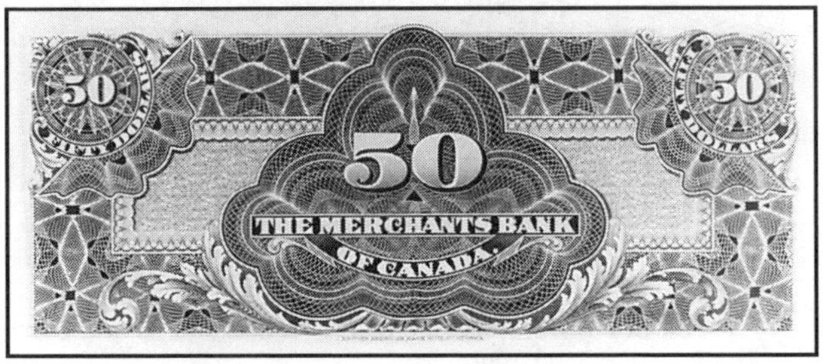

Back Design: Lathework, counters and bank name
Colour Green

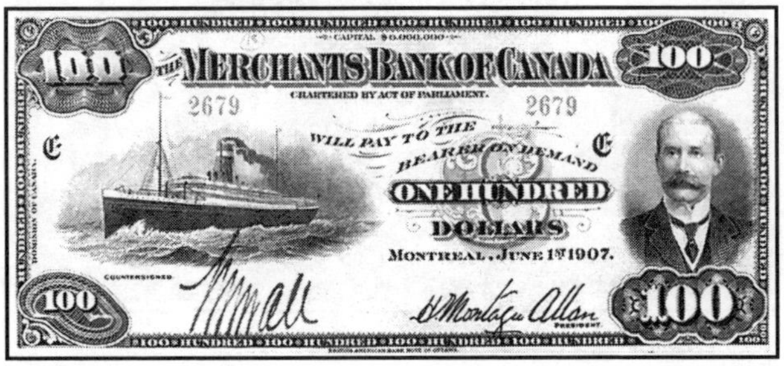

460-16-10
$100 Face Design: Steamship/-/H. Montagu Allan
Colour: Black with overall green tint

Back Design: Lathework, counters, bank name and youth painting jug
Colour: Green

IMPRINT

British American Bank Note Co. Ottawa

SIGNATURES

left	right
mss. various	engr. H. Montagu Allan

ISSUE DATING

Engraved

Feb 1st 1906
June 1st 1907

Cat. No.	Denom.	Date	Variety	G	VG	F	VF	EF	AU
16-02	$5	1906		90.	185.	275.	450.	750.	—
16-04	$10	1906		90.	185.	275.	450.	750.	—
16-06	$20	1907		325.	650.	900.	1,350.	—	—
16-08	$50	1907	Type I	800.	1,600.	2,300.	3,400.	4,800.	—
16-09	$50	1907	Type II	750.	1,500.	2,150.	3,200.	—	—
16-10	$100	1907		1,000.	2,000.	2,500.	—	—	—

460-18 ISSUE OF 1916

DESIGNS AND COLOURS

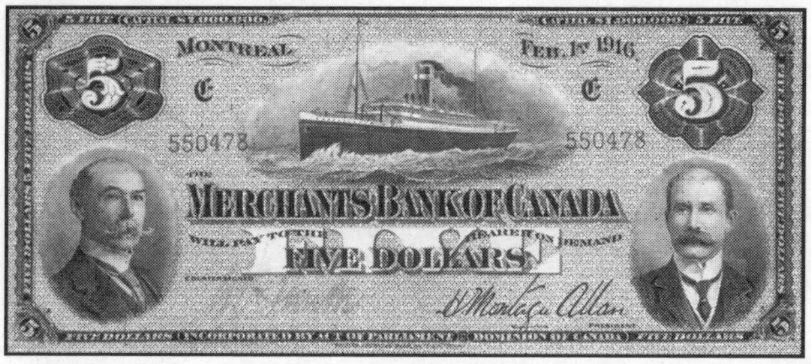

460-18-02

$5 Face Design: D.C. Macarow/steamship/H. Montague Allan
Colour: Black with overall green tint

Back Design Lathework, counters, bank name and two beavers
Colour: Green

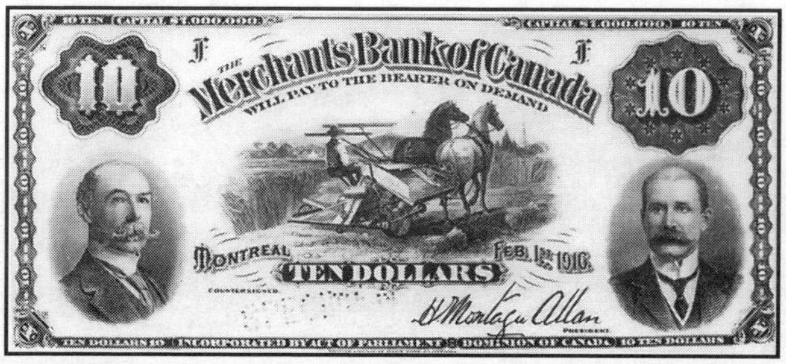

460-18-04

$10 Face Design: D.C. Macarow/horse-drawn reaper/ H. Montague Allan
Colour: Black with overall green tint

Back Design: Lathework, counters, bank name and sailor "On the look out"
Colour: Green

IMPRINT

British American Bank Note Co. Ottawa

SIGNATURES

left	right
mss. various	engr. H. Montague Allan

ISSUE DATING

Engraved

Feb. 1st 1916

Cat. No.	Denom.	Date	G	VG	F	VF	EF	AU
18-02	$5	1916	85.	175.	250.	400.	700.	—
18-04	$10	1916	85.	175.	250.	400.	700.	—

460-20 ISSUE OF 1917

DESIGNS AND COLOURS

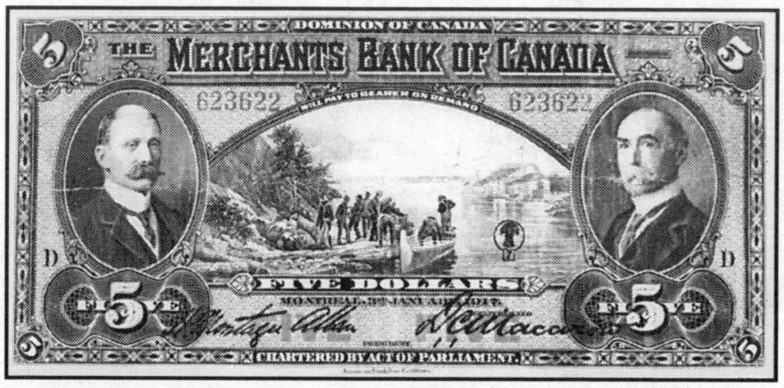

460-20-04

$5 Face Design: H. Montague Allan/men loading canoes/ E.F. Hebden
Colour: Black with overall green tint

Back Design: Lathework, counters, bank name and Bank Crest
Colour: Green

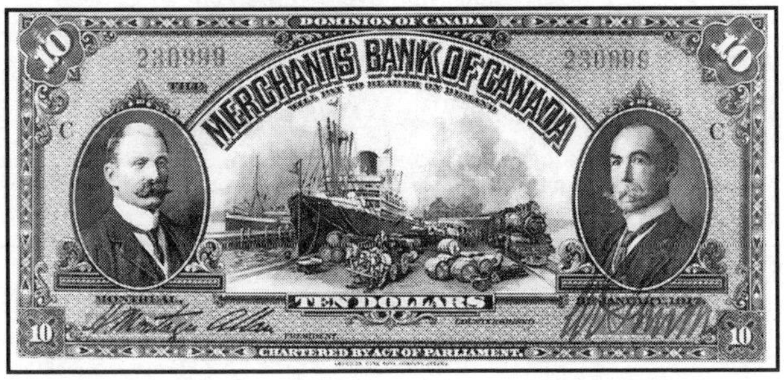

460-20-06
$10 Face Design: H. Montague Allan/steamship, train at dock/E.F. Hebden
Colour: Black with overall green tint

Back Design: Lathework, counters, bank name and Bank Crest
Colour: Green

460-20-10
$20 Face Design: Steer's head (after Landseer)/—/—
Colour: Black with overall green tint

Back Design: Lathework, counters, bank name and Bank Crest
Colour: Green

460-20-14
$50 Face Design: Stag "Monarch of the Glen" Landseer/—/young woman "Reverie"
Colour: Black with overall green tint

Back Design: Lathework, counters, bank name and Bank Crest
Colour: Green

460-20-20
$100 Face Design: H. Montague Allan/seated female with winged wheel and books "Allegory"/ E.F. Hebden
Colour: Black with overall green tint

Back Design: Lathework, counters, bank name and Bank Crest
Colour: Green

IMPRINT

American Bank Note Co. Ottawa
American Bank Note Company, Ottawa

SIGNATURES

left	right
$5, $10 and $100:	
typed H. Montague Allan	mss. various
typed H. Montague Allan	typed D.C. Macarow
$20 and $50:	
mss. various	typed H. Montague Allan
typed D.C. Macarow	typed H. Montague Allan

ISSUE DATING

Engraved

3rd January 1917

CIRCULATING NOTES

Cat. No.	Denom.	Date	Variety	G	VG	F	VF	EF	AU
20-02	$5	1917	Mss. sig., r.	250.	500.	750.	1,200.	1,750.	—
20-04	$5	1917	D.C. Macarow, r.	250.	500.	750.	1,200.	1,750.	—
20-06	$10	1917	Mss. sig., r.	250.	500.	750.	1,200.	1,750.	—
20-08	$10	1917	D.C. Macarow, r.	250.	500.	750.	1,200.	1,750.	—
20-10	$20	1917	Mss. sig., l.	750.	1,200.	1,600.	2,100.	—	—
20-12	$20	1917	D.C. Macarow, l.	750.	1,200.	1,600.	2,100.	—	—
20-14	$50	1917	Mss. sig., l.	1,000.	1,800.	2,400.	3,000.	—	—
20-16	$50	1917	D.C. Macarow, l.	1,000.	1,800.	2,400.	3,000.	—	—
20-18	$100	1917	Mss. sig., r.	1,100.	2,000.	2,750.	3,500.	—	—
20-20	$100	1917	D.C. Macarow, r.	1,100.	2,000.	2,750.	3,500.	5,000.	—

PROOF NOTES

Cat. No.	Denom.	Date	Variety		Unc
20-02P	$5	1917	B & W	FACE PROOF	200.
20-02Pa	$5	1917	Coloured	FACE PROOF	350.
20-06P	$10	1917	B & W	FACE PROOF	200.
20-06Pa	$10	1917	Coloured	FACE PROOF	350.
20-18P	$100	1917	B & W	FACE PROOF	300.
20-18Pa	$100	1917	Coloured	FACE PROOF	500.

460-22 ISSUE OF 1919

DESIGNS AND COLOURS

460-22-02

$5 Face Design: —/Prince of Wales/—
Colour: Black with green tint

Back Design: Lathework, counters, bank name and Bank Crest
Colour: Green

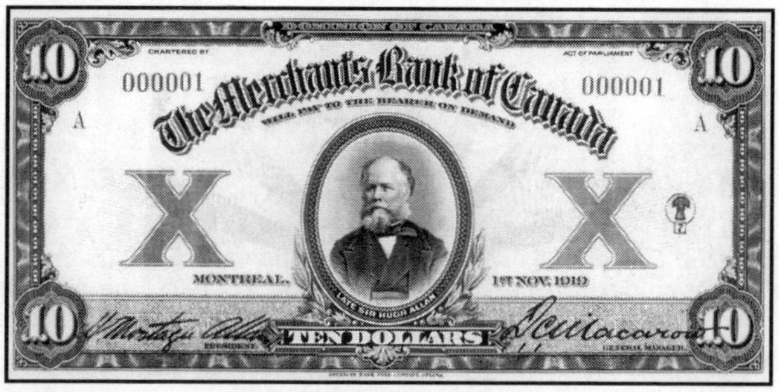

460-22-04

$10 Face Design: —/Late Sir Hugh Allan/—
Colour: Black with blue tint

Back Design: Lathework, counters, bank name and Bank Crest
Colour: Blue

IMPRINT

American Bank Note Company, Ottawa

SIGNATURES

	left	right
$5:	typed D.C. Macarow	typed H. Montague Allan
$10:	typed H. Montague Allan	typed D.C. Macarow

ISSUE DATING

Engraved

1st Nov. 1919

CIRCUATING NOTES

Cat. No.	Denom.	Date	VG	F	VF	EF	AU	Unc
22-02	$5	1919	300.	400.	700.	1,100.	1,650.	2,200.
22-04	$10	1919	550.	700.	1,000.	1,400.	2,100.	2,800.

PROOF NOTES

Cat. No.	Denom	Date		Unc
22-02P	$5	1919	FACE PROOF	500.
22-04P	$10	1919	FACE PROOF	500.

THE MERCHANTS BANK OF HALIFAX

1864-1901

HALIFAX, NOVA SCOTIA

BANK NUMBER 465 ***REDEEMABLE***

This bank was established in 1864 in Halifax, Nova Scotia, with an authorized capital of $1 million in 10,000 shares of $100.00 each. Its name was changed to the Royal Bank of Canada in 1901. The latter bank is now active as the largest bank in Canada and as one of the largest banks in the world.

465-10 MERCHANTS BANK $20, NO FRAME ISSUE, 1864

The bank title was rendered as MERCHANTS BANK, and the face design lacks a frame.

DESIGNS AND COLOURS

465-10-02

$20 Face Design: —/steamship/—
Colour: Black with orange "TWENTY DOLLARS" tint

Back Design: Lathework and counter
Colour: Black

IMPRINT

Blades, East & Blades, London

SIGNATURES

left	**right**
mss. Geo. Maclean	mss. J.W. Merkel

ISSUE DATING

Engraved

31st March, 1864

Cat. No.	Denom.	Date	Variety	G	VG	F	VF	EF	AU
10-02	$20	1864	No frame	2,000.	3,500.	5,000.	—	—	—

465-12 MERCHANTS BANK $20, FRAME ISSUE, 1864

Bank title rendered as MERCHANTS BANK, and the face design includes a frame.

DESIGNS AND COLOURS

465-12-02

$20 Face Design: —/steamship/—
Colour: Black with orange "TWENTY DOLLARS" tint

Back Design: Lathework and counters
Colour: Black

IMPRINT

Blades, East & Blades, London

SIGNATURES

left	**right**
mss. various	engr. T.E. Kenny

ISSUE DATING

Engraved

1st October, 1864

Cat. No.	Denom.	Date	Variety	G	VG	F	VF	EF	AU
12-02	$20	1864	Frame	2,000.	3,500.	5,000.	—	—	—

465-14 MERCHANTS' BANK OF HALIFAX, 1869 AND 1870 ISSUES

Bank title rendered as MERCHANTS' BANK OF HALIFAX.

DESIGNS AND COLOURS

465-14-04-02

$4 Face Design: Steamship/steamship/steamship
Colour: Black with "Four dollars" in green panel

Back Design: Lathework and counter
Colour: Unknown

465-14-04-04

$5 Face Design: —/steamship/—
Colour: Black with orange "FIVE DOLLARS" tint

Back Design: Lathework and counter
Colour: Green

465-14-04-06

$20 Face Design: —/steamship/—
Colour: Black with orange "TWENTY DOLLARS" tint

Back Design: Lathework and counter
Colour: Black

IMPRINT

Blades, East & Blades, London

SIGNATURES

left	right
mss. various	engr. T.E. Kenny

ISSUE DATING

Engraved

1st October 1869
July 1st 1870

2. NO GREEN OVERPRINT

Cat. No.	Denom.	Date	G	VG	F	VF	EF	AU
14-02-02	$5	1870	1,800.	3,000.	4,000.	—	—	—
14-02-04	$20	1869	1,800.	3,000.	4,000.	—	—	—

4. GREEN OVERPRINT

OVERPRINT

"CANADIAN CURRENCY, 1 JULY, 1871" in green

Cat. No.	Denom.	Date	G	VG	F	VF	EF	AU
14-04-02	$4	1870	1,800.	3,000.	4,000.	—	—	—
14-04-04	$5	1870	1,800.	3,000.	4,000.	—	—	—
14-04-06	$20	1869	Institutional collection only					

465-16 "CANADA CURRENCY" ISSUES, 1871-1874

DESIGNS AND COLOURS

$4 and $5: "CANADA CURRENCY" engraved in frame at top and ends
$10 and $20: "CANADA CURRENCY" engraved at top only

465-16-06

$4 Face Design: —/steamship/steamship/steamship/—
Colour: Black with green "FOUR DOLLARS" and orange "4 4" tint

Back Design: Lathework and counter
Colour: Orange

465-16-08

$5 Face Design: —/steamship/—
Colour: Black with orange "FIVE DOLLARS" tint

Back Design: Lathework and counter
Colour: Green

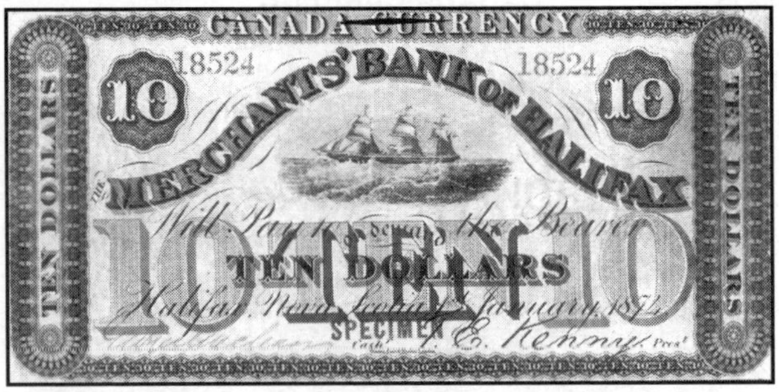

465-16-14

$10 Face Design: —/steamship/—
Colour: Black with green "TEN" and orange "10 10" tint

Back Design: Lathework and counter
Colour: Orange

465-16-16

$20 Face Design: —/steamship/—
Colour: Black with orange: "TWENTY DOLLARS" tint

Back Design: Lathework and counter
Colour: Black

IMPRINT
Blades, East & Blades, London

SIGNATURES

	left	right
1871:	mss. Geo. Maclean	mss. Jeremiah Northup
	mss. Geo. Maclean	mss. T.E. Kenny
1871-1874:	mss. Geo. Maclean	engr. T.E. Kenny

ISSUE DATING
Engraved
July 1st 1871
1st Jany. 1872
1st Octr. 1873
1st January 1874

OVERPRINT
"SUMMERSIDE"

Cat. No.	Den.	Date	Variety	G	VG	F	VF	EF	AU
16-02	$4	1871		1,500.	2,500.	3,500.	—	—	—
16-04	$4	1872		1,500.	2,500.	3,500.	—	—	—
16-06	$4	1873		1,500.	2,500.	3,500.	—	—	—
16-06a	$4	1873	SUMMERSIDE o/p	Institutional collection only					
16-08	$5	1871		1,500.	2,500.	3,500.	—	—	—
16-10	$5	1872		1,500.	2,500.	3,500.	—	—	—
16-12	$5	1873		Institutional collection only					
16-14	$10	1874		Institutional collection only					
16-16	$20	1873		Institutional collection only					

465-18 "DOMINION OF CANADA," ISSUES OF 1878 AND 1879

DESIGNS AND COLOURS

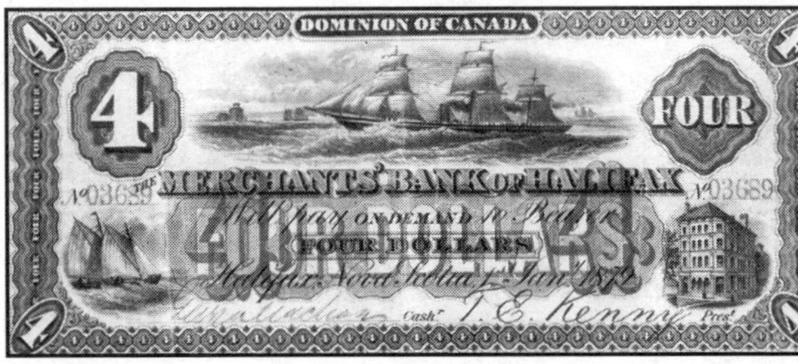

465-18-02

$4 Face Design: Sloop/steamship, entrance to Halifax harbour/bank building
Colour: Black with chartreuse "FOUR DOLLARS" and red "4 4" tint

Back Design: Lathework and counter
Colour: Orange

465-18-04

$10 Face Design: —/steamship/—
Colour: Black with green "TEN" and orange "10 10" tint

Back Design: Lathework and counter
Colour: Orange

IMPRINT

Blades, East & Blades, London E.C.

SIGNATURES

	left	right
	mss. Geo. Maclean	engr. T.E. Kenny

ISSUE DATING

Engraved

1st January 1878
1st Jany 1879

CIRCULATING NOTES

Cat. No.	Denom.	Date	G	VG	F	VF	EF	AU
18-02	$4	1879	Institutional collection only					
18-04	$10	1878	Institutional collection only					

PROOF NOTES

Cat. No.	Denom.	Date	Unc
18-02P	$4	1879	FACE PROOF 1,000.

465-20 "NO PORTRAIT" ISSUES, 1880-1898

DESIGNS AND COLOURS

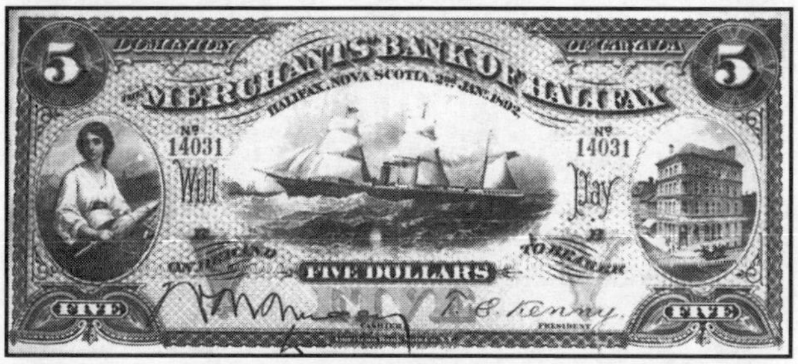

465-20-06

$5 Face Design: Seated allegorical female/steamship/bank building
Colour: Black with orange and green tint

Back Design: Lathework, counters and bank name
Colour: Brown

465-20-10P

$10 Face Design: Small ship sailing away from larger ship "Pilot leaving vessel"/—/bank building
Colour: Black with yellow-orange and blue tint

Back Design: Lathework, counters and bank name
Colour: Green

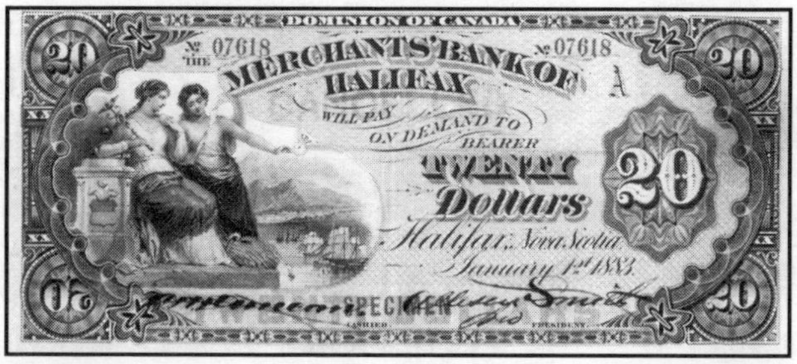

465-20-16

$20 Face Design: Seated "Agriculture" and "Commerce" figures, ships in harbour/—/—
Colour: Black with blue and orange tint

Back Design: Lathework, counters and bank name
Colour: Brown

IMPRINT

American Bank Note Co. N.Y.
American Bank Note Co., Ottawa

SIGNATURES

	left	right
1880:	mss. various	engr. T.E. Kenny
1883:	mss. D.H. Duncan	mss. Allison Smith
1888-1892:	mss. various	engr. T.E. Kenny
1893:	none	engr. T.E. Kenny
1896:	mss. various	engr. T.E. Kenny
1898:	none	none

ISSUE DATING

Engraved

1st July, 1880
January 1st 1883
2nd July 1888
1st. May. 1890
2nd. Jany. 1892
2nd. Jany. 1893
2nd. Jany. 1896
January 1st 1898

CIRCULATING NOTES

Cat. No.	Denom.	Date	G	VG	F	VF	EF	AU
20-02	$5	1880	1,000.	1,800.	2,400.	3,600.	—	—
20-03	$5	1888			Fair $300.			
20-04	$5	1890	1,000.	1,800.	2,400.	3,600.	—	—
20-06	$5	1892	1,050.	1,900.	2,500.	3,800.	—	—
20-08	$5	1896			No known issued notes			
20-10	$10	1880			No known issued notes			
20-12	$10	1893	1,200.	2,200.	3,000.	—	—	—
20-14	$10	1896	1,200.	2,200.	3,000.	—	—	—
20-16	$20	1883	1,400.	2,500.	3,500.	—	—	—
20-18	$20	1898			No known issued notes			

PROOF NOTES

Cat. No.	Denom.	Date		Unc.
20-02P	$5	1880	FACE PROOF	600.
20-08P	$5	1896	FACE PROOF	700.
20-10P	$10	1880	FACE PROOF	600.
20-16P	$20	1883	FACE PROOF	800.
20-18P	$20	1898	FACE PROOF	800.

SPECIMEN NOTES

Cat. No.	Denom.	Date		Unc
20-02S	$5	1880	SPECIMEN	1,000.
20-10S	$10	1880	SPECIMEN	1,000.
20-16S	$20	1883	SPECIMEN	1,200.
20-18S	$20	1898	SPECIMEN	1,200.

465-22

"PORTRAIT" ISSUES 1894-1899

DESIGNS AND COLOURS

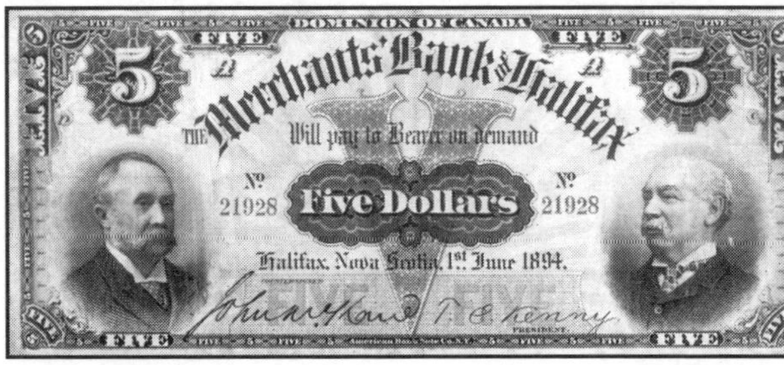

465-22-04P

$5 Face Design: D.H. Duncan/—/T.E. Kenny
Colour: Black with green tint

Back Design: Lathework, counters, bank name and bank building
Colour: Green

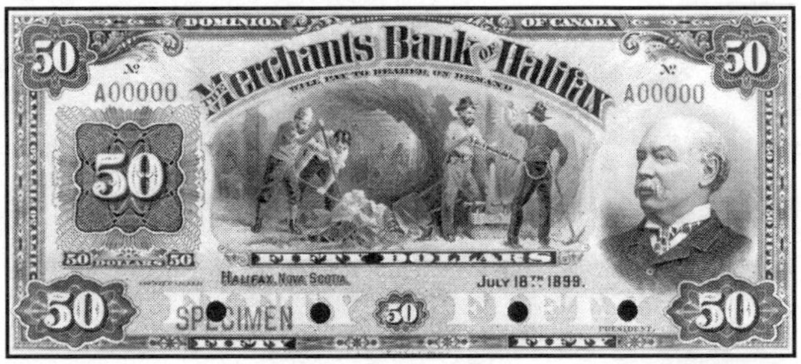

465-22-08S

$50 Face Design: —/miners/T.E. Kenny
Colour: Black with yellow and blue tint

Back Design: Lathework, counters, bank name and bank building
Colour: Blue

465-22-10S

$100 Face Design: Seated woman and baby "History"/—/ T.E. Kenny

Colour: Black with yellow and orange tint

Back Design: Lathework, counters, bank name and bank building

Colour: Orange

IMPRINT

American Bank Note Co. Ottawa

SIGNATURES

	left	right
1894:	mss. John W. Kane	engr. T.E. Kenny
1896-1899:	none	engr. T.E. Kenny

ISSUE DATING

Engraved

1st June 1894
Jan. 2, 1896
2nd Jany. 1899

Letterpress

$50: July 18th 1899
$100: July 3, 1899

CIRCULATING NOTES

Cat. No.	Denom.	Date	G	VG	F	VF	EF	AU
22-02	$5	1894	1,000.	1,800.	2,500.	3,500.	6,000.	—
22-04	$5	1896	No known issued notes					
22-06	$5	1899	1,000.	1,800.	2,500.	3,500.	6,000.	—
22-08	$50	1899	No known issued notes					
22-10	$100	1899	No known issued notes					

PROOF NOTES

Cat. No.	Denom.	Date			Unc
22-02P	$5	1894		FACE PROOF	700.
22-04P	$5	1896		FACE PROOF	700.
22-08P	$50	1899		FACE PROOF	700.
22-10P	$100	1899	B & W	FACE PROOF	500.
22-10Pa	$100	1899	Coloured	FACE PROOF	800.

SPECIMEN NOTES

Cat. No.	Denom.	Date		Unc
22-08S	$50	1899	SPECIMEN	1,000.
22-10S	$100	1899	SPECIMEN	1,000.

THE MERCHANTS BANK OF HALIFAX PROPOSED BRITISH WEST INDIES ISSUE

465-24 HAMILTON, BERMUDA, PROPOSED ISSUE, 1880

DESIGNS AND COLOURS

465-24-02S

$5 Face Design: Seated allegorical female/steamship/ bank building

Colour: Black with orange and green tint

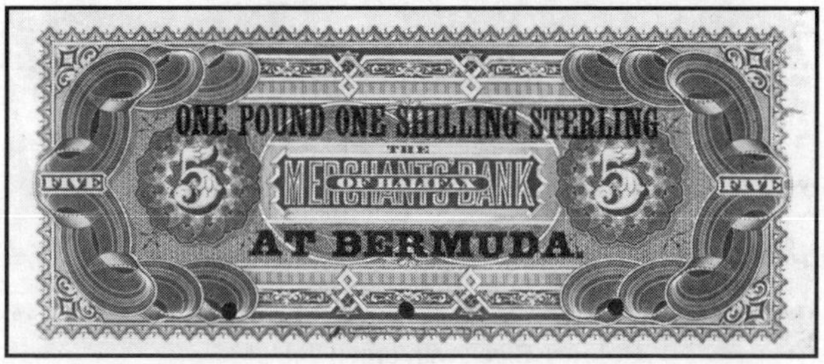

Back Design: Lathework, counters and bank name

Colour: Brown

IMPRINT

American Bank Note Co. N.Y.

SIGNATURES

left	right
none	engr. T.E. Kenny

ISSUE DATING

Engraved

1st July 1880

Note: Proofs known with notation "Oct. 6, 1882."

OVERPRINT

"1.1" on upper counters and "The Agency at Hamilton, Bermuda will exchange this note for/ONE POUND ONE SHILLING ST'G." on front and "ONE POUND ONE SHILLING STERLING/AT BERMUDA" on back, all in blue

SPECIMEN NOTES

Cat. No.	Denom.	Date		Unc
24-02S	$5	1880	SPECIMEN	1,500.

THE MERCHANTS BANK OF PRINCE EDWARD ISLAND, 1871 - 1906

CHARLOTTETOWN, PRINCE EDWARD ISLAND

BANK NUMBER 470 ***REDEEMABLE***

This bank was chartered in 1871 with a capital of £30,000 P.E.I. currency, of which one-third was paid in prior to the commencement of business. The failure of a large shipping firm, James Duncan & Co., brought about the suspension of the bank in 1878. Further calls on the shareholders were necessary for the bank to resume business at that time, and again in 1884. Thereafter the bank expanded and prospered, as the other P.E.I. banks vanished one by one. The paid-up capital passed $350,000, and there were six branches when the bank was absorbed by the Canadian Bank of Commerce in 1906.

470-10 **ISSUES OF 1871-1892**

DESIGNS AND COLOURS

470-10-04-04
$1 Face Design: Farmer ploughing with a team of horses/—/ sailor standing by rail of ship "Charlies Sailor"
Colour: Black with green tint

Back Design: Lathework, counters and bank name
Colour: Green

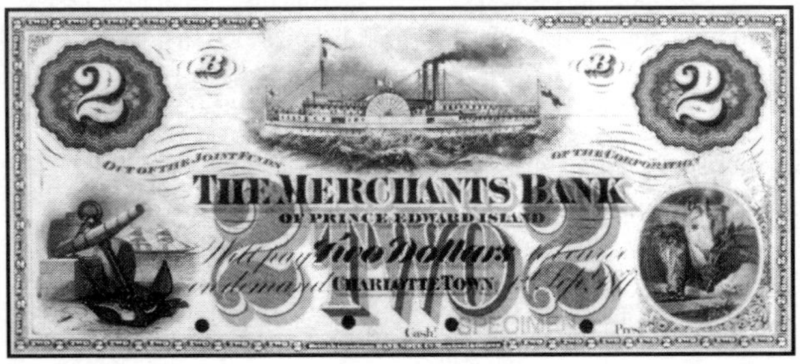

470-10-04-06
$2 Face Design: Anchor with box and bales/ "Steamboat Canada"/ three horses' heads in oval
Colour: Black with green tint

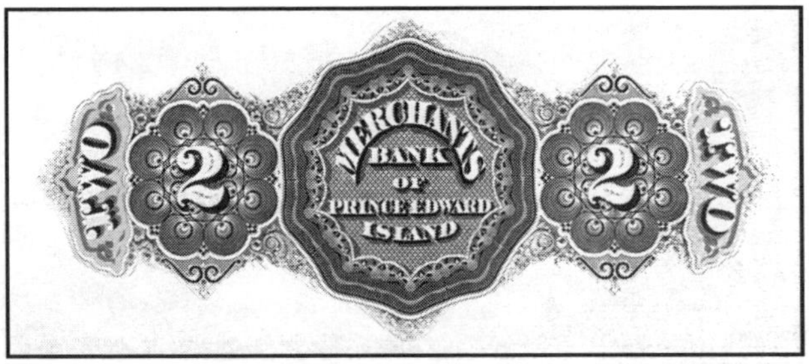

Back Design: Lathework, counters and bank name
Colour: Green

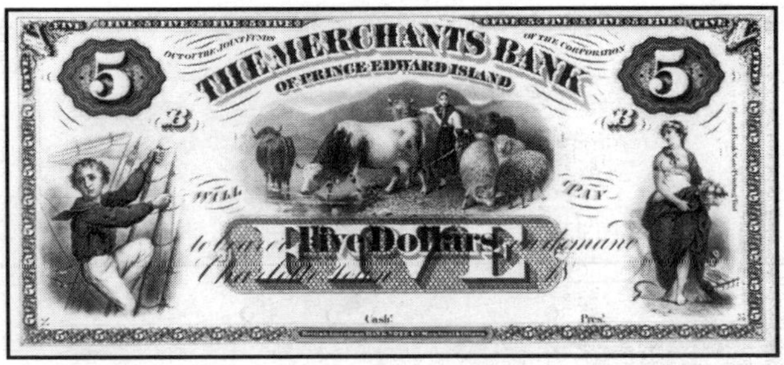

470-10-02-06P
$5 Face Design: Young sailor climbing ship's rigging "Going aloft"/woman with cattle and sheep "Vogts cattle"/allegorical female
Colour: Black with green tint

Back Design: Lathework, counters and bank name
Colour: Green

470-10-02-08P
$10 Face Design: Portrait of young woman "Adrienne"/train emerging from tunnel/Prince of Wales
Colour: Black with green tint

Back Design: Lathework, counters and bank name
Colour: Green

470-10-02-10P
$20 Face Design: —/Queen Victoria in widow's weeds/—
Colour: Black with green tint

Back Design: Lathework, counters and bank name
Colour: Green

IMPRINT

British American Bank Note Co. Montreal & Ottawa

SIGNATURES

left	right
mss. Wm. McLean	mss. Robt. Longworth
mss. Wm. McLean	mss. B. Heartz (P)
mss. Wm. McLean	mss. L.H. Davies
mss. J.M. Davison	mss. Benjamin Heartz
mss. J.M. Davison	mss. W.A. Weeks (pro)
mss. J.M. Davison	mss. W.A. Weeks

2. PARTIALLY ENGRAVED DATE, 1871

ISSUE DATING

Partially engraved ___ 18___:

$1, 1871: Nov. 6
$2, 1871: Sept. 1

OVERPRINT

"CANADA CURRENCY" in red

CIRCULATING NOTES

Cat. No.	Denom.	Date	G	VG	F	VF	EF	AU
10-02-02	$1	1871	2,000.	3,500.	4,750.	—	—	—
10-02-04	$2	1871	2,250.	3,750.	—	—	—	—
10-02-06	$5	18_	No known issued notes					
10-02-08	$10	18_	No known issued notes					
10-02-10	$20	18_	No known issued notes					

PROOF NOTES

Cat. No.	Denom.	Date		Unc
10-02-02P	$1	18__	FACE PROOF	700.
10-02-04P	$2	18__	FACE PROOF	700.
10-02-06P	$5	18__	FACE PROOF	700.
10-02-08P	$10	18__	FACE PROOF	700.
10-02-10P	$20	18__	FACE PROOF	700.

4. FULLY ENGRAVED DATE, 1877-1892

ISSUE DATING

Engraved

1st Sept. 1877
1st September, 1877
1st August 1889
6 November 1891
1st March 1892

OVERPRINT

"CANADA CURRENCY" in red

CIRCULATING NOTES

Cat. No.	Den.	Date	Variety	G	VG	F	VF	EF	AU
10-04-02	$1	1877	no o/p	2000.	3,500.	—	—	—	—
10-04-02a	$1	1877	Canada currency o/p	2,000.	3,500.	—	—	—	—
10-04-04	$1	1889		2,000.	3,500.	4,750.	—	—	—
10-04-06a	$2	1877	Canada currency o/p	2,000.	3,500.	4,750.	—	—	—
10-04-08	$5	1877		Institutional collection only					
10-04-10	$5	1892		Institutional collection only					
10-04-12	$10	1891		Institutional collection only					
10-04-14	$10	1892		4,500.	—	—	—	—	—
10-04-16	$20	1891		Institutional collection only					
10-04-18	$20	1892		Institutional collection only					

SPECIMEN NOTES

Cat. No.	Den.	Date		Unc
10-04-10S	$5	1892	SPECIMEN	1,200.
10-04-12S	$10	1891	SPECIMEN	1,200.
10-04-14S	$10	1892	SPECIMEN	1,200.
10-04-16S	$20	1891	SPECIMEN	1,200.
10-04-18S	$20	1892	SPECIMEN	1,200.

470-12 **$5 ISSUE OF 1900**

DESIGNS AND COLOURS

470-12-02P

$5 Face Design: Two allegorical women "The Reapers"/ steamship at anchor/Indian maiden with spear, leaning on "V" counter
Colour: Black with pink and green tint

Back Design: Lathework, counters and bank name
Colour: Green

IMPRINT

British American Bank Note Co. Ottawa

SIGNATURES

left	right
none	none

ISSUE DATING

Engraved

Jan. 2nd 1900

CIRCULATING NOTES

Cat. No.	Denom.	Date	G	VG	F	VF	EF	AU
12-02	$5	1900	No known issued notes					

PROOF NOTES

Cat. No.	Denom.	Date	Unc
12-02P	$5	1900	1,000.

MERCHANTS EXCHANGE BANK

1853

GODERICH, CANADA WEST

BANK NUMBER 475 ***NONREDEEMABLE***

This was probably a spurious issue, using the plate from the United States note illustrated below.

475-10 **ISSUE OF 1853**

DESIGNS AND COLOURS

475-10-02

$1 Face Design: Eagle and shield in oval/"Agriculture" and "Justice" figures with eagle and shield; small paddlewheeler below/ship sailing toward viewer Engraved "Will pay ONE DOLLAR on demand to the bearer at their agency in New York"
Colour: Black with no tint

Back Design: Plain

IMPRINT

Wellstood, Hanks, Hay and Whiting, New York

SIGNATURES

left	right
none	mss. illegible

ISSUE DATING

Engraved

January 1st 1853

Cat. No.	Denom.	Date	G	VG	F	VF	EF	AU
10-02	$1	1853	400.	800.	1,200.	—	—	—

The illustration above of the Merchants Exchange Bank, Anacostia, D.C., is almost identical, except for the placement of the date, the domicile and the red protectors.

THE METROPOLITAN BANK

1871-1876

MONTREAL (QUEBEC)

BANK NUMBER 480 ***NONREDEEMABLE***

Established in Montreal in 1871, this bank engaged largely in making loans on bank stock and in taking exceptional risks at high rates of interest. The bank did not suspend, but liquidated in 1876. Notes were redeemed at face value at the time of closure, and there was no loss to the creditors. Shareholders received about 75 cents on the dollar.

480-10 **ISSUE OF 1872**

DESIGNS AND COLOURS

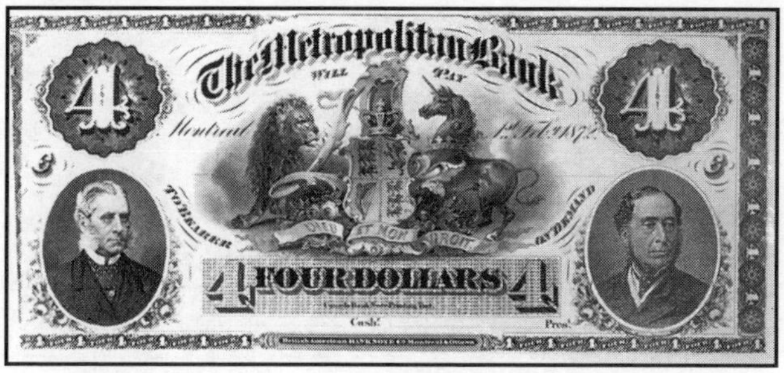

480-10-02
$4 Face Design: Maurice Cuvillier/lion, shield, unicorn and ornate 4/Henry Starnes
Colour: Black with green tint

Back Design: Lathework, counters and bank name
Colour: Green

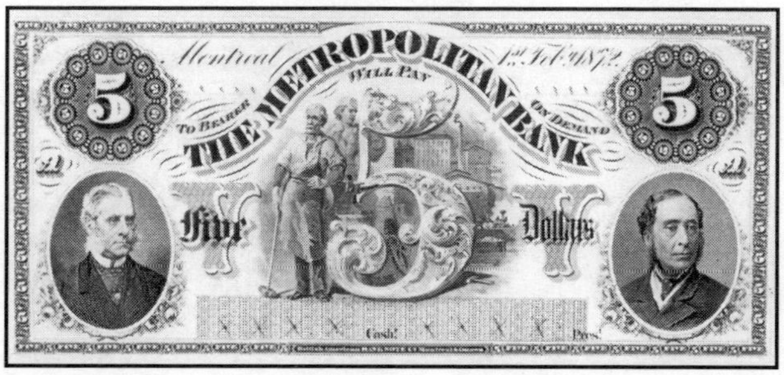

480-10-04
$5 Face Design: Maurice Cuvillier/two blacksmiths and ornate 5/Henry Starnes
Colour: Black with green tint

Back Design: Lathework, counters and bank name
Colour: Green

480-10-06
$10 Face Design: Maurice Cuvillier/two seated allegorical women and ornate X/Henry Starnes
Colour: Black with green tint

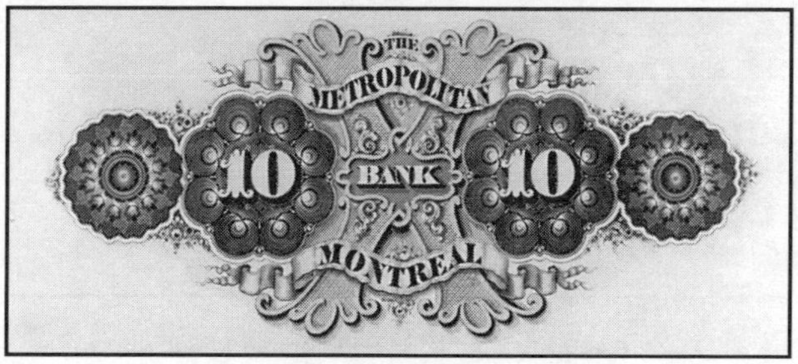

Back Design: Lathework, counters and bank name
Colour: Green

480-10-08P
$50 Face Design: Maurice Cuvillier/—/Henry Starnes
Colour: Black with green tint

Back Design: Lathework, counters and bank name
Colour: Green

480-10-10P
$100 Face Design: Maurice Cuvillier/—/Henry Starnes
Colour: Black with green tint

Back Design: Lathework, counters and bank name
Colour: Green

IMPRINT
British American Bank Note Co. Montreal & Ottawa

SIGNATURES

left	right
mss. A.S. Hincks	mss. H. Starnes

ISSUE DATING
Engraved
$4 and $5: 1st Feby. 1872
$10, $50 and $100: 1st May 1872

OVERPRINT
$5: "O B" in red

CIRCULATING NOTES

Cat. No.	Denom.	Date	G	VG	F	VF	EF	AU
10-02	$4	1872	Institutional collection only					
10-04	$5	1872	Institutional collection only					
10-06	$10	1872	Institutional collection only					
10-08	$50	1872	No known issued notes					
10-10	$100	1872	No known issued notes					

PROOF NOTES

Cat. No.	Denom.	Date	Unc
10-02P	$4	1872	700.
10-04P	$5	1872	700.
10-06P	$10	1872	700.
10-08P	$50	1872	800.
10-10P	$100	1872	1,200.

THE METROPOLITAN BANK

1902-1914

TORONTO (ONTARIO)

BANK NUMBER 485 ***REDEEMABLE***

Established in Toronto in 1902 by a group of financiers, the Metropolitan Bank was the first and only Canadian bank to offer its shares at a $100.00 premium. This meant that its authorized capital was, from the beginning, reinforced by an equal sum in reserve fund. In 1914 the bank merged with the Bank of Nova Scotia.

485-10 **ISSUES OF 1902-1912**

DESIGNS AND COLOURS

485-10-06
$5 Face Design: —/two seated women flanking a standing child/—
Colour: Black with yellow and red tint

Back Design: Lathework, counters, bank name and Royal Crest
Colour: Green

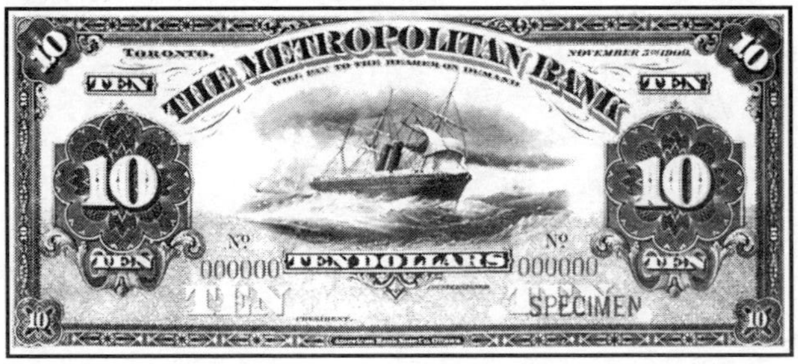

485-10-14S
$10 Face Design: —/steamship/—
Colour: Black with yellow-green and green tint

Back Design: Lathework, counters, bank name and Royal Crest
Colour: Brown

485-10-16S

$20 Face Design: —/streetcar/—
Colour: Black with yellow-green and green tint

Back Design: Lathework, counters, bank name and Royal Crest
Colour: Olive green

485-10-22S

$50 Face Design: —/trains, station at left/—
Colour: Black with brown tint

Back Design: Lathework, counters, bank name and Royal Crest
Colour: Orange

485-10-24S

$100 Face Design: —/mining scene/—
Colour: Black with yellow-green and red tint

Back Design: Lathework, counters, bank name and Royal Crest
Colour: Slate

IMPRINT

American Bank Note Co. Ottawa

SIGNATURES

	Left	right
$5 and $10, 1902:	typed A.E. Ames	mss. various
	typed Robt. H. Warden	mss. various
	typed S.J. Moore	mss. various
$20, $50 1902: and $100	typed Robt. H. Warden	none
1909:	typed S.J. Moore	mss. various
1912:	typed S.J. Moore	mss. various

ISSUE DATING

Engraved

November 5th 1902
November 5th 1909
November 5th 1912

OVERPRINT

$5 and $10, 1902: "S S" in red
$5 and $10, 1902: "Q Q" in red

CIRCULATING NOTES

Cat. No.	Denom.	Date	Variety	G	VG	F	VF	EF	AU
10-02	$5	1902	Ames, l.	—	2,300.	—	—	5,000.	7,000.
10-04	$5	1902	Warden, l.	No known issued notes					
10-06	$5	1902	Moore, l.	1,050.	2,100.	2,800.	—	—	—
10-08	$10	1902	Ames, l.	No known issued notes					
10-10	$10	1902	Warden, l.	Institutional collection only					
10-12	$10	1902	Moore, l.	No known issued notes					
10-14	$10	1909		1,250.	2,500.	—	—	—	—
10-16	$20	1902		No known issued notes					
10-18	$20	1909		Institutional collection only					
10-20	$50	1902		No known issued notes					
10-22	$50	1909		No known issued notes					
10-24	$100	1902		No known issued notes					
10-26	$100	1912		No known issued notes					

PROOF NOTES

Cat. No.	Denom.	Date		Unc
10-02P	$5	1902	FACE PROOF	500.
10-08P	$10	1902	FACE PROOF	500.
10-16P	$20	1902	FACE PROOF	750.
10-20P	$50	1902	FACE PROOF	750.
10-22P	$50	1909	FACE PROOF	750.
10-24P	$100	1902	FACE PROOF	750.

* Some 1902-dated proofs exist in colours differing from issued notes: $5 with orange back; $10 with red-brown or green back; $20 with face tint and back in gray; $50 with red-orange face tint; $100 with yellow and orange, yellow and blue or yellow and red face tints.

SPECIMEN NOTES

Cat. No.	Denom.	Date		Unc
10-14S	$10	1909	SPECIMEN	1,200.
10-16S	$20	1902	SPECIMEN	1,200.
10-20S	$50	1902	SPECIMEN	1,200.
10-22S	$50	1909	SPECIMEN	1,200.
10-24S	$100	1902	SPECIMEN	1,200.
10-26S	$100	1912	SPECIMEN	1,200.

Note: The 1902 notes are extremely rare in fine or better.

THE MOLSONS BANK

1837-1925

MONTREAL (CANADA EAST)

BANK NUMBER 490 ***REDEEMABLE***

The Molsons Bank operated briefly as a private bank from 1837 to 1838. On August 16, 1837, William Molson went to New York to take delivery of some 12,000 bank notes in $1, $2 and $5 denominations, although pounds, shillings and pence were still the official currency in Canada. The government, however, began restricting note issue to chartered banks not engaged in any other business but banking. In response to this policy, Thomas and William Molson applied for a license in March 1839 to engage in the general banking business. Although they had outstanding notes in excess of £6,345 and a capital stock amounting to £120,000, the Molson application was turned down. The government felt that it was not in keeping with the ordinance, as the Molsons were "already being engaged in extensive business as brewers and distillers."

In 1853 the Molsons again entered the banking business under the Free Banking Act. The Molsons Bank operated as a free bank until 1855, when it received a provincial charter. When the Molsons Bank was acquired by the Bank of Montreal in 1925, the purchase price was two shares of Bank of Montreal stock and $10 cash for three shares of the Molsons Bank stock, about $170.00. This transaction was in line with the evolution of Canadian banking, which brought about the disappearance of all but eight major institutions.

490-10 ISSUE OF 1837

DESIGNS AND COLOURS

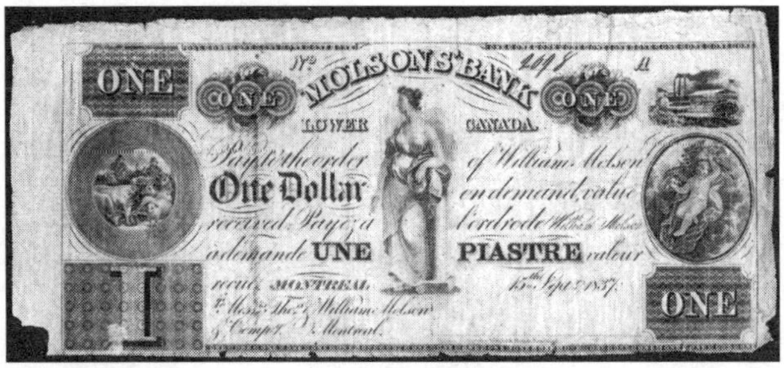

490-10-02R

$1 Face Design: Men and livestock/allegorical female/paddlewheel steamer; cherub with fruit basket. Engraved "To Messrs. Thos. & William Molson & Compy. Montreal."

Photo Not Available

490-10-04R

$2 Face Design: Unknown
Engraved "To Messrs. Thos. & William Molson & Compy. Montreal."
Colour: Black with no tint

Back Design: Unknown
Colour: Brown

490-10-06R

$5 Face Design: Steamship/Royal Crest/Archimedes lifting globe with lever
Colour: Black with no tint

Back Design: Lathework
Colour: Brown

IMPRINT

Rawdon Wright & Hatch, New-York

SIGNATURES

left	right
none	none

ISSUE DATING

Engraved

15 Septr. 1837.

Cat. No.	Denom.	Date	Variety	G	VG	F	VF	EF	AU
10-02R	$1	1837	Remainder*	—	—	1,400.	2,000.	3,000.	—
10-04R	$2	1837	Remainder*	—	—	1,500.	2,200.	3,400.	—
10-06R	$5	1837	Remainder*	—	—	1,450.	2,100.	3,200.	—

*Numbered, but unsigned

490-12 "FREE BANKING" ISSUE, 1853

DESIGNS AND COLOURS

Some notes have engraved on them "Secured by deposit of Provincial Securities."

490-12-02

$1 (5s) Face Design: Seated allegorical woman "Agriculture," 1 in oval/three ships/1 in oval, seated allegorical woman, "Commerce"
Colour: Black with no tint

Back Design: Lathework, space for Inspector General's registration signature
Colour: Brown

490-12-04

$2 (10s) Face Design: Prince Consort in oval in medallion 2/ seated allegorical woman, harvesting scene in background/Queen Victoria (Chalon portrait) in oval
Colour: Black with no tint

Back Design: Lathework, space for Inspector General's registration signature
Colour: Olive

490-12-06

$5 (25s) Face Design: Three women and anchor/seated woman, cattle/—
Colour: Black with no tint

Back Design: Lathework, space for Inspector General's registration signature
Colour: Brown

490-12-08R

$20 (£5) Face Design: Indian standing in shield/paddlewheel steamship and sailing ships/habitant
Colour: Black with no tint

Back Design: Lathework and counters
Colour: Brown

Photo Not Available

490-12-10P

$50 (£12.10) Face Design: Harvesting scene/Queen Victoria (Chalon portrait) in oval/train approaching viewer
Colour: Black with no tint
Back Design: Lathework, space for Inspector General's registration signature
Colour: Brown

IMPRINT

Toppan, Carpenter, Casilear & Co, Montreal

SIGNATURES

left	right
mss. Wm. Sache	mss. Molson & Co.

ISSUE DATING

Engraved

October 1st 1853

OVERPRINT

"PAYABLE AT MONTREAL" in red
"ST. C" in blue

CIRCULATING NOTES

Cat. No.	Den.	Date	Variety	G	VG	F	VF	EF	AU
12-02	$1 (5s)	1853		450.	900.	1,250.	—	—	—
12-04	$2 (10s)	1853		500.	1,000.	1,400.	—	—	—
12-06	$5 (25s)	1853		550.	1,100.	1,500.	—	—	—
12-08	$20 (£5)	1853		No known issued notes					
12-08R	$20 (£5)	1853	Remainder	—	—	—	1,000.	—	—
12-10	$50 (£12.10)	1853		No known issued notes					

PROOF NOTES

Cat. No.	Den.	Date	Unc
12-10P	$50 (£12.10)	1853	FACE PROOF 1,000.

FIRST CHARTERED BANK ISSUE, 1855

DESIGNS AND COLOURS

These notes have engraved on them "Chartered by Act of Parliament" at the top or bottom.

490-16-04-02

$1 (5s) Face Design: Seated allegorical woman, "Agriculture," 1 in oval/three ships/1 in oval, seated allegorical woman, "Commerce"

Back Design: Lathework, counters and bank name

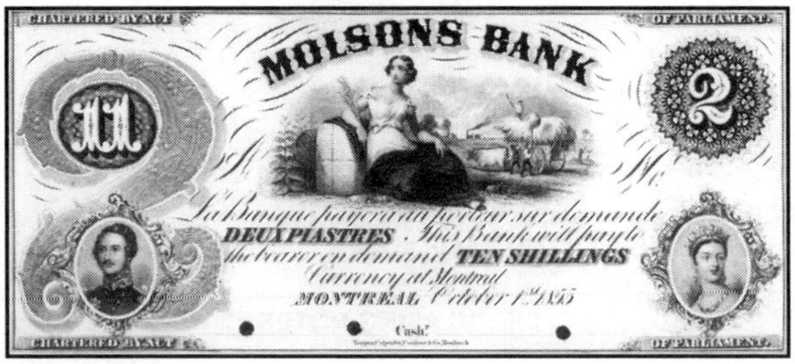

490-14-02-04P
$2 (10s) Face Design: Prince Consort in oval in medallion 2/ seated allegorical woman, "Harvesting" allegory in background/Queen Victoria (Chalon portrait) in oval

Back Design: Lathework, counters and bank name

490-16-04-04
$4 (£1) Face Design: Portrait of young woman/cherubs and ornate 4; small train below/ three allegorical women and 4

Back Design: Lathework, counters and bank name

490-14-04-06
$5 (25s) Face Design: Three women and anchor/ seated woman, cattle; agricultural tools and sheaves below/—

Back Design: Lathework, counters and bank name

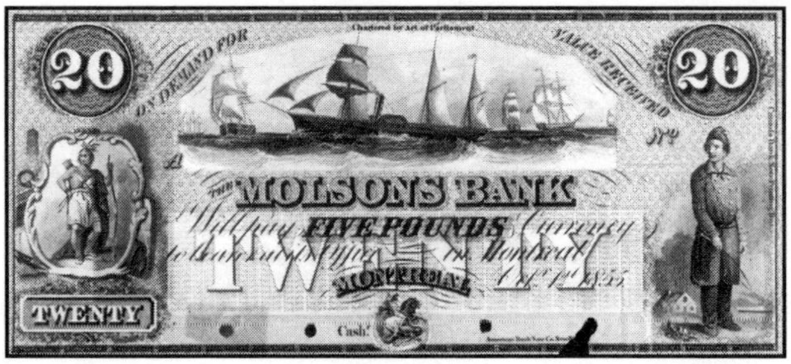

490-14-06-02P
$20 (£5) Face Design: Indian standing in shield/paddlewheel steamer, ships; St. George and Dragon below/habitant

Back Design: Lathework, counters and bank name

490-14-06-04P
$50 (£12.10) Face Design: Harvesting scene/Queen Victoria (Chalon portrait) in oval/train approaching viewer

Back Design: Lathework, counters and bank name

IMPRINT

Toppan, Carpenter, Casilear & Co. Montreal
Toppan, Carpenter & Co. Montreal
American Bank Note Co. New York.

SIGNATURES

left	right
mss. Wm. Sache	mss. Wm. Molson (pres)
mss. F.J. Foy (p)	mss. Jno. Molson (p)
mss. F.W. Thomas	mss. Jno. Molson (p)

ISSUE DATING

Engraved

October 1st 1855
Octr. 1st 1855

490-14 MONTREAL ISSUE

$1: Branch name engraved at lower left and lower right
$4: Branch name engraved at upper left
$5, $20: Branch name engraved at bottom centre
$50: Branch name engraved at lower left

COLOURS

$1 (5s) Face Colour: Black with no tint
Back Colour: Orange
$2 (10s) Face Colour: Black with no tint
Back Colour: Unknown
$4 (£1) Face Colour: Black with no tint
Back Colour: Green
$5 (25s) Face Colour: Black with no tint
Back Colour: Green
$20 (£5) Face Colour: See subheadings
Back Colour: Orange
$50 (£12.10) Face Colour: See subheadings
Back Colour: Orange

2. No Protector, No Face Tint

CIRCULATING NOTES

Cat. No.	Denom.	Date	Variety	G	VG	F	VF	EF	AU
14-02-02	$1 (5s)	1855	Montreal, B&W	500.	1,000.	1,400.	—	—	—
14-02-04	$2 (10s)	1855	Montreal, B&W	700.	1,400.	1,900.	—	—	—
14-02-08	$5 (25s)	1855	Montreal, B&W	700.	1,400.	1,900.	—	—	—
14-02-10	$20 (£5)	1855	Montreal, B&W	No known issued notes					
14-02-12	$50 (£12.10)	1855	Montreal, B&W	No known issued notes					

Note: $1 note is known raised to a $5 note.

PROOF NOTES

Cat. No.	Denom	Date			Unc
14-02-04P	$2 (10s)	1855	Montreal, B & W	FACE PROOF	650.
14-02-10P	$20 (£5)	1855	Montreal, B & W	FACE PROOF	650.
14-02-12P	$50 (£12.10)	1855	Montreal, B & W	FACE PROOF	650.

4. Green Word Protector, No Face Tint

PROTECTOR

Green "word" on face and back

Cat. No.	Denom.	Date	Variety	G	VG	F	VF	EF
14-04-02	$1 (5s)	1855	Montreal, green ONE	500.	1,000.	1,400.	—	—
14-04-04	$4 (£1)	1855	Montreal, green FOUR	700.	1,400.	1,900.	—	—
14-04-06	$5 (25s)	1855	Montreal, green FIVE	700.	1,400.	1,900.	—	—

6. No Protector, Green Overall Face Tint

PROOF NOTES

Cat. No.	Denom.	Date	Variety		Unc
14-06-02P	$20 (£5)	1855	Montreal, green tint	FACE PROOF	500.
14-06-04P	$50 (£12.10)	1855	Montreal, green tint	FACE PROOF	500.

490-16 TORONTO ISSUE, BRANCH NAME ENGRAVED

COLOURS

$1 (5s) Face Colour: Black with no tint
Back Colour: Blue
$4 (£1) Face Colour: Black with no tint
Back Colour: Blue

2. No Protectors

Cat. No.	Denom.	Date	Variety	G	VG	F	VF	EF	AU
16-02-06	$1 (5s)	1855	Toronto, B&W	500.	1,000.	1,400.	—	—	—
16-02-04	$4 (£1)	1855	Toronto, B&W	700.	1,400.	1,900.	—	—	—

4. Green Word Protectors

PROTECTOR

Green "word" on face and back

OVERPRINT

$1: "LONDON" and "PAYABLE/AT/LONDON" in blue near ends "PAYABLE AT MONTREAL" in red near ends
$4: "PAYABLE AT LONDON" in blue near ends
$5: "PAYABLE AT LONDON" in blue near ends

Cat. No.	Denom.	Date	Variety	G	VG	F	VF	EF
16-04-02	$1 (5s)	1855	Toronto, green ONE	500.	1,000.	1,400.	—	—
16-04-04	$4 (£1)	1855	Toronto, green FOUR	700.	1,400.	1,900.	—	—
16-04-06	$5 (25s)	1855	Toronto, green FIVE	700.	1,400.	1,900.	—	—

490-18 GREEN TINT ISSUE OF 1857

DESIGNS AND COLOURS

490-18-02

$1 Face Design: Portrait of young woman/reclining woman holding ornate 1/sailor with sextant
Colour: Black with overall green tint

Back Design: Lathework, counters and bank name
Colour: Green

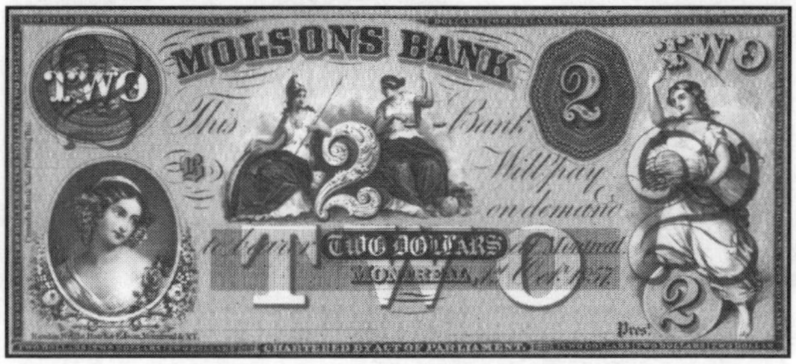

490-18-04

$2 Face Design: Portrait of young woman/—/Britannia and "Justice" figure flanking ornate 2/—/woman with sheaf and sickle
Colour: Black with overall green tint

Back Design: Lathework, counters and bank name
Colour: Green

IMPRINT

Rawdon, Wright, Hatch & Edson, Montreal & N.Y.

SIGNATURES

left	right
mss. F.W. Thomas	mss. Jno. Molson (p)

ISSUE DATING

Engraved

1st Oct. 1857

Cat. No.	Denom.	Date	G	VG	F	VF	EF	AU
18-02	$1	1857	500.	1,000.	1,400.	—	—	—
18-04	$2	1857	600.	1,200.	1,700.	—	—	—

490-20 — ## ISSUE OF 1871

DESIGNS AND COLOURS

490-20-02

$6 Face Design: F. W. Thomas/two beavers/Wm. Molson
Colour: Black with green tint

Back Design: Lathework, counters and bank name
Colour: Green

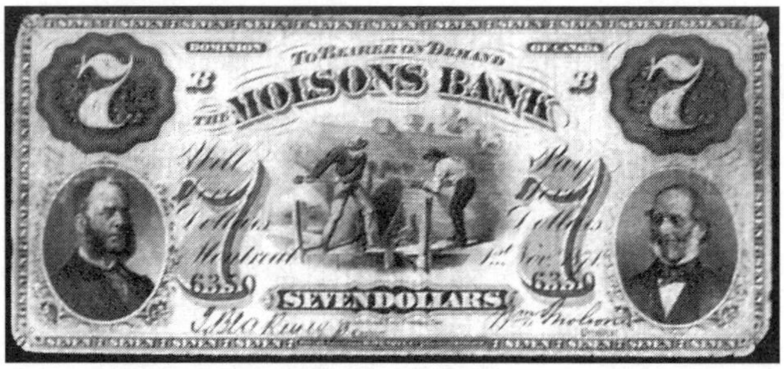

490-20-04

$7 Face Design: F. W. Thomas/men working on ship's hull "Ship Building"/Wm. Molson
Colour: Black with green tint

Back Design: Lathework, counters and bank name
Colour: Green

IMPRINT

British American Bank Note Co. Montreal & Ottawa

SIGNATURES

left	**right**
mss. various	engr. Wm. Molson

ISSUE DATING

Engraved

1st Nov. 1871

OVERPRINT

"TORONTO" in blue

Cat. No.	Denom.	Date	Variety	G	VG	F	VF	EF	AU
20-02	$6	1871		—	8,500.	11,000.	—	—	—
20-04	$7	1871		5,000.	8,000.	—	—	—	—
20-04a	$7	1871	TORONTO o/p	5,500.	8,500.	—	—	—	—

490-22 — ## ISSUES OF 1872-1901

DESIGNS AND COLOURS

490-22-04

$4 Face Design: F. W. Thomas/cherubs and ornate 4/ Wm. Molson
Colour: Black with green tint

Back Design: Lathework, counters and bank name
Colour: Green

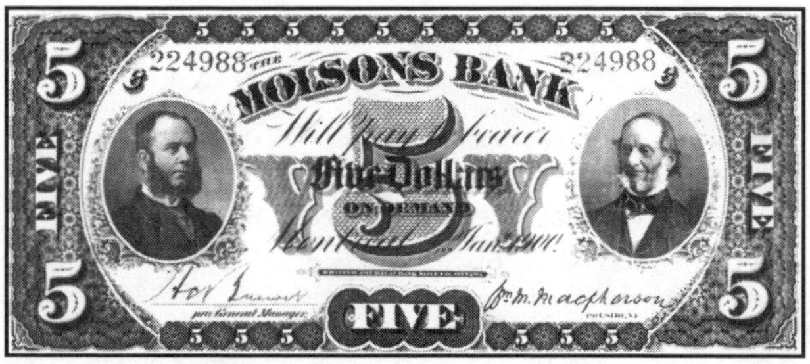

490-22-18

$5 Face Design: F. W. Thomas/—/Wm. Molson
Colour: Black with green tint

Back Design: Lathework, counters and bank name
Colour: Green

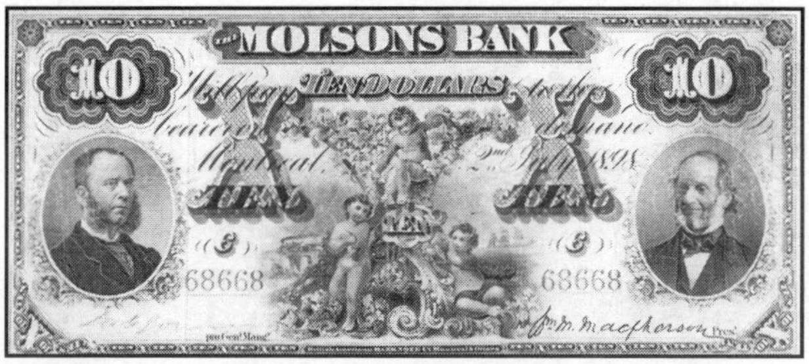

490-22-28

$10 Face Design: F. W. Thomas/cherubs and ornate X/ Wm. Molson
Colour: Black with green tint

Back Design: Lathework, counters and bank name
Colour: Green

IMPRINT

British American Bank Note Co. Montreal & Ottawa
British American Bank Note Co., Ottawa

SIGNATURES

	left	right
1872:	mss. various	engr. Wm. Molson
1875:	mss. various	engr. Jno. Molson
1880:	mss. various	engr. Thomas Workman
1890-1893:	mss. various	engr. John H.R. Molson
1898-1901:	mss. various	engr. Wm. M. Macpherson

ISSUE DATING

Engraved

1st June 1872	3rd Jany. 1893
June 1st 1872	2nd July 1898
June 1st 1875	3rd July 1899
1st June 1880	2nd Jany. 1900
2nd July 1890	2nd July 1901

CIRCULATING NOTES

Cat. No.	Denom.	Date	G	VG	F	VF	EF	AU
22-02	$4	1872	800.	1,600.	2,100.	—	—	—
22-04	$4	1875	800.	1,600.	2,100.	—	—	—
22-06	$5	1872	No known issued notes					
22-08	$5	1880	600.	1,200.	1,600.	—	—	—
22-10	$5	1890	675.	1,350.	1,750.	—	—	—
22-12	$5	1893	675.	1,350.	1,750.	—	—	—
22-14	$5	1898	450.	900.	1,300.	—	—	—
22-16	$5	1899	300.	600.	850.	1,250.	—	—
22-18	$5	1900	300.	600.	850.	1,250.	—	—
22-20	$5	1901	300.	600.	850.	1,250.	—	—
22-22	$10	1872	No known issued notes					
22-24	$10	1880	675.	1,350.	1,750.	—	—	—
22-26	$10	1890	525.	1.050.	1,450.	—	—	—
22-28	$10	1898	450.	900.	1,300.	—	—	—
22-30	$10	1899	450.	900.	1,300.	—	—	—
22-32	$10	1900	300.	600.	850.	1,250.	—	—
22-34	$10	1901	300.	600.	850.	1,250.	—	—

PROOF NOTES

Cat. No.	Denom.	Date		Unc
22-06P	$5	1872	FACE PROOF	650.
22-22P	$10	1872	FACE PROOF	650.

490-24 LATE ISSUES OF OLD RWH 1855 DESIGNS, 1891, 1899 AND 1901

DESIGNS AND COLOURS

490-24-02

$20 Face Design: Indian standing on shield/ paddlewheel steamer; St. George and Dragon below/habitant
Colour: Black with green tint

Back Design: Lathework, counters and bank name
Colour: Green

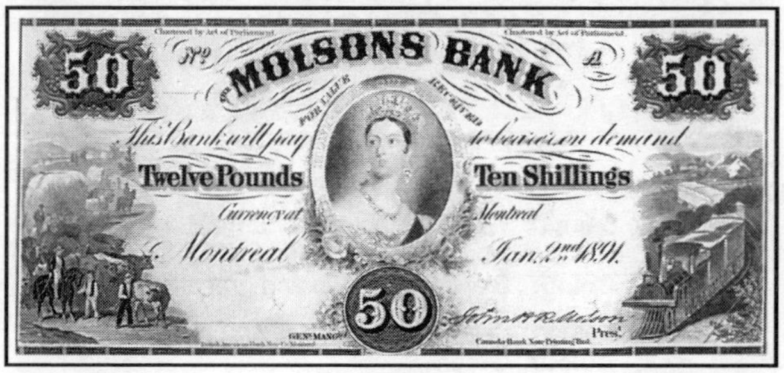

490-24-06

$50 (£12.10) Face Design: Harvesting scene/Queen Victoria/train
Colour: Black with no tint
Back Design: Lathework, counters and bank name
Colour: Unknown

490-24-058

$50 Face Design: Harvesting scene/Queen Victoria (Chalon portrait)/train approaching viewer
Colour: Black with green tint
Back Design: Lathework, counters and bank name
Colour: Green

IMPRINT
British American Bank Note Co. Montreal

SIGNATURES

	left	right
1891:	mss. Jas. Elliot	engr. John H.R. Molson
1899:	mss. Jas. Elliot	engr. Wm. M. Macpherson
1901:	mss. Jas. Elliot	engr. Wm. M. Macpherson

ISSUE DATING
Engraved
Jan. 2nd 1891
3rd. July, 1899
1st Oct, 1901

OVERPRINT
ST.T.

CIRCULATING NOTES

Cat. No.	Denom.	Date	G	VG	F	VF	EF	AU
24-02	$20	1899	1,000.	2,000.	2,500.	—	—	—
24-04	$20	1901	1,000.	2,000.	2,500.	—	—	—
24-06	$50(£12.10)	1891	No known issued notes					
24-08	$50	1891	1,500.	2,500.	3,500.	—	—	—

PROOF NOTES

Cat. No.	Denom.	Date		Unc
24-06P	$50 (£12.10)	1891	FACE PROOF	750.

490-26 ISSUES OF 1903 AND 1904

DESIGNS AND COLOURS

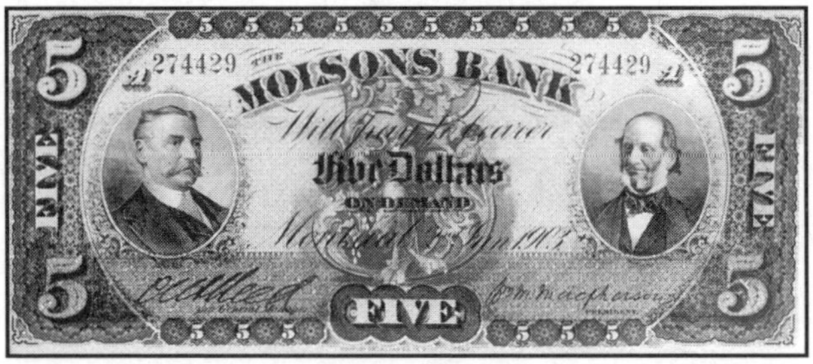

490-26-02
$5 Face Design: Wm. M. Macpherson/ornate 5, woman, cherub/Wm. Molson
Colour: Black with brown and green tint

Back Design: Lathework, counters and bank name
Colour: Green

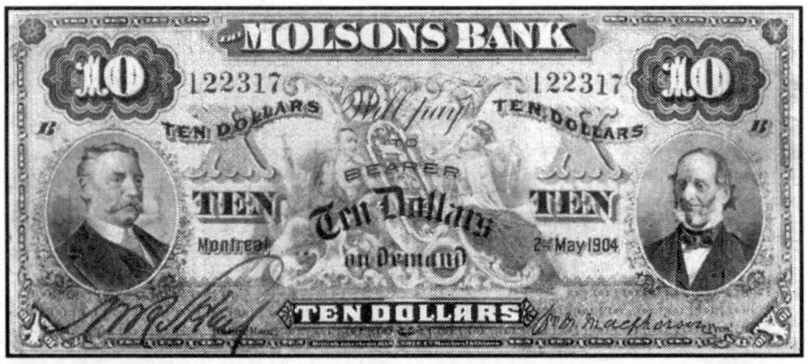

490-26-06
$10 Face Design: Wm. M. Macpherson/ornate X, Indian, woman/Wm. Molson
Colour: Black with brown and green tint

Back Design: Lathework, counters and bank name
Colour: Green

490-26-10
$20 Face Design: Blacksmith leaning on 20 counter/ steam sailing ship "C.P. LAKE. STEAMER"/ woman with basket of flowers
Colour: Black with green and orange tint

Back Design: Lathework, counters and bank name
Colour: Green

IMPRINT
British American Bank Note Co. Ottawa
British American Bank Note Co. Montreal & Ottawa

SIGNATURES

left	right
mss. various	engr. Wm. M. Macpherson

ISSUE DATING
Engraved
2nd Jan. 1903
2nd May 1904
Jan. 2nd 1904

CIRCULATING NOTES

Cat. No.	Denom.	Date	G	VG	F	VF	EF	AU
26-02	$5	1903	200.	400.	600.	900.	—	—
26-04	$5	1904	200.	400.	600.	900.	—	—
26-06	$10	1903	325.	650.	900.	1,350.	—	—
26-08	$10	1904	325.	650.	900.	1,350.	—	—
26-10	$20	1904	350.	700.	1,000.	1,500.	2,400.	4,500.

PROOF NOTES

Cat. No.	Denom.	Date	Variety		Unc
26-10P	$20	1904	B & W	FACE PROOF	500.

490-28 ISSUE OF 1905

DESIGN AND COLOURS

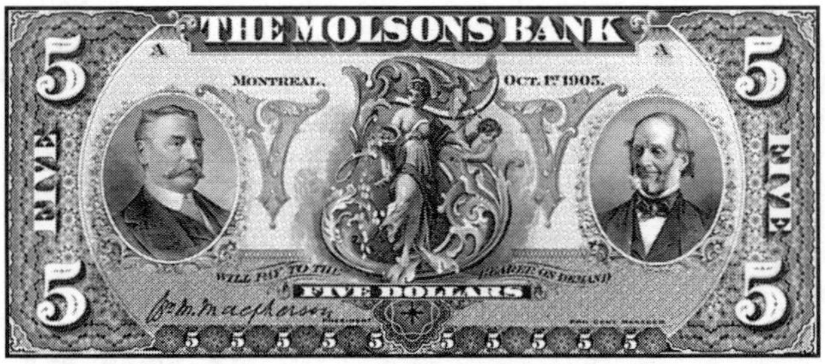

490-28-01P
$5 Face Design: Wm. M. MacPherson, shoulder turned to right/woman, cherub, ornate 5/Wm. Molson
Colour: Black with yellow and green tint

Back Design: Lathework, counters and bank name
Colour: Green

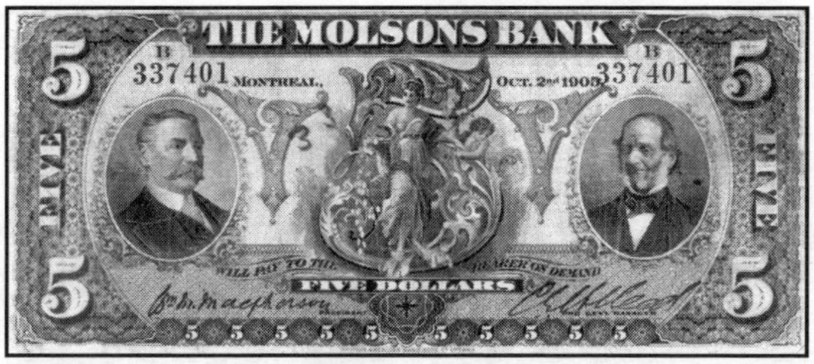

490-28-02

$5 Face Design: Wm. M. Macpherson, shoulder turned to right/woman, cherub and ornate 5/ Wm. Molson

Colour: Black with yellow and green tint

Back Design: Lathework, counters and bank name

Colour: Green

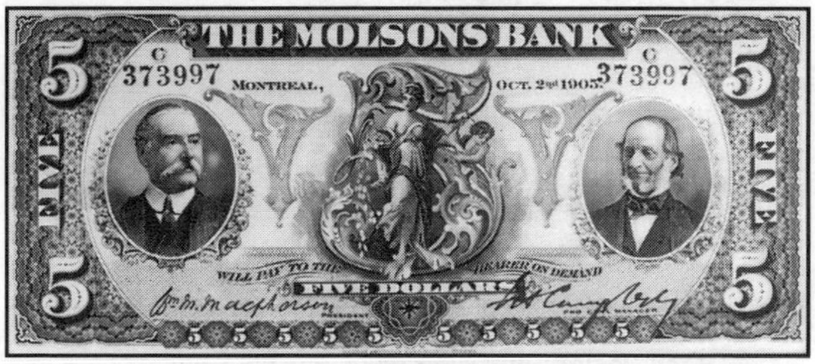

490-28-04

$5 Face Design: Wm. M. Macpherson, shoulders turned to front/woman, cherub and ornate 5/ Wm. Molson

Colour: Black with yellow and green tint

Back Design: Lathework, counters and bank name

Colour: Green

490-28-05P

$10 Face Design: Wm. M. MacPherson, shoulders turned to right/Indian and woman flanking ornate X/Wm. Molson

Colour: Black with yellow and green tint

Back Design: Lathework, counters and bank name

Colour: Green

Photo Not Available

490-28-06

$10 Face Design: Wm. M. Macpherson, shoulders turned to right/Indian and woman flanking ornate X/ Wm. Molson

Colour: Black with yellow and green tint

Back Design: Lathework, counters and bank name

Colour: Green

490-28-08

$10 Face Design: Wm. M. Macpherson, shoulders turned to front/Indian and woman flanking ornate X/ Wm. Molson

Colour: Black with yellow and green tint

Back Design: Lathework, counters and bank name

Colour: Green

IMPRINT

British American Bank Note Co. Ottawa

SIGNATURES

left	**right**
engr. Wm. M. Macpherson	mss. various

ISSUE DATING

Engraved

Oct. 1st 1905
Oct. 2nd 1905

VARIETIES

Face Design: Shoulders turned right in Macpherson portrait
Face Design: Shoulders turned front in Macpherson portrait

CIRCULATING NOTES

Cat. No.	Denom.	Date	Variety	G	VG	F	VF	EF	Unc
28-01	$5	1905	Oct. 1	No known issued notes					
28-02	$5	1905	Shoulders right	160.	325.	450.	700.	—	—
28-04	$5	1905	Shoulders front	135.	275.	375.	550.	—	—
28-05	$10	1905	Oct. 1	No known issued notes					
28-06	$10	1905	Shoulders right	185.	375.	525.	800.	—	—
28-08	$10	1905	Shoulders front	150.	300.	425.	650.	—	—

PROOF NOTES

Cat. No.	Denom.	Date	Variety		Unc
28-01P	$5	1905	Oct. 1	FACE PROOF	700.
28-05P	$10	1905	Oct. 1	FACE PROOF	700.

490-30 ISSUE OF 1908

DESIGNS AND COLOURS

490-30-02

$5 Face Design: Sir William Molson Macpherson/—/ Wm. Molson

Colour: Black with olive green tint

Back Design: Lathework, counters and Bank Crest
Colour: Green

490-30-04S
$10 Face Design: Sir William Molson Macpherson/—/ Wm. Molson
Colour: Black with olive green tint

Back Design: Lathework, counters and Bank Crest
Colour: Green

IMPRINT
American Bank Note Co. Ottawa

SIGNATURES

left	right
typed Wm. M. Macpherson	mss. various

ISSUE DATING
Engraved
2d. January 1908
2nd. January 1908

CIRCULATING NOTES

Cat. No.	Denom.	Date	G	VG	F	VF	EF	AU
30-02	$5	1908	100.	200.	275.	425.	—	—
30-04	$10	1908	110.	220.	300.	460.	—	—

PROOF NOTES

Cat. No.	Denom.	Date	Variety		Unc
30-02P	$5	1908	B & W	FACE PROOF	250.
30-02Pa	$5	1908	Coloured	FACE PROOF	400.
30-04P	$10	1908	B & W	FACE PROOF	250.
30-04Pa	$10	1908	Coloured	FACE PROOF	400.

SPECIMEN NOTES

Cat. No.	Denom.	Date		Unc
30-02S	$5	1908	SPECIMEN	600.
30-04S	$10	1908	SPECIMEN	600.

490-32 **ISSUE OF 1912**

DESIGNS AND COLOURS

490-32-02
$5 Face Design: Two beehives/Wm. Molson/two steers
Colour: Black with green tint

Back Design: lathework, counters, bank name and Bank Crest
Colour: Green

490-32-04
$10 Face Design: Steamship/Sir William Molson Macpherson/ train
Colour: Black with lilac tint

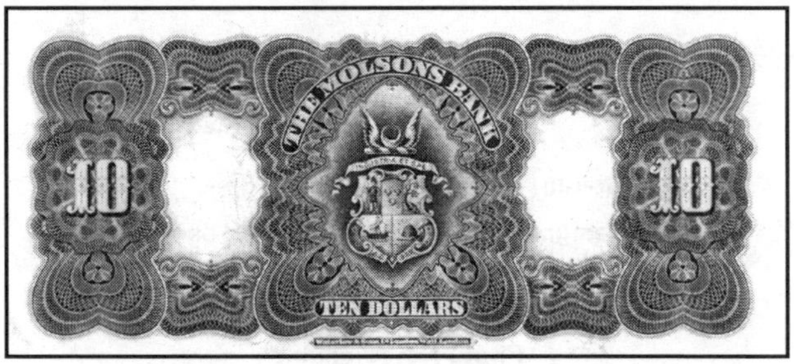

Back Design: Lathework, counters, bank name and Bank Crest
Colour: Blue-green

IMPRINT
Waterlow & Sons Ld, London Wall, London

SIGNATURES

left	right
engr. Wm. M. Macpherson	mss. various

ISSUE DATING

Engraved

2nd. January, 1912

CIRCULATING NOTES

Cat. No.	Denom.	Date	G	VG	F	VF	EF	AU
32-02	$5	1912	70.	140.	200.	325.	600.	800.
32-04	$10	1912	110.	225.	300.	450.	800.	1,200.

SPECIMEN NOTES

Cat. No.	Denom.	Date		Unc
32-02S	$5	1912	SPECIMEN	600.
32-04S	$10	1912	SPECIMEN	600.

Note: Specimen notes are known with different tints:
- **$5:** Lilac face, black back
- **$10:** Blue face, brown back
- **$10:** Blue-green face, carmine back

490-34 ISSUE OF 1914

DESIGNS AND COLOURS

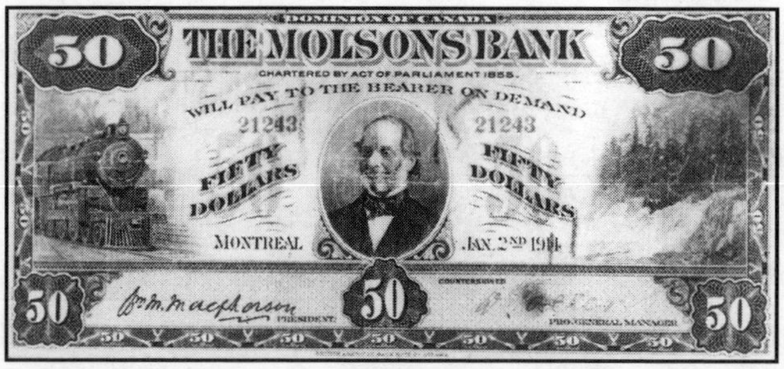

490-34-02

$50 Face Design: Locomotive under bridge/ Wm. Molson/waterfall and forest
Colour: Black with green tint

Back Design: Lathework, counters, bank name and Bank Crest
Colour: Green

490-34-04E

$100 Face Design: —/King George V/—
Colour: Black with orange tint

Back Design: Lathework, counters, bank name and Bank Crest
Colour: Green

490-34-06

$100 Face Design: —/S.H. Ewing/—
Colour: Black with green tint

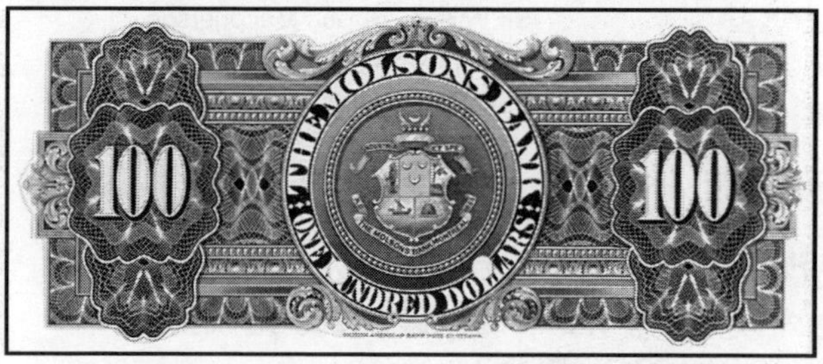

Back Design: Lathework, counters, bank name and Bank Crest
Colour: Green

IMPRINT

British American Bank Note Co. Ottawa

SIGNATURES

left	right
engr. Wm. M. Macpherson	mss. various

ISSUE DATING

Engraved

Jan. 2nd 1914

CIRCULATING NOTES

Cat. No.	Denom.	Date	G	VG	F	VF	EF	AU
34-02	$50	1914	—	5,000.	6,500.	—	—	—
34-04	$100	1914	No known issued notes					
34-06	$100	1914	—	8,800.	—	—	—	—

PROOF NOTES

Cat. No.	Denom.	Date		Unc
34-02P	$50	1914	FACE PROOF	800.

ESSAY NOTES

Cat. No.	Denom	Date		Unc
34-04E	$100	1914	ESSAY	1,500.

490-36 ISSUE OF 1916

DESIGNS AND COLOURS

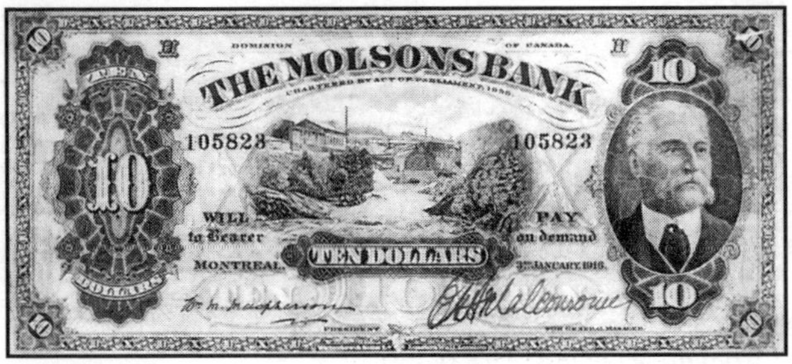

490-36-02

$10 Face Design: —/river and factories/
Sir William Molson Macpherson
Colour: Black with green tint

Back Design: —/Bank Crest/—
Colour: Blue

IMPRINT

Waterlow and Sons Ld, London Wall, London

SIGNATURES

left	**right**
engr. Wm. M. Macpherson	mss. various

ISSUE DATING

Engraved

3rd. January, 1916

Cat. No.	Denom.	Date	G	VG	F	VF	EF	AU
36-02	$10	1916	85.	175.	250.	375.	700.	1,000.

490-38 1908 DESIGNS RESUMED 1918

DESIGNS AND COLOURS

490-38-02

$5 Face Design: Wm. M. Macpherson/—/Wm. Molson
Colour: Black with green tint

Back Design: Lathework, counters and Bank Crest
Colour: Green

490-38-04

$10 Face Design: Wm. M. Macpherson/—/Wm. Molson
Colour: Black with orange tint

Back Design: Lathework, counters and Bank Crest
Colour: Orange

IMPRINT

American Bank Note Co. Ottawa

SIGNATURES

left	**right**
typed Wm. M. Macpherson	mss. various

ISSUE DATING

Engraved

2d. July 1918
2nd July 1918

CIRCULATING NOTES

Cat. No.	Denom.	Date	G	VG	F	VF	EF	Unc
38-02	$5	1918	85.	175.	250.	375.	700.	—
38-04	$10	1918	70.	145.	210.	325.	600.	—

PROOF NOTES

Cat. No.	Denom.	Date		Unc
38-02P	$5	1918	FACE PROOF	500.
38-04P	$10	1918	FACE PROOF	500.

490-40 ISSUE OF 1922

DESIGNS AND COLOURS

490-40-02

$5 Face Design: —/—/F.W. Molson
Colour: Black with green tint

Back Design: Lathework, counters, bank name and Bank Crest
Colour: Green

490-40-04

$10 Face Design: —/Wm. Molson/—

Colour: Black with green tint

Back Design: Lathework, counters, bank name and Bank Crest

Colour: Green

IMPRINT

British American Bank Note Co. Ottawa

SIGNATURES

left	right
typed E.C. Pratt	engr. F.W. Molson

ISSUE DATING

Engraved

July 3rd. 1922

Cat. No.	Denom.	Date	VG	F	VF	EF	AU	Unc
40-02	$5	1922	75.	100.	150.	250.	350.	450.
40-04	$10	1922	90.	125.	200.	350.	475.	600.

Note: Proof of $10 exists with yellow tint.

THE MONTREAL BANK

1840s-1850s

MONTREAL, CANADA WEST

BANK NUMBER 495 ***NONREDEEMABLE***

This was a phantom bank, trading on the colloquial name for the Bank of Montreal.

495-10 **ISSUE OF 1848**

DESIGNS AND COLOURS

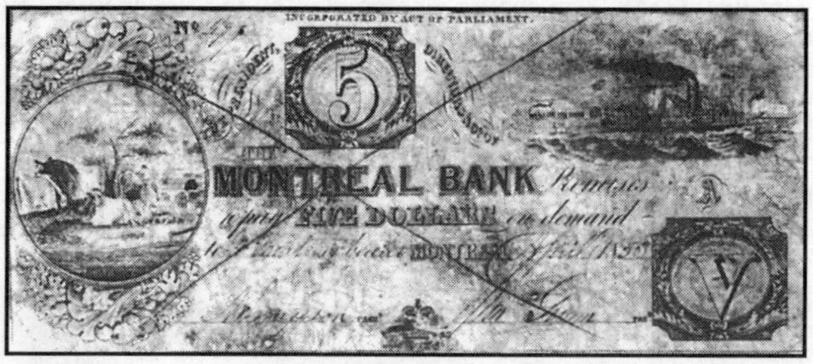

495-10-02

$5 Face Design: Livestock and farmer by tree in circle/—; seated crown below/paddlewheel steamer

Colour: Black with no tint

Back Design: Plain

IMPRINT

None

SIGNATURES

left	right
mss. Th. Holmes	mss. J.P. Simm

ISSUE DATING

Partially engraved ___ 18___:

1848: Oct. 10

1853: Apr. 1

Cat. No.	Denom.	Date	G	VG	F	VF	EF	AU
10-02	$5	1848-1853	150.	300.	400.	600.	—	—

MONTREAL BANK

1817-1822

MONTREAL, LOWER CANADA

BANK NUMBER 500 ***REDEEMABLE***

After failing to obtain a charter for 25 years, the founders of the Montreal Bank decided in May 1817 to form a private joint-stock banking corporation. Start-up capital was £250,000, half of which had been raised by sales of stock in the United States. The bank opened its doors for business on November 3, 1817, at 32 Paul Street, Montreal. This institution was the first in British North America to give full banking service.

On July 22, 1822, a charter was granted by the Province of Lower Canada under the name "The President, Directors and Company of the Bank of Montreal."

500-10 REED ISSUE, 1817-1819

DESIGN AND COLOURS

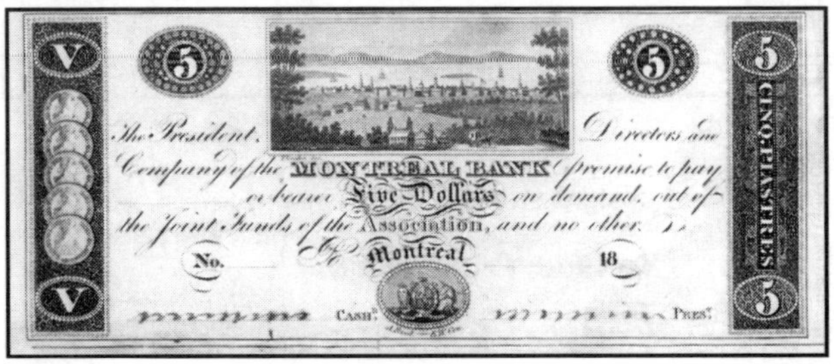

500-10-02P

$5 Face Design: Five coins/view of Montreal, crest in oval below/—

Colour: Black with no tint

Back Design: Plain

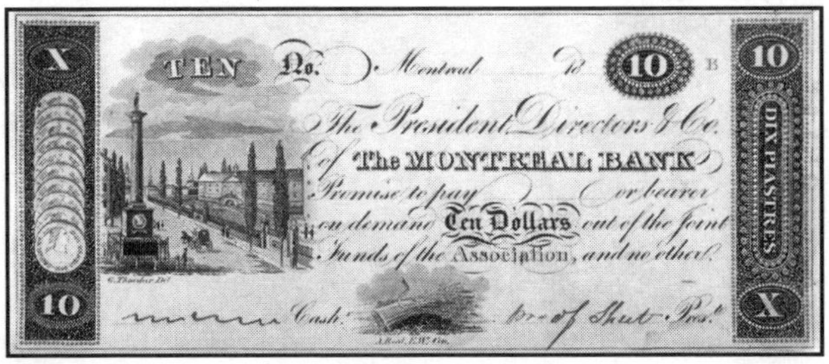

500-10-10

$10 Face Design: Nelson's monument/sickle and sheaves below/—

Colour: Black with no tint

Back Design: Plain

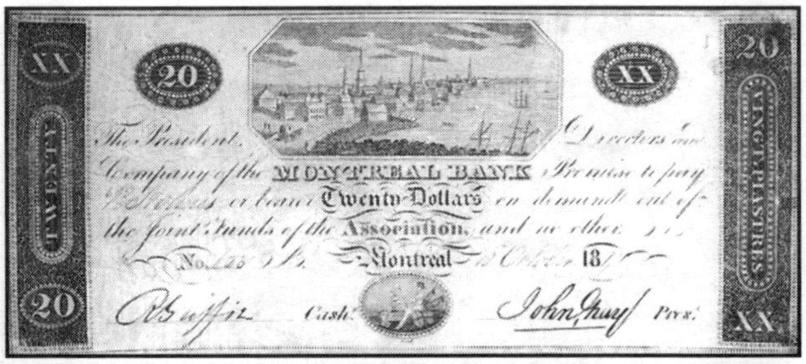

500-10-20

$20 Face Design: —/Montreal harbour with ships; Britannia, ship and lion in oval below/—

Colour: Black with no tint

Back Design: Plain

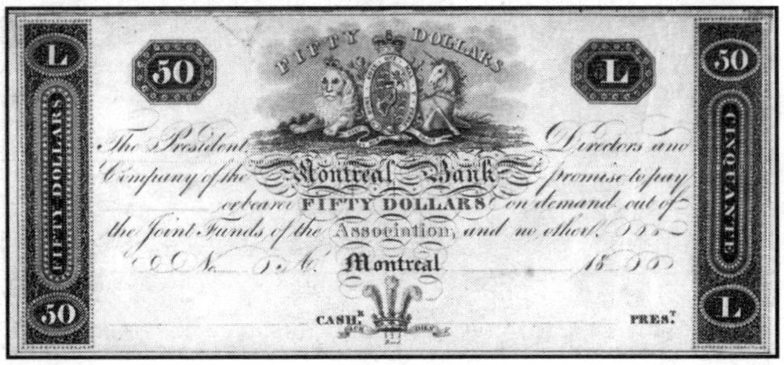

500-10-30P

$50 Face Design: —/Royal Crest/—

Colour: Black with no tint

Back Design: Plain

IMPRINT

A. Reed E.W. Con.

SIGNATURES

left	right
mss. R. Griffin	mss. John Gray

ISSUE DATING

Partially engraved ___ 18___:

1817: 10th October
1818: 1st Jany
1819: 1st January

Note: The Reed, Leney & Rollinson and Reed & Stiles issues were extensively counterfeited, causing them to be withdrawn by the bank. Counterfeits probably outnumber the genuine notes still in existence. Some, like 14-08C, are fairly obvious counterfeits, while others are well done and very deceptive. Notes of the Graphic issue were sometimes altered by raising them to higher denominations, but there is no record that they were ever counterfeited.

CIRCULATING NOTES

Cat. No.	Denom.	Date Variety	G	VG	F	VF	EF	AU
10-02	$5	18__		No known issued notes				
10-10	$10	1818	600.	1,200.	1,700.	—	—	—
10-10C	$10	1817-19 Counterfeit	75.	150.	200.	—	—	—
10-20	$20	1817-1818	600.	1,200.	1,700.	—	—	—
10-20C	$20	1817-1819 Counterfeit	75.	150.	200.	—	—	—
10-30	$50	18__		No known issued notes				

PROOF NOTES

Cat. No.	Denom.	Date		Unc
10-02P	$5	18__	PROOF	400.
10-10P	$10	18__	PROOF	400.
10-20P	$20	18__	PROOF	400.
10-30P	$50	18__	PROOF	400.

500-12 LENEY & ROLLINSON ISSUE, 1818-1820

DESIGNS AND COLOURS

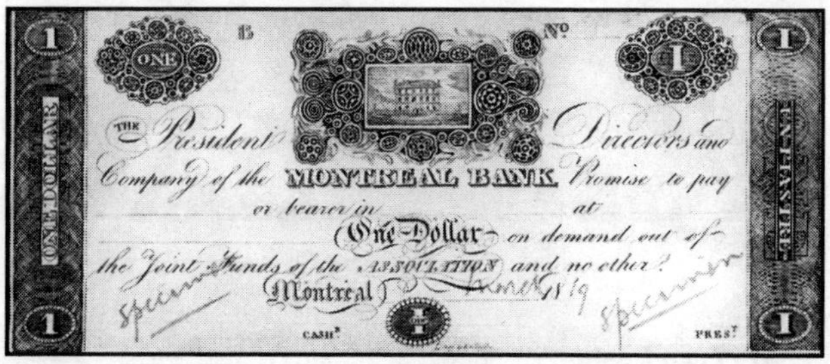

500-12-04

$1 Face Design: —/Montreal prison/—
Colour: Black with no tint

Back Design: Plain

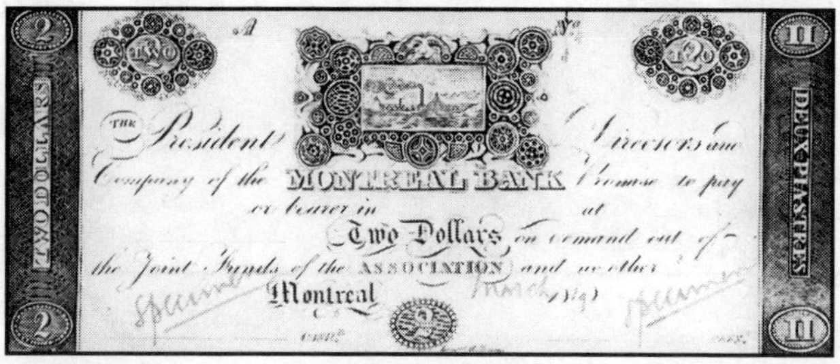

500-12-10

$2 Face Design: —/paddlewheel steamboat on the St. Lawrence/—
Colour: Black with no tint

Back Design: Plain

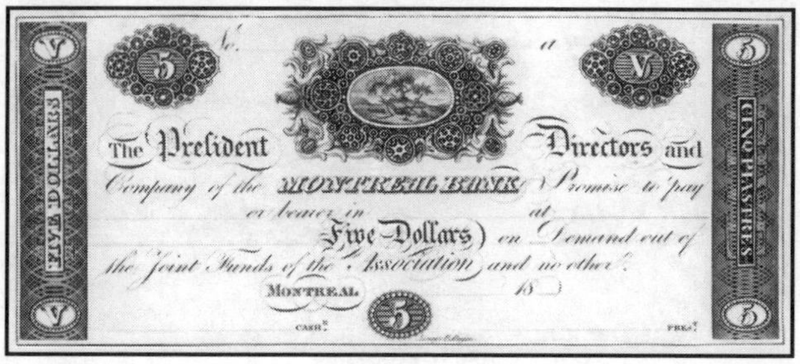

500-12-20

$5 Face Design: —/tree and agricultural implements/—
Colour: Black with no tint

Back Design: Plain

500-12-30

$10 Face Design: —/Indian hunting game in forest/—
Colour: Black with no tint

Back Design: Plain

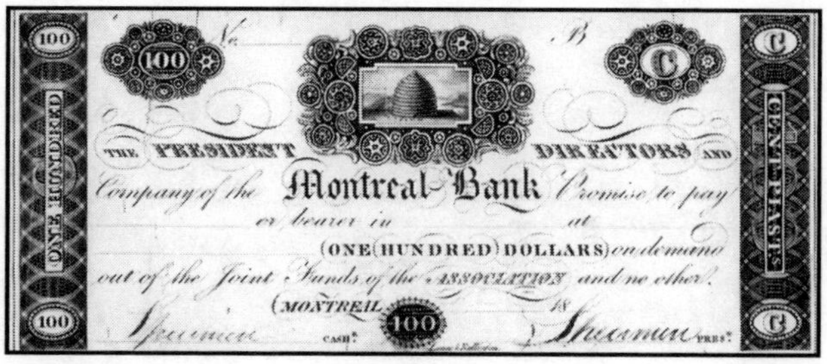

500-12-40P

$100 Face Design: —/beehive/—
Colour: Black with no tint

Back Design: Plain

IMPRINT

Leney & Rollinson.

SIGNATURES

	left	right
$1:	mss. R. Griffin	mss. G. Garden (v)
$5-$100:	mss. R. Griffin	mss. John Gray

ISSUE DATING

Partially engraved _ 18_:

$1, 1819: 1 Mar., Apr. 1
$2, 1818: 1 Dec
1819: 1 Mar, 1 April
1820: Jany 5
$5, 1819: January 4, 1 Feby, 1 Mar, Mar 5, Mar 11
$10, 1818: Jan. 1

CIRCULATING NOTES

Cat. No.	Denom.	Date	G	VG	F	VF	EF	AU
12-04	$1	1819	500.	1,000.	1,400.	—	—	—
12-10	$2	1818-1820	400.	800.	1,150.	—	—	—
12-10C	$2	1818-1820 Counterfeit	75.	150.	250.	—	—	—
12-20	$5	1819	400.	800.	1,150.	—	—	—
12-20C	$5	1819 Counterfeit	75.	150.	250.	—	—	—
12-30	$10	1818	600.	1,200.	1,700.	—	—	—
12-40	$100	18__	No known issued notes					

PROOF NOTES

Cat. No.	Denom.	Date		Unc
12-04P	$1	18__	PROOF	400.
12-10P	$2	18__	PROOF	400.
12-20P	$5	18__	PROOF	400.
12-30P	$10	18__	PROOF	400.
12-40P	$100	18__	PROOF	400.

500-14 REED & STILES PRINTING, 1821-1822

DESIGNS AND COLOURS

500-14-04P

$1 Face Design: —/standing Britannia in front of ships and harbour; coin on ornate ONE below/—
Colour: Black with no tint

Back Design: Plain

500-14-08C

$5 Face Design: —/woman on shell drawn by sea horses; coin below/—
Colour: Black with no tint

Back Design: Plain

IMPRINT

Reed & Stiles

SIGNATURES

left	right
mss. R. Griffin	mss. S. Gerrard

ISSUE DATING

Partially engraved ___ 18___:

1821: 7 July, 2 Oct.

STAMP

Some notes have "PAYABLE AT QUEBEC" stamped vertically near left end.

CIRCULATING NOTES

Cat. No.	Denom.	Date	Variety	G	VG	F	VF	EF	AU
14-04	$1	18_		500.	1,000.	1,400.	—	—	—
14-08	$5	1821		500.	1,000.	1,400.	—	—	—
14-08C	$5	1821	Counterfeit	60.	125.	150.	200.	250.	300.

PROOF NOTES

Cat. No.	Denom.	Date		Unc
14-04P	$1	18__	PROOF	400.

Note: Beware of counterfeit issues of these notes as in illustration 550-14-08

500-16 GRAPHIC PRINTING 1820 - 1829

DESIGNS AND COLOURS

500-16-05R

$5 Face Design: —/hunters, seals/—
Colour: Black with no tint

Back Design: Plain

500-16-10R

$10 Face Design: —/sheep, shepherd, woman/—
Colour: Black with no tint

Back Design: Plain

500-16-20

$10 Face Design: —/sailing ships/—
Colour: Black with no tint

Back Design: Plain

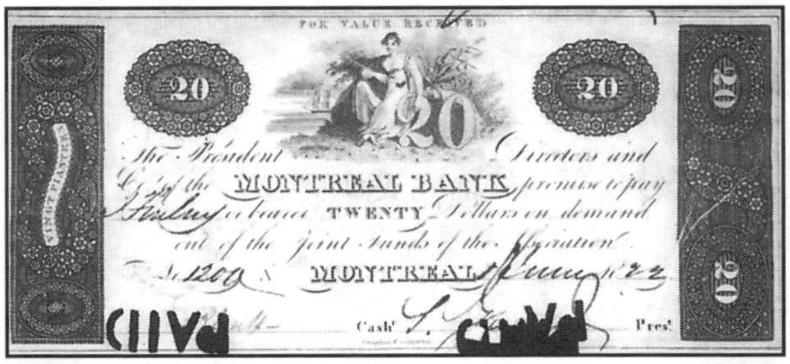

500-16-40

$20 Face Design: —/seated woman with/—
Colour: Black with no tint

Back Design: Plain

500-16-60R

$50 Face Design: —/seated "Commerce" figure and L/—
Colour: Black with no tint

Back Design: Plain

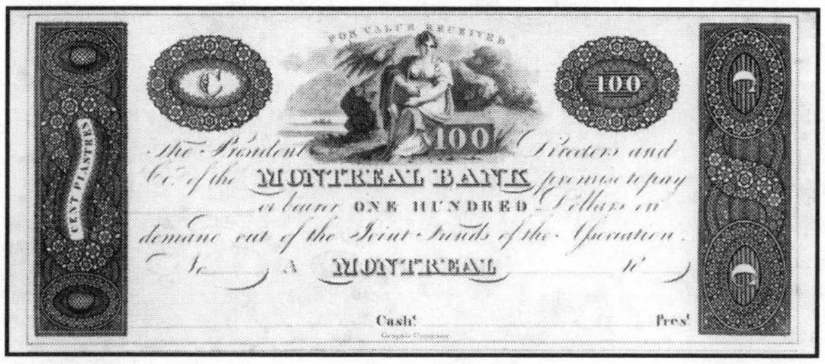

500-16-80

$100 Face Design: —/woman seated on block/—
Colour: Black with no tint

Back Design: Plain

IMPRINT

Graphic Company

SIGNATURES

	left	right
$10:	mss. B. Holmes	mss. J. Molson
$20:	mss. illegible	mss. S. Gerrard
$100:	mss. R. Griffin	mss. S. Gerrard

ISSUE DATING

Partially engraved ___ 18___:

1822: June 1
1829: 1 July

STAMP

Some notes are stamped "PAYABLE IN QUEBEC" vertically at the right end.

Cat. No.	Denom.	Date	Variety	G	VG	F	VF	EF	AU
16-05R	$5	18__	Remainder*	—	—	—	900.	—	—
16-10R	$10	18__	Remainder*	—	—	—	900.	—	—
16-20	$10	1829		500.	1,000.	1,400.	—	—	—
16-40	$20	1822		500.	1,000.	1,400.	—	—	—
16-60R	$50	18_	Remainder*	—	—	—	1,000.	—	—
16-80	$100	1822		500.	1,000.	1,400.	—	—	—

* Unsigned, undated and unnumbered.

THE BANK OF MONTREAL
1822 To Date

MONTREAL, LOWER CANADA

BANK NUMBER 505 ***REDEEMABLE***

In 1817 nine Montreal merchants signed articles of association of the Montreal Bank, as it was initially called, thereby establishing the first permanent bank in Canada. Under its auspices, the first domestic currency that Canada had known was introduced. Despite its relatively small capital, the bank stood ready to redeem in specie its issue of bank notes at all times. It was also able to bring a degree of order to the market for foreign exchange that had never existed before.

Within a month of its founding, the bank opened an agency in Quebec City to serve two of its most important customers - the government of Lower Canada and the British Army. At the same time, the opening of additional agencies in Toronto, Kingston and elsewhere, set the pattern for branch banking in Canada.

The bank shared in the decline of the fur trade in the late 1820s, but overcame other pre-Confederation upheavals. By buying the Toronto-based Bank of the People in 1840, it expanded its operations to Upper Canada. The bank's entire branch system was centralized by the adoption of the telegraphic message transmission, which had recently been introduced. In 1859 it established its first office in the United States, in New York City. Its first overseas office was opened in London, England, in 1870. In the year of Confederation, on the 50th anniversary of its establishment, the bank found itself acting as the government's depository and fiscal agent and subsequently enjoyed special advantages as the sole issuer of provincial notes.

After Confederation the Dominion of Canada assumed the financial obligations of the various provinces, and while the Bank of Montreal became the federal government's banker, the Dominion took over the sole right to issue notes in denominations of less than four dollars.

When the gigantic project for the building of the Canadian Pacific Railway from Montreal to the Pacific coast was taken up in the 1880s, the bank gave the project its financial support. As western Canada was settled following the building of the railway, local branches were established. The bank's operations then reached from coast to coast.

In 1892 the government of the Dominion withdrew its London fiscal agency from the British houses that had held the Canadian account since the 1830s and awarded it to the Bank of Montreal. From then on the bank not only handled the government's domestic business, but was also responsible for floating Dominion bond issues on the London market. After the turn of the century, British investor confidence in Canada was revived, and the bank's operations through its London branch reached what were then considered immense proportions.

In addition to its underwriting operations, the bank took steps during the first decade of the new century to improve its position in eastern Canada, alongside emerging Canadian industries. To this end, amalgamations were effected with several existing institutions: the Exchange Bank of Yarmouth (1903), the People's Bank of Halifax (1905) and the People's Bank of New Brunswick (1907), all of which had well-established branches and provided the Bank of Montreal with important outlets in the Maritimes and in Quebec. Another acquisition, the Ontario Bank, took place in 1906.

When World War I broke out, the bank was the largest financial institution in Canada. The departure of several staff members to join the armed forces put a strain on the bank at a time when its volume of business was increasing, particularly in connection with its role as the government's banker and fiscal agent in London. This staff depletion led to the hiring of women in large numbers. While mergers effected by the bank in the first decade of the century had greatly strengthened its position in the East, the acquisition of the Bank of British North America in 1918 and the Merchants Bank of Canada in 1922 brought two banks under its direction that had led the way in the opening of the West. In 1925 the Molsons Bank, a Montreal-based institution with good rural representation in Quebec and Ontario, was also absorbed.The drastic deterioration of the economy during the Great Depression was reflected in the balance sheet of the bank, and its assets decreased. All other banks experienced similar declines at this time. For the Bank of Montreal, the establishment of the Bank of Canada had further significance. Since the formation of the Dominion nearly seventy years earlier, the Bank of Montreal had served as banker to the federal government, but after 1935 all chartered banks shared the government account.

During World War II, the bank shared the burden of Canada's war effort with other banks. After the wartime controls were lifted in 1950, Canada entered a period of rapid economic development that has continued, with minor setbacks, to the present day. The bank shared in this development and is now one of the largest banks in Canada.

505-10 GRAPHIC PRINTING, 1820s

DESIGNS AND COLOURS

505-10-04

$1 Face Design: —/seated Britannia, ship, figure 1, female head in oval/—
Colour: Black with no tint

Back Design: Plain

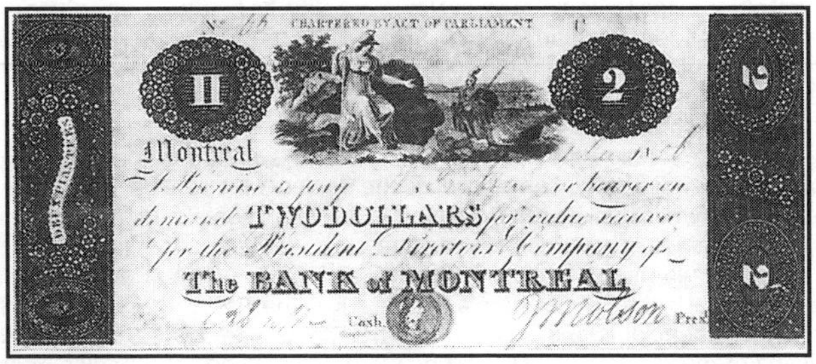

505-10-24

$2 Face Design: —/seated Britannia and Indian; female head in oval below/—
Colour: Black with no tint

Back Design: Plain

505-10-30P

$5 Face Design: —/seated woman, ship, figure 5/—
Colour: Black with no tint

Back Design: Plain

IMPRINT
Graphic Co.

SIGNATURES

left	right
mss. R. Griffin	mss. S. Gerrard

ISSUE DATING
Partially engraved ___ 18___:

1823: Aug. 1
1824: July 2
1825: 1 Mar, Mar. 1, May 1
1826: Dec. 1

OVERPRINT
"PAYABLE AT QUEBEC" vertically at left end

CIRCULATING NOTES

Cat. No.	Denom.	Date	G	VG	F	VF	EF	AU
10-04	$1	1823-1825	500.	1,000.	1,400.	—	—	—
10-24	$2	1826	500.	1,000.	1,400.	—	—	—
10-30	$5	18__	No known issued notes					

PROOF NOTES

Cat. No.	Denom.	Date		Unc
10-30P	$5	18__	PROOF	500.

505-12 FAIRMAN, DRAPER & UNDERWOOD PRINTING, 1830s

DESIGNS AND COLOURS

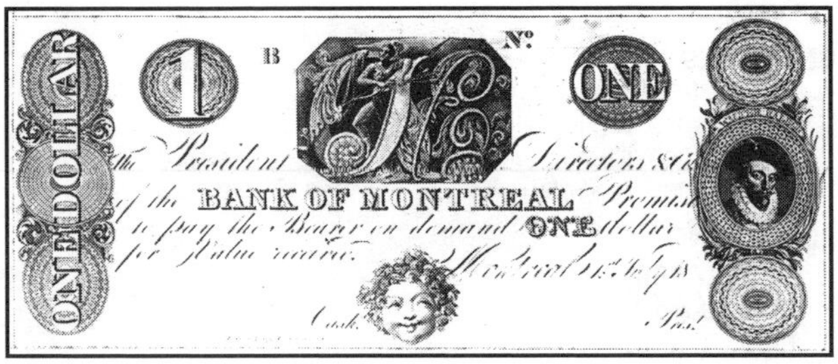

505-12-02-10P

$1 Face Design: —/Indian and ornate ONE; child's head below/Walter Ralegh
Colour: Black with no tint

Back Design: Plain

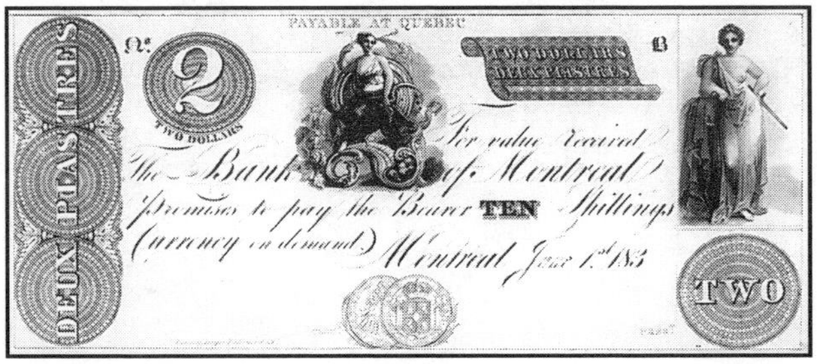

505-12-04-14P

$2 Face Design: —/woman on ornate 2, two coins below/standing justice figure
Colour: Black with no tint

Back Design: Plain

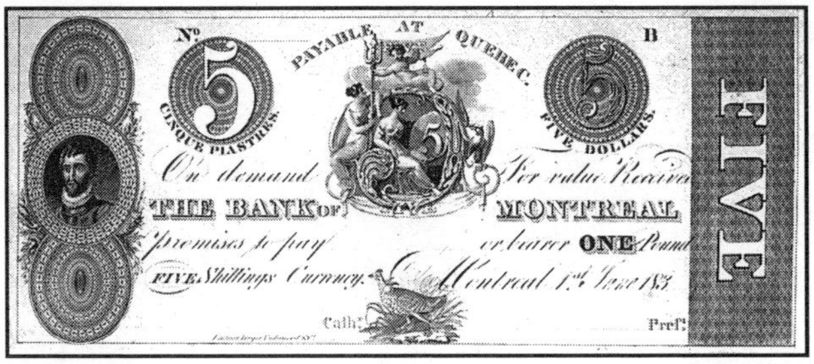

505-12-04-18P

$5 Face Design: Columbus/two women, child, eagle on ornate 5, bird below/—
Colour: Black with no tint

Back Design: Plain

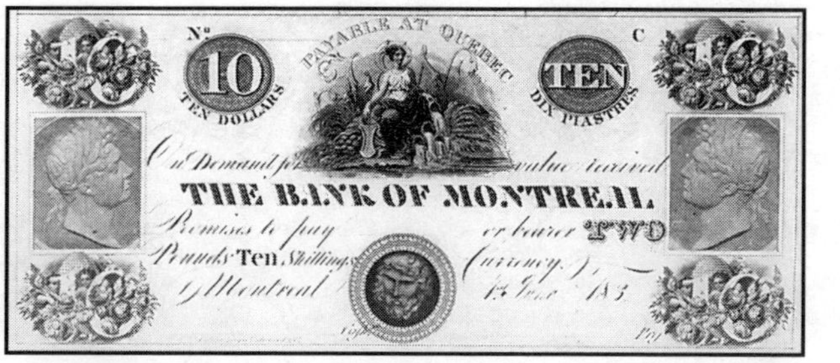

505-12-04-20P

$10 (£2.10) Face Design: Medallion engraved bust/seated woman with ornate TEN; man's head in oval below/medallion engraved bust

Colour: Black with no tint

Back Design: Plain

IMPRINT

Fairman, Draper, Underwood & Co.

SIGNATURES

left	right
mss. B. Holmes	mss. J. Molson (v)
mss. B. Holmes	mss. John Fleming

ISSUE DATING

Partially engraved

1831: 1st July
1835: June 1st 183_
1st June 183_

2. MONTREAL ISSUE

$1: Branch name is engraved at the lower right
$10: Branch name is engraved at the lower left

CIRCULATING NOTES

Cat. No.	Denom.	Date	G	VG	F	VF	EF	AU
12-02-10	$1	1831	500.	1,000.	1,400.	—	—	—
12-02-20	$10 (£2.10)	1835	Institutional collection only					

PROOF NOTES

Cat. No.	Denom.	Date		Unc
12-02-10P	$1	18_	PROOF	600.

4. QUEBEC ISSUE

Engraved "PAYABLE AT QUEBEC" at the top.

CIRCULATING NOTES

Cat. No.	Denom.	Date	G	VG	F	VF	EF	AU
12-04-10	$1	1831	500.	1,000.	1,400.	—	—	—
12-04-14	$2 (10s)	183_ June 1st	No known issued notes					
12-04-18	$5 (£1.5)	183_ June 1st	No known issued notes					
12-04-20	$10 (£2.10)	1835	Institutional collection only					

PROOF NOTES

Cat. No.	Denom.	Date	Unc
12-04-14P	$2 (10s)	183_ June 1st	600.
12-04-18P	$5 (£1.5)	183_ June 1st	600.
12-04-20P	$10 (£2.10)	183_	600.

505-14 RAWDON, WRIGHT, HATCH PRINTING, 1830s

DESIGNS AND COLOURS

505-14-04-02

$1 (5s) Face Design: Two men and livestock/King William IV; small boat at bottom/St. George slaying the dragon

Colour: Black with no tint

Back Design: Plain

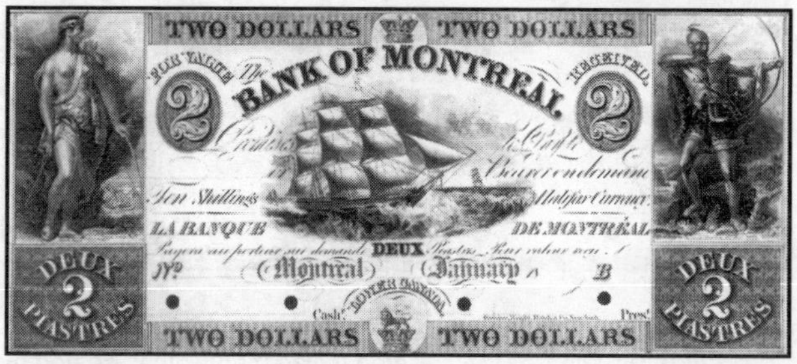

505-14-02-16P

$2 (10s) Face Design: Indian woman/small crown; sailing ships; small lion on crown below/ Indian shooting arrow

Colour: Black with no tint

Back Design: Plain

505-14-04-40P

$5 (£1.5) Face Design: —/small crown, Greek god seated by fountain; small lion on crown below/—

Colour: Black with no tint

Back Design: Plain

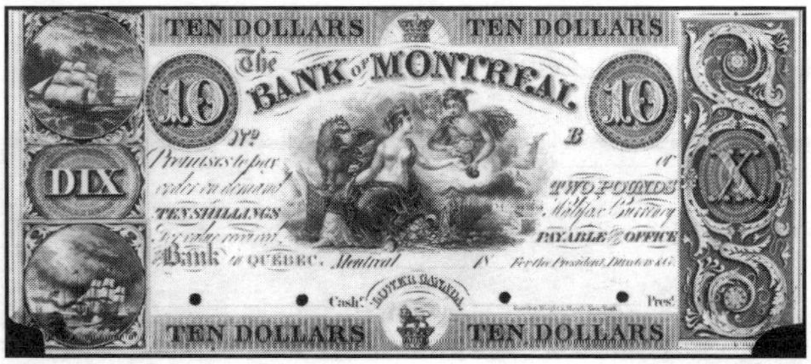

505-14-04-50P

$10 (£2.10) Face Design: Two ships in circles/small crown; griffin, allegorical man and woman; small lion on crown below/—

Colour: Black with no tint

Back Design: Plain

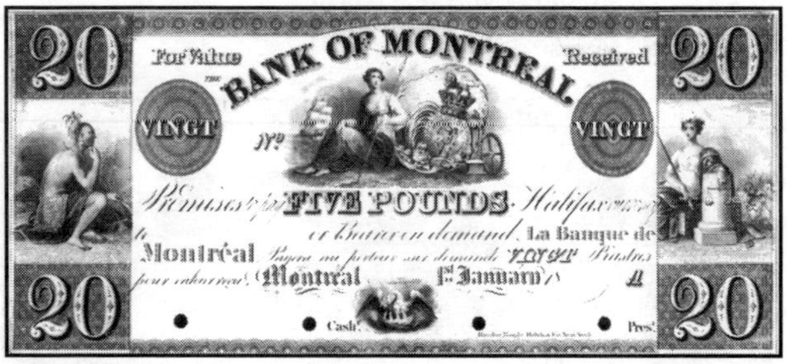

505-14-02-40P

$20 (£5) Face Design: Seated Indian man/woman seated by shield; swan feeding its young below/seated "Justice" figure, lion

Colour: Black with no tint

Back Design:

Photo Not Available

505-14-02-50P

$50 (£12.10) Face Design: Unknown

Colour: Unknown

Back Design: Unknown

Photo Not Available

505-14-02-60P

$100 (£25) Face Design: Unknown

Colour: Unknown

Back Design: Unknown

505-14-02-70P

£ (Postnote) Face Design: Standing "Commerce" figure/child riding deer, female in chariot pulled by lions, child riding deer/standing "Commerce" figure

Colour: Black with no tint

Back Design: Plain

IMPRINT

Rawdon, Wright, Hatch & Co. New York.
Rawdon, Wright & Hatch New-York

SIGNATURES

left	right
mss. B. Holmes	mss. J. Molson
mss. A. Simpson	mss. J. Molson
mss. B. Holmes	mss. P. McGill

ISSUE DATING

Partially engraved ___ 18___:

$1: 1st January 18__:
1st January 1835
1st January 1836

$2: 1837: June 3

2. MONTREAL ISSUE

STAMP

$1 (5s) and $2 (10s): "PAYABLE AT QUEBEC" in black

CIRCULATING NOTES

Cat. No.	Denom.	Date	G	VG	F	VF	EF	AU
14-02-02	$1 (5s)	1835-1837	425.	850.	1,200.	—	—	—
14-02-16	$2 (10s)	1837	425.	850.	1,200.	—	—	—
14-02-20	$5 (£1.5)	18__		No known issued notes				
14-02-30	$10 (£2.10)	18__		No known issued notes				
14-02-40	$20 (£5)	18__		No known issued notes				
14-02-50	$50 (£12.10)	18__		No known issued notes				
14-02-60	$100 (£25)	18__		No known issued notes				
14-02-70	Postnote (£)	18__		No known issued notes				

PROOF NOTES

Cat. No.	Denom.	Date		Unc
14-02-02P	$1 (5s)	18__	PROOF	500.
14-02-16P	$2 (10s)	18__	PROOF	500.
14-02-20P	$5 (£1.5)	18__	PROOF	500.
14-02-30P	$10 (£2.10)	18__	PROOF	500.
14-02-40P	$20 (£5)	18__	PROOF	500.
14-02-50P	$50 (£12.10)	18__	PROOF	500.
14-02-60P	$100 (£25)	18__	PROOF	500.
14-02-70P	Postnote (£)	18__	PROOF	500.

4. QUEBEC ISSUE

VARIETIES

The notes are engraved "PAYABLE AT QUEBEC" at the top. They are engraved with "PAYABLE AT THE OFFICE OF THE BANK IN QUEBEC" at the bottom.

CIRCULATING NOTES

Cat. No.	Denom.	Date	Variety	G	VG	F	VF	EF	AU
14-04-02	$1 (5s)	18_	At top	425.	850.	1,200.	—	—	—
14-04-10	$1 (5s)	18_	At bottom	425.	850.	1,200.	—	—	—
14-04-20	$2 (10s)	18_	At top	425.	850.	1,200.	—	—	—
14-04-30	$2 (10s)	18_	At bottom	425.	850.	1,200.	—	—	—
14-04-40	$5 (£1.5)	18_	At bottom	No known issued notes					
14-04-50	$10 (£2.10)	18_	At bottom	No known issued notes					

PROOF NOTES

Cat. No.	Denom.	Date	Variety		Unc
14-04-40P	$5 (£1.5)	18__	At bottom	PROOF	500.
14-04-50P	$10 (£2.10)	18__	At bottom	PROOF	500.

6. BLUE LATHEWORK BACK ISSUE PAYABLE AT MONTREAL BUT ISSUED BY QUEBEC BRANCH

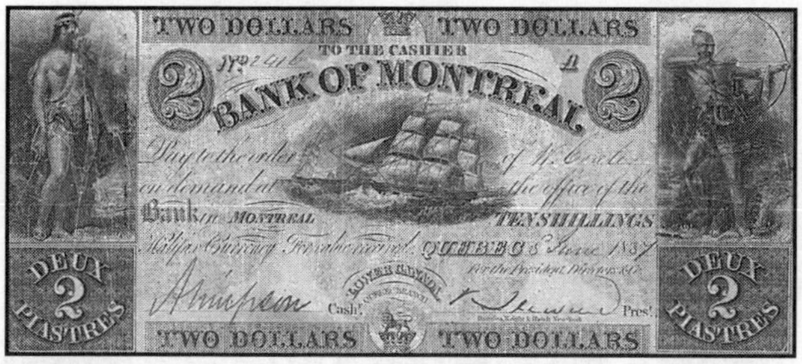

505-14-06-20

$2 (10s) Face Design: Indian woman/ship sailing left; small lion on crown below/Indian shooting arrow
Colour: Black with no tint

Back Design: Lathework; denomination spelled out
Colour: Blue

IMPRINT:

Rawdon, Wright & Hatch New-York

SIGNATURES:

left	**right**
Mss A. Simpson	mss. Illegible

ISSUE DATING:

Partially Engraved, __________18___
$2: 1837: 5 June

Cat. No.	Denom.	Date	G	VG	F	VF	EF	AU
14-06-20	$2 (10s)	1837	Institutional collection only					

"MONTREAL ARMS" ISSUE, ISSUES 505-16, 18 AND 20

The notes have a miniature Montreal Coat of Arms at the bottom centre.

DESIGNS AND COLOURS

505-18-02-02

$1 (5s) Face Design: Woman with anchor in ornate 1/ships in harbour/woman with sheaf and sickle in ornate 1
Colour: Black with no tint
Back Design: Plain

505-20-06-02

$2 (10s) Face Design: Woman with spear and cornucopia standing on ornate 2/Britannia and "Justice" figure flanking ornate 2/woman with sheaf and sickle standing on ornate 2
Colour: Black with no tint
Back Design: Plain

505-16-04-30

$3 (15s) Face Design: Woman standing in ornate 3/allegorical woman with Crest/woman standing in ornate 3
Colour: Black with no tint
Back Design: Plain

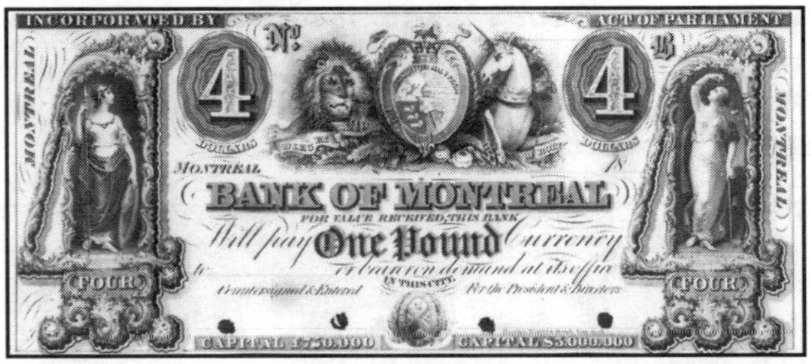

505-16-02-30P

$4 (£1) Face Design: Britannia standing in ornate 4/ Royal Crest/"Justice" figure standing in ornate 4

Colour: Black with no tint

Back Design: Plain

505-16-02-40

$5 (£1.5) Face Design: Young woman with wheat stalks/ woman seated in ornate V/ young woman with sickle

Colour: Black with no tint

Back Design: Plain

505-16-02-50

$10 (£2.10) Face Design: Semi-nude seated woman/two women in ornate X/semi-nude seated woman

Colour: Black with no tint

Back Design: Plain

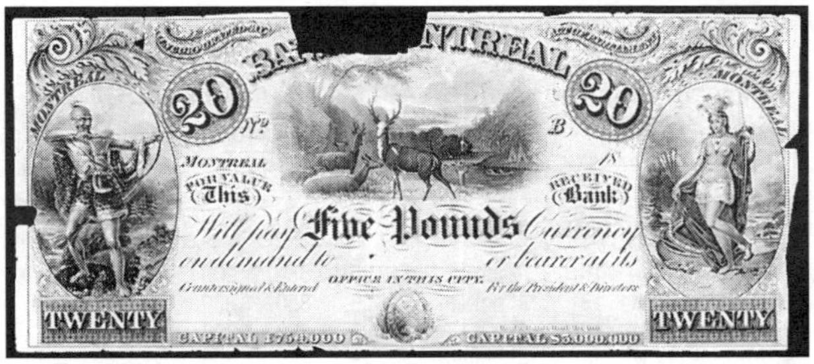

505-16-02-60P

$20 (£5) Face Design: Standing Indian man with drawn bow/ wilderness scene with deer and Indians/standing Indian princess with bow and arrows

Colour: Black with no tint

Back Design: Plain

Photo Not Available

505-16-02-70P

$50 (£12.10) Face Design: Queen Victoria (Chalon portrait)/ ship/Prince Consort

Colour: Black with no tint

Back Design: Plain

505-16-02-80

$100 (£25) Face Design: Standing "Justice" figure in oval/ Queen Victoria seated on throne/ seated "Commerce" figure

Colour: Black with no tint

Back Design: Plain

505-16 PARTIALLY ENGRAVED DATE, 1844-1860s

IMPRINT

Rawdon, Wright & Hatch New-York

SIGNATURES

left	right
mss. illegible	mss. J. Bolton
mss. C.G. Brown	mss. R. Angus
mss. J. Bolton	mss. A. Simpson

2. MONTREAL ISSUE, 1844-1861

The branch name is engraved at the ends or at the top.

ISSUE DATING

Partially engraved ___ 18___:

1844: Jan. 1
1849: Jan. 1
1861: 1 Augt.

PROTECTOR

$5: Red "numeral" on face and back
$10 and $100: Green "word" on face and back

OVERPRINT

$10: "T T" in blue and "M" in green

CIRCULATING NOTES

Cat. No.	Denom.	Date	G	VG	F	VF	EF	AU
16-02-02	$1 (5s)	18__	No known issued notes					
16-02-10	$2 (10s)	18__	No known issued notes					
16-02-20	$3 (15s)	1844	1,300.	2,600.	3,400.	—	—	—
16-02-30	$4 (£1)	18__	No known issued notes					
16-02-40	$5 (£1.5)	1844	500.	1,000.	1,300.	—	—	—
16-02-50	$10 (£2.10)	1849	500.	1,000.	1,300.	—	—	—
16-02-60	$20 (£5)	18__	No known issued notes					
16-02-70	$50 (£12.10)	18__	No known issued notes					
16-02-80	$100 (£25)	1861	Intitutional collection only					

PROOF NOTES

Cat. No.	Denom.	Date		Unc
16-02-02P	$1 (5s)	18__	PROOF	600.
16-02-10P	$2 (10s)	18__	PROOF	600.
16-02-20P	$3 (15s)	18__	PROOF	600.
16-02-30P	$4 (£1)	18__	PROOF	600.
16-02-40P	$5 (£1.5)	18__	PROOF	600.
16-02-50P	$10 (£2.10)	18__	PROOF	600.
16-02-60P	$20 (£5)	18__	PROOF	600.
16-02-70P	$50 (£12.10)	18__	PROOF	600.
16-02-80P	$100 (£25)	18__	PROOF	600.

4. QUEBEC ISSUE, 1844-1852

The branch name is engraved vertically at the ends.

505-16-04-40

ISSUE DATING

Partially engraved _ 18_:

1 May 1844
1 May 1846
1 May 1852

PROTECTOR

$1 (5s) and $2 (10s): Red "numeral" on face and back

Cat. No.	Denom.	Date	G	VG	F	VF	EF	AU
16-04-10	$1 (5s)	1846	350.	700.	1,000.	—	—	—
16-04-20	$2 (10s)	1846	350.	700.	1,000.	—	—	—
16-04-30	$3 (15s)	1844	1,250.	2,500.	3,300.	—	—	—
16-04-40	$10 (£2.10)	1846-1852	500.	1,000.	1,300.	—	—	—

505-18 ENGRAVED DATE, RED PROTECTOR, TWO SIGNATURES, 1849

These notes have a miniature Montreal Coat of Arms at the bottom centre. The branch names are engraved vertically at the ends.

505-18-04-02

505-18-02-04

505-18-02-06

IMPRINT

Rawdon, Wright & Hatch, New York

SIGNATURES

left	right
mss. various	mss. various

ISSUE DATING

Engraved

Jany. 1st 1849

PROTECTOR

Red "word" on face and back

2. MONTREAL ISSUE

Cat. No.	Denom.	Date	G	VG	F	VF	EF	AU
18-02-02	$1 (5s)	1849	350.	700.	1,000.	—	—	—
18-02-04	$2 (10s)	1849	350.	700.	1,000.	—	—	—
18-02-06	$4 (£1)	1849	Institutional collection only					

4. QUEBEC ISSUE

Cat. No.	Denom.	Date	G	VG	F	VF	EF	AU
18-04-02	$1 (5s)	1849	260.	525.	750.	—	—	—

505-20 ENGRAVED DATE, GREEN PROTECTOR, ONE SIGNATURE, 1849

The green protector notes were issued considerably later than the 1849 engraved date they bear, Chronologically, they followed the blue back issue of 1853 - 1857.

These notes have a miniature Montreal Coat of Arms at the bottom centre. The branch names are engraved vertically at the ends. Red printed numbers are to the right of the centre vignette, near the left signature space or above the right signature space.

IMPRINT

Rawdon, Wright, Hatch & Edson, Montreal & N.Y.
"ABNCo." Monogram on some notes

SIGNATURES

right only

mss. C.J. Brown
mss. R. Angus

ISSUE DATING

Engraved

Jany. 1st 1849

505-20-06-02

PROTECTOR

Green "word" on face and back
Green "word" and "numeral" on face of some notes.

2. COBOURG ISSUE

OVERPRINT
"LINDSAY" in red

Cat. No.	Denom.	Date	Variety	G	VG	F	VF	EF	AU
20-02-02	$2 (10s)	1849	no o/p	275.	550.	800.	—	—	—
20-02-02a	$2 (10s)	1849	LINDSAY o/p	325.	650.	1,000.	—	—	—

4. HAMILTON ISSUE

OVERPRINT
"BRANTFORD" in red

Cat. No.	Denom.	Date	Variety	G	VG	F	VF	EF	AU
20-04-02	$1 (5s)	1849	no o/p	225.	450.	650.	—	—	—
20-04-02a	$1 (5s)	1849	BRANTFORD o/p	275.	550.	800.	—	—	—

6. MONTREAL ISSUE

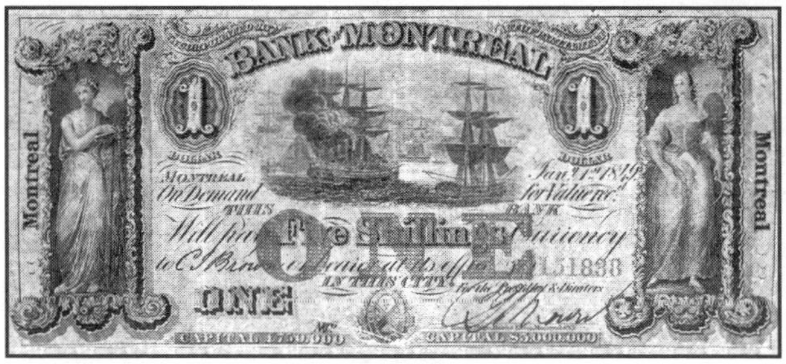

505-20-06-04

OVERPRINT

$1 (5s): "LONDON" in green, in medium or in large letters

STAMP

$1 (5s), with overprint: "S" in blue

Cat. No.	Denom.	Date	Variety	G	VG	F	VF	EF	AU
20-06-02	$1 (5s)	1849	no o/p	250.	500.	750.	—	—	—
20-06-02a	$1 (5s)	1849	LONDON o/p	300.	600.	950.	—	—	—
20-06-04	$2 (10s)	1849	no o/p	250.	500.	750.	—	—	—

8. QUEBEC ISSUE

505-20-08-04

Cat. No.	Denom.	Date	G	VG	F	VF	EF	AU
20-08-02	$1 (5s)	1849	250.	500.	750.	—	—	—
20-08-04	$2 (10s)	1849	250.	500.	750.	—	—	—

10. TORONTO ISSUE

505-20-10-02

OVERPRINT

$1 (5s): "BRANTFORD" twice in red
"COBOURG" in red

$2 (10s): "SIMCOE" in red
"HAMILTON" in green

Cat. No.	Denom.	Date	Variety	G	VG	F	VF	EF	AU
20-10-02	$1 (5s)	1849	no o/p	250.	500.	750.	—	—	—
20-10-02a	$1 (5s)	1849	town o/p	300.	600.	950.	—	—	—
20-10-04	$2 (10s)	1849	no o/p	250.	500.	750.	—	—	—
20-10-04a	$2 (10s)	1849	town o/p	300.	600.	950.	—	—	—

"DOG AND SAFE" ISSUES

Numbers 505-22 and 505-24 were issued for the Toronto branch. There is a vignette of a small dog and a safe on the bottom centre of all denominations.

DESIGNS AND COLOURS

505-22 PARTIALLY ENGRAVED DATE NO PROTECTOR, 1842-1847

2. RAWDON, WRIGHT, HATCH PRINTINGS 2nd APRIL 184—

505-22-02-04P

$2 (10s) Face Design: —/seated Mercury, lion/—
Colour: Black with no tint

Back Design: Plain

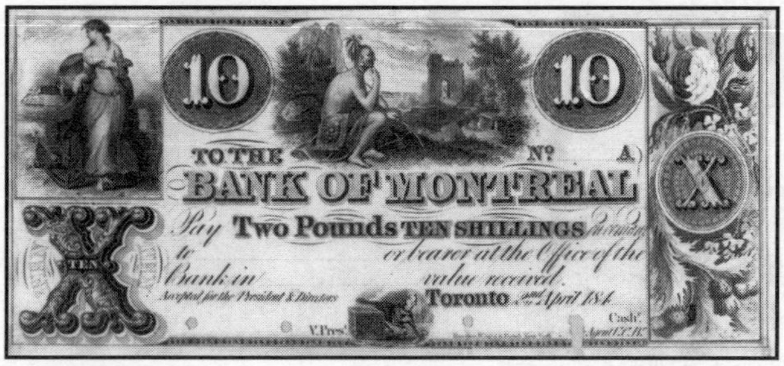

505-22-02-08P

$10 (£2.10) Face Design: Allegorical female, anchor/seated Indian (from Death of Wolfe by West) and "Ruins of Jamestown"/ roses, shamrocks, thistles, counter
Colour: Black with no tint

Back Design: Plain

IMPRINT

Rawdon, Wright & Hatch, New York

SIGNATURES

left	right
none	none

ISSUE DATING

Partially Engraved 2nd April 184__

PROOF NOTES

Cat.No.	Demon	Date		Unc
22-02-02P	$1 (5s)	184_	PROOF	750.
22-02-04P	$2 (10s)	184_	PROOF	750.
22-02-06P	$5(£1.5)	184_	PROOF	750.
22-02-08P	$10(£2.10)	184_	PROOF	750.

4. RAWDON, WRIGHT, HATCH PRINTINGS 2nd AUGT 184__

Photo Not Available

IMPRINT

Rawdon, Wright, Hatch New York

SIGNATURES

left	right
mss. B. Thorne	mss. W. Wilson

ISSUE DATING

Partially Engraved 2nd Augt. 184___

1842
1843

STAMP

"BELLEVILLE" in red

CIRCULATING NOTES

Cat.No.	Denom	Date	G	VG	F	VF	EF	AU
22-04-02	$1(5s)	1842	400.	800.	1,125.	—	—	—
22-04-10	$2(10s)	184_	No known issued notes					
22-04-20	$5(£1.5)	184_	No known issued notes					
22-04-30	$10(£2.10)	1842	400.	800.	1,125.	—	—	—

PROOF NOTES

Cat. No.	Denom.	Date	Unc
22-04-10P	$2 (10s)	184_	750.
22-04-20P	$5 (£1.5)	184_	750.

6. DANFORTH/UNDERWOOD PRINTINGS, 2ND AUGT. 184_

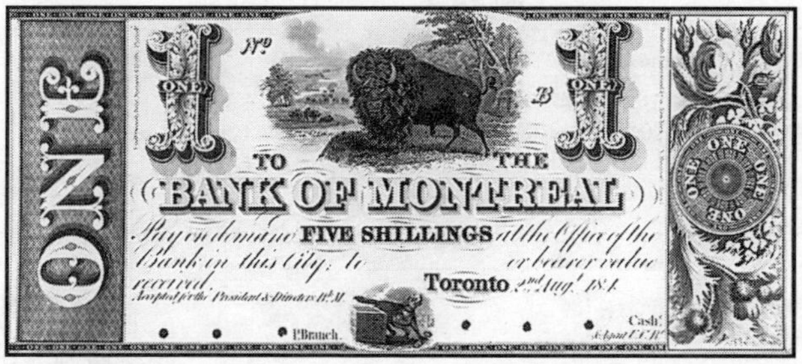

505-22-06-10P

$1 (5s) Face Design: —bison/roses, shamrocks, thistles, counter
Colour: Black with no tint

Back Design: Plain

505-22-06-20P

$2 (10s) Face Design: —/seated Mercury, lion/—
Colour: Black with no tint

Back Design: Plain

505-22-06-30P

$5 Face Design: Roses, shamrocks, thistles, counter/ Royal Crest/roses, shamrocks, thistles, counter

Colour: Black with no tint

Back Design: Plain

IMPRINT

Underwood, Bald, Spencer & Hufty, Philada
Danforth, Underwood & Co. New York-A.Bourne Agent
Danforth, Spencer & Hufty. New York-A.Bourne Agent and
Spencer, Hufty & Danforth, Philada.

SIGNATURES

left	right
J.S. Smith	W. Wilson

ISSUE DATING

Partially Engraved 2nd Augt. 184__:

1843
1847

STAMP

"BELLEVILLE" in red

CIRCULATING NOTES

Cat.No.	Denom.	Date	G	VG	F	VF	EF	AU
22-06-10	$1(5s)	1847	450.	900.	1,300.	—	—	—
22-06-20	$2(10s)	1843-1847	450.	900.	1,300.	—	—	—
22-06-30	$5(£1.5)	1843-1847	450.	900.	1,300.	—	—	—

PROOF NOTES

Cat. No.	Denom.	Date		Unc
22-06-10P	$1 (5s)	184_	PROOF	600.
22-06-20P	$2 (10s)	184_	PROOF	600.
22-06-30P	$5 (£1.5)	184_	PROOF	600.

505-24 ENGRAVED DATE, RED PROTECTORS, 1849

505-24-04a

505-24-06

$5 (£1.5) Face Design: Roses, shamrocks, thistles, counter/ Royal Crest/roses, shamrocks, thistles, counter

Colour: Black with no tint

Back Design: Plain

IMPRINT

Rawdon, Wright, Hatch & Edson, New York

SIGNATURES

left	right
mss. illegible	mss. W. Wilson
mss. G.H. Wilson	mss. J.F. Smith

ISSUE DATING

Engraved

1st MAY, 1849

PROTECTOR

Red "word" on face and back

ENGRAVED PAYABLE

John G. Horne
J.G. Horne

OVERPRINT

"BROCKVILLE" in red
"BYTOWN" in red
"COBOURG" in red
"HAMILTON" in red
"LONDON" in red
"ST. THOMAS" in red

Cat. No.	Den.	Date	Variety	G	VG	F	VF	EF	AU
24-02	$1 (5s)	1849	no o/p	475.	950.	1,400.	—	—	—
24-02a	$1 (5s)	1849	town o/p	500.	1,000.	1,500.	—	—	—
24-04	$2 (10s)	1849	no o/p	475.	950.	1,400.	—	—	—
24-04a	$2 (10s)	1849	town o/p	500.	1,000.	1,500.	—	—	—
24-06	$5 (£1.5)	1849	no o/p	425.	850.	1,200.	—	—	—
24-06a	$5 (£1.5)	1849	town o/p	450.	900.	1,300.	—	—	—
24-08	$10 (£2.10)	1849	no o/p	475.	950.	1,400.	—	—	—
24-08a	$10 (£2.10)	1849	town o/p	500.	1,000.	1,500.	—	—	—

505-26 "BANK CREST" ISSUE, 1852-1856

These notes were printed on watermarked paper, with the date and the branch in red, blue or black letterpress. All notes of these designs dated 1858 or 1864 are counterfeits, and there are counterfeits of other dates as well. The notes have the bank crest design at the top left corner.

1. Branch name at centre
   Montreal, Quebec, Toronto
2. Branch name at ends
   Brantford, Bytown, Hamilton, Kingston, London, Montreal, Perth, Peterboro, Quebec, St. Thomas, Toronto

DESIGNS AND COLOURS

Type I (1852)

505-26-04

$1 (5s) Face Design: Bank Crest/—/sailing ships and 1 counter
Colour: Black with no tint

Back Design: Plain

Type II (1852)

505-26-02-10

Type I (1851)

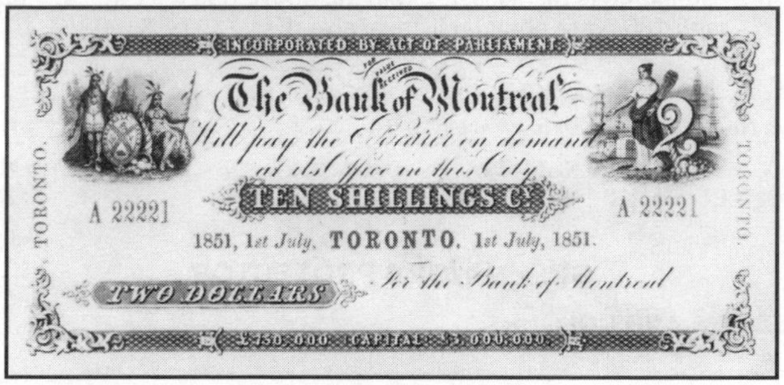

505-26-02-16E

$2 (10s) Face Design: Bank Crest/—/allegorical female, ships, 2 counter
Colour: Black with no tint

Back Design: Plain

Type I (1852)

505-26-02-18

Type I (1851)

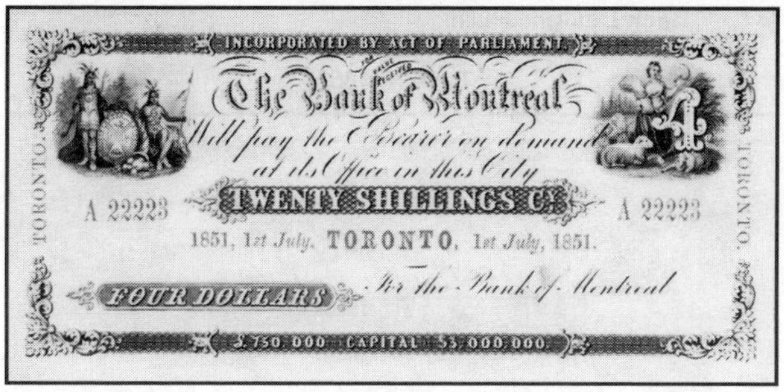

505-26-02-30E

$4 (20s) Face Design: Bank Crest/—/allegorical female, sheep, 4 counter
Colour: Black with no tint

Back Design: Plain

Type I (1852)

505-26-02-32

Type II (1856)

Photo Not Available

505-26-02-42

Type I (1852)

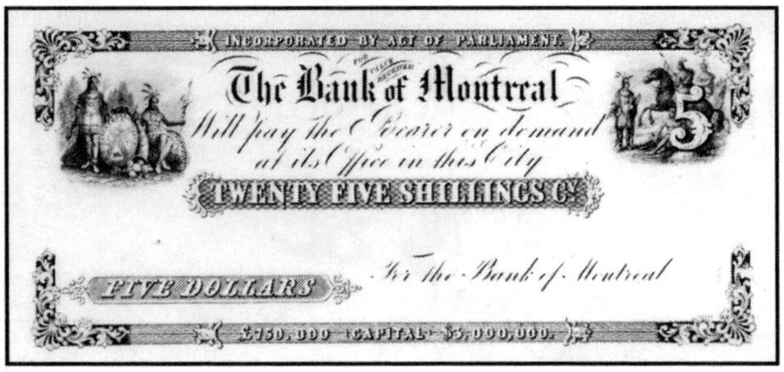

505-26-02-46

$5 (25s) Face Design: Bank Crest/—/Indians and 5 counter
Colour: Black with no tint

Back Design: Plain

Type II (1852)

505-26-02-52

Type I (1852)

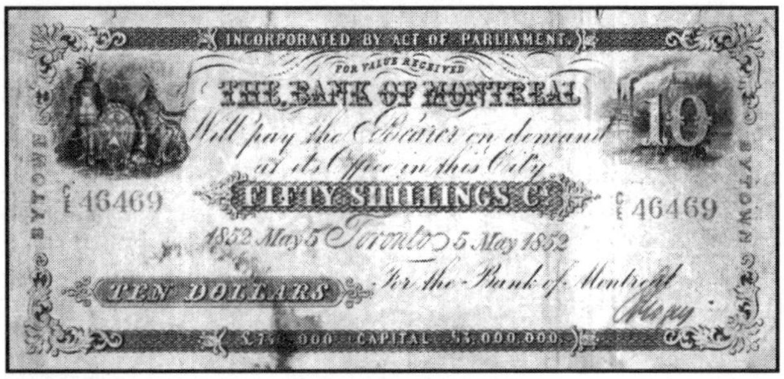

505-26-02-60

$10 (50s) Face Design: Bank Crest /—/paddlewheel steamboat and 10 counter
Colour: Black with no tint

Back Design: Plain

Type II (1852)

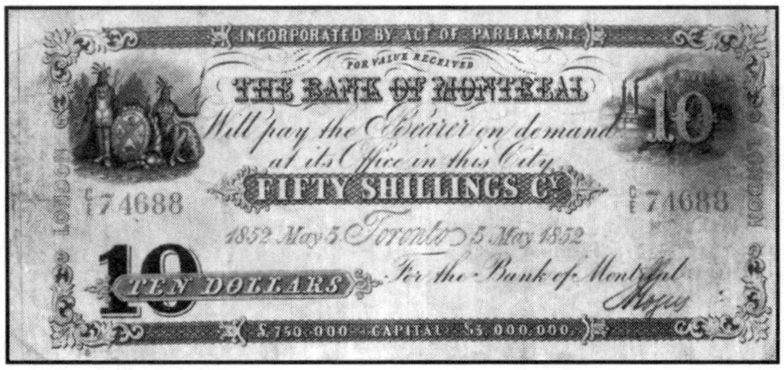

505-26-02-66

IMPRINT

Perkins, Bacon & Co. London

SIGNATURES

right only
mss. J. Reed
mss. R. Angus

2. NO PROTECTOR

ISSUE DATING

The entire date added letterpress with serial number:

$1 (5s): 3 Jan 1852; 6 June 1852
$2 (10s): 5 Mar 1852; 1 July 1852
$4 (20s): 1 Apr 1852; 1 Aug 1856
$5 (25s): 3 Apr., 1852; 5 Apr., 1852; 1 Sept 1852; 1 Mar 1853
$10 (50s): 5 May 1852

OVERPRINT

"THREE RIVERS" twice vertically in red

VARIETIES

Type I: Notes have denominations spelled out in a panel at the lower left.
Type II: Notes have a numeral engraved at the left end of the type I panel.

Cat. No.	Denom.	Date	Variety	G	VG	F	VF	EF	AU
26-02-04	$1 (5s)	1852	Type I	375.	750.	1,100.	—	—	—
26-02-10	$1 (5s)	1852	Type II	375.	750.	1,100.	—	—	—
26-02-16	$2 (10s)	1851	Type I	No known issued notes					
26-02-18	$2 (10s)	1852	Type I	375.	750.	1,100.	—	—	—
26-02-30	$4 (20s)	1851	Type I	No known issued notes					
26-02-32	$4 (20s)	1852	Type I	500.	1,000.	1,450.	—	—	—
26-02-38	$4 (20s)	1852	Type II	500.	1,000.	1,450.	—	—	—
26-02-42	$4 (20s)	1856	Type II	NOT CONFIRMED					
26-02-46	$5 (25s)	1852	Type I	375.	750.	1,100.	—	—	—
26-02-48	$5 (25s)	1853	Type I	375.	750.	1,100.	—	—	—
26-02-52	$5 (25s)	1852	Type II	375.	750.	1,100.	—	—	—
26-02-54	$5 (25s)	1853	Type II	375.	750.	1,100.	—	—	—
26-02-60	$10 (50s)	1852	Type I	500.	1,000.	1,450.	—	—	—
26-02-66	$10 (50s)	1852	Type II	500.	1,000.	1,450.	—	—	—

Note: Counterfeits of this issue, with the above dates as well as 1858 and 1864, are abundantly available. Est. $50 G; $100 VG.

ESSAY NOTES

Cat. No.	Denom.	Date	Variety	Unc
26-02-16E	$2 (10s)	1851	Type I	600.
26-02-30E	$4 (20s)	1851	Type I	600.

4. GREEN WORD PROTECTOR

DESIGNS AND COLOURS

505-26-04-02

$2 (10s) Face Design: Bank Crest/—/allegorical female, ships, 2 counter
Colour: Black with no tint
Back Design: Plain

ISSUE DATING

The entire date added letterpress with serial numbers:

$2 (10s): 1 Mar. 1852

OVERPRINT

"LONDON" in green

PROTECTOR

Green "word" on face

Cat. No.	Denom.	Date	Variety	G	VG	F	VF	EF	AU
26-04-02	$2 (10s)	1852	Type II		Institutional collection only				

505-28 "BLUE BACK" ISSUE, 1853-1857

The principal branch name is engraved vertically in black at the ends of the centre panel. Sometimes an additional branch name is overprinted horizontally below the bank title.

DESIGNS AND COLOURS

505-28-60-02R

$1 Face Design: Bank Crest/—/Queen Victoria (Winterhalter portrait)

Colour: Black with no tint

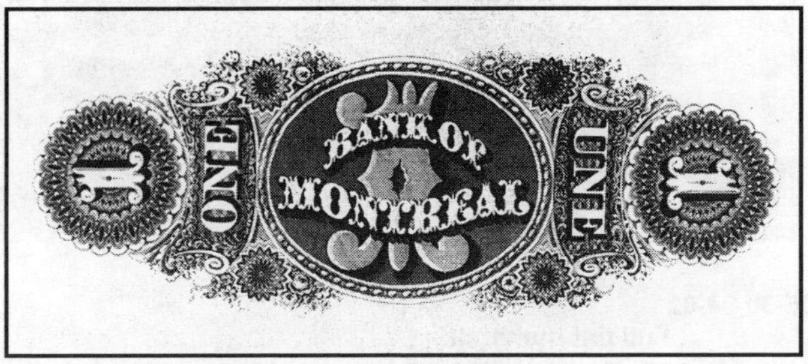

Back Design: Lathework, counters and bank name

Colour: Blue

505-28-56-02

$2 Face Design: Bank Crest/—/Prince Consort

Colour: Black with no tint

Back Design: Lathework, counters and bank name

Colour: Blue

IMPRINT

Toppan, Carpenter, Casilear & Co.
Toppan, Carpenter & Co. Montreal

SIGNATURES

right only
none
mss. R. Angus

ISSUE DATING

The entire date added letterpress in red with serial numbers:

1 Feb 1853
1 Aug 1856
2 Jan 1857
2 Feb 1857

2. ENGRAVED "BROCKVILLE"

The letterpress "BROCKVILLE" is in red in the date.

Cat. No.	Denom.	Date	G	VG	F	VF	EF	AU
28-02-02	$1	1857	350.	700.	950.	—	—	—

12. ENGRAVED "GODERICH"

"LONDON" is overprinted in red in the date.

OVERPRINT

"BRANTFORD" in green

Cat. No.	Denom.	Date	G	VG	F	VF	EF	AU
28-12-02	$1	1856	350.	700.	950.	—	—	—

22. ENGRAVED "LONDON"

The letterpress "LONDON" is in red in the date, with "T T" at the top.

Cat. No.	Denom.	Date	G	VG	F	VF	EF	AU
28-22-02	$1	1857	350.	700.	950.	—	—	—
28-22-04	$2	1856	350.	700.	950.	—	—	—

30. ENGRAVED "MONTREAL"

There is no overprinted branch name.

PROOF NOTES

Cat. No.	Denom.	Date		Unc
28-30-02P	$1	Undated	FACE PROOF	500.

36. ENGRAVED "OTTAWA"

"OTTAWA" is overprinted in red in the date.

Cat. No.	Denom.	Date	G	VG	F	VF	EF	AU
28-36-02	$1	1857	350.	700.	950.	—	—	—
28-36-04	$2	1857	350.	700.	950.	—	—	—

40. ENGRAVED "PERTH"

"OTTAWA" is overprinted in red in the date.

Cat. No.	Denom.	Date	G	VG	F	VF	EF	AU
28-40-02	$2	1856	350.	700.	950.	—	—	—

44. ENGRAVED "PICTON"

"KINGSTON" is overprinted in red in the date.

Cat. No.	Denom.	Date	G	VG	F	VF	EF	AU
28-44-02	$1	1856	350.	700.	950.	—	—	—
28-44-04	$2	1856	350.	700.	950.	—	—	—

48. ENGRAVED "PORT HOPE"

The letterpress "COBOURG" is in red in the date.

OVERPRINT

"LINDSAY" in red

Cat. No.	Denom.	Date	G	VG	F	VF	EF	AU
28-48-02	$1	1857	350.	700.	950.	—	—	—

52. ENGRAVED "QUEBEC"

No overprinted branch name.

PROOF NOTES

Cat. No.	Denom.	Date		Unc
28-52-02P	$2	Undated	FACE PROOF	400.

56. ENGRAVED "SIMCOE"

"BRANTFORD" is overprinted in red in the date.

Cat. No.	Denom.	Date	G	VG	F	VF	EF	AU
28-56-02	$2	1856	350.	700.	950.	—	—	—

60. ENGRAVED "TORONTO"

"TORONTO" is overprinted in red in the date.

Cat. No.	Denom.	Date	Variety	G	VG	F	VF	EF	AU
28-60-02R	$1	1853	Remainder*	—	—	—	—	1,000.	—

*Unsigned, dated and numbered.

64. ENGRAVED "WHITBY"

The letterpress "BOWMANVILLE" is in red in the date.

Cat. No.	Denom.	Date	G	VG	F	VF	EF	AU
28-64-02	$1	1856	350.	700.	950.	—	—	—

68. ENGRAVED "WOODSTOCK"

"LONDON" is overprinted in red in the date.

Cat. No.	Denom.	Date	G	VG	F	VF	EF	AU
28-68-02	$1	1856	350.	700.	950.	—	—	—

505-30 "GREEN" ISSUE OF 1859

The branch name was added letterpress in red or blue across the lower centre. Additional branch names may be overprinted vertically at each end of the note and in larger print below the bank title.

1. Branch name at centre

Belleville	Kingston	Peterboro
Brantford	Lindsay	Quebec
Brockville	London	Toronto
Cobourg	Montreal	Waterloo
Hamilton	Ottawa	Whitby

2. Branch name above the date line, at the ends or both places.

Cornwall	Perth	Stratford
Goderich	Peterboro	Waterloo
Guelph	Picton	Whitby
Lindsay	Quebec	

DESIGNS AND COLOURS

505-30-02-02

White outlined numerals

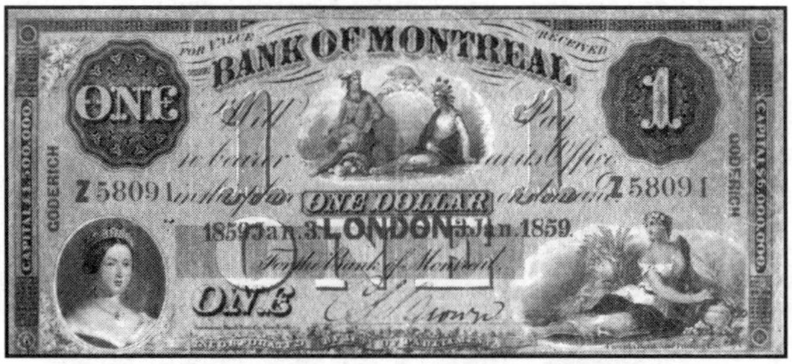

505-30-04-02

Full tint numerals

$1 Face Design: Portrait of Queen Victoria/Bank Crest/reclining woman with produce "Ceres"

Colour: Black with overall green tint

Back Design: See subheadings

Colour: See subheadings

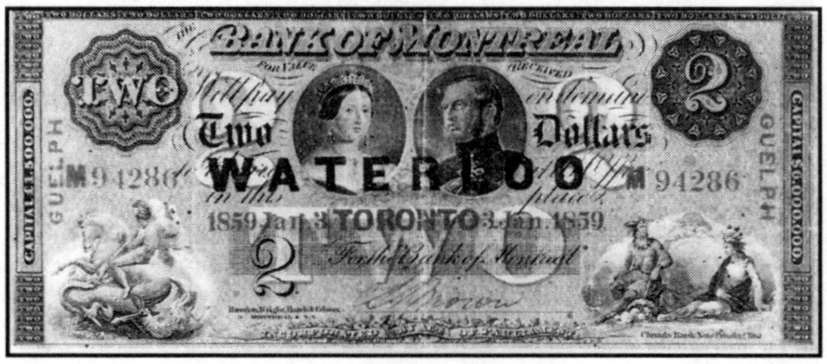

505-30-02-04

$2 Face Design: St. George slaying the dragon/Victoria and Albert/Bank Crest

Colour: Black with overall green tint

Back Design: See subheadings

Colour: See subheadings

505-30-04-06

$4 Face Design: Bank Crest/Wellington/seated Britannia
Colour: Black with overall green tint

Back Design: See subheadings
Colour: See subheadings

505-30-04-08

$5 Face Design: Bank Crest/front view of head office building/ seated blacksmith
Colour: Black with overall green tint

Back Design: See subheadings
Colour: See subheadings

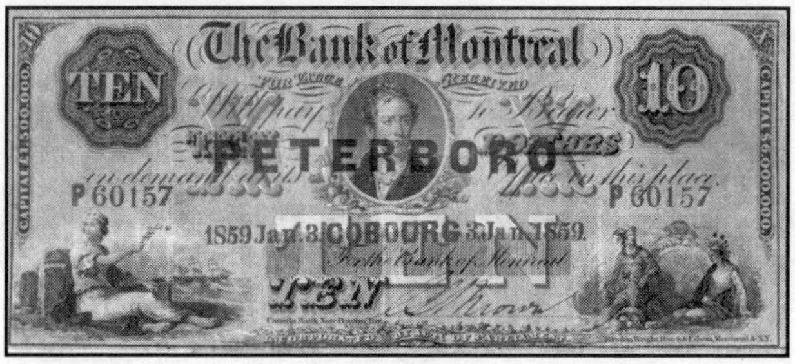

505-30-04-10

$10 Face Design: Seated female on dock "Commerce"/ Robert Peel/Bank Crest
Colour: Black with overall green tint

Back Design: St. George slaying the dragon
Colour: Green

IMPRINT

Rawdon, Wright, Hatch & Edson
Rawdon, Wright, Hatch & Edson, Montreal & N.Y.
American Bank Note Co.
American Bank Note Co. New York

SIGNATURES

right only
mss. R. Angus
mss. C.G. Brown

ISSUE DATING

Entire date added letterpress:
3 Jan. 1859

2. WHITE OUTLINED NUMERALS, ST. GEORGE BACK DESIGNS

Cat. No.	Denom.	Date	G	VG	F	VF	EF	AU
30-02-02	$1	1859	500.	1,000.	1,400.	2,200.	—	—
30-02-04	$2	1859	500.	1,000.	1,400.	2,200.	—	—
30-02-06	$4	1859	550.	1,100.	1,500.	2,400.	—	—
30-02-08	$5	1859	500.	1,000.	1,400.	2,200.	—	—
30-02-10	$10	1859	550.	1,100.	1,500.	2,400.	—	—

4. FULL TINT NUMERALS, ST. GEORGE BACK DESIGNS

Cat. No.	Denom.	Date	G	VG	F	VF	EF	AU
30-04-02	$1	1859	500.	1,000.	1,400.	2,200.	—	—
30-04-04	$2	1859	500.	1,000.	1,400.	2,200.	—	—
30-04-06	$4	1859	550.	1,100.	1,500.	2,400.	—	—
30-04-08	$5	1859	500.	1,000.	1,400.	2,200.	—	—
30-04-10	$10	1859	550.	1,100.	1,500.	2,400.	—	—

6. WHITE OUTLINED NUMERALS, PLAIN BACKS

Cat. No.	Denom.	Date	G	VG	F	VF	EF	AU
30-06-02	$1	1859	475.	950.	1,300.	2,000.	—	—
30-06-04	$2	1859	475.	950.	1,300.	2,000.	—	—
30-06-06	$4	1859	500.	1,000.	1,400.	2,200.	—	—
30-06-08	$5	1859	475.	950.	1,300.	2,000.	—	—

8. FULL TINT NUMERALS, PLAIN BACKS

Cat. No.	Denom.	Date	G	VG	F	VF	EF	AU
30-08-02	$1	1859	475.	950.	1,300.	2,000.	—	—
30-08-04	$2	1859	475.	950.	1,300.	2,000.	—	—
30-08-06	$4	1859	500.	1,000.	1,400.	2,200.	—	—
30-08-08	$5	1859	475.	950.	1,300.	2,000.	—	—

505-32 ISSUE OF 1862

The branch names were added letterpress across the lower centre in red or blue. Sometimes an additional branch name is added vertically at the ends or across the upper centre.

1. Branch names added across lower centre

Brantford	Quebec
London	Toronto

2. Branch names added vertically at ends

Goderich	Whitby

DESIGNS AND COLOURS

The tint in this issue is greatly reduced from the 1859 issue to become a panel and two counters.

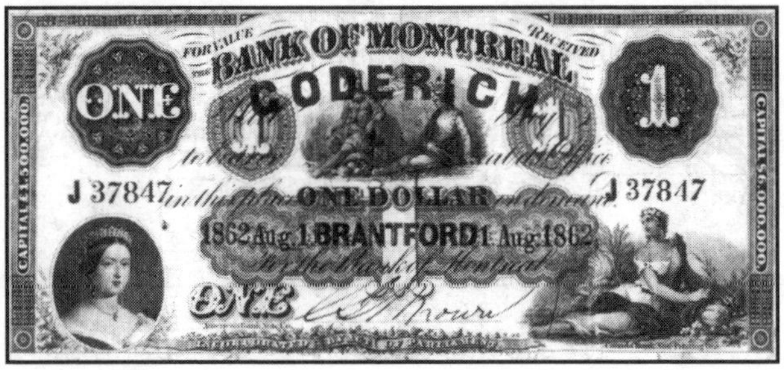

505-32-02

$1 Face Design: Portrait of Queen Victoria/Bank Crest/ reclining woman with produce "Ceres"
Colour: Black with green tint

Back Design: Plain

505-32-04

$2 Face Design: St. George slaying the dragon/ Victoria and Albert/Bank Crest
Colour: Black with green tint

Back Design: Plain

505-32-06

$5 Face Design: Bank Crest/corner view of head office building/seated blacksmith
Colour: Black with green tint

Back Design: Plain

505-32-08

$10 Face Design: Seated female on dock "Commerce"/ Robert Peel/Bank Crest
Colour: Black with green tint

Back Design: Plain

IMPRINT

American Bank Note Co.

SIGNATURES

right only
mss. C.G. Brown
mss. R. Angus

ISSUE DATING

Entire date added letterpress:

1 Aug. 1862

Cat. No.	Denom.	Date	G	VG	F	VF	EF	AU
32-02	$1	1862	350.	700.	1,000.	1,600.	—	—
32-04	$2	1862	550.	1,100.	1,500.	2,500.	—	—
32-06	$5	1862	475.	950.	1,300.	2,000.	3,500.	—
32-08	$10	1862	550.	1,100.	1,500.	2,500.	—	—

505-34 ISSUE OF 1871

DESIGNS AND COLOURS

505-34-02

$4 Face Design: R.B. Angus/woman, cherubs and ornate 4/ E.H. King
Colour: Black with green tint

Back Design: Lathework, counters and bank name, St. George slaying the dragon
Colour: Green

505-34-04

$5 Face Design: Hon. T. Ryan/Britannia, lion and ornate V/ E.H. King
Colour: Black with green tint

Back Design: Lathework, counters, bank name and crest
Colour: Green

505-34-06

$10 Face Design: Hon. T. Ryan/cherubs and ornate X/E.H. King
Colour: Black with green tint

Back Design: Lathework, counters, bank name and crest
Colour: Green

505-34-08

$20 Face Design: —/E.H. King/—
Colour: Black with green tint

Back Design: Lathework, counters, bank name and crest
Colour: Green

505-34-10

$50 Face Design: R.B. Angus/allegorical female and ornate L/ E.H. King
Colour: Black with green tint

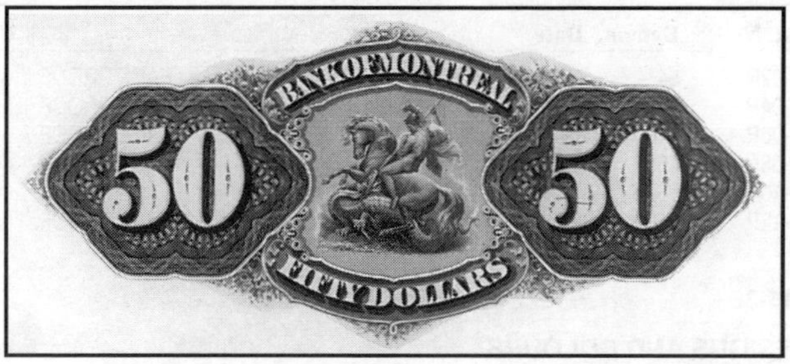

Back Design: Lathework, counters, bank name and crest
Colour: Green

505-34-12

$100 Face Design: R.B. Angus/"Justice" figure seated in ornate C/E.H. King
Colour: Black with green tint

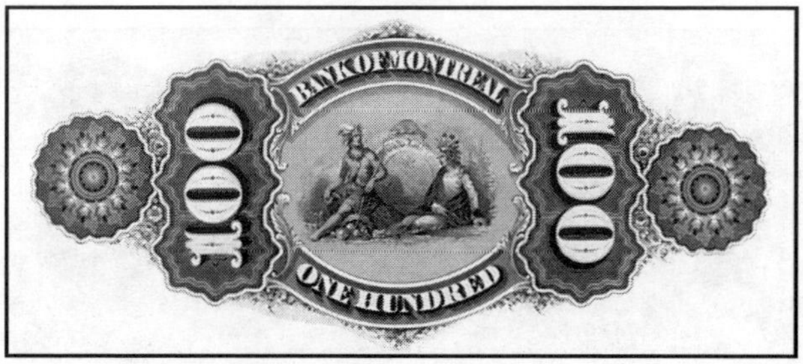

Back Design: Lathework, counters, bank name and crest
Colour: Green

IMPRINT

British American Bank Note Co. Montreal & Ottawa

SIGNATURES

left	**right**
mss. various	engr. E.H. King

ISSUE DATING

Engraved

$4: 6th Feby 1871
$5: 2nd Jany 1871
$10: 1st March 1871
$20: 3rd April 1871
$50: 5th May 1871
$100: 6th June 1871

CIRCULATING NOTES

Cat. No.	Denom.	Date	G	VG	F	VF	EF	AU
34-02	$4	1871	550.	1,100.	1,600.	—	—	—
34-04	$5	1871	600.	1,200.	1,750.	—	—	—
34-06	$10	1871	650.	1,300.	1,900.	—	—	—
34-08	$20	1871	800.	1,600.	2,100.	—	—	—
34-10	$50	1871	800.	1,600.	2,100.	—	—	—
34-12	$100	1871	800.	1,600.	2,100.	—	—	—

PROOF NOTES

Cat. No.	Denom.	Date		Unc
34-02P	$4	1871	FACE PROOF	500.
34-04P	$5	1871	FACE PROOF	500.
34-06P	$10	1871	FACE PROOF	500.
34-08P	$20	1871	FACE PROOF	600.
34-10P	$50	1871	FACE PROOF	600.
34-12P	$100	1871	FACE PROOF	600.

505-36 ISSUE OF 1882

DESIGNS AND COLOURS

505-36-02

$5 Face Design: W.J. Buchanan/Britannia, lion and ornate V/ C.F. Smithers
Colour: Black with green tint

Back Design: Lathework, counters and bank name, St. George slaying the dragon
Colour: Green

505-36-04

$10 Face Design: Dr. G.W. Campbell/cherubs and ornate X/ C.F. Smithers
Colour: Black with green tint

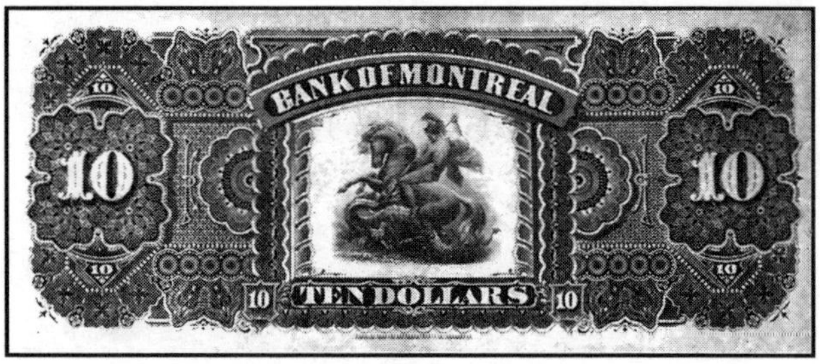

Back Design: Lathework, counters and bank name, St. George slaying the dragon
Colour: Green

505-36-06

$20 Face Design: C.F. Smithers
Colours: Black with green tint

Back Design: Lathework, counters and bank name, St. George slaying the dragon
Colour: Green

IMPRINT

British American Bank Note Co. Montreal
British American Bank Note Co. Monteal & Ottawa

SIGNATURES

left	right
mss. various	engr. C.F. Smithers

ISSUE DATING

Engraved

2nd January 1882
Jany. 2nd 1882

Cat. No.	Denom.	Date	G	VG	F	VF	EF	AU
36-02	$5	1882	850.	1,700.	—	—	—	—
36-04	$10	1882	600.	1,200.	1,700.	2,500.	—	—
36-06	$20	1882	1,000.	2,000.	—	—	—	—

505-38 ISSUE OF 1888

DESIGNS AND COLOURS

505-38-02

$5 Face Design: W.J. Buchanan/Britannia, lion and ornate V/Donald Smith
Colour: Black with green tint

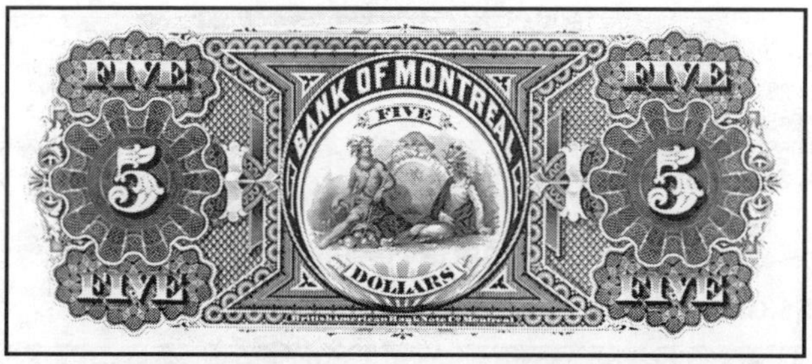

Back Design: Lathework, counters, bank name and crest
Colour: Green

505-38-04

$10 Face Design: Geo. Drummond/cherubs and ornate X/Donald Smith
Colour: Black with green tint

Back Design: Lathework, counters, bank name and crest
Colour: Green

IMPRINT

British American Bank Note Co. Montreal

SIGNATURES

left	right
mss. various	engr. Donald Smith

ISSUE DATING

Engraved

Jany. 2nd 1888

Cat. No.	Denom.	Date	G	VG	F	VF	EF	AU
38-02	$5	1888	600.	1,200.	1,700.	—	—	—
38-04	$10	1888	900.	1,800.	2,250.	—	—	—

505-40 **ISSUE OF 1891**

DESIGNS AND COLOURS

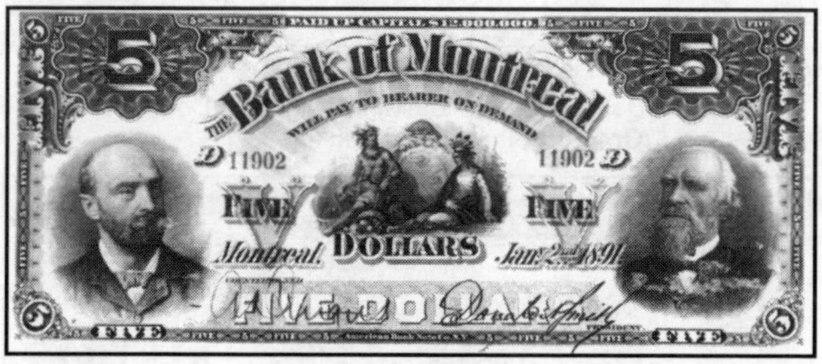

505-40-02

$5 Face Design: Edw. Clouston/Bank Crest/Donald Smith
Colour: Black with green tint

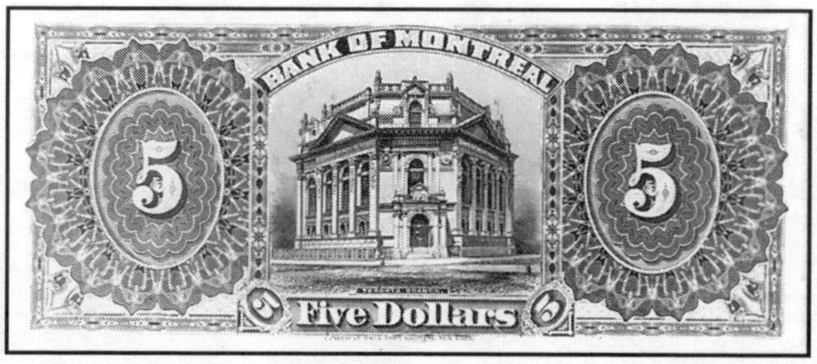

Back Design: Lathework, counters, bank name and Toronto branch building
Colour: Green

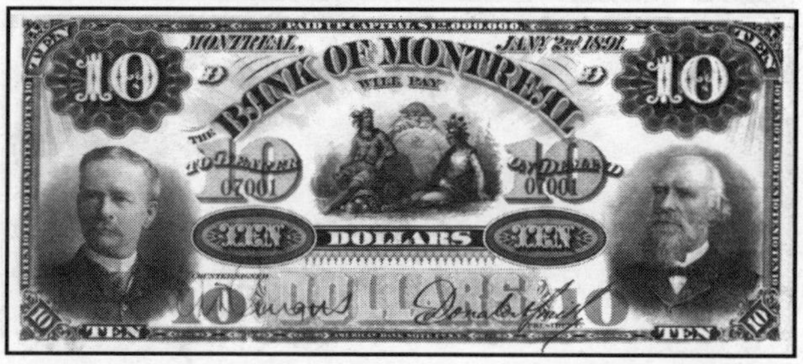

505-40-04

$10 Face Design: Geo. Drummond/Bank Crest/Donald Smith
Colour: Black with green tint

Back Design: Lathework, counters, bank name and head office
Colour: Green

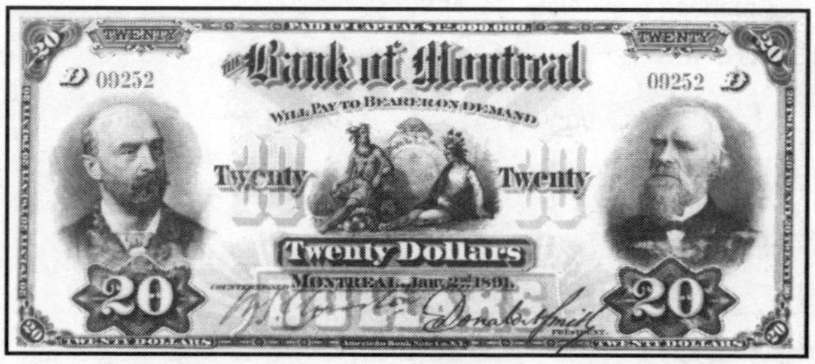

505-40-06

$20 Face Design: Edw. Clouston/Bank Crest/Donald Smith
Colour: Black with green tint

Back Design: Lathework, counters, bank name and head office
Colour: Green

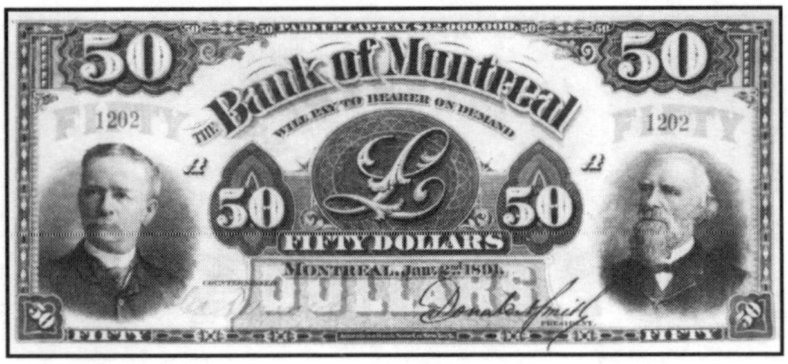

505-40-08
$50 Face Design: Geo. Drummond/—/Donald Smith
Colour: Black with green tint

Back Design: Lathework, counters, bank name and head office
Colour: Green

IMPRINT

American Bank Note Co. N.Y.

SIGNATURES

left	right
mss. various	engr. Donald Smith

ISSUE DATING

Engraved

Jany. 2nd 1891

CIRCULATING NOTES

Cat. No.	Denom.	Date	G	VG	F	VF	EF	AU
40-02	$5	1891	600.	1,200.	1,800.	2,400.	—	—
40-04	$10	1891	750.	1,500.	2,100.	2,700.	—	—
40-06	$20	1891	750.	1,500.	2,100.	2,700.	—	—
40-08	$50	1891	Institutional collection only					

PROOF NOTES

Cat. No.	Denom.	Date		Unc
40-02P	$5	1891	FACE PROOF	250.
40-04P	$10	1891	FACE PROOF	250.
40-06P	$20	1891	FACE PROOF	250.
40-08P	$50	1891	FACE PROOF	250.

Untinted (black and white) uncut sheets of the above proofs exist.

SPECIMEN NOTES

Cat. No.	Denom.	Date		Unc
40-02S	$5	1891	SPECIMEN	500.
40-04S	$10	1891	SPECIMEN	500.
40-06S	$20	1891	SPECIMEN	600.
40-08S	$50	1891	SPECIMEN	600.

505-42 ISSUE OF 1892

DESIGNS AND COLOURS

505-42-04
$50 Face Design: E.S. Clouston/Donald Smith/Bank Crest
Colour: Black with green tint

Back Design: Lathework, counters, bank name and head office
Colour: Green

505-42-08
$100 Face Design: E.S. Clouston/Bank Crest/Donald Smith
Colour: Black with green tint

Back Design: Lathework, counters, bank name and head office between ornate pillars
Colour: Green

IMPRINT
Canada Bank Note Co. Montreal

SIGNATURES

left	right
mss. various	engr. Donald Smith

ISSUE DATING
Engraved
Jan. 2nd, 1892

CIRCULATING NOTES

Cat. No.	Denom.	Date	G	VG	F	VF	EF	AU
42-04	$50	1892	Institutional collection only					
42-08	$100	1892	Institutional collection only					

PROOF NOTES

Cat. No.	Denom.	Date		Unc
42-04P	$50	1892	FACE PROOF	750.
42-08P	$100	1892	FACE PROOF	750.

Note: $100 proof notes exist with the face tint in gold and the back tint in red-brown.

505-44 ISSUE OF 1895

DESIGNS AND COLOURS

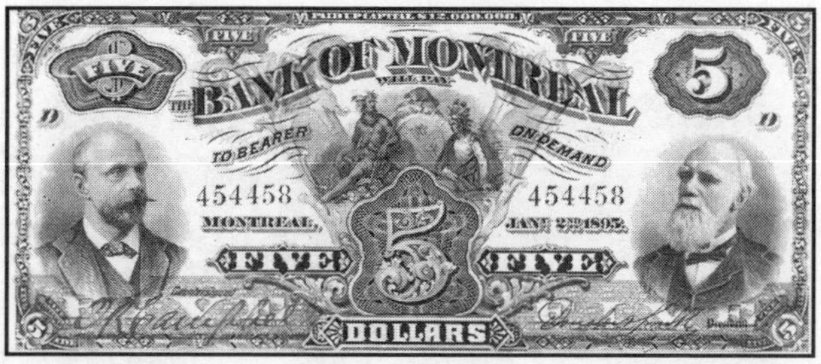

505-44-02
$5 Face Design: E.S. Clouston/counter and Bank Crest/ Donald Smith
Colour: Black with green tint

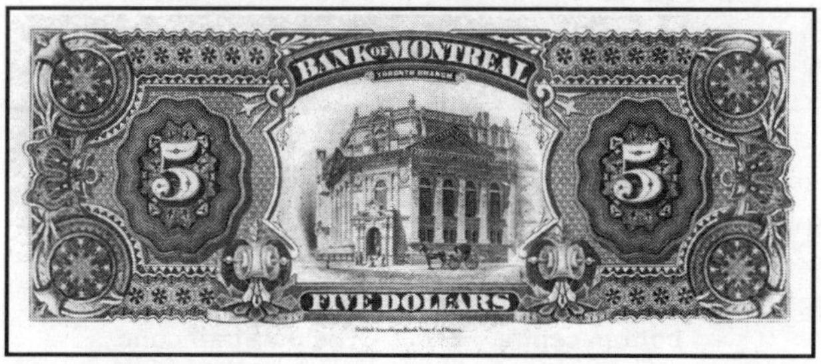

Back Design: Latheworks, counters, bank name and Toronto branch building
Colour: Green

505-44-04
$10 Face Design: Bank Crest and Donald Smith/—/George Drummond
Colour: Black with green tint

Back Design: Lathework, counters, bank name and head office
Colour: Green

505-44-06
$20 Face Design: Donald Smith/Bank Crest and ornate XX/ E.S. Clouston
Colour: Black with green tint

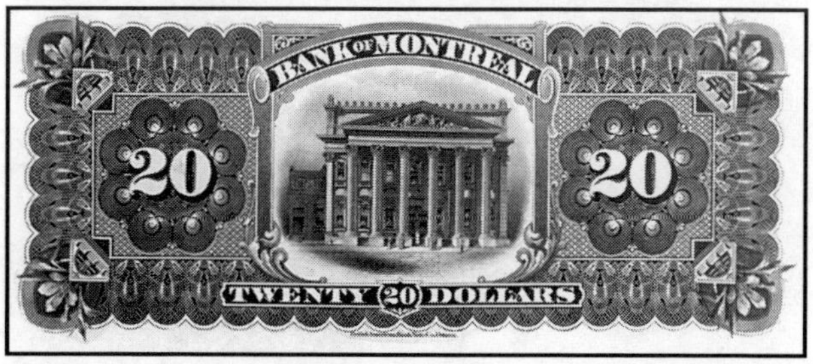

Back Design: Lathework, counters, bank name and head office
Colour: Green

IMPRINT
British American Bank Note Co. Ottawa

SIGNATURES

left	right
mss. various	engr. Donald Smith

ISSUE DATING
Engraved
Jan. 2nd 1895
Jany. 2nd 1895

Cat. No.	Denom.	Date	G	VG	F	VF	EF	AU
44-02	$5	1895	225.	450.	600.	900.	1,500.	2,000.
44-04	$10	1895	600.	1,200.	1,600.	2,400.	4,000.	—
44-06	$20	1895	750.	1,500.	2,100.	—	—	—

505-46 "DOUBLE-SIZE" NOTE (19.5 CM. X 16.5 CM.), ISSUE OF 1903

DESIGNS AND COLOURS

505-46-02
$50 Face Design: Donald Smith/Bank Crest/Geo. Drummond
Colour: Black with orange and green tint

Back Design: Head office/—/Toronto branch
Colour: Black with green

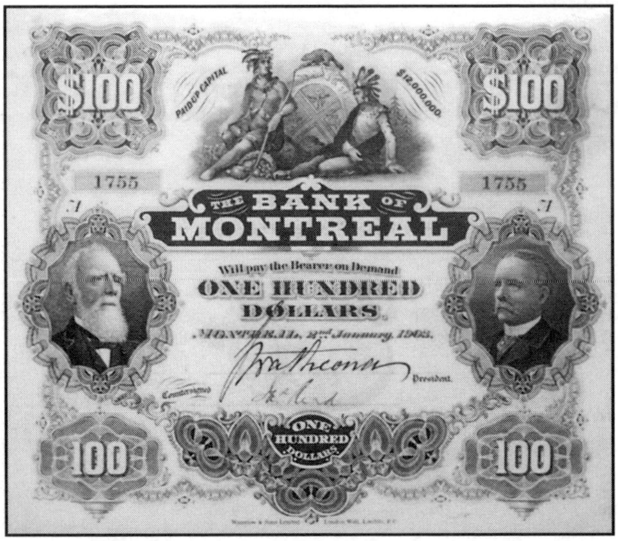

505-46-04
$100 Face Design: Donald Smith/Bank Crest/Geo. Drummond
Colour: Black with gold and rose tint

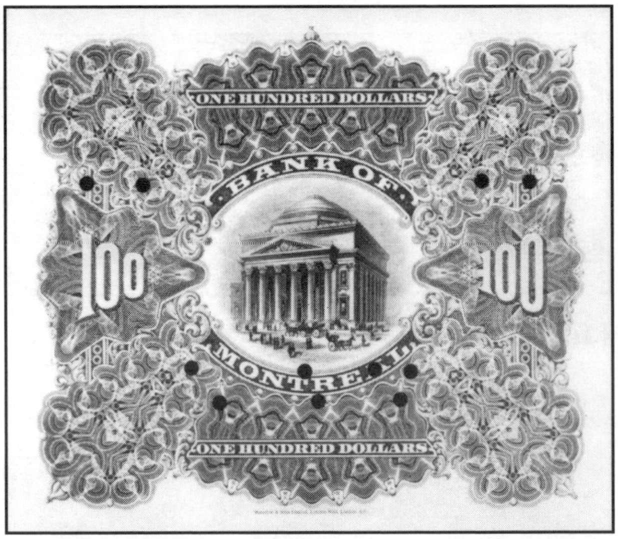

Back Design: —/head office/—
Colour: Black and green

IMPRINT
Waterlow & Sons, Ld. London Wall, London

SIGNATURES

bottom centre	below strathcona
engr. (Donald Smith) Lord Strathcona	mss. various

ISSUE DATING
Engraved
2nd, January, 1903

CIRCULATING NOTES

Cat. No.	Denom.	Date	G	VG	F	VF	EF	AU
46-02	$50	1903	—	7,000.	10,000.	15,000.	—	—
46-04	$100	1903	—	7,500.	10,500.	16,000.	—	—

SPECIMEN NOTES

Cat. No.	Denom.	Date	Unc
46-02S	$50	1903	SPECIMEN 5,000.
46-04S	$100	1903	SPECIMEN 6,000.

505-48 ISSUE OF 1904

DESIGNS AND COLOURS

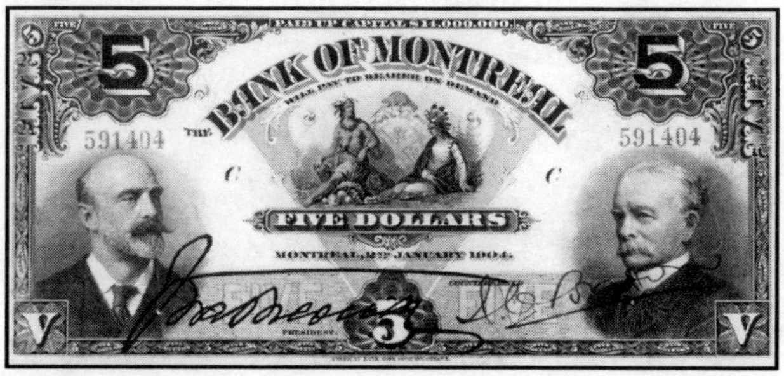

505-48-02

$5 Face Design: E.S. Clouston/Bank Crest/Geo. Drummond
Colour: Black with olive green tint

Back Design: Lathework, counters, bank name and head office
Colour: Green

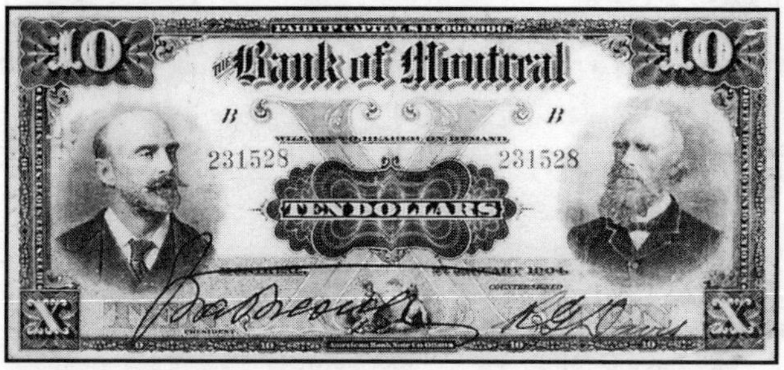

505-48-04

$10 Face Design: E.S. Clouston/Bank Crest/Donald Smith
Colour: Black with olive green tint

Back Design: Lathework, counters, bank name and Toronto branch
Colour: Green

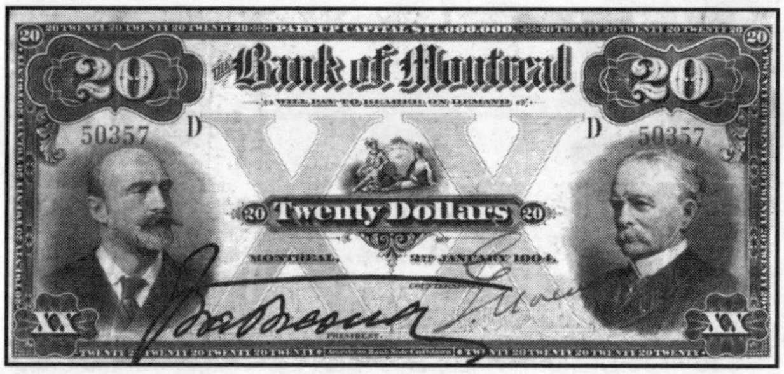

505-48-06

$20 Face Design: E.S. Clouston/Bank Crest/Geo. Drummond
Colour: Black with olive green tint

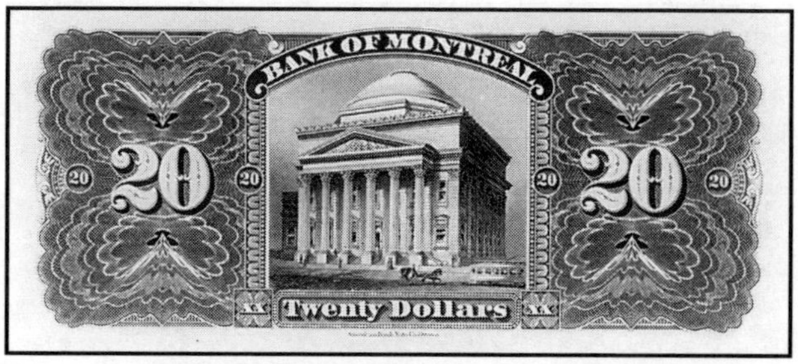

Back Design: Lathework, counters, bank name and head office
Colour: Green

IMPRINT

American Bank Note Company, Ottawa

SIGNATURES

left	right
typed Donald Smith (as Lord Strathcona)	mss. various

ISSUE DATING

Engraved

2d January 1904
2nd January 1904

CIRCULATING NOTES

Cat. No.	Denom.	Date	G	VG	F	VF	EF	AU
48-02	$5	1904	60.	120.	200.	300.	500.	800.
48-04	$10	1904	75.	150.	250.	375.	600.	—
48-06	$20	1904	150.	300.	450.	700.	1,100.	1,700.

PROOF NOTES

Cat. No.	Denom.	Date		Unc
48-02P	$5	1904	FACE PROOF	250.
48-04P	$10	1904	FACE PROOF	250.
48-06P	$20	1904	FACE PROOF	300.

SPECIMEN NOTES

Cat. No.	Denom.	Date		Unc
48-02S	$5	1904	SPECIMEN	600.
48-04S	$10	1904	SPECIMEN	600.
48-06S	$20	1904	SPECIMEN	700.

505-50 ISSUE OF 1911

DESIGNS AND COLOURS

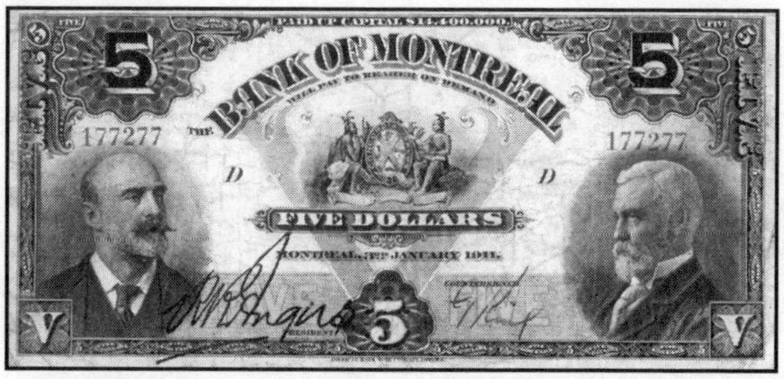

505-50-02

$5 Face Design: E.S. Clouston/Bank Crest/R.B. Angus
Colour: Black with olive green tint

Back Design: Lathework, counters, bank name and head office
Colour: Olive green

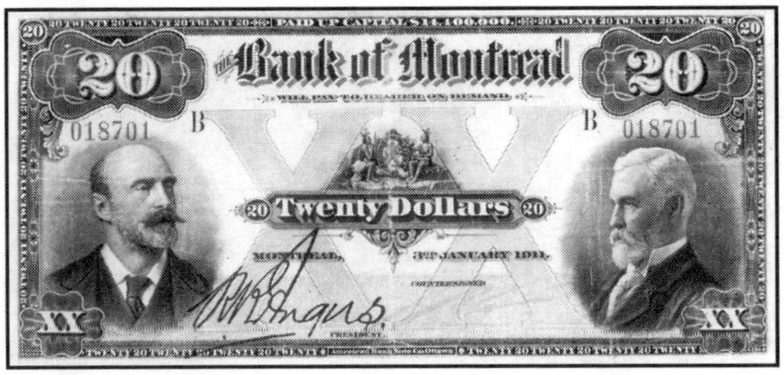

505-50-04

$20 Face Design: E.S. Clouston/Bank Crest/R.B. Angus
Colour: Black with olive green tint

Back Design: Lathework, counters, bank name and head office
Colour: Olive green

IMPRINT

American Bank Note Company. Ottawa

SIGNATURES

left	**right**
typed R.B. Angus	mss. various

ISSUE DATING

Engraved

3rd January 1911

CIRCULATING NOTES

Cat. No.	Denom.	Date	G	VG	F	VF	EF	AU
50-02	$5	1911	200.	400.	550.	800.	1,400.	—
50-04	$20	1911	375.	750.	1,000.	—	—	—

PROOF NOTES

Cat. No.	Denom.	Date	Variety		Unc
50-01P	$5	1911	2nd January	FACE PROOF	300.
50-02P	$5	1911	3rd January	FACE PROOF	300.
50-03P	$20	1911	2nd January	FACE PROOF	400.
50-04P	$20	1911	3rd January	FACE PROOF	400.

SPECIMEN NOTES

Cat. No.	Denom.	Date		Unc
50-02S	$5	1911	SPECIMEN	600.
50-04S	$20	1911	SPECIMEN	600.

505-52 ISSUE OF 1912

DESIGNS AND COLOURS

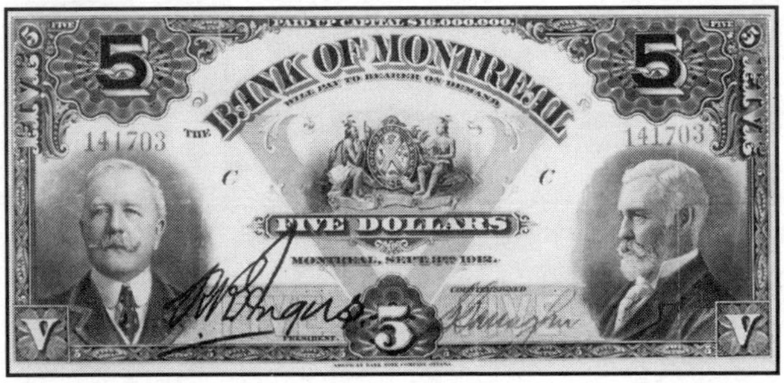

505-52-02

$5 Face Design: Vincent Meredith/Bank Crest/R.B. Angus
Colour: Black with olive green tint

Back Design: Lathework, counters, bank name and head office
Colour: Green

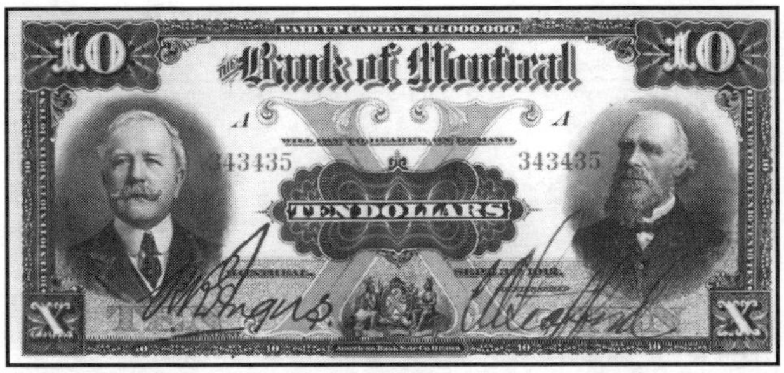

505-52-04

$10 Face Design: Vincent Meredith/Bank Crest/Donald Smith
Colour: Black with olive green tint

Back Design: Lathework, counters, bank name and Toronto branch
Colour: Green

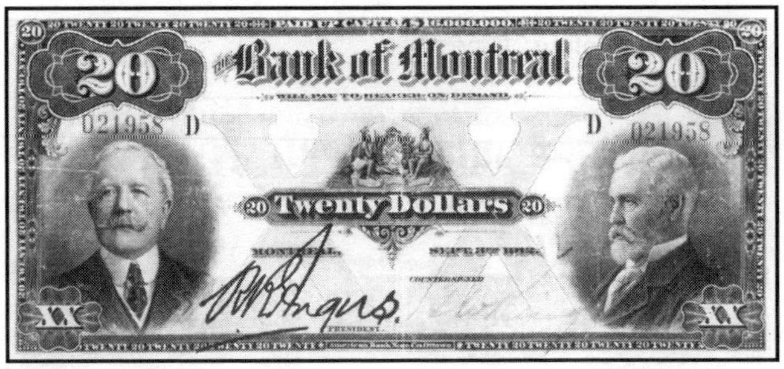

505-52-06

$20 Face Design: Vincent Meredity/Bank Crest/R.B. Angus
Colour: Black with olive green tint

Back Design: Lathework, counters, bank name and head office
Colour: Green

505-52-08

$50 Face Design: Vincent Meredith/Bank Crest/Donald Smith
Colour: Black with olive green tint

Back Design: Lathework, counters, bank name and bank building (Toronto branch)
Colour: Green

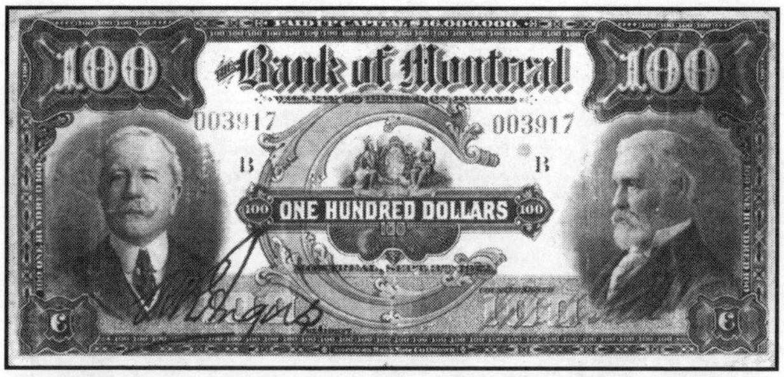

505-52-10

$100 Face Design: Vincent Meredith/Bank Crest/R.B. Angus
Colour: Black with olive green tint

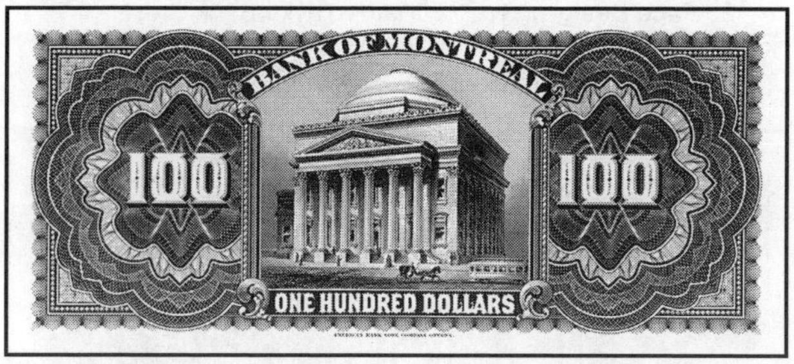

Back Design: Lathework, counters, bank name and head office
Colour: Green

IMPRINT

American Bank Note Company, Ottawa.

SIGNATURES

left	**right**
typed R.B. Angus	mss. various

ISSUE DATING

Engraved

Sept. 3rd 1912

CIRCULATING NOTES

Cat. No.	Denom.	Date	G	VG	F	VF	EF	AU
52-02	$5	1912	125.	250.	350.	500.	800.	—
52-04	$10	1912	200.	400.	550.	800.	—	—
52-06	$20	1912	200.	400.	550.	800.	—	—
52-08	$50	1912		Institutional collection only				
52-10	$100	1912		Institutional collection only				

PROOF NOTES

Cat. No.	Denom.	Date	Variety		Unc
52-01P	$5	1912	2nd January	FACE PROOF	400.
52-02P	$5	1912	Sept. 3rd	FACE PROOF	300.
52-04P	$10	1912		FACE PROOF	300.
52-06P	$20	1912		FACE PROOF	300.
52-08P	$50	1912		FACE PROOF	400.
52-10P	$100	1912		FACE PROOF	400.

Note: $5 back proofs in yellow-orange and yellow exist.

505-54 ISSUE OF 1914

DESIGNS AND COLOURS

505-54-04

$5 Face Design: Sir Frederick Williams-Taylor/ Bank Crest in large V/Vincent Meredith
Colour: Black with olive green tint

Back Design: Lathework, counters, bank name and head office
Colour: Green

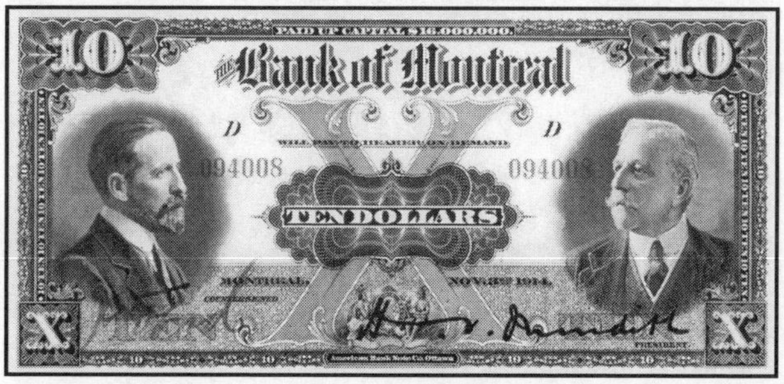

505-54-06

$10 Face Design: Sir Frederick Williams-Taylor/ Bank Crest under large X/Vincent Meredith
Colour: Black with olive green tint

Back Design: Lathework, counters, bank name and Toronto branch
Colour: Green

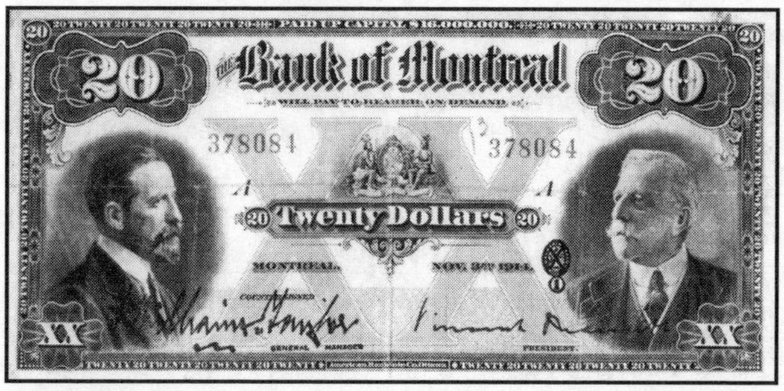

505-54-12

$20 Face Design: Sir Frederick Williams-Taylor/Bank Crest between large XX/Vincent Meredith
Colour: Black with olive green tint

Back Design: Lathework, counters, bank name and head office
Colour: Green

505-54-16

$50 Face Design: Sir Frederick Williams-Taylor/ Bank Crest under large L/Vincent Meredith
Colour: Black with olive green tint

Back Design: Lathework, counters, bank name and Toronto branch
Colour: Green

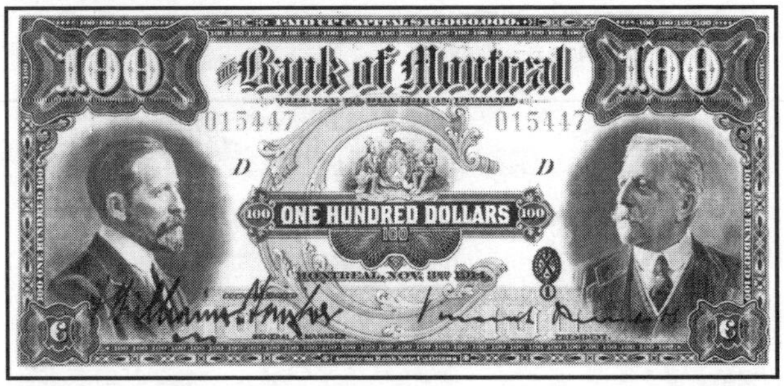

505-54-20

$100 Face Design: Sir Frederick Williams-Taylor/ Bank Crest inside large C/Vincent Meredith
Colour: Black with olive green tint

Back Design: Lathework, counters, bank name and head office
Colour: Green

IMPRINT

American Bank Note Company, Ottawa
American Bank Note Co. Ottawa

SIGNATURES

left	right
mss. various	typed H.V. Meredith
typed F. Williams-Taylor	typed Vincent Meredith

ISSUE DATING

Engraved

Nov. 3rd 1914

Cat. No.	Denom.	Date	Variety	G	VG	F	VF	EF	AU
54-02	$5	1914	Mss. sig., l.	20.	40.	55.	100.	170.	375.
54-04	$5	1914	Typed sig., l.	15.	35.	50.	90.	160.	350.
54-06	$10	1914	Mss. sig., l.	20.	45.	60.	110.	180.	425.
54-08	$10	1914	Typed sig., l.	20.	40.	55.	100.	170.	400.
54-10	$20	1914	Mss. sig., l.	55.	110.	150.	215.	425.	635.
54-12	$20	1914	Typed sig., l.	50.	100.	140.	200.	400.	600.
54-14	$50	1914	Mss. sig., l.	185.	370.	525.	825.	—	—
54-16	$50	1914	Typed sig., l.	175.	350.	500.	800.	1,150.	—
54-18	$100	1914	Mss. sig., l.	210.	420.	700.	1,000.	—	—
54-20	$100	1914	Typed sig., l.	200.	400.	675.	950.	1,400.	—

505-56 ISSUE OF 1923

DESIGNS AND COLOURS

This issue is similar to that of 1914.

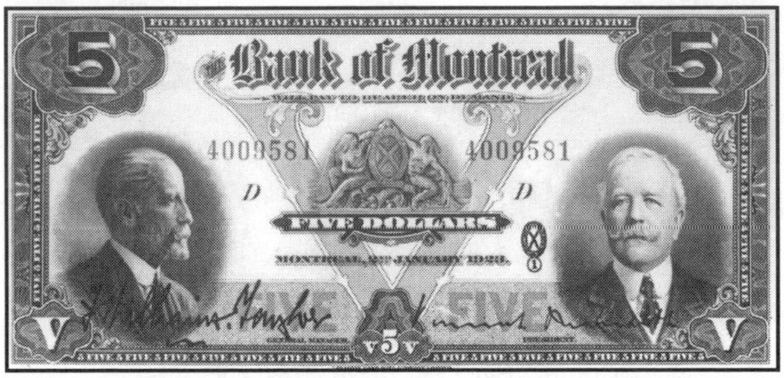

505-56-02

$5 Face Design: Sir F. Williams-Taylor/Bank Crest, in large V/Vincent Meredith
Colour: Black with olive green tint

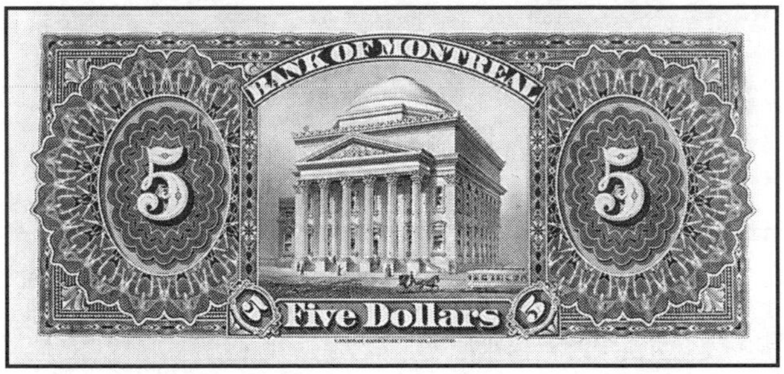

Back Design: Lathework, counters, bank name and head office
Colour: Green

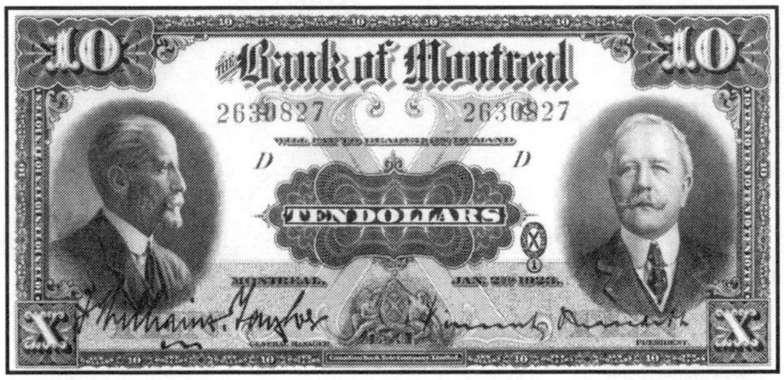

505-56-04

$10 Face Design: Sir F. Williams-Taylor/Bank Crest under large X/Vincent Meredith
Colour: Black with olive green tint

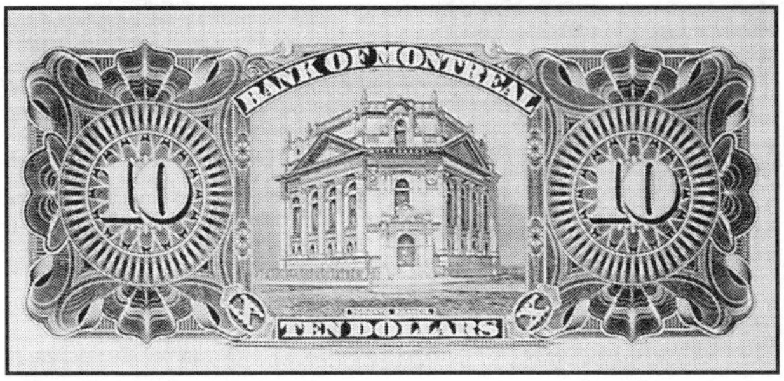

Back Design: Lathework, counters, bank name, and Toronto branch
Colour: Green

505-56-06

$20 Face Design: Sir F. Williams-Taylor/Bank Crest between large XX/Vincent Meredith
Colour: Black with olive green tint

Back Design: Lathework, counters, bank name and head office
Colour: Green

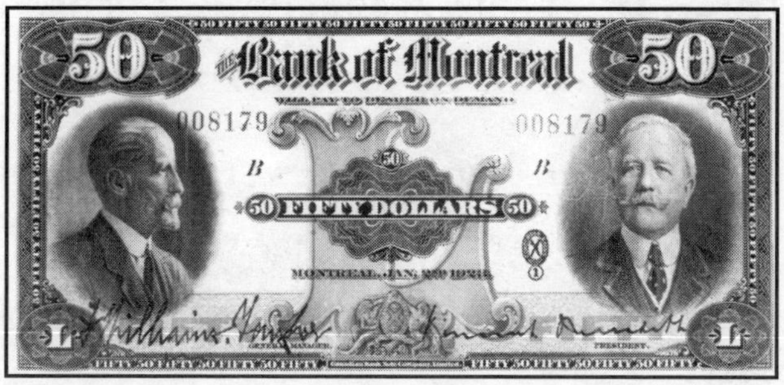

505-56-08

$50 Face Design: Sir F. Williams-Taylor/Bank Crest under large L/Vincent Meredith
Colour: Black with olive green tint

Back Design: Lathework, counters, bank name and Toronto branch
Colour: Green

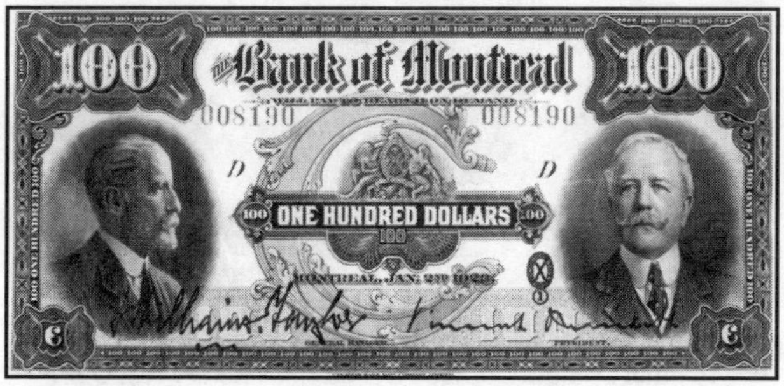

505-56-10

$100 Face Design: Sir F. Williams-Taylor/Bank Crest inside large C/Vincent Meredith
Colour: Black with olive green tint

Back Design: Lathework, counters, bank name and head office
Colour: Green

IMPRINT

Canadian Bank Note Company, Limited

SIGNATURES

left	right
typed R. Williams-Taylor	typed Vincent Meredith

ISSUE DATING

Engraved

2nd January 1923
Jan. 2nd 1923

Cat. No.	Denom.	Date	VG	F	VF	EF	AU	Unc
56-02	$5	1923	35.	45.	70.	150.	225.	300.
56-04	$10	1923	45.	60.	80.	175.	250.	350.
56-06	$20	1923	60.	75.	110.	250.	375.	500.
56-08	$50	1923	275.	400.	700.	1,100.	—	—
56-10	$100	1923	400.	600.	875.	1,200.	1,600.	—

505-58 ISSUE OF 1931

DESIGNS AND COLOURS

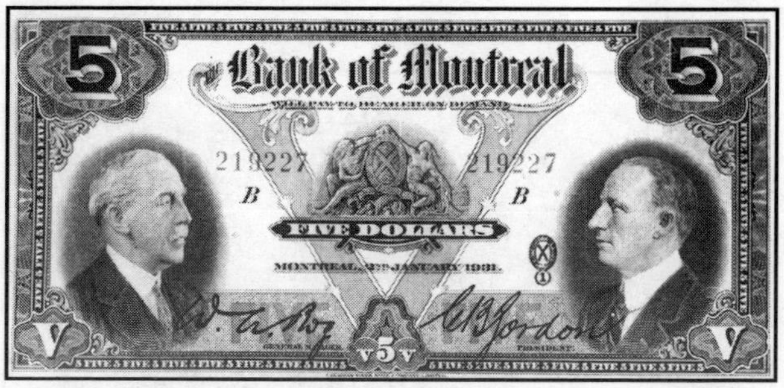

505-58-02

$5 Face Design: W.A. Bog/Bank Crest in large V/C.B. Gordon
Colour: Black with olive green tint

Back Design: —/head office/—
Colour: Green

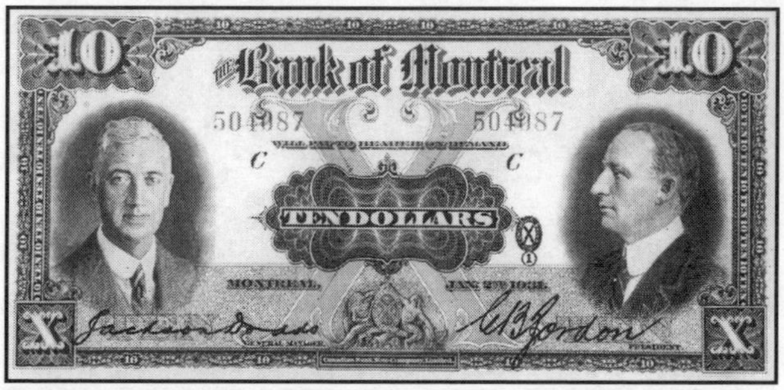

505-58-04

$10 Face Design: Jackson Dodds/Bank Crest under large X/ C.B. Gordon
Colour: Black with olive green tint

Back Design: —/Toronto branch/—
Colour: Green

505-58-06

$20 Face Design: Jackson Dodds/small Bank Crest/C.B. Gordon
Colour: Black with olive green tint

Back Design: —/head office/—
Colour: Green

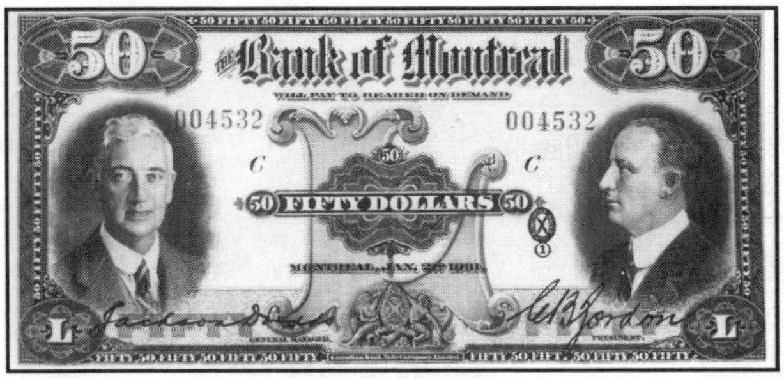

505-58-08

$50 Face Design: Jackson Dodds/small Bank Crest/C.B. Gordon
Colour: Black with olive green tint

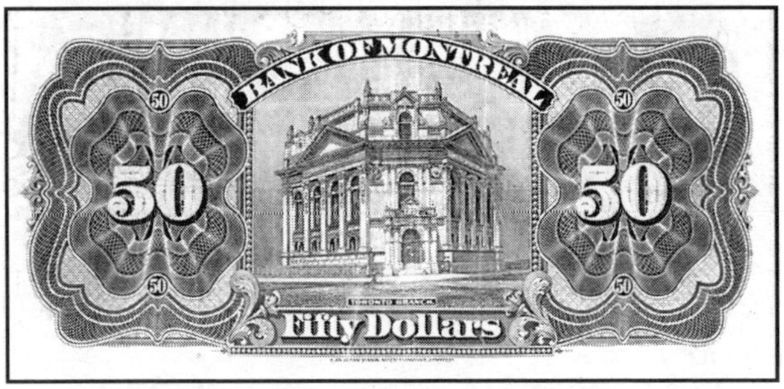

Back Design: Lathework, counters, bank name and Toronto branch
Colour: Green

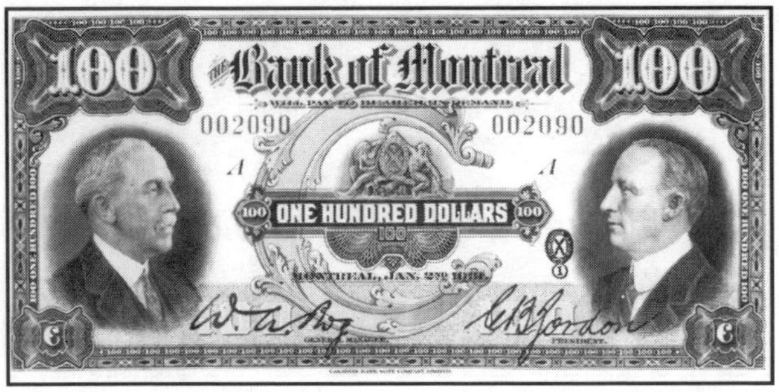

505-58-10

$100 Face Design: W.A. Bog/small Bank Crest/C.B. Gordon
Colour: Black with olive green tint

Back Design: Lathework, counters, bank name and head office
Colour: Green

IMPRINT

Canadian Bank Note Company, Limited

SIGNATURES

left	right
typed W.A. Bog	typed C.B. Gordon
typed Jackson Dodds	typed C.B. Gordon

ISSUE DATING

Engraved

2nd January 1931
Jan. 2nd 1931

CIRCULATING NOTES

Cat. No.	Denom.	Date		VG	F	VF	EF	AU	Unc
58-02	$5	1931		30.	40.	65.	125.	210.	300.
58-02a	$5	1931	prefix "S"	Rare. Market value not yet established					
58-04	$10	1931		30.	40.	65.	125.	185.	250.
58-06	$20	1931		350.	550.	800.	1,200.	—	—
58-08	$50	1931		175.	250.	375.	600.	950.	1,300.
58-10	$100	1931		215.	300.	450.	750.	1,125.	1,500.

Note: The $5 of this issue with prefix S preceeding a seven-digit sheet number has only recently been discovered. At the time of writing, a single example is known (Fine Condition). It obviously represents a special issue, but no further information concerning this note, or the reason for its issue, is currently available.

505-60 FIRST SMALL-SIZE NOTE, ISSUE 1935

DESIGNS AND COLOURS

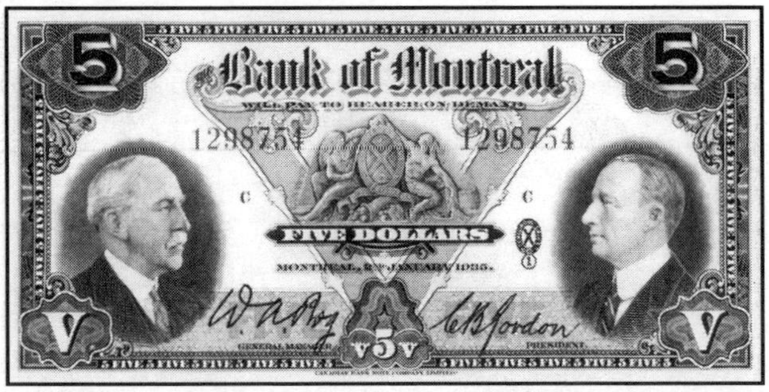

505-60-02

$5 Face Design: W.A. Bog/Bank Crest/C.B. Gordon
Colour: Black with olive green tint

Back Design: Lathework, counters, bank name and head office
Colour: Green

505-60-04

$10 Face Design: Jackson Dodds/small Bank Crest/C.B. Gordon
Colour: Black with olive green tint

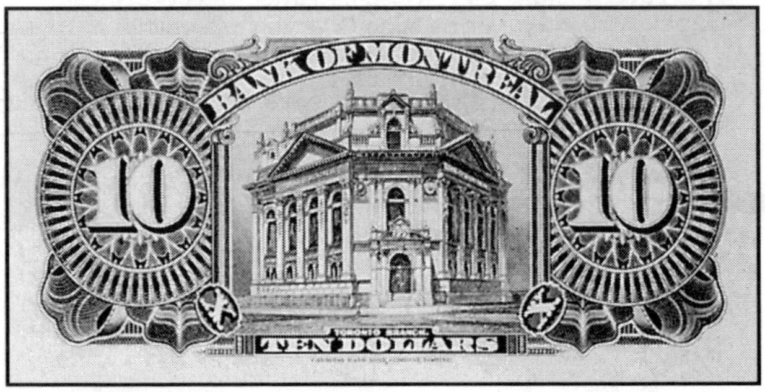

Back Design: Lathework, counters, bank name and Toronto branch
Colour: Green

505-60-06

$20 Face Design: Jackson Dodds/Bank Crest/C.B. Gordon
Colour: Black with olive green tint

Back Design: Lathework, counters, bank name and head office
Colour: Green

IMPRINT

Canadian Bank Note Company

SIGNATURES

left	right
typed W.A. Bog	typed C.B. Gordon
typed Jackson Dodds	typed C.B. Gordon

ISSUE DATING

Engraved

2nd Jan. 1935
2nd January 1935

Cat. No.	Denom.	Date	VG	F	VF	EF	AU	Unc
60-02	$5	1935	40.	60.	95.	190.	270.	350.
60-04	$10	1935	35.	55.	85.	180.	240.	300.
60-06	$20	1935	40.	60.	95.	200.	280.	375.

505-62 ISSUE OF 1938

DESIGNS AND COLOURS

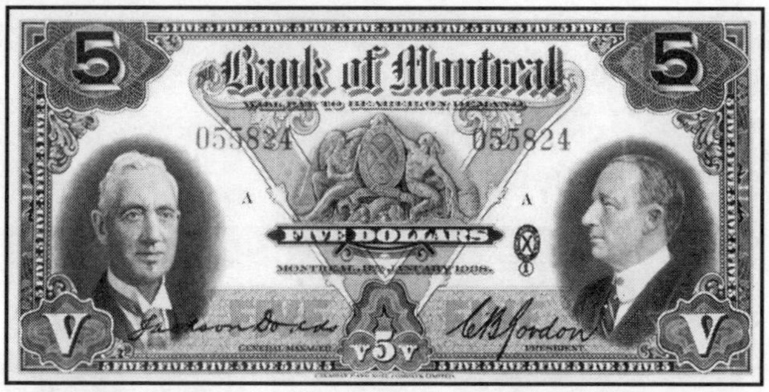

505-62-02

$5 Face Design: Jackson Dodds/Bank Crest/C.B. Gordon
Colour: Black with olive green tint
Back Design: Lathework, counters, bank name and head office
Colour: Green

505-62-04

$10 Face Design: G.W. Spinney/small Bank Crest/C.B. Gordon
Colour: Black with olive green tint

Back Design: Lathework, counters, bank name and Toronto branch
Colour: Green

505-62-06

$20 Face Design: G.W. Spinney/Bank Crest/C.B. Gordon
Colour: Black with olive green tint

Back Design: Lathework, counters, bank name and head office
Colour: Green

IMPRINT

Canadian Bank Company Limited

SIGNATURES

left	right
typed Jackson Dodds	typed C.B. Gordon
typed G.W. Spinney	typed C.B. Gordon

ISSUE DATING

Engraved

3rd January 1938
3rd Jan. 1938

Cat. No.	Denom.	Date	VG	F	VF	EF	AU	Unc
62-02	$5	1938	35.	55.	85.	175.	230.	300.
62-04	$10	1938	35.	55.	85.	175.	230.	300.
62-06	$20	1938	40.	60.	95.	180.	230.	300.

505-64 **ISSUE OF 1942**

DESIGNS AND COLOURS

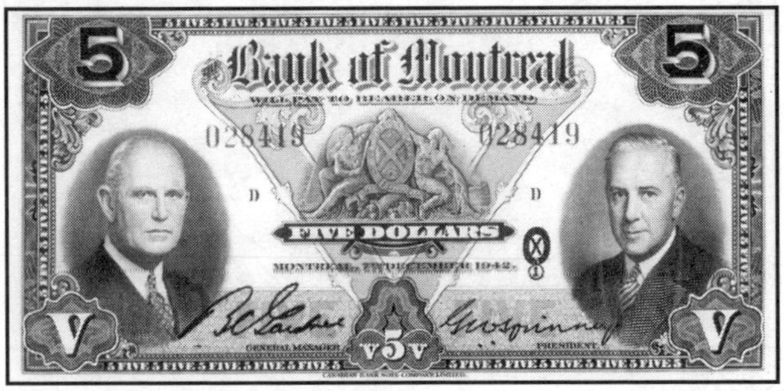

505-64-02

$5 Face Design: B.C. Gardner/Bank Crest/G.W. Spinney
Colour: Black with olive green tint

Back Design: Lathework, counters, bank name and head office
Colour: Green

IMPRINT

Canadian Bank Note Company, Limited

SIGNATURES

left	**right**
typed B.C. Gardner	typed G.W. Spinney

ISSUE DATING

Engraved

7th December 1942

Cat. No.	Denom.	Date	VG	F	VF	EF	AU	Unc
64-02	$5	1942	70.	100.	150.	315.	425.	550.

LA BANQUE NATIONALE

1860-1925

QUEBEC CITY, QUEBEC

BANK NUMBER 510 ***REDEEMABLE***

La Banque Nationale was founded in 1860 with 1,456 shareholders, all with the double liability on the existing 30,000 shares. After World War I, the bank appeared to be failing, despite the fact that it had 230,000 customers, $6 million in circulating notes and over $40 million in deposits. Rather than declaring bankruptcy, an attempt was made to merge La Banque Nationale, La Banque d'Hochelaga and the Provincial Bank. The Provincial Bank declined, the directors of the other two banks asked the premier of Quebec for assistance.

On January 31, 1924, the Legislative Council granted a $15-million provincial bond to assist the merger. It was sanctioned by the Lieutenant-Governor on February 15, 1924.

The merged banks were to be given 40 years to reimburse the bonds. La Banque d'Hochelaga was to assume the liabilities of La Banque Nationale, as well as its assets, and in February 1925 the two banks formally merged under the name La Banque Canadienne Nationale.

Despite the market crash and the depression of the 1930s, the new bank was able to reimburse the government in 20 years, half the time originally allotted.

510-10 **ISSUE OF 1860**

DESIGNS AND COLOURS

510-10-04-02

$1 Face Design: Habitant/Arms of Quebec City/ Jacques Cartier
Colour: Black with overall green tint

Back Design: Plain

510-10-04-08

$2 Face Design: Two allegorical women, "The Reapers"/ Arms of Quebec City/ bust of Jacques Cartier in oval
Colour: Black with overall green tint

Back Design: Plain

510-10-04-10

$5 Face Design: Agricultural implements/two men ploughing/ young woman with cornucopia
Colour: Black with overall green tint

Back Design: Plain

510-10-04-12

$10 Face Design: St. John the Baptist/train/ Britannia, Arms of Upper Canada
Colour: Black with overall green tint

Back Design: Plain

IMPRINT

American Bank Note Company

SIGNATURES

left	**right**
mss. various	mss. various

2. PARTIALLY ENGRAVED DATE, MSS. SHEET NUMBERS

ISSUE DATING

Partially engraved ___ 18___:

28 Avril 1860

Notes of this group are quite rare. Those in private collections are mostly, if not all, cancelled. Values given below are for cancelled notes.

Cat. No.	Denom.	Date	G	VG	F	VF	EF	AU
10-02-02	$1	1860	400.	800.	1,000.	1,400.	2,200.	—
10-02-04	$2	1860	400.	800.	1,000.	1,400.	—	—
10-02-06	$5	1860	Institutional collection only					
10-02-08	$10	1860	Institutional collection only					

4. ENGRAVED DATE, PRINTED SHEET NUMBERS

ISSUE DATING

Engraved

28 Avril 1860
25 Mai 1860

OVERPRINT

$10: "G G" twice at ends and "OTTAWA" twice vertically in red
$1: Red A at top right

Note: The majority of surviving notes of this issue have a large X pen cancellation, or punch cancellation, or both.

Cat. No.	Den.	Date	Variety	G	VG	F	VF	EF	AU
10-04-02	$1	1860	Avril, uncancelled	400.	800.	1,000.	—	—	—
10-04-02	$1	1860	Avril, cancelled	300.	600.	800.	—	—	—
10-04-04	$1	1860	Mai, uncancelled	300.	600.	800.	—	—	—
10-04-04	$1	1860	Mai, cancelled	200.	400.	500.	750.	—	—
10-04-06	$2	1860	Avril, uncancelled	550.	1,100.	1,400.	—	—	—
10-04-06	$2	1860	Avril, cancelled	450.	900.	1,100.	—	—	—
10-04-08	$2	1860	Mai, uncancelled	475.	950.	1,200.	—	—	—
10-04-08	$2	1860	Mai, cancelled	350.	700.	900.	1,350.	—	—
10-04-10	$5	1860	Avril, uncancelled	550.	1,100.	—	—	—	—
10-04-10	$5	1860	Avril, cancelled	400.	800.	1,000.	—	—	—
10-04-12	$10	1860	Avril, uncancelled	Institutional collection only					
10-04-12	$10	1860	Avril, cancelled	500.	1,000.	1,250.	—	—	—

510-12 ISSUES OF 1870 AND 1871

DESIGNS AND COLOURS

510-12-02

$4 Face Design: Beehive and flowers/ paddlewheel steamer "Quebec"/ sailor leaning on sail, "Charlies Sailor"
Colour: Black with green tint

Back Design: Plain

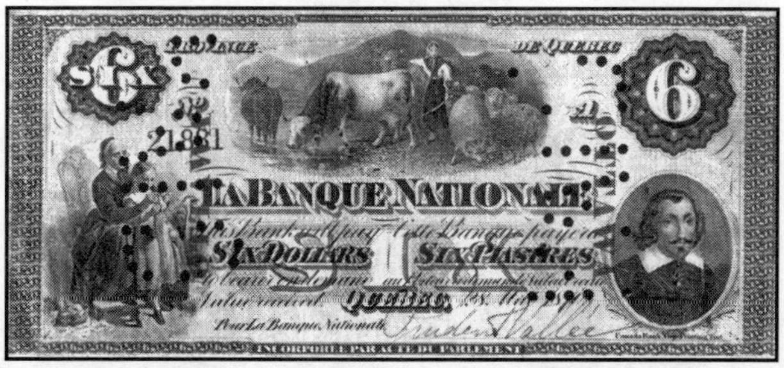

510-12-06a

$6 Face Design: Woman teaching granddaughter to knit "The first lesson"/ girl watering livestock "Vogts cattle"/ Samuel de Champlain
Colour: Black with green tint

Back Design: Plain

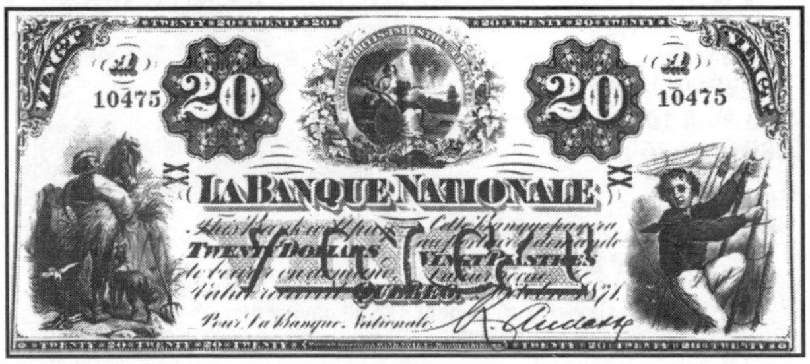

510-12-08

$20 Face Design: Farmer feeding horses "Old Burhans"/ Crest/boy climbing rigging "Going Aloft"
Colour: Black with green tint

Back Design: Lathework, counters and bank name
Colour: Green

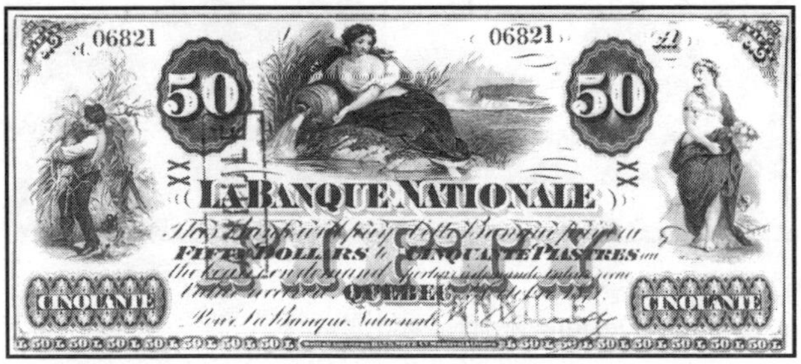

510-12-10

$50 Face Design: Farmer with cornstalks/reclining female with water jar, Niagara Falls "Power"/ "Agriculture" figure
Colour: Black with green tint

Back Design: Lathework, counters and bank name
Colour: Green

510-12-12

$100 Face Design: —/sailors looking to sea "Coast scene"/—
Colour: Black with green tint

Back Design: Lathework, counters and bank name
Colour: Green

IMPRINT

British American Bank Note Co. Montreal & Ottawa

SIGNATURES

	left	right
$4 and $6:	none	mss. various
$20, $50 and $100:	none	mss. R. Audette

ISSUE DATING

Engraved

28 Mai 1870
28 Mai 1871
2 Octobre 1871

OVERPRINT

$4 and $6: "SHERBROOKE" in red
"OTTAWA" in red
"M M" in black
"DD" in red

$20, $50 and $100: "XX XX" vertically in black

VARIETIES

$6 1870: Small green tint does not cover signature areas
Large green tint covers signature areas

Most $6 notes in private collections are overprinted, and are all pen and/or punch cancelled. $50 and $100 notes are punch cancelled or stamped, ANNULE.

CIRCULATING NOTES

Cat. No.	Den.	Date	Variety	G	VG	F	VF	EF	AU
12-02	$4	1870	uncancelled	350.	700.	1,000.	—	—	—
12-02	$4	1870	cancelled	250.	500.	750.	1,100.	1,600.	—
12-02a	$4	1870	town o/p	Institutional collection only					
12-04	$4	1871		No known issued notes					
12-06	$6	1870	small tint; no o/p	2,000.	4,000.	5,000.	6,000.	7,500.	—
12-06a	$6	1870	small tint; town o/p	2,000.	4,000.	5,000.	6,000.	7,500.	—
12-07	$6	1870	large tint; no o/p	2,000.	4,000.	5,000.	6,000.	7,500.	—
12-07a	$6	1870	large tint; town o/p	2,000.	4,000.	5,000.	6,000.	7,500.	—
12-08	$20	1871	uncancelled	—	—	1,750.	2,400.	3,500.	—
12-08a	$20	1871	cancelled	—	—	1,500.	2,000.	3,000.	—
12-10	$50	1871	cancelled	—	—	1,750.	2,400.	3,500.	4,500.
12-12	$100	1871	cancelled	—	—	2,000.	2,750.	3,750.	5,000.

PROOF NOTES

Cat. No.	Denom.	Date		Unc
12-04P	$4	1871	PROOF	400.

510-14 ISSUE OF 1873

DESIGNS AND COLOURS

510-14-02

$5 Face Design: Agricultural produce and implements/ shipbuilders at work "Ship Building"/ Britannia and 5 counter
Colour: Black with green tint

Back Design: Lathework, counters and bank name
Colour: Green

510-14-04P

$10 Face Design: St. John the Baptist/agricultural produce and implements/anchor
Colour: Black with green tint

Back Design: Lathework, counters and bank name
Colour: Green

IMPRINT

British American Bank Note Co. Montreal & Ottawa

SIGNATURES

left	**right**
none	mss. Ol. Robitaille

ISSUE DATING

Engraved

2 Janvier 1873

Notes of the 1873 issue are seldom offered. Those in private collections are generally well preserved but punch cencelled.

Cat. No.	Denom.	Date	Variety	G	VG	F	VF	EF	AU
14-02	$5	1873	cancelled	—	—	900.	1,400.	2,000.	3,000.
14-04	$10	1873	cancelled	—	—	900.	1,400.	2,000.	3,000.

510-16 ISSUE OF 1883

DESIGNS AND COLOURS

510-16-02

$5 Face Design: Samuel de Champlain/paddlewheel steamer "Quebec"/J.R. Thibaudeau
Colour: Black with green tint

Back Design: Lathework, counters and bank name
Colour: Green

510-16-04

$10 Face Design: Jacques Cartier/farmer ploughing/ J.R. Thibaudeau
Colour: Black with green tint

Back Design: Lathework, counters and bank name
Colour: Green

IMPRINT

British American Bank Note Co. Montreal

SIGNATURES

left	right
mss. various	engr. J. Thibaudeau

ISSUE DATING

Engraved

1er Mars 1883

OVERPRINT

"A D" twice in red

Notes of the 1883 issue are seldom offered. Most have the red "A D" overprint, and all known examples are punch cancelled.

CIRCULATING NOTES

Cat. No.	Denom.	Date	Variety	G	VG	F	VF	EF	AU
16-02	$5	1883	cancelled	—	—	900.	1,400.	2,000.	3,000.
16-04	$10	1883	cancelled	—	—	1,000.	1,550.	2,200.	3,300.

PROOF NOTES

Cat. No.	Denom.	Date	Variety		Unc
16-02P	$5	1883	B & W	FACE PROOF	500.

510-18 ISSUE OF 1891

DESIGNS AND COLOURS

510-18-02

$5 Face Design: Samuel de Champlain/train/A. Gaboury
Colour: Black with green tint

Back Design: Lathework, counters, bank name and the Arms of the City of Quebec
Colour: Green

510-18-04

$10 Face Design: Jacques Cartier/farmer ploughing/A. Gaboury
Colour: Black with green tint

Back Design: Lathework, counters, bank name and the Arms of the City of Quebec
Colour: Green

IMPRINT

British American Bank Note Co. Montreal

SIGNATURES

left	right
mss. various	engr. A. Gaboury

ISSUE DATING

Engraved

Le 2 Janvier 1891

OVERPRINT

"A D" twice in red
"R" twice in red
"P" twice in blue

Notes of the 1891 issue are seldom offered. Most have a letter overprint, and all known examples are punch cancelled.

Cat. No.	Denom.	Date	Variety	G	VG	F	VF	EF	AU
18-02	$5	1891	cancelled	—	750.	1,000.	1,600.	—	—
18-04	$10	1891	cancelled	—	750.	1,000.	1,600.	—	—

510-20 ISSUE OF 1897

DESIGNS AND COLOURS

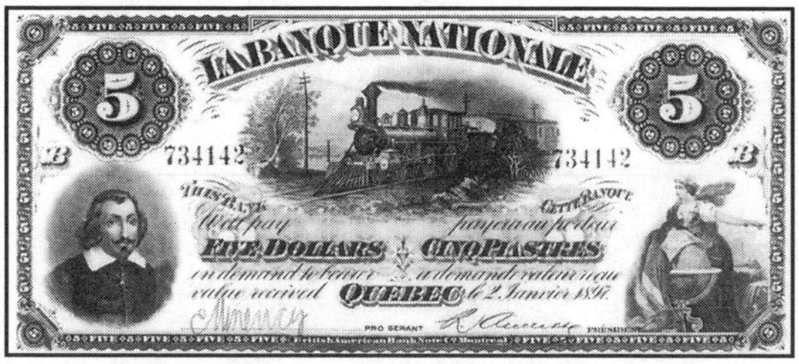

510-20-02

$5 Face Design: Samuel de Champlain/train/ Britannia standing by globe and flag
Colour: Black with orange tint (tends to oxidize to brown or yellow)

Back Design: Lathework, counters, bank name and the Arms of the City of Quebec
Colour: Green

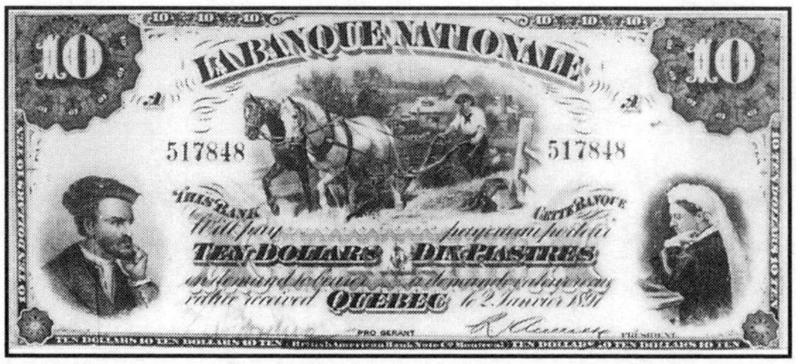

510-20-06

$10 Face Design: Jacques Cartier/farmer ploughing/ Queen Victoria in "widow's weeds"
Colour: Black with orange tint (tends to oxidize to brown or yellow)

Back Design: Lathework, counters, bank name and the Arms of the City of Quebec
Colour: Green

IMPRINT

British American Bank Note Co. Montreal

SIGNATURES

left	**right**
mss. various	engr. R. Audette

ISSUE DATING

Engraved

Le 2 Janvier 1897

VARIETIES

Both denominations were initally printed from rather poorly engraved plates and later from greatly improved plates. Apart from the obvious difference in the the quality of the engraving, there are numerous subtle differences.

The first plate lacks the acute accent over the first E of PRESIDENT at the lower-right signature space and has thin date figures. The second plate includes the accent in PRESIDENT and has thick date figures. The characteristic by which the varieties can be most easily identified is the presence of engraved lines below the sheet numbers on the poorly engraved plate and the absence of such lines on the well-engraved plate.

$5: lines under sheet numbers
$5: no lines under sheet numbers, accent over E
$10: lines under sheet numbers
$10: no lines under sheet numbers, accent over E

Note: Back proofs exist in green, as well as in brown tints.

CIRCULATING NOTES

Cat. No.	Denom.	Date	Variety	G	VG	F	VF	EF	AU
20-02	$5	1897	Lines	100.	200.	300.	500.	1,000.	—
20-02	$5	1897	cancelled	—	—	—	250.	500.	750.
20-04	$5	1897	No lines	85.	175.	250.	400.	800.	—
20-06	$10	1897	Lines	110.	225.	350.	600.	—	—
20-06	$10	1897	cancelled	—	—	—	250.	500.	750.
20-08	$10	1897	No lines	100.	200.	300.	500.	1,000.	—

PROOF NOTES

Cat. No.	Denom.	Date	Variety		Unc
20-04P	$5	1897	B & W	FACE PROOF	300.
20-08P	$10	1897	B & W	FACE PROOF	300.

510-22 **ISSUE OF 1922**

DESIGNS AND COLOURS

510-22-02

$5 Face Design: Monument/—/Geo. E. Amyot
Colour: Black with olive tint

Back Design: Lathework, counters, bank name and the Arms of the City of Quebec
Colour: Green

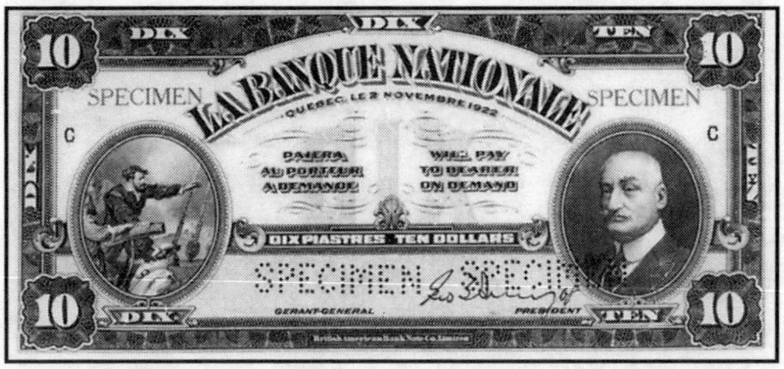

510-22-04S

$10 Face Design: Cartier sighting land/—/Geo. E. Amyot
Colour: Black with orange tint

Back Design: Lathework, counters, bank name and the Arms of the City of Quebec
Colour: Green

510-22-06S

$20 Face Design: "Quebec Citadel"/—/Geo. E. Amyot
Colour: Black with orange tint

Back Design: Lathework, counters, bank name and the Arms of the City of Quebec
Colour: Green

510-22-08S

$50 Face Design: —/Geo. E. Amyot/—
Colour: Black with brown tint

Back Design: Lathework, counters, bank name and the Arms of the City of Quebec
Colour: Green

510-22-10S

$100 Face Design: —/—/Geo. E. Amyot
Colour: Black with brown tint

Back Design: Lathework, counters, bank name and the Arms of the City of Quebec
Colour: Green

IMPRINT

British American Bank Note Co. Limited
British American Bank Note Co. Limited, Ottawa

SIGNATURES

left	right
typed H. des Rivieres	engr. Geo. E. Amyot

ISSUE DATING

Engraved

Le 2 Novembre 1922

CIRCULATING NOTES

Cat. No.	Denom.	Date	G	VG	F	VF	EF	AU
22-02	$5	1922	400.	800.	1,100.	1,600.	—	—
22-04	$10	1922	—	—	2,200.	—	—	—
22-06	$20	1922	600.	—	—	2,500.	—	—
22-08	$50	1922	No known issued notes					
22-10	$100	1922	No known issued notes					

SPECIMEN NOTES

Cat. No.	Denom.	Date		Unc
20-02S	$5	1922	SPECIMEN	200.
22-04S	$10	1922	SPECIMEN	200.
22-06S	$20	1922	SPECIMEN	250.
22-08S	$50	1922	SPECIMEN	250.
22-10S	$100	1922	SPECIMEN	300.

THE BANK OF NEW BRUNSWICK

1820-1913

SAINT JOHN, NEW BRUNSWICK

BANK NUMBER 515 ***REDEEMABLE***

The Bank of New Brunswick was established in 1820 in Saint John, New Brunswick. The first bank in Canada to operate under a charter, it started business with an initial capital of £50,000, and its charter was for 20 years. The bank's total liabilities were restricted to twice the paid-up capital, instead of three times, as in the other provinces.

The bank absorbed the City Bank, Saint John, in 1839 and the Summerside Bank in 1901, but remained a small institution. Its expansion was hindered by difficulties in raising more capital, and the directors offered to sell out to the Bank of Nova Scotia. This offer was accepted in 1913.

515-10 **PERKINS FAIRMAN HEATH**
1820-1832
POUNDS AND SHILLINGS PRINTINGS
LARGE SIZE NOTES
(10 CM. X 18.5 CM.)

DESIGNS AND COLOURS

Note: All the notes up to and including 1884 have two cherubs, a cask and a bale at the bottom.

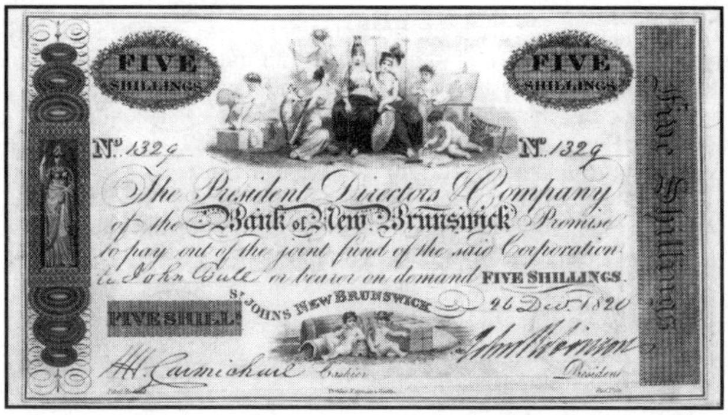

515-10-02

5s Face Design: Small Britannia in lathework/seated Brittania flanked by women and cherubs/—
Colour: Black with green tint

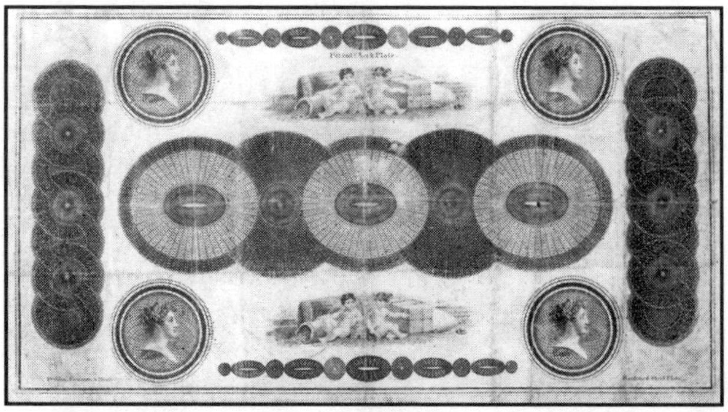

Back Design: Two women's heads on lathework circles/cherubs, cask and bale twice/two women's heads on lathework circles
Colour: Blue

515-10-14

£1 Face Design: Small Britannia in lathework/seated Brittania flanked by women and cherubs/—
Colour: Black with no tint
Back Design: Two women's heads on lathework circles/ cherubs, cask and bale twice/ two women's heads on lathework circles
Colour: Blue

515-10-24P

£2 Face Design: Small Britannia in lathework/seated Brittania flanked by women and cherubs, two cherubs, casks and bale below/—
Colour: Black with no tint
Back Design: Two women's heads on lathework circles/cherubs, cask and bale twice/two women's heads on lathework circles
Colour: Blue

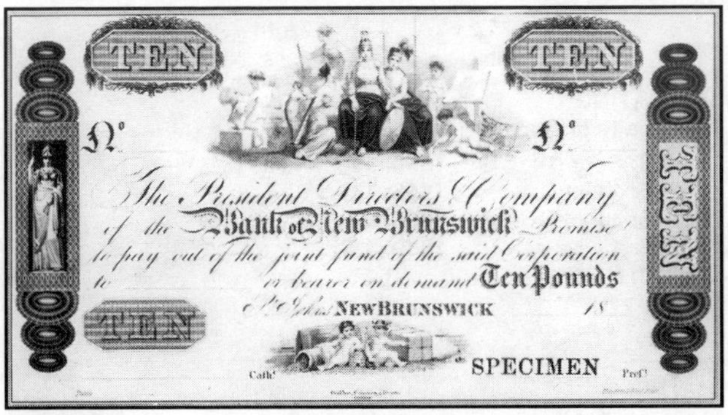

515-10-34P

£2 Face Design: Small Britannia in lathework/seated Brittania flanked by women and cherubs, two cherubs, casks and bale below/—
Colour: Black with no tint
Back Design: Two women's heads on lathework circles/ cherubs, cask and bale twice/ two women's heads on lathework circles
Colour: Blue

IMPRINT

Perkins, Fairman & Heath London

SIGNATURES

	left	right
1820:	mss. H.H. Carmichael	mss. John Robinson
1831:	mss. Z. Wheeler	mss. H. Gilbert

ISSUE DATING

Partially engraved ___ 18___:

1820: 26 Dec.
1831: 1 Jany.
1832: 1 Octr.

CIRCULATING NOTES

Cat. No.	Denom.	Date	G	VG	F	VF	EF	AU
10-02	5s	1820-1821	1,500.	2,500.	3,500.	—	—	—
10-14	£1	1831	1,500.	2,500.	3,500.	—	—	—
10-24	£2	1832	Institutional collection only					
10-28	£5	18__	No known issued notes					
10-34	£10	18__	No known issued notes					

PROOF NOTES

Cat. No.	Denom.	Date	Unc
10-28P	£5	18__	FACE PROOF 1,000.
10-34P	£10	18__	FACE PROOF 800.

515-12 NEBN CO. 1838 - 1859 POUNDS AND SHILLINGS PRINTINGS REGULAR-SIZE NOTES (7.2 CM. X 17 CM.)

DESIGNS AND COLOURS

515-12-12

5s Face Design: Small Britannia in lathework/seated Brittania flanked by women and cherubs, two cherubs, casks and bale below/—
Colour: Black with no tint
Back Design: Two women's heads on lathework circles/cherubs, cask and bale twice/two women's heads on lathework circles
Colour: Blue

515-12-22

£1 Face Design: Small Britannia in lathework/seated Brittania flanked by women and cherubs, two cherubs, casks and bale below/—
Colour: Black with no tint

Back Design: Two women's heads on lathework circles/cherubs, cask and bale twice/two women's heads on lathework circles
Colour: Blue

515-12-32P

£2 Face Design: Small Britannia in lathework/seated Brittania flanked by women and cherubs, two cherubs, casks and bale below/—
Colour: Black with no tint

Back Design: Two women's heads on lathework circles/cherubs, cask and bale twice/two women's heads on lathework circles
Colour: Blue

515-12-42P

£5 Face Design: Small Britannia in lathework/seated Brittania flanked by women and cherubs, two cherubs, casks and bale below/—
Colour: Black with no tint

Back Design: Two women's heads on lathework circles/cherubs, cask and bale twice/two women's heads on lathework circles
Colour: Blue

515-12-50P

£10 Face Design: Small Britannia in lathework/seated Brittania flanked by women and cherubs, two cherubs, casks and bale below/—
Colour: Black with no tint

Back Design: Two women's heads on lathework circles/cherubs, cask and bale twice/two women's heads on lathework circles
Colour: Blue

515-12-60P

£25 Face Design: Small Britannia in lathework/seated Brittania flanked by women and cherubs, two cherubs, casks and bale below/—
Colour: Black with no tint
Back Design: Two women's heads on lathework circles/cherubs, cask and bale twice/two women's heads on lathework circles
Colour: Blue

IMPRINT

New England Bank Note Co. Boston
New England Bank Note Co. Boston and ABN Co. Logo

SIGNATURES

left	right
mss. illegible	mss. J.D. Lewin

ISSUE DATING

Partially engraved___ 18___:

1838: Sept. 14	**1853:** July 1, Oct. 1
1845: 1 Oct.	**1856:** 1 Oct.
1849: June 1, Sept. 1	**1858:** Dec. 1, Apr. 21
1852: 1July	**1859:** 1 Oct.
1860: Novr. 1	

PROTECTOR

5s, 1858-1859: Red "ONE DOLLAR" on face only
£25, 1860: Red "ONE HUNDRED DOLLARS" on face only

Note: All known £5 issued notes that were dated and signed are counterfeit.

Cat. No.	Den.	Date	Variety	G	VG	F	VF	EF	AU
12-02	5s	1849-56	No ptr.	1,350.	2,250.	3,000.	—	—	—
12-12	5s	1858-59	Red ptr.	1,350.	2,250.	3,000.	—	—	—
12-22	£1	1845-52		1,500.	2,500.	3,500.	—	—	—
12-32	£2	18__			No known issued notes				
12-42C	£5	1838	Counterfeit	75.	150.	200.	—	—	—
12-50	£10	18_			No known issued notes				
12-60	£25	1860			Institutional collection only				

PROOF NOTES

Cat. No.	Den.	Date		Unc
12-02P	5s	18__	FACE PROOF	600.
12-22P	£1	18__	FACE PROOF	600.
12-32P	£2	18__	FACE PROOF	600.
12-42P	£5	18__	FACE PROOF	600.
12-50P	$10	18__	FACE PROOF	600.
12-60P	$25	18__	FACE PROOF	1,000.
Full sheet £1.2.5.10		18__	FACE PROOF	4,000.

515-14 DOLLAR ISSUES OF 1860-1884

Counters at top

A: Have $ no. and words
B: Have $ no. and $ no.
C: Have words and $ no.

DESIGNS AND COLOURS

515-14-02

515-14-10

$1 Face Design: Small Britannia in lathework/seated Brittania flanked by women and cherubs, two cherubs, casks and bale below/—
Colour: Black with green tint

Back Design: Two women's heads on lathework circles/ cherubs, cask and bale twice/two women's heads on lathework circles
Colour: Blue

515-14-14P

$2 Face Design: Small Britannia in lathework/seated Brittania flanked by women and cherubs, two cherubs, casks and bale below/—
Colour: Black with green tint

Back Design: Two women's heads on lathework circles/ cherubs, cask and bale twice/two women's heads on lathework circles
Colour: Blue

515-14-18

515-14-22

$5 Face Design: Small Britannia in lathework/seated Brittania flanked by women and cherubs, two cherubs, casks and bale below/—
Colour: Black with green tint

Back Design: Two women's heads on lathework circles/ cherubs, cask and bale twice/two women's heads on lathework circles
Colour: Blue

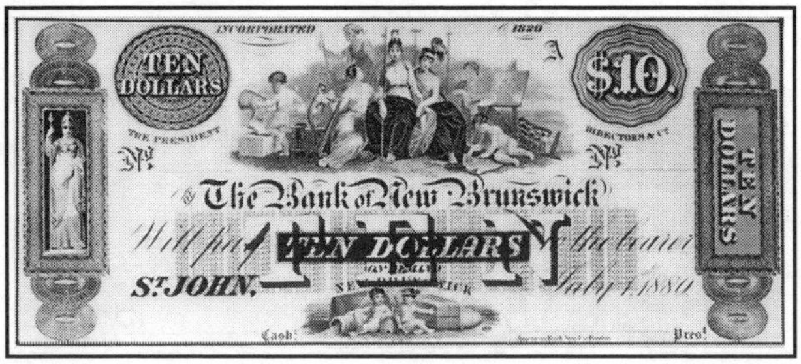

515-14-38P

$10 Face Design: Small Britannia in lathework/seated Brittania flanked by women and cherubs, two cherubs, casks and bale below/—

Colour: Black with green tint

Back Design: Two women's heads on lathework circles/ cherubs, cask and bale twice/two women's heads on lathework circles

Colour: Blue

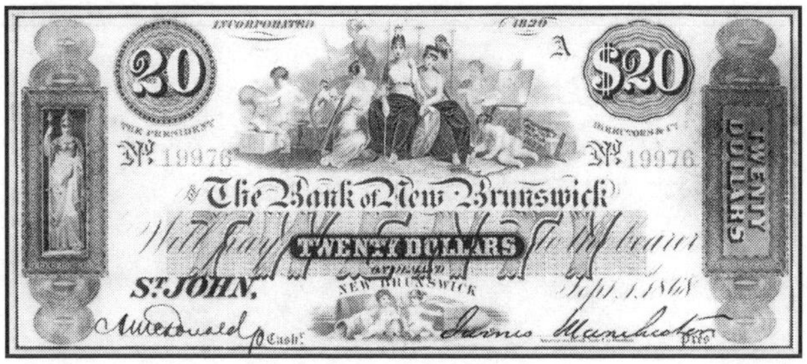

515-14-50

$20 Face Design: Small Britannia in lathework/seated Brittania flanked by women and cherubs, two cherubs, casks and bale below/—

Colour: Black with green tint

Back Design: Two women's heads on lathework circles/ cherubs, cask and bale twice/two women's heads on lathework circles

Colour: Blue

515-14-54

$50 Face Design: Small Britannia in lathework/seated Brittania flanked by women and cherubs, two cherubs, casks and bale below/—

Colour: Black with green tint

Back Design: Two women's heads on lathework circles/ cherubs, cask and bale twice/two women's heads on lathework circles

Colour: Blue

Photo Not Available

515-14-58

$100 Face Design: Small Britannia in lathework/seated Brittania flanked by women and cherubs, two cherubs, casks and bale below/—

Colour: Black with green tint

Back Design: Two women's heads on lathework circles/ cherubs, cask and bale twice/ two women's heads on lathework circles

Colour: Blue

IMPRINT

American Bank Note Co. Boston

SIGNATURES

	left	right
1860-1863:	mss. Tho. A. Sancton	mss. J.D. Lewin
	mss. W. Girvan	mss. J.D. Lewin
$1 & $5, 1868:	engr. J.D. Lewin	mss. various
$1 & $2, 1868:	mss	engr. J.D. Lewin
$20, 1868:	engr. J.D. Lewin	mss. various
	mss. A. McDonald	typed James Manchester
1880:	engr. J.D. Lewin	mss. various

ISSUE DATING

Engraved

November 1st 1860
July 1st 1863
Sept. 1st 1868
July 1, 1880
Jan. 1, 1884

STAMP

$5, 1860: "$5" in red at right

Note: The counters at the top right and left are different on the 1860 $1 and $5 notes. Most of the later issues seem to have both counters at the top as numerals, except the $10 of 1880.

CIRCULATING NOTES

Cat. No.	Denom.	Date	Variety	G	VG	F	VF	EF	AU
14-02	$1	1860		1,000.	2,000.	2,500.	—	—	—
14-06	$1	1863		1,250.	2,500.	—	—	—	—
14-10	$1	1868		900.	1,800.	2,250.	—	—	—
14-14	$2	1868			No known issued notes				
14-18	$5	1860		1,125.	2,250.	2,750.	—	—	—
14-22	$5	1863		1,125.	2,250.	2,750.	—	—	—
14-26	$5	1868		—	—	3,000.	—	—	—
14-30	$5	1884			No known issued notes				
14-34	$10	1860			Institutional collection only				
14-38	$10	1880			No known issued notes				
14-42	$20	1860		1,250.	2,500.	3,200.	—	—	—
14-46	$20	1868	Lewin, l.		Institutional collection only				
14-50	$20	1868	Mnchstr, r.	1,250.	2,500.	3,200.	4,500.	—	—
14-54	$50	1860			Institutional collection only				
14-58	$100	1860			Institutional collection only				

PROOF NOTES

Cat. No.	Denom.	Date		Unc
14-14P	$2	1868	FACE PROOF	600.
14-30P	$5	1884	FACE PROOF	600.
14-38P	$10	1880	FACE PROOF	600.
14-54P	$50	1860	FACE PROOF	700.

Note: Proof sheets in ABN archive sale. $1 (1868), $1 (1868), $5 (1884), $5 (1885), $10 (1880), $20 (1868), $50 (1860)

515-16 ISSUE OF 1892

DESIGNS AND COLOURS

515-16-02

$5 Face Design: J.D. Lewin/seated Britannia flanked by women and cherubs/Griffin over Bank Crest

Colour: Black with green and yellow tint

Back Design: —/bank building/—

Colour: Blue

515-16-06

$10 Face Design: Sailor beside Provincial Crest/seated Britannia flanked by women and cherubs/J.D. Lewin

Colour: Black with green and yellow tint

Back Design: —/bank building/—

Colour: Green

IMPRINT

American Bank Note Co. New York

SIGNATURES

left	right
mss. J. Clawson	mss. J.D. Lewin

ISSUE DATING

Engraved

March 25th 1892

October 1st 1902 ($5 proof only)

PROTECTOR

Some $5 notes: "V V" in red on face only

Some $10 notes: "X X" in red on face only

CIRCULATING NOTES

Cat. No.	Denom.	Date	Variety	VG	F	VF	EF	Unc	
16-02	$5	1892	No ptr.	1,250.	2,500.	—	—	—	—
16-04	$5	1892	Red ptr.	1,500.	3,000.	4,000.	—	—	—
16-06	$10	1892	No ptr.		Institutional collection only				
16-08	$10	1892	Red ptr.		Institutional collection only				
16-08R	$10	1892	Remainder	—	—	—	1,500.	2,500.	—

PROOF NOTES

Cat. No.	Denom.	Date		Unc
16-02P	$5	189_	FACE PROOF	600.
16-03P	$5	1902	FACE PROOF	700.
16-06P	$10	1892	FACE PROOF	700.

SPECIMEN NOTES

Cat. No.	Denom.	Date	Variety		Unc
16-04S	$5	1892	Red ptr.	SPECIMEN	1,000.

515-18 ISSUES OF 1903-1906

DESIGNS AND COLOURS

515-18-02

$5 Face Design: James Manchester/view of Saint John/Griffin over Bank Crest

Colour: Black with yellow-green and rose tint

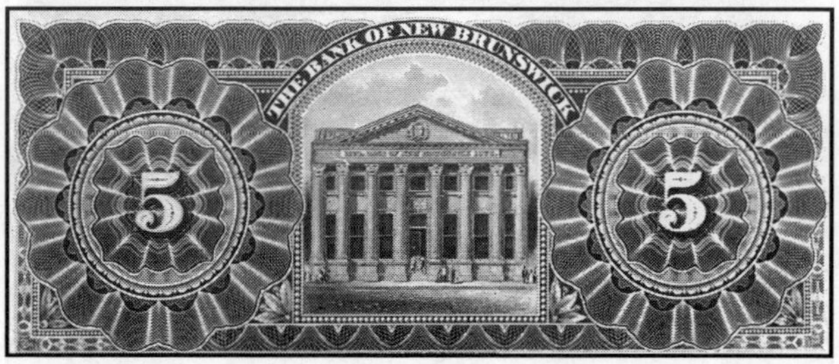

Back Design: —/head office/—

Colour: Green

515-18-06

$10 Face Design: Sailor beside Provincial Crest/seated Britannia flanked by women and cherubs/ James Manchester
Colour: Black with yellow-green and green tint

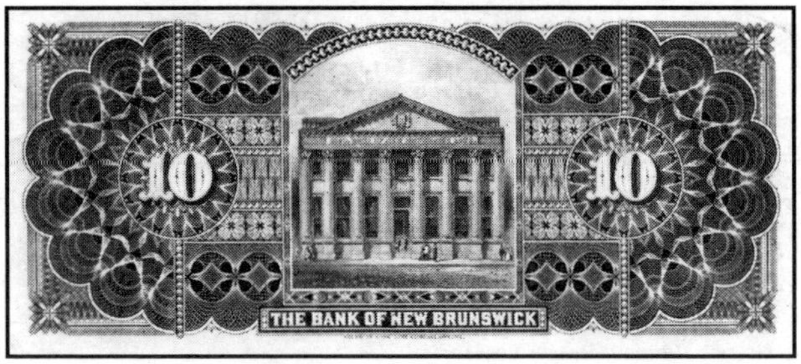

Back Design: —/head office/—
Colour: Olive

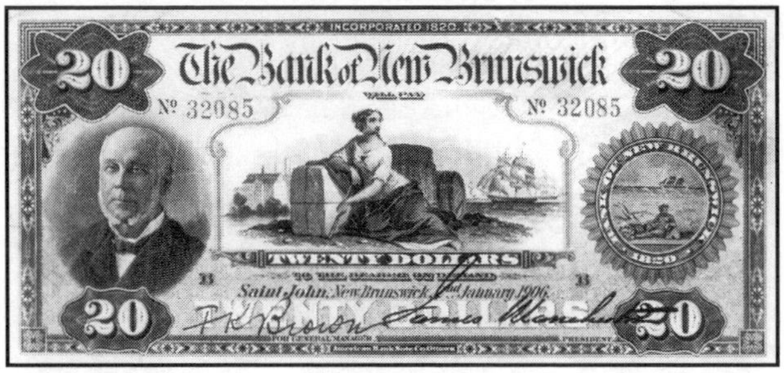

515-18-12

$20 Face Design: James Manchester/ woman seated by casks and bale/Bank Crest
Colour: Black with blue tint

Back Design: —/head office/—
Colour: Blue

515-18-16S

$50 Face Design: Seated "Commerce" figure and cornucopia/Bank Crest/James Manchester
Colour: Black with green tint

Back Design: —/head office/—
Colour: Green

IMPRINT

American Bank Note Co. Ottawa

SIGNATURES

left	**right**
mss. various	typed James Manchester

ISSUE DATING

Engraved

1st September 1903
2nd January 1904
2nd January 1906

VARIETIES

Left signature space is labelled "MANAGER."
Left signature space is labelled "FOR GENERAL MANAGER."

CIRCULATING NOTES

Cat. No.	Denom.	Date	Variety	G	VG	F	VF	EF	AU
18-02	$5	1904	Manager	1,250.	2,500.	3,500.	5,000.	6,500.	—
18-04	$5	1904	Gen. Mgr.	1,250.	2,500.	3,500.	5,000.	6,500.	—
18-06	$10	1903	Manager	1,500.	3,000.	4,000.	5,750.	7,500.	—
18-08	$10	1903	Gen. Mgr.	1,500.	3,000.	4,000.	5,750.	7,500.	—
18-10	$20	1906	Manager	Institutional collection only					
18-12	$20	1906	Gen. Manager	Institutional collection only					
18-14	$50	1906	Manager	No known issued notes					
18-16	$50	1906	Gen. Manager	No known issued notes					

PROOF NOTES

Cat. No.	Denom.	Date	Variety		Unc
18-12P	$20	1906	B & W	FACE PROOF	400.
18-14P	$50	1906	Manager	FACE PROOF	400.

SPECIMEN NOTES

Cat. Np.	Denom.	Date	Variety		Unc
18-12S	$20	1906	Gen. Manager	SPECIMEN	800.
18-16S	$50	1906	Gen. Manager	SPECIMEN	800.

Note: $50 face and back proofs in blue (unissued colour) exist.

THE NEWCASTLE BANKING COMPANY

1836

AMHERST, NEWCASTLE DISTRICT, UPPER CANADA

BANK NUMBER 520 ***NONREDEEMABLE***

This bank was established in 1836 at Amherst, Upper Canada, as a private institution. It issued notes, but its application for a charter was refused.

520-10 **ISSUE OF 1836**

This issue was in reality a post note. The notes were not convertible into specie until a year after the issue date. They were typographed.

DESIGNS AND COLOURS

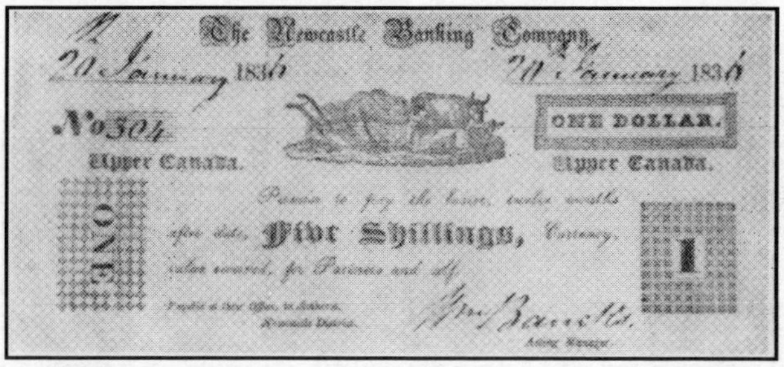

520-10-02
$1 (5s) Face Design: —/Plough and cattle/—
Colour: Black with no tint

Back Design: Plain

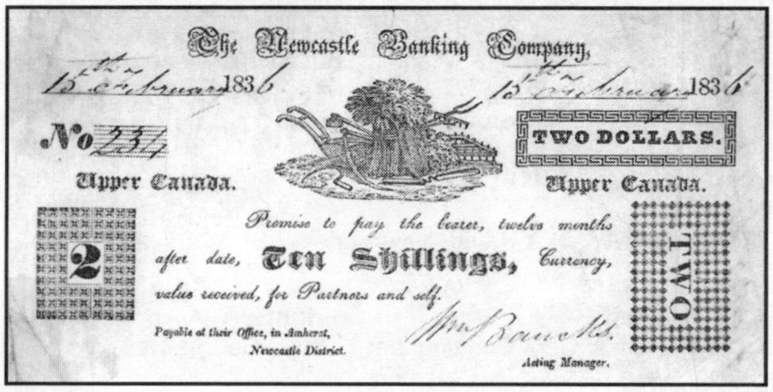

520-10-04
$2 (10s) Face Design: —/sheaves of wheat and agricultural implements/—
Colour: Black with no tint

Back Design: Plain

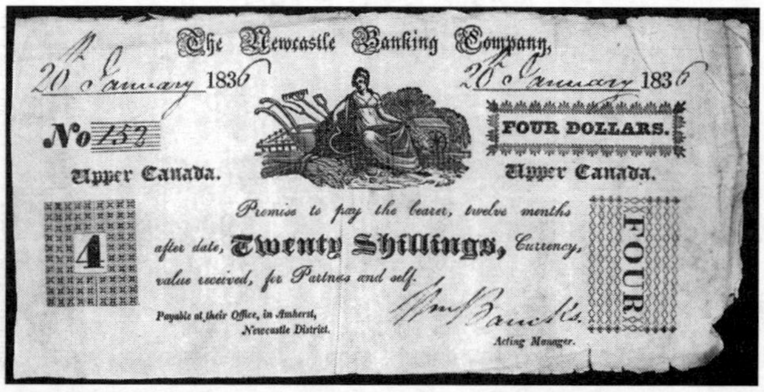

520-10-06
$4 (20s) Face Design: —/seated woman with agricultural implements and produce/—
Colour: Black with no tint

Back Design: Plain

IMPRINT
None

SIGNATURES

left	right
none	mss. Wm. Bancks

ISSUE DATING
Partially engraved ___ 18___:
1836: 20th January
15th February

Cat. No.	Denom.	Date	G	VG	F	VF	EF	AU
10-02	$1(5s)	1836	—	350.	475.	700.	1,150.	—
10-04	$2(10s)	1836	—	250.	350.	550.	900.	—
10-06	$4(20s)	1836	—	250.	350.	550.	900.	—

THE NEWCASTLE DISTRICT LOAN COMPANY

1836

PETERBOROUGH, UPPER CANADA

BANK NUMBER 525 ***NONREDEEMABLE***

525-10 ISSUE OF 1836

These were post notes, payable 12 months after the issue date.

DESIGNS AND COLOURS

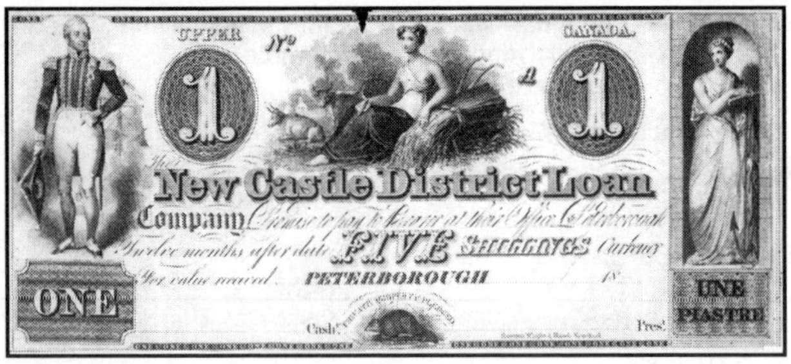

525-10-02R

$1 (5s) Face Design: Naval figure/seated "Agriculture" figure; beaver below/allegorical female, anchor

Colour: Black with no tint

Back Design: Plain

525-10-04

$2 (10s) Face Design: King William IV; man with cradle cutting grain/reclining woman, flowers; arm and hammer below/—

Colour: Black with no tint

Back Design: Plain

525-10-06

$4 (20s, £1) Face Design: Men, cattle and sheep/ King William IV on Royal Crest; ship, cask and bale below/ blacksmith with tools

Colour: Black with no tint

Back Design: Plain

525-10-08

$10 (50s) Face Design: Men, cattle and sheep/ St. George slaying the dragon small paddlewheel steamboat below/ Indian with drawn bow

Colour: Black with no tint

Back Design: Plain

IMPRINT

Rawdon, Wright & Hatch, New-York.

SIGNATURES

left	**right**
mss. Geo. Cunningham	mss. George Hall

ISSUE DATING

Partially engraved ___ 18___:

$2, 1836: 27 Augt., 8th Octr

$4, 1836: Feb. 15, 6 Augt, 13th Augt, 20 Augt, 27 August, 27 Augt.

$10, 1836: 6 Augt, 13th Augt, 20 Augt, 27 August

Cat. No.	Denom.	Date	Variety	G	VG	F	VF	EF	AU
10-02R	$1 (5s)	18_	Remainder*	125.	250.	325.	—	—	—
10-04	$2 (10s)	1836		125.	250.	325.	—	—	—
10-04R	$2 (10s)	18_	Remainder*	—	—	—	350.	500.	—
10-06	$4 (20s, £1)	1836		45.	90.	120.	175.	275.	—
10-08	$10 (50s)	1836		60.	120.	150.	225.	350.	—

* Unsigned, undated and unnumbered.

THE NIAGARA DISTRICT BANK

1853-1875

ST. CATHARINES, CANADA WEST

BANK NUMBER 530 ***REDEEMABLE***

The "Bank of the Niagara District" was chartered in 1841, but did not go into operation, being unable to raise sufficient capital. Under the name of the Niagara District Bank it finally went into business in 1853, under the Free Banking Act. In 1855 a charter was applied for and received from the legislature.

The bank operated successfully, with Ontario branches in St. Catharines, Ingersoll and Port Colborne, until it incurred heavy losses through the failure of American correspondents in 1873. It was also affected by the decaying fortunes of St. Catharines, the city in which it had its principal branch. Late in 1874 negotiations began for a merger between the Niagara District Bank and the Imperial Bank of Canada. They officially merged on July 2, 1875, the amalgamation being the first of its kind under the new Bank Act of 1871.

530-10 FREE BANKING ISSUE, 1854-1855

DESIGNS AND COLOURS

530-10-04

$1 Face Design: Milkmaid/royal Crest/—

Colour: Black with no tint

Back Design: Plain

530-10-10

Note: The note shown above is a $1 raised to $10.

530-10-12P

$2 Face Design: Prince Consort/—/—

Colour: Black with no tint

Back Design: Plain

530-10-14P

$5 Face Design: Shipbuilding scene/Queen Victoria (Chalon portrait)/—

Colour: Black with no tint

Back Design: Plain

IMPRINT

Danforth, Wright & Co., New York & Philada

SIGNATURES

left	right
mss. J.R. Andy	mss. Jno. Smart, Cashr and mss. Thomas C. Street, Prest.

ISSUE DATING

Partially engraved ___ 18___:

1854: Unknown

1855: Unknown

CIRCULATING NOTES

Cat. No.	Denom.	Date Variety	G	VG	F	VF	EF	AU
10-04	$1	1854-55	Institutional collection only					
10-08	$1	1854-55 Raised to $5	Institutional collection only					
10-10	$1	1854-55 Raised to $10	900.	1,500.	2,000.	—	—	—
10-12	$2	18__	No known issued notes					
10-14	$5	18__	No known issued notes					

PROOF NOTES

Cat. No.	Denom.	Date		Unc
10-04P	$1	18__	PROOF	700.
10-12P	$2	18__	PROOF	700.
10-14P	$5	18__	PROOF	700.

530-12 CHARTERED BANK ISSUES 1855 - 1862

DESIGNS AND COLOURS

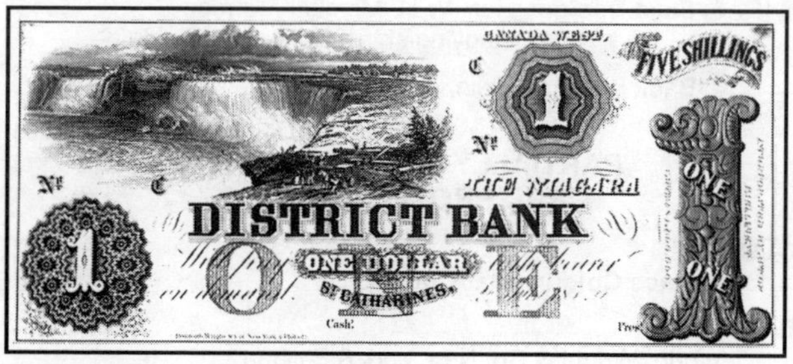

530-12-02-02P

$1 (5s) Face Design: Niagara Falls/—/—

Back Design: Plain

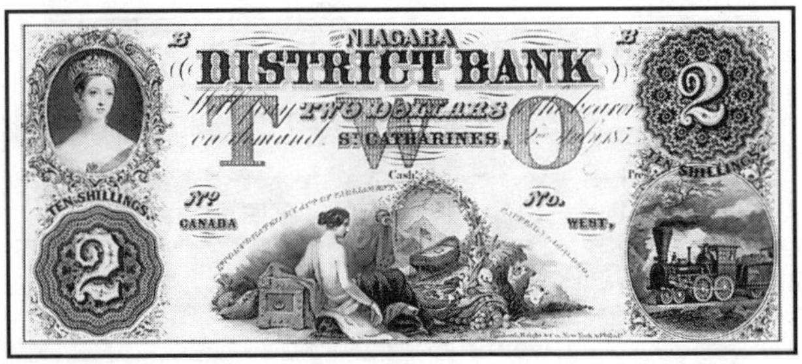

530-12-02-04P

$2 (10s) Face Design: Queen Victoria/woman and plaque with shipbuilding scene/locomotive and tender in oval

Back Design: Plain

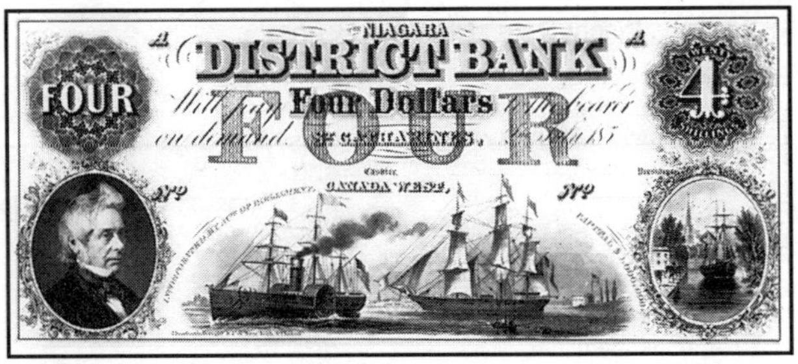

530-12-02-06P

$4 (20s) Face Design: Hon. W.H. Merritt/ steamboat and sailing ships/ ship in canal and town in oval

Back Design: Plain

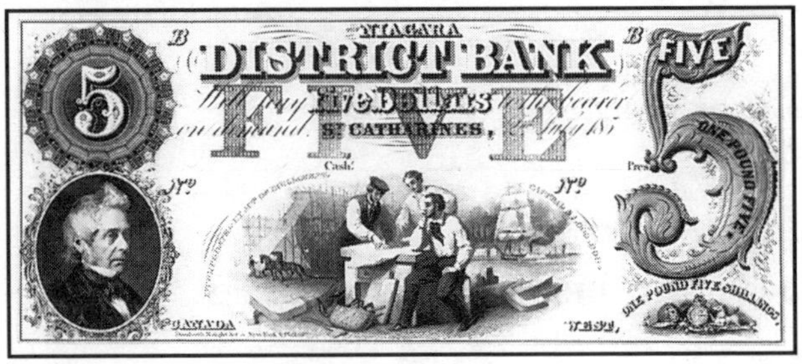

530-12-02-08P

$5 (£1.5) Face Design: Hon. W.H. Merritt/three men studying ships' plans at dockside/—

Back Design: Plain

2. PARTIALLY ENGRAVED DATE, RED PROTECTOR, 1855

COLOURS

Face Colour: Black with no tint

IMPRINT

Danforth, Wright & Co. New York & Philada

SIGNATURES

left	**right**
mss. various	mss. various
none	none

ISSUE DATING

Partially engraved 2nd July 185_:

1855

PROTECTOR

Red "word" on face and back

CIRCULATING NOTES

Cat. No.	Denom.	Date	G	VG	F	VF	EF	AU
12-02-02	$1 (5s)	1855	Institutional collection only					
12-02-04	$2 (10s)	185_	No known issued notes					
12-02-06	$4 (20s)	1855	Institutional collection only					
12-02-08	$5 (£1.5)	185_	No known issued notes					

PROOF NOTES

Cat. No.	Denom.	Date	Unc
12-02-02P	$1 (5s)	185_	750.
12-02-04P	$2 (10s)	185_	750.
12-02-06P	$4 (20s)	185_	750.
12-02-08P	$5 (£1.5)	185_	750.

4. PARTIALLY ENGRAVED DATE GREEN TINT, 1860s

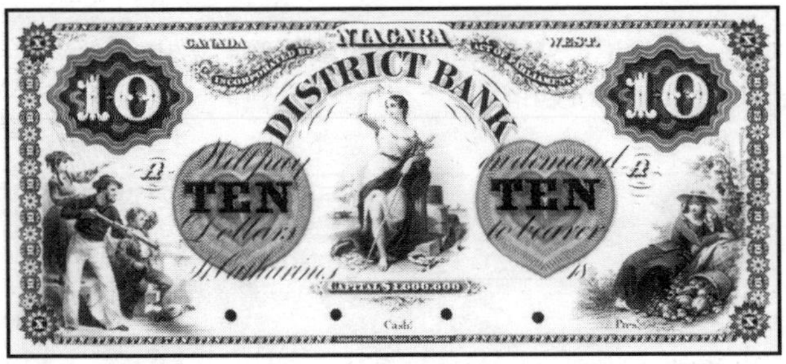

530-12-04-02P

$10 Face Design: Sailor, woman and child "Land Ho!"/ "Justice" figure/reclining woman with basket of produce

Back Design: Plain

COLOURS

Face Colour: Black with green tint

IMPRINT

American Bank Note Co. New York.

SIGNATURES

left	**right**
none	none

ISSUE DATING

Partially engraved ___ 18___:

CIRCULATING NOTES

Cat. No.	Denom.	Date	G	VG	F	VF	EF	AU
12-04-02	$10	18__	No known issued notes					

PROOF NOTES

Cat. No.	Denom.	Date	Variety		Unc
12-04-02P	$10	18__	B & W	PROOF	500.
12-04-02Pa	$10	18__	Green tint	PROOF	750.

6 FULLY ENGRAVED DATE 1862

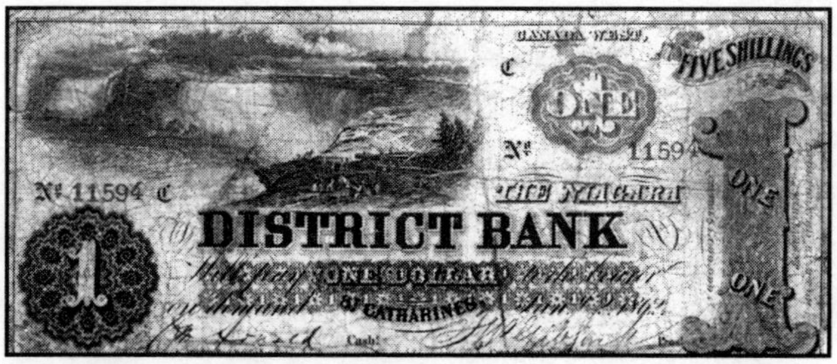

530-12-06-02
$1 (5s) Face Design: Niagara Falls/—/—
Back Design: Plain

530-12-06-04
$2 (10s) Face Design: Queen Victoria/woman and plaque with shipuilding scene/locomative and tender in oval
Back Design: Plain

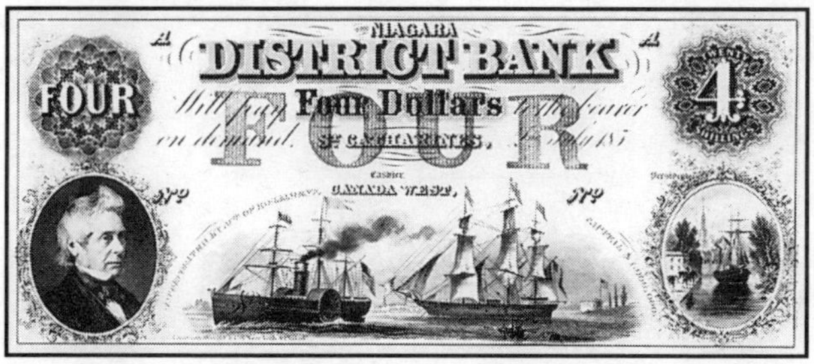

530-12-06-06P
$4 (20s) Face Deisgn: Hon. W.H. Merritt/steamboat and sailing ships/ship in canal and town in oval
Back Design: Plain

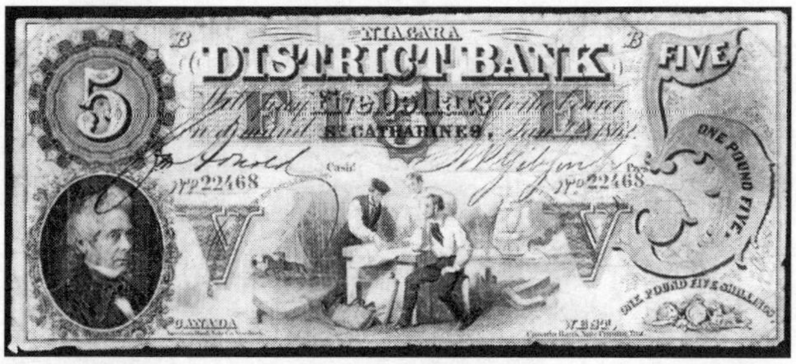

530-12-06-08
$5 (£1.5) Face Design: Hon. W.H. Merritt/three men studing ships plans at dock-side/—
Back Design: Plain

COLOURS
Face Colour: Black with green tint

IMPRINT
Danforth, Wright & Co. New York & Philada and ABNCo. Mono American Bank Note Co. New York

SIGNATURES

left	right
mss. F.W. Gibson	engr. James R. Benson
mss. C.M. Arnold	mss. F.W. Gibson

ISSUE DATING
Engraved
Jan'y. 2 1862.

CIRCULATING NOTES

Cat. No.	Denom.	Date	Variety	G	VG	F	VF	EF	AU
12-06-02	$1 (5s)	1862		Institutional collection only					
12-06-04	$2 (10s)	1862		Institutional collection only					
12-06-06	$4 (20s)	1862		1,500.	2,500.	—	—	—	—
12-06-06C	$4 (20s)	1862	Counterfeit	75.	150.	200.	—	—	—
12-06-08	$5 (£1.5)	1862		Institutional collection only					

* Most of the surviving $4 notes are counterfeits, with scratchy engraving and engraved signatures.

PROOF NOTES

Cat. No.	Denom.	Date		Unc
12-06-02P	$1 (5s)	1862	PROOF	600.
12-06-04P	$2 (10s)	1862	PROOF	600.
12-06-06P	$4 (20s)	1862	PROOF	600.
12-06-08P	$5 (£1.5)	1862	PROOF	600.

530-14 ISSUE OF 1872

DESIGNS AND COLOURS

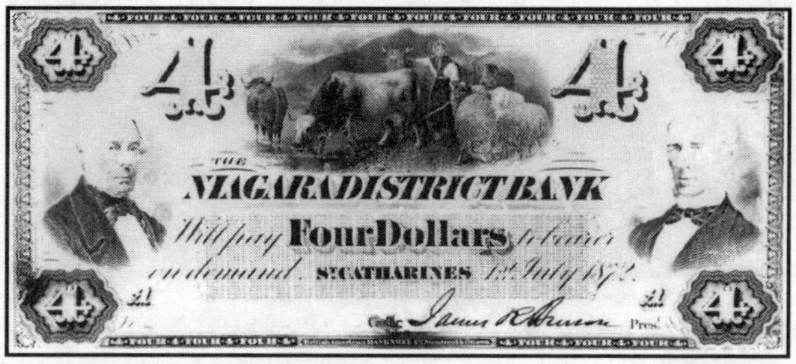

530-14-02 (modern reprint)
$4 Face Design: Hon. W.H. Merritt/girl watering livestock "Vogt's cattle"/Hon. Jas. R. Benson
Colour: Black with green tint

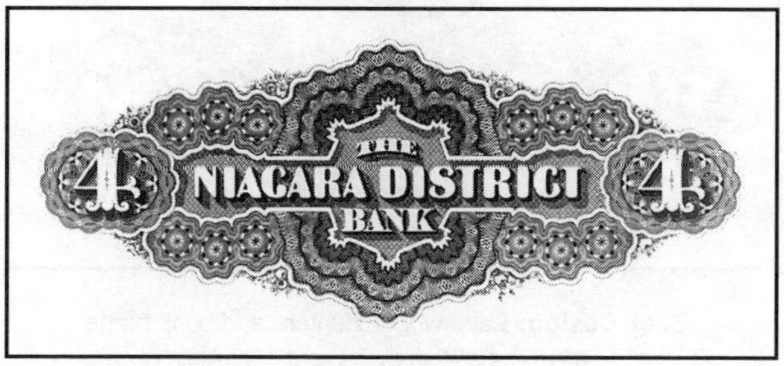

Back Design: Lathework, counters and bank name
Colour: Green

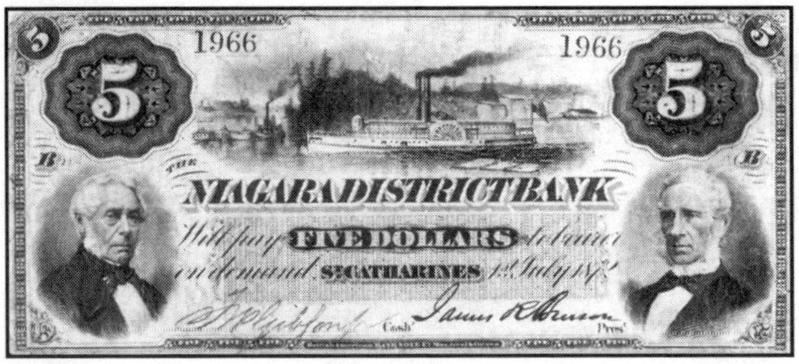

530-14-04

$5 Face Design: Hon. W.H. Merritt/paddlewheel steamer/ Hon. Jas. R. Benson
Colour: Black with green tint

Back Design: Lathework, counters and bank name
Colour: Green

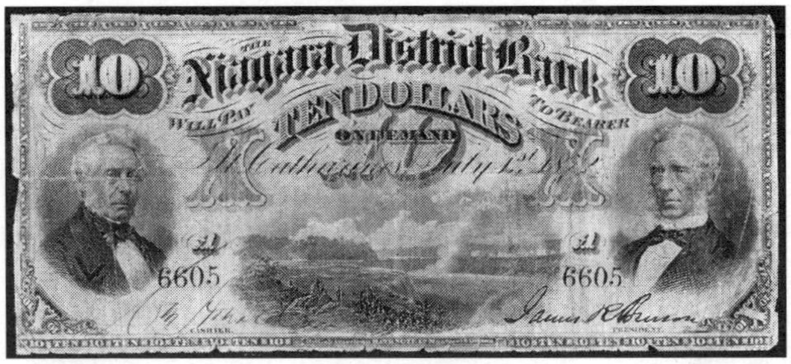

530-14-06

$10 Face Design: Hon. W.H. Merritt/Niagara Falls/ Hon. Jas. R. Benson
Colour: Black with green tint

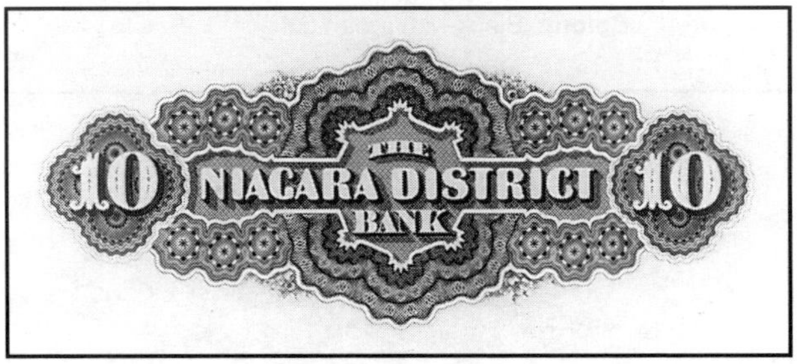

Back Design: Lathework, counters and bank name
Colour: Green

IMPRINT

British American Bank Note Co. Montreal & Ottawa

SIGNATURES

left	right
mss. F.W. Gibson	engr. James R. Benson
mss. C.M. Arnold	engr. James R. Benson

ISSUE DATING

Engraved

July 1st 1872
1st July 1872

Cat. No.	Denom.	Date	Variety	G	VG	F	VF	EF	AU
14-02	$4*	1872		Institutional collection only					
14-04	$5*	1872		1,200.	2,000.	3,000.	—	—	—
14-06	$10*	1872		Institutional collection only					

* Beware of modern lithographic reproductions of this issue in single notes or in sheets.

THE NIAGARA SUSPENSION BRIDGE BANK

1836-1841

QUEENSTON, UPPER CANADA

BANK NUMBER 535 ***NONREDEEMABLE***

This bank went into business on December 20, 1836, as an unincorporated joint-stock bank, at Queenston, Upper Canada. It began with a capital of £7,700, subscribed by a small number of shareholders, most of whom were Americans. It had agencies in Chippewa, Upper Canada, and in Lockport, New York, and did most of its business on the American side of the border. The bank was recognized by the government, and its note issues were taxed. When the bank failed in December 1841, there were $62,384 of its notes in circulation.

535-10 ISSUE OF 1836-1841

DESIGNS AND COLOURS

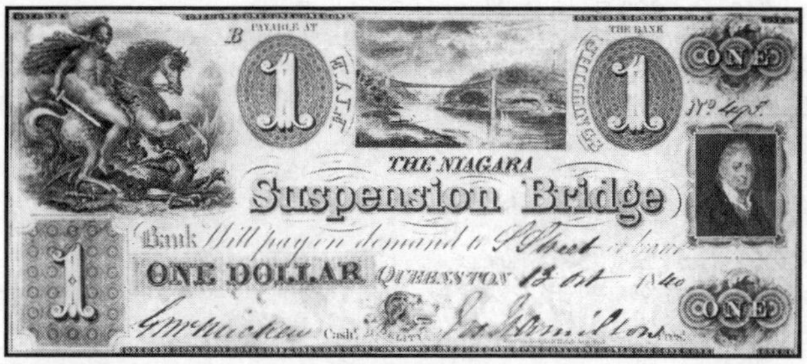

535-10-06-02

$1 (5s) Face Design: St. George slaying the dragon/ Niagara suspension bridge; dog's head below/King William IV
See subheadings
Colour: Black with green tint

Back Design: See subheadings
Colour: See subheadings

535-10-02-04

$3 (15s) Face Design: Woman standing with anchor/Niagara suspension bridge; dog's head below/ Indian paddling canoe
See subheadings
Colour: Black with no tint

Back Design: See subheadings
Colour: See subheadings

535-10-08-12

$5 (25s) Face Design: —/Niagara suspension bridge; steamboat below/Indian with drawn bow
See subheadings
Colour: Black with no tint

Back Design: See subheadings
Colour: See subheadings

535-10-08-18

$10 Face Design: —/Niagara suspension bridge/ St. George slaying the dragon
See subheadings
Colour: Black with no tint

Back Design: Plain

535-10-08-30

$20 Face Design: Niagara suspension bridge (side view)/ goddess rising from the waves/ Greek god reclining by fountain
See subheadings
Colour: Black with no tint

Back Design: Plain

IMPRINT

Rawdon, Wright & Hatch, New York

2. MSS. "PAYABLE AT THE BANK" VERTICALLY AT LEFT, PLAIN BACK, 1836-1837

SIGNATURES

left	right
mss. P.C.H. Brotherson	mss. Bates Cooke

ISSUE DATING

Partially engraved ___ 18___:

1836: Dec. 20
1837: Aug. 31

Cat. No.	Denom.	Date	G	VG	F	VF	EF	AU
10-02-02	$1 (5s)	1836-37	75	150.	200.	—	—	—
10-02-04	$3 (15s)	1836	Institutional collection only					
10-02-06	$5 (25s)	1836	75.	150.	200.	—	—	—

4. ENGRAVED "PAYABLE AT THE BANK" AT TOP, PLAIN BACK, 1837-1839

SIGNATURES

left	right
mss. P.C.H. Brotherson	mss. Bates Cooke

ISSUE DATING

Partially engraved ___ 18___:

1837: Apr. 3
1839: July 20

Cat. No.	Denom.	Date	G	VG	F	VF	EF	AU
10-04-02	$1 (5s)	1837	60.	125.	175.	—	—	—
10-04-04	$3 (15s)	18__	75.	150.	200.	—	—	—
10-04-06	$3 (15s)	1839	60.	125.	175.	—	—	—

6. ENGRAVED "PAYABLE AT THE BANK" AT TOP, ORANGE LATHEWORK ON BACK, 1840

SIGNATURES

left	right
mss. G. McMicken	mss. Jos. Hamilton

ISSUE DATING

Partially engraved ___ 18___:

1840: Oct. 13, 13 Oct.

Cat. No.	Denom.	Date	G	VG	F	VF	EF	AU
10-06-02	$1 (5s)	1840	35.	70.	120.	200.	—	—
10-06-04	$3 (15s)	1840	50.	100.	150.	250.	—	—
10-06-06	$5 (25s)	1840	35.	70.	120.	200.	—	—

8. PLAIN BACK ISSUE 1841

SIGNATURES

left	right
mss. G. McMicken	mss. Jos. Hamilton

ISSUE DATING

Partially engraved ___ 18___:

$1, 1841: 1 July
$3, 1841: 1 Mar., 1 May, May 1, 1 July
$5: See varieties
$10, 1841: Jan. 4, 4 Jany
$20, 1841: 4 Jany.

VARIETIES

$5 Issue Dating: Engraved "QUEENSTON" on bottom, at left of miniature ship; U.C.: 1841: 1 Mar., May 1, 1 July
$5 Issue Dating: Engraved "QUEENSTON" at bottom, above miniature ship; U.C.: 1841: 4 Jany
$5 Issue Dating: Engraved "QUEENSTON" at bottom, above miniature ship; Upper Canada 18__: Undated remainder
$10 and $20 Face Design: U.C. at bottom
$10 and $20 Face Design: UPPER CANADA at bottom

Cat. No.	Denom.	Date	Variety	G	VG	F	VF	EF	AU
10-08-02	$1 (5s)	1841		35.	70.	120.	200.	—	—
10-08-06	$3 (15s)	1841		50.	100.	150.	250.	400.	—
10-08-10	$5 (25s)	1841	QUEENSTON above; U.C.	80.	160.	225.	375.	—	—
10-08-10R	$5 (25s)	1841	Remainder	50.	100.	150.	250.	—	—
10-08-12	$5 (25s)	1841	QUEENSTON left; U.C.	35.	70.	120.	200.	—	—
10-08-14R	$5 (25s)	1841	QUEENSTON UPPER CANADA	Institutional collection only					
10-08-18	$10 (50s)	1841	U.C.	100.	200.	300.	500.	—	—
10-08-18R	$10 (50s)	1841	Remainder	50.	100.	150.	250.	—	—
10-08-22	$10 (50s)	1841	UPPER CANADA	100.	200.	300.	500.	—	—
10-08-22R	$10 (50s)	1841	Remainder	50.	100.	150.	200.	—	—
10-08-26	$20 (£5)	1841	U.C.	135.	275.	400.	750.	—	—
10-08-26R	$20 (£5)	1841	Remainder	100.	200.	275.	450.	—	—
10-08-30	$20 (£5)	1841	UPPER CANADA	135.	275.	400.	750.	—	—
10-08-30R	$20 (£5)	1841	Remainder	100.	200.	275.	450.	—	—

THE NORTHERN BANK

1905-1908

WINNIPEG, MANITOBA

BANK NUMBER 540 ***REDEEMABLE***

Established in Winnipeg, Manitoba, in 1905, this bank amalgamated with the Crown Bank of Canada to become the Northern Crown Bank in 1908.

540-10 **ISSUE OF 1905**

DESIGNS AND COLOURS

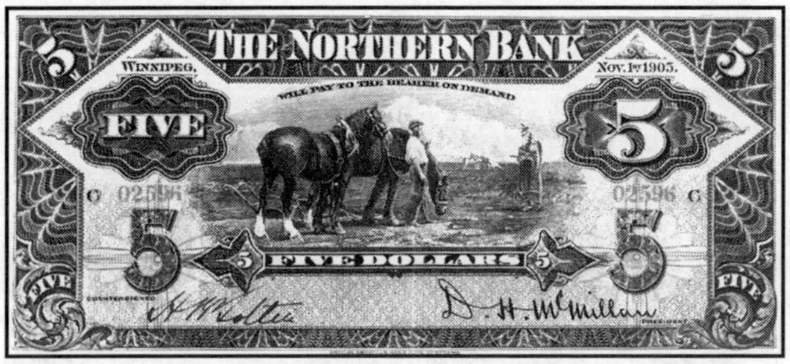

540-10-02
$5 Face Design: —/farmer, horses and native on prairies/—
Colour: Black with green tint

Back Design: Lathework, counters and bank name
Colour: Green

540-10-04
$10 Face Design: —/farmer cutting wheat with binder/—
Colour: Black with red-brown tint

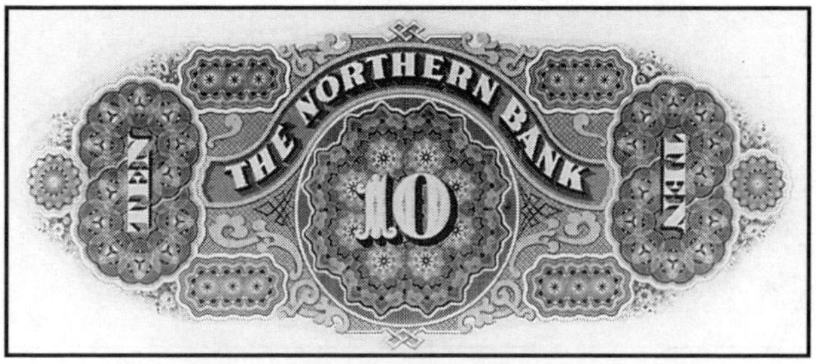

Back Design: Lathework, counters and bank name
Colour: Green

540-10-06
$20 Face Design: —/bison on prairies/—
Colour: Black with brown tint

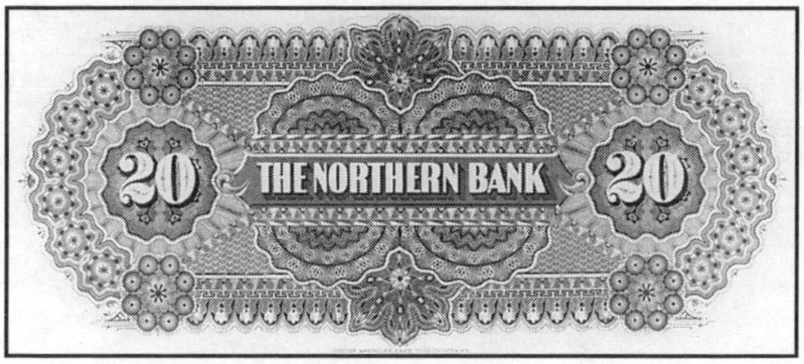

Back Design: Lathework, counters and bank name
Colour: Green

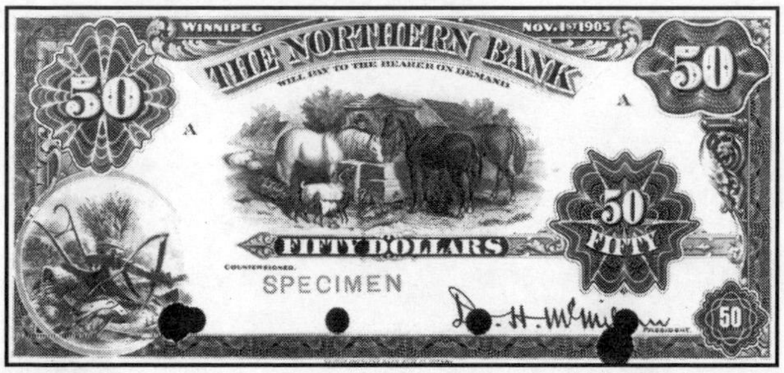

540-10-08P
$50 Face Design: Agricultural produce and implements/ farmer watering horses at trough/—
Colour: Black with ochre tint

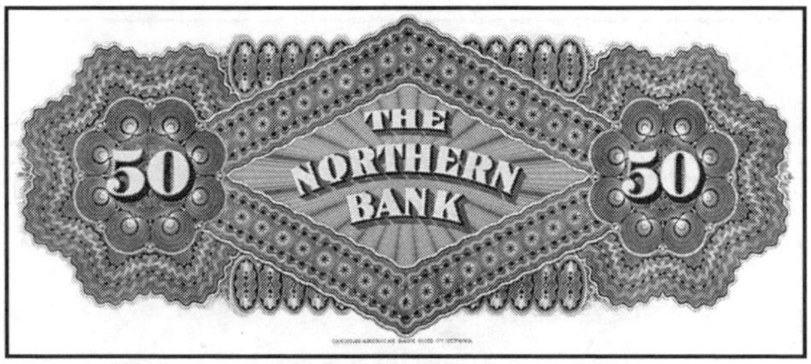

Back Design: Lathework, counters and bank name
Colour: Green

IMPRINT
British American Bank Note Co. Ottawa

SIGNATURES

left	**right**
mss. various	engr. D.H. McMillan

ISSUE DATING
Engraved
Nov. 1st 1905

Note: A back proof of the $5 note is known with brown tint.

CIRCULATING NOTES

Cat. No.	Denom.	Date	G	VG	F	VF	EF	AU
10-02	$5	1905	—	4,500.	6,500.	9,000.	—	—
10-04	$10	1905	—	5,000.	—	—	—	—
10-06	$20	1905	Institutional collection only					
10-08	$50	1905	No known issued notes					

PROOF NOTES

Cat. No.	Denom.	Date		Unc
10-02P	$5	1905	FACE PROOF	650.
10-04P	$10	1905	FACE PROOF	700.
10-06P	$20	1905	FACE PROOF	750.
10-08P	$50	1905	FACE PROOF	850.

THE NORTHERN CROWN BANK

1908-1918

WINNIPEG, MANITOBA

BANK NUMBER 545 ***REDEEMABLE***

Established in Winnipeg, Manitoba, in 1905 as the Northern Bank, this bank became the Northern Crown Bank upon amalgamation with the Crown Bank of Canada (Toronto) in 1908. It was taken over by the Royal Bank of Canada in July 1918 for 10,883 shares of Royal Bank stock and $576,970 cash. The total assets of the bank at the time of sale were about $28 million. The bank had 111 branches and one sub-branch.

545-10 **ISSUES OF 1908-1914**

DESIGNS AND COLOURS

545-10-02
$5 Face Design: —/farmer and horses on prairies/—
Colour: Black with olive and red tint

Back Design: Lathework, counters, bank name and floral emblems and crown
Colour: Red-brown

545-10-06
$10 Face Design: —/farmer cutting wheat with binder/—
Colour: Black with yellow and green tint

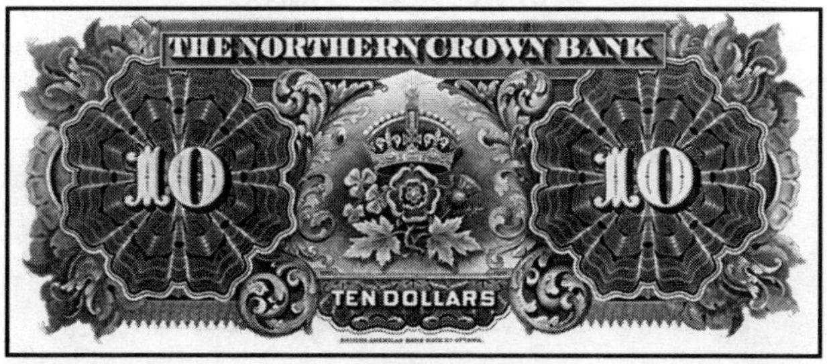

Back Design: Lathework, counters, bank name and floral emblems and crown
Colour: Blue

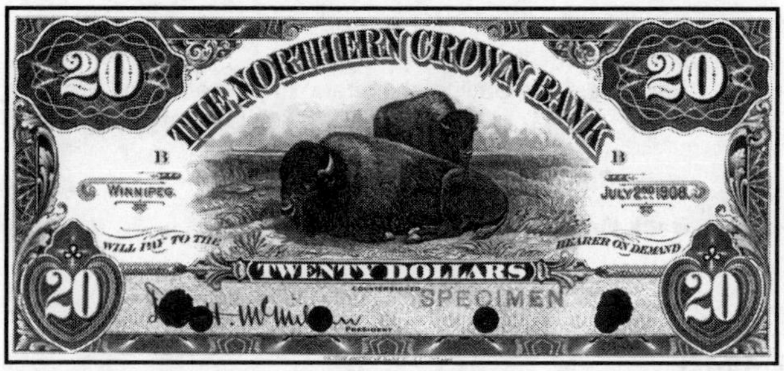

545-10-10S
$20 Face Design: —/bison on prairies/—
Colour: Black with peach and blue tint

Back Design: Lathework, counters, bank name and floral emblems and crown
Colour: Orange

545-10-12P
$50 Face Design: —/lion in mountains/—
Colour: Black with yellow and red tint
Back Design: Lathework, counters, bank name and floral emblems and crown
Colour: Purple

IMPRINT
British American Bank Note Co. Ottawa

SIGNATURES

left	right
engr. D.H. McMillan	mss. various

ISSUE DATING
Engraved
July 2nd 1908
July 2nd 1914

Note: A back proof of the $5 note is known with maroon tint.

CIRCULATING NOTES

Cat. No.	Denom.	Date	G	VG	F	VF	EF	AU
10-02	$5	1908	750.	1,500.	2,000.	3,200.	4,800.	—
10-04	$5	1914	800.	1,600.	2,400.	3,500.	—	—
10-06	$10	1908	800.	1,600.	2,400.	3,500.	—	—
10-08	$10	1914	900.	1,800.	2,600.	3,800.	—	—
10-10	$20	1908	2,000.	3,500.	4,500.	—	—	—
10-12	$50	1908	No known issued notes					

PROOF NOTES

Cat. No.	Denom.	Date		Unc
10-02P	$5	1908	FACE PROOF	700.
10-06P	$10	1908	FACE PROOF	700.
10-10P	$20	1908	FACE PROOF	800.
10-12P	$50	1908	FACE PROOF	1,000.

THE BANK OF NOVA SCOTIA

1832 TO DATE

HALIFAX, NOVA SCOTIA

BANK NUMBER 550 ***REDEEMABLE***

On December 13, 1831, a group of merchants, ship owners and citizens assembled in Halifax for the purpose of organizing a public bank. After argument, amendment and compromise in the legislature, the bill to incorporate the Bank of Nova Scotia passed on March 30, 1832.

For the first 40-odd years of its existence, the bank was a very small institution by modern standards, but it was by no means unenterprising. For example, it opened the first bank branches in Nova Scotia. The first agency was established in Windsor, Nova Scotia, in 1837, and by the end of 1839, Pictou, Annapolis, Liverpool and Yarmouth also had agencies of the bank. During these early years connections were established with mercantile and private banking firms in Saint John, New Brunswick, New York, Boston and London, England.

The first presidents of the bank were merchants whose businesses, like those of so many of their contemporaries, were founded on the exchange of lumber and fish for West Indian sugar and rum. With the building of the Canadian Pacific Railway in the 1880s, the bank established branches in Winnipeg and Minneapolis. Branches were added in Chicago in 1892 and in Boston in 1899.

During the first two decades of the present century, the bank extended its Caribbean business to Cuba and Puerto Rico and opened its own agency in New York, as well as branches in London, England, and in the Dominican Republic. Business was conducted in Cuba through branches in Havana and at other points on the island, until all foreign banks were closed by arrangement with the Castro government in December 1960.

Mergers with other banks played an important role in the bank's continuing growth as market forces began to reduce the number of Canadian chartered banks. After absorbing the Union Bank of Prince Edward Island in 1883, three additional mergers took place, with the Bank of New Brunswick in 1913, the Metropolitan Bank in 1914 and the Bank of Ottawa in 1919. As the 1920s began, the Bank of Nova Scotia was active in every Canadian province and maintained 30 branches outside Canada. From a sturdy regional bank, it had become an enterprising and responsible national institution, which served international as well as local needs.

After a consolidation of operations during the Depression and World War II, expansion was renewed through new branches and additional services. In 1958 the bank entered a new phase of business by joining with three British firms to establish the Bank of Nova Scotia Trust Company (Bahamas) Limited, with headquarters in Nassau. The Bahamas Trust has become the parent company for several subsidiaries, and new companies with similar operations have been founded.

A noteworthy feature of the international postwar financial situation was the revival of interest in gold. To facilitate the holding of gold, in 1958 the Bank of Nova Scotia introduced a unique gold certificate, designed as a transferable receipt for gold ingots and bars held for safekeeping in the bank's own vaults. Owners of the certificates made arrangements to take delivery of the metal in Canada, or when conditions permitted at any other office of the bank, or at the office of a correspondent bank in any major gold-trading centre outside Canada where the bank had no office. The bank quickly became Canada's largest gold trader, in both certificates and in bullion, and maintains that position today.

During the 1960s even greater emphasis was placed on international representation. The 1970s saw even further international expansion, with new offices opened in the Middle and Far East. The Pacific Rim continues as a very important area to the bank. Today the Bank of Nova Scotia is recognized as one of the world's leading international financial institutions.

550-10 RAWDON, WRIGHT, HATCH & CO. POUNDS & SHILLINGS PRINTINGS 1832-1852

DESIGNS AND COLOURS

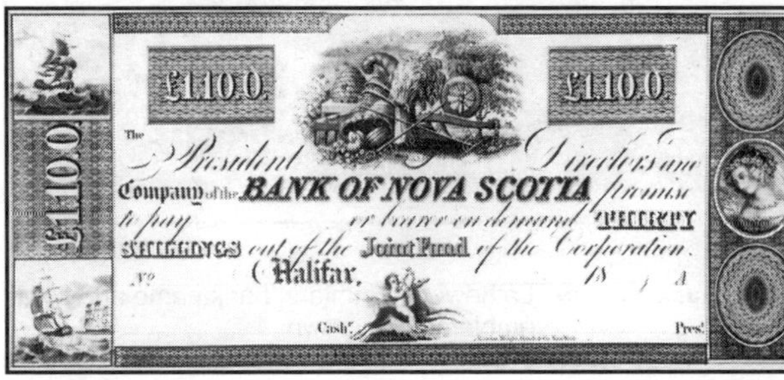

550-10-02P
£1.10.0 (30s)

Face Design: Sailing ships/farm implements and produce; child riding deer below/bust of young woman "Ceres, Goddess of Corn"
Colour: Black with no tint

Back Design: Plain

Photo Not Available

550-10-12P
£2 Face Design: Unknown
Colour: Black with no tint

Back Design: Plain

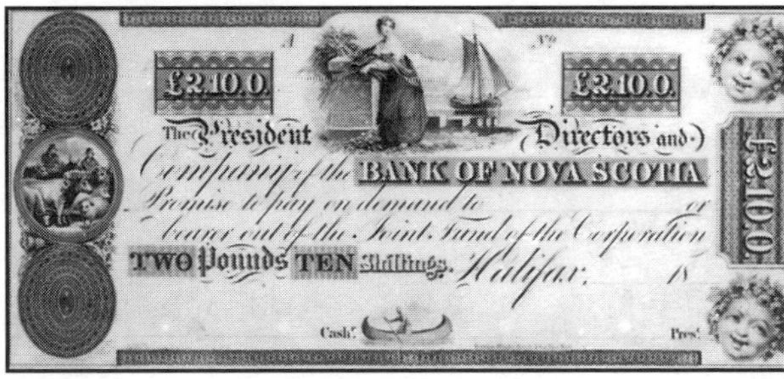

550-10-22P
£2.10.0 Face Design: Two men and livestock/ woman; ship; man in canoe below/ cherubs face top and bottom
Colour: Black with no tint

Back Design: Plain

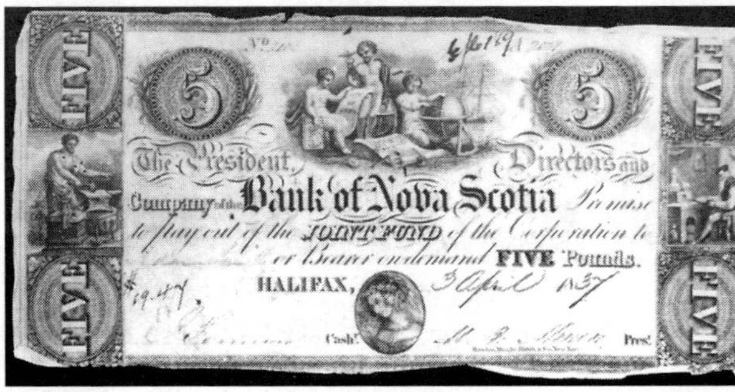

550-10-32
1837 Issue
£5 Face Design: Blacksmith/three cherubs and counters; bust of young woman "Ceres, Goddess of Corn" below/alchemist
Colour: Black with no tint

Back Design: Plain

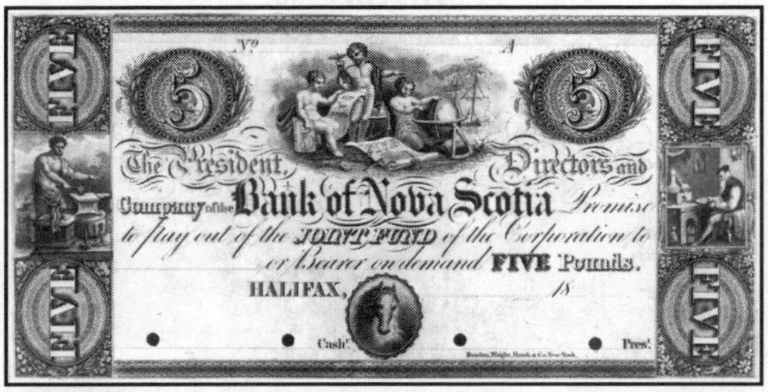

550-10-42
1834, 1839 and 1852 Issues

£5 Face Design: Blacksmith/three cherubs and counters; horse's head below/alchemist
Colour: Black with no tint

Back Design: Plain

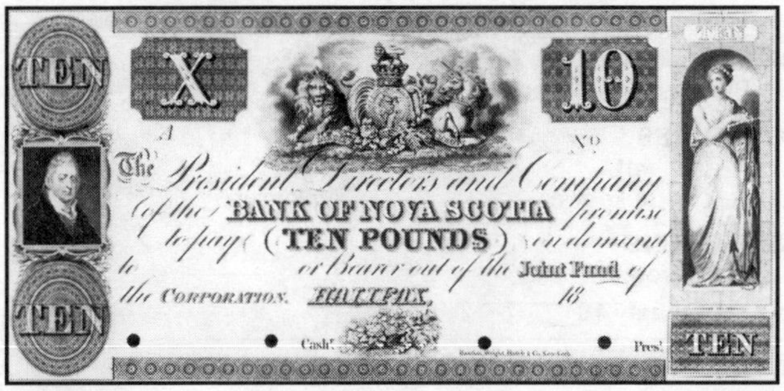

550-10-52

£10 Face Design: King William IV/Royal Crest; flowers below/woman standing with anchor
Colour: Black with no tint

Back Design: Plain

IMPRINT

Rawdon, Wright, Hatch & Co. New York

SIGNATURES

left	right
mss. James Forman	mss. William Lawson
mss. J. Forman	mss. M.B. Almon

ISSUE DATING

Partially engraved ___ 18___:

1832: Aug. 6
1834: 2nd June
1837: 3rd April
1839: 1 Jany

Engraved

January 1st 1852

CIRCULATING NOTES

Cat. No.	Denom.	Date	Variety	G	VG	F	VF	EF	AU
10-02	£1.10	18__	No known issued notes						
10-12	£2	18__	No known issued notes						
10-22	£2.10	18__	No known issued notes						
10-32	£5	1837	Woman vign. Institutional collection only						
10-42	£5	1832-52	Horse vign. Institutional collection only						
10-52	£10	1839-52	Horse vign. Institutional collection only						

PROOF NOTES

Cat. No.	Denom.	Date	Variety		Unc
10-02P	£1.10	18__		PROOF	750.
10-12P	£2	18__		PROOF	750.
10-22P	£2.10	18__		PROOF	750.
10-32P	£5	18__	Woman vign.	PROOF	750.
10-42P	£5	18__	Horse vign.	PROOF	750.
10-52P	£10	18__	Horse vign.	PROOF	750.

550-12 NEBN PRINTINGS POUNDS & SHILLINGS 1840

DESIGNS AND COLOURS

550-12-02P

£5.5 Face Design: Man and boy in shop/ St. George slaying the dragon; man and horses below/sailing ship
Colour: Black with no tint

Back Design: Plain

550-12-04

£6 Face Design: Men harvesting wheat/ allegorical male on chariot; steamboat below/ man on horse talking to farmer
Colour: Black with no tint

Back Design: Plain

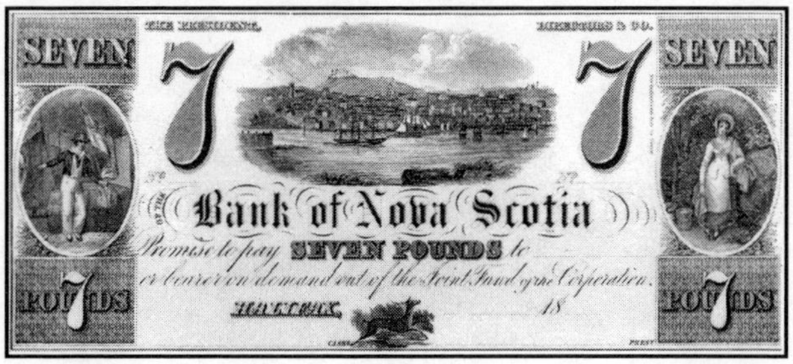

550-12-06

£7 Face Design: Sailor holding flag/Halifax harbour; deer leaping below/dairymaid
Colour: Black with no tint

Back Design: Plain

550-12-08

£7.10 Face Design: "Justice" figure/Crest; dog with key below/ woman supporting lyre

Colour: Black with no tint

Back Design: Plain

IMPRINT

New England Bank Note Co. Boston

SIGNATURES

left	right
unknown	unknown

ISSUE DATING

Partially engraved ___ 18___:

£5.5 1840: May 2

Engraved

£6: 1 July 1840
£7: 1 Augt 1840
£7.10: 1 August 1840

Cat. No.	Denom.	Date	G	VG	F	VF	EF	AU
12-02	£5.5	1840	Institutional collection only					
12-04	£6	1840	Institutional collection only					
12-06	£7	1840	Institutional collection only					
12-08	£7.10	1840	Institutional collection only					

550-14 BLADES, EAST & BLADES PRINTINGS, 1864

DESIGNS AND COLOURS

550-14-02

$20 Face Design: —/Royal Crest/—

Colour: Black with green tint

Back Design: Lathework and bank Crest

Colour: Unknown

IMPRINT

Blades, East & Blades, London

SIGNATURES

left	right
unknown	unknown

ISSUE DATING

Engraved

1st January 18__

Cat. No.	Denom.	Date	G	VG	F	VF	EF	AU
14-10	$20	18_	Institutional collection only					

550-16 $4, $5 AND $20 ISSUES OF 1870-1877

DESIGNS AND COLOURS

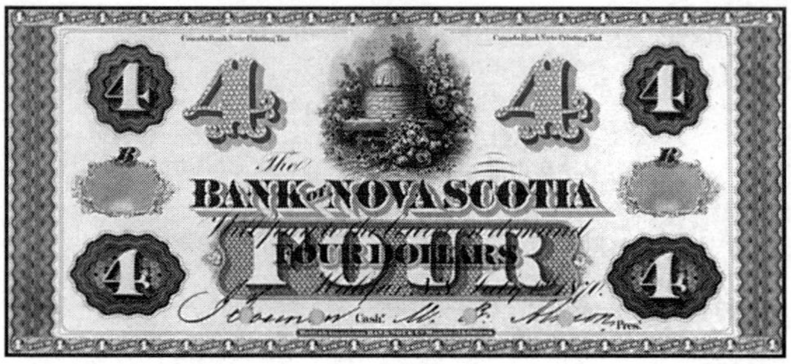

550-16-02

$4 Face Design: —/beehive and flowers/— plain green 4's at top

Colour: Black with green tint

550-16-03
$4 Face Design: —/beehive and flowers/— green four over 4's at top
Colour: Black with green tint

550-16-06
$4 Face Design: —/beehive and flowers/— four over 4 and Province of Nova Scotia at top
Colour: Black with green tint

Back Design: Lathework, counters, bank name and Crest
Colour: Green

550-16-08a
$5 Face Design: —/St. George slaying the dragon/—
Colour: Black with green tint

Back Design: Lathework, counters, bank name and Crest
Colour: Green

Photo Not Available

550-16-14
$20 Face Design: Unknown
Colour: Black with green tint

Back Design: Lathework, counters and bank name
Colour: Green

IMPRINT
$4 and $5: British American Bank Note Co. Montreal and Ottawa
$20: American Bank Note Company

SIGNATURES

left	right
mss. various	mss. various

ISSUE DATING
Engraved
$4 and $5: July 1st 1870
$4 and $5: July 1st 1871
$4 and $5: July 2nd 1877
$20: Jan. 1 1877

OVERPRINT
1870 or 1871: "CANADA CURRENCY" twice in red

Cat. No.	Denom.	Date	Variety	G	VG	F	VF	EF	AU
16-02	$4	1870	No o/p	1,500.	2,400.	3,200.	—	—	—
16-02a	$4	1870	Red o/p	1,500.	2,400.	3,200.	—	—	—
16-03	$4	1870	Four/4	1,500.	2,400.	3,200.	—	—	—
16-04	$4	1871		1,500.	2,400.	3,200.	—	—	—
16-06	$4	1877		1,500.	2,400.	3,200.	—	—	—
16-08	$5	1870	No o/p	1,500.	2,400.	3,200.	4,500.	—	—
16-08a	$5	1870	Red o/p	1,500.	2,400.	3,200.	—	—	—
16-10	$5	1871	Red o/p	1,500.	2,400.	3,200.	—	—	—
16-12	$5	1877		Institutional collection only					
16-14	$20	1871		Surviving Notes Not Confirmed					
16-16	$20	1877		Surviving Notes Not Confirmed					

550-18 $10 ISSUES OF 1877-1929

DESIGNS AND COLOURS

550-18-08
$10 Face Design: Mining scene/unicorn, shield and Indian "Arms of Nova Scotia"/ sailing ship
Colour: Black with ochre and blue tint

Back Design: Lathework, counters and bank name
1877-1919 Colour: Green
Back Design: Lathework, counters, bank name and bank seal
1924 Colour: Blue
1929 Colour: Slate

IMPRINT

American Bank Note Co. N.Y.
American Bank Note Co. Ottawa
Canadian Bank Note Company Limited

SIGNATURES

	left	right
1877:	mss. various	engr. Jno. Y. Payzant
	mss. various	engr. Jairus Hart
	mss. various	engr. John Doull
1903:	mss. various	typed Jno. Y. Payzant
1917:	mss. various	typed Jno. Y. Payzant
	typed H.A. Richardson	typed Jno. Y. Payzant
1919:	typed H.A. Richardson	typed Charles Archibald
1924:	typed G.S. Campbell	typed J.S. McLeod
1929:	typed S.J. Moore	typed J.A. McLeod

ISSUE DATING

Engraved

July 2nd 1877
Jany. 2nd 1903
Jany. 2nd 1917
Jany. 2nd 1919
Jany. 2nd 1924
Jany. 2nd 1929

CIRCULATING NOTES

Cat. No.	Denom.	Date	Variety	VG	F	VF	EF	AU	Unc
18-02	$10	1877	Payzant, r.	1,200.	1,600.	2,400.	—	—	—
18-04	$10	1877	Hart, r.	1,200.	1,600.	2,400.	—	—	—
18-06	$10	1877	Doull, r.	1,200.	1,600.	2,400.	—	—	—
18-08	$10	1903		200.	275.	400.	750.	1,150.	—
18-12	$10	1917	Mss. sig., l.	100.	125.	200.	375.	550.	750.
18-14	$10	1917	Richardson, l.	100.	125.	200.	375.	550.	750.
18-16	$10	1919		75.	100.	160.	275.	400.	550.
18-18	$10	1924		75.	100.	160.	275.	400.	550.
18-20	$10	1929		60.	80.	125.	225.	325.	450.

PROOF NOTES

Cat. No.	Denom.	Date		Unc
18-02P	$10	1877	FACE PROOF	600.

550-20 $5 ISSUES OF 1881

DESIGNS AND COLOURS

550-20-02

$5 Face Design: The Greek goddess Pallas/ Hon. Joseph Howe/Bank seal
Colour: See varieties

550-20-06a

Back Design: Lathework, counters and bank name
Colour: See varieties

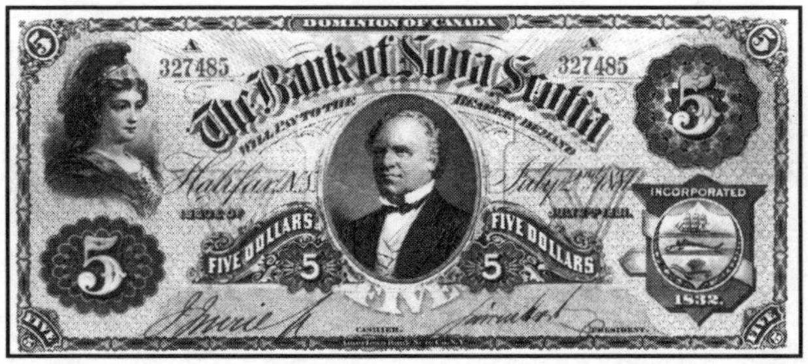

550-20-10

IMPRINT

American Bank Note Co. N.Y.

SIGNATURES

left	right
mss. various	mss. Jairus Hart
mss. various	mss. Adam Burns
mss. various	mss. John Doull

ISSUE DATING

Engraved

July 2nd 1881

VARIETIES

1. Face Colour: Black with overall blue tint, "FIVE" twice at bottom
   Back Colour: Green
2. Face Colour: Black with blue tint, no 5 outlined at bottom
   Back Colour: Brown
3. Face Colour: Black with blue, green and ochre tint, "FIVE" under portrait
   Back Colour: Brown
4. Face Colour: Black with green and red tint, No "FIVE" under portrait
   Back Colour: Brown

OVERPRINT

"WINNIPEG" twice in red

CIRCULATING NOTES

Cat. No.	Denom.	Date	Variety	G	VG	F	VF	EF	AU
20-02	$5	1881	Var. 1	No known issued notes					
20-06	$5	1881	Var. 2	—	2,500.	3,500.	5,000.	—	—
20-06a	$5	1881	Var. 2, Winn.	—	3,000.	4,100.	—	—	—
20-10	$5	1881	Var. 3	1,500.	2,500.	3,500.	5,000.	—	—
20-12	$5	1881	Var. 4	—	2,500.	3,500.	5,000.	—	—

PROOF NOTES

Cat. No.	Denom.	Date			Unc
20-02P	$5	1881	Var. 1	FACE PROOF	750.
20-06P	$5	1881	Var. 2	FACE PROOF	750.
20-10P	$5	1881	Var. 3	FACE PROOF	750.
20-12P	$5	1881	Var. 4	FACE PROOF	750.

550-22 $20 ISSUE OF 1882

DESIGNS AND COLOURS

Photo Not Available

550-22-02P

$20 Face Design: Unknown
Colour: Unknown

Back Design: Unknown
Colour: Unknown

IMPRINT

American Bank Note Company

SIGNATURES

left	right
unknown	unknown

ISSUE DATING

Engraved

Jan. 1, 1882

PROOF NOTES

Cat. No.	Denom.	Date		Unc
22-02P	$20	1882	FACE PROOF	900.

550-24 $20 ISSUE OF 1896

DESIGNS AND COLOURS

550-24-02

$20 Face Design: —/allegorical female and cherub/—
Colour: Black with pink and blue tint

Back Design: —/bank seal/—
Colour: Blue

IMPRINT

American Bank Note Company, New York

SIGNATURES

left	right
mss. various	engr. John Doull

ISSUE DATING

Engraved

July 2nd 1896

CIRCULATING NOTES

Cat. No.	Denom.	Date	G	VG	F	VF	EF	AU
24-02	$20	1896	1,200.	2,000.	3,000.	4,200.	—	—

PROOF NOTES

Cat. No.	Denom.	Date		Unc
24-02P	$20	1896	FACE PROOF	700.

SPECIMEN NOTES

Cat. No.	Denom.	Date		Unc
24-02S*	$20	1896	SPECIMEN	1,000.

* Colour trial, salmon colour tint on face, orange back.

550-26 $20 ISSUE OF 1897

DESIGNS AND COLOURS

550-26-02

$20 Face Design: Allegorical female writing, child "History"/portrait of young woman/allegorical female
Colour: Black with yellow-green and rose tint

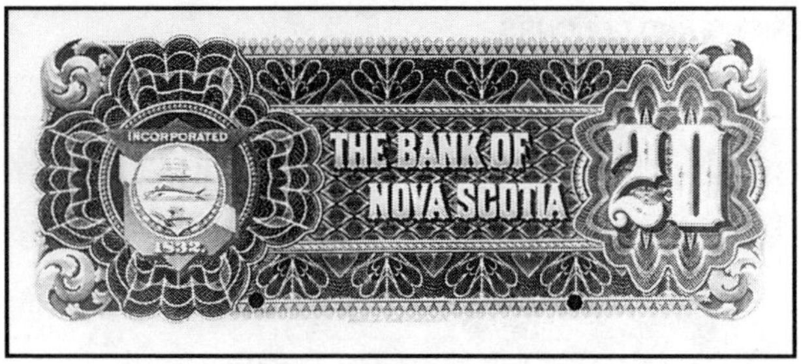

Back Design: Lathework, counters, bank name and bank seal
Colour: Olive green

IMPRINT

American Bank Note Company. New York

SIGNATURES

left	right
mss. various	engr. John Doull

ISSUE DATING

Engraved

Novr 1st, 1897

CIRCULATING NOTES

Cat. No.	Denom.	Date	G	VG	F	VF	EF	AU
26-02	$20	1897	1,200.	2,000.	3,000.	4,200.	—	—

SPECIMEN NOTES

Cat. No.	Denom.	Date	Unc
26-02S	$20	1897	SPECIMEN 1,000.

550-28 SCENIC ISSUES OF 1898-1929

DESIGNS AND COLOURS

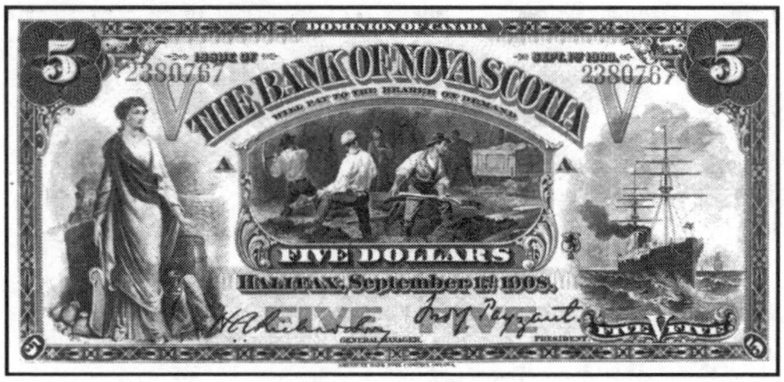

550-28-12a

$5 Face Design: Allegorical female/mining scene/ steamship approaching viewer
Colour: Black with yellow-green and orange tint
See varieties

Back Design: Lathework, counters, bank name and bank seal
Colour: Olive

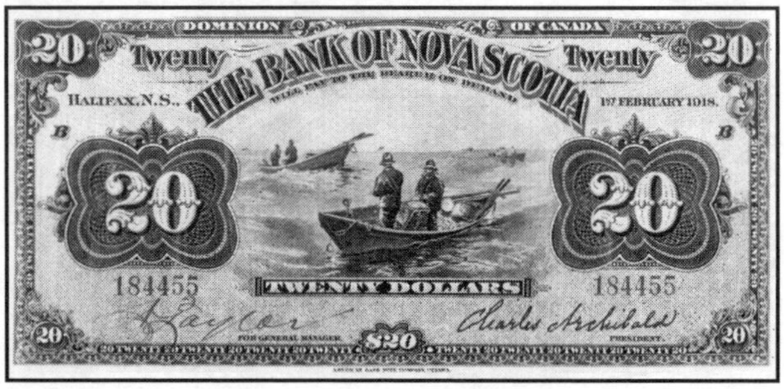

550-28-16

$20 Face Design: —/men fishing from two dories/—
Colour: Black with yellow-green and rose tint

Back Design: Lathework, counters, bank name and bank seal
Colour: Rose, green and brown
1925 Colour: Green
1929 Colour: Orange

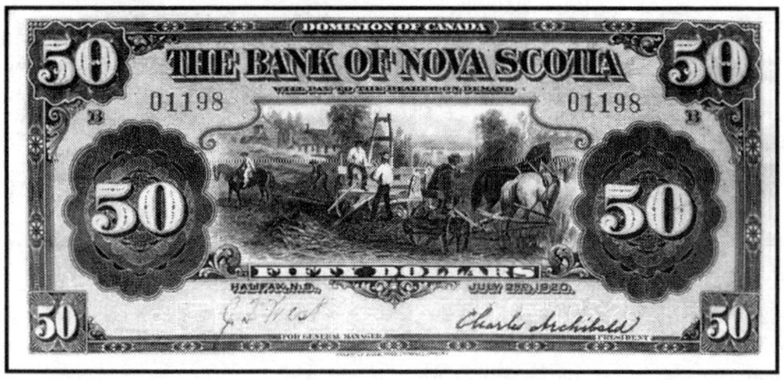

550-28-26

$50 Face Design: —/threshing scene/—
Colour: Black with olive and red tint

Back Design: Lathework, counters, bank name and bank seal
Colour: Slate

550-28-38

$100 Face Design: —/100 counter flanked by Liberty and a lion, and by art and industry figure/—
Colour: Black with yellow-green and rose tint

Back Design: Lathework, counters, bank name and bank seal
Colour: Brown

IMPRINT

American Bank Note Company, Ottawa
Canadian Bank Note Company Limited
American Bank Note Co. Ottawa

SIGNATURES

	left	right
1898:	mss. various	engr. Jairus Hart
	mss. various	typed Jno. Y. Payzant
	mss. various	engr. John Doull
1899:	mss. various	engr. John Doull
1903-1906:	mss. various	typed Jno. Y. Payzant
1908:	mss. various	typed Jno. Y. Payzant
	typed H.A. Richardson	typed Jno. Y. Payzant
1911:	mss. various	typed Jno. Y. Payzant
1918-1920:	mss. various	typed Charles Archibald
	typed Charles Archibald	typed H.A. Richardson
	mss. various	typed G.S. Campbell
1925:	typed J.A. McLeod	typed G.S. Campbell
	mss. various	typed G.S. Campbell
1929:	typed J.A. McLeod	typed S.J. Moore

ISSUE DATING

Engraved

June 1st 1898	1st February 1918
August 1st 1899	January 2nd 1919
January 2nd 1903	July 2nd 1920
May 1st 1906	January 2nd 1925
September 1st 1908	January 2nd 1929
January 3rd 1911	

VARIETIES

$5, 1908 Face Tint: No orange Vs
$5, 1908 Face Tint: Orange Vs at top and "FIVE" twice at bottom

OVERPRINT

$5, 1898: "S S" in red

CIRCULATING NOTES

Cat. No.	Denom.	Date	Variety	G	VG	F	VF	EF	Unc
28-02	$5	1898	Hart, r.	300.	500.	700.	1,000.	—	—
28-04	$5	1898	Doull,r	350.	600.	850.	1,200.	—	—
28-06	$5	1898	Payzant, r.	125.	250.	325.	500.	750.	—
28-06a	$5	1898	SS o/p	125.	250.	325.	500.	750.	—
28-08	$5	1908	No Vs	75.	150.	200.	350.	650.	—
28-12	$5	1908	Orange V's mss. l.	75.	150.	200.	350.	650.	—
28-12a	$5	1908	Orange V's typed l.	75.	150.	200.	350.	650.	1,250.
28-14	$20	1903		125.	250.	350.	500.	—	—
28-16	$20	1918	mss. l.	75.	150.	200.	300.	550.	1,100.
28-16a	$20	1918	typed l.	125.	250.	350.	—	—	—
28-18	$20	1925		60.	125.	175.	250.	450.	900.
28-22	$20	1929		60.	125.	175.	250.	450.	900.
28-24	$50	1906		550.	1,100.	1,600.	2,500.	—	—
28-26	$50	1920		350.	700.	1,000.	1,500.	2,500.	5,000.
28-28	$50	1925		600.	1,200.	1,800.	2,800.	—	—
28-32	$100	1899		Institutional collection only					
28-34	$100	1911		Institutional collection only					
28-36	$100	1919		950.	1,900.	2,700.	3,500.	4,600.	—
28-38	$100	1925		—	—	2,700.	3,500.	4,600.	—
28-38	$100	1929		—	—	2,700.	3,500.	4,600.	—

SPECIMEN NOTES

Cat. No.	Denom.	Date		Unc
28-22S	$20	1929	SPECIMEN	500.
28-24S	$50	1906	SPECIMEN	600.

550-30 $5 ISSUE OF 1918

DESIGNS AND COLOURS

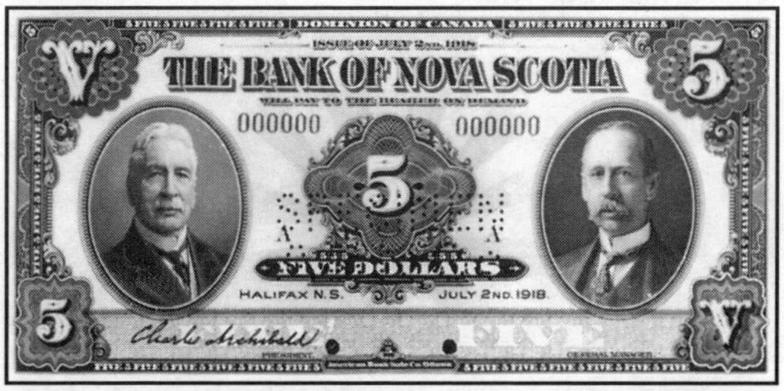

550-30-02S

$5 Face Design: John Y. Payzant/—/H.A. Richardson
Colour: Black with green tint

Back Design: Lathework, counters, bank name and bank seal
Colour: Green

IMPRINT

American Bank Note Co. Ottawa

SIGNATURES

left	right
typed Charles Archibald	typed H.A. Richardson

ISSUE DATING

Engraved

July 2nd 1918

CIRCULATING NOTES

Cat. No.	Denom.	Date	VG	F	VF	EF	AU	Unc
30-02	$5	1918	90.	125.	200.	350.	—	—

SPECIMEN NOTES

Cat. No.	Denom.	Date		Unc
30-02S	$5	1918	SPECIMEN	500.

550-32 **$5 ISSUE OF 1924**

DESIGNS AND COLOURS

550-32-02

$5 Face Design: G.S. Campbell/—/John A. McLeod
Colour: Black with red and green tint

Back Design: Lathework, counters, bank name and bank seal
Colour: Brown

IMPRINT

Canadian Bank Note Company Limited

SIGNATURES

left	**right**
typed G.S. Campbell	typed J.A. McLeod

ISSUE DATING

Engraved

January 2nd 1924

Cat. No.	Denom.	Date	VG	F	VF	EF	AU	Unc
32-02	$5	1924	60.	75.	125.	200.	350.	500.

550-34 **$5 ISSUE OF 1929**

DESIGNS AND COLOURS

550-34-02

$5 Face Design: S.J. Moore/—/John A. McLeod
Colour: Black with red and green tint

Back Design: Lathework, counters, bank name and Bank Seal
Colour: Green

IMPRINT

Canadian Bank Note Company Limited

SIGNATURES

left	**right**
typed S.J. Moore	typed J.A. McLeod

ISSUE DATING

Engraved

January 2nd 1929

Cat. No.	Denom.	Date	VG	F	VF	EF	AU	Unc
34-02	$5	1929	60.	80.	125.	225.	325.	450.

550-36 **ISSUE OF 1935, SMALL-SIZE NOTES**

DESIGNS AND COLOURS

550-36-02

$5 Face Design: John A. McLeod/—/Harry F. Patterson
Colour: Black with red and green tint

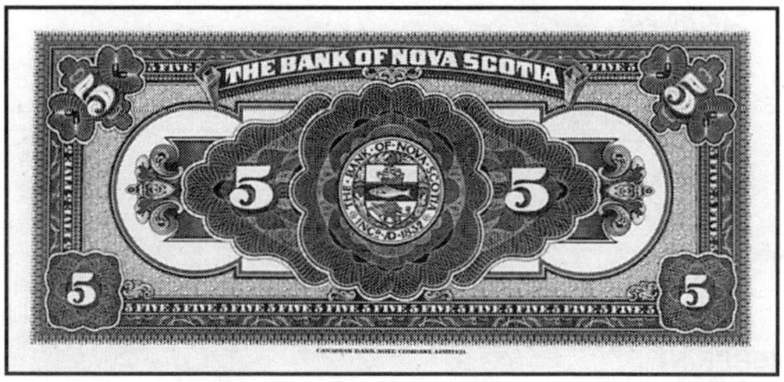

Back Design: Lathework, counters, bank name and Bank Seal
Colour: Green

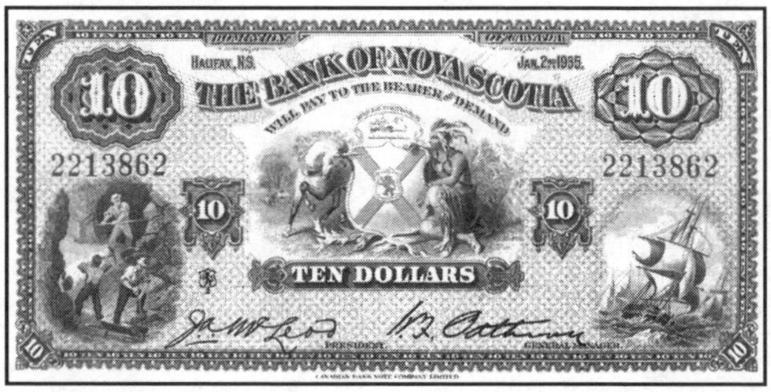

550-36-04

$10 Face Design: Mining scene/unicorn, shield and lion "Arms of Nova Scotia"/ sailing ship
Colour: Black with ochre and blue tint

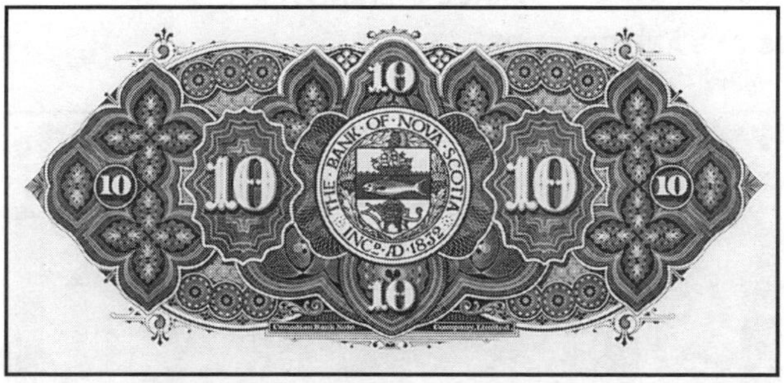

Back Design: Lathework, counters, bank name and Bank Seal
Colour: Slate

IMPRINT

Canadian Bank Note Co. Limited
Canadian Bank Note Company Limited

SIGNATURES

left	right
typed J.A. McLeod	typed H.F. Patterson

ISSUE DATING

Engraved

Jan. 2nd 1935.

Cat. No.	Denom.	Date	VG	F	VF	EF	AU	Unc
36-02	$5	1935	45.	65.	110.	175.	275.	400.
36-04	$10	1935	40.	60.	100.	150.	200.	250.

THE BANK OF NOVA SCOTIA BRITISH WEST INDIES ISSUES

The trade between the Province of Nova Scotia and the West Indies had always been active, as far back as the 1820s. An act of Parliament, passed in July 1899, enabled Canadian banks to issue notes in any British colony other than Canada, and the Bank of Nova Scotia was the first Canadian bank to establish a branch outside Canada.

The Caribbean branch opened in Kingston, Jamaica, in 1889. The notes issued for Jamaica were in denominations of £1 and £5 and were redeemable in that colony. The Bank of Nova Scotia was also the first to open a savings-account business on the island.

550-38 KINGSTON, JAMAICA, 1900-1930

2. LARGE-SIZE NOTES

DESIGNS AND COLOURS

550-38-02-02P

£1 Face Design: —/two seated allegorical figures flanking counter/—
Colour: Black with green and yellow-green tint

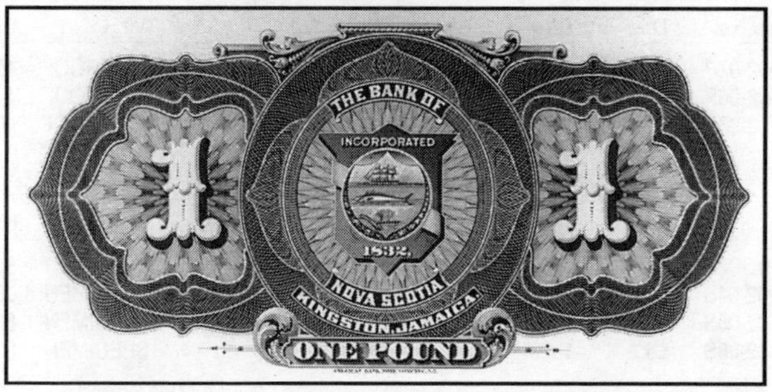

Back Design: Lathework, counters, bank name and Bank Crest
Colour: Green

550-38-02-08

£5 Face Design: —/two allegorical women seated on globe/—
Colour: Black with orange and yellow-green tint

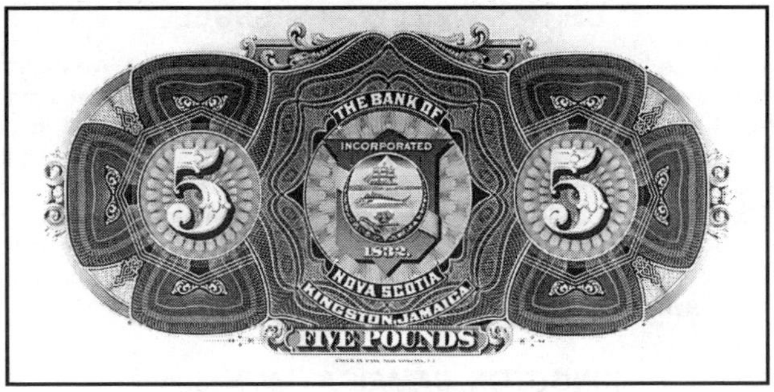

Back Design: Lathework, counters, bank name and bank crest
Colour: Brown

IMPRINT

American Bank Note Company, N.Y.

SIGNATURES

	left	right
1900:	mss. various	typed Jno. Y. Payzant
1919-1920:	mss. various	typed Charles Archibald

ISSUE DATING

Engraved

January 2nd 1900
January 2nd 1919
Jan. 2, 1920

CIRCULATING NOTES

Cat. No.	Denom.	Date	G	VG	F	VF	EF	AU
38-02-02	£1	1900	—	—	—	5,000.	—	—
38-02-04	£1	1919	No known issued notes					
38-02-06	£5	1900	—	1,000.	1,500.	2,500.	—	—
38-02-08	£5	1920	—	750.	1,000.	1,600.	—	—

PROOF NOTES

Cat. No.	Denom.	Date		Unc
38-02-02P	£1	1900	FACE PROOF	400.
38-02-06P	£5	1900	FACE PROOF	400.
38-02-08P	£5	1920	FACE PROOF	400.

SPECIMEN NOTES

Cat. No.	Denom.	Date		Unc
38-02-02S	£1	1900	SPECIMEN	850.
38-02-04S	£1	1919	SPECIMEN	1,000.
38-02-06S	£5	1900	SPECIMEN	850.
38-02-08S	£5	1920	SPECIMEN	850.

4. SMALL-SIZE NOTES

DESIGNS AND COLOURS

550-38-04-04

£1 Face Design: —/woman seated on throne with produce/—
Colour: Black with green, blue and yellow tint

Back Design: Lathework, counters, bank name and Bank Crest
Colour: Green

IMPRINT

Canadian Bank Note Company Limited

SIGNATURES

left	right
typed S.J. Moore	typed John A. McLeod
typed J.A. McLeod	typed Henry F. Patterson

ISSUE DATING

Engraved

January 2nd 1930.

CIRCULATING NOTES

Cat. No.	Denom.	Date	Variety	G	VG	F	VF	EF	AU
38-04-02	£1	1930	McLeod, r.	175.	350.	450.	800.	1,300.	1,750.
38-04-04	£1	1930	Patterson, r.	175.	350.	450.	800.	1,300.	1,750.

PROOF NOTES

Cat. No.	Denom.	Date		Unc
38-04-02P	£1	1930	FACE PROOF	400.

THE ONTARIO BANK

1857-1906

BOWMANVILLE, PROVINCE OF CANADA

BANK NUMBER 555 ***REDEEMABLE***

The Ontario Bank was established in Bowmanville, Canada West, in 1857 (and later in Toronto). It was discovered in 1905 that the general manager had been falsifying the books to hide Wall Street losses that had obliterated the bank's reserves. The bank did not suspend payment, but when difficulties were encountered through some of its lumber accounts, an arrangement was made in 1906 whereby all liabilities were taken over by the Bank of Montreal. Together with certain other banks, the Bank of Montreal assumed all liabilities and paid depositors in full. Criminal charges were laid against the general manager and the president. The former was sentenced to the Kingston Penitentiary, but the president was exonerated of complicity.

555-10 ISSUES OF 1857 AND 1861

DESIGNS AND COLOURS

555-10-02-02a

$1 Face Design: Agricultural produce/cattle/ sheep shearing scene
See subheadings
Colour: Black with overall green tint

Back Design: Lathework and bank name
Colour: Green

555-10-08-04a

$2 Face Design: Blacksmith and anvil/ seated woman with dog and cattle/-
See subheadings
Colour: Black with overall green tint

Back Design: Lathework and bank name
Colour: Green

555-10-06-06P

$5 Face Design: Jacques Cartier/farmer sharpening scythe in grain field/bull's head
See subheadings
Colour: Black with overall green tint

Back Design: Lathework and bank name
Colour: Green

555-10-02-08P

$10 Face Design: Barges and bridge/ seated Indian and Crest/cattle driving scene
See subheadings
Colour: Black with overall green tint

Back Design: Lathework and bank name
Colour: Green

IMPRINT

Rawdon, Wright, Hatch & Edson Montreal & N.Y. and American Bank Note Co. "mono"

SIGNATURES

left	right
mss. various	mss. various

2. ENGRAVED "BOWMANVILLE" ONE BLUE SHEET NUMBER (AT BOTTOM) 1857

ISSUE DATING

Engraved

Aug't. 15th 1857

OVERPRINT

"GUELPH" twice in red
"MONTREAL" twice in red
"PRESCOTT" in blue
"TORONTO" twice in blue
"ALEXANDRIA" in blue

CIRCULATING NOTES

Cat. No.	Denom.	Date	Variety	G	VG	F	VF	EF	AU
10-02-02	$1	1857	no o/p	450.	900.	—	—	—	—
10-02-02a	$1	1857	town o/p	500.	1,000.	1,300.	—	—	—
10-02-04a	$2	1857	town o/p	550.	1,100.	—	—	—	—
10-02-06	$5	1857		No known issued notes					
10-02-08	$10	1857		No known issued notes					

PROOF NOTES

Cat. No.	Denom.	Date		Unc
10-02-02P	$1	1857	FACE PROOF	500.
10-02-04P	$2	1857	FACE PROOF	500.
10-02-06P	$5	1857	FACE PROOF	500.
10-02-08P	$10	1857	FACE PROOF	500.

Note: A $1 1857 face proof is known with red-orange tint.

4. ENGRAVED "MONTREAL" ONE BLUE SHEET NUMBER (AT BOTTOM) 1857

ISSUE DATING

Engraved

Augt. 15 1857

OVERPRINT

"OSHAWA" twice in red
"TORONTO" in blue

CIRCULATING NOTES

Cat. No.	Denom.	Date	Variety	G	VG	F	VF	EF	AU
10-04-02	$1	1857	no o/p	450.	900.	—	—	—	—
10-04-02a	$1	1857	town o/p	500.	1,000.	1,300.	—	—	—
10-04-04a	$2	1857	town o/p	550.	1,100.	—	—	—	—
10-04-06	$5	1857		No known issued notes					
10-04-08	$10	1857		No known issued notes					

PROOF NOTES

Cat. No.	Denom.	Date		Unc
10-04-02P	$1	1857	FACE PROOF	500.
10-04-04P	$2	1857	FACE PROOF	500.
10-04-06P	$5	1857	FACE PROOF	500.
10-04-08P	$10	1857	FACE PROOF	500.

6. ENGRAVED "BOWMANVILLE" ONE RED SHEET NUMBER (AT BOTTOM) 1861

ISSUE DATING

Engraved

Augt. 15th 1861

OVERPRINT

"GUELPH" twice in red
"DUNDAS" twice in red
"TORONTO" twice in blue

CIRCULATING NOTES

Cat. No.	Denom.	Date	Variety	G	VG	F	VF	EF	AU
10-06-02a	$1	1861	town o/p	500.	1,000.	1,300.	—	—	—
10-06-04a	$2	1861	town o/p	550.	1,100.	—	—	—	—
10-06-06	$5	1861		Institutional collection only					
10-06-08	$10	1861		Institutional collection only					

PROOF NOTES

Cat. No.	Denom.	Date		Unc
10-06-02P	$1	1861	FACE PROOF	500.
10-06-04P	$2	1861	FACE PROOF	500.
10-06-06P	$5	1861	FACE PROOF	500.
10-06-08P	$10	1861	FACE PROOF	500.

8. ENGRAVED "BOWMANVILLE" TWO RED SHEET NUMBERS (AT TOP) 1861

ISSUE DATING

Engraved

Augt. 15th 1861

OVERPRINT

"HAMILTON" twice in blue
"LINDSAY" twice in red

Cat. No.	Denom.	Date	Variety	G	VG	F	VF	EF	AU
10-08-02a	$1	1861	town o/p	500.	1,000.	1,300.	—	—	—
10-08-04a	$2	1861	town o/p	550.	1,100.	—	—	—	—
10-08-06	$5	1861		No known issued notes					
10-08-08	$10	1861		No known issued notes					

10. ENGRAVED "BOWMANVILLE" TWO BLUE SHEET NUMBERS (AT TOP) 1861

ISSUE DATING

Engraved

Augt. 15th 1861

OVERPRINT

"GUELPH" twice in red
"WHITBY" twice in blue
"MONTREAL" twice in red

CIRCULATING NOTES

Cat. No.	Denom.	Date	Variety	G	VG	F	VF	EF	AU
10-10-02a	$1	1861	town o/p	500.	1,000.	1,300.	—	—	—
10-10-04a	$2	1861	town o/p	550.	1,100.	—	—	—	—
10-10-06	$5	1861		No known issued notes					
10-10-08	$10	1861		No known issued notes					

555-12 **ISSUE OF 1860**

DESIGNS AND COLOURS

555-12-02P

$20 Face Design: Young woman resting on hay/—/ farm boy sitting with sheep; Prince Albert
Colour: Black with green tint

Back Design: Lathework, counters and bank name
Colour: Green

555-12-04P

$50 Face Design: Allegorical women with beehive, cornucopia/ Prince of Wales/allegorical woman with cornucopia, grapes
Colour: Black with green tint

Back Design: Lathework, counters and bank name
Colour: Green

555-12-06P

$100 Face Design: Prince of Wales/two seated allegorical women "Prosperity"/—
Colour: Black with green tint

Back Design: Lathework, counters and bank name
Colour: Green

IMPRINT

American Bank Note Company

SIGNATURES

left	**right**
none	none

ISSUE DATING

Engraved

Aug. 3rd 1860
Aug't 3rd 1860

PROOF NOTES

Cat. No.	Denom.	Date		Unc
12-02P	$20	1860	FACE PROOF	600
12-04P	$50	1860	FACE PROOF	750
12-06P	$100	1860	FACE PROOF	900

555-14 **ISSUES OF 1870**

DESIGNS AND COLOURS

555-14-02a

$4 Face Design: Farmer ploughing/—/Prince Arthur
Colour: Black with green tint

Back Design: Lathework, counters and bank name
Colour: Green

555-14-04a

$5 Face Design: Prince Arthur/farm woman with sickle/ portrait of woman "Adrienne"
Colour: Black with green tint

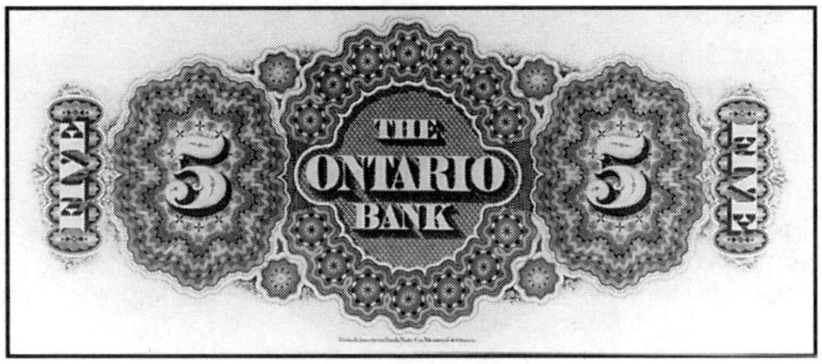

Back Design: Lathework, counters and bank name
Colour: Green

555-14-06a
$10 Face Design: Woodsman felling tree/—/
girl holding scroll of Confederation
Colour: Black with green tint

Back Design: Lathework, counters and bank name
Colour: Green

IMPRINT

British American Bank Note Co. Montreal & Ottawa

SIGNATURES

	left	right	
$4:	none	mss. illegible	
$5 and $10:		mss. various	engr. J. Simpson

ISSUE DATING

Engraved

$4: Augt 1st 1870
$5 and $10: Novr. 1st 1870

OVERPRINT

"LINDSAY" twice in blue
"PETERBORO" twice in blue
"MONTREAL" twice in blue
"OSHAWA" twice in blue

Note: Beware of counterfeits, some with overprints, that have a crude imprint of the British American Bank Note Co. on the bottom.

CIRCULATING NOTES

Cat. No.	Denom.	Date	Variety	G	VG	F	VF	EF	AU
14-02a	$4	1870	town o/p	400.	800.	1,200.	—	—	—
14-04a	$5	1870	town o/p	400.	800.	1,200.	—	—	—
14-06	$10	1870	no o/p	350.	700.	1,000.	—	—	—
14-06a	$10	1870	town o/p	400.	800.	1,200.	—	—	—
14-06C	$10	1870	Counterfeit	50.	100.	150.	—	—	—
14-06Ca	$10	1870	Counterfeit o/p PETERBORO	60.	125.	275.	—	—	—

PROOF NOTES

Cat. No.	Denom.	Date		Unc
14-02P	$4	1870	FACE PROOF	500.
14-04P	$5	1870	FACE PROOF	500.
14-06P	$10	1870	FACE PROOF	500.

555-16 ISSUE OF 1882

DESIGNS AND COLOURS

555-16-02
$5 Face Design: Portrait of woman "Lucy"/
Indian girl and Crest/train at station
Colour: Black with green tint

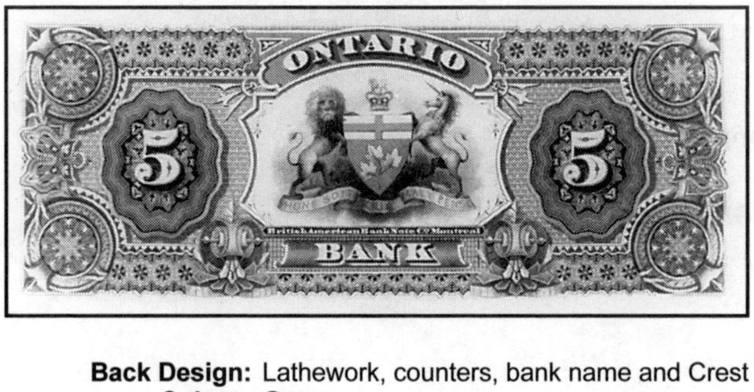

Back Design: Lathework, counters, bank name and Crest
Colour: Green

555-16-04P

$10 Face Design: Prince Arthur/dockside scene/ girl with agricultural emblems
Colour: Black with green tint

Back Design: Lathework, counters, bank name and Crest
Colour: Green

555-16-06P

$10 Face Design: Cattle grazing/—/ girl with agricultural emblems
Colour: Black with green tint

Back Design: Lathework, counters, bank name and Crest
Colour: Green

555-16-08

$100 Face Design: Prince of Wales/ allegorical females "Prosperity"/—
Colour: Black with green tint

Back Design: Lathework, counters, bank name and Crest
Colour: Green

IMPRINT

British American Bank Note Co. Monteal

SIGNATURES

left	right
engr. W.P. Howland	mss. various

ISSUE DATING

Engraved

July 3rd 1882
1st September 1882 ($100)

CIRCULATING NOTES

Cat. No.	Denom.	Date	Variety	G	VG	F	VF	EF	AU
16-02	$5	1882		Institutional collection only					
16-04	$10	1882	Prince Arthur vign.	No known issued notes					
16-06	$10	1882	Cattle grazing vign.	No known issued notes					
16-08	$100	1882		No known issued notes					

PROOF NOTES

Cat. No.	Denom.	Date	Variety		Unc
16-02P	$5	1882		FACE PROOF	500.
16-04P	$10	1882	Prince Arthur vign.	FACE PROOF	500.
16-06P	$10	1882	Cattle grazing vign.	FACE PROOF	500.
16-08P	$100	1882		FACE PROOF	800.

555-18 ISSUE OF 1888

DESIGNS AND COLOURS

555-18-02

$5 Face Design: Farmer feeding hay to horse "Old Burhans"/ Indian brave/woman with hand on wheel
Colour: Black with yellow and orange tint

Back Design: Lathework, counters and bank name
Colour: Orange

555-18-04
$5 Face Design: Farmer feeding hay to horse "Old Burhans"/ Indian brave/woman with hand on wheel (1903 overprint)
Colour: Black with yellow and orange tint

Back Design: Lathework, counters and bank name
Colour: Orange

555-18-06
$10 Face Design: Baby and young girl "Calmady children"/ seated allegorical female/sailor boy holding hat
Colour: Black with yellow-green and orange tint

Back Design: Lathework, counters, bank name and flowers
Colour: Olive

555-18-10P
$20 Face Design: Laureate busts of two allegorical women "Reapers"/seated woman and sheep/—
Colour: Black with yellow and blue tint

Back Design: Lathework, counters and bank name
Colour: Green

555-18-12P
$50 Face Design: Seated woman with water jar "River Source"/—/sailor, anchor and small boat
Colour: Black with yellow-green and red tint

Back Design: Lathework, counters and bank name
Colour: Brown

IMPRINT

American Bank Note Co. Ottawa
American Bank Note Co. N.Y.
American Bank Note Co. New York

OVERPRINTS
"1903" twice in red

SIGNATURES

	left	right
1888:	engr. W.P. Howland	mss. various
1903:	engr. George R.R. Cockburn	mss. various

ISSUE DATING
Engraved
1st June 1888

CIRCULATING NOTES

Cat. No.	Denom.	Date	Variety	G	VG	F	VF	EF	AU
18-02	$5	1888		800.	1,600.	2,400.	3,500.	—	—
18-04	$5	1888	Red o/p, 1903	950.	1,900.	—	—	—	—
18-06	$10	1888		1,000.	2,000.	3,000.	—	—	—
18-08	$10	1888	Red o/p, 1903	Institutional collection only					
18-10	$20	1888		No known issued notes					
18-12	$50	1888		No known issued notes					

PROOF NOTES

Cat. No	Denom.	Date	Variety		Unc
18-02P	$5	1888	B & W	FACE PROOF	300.
18-02Pa	$5	1888	Coloured	FACE PROOF	600.
18-06P	$10	1888	B & W	FACE PROOF	300.
18-06Pa	$10	1888	Coloured	FACE PROOF	600.
18-10P	$20	1888	B & W	FACE PROOF	300.
18-10Pa	$20	1888	Coloured	FACE PROOF	600.
18-12P	$50	1888	B & W	FACE PROOF	400.
18-12Pa	$50	1888	Coloured	FACE PROOF	800.

SPECIMEN NOTES

Cat. No.	Denom.	Date		Unc
18-02S	$5	1888	SPECIMEN	900.
18-06S	$10	1888	SPECIMEN	900.
18-10S	$20	1888	SPECIMEN	900.
18-12S	$50	1888	SPECIMEN	1,100.

555-20 $5 ISSUE OF 1898

DESIGNS AND COLOURS

555-20-02

$5 Face Design: Portrait of woman "Lucy"/ female figure and cherubs, ornate V/ bull's head
Colour: Black with green tint

Back Design: Lathework, counters and bank name
Colour: Green

IMPRINT
British American Bank Note Co. Ottawa

SIGNATURES

left	right
engr. George R.R. Cockburn	mss. various

ISSUE DATING
Engraved
Jan. 1st 1898.

CIRCULATING NOTES

Cat. No.	Denom.	Date	G	VG	F	VF	EF	AU
20-02	$5	1898	850.	1,700.	2,500.	—	—	—

PROOF NOTES

Cat. No.	Denom.	Date		Unc
20-02P	$5	1898	FACE PROOF	600.

Note: Face proof exists with red-brown face tint.

THE BANK OF OTTAWA

1837

MONTREAL, LOWER CANADA

BANK NUMBER 560 ***NONREDEEMABLE***

This "spurious" bank was established in 1837 by a group of New York swindlers. Ottawa was known as Bytown until the 1860s.

560-10 DRAFT ISSUE OF 1837 FRENCH TEXT

DESIGNS AND COLOURS

560-10-02

$5 Face Design: —/Royal Crest; small horse's head at bottom/ King William IV
Colour: Black with no tint

Back Design: Lathework, miniature vignettes and "steel plate"
Colour: Blue

IMPRINT

Burton, Gurley & Edmonds, N. York

SIGNATURES

left	right
mss. D. Moir Thom	mss. A. Sears

ISSUE DATING

Partially engraved _ 18_:

1837: April 1, Apr. 15, May 15

Cat. No.	Denom.	Date	G	VG	F	VF	EF	AU
10-02	$5	1837	175.	350.	500.	—	—	—

560-12 DRAFT ISSUE OF 1837 ENGLISH TEXT

DESIGNS AND COLOURS

560-12-02-02

$1 Face Design: Woman pouring wine "Temperance"/ three allegorical women; small crown at bottom/helmeted woman with eagle "Prudence"
Colour: Black with no tint

Back Design: See subheadings
Colour: See subheadings

560-12-04-04

$3 Face Design: Allegorical female with foot on globe/ mill scene, small horse's head at bottom/ bust of young woman
Colour: Black with no tint

Back Design: See subheadings
Colour: See subheadings

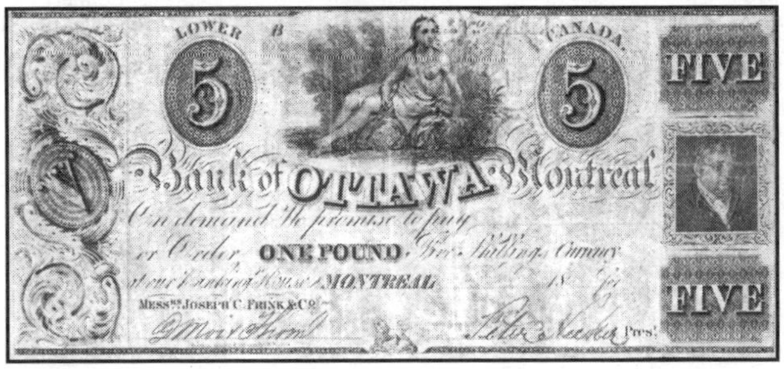

560-12-02-04R

$5 (£1.5) Face Design: Floral panel/semi-nude, reclining Indian maiden; small lion on crown at bottom/ James Fox
See subheadings
Colour: Black with no tint

Back Design: See subheadings
Colour: See subheadings

IMPRINT

Burton, Gurley & Edmonds, N. York

2. "ACCEPTED FOR MESSRS. JOSEPH C. FRINK & CO." AT BOTTOM, BLUE BACK

DESIGNS AND COLOURS

Back Design: Lathework, miniature vignettes of horsehead, deer head, small train, steamboat and "steel plate"

Colour: Blue

SIGNATURES

left	right
mss. D. Moir Thom	mss. Peter Hicker

ISSUE DATING

Partially engraved ___ 18___:

1837: Aug. 10; Oct. 11
1844: Jany

Cat. No.	Denom.	Date	Variety	G	VG	F	VF	EF	AU
12-02-02	$1	1837		175.	350.	500.	—	—	—
12-02-04R	$5 (£1.5)	18_	Remainder*	150.	300.	400.	—	—	—

* Signed and numbered, but undated.

3. "ACCEPTED FOR D.F. MERRILL & CO" AT BOTTOM

DESIGNS AND COLOURS

Back Design: Plain

SIGNATURES

left	right
mss. D. Moir Thom	—

ISSUE DATING

Partially Engraved ___ 18___:

1837: May 10, May 18

Cat.No.	Denom.	Date	G	VG	F	VF	EF	AU
12-03-02	$1	1837	160.	325.	425.	—	—	—

4. "ACCEPTED FOR ____" AT BOTTOM, PLAIN BACK

DESIGNS AND COLOURS

Back Design: Plain

SIGNATURES

left	right
mss. A. Keith	mss. H. Fitch

ISSUE DATING

Partially engraved _ 18_:

1837: Nov. 1
1838: Jan. 4

STAMP

"SECURED BY REAL ESTATE" in black

Cat. No.	Denom.	Date	G	VG	F	VF	EF	AU
12-04-02	$1	1837	160.	325.	425.	—	—	—
12-04-04	$3	1838	225.	450.	600.	—	—	—

Note: On some notes the space designated "Accepted for" has been filled in with the inscription, "the stockholders".

560-14 ISSUE OF 1837

DESIGNS AND COLOURS

560-14-02

$10 Face Design: Three cherubs with slab bearing "TEN"/ small lion on crown below/ woman with spear

Colour: Black with no tint

Back Design: Lathework, miniature vignettes and steel plate

Colour: Blue

IMPRINT

Burton, Gurley & Edmonds, N. York

SIGNATURES

left	right
mss. D. Moir Thom	mss. A. Sears

ISSUE DATING

Partially engraved ___ 18___:

1837: April 1

Cat. No.	Denom.	Date	G	VG	F	VF	EF	AU
14-02	$10	1837	235.	475.	650.	—	—	—

THE BANK OF OTTAWA

1874-1919

OTTAWA (ONTARIO) DOMINION OF CANADA

BANK NUMBER 565 ***REDEEMABLE***

Established in 1874 in Ottawa, this bank dominated the banking facilities in that city. The Bank of Ottawa had been founded by men who were pioneers in the Ottawa Valley lumber industry. After World War I the bank had reached a point where new capital and vigorous expansion were necessary to maintain its earnings. The offer made by the Bank of Nova Scotia to absorb the bank looked attractive, and the merger was finalized in 1919.

565-10 ISSUE OF 1874

DESIGNS AND COLOURS

565-10-02

$4 Face Design: Hon. George Bryson/Crest of Ottawa/ James Maclaren
Colour: Black with green tint

Back Design: Lathework, counters and bank name
Colour: Green

565-10-04

$5 Face Design: Hon. George Bryson/Crest of Ottawa/ James Maclaren
Colour: Black with green tint

Back Design: Lathework, counters and bank name
Colour: Green

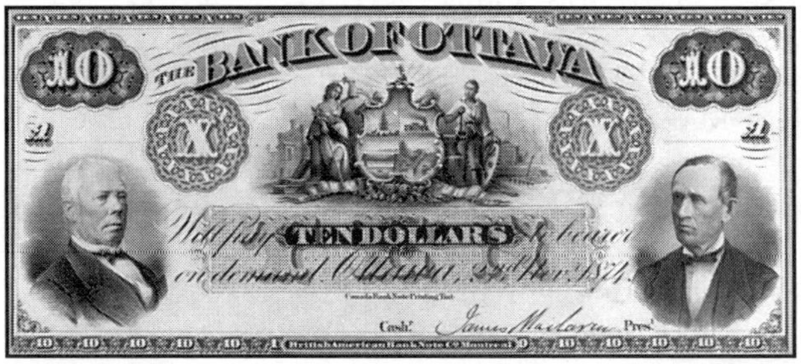

565-10-06P

$10 Face Design: Hon. George Bryson/Crest of Ottawa/ James Maclaren
Colour: Black with green tint

Back Design: Lathework, counters and bank name
Colour: Green

IMPRINT

British American Bank Note Co. Montreal

SIGNATURES

left	right
mss. P. Robinson	engr. James Maclaren
mss. Geo. Burn	engr. James Maclaren

ISSUE DATING

Engraved

2nd Novr. 1874

CIRCULATING NOTES

Cat. No.	Denom.	Date	G	VG	F	VF	EF	AU
10-02	$4	1874	1,250.	2,200.	2,750.	4,000.	—	—
10-04	$5	1874	1,100.	2,000.	2,500.	3,600.	—	—
10-06	$10	1874	No known issued notes					

PROOF NOTES

Cat. No.	Denom.	Date		Unc
10-06P	$10	1874	FACE PROOF	750.

565-12 ISSUE OF 1880

DESIGNS AND COLOURS

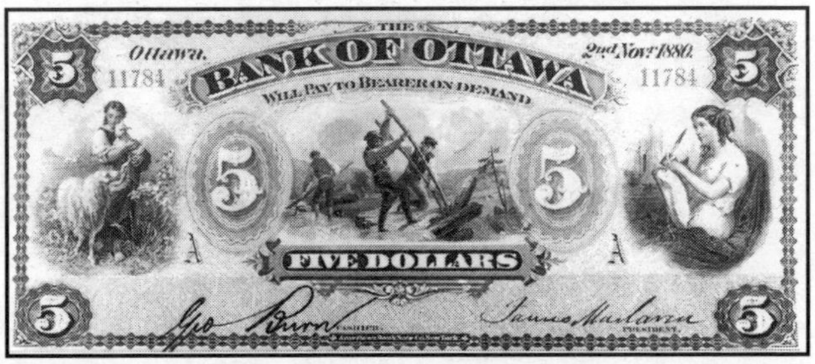

565-12-02

$5 Face Design: Shepherd girl with lamb, ewe/logging scene/seated woman with pen and book "Trade"

Colour: Black with olive tint

Back Design: —/rafting scene/—

Colour: Brown

565-12-04

$10 Face Design: Bust of blacksmith in oval/"Justice" figure flanked by Crest in oval and loggers in oval/bust of sailor

Colour: Black with olive tint

Back Design: —/Indian maiden/—

Colour: Brown

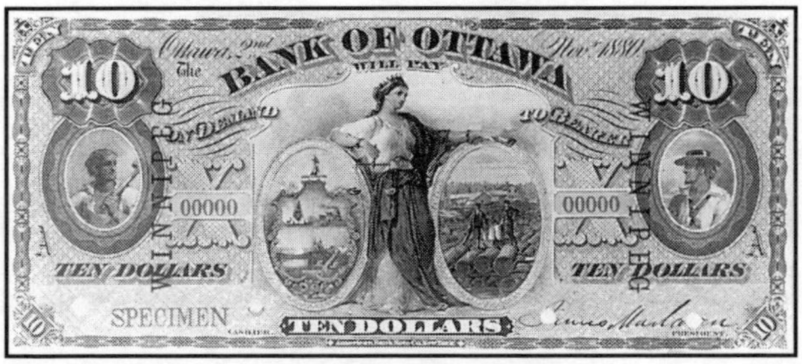

565-12-04aS

$10 Face Deisgn: Bust of blacksmith in oval/"Justice" figure flanked by Crest in oval and loggers in oval/bust of sailor

Colour: Black with olive tint

IMPRINT

American Bank Note Co. New York

SIGNATURES

left	right
mss. Geo. Burn	engr. James Maclaren

ISSUE DATING

Engraved

2nd Novr. 1880

OVERPRINT

"WINNIPEG" twice vertically in blue

CIRCULATING NOTES

Cat. No.	Denom.	Date	Variety	G	VG	F	VF	EF	AU
12-02	$5	1880		1,000.	1,800.	2,250.	3,250.	4,500.	5,500.
12-02a	$5	1880	Winnipeg	No known issued notes					
12-04	$10	1880		1,050.	1,900.	2,350.	3,500.	4,800.	—
12-04a	$10	1880	Winnipeg	No known issued notes					

PROOF NOTES

Cat. No.	Denom.	Date		Unc
12-02P	$5	1880	FACE PROOF	400.

SPECIMEN NOTES

Cat. No.	Denom.	Date	Variety		Unc
12-02S	$5	1880		SPECIMEN	600.
12-02aS	$5	1880	Winnipeg	SPECIMEN	900.
12-04S	$10	1880		SPECIMEN	600.
12-04aS	$10	1880	Winnipeg	SPECIMEN	900.

Note: Proofs and specimens of this issue (without "Winnipeg") occur with ochre brown face tint as well as with the issued olive tint.

565-14 ISSUES OF 1888 AND 1891

DESIGNS AND COLOURS

565-14-02P

$5 Face Design: Lumberjack felling tree/cattle/James Maclaren

Colour: Black with red-brown tint

Back Design: Lathework, counters, bank name and crest
Colour: Green

565-14-04P
$10 Face Design: —/James Maclaren/—
Colour: Black with red-brown tint

Back Design: Lathework, counters, bank name and crest
Colour: Green

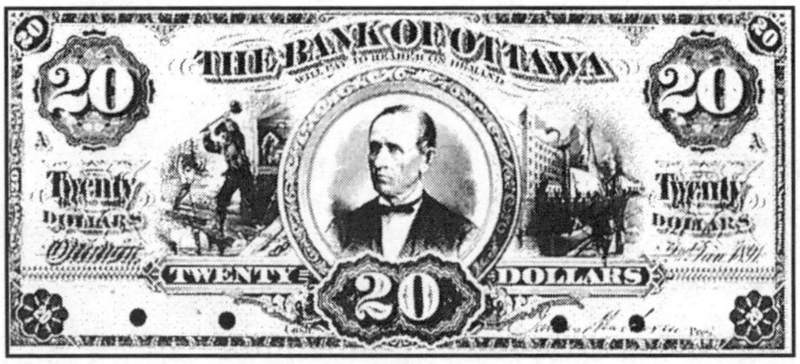

565-14-06P
$20 Face Design: —/loggers at work, James Maclaren, "Canal Locks No. 2"/—
Colour: Black with overall green tint

Back Design: lathework, counters, bank name and Crest of Ottawa
Colour: Green

565-14-08P
$50 Face Design: Farmer with dog/Parliament buildings, James McLaren/three horses heads
Colour: Black with overall green tint

Back Design: Unknown
Colour: Green

IMPRINT

British American Bank Note Company

SIGNATURES

left	**right**
mss. various	engr. James Maclaren

ISSUE DATING

Engraved

Jan. 2, 1888
Jan. 2, 1891
2nd Jan. 1891

CIRCULATING NOTES

Cat. No.	Denom.	Date	G	VG	F	VF	EF	AU
14-02	$5	1888	Institutional collection only					
14-04	$10	1888	No known issued notes					
14-06	$20	1891	No known issued notes					
14-08	$50	1891	No known issued notes					

PROOF NOTES

Cat. No.	Denom.	Date		Unc
14-02P	$5	1888	FACE PROOF	650.
14-04P	$10	1888	FACE PROOF	650.
14-06P	$20	1891	FACE PROOF	650.
14-08P	$50	1891	FACE PROOF	650.

565-16 ISSUES OF 1895 AND 1900

DESIGNS AND COLOURS

565-16-02

$5 Face Design: Charles Magee/Parliament Buildings/—

Back Design: Lathework, counters, bank name and Crest of Ottawa

565-16-04

$5 Face Design: Charles Magee/Parliament Buildings/—Dominion of Canada at top

Back Design: Lathework, counters, bank name and Crest of Ottawa

565-16-06P

$5 Face Design: Charles Magee/allegorical female/ Parliament Buildings, East Block

Back Design: Lathework, counters, bank name and Crest of Ottawa

1895 Face Colour: Black with green tint

Back Colour: Green

565-16-08

$10 1900 Face Colour: Black with enlarged ochre or olive tint "Dominion of Canada" at the top

Back Colour: Green

IMPRINT

British American Bank Note Co. Ottawa

SIGNATURES

left	**right**
mss. various	engr. Charles Magee

ISSUE DATING

Engraved

Jan. 2nd 1895
June 1st 1900

Note: The tint design and location in the 1900 issues differs from 1895 issues. Also "Dominion of Canada" is engraved at the top of the 1900 issues.

CIRCULATING NOTES

Cat. No.	Denom.	Date	G	VG	F	VF	EF	AU
16-02	$5	1895	—	1,750.	2,250.	3,500.	—	—
16-04	$5	1900	—	1,750.	2,250.	3,500.	—	—
16-06	$10	1895	Institutional collection only					
16-08	$10	1900	Institutional collection only					

PROOF NOTES

Cat. No.	Denom.	Date		Unc
16-02P	$5	1895	FACE PROOF	500.
16-04P	$10	1900	FACE PROOF	500.
16-06P	$20	1895	FACE PROOF	500.
16-08P	$50	1900	FACE PROOF	500.

565-18 ISSUE OF 1903

DESIGNS AND COLOURS

565-18-02

$5 Face Design: Locomotive/Parliament Buildings/—

Colour: Black with ochre tint

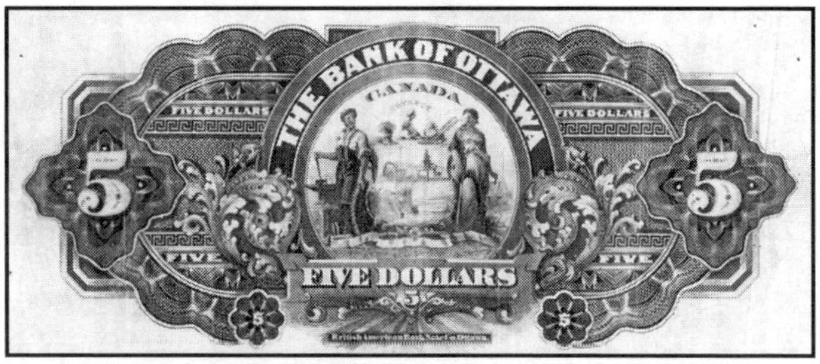

Back Design: —/Crest/—
Colour: Green

565-18-03

Photo Not Available

$5 Face Design: Locomotive/Parliament Buildings/—
Colour: Black with larger ochre tint (large tint variety)

Back Design: Lathework, counters, bank name and Crest
Colour: Green

565-18-04
$10 Face Design: Head office/cattle scene/ Parliament Buildings, East Block
Colour: Black with enlarged olive tint

565-18-06
$10 Face Design: Head office/cattle scene/ Parliament buildings, east block
Colour: Black with modified (less) tint

Back Design: Lathework, counters, bank name and Crest See varieties
Colour: Green

565-18-11E
$20 Face Design: —/logger at work, Hon. George Bryson, canal locks "Canal Locks No. 2"/—
Colour: Black with green tint

Back Design: Lathework, counters, bank name and Crest
Colour: Green

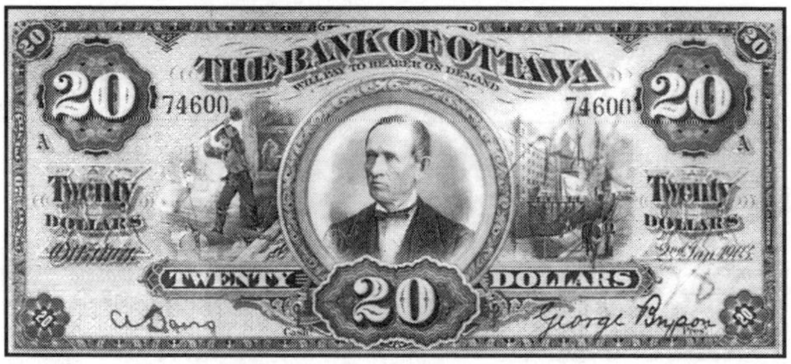

565-18-12
$20 Face Design: —/loggers at work, James McLaren, canal locks "Canal Locks No. 2"/—
Colour: Black with green tint

Back Design: Lathework, counters, bank name and Crest
Colour: Green

565-18-16
$50 Face Design: Farmer with horse, dog and hay "Old Burhans"/Parliament Buildings, James Mclaren/three horses' heads
Colour: Black with green tint

Back Design: —/Crest/—
Colour: Green

565-18-18P

$50 Face Design: Farmer with horse, dog and hay, "Old Burhans"/Parliament buildings James McLaren/three horses' heads
Colour: Black with overall green tint

Back Design: lathework, counters, bank name and Crest
Colour: Green

IMPRINT

British American Bank Note Co. Ottawa

SIGNATURES

left	right
mss. various	engr. Geo. Hay
mss. various	engr. David Maclaren
mss. various	engr. George Bryson

ISSUE DATING

Engraved

Jan. 2nd 1903
2nd Jan 1903

VARIETIES

$10 Face Colour: Large olive tint
$10 Face Colour: Modified olive tint (reduced)

CIRCULATING NOTES

Cat. No.	Denom.	Date	Variety	G	VG	F	VF	EF	AU
18-02	$5	1903		750.	1,500.	2,000.	3,000.	—	—
18-03	$5	1903	Large tint	No known issued notes					
18-04	$10	1903	Large tint	850.	1,700.	2,250.	3,500.	—	—
18-06	$10	1903	Modified tint	850.	1,700.	2,250.	3,500.	—	—
18-08	$20	1903	Hay, r.	Institutional collection only					
18-10	$20	1903	Maclaren, r.	950.	—	—	—	—	—
18-12	$20	1903	Bryson, r.	950.	1,900.	2,500.	4,000.	—	—
18-14	$50	1903	Hay, r.	Institutional collection only					
18-16	$50	1903	Maclaren, r.	Institutional collection only					
18-18	$50	1903	Bryson, r.	Institutional collection only					

PROOF NOTES

Cat. No.	Denom.	Date	Variety		Unc
18-03P	$5	1903	Large tint	FACE PROOF	600.
18-12P	$20	1903	Bryson, r.	FACE PROOF	600.

ESSAY NOTES

Cat. No.	Denom.	Date	Variety		Unc
18-11E	$20	1903	Bryson, r.	ESSAY	2,000.

565-20 **ISSUE OF 1906**

DESIGNS AND COLOURS

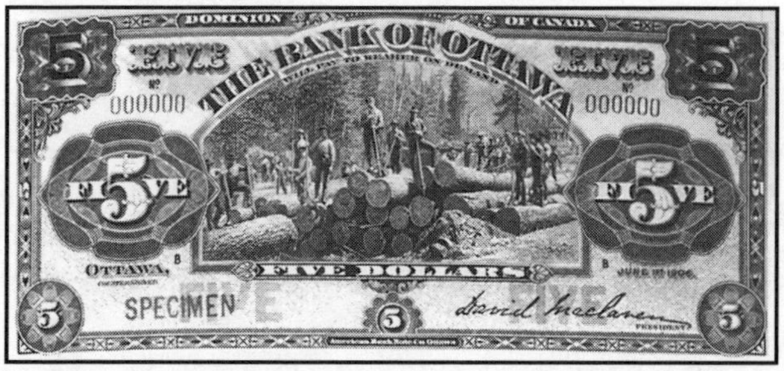

565-20-04

$5 Face Design: logging camp scene
Colour: See varieties

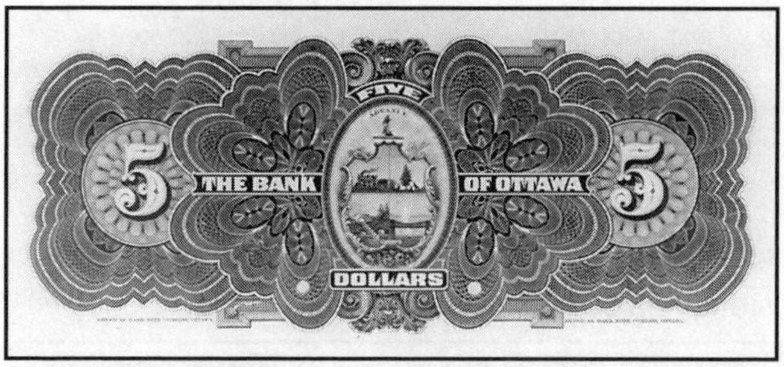

Back Design: lathework, counters, bank name and Crest of Ottawa
Colour: Green

565-20-10

$10 Face Design: —/dairy farm scene/—
Colour: See varieties

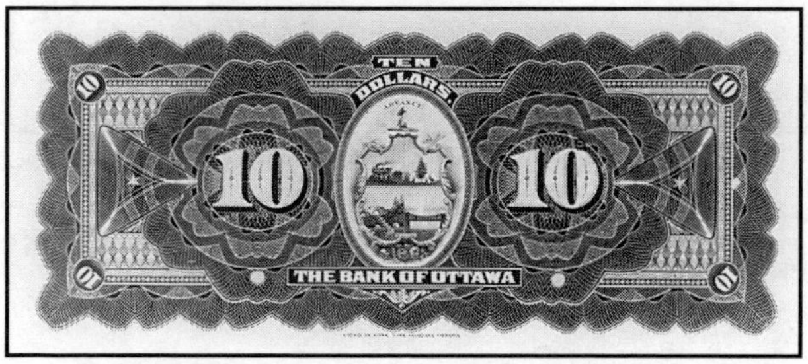

Back Design: Lathework, counters, bank name and Crest of Ottawa
Colour: Green

IMPRINT

American Bank Note Co. Ottawa

SIGNATURES

left	right
mss. various	typed Geo. Hay
mss. various	typed David Maclaren

ISSUE DATING

Engraved

June 1st 1906

VARIETIES

Face Colour: Black with green tint; Hay signature
Black with green tint; Maclaren signature
Black with yellow and green tint; Maclaren signature

CIRCULATING NOTES

Cat. No.	Den.	Date	Variety	G	VG	F	VF	EF	AU
20-02	$5	1906	Hay, r.	600.	1,250.	1,600.	—	—	—
20-04	$5	1906	Maclaren, r., green	500.	1,000.	1,350.	2,000.	—	—
20-06	$5	1906	Maclaren, r., yellow	500.	1,000.	1,350.	2,000.	—	—
20-08	$10	1906	Hay, r., green	600.	1,200.	1,600.	2,300.	—	—
20-10	$10	1906	Maclaren, r., green	500.	1,000.	1,350.	2,000.	—	—
20-12	$10	1906	Maclaren, r., yellow	500.	1,000.	1,350.	2,000.	—	—

SPECIMEN NOTES

Cat. No.	Den.	Date			Unc
20-02	$5	1906	Hay, r.	SPECIMEN	800.

565-22 ISSUE OF 1912

DESIGNS AND COLOURS

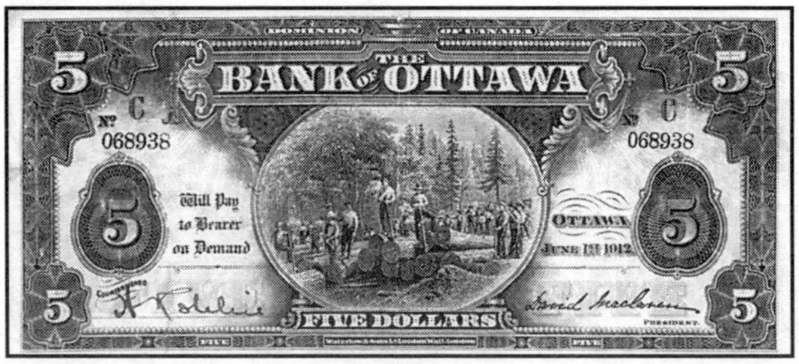

565-22-02

$5 Face Design: —/logging camp scene/—
Colour: Black with blue tint

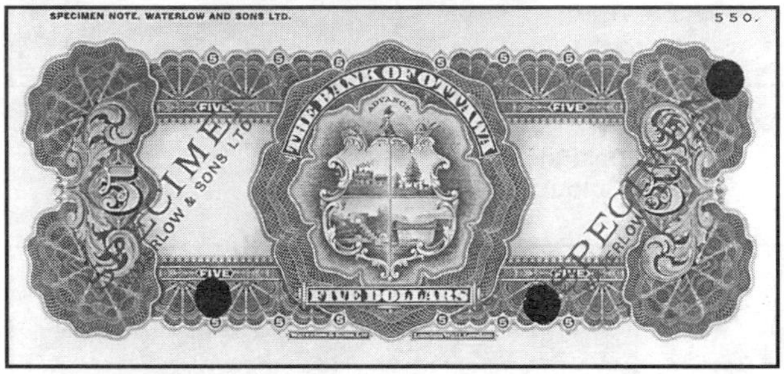

Back Design: Lathework, counters, bank name and Ottawa Crest
Colour: Olive

IMPRINT

Waterlow & Sons, Ld. London Wall, London

SIGNATURES

left	right
mss. various	engr. David Maclaren

ISSUE DATING

Engraved

June 1st, 1912

Note: A specimen of this issue is known with red face tint and brown back tint.

Cat. No.	Denom.	Date	G	VG	F	VF	EF	AU
22-02	$5	1912	550.	1,100.	1,500.	2,400.	—	—

565-24 ISSUE OF AUGUST 1, 1913

DESIGNS AND COLOURS

565-24-02

$10 Face Design: —/dairy farm scene/—
Colour: See varieties

Back Design: —/Crest of Ottawa/—
Colour: Green

IMPRINT

American Bank Note Co. Ottawa

SIGNATURES

left	right
mss. various	typed George Bryson

ISSUE DATING

Engraved

August 1st, 1913

VARIETIES

Face Colour: Black with green tint
Face Colour: Black with ochre and green tint

Cat. No.	Denom.	Date	Variety	G	VG	F	VF	EF	AU
24-02	$10	1913	Green tint	500.	1,000.	1,350.	—	—	—
24-04	$10	1913	Ochre tint	550.	1,100.	1,500.	—	—	—

565-26 ISSUE OF SEPTEMBER 1, 1913

DESIGNS AND COLOURS

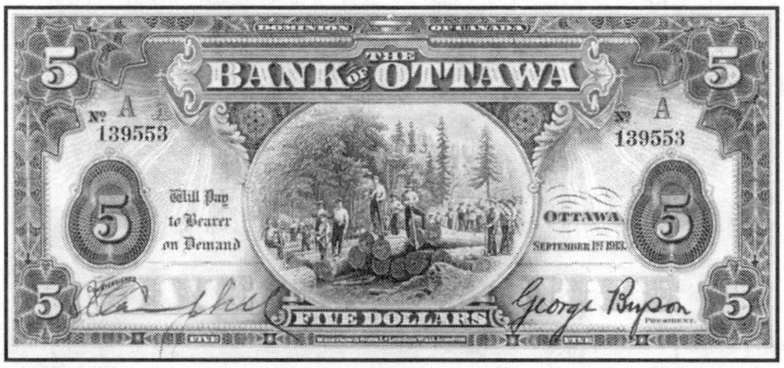

565-26-02

$5 Face Design: —/logging camp scene/—
Colour: Black with blue-green plate and ochre tint

Back Design: —/Crest of Ottawa/—
Colour: Brown

565-26-04

$10 Face Design: —/cattle herded under trees/—
Colour: Black with green tint

Back Design: —/Crest of Ottawa/—
Colour: Green

IMPRINT

$5: Waterlow & Sons, Ld. London Wall, London
$10: British American Bank Note Co. Ottawa

SIGNATURES

left	right
mss. various	engr. George Bryson

ISSUE DATING

Engraved

September 1st 1913
Sep. 1st 1913

Note: Specimens of the $5 issue are known with orange face tint and brown back tint and also lilac face plate with orange and green tint and red-brown back tint.

Cat. No.	Denom.	Date	G	VG	F	VF	EF	AU
26-02	$5	1913	250.	500.	800.	1,200.	2,000.	—
26-04	$10	1913	500.	1,000.	1,350.	2,000.	—	—

565-28 $5 DESIGN OF 1906 RESUMED 1917

DESIGNS AND COLOURS

565-28-02

$5 Face Design: —/logging camp scene/—
Colour: Black with yellow and green tint

Back Design: —/Crest of Ottawa/—
Colour: Green

IMPRINT

American Bank Note Co. Ottawa

SIGNATURES

left	right
mss. various	typed George Bryson

ISSUE DATING

Engraved

June 1st 1917

Cat. No.	Denom.	Date	G	VG	F	VF	EF	AU
28-02	$5	1917	550.	1,100.	1,500.	2,400.	3,500.	—

THE BANK OF THE PEOPLE

1835-1841

TORONTO, UPPER CANADA

BANK NUMBER 570 ***REDEEMABLE***

Established in Toronto in 1835 as a joint-stock bank by supporters of the Reform Movement, this institution was the only bank in Canada that did not suspend specie payment in 1837. Its entire capital stock of £50,000 was bought up by the Bank of Montreal in 1840, giving the latter access to business in Upper Canada through the agency of the Bank of the People. When Upper and Lower Canada were united in 1841, the Bank of Montreal was able to operate in the upper province in its own name, and the process of the absorption of the Bank of the People was completed.

DESIGNS AND COLOURS

570-10 DRAPER, TOPPAN, LONGACRE ISSUE

570-10-02

$1 (5s) Face Design: Three standing women/ships and paddlewheeler, small primitive train below/three standing women
Colour: Black with no tint

Back Design: Plain

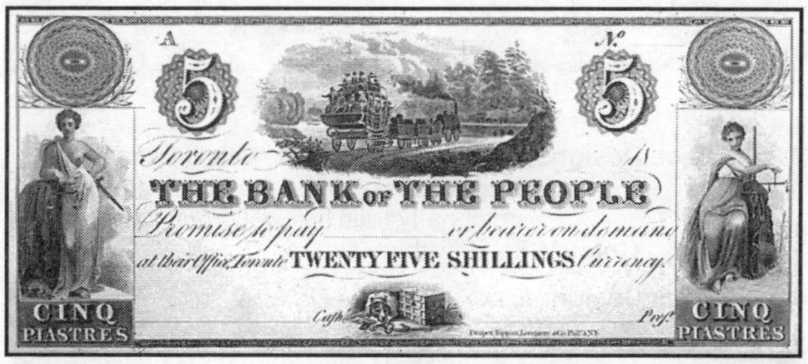

570-10-10

$5 (25s) Face Design: Standing justice figure/primitive train pulling stagecoach, dog, safe and key below/seated justice figure
Colour: Black with no tint

Back Design: Plain

IMPRINT

Draper, Toppan, Longacre & Co. Phila & N.Y.

SIGNATURES

Left	Right
Unknown	Unknown

ISSUE DATING

Partially Engraved ___18___:

PROOF NOTES

Cat. No.	Denom.	Date	Unc
10-02P	$1 (5s)	18__	Institutional collection only
10-10P	$5 (25s)	18__	Institutional collection only

570-12 ISSUE OF 1836-1840

Note I: Denominations are listed in English, French and in German.

Note II: Written in light purple ink on the $10 proof is "April 9, 1842" with sheet number 1106. The left signature is J.C. Walsh and the right signature is illegible.

Note III: A spurious $10 note with almost the same design and bank title is known. See United States Obsolete Bank Notes, Haxby, NY, 1275-S5

Note IV: 10-02R exists with spurious dates and signatures.

570-12-02
$1 (5s) Face Design: Allegorical woman seated beside hay/ view of Toronto from harbour; small steamboat below/seated allegorical male with chest and anchor
Colour: Black with no tint

Back Design: Plain

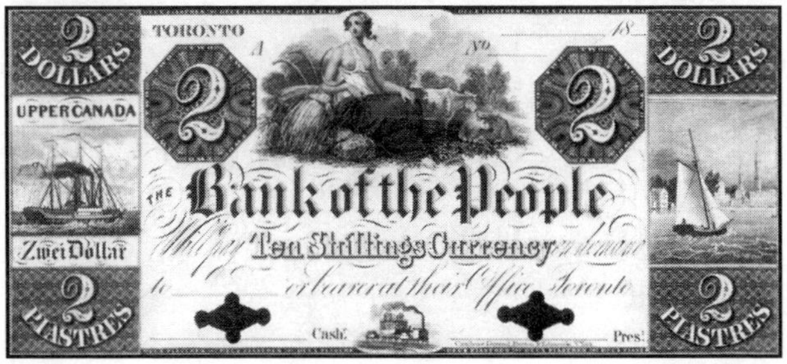

570-12-04P
$2 (10s) Face Design: Paddlewheel steamer with U.S. flag/ allegorical woman seated beside hay, cattle; small early train below/Toronto harbour
Colour: Black with no tint

Back Design: Plain

570-12-05
$3 (15s) Face Design: —/Three seated allegorical women, crown below/—
Colour: Black with no tint

Back Design: Plain

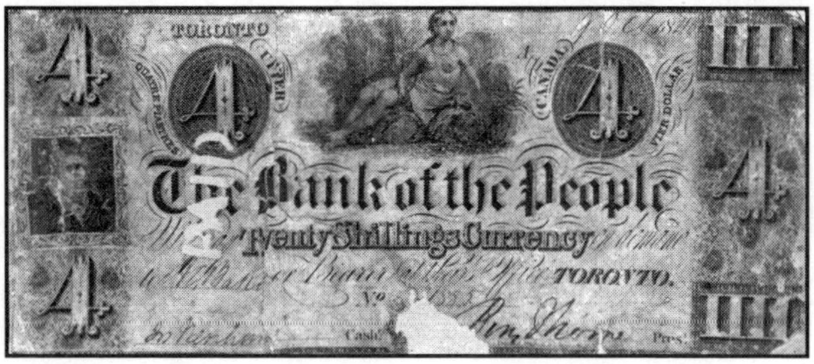

570-12-08
$4 (20s) Face Design: James Fox/reclining Indian maiden/—
Colour: Black with no tint

Back Design: Plain

570-12-10
$8 (£2) Face Design: —/royal Crest/—
Colour: Black with no tint

Back Design: Plain

570-12-12P
$10 Face Design: James Fox/farm tools, lion in shield, ships/ young farm girl
Colour: Black with no tint

Back Design: Plain

IMPRINT

Casilear, Durand, Burton & Edmonds N. York

SIGNATURES

left	right
mss. F. Hincks	mss. J. Leslie
mss. J.N. Wenham	mss. Benj. Thorne
mss. J. Hastings	mss. F. Wright

ISSUE DATING
Partially Engraved ___ 18___:

$1, 1836: 12 Dec.
1840: April
$3 1840: 9 Oct
$4 1840: 9 Oct.
$8 1840: 8 June
$10 1842: April 9

CIRCULATING NOTES

Cat. No.	Denom.	Date	G	VG	F	VF	EF	AU
12-02	$1 (5s)	1836	1,000.	1,750.	2,400.	—	—	—
12-02R	$1 (5s)	18__ Remainder	850.	1,500.	2,000.	—	—	—
12-04	$2 (10s)	18__	No known issued notes					
12-06	$3 (15s)	1840	Institutional collection only					
12-08	$4 (20s)	1840	Institutional collection only					
12-10	$8 (£2)	1840	Institutional collection only					
12-12	$10	1842	Institutional collection only					
12-20	$20	18__	SURVIVING EXAMPLES NOT CONFIRMED					
12-30	$50	18__	SURVIVING EXAMPLES NOT CONFIRMED					

PROOF NOTES

Cat. No.	Denom.	Date	Unc
12-02P	$1 (5s)	18__	PROOF 900.
12-04P	$2 (10s)	18__	PROOF 900.
12-12P	$10	18__	PROOF 1,200.

LA BANQUE DU PEUPLE

1835-1895

MONTREAL, LOWER CANADA

BANK NUMBER 575 ***REDEEMABLE***

Founded in 1835 by Viger, deWitt & Cie, this bank was organized on the en commandite principle, whereby the 12 partners had unlimited liability, while their stockholders were liable only to the extent of their equity. A charter was granted in 1844, setting the authorized capital at £200,000. The failure of several of its debtors precipitated the collapse of the bank in 1895, in which the creditors lost $1,718,284. There followed a wave of failures of Quebec industries that had been supported by the bank.

575-10 **ISSUE OF 1835-1836**

DESIGNS AND COLOURS

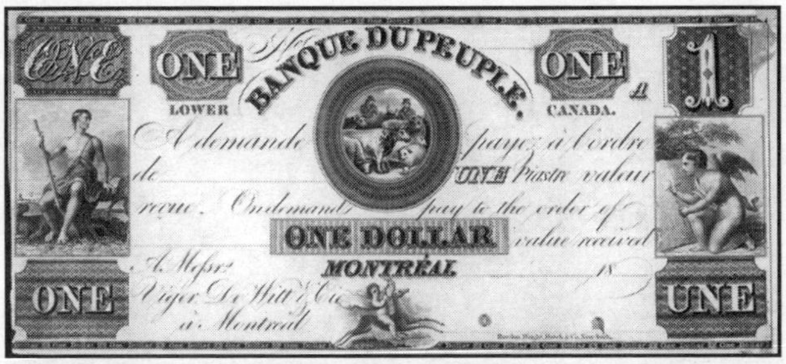

575-10-02-02
$1 Face Design: Seated shepherd boy/two men, cattle and sheep; child riding deer below/ kneeling cherub engraving stone
Colour: Black with no tint

Back Design: Lathework/habitant/lathework
Colour: Blue

575-10-02-06
$2 Face Design: Portrait of man; two allegorical women in clouds; man in canoe below/ seated allegorical female
Colour: Black with no tint

Back Design: Lathework/habitant/lathework
Colour: Blue

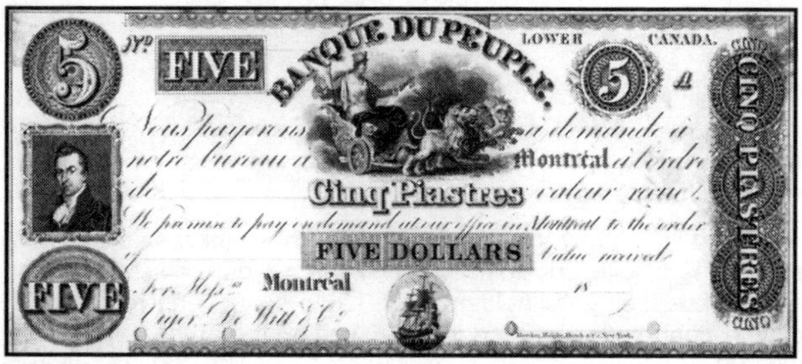

575-10-02-10R

$5 Face Design: Louis-Joseph Papineau/ woman in chariot drawn by lions; small sailing ship below/—
Colour: Black with no tint

Back Design: Lathework/habitant/lathework
Colour: Blue

575-10-04-04

$10 Face Design: —/ship and seated allegorical male "Commerce"; small steamboat below/Louis-Joseph Papineau
Colour: Black with no tint

Back Design: Lathework/habitant/lathework
Colour: Blue

IMPRINT

Rawdon, Wright, Hatch & Co. New York

2. DRAFTS: "Messrs. Viger, Dewitt & Cie" ENGRAVED AT LOWER LEFT

The company name is also endorsed vertically across the face on fully completed drafts.

SIGNATURES

	left	right
$1 and $2:	mss. E.R. Fabré,	mss. various
	none	mss. Jogn Donegani
$5 and $10:	none	mss. various

ISSUE DATING

Partially engraved ___ 18___:

1835: 11 Juillet
1836: 2 Aout

Note: Back proofs known in black.

Cat. No.	Denom.	Date	Variety	G	VG	F	VF	EF	Unc
10-02-02	$1	1835-36		300.	600.	800.	—	—	—
10-02-06	$2	1835		375.	750.	1,000.	—	—	—
10-02-10R	$5	18_	Remainder*	—	—	—	—	350.	700.
10-02-14R	$10	18_	Remainder*	—	—	—	—	350.	700.
Full sheet	$1,2,5,10	18_	Remainder*	—	—	—	—	—	3,000.

* Unsigned, undated and unnumbered.

4. NOTES: COMPANY NAME REPLACED BY "_______ CAISSIER"

SIGNATURES

left	right
mss. B.H. Lemoine	mss. Viger DeWitt & Cie

ISSUE DATING

Partially engraved ___ 18___:

1835: 11 Juillet
1836: 1 Mars, 2 Mai

Cat. No.	Denom.	Date	G	VG	F	VF	EF	AU
10-04-02	$5	1835	400.	800.	1,100.	—	—	—
10-04-04	$10	1836	400.	800.	1,100.	—	—	—

575-12 $5 ISSUE OF 1838

DESIGNS AND COLOURS

575-12-02

$5 Face Design: Seated woman, lamb/ farm family eating by wheat field/ five Spanish dollars
Colour: Black with no tint

Back Design: Habitant/lathework and counters/ man picking corn
Colour: Blue

IMPRINT

Rawdon, Wright & Hatch, New York

SIGNATURES

left	right
mss. B. Lemoine	mss. Viger DeWitt & Cie

ISSUE DATING

Engraved

1st July 1838

Note: Back proof is known in red and black.

Cat. No.	Denom.	Date	Variety	G	VG	F	VF	EF	AU
12-02R	$5	18__	Remainder	135.	275.	450.	—	—	—
12-02	$5	1838		400.	800.	1,100.	—	—	—

575-14 **DURAND & CO. PRINTINGS 1839-1845**

DESIGNS AND COLOURS

575-14-02-02

$1 (5s) Face Design: Christ child/angel with cherub and Britannia in shield; agricultural tools below/Christ child
See subheadings

Colour: Black with no tint

Back Design: Spanish dollar/
seated "Agriculture" figure/habitant

Colour: Blue

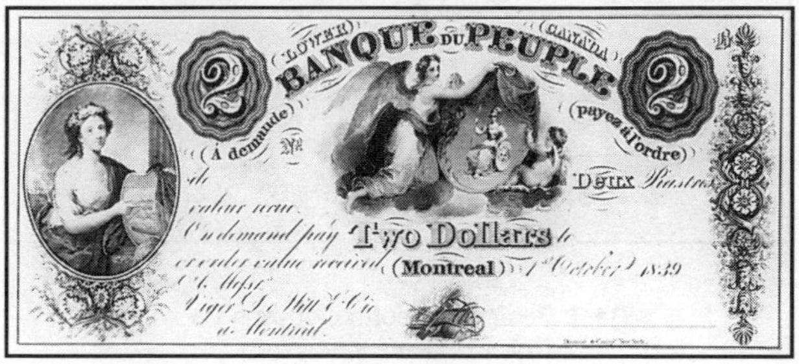

575-14-02-04

$2 Face Design: Woman seated by shield/ angel with cherub and Britannis in shield; agricultural tools below/—
See subheadings

Colour: Black with no tint

Back Design: Reverses of two Spanish dollars/
seated "Agriculture" figure/habitant

Colour: Blue

575-14-04-04

$2 (10s) Face Design: Woman seated by shield/
angel with cherub and Britannia in shield;
agricultural tools below/—
See subheadings

Colour: Black with no tint

Back Design: Reverses of two Spanish dollars/
seated "Agriculture" figure/habitant

Colour: Blue

IMPRINT

Durand & Compy New York

2. DRAFTS "A Messrs. Viger Dewitt & Cie" ENGRAVED AT LOWER LEFT 1839 DOLLARS ONLY

The company name is also endorsed vertically across the right end of the face.

SIGNATURES

right only
mss. Jogn Donegani

ISSUE DATING

Engraved

1st October 1839

Cat. No.	Denom.	Date	G	VG	F	VF	EF	AU
14-02-02	$1	1839	325.	650.	900.	—	—	—
14-02-04	$2	1839	350.	700.	1,000.	—	—	—

4. NOTES: COMPANY NAME REPLACED BY "__________ CASH", 1845 DOLLARS/POUNDS & SHILLINGS

The text is slightly modified to include dual denominations.

SIGNATURES

left	right
mss. B.H. Lemoine	mss. J. DeWitt (v)

ISSUE DATING

Partially engraved ___ 184_:

1845: 1 Mars

Cat. No.	Denom.	Date	G	VG	F	VF	EF	AU
14-04-02	$1 (5s)	1845	325.	650.	900.	—	—	—
14-04-04	$2 (10s)	1845	350.	700.	1,000.	—	—	—

TOPPAN CARPENTER PRINTINGS
1845-1892

The basic designs are the same for 575-16, 18 and 20. Only the denominations, tints and imprints change.

DESIGNS AND COLOURS

575-16-02-04
$1 (5s) Face Design: Man constructing barrel/
boy carrying sheaf of wheat and cradle/
four cherubs with numeral 1
Colour: See subheadings

Back Design: Habitant/lathework and counter/habitant
Colour: See subheadings

575-16-02-16
$2 (10s) Face Design: Man sharpening scythe/
two men with sledge and axe/
dog lying by strong box
Colour: See subheadings

Back Design: Lathework and counters/habitant/
lathework and counters
Colour: See subheadings

575-16-02-22P
$4 (20s) Face Design: Seated carpenter/milkmaids and cows, ships; dog's head below/blacksmith
Colour: See subheadings

Back Design: —/portrait of young woman in oval/—
Colour: See subheadings

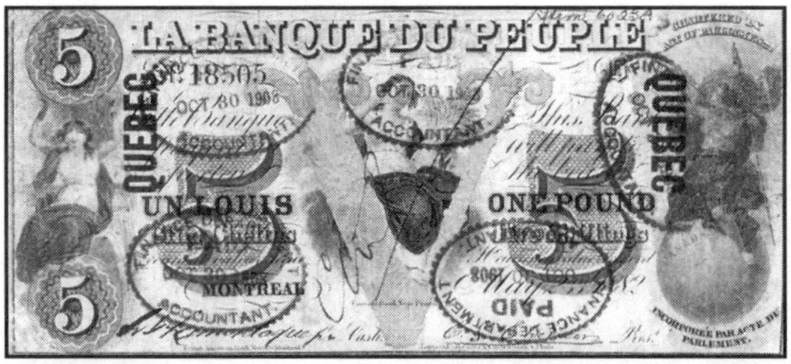

575-20-02-02
$5 (£1.5) Face Design: "Commerce" figure holding counter/
seated woman with sheaves in ornate V/
allegorical female seated on globe and blowing trumpet
Colour: See subheadings

Back Design: —/man and woman seated by ornate 5/—
Colour: See subheadings

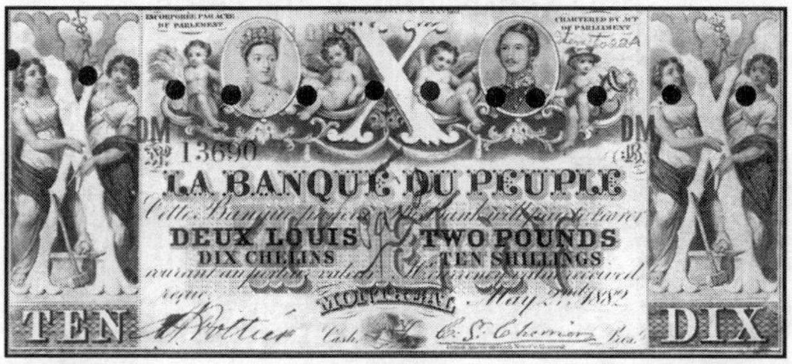

575-20-02-04
$10 (£2.10) Face Design: Two women and ornate X/four cherubs and ornate X, portraits of Victoria and Albert in ovals; sheaves and agricultural tools below/ two women and ornate X
Colour: See subheadings
Back Design: —/six cherubs and 10 counter/—
Colour: See subheadings

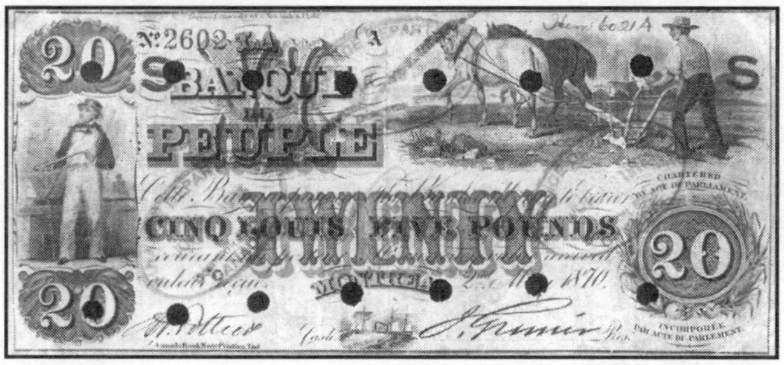

575-18-08
$20 (£5) Face Design: Sailor holding telescope/—; small steamboat with sails below/ man ploughing with horses
Colour: See subheadings
Back Design: —/ornate 20/—
Colour: See subheadings

575-16-02-64
$50 (£12.10) Face Design: Canal boat/seated sailor with flag; bust of young girl below/ paddlewheel steamship in oval
Colour: See subheadings
Back Design: Blue 50 counter
Colour: See subheadings

Photo Not Available

575-20-04-22P
$100 (£25) Face Design: Portrait of woman/Montreal harbour scene; small shield below/portrait of woman
Colour: See subheadings
Back Design: Lathework, counters and bank name
Colour: See subheadings

575-16 BLUE BACKS 1845 - 1870 DOLLARS/POUNDS & SHILLINGS

2. NO PROTECTORS 1845-1850

DESIGNS AND COLOURS
Face Colour: Black with no tint
Back Colour: Blue

IMPRINT
Toppan, Carpenter & Co. Philada and New York
Toppan Carpenter & Co. New York & Phila

SIGNATURES

left	right
mss. B.H. Lemoine	mss. J. DeWitt (v)
mss. G. Peltier	mss. J. DeWitt (v)

ISSUE DATING
Partially engraved _ 18_:
$1 and $2, 1846: 1 Septr.
$1 and $2, 1850: 1 Mars
Partially engraved _ 184_:
$4, 1847: 1 Mai.
$20 and $50, 1845: 1 Mars

OVERPRINT

"TORONTO" in blue

CIRCULATING NOTES

Cat. No.	Denom.	Date	G	VG	F	VF	EF	AU
16-02-04	$1 (5s)	1846-50	325.	650.	900.	—	—	—
16-02-16	$2 (10s)	1846-50	350.	700.	1,000.	—	—	—
16-02-22	$4 (20s)	1847	400.	800.	1,100.	—	—	—
16-02-30	$5 (£1.5)	184_	No known issued notes					
16-02-40	$10 (£2.10)	184_	No known issued notes					
16-02-52	$20 (£5)	1845	500.	1,000.	1,500.	—	—	—
16-02-64	$50 (£12.10)	1845	500.	1,000.	1,500.	—	—	—
16-02-76	$100 (£25)	184_	No known issued notes					

PROOF NOTES

Cat. No.	Denom.	Date		Unc
16-02-04P	$1 (5s)	18__	PROOF	500.
16-02-16P	$2 (10s)	18__	PROOF	500.
16-02-22P	$4 (20s)	184_	PROOF	500.
16-02-30P	$5 (£1.5)	184_	PROOF	500.
16-02-40P	$10 (£2.10)	184_	PROOF	500.
16-02-76P	$100 (£25)	184_	PROOF	500.

4. GREEN PROTECTORS 1854, 1870

575-16-04-08

$1 Face Design: Man constructing barrel/boy carrying sheaf of wheat and cradle/four cherubs with numeral 1

Colour: See subheadings

DESIGNS AND COLOURS

Face Colour: Black with no tint

Back Colour: Blue

IMPRINT

Toppan, Carpenter & Co. Philada & New York

Toppan, Carpenter & Co. New York & Phila.

SIGNATURES

	left	right
$1 (5s):	mss illegible	mss. J.A. Trottier
	none	mss. L.J. Lamontagne
$2 (10s):	mss. Ed. Fournier	mss. J.A. Trottier
$4 (20s):	mss. J.A. Trottier (cashr)	mss. John Pratt

ISSUE DATING

Partially engraved ___ 18___:

$1 (5s), 1870: 2 May

$2 (10s), 1870: May 2

Engraved

$4 (20s): 2eme Janvier 1854

PROTECTOR

Green "word" on face only

VARIETIES

$1: "Countersigned and Entered/For La Banque de Peuple" inscribed above signature spaces. Blue printed sheet numbers.

$1: Inscriptions deleted above signature spaces. Mss. sheet numbers.

Cat. No.	Denom.	Date	G	VG	F	VF	EF	AU
16-04-04	$1 (5s)	1870*	275.	550.	800.	1,350.	—	—
16-04-08	$1 (5s)	1870**	275.	550.	800.	1,350.	—	—
16-04-12	$2 (10s)	1870*	350.	700.	1,000.	—	—	—
16-04-14	$4 (20s)	1854**	400.	800.	1,100.	—	—	—

* Inscription above signature.

** Inscription deleted.

575-18 GREEN FACE TINTS, GREEN BACKS 1870 DOLLARS/ POUNDS & SHILLINGS

Blue printed sheet numbers.

DESIGNS AND COLOURS

575-18-02

$4 Face Colour: Black with green tint

Back Colour: Green

IMPRINT

$4 (20s): Toppan, Carpenter & Co. New York & Phila.
British American Bank Note Co. Montreal

$20 (£5): Toppan, Carpenter & Co. New York & Phila.

SIGNATURES

	left	right
$4 (20s):	mss. J.A. Trottier	mss. Geo. S. Brush (v.)
$20 (£5):	mss. J.A. Trottier	engr. J. Grenier

ISSUE DATING

Engraved

2eme Mai 1870

2nd May 1870

OVERPRINT

$20 (£5): "S" twice in red

Cat. No.	Denom.	Date	G	VG	F	VF	EF	AU
18-02	$4 (20s)	1870	400.	800.	1,100.	—	—	—
18-04	$5 (£1.5)	1870	NOT YET CONFIRMED					
18-06	$10 (£2.10)	1870	NOT YET CONFIRMED					
18-08	$20 (£5)	1870	450.	900.	1,250.	—	—	—

570-20

GREEN FACE TINTS
BLUE BACKS
1882-1892

2. DOLLAR/POUNDS & SHILLINGS ISSUE BLUE NUMBERS

DESIGNS AND COLOURS

Face Colour: Black with green tint
Back Colour: Blue

IMPRINT

Toppan, Carpenter & Co. New York and
British American Bank Note Co. Montreal

SIGNATURES

left	**right**
mss. various	engr. C.S. Cherrier

ISSUE DATING

Engraved

May 2nd 1882

OVERPRINT

$5 (£1.5): "QUEBEC" twice in blue
$10 (£2.10): "DM" twice in red

Cat. No.	Denom.	Date	G	VG	F	VF	EF	Unc
20-02-02	$5 (£1.5)	1882	400.	800.	1,100.	—	—	—
20-02-04	$10 (£2.10)	1882	450.	900.	1,250.	—	—	—

4. DOLLAR ONLY ISSUES BLUE NUMBERS

DESIGNS AND COLOURS

575-20-04-02

$5 Face Design: "Commerce" figure holding counter/ seated woman in ornate V/allegorical female seated on globe and blowing trumpet
Colour: Black with green tint

Back Design: Counters, bank name and man and woman seated by ornate 5/—
Colour: Blue

575-20-04-8

$5 Face Design: "Commerce" figure holding counter/ seated woman in ornate V/allegorical female blowing trumpet seated on globe
Colour: Black with green tint

Back Design: Counters, bank name and man and women seated by ornate 5/—
Colour: Blue

Note: Central V in this bank note has numerous differences with fancy scrollwork.

575-20-04-12P

$10 Face Design: Two women and ornate X/four cherubs and ornate X, portraits of Victoria and Albert in ovals; sheaves and agricultural tools below/two women and ornate X
Colour: Blue

Back Design: —/six cherubs and 10 counter/—
Colour: Blue

575-20-06-04

$50 Face Design: Canal boat/seated sailor with flag; bust of young girl below/ paddlewheel steamship in oval
Colour: Black with green tint

Back Design: Lathework, counters and bank name
Colour: Blue

575-20-06-06P

$100 Face Design: Portrait of woman/Montreal harbour scene; small shield below/portrait of woman
Colour: Black with green tint

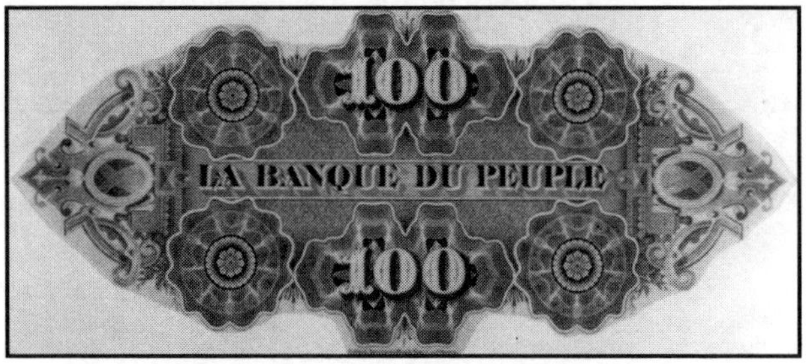

Back Design: Lathework, counters and bank name
Colour: Blue

IMPRINT

Toppan, Carpenter & Co. New York and Phila.
British American Bank Note Co. Montreal
British American Bank Note Co. Ottawa

SIGNATURES

left	right
mss. various	engr. J. Grenier

ISSUE DATING

Engraved

November 6th, 1885
May 2, 1888
July 2, 1892

OVERPRINT

F.D. twice in blue
$5: "QUEBEC" twice in blue

CIRCULATING NOTES

Cat. No.	Denom.	Date	G	VG	F	VF	EF	AU
20-04-02	$5	1885	400.	800.	1,100.	—	—	—
20-04-08	$5	1892	450.	900.	1,250.	—	—	—
20-04-12	$10	1888	No known issued notes					
20-04-16	$50	1885	No known issued notes					
20-04-22	$100	1885	No known issued notes					

PROOF NOTES

Cat. No.	Denom.	Date		Unc
20-04-02P	$5	1885	PROOF	500.
20-04-08P	$5	1892	PROOF	500.
20-04-12P	$10	1888	PROOF	500.
20-04-16P	$50	1885	PROOF	500.
20-04-22P	$100	1885	PROOF	500.

6. DOLLAR ONLY ISSUES RED NUMBERS

575-20-06-02

IMPRINT

Toppan, Carpenter & Co. New York & Phila
Canada Bank Note Co. Montreal.

SIGNATURES

left	right
mss. various	engr. J. Grenier

ISSUE DATING

Engraved

November 6th, 1885

OVERPRINT

$5: "S S" in red

CIRCULATING NOTES

Cat. No.	Denom.	Date	G	VG	F	VF	EF	AU
20-06-02	$5	1885	400.	800.	1,100.	—	—	—
20-06-04	$50	1885	550.	1,100.	1,600.	—	—	—
20-06-06	$100	1885	No known issued notes					

PROOF NOTES

Cat. No.	Denom.	Date		Unc
20-06-02P	$5	1885	PROOF	500.
20-06-04P	$50	1885	PROOF	500.
20-06-06P	$100	1885	PROOF	500.

THE PEOPLE'S BANK OF HALIFAX

1864-1905

HALIFAX, NOVA SCOTIA

BANK NUMBER 580 ***REDEEMABLE***

Established in 1864 in Halifax, Nova Scotia, this bank was absorbed by the Bank of Montreal in 1905. The bank was well managed, and all of its assets were sold to the Bank of Montreal with "the good will of the banking business." With its 26 branches, the People's Bank of Halifax provided a valuable addition to the Bank of Montreal expansion in Nova Scotia and New Brunswick.

Employees of the bank were guaranteed a minimum of one year of employment at their existing salaries, after which those remaining in the service of the Bank of Montreal were added to its pension list with credit for time spent with both banks.

580-10 $20 ISSUES OF 1864 - 1903

DESIGNS AND COLOURS

580-10-04

$20 Face Design: Princess of Wales/lion and Indian woman flanking bust of Victoria/two sailors on shore, one with telescope "Looking Out"

Colour: Black with green tint

Back Design: Lathework, counters and bank name

Colour: Blue

580-10-06P

$20 Face Design: Princess of Wales/lion and Indian woman flanking bust of Victoria/two sailors on shore, one with telescope "Looking Out"

Colour: Black with green tint

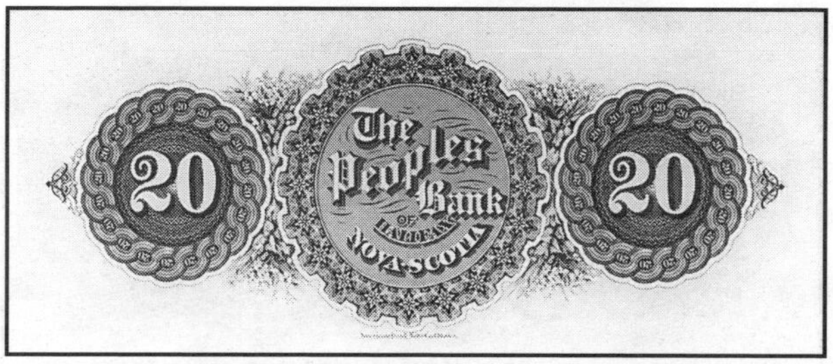

Back Design: Lathework, counters and bank name

Colour: Blue

Note: The 1903 issue has "of Halifax" added to "The Peoples Bank."

IMPRINT

American Bank Note Co. N.Y.
American Bank Note Co. Ottawa

SIGNATURES

	left	right
1864:	none	none
1898:	mss. various	typed Patrick O'Mullin
1903:	mss. various	typed J.J. Stewart

ISSUE DATING

Engraved

25th May 1864 2nd July 1903.
1st November 1898.

CIRCULATING NOTES

Cat. No.	Denom.	Date	G	VG	F	VF	EF	AU
10-02	$20	1864	No known issued notes					
10-04	$20	1898	—	—	4,200.	—	—	—
10-06	$20	1903	No known issued notes					

PROOF NOTES

Cat. No.	Denom.	Date		Unc
10-02P	$20	1864	FACE PROOF	800.
10-06P	$20	1903	FACE PROOF	800.

580-12 $4, $5 AND $10 ISSUES OF 1870-1903

DESIGNS AND COLOURS

Note: The designs, wording and tints of the issues starting in 1900 vary slightly from previous issues.

580-12-02a

$4 Face Design: Seated "Commerce" figure "Export"/—/ Royal Crest

Colour: Black with green tint

Back Design: Lathework, counters and bank name
Colour: Green

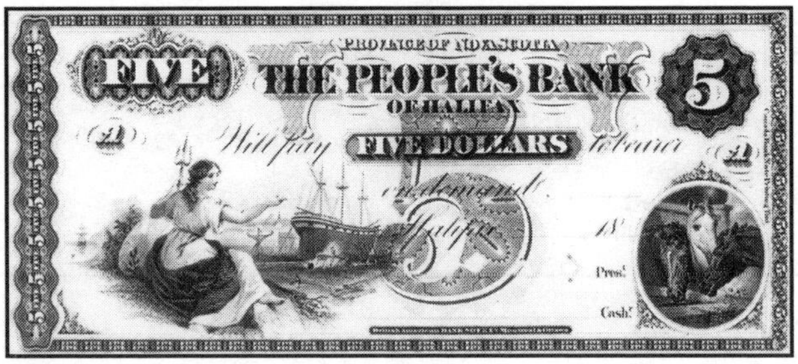

580-12-04P
$5 Face Design: Seated woman, ship in drydock/—/ three horses' heads/end frame has "5-fives"
Colour: Green V's and five

Back Design: lathework counters and bank name
Colour: Green

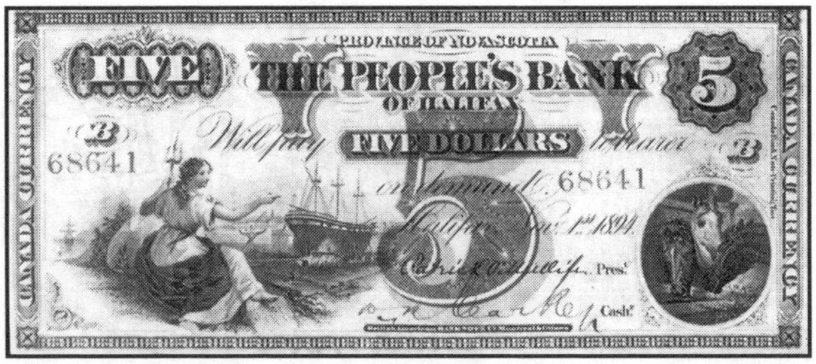

580-12-10
$5 Face Design: Seated woman holding trident, ship in drydock "Ship building"/three horses' heads
Colour: green Vs and 5

Back Design: Lathework, counters and bank name
Colour: Green

580-12-16
$5 Face Design: Seated woman holding trident, ship in drydock "Ship building"/ three horses' heads
Colour: overall green tint

Back Design: Lathework, counters and bank name
Colour: Green

580-12-18P
$10 Face Design: —/female operating telegraphic equipment/—

Colour: overall green tint

Back Design: Lathework, counters and bank name
Colour: Green

580-12-24
$10 Face Design: —/female operating telegraphic equipment/—

Colour: Green tint

Back Design: Lathework, counters and bank name
Colour: Green

Face Colour:
$4 and $5, 1870-1871: Black with green tint
$5 and $10, 1882-1899: Black with green tint
$5, 1900: Black with orange tint
$5, 1901: Black with overall green tint
$10, 1880: Black with overall orange tint
$10, 1900: Black with red-brown tint
$10, 1901: Black with overall orange tint
$10, 1903: Black with green tint

IMPRINT
British American Bank Note Co. Montreal & Ottawa
British American Bank Note Co. Ottawa
British American Bank Note Co. Montreal

SIGNATURES

	left (only)	right (only)
1870-1871:	mss. Geo. H. Starr and mss. Peter Jack	
1880:	none	none
1882:		engr. Augustus W. West and mss. Various
1894-1900:	mss. various	engr. Patrick O'Mullin
1901, 1903:	mss. various	engr. J.J. Stewart

ISSUE DATING
Engraved

July 1st 1870	April 1st 1899
July 1st 1871	2nd Jan 1900
1st Sept 1880	1st Oct, 1900
July 1st 1882	1st Oct. 1901
Nov. 1st 1894	July 2, 1903
1st Nov 1894	

OVERPRINT
The bank name and "CANADA CURRENCY issue of July 1871" is in a red seal and "CANADA CURRENCY" appears vertically at the right end.

CIRCULATING NOTES

Cat. No.	Denom.	Date	Variety	G	VG	F	VF	EF	AU
12-02	$4	18__	no o/p	No known issued notes					
12-02a	$4	1870	red seal o/p	1,200.	2,200.	—	—	—	—
12-04	$5	18__	no o/p	No known issued notes					
12-04a	$5	1870	red seal o/p	1,200.	2,200.	2,800.	4,250.	—	—
12-06	$5	1871	no o/p	1,400.	2,500.	3,700.	5,500.	—	—
12-08	$5	1882		1,400.	2,500.	3,700.	5,500.	—	—
12-10	$5	1894		Institutional collection only					
12-12	$5	1899		1,400.	2,500.	3,700.	5,500.	—	—
12-14	$5	1900		1,400.	2,500.	3,700.	5,500.	—	—
12-16	$5	1901		1,400.	2,500.	3,700.	5,500.	—	—
12-18	$10	1880		No known issued notes					
12-20	$10	1894		1,800.	3,200.	—	—	—	—
12-22	$10	1900		1,800.	3,200.	—	—	—	—
12-24	$10	1901		Institutional collection only					
12-26	$10	1903		No known issued notes					

PROOF NOTES

Cat. No.	Denom.	Date	Variety		Unc
12-02P	$4	18__	no o/p	FACE PROOF	800.
12-04P	$5	18__	no o/p	FACE PROOF	800.
12-18P	$10	1880		FACE PROOF	800.
12-26P	$10	1903		FACE PROOF	800.

THE PEOPLE'S BANK OF NEW BRUNSWICK

1864-1907

FREDERICTON (NEW BRUNSWICK)

BANK NUMBER 585 ***REDEEMABLE***

Established in Fredericton, New Brunswick, in 1864, this bank was absorbed by the Bank of Montreal in 1907. The principal shareholders of this small bank, the Randolph family, accepted the offer of the Bank of Montreal of a "very generous price of $350.00 per share."

585-10 **ABNC PRINTINGS**
1864 - 1873

DESIGNS AND COLOURS

585-10-02
$1 Face Design: Henry George Clopper/lion and shield/ Victoria (Winterhalter portrait) in oval
Colour: Black with green tint
Back Design: Plain

Photo Not Available

585-10-24
$2 Face Design: Henry George Clopper/Britannia and "Justice" figure flanking numeral 2/ oval portrait of Queen Victoria
Colour: Black with green tint
Back Design: Plain

Photo Not Available

585-10-40P
$5 Face Design: Henry George Clopper/Royal Crest/sailboat
Colour: Black with green tint
Back Design: Plain

IMPRINT
American Bank Note Co. New York

SIGNATURES

left	right
mss. S.W. Babbitt	mss. A.F. Randolph

ISSUE DATING

Partially engraved ___ 1st, 18___:

1864: Sep.
1867: May
1873: Apr.

CIRCULATING NOTES

Cat. No.	Denom.	Date	G	VG	F	VF	EF	AU
10-02	$1	1864	1,600.	2,500.	3,250.	—	—	—
10-10	$1	1867	1,400.	2,200.	2,800.	—	—	—
10-24	$2	1873	—	3,000.	—	—	—	—
10-40	$5	18_	No known issued notes					

PROOF NOTES

Cat. No.	Denom.	Date		Unc
10-40P	$5	18__	PROOF	800.

585-12 ABNC AND BABN PRINTINGS 1874 AND 1881

DESIGNS AND COLOURS

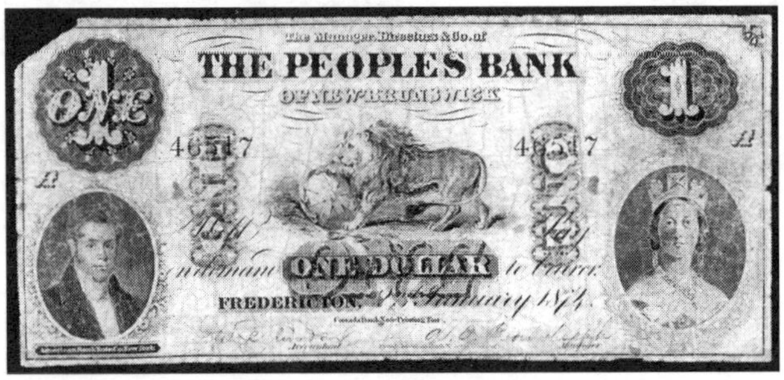

585-12-02
$1 Face Design: Like previous issue, but counters, lathework and tint are different
Colour: Green

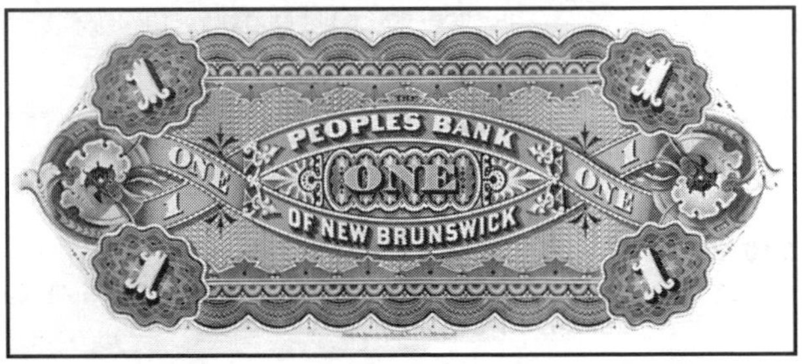

Back Design: Lathework, counters and bank name
Colour: Green

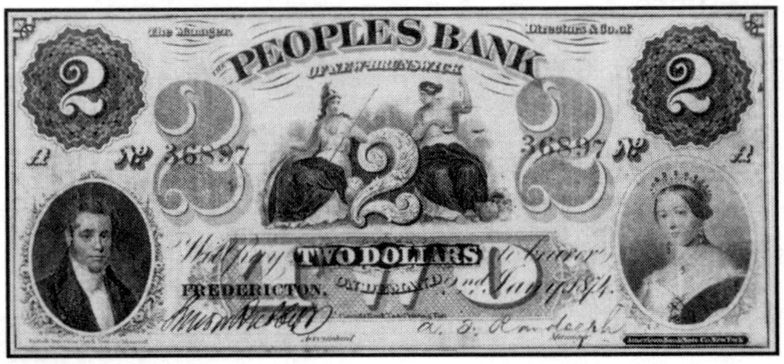

585-12-06
$2 Face Design: Like previous issue 585-10
Colour: Green

Back Design: Lathework, counters and bank name
Colour: Green

585-12-10P
$5 Face Design: Henry George Clopper/Royal Crest/sailboat
Colour: Black with green tint

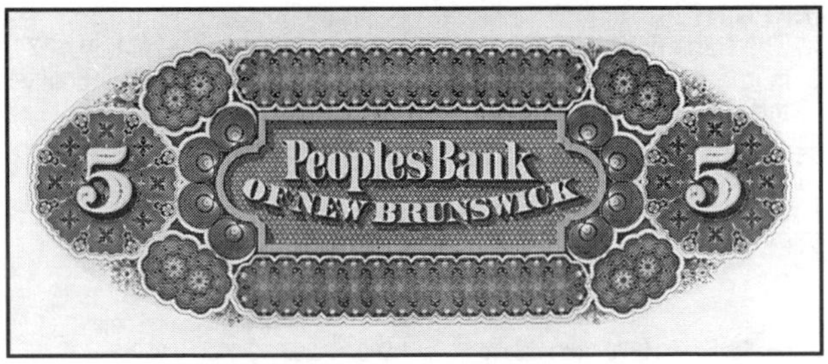

Back Design: latherwork, counters and bank name
Colour: Green

585-12-16
$10 Face Design: Prince of Wales in Highland dress/ seated woman with book and torch/ ship/George Clopper
Colour: Black with green tint

Back Design: Lathework, counters and bank name
Colour: Green

IMPRINT

American Bank Note Co. New York and British American Bank Note Co. Montreal

SIGNATURES

	left	right
1874:	mss. S.W. Babbitt	mss. A.F. Randolph
	mss. J.W. Spurden	mss. A.F. Randolph
1881:	mss. J.W. Spurden	engr. A.F. Randolph

ISSUE DATING

Engraved

2nd Jany 1874
2nd January 1874
1st December 1881
1st Decr 1881

Cat. No.	Denom.	Date	G	VG	F	VF	EF	AU
12-02	$1	1874	1,100.	1,800.	2,300.	—	—	—
12-04	$1	1881	1,400.	2,200.	2,800.	—	—	—
12-06	$2	1874	1,200.	2,000.	2,600.	—	—	—
12-08	$2	1881	1,400.	2,200.	2,800.	—	—	—
12-10	$5	1874	Institutional collection only					
12-14	$10	1874	1,500.	2,350.	3,000.	—	—	—
12-16	$10	1881	1,500.	2,350.	3,000.	—	—	—

585-14 QUEEN VICTORIA "WIDOW'S WEEDS" ISSUE 1885

DESIGNS AND COLOURS

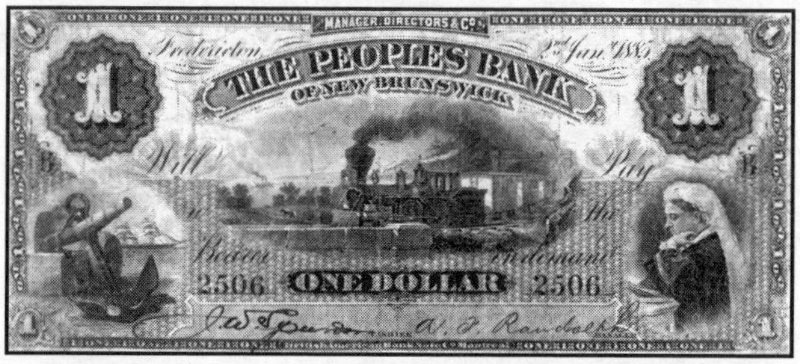

585-14-02

$1 Face Design: Anchor with box and kegs/train emerging from tunnel "Through the tunnel"/ Queen Victoria in widow's weeds
Colour: Black with green tint

Back Design: Lathework, counters and bank name
Colour: Green

585-14-04

$5 Face Design: Oval portrait of Prince Arthur/sailing ship, "Clipper"/Queen Victoria in widow's weeds
Colour: Black with green tint

Back Design: Lathework, counters and bank name
Colour: Green

IMPRINT

British American Bank Note Co. Montreal

SIGNATURES

left	right
mss. J.W. Spurden	engr. A.F. Randolph

ISSUE DATING

Engraved

$1: 2nd Jany 1885
$5: 2nd Nov 1885

STAMPS

Red "A"s left and right

Cat. No.	Denom.	Date	G	VG	F	VF	EF	AU
14-02	$1	1885	900.	1,600.	2,000.	3,000.	—	—
14-04	$5	1885	1,400.	2,200.	2,800.	—	—	—

585-16 "RANDOLPH PORTRAIT" ISSUES 1897 AND 1904

DESIGNS AND COLOURS

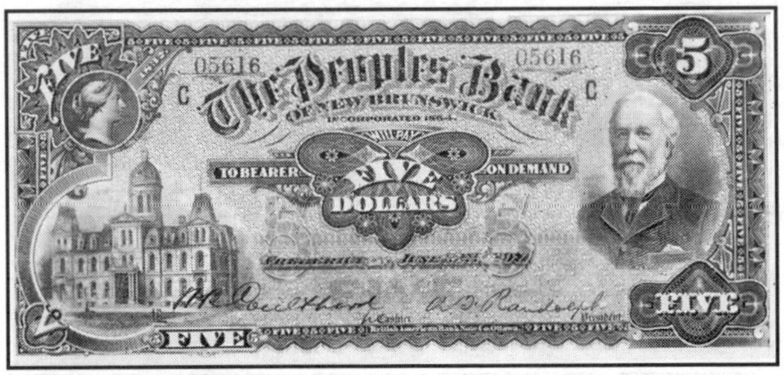

585-16-02
$5 Face Design: Queen Victoria; N.B. legislative building/—/A.F. Randolph

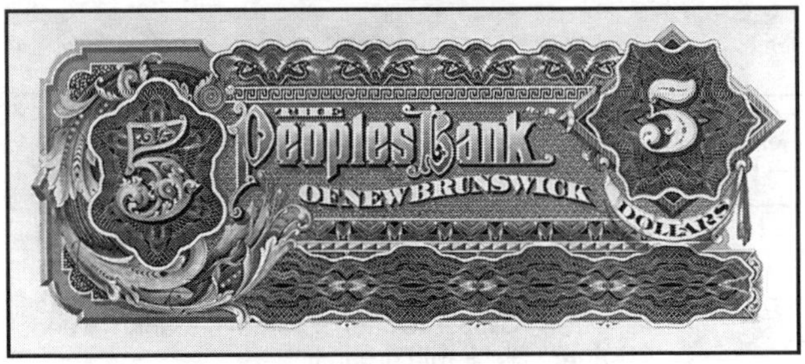

Back Design: Lathework, counters and bank name

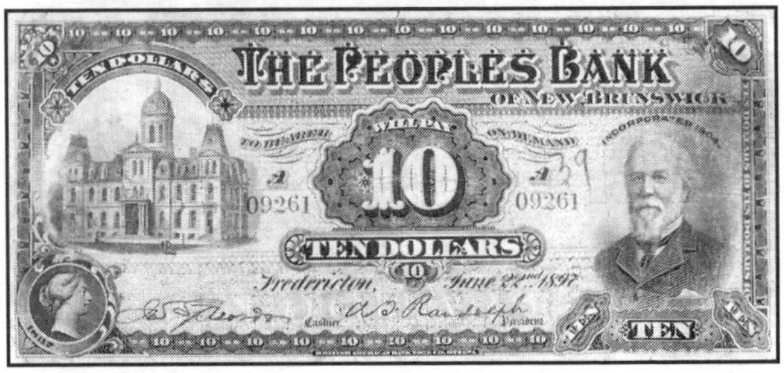

585-16-06
$10 Face Design: N.B. legislative building; Queen Victoria/—/A.F. Randolph

Back Design: Lathework, counters and bank name

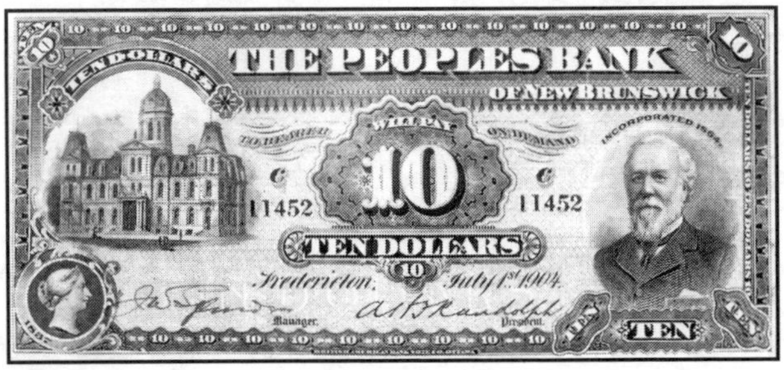

585-16-08
$10 Face Design: N.B. legislative building; Queen Victoria/—/A.F. Randolph

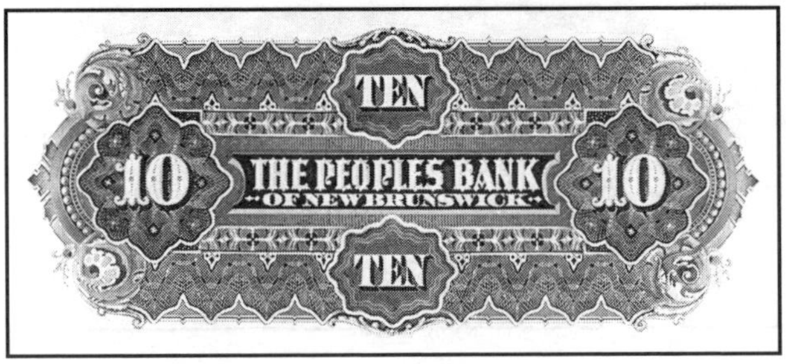

Back Design: Lathework, counters and bank name

1897 Face Colour: Black with red-brown tint
Back Colour: Green
Proofs of the 1897 $5 and $10 exist with blue tint

1904 Face Colour: Black with ochre tint
Back Colour: Green

IMPRINT

British American Bank Note Co. Ottawa

SIGNATURES

	left	right
1897:	mss. J.W. Spurden	engr. A.F. Randolph
	mss. W.B. Coulthard	engr. A.F. Randolph
1904:	mss. J.W. Spurden	engr. A.H.F. Randolph

ISSUE DATING

Engraved

June 22nd, 1897
July 1st, 1904

Cat. No.	Denom.	Date	G	VG	F	VF	EF	AU
16-02	$5	1897	Institutional collection only					
16-04	$5	1904	1,800.	3,000.	4,000.	5,500.	—	—.
16-06	$10	1897	Institutional collection only					
16-08	$10	1904	1,800.	3,000.	—	—	—	—.

585-18 ABNC PRINTINGS 1897 AND 1905

DESIGNS AND COLOURS

585-18-02-02
$20 Face Design: "Justice" figure/ St. George slaying the dragon/ oval portrait of the Duke of Wellington

Back Design: Lathework, counters and bank name

585-18-02-04P

$50 Face Design: Queen Victoria (Chalon portrait) in oval/ ship and seated "Commerce" figure with cornucopia full of produce/train on bridge with cattle being driven beneath, "The Drove"

Back Design: Lathework, counters and bank name

2. FULLY ENGRAVED DATE, 1897

DESIGNS AND COLOURS

Face Colour: Black with blue tint
Back Colour: Blue

IMPRINT

American Bank Note Company and
British American Bank Note Company

SIGNATURES

left	right
mss. J.W. Spurden	engr. A.F. Randolph

ISSUE DATING

Engraved

June 22nd 1897

CIRCULATING NOTES

Cat. No.	Denom.	Date	G	VG	F	VF	EF	AU
18-02-02	$20	1897			Institutional collection only			
18-02-04	$50	1897			No known issued notes			

PROOF NOTES

Cat. No.	Denom.	Date		Unc
18-02-04P	$50	1897	FACE PROOF	800.

4. PARTIALLY ENGRAVED DATE, COMPLETED BY RED STAMP, 1905

DESIGNS AND COLOURS

585-18-04-02

Face Colour: Black with green tint
Back Colour: Green

IMPRINT

American Bank Note Co. New York and British American Bank Note Company

SIGNATURES

left	right
mss. J. W. Spurdon (p)	mss. A.H.F. Randolph
mss. W.B. Coulthard	mss. A.H.F. Randolph

ISSUE DATING

Partially engraved _ 18_:

1905: Oct. 6 (stamped in red)

Cat. No.	Denom.	Date	G	VG	F	VF	EF	AU
18-04-02	$50	1905			Institutional collection only			
18-04-06	$50	18__ (no red date stamp)			Institutional collection only			

THE PHENIX BANK

1837-1841

PHILLIPSBURGH, LOWER CANADA

BANK NUMBER 590 ***NONREDEEMABLE***

The Phenix Bank is thought to have been a spurious bank of the type that proliferated during the financial crisis of 1837 to 1839. It existed to circulate its paper money at the expense of the public. In the title on the notes there appears the word, "adjoining" in very small letters beside Phillipsburgh, L.C. "The State of Vermont," which led the unwary to believe that these notes were from a U.S. bank. See Haxby VT-170G2, 4 and 6.

590-10 HARRIS ISSUE, 1837-1841

DESIGNS AND COLOURS

590-10-02-02
$1 (5s) Face Design: Steamboat in oval (sideways)/ dog by safe below/Phoenix rising from flames See subheadings
Colour: Black with no tint

Back Design: Plain

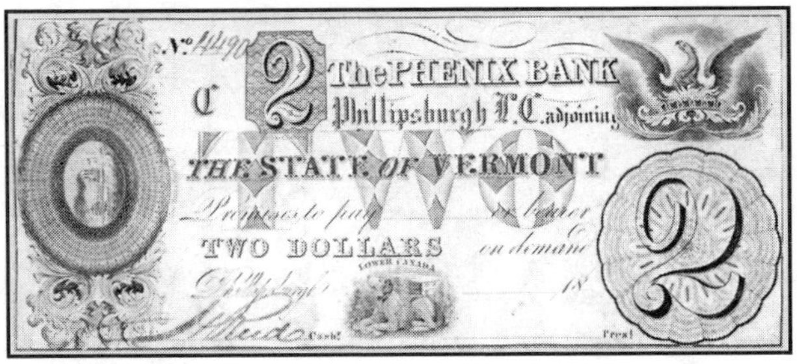

590-10-02-04R
$2 Face Design: Steamboat in oval (sideways)/ dog by safe below/Phoenix rising from flames
Colour: Black with no tint

Back Design: Plain

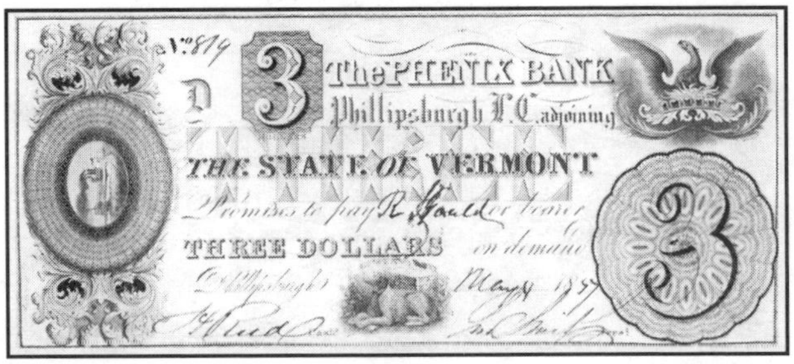

590-10-02-06
$3 Face Design: Steamboat in oval (sideways)/ dog by safe below/Phoenix rising from flames
Colour: Black with no tint

Back Design: Plain

IMPRINT
Jas. Harris Eng. N.Y.

SIGNATURES

left	right
mss. H. Reed	mss. Jno. Smith

2. DENOMINATION IN DOLLARS ONLY 1837

ISSUE DATING
Partially engraved ___ 18___:
1837: May 4

Cat. No.	Denom.	Date	Variety	G	VG	F	VF	EF	AU
10-02-02	$1	1837		200.	400.	550.	800.	—	—
10-02-04R	$2	18_	Remainder*	250.	500.	700.	950.	—	—
10-02-06	$3	1837		300.	600.	800.	1,200.	—	—

* Partially signed, undated and unnumbered.

4. DENOMINATION IN DOLLARS AND SHILLINGS 1841

ISSUE DATING
Partially engraved ___ 18___:
1841: Oct. 8

Cat. No.	Denom.	Date	G	VG	F	VF	EF	AU
10-04-02	$1 (5s)	1841	250.	500.	700.	950.	—	—

THE PICTOU BANK

1873-1887

PICTOU, NOVA SCOTIA

BANK NUMBER 595 ***NONREDEEMABLE***

This bank received its charter in 1873. At the time of its collapse, its paid-up capital was $200,000. A series of losses by its main debtors led to lockups. The principal account was with a tannery that used its loans for buildings and equipment. Depositors and noteholders were fully reimbursed, but the shareholders lost $163,970.

595-10 ISSUES OF 1874 AND 1882

DESIGNS AND COLOURS

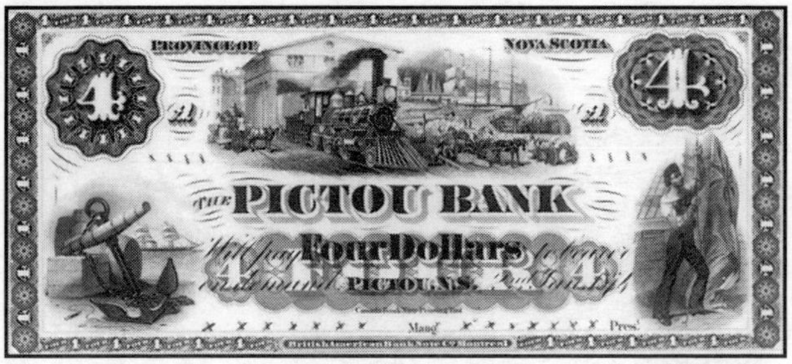

595-10-02R
$4 Face Design: Anchor/train and ships at dockside "Wharf scene"/ sailor raising flag "Show your colours"
Colour: Black with green tint

Back Design: Lathework, counters and bank name
Colour: Green

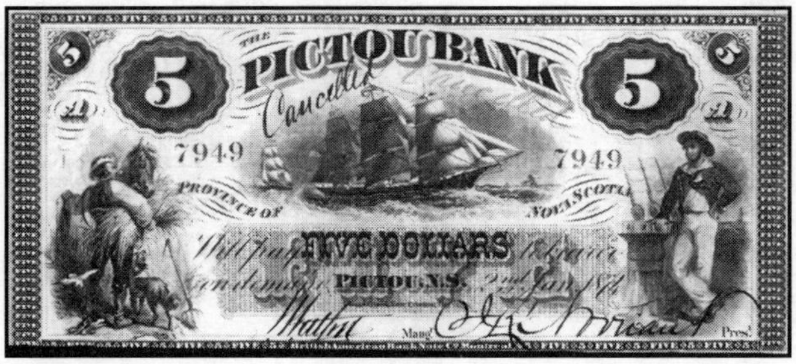

595-10-04
$5 Face Design: Farmer feeding horse "Old Burhans"/ sailing ships "Clipper"/ sailor aboard ship "Charlies Sailor"
Colour: Black with green tint

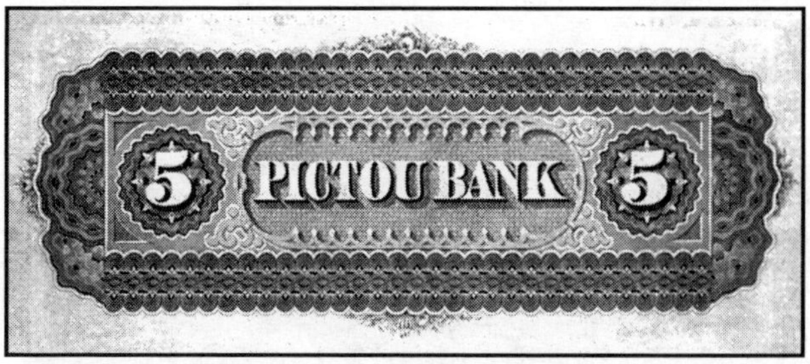

Back Design: Lathework, counters and bank name
Colour: Green

595-10-10R
$10 Face Design: —/mining scene "coal mining"/sailing ship
Colour: Black with green tint

Back Design: Lathework, counters and bank name
Colour: Green

IMPRINT
British American Bank Note Co. Montreal

SIGNATURES

	left	right
1874:	mss. T. Wilson	mss. John Crerar
	mss. T. Watson	mss. J. R. Noonan
	mss. T. Watson	mss. R. A. Grant
1882:	mss. T. Watson	mss. J. R. Noonan
	mss. T. Watson	mss. R. P. Grant
	mss. D. M. Fraser	mss. Illegible

ISSUE DATING
Engraved

2nd. Jan. 1874
2nd. Jan. 1882

CIRCULATING NOTES

Cat. No.	Denom.	Date	Variety	G	VG	F	VF	EF	Unc
10-02	$4	1874		Institutional collection only					
10-02R	$4	1874*	Remainder	—	—	—	—	1,100.	1,600.
10-04	$5	1874		1,500.	2,500.	3,500.	—	—	—
10-04R	$5	1874*	Remainder	—	—	—	—	900.	1,200.
10-06	$5	1882		1,200.	2,000.	2,800.	4,000.	—	—
10-06R	$5	1882*	Remainder	—	—	—	—	750.	1,000.
10-08	$10	1874		One known, poor. Est., $800					
10-08R	$10	1874*	Remainder	—	—	—	—	1,100.	1,600.
10-10	$10	1882		1,800.	3,000.	4,000.	5,500.	—	—
10-10R	$10	1882*	Remainder	—	—	—	—	850.	1,100.
Full sheet	$4,5,5,10	1874*		—	—	—	—	—	8,500.
Part sheet	$5,5,10	1882*		—	—	—	—	3,200.	4,500.

* Unsigned remainders.

PROOF NOTES

Cat. No.	Denom.	Date		Unc
10-02P	$4	1874	FACE PROOF	750.
10-04P	$5	1874	FACE PROOF	750.
10-08P	$10	1874	FACE PROOF	750.

THE BANK OF PRINCE EDWARD ISLAND

1856-1881
CHARLOTTE TOWN, (PRINCE EDWARD ISLAND)

BANK NUMBER 600 ***NONREDEEMABLE***

The first bank in the colony to be incorporated under provincial charter, the Bank of Prince Edward Island was established in 1856. With a capital stock of £30,000 and through conservative management, the bank was prosperous over the next 20 years, until a change of cashiers in 1876 resulted in large advances being made under false pretences. The bank became insolvent as a result and in 1881 was liquidated by the courts, with the Bank of Nova Scotia as liquidator.

600-10 POUNDS, SHILLINGS AND PENCE ISSUE, 1856-1868

DESIGNS AND COLOURS

600-10-02

5s cy. Face Design Ship sailing toward viewer/
(3s 4d stg.): seated woman with dog and cattle/—
Colour: Black with no tint
Back Design: Plain

600-10-18

10s cy. Face Design —/man ploughing field; small sailing ship below/—
(6s 8d stg.):
Colour: Black with no tint
Back Design: Plain

600-10-34

£1 cy. Face Design (13s 4d stg.): Floral panel/ seated "Agriculture" figure/—
Colour: Black with no tint
Back Design: Plain

600-10-48

£2 cy. Face Design (1.6.8 stg.): —/seated farmer with produce; small sailing ship below/—
Colour: Black with no tint
Back Design: Plain

600-10-64

£5 cy. Face Design (3.6.8 stg.): Queen Victoria (Chalon portrait)/ Royal Crest/Prince Consort
Colour: Black with no tint
Back Design: Plain

IMPRINT

1856-1857: New England Bank Note Co. Boston and Rawdon, Wright, Hatch & Edson. New York
1859-1863: New England Bank Note Co. Boston and Rawdon, Wright, Hatch & Edson, New York and American Bank Note Company (monogram)

SIGNATURES

	left	right
1856-1857:	mss. Wm. Cundall	mss. R. Brecken
1859-1863:	mss. Wm. Cundall	mss. T.H. Haviland
1868:	mss. Wm. Cundall	mss. Daniel Brenan

ISSUE DATING

Partially engraved _18_:

5s cy.,	**1856:**	18 Aug.	**£1 cy.,**	**1856:**	18 Aug.
	1857:	7 April		**1857:**	Jany. 1st
	1859:	1 Jan.		**1860:**	2 Jan.
	1863:	Dec. 1	**£2 cy.,**	**1856:**	13 Aug., 13 Oct.
	1868:	2 Nov.		**1859:**	1 Jan.
10s cy.,	**1856:**	13 Aug.		**1863:**	Jan. 1st
	1857:	7 April	**£5 cy.,**	**1856:**	13 Aug.
	1859:	1 Jan.			
	1860:	Jan. 2			
	1862:	Jan. 1			

PROTECTOR

Red word on face and mirror image on the back.

Cat. No.	Denom.	Date	G	VG	F	VF	EF	AU
10-02	5s	1856-1868	900.	1,500.	2,000.	—	—	—
10-18	10s	1856-1862	800.	1,350.	1,800.	—	—	—
10-34	£1	1856-1860	1,200.	2,000.	2,500.	—	—	—
10-48	£2	1856-1863	700.	1,100.	1,500.	—	—	—
10-64	£5	1856	Institutional collection only					

600-12 DOLLAR ISSUES, 1872 AND 1877

DESIGNS AND COLOURS

600-12-04

$1 Face Design: —/woman cutting grain with sickle/—
Colour: Black with green tint

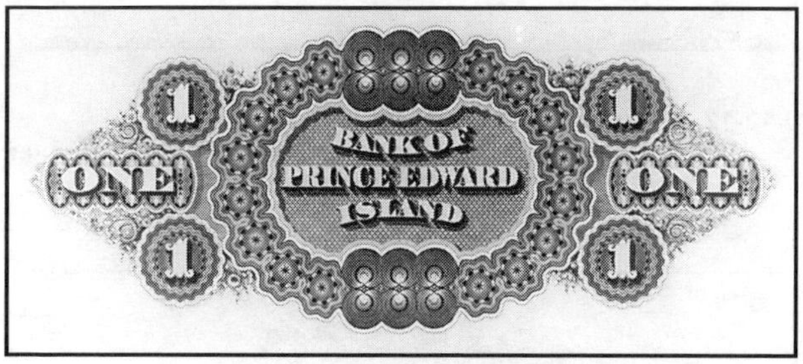

Back Design: Lathework, counters and bank name
Colour: Green

600-12-06a

$2 Face Design: Anchor/horse being watered at stream "At the Brook"/animals at barn door "Farm Stock"

Colour: Black with green tint

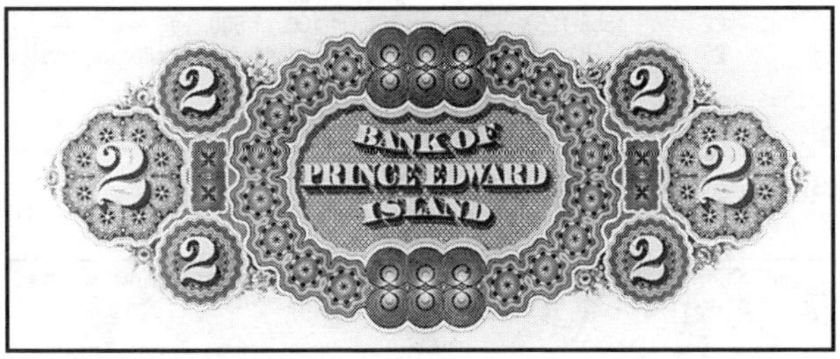

Back Design: Lathework, counters and bank name

Colour: Green

600-12-12

$5 Face Design: —/farmer watering livestock at pump; young girls head below "Autumn"/—

Colour: Black with green tint

Back Design: Lathework, counters and bank name

Colour: Green

600-12-14R

$10 Face Design: Sailor aboard ship/fishermen and sailing ships "On the Banks"/beehive and flowers

Colour: Black with green tint

Back Design: Lathework, counters and bank name

Colour: Green

600-12-16R

$20 Face Design: Queen Victoria/seated Britannia and ship in dry dock "Ship Building"/Prince of Wales

Colour: Black with green tint

Back Design: Lathework, counters and bank name

Colour: Green

IMPRINT

British American Bank Note Co. Montreal & Ottawa

SIGNATURES

	left	right
1872:	mss. Wm. Cundall	mss. Daniel Brenan
	mss. J.R. Brecken	mss. Joseph Hensley
	mss. J.R. Brecken	mss. Daniel Brenan
1877:	mss. Leslie S. McNutt	mss. T. Heath Haviland (p)
	mss. John A. Moore	mss. T. Heath Haviland
	mss. Leslie S. McNutt	mss. Joseph Hensley
	mss. J.R. Brecken	mss. J. Longworth
	mss. John A. Moore	mss. J. Longworth
	mss. J.R. Brecken	mss. Joseph Hensley
	mss. J.R. Brecken	mss. T. Heath Haviland
	mss. Leslie S. McNutt	mss. J. Longworth

ISSUE DATING

Engraved

1st Jany. 1872
1st Jany. 1877

OVERPRINT

CANADA CURRENCY in red

CIRCULATING NOTES

Cat. No.	Denom.	Date	Variety	G	VG	F	VF	EF	Unc
12-02	$1	1872	No o/p	300.	500.	700.	—	—	—
12-02a	$1	1872	Red o/p	350.	600.	—	—	—	—
12-04	$1	1877	No o/p	50.	100.	125.	175.	250.	500.
12-04a	$1	1877	Red o/p	60.	125.	175.	250.	450.	900.
12-06	$2	1872	No o/p	125.	200.	300.	—	—	—
12-06a	$2	1872	Red o/p	150.	250.	350.	—	—	—
12-08	$2	1877	No o/p	60.	110.	140.	200.	300.	600.
12-08a	$2	1877	Red o/p	60.	125.	175.	275.	500.	1,000.
12-10	$5	1872	No o/p	350.	600.	800.	—	—	—
12-10a	$5	1872	Red o/p	300.	500.	700.	—	—	—
12-12	$5	1877	No o/p	200.	400.	550.	800.	—	—
12-12a	$5	1877	Red o/p	250.	500.	700.	1,000.	—	—
12-14	$10	1872	Fully issued	200.	400.	550.	—	—	—
12-14R	$10	1872	Remainder*	100.	200.	250.	400.	600.	1,200.
12-16	$20	1872	Fully issued	175.	350.	450.	700.	—	—
12-16R	$20	1872	Remainder*	100.	200.	250.	400.	600.	1,200.

* Remainder with one signature only.

Note: Some $10 and $20 remainder notes have spurious signatures, such as "Sam Finlay".

PROOF NOTES

Cat. No.	Denom.	Date		Unc
12-02P	$1	1872	FACE PROOF	700.
12-06P	$2	1872	FACE PROOF	700.
12-10P	$5	1872	FACE PROOF	700.
12-14P	$10	1872	FACE PROOF	700.
12-16P	$20	1872	FACE PROOF	700.

THE PROVINCIAL BANK

1884

LONDON, ONTARIO

BANK NUMBER 605 ***NONREDEEMABLE***

The Provincial Bank was incorporated in 1884 in London, Ontario, but did not open for business.

605-10 DESIGNS OF 1884

DESIGNS AND COLOURS

605-10-02P

$5 Face Design: Lord Dufferin/farmer watering livestock at pump/barge in locks

Colour: Black with green tint

Back Design: Lathework, counters and bank name

Colour: Green

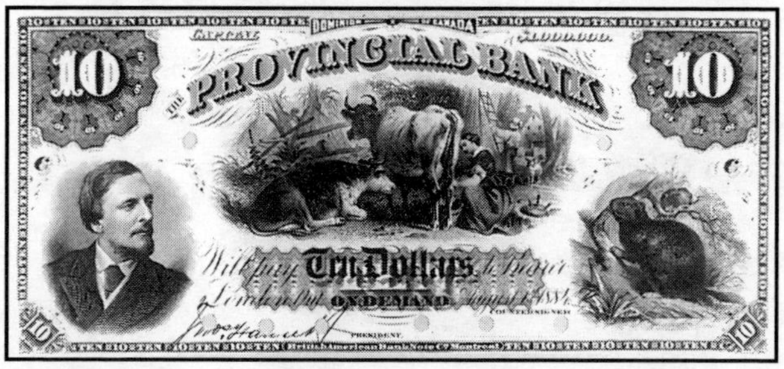

605-10-04P

$10 Face Design: Lord Dufferin/farm scene "Dairy Maid"/beavers

Colour: Black with green tint

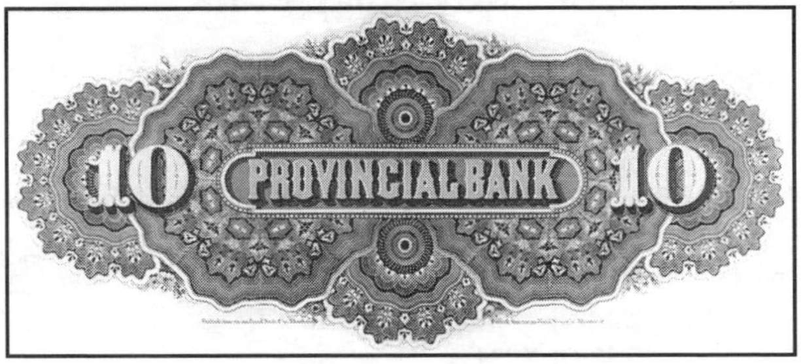

Back Design: Lathework, counters and bank name
Colour: Green

IMPRINT
British American Bank Note Company

SIGNATURES

left	right
none	engr. Thos. Fawcett

ISSUE DATING
Engraved
Aug. 1, 1884

PROOF NOTES

Cat. No.	Denom.	Date		Unc
10-02P	$5	1884	FACE PROOF	500.
10-04P	$10	1884	FACE PROOF	500.

THE PROVINCIAL BANK OF CANADA

1856-1863

STANSTEAD, PROVINCE OF CANADA

BANK NUMBER 610 ***NONREDEEMABLE***

This bank was established under the Free Banking Act of Canada in June 1856 in Stanstead, Canada East. The office was moved to Montreal in 1859. Capital, supplied by a New York firm, was to be $100,000, secured by a deposit of Canada 6-percent debentures. George W. McCollum purchased $100,000 in municipal debentures and had them deposited with the receiver general of Canada. The notes were printed in New York and Philadelphia and were first shipped to the bank in 1856. Shipments of the notes continued until fall 1860, when approximately $166,500 in face value had been sent.

Even before opening, the bank was under attack. Notes of the bank were placed in circulation in Toronto, Montreal, points in between and the Eastern Townships before the people of Stanstead were aware that a bank had been established. Although notes were in circulation, no office had been set up to redeem them. However, McCollum challenged those concerned to send their notes to Stanstead for redemption. The notes were, in fact, redeemed and confidence in the bank was restored.

In March 1859 a move was made to change the status of the institution, to incorporate it as a chartered bank. McCollum was required to state that he had no interest, past or present, in any bank except the Provincial Bank of Canada. This, however, proved not to be the case, and the application for charter was withdrawn. On December 15, 1863, the receiver general accepted a bond jointly given by J.D. Nutter, Robert Millard and George Warner of Montreal for $12,000 to guarantee the redemption of notes during the time required by law.

Withdrawal of their paper money began in 1862, and the negligible amount not returned became worthless on December 15, 1865.

610-10 **ISSUE OF 1856**

DESIGNS AND COLOURS

610-10-02
$1 (5s) Face Design:
Colour: Black with no tint
Back Design: Plain

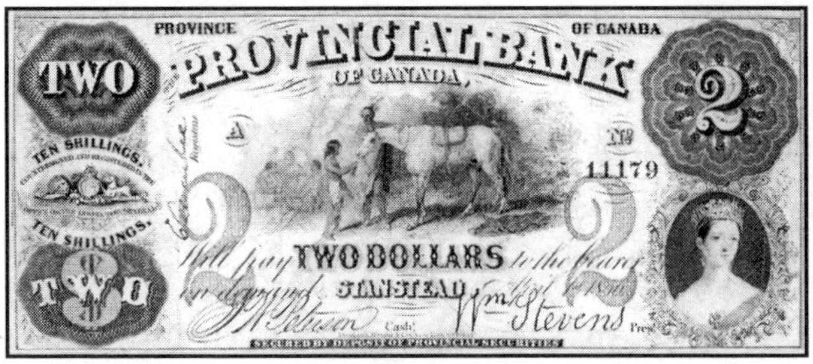

610-10-04
$2 (10s) Face Design: Small crest/Indians with horse/Queen Victoria (Chalon portrait)
Colour: Black with no tint
Back Design: Plain

610-10-06

$5 (L1.5) Face Design: Three Indians overlooking town/bust of Prince Consort in ornate 5/small crest

Colour: Black with no tint

Back Design: Plain

IMPRINT

Danforth Wright & Co. New York & Philada

SIGNATURES

left	**vertically right**
engr. F.W. Peterson	mss. C. Cambie
	engr. Wm. Stevens

ISSUE DATING

Engraved

April 1st 1856.

PROTECTOR

$1 and $2: Red numeral on face and back

$5: Red Roman numeral on face and back

CIRCULATING NOTES

Cat. No.	Denom.	Date	Variety	G	VG	F	VF	EF	Unc
10-02	$1	1856		225.	450.	650.	1,200.	—	—
10-04	$2	1856		200.	400.	600.	1,100.	—	—
10-06	$5	1856		250.	500.	700.	1,300.	—	—
10-06a	$5	1856	o/p MONTREAL	400.	800.	—	—	—	—

PROOF NOTES

Cat. No.	Denom.	Date	Variety		Unc
10-02P	$1	1856	B & W	PROOF	300.
Full sheet	$1,2,1,5	1856	Coloured	PROOF	2,500.

LA BANQUE PROVINCIALE DU CANADA

1900-1979

MONTREAL, QUEBEC

BANK NUMBER 615 ***REDEEMABLE***

This bank was established in Montreal in 1862 as La Banque Jacques Cartier and changed its name in 1900 to La Banque Provinciale du Canada. By the end of the century it had 15 branches, mainly in Quebec, and was growing slowly but successfully despite strong competition from several other banks. Although this bank operated chiefly in Quebec, it had branches in Prince Edward Island, New Brunswick and the French-speaking districts of Ontario.

The bank expanded its operations in Quebec by absorbing the Peoples Bank in 1970. In Ontario and other provinces expansion occurred through a merger with the Unity Bank of Canada in 1977. On November 1, 1979, La Banque Provinciale du Canada and La Banque Canadienne Nationale amalgamated to form the National Bank (La Banque Nationale). Despite the large assets of the combined institution, it was endangered by having committed funds previously on a long-term basis at a relatively low rate of interest and then, when interest rates soared, having to pay depositors a higher rate than it was receiving.

615-10 **ISSUE OF 1900**

DESIGNS AND COLOURS

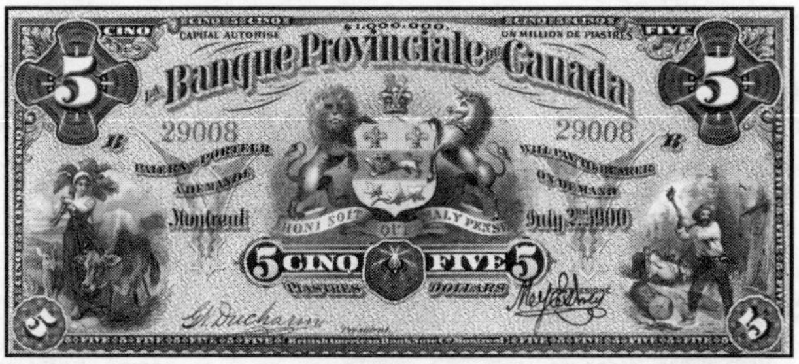

615-10-02

$5 Face Design: Woman with cow and calf "Alderney"/ bank crest/man chopping tree, cattle "Logging No. 2"

Colour: Black with green tint

Back Design: —/Indians on bluff/—

Colour: Green

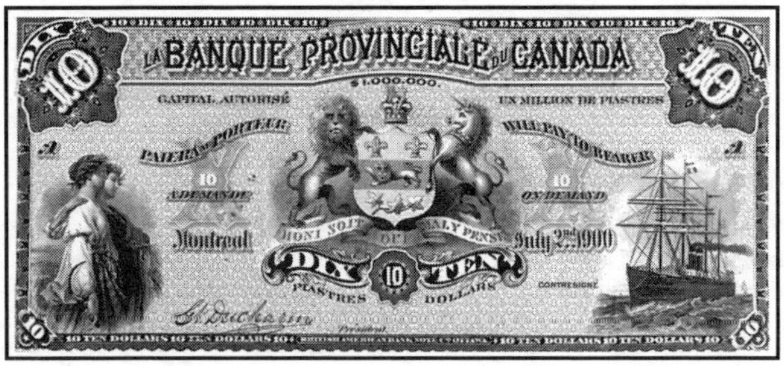

615-10-04P

$10 Face Design: Two women "The Reapers"/Bank Crest/ship
Colour: Black with green tint

Back Design: Unknown
Colour: Green

IMPRINT
British American Bank Note Co. Montreal

SIGNATURES

left	right
engr. G.V. Ducharme	mss. various

ISSUE DATING
Engraved
July 2nd 1900

Note: A proof of the $5 issue exists with ochre tint

CIRCULATING NOTES

Cat. No.	Denom.	Date	G	VG	F	VF	EF	AU
10-02	$5	1900	Institutional collection only					
10-04	$10	1900	No known issued notes					

PROOF NOTES

Cat. No.	Denom.	Date		Unc
10-02P	$5	1900	FACE PROOF	500.
10-04P	$10	1900	FACE PROOF	500.

SPECIMEN NOTES

Cat. No.	Denom.	Date		Unc
10-02S	$5	1900	SPECIMEN	1,000.
10-04S	$10	1900	SPECIMEN	1,000.

615-12 ISSUE OF 1907

DESIGNS AND COLOURS

615-12-02

$5 Face Design: Tancrède Bienvenu/train in station/ H. Laporte
Colour: Black with green tint

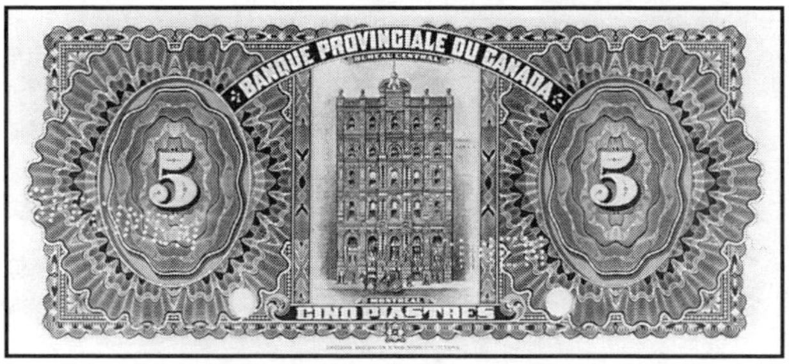

Back Design: Lathework, counters, bank name and head office
Colour: Green

615-12-06

$10 Face Design: Tancrède Bienvenu/ steamboat Montreal/H. Laporte
Colour: Black with green tint

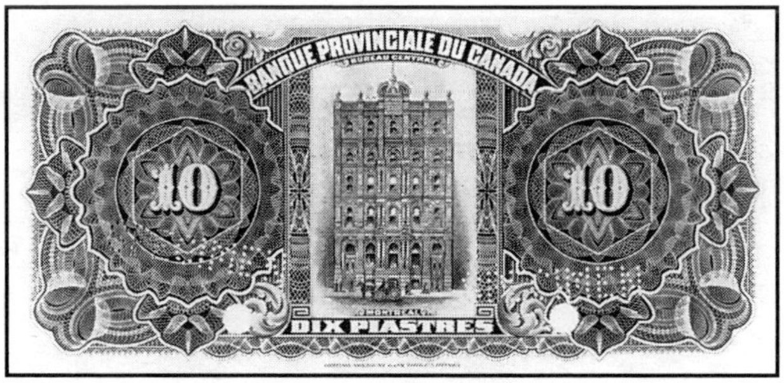

Back Design: Lathework, counters, bank name and head office
Colour: Green

IMPRINT
British American Bank Note Co. Ottawa

SIGNATURES

left	right
mss. various	engr. H. Laporte

ISSUE DATING
Engraved
Le 1er. Juin 1907

CIRCULATING NOTES

Cat. No.	Denom.	Date	G	VG	F	VF	EF	AU
12-02	$5	1907	300.	600.	900.	1,300.	—	—
12-06	$10	1907	750.	1,500.	—	—	—	—

PROOF NOTES

Cat. No.	Denom.	Date	Variety		Unc
10-04P	$5	1907	Brown tint	FACE PROOF	500.

615-14 ISSUE OF 1913-1928

DESIGNS AND COLOURS

615-14-08

$5 Face Design: H. Laporte/ornate V/Tancrède Bienvenu

Back Design: Lathework, counters, bank name and head office

615-14-10

$10 Face Design: Ornate X/H. Laporte and Tancrède Bienvenu/ornate X

Back Design: Lathework, counters, bank name and head office

615-14-18

$20 Face Design: H. Laporte/ornate XX/J.B. Rolland

Back Design: Lathework, counters, bank name and head office

$5, 1913 Face Colour: Black with predominantly orange and green tint
Back Colour: Green
1919 Face Colour: See Varieties
Back Colour: See Varieties
1928 Face Colour: Black with predominantly green and yellow tint
Back Colour: Green

$10, 1913 Face Colour: Black with predominantly orange and yellow-green tint
Back Colour: Orange
1919 Face Colour: See Varieties
Back Colour: See Varieties
1928 Face Colour: Black with predominantly brownabd yellow tint
Back Colour: Brown

$20, 1928 Face Colour: Black with blue tint
Back Colour: Blue

IMPRINT

American Bank Note Co. Ottawa
Canadian Bank Note Company, Limited

SIGNATURES

left	right
typed H. Laporte	mss. various

ISSUE DATING

Engraved

Le 2 Janvier 1913
Le 31 Janvier 1919
Le 1er Aout. 1928

VARIETIES

$5, 1919 Face Colour: Black with predominantly orange and green tint
Back Colour: Green
$5, 1919 Face Colour: Black with predominantly green and yellow tint
Back Colour: Green
$10, 1919 Face Colour: Black with predominantly orange and yellow-green tint
Back Colour: Orange
$10, 1919 Face Colour: Black with predominantly brown and yellow tint
Back Colour: Brown

CIRCULATING NOTES

Cat. No.	Denom.	Date	Variety	G	VG	F	VF	EF	Unc
14-02	$5	1913		350.	700.	950.	1,400.	—	—
14-04	$5	1919	Orange tint	100.	200.	300.	500.	—	—
14-06	$5	1919	Green tint	40.	80.	110.	175.	300.	600.
14-08	$5	1928		30.	60.	80.	125.	225.	500.
14-10	$10	1913		200.	400.	550.	750.	—	—
14-12	$10	1919	Orange tint	85.	175.	250.	400.	—	—
14-14	$10	1919	Brown tint	30.	60.	80.	125.	225.	500.
14-16	$10	1928		30.	60.	85.	150.	300.	600.
14-18	$20	1928		55.	110.	150.	225.	400.	850.

PROOF NOTES

Cat. No.	Denom.	Date	Variety		Unc
14-06P	$5	1919	B & W	FACE PROOF	300.
14-06Pa	$5	1919	Coloured	FACE PROOF	450.
14-08P	$5	1928		FACE PROOF	450.
14-12P	$10	1919	B & W	FACE PROOF	300.
14-16P	$10	1928		FACE PROOF	450.
14-18P	$20	1928		FACE PROOF	450.

SPECIMEN NOTES

Cat. No.	Denom.	Date		Unc
14-02S	$5	1913	SPECIMEN	750.
14-08S	$5	1928	SPECIMEN	750.
14-16S	$10	1928	SPECIMEN	750.
14-18S	$20	1928	SPECIMEN	750.

615-16 ISSUE OF 1935 SMALL-SIZE NOTES

DESIGNS AND COLOURS

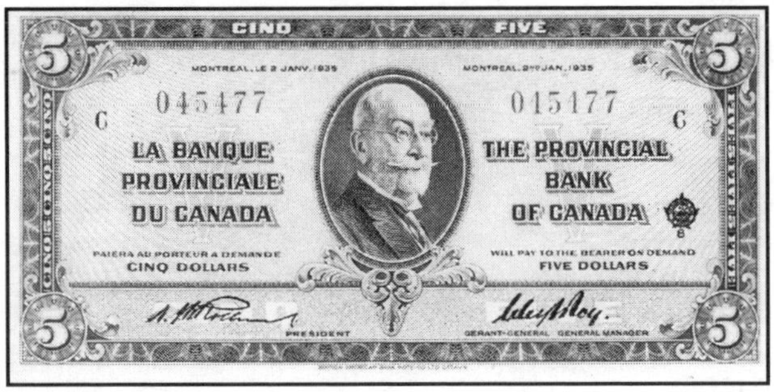

615-16-02

$5 Face Design: —/J.B. Rolland/—

Colour: Brown tint

Back Design: Lathework, counters, bank name and bank building

Colour: Green

615-16-04

$10 Face Design: —/J.B. Rolland/—

Colour: Black tint

Back Design: Lathework, counters, bank name and bank building

Colour: Olive green

IMPRINT

British American Bank Note Co Ltd Ottawa

SIGNATURES

left	right
typed S.J.B. Rolland	typed Chs. A. Roy

ISSUE DATING

Engraved

Le 2 Janv. 1935
2nd Jan. 1935

CIRCULATING NOTES

Cat. No.	Denom.	Date	VG	F	VF	EF	AU	Unc
16-02	$5	1935	45.	65.	100.	210.	325.	450.
16-04	$10	1935	45.	65.	100.	210.	325.	450.

SPECIMEN NOTES

Cat. No.	Denom.	Date		Unc
16-02S	$5	1935	SPECIMEN	750.
16-04S	$10	1935	SPECIMEN	750.

615-18 ISSUE OF 1936 SMALL-SIZE NOTES

DESIGNS AND COLOURS

615-18-04

$5 Face Design: Charles Arthur Roy

Colour: Black with yellow and blue tint

Back Design: Lathework, counters, bank name and bank building
Colour: See varieties

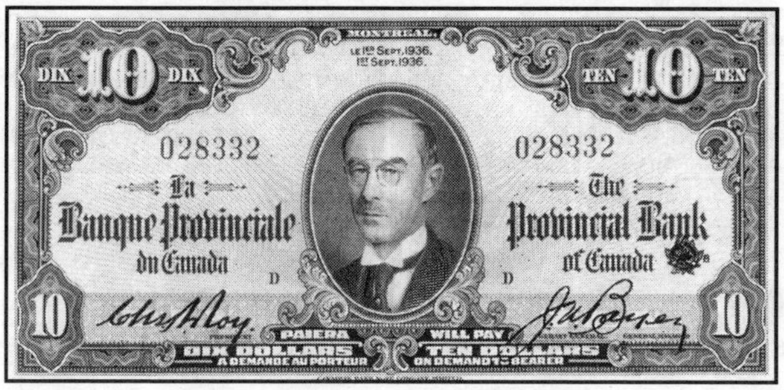

615-18-08
$10 Face Design: Charles Arthur Roy
Colour: Black with yellow and orange tint

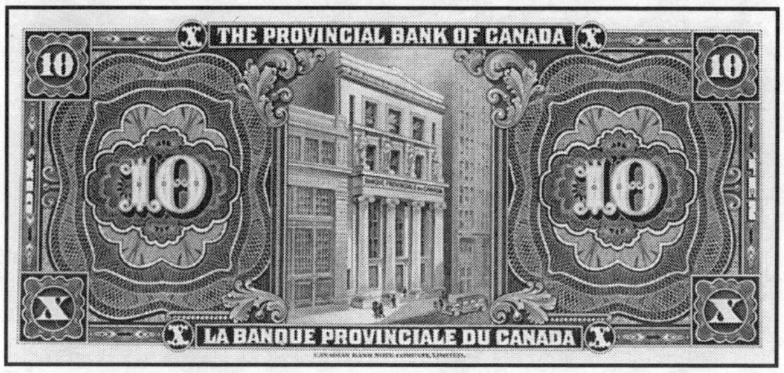

Back Design: lathework, counters, bank name and bank building
Colour: Orange

615-18-08
$10 Face Design: Charles Arthur Roy
Colour: Black with green tint and X's
Back Design: Lathework, counters, bank name and bank building
Colour: Green

IMPRINT
Canadian Bank Note Company Limited

SIGNATURES

left	**right**
typed Charles A. Roy	typed J.U. Bayer

ISSUE DATING
Engraved
Le 1er Sept. 1936
1st Sept. 1936

VARIETIES
$5 Back Colour: Blue
$5 Back Colour: Green
$10 Back Colour: Orange
$10 Back Colour: Green

CIRCULATING NOTES

Cat. No.	Denom.	Date	Variety	VG	F	VF	EF	AU	Unc
18-02	$5	1936	Blue back	55.	80.	120.	240.	350.	475.
18-04	$5	1936	Green back	80.	115.	175.	350.	500.	700.
18-06	$10	1936	Orange back	55.	80.	120.	240.	350.	475.
18-08	$10	1936	Green back	70.	100.	150.	315.	475.	650.

SPECIMEN NOTES

Cat. No.	Denom.	Date	Variety		Unc
18-02S	$5	1936	Blue back	SPECIMEN	750.
18-04S	$5	1936	Green back	SPECIMEN	750.
18-06S	$10	1936	Orange back	SPECIMEN	750.
18-08S	$10	1936	Green back	SPECIMEN	750.

Note: The $5 note with green back was prepared Jan. 24, 1941; the $10 note with green back was prepared Jan. 17, 1941.

THE QUEBEC BANK

1818-1917
QUEBEC, LOWER CANADA

BANK NUMBER 620 ***REDEEMABLE***

Started as a private partnership in October 1818 in Quebec, Lower Canada, this bank obtained a charter in 1822 from the Province of Lower Canada and obtained a royal charter in May 1837. Its charter from the province was the last one granted by that government. After successful operations as one of the oldest banks in Canada, it merged with the Royal Bank of Canada in 1917, with assets of $22 million and 58 branches. The merger enabled the Royal Bank to expand its operations in Quebec.

620-10 "MAVERICK" PRINTING "ARMY-BILL" TYPE NOTES 1818-1819

DESIGNS AND COLOURS

Photo Not Available

620-10-02
$1 Face Design: Unknown
Colour: Black with no tint
Back Design: Plain

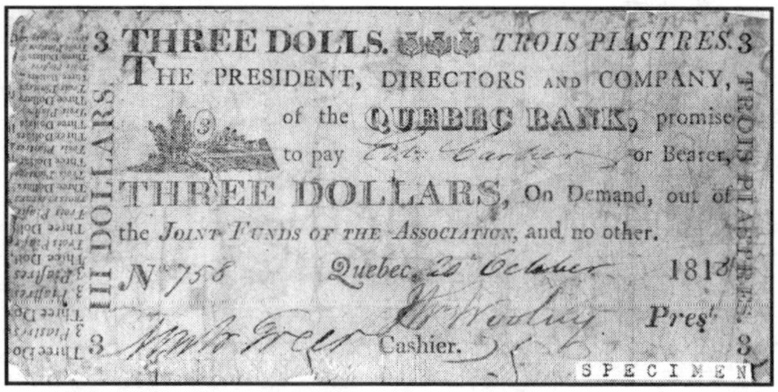

620-10-06
$3 Face Design: Farm and 3/—/—
Colour: Black with no tint
Back Design: Plain

Photo Not Available

620-10-10
$5 Face Design: Unknown
Colour: Black with no tint
Back Design: Plain

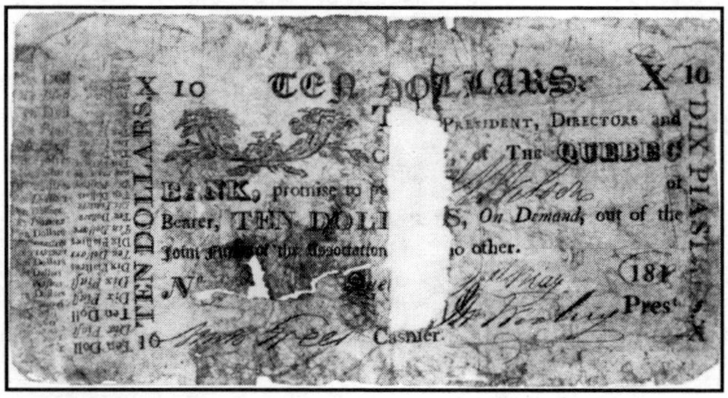

620-10-14
$10 Face Design: Crossed cornucopias/—/—
Colour: Black with no tint
Back Design: Plain

Photo Not Available

620-10-18
$100 Face Design: Unknown
Colour: Black with no tint
Back Design: Plain

IMPRINT
Maverick

SIGNATURES

left	right
mss. Noah Freer	mss. J.W. Woolsey

ISSUE DATING
Partially engraved __ 18__:
$3, 1818: 20th October

Cat. No.	Denom.	Date	G	VG	F	VF	EF	AU
10-02	$1	1818-1819		GENUINE NOTES NOT KNOWN				
10-06	$3	1818	1,000.	2,000.	2,750.	—	—	—
10-10	$5	1818-1819		GENUINE NOTES NOT KNOWN				
10-14	$10	1818-1819		GENUINE NOTES NOT KNOWN				
10-14C	$10	1819 Counterfeit	50.	100.	125.	175.	—	—
10-18	$100	1818-1819		ALL NOTES REDEEMED				

620-12 GRAPHIC PRINTINGS, 1819-1830s

DESIGNS AND COLOURS

620-12-02R
$1 Face Design: —/Wheat sheaves, ONE; squirrel below/—
Colour: Black with no tint
Back Design: Plain

620-12-04R
$2 Face Design: —/TWO, ship, justice figure, 2; racoon below/—
Colour: Black with no tint
Back Design: Plain

620-12-06R

$5 Face Design: —/Ship, female, 5 on pillar, wheat sheaves; fox below/—
Colour: Black with no tint
Back Design: Plain

6

20-12-08R

$10 Face Design: —/Buildings, TEN over paddlewheel steamer; beaver below/—
Colour: Black with no tint
Back Design: Plain

Photo Not Available

620-12-10R

$20 Face Design: Unknown
Colour: Black with no tint

Back Design: Plain

620-12-12R

$50 Face Design: —/Citadel from south shore; bear below/—
Colour: Black with no tint

Back Design: Plain

620-12-14R

$100 Face Design: —/Royal Coat of Arms; Ox below/—
Colour: Black with no tint
Back Design: Plain

620-12-16R

Post Note Design: —/Stagecoach and horses going left; jumping deer below/—
Colour: Black with no tint

Back Design: Plain

IMPRINT

Graphic Company

SIGNATURES

left	right
unknown	unknown

ISSUE DATING

Partially engraved __ 18__:

1819-1837

Cat. No.	Denom.	Date		VG	F	VF	EF	Unc
12-02R	$1	18__	Remainder					500.
12-04R	$2	18__	Remainder					500.
12-06R	$5	18__	Remainder					500.
12-08R	$10	18__	Remainder					500.
12-10R	$20	18__	Remainder	SURVIVING EXAMPLE NOT CONFIRMED				
12-12R	$50	18__	Remainder					500.
12-14R	$100	18__	Remainder					500.
12-16R	Post Note	18__	Remainder					300.

620-14 ISSUES OF 1833-1841

DESIGNS AND COLOURS

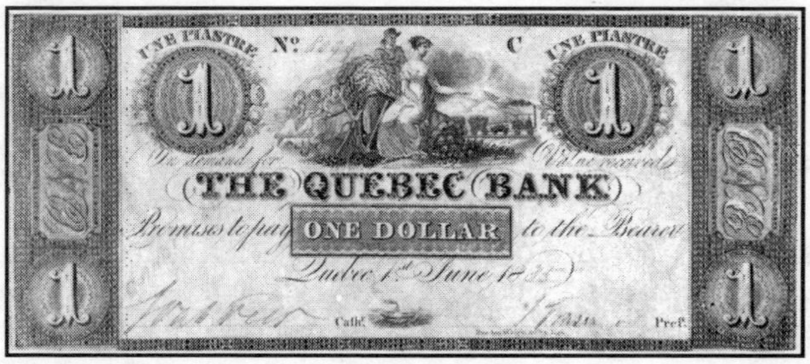

620-14-02

$1 Face Design: —/three children, man, seated woman, train; small ship below/—
Colour: Black with no tint

Back Design: Plain

Photo Not Available

620-14-06P

$5 Face Design: Unknown
Colour: Black with no tint

Back Design: Plain

IMPRINT

Rawdon, Wright, & Co. N. York

SIGNATURES

left	right
mss. Noah Freer	mss. J. Fraser (v)
mss. Noah Freer	mss. illegible

ISSUE DATING

Partially engraved 1st June, 18_:

1835
1836

CIRCULATING NOTES

Cat. No.	Denom.	Date	G	VG	F	VF	EF	AU
14-02	$1	1835-1836	550.	1,100.	1,400.	2,400.	—	—
14-06	$5	18__	No known issued notes					

PROOF NOTES

Cat. No.	Denom.	Date		Unc
14-02P	$1	18__	PROOF	400.
14-06P	$5	18__	PROOF	400.

620-16 JONES PRINTING, 1837

DESIGNS AND COLOURS

620-16-02

6d (12 sous) Face Design: No vignettes, all text
Colour: Black with no tint

Back Design: Plain

IMPRINT

Jones

SIGNATURES

left	right
none	mss. Jas. Gibb

ISSUE DATING

Partially engraved 1er Juin 183_:

1837

Cat. No.	Denom.	Date	G	VG	F	VF	EF	AU
16-02	6d (12 sous)	1837	450.	900.	1,250.	—	—	—

620-18 RAWDON, WRIGHT & HATCH PRINTINGS

DESIGNS AND COLOURS

620-18-02

$1/4 Face Design: Cherub with full basket/woman in waves;
(15d, 30 sous) sheaves and farm tools below/cherub with fruit basket/reverse of Spanish-American 2 reales coin
Colour: Black with no tint

Back Design: Plain

620-18-04

$1/2 Face Design: Reverse of Spanish-American 4 reales
(2s 6d, 1ecu, coin/woman in waves, ship, woman in
3 francs) waves/—
Colour: Black with no tint

Back Design: Plain

IMPRINT

Engr by Rawdon, Wright & Hatch New-York

SIGNATURES

left	right
none	mss. Jas. Gibb
none	mss. illegible

ISSUE DATING

Engraved

1er Octobre 1837

Cat. No.	Denom.	Date	G	VG	F	VF	EF	AU
18-02	$1/4	1837	550.	1,100.	1,450.	2,100.	—	—
18-04	$1/2	1837	550.	1,100.	1,450.	2,100.	—	—

ISSUE OF 1837-1860s

Note: For the spurious $2 notes of 1857 to 1859 (with royal crest at centre), see issue 620-52.

DESIGNS AND COLOURS

Photo Not Available

620-20-02P
$1 Face Design: Unknown
Colour: Black with no tint
Back Design: Plain

Photo Not Available

620-20-14P
$2 Face Design: Unknown
Colour: Black with no tint
Back Design: Plain

Photo Not Available

620-20-28P
$5 Face Design: Unknown
Colour: Black with no tint
Back Design: Plain

Photo Not Available

620-20-42P
$10 Face Design: Unknown
Colour: Black with no tint
Back Design: Plain

620-22-20R
$20 Face Design: Ships (whaling scene) in circle/ allegorical women and two men; factory and ship below/ship in circle
Colour: Black with no tint
Back Design: See subheadings
Colour: See subheadings

620-22-40R
$50 Face Design: Dock scene/griffin, allegorical man and women; dog by safe below/—
Colour: Black with no tint
Back Design: See subheadings
Colour: See subheadings

620-22-60R
$100 Face Design: Dock scene/seahorses drawing Neptune and woman/schooner
Colour: Black with no tint
Back Design: See subheadings
Colour: See subheadings

IMPRINT
Rawdon, Wright & Hatch New York

SIGNATURES

left	right
mss. Jas. Stevenson	mss. D.D. Young

620-20 ISSUES OF 1837-1842 PLAIN BACK

ISSUE DATING
Partially engraved Nov. 1, 18_:
1837-1842

PROOF NOTES

Cat. No.	Denom.	Date		Unc
20-02P	$1	18_	PROOF	400.
20-14P	$2	18_	PROOF	400.
20-28P	$5	18_	PROOF	400.
20-42P	$10	18_	PROOF	400.
20-56P	$20	18_	PROOF	400.
20-70P	$50	18_	PROOF	400.
20-84P	$100	18_	PROOF	400.

620-22 ISSUES OF 1860s GREEN LATHEWORK BACK

ISSUE DATING
Partially engraved 1st Novr. 18_
1860s

PROTECTOR
Olive green "word" on face only

OVERPRINT
"OTTAWA" twice in blue

Cat. No.	Denom.	Date Variety	Unc
22-20R	$20	18_Remainder*	800.
22-40R	$50	18_Remainder*	800.
22-60R	$100	18_Remainder*	800.

*Unsigned and undated; blue printed numbers.

620-24 ISSUES OF 1843-1861

Note: For the spurious $2 notes of 1857 to 1859 (with the royal crest in the centre), see issue 620-52.

2. ISSUES OF 1843-1860, PLAIN BACK NO PROTECTOR

DESIGNS AND COLOURS

Photo Not Available

620-24-02-02P

$1 (5s) Face Design: —/two women and crowned shield; dogs head "Fidelity" below/—
Colour: Black with no tint

Back Design: Plain

620-24-02-20

$2 (10s) Face Design: Britannia/seated allegorical man and woman/milkmaid with bucket
Colour: Black with no tint

Back Design: Plain

Photo Not Available

620-24-02-40P

$5 (£1.5) Face Design: Seated woman with shield bearing 5/ two men, shield and beehive; 2 small ships below/three cherubs in small oval
Colour: Black with no tint

Back Design: Plain

Photo Not Available

620-24-02-50P

$10 (£2.10) Face Design: Bust of helmeted soldier/sailing ships; dogs head "Fidelity" below/cherub in ornate 10/royal crest over Queen Victoria (Chalon portrait)
Colour: Black with no tint

Back Design: Plain

IMPRINT

Rawdon, Wright & Hatch New York
Rawdon Wright Hatch & Edson. New York

SIGNATURES

	left	right
1852:	mss. C. Gethings	mss. Jas. Gibb
1858-1860:	mss. C. Gethings	mss. W.H. Anderson

ISSUE DATING

Partially engraved Nov. 1st, 18_:

1852
1858-1860

CIRCULATING NOTES

Cat. No.	Denom.	Date	G	VG	F	VF	EF	AU
24-02-02	$1 (5s)	18__		No known issued notes				
24-02-20	$2 (10s)	1852-60	400.	800.	1,100.	1,600.	—	—
24-02-40	$5 (£1.5)	18__		No known issued notes				
24-02-50	$10 (£2.10)	18__		No known issued notes				

PROOF NOTES

Cat. No.	Denom.	Date		Unc
24-02-02P	$1 (5s)	18__	PROOF	500.
24-02-20P	$2 (10s)	18__	PROOF	500.
24-02-40P	$5 (£1.5)	18__	PROOF	500.
24-02-50P	$10 (£2.10)	18__	PROOF	500.

4. ISSUES OF 1847-1861 PLAIN BACK, RED PROTECTOR

DESIGNS AND COLOURS

See 620-24-02

620-24-04-02

620-24-04-20

620-24-04-40

Photo Not Available

620-24-04-50

IMPRINT
Rawdon, Wright & Hatch New York
Rawdon Wright Hatch & Edson New York and ABNCo Mono.

SIGNATURES

	left	right
1847:	mss. Noah Freer	mss. illegible (v)
1849:	mss. Noah Freer	mss. Jas. Gibb
1850:	mss. Noah Freer	mss. Jas Gibb
1855-1859:	mss. C. Gethings	mss. W.H. Anderson
1860-1861:	mss. W. Dunn	mss. C. Gethings (p)

ISSUE DATING
Partially engraved
1847-1861: November 1st 18_
Novr. 1st 18_

PROTECTOR
Red "word" on face, and red "word" on back in mirror image.

STAMP
"OTTAWA" in blue

Cat. No.	Denom.	Date	G	VG	F	VF	EF	AU
24-04-02	$1 (5s)	1855-61	325.	650.	900.	1,300.	2,100.	—
24-04-20	$2 (10s)	1850	425.	850.	1,200.	1,800.	2,700.	—
24-04-40	$5 (£1.5)	1847, 1860-61	375.	750.	1,000.	1,500.	—	—
24-04-50	$10 (£2.10)	1849	425.	850.	1,200.	—	—	—

620-26 ISSUES OF 1865 WITH GREEN LATHEWORK BACK TORONTO ISSUE

620-26-10

IMPRINT
Rawdon, Wright, Hatch & Edson New York

SIGNATURES

left	right
none	mss. J. Price

ISSUE DATING
Partially engraved Nov. 1st, 18_:
1865

PROTECTOR
Red "word" and green "numeral" on face and back
Green "word" and green "numeral" on face only

OVERPRINT
"Payable in Toronto" at top, "TORONTO" at ends and
"For the Quebec Bank" in the left signature space, all in black

Cat. No.	Denom.	Date	G	VG	F	VF	EF	AU
26-10	$2 (10s)	1865	475.	950.	1,300.	—	—	—

620-28 ISSUES OF 1843-1862

Note: For the spurious $2 notes of 1857 to 1859 (with the royal crest in the centre), see issue 620-22.

DESIGNS AND COLOURS

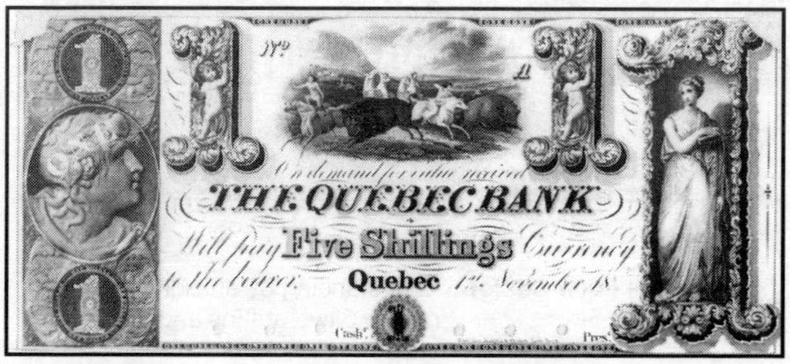

620-28-02-02P
$1 (5s) Face Design: Head of Greek god/cherub in ornate 1/ Indians hunting buffalo "Buffalo chase" (after Catlin)/cherub in ornate 1/ woman and anchor in ornate 1
Colour: Black with no tint
Back Design: Plain

620-28-02-06P
$2 (10s) Face Design: —/radiant royal crest/bust of helmeted soldier
Colour: Black with no tint
Back Design: Plain

620-28-02-10P
$4 (£1) Face Design: Bust of helmeted soldier/ ships in harbour; mermaid and sea creature below/bust of helmeted soldier
Colour: Black with no tint
Back Design: Plain

620-28-02-14

$5 (£1.5) Face Design: Man standing by shield/cherubs in ornate 5/two griffins and shield; two small ships below/cherub in ornate 5/royal crest over Queen Victoria (Chalon portrait)

Colour: Black with no tint

Back Design: Plain

620-28-06-32

$10 (£2.10) Face Design: Bust of helmeted soldier/sailing ships; dogs head "Fidelity" below/cherub in ornate 10/royal crest over Queen Victoria (Chalon portrait)

Colour: Black with no tint

Back Design: Plain

2. ISSUE WITH NO PROTECTOR DATED NOVEMBER 1843-1853

IMPRINT

Rawdon, Wright & Hatch, New-York

SIGNATURES

left	right
mss. C. Gethings	mss. W.H. Anderson
mss. C. Gethings	mss. Jas. Gibb

ISSUE DATING

Partially engraved

1852-1853: 1st November 18__
1st Novr. 18__

STAMP

"BYTOWN" in blue

CIRCULATING NOTES

Cat. No.	Denom.	Date	G	VG	F	VF	EF	AU
28-02-02	$1 (5s)	18__		No known issued notes				
28-02-06	$2 (10s)	18__		No known issued notes				
28-02-10	$4 (£1)	18__		No known issued notes				
28-02-14	$5 (£1.5)	1852-53	375.	750.	1,150.	—	—	—
28-02-18	$10 (£2.10)	1853	375.	750.	1,150.	—	—	—

PROOF NOTES

Cat. No.	Denom.	Date		Unc
28-02-02P	$1 (5s)	18__	PROOF	500.
28-02-06P	$2 (10s)	18__	PROOF	500.
28-02-10P	$4 (£1)	18__	PROOF	500.

Note: Most notes are pen or punch cancelled.

4. ISSUE WITH RED PROTECTOR DATED NOVEMBER 1849-1852

DESIGNS AND COLOURS

Same as previous

620-28-04-02

620-28-04-20

IMPRINT

Rawdon, Wright & Hatch, New York

SIGNATURES

left	right
mss. C. Gethings	mss. illegible (v)

ISSUE DATING

Partially engraved

1849-1852: 1st November 18__
1st Novr

PROTECTOR

Red "word" on face and back

Cat. No.	Denom.	Date	G	VG	F	VF	EF	AU
28-04-02	$4	1849-52	375.	750.	1,150.	—	—	—
28-04-10	$5	1849-52			NOT CONFIRMED			
28-04-20	$10	1849-52	375.	750.	1,150.	—	—	—

6. ISSUE WITH NO PROTECTOR DATED FEBRUARY 1854-1862

DESIGNS AND COLOURS

See previous

620-28-06-14

620-28-06-16

620-28-06-32

IMPRINT

Rawdon, Wright, Hatch & Edson. New York

SIGNATURES

left	right
mss. C. Gethings	mss. W.H. Anderson
mss. W. Dunn	mss. W.H. Anderson
mss. W. Dunn	mss. C. Gethings

ISSUE DATING

Partially engraved

1854 and 1862: 1st February 18__

1st Feby 18_

Cat. No.	Denom.	Date	G	VG	F	VF	EF	AU
28-06-14	$4 (£1)	1862	375.	750.	1,100.	1,550.	—	—
28-06-16	$5 (£1.5)	1854	375.	750.	1,100.	1,550.	—	—
28-06-32	$10 (£2.10)	1862	375.	750.	1,100.	1,550.	—	—

620-30 TOPPAN CARPENTER CASILEAR PRINTING, 1850s ENGRAVED "PAYABLE IN TORONTO" AT TOP

Note: For the spurious $2 notes of 1857 to 1859 (with the royal crest at the centre), see issue 620-52.

2. TORONTO ISSUE, NO TINT, NO PROTECTOR, 1856

DESIGNS AND COLOURS

Photo Not Available

620-30-02-02P

$1 (5s) Face Design: Anchor with box, bale and barrel/ wood chopper; St. George slaying the dragon below/beehive and flowers
Colour: See subheadings
Back Design: Plain

620-30-02-04

$4 (£1) Face Design: Men, cattle and wagons/ men standing with cattle/ train coming toward viewer
Colour: See subheadings
Back Design: Plain

Photo Not Available

620-30-02-06P

$10 (£2.10) Face Design: Sailor with capstan/—/wood chopper
Colour: See subheadings
Back Design: Plain

IMPRINT

Toppan Carpenter Casilear & Co. Montreal

SIGNATURES

left	right
mss. Wm. Manson	mss. Jas. Gibb

ISSUE DATING

Partially engraved Jany. 2nd, 185_:

1856

CIRCULATING NOTES

Cat. No.	Denom.	Date	Variety	G	VG	F	VF	EF	AU
30-02-02	$1 (5s)	18__	B&W	No known issued notes					
30-02-04	$4 (£1)	1856	B&W	375.	750.	1,150.	—	—	—
30-02-06	$10 (£2.10)	18__	B&W	No known issued notes					

PROOF NOTES

Cat. No.	Denom.	Date		Unc
30-02-02P	$1 (5s)	18__	PROOF	500.
30-02-04P	$4 (£1)	18__	PROOF	500.
30-02-06P	$10 (£2.10)	18__	PROOF	500.

4. TORONTO ISSUE, NO TINT, GREEN PROTECTOR

SIGNATURES

left	right
mss. unknown	mss. unknown

ISSUE DATING

Partially engraved Jany. 2nd 185_:

PROTECTOR

Green "word" on face only

Note: A $4 note is known with a green FIVE protector.

Cat. No.	Denom.	Date	Variety	G	VG	F	VF	EF	Unc
32-04-02	$1 (5s)	185_	Green ptr.		No known issued notes				
32-04-04	$4 (£1)	185_	Green ptr.		No known issued notes				
32-04-06	$10 (£2.10)	185_	Green ptr.		No known issued notes				

620-32 TOPPAN CARPENTER CASILEAR GREEN TINT PRINTINGS OF 1859 ENGRAVED "PAYABLE IN TORONTO" AT TOP

DESIGNS AND COLOURS

Designs: Same as previous issue
Colour: Overall green face tint

620-32-02

620-32-04

SIGNATURES

left	right
mss. Wm. Manson	mss. W.H. Anderson

ISSUE DATING

Partially engraved Jany. 2nd 185_:
1859

Cat. No.	Denom.	Date	Variety	G	VG	F	VF	EF	AU
32-02	$1 (5s)	1859	Green tint	450.	900.	1,400.	—	—	—
32-04	$4 (£1)	1859	Green tint	450.	900.	1,400.	—	—	—
32-06	$10 (£2.10)	185_	Green tint		No known issued notes				

620-34 ISSUE OF 1863 BACK DESIGN LATHEWORK AND BANK NAME ONLY

DESIGNS AND COLOURS

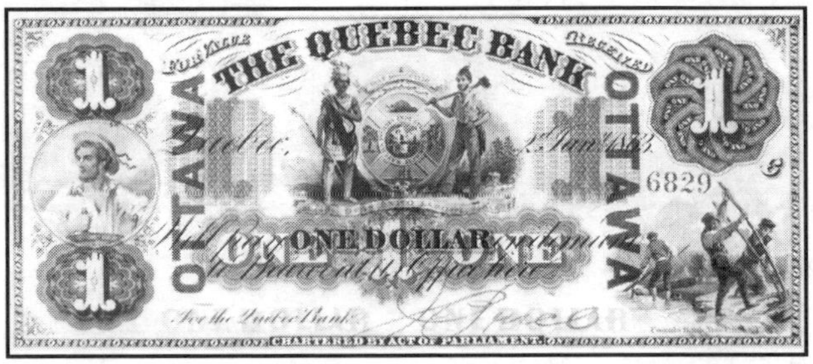

620-34-02

$1 Face Design: Sailor at ship's wheel/bank crest/three loggers in river
Colour: Black with green tint

Back Design: Lathework and bank name
Colour: Green

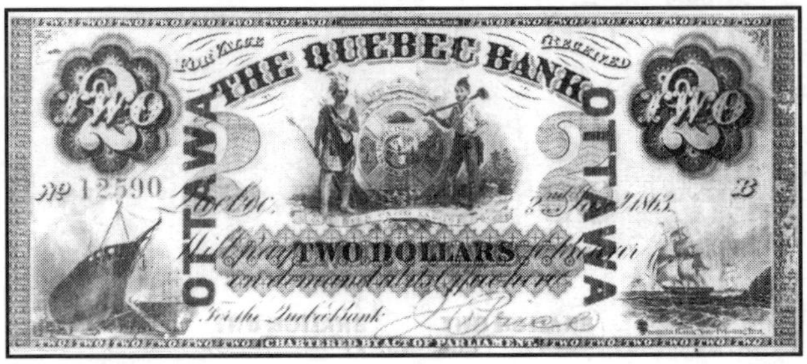

620-34-04

$2 Face Design: Shipbuilding scene/Bank Crest/three ships
Colour: Black with green tint

Back Design: Lathework and bank name
Colour: Green

620-34-06

$4 Face Design: Sailor, woman and child on shore with telescope "Land Ho!"/Bank Crest/seated Britannia, shield bearing FOUR and 4
Colour: Black with green tint

Back Design: Lathework and bank name
Colour: Green

620-34-08

$5 Face Design: Two beavers/Bank Crest/ seated woman with telescope and 5
Colour: Black with green tint

Back Design: Lathework and bank name
Colour: Green

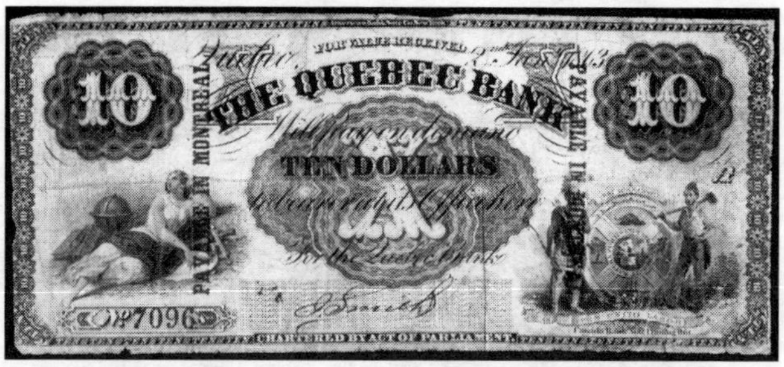

620-34-10

$10 Face Design: Reclining woman with navigational equipment/—/Bank Crest
Colour: Black with green tint

Back Design: Lathework and bank name
Colour: Green

IMPRINT

American Bank Note Co. New York

SIGNATURES

Centre on $10
right only on $1,2,4 and 5
mss. various

ISSUE DATING

Engraved

2nd Jany. 1863
2d Jany. 1863

OVERPRINT

Twice vertically towards ends
"GASPE" in blue
"OTTAWA" in blue
"PAYABLE IN TORONTO" in blue
"ST. CATHARINES/PAYABLE IN TORONTO" in blue
"PAYABLE IN MONTREAL" in blue
"THREE RIVERS" in blue
"OTTAWA/PAYABLE IN MONTREAL" in blue

CIRCULATING NOTES

Cat. No.	Denom.	Date	Variety	G	VG	F	VF	EF	AU
34-02	$1	1863		250.	500.	700.	1,100.	—	—
34-02a	$1	1863	town o/p	300.	600.	850.	1,300.	—	—
34-04	$2	1863		425.	850.	1,250.	1,600.	—	—
34-04a	$2	1863	town o/p	500.	1,000.	1,400.	1,900.	—	—
34-06	$4	1863		450.	900.	1,250.	1,700.	—	—
34-06a	$4	1863	town o/p	500.	1,000.	1,400.	1,900.	—	—
34-08	$5	1863		600.	1,200.	1,600.	2,300.	—	—
34-08a	$5	1863	town o/p	700.	1,400.	1,900.	2,750.	—	—
34-10	$10	1863		600.	1,200.	1,600.	2,300.	—	—
34-10a	$10	1863	town o/p	700.	1,400.	1,900.	2,750.	—	—

PROOF NOTES

Cat. No.	Denom.	Date		Unc
34-02P	$1	1863	FACE PROOF	400.
34-04P	$2	1863	FACE PROOF	400.
34-08P	$5	1863	FACE PROOF	400.
34-10P	$10	1863	FACE PROOF	400.

620-36

ISSUE OF 1863
BACK DESIGN LATHEWORK COUNTERS AND BANK NAME

DESIGNS AND COLOURS

620-36-02

This issue is the same as 620-34, except for the large green 4s near the top centre, and the green around the 4s in the corners is different.

Photo Not Available

620-36-10

$10 Face Design: As 34-10 but top XX counters are like 40-08

Back Design: Lathework, counters and bank name

IMPRINT

American Bank Note Co. New York
British American Bank Note Co. Montreal - Ottawa on the back

SIGNATURES

right only
mss. various

ISSUE DATING

Engraved

2nd Jany. 1863

OVERPRINT

"TORONTO" twice in blue

Cat. No.	Denom.	Date	G	VG	F	VF	EF	AU
36-02	$4	1863	450.	900.	1,200.	1,700.	—	—
36-10	$10	1863	Institutional collection only					

620-38 **ISSUE OF 1870**

DESIGNS AND COLOURS

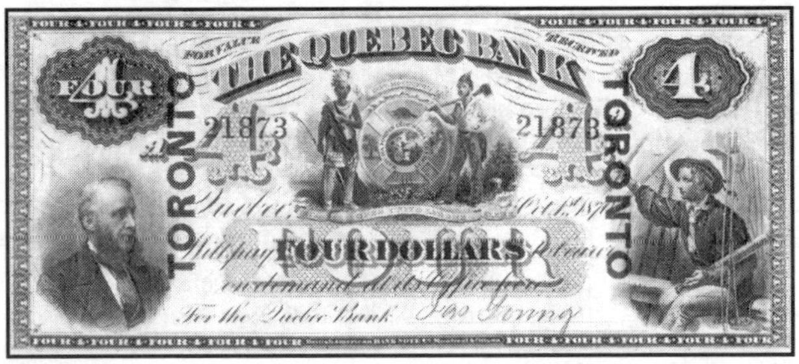

620-38-02

$4 Face Design: Sir N.F. Belleau/Bank Crest/ sailor with telescope
Colour: Black with green tint

Back Design: Lathework, counters and bank name
Colour: Green

IMPRINT

British American Bank Note Co. Montreal & Ottawa

SIGNATURES

right only
mss. various

ISSUE DATING

Engraved

Oct. 1st 1870

OVERPRINT

Twice vertically near ends
"OTTAWA" in blue
"TORONTO" in blue
"THREE RIVERS" in blue

Cat. No.	Denom.	Date	Variety	G	VG	F	VF	EF	AU
38-02	$4	1870		450.	900.	1,250.	1,700.	—	—
38-02a	$4	1870	town o/p	500.	1,000.	1,400.	1,900.	—	—

620-40 **ISSUES OF 1873 AND 1888**
GREEN FACE AND BACK TINT

DESIGNS AND COLOURS

620-40-02

$4 Face Design: Sailor with telescope, woman and child on ship "Land Ho!"/Bank Crest/ seated Britannia, shield bearing FOUR and 4
Colour: Green tint

Back Design: Lathework, counters and bank name
Colour: Green tint

620-40-04

$5 Face Design: Two beavers/Bank Crest/ seated woman with telescope and 5
Colour: Green tint

Back Design: Lathework, counters and bank name
Colour: Green tint

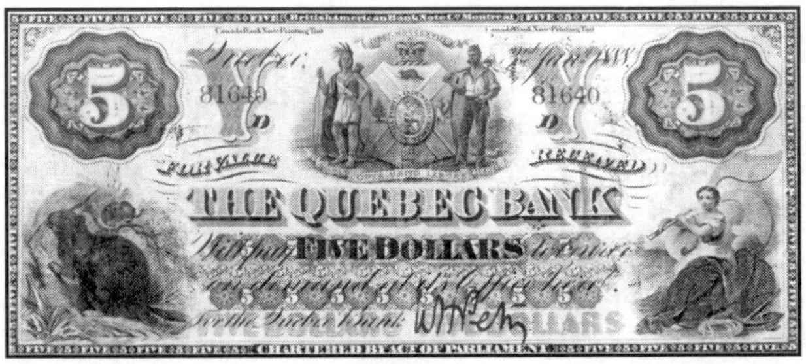

620-40-06

$5 Face Design: Two beavers/Bank Crest/ seated woman with telescope and 5
Colour: Green tint, but design around 5s at top is different from 1863 and 1873 designs

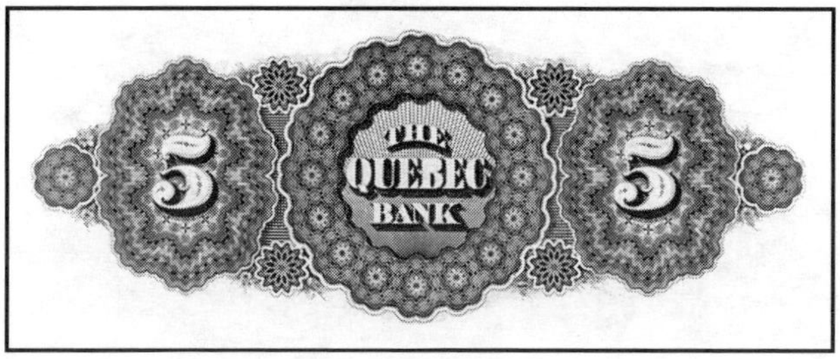

Back Design: Lathework, counters and bank name
Colour: Green tint

620-40-08

$10 Face Design: Reclining woman with navigational equipment/—/modified bank crest
Colour: Green tint

Back Design: Lathework, counters and bank name
Colour: Green tint

IMPRINT

American Bank Note Co., New York
British American Bank Note Co. Montreal

SIGNATURES

centre on $10	**right only on $4 and $5**
mss. various	mss. various

ISSUE DATING

Engraved

2d. Jany. 1873.
1st Oct/ 1873
3rd Jany. 1888.

OVERPRINT

1888: "A A" in red
"B B" in blue

STAMP

1888: "D" in purple
"B" in purple

Cat. No.	Denom.	Date	G	VG	F	VF	EF	AU
40-02	$4	1873	450.	900.	1,200.	1,700.	—	—
40-04	$5	1873 2nd Jan	550.	1,100.	1,500.	2,100.	—	—
40-05	$5	1873 1st Oct.	550.	1,100.	1,500.	2,100.	—	—
40-06	$5	1888	550.	1,100.	1,500.	2,100.	—	—
40-08	$10	1888	650.	1,300.	1,700.	2,500.	—	—

620-42 **ISSUE OF 1888**

BROWN FACE AND BACK TINT

DESIGNS AND COLOURS

Design: Same as 620-40 issue
Colours: The tint colour for this issue is brown

Cat. No.	Denom.	Date	G	VG	F	VF	EF	AU
42-02	$5	1888	575.	1,150.	1,550.	2,300.	—	—

620-44 **ISSUE OF 1898**

DESIGNS AND COLOURS

620-44-02

$5 Face Design: —/paddlewheel and modern ship with Quebec Citadel in background/—
Colour: Black with green tint

Back Design: Lathework. counters, bank name and Bank Crest
Colour: Green

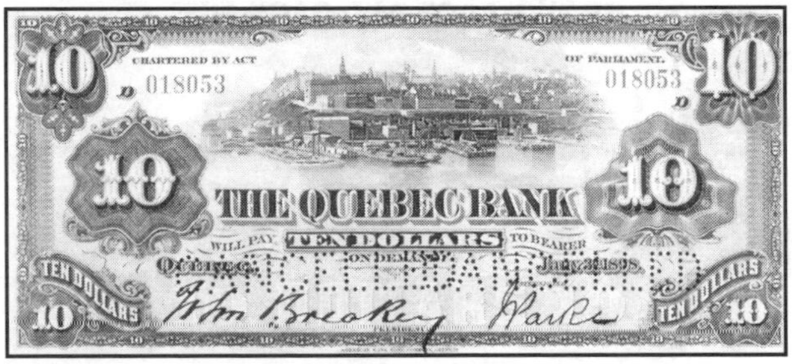

620-44-04

$10 Face Design: —/docks at Quebec City/—
Colour: See varieties

Back Design: Lathework, counters, bank name and Bank Crest
Colour: See varieties

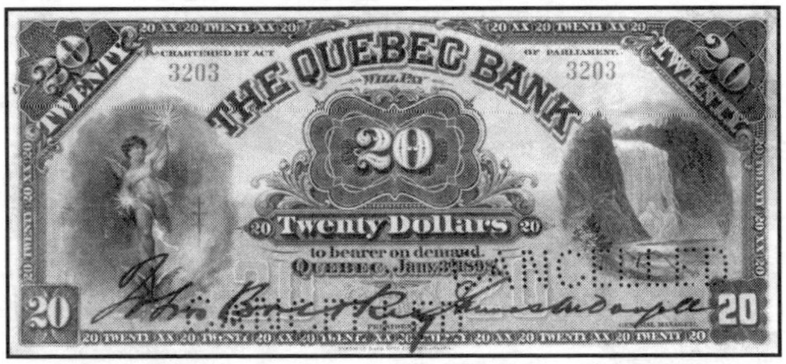

620-44-08

$20 Face Design: Cherub on winged wheel and power lines "Coming Light"/—/Montmorency Falls
Colour: Black with yellow and olive tint

Back Design: Lathework, counters, bank name and Quebec City, Prescott Gate
Colour: Olive

620-44-12

$50 Face Design: —/seated woman with globe, lyre and fountain globe/—
Colour: Black with yellow and olive tint

Back Design: Lathework, counters, bank name and Quebec City, Kent Gate
Colour: Olive

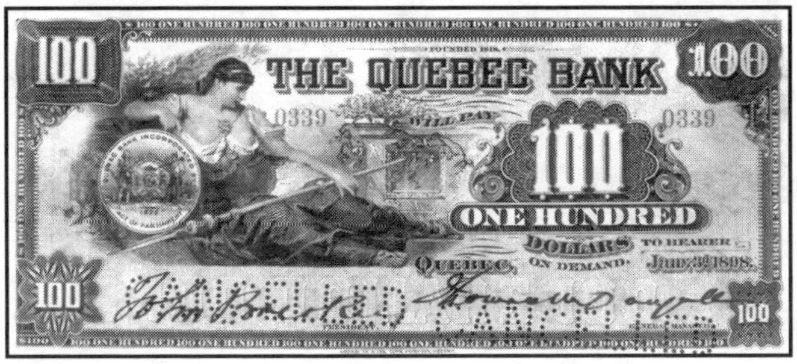

620-44-16

$100 Face Design: Bank crest in circle, reclining woman with spear "Clione"/—/—
Colour: Black with yellow and olive tint

Back Design: Lathework, counters, bank name and Quebec City, Hope Gate
Colour: Olive

IMPRINT

American Bank Note Company, Ottawa

SIGNATURES

	left	right
$5 and $10:		engr. John Breakey mss. various
$20, $50:	mss. John Breakey	mss. various
and $100:	typed John Breakey	mss. various

ISSUE DATING

Engraved

Jany. 3d, 1898

VARIETIES

$10 Face Colour: Black with olive tint
Back Colour: Blue
$10 Face Colour: Black with yellow and olive tint
Back Colour: Green

Cat. No.	Denom.	Date	Variety	G	VG	F	VF	EF	AU
44-02	$5	1898		500.	1,000.	1,400.	2,500.	—	—
44-04	$10	1898	Blue back	Insitutional collection only					
44-06	$10	1898	Green back	Institutional collection only					
44-08	$20	1898	Mss. Breakey, l.	Institutional collection only					
44-10	$20	1898	Typed Breakey, l.	Institutional collection only					
44-12	$50	1898	Mss. Breakey, l.	Institutional collection only					
44-14	$50	1898	Typed Breakey, l.	Institutional collection only					
44-16	$100	1898	Mss. Breakey, l.	Institutional collection only					
44-18	$100	1898	Typed Breakey, l.	Institutional collection only					

620-46 ISSUE OF 1901

DESIGNS AND COLOURS

620-46-02

$5 Face Design: —/ships, seated woman with shield, lion and globe/—
Colour: Black with yellow and olive tint

Back Design: Lathework, counters, bank name and Bank Crest
Colour: Green

IMPRINT

American Bank Note Company, Ottawa

SIGNATURES

left	right
engr. John Breakey	mss. various

ISSUE DATING

Engraved

2nd July 1901

OVERPRINT

V V in red

Cat. No.	Denom.	Date	G	VG	F	VF	EF	AU
46-02	$5	1901	500.	1,000.	1,400.	2,500.	3,500.	—

620-48 ISSUES OF 1908 AND 1911

DESIGNS AND COLOURS

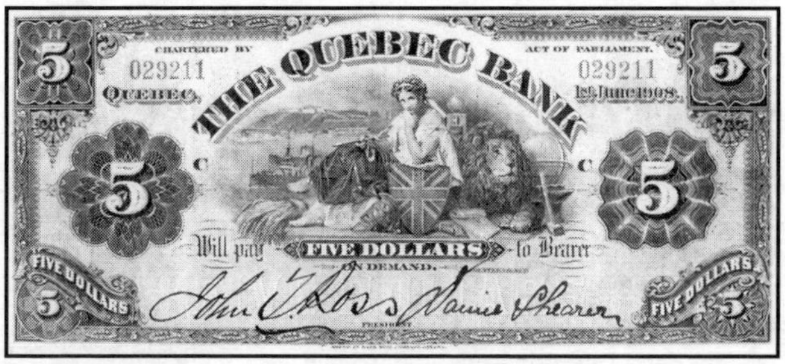

620-48-02-02

$5 Face Design: —/ships, seated woman with shield and (altered) lion and scroll (improved design)/—
Colour: Black with yellow and olive tint

Back Design: See subheadings
Colour: Green

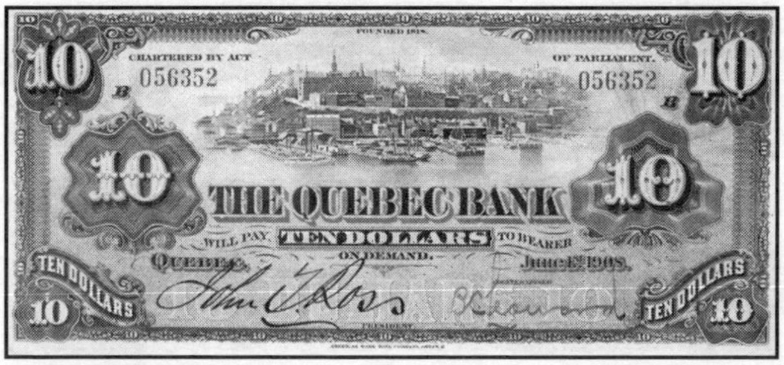

620-48-04-04

$10 Face Design: —/docks at Quebec City/—
See subheadings
Colour: Black with yellow and olive tint

Back Design: See subheadings
Colour: Green

620-48-04-06S

$20 Face Design: Cherub on winged wheel and power lines "Coming Light"/—/Montmorency Falls
See subheadings
Colour: Black with olive and yellow tint

Back Design: See subheadings
Colour: Olive

620-48-04-08S

$50 Face Design: —/seated woman with globe, lyre and fountain/—
See subheadings
Colour: Black with yellow and olive tint

Back Design: Lathework, counters, bank name and "Kent Gate"
Colour: Olive

620-48-04-10S

$100 Face Design: Bank crest in circle, reclining woman and spear "Clione"/—/—
See subheadings
Colour: Black with yellow and olive tint

Back Design: Lathework, counters, bank name and "Hope Gate"
Colour: Olive

IMPRINT

American Bank Note Company, Ottawa

SIGNATURES

left	right
typed John T. Ross	mss. various

ISSUE DATING

Engraved

June 1st 1908.
Jany. 3d. 1911

2. FACE DESIGNS LACKING "FOUNDED 1818" AT TOP

DESIGNS AND COLOURS

$5 Back Design: Bank crest
$10 Back Design: Bank crest

OVERPRINT

$5: "M" twice in red

Cat. No.	Denom.	Date	G	VG	F	VF	EF	AU
48-02-02	$5	1908	500.	1,000.	1,400.	—	—	—
48-02-04	$10	1908	750.	1,500.	2,000.	—	—	—

4. FACE DESIGNS HAVING "FOUNDED 1818" AT TOP

BACK DESIGNS

$5 Back Design: —/bank crest/—
$10 Back Design: —/bank crest/—
$20 Back Design: —/Quebec City, Prescott Gate/—
$50 Back Design: —/Quebec City, Kent Gate/—
$100 Back Design: —/Quebec City, Hope Gate/—

CIRCULATING NOTES

Cat. No.	Denom.	Date	G	VG	F	VF	EF	AU
48-04-02	$5	1908	500.	1,000.	1,400.	2,500.	3,500.	—
48-04-04	$10	1908	450.	900.	1,200.	2,000.	3,000.	4,500.
48-04-06	$20	1911	750.	1,500.	—	—	—	—
48-04-08	$50	1911	Institutional collection only					
48-04-10	$100	1911	Institutional collection only					

SPECIMEN NOTES

Cat. No.	Denom.	Date		Unc
48-04-02S	$5	1908	SPECIMEN	800.
48-04-04S	$10	1908	SPECIMEN	800.
48-04-06S	$20	1911	SPECIMEN	800.
48-04-08S	$50	1911	SPECIMEN	800.
48-04-10S	$100	1911	SPECIMEN	800.

620-50 ISSUE OF 1908 AND 1911 "FOUNDED 1818" AT TOP NEW BACK DESIGNS

BACK DESIGNS

620-50-02

Back Design: Lathework, counters, bank name and Quebec City, Prescott Gate
Colour: Green

620-50-04

$10 Back Design Lathework, counters, bank name and Quebec City, Hope Gate
Colour: Green

620-50-06

$20 Back Design: Lathework, counters, bank name and Bank Crest
Colour: Green

CIRCULATING NOTES

Cat. No.	Denom.	Date	G	VG	F	VF	EF	AU
50-02	$5	1908	550.	1,100.	1,500.	—	—	—
50-04	$10	1908	Institutional collection only					
50-06	$20	1911	Institutional collection only					

SPECIMEN NOTES

Cat. No.	Denom.	Date		Unc
50-02S	$5	1908	SPECIMEN	800.
50-04S	$10	1908	SPECIMEN	800.
50-06S	$20	1911	SPECIMEN	800.

620-52 SPURIOUS $2 ISSUE, 1857-1859

DESIGNS AND COLOURS

620-52-02

$2 Face Design: Beehive and agricultural implements/ radiant royal crest; Indian paddling canoe below/Britannia with spear and shield
Colour: Black with no tint
Back Design: Plain

IMPRINT
Harris & Sealey Engravers N. York

SIGNATURES

left	right
mss. Chas. Gething	mss. G. Gibb

ISSUE DATING
Partially engraved _ 18_:
1859: Not completed

OVERPRINT
"QUEBEC" and "C.E." in green

PROTECTOR
Green word on face only

Cat. No.	Denom.	Date	Variety	G	VG	F	VF	EF	AU
52-02	$2	1858-59	Spurious	75.	150.	200.	325.	—	—

BANK OF QUEBEC LOWER CANADA

1841

QUEBEC, LOWER CANADA

BANK NUMBER 625 ***NONREDEEMABLE***

This was undoubtedly a phantom bank. These notes were printed from the same plate as the spurious $2 notes for the Quebec Bank and for the Bank of Lower Canada.

625-10 DESIGN OF 1841

DESIGNS AND COLOURS

625-10-02R

$2 Face Design: Beehive and agricultural implements/ radiant royal crest; Indian paddling canoe below/Britannia with spear and shield
Colour: Black with no tint
Back Design: Plain

IMPRINT
Harris & Sealey Engravers N. York

SIGNATURES

left	right
none	none

ISSUE DATING
Partially engraved _ 18_:
1841: Jany. 2

Cat. No.	Denom.	Date	Variety	G	VG	F	VF	EF	AU
10-02R	$2	1841	Remainder	125.	250.	325.	500.	—	—

THE ROYAL BANK OF CANADA

1901 TO DATE

MONTREAL, QUEBEC

BANK NUMBER 630 ***REDEEMABLE***

The Royal Bank of Canada is the largest Canadian chartered bank in terms of assets and one of the largest in the world.

In April 1864 eight well-to-do merchants in Halifax, Nova Scotia, joined together in a co-partnership called the Merchants Bank, with a capital of $200,000, of which $160,000 was paid up. After Confederation full banking privileges were confirmed by the Royal assent given on June 22, 1869, to a federal charter for the Merchants Bank of Halifax. The new bank had an authorized capital of $1,000,000 in 10,000 shares of $100 each.

Until 1887 the bank's operations were "acceptably profitable," but a marked improvement in business conditions from that date until 1892 lifted the bank from being a small institution of provincial importance to being a large one with some 25 branches in four provinces.

At the 1900 annual general meeting, the president of the bank stated that the expansion of the bank's business throughout Canada and abroad was such that the time had come to adopt a more distinctive and comprehensive designation. Upon the completion of necessary formalities, the name of the bank was changed to the Royal Bank of Canada, effective January 2, 1901. During the period of 1869 to 1900, the bank's growth was cautious, but steady. Rapid expansion came during 1901 to 1913, when Canada experienced a wave of development.

The bank greatly expanded its operations in other provinces and the Caribbean by absorbing other institutions, including a Cuban bank in 1904. Also in 1904, the bank changed its head office from Halifax to Montreal.

During World War 1, the bank gave considerable assistance to the government, and despite a preoccupation with the problems of operating under war conditions, expansion continued. Between 1914 and 1918, the number of its branches in Canada increased by 147, but of these, 134 were through the takeovers of two other banks. In terms of total assets, the bank became the second largest bank in Canada by the end of 1918.

The wartime prosperity, which had continued almost uninterrupted through 1919, turned into a depression in 1921 and 1922, during which the bank's assets declined, but its profits kept up remarkably well. With the improvement in business conditions in 1925, prosperity returned until the last quarter of 1929. When the market collapsed in 1929, both the total assets and profits of the bank were at a record high, and it had become the largest bank in Canada. However, like other banks, the Royal Bank was greatly affected by the Depression. Its assets shrunk, and some of its branches were closed. By 1935 the upward trend in business was firmly established and, in general, continued in that direction during the remainder of the 1930s.

Following the outbreak of war in September 1939, the bank cooperated fully in the execution of the country's war efforts. In this it played its part equally with the other banks and under similar difficulties. Since the end of World War II. the Royal Bank has continued to expand, both in Canada and abroad.

630-10 ISSUES OF 1901 AND 1909

2 1901 ISUES.

DESIGNS AND COLOURS

630-10-02-02

$5 Face Design: Seated woman with two childred and dove "Peace"/—/—
Colour: See varieties

Back Design: —/Royal Crest/—
Colour: See varieties

630-10-02-04

630-10-02-08

$10 Face Design: —/—/seated allegorical female
Colour: Black with blue, violet, yellow-brown and yellow-green tint

Back Design: —/Royal Crest/—
Colour: Blue, violet, yellow-brown and yellow-green

630-10-02-12

$20 Face Design: —/seated woman with globe, shield and lion/—
Colour: Black, yellow-brown, green, lilac adn gold tint

Back Design: —/Royal Crest/—
Colour: Yellow-brown, green, lilac and gold

630-10-02-16S

$50 Face Design: —/—/ships at sea
Colour: Black with yellow-brown, green, lilac and gold tint

Back Design: —/Royal Crest/—
Colour: Yellow-brown, green, lilac and gold

IMPRINT

American Bank Note Co. Ottawa

SIGNATURES

left	right
mss. various	engr. T.E. Kenny
mss. various	typed T.E. Kenny

ISSUE DATING

Engraved

Jan. 2nd 1901

VARIETIES

Multicoloured Frame - Kenny, engraved right

Face Colour: Black with green, yellow-green, yellow-brown and lilac tint
Back Colour: Green, yellow-green, yellow-brown and lilac

Green Frame - Kenny, typed right

Face Colour: Black with green and yellow-green tint
Back Colour: Green

CIRCULATING NOTES

Cat. No.	Den.	Date	Variety	G	VG	F	VF	EF	AU
10-02-02	$5	1901	Kenny engr. r, multi	—	2,800.	3,500.	4,500.	—	—
10-02-04	$5	1901	Kenny typed r, green	—	1,000.	1,500.	2,000.	—	—
10-02-06	$10	1901	Kenny engr. r	1,500.	3,000.	4,000.	—	7,000.	—
10-02-08	$10	1901	Kenny typed r	1,500.	3,000.	4,000.	—	—	—
10-02-10	$20	1901	Kenny, engr. r		No known issued notes				
10-02-12	$20	1901	Kenny, typed r	2,250.	4,500.	—	—	—	—
10-02-14	$50	1901	Kenny, engr. r		No known issued notes				
10-02-16	$50	1901	Kenny, typed r		No known issued notes				

PROOF NOTES

Cat. No.	Den.	Date	Variety		Unc
10-02-02P	$5	1901	Kenny engr. r, B & W	FACE PROOF	500.
10-02-10p	$20	1901	Kenny engr. R.	FACE PROOF	600.
10-02-14P	$50	1901	Kenny engr. R.	FACE PROOF	700.

SPECIMEN NOTES

Cat. No.	Den.	Date	Variety		Unc
10-02-02S	$5	1901	Kenny engr. r, multi	SPECIMEN	800.
10-02-14S	$50	1901	Kenny engr. R.	SPECIMEN	1,250.
10-02-16S	$50	1901	Kenny typed. R.	SPECIMEN	1,250.

4. 1909 ISSUES

DESIGNS AND COLOURS

630-10-04-02

$5 Face Design: Seated woman with two children and dove "Peace"/—/—
Colour: Black with green and yellow tint, black outlined 5s

Back Design: —/Royal Crest/—
Colour: Black with green tint

630-10-04-06

$5 Face Design: Seated woman with two children and dove "Peace"/—/—
Colour: Black with green and yellow tint, green outlined 5s

Back Design: —/Royal Crest/—
Colour: Black with green tint

630-10-04-10
$10 Face Design: —/—/seated allegorical female
Multicoloured Frame:
Colour: Black with green, yellow-green, yellow-brown and lilac tint

Back Design: —/Royal Crest/—
Colour: Green, yellow-green, yellow-brown and lilac

630-10-04-14
$10 Face Design: —/—/seated allegorical female
Black Frame:
Colour: Black with green-yellow tint

Back Design: —/Royal Crest/—
Colour: Olive and yellow

630-10-04-18S
$20 Face Design: —/seated woman with globe, shield and lion/—
Multicoloured Frame:
Colour: Black with green, yellow-green, yellow-brown and lilac tint

Back Design: —/Royal Crest/—
Colour: Green, yellow-green, yellow-brown and lilac

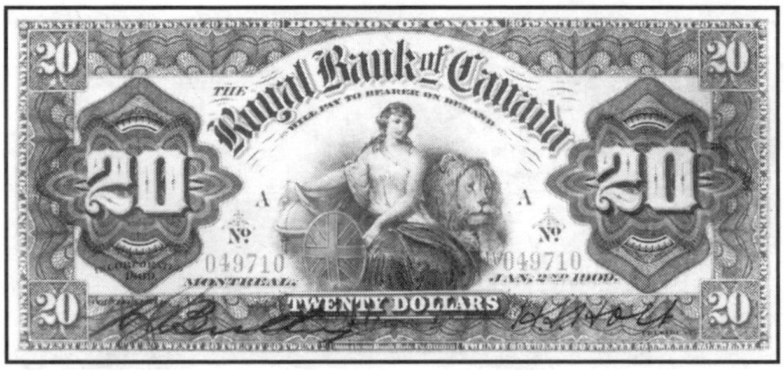

630-10-04-22
$20 Face Design: —/seated woman with globe, shield and lion/—
Black Frame:
Colour: Black with blue and yellow tint

Back Design: —/Royal Crest/—
Colour: Blue and yellow

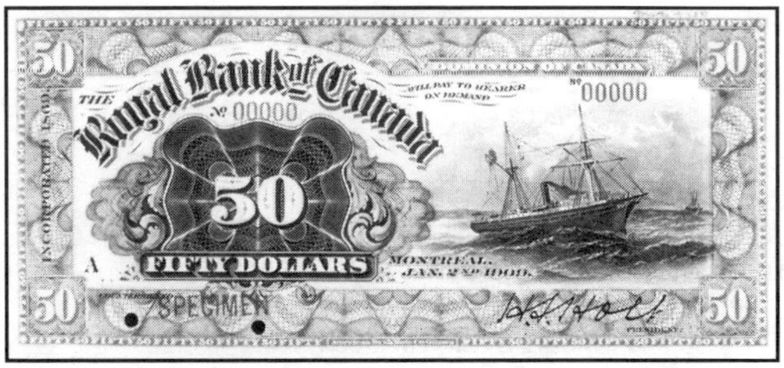

630-10-04-26S
$50 Face Design: —/—/ships at sea
Colour: Black with yellow-brown, green, lilac and gold tint

Back Design: —/Royal Crest/—
Colour: Yellow-brown, green, lilac and gold

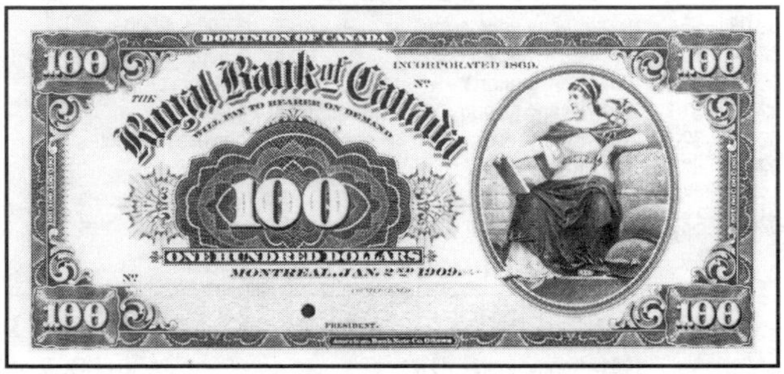

630-10-04-34P
$100 Face Design: —/—/seated "Commerce" figure
Colour: Black with orange tint

Back Design: —/Royal Crest/—
Colour: Red-orange

IMPRINT
American Bank Note Co. Ottawa

SIGNATURES

left	right
mss. various	typed H.S. Holt
typed H.S. Holt	mss. various

ISSUE DATING
Engraved
Jan. 2nd 1909

VARIETIES

$5, 1909 Face Design: Black outlined 5s
$5, 1909 Face Design: Green outlined 5s
Back Colour: Green

Multicoloured Frame:
Face Colour: Black with green, yellow-green, yellow-brown and lilac tint
Back Colour: Green, yellow-green, yellow-brown and lilac

Green Frame:
Face Colour: Black with green and yellow-green tint
Back Colour: Green

Black Frame:
Face Colour: Black with green and yellow tint
Back Colour: Olive and yellow

Blue Frame:
Face Colour: Black with blue and yellow tint
Back Colour: Blue and yellow

CIRCULATING NOTES

Cat. No.	Denom.	Date	Variety	G	VG	F	VF	EF	AU
10-04-02	$5	1909	Black, Holt, r.	400.	800.	1,200.	1,800.	3,000.	—
10-04-06	$5	1909	Green, Holt, l.	125.	250.	450.	750.	—	—
10-04-10	$10	1909	Multi, Holt, r.	1, 250.	2,500.	3,500.	4,500.	—	—
10-04-14	$10	1909	Black, Holt, l.	200.	400.	650.	1,000.	2,000.	—
10-04-18	$20	1909	Multi, Holt, l.	Intitutional collection only					
10-04-22	$20	1909	Blue, Holt, r.	500.	1,000.	1,400.	2,000.	3,500.	—
10-04-26	$50	1909	Holt, r.	No known issued notes					
10-04-34	$100	1909		No known issued notes					

PROOF NOTES

Cat. No.	Denom.	Date			Unc
10-04-02P	$5	1909	Black, Holt r.	FACE PROOF	600.
10-04-06P	$5	1909	Green, Holt l.	FACE PROOF	600.
10-04-10P	$10	1909	Multi, Holt r.	FACE PROOF	600.
10-04-18P	$20	1909	Multi, Holt l.	FACE PROOF	700.
10-04-22P	$20	1909	Blue, Holt r.	FACE PROOF	600.
10-04-26P	$50	1909		FACE PROOF	700.
10-04-34P	$100	1909		FACE PROOF	800.

SPECIMEN NOTES

Cat. No.	Denom.	Date	Variety		Unc
10-04-06S	$5	1909	Green	SPECIMEN	1,000.
10-04-10S	$10	1909	Multi	SPECIMEN	1,000.
10-04-18S	$20	1909	Multi	SPECIMEN	1,250.
10-04-26S	$50	1909	Multi	SPECIMEN	1,250.

630-12 ISSUES OF 1913

DESIGNS AND COLOURS

630-12-04
$5 Face Design: Edson L. Pease/Canadian coat of arms/Herbert S. Holt
Colour: Black with green tint

Back Design: Lathework, counters, bank name and Royal Crest
Colour: Green

630-12-08
$10 Face Design: —/battleship Bellerophon/—
Colour: Black with yellow-green and blue tint

Back Design: —/Royal Crest/—
Colour: Yellow-orange

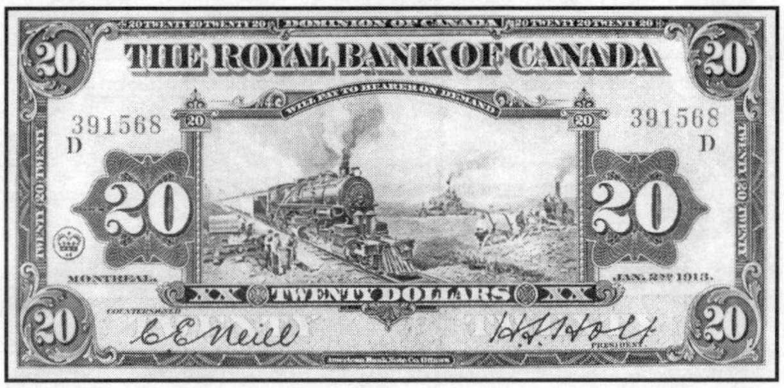

630-12-12
$20 Face Design: —/train on prairies/—
Colour: Black with blue tint

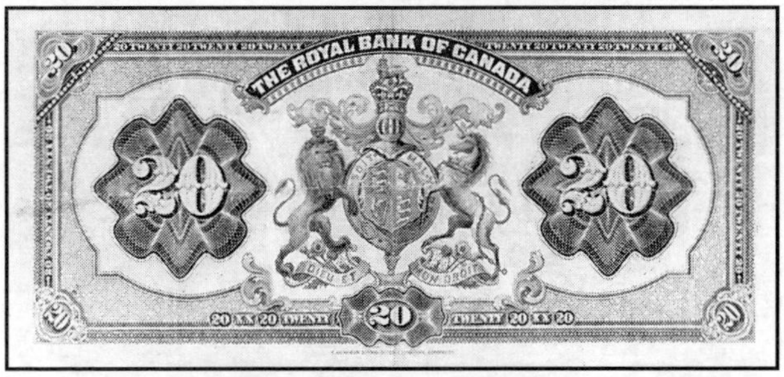

Back Design: Lathework, counters, bank name and Royal Crest
Colour: Blue

630-12-14E
$50 Face Design: —/Vincent Meredith/—
Colour: Black with yellow and red tint

Back Design: Unknown
Colour: Unknown

630-12-18
$50 Face Design: Edson L. Pease/—/—
Colour: Black with green and yellow tint

Back Design: Lathework, counters, bank name and Royal Crest
Colour: Olive

630-12-20
$100 Face Design: —/—/Herbert S. Holt
Colour: Black with orange and yellow-green tint

Back Design: Lathework, counters, bank name and Royal Crest
Colour: Red

IMPRINT
American Bank Note Co. Ottawa or Canadian Bank Note Company, Limited.

SIGNATURES

left	right
mss. various	typed H.S. Holt
typed C.E. Neill	typed H.S. Holt

ISSUE DATING
Engraved
Jan. 2nd 1913

CIRCULATING NOTES

Cat. No.	Denom.	Date	Variety	G	VG	F	VF	EF	AU
12-02	$5	1913	Mss. signature, l.	45.	90.	125.	200.	350.	500.
12-04	$5	1913	Typed Neill, l.	35.	75.	100.	175.	300.	450.
12-06	$10	1913	Mss. signature, l.	85.	175.	300.	600.	1,050.	1,400.
12-08	$10	1913	Typed Neill, l.	75.	150.	250.	500.	900.	1,200.
12-10	$20	1913	Mss. signature, l.	85.	170.	275.	550.	1,000.	1,300.
12-12	$20	1913	Typed Neill, l.	75.	150.	250.	500.	900.	1,200.
12-16	$50	1913	Mss. signature, l.	—	1,000.	1,250.	1,900.	—	—
12-18	$50	1913	Typed Neill, l.	—	800.	1,000.	1,500.	2,500.	—
12-20	$100	1913	Mss. signature, l.	—	1,300.	1,700.	—	—	—
12-22	$100	1913	Typed Neill, l.	—	1,100.	1,500.	2,200.	—	—

SPECIMEN NOTES

Cat. No.	Denom.	Date		Unc
12-02S	$5	1913	SPECIMEN	700.
12-06S	$10	1913	SPECIMEN	700.
12-10S	$20	1913	SPECIMEN	700.
12-16S	$50	1913	SPECIMEN	700.
12-20S	$100	1913	SPECIMEN	700.

ESSAY NOTES

Cat. No.	Denom.	Date		Unc
12-14E	$20	1913	ESSAY	2,000.

630-14 ISSUE OF 1927

DESIGNS AND COLOURS

630-14-04
$5 Face Design: C.E. Neill/coat of arms/Herbert S. Holt
Colour: Black with green tint
Back Design: —/Royal Crest/—
Colour: Green

630-14-08
$10 Face Design: C.E. Neill/coat of arms/Herbert S. Holt
Colour: Black with orange tint
Back Design: —/Royal Crest/—
Colour: Orange

630-14-12

$20 Face Design: C.E. Neill/coat of arms/Herbert S. Holt
Colour: Black with blue tint

Back Design: —/Royal Crest/—
Colour: Blue

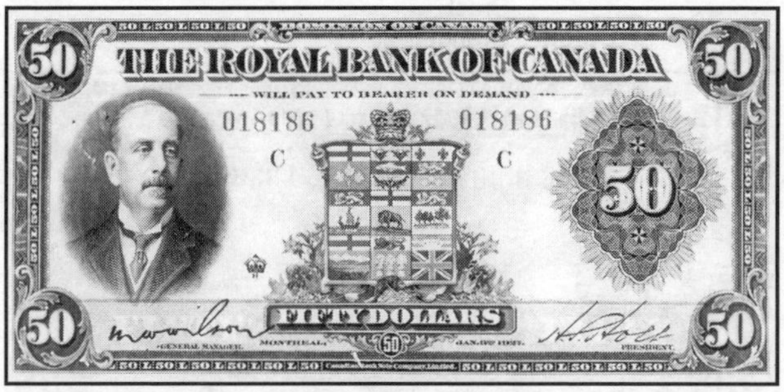

630-14-16

$50 Face Design: Edson L. Pease/coat of arms/—
Colour: Black with purple tint

Back Design: —/Royal Crest/—
Colour: Purple

630-14-20

$100 Face Design: —/Canadian coat of arms/Herbert S. Holt
Colour: Black with olive green tint

Back Design: —/Royal Crest/—
Colour: Olive

IMPRINT

Canadian Bank Note Company, Limited

SIGNATURES

left	right
typed C.E. Neill	typed H.S. Holt
typed M.W. Wilson	typed H.S. Holt

ISSUE DATING

Engraved

Jan. 3rd 1927

CIRCULATING NOTES

Cat. No.	Denom.	Date	Variety	VG	F	VF	EF	AU	Unc
14-02	$5	1927	Neill, l.	45.	70.	120.	200.	400.	600.
14-04	$5	1927	Wilson, l.	40.	60.	100.	170.	335.	500.
14-06	$10	1927	Neill, l.	50.	75.	130.	220.	450.	—
14-08	$10	1927	Wilson, l.	40.	60.	100.	170.	335.	500.
14-10	$20	1927	Neill, l.	200.	275.	400.	—	—	—
14-12	$20	1927	Wilson, l.	60.	80.	130.	220.	450.	700.
14-14	$50	1927	Neill, l.	750.	1,000.	—	—	—	—
14-16	$50	1927	Wilson, l.	250.	325.	475.	750.	1,250.	—
14-18	$100	1927	Neill, l.	400.	550.	750.	1,200.	—	—
14-20	$100	1927	Wilson, l.	300.	400.	550.	900.	1,500.	—

SPECIMEN NOTES

Cat. No.	Denom.	Date		Unc
14-10S	$20	1927	SPECIMEN	600.

630-16 ISSUE OF 1933

DESIGNS AND COLOURS

630-16-02

$5 Face Design: Morris W. Wilson/coat of arms/
Sir Herbert Holt
Colour: Black with green tint

Back Design: Lathework, counters, bank name and Royal Crest
Colour: Green

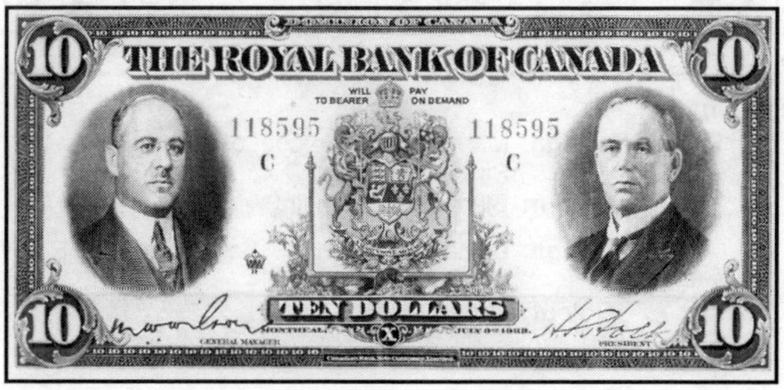

630-16-04

$10 Face Design: Morris W. Wilson/coat of arms/
Sir Herbert Holt
Colour: Black with orange tint

Back Design: —/Royal Crest/—
Colour: Orange

630-16-06S

$20 Face Design: Morris W. Wilson/coat of arms/ Sir Herbert Holt
Colour: Black with blue tint

Back Design: —/Royal Crest/—
Colour: Blue

IMPRINT

Canadian Bank Note Company. Limited

SIGNATURES

left	right
typed M.W. Wilson	typed H.S. Holt

ISSUE DATING

Engraved

July 3rd 1933

CIRCULATING NOTES

Cat. No.	Denom.	Date	VG	F	VF	EF	AU	Unc
16-02	$5	1933	75.	100.	160.	250.	375.	500.
16-04	$10	1933	85.	115.	180.	300.	475.	650.
16-06	$20	1933	No known issued notes					

SPECIMEN NOTES

Cat. No.	Denom.	Date		Unc
16-06	$20	1933	SPECIMEN	750.

630-18 **ISSUE OF 1935**
SMALL-SIZE NOTES

DESIGNS AND COLOURS

630-18-02

$5 Face Design: Morris W. Wilson/coat of arms/ Sir Herbert Holt
Colour: Black with green tint

Back Design: Lathework, counters, bank name and Royal Crest
Colour: Green

630-18-04a

$10 Face Design: Morris W. Wilson/coat of arms/ Sir Herbert Holt
Colour: Black with orange tint

Back Design: Lathework, counters, bank name and Royal Crest
Colour: Orange

630-18-06a

$20 Face Design: Morris W. Wilson/coat of arms/ Sir Herbert Holt
Colour: Black with blue tint

Back Design: Lathework, counters, bank name and Royal Crest
Colour Blue

IMPRINT

British American Bank Note Co. Ltd Ottawa

SIGNATURES

left	right
typed S.G. Dobson	typed M.W. Wilson

VARIETIES

Small signatures: Left signature (Dobson) does not reach "MONTREAL"
Large signatures: Left signature (Dobson) ends superimposed on first letters of "MONTREAL"

ISSUE DATING

Engraved

Jan. 2nd 1935

Cat. No.	Denom.	Date	Variety	VG	F	VF	EF	AU	Unc
18-02	$5	1935	small signatures	45.	65.	100.	210.	285.	375.
18-02a	$5	1935	large signatures	35.	55.	85.	175.	230.	300.
18-04	$10	1935	small signatures	45.	65.	100.	210.	285.	375.
18-04a	$10	1935	large signatures	35.	55.	85.	175.	230.	300.
18-06	$20	1935	small signatures	60.	85.	130.	280.	375.	475.
18-06a	$20	1935	large signatures	45.	65.	100.	210.	285.	375.

630-20

ISSUE OF 1943

These notes bear the last date of issue of any chartered bank.

DESIGNS AND COLOURS

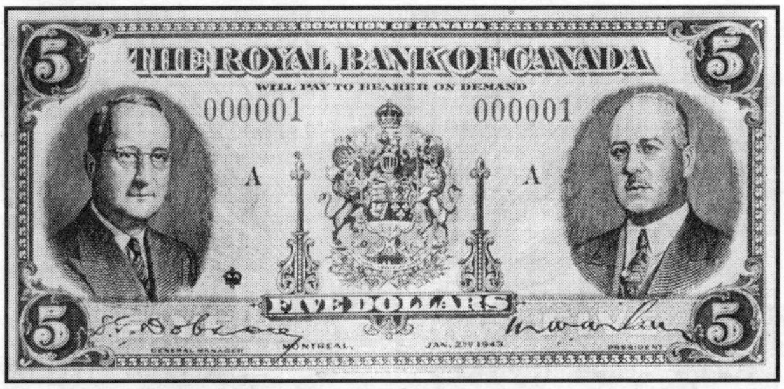

630-20-02

$5 Face Design: S.G. Dobson/Coat of Arms/Morris W. Wilson
Colour: Black with green tint

Back Design: Lathework, counters, bank name and Royal Crest
Colour: Green

IMPRINT

British American Bank Note Company Limited

SIGNATURES

left	**right**
typed S.G. Dobson	typed M.W. Wilson

ISSUE DATING

Engraved

Jan. 2nd 1943

Cat. No.	Denom.	Date	VG	F	VF	EF	AU	Unc
20-02	$5	1943	60.	90.	140.	280.	400.	500.

BRITISH WEST INDIES ISSUES

In 1902 the Union Bank of Halifax opened a branch in Port of Spain, Trinidad. The Royal Bank took over the Union Bank in 1910 and continued the Caribbean operations. The Royal Bank issued notes dated as early as January 2, 1909, payable on various Caribbean islands.

ISSUES FOR ST. JOHN'S, ANTIGUA

630-22

DESIGNS FOR OVERPRINTED CANADIAN NOTES, 1913

DESIGNS AND COLOURS

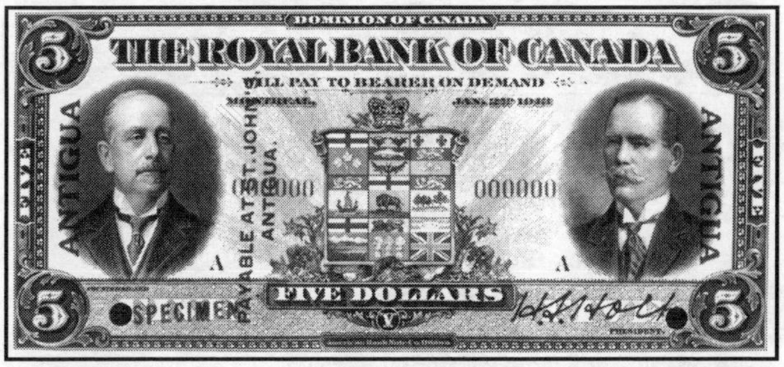

630-22-02S

$5 Face Design: Edson L. Pease/Canadian Coat of Arms/ H.S. Holt
Colour: Black with green tint

Back Design: Lathework, counters, bank name and Royal Crest
Colour: Green

IMPRINT

American Bank Note Co. Ottawa

SIGNATURES

left	**right**
none	typed H.S. Holt

ISSUE DATING

Engraved

Jan. 2nd 1913

OVERPRINT

"ANTIGUA" at ends and "PAYABLE AT ST. JOHN'S/ANTIGUA" at left centre, all in blue

CIRCULATING NOTES

Cat. No.	Denom.	Date	G	VG	F	VF	EF	AU
22-02	$5	1913	No known issued notes					

SPECIMEN NOTES

Cat. No.	Denom.	Date		Unc
22-02S	$5	1913	SPECIMEN	750.

630-24 NOTES DESIGNED SPECIFICALLY FOR WEST INDIES, ANTIGUA LARGE SIZE NOTES, 1920

DESIGNS AND COLOURS

630-24-02

$5 (£1.0.10) Face Design: —/steamships and sailboat/—
Colour: Black with green tint

Back Design: —/Royal Crest/—
Colour: Green

IMPRINT

American Bank Note Company, Ottawa

SIGNATURES

left	right
typed C.E. Neill	typed H.S. Holt

ISSUE DATING

Engraved

January 2nd 1920

Cat. No.	Denom.	Date	G	VG	F	VF	EF	AU
24-02	$5 (£1.0.10)	1920	—	1,000..	1,400.	—	—	—

630-26 WEST INDIES ANTIGUA DESIGNS SMALL-SIZE NOTES, 1938

DESIGNS AND COLOURS

630-26-02

$5 (£1.0.10) Face Design: —/steamships and sailboat/—
Colour: Black with green tint

Back Design: —/Royal Crest/—
Colour: Green

IMPRINT

Canadian Bank Note Company Limited

SIGNATURES

left	right
typed S.G. Dobson	typed M.W. Wilson

ISSUE DATING

Engraved

January 3rd 1938

Cat. No.	Denom.	Date	G	VG	F	VF	EF	AU
26-02	$5 (£1.0.10)	1938	200.	400.	550.	900.	1,400.	—

ISSUES FOR BRIDGETOWN, BARBADOS

630-28 OVERPRINTED CANADIAN NOTES, 1909

DESIGNS AND COLOURS

630-28-02S

$5 Face Design: Seated woman with two children and dove "peace"/—/—
Colour: Black with green and yellow tint
Back Design: —/Royal Crest/—
Colour: Green and yellow

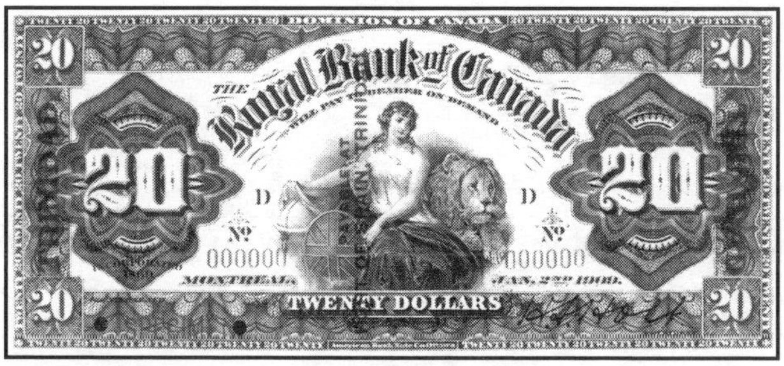

630-28-04S

$20 Face Design: —/seated woman and lion/—
Colour: Blue frame, black with blue and yellow tint
Back Design: —/Royal Crest/—
Colour: Blue and yellow

630-28-06S

$100 Face Design: —/—/seated "Commerce" figure
Colour: Black with red-orange, yellow and olive tint
Back Design: —/Royal Crest/—
Colour: Red-orange

IMPRINT

American Bank Note Co. Ottawa

SIGNATURES

	left	right
$5:	typed H.S. Holt	mss. various
$20:	mss. various	typed H.S. Holt
$100:	typed H.S. Holt	none

ISSUE DATING

Engraved

Jan. 2nd 1909.

OVERPRINT

"BARBADOS" at ends and "PAYABLE AT/BRIDGETOWN, "BARBADOS" in centre, all in blue

CIRCULATING NOTES

Cat. No.	Denom.	Date	G	VG	F	VF	EF	AU
28-02	$5	1909	—	—	—	2,000.	3,300.	—
28-04	$20	1909	Institutional collection only					
28-06	$100	1909	No known issued notes					

SPECIMEN NOTES

Cat. No.	Denom.	Date		Unc
28-06S	$100	1909	SPECIMEN	850.

630-30 NOTES DESIGNED SPECIFICALLY FOR WEST INDIES, BARBADOS LARGE SIZE NOTE DESIGNS, 1920

DESIGNS AND COLOURS

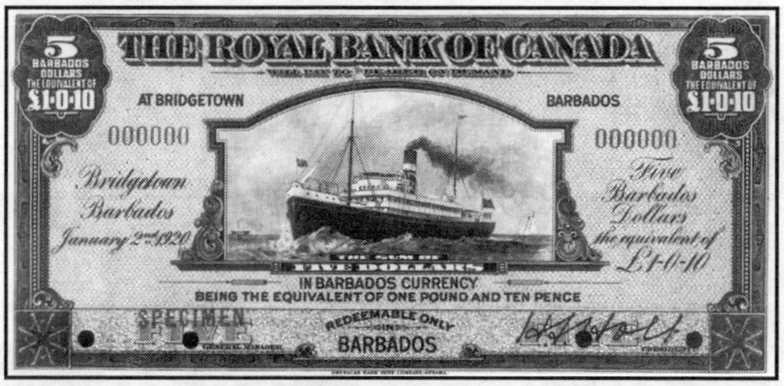

630-30-02

$5 (£1.0.10) Face Design: —/steamships and sailboat/—
Colour: Black with green tint

Back Design: —/Royal Crest/—
Colour: Green

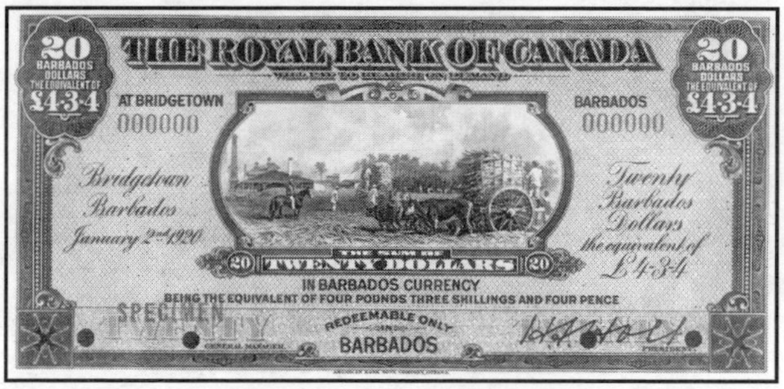

630-30-04S

$20 (£4.3.4) Face Design: —/harvesting sugar cane/—
Colour: Black with blue tint

Back Design: —/Royal Crest/—
Colour: Blue

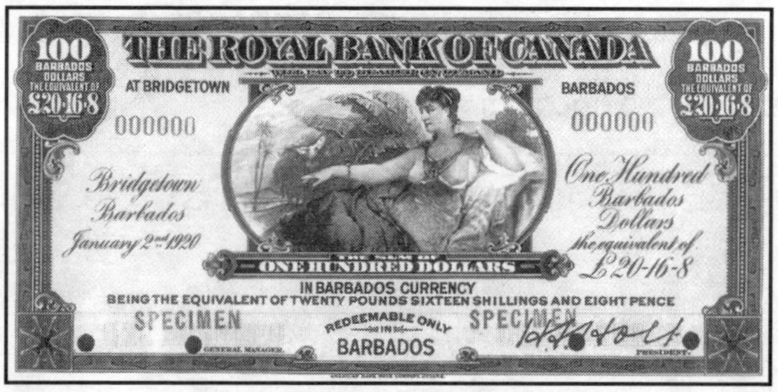

630-30-06S

$100 (£20.16.8) Face Design: —/seated "Cleopatra" with tropical island in background,/—
Colour: Black with orange tint

Back Design: —/Royal Crest/—
Colour: Orange

IMPRINT

American Bank Note Company, Ottawa

SIGNATURES

left	right
typed C.E. Neill	typed H.S. Holt
typed S.G. Dobson	typed H.S. Holt

ISSUE DATING

Engraved

January 2nd 1920

CIRCULATING NOTES

Cat. No.	Denom.	Date	G	VG	F	VF	EF	AU
30-02	$5 (£1.0.10)	1920	—	—	1,300.	—	—	4,250.
30-04	$20 (£4.3.4)	1920	No known issued notes					
30-06	$100 (£20.16.8.)	1920	No known issued notes					

PROOF NOTES

Cat. No.	Denom.	Date		Unc
30-02P	$5 (£1.0.10)	1920	FACE PROOF	500.
30-04P	$20 (£4.3.4)	1920	FACE PROOF	500.
30-06P	$100 (£20.16.8)	1920	FACE PROOF	500.

SPECIMEN NOTES

Cat. No.	Denom.	Date		Unc
30-02S	$5 (£1.0.10)	1920	SPECIMEN	1,000.
30-04S	$20 (£4.3.4)	1920	SPECIMEN	1,000.
30-06S	$100 (£20.16.8)	1920	SPECIMEN	1,000.

630-32 NOTES DESIGNED SPECIFICALLY FOR WEST INDIES, BARBADOS SMALL SIZE NOTES, 1938

DESIGNS AND COLOURS

630-32-02
$5 (£1.0.10) Face Design: —/steamship/—
Colour: Black with green tint

Back Design: —/Royal Crest/—
Colour: Green

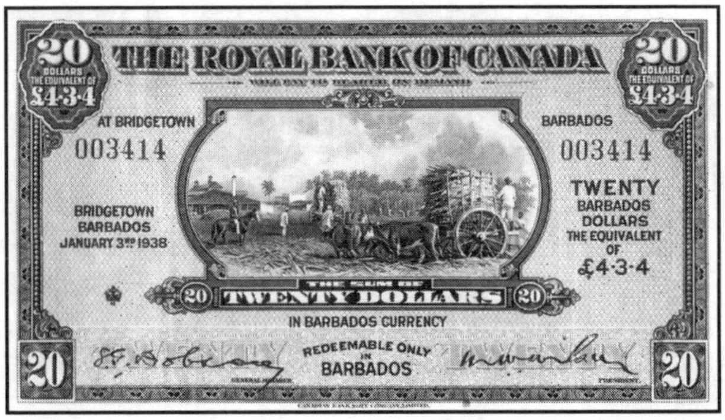

630-32-04
$20 (£4.3.4) Face Design: —/harvesting sugar cane/—
Colour: Black with orange tint

Back Design: —/Royal Crest/—
Colour: Rose

IMPRINT

Canadian Bank Note Company Limited

SIGNATURES

left	right
typed S.G. Dobson	typed M.W. Wilson

ISSUE DATING

Engraved

January 3rd 1938

CIRCULATING NOTES

Cat. No.	Denom.	Date	G	VG	F	VF	EF	AU
32-02	$5 (£1.0.10)	1938	—	200.	275.	450.	750.	—
32-04	$20 (£4.3.4)	1938	—	—	—	1,750.	2,500.	—

PROOF NOTES

Cat. No.	Denom.	Date		Unc
32-02P	$5 (£1.0.10)	1938	FACE PROOF	500.
32-04P	$20 (£4.3.4)	1938	FACE PROOF	500.

ISSUES FOR GEORGETOWN, BRITISH GUIANA

630-34 OVERPRINTED CANADIAN NOTES 1909 AND 1913

DESIGNS AND COLOURS

630-34-02
$5 Face Design: Edson L. Pease/Canadian coat of arms/ H.S. Holt
Colour: Black with green tint

Back Design: —/Royal Crest/—
Colour: Green

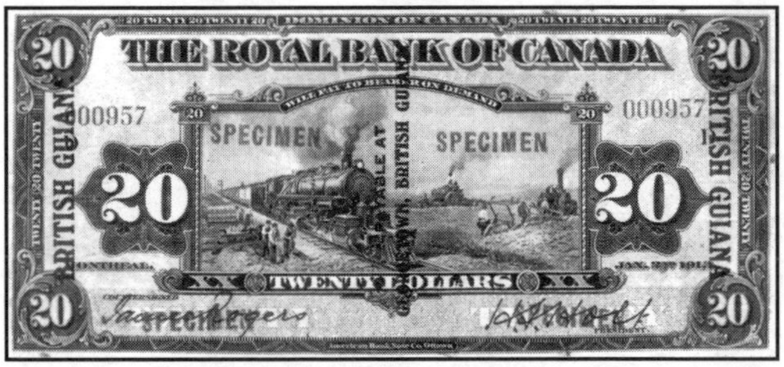

630-34-04
$20 Face Design: —/train on prairie/—
Colour: Black with blue tint
Back Design: —/Royal Crest/—
Colour: Blue

Photo Not Available

630-34-06
$100 Face Design: —/—/seated "Commerce" figure
Colour: Black with red-orange tint

Back Design: —/Royal Crest/—
Colour: Red-orange

630-34-08S
$100 Face Design: —/—/H.S. Holt
Colour: Black with orange and yellow-green tint

Back Design: —/Royal Crest/—
Colour: Red

IMPRINT

American Bank Note Co. Ottawa

SIGNATURES

	left	right
$5 and $20:	mss. various	typed H.S. Holt
$100:	none	typed H.S. Holt

ISSUE DATING

Engraved

Jan. 2, 1909

Jan. 2nd 1913

OVERPRINT

"BRITISH GUIANA" at ends and "PAYABLE AT/GEORGETOWN, "BRITISH GUIANA" in centre, all in blue

CIRCULATING NOTES

Cat. No.	Denom.	Date	G	VG	F	VF	EF	AU
34-02	$5	1913	300.	600.	800.	1,300.	—	—
34-04	$20	1913	Institutional collection only					
34-06	$100	1909	No known issued notes					
34-08	$100	1913	No known issued notes					

SPECIMEN NOTES

Cat. No.	Denom.	Date	Unc
34-06S	$100	1909	850.
34-08S	$100	1913	750.

630-36 NOTES DESIGNED SPECIFICALLY FOR WEST INDIES, BRITISH GUIANA LARGE SIZE NOTES, 1920

DESIGNS AND COLOURS

630-36-02

$5 (£1.0.10) Face Design: —/steamship and sailboat/—

Colour: Black with green tint

Back Design: —/Royal Crest/—

Colour: Green

630-36-04S

$20 (£4.3.4) Face Design: —/harvesting sugar cane/—

Colour: Black with blue tint

Back Design: —/Royal Crest/—

Colour: Green

630-36-06S

$100 (£20.16.8) Face Design: —/seated semi-nude "Cleopatra" with tropical island in background/—

Colour: Black with orange tint

Back Design: —/Royal Crest/—

Colour: Orange

IMPRINT

American Bank Note Company, Ottawa

SIGNATURES

left	right
typed C.E. Neill	typed H.S. Holt
typed M.W. Wilson	typed H.S. Holt

ISSUE DATING

Engraved

January 2nd 1920

CIRCULATING NOTES

Cat. No.	Denom.	Date	G	VG	F	VF	EF	AU
36-02	$5 (£1.0.10)	1920	300.	600.	800.	1,300.	2,000.	—
36-04	$20 (£4.3.4)	1920	Institutional collection only					
36-06	$100 (£20.16.8)	1920	—	—	2,000.	3,000.	—	—

PROOF NOTES

Cat. No.	Denom.	Date		Unc
36-02P	$5 (£1.0.10)	1920	FACE PROOF	500.
36-04P	$20 (£4.3.4)	1920	FACE PROOF	500.
36-06P	$100 (£20.16.8)	1920	FACE PROOF	500.

SPECIMEN NOTES

Cat. No.	Denom.	Date		Unc
36-02S	$5 (£1.0.10)	1920	SPECIMEN	600.
36-04S	$20 (£4.3.4)	1920	SPECIMEN	750.
36-06S	$100 (£20.16.8)	1920	SPECIMEN	850.

630-38 NOTES DESIGNED SPECIFICALLY FOR WEST INDIES, BRITISH GUIANA SMALL SIZE NOTES 1938

DESIGNS AND COLOURS

630-38-02

$5 (£1.0.10) Face Design: —/steamship and sailboat/—
Colour: Black with green tint
Back Design: Lathework, counters, bank name and Royal Crest
Colour: Green

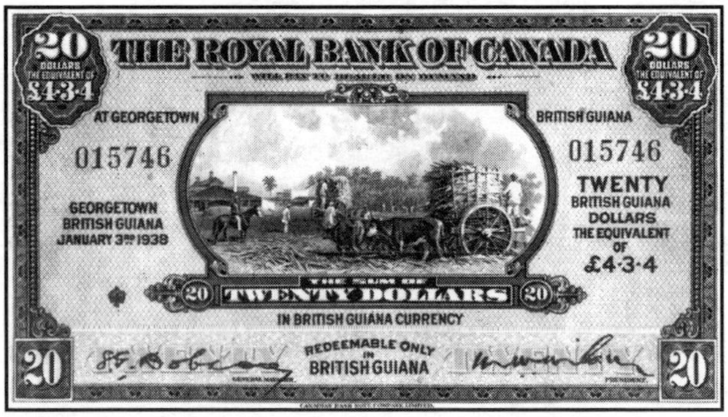

630-38-04

$20 (£4.3.4) Face Design: —/harvesting sugar cane/—
Colour: Black with orange tint
Back Design: Lathework, counters, bank name and Royal Crest
Colour: Rose

IMPRINT

Canadian Bank Note Company. Limited

SIGNATURES

left	right
typed S.G. Dobson	typed M.W. Wilson

ISSUE DATING

Engraved

January 3rd 1938

CIRCULATING NOTES

Cat. No.	Denom.	Date	G	VG	F	VF	EF	AU
38-02	$5 (£1.0.10)	1938	—	325.	450.	700.	—	—
38-04	$20 (£4.3.4)	1938	—	—	500.	800.	1,250.	—

PROOF NOTES

Cat. No.	Denom.	Date		Unc
38-02P	$5 (£1.0.10)	1938	FACE PROOF	500.
38-04P	$20 (£4.3.4)	1938	FACE PROOF	500.

ISSUES FOR ROSEAU, DOMINICA

630-40 OVERPRINTED CANADIAN NOTES 1913

DESIGNS AND COLOURS

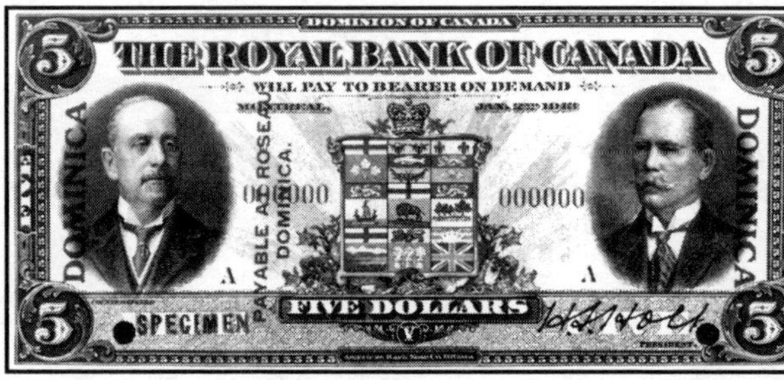

630-40-02

$5 Face Design: Edson L. Pease/ Canadian Coat of Arms/H.S. Holt
Colour: Black with green tint
Back Design: Lathwork, counters, bank name and Royal Crest
Colour: Green

IMPRINT

American Bank Note Co. Ottawa

SIGNATURES

left	right
mss. various	typed H.S. Holt

ISSUE DATING

Engraved

Jan. 2nd 1913

OVERPRINT

"DOMINICA" at ends and "PAYABLE AT ROSEAU/DOMINICA" at left centre, all in blue

CIRCULATING NOTES

Cat. No.	Denom.	Date	G	VG	F	VF	EF	AU
40-02	$5	1913	Institutional collection only					

SPECIMEN NOTES

Cat. No.	Denom.	Date		Unc
40-02S	$5	1913	SPECIMEN	850.

630-42 NOTES DESIGNED SPECIFICALLY FOR WEST INDIES, DOMINICA LARGE SIZE NOTES 1920

DESIGNS AND COLOURS

630-42-02

$5 (£1.0.10) Face Design: —/steamships and sailboat/—
Colour: Black with green tint
Back Design: —/Royal Crest/—
Colour: Green

IMPRINT
American Bank Note Company, Ottawa

SIGNATURES

Left	right
typed C.E. Neill	typed H.S. Holt
typed S.G. Dobson	typed H.S. Holt

ISSUE DATING
Engraved
January 2nd 1920

Cat. No.	Denom.	Date	G	VG	F	VF	EF	AU
42-02	$5 (£1.0.10)	1920	450.	900.	1,200.	1,800.	—	—

630-44 NOTES DESIGNED SPECIFICALLY FOR WEST INDIES, DOMINICA SMALL SIZE NOTES, 1938

DESIGNS AND COLOURS

630-44-02
$5 (£1.0.10) Face Design: —/steamships and sailboat/—
Colour: Black with green tint

Back Design: —/Royal Crest/—
Colour: Green

IMPRINT
Canadian Bank Note Company Limited

SIGNATURES

left	right
typed S.G. Dobson	typed M.W. Wilson

ISSUE DATING
Engraved
January 3rd 1938

Cat. No.	Denom.	Date	G	VG	F	VF	EF	AU
44-02	$5(£1.0.10)	1938	450.	900.	1,200.	1,800.	—	—

ISSUES FOR ST. GEORGE'S, GRENADA

630-46 DESIGNS FOR OVERPRINTED CANADIAN NOTES 1909

DESIGNS AND COLOURS

630-46-02s
$5 Face Design: Seated woman with two children and dove "Peace"/—/—
Colour: Black with green and yellow tint

Back Design: —/Royal Crest/—
Colour: Green and yellow

IMPRINT
American Bank Note Co. Ottawa

SIGNATURES

left	right
none	none

ISSUE DATING
Engraved
Jan. 2nd 1909

OVERPRINT
"GRENADA" at ends and "PAYABLE AT/ST. GEORGE'S, "GRENADA" in centre, all in blue

CIRCULATING NOTES

Cat. No.	Denom.	Date	G	VG	F	VF	EF	AU
46-02	$5	1909		No known issued notes				

SPECIMEN NOTES

Cat. No.	Denom.	Date		Unc
46-02S	$5	1909	SPECIMEN	850

630-48 NOTES DESIGNED SPECIFICALLY FOR WEST INDIES, GRENADA LARGE SIZE NOTE DESIGNS 1920

DESIGNS AND COLOURS

630-48-02S
$5 (£1.0.10) Face Design: —/steamships and sailboat/—
Colour: Black with green tint

Back Design: —/Royal Crest/—
Colour: Green

IMPRINT
American Bank Note Company, Ottawa

SIGNATURES

left	right
none	typed H.S. Holt

ISSUE DATING
Engraved
January 2nd 1920

CIRCULATING NOTES

Cat. No.	Denom.	Date	G	VG	F	VF	EF	AU
48-02	$5 (£1.0.10)	1920	No known issued notes					

SPECIMEN NOTES

Cat. No.	Denom.	Date		Unc
48-02S	$5 (£1.0.10)	1920	SPECIMEN	850.

630-50 NOTES DESIGNED SPECIFICALLY FOR WEST INDIES, GRENADA SMALL SIZE NOTES 1938

DESIGNS AND COLOURS

630-50-02
$5 (£1.0.10) Face Design: —/steamships and sailboat/—
Colour: Black with green tint

Back Design: —/Royal Crest/—
Colour: Green

IMPRINT
Canadian Bank Note Company, Limited

SIGNATURES

left	right
typed S.G. Dobson	typed M.W. Wilson

ISSUE DATING
Engraved
January 3rd 1938

Cat. No.	Denom.	Date	G	VG	F	VF	EF	AU
50-02	$5 (£1.0.10)	1938	500.	1,000.	—	2,000.	—	—

630-52 ISSUES FOR KINGSTON, JAMAICA LARGE SIZE NOTES 1911

DESIGNS AND COLOURS

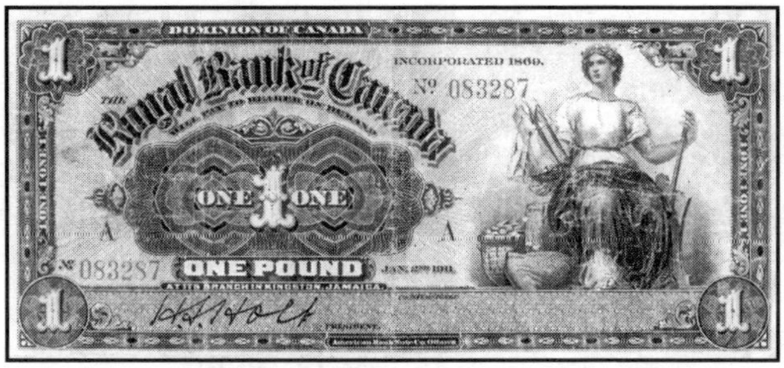

630-52-02
£1 Face Design: —/—/seated woman with lyre and model ship
Colour: Black with orange, yellow and olive tint

Back Design: Lathework, counters, bank name and Royal Crest
Colour: Green

630-52-04S
£5 Face Design: Seated woman with pad and palette "Study"/—/—
Colour: Black with red-orange and yellow-green tint

Back Design: —/Royal Crest/—
Colour: Olive

IMPRINT
American Bank Note Co. Ottawa

SIGNATURES

left	right
typed H.S. Holt	mss. various
typed H.S. Holt	none

ISSUE DATING
Jan. 2nd 1911

CIRCULATING NOTES

Cat. No.	Denom.	Date	G	VG	F	VF	EF	AU
52-02	£1	1911	500.	1,000.	1,300.	2,000.	—	—
52-04	£5	1911	600.	1,200.	—	—	—	—

PROOF NOTES

Cat. No.	Denom.	Date		Unc
52-02P	£1	1911	FACE PROOF	500.
52-04P	£5	1911	FACE PROOF	850.

630-54 ISSUES FOR KINGSTON, JAMAICA SMALL SIZE NOTES 1938

DESIGNS AND COLOURS

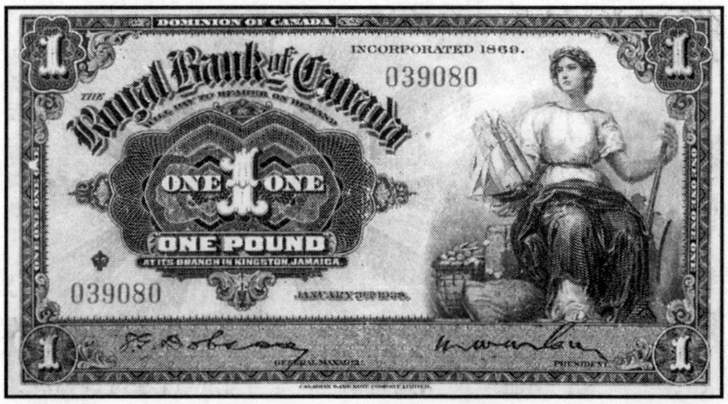

630-54-02

£1 Face Design: —/—/seated woman with lyre and model ship
Colour: Black with green and orange tint

Back Design: —/Royal Crest/—
Colour: Green

630-54-04

£5 Face Design: Seated woman with pad and palette "Study"/—/—
Colour: Black with red-orange and yellow-green tint

Back Design: —/Royal Crest/—
Colour: Olive

IMPRINT

Canadian Bank Note Company, Limited

SIGNATURES

left	right
typed S.G. Dobson	typed M.W. Wilson

ISSUE DATING

Engraved

January 3rd, 1938

CIRCULATING NOTES

Cat. No.	Denom.	Date	G	VG	F	VF	EF	AU
54-02	£1	1938	400.	800.	1,100.	1,700.	—	—
54-04	£5	1938	—	—	1,750.	2,250.	3,000.	—

PROOF NOTES

Cat. No.	Denom.	Date		Unc
54-02	£1	1938	FACE PROOF	500.
54-04	£5	1938	FACE PROOF	500.

ISSUES FOR BASSETERRE, ST. KITTS

630-56 OVERPRINTED CANADIAN NOTES 1913

DESIGNS AND COLOURS

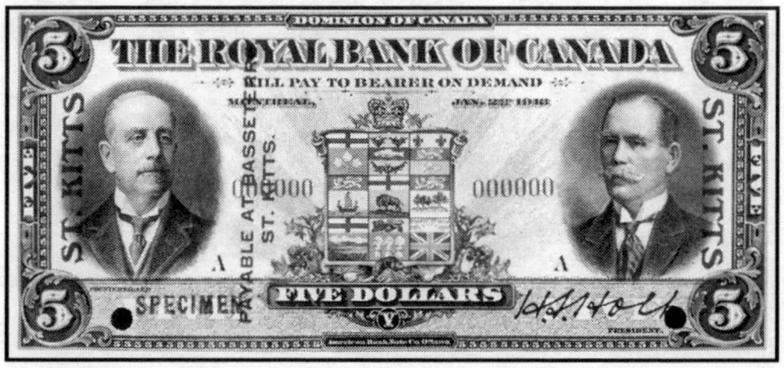

630-56-02

$5 Face Design: Edson L. Pease/Canadian coat of arms/ H.S. Holt
Colour: Black with green tint

Back Design: Lathework, counters, bank name and Royal Crest
Colour: Green

IMPRINT

American Bank Note Co. Ottawa

SIGNATURES

left	right
mss. various	typed H.S. Holt

ISSUE DATING

Engraved

Jan. 2nd, 1913

OVERPRINT

"ST. KITTS" at ends and "PAYABLE AT BASSETERRE,/ ST. KITTS" at left centre, all in blue

Cat. No.	Denom.	Date	G	VG	F	VF	EF	AU
56-02	$5	1913	—	—	2,000.	—	—	—

630-58 NOTES DESIGNED SPECIFICALLY FOR WEST INDIES, ST. KITTS LARGE SIZE NOTE DESIGNS, 1920

DESIGNS AND COLOURS

630-58-02S

$5 (£1.0.10) Face Design: —/steamships and sailboat/—
Colour: Black with green tint

Back Design: —/Royal Crest/—
Colour: Green

IMPRINT
American Bank Note Company, Ottawa

SIGNATURES

left	right
none	typed H.S. Holt

ISSUE DATING
Engraved
January 2nd, 1920

CIRCULATING NOTES

Cat. No.	Denom.	Date	G	VG	F	VF	EF	AU
58-02	$5 (£1.0.10)	1920	—	1,500.	—	—	—	—

SPECIMEN NOTES

Cat. No.	Denom.	Date		Unc
58-02S	$5 (£1.0.10)	1920	SPECIMEN	750.

630-60 NOTES DESIGNED SPECIFICALLY FOR WEST INDIES, ST. KITTS SMALL SIZE NOTES, 1938

DESIGNS AND COLOURS

630-60-02

$5 (£1.0.10) Face Design: —/steamships and sailboat/—
Colour: Black with green tint

Back Design: —/Royal Crest/—
Colour: Green

IMPRINT
Canadian Bank Note Company Limited

SIGNATURES

left	right
typed S.G. Dobson	typed M.W. Wilson

ISSUE DATING
Engraved
January 3rd 1938

Cat. No.	Denom.	Date	G	VG	F	VF	EF	AU
60-02	$5 (£1.0.10)	1938	400.	800.	1,100.	1,700.	—	—

630-62 ISSUE FOR CASTRIES, ST. LUCIA

These designs were for large-size notes and were designed specifically for the West Indies.

DESIGNS AND COLOURS

630-62-02S

$5 (£1.0.10) Face Design: —/steamships and sailboat/—
Colour: Black with green tint

Back Design: —/Royal Crest/—
Colour: Green

IMPRINT
American Bank Note Company, Ottawa

SIGNATURES

left	right
none	typed H.S. Holt

ISSUE DATING
Engraved
January 2nd 1920

CIRCULATING NOTES

Cat. No.	Denom.	Date	G	VG	F	VF	EF	AU
62-02	$5 (£1.0.10)	1920	No known issued notes					

PROOF NOTES

Cat. No.	Denom.	Date		Unc
62-02P	$5 (£1.0.10)	1920	FACE PROOF	600.

SPECIMEN NOTES

Cat. No.	Denom.	Date		Unc
62-02S	$5 (£1.0.10)	1920	SPECIMEN	1,000.

ISSUES FOR PORT OF SPAIN, TRINIDAD

630-64 OVERPRINTED CANADIAN NOTES 1909

DESIGNS AND COLOURS

630-64-02

$5 Face Design: Seated woman with two children and dove "peace"/—/—
Colour: Black with green and yellow tint

Back Design: —/Royal Crest/—
Colour: Green and yellow

630-64-04S

$20 Face Design: —/seated woman, lion, shield and globe/—
Colour: Blue frame, black with blue and yellow frame

Back Design: —/Royal Crest/—
Colour: Blue and yellow

630-64-06S

$100 Face Design: —/—/seated "Commerce" figure
Colour: Black with red-orange, yellow and olive tint

Back Design: —/Royal Crest/—
Colour: Red-orange

IMPRINT

American Bank Note Co. Ottawa

SIGNATURES

	left	right
$5:	typed H.S. Holt	mss. various
	typed H.S. Holt	none
$20:	none	typed H.S. Holt
$100:	typed H.S. Holt	none

ISSUE DATING

Engraved

Jan. 2nd 1909

OVERPRINT

"TRINIDAD" at ends and "PAYABLE AT/PORT OF SPAIN, TRINIDAD" in centre, all in red

CIRCULATING NOTES

Cat. No.	Denom.	Date	G	VG	F	VF	EF	AU
64-02	$5	1909	400.	800.	1,100.	1,700.	—	—
64-04	$20	1909		No known issued notes				
64-06	$100	1909		No known issued notes				

SPECIMEN NOTES

Cat. No.	Denom.	Date		Unc
64-04S	$20	1909	SPECIMEN	850.
64-06S	$100	1909	SPECIMEN	850.

630-66 NOTES DESIGNED SPECIFICALLY FOR WEST INDIES, TRINIDAD LARGE SIZE NOTES 1920

DESIGNS AND COLOURS

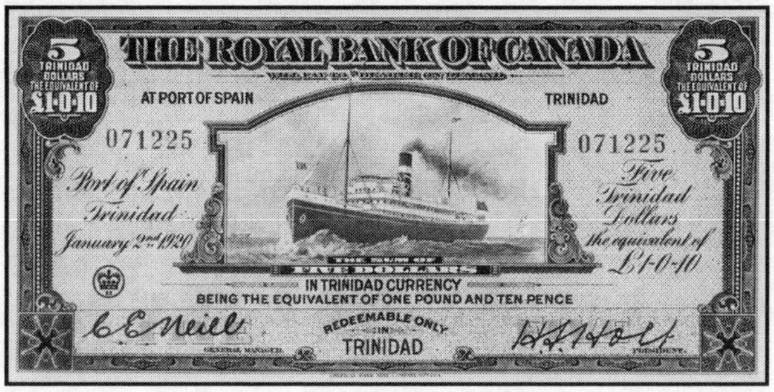

630-66-02

$5 (£1.0.10) Face Design: —/steamships and sailboat/—
Colour: Black with green tint
Back Design: Lathework, counters, bank name and Royal Crest
Colour: Green

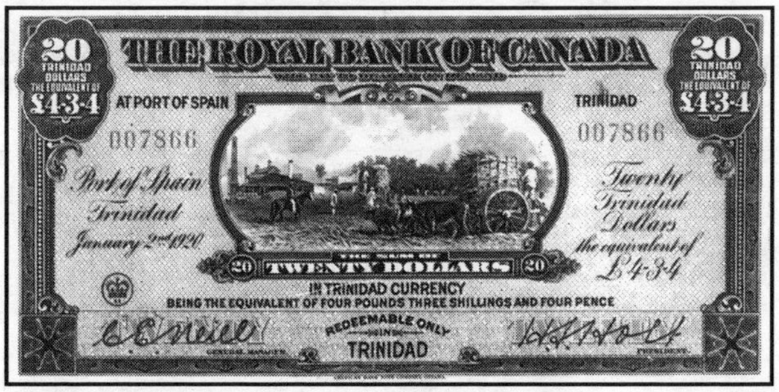

630-66-04

$20 (£4.3.4) Face Design: —/harvesting sugar cane/—
Colour: Black with blue tint

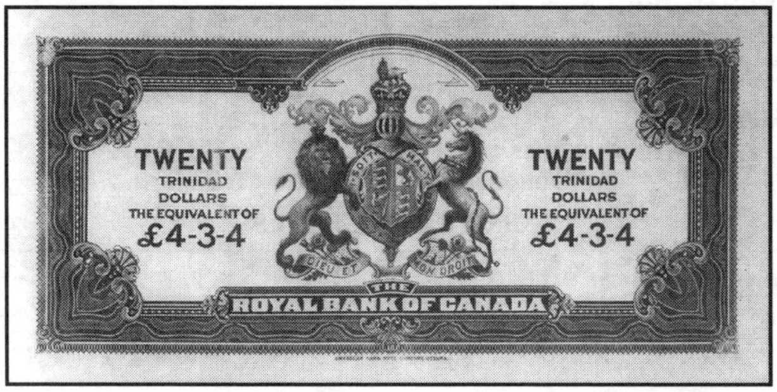

Back Design: Lathework, counters, bank name and Royal Crest
Colour: Blue

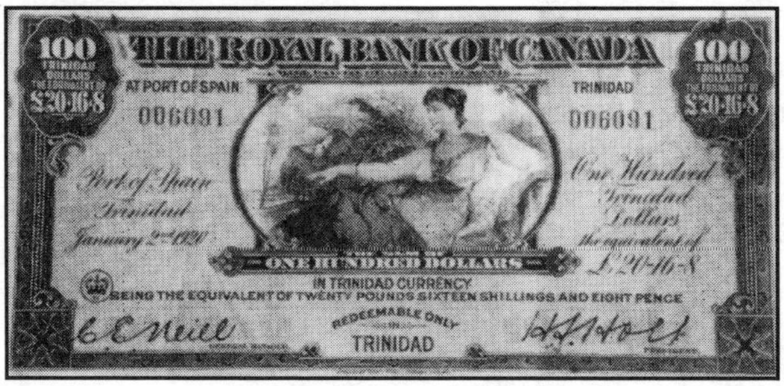

630-66-06
$100 (£20.16.8) Face Design: —/seated semi-nude "Cleopatra" with tropical island in background /—
Colour: Black with orange tint

Back Design: Lathework, counters, bank name and Royal Crest
Colour: Orange

IMPRINT
American Bank Note Company, Ottawa

SIGNATURES

left	right
mss. various	typed H.S. Holt
typed C.E. Neill	typed H.S. Holt
typed M.W. Wilson	typed H.S. Holt
typed S.G. Dobson	typed H.S. Holt
typed S.G. Dobson	typed M.W. Wilson

ISSUE DATING
Engraved
January 2nd 1920

Cat. No.	Denom.	Date	G	VG	F	VF	EF	Unc
66-02	$5 (£1.0.10)	1920	135.	275.	375.	600.	1,000.	2,000.
66-04	$20 (£4.3.4)	1920	—	—	—	1,500.	—	—
66-06	$100 (£20.16.8)	1920	—	1,000.	1,400.	2,150.	—	—

630-68 **NOTES DESIGNED SPECIFICALLY FOR WEST INDIES, TRINIDAD SMALL SIZE NOTES 1938**

DESIGNS AND COLOURS

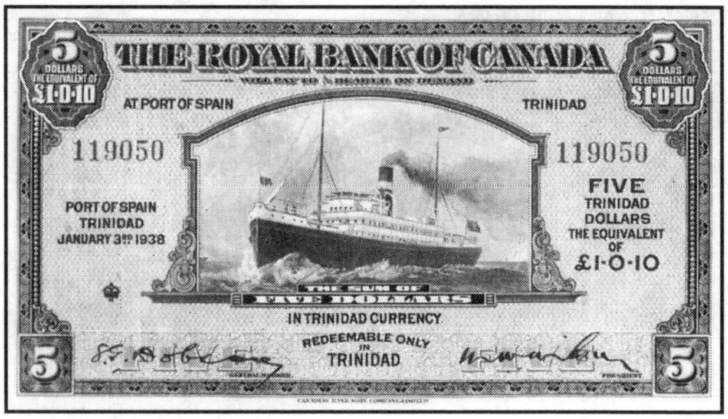

630-68-02
$5 (£1.0.10) Face Design: —/steamships and sailboat/—
Colour: Black with green tint

Back Design: —/Royal Crest/—
Colour: Green

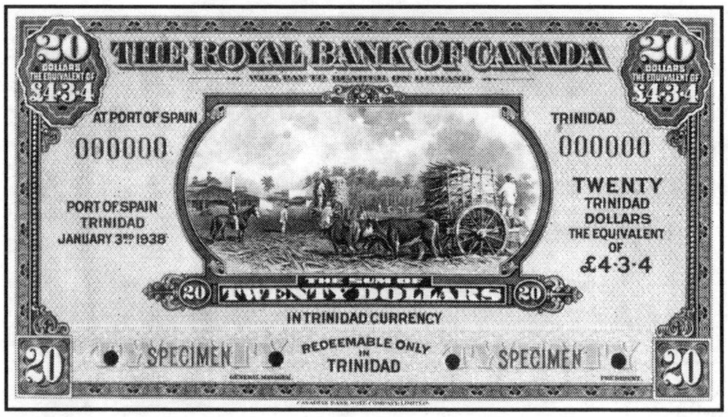

630-68-04
$20 (£4.3.4) Face Design: —/harvesting sugar cane/—
Colour: Black with orange tint

Back Design: —/Royal Crest/—
Colour: Rose

IMPRINT
Canadian Bank Note Company, Limited

SIGNATURES

left	right
typed S.G. Dobson	typed M.W. Wilson

ISSUE DATING
Engraved
January 3rd 1938

CIRCULATING NOTES

Cat. No.	Denom.	Date	G	VG	F	VF	EF	AU
68-02	$5 (£1.0.10)	1938	100.	200.	275.	450.	750.	—
68-04	$20 (£4.3.4)	1938	—	500.	700.	1,050.	—	—

SPECIMEN NOTES

Cat. No.	Denom	Date	Unc
68-04S	$20 (£4.3.4)	1938	SPECIMEN 750.

THE ROYAL CANADIAN BANK

1864-1876

TORONTO, CANADA WEST

BANK NUMBER 635 ***NONREDEEMABLE***

Established in Toronto in 1864, this bank had an aggressive management and expanded very rapidly, but soon found dissension and rivalry among its directors. The bank incurred heavy losses through unprofitable branches, fraudulent managers, bad loans and improper favours to political figures. It was reorganized in 1869 and enjoyed prosperity for some time, but again accumulated a substantial number of bad debts. The institution was saved from liquidation by merging with the City Bank in 1876 to become the Consolidated Bank of Canada.

635-10 ABNC PRINTINGS 1865

DESIGNS AND COLOURS

635-10-04-04

$1 Face Design: Wellington/bank seal flanked by lion and unicorn/sailor standing by capstan
Colour: Black with green tint

Back Design: Lathework and bank name
Colour: Brown

635-10-04-08a

$2 Face Design: Prince of Wales/bank seal flanked by lion and unicorn/seated woman with basket of produce
Colour: Black with green tint

Back Design: Lathework and bank name
Colour: Brown

635-10-04-10

$5 Face Design: Princess of Wales/bank seal flanked by lion and unicorn/seated woman with telescope and large 5
Colour: Black with green tint

Back Design: Lathework and bank name
Colour: Brown

Photo Not Available

635-10-02-08P

$10 Face Design: Queen Victoria/bank seal, lion and unicorn/woman with scale and sword on dock
Colour: Black with green tint

Back Design: Lathework and bank name
Colour: Brown

IMPRINT

American Bank Note Co. New York
American Bank Note Co. New York and Continental Bank Note Co. N.Y. print

2. PARTIALLY ENGRAVED DATE

635-10-02-02

SIGNATURES

left	right
mss. T. Woodside	mss. Jas. Metcalfe (v)
mss. T. Woodside	mss. A.M. Smith (p)

ISSUE DATING

Partially engraved ___ 18___:

1865: 4 July

OVERPRINT
"C" in red

STAMP
"K" in black

CIRCULATING NOTES

Cat. No.	Denom.	Date	G	VG	F	VF	EF	AU
10-02-02	$1	1865	450.	900.	1,200.	1,700.	—	—
10-02-04	$2	1865	450.	900.	1,200.	1,700.	—	—
10-02-06	$5	18__		No known issued notes				
10-02-08	$10	18__		No known issued notes				

PROOF NOTES

Cat. No.	Denom.	Date		Unc
10-02-02P	$1	18__	FACE PROOF	500.
10-02-04P	$2	18__	FACE PROOF	500.
10-02-06P	$5	18__	FACE PROOF	500.
10-02-08P	$10	18__	FACE PROOF	500.

SPECIMEN NOTES

Cat. No.	Denom.	Date		Unc
10-02-02S	$1	18__	SPECIMEN	850.
10-02-04S	$2	18__	SPECIMEN	850.

Note: A back for $5 (10-02-06) is known in green.

4. ENGRAVED DATE

SIGNATURES

left	right
mss. T. Woodside	mss. Jas. Metcalfe
mss. T. Woodside	mss. A.M. Smith
engr. T. Woodside	mss. A.M. Smith

ISSUE DATING
Engraved
26th July 1865

OVERPRINT
"COBOURG" twice in red
"COBOURG" twice in blue
"PARIS" twice in red
"WOODSTOCK" in blue
"OTTAWA" in blue

STAMP
"T T" in blue

VARIETIES
Mss. signature at left: blue sheet number
Engr. signature at left: red sheet number

Note: Some of the $1, $5 notes with engraved date and small blue serial numbers have both the ABN and CON.B.N imprints

Cat. No.	Denom.	Date	Variety	G	VG	F	VF	EF	AU
10-04-02	$1	1865	Blue sheet #s	500.	1,000.	1,300.	1,900.	—	—
10-04-02a	$1	1865	Blue #s; town o/p	550.	1,100.	1,450.	2,100.	—	—
10-04-04	$1	1865	Red sheet #s	500.	1,000.	1,300.	1,900.	—	—
10-04-04a	$1	1865	Red #s; town o/p	550.	1,100.	1,450.	2,100.	—	—
10-04-06	$2	1865	Blue sheet #s	500.	1,000.	1,300.	1,900.	—	—
10-04-06a	$2	1865	Blue #s; town o/p	550.	1,100.	1,450.	2,100.	—	—
10-04-08	$2	1865	Red sheet #s	500.	1,000.	1,300.	1,900.	—	—
10-04-08a	$2	1865	Red #s; town o/p	550.	1.100.	1,450.	2,100.	—	—
10-04-10	$5	1865	Blue sheet #s	600.	1,200.	1,600.	2,400.	—	—
10-04-10a	$5	1865	Blue #s, town o/p	650.	1,300.	1,750.	2,600.	—	—

635-12 CONTINENTAL BANK NOTE COMPANY ISSUE OF 1865

DESIGNS AND COLOURS

635-12-02-01
$1 Face Design: Duke of Wellington/arms of bank/ blacksmith with anvil
Colour: Black with green tint

Back Design: Bank name, lathework and counters
Colour: Green

635-12-02-02
$2 Face Design: Prince Albert/bank seal/farmer with scythe
Colour: Black with green tint

Back Design: Bank name, lathework and counters
Colour: Green

635-12-02-04
$5 Face Design: Portrait of young woman/bank seal flanked by lion and unicorn/Indian riding horse
Colour: Black with green tint

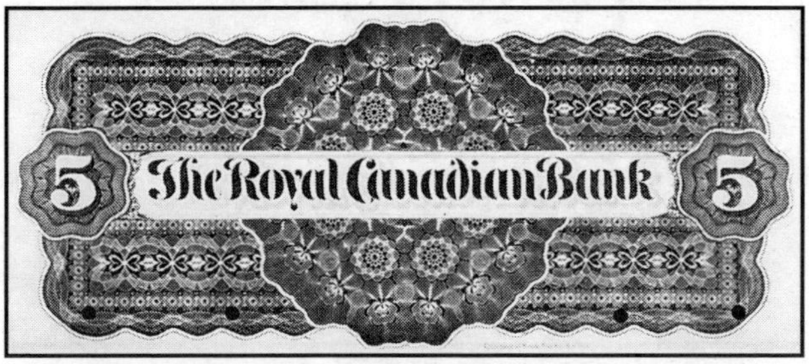

Back design: Bank name, lathework and counters
Colour: Green

635-12-04-06S
$10 Face Design: Queen Victoria (Chalon portrait)/ bank seal flanked by lion and unicorn/ crouching Indian (after F.O.C. Darley)
Colour: Black with green tint

Back Design: Bank name, lathework and counters
Colour: Green

IMPRINT
Continental Bank Note Co. New York

SIGNATURES

left	right
engr. T. Woodside	mss. G.M. Knight
engr. T. Woodside	mss. M.H. Gault (per)
engr. T. Woodside	mss. A.M. Smith
mss. T. Woodside	engr. Hon. J. Crawford

ISSUE DATING
Engraved
26th July 1865

STAMP
"T" twice in blue on face and back

2. "AT ITS BANKING HOUSE IN TORONTO" ABOVE BANK SEAL

Cat. No.	Denom.	Date	G	VG	F	VF	EF	AU
12-02-01	$1	1865	750.	—	—	—	—	—
12-02-02	$2	1865	625.	1,250.	1,700.	2,500.	—	—
12-02-04	$5	1865	625.	1,250.	1,700.	2,500.	—	—
12-02-06	$10	1865	NOT CONFIRMED					

4. "AT ITS BANKING HOUSE IN MONTREAL" ABOVE BANK SEAL

CIRCULATING NOTES

Cat. No.	Denom.	Date	G	VG	F	VF	EF	AU
12-04-01	$1	1865	NOT CONFIRMED					
12-04-02	$2	1865	NOT CONFIRMED					
12-04-04	$5	1865*	500.	1,000.	1,300.	1,900.	—	—
12-04-06	$10	1865*	No known issued notes					

* Note: $5 and $10 SPECIMEN notes exist having very low sheet numbers (see illustrated $10) instead if the usual zeroes. As a result, these have sometimes been classified as remainders.

SPECIMEN NOTES

Cat. No.	Denom.	Date		Unc
12-04-04S	$5	1865	SPECIMEN	850.
12-04-06S	$10	1865	SPECIMEN	850.

635-14 BRITISH AMERICAN BANK NOTE COMPANY ISSUE 1870 - 1872

DESIGNS AND COLOURS

635-14-02
$4 Face Design: Sailors at dockside "Mech's & Commerce"/ Crest/beaver
Colour: Black with green tint
See varieties: top left 4 in round lathework

Back Design: Lathework, counters and bank name
Colour: Green

635-14-04

$4 Face Design: Sailors at dockside "Mech's & Commerce"/ Crest/beaver
Colour: Black with green tint
See varieties: top left 4 in oval lathework

Back Design: Lathework, counters and bank name
Colour: Green

635-14-06

$5 Face Design: T. McCracken/Crest/—
Colour: Black with green tint

Back Design: Lathework, counters and bank name
Colour: Green

635-14-08a

$10 Face Design: Crest/—/Hon. J. Crawford
Colour: Black with green tint

Back Design: Lathework, counters and bank name
Colour: Green

635-14-10P

$20 Face Design: Allegorical female/Crest/sailor aboard ship
Colour: Black with green tint

Back Design: Lathework, counters and bank name
Colour: Green

635-14-12P

$50 Face Design: —/Crest/—
Colour: Black with green tint

Back Design: Lathework, counters and bank name
Colour: Green

635-14-14P

$100 Face Design: —/Crest/—
Colour: Black with green tint

Back Design: Lathework, counters and bank name
Colour: Green

IMPRINT

British American Bank Note Co. Montreal & Ottawa

SIGNATURES

left	right
mss. M. Lang (pro)	engr. Hon. J. Crawford, Jr.

ISSUE DATING

Engraved

July 1st, 1870
2nd Oct. 1871
1st July 1872

OVERPRINT

"MONTREAL" twice in blue
"BELLEVILLE" in red
"BELLEVILLE" twice in red and "THE CONSOLIDATED BANK OF CANADA" in red

STAMP

"A" in black

VARIETIES

$4: two sheet numbers, 4 in round lathework at top left
$4: one sheet number (modified tint), 4 in oval lathework at top left

CIRCULATING NOTES

Cat. No.	Denom.	Date	Variety	G	VG	F	VF	EF	AU
14-02	$4	1870	Two sheet #s	500.	1,000.	1,300.	1,900.	—	—
14-04	$4	1870	One sheet #	500.	1,000.	1,300.	1,900.	—	—
14-04a	$4	1870	One #; town o/p	550.	1,100.	1,450.	2,100.	—	—
14-06	$5	1872		625.	1,250.	1,700.	2,500.	—	—
14-06R	$5	1872	Remainder	—	—	1,000.	1,500.	—	—
14-08	$10	1872		700.	1,400.	1,900.	2,900.	—	—
14-08a	$10	1872	Town o/p	750.	1,500.	2,050.	3,100.	—	—
14-08b	$10	1872	dual o/p	800.	1,600.	2,200.	3,300.	—	—
14-10	$20	1871			No known issued notes				
14-12	$50	1871			No known issued notes				
14-14	$100	1871			No known issued notes				

PROOF NOTES

Cat. No.	Denom.	Date		Unc
14-04P	$4	1870	FACE PROOF	600.
14-06P	$5	1872	FACE PROOF	600.
14-08P	$10	1872	FACE PROOF	600.
14-10P	$20	1871	FACE PROOF	600.
14-12P	$50	1871	FACE PROOF	600.
14-14P	$100	1871	FACE PROOF	600.

THE SAINT FRANCIS BANK

1855

STANSTEAD, PROVINCE OF CANADA

BANK NUMBER 640 ***NONREDEEMABLE***

Intending to have its head office in Stanstead, Canada East, this bank never used its charter and did not operate.

640-10 **TC PRINTINGS**

"MONTREAL" was engraved twice vertically across the note, flanking the central vignette.

DESIGNS AND COLOURS

640-10-02P

$5 Face Design: Seated Indian brave in oval/Queen Victoria (Chalon portrait) in oval on Royal Crest/Prince Consort in oval

Colour: Black with overall red tin

Back Design: Lathework, counters and bank name

Colour: Blue

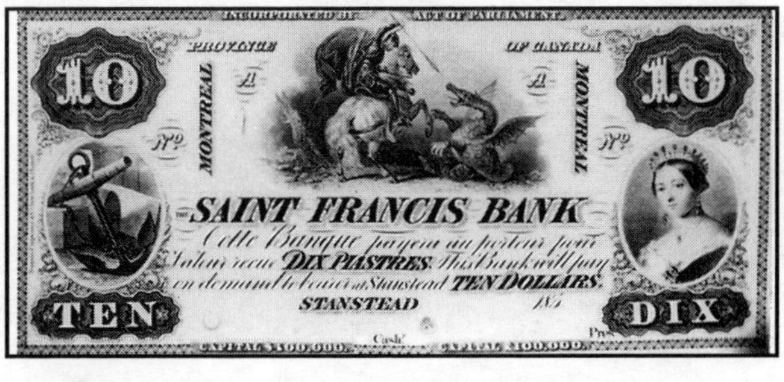

640-10-04P

$10 Face Design: Anchor with box, bale and barrel in oval/St. George slaying the dragon/Queen Victoria in oval

Colour: Black with overall red tint

Back Design: Lathework, counters and bank name

Colour: Blue

IMPRINT
Toppan, Carpenter & Co. New York and Phila.

SIGNATURES

left	right
none	none

ISSUE DATING
Partially engraved ___ 185___:

PROOF NOTES

Cat. No.	Denom.	Date		Unc
10-02P	$5	185_	FACE PROOF	600.
10-04P	$10	185_	FACE PROOF	600.

LA BANQUE DE ST. HYACINTHE

1873-1908

ST. HYACINTHE, QUEBEC

BANK NUMBER 645 ***REDEEMABLE***

Established in St. Hyacinthe, Quebec, this bank was small in size and in operating area. In 1908 the bank's large loans to the Southern Counties Railway became generally known, and this raised doubts about its actual strength. The bank was then obliged to suspend payment pending the result of suits against another company that took over this railway. However, the bank failed in the same year, with about $250,000 of notes still in circulation. They were redeemed, but both the creditors and shareholders lost substantial amounts.

645-10 **ISSUE OF 1874**

DESIGNS AND COLOURS

645-10-02P
$4 Face Design: Farmer with corn stalks/"John Baptist"/ P. Bachand
Colour: Black with green tint

Back Design: Lathework, counters and bank name
Colour: Green

645-10-04P
$5 Face Design: Allegorical female/farmer watering livestock at pump/P. Bachand
Colour: Black with green tint

Back Design: Lathework, counters and bank name
Colour: Green

645-10-06P

$10 Face Design: Shepherd boy/ploughing scene/P. Bachand
Colour: Black with green tint

Back Design: Lathework, counters and bank name
Colour: Green

IMPRINT

British American Bank Note Company

SIGNATURES

left	right
none	none

ISSUE DATING

Engraved

2 Janvier, 1874
2 Jan. 1874

CIRCULATING NOTES

Cat. No.	Denom.	Date	G	VG	F	VF	EF	AU
10-02	$4	1874	No known issued notes					
10-04	$5	1874	No known issued notes					
10-06	$10	1874	No known issued notes					

PROOF NOTES

Cat. No.	Denom.	Date		Unc
10-02P	$4	1874	FACE PROOF	700.
10-04P	$5	1874	FACE PROOF	700.
10-06P	$10	1874	FACE PROOF	700.

645-12 **ISSUES OF 1880 AND 1892**

DESIGNS AND COLOURS

645-12-02

$5 Face Design: Allegorical female/farmer watering livestock at pump/G.C. Dessaulles
Colour: Black with green tint

Back Design: Lathework, counters and bank name
Colour: Green

645-12-04

$10 Face Design: Shepherd boy "John Baptist"/ploughing scene/G.C. Dessaulles
Colour: Black with green tint

Back Design: Lathework, counters and bank name
Colour: Green

645-12-06

$20 Face Design: Shepherdess/Canadian Coat of Arms/allegorical female "Medea"
Colour: Black with yellow-green and green tint

Back Design: Lathework, counters and bank name
Colour: Brown

IMPRINT

1880: British American Bank Note Co. Montreal
1892: Canada Bank Note Co. Montreal and British American Bank Note Company

SIGNATURES

	left	right
1880:	mss. illegible	engr. G.C. Dessaulles
1892:	mss. E.R. Blanchard	engr. G.C. Dessaulles

ISSUE DATING

Engraved

1 Juillet 1880
1 Juil. 1880
2 Janvier 1892

CIRCULATING NOTES

Cat. No.	Denom.	Date	Variety	G	VG	F	VF	EF	Unc
12-02	$5	1880		1,800.	3,600.	—	—	—	7,500.
12-04	$10	1880		—	3,600.	—	—	—	7,500.
12-06	$20	1892		Institutional collection only					
Full sheet	$5,5,5,10	1880	Remainder*	—	—	—	—	10,000.	—

* No signature at left.

PROOF NOTES

Cat. No.	Denom.	Date		Unc
12-02P	$5	1880	FACE PROOF	700.
12-04P	$10	1880	FACE PROOF	700.
12-06P	$20	1892	FACE PROOF	800.

LA BANQUE DE ST. JEAN

1873-1908

ST. JEAN, QUEBEC

BANK NUMBER 650 ***REDEEMABLE***

Established at St. Jean, Quebec, in 1873, this small bank experienced serious exploitation by its president, who was later sentenced to five years in the penitentiary for making false returns. An amount of $162,000 was collected in respect of double liability, and note holders were paid in full when the bank failed in 1908.

650-10 **ISSUES OF 1873 - 1900**

DESIGNS AND COLOURS

650-10-02P
$4 Face Design: Crest over ornate 4/L. Molleur/"John Baptist"
Colour: Black with green tint

Back Design: Lathework, counters and bank name
Colour: Green

650-10-06
$5 Face Design: L. Molleur/factories, workers and ornate 5/ "John Baptist"
Colour: Black with green tint

Back Design: Lathework, counters and bank name
Colour: Green

650-10-10
$10 Face Design: L. Molleur/allegorical women and ornate X/ “John Baptist”
Colour: Black with green tint

Back Design: Lathework, counters and bank name
Colour: Green

IMPRINT

British American Bank Note Co. Montreal

SIGNATURES

	left	right
1873:	mss. J. L’Ecuyer	engr. Louis Molleur fils’
1881:	mss. Ph. Baudouin	engr. Louis Molleur fils’
1900:	mss. P.J. L’Heureux	engr. Louis Molleur

ISSUE DATING

Engraved

1 Septembre 1873
1 Septe 1873
1 Avril 1881
1 Avril 1900

CIRCULATING NOTES

Cat. No.	Denom.	Date	Variety	G	VG	F	VF	EF	AU
10-02	$4	1873		2,000.	3,600.	—	—	—	—
10-04	$5	1873		Institutional collection only					
10-06	$5	1900	cancelled”	—	2,400.	—	—	—	—
10-08	$10	1873		Institutional collection only					
10-10	$10	1881	cancelled”	—	2,400.	—	—	—	—

Note: Some denominations occur with punch cancellations, and are priced as such.

PROOF NOTES

Cat. No.	Denom.	Date		Unc
10-02P	$4	1873	FACE PROOF	600.
10-04P	$5	1873	FACE PROOF	600.
10-08P	$10	1873	FACE PROOF	600.

650-12 ISSUE OF 1906

DESIGNS AND COLOURS

650-12-02
$5 Face Design: Jacques Cartier/factories, workers and ornate 5/shepherd boy “John Baptist”
Colour: Black with green tint

Back Design: Lathework, counters and bank name
Colour: Green

650-12-04
$10 Face Design: Jacques Cartier/allegorical women and ornate X/"John Baptist"
Colour: Black with green tint

Back Design: Lathework, counters and bank name
Colour: Green

IMPRINT

British American Bank Note Co. Montreal

SIGNATURES

left	right
mss. P.J. L’Heureux	engr. P.H. Roy

ISSUE DATING

Engraved

1 Avril 1906

Cat. No.	Denom.	Date	Variety	G	VG	F	VF	EF	AU
12-02	$5	1906		—	3,600.	4,800.	—	—	—
12-04	$10	1906	cancelled*	—	2,400.	—	—	—	—

BANQUE ST. JEAN BAPTISTE

1875

MONTREAL, QUEBEC

BANK NUMBER 655 ***NONREDEEMABLE***

The founders of this bank did not use their charter, and the bank never opened for business.

655-10 DESIGNS OF 1875

DESIGNS AND COLOURS

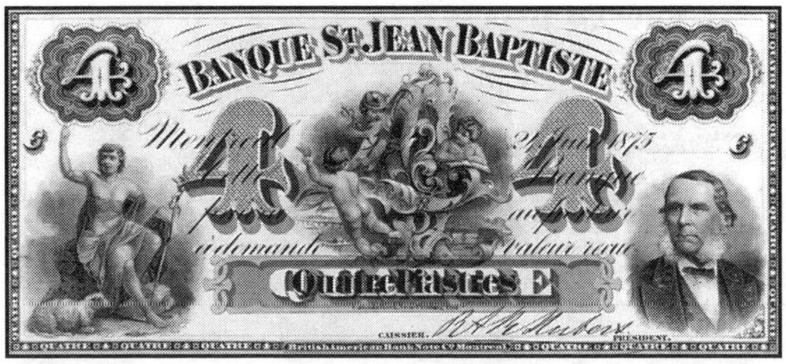

655-10-02P
$4 Face Design: "St. John Baptiste No. 2"/cupids and ornate 4/
R.A.R. Hubert
Colour: Black with green tint

Back Design: Lathework, counters and bank name
Colour: Green

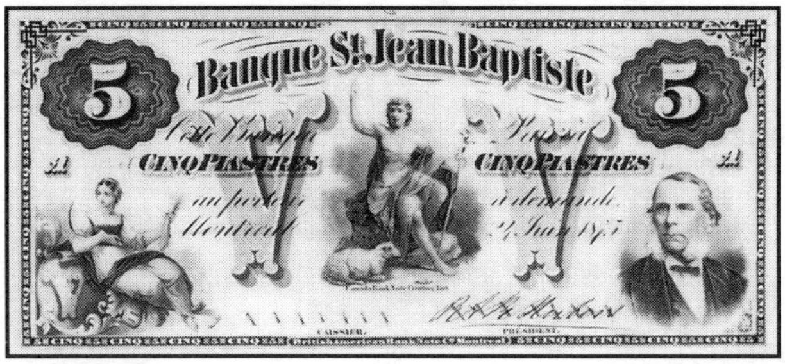

655-10-04P
$5 Face Design: Allegorical female/"St. Jean Baptiste No. 2"/R.A.R. Hubert
Colour: Black with green tint

Back Design: Lathework, counters and bank name
Colour: Green

655-10-06P
$10 Face Design: —/"St. Jean Baptiste No. 2"/R.A.R. Hubert
Colour: Black with green tint

Back Design: Lathework, counters and bank name
Colour: Green

IMPRINT

British American Bank Note Co. Montreal

SIGNATURES

left	right
none	engr. R.A.R. Hubert

ISSUE DATING

Engraved

24 Juin 1875

PROOF NOTES

Cat. No.	Denom.	Date		Unc
10-02P	$4	1875	FACE PROOF	600.
10-04P	$5	1875	FACE PROOF	600.
10-06P	$10	1875	FACE PROOF	600.

THE ST. LAWRENCE BANK

1872-1876

TORONTO (ONTARIO)

BANK NUMBER 660 ***REDEEMABLE***

The charter for the St. Lawrence bank was given Royal assent on June 14, 1872, but when it opened for business in Toronto on March 23, 1873, it became apparent that some bad choices had been made regarding staff and the location of the premises. In addition, the bank's haste in opening other branches in its first year of operation let to early troubles. By June 1874 the bank had 11 agencies in operation, despite the fact that the previous year had seen most banks restricting their loans due to the financial crisis of 1873. The new bank acquired a number of bad risks, and in the latter part of 1874 and the beginning of 1875, Canadian conditions grew worse and the usual dividend was not forthcoming.

At the annual general meeting in June 1875, it was reported that $200,000 was still in arrears on the subscribed stock. At this meeting two directors resigned and a new president, the Honourable Thomas N. Gibbs, who had served as minister of Inland Revenue in the Macdonald Government, was elected to take over from Mr. Fitch, the bank's first president. A new cashier was also engaged. On May 31, 1876, the St. Lawrence Bank changed its name to the Standard Bank of Canada. It was felt the new name would give the bank a fresh start. Permission was granted to reissue St. Lawrence Bank notes until the Standard Bank notes were ready, which took about nine months.

660-10 LOCKHART, FITCH PORTRAIT ISSUE

DESIGNS AND COLOURS

660-10-02P

$4 Face Design: Deer on hillside/oval portrait of K.F. Lockhart/train and ships at dock/—
Colour: Black with green tint

Back Design: Lathework, counters and bank name
Colour: Green

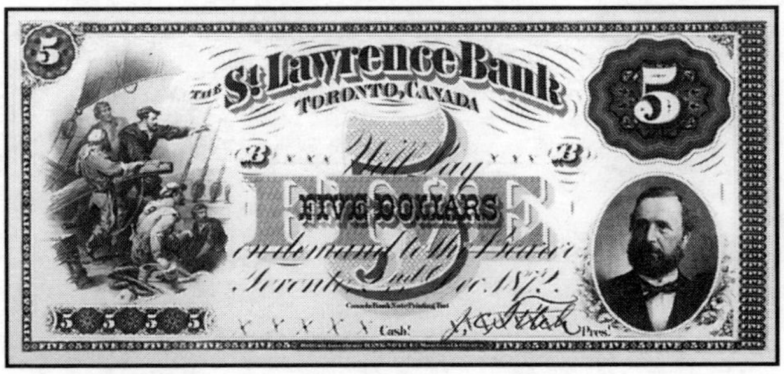

660-10-04P

$5 Face Design: Cartier approaching land "Quebec"/—/ oval portrait of J.C. Fitch
Colour: Black with green tint

Back Design: Unknown
Colour: Unknown

660-10-06P

$10 Face Design: Oval portrait of K.F. Lockhart/ three cherubs and ornate X/ oval portrait of J.C. Fitch
Colour: Black with green tint

Back Design: Lathework, counters and bank name
Colour: Green

IMPRINT

British American Bank Note Co. Montreal & Ottawa

SIGNATURES

left	right
mss. K.F. Lockhart	engr. J.C. Fitch

ISSUE DATING

Engraved

2nd Dec. 1872

PROOF NOTES

Cat. No.	Denom.	Date		Unc
10-02P	$4	1872	FACE PROOF	800.
10-04P	$5	1872	FACE PROOF	800.
10-06P	$10	1872	FACE PROOF	800.

660-12 LOCKHART, FITCH PORTRAITS REMOVED

DESIGNS AND COLOURS

660-12-02P

$4 Face Design: Deer on hillside/train and ships at dock/—
Colour: Black with green tint

Back Design: Lathework, counters and bank name
Colour: Green

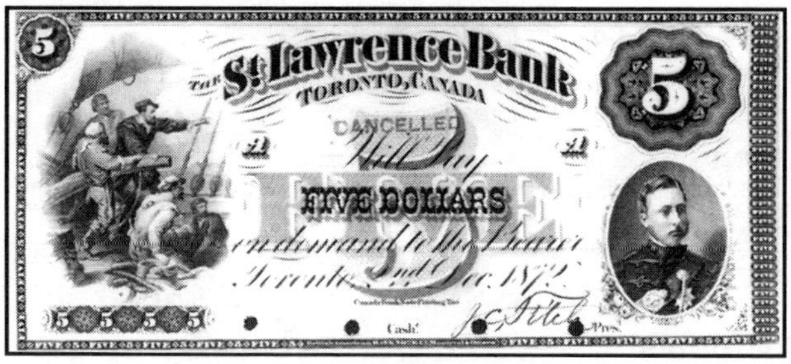

660-12-04P
$5 Face Design: Cartier approaching land “Quebec”/—/oval portrait of Prince Arthur
Colour: Black with green tint

Back Design: Lathework, counters and bank name
Colour: Green

660-12-06P
$10 Face Design: Portrait of allegorical female/three cherubs and ornate X/—
Colour: Black with green tint

Back Design: Lathework, counters and bank name
Colour: Green

IMPRINT
British American Bank Note Co. Montreal & Ottawa

SIGNATURES

left	right
mss. K.F. Lockhart	engr. J.C. Fitch

ISSUE DATING
Engraved
2nd Dec. 1872

PROOF NOTES

Cat. No.	Denom.	Date		Unc
12-02P	$4	1872	FACE PROOF	800.
12-04P	$5	1872	FACE PROOF	800.
12-06P	$10	1872	FACE PROOF	800.

THE ST. LAWRENCE BANK & LUMBER CO.

1837

MALBAY, LOWER CANADA

BANK NUMBER 665 ***NONREDEEMABLE***

This spurious bank was a fraud perpetuated by some rogues from Buffalo during the summer of 1837. Their paper circulated to some extent in the Buffalo area, but not in Canada.

665-10 **ISSUE OF 1837**

DESIGNS AND COLOURS

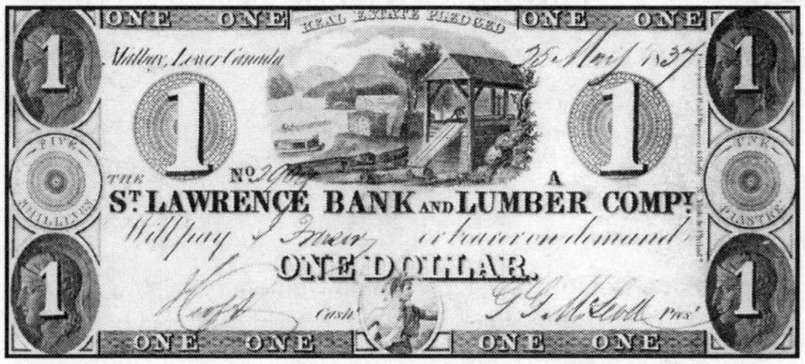

665-10-02

$1 (5s) Face Design: 1 over Roman bust twice/sawmills; Indian pointing at bottom/1 over Roman bust twice

Colour: Black with no tint

Back Design: Plain

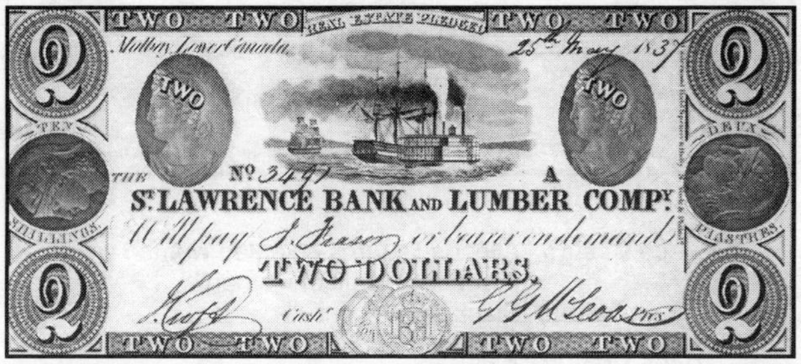

665-10-04

$2 (10s) Face Design: 2 Roman bust (sideways), 2/TWO over Roman bust/steamship St. Lawrence and two sailing ships, two Spanish dollars below/TWO over Roman bust/2, Roman bust (sideways), 2

Colour: Black with no tint

Back Design: Plain

IMPRINT

Underwood, Bald, Spencer & Hufty N. York & Philada

SIGNATURES

left	right
mss. J. Croft	mss. G.G. McLeod

ISSUE DATING

Partially engraved ___ 18___:

1837: 25th May

Cat. No.	Denom.	Date	VG	F	VF	EF	AU	Unc
10-02	$1	1837	—	—	50.	100.	150.	200.
10-04	$2	1837	—	—	50.	100.	150.	200.

ST. STEPHENS JOINT STOCK BANKING COMP'Y

1830's

ST. STEPHEN, NEW BRUNSWICK

BANK NUMBER 670 ***NONREDEEMABLE***

This bank may have been the forerunner of the St. Stephens Bank.

670-10 **DOLLAR ISSUE, 1830s**

DESIGNS AND COLOURS

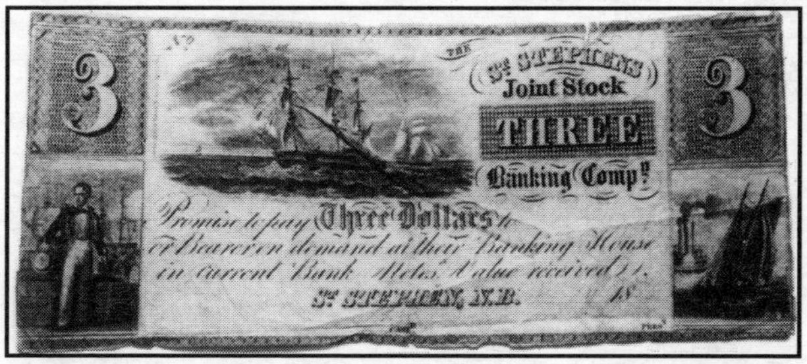

670-10-02

$3 Face Design: Man standing on wharf "Lord Byron"/sailing ships/steamboat and sailboat

Colour: Black with no tint

Back Design: Plain

IMPRINT

New England Bank Note Co. Boston

SIGNATURES

left	right
none	none

ISSUE DATING

Partially engraved ___ 18___:

Cat. No.	Denom.	Date	Variety	G	VG	F	VF	EF	AU
10-02R	$3	18_	Remainder	2,000.	3,500.	—	—	—	—

THE ST. STEPHEN'S BANK

1836-1910

ST. STEPHEN, NEW BRUNSWICK

BANK NUMBER 675 — ***REDEEMABLE***

This bank was established in St. Stephen, New Brunswick, in 1836, with a charter that contained a provision that no shareholder should own more than 20 percent of the capital stock. The bank operated successfully as a small local institution, but found competition with the larger banks difficult. Upon failing in 1910, its assets were sold to the Bank of British North America, and the president of that bank advanced sufficient funds to permit all liabilities to be paid in full, without resorting to the double liability of its shareholders.

675-10 POUNDS ISSUE 1830's

DESIGNS AND COLOURS

675-10-02P

£1 Face Design: Shipbuilding scene/
Royal Crest; harbour scene below/—
Colour: Black with no tint

Back Design: Plain

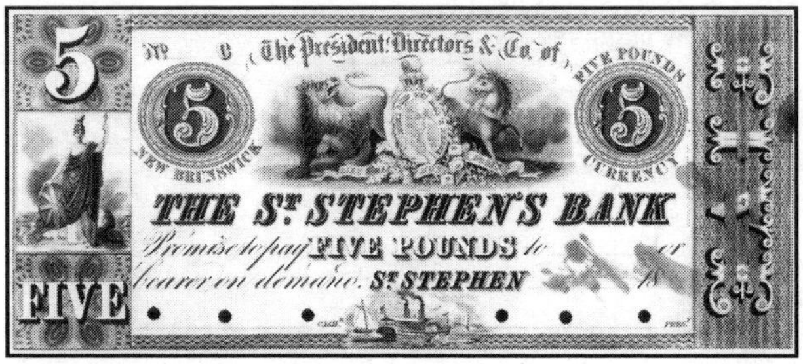

675-10-04P

£5 Face Design: Standing Britannia/
Royal Crest; small ships below/—
Colour: Black with no tint

Back Design: Plain

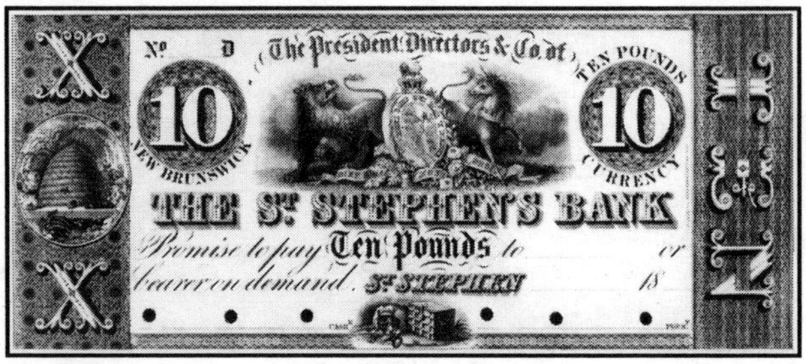

675-10-06P

£10 Face Design: Beehive and flowers/
Royal Crest; dog, key and safe below/—
Colour: Black with no tint

Back Design: Plain

IMPRINT

New England Bank Note Co. Boston

SIGNATURES

left	right
none	none

ISSUE DATING

Partially engraved ___18___:

PROOF NOTES

Cat. No.	Denom.	Date		Unc
10-02P	£1	18_	PROOF	500.
10-04P	£5	18_	PROOF	500.
10-06P	£10	18_	PROOF	500.

675-12 FIRST DOLLAR ISSUE 1830s

DESIGNS AND COLOURS

Photo Not Available

675-12-02P

$1 Face Design: —/ships/seated women
Colour: Black with no tint

Back Design: Plain

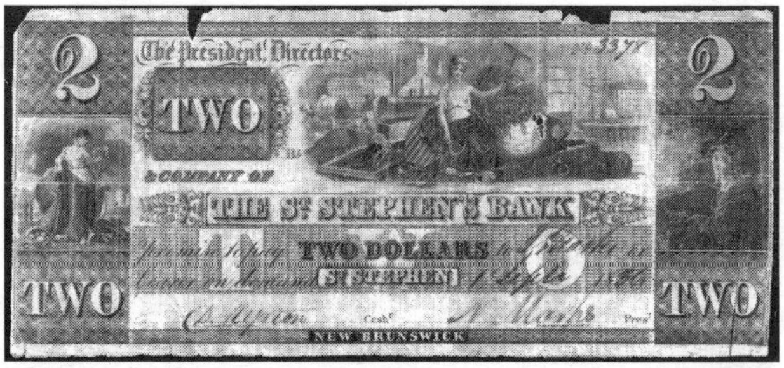

675-12-04

$2 Face Design: Allegorical female/seated woman with produce/portrait of woman
Colour: Black with no tint

Back Design: Plain

IMPRINT

New England Bank Note Co. Boston

SIGNATURES

left	right
mss. D. Upton	mss. N. Marks

ISSUE DATING

Partially engraved ___ 18___:

1836: Sept. 1

CIRCULATING NOTES

Cat. No.	Denom.	Date	G	VG	F	VF	EF	AU
12-02	$1	18__	No known issued notes					
12-04	$2	1836	1,200.	2,000.	—	—	—	—

PROOF NOTES

Cat. No.	Denom.	Date		Unc
12-02P	$1	18__	PROOF	600.

675-14 ORNATE COUNTER ISSUE 1846-1853

DESIGNS AND COLOURS

675-14-02-02
$1 Face Design: Ships, ornate 1/seated Indian woman
Colour: Black with no tint
Back Design: Plain

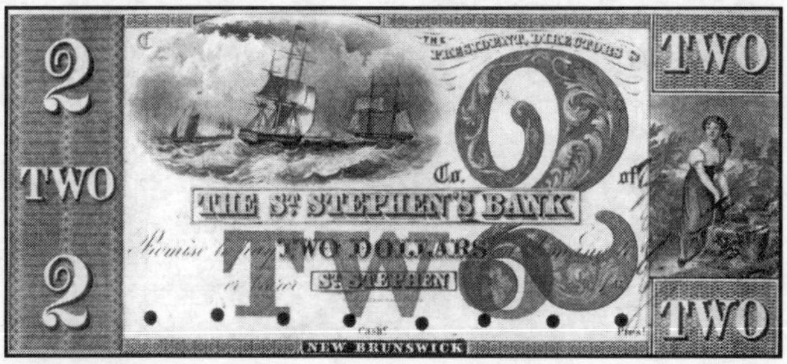

675-14-04-10R
$2 Face Design: Ships/ornate 2/
young woman standing by well
Colour: Black with no tint
Back Design: Plain

Photo Not Available

675-14-02-26P
$3 Face Design: Harvest scene/ornate 3/steamboat
Colour: Black with no tint
Back Design: Plain

IMPRINT
New England Bank Note Company, Boston

SIGNATURES

	left	right
1846:	mss. illegible	mss G.D. King
1853:	none	mss. Wm. Todd
	none	none

ISSUE DATING
Partially engraved ___ 18___:
1846: January 1
1853: Sept. 1

2. NO PROTECTOR

CIRCULATING NOTES

Cat. No.	Denom.	Date	G	VG	F	VF	EF	AU
14-02-02	$1	1846	1,000.	1,700.	—	—	—	—
14-02-16	$2	18_	No known issued notes					
14-02-26	$3	18_	No known issued notes					

PROOF NOTES

Cat. No.	Denom.	Date		Unc
14-02-02P	$1	18__	PROOF	600.
14-02-16P	$2	18__	PROOF	600.
14-02-26P	$3	18__	PROOF	600.

4. RED PROTECTOR

PROTECTOR
Red "word" protector on face and back

Cat. No.	Denom.	Date	Variety	G	VG	F	VF	EF	AU
14-04-02	$1	18__	Red ptr.	No surviving notes known					
14-04-10R	$2	18__	Red ptr.	Institutional collection only					
14-04-16	$3	18__	Red ptr.	No surviving notes known					

* Unsigned, undated and unnumbered.

675-16 BOSTON BANK NOTE CO. PRINTINGS, 1852

DESIGNS AND COLOURS

675-16-04R
$5 Face Design: Tug and sailing ships/two Indians, falls in background; ships below/ farmer holding sheaf and sickle
Colour: Black with no tint

Back Design: Lathework and bank name
Colour: Brown

675-16-08P
$10 Face Design: Indian paddling canoe; spread eagle below/ shipbuilding scene
Colour: Black with no tint

Back Design: Lathework
Colour: Brown

IMPRINT

Boston Bank Note Co. 39 State St.

SIGNATURES

left	right
none	mss. Wm. Todd
none	none

ISSUE DATING

Partially engraved ___ 18___:

Engraved

June 1st, 1852

CIRCULATING NOTES

Cat. No.	Denom.	Date	G	VG	F	VF	EF	AU
16-02	$5	18_		No known issued notes				
16-04R	$5	1852* *		Institutional collection only				
16-06	$10	18_		No known issued notes				
16-08	$10	1852		No known issued notes				

* Unnumbered and unsigned at left.

** Engraved "WILL PAY ___ ON DEMAND TO CHA'S SPRAGUE OR BEARER."

PROOF NOTES

Cat. No.	Denom.	Date		Unc
16-02P	$5	18__	FACE PROOF	600.
16-04P	$5	1852	FACE PROOF	600.
16-06P	$10	18__	FACE PROOF	600.
16-08P	$10	1852	FACE PROOF	600.

CANADIAN FUNDS ISSUES OF 1860-1886

DESIGNS AND COLOURS

675-18-02

$1 Face Design: Wm. Todd/polar bear attacking hunters in boat "The White Bear"/sailor boy holding hat

Colour: Black with green tint

Back Design: See subheadings

Colour: See subheadings

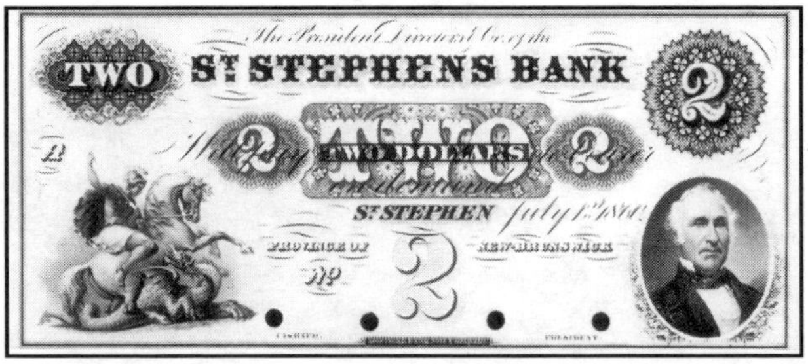

675-18-04P

$2 Face Design: St. George slaying the dragon/—/Wm. Todd

Colour: Black with green tint

Back Design: See subheadings

Colour: See subheadings

675-18-06P

$3 Face Design: Woman writing on tablet, child "History"/Queen Victoria (Winterhalter portrait)/seated Britannia with 3

Colour: Black with green tint

Back Design: See subheadings

Colour: See subheadings

675-18-08P

$5 Face Design: Two sailors on dock "Mech's & Commerce"/lion and shield/portrait of Queen Victoria

Colour: Black with green tint

Back Design: See subheadings
Colour: See subheadings

675-18-10P

$10 Face Design: Beehive and flowers/sailor at ship's rail with horn "The Hail"/Royal Crest
Colour: Black with green tint

Back Design: See subheadings
Colour: See subheadings

675-18 ISSUE OF 1860: PLAIN BACK

DESIGNS AND COLOURS
Back Design: Plain

IMPRINT
American Bank Note Company
American Bank Note Co. New-York

SIGNATURES

left	right
mss. R. Watson	mss. Wm. Todd

ISSUE DATING
Engraved
July 1st 1860.

CIRCULATING NOTES

Cat. No.	Denom.	Date	G	VG	F	VF	EF	AU
18-02	$1	1860	Institutional collection only					
18-04	$2	1860	No known issued notes					
18-06	$3	1860	Institutional collection only					
18-08	$5	1860	No known issued notes					
18-10	$10	1860	No known issued notes					

PROOF NOTES

Cat. No.	Denom.	Date		Unc
18-02P	$1	1860	FACE PROOF	600.
18-04P	$2	1860	FACE PROOF	600.
18-06P	$3	1860	FACE PROOF	600.
18-08P	$5	1860	FACE PROOF	600.
18-10P	$10	1860	FACE PROOF	600.

675-20 ISSUES OF 1860-1886

2. ISSUE OF 1860: GREEN BACK, SMALL RED SHEET NUMBERS

DESIGNS AND COLOURS
$1, $2 and $3 Back Design: Lathework, counters and bank name
$5 and $10 Back Design: Lathework and counters
Colour: Green

IMPRINT
American Bank Note Co. New York

ISSUE DATING
Engraved
July 1 1860.

Note: A $3 note dated July 1, 1860, has been reported with a brown back.

CIRCULATING NOTES

Cat. No.	Denom.	Date	G	VG	F	VF	EF	AU
20-02-02	$1	1860	Institutional collection only					
20-02-04	$2	1860	No surviving notes known					
20-02-06	$3	1860	No surviving notes known					
20-02-08P	$5	1860	No known issued notes					
20-02-10P	$10	1860	No known issued notes					

PROOF NOTES

Cat. No.	Denom.	Date		Unc
20-02-08P	$5	1860	FACE PROOF	600.
20-02-10P	$10	1860	FACE PROOF	600.

4. LATER ISSUES 1873 - 1886 GREEN BACK, LARGE BLUE SHEET NUMBERS

DESIGNS AND COLOURS
These notes are identical to those of subheading 2, except the face tints are slightly modified.

675-20-04-06

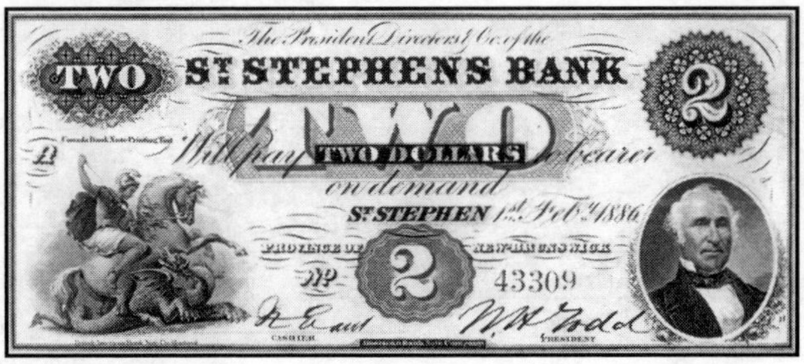

675-20-04-12

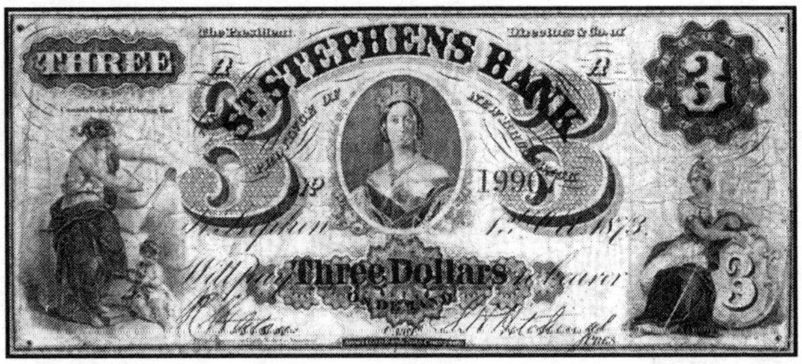

675-20-04-14

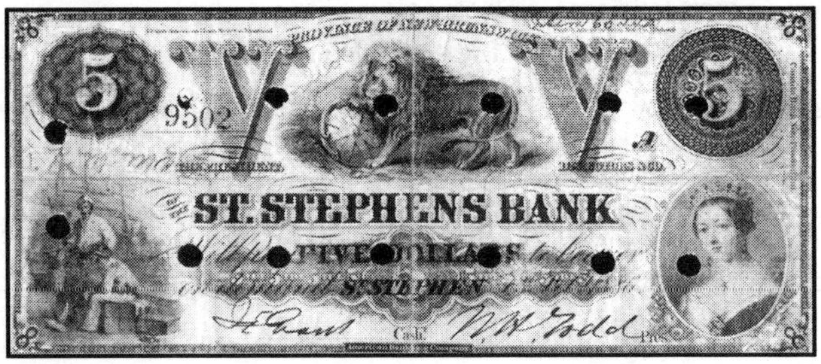

675-20-04-20

IMPRINT

American Bank Note Company
British American Bank Note Co. Montreal

SIGNATURES

	left	right
1873:	mss. R. Watson	engr. S.H. Hitchings
	mss. J.F. Grant	engr. F.H. Todd
1880 and	mss. J.F. Grant	engr. W.H. Todd
1886:	mss. R. Watson	engr. F.H. Todd

ISSUE DATING

Engraved

1st Oct. 1873.
1st March 1880.
1st Feby. 1886.

CIRCULATING NOTES

Cat. No.	Denom.	Date	G	VG	F	VF	EF	AU
20-04-02	$1	1873	900.	1,500.	2,000.	—	—	—
20-04-04	$1	1880	1,000.	1,700.	—	—	—	—
20-04-06	$1	1886	1,000.	1,700.	2,250.	3,000.	4,000.	6,000.
20-04-08	$2	1873	1,500.	2,500.	—	—	—	—
20-04-10	$2	1880	Institutional collection only					
20-04-12	$2	1886	Institutional collection only					
20-04-14	$3	1873	1,000.	1,700.	2,250.	—	—	—
20-04-16	$3	1880	1,000.	1,700.	2,250.	—	—	—
20-04-18	$3	1886	1,100.	1,800.	2,400.	3,200.	4,500.	6,600.
20-04-20	$5	1886	—	2,250.	3,000.	—	—	—
20-04-22	$10	1886	Institutional collection only					

PROOF NOTES

Cat. No.	Denom.	Date		Unc
20-04-02P	$1	1873	FACE PROOF	600.
20-04-08P	$2	1873	FACE PROOF	600.
20-04-14P	$3	1873	FACE PROOF	600.

675-22 "U.S. FUNDS" ISSUES OF 1863

2. BANK OF NEW YORK ISSUE

Engraved: "To the/BANK OF NEW YORK/New York/Pay . . . in Current/funds of the United States."

DESIGNS AND COLOURS

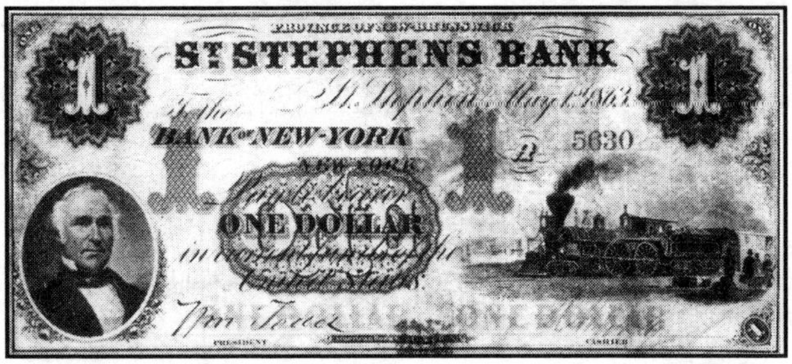

675-22-02-02

$1 Face Design: Wm. Todd/—/train
Colour: Black with green tint

Back Design: Lathework, counters and bank name
Colour: Green

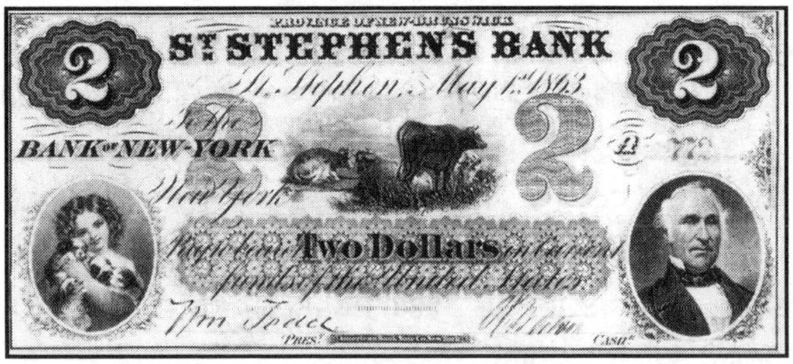

675-22-02-04

$2 Face Design: Girl with puppies/cattle/Wm. Todd
Colour: Black with green tint

Back Design: Lathework, counters and bank name
Colour: Green

675-22-02-06

$3 Face Design: Woodcutters/—/Wm. todd
Colour: Black with green tint

Back Design: Lathework, counters and bank name
Colour: Green

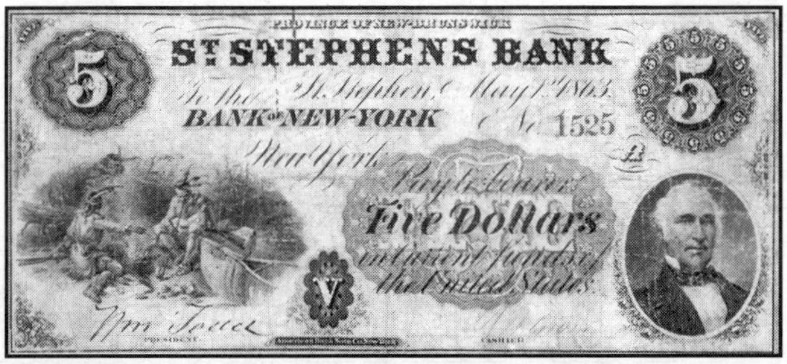

675-22-02-08

$5 Face Design: Three Indians by campfire "Indian Camp" (F.O.C. Darley)/—/Wm. Todd
Colour: Black with green tint

Back Design: Lathework, counters and bank name
Colour: Green

IMPRINT

American Bank Note Co. New York

SIGNATURES

left	**right**
engr. Wm. Todd	mss. R. Watson

ISSUE DATING

Engraved

May 1st 1863

Cat. No.	Denom.	Date	G	VG	F	VF	EF	AU
22-02-02	$1	1863	1,100.	1,800.	2,300.	—	—	—
22-02-04	$2	1863	1,100.	1,800.	2,300.	—	—	—
22-02-06	$3	1863	1,100.	1,800.	2,300.	—	—	—
22-02-08	$5	1863	1,100.	1,800.	2,300.	—	—	—

4. Z. CHIPMAN ISSUE

Engraved:"To/Z. Chipman/St. Stephen, N.B. [or New Brunswick]/ Pay in Current/funds of the United States."

DESIGNS AND COLOURS

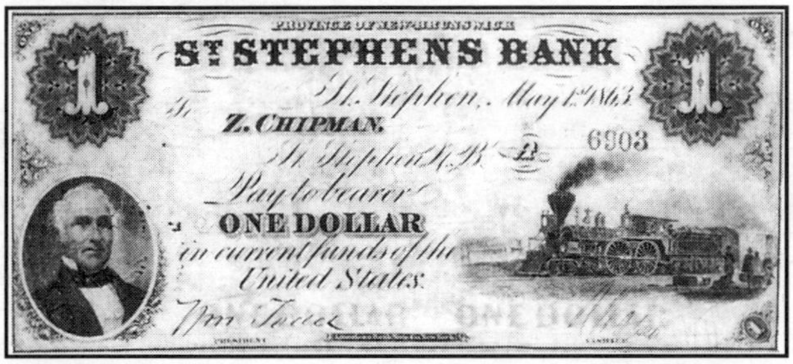

675-22-04-02

$1 Face Design: Wm. Todd/—/train
Colour: Black with no tint

Back Design: Lathework and counters
Colour: Green

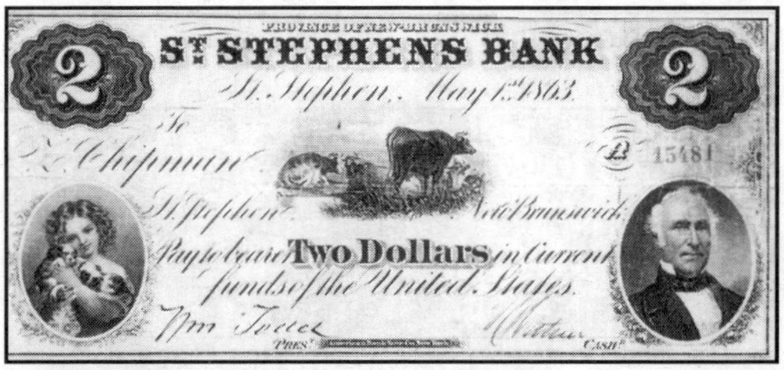

675-22-04-04

$2 Face Design: Girl with puppies/cattle/Wm. Todd
Colour: Black with no tint

Back Design: Lathework and counters
Colour: Green

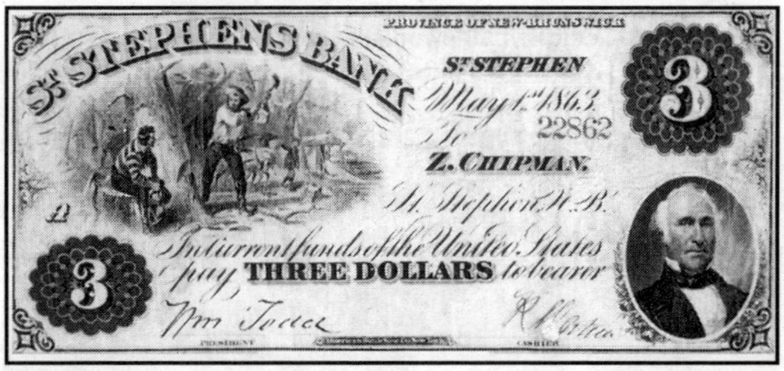

675-22-04-10

$3 Face Design: Woodcutters/—/Wm Todd
Colour: Black with no tint

Back Design: Lathework and counters
Colour: Green

675-22-04-14

$5 Face Design: Three Indians by campfire "Indian Camp" (F.O.C. Darley)/—/Wm. Todd
Colour: Black with no tint

Back Design: Lathework and counters
Colour: Green

IMPRINT

American Bank Note Co. New York

SIGNATURES

left	**right**
engr. Wm. Todd	mss. R. Watson

ISSUE DATING

Engraved

May 1st 1863

Note: Notes exist with small and large sheet numbers.

Cat. No.	Denom.	Date	G	VG	F	VF	EF	AU
22-04-02	$1	1863	850.	1,400.	1,850.	—	—	—
22-04-06	$2	1863	1,100.	1,800.	2,300.	—	—	—
22-04-10	$3	1863	900.	1,500.	2,000.	—	—	—
22-04-14	$5	1863	Institutional collection only					

675-24 ISSUES OF 1892 AND 1903

DESIGNS AND COLOURS

675-24-02

$5 Face Design: Lighthouse and ships "Lighthouse"/ allegorical female "Arts"/train at station
Colour: Black with green tint

Back Design: Lathework and counters
Colour: Green

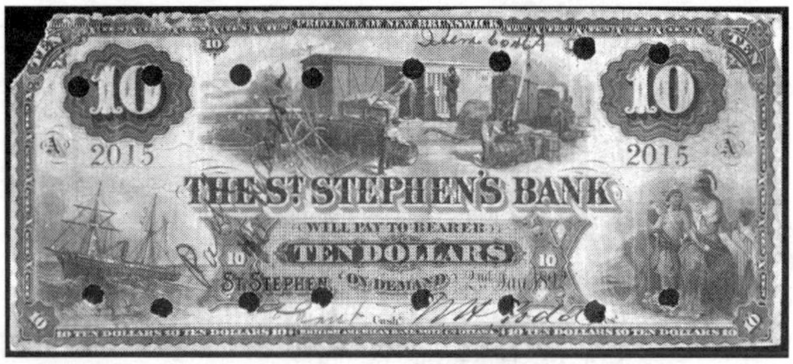

675-24-06

$10 Face Design: Ships "Propeller Brig"/C.P.R. train, men unloading boxcar no. 43 "The Freight Car"/ Britannia and young Indian girl "Protection"
Colour: Black with green tint

Back Design: Lathework and counters
Colour: Green

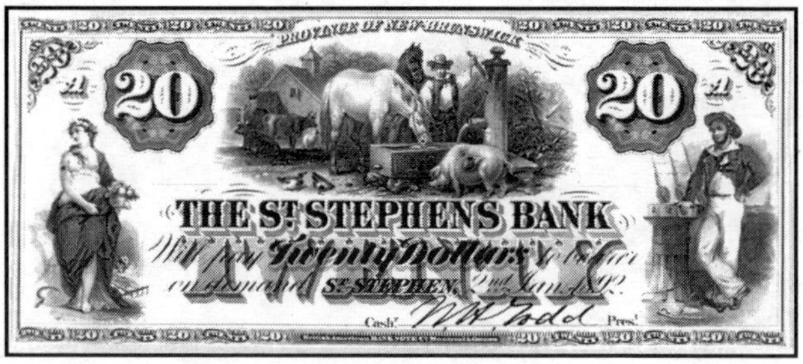

675-24-10

$20 Face Design: Allegorical female/farmer watering livestock at pump/sailor
Colour: Black with green tint

Back Design: Lathework and counters
Colour: Green

IMPRINT

British American Bank Note Company and American Bank Note Company
British American Bank Note Co. Ottawa
British American Bank Note Co. Montreal and Ottawa

SIGNATURES

	left	right
1892:	mss. J.F. Grant	mss. W.H. Todd
	engr. J.F. Grant	engr. W.H. Todd
1903:	mss. J.F. Grant	engr. Frank Todd

ISSUE DATING

Engraved

2nd Jan 1892
2nd Jan 1903

CIRCULATING NOTES

Cat. No.	Denom.	Date	G	VG	F	VF	EF	AU
24-02	$5	1892	—	2,000.	2,500.	—	—	—
24-04	$5	1903	—	2,000.	2,500.	—	—	—
24-06	$10	1892	—	—	2,500.	—	—	—
24-08	$10	1903	Institutional collection only					
24-10	$20	1892	No known issued notes					
24-12	$20	1903	No known issued notes					

PROOF NOTES

Cat. No.	Denom.	Date		Unc
24-02P	$5	1892	FACE PROOF	600.
24-06P	$10	1892	FACE PROOF	600.
24-10P	$20	1892	FACE PROOF	600.
24-14P	$20	1903	FACE PROOF	600.

THE BANK OF SASKATCHEWAN

1913

MOOSE JAW (SASKATCHEWAN)

BANK NUMBER 680 ***NONREDEEMABLE***

It appears that the Bank of Saskatchewan was meant to be established in 1912 or 1913; however, the charter was never used.

680-10 DESIGNS OF 1913

DESIGNS AND COLOURS

680-10-02P

$5 Face Design: —/discing and prairies, train/—
Colour: Black with yellow and dark green tint

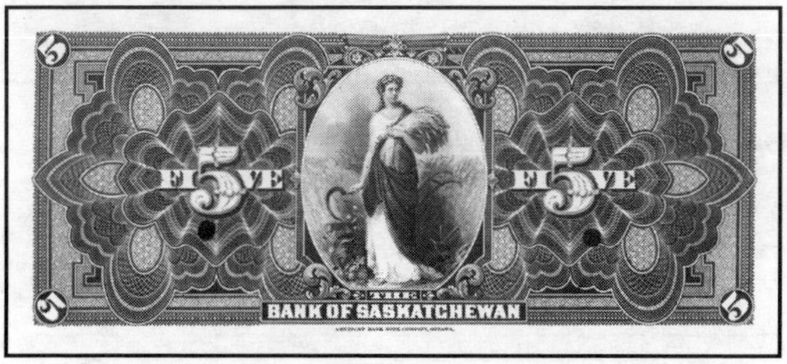

Back Design: Lathework, counters, bank name and allegorical female in hayfield
Colour: Green

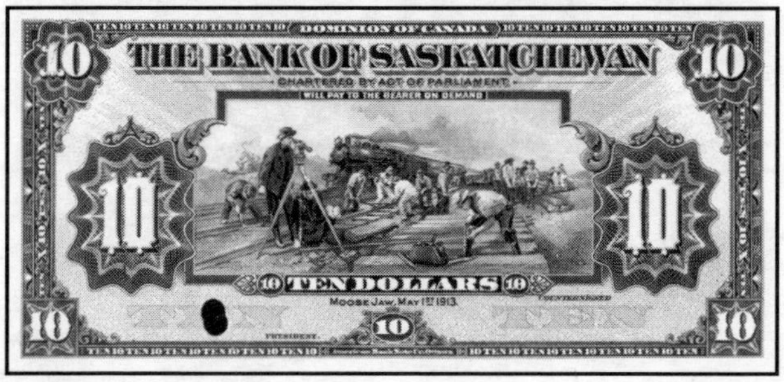

680-10-04P

$10 Face Design: —/railroad construction/—
Colour: Black with brown and yellow tint

Back Design: Counters, Lathework and bank name
Colour: Green

680-10-06P

$20 Face Design: —/train in grain-storage yard/—
Colour: Black with red and yellow tint

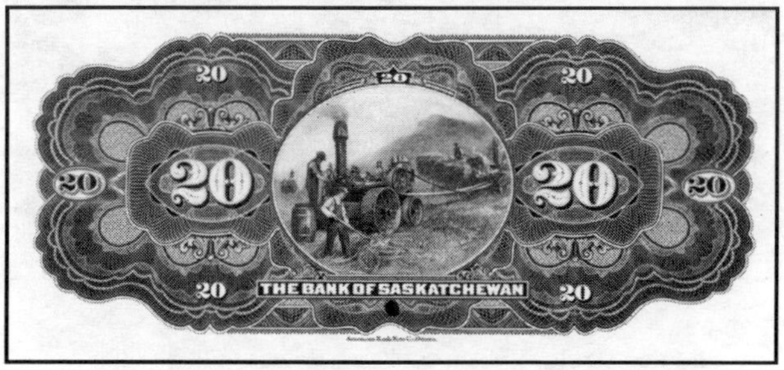

Back Design: Lathework, counters, bank name and threshing scene
Colour: Green

IMPRINT

American Bank Note Co. Ottawa

SIGNATURES

left	right
none	none

ISSUE DATING

Engraved

May 1st 1913.

PROOF NOTES

Cat. No.	Denom.	Date		Unc
10-02P	$5	1913	FACE PROOF	1,000.
10-04P	$10	1913	FACE PROOF	1,000.
10-06P	$20	1913	FACE PROOF	1,000.

Note: Back proofs of the $10 in brown and $20 in orange are known.

THE SOVEREIGN BANK OF CANADA

1901-1908

TORONTO, ONTARIO

BANK NUMBER 685 ***REDEEMABLE***

Established in 1901 in Montreal by Sir Herbert Holt, in collaboration with J.P. Morgan, the Sovereign Bank of Canada had a brief but spectacular existence. In haste its sponsors succeeded in selling enough shares at a premium to give the bank a paid-up capital of $4 million and a reserve of $1,250,000. Branches opened rapidly until there were over eighty. Among the bank's new and aggressive methods to attract business was the paying of quarterly interest on savings accounts. This was a first in Canadian banking history.

However, the bank sacrificed safety and accumulated a substantial number of bad loan accounts in its drive to attain volume. Inevitably confidence in the bank was weakened and subsequently shattered in the financial crisis precipitated by the Knickerbocker Trust failure of 1907. In January 1908 it was arranged that 12 of the major banks would guarantee the liabilities of the Sovereign Bank of Canada and liquidate its affairs. In carrying out the liquidation, each of the guaranteeing banks took over allotted branches of the failed bank. The depositors and other creditors experienced neither loss nor delay. The notes were redeemable at $1.0056 per dollar.

685-10 ISSUES OF 1902-1907

DESIGNS AND COLOURS

685-10-02

$5 Face Design: Bank seal/King Edward VII/—
Colour: Black with green and yellow-green tint

Back Design: Lathework, counters, bank name and Bank Crest
Colour: Black with yellow-brown, green and lilac tint

685-10-08

$10 Face Design: —/Britannia with laurel crown, lion and produce/—
Colour: Black with red-orange and yellow-green tint

Back Design: Lathework, counters, bank name and bank crest
Colour: Black with red-brown, yellow-brown and lilac tint

685-10-12S

$20 Face Design: Bank seal/—/King Edward VII
Colour: Black with green tint

Back Design: Lathework, counters and bank name
Colour: Orange

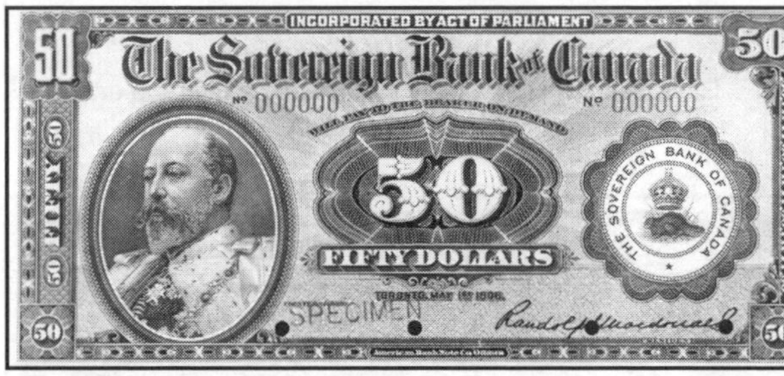

685-10-14S

$50 Face Design: King Edward VII/—/bank seal
Colour: Black with blue and yellow-green tint

Back Design: Lathework, counters, bank name and bank building
Colour: Green

IMPRINT

American Bank Note Co. Ottawa

SIGNATURES

	left	right
1902:	typed H.S. Holt	mss. various
1905 &	typed	mss. various
1906:	Randolph Macdonald	
1907:	typed Aemllus Jarvis	mss. various

ISSUE DATING

Engraved

May 1st 1902
May 1st 1905
May 1st 1906
May 1st 1907

OVERPRINT

1902: Large "M" twice in red

CIRCULATING NOTES

Cat. No.	Denom.	Date	G	VG	F	VF	EF	AU
10-02	$5	1902	—	1,800.	2,400.	3,300.	—	—
10-04	$5	1905	900.	1,900.	2,600.	3,500.	4,500.	—
10-06	$10	1902	No known issued notes					
10-08	$10	1905	—	3,500.	4,500.	7,000.	—	—
10-10	$10	1907	No known issued notes					
10-12	$20	1907	No known issued notes					
10-14	$50	1906	No known issued notes					
10-16	$50	1907	No known issued notes					

PROOF NOTES

Cat. No.	Denom.	Date		Unc
10-06P	$10	1902	FACE PROOF	750.
10-10P	$10	1907	FACE PROOF	750.
10-12P	$20	1907	FACE PROOF	750.
10-14P	$50	1906	FACE PROOF	900.
10-16P	$50	1907	FACE PROOF	900.

SPECIMEN NOTES

Cat. No.	Denom.	Date		Unc
10-06S	$10	1902	SPECIMEN	1,000.
10-10S	$10	1907	SPECIMEN	1,000.
10-12S	$20	1907	SPECIMEN	1,200.
10-14S	$50	1906	SPECIMEN	1,200.
10-16S	$50	1907	SPECIMEN	1,200.

THE STADACONA BANK

1872-1879

QUEBEC CITY, QUEBEC

BANK NUMBER 690 ***NONREDEEMABLE***

This bank was established in Quebec City in 1872. There was a general panic in Canada in the years that followed and a deep depression set in, notably in the timber market. The bank went into voluntary liquidation in 1879. All creditors and shareholders were paid in full.

690-10 **ISSUE OF 1874**

DESIGNS AND COLOURS

690-10-02

$4 Face Design: Sailing ship/crest on ornate 4/A. Joseph

Colour: Black with green tint

Back Design: Lathework, counters and bank name

Colour: Green

690-10-04P

$5 Face Design: Samuel de Champlain/steamboat "Quebec"/ A. Joseph

Colour: Black with green tint

Back Design: Lathework, counters and bank name
Colour: Green

690-10-06P
$6 Face Design: Train rounding curve/—/A. Joseph
Colour: Black with green tint

Back Design: Lathework, counters and bank name
Colour: Green

690-10-08P
$10 Face Design: Jacques Cartier/—/A. Joseph
Colour: Black with green tint

Back Design: Lathework, counters and bank name
Colour: Green

IMPRINT
British American Bank Note Co. Montreal

SIGNATURES

left	right
mss. G. Holt (p)	engr. A. Joseph
mss. Wm. R. Dean	engr. A. Joseph

ISSUE DATING
Engraved
2nd April 1874

OVERPRINT
$4: "E" twice in red
$4: "L" twice in red
$4: "P" twice in red
$4: "ST. SAUVEUR" twice in red
$5: "E" twice in red
$10: "FRASERVILLE" twice in red

CIRCULATING NOTES

Cat. No.	Denom.	Date	G	VG	F	VF	EF	AU
10-02	$4	1874	800.	1,600.	2,250.	—	—	—
10-04	$5	1874	900.	1,800.	—	—	—	—
10-06	$6	1874	No known issued notes					
10-08	$10	1874	900.	1,800.	2,500.	—	—	—

PROOF NOTES

Cat. No.	Denom.	Date		Unc
10-02P	$4	1874	FACE PROOF	600.
10-04P	$5	1874	FACE PROOF	600.
10-06P	$6	1874	FACE PROOF	1,000.
10-08P	$10	1874	FACE PROOF	600.

THE STANDARD BANK OF CANADA

1876-1928

TORONTO, ONTARIO

BANK NUMBER 695 ***REDEEMABLE***

On May 31,1876, the St. Lawrence Bank changed management and became known as the Standard Bank of Canada. Deposits doubled during the next five years of operation, making it possible to establish a small reserve fund. The bank survived another depression from 1896 to 1897, and at the turn of the century, it enjoyed a period of development never before experienced.

By 1907 the assets of the bank reached $20 million, and it was represented by nearly fifty branches. Within another year negotiations had commenced that led to an amalgamation with the Western Bank of Canada, which at that time operated entirely in Ontario. The Standard Bank officially absorbed the Western Bank of Canada in 1909.

In the fall of 1924, the bank amalgamated with the Sterling Bank of Canada and acquired 70 more branches, bringing its total number of offices to 243. Profits for the bank in 1927 were the highest since its inception, with assets reaching $100 million. In 1928 the minister of Finance consented to the union of the Standard Bank of Canada with the Canadian Bank of Commerce on a share for share basis.

695-10 ISSUES OF 1876 AND 1881

DESIGNS AND COLOURS

695-10-02P

$4 Face Design: Hon. Thos. N. Gibbs/train and ships at dockside/—

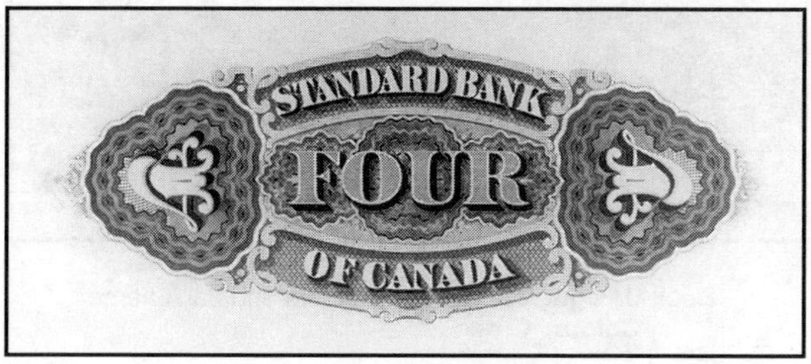

Back Design: Lathework, counters and bank name
Colour: Green

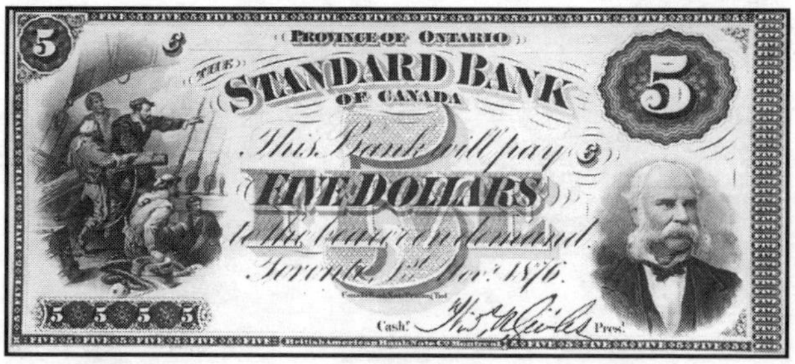

695-10-04P

$5 Face Design: Jacques Cartier approaching land "Quebec"/—/Hon. Thos. N. Gibbs
Colour: Black with green tint

Back Design: Lathework, counters and bank name
Colour: Green

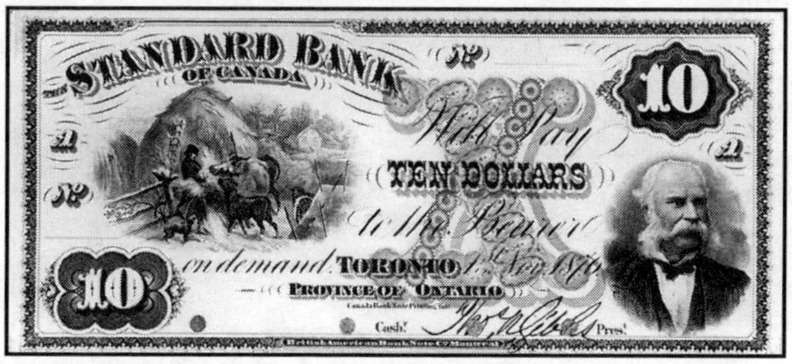

695-10-06P

$10 Face Design: Farmer feeding cattle "Christmas in the fields"/—/Hon. Thos. N. Gibbs
Colour: Black with green tint

Back Design: Lathework, counters and bank name
Colour: Green

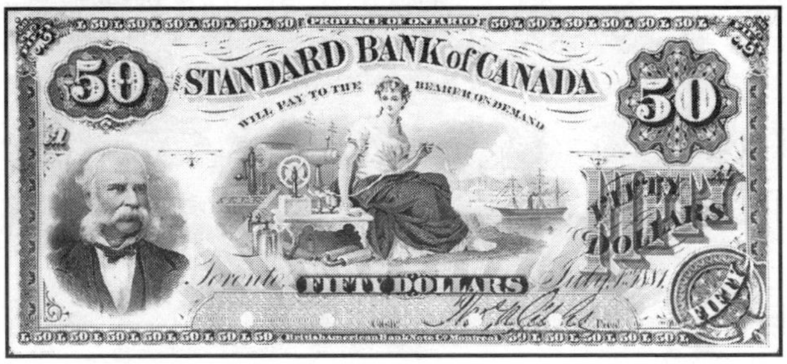

695-10-08P

$50 Face Design: Hon. Thos. N. Gibbs/female operating telegraphic equipment/—
Colour: Black with green tint

Back Design: Lathework, counters and bank name
Colour: Green

IMPRINT

British American Bank Note Co. Montreal

SIGNATURES

left	**rlght**
mss. various	engr. Thos. N. Gibbs

ISSUE DATING

Engraved

1st Nov. 1876
1st Dec. 1881

CIRCULATING NOTES

Cat. No.	Denom.	Date	G	VG	F	VF	EF	AU
10-02	$4	1876	1,800.	3,000.	—	—	—	—
10-04	$5	1876	Institutional collection only					
10-06	$10	1876	Institutional collection only					
10-08	$50	1881	No known issued notes					

PROOF NOTES

Cat. No.	Denom.	Date		Unc
10-02P	$4	1876	FACE PROOF	600.
10-04P	$5	1876	FACE PROOF	600.
10-06P	$10	1876	FACE PROOF	600.
10-08P	$50	1881	FACE PROOF	750.

695-12 ISSUE OF 1890

DESIGNS AND COLOURS

695-12-02

$10 Face Design: Farmer feeding cattle "Christmas in the fields"/—/Hon. Thos. N. Gibbs
Colour: Black with green tint

Back Design: Lathework, counters and bank name
Colour: Green

695-12-04

$50 Face Design: W.F. Cowan/female operating telegraphic equipment/—
Colour: Black with green tint

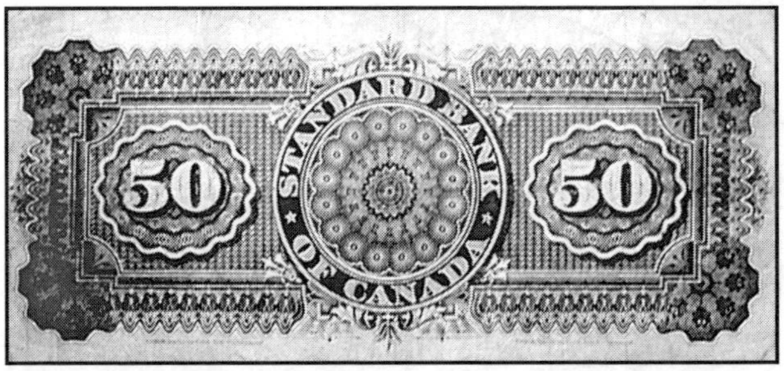

Back Design: Lathework, counters and bank name
Colour: Green

IMPRINT

British American Bank Note Co. Montreal

SIGNATURES

left	**right**
mss. various	engr. W.F. Cowan
typed Houston	engr. W.F. Cowan

ISSUE DATING

Engraved

1st Dec. 1890

Cat. No.	Denom.	Date	Variety	G	VG	F	VF	EF	AU
12-02	$10	1890		Institutional collection only					
12-04	$50	1890	Mss. Sig., l.	2,000.	4,000.	5,000.	6,500.	—	—
12-06	$50	1890	Typed sig., l.	Institutional collection only					

695-14 $5 ISSUE OF 1891

DESIGNS AND COLOURS

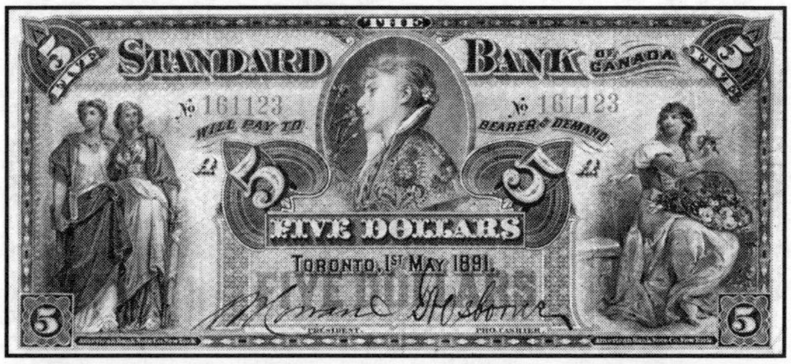

695-14-02

$5 Face Design: Two women/woman smelling flowers, "Innocence"/seated woman with basket of flowers
Colour: See varieties

Back Design: Lathework, counters, bank name, bank crest and "Justice" figure
Colour: See varieties

IMPRINT
American Bank Note Co. New York

SIGNATURES

left	right
engr. W.F. Cowan	mss. various

ISSUE DATING
Engraved
1st May 1891

VARIETIES

Face Colour: Black with yellow and blue tint
Back Colour: Brown

Face Colour: Black with yellow and green tint
Back Colour: Green

Face Colour: Black with yellow and red tint
Back Colour: Green

Face Colour: Black with yellow and red tint
Back Colour: Red

CIRCULATING NOTES

Cat. No.	Denom.	Date	Variety	G	VG	F	VF	EF	AU
14-02	$5	1891	Blue/brown	Institutional collection only					
14-04	$5	1891	Green/green	1,000.	2,000.	—	—	—	—
14-06	$5	1891	Red/green	400.	—	—	—	—	—
14-08	$5	1891	Red/red	200.	400.	750.	1,500.	2,500.	—

PROOF NOTES

Cat. No.	Denom.	Date	Variety		Unc
14-02P	$5	1891	Blue	FACE PROOF	500.
14-04P	$5	1891	Green	FACE PROOF	500.
14-06P	$5	1891	Red	FACE PROOF	500.

SPECIMEN NOTES

Cat. No.	Denom.	Date	Variety		Unc
14-08S	$5	1891	Red/red	SPECIMEN	1,500.

695-16 $10 ISSUE OF 1900

DESIGNS AND COLOURS

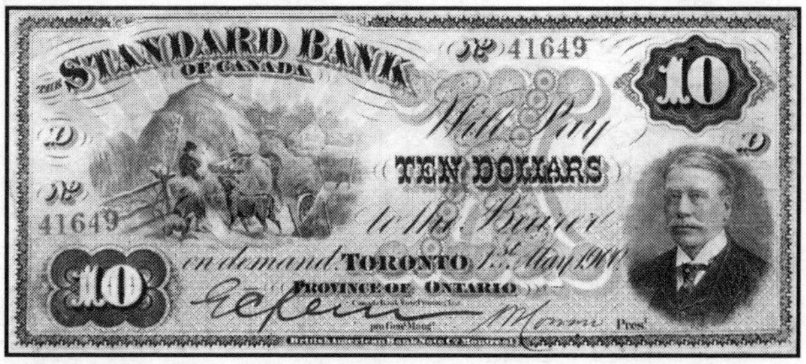

695-16-02

$10 Face Design: Farmer feeding cattle "Christmas in the fields"/—/W.F. Cowan
Colour: Black with gold tint

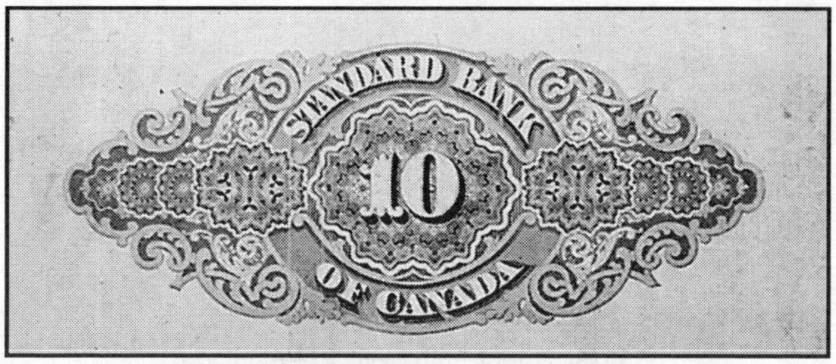

Back Design: Lathework, counters and bank name
Colour: Green

IMPRINT
British American Bank Note Co. Montreal

SIGNATURES

left	right
mss. various	engr. W.F. Cowan

ISSUE DATING
Engraved
1st May 1900

Cat. No.	Denom.	Date	G	VG	F	VF	EF	AU
16-02	$10	1900	300.	600.	1,000.	1,800.	3,000.	—

695-18 ISSUES OF 1914-1919

DESIGNS AND COLOURS

695-18-10

$5 Face Design: —/allegorical woman wearing wreath/—
Colour: Black with orange tint

Bank Design: Lathework, counters, bank name and bank crest
Colour: Green

695-18-22
$10 Face Design: —/W.F. Cowan/—
Colour: Black with olive green tint

Back Design: Lathework, counters, bank name and Bank Crest
Colour: Brown

695-18-32
$20 Face Design: —/two allegorical women, one wearing mantilla, the other wearing a wreath of roses/—
Colour: Black with green tint

Back Design: Lathework, counters, bank name and Bank Crest
Colour: Olive green

695-18-34S
$100 Face Design: —/W.F. Cowan/—
Colour: Black with yellow-brown tint

Back Design: Lathework, counters, bank name and Bank Crest
Colour: Purple-brown

IMPRINT

American Bank Note Company, Ottawa
Canadian Bank Note Company, Limited

SIGNATURES

	left	right
1914:	typed W.F. Cowan	typed George P. Scholfield
	typed W.F. Cowan	typed C.H. Easson
1918:	typed W.F. Cowan	typed C.H. Easson
1919:	typed W. Francis	typed C.H. Easson
	typed W. Francis	typed N.L. McLeod
	typed A.F. White	typed N.L. McLeod

ISSUE DATING

Engraved

2nd January 1914
2nd January 1918
2nd January 1919

Cat. No.	Denom.	Date	Variety	G	VG	F	VF	EF	AU
18-02	$5	1914	Cowan-Schofield	175.	350.	450.	700.	—	—
18-04	$5	1914	Cowan-Easson	200.	400.	600.	—	—	—
18-06	$5	1918		150.	300.	400.	650.	—	—
18-08	$5	1919	Francis-Easson	100.	200.	275.	—	—	—
18-10	$5	1919	Francis-McLeod	75.	150.	200.	325.	—	—
18-12	$5	1919	White-McLeod	60.	125.	175.	275.	400.	800.
18-14	$10	1914	Cowan-Schofield	225.	450.	—	—	—	—
18-16	$10	1914	Cowan-Easson	225.	450.	—	—	—	—
18-18	$10	1918		175.	350.	450.	700.	1,100.	—
18-20	$10	1919	Francis-Easson	125.	250.	350.	550.	950.	—
18-22	$10	1919	Francis-McLeod	125.	250.	350.	550.	—	—
18-24	$20	1914	Cowan-Easson	600.	1,200.	1,600.	—	—	—
18-26	$20	1918		No known issued notes					
18-28	$20	1919	Francis-Easson	350.	700.	950.	1,400.	—	—
18-30	$20	1919	Francis-McLeod	550.	1,100.	—	—	—	—
18-32	$20	1919	White-McLeod	—	450.	700.	1,100.	—	—
18-34	$100	1914	Cowan-Easson	—	—	4,000.	6,000.	—	—
18-36	$100	1918		No known issued notes					

PROOF NOTES

Cat. No.	Denom.	Date		Unc
18-26P	$20	1918	FACE PROOF	500.
18-36P	$100	1918	FACE PROOF	500.

SPECIMEN NOTES

Cat. No.	Denom.	Date		Unc
18-14S	$10	1914	SPECIMEN	800.
18-24S	$20	1914	SPECIMEN	800.
18-34S	$100	1914	SPECIMEN	800.

695-20 ISSUE OF 1924

DESIGNS AND COLOURS

695-20-04

$10 Face Design: "Industry" figure in panel/seated "Britannia No. 2"/"Agriculture" figure in panel

Colour: See varieties

Back Design: Lathework, counters, bank name and Bank Crest

Colour: Green

IMPRINT

British American Bank Note Co. Limited. Ottawa

SIGNATURES

left	right
signed W. Francis	signed N.L. McLeod
signed A.F. White	signed N.L. McLeod

ISSUE DATING

Engraved

2nd January 1924

VARIETIES

Face Colour: Black with yellow-brown tint
Face Colour: Black with yellow-orange tint

CIRCULATING NOTES

Cat. No.	Denom.	Date	Variety	G	VG	F	VF	EF	AU
20-02	$10	1924	Francis, I.	85.	175.	250.	—	—	—
20-04	$10	1924	White, I.	60.	125.	175.	300.	550.	—

PROOF NOTES

Cat. No.	Denom.	Date		Unc
20-02P	$10	1924	FACE PROOF	500.

THE STERLING BANK OF CANADA

1905-1924

TORONTO, ONTARIO

BANK NUMBER 700 ***REDEEMABLE***

The Sterling Bank of Canada received its charter 1905 and opened for business in the summer of 1906. The principal men behind the bank were Gabriel T. Somers, a private banker and grain exporter, and George B. Woods, managing director of the Continental Life Insurance Company. The bank started with a capital of $1 million, but the failure of some smaller banks at the time caused apprehension with regard to the Sterling's strength in competing with larger and stronger institutions.

In 1922 the bank established its own bond division and is noted for introducing a profit-sharing plan for its employees for the first time in Canadian banking history. The failure of the Home Bank of Canada, coupled with a sizable bank robbery, both in 1923, diminished the Sterling's earning power through the loss of deposits to the point where the ability to continue the existing dividend was uncertain.

On November 17, 1924, a meeting was called at which an offer of merger was presented by the Standard Bank of Canada. This merger came into effect on December 31, 1924, on the basis of two shares of Standard stock for every three shares of Sterling stock.

700-10 ISSUE OF 1906

DESIGNS AND COLOURS

700-10-02

$5 Face Design: —/steamships and sailing vessels/—
Colour: Black with green tint

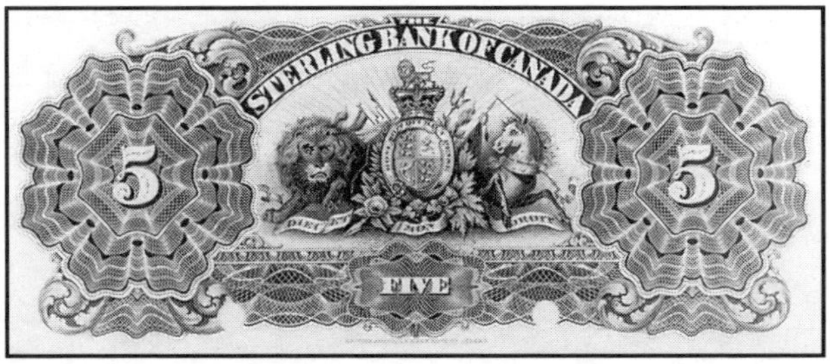

Back Design: Lathework, counters, bank name and Royal Crest
Colour: Green

700-10-04

$10 Face Design: Seated woman holding flag "Exports"/—/—
Colour: Black with yellow and orange-yellow tint

Back Design: Lathework, counters, bank name and seated Britannia
Colour: Green

700-10-06P

$20 Face Design: —/lion and lioness/—
Colour: Black with green tint

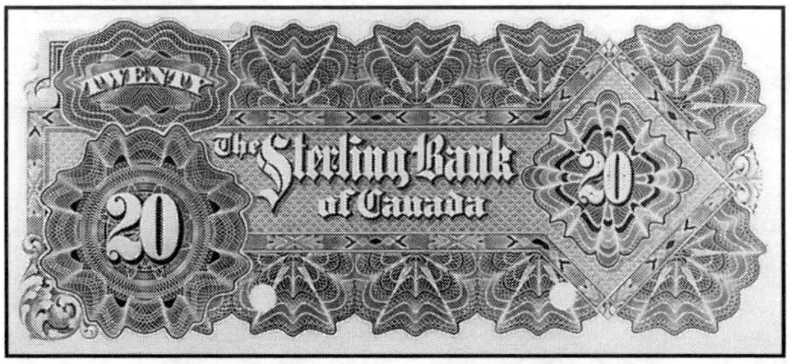

Back Design: Lathework, counters and bank name
Colour: Green

700-10-08P

$50 Face Design: —/Ontario Parliament Buildings, allegorical female with Crest, Niagara Falls/—
Colour: Black with blue tint

Back Design: Lathework, counters and bank name
Colour: Green

IMPRINT

British American Bank Note Co. Ottawa

SIGNATURES

left	**right**
mss. various	engr. G.T. Somers

ISSUE DATING

Engraved

April 25th, 1906

CIRCULATING NOTES

Cat. No.	Denom.	Date	G	VG	F	VF	EF	AU
10-02	$5	1906	500.	1,000.	1,400.	—	—	—
10-04	$10	1906	375.	750.	1,000.	2,000.	3,500.	—
10-06	$20	1906	1,800.	3,000.	4,000.	—	—	—
10-08	$50	1906	No known issued notes					

PROOF NOTES

Cat. No.	Denom.	Date		Unc
10-02P	$5	1906	B & W	500.
10-08P	$50	1906		Institutional collection only

SPECIMEN NOTES

Cat. No.	Denom.	Date	Unc
10-08S	$50	1906	Institutional collection only

700-12 **$5 ISSUE OF 1914**

DESIGNS AND COLOURS

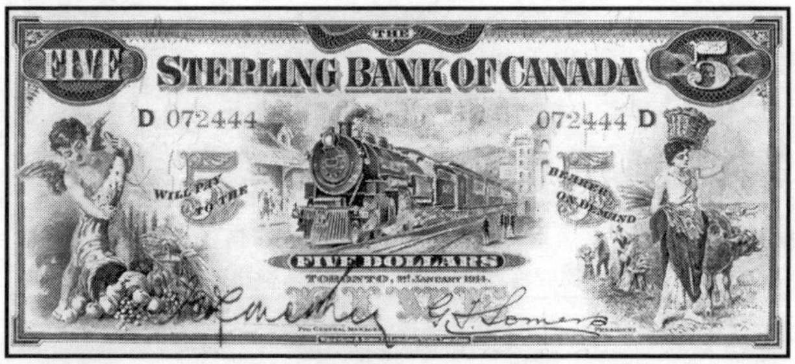

700-12-02

$5 Face Design: Cupid emptying cornucopia/train and station/ farm scene with woman in field carrying basket and sheaf
Colour: Black with overall yellow tint

Back Design: —/Princess Patricia of Connaught/—
Colour: Orange-red

IMPRINT

Waterlow & Sons Ld. London Wall, London

SIGNATURES

left	**right**
mss. various	engr. G.T. Somers

ISSUE DATING

Engraved

1st January 1914

Note: Proofs of the $5 1914 issue are known with yellow face tint and green back tint.

Cat. No.	Denom.	Date	G	VG	F	VF	EF	AU
12-02	$5	1914	375.	750.	1,000.	1,750.	3,000.	4,500.

700-14 **$10 ISSUE OF 1921**

700-14-02

$10 Face Design: Female with anchor/—/ female with cornucopia

Colour: Black with gold tint

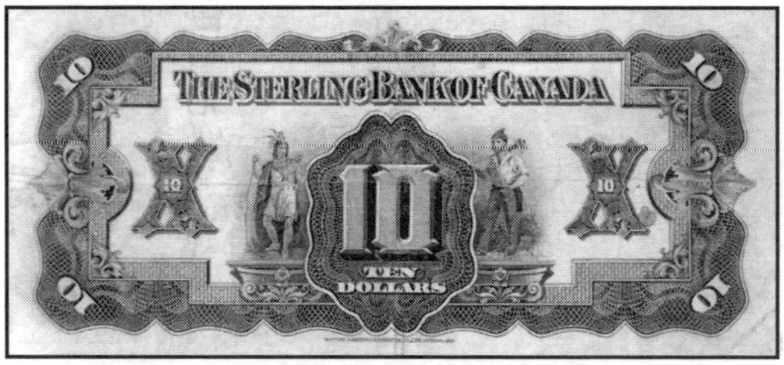

Back Design: Lathework, counters, bank name and Indian and woodsman flanking counter

Colour: Blue

IMPRINT

British American Bank Note Co. Ltd. Ottawa Can.

SIGNATURES

left	right
mss. various	engr. G.T. Somers

ISSUE DATING

Engraved

Jan. 3rd 1921

Cat. No.	Denom.	Date	G	VG	F	VF	EF	AU
14-02	$10	1921	—	1,200.	1,700.	—	—	—

THE SUMMERSIDE BANK OF PRINCE EDWARD ISLAND

1866-1901

SUMMERSIDE, PRINCE EDWARD ISLAND

BANK NUMBER 705 ***REDEEMABLE***

Established in 1866 at Summerside, Prince Edward Island, this institution was a small but successful local bank with capital of $48,667. It was one of the few banks to issue notes of $8 denomination. It expanded but could not meet the competition of other, larger banks and was absorbed by the Bank of New Brunswick in 1901.

Records of the Bank of Canada report only $43 in face value of its issue remains outstanding, but this is believed to be lower than the true amount.

ABNC PRINTINGS 1866-1872

DESIGNS AND COLOURS

705-10-02

$1 (4s 2d) Face Design: Three children with a colt; "Feeding the colt"/farmer watching dairymaid milking cow/boy tending sheep in snow; "Sheep feeding"

Colour: Black with no tint

Back Design: Lathework, counters and bank name

Colour: Brown

705-12-04P

$2 (8s 4d) Face Design: Shipbuilding scene/Royal Crest/ dog and strongbox

Colour: Black with no tint

Back Design: Lathework, counters and bank name

Colour: Brown

Photo Not Available

705-10-06

$4 (16s 8d) Face Design: Sailor with flag and lion at wharf/ paddlewheel steamer/seated Britannia holding shield bearing 4
Colour: Black with no tint

Back Design: Lathework, counters and bank name
Colour: Brown

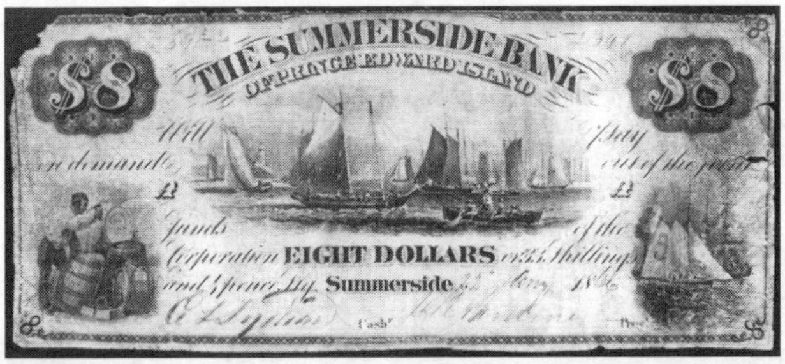

705-10-08

$8 (33s 4d) Face Design: Man with barrels/fishing boats/ two sailing ships, one with 5 on sail
Colour: Black with no tint

Back Design: Lathework, counters and bank name
Colour: Brown

IMPRINT

American Bank Note Co. N.Y. & Boston on face
American Bank Note Co. New York and Boston on back

705-10 ABNC PRINTINGS DOLLARS/STERLING

SIGNATURES

left	right
mss. E.L. Lydiard	mss. J.R. Gardner

ISSUE DATING

Partially engraved ___ 18 ___:

$1 (4s 2d stg), 1866: 2nd April
$8 (33s 4d stg), 1866: 22nd Jany.

CIRCULATING NOTES

Cat. No.	Denom.	Date	G	VG	F	VF	EF	AU
10-02	$1 (4s 2d)	1866	Institutional collection only					
10-04	$2 (8s 4d)	18__	No known issued notes					
10-06	$4 (16s 8d)	1866*	—	9,000.	—	—	—	—
10-08	$8 (33s 4d)	1866	Institutional collection only					

* Only one $4 note of this bank is known to have survived. It has a phony typewritten date.

PROOF NOTES

Cat. No.	Denom. Date		Unc
10-02P	$1 (4s2d) 18__	FACE PROOF	800.
10-04P	$2 (8s4d) 18__	FACE PROOF	800.

705-12 ABNC PRINTINGS DOLLAR ONLY

DESIGNS AND COLOURS

705-12-02a

$1 Face Design: Three children with a colt "Feeding the colt"/ farmer watching dairymaid milking a cow/boy tending sheep in snow "Sheep feeding"
Colour: Black with no tint

Back Design: Lathework, counters and bank name
Colour: Brown

705-12-04

$2 Face Design: Shipbuilding scene/Royal Crest/ dog and strongbox
Colour: Black with no tint

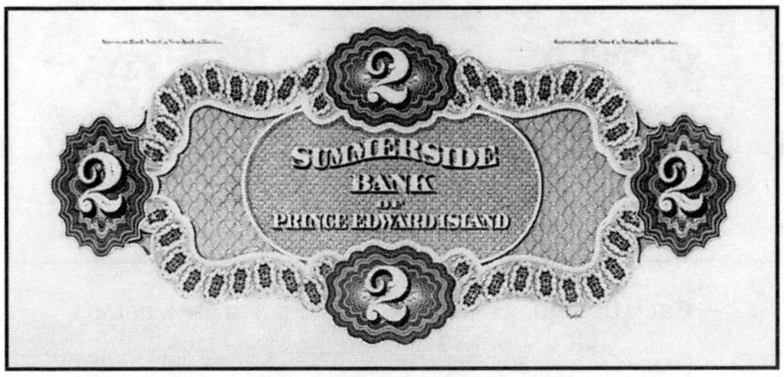

Back Design: Lathework, counters and bank name
Colour: Brown

705-12-06P

$5 Face Design: Sailor with flag, bales and lion/ paddlewheel steamship/ seated Britannia holding shield bearing 5
Colour: Black with no tint

Back Design: Lathework, counters and bank name
Colour: Brown

705-12-08

$10 Face Design: Man with barrels/fishing boats/ two sailing ships, one with 5 on sail
Colour: Black with no tint

Back Design: Lathework, counters and bank name
Colour: Brown

SIGNATURES

left	right
mss. Robt. Mc C. Stavert	mss. Angus McMillan
mss. Robt. Mc C. Stavert	mss. G. Holman

ISSUE DATING
Engraved
Feby. 1st 1872

PROTECTOR
Green "word" and numeral on face only

OVERPRINT
$1: "CANADA CURRENCY" vertically at ends in red

Cat. No.	Denom.	Date	Variety	G	VG	F	VF	EF	AU
12-02	$1	1872	No o/p	2,700.	4,500.	—	—	—	—
12-02a	$1	1872	Red o/p	2,400.	4,000.	7,000.	9,000.	12,000.	—
12-04	$2	1872	No o/p	Institutional collection only					
12-06	$5	1872	No o/p	5,500.	9,000.	—	—	—	—
12-08	$10	1872	No o/p	—	—	9,000.	—	—	—

705-14 BABN PRINTINGS, 1884

DESIGNS AND COLOURS

705-14-02

$1 Face Design: Farm girl with cow and calf, "Alderney"/boy on horse with dog at stream "At the Brook"/sailors, one with telescope at seashore "Looking Out"
Colour: Black with green tint

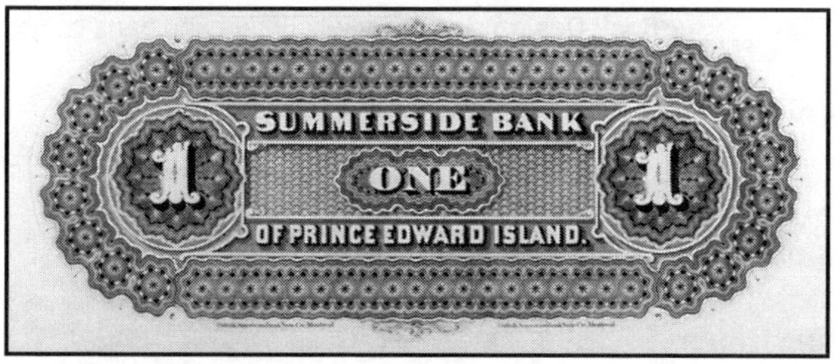

Back Design: See varieties
Colour: See varieties

IMPRINT
British American Bank Note Co. Montreal
British American Bank Note Co. OTTAWA

SIGNATURES

left	right
mss. Robt. Mc C. Stavert	mss. Angus McMillan

ISSUE DATING
Engraved
December 1st 1884

VARIETIES
$1 Back Design: Lathework, counters and bank name
Back Colour: Green
$1 Back Design: Plain

Cat. No.	Denom.	Date	Variety	G	VG	F	VF	EF	AU
14-02	$1	1884	Green back	3,000.	5,000.	8,000.	—	—	—
14-04	$1	1884	Plain back	2,400.	4,000.	7,000.	9,000.	12,500.	—

705-16

BABN PRINTINGS
1891

DESIGNS AND COLOURS

705-16-02P

$5 Face Design: Farm implements/fishermen and ships;"On the Banks"/seated Britannia and shield bearing 5

Colour: Black with green tint

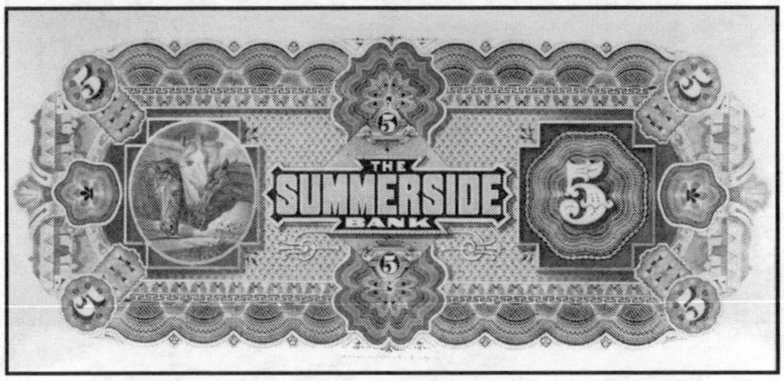

Back Design: Lathework, counters, bank name and heads of three horses at left

Colour: Green

IMPRINT

British American Bank Note Co. Ottawa

SIGNATURES

left	right
none	engr. Angus McMillan

ISSUE DATING

Engraved

July 1st 1891

CIRCULATING NOTES

Cat. No.	Denom.	Date	G	VG	F	VF	EF	AU
16-02	$5	1891	4,000.	7,000.	9,000.	—	—	—

PROOF NOTES

Cat. No.	Denom.	Date		Unc
16-02P	$5	1891	FACE PROOF	900.

705-18

BABN PRINTINGS
1900

DESIGNS AND COLOURS

705-18-02P

$10 Face Design: Seated woman with cornucopia/ grazing sheep/steamships and sailboats

Colour: Black with olive green tint

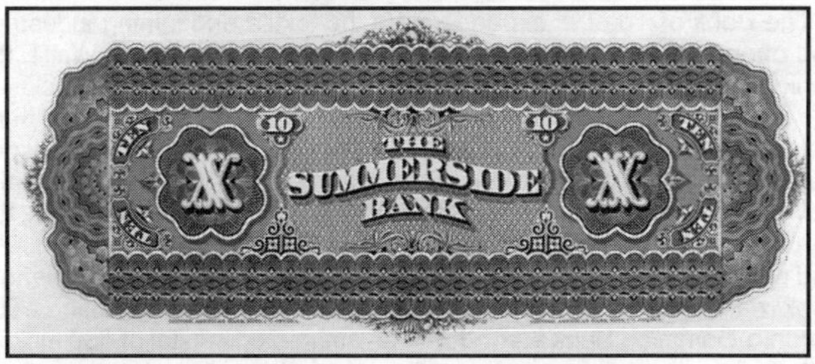

Back Design: Lathework, counters and bank name

Colour: Green

IMPRINT

British American Bank Note Co. Ottawa

SIGNATURES

left	right
none	engr. Angus McMillan

ISSUE DATING

Engraved

Sept. 1st 1900

PROOF NOTES

Cat. No.	Denom.	Date		Unc
18-02P	$10	1900	FACE PROOF	900.

THE BANK OF TORONTO

1855-1954

TORONTO, PROVINCE OF CANADA

BANK NUMBER 715 ***REDEEMABLE***

Toronto was an over-banked city, but for the most part, the rural areas were poorly served. The Millers Association of Canada West, as the bank was known before incorporation, comprised millers, wheat merchants and grain marketers from southern Ontario. They sought to establish a bank with powers to carry on a flour, grain and produce agency, an insurance agency and a banking company. The petition to establish such an institution failed initially, but a charter was finally granted on March 8, 1855, in the name of the Bank of Toronto. It faced difficulties in raising the necessary capital in its first year and did not open its doors to the public until July 8, 1856. Once in operation it completed its first year "with much pleasure" to the shareholders.

The bank was wary of real estate and directed its financing towards the staple industries. From the mid 1850s to the mid 1890s, this policy proved wise in the face of the collapse of the land boom and other national economic failures that saw the demise of some 14 banks.

The Bank of Toronto expanded into the textile and mining industries and opened new branches in other provinces. During World War I, the bank cooperated with the government in raising public loans and closed some of its branches. From 1930 to 1934, the Depression years, the bank was almost at a standstill, but recovered strongly from 1938 on, despite playing its part, as did the other banks, during World War II. Between the end of the war and the amalgamation in 1955 with the Dominion Bank, the bank expanded rapidly. The amalgamation was a "marriage of equals" and was unique in that, of the nine major banks then in operation, neither bank had ever taken over or merged with another institution. The Toronto-Dominion Bank started with an authorized capital of $30 million, with $15 million paid-up, a reserve fund of $30 million, total assets in excess of $1 billion and 450 branches. It is now one of the largest banks in Canada, with operations across Canada and in several other countries.

"PROVINCE OF CANADA" ISSUES OF 1856-1865

DESIGNS AND COLOURS

715-14-02a

$1 Face Design: "Justice" figure/reclining farmer, haying in background; small crest of Toronto below/ Indian seated by ornamental 1
Colour: Black with no tint

Back Design: See subheadings
Colour: See subheadings

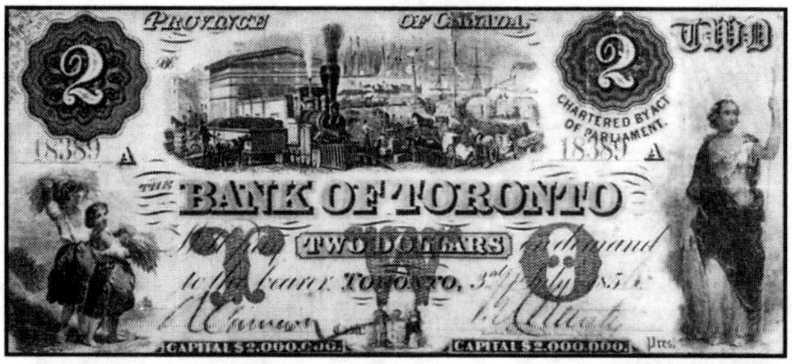

715-10-04

$2 Face Design: Two children with sheaves/train and wagons at wharf; small crest of Toronto below/ allegorical female
Colour: Black with no tint

Back Design: See subheadings
Colour: See subheadings

715-14-06a

$4 Face Design: Man with scythe/three allegorical women; small crest of Toronto below/ Indian chief "Red Jacket"
Colour: Black with no tint

Back Design: See Subheadings
Colour: See Subheadings

715-12-02R

$5 Face Design: Laureated woman/Royal Crest; small crest of Toronto below/ seated "Commerce" figure and 5, (sideways)
Colour: Black with no tint

Back Design: See subheadings
Colour: See subheadings

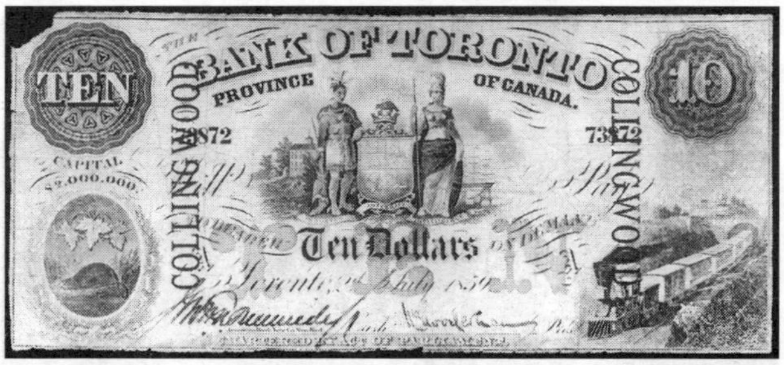

715-14-10a

$10 Face Design: Beaver and maple leaves/ crest of Toronto/train
Colour: Black with no tint

Back Design: See subheadings
Colour: See subheadings

715-10 ISSUE OF 1856 PARTIALLY ENGRAVED DATE ORANGE BACK, "WORD" PROTECTOR

DESIGNS AND COLOURS

Back Design: Lathework, counters, bank name and Medallion engraved portraits of Queen Victoria and Prince Albert
Colour: Orange

IMPRINT
Rawdon, Wright Hatch & Edson, New York

SIGNATURES

left	right
mss. various	mss. J.G. Chewett

ISSUE DATING
Partially engraved 3rd July 185_:
1856

PROTECTOR
Blue "word" on face only
Green "word" on face only

OVERPRINT
"BARRIE"
"PORT HOPE"

CIRCULATING NOTES

Cat. No.	Denom.	Date	Variety	G	VG	F	VF	EF	AU
10-02	$1	1856		550.	1,100.	1,500.	—	—	—
10-02a	$1	1856	Port Hope o/p	Institutional collection only					
10-04	$2	1856		Institutional collection only					
10-06	$4	1856		650.	1,300.	1,800.	—	—	—
10-08	$5	1856		Institutional collection only					
10-10	$10	185_		No known issued notes					

PROOF NOTES

Cat. No.	Denom.	Date		Unc
10-10P	$10	185_	FACE PROOF	750.

715-12 ISSUE OF 1857 PRINTED DATE, ORANGE BACK ROMAN NUMERAL PROTECTOR COBOURG BRANCH

DESIGNS AND COLOURS

Back Design: Lathework, counters, bank name and Medallion engraved portraits of Queen Victoria and Prince Albert
Colour: Orange

IMPRINT
Rawdon, Wright, Hatch & Edson, New York

SIGNATURES

right only
mss. J.G. Chewett

ISSUE DATING
Letterpress
3 Jany, 1857

PROTECTOR
Blue Roman Numeral on face only

OVERPRINT
3rd Jan'y COBOURG, 1857

Cat. No.	Denom.	Date	Variety	G	VG	F	VF	EF	AU
12-02R	$5	1857	Remainder	Institutional collection only					

715-14 ISSUE OF 1859 ENGRAVED DATE, PLAIN BACK "WORD" PROTECTOR

DESIGNS AND COLOURS

Back Design: Plain

IMPRINT
American Bank Note Co. New-York

SIGNATURES

left	right
mss. various	mss. J.G. Chewett
mss. various	mss. Wm. Gooderham
mss. various	mss. Jas. G. Worts

ISSUE DATING
Engraved
July 2nd, 1859
2d July 1859

PROTECTOR
Green "word" on face and back

OVERPRINTS
"BARRIE" twice in blue
"COBOURG" twice in blue
"COLLINGWOOD" twice in blue
"MONTREAL" twice in blue
"PETERBORO" twice in red
"PORT HOPE" twice in blue
"ST. CATHARINES" twice in blue

Cat. No.	Denom.	Date	Variety	G	VG	F	VF	EF	AU
14-02	$1	1859	no o/p	275.	550.	750.	1,100.	—	—
14-02a	$1	1859	town o/p	350.	700.	900.	1,350.	—	—
14-04	$2	1859	no o/p	Institutional collection only					
14-04a	$2	1859	town o/p	500.	1,000.	1,400.	—	—	—
14-06	$4	1859	no o/p	Institutional collection only					
14-06a	$4	1859	town o/p	500.	1,000.	1,400.	—	—	—
14-08	$5	1859	no o/p	500.	1,000.	1,400.	2,100.	—	—
14-10	$10	1859	no o/p	No known issued notes					
14-10a	$10	1859	town o/p	Institutional collection only					

715-16 ISSUE OF 1865
ENGRAVED DATE, PLAIN BACK
"WORD" PROTECTOR

DESIGNS AND COLOURS

Back Design: Plain

IMPRINT

American Bank Note Co. New-York

SIGNATURES

left	right
mss. various	mss. Wm. Gooderham

ISSUE DATING

Engraved

July 3rd, 1865

PROTECTOR

Blue "word" on face and back

Cat. No.	Denom.	Date	G	VG	F	VF	EF	AU
16-02	$5	1865	Institutional collection only					

715-18 DOMINION OF CANADA
ISSUE OF 1876

DESIGNS AND COLOURS

715-18-02

$4 Face Design: J.G. Worts/allegorical female and two children/Wm. Gooderham
Colour: Black with green and pink tint

Back Design: Plain

IMPRINT

American Bank Note Co. New York

SIGNATURES

left	right
mss. various	mss. Wm. Gooderham

ISSUE DATING

Engraved

1st January 1876

OVERPRINTS

"COLLINGWOOD" twice in blue
"ST. CATHARINES" twice in blue

CIRCULATING NOTES

Cat. No.	Denom.	Date	Variety	G	VG	F	VF	EF	AU
18-02	$4	1876	no o/p	Institutional collection only					
18-02a	$4	1876	town o/p	650.	1,300.	1,800.	—	—	—

PROOF NOTES

Cat. No.	Denom.	Date		Unc
18-02P	$4	1876	FACE PROOF	500.

715-20 DOMINION OF CANADA
ISSUE OF 1880

DESIGNS AND COLOURS

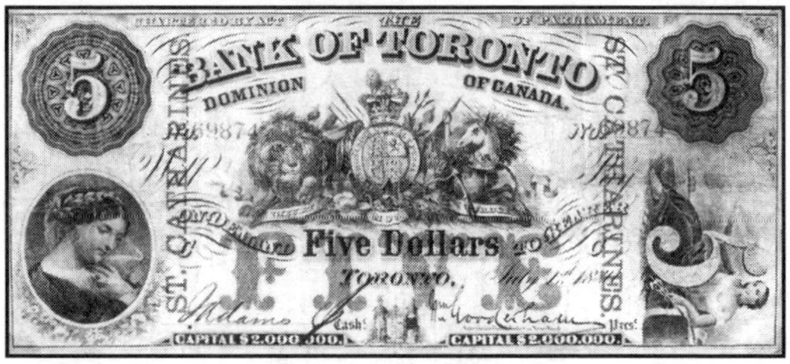

715-20-02a

$5 Face Design: Woman with laureate/ Royal Crest; small crest of Toronto below/ seated "Commerce" figure and 5 (sideways)
Colour: Black with no tint

Back Design: Lathework, counters, bank name and Medallion engraved portraits of Queen Victoria and Prince Albert
Colour: Blue

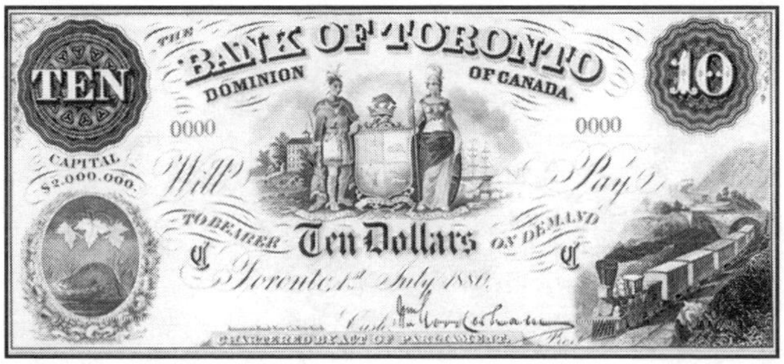

715-20-04P

$10 Face Design: Beaver and maple leaves/ crest of Toronto/train
Colour: Black with no tint

Back Design: Lathework, counters, bank name and Medallion engraved portraits of Queen Victoria and Prince Albert
Colour: Blue

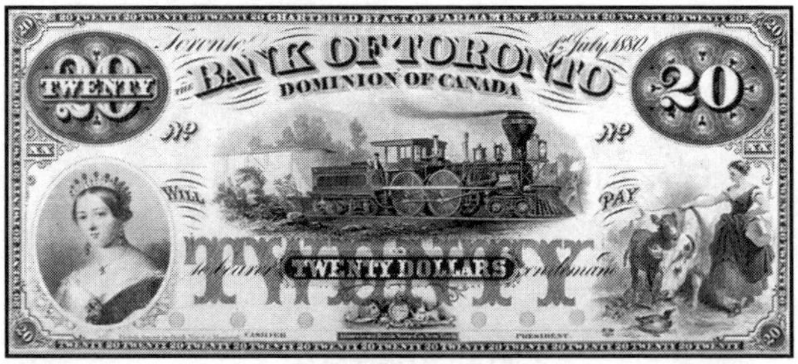

715-20-06P

$20 Face Design: Portrait of Queen Victoria/train; small crest below/milkmaid standing beside cow and calf
Colour: Black with no tint

Back Design: Lathework, counters, bank name and Medallion engraved portraits of Queen Victoria and Prince Albert
Colour: Blue

IMPRINT
American Bank Note Co. New York
British American Bank Note Co. Montreal

SIGNATURES

left	right
mss. J. Adams (p)	engr. Wm. Gooderham
mss. various	engr. Wm. Gooderham

ISSUE DATING
Engraved
July 1st 1880
1st July 1880

PROTECTOR
Green "word" on face only

OVERPRINTS
"ST. CATHARINES" twice in blue

CIRCULATING NOTES

Cat. No.	Denom.	Date	Variety	G	VG	F	VF	EF	AU
20-02	$5	1880	no o/p		No known issued notes				
20-02a	$5	1880	town o/p		Institutional collection only				
20-04	$10	1880			No known issued notes				
20-06	$20	1880			No known issued notes				

PROOF NOTES

Cat. No.	Denom.	Date		Unc
20-02P	$5	1880	FACE PROOF	600.
20-04P	$10	1880	FACE PROOF	700.
20-06P	$20	1880	FACE PROOF	700.
Full sheet	$5,$5,$5,$5, 1880		FACE PROOF	3,000.

SPECIMEN NOTES

Cat. No.	Denom.	Date		Unc
20-02S	$5	1880	SPECIMEN	600.
20-04S	$10	1880	SPECIMEN	600.

715-22

YELLOW ISSUES OF 1887-1929

DESIGNS AND COLOURS

715-22-02a
$5 Face Design: Woman with laureate/Royal Crest; small crest of Toronto below/seated "Commerce" figure and 5 (sideways)
Colour: Black with yellow tint
Back Design: Lathework, counters, bank name and Medallion engraved portraits of Queen Victoria and Prince Albert
Colour: Orange

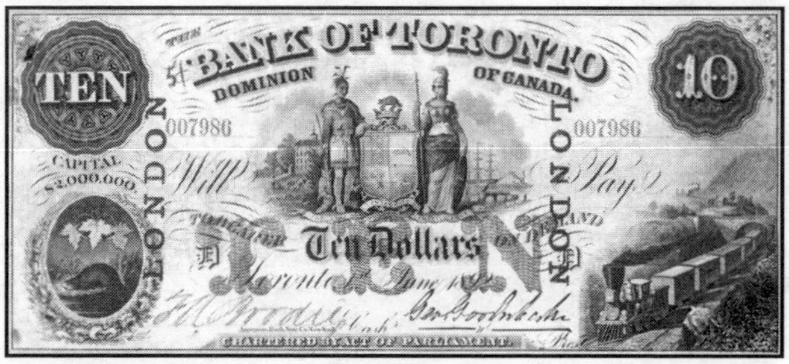

715-22-26a
$10 Face Design: Beaver and maple leaves/crest of Toronto/train
Colour: Black with yellow tint
Back Design: Lathework, counters, bank name and Medallion engraved portraits of Queen Victoria and Prince Albert
Colour: Orange

715-22-58
$20 Face Design: Queen Victoria/train; small crest below/milkmaid standing beside cow and calf
Colour: Black with yellow tint
Back Design: Lathework, counters, bank name and Medallion engraved portraits of Queen Victoria and Prince Albert
Colour: Orange

715-22-76

$50 Face Design: Bull's head/City Hall/herd of cattle
Colour: Black with yellow tint

Back Design: Lathework, counters, bank name and Medallion engraved portraits of Queen Victoria and Prince Albert
Colour: Orange

IMPRINT

American Bank Note Co. New York
Canadian Bank Note Company Limited
American Bank Note Co. Ottawa

SIGNATURES

	left	right
1887-1892:	mss. various	engr. Geo. Gooderham
	mss. J.A. Adams	engr. Geo. Gooderham
1906:	mss. various	engr. W.H. Beatty
1911-1914:	mss. various	typed D. Coulson
1917:	mss. various	typed.W.G. Gooderham
	typed Jno. R. Lamb	typed W.G. Gooderham
1920:	mss. various	typed W.G. Gooderham
	typed Jno. R. Lamb	typed W.G. Gooderham
	typed H.B. Henwood	typed W.G. Gooderham
1923:	mss various	typed W.G. Gooderham
	typed Jno. R. Lamb	typed W.G. Gooderham
	typed H.B. Henwood	typed W.G. Gooderham
1929:	typed H.B. Henwood	typed W.G. Gooderham

ISSUE DATING

Engraved

July 1st 1887	1st Feby 1913
1st July 1887	Feb 1 1914
1st July 1890	2nd February 1914
July 1st, 1890	2nd Feb'y 1914
1st June 1892	1st February 1917
1st June 1902	1st Feb. 1917
1st Feb'y 1906	2nd Feb'y 1920
1st February 1906	1st February 1923
1st February 1911	1st Feb'y 1923
Feb 1, 1911	1st October 1929
1st February 1912	1st Oct. 1929
1st Feb'y 1912	Feb 2 1913

PROTECTOR

Green "word" on face only

OVERPRINTS

Issue of 1887:

"LONDON" twice in blue
"LONDON" and "F" twice in blue
"PARRY SOUND" twice in blue
"POINT ST. CHARLES" twice in blue
"WINNIPEG" twice in blue

Issue of 1890:

"BRANTFORD" twice in blue
"CARDINAL" twice in blue
"COLDWATER" twice in blue
"CREEMORE" twice in blue
"ELMVALE" twice in blue
"GANANOQUE" twice in blue
"KEENE" twice in blue
"LONDON" twice in blue
"MILLBROOK" twice in blue
"MONTREAL" twice in blue
"NIAGARA FALLS CENTRE" twice in blue
"OIL SPRINGS" twice in blue
"OMEMEE" twice in blue
"PETERBORO" twice in blue
"POINT ST. CHARLES" twice in blue
"PORT HOPE" twice in blue
"ST. CATHARINES" twice in blue
"SUDBURY" twice in blue
"VICTORIA HARBOUR" twice in blue
"WINNIPEG" twice in blue

Issue of 1892:

"CARTWRIGHT" twice in blue
"COPPER CLIFF" twice in blue
"KING ST. WEST BR." twice in blue
"LONDON" twice in blue

Issue of 1906:

"GASPE" twice in blue
"POINT ST. CHARLES" twice in blue
"ST. CATHARINES" twice in blue
"WATERLOO" twice in blue

CIRCULATING NOTES

Cat. No.	Denom.	Date	Variety	G	VG	F	VF	EF	AU
22-01	$5	1887		No known issued notes					
22-02a	$5	1890	town o/p	500.	1,000.	1,500.	2,200.	—	—
22-06	$5	1906		150.	300.	450.	700.	—	—
22-06a	$5	1906	town o/p	750.	1,500.	2,100.	—	—	—
22-08	$5	1911		250.	500.	700.	1, 000.	—	—
22-10	$5	1912		85.	175.	250.	375.	650.	—
22-12	$5	1914		100.	200.	300.	450.	—	—
22-14	$5	1917	Mss. signature, l.	40.	80.	125.	200.	375.	550.
22-16	$5	1917	Typed Lamb, l.	40.	80.	125.	200.	375.	550.
22-18	$5	1923	Typed Lamb,l.	30.	60.	90.	175.	275.	400.
22-20	$5	1923	Typed Henwood,l.	30.	60.	90.	175.	275.	400.
22-22	$5	1929		30.	60.	90.	175.	275.	400.
22-24a	$10	1887	LONDON o/p	600.	1,200.	1,800.	—	—	—
22-26a	$10	1892	LONDON o/p	500.	1,000.	1,500.	2,200.	—	—
22-26b	$10	1892	other town o/p	600.	1,200.	1,800.	—	—	—
22-27	$10	1902		300.	600.	900.	—	—	—
22-28	$10	1906		300.	600.	900.	—	—	—
22-28a	$10	1906	town o/p	800.	1,600.	2,200.	—	—	—
22-30	$10	1911		300.	600.	900.	—	—	—
22-32	$10	1912		125.	250.	375.	—	—	—
22-34	$10	1914		100.	200.	300.	450.	750.	—
22-36	$10	1917	Mss. sign., l.	45.	90.	135.	225.	400.	600.
22-38	$10	1917	Typed Lamb, l.	45.	90.	135.	225.	400.	600.
22-39	$10	1923	mss. sign,.l.	45.	90.	135.	225.	400.	600.
22-40	$10	1923	Typed Lamb, l.	45.	90.	135.	225.	400.	600.
22-42	$10	1923	Typed Henwood, l.	45.	90.	135.	225.	400.	600.
22-44	$10	1929		35.	70.	100.	175.	300.	450.
22-46a	$20	1887	town o/p	900.	1,800.	2,500.	—	—	—
22-48	$20	1906		300.	600.	900.	—	—	—
22-50	$20	1913		300.	600.	900.	—	—	—
22-52	$20	1914		No known issued notes					
22-54	$20	1917	Mss. signature, l.	100.	200.	300.	450.	700.	—
22-56	$20	1917	Typed Lamb, l.	100.	200.	300.	450.	700.	—
22-58	$20	1923	Typed Lamb, l.	110.	225.	350.	480.	750.	1,000.
22-60	$20	1923	Typed Henwood, l.	100.	200.	300.	450.	700.	950.
22-62	$20	1929		100.	200.	275.	400.	600.	800.
22-64	$50	1890		No known issued notes					
22-66	$50	1906		550.	1,100.	1,600.	—	—	—
22-68	$50	1913		No known issued notes					
22-70	$50	1914		550.	1,100.	1,600.	—	—	—
22-72	$50	1920	Mss. signature, l.	275.	550.	750.	1,150.	—	—
22-74	$50	1920	Typed Lamb, l.	275.	550.	750.	1,150.	—	—
22-76	$50	1920	Typed Henwood, l.	250.	500.	700.	1,050.	1,800.	—
22-78	$50	1929		300.	600.	850.	—	—	—

PROOF NOTES

Cat. No.	Denom.	Date	Variety		Unc
22-01P	$5	1887		FACE PROOF	400.
22-02P	$5	1890		FACE PROOF	250.
22-06P	$5	1906	B & W	FACE PROOF	200.
22-10P	$5	1912	B & W	FACE PROOF	200.
22-24P	$10	1887		FACE PROOF	400.
22-26P	$10	1892	B & W	FACE PROOF	250.
22-26Pa	$10	1892	Coloured	FACE PROOF	350.
22-28P	$10	1906	B & W	FACE PROOF	250.
22-30P	$10	1911		FACE PROOF	400.
22-32P	$10	1912		FACE PROOF	350.
22-46P	$20	1887	B & W	FACE PROOF	250.
22-46Pa	$20	1887	Coloured	FACE PROOF	400.
22-52P	$20	1914		FACE PROOF	400.
22-64P	$50	1890	B & W	FACE PROOF	300.
22-64Pa	$50	1890	Coloured	FACE PROOF	450.
22-68P	$50	1913		FACE PROOF	450.

SPECIMEN NOTES

Cat. No.	Denom.	Date		Unc
22-24S	$10	1887	SPECIMEN	600.
22-46S	$20	1887	SPECIMEN	700.
22-64S	$50	1890	SPECIMEN	800.

715-24 SMALL-SIZE ISSUES OF 1935 AND 1937

DESIGNS AND COLOURS

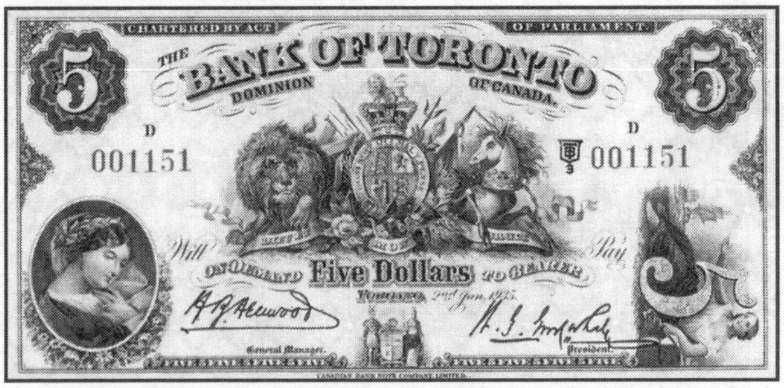

715-24-02

$5 Face Design: Woman with laureate/Royal Crest/ seated “Commerce” figure and 5 (sideways)
Colour: Black with yellow tint

Back Design: Lathework, counters, bank name and Medallion engraved portraits of Queen Victoria and Prince Albert
Colour: Orange

715-24-08

$10 Face Design: Beaver and maple leaves/ crest of Toronto/train
Colour: Black with yellow tint

Back Design: Lathework, counters, bank name and Medallion engraved portraits of Queen Victoria and Prince Albert
Colour: Orange

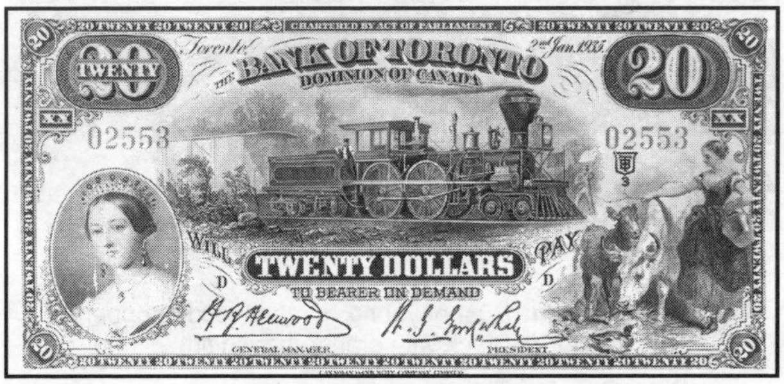

715-24-14

$20 Face Design: Queen Victoria/train/dairymaid with cattle
Colour: Black with yellow tint

Back Design: Lathework, counters, bank name and Medallion engraved portraits of Queen Victoria and Prince Albert
Colour: Orange

IMPRINT

Canadian Bank Note Company, Limited

SIGNATURES

	left	right
1935:	typed H.B. Henwood	typed W.G. Gooderham
1937:	typed H.B. Henwood	typed Jno. R. Lamb
	typed F.H. Marsh	typed Jno. R. Lamb

ISSUE DATING

Engraved

2nd Jan. 1935 — 2nd Jan. 1937

2nd January, 1935 — 2nd January, 1937

CIRCULATING NOTES

Cat. No.	Denom.	Date	Variety	VG	F	VF	EF	AU	Unc
24-02	$5	1935		50.	70.	110.	225.	350.	475.
24-04	$5	1937	Henwood, l.	50.	70.	110.	225.	350.	475.
24-06	$5	1937	Marsh, l.	50.	70.	110.	225.	350.	475.
24-08	$10	1935		50.	70.	110.	225.	350.	475.
24-10	$10	1937	Henwood, l.	50.	70.	110.	225.	350.	475.
24-12	$10	1937	Marsh, l.	50.	70.	110.	225.	350.	475.
24-14	$20	1935		80.	115.	175.	350.	525.	700.

PROOF NOTES

Cat. No.	Denom.	Date		Unc
24-02P	$5	1935	FACE PROOF	300.
24-08P	$10	1935	FACE PROOF	300.
24-14P	$20	1935	FACE PROOF	300.

715-26 NOTES ALTERED FROM THE COLONIAL BANK OF CANADA

DESIGNS AND COLOURS

715-26-02

$1 Face Design: Bust of young women/wood chopper/—

Colour: Black with orange-brown tint

Back Design: Plain

Photo Not Available

715-26-04

$4 Face Design: Helmeted "Justice" figure/ Queen Victoria (Winterhalter portrait)/—

Colour: Black with pink tint

Back Design: Plain

IMPRINT

$1: Jocelyn, Draper, Welch & Co. and American Bank Note Company. New York

$4: Jocelyn, Draper & Welch and American Bank Note Co. (monogram)

SIGNATURES

left	right
mss. A. Cameron	mss. J.C. Chewett

ISSUE DATING

Partially engraved ___ 18___:

$1: 1862

Engraved

$4: May 4, 1859

Cat. No.	Denom.	Date	Variety	G	VG	F	VF	EF	AU
26-02	$1	1862	Altered	125.	250.	400.	—	—	—
26-04	$4	1859	Altered	150.	300.	475.	—	—	—

715-28 NOTES ALTERED FROM THE INTERNATIONAL BANK OF CANADA

DESIGNS AND COLOURS

715-28-02

$2 Face Design: Allegorical woman/Royal Crest/—

Colour: Black with no tint

Back Design: Plain

IMPRINT

Danforth, Wright & Co.

SIGNATURES

right only

mss. J.C. Fitch

ISSUE DATING

Engraved

Sept. 15, 1858

March 15, 1861

PROTECTOR

Red "word" on face and back

Cat. No.	Denom.	Date	Variety	G	VG	F	VF	EF	AU
28-01	$1	1861	Altered	135.	275.	450.	—	—	—
28-02	$2	1858	Altered	135.	275.	450.	—	—	—

THE TRADERS BANK OF CANADA

1885-1912

TORONTO, ONTARIO

BANK NUMBER 720 ***REDEEMABLE***

The Traders Bank opened for business in 1885 with limited capital, but with proper management over a period of years, assets increased and the financial and business communities gained a substantial regard for it. At the time of its takeover by the Royal Bank of Canada in 1912, the Traders Bank of Canada had reserves and capital of $7 million, with total assets of $52 million. The smaller bank also had 126 branches and agencies in operation. A reorganization followed the merger, which saw final acquisition of 90 new branches for the Royal Bank in Ontario, 13 in Alberta, five in Saskatchewan and one in British Columbia. Both the extensive representation of the Traders Bank and its high reputation in Ontario were of particular importance to the purchasing bank, since at this time, the Royal Bank was represented in only 36 places in Ontario.

720-10 ISSUES OF 1885 AND 1886

DESIGNS AND COLOURS

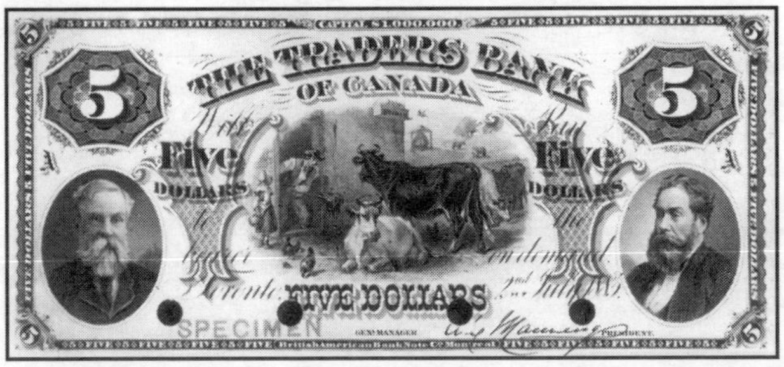

720-10-02P

$5 Face Design: H.S. Strathy/farmer and cattle at barn door, "Milk Producers"/A. Manning
Colour: Black with green tint

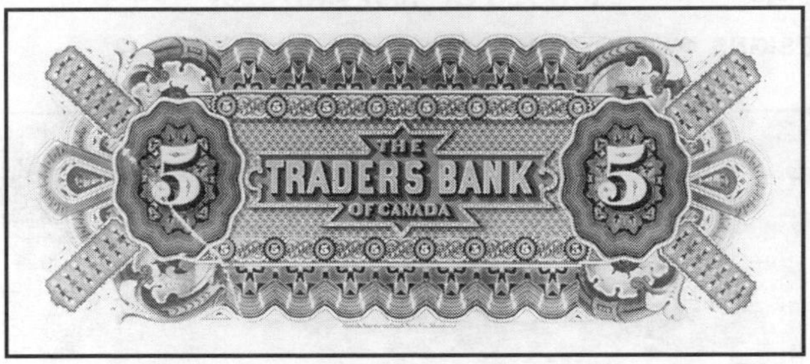

Back Design: Lathework, counters and bank name
Colour: Green

720-10-04P

$10 Face Design: H.S. Strathy/allegorical figures and ornate X/ A. Manning
Colour: Black with green tint

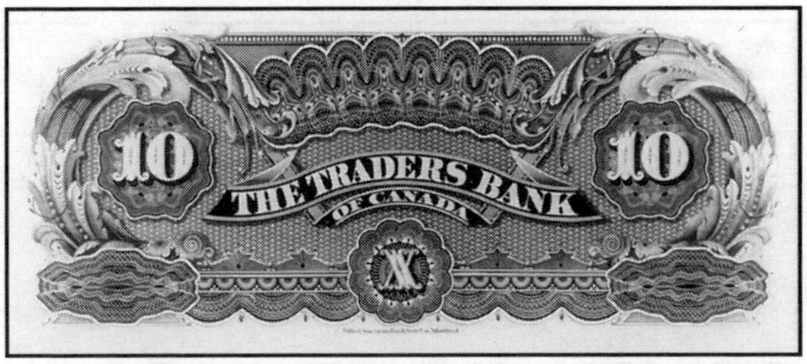

Back Design: Lathework, counters and bank name
Colour: Green

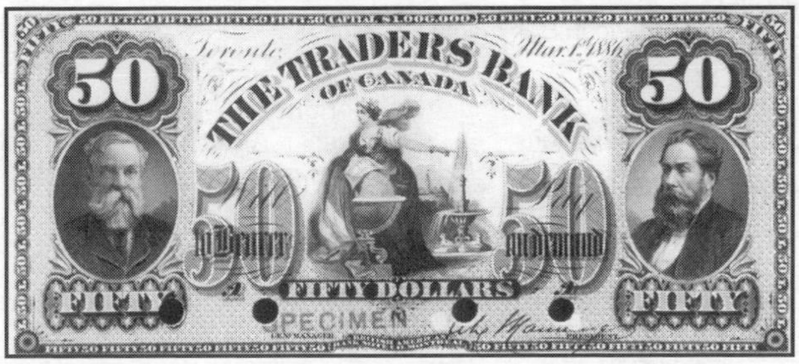

720-10-06P

$50 Face Design: H.S. Strathy/allegorical female and globe "Confederation"/A. Manning
Colour: Black with green tint

Back Design: Lathework, counters and bank name
Colour: Green

720-10-08P

$100 Face Design: H.S. Strathy/ships at dock "Allan Line Wharves"/A. Manning
Colour: Black with green tint

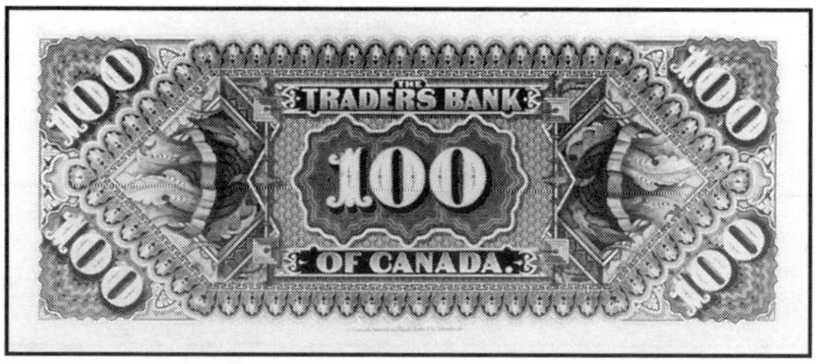

Back Design: Lathework, counters and bank name
Colour: Green

IMPRINT

British American Bank Note Co. Montreal

SIGNATURES

left	right
mss. various	engr. Alex Manning

ISSUE DATING

Engraved

2nd July 1885
Mar. 1st 1886

PROOF NOTES

Cat. No.	Denom.	Date		Unc
10-02P	$5	1885	FACE PROOF	350.
10-04P	$10	1885	FACE PROOF	350.
10-06P	$50	1886	FACE PROOF	700.
10-08P	$100	1886	FACE PROOF	800.

720-12 ISSUES OF 1890 AND 1893

DESIGNS AND COLOURS

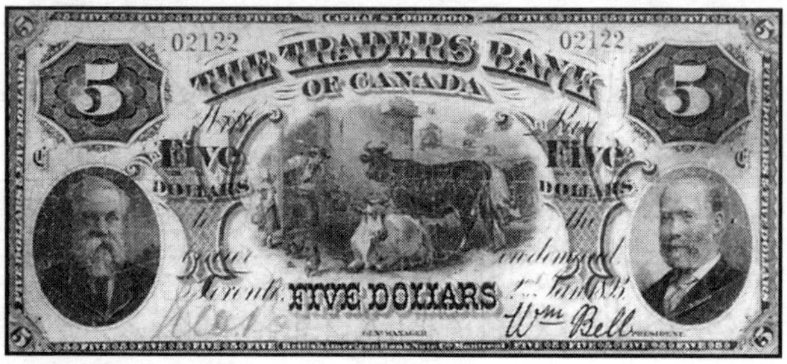

720-12-02

$5 Face Design: H.S. Strathy/farmer and cattle at barn door "Milk Producers"/Wm. Bell
Colour: Black with green tint

Back Design: Lathework, counters and bank name
Colour: Green

720-12-04P

$20 Face Design: H.S. Strathy/seated allegorical female and machinery/Wm. Bell
Colour: Black with green tint

Back Design: Lathework, counters and bank name
Colour: Green

IMPRINT

British American Bank Note Co. Ottawa

SIGNATURES

left	right
mss. various	engr. Wm. Bell

ISSUE DATING

Engraved

Jan. 2, 1890
2nd Jan. 1893

CIRCULATING NOTES

Cat. No.	Denom.	Date	G	VG	F	VF	EF	AU
12-02	$5	1893	400.	800.	—	—	—	—
12-04	$20	1890	No known issued notes					

PROOF NOTES

Cat. No.	Denom.	Date		Unc
12-04P	$20	1890	FACE PROOF	500.

720-14 ISSUES OF 1897 AND 1907

DESIGNS AND COLOURS

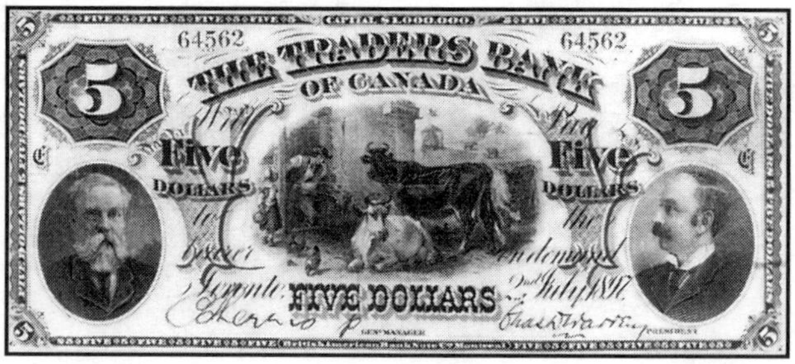

720-14-02a

$5 Face Design: H.S. Strathy/farmer and cattle at barn door "Milk Producers"/Chas. D. Warren
Colour: Black with green tint

Back Design: Lathework, counters and bank name
Colour: Green

720-14-08

$10 Face Design: H.S. Strathy/allegorical figures and ornate X/ Chas. D. Warren

Colour: Black with green tint

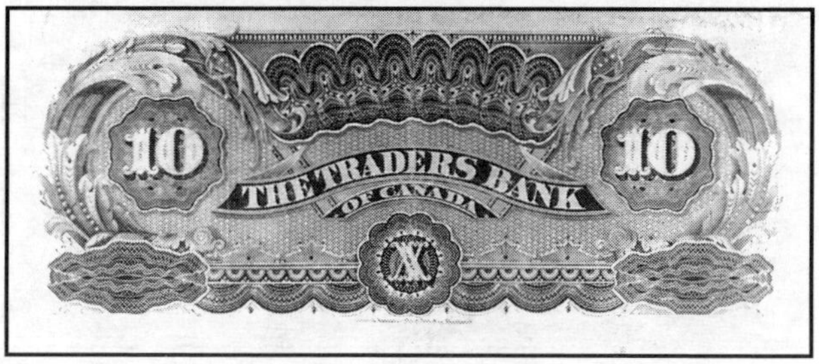

Back Design: Lathework, counters and bank name

Colour: Green

720-14-10P

$20 Face Design: H.S. Strathy/seated allegorical woman and machinery/Chas. D. Warren

Colour: Black with green tint

Back Design: Lathework, counters and bank name

Colour: Green

720-14-12P

$50 Face Design: H.S. Strathy/allegorical female and globe "Confederation"/Chas. D. Warren

Colour: Black with green tint

Back Design: Lathework, counters and bank name

Colour: Green

720-14-14P

$100 Face Design: H.S. Strathy/ships at dock, part of "Allan Line Wharves"/Chas. D. Warren

Colour: Black with green tint

Back Design: Lathework, counters and bank name

Colour: Green

IMPRINT

British American Bank Note Co. Montreal

SIGNATURES

left	**right**
mss. various	engr. Chas. D. Warren

ISSUE DATING

Engraved

Jan. 2, 1897
2nd July, 1897
1st Nov. 1907

VARIETIES

14-02a $5 1897 Capital $1,000,000 on the note;
14-02b $5 1897 Capital $2,000,000 on the note;
14-02c $5 1897 Capital $3,000,000 on the note.

CIRCULATING NOTES

Cat. No.	Denom.	Date	G	VG	F	VF	EF	AU
14-02a	$5	1897	225.	500.	700.	1,200.	2,000.	4,000.
14-02b	$5	1897	250.	550.	750.	1,300.	—	—
14-02c	$5	1897	235.	525.	725.	1.250.	—	—
14-04	$5	1907	250.	550.	750.	1,300.	—	—
14-06	$10	1897	350.	700.	1,250.	1,750.	—	—
14-08	$10	1907	400.	800.	1,500.	2,000.	3,000.	—
14-10	$20	1907	No known issued notes					
14-12	$50	1897	No known issued notes					
14-14	$100	1897	No known issued notes					

PROOF NOTES

Cat. No.	Denom.	Date		Unc
14-10P	$20	1907	FACE PROOF	500.
14-12P	$50	1897	FACE PROOF	750.
14-14P	$100	1897	FACE PROOF	750.

720-16 ## ISSUE OF 1909

DESIGNS AND COLOURS

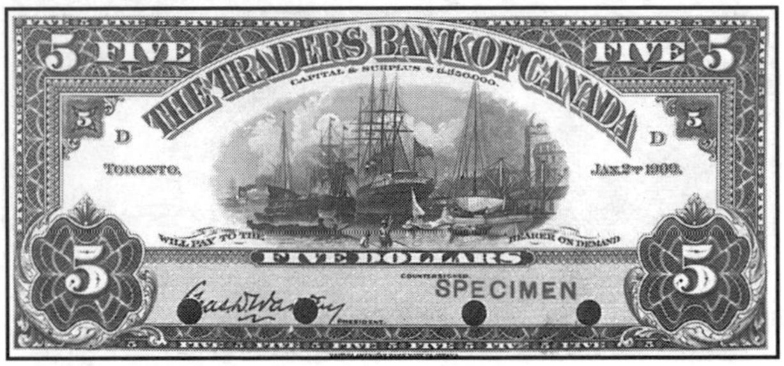

720-16-02P
$5 Face Design: —/"Allan Line Wharves"/—
Colour: Black with yellow and green tint

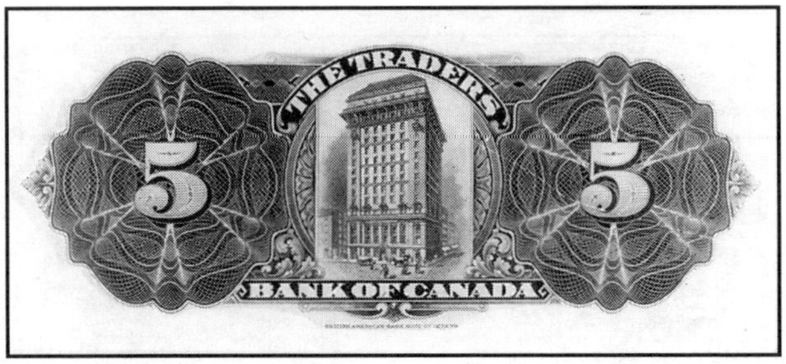

Back Design: Lathework, counters bank name and bank building
Colour: Green

720-16-04
$10 Face Design: —/men cutting logs/—
Colour: Black with brown, blue and purple tint
Back Design: Lathework, counters, bank name and bank building
Colour: Green, red and brown

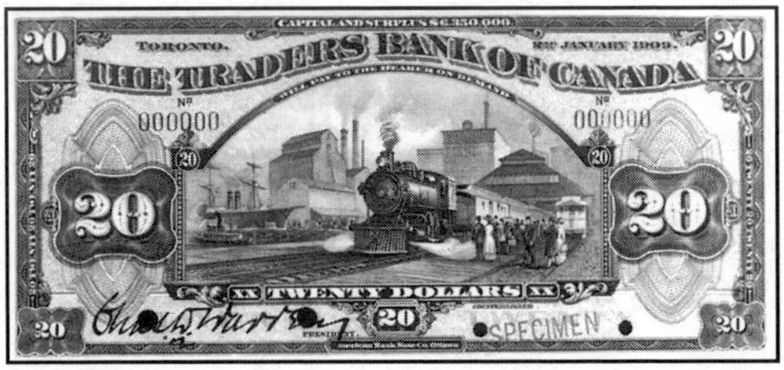

720-16-06P
$20 Face Design: —/train at station/—
Colour: Black with brown, green and red tint

Back Design: Lathework, counters, bank name and bank building
Colour: Brown, green and red

720-16-08P
$50 Face Design: —/steamship in storm/—
Colour: Black with green, brown and red tint

Back Design: Lathework, counters, bank name and bank building
Colour: Blue with brown and purple

720-16-10P
$100 Face Design: —/cattle roundup/—
Colour: Black with yellow-brown, green and brown tint

Back Design: Lathework, counters, bank name and bank building
Colour: Orange with red, green and brown

IMPRINT

American Bank Note Co. Ottawa — $10,20,50,100.
British American Bank Note Co. Ottawa — $5

SIGNATURES

left	right
engr. Chas. D. Warren	mss. various

ISSUE DATING

Engraved

Jan. 2nd 1909
2nd January 1909

Note: Proofs of this issue are known to exist with various coloured faces and backs.

CIRCULATING NOTES

Cat. No.	Denom.	Date	G	VG	F	VF	EF	AU
16-02	$5	1909	No known issued notes					
16-04	$10	1909	—	1,500.	2,100.	—	—	—
16-06	$20	1909	No Known issued notes					
16-08	$50	1909	No known issued notes					
16-10	$100	1909	No known issued notes					

PROOF NOTES

Cat. No.	Denom.	Date		Unc
16-02P	$5	1909	FACE PROOF	600.
16-04P	$10	1909	FACE PROOF	500.
16-06P	$20	1909	FACE PROOF	500.
16-08P	$50	1909	FACE PROOF	700.
16-10P	$100	1909	FACE PROOF	750.

720-18 $5 ISSUE OF 1910

DESIGNS AND COLOURS

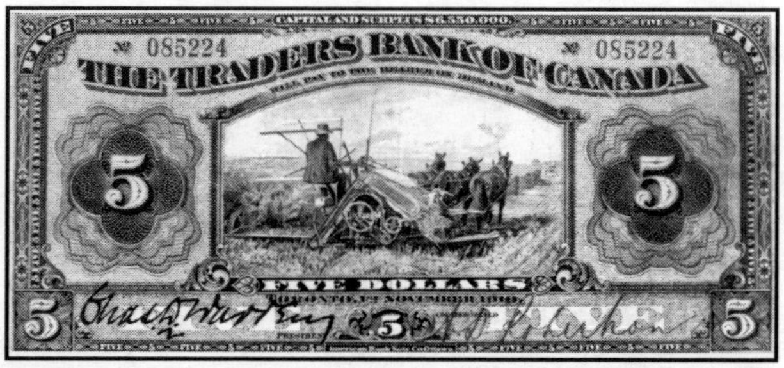

720-18-02

$5 Face Design: —/farmers reaping grain with horses/—
Colour: Black with red, green and purple tint

Back Design: Lathework, counters, bank name and bank building
Colour: Olive with blue and brown

IMPRINT

American Bank Note Co. Ottawa

SIGNATURES

left	right
engr. Chas. D. Warren	mss. various

ISSUE DATING

Engraved

1st November 1910

CIRCULATING NOTES

Cat. No.	Denom.	Date	G	VG	F	VF	EF	AU
18-02	$5	1910	700.	1,400.	2,000.	3,000.	4,500.	—

PROOF NOTES

Cat. No.	Denom.	Date		Unc
18-02P	$5	1910	FACE PROOF	500.

THE UNION BANK

1838 - CA. 1840

MONTREAL, LOWER CANADA

BANK NUMBER 725 ***NONREDEEMABLE***

Established in Montreal, Lower Canada, in 1838 as a private bank, it later became the Union Bank of Montreal.

BURTON & GURLEY PRINTING, 1838

DESIGNS AND COLOURS

Some notes are endorsed vertically across the left end of the face with "H. Gray & Co."

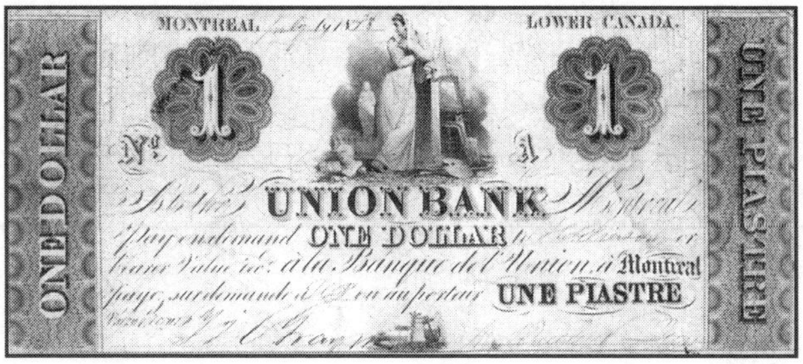

725-10-02

$1 Face Design: —/posing female with sculptures, palette and easel; caduceus, anchor and ship below/—
Colour: Black with no tint

Back Design: See subheadings
Colour: See subheadings

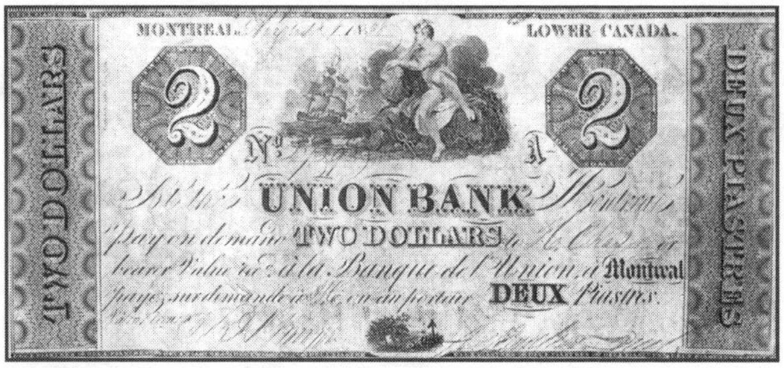

725-10-04

$2 Face Design: —/seated Mercury, ship in background; road and signpost below/—
Colour: Black with no tint

Back Design: See subheadings
Colour: See subheadings

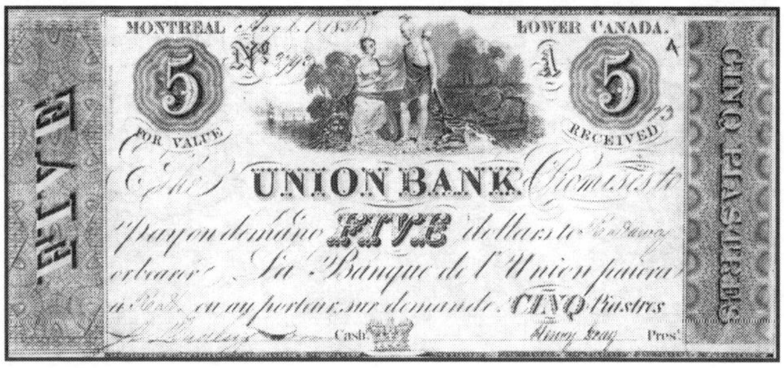

725-14-06

$5 Face Design: —/seated allegorical female and Indian; crown below/—
Colour: Black with no tint

Back Design: See subheadings
Colour: See subheadings

IMPRINT

Burton & Gurley. New York

SIGNATURES

left	right
To H. Gray & Co.	mss. A. Dudley

725-10 BURTON GURLEY PRINTINGS ISSUE OF 1838 WITH PLAIN BACKS

DESIGNS AND COLOURS

Back Design: Plain

ISSUE DATING

Partially engraved ___ 18___:

$1, 1838: July 14, Aug. 1

$2 and $5, 1838: July 14

Cat. No.	Denom.	Date	G	VG	F	VF	EF	AU
10-02	$1	1838	100.	200.	300.	—	—	—
10-04	$2	1838	100.	200.	300.	—	—	—
10-06	$5	1838	125.	250.	400.	—	—	—

725-12 ISSUE OF 1838 WITH GREEN BACKS

DESIGNS AND COLOURS

Back Design: Lathework, miniature vignettes and "STEEL PLATE"
Back Colour: Green

ISSUE DATING

Partially engraved ___ 18___:

1838: Aug. 1
August 1

STAMP:

"G" in red

Cat. No.	Denom.	Date	G	VG	F	VF	EF	AU
12-02	$1	1838	125.	250.	375.	—	—	—
12-04	$2	1838	125.	250.	375.	—	—	—
12-06	$5	1838	160.	325.	425.	—	—	—

725-14

ISSUE OF 1838
WITH BLUE BACKS

DESIGNS AND COLOURS

Back Design: Lathework, miniature vignettes and “STEEL PLATE”
Back Colour: Blue

ISSUE DATING

Partially engraved ___ 18___:

1838: August 1, Augt 1.

Cat. No.	Denom.	Date	G	VG	F	VF	EF	AU
14-02	$1	1838	125.	250.	375.	—	—	—
14-04	$2	1838	125.	250.	375.	—	—	—
14-06	$5	1838	160.	325.	425.	—	—	—

RWH PRINTINGS
1838

DESIGNS AND COLOURS

725-16-02

$1 Face Design: —/Indian buffalo-hunting scene “Buffalo chase” (Catlin), man with hammer below/ Indian with drawn bow
Colour: Black with no tint

Back Design: Lathework
Colour: See subheadings

725-16-04

$2 Face Design: —/Indian in canoe; clasped hands in wreath below/ woman with wheat stalks, leaning on pillar
Colour: Black with no tint

Back Design: Lathework
Colour: See subheadings

725-16-06R

$3 Face Design: —/allegorical figures in clouds; small train below/Indian woman
Colour: Black with no tint

Back Design: Lathework
Colour: See subheadings

725-16-08

$5 Face Design: —/train; Mercury’s head below/farmer with agricultural implements and plaque
Colour: Black with no tint

Back Design: Lathework
Colour: See subheadings

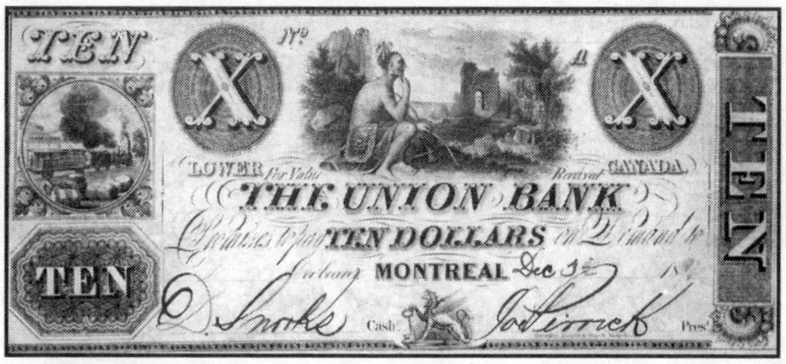

725-16-10R

$10 Face Design: Train, bales and barrels/ seated “Wolfes Indian” and “Ruins of Jamestown,” griffin with key below/—
Colour: Black with no tint

Back Design: Lathework
Colour: See subheadings

725-16-12R

$20 Face Design: Kneeling woman with grain/ train at wharf; reclining woman with sheaves below/allegorical female
Colour: Black with no tint

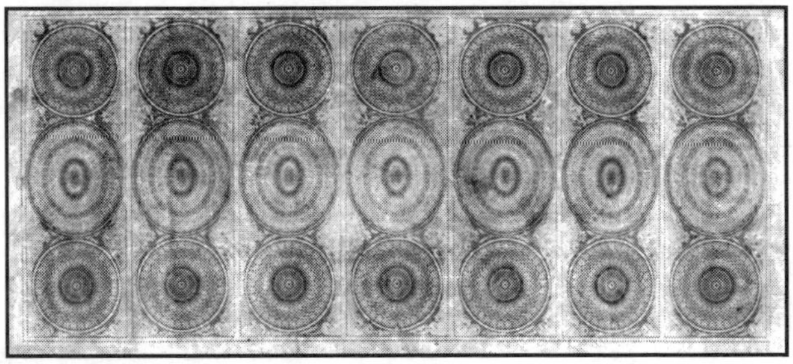

Back Design: Lathework
Colour: See subheadings

IMPRINT
Rawdon, Wright & Hatch. New-York

SIGNATURES

left	**right**
mss. A. Dudley	mss. Henry Gray

ISSUE DATING
Partially engraved ___ 18___:
1838: August 1
1839: August 1

STAMPS AND OVERPRINTS
"COUNTERSIGNED" vertically in black near the left bottom

725-16 ORANGE BACKS

Cat. No.	Denom.	Date	G	VG	F	VF	EF	AU
16-02	$1	1838	60.	125.	175.	225.	325.	—
16-04	$2	1838	50.	100.	140.	185.	275.	—
16-06	$3	1838	85.	175.	250.	—	—	—
16-06R	$3	18_*	75.	150.	200.	300.	450.	600.
16-08	$5	1838	75.	150.	200.	—	—	—
16-08R	$5	18_*	50.	100.	125.	200.	300.	400.
16-10R	$10	18_*	175.	350.	500.	700.	1,100.	—
16-12	$20	1839	—	—	—	450.	600.	—
16-12R	$20	18_*	85.	175.	250.	350.	500.	—

*These notes are remainders that are unsigned and undated or numbered and dated with no signature or have spurious dates and signatures.

725-18 BLUE BACKS

Cat. No.	Denom.	Date	G	VG	F	VF	EF	AU
18-02	$1	1838	50.	100.	140.	—	—	—
18-04	$2	1838	50.	100.	140.	—	—	—
18-06	$3	1838	70.	140.	200.	—	—	—
18-08	$5	1838	100.	200.	350.	—	—	—

Note: The red-brown backs are believed to be oxidized orange backs, and blue-green backs slightly changed blue backs.

THE UNION BANK OF CANADA

1886-1925

QUEBEC CITY, QUEBEC

BANK NUMBER 730 ***REDEEMABLE***

This bank commenced business in 1865, under a provincial charter as the Union Bank of Lower Canada; the name was changed to the Union Bank of Canada in 1886. In 1911 the bank acquired the United Empire Bank of Toronto, and the following year it moved its head office to Winnipeg. It was the first chartered bank to open a branch in Alberta. At its peak the bank had 329 branches, with good representation in western Canada. In 1906 negotiations with the Royal Bank of Canada began, but fell through. However, in May 1925 the Royal Bank concluded an agreement with the directors of the Union Bank to purchase that bank for a consideration of 40,000 shares of Royal Bank stock at a par value of $100 each. After all necessary formalities, the purchase was completed and the actual transfer took place on September 1, 1925.

730-10 ISSUE OF 1886

DESIGNS AND COLOURS

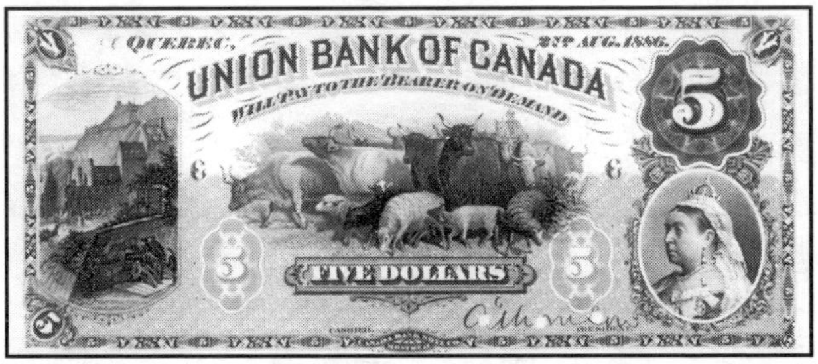

730-10-02P

$5 Face Design: Quebec Citadel/farmer herding cattle and sheep "The Herd"/Queen Victoria
Colour: Black with red-brown tint

Back Design: Lathework, corner counters and counters with griffins flanking bank name
Colour: Green

730-10-04
$10 Face Design: Quebec Citadel/farmer reaping grain/ Queen Victoria
Colour: Black with ochre tint

Back Design: lathework, corner counters and counters with griffins flanking bank name
Colour: Blue

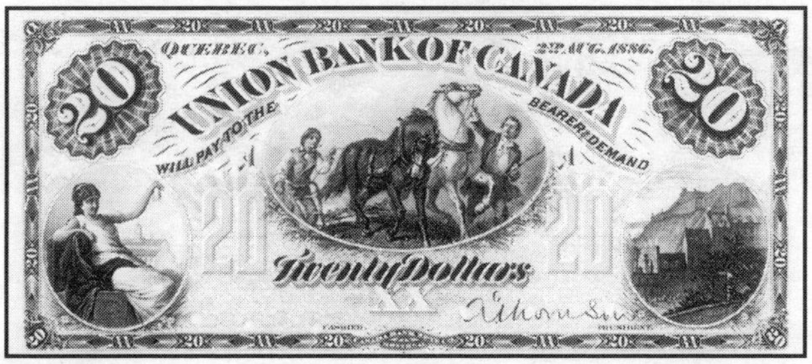

730-10-06P
$20 Face Design: Seated allegorical female/ two farmers plowing/Quebec Citadel
Colour: Black with red-orange tint

Back Design: Lathework, counters and bank name
Colour: Brown

730-10-08P
$50 Face Design: Raphael's angel (minus wings)/—/ Quebec Citadel
Colour: Black with red-orange tint

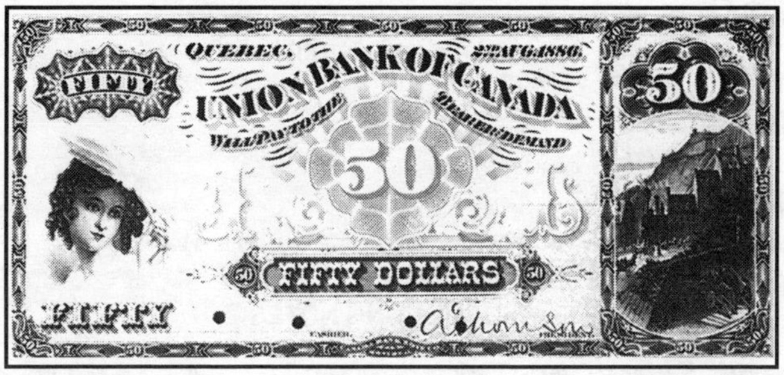

730-10-09P
$50 Face Design: Girl holding feather over head "Juanita"/—/ Quebec Citadel
Colour: Unknown

Back Design: Lathework, counters, flowers and bank name
Colour: Brown

730-10-10P
$100 Face Design: Allegorical female/winged sphinx-like bust of two women flanking counter/ allegorical female
Colour: Black with red-orange tint

Back Design: Lathework, counters and bank name
Colour: Brown

IMPRINT

Canada Bank Note Co. Montreal

SIGNATURES

left	right
mss. various	engr. A. Thomson

ISSUE DATING

Engraved

2nd Aug. 1886

Note: Proofs are known of $10 notes with an olive face tint and backs with a brown tint and $50 backs in green.

CIRCULATING NOTES

Cat. No.	Denom.	Date	Variety	G	VG	F	VF	EF	AU
10-02	$5	1886		No known issued notes					
10-04	$10	1886		1,500.	2,500.	3,500.	—	—	—
10-06	$20	1886		No known issued notes					
10-08	$50	1886	Angel	No known issued notes					
10-09	$50	1886	"Juanita"	No known issued notes					
10-10	$100	1886		No known issued notes					

PROOF NOTES

Cat. No.	Denom.	Date	Variety		Unc
10-02P	$5	1886		FACE PROOF	600.
10-04P	$10	1886		FACE PROOF	600.
10-06P	$20	1886		FACE PROOF	600.
10-08P	$50	1886	Angel	FACE PROOF	700.
10-09P	$50	1886	"Juanita"	FACE PROOF	700.
10-10P	$100	1886		FACE PROOF	800.

730-12 ISSUE OF 1893

DESIGNS AND COLOURS

730-12-02P

$5 Face Design: Sailing ship/Bank Crest/A. Thomson
Colour: Black with overall green tint

Back Design: Lathework, counters and bank name
Colour: Green

730-12-04

$10 Face Design: Farm implements/Bank Crest/A. Thomson
Colour: Black with overall green tint

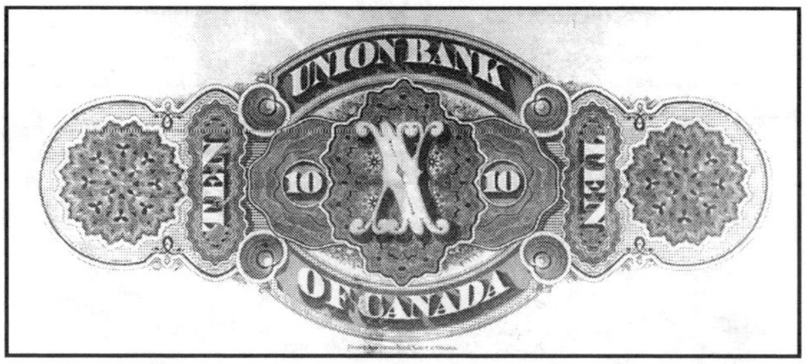

Back Design: Lathework, counters and bank name
Colour: Green

730-12-06P

$20 Face Design: Three horses' heads/Bank Crest/A. Thomson
Colour: Black with overall green tint

Back Design: Lathework, counters and bank name
Colour: Green

730-12-08P
$50 Face Design: —/Bank Crest/A. Thomson
Colour: Black with overall green tint

Back Design: Lathework, counters and bank name
Colour: Green

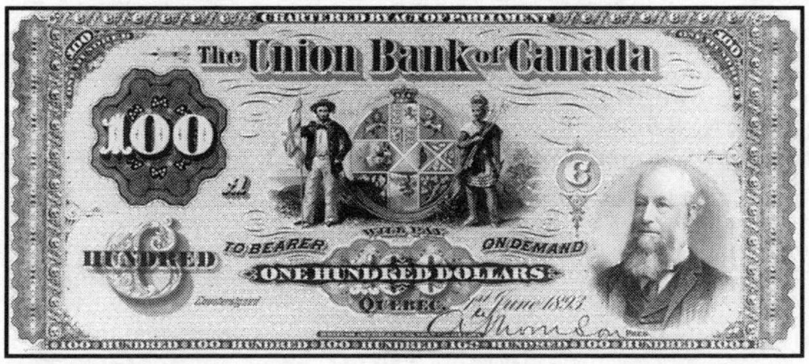

730-12-10P
$100 Face Design: —/Bank Crest/A. Thomson
Colour: Black with overall green tint

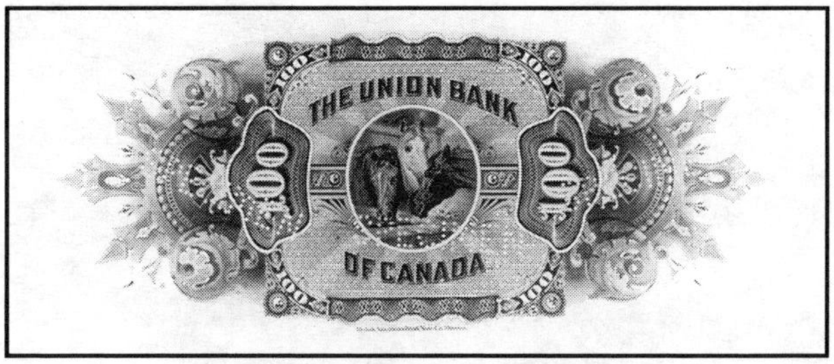

Back Design: Lathework, counters, bank name and three horses' heads
Colour: Green

IMPRINT

British American Bank Note Co. Ottawa

SIGNATURES

left	right
mss. various	engr. A. Thomson

ISSUE DATING

Engraved

1st June 1893

CIRCULATING NOTES

Cat. No.	Denom.	Date	G	VG	F	VF	EF	AU
12-02	$5	1893	300.	600.	800.	1,200.	2,200.	—
12-04	$10	1893	—	—	—	—	1,800.	2,750.
12-06	$20	1893	No known issued notes					
12-08	$50	1893	No known issued notes					
12-10	$100	1893	No known issued notes					

PROOF NOTES

Cat. No.	Denom.	Date		Unc
12-02P	$5	1893	PROOF	600.
12-04P	$10	1893	PROOF	600.
12-06P	$20	1893	PROOF	600.
12-08P	$50	1893	PROOF	700.
12-10P	$100	1893	PROOF	800.

730-14 "QUEBEC" $5 AND $10 ISSUES OF 1903 AND 1907

DESIGNS AND COLOURS

730-14-04
$5 Face Design: —/farmers harvesting with horses "Harvesting"/—

Back Design: Lathework, counters, bank name and Bank Crest

730-14-08

$10 Face Design: —/cowboy roping steers "A Round Up"/—

Back Design: Lathework, counters, bank name and Bank Crest

1903 $5 Face Colour: Black with brown frame and brown, olive, red and yellow-green tint

Back Colour: Black with brown, olive, red and yellow-green tint

1907 $5 Face Colour: Black with green frame and blue-green, olive, green and yellow-green tint

Back Colour: Black with blue-green, olive, green and yellow-green tint

$10 Face Colour: Black with black frame and blue, brown, green and yellow-green tint

Back Colour: Black with blue, brown, green and yellow-green tint

IMPRINT

American Bank Note Co. Ottawa
American Bank Note Company, Ottawa

SIGNATURES

	left	right
1903:	typed A. Thomson	mss. various
1907:	typed John Sharples	mss. various

ISSUE DATING

Engraved

1st June 1903
1st June 1907

CIRCULATING NOTES

Cat. No.	Denom.	Date	Variety	G	VG	F	VF	EF	AU
14-02	$5	1903*	Blue numbers	325.	650.	900.	1,500.	2,400.	—
14-02a	$5	1903*	Red numbers	325.	650.	900.	1,500.	2,400.	—
14-04	$5	1907		150.	300.	400.	600.	1,100.	—
14-06	$10	1903		600.	1,200.	1,500.	2,500.	3,500.	—
14-08	$10	1907		500.	1,000.	1,250.	2,000.	3,000.	4,000.

PROOF NOTES

Cat. No.	Denom.	Date		Unc
14-02P	$5	1903	FACE PROOF	500.
14-04P	$5	1907	FACE PROOF	500.
14-06P	$10	1903	FACE PROOF	500.
14-08P	$10	1907	FACE PROOF	500.

730-16 "WINNIPEG" $5 AND $10 ISSUE OF 1912

The head office of the bank changed its location from Quebec City to Winnipeg.

DESIGNS AND COLOURS

730-16-04a

$5 Face Design: —/farmers "Harvesting" with horses/—

Colour: See varieties

Back Design: Lathework, counters, bank name and bank crest

Colour: See varieties

730-16-07a

$10 Face Design: —/cowboy roping steers "A Round Up"/—

Colour: Black with blue, olive, green and yellow-green tint

Back Design: Lathework, counters, bank name and bank crest

Colour: Black with blue, olive, green and yellow-green tint

IMPRINT

American Bank Note Co. Ottawa
Canadian Bank Note Company, Limited

VARIETIES

$5 Face Colour: Black frame, black with black, green, olive and yellow-green tint

Back Colour: Black frame, black with black, green, olive and yellow-green tint

$5 Face Colour: Green frame, black with dark green, green, olive and yellow-green tint

Back Colour: Green frame, black with dark green, green, olive and yellow-green tint

SIGNATURES

	left	right
$5, black frame:	typed John Galt	mss. various
	typed John Galt	typed H.B.Shaw
$5, green frame:	typed John Galt	mss. various
	typed John Galt	typed H.B. Shaw
	typed W.R. Allan	typed J.W. Hamilton
$10, green frame:	typed John Galt	mss. various
	typed John Galt	typed H.B. Shaw
	typed W.R. Allan	typed J.W. Hamilton

ISSUE DATING

Engraved

July 1st 1912

OVERPRINT

$5, green frame: Galt signature, "NORTHWEST TERRITORIES" twice vertically in blue

CIRCULATING NOTES

Cat. No.	Den.	Date	Variety	G	VG	F	VF	EF	AU
16-02	$5	1912	Black frame, mss r.	85.	175.	250.	400.	750.	1,000.
16-03	$5	1912	Black frame, Shaw r.	85.	175.	250.	400.	750.	1,000.
16-04	$5	1912	Green frame, mss r.	75.	150.	225.	350.	675.	900.
16-04a	$5	1912	Green frame, blue o/p	—	1,500.	2,000.	3,000.	4,500.	—
16-05	$5	1912	Green frame, Shaw r.	75.	150.	225.	350.	675.	900.
16-05a	$5	1912	Green frame, Hamilton r.	75.	150.	225.	350.	675.	900.
16-06	$10	1912	Mss r.	100.	200.	275.	450.	800.	1,100.
16-07	$10	1912	Shaw r.	100.	200.	275.	450.	800.	1,100.
16-07a	$10	1912	Hamilton r.	100.	200.	275.	450.	800.	1,100.

PROOF NOTES

Cat. No.	Den.	Date	Variety		Unc
16-02P	$5	1912	Black frame	FACE PROOF	500.
16-04P	$5	1912	Green frame	FACE PROOF	500.
16-06P	$10	1912		FACE PROOF	500.

SPECIMEN NOTES

Cat. No.	Den.	Date	Variety		Unc
16-05Sa	$5	1912	Allan, 1.	SPECIMEN	750.
16-07Sa	$10	1912	Allan, 1.	SPECIMEN	750.

730-18 $20, $50 AND $100 DESIGNS SIMILAR TO THE 1886 ISSUE RESUMED 1907 AND 1912

DESIGNS AND COLOURS

730-18-04

$20 Face Design: Seated allegorical female/farmers and horses plowing/Quebec Citadel

Colour: Black with green tint

Back Design: Lathework, counters and bank name

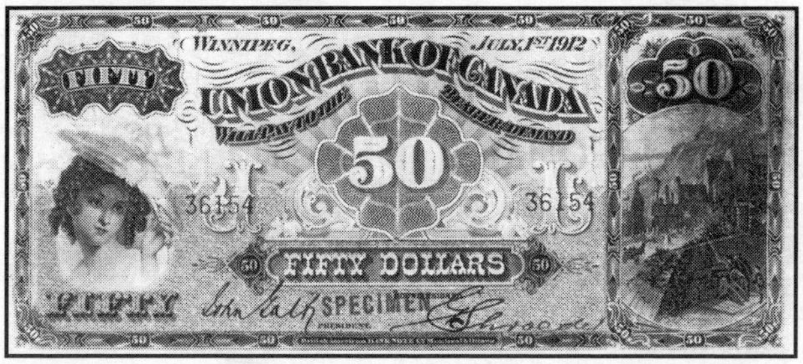

730-18-08

$50 Face Design: Girl holding feather fan over head "Juanita"/—/Quebec Citadel

Colour: Black with green tint

Back Design: Lathework, counters, flowers and bank name

730-18-12

$100 Face Design: Allegorical female/winged sphinx-like bust of two women flanking counter/ allegorical female

Colour: Black with green tint

Back Design: Lathework, counters and bank name

BACK COLOURS

1907: Back Colour: Brown
1912: Back Colour: Green

IMPRINT

British American Bank Note Co. Montreal & Ottawa

SIGNATURES

	left	right
1907:	engr. John Sharples	mss. various
1912:	engr. John Galt	mss. various

ISSUE DATING

Engraved

1st June, 1907
July, 1st 1912

Note: 1907 issues are domiciled in Quebec, later issues in Winnipeg.

CIRCULATING NOTES

Cat. No.	Denom.	Date	Variety	G	VG	F	VF	EF	AU
18-02	$20	1907	Quebec	No known issued notes					
18-04	$20	1912	Winnipeg	400.	800.	1,150.	1,600.	—	—
18-06	$50	1907	Quebec	No known issued notes					
18-08	$50	1912	Winnipeg	750.	1,500.	2,200.	—	—	—
18-10	$100	1907	Quebec	No known issued notes					
18-12	$100	1912	Winnipeg	650.	1,300.	1,800.	2,600.	—	—

PROOF NOTES

Cat. No.	Denom.	Date	Variety		Unc
18-02P	$20	1907	Quebec	FACE PROOF	500.
18-04P	$20	1912	Winnipeg	FACE PROOF	500.
18-06P	$50	1907	Quebec	FACE PROOF	650.
18-08P	$50	1912	Winnipeg	FACE PROOF	650.
18-10P	$100	1907	Quebec	FACE PROOF	750.
18-12P	$100	1912	Winnipeg	FACE PROOF	750.

730-20 ISSUE OF 1921

DESIGNS AND COLOURS

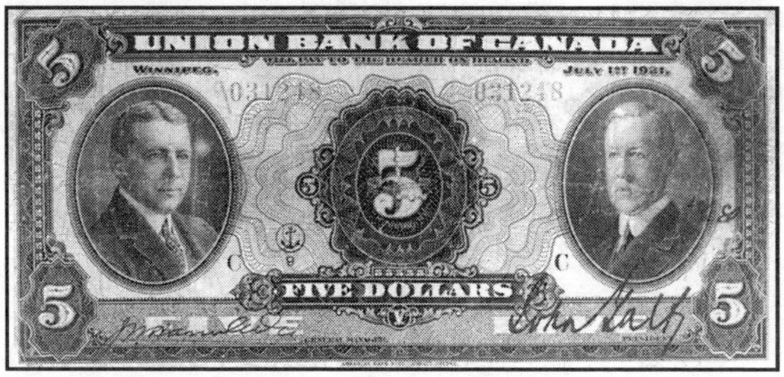

730-20-02

$5 Face Design: H.B. Shaw/—/John Galt
Colour: Black with lilac, green, gold, red and blue tint

Back Design: Lathework, counters and bank name
Colour: Green

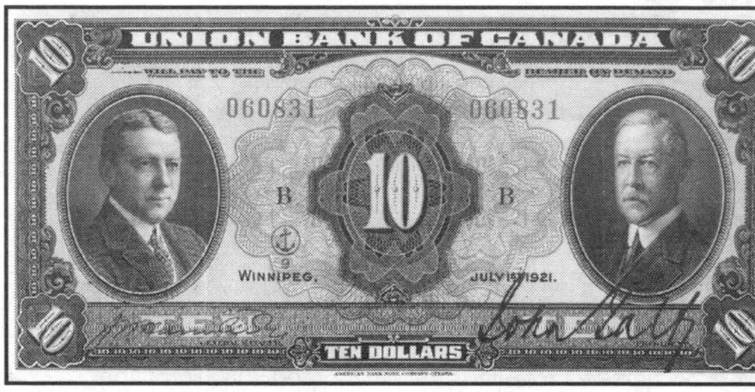

730-20-04

$10 Face Design: H.B. Shaw/—/John Galt
Colour: Black with red, lilac, green, orange and blue tint

Back Design: Lathework, counters and bank name
Colour: Red

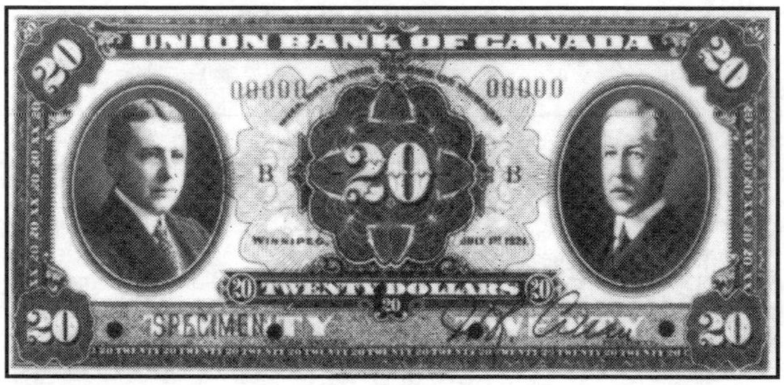

730-20-06S

$20 Face Design: H.B. Shaw/—/John Galt
Colour: Black with orange, green, red, blue and lilac tint

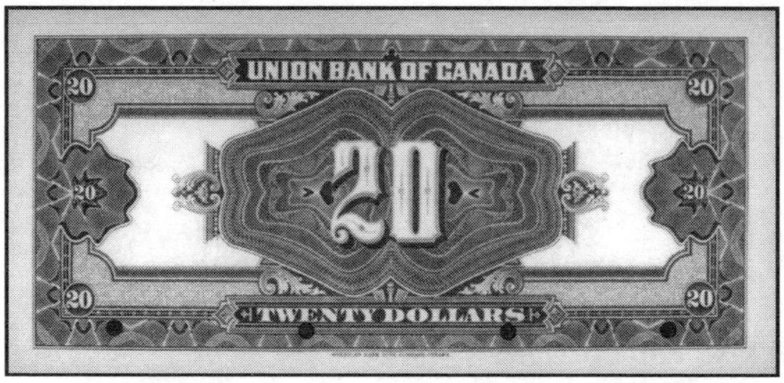

Back Design: Lathework, counters and bank name
Colour: Blue

730-20-08S

$50 Face Design: —/John Galt/—
Colour: Black with blue, lilac, yellow-green, orange and yellow-brown tint

Back Design: Lathework, counters and bank name
Colour: Brown

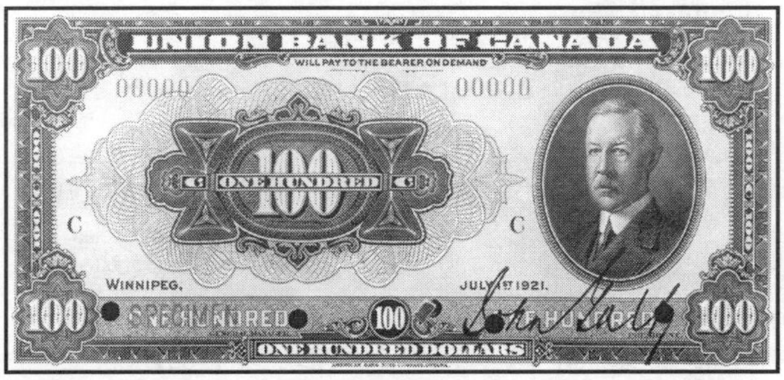

730-20-10S

$100 Face Design: —/—/John Galt
Colour: Black with yellow-green, orange, blue, magenta and green tint

Back Design: Lathework, counters and bank name
Colour: Olive green

IMPRINT

American Bank Note Company, Ottawa

SIGNATURES

left	right
typed J.W. Hamilton	typed John Galt
typed J.W. Hamilton	typed W.R. Allan

ISSUE DATING

Engraved

July 1st 1921.

CIRCULATING NOTES

Cat. No.	Denom.	Date	Variety	G	VG	F	VF	EF	AU
20-02	$5	1921	Galt, r.	175.	350.	450.	750.	1,200.	—
20-03	$5	1921	Allan, r.	185.	375.	500.	800.	1,300.	—
20-04	$10	1921	Galt, r.	125.	250.	300.	400.	750.	—
20-05	$10	1921	Allan, r.	125.	250.	300.	400.	750.	—
20-06	$20	1921		No known issued notes					
20-08	$50	1921		No known issued notes					
20-10	$100	1921		No known issued notes					

PROOF NOTES

Cat. No.	Denom.	Date		Unc
20-02P	$5	1921	FACE PROOF	300.
20-04P	$10	1921	FACE PROOF	300.
20-06P	$20	1921	FACE PROOF	300.
20-08P	$50	1921	FACE PROOF	300.
20-10P	$100	1921	FACE PROOF	300.

SPECIMEN NOTES

Cat. No.	Denom.	Date		Unc
20-02S	$5	1921	SPECIMEN	700.
20-04S	$10	1921	SPECIMEN	700.
20-06S	$20	1921	SPECIMEN	700.
20-08S	$50	1921	SPECIMEN	700.
20-10S	$100	1921	SPECIMEN	700.

THE UNION BANK OF HALIFAX

1856-1910

HALIFAX, NOVA SCOTIA

BANK NUMBER 735 ***REDEEMABLE***

Established in Halifax, Nova Scotia, in 1856, negotiations regarding an amalgamation of this bank with the Merchants Bank of Halifax in 1882 came to nothing. The Union Bank took over the Commercial Bank of Windsor in 1902 and prospered. In 1910 the Union Bank was absorbed by the Royal Bank of Canada, thus expanding the representation of the Royal Bank in the Atlantic provinces and in the Caribbean.

735-10 **POUNDS ISSUE, 1861**

DESIGNS AND COLOURS

735-10-02

£5 Face Design: Shipping cargoes top and bottom/ two allegorical women; Queen Victoria (Chalon portrait) below/flowers
Colour: Black with no tint

Back Design: Lathework, counters, bank name and Medallion engraved portraits of Victoria and Albert
Colour: Red-brown

IMPRINT

Rawdon, Wright, Hatch & Edson, New-York

SIGNATURES

left	right
mss. W.S. Stirling	mss. J.A. Moren

ISSUE DATING

Partially engraved 1st September 18___:___

1861

PROTECTOR

Red "word" on face only

CIRCULATING NOTES

Cat. No.	Denom.	Date	G	VG	F	VF	EF	AU
10-02	£5	1861	Institutional collection only					

PROOF NOTES

Cat. No.	Denom.	Date		Unc
10-02P	£5	1861	FACE PROOF	700.

735-12

ISSUE OF 1870

DESIGNS AND COLOURS

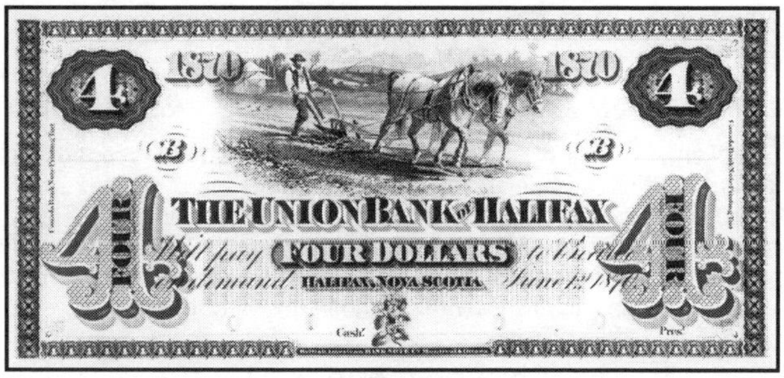

735-12-02P

$4 Face Design: —/ploughing scene; flower below/—
Colour: Black with green tint

Back Design: Lathework, counters and bank name
Colour: Green

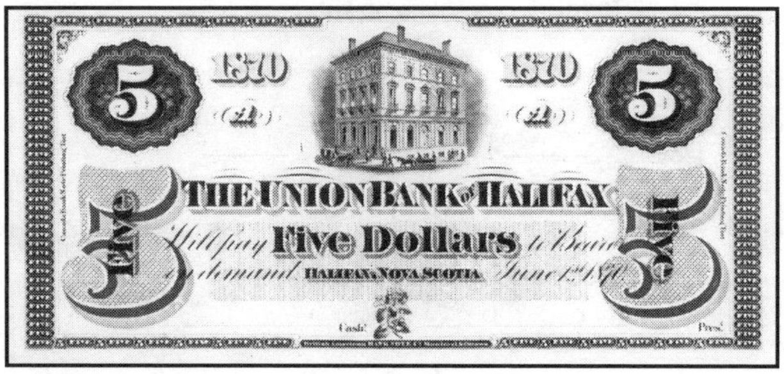

735-12-04P

$5 Face Design: —/head office; flower below/—
Colour: Black with green tint

Back Design: Lathework, counters and bank name
Colour: Green

IMPRINT

British American Bank Note Co. Montreal & Ottawa

SIGNATURES

left	right
none	none

ISSUE DATING

Engraved

June 1st, 1870

CIRCULATING NOTES

PROOF NOTES

Cat. No.	Denom.	Date	G	VG	F	VF	EF	AU
12-02	$4	1870	No known issued notes					
12-04	$5	1870	No known issued notes					

Cat. No.	Denom.	Date		Unc
12-02P	$4	1870	FACE PROOF	700.
12-04P	$5	1870	FACE PROOF	700.

ISSUES OF 1871-1909

DESIGNS AND COLOURS

735-14-02P

$4 Face Design: Steamship/—/ dog's head "My Dog" (after Landseer)
Colour: Black with green tint

Back Design: Plain

735-14-04P

$5 Face Design: —/head office/—
Colour: Black with green tint

Back Design: Lathework, counters, bank name and fishermen "Cod Fishing"
Colour: Green

735-14-09M

$5 Face Design: Three sailing vessels and one propeller brig in rough seas/—/Halifax crest (no imprint)
Colour: Black with green wash tint

Back Design: Plain

735-14-12P

$10 Face Design: —/Royal Crest/—
Colour: Black with green tint

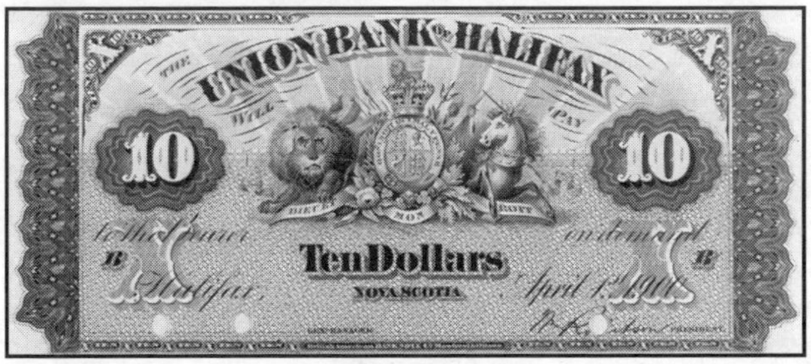

735-16-04P

$10 Face Design: —/Royal Crest/—
Colour: Black with ochre tint

Back Design: Lathework, counters, bank name and fishermen "Cod Fishing"
Colour: Green

735-14-14P

$20 Face Design: Seated female on deck, ship "Exports"/ fishermen and ship "Union" "Cod Fishing"/ anchor, box, cask and ship
Colour: Black with green tint

735-16-06P

$20 Face Design: Seated female on deck, ship "Exports "/ fishermen and ship "Union" "Cod Fishing"/ anchor, box, cask and ship
Colour: Black with ochre tint

Back Design: Lathework, counters, bank name and boy, fish and dog on ship
Colour: Green

735-16-08P

$50 Face Design: "Landing Trinidad"/ Indian and sailor with crest/—
Colour: Black with overall blue tint

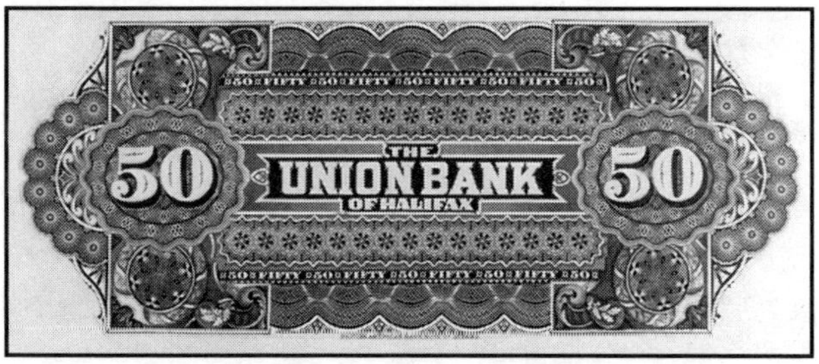

Back Design: Lathework, counters and bank name
Colour: Green

735-16-10P

$100 Face Design: Fishermen and wife with baby looking out to sea "An Old Salt"/sailor "Young Tar"/—
Colour: Black with overall brown tint

Back Design: Lathework, counters and bank name
Colour: Green

IMPRINT

British American Bank Note Co. Montreal & Ottawa
British American Bank Note Co. Ottawa

SIGNATURES

	left	right
1871:	mss. W.S. Stirling	mss. James A. Moren
1882:	mss. various	engr. James A. Moren
1886:	mss. E.L. Thorne	mss. various
1900-1909:	mss. various	engr. Wm. Robertson

735-14 ISSUES OF 1871 - 1895
GREEN DENOMINATIONAL FACE TINT

ISSUE DATING

Engraved

1st July 1871
July 1st 1871
1st July, 1882
May 1, 1886
April 1st 1900

Note: These notes all have plate letter u.

CIRCULATING NOTES

Cat. No.	Denom.	Date	G	VG	F	VF	EF	AU
14-02	$4	1871	Institutional collection only					
14-04	$5	1871	No known issued notes					
14-06	$5	1882	No known issued notes					
14-08	$5	1886	2,100.	3,500.	5,000.	7,000.	—	—
14-12	$10	1871	No known issued notes					
14-14	$20	1871	No known issued notes					
14-16	$20	1886	—	9,500.	—	—	—	—

PROOF NOTES

Cat. No.	Denom.	Date		Unc
14-02P	$4	1871	FACE PROOF	600.
14-04P	$5	1871	FACE PROOF	600.
14-06P	$5	1882	FACE PROOF	600.
14-12P	$10	1871	FACE PROOF	600.
14-14P	$20	1871	FACE PROOF	700.

SPECIMEN NOTES

Cat. No.	Denom.	Date		Unc
14-04S	$5	1871	SPECIMEN	1,000.

MODEL NOTES

Cat. No.	Denom.	Date		Unc
14-09M	$5	1895	MODEL	2,000.

735-16

ISSUES OF 1900-1909
GENERAL FACE TINTS

DESIGNS AND COLOURS

For designs see previous issues.

735-16-01P

735-16-02P

$5 Face Design: —/Head office building (different view from earlier issues)/—lathework around inside border has differences.

FACE COLOURS

1900 $5: Black with green V — V and panel
1909 $5: Black with overall green tint
$10: Black with overall ochre tint
$20: Black with ochre tint
$50: Black with overall blue tint
$100: Black with overall brown tint

ISSUE DATING

Engraved

April 1st 1900
Sept. 1st 1904
May 1st 1909

CIRCULATING NOTES

Cat. No.	Denom.	Date	G	VG	F	VF	EF	AU
16-01	$5	1900	2,100.	3,500.	—	—	—	—
16-02	$5	1909	No known issued notes					
16-04	$10	1900	—	—	5,500.	7,500.	—	—
16-06	$20	1900	No known issued notes					
16-08	$50	1904	No known issued notes					
16-10	$100	1904	No known issued notes					

PROOF NOTES

Cat. No.	Denom.	Date		Unc
16-01P	$5	1900	FACE PROOF	500.
16-02P	$5	1909	FACE PROOF	500.
16-04P	$10	1900	FACE PROOF	500.
16-06P	$20	1900	FACE PROOF	600.
16-08P	$50	1904	FACE PROOF	700.
16-10P	$100	1904	FACE PROOF	800.

THE UNION BANK OF HALIFAX
BRITISH WEST INDIES ISSUE

735-18

DESIGNS FOR PORT OF SPAIN
TRINIDAD, 1904

DESIGNS AND COLOURS

Notes were put into circulation beginning on 3 January 1905, but no issued notes are known to have survived.

735-18-02P

$5 Face Design: —/bank building/—
Colour: Black with green tint

Back Design: lathework, counters, bank name and men fishing from end of ship "Cod Fishing"
Colour: Green

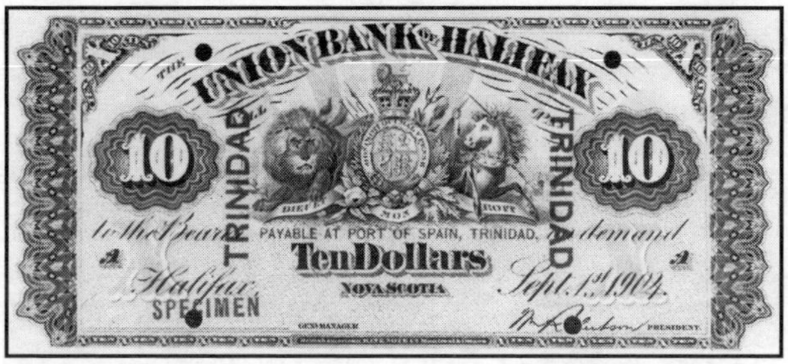

735-18-04P

$10 Face Design: —/Royal Crest/—
Colour: Black with ochre tint

Back Design: Lathework, counters, bank name and men fishing from end of ship "Cod Fishing"
Colour: Yellow-orange

735-18-06P

$20 Face Design: woman with flag seated on bale "Exports"/ men fishing from end of ship "Cod Fishing"/ anchor, box and barrels
Colour: Black with modified blue tint

Back Design: Lathework, counters, bank name and boy and dog looking over side of ship
Colour: Blue

735-18-08P

$50 Face Design: Dock and tower "Landing, Trinidad"/ Crest with Indian and sailor/—
Colour: Black with red-brown tint

Back Design: Lathework, counters and bank name
Colour: Red-brown

735-18-10P

$100 Face Design: Fishermen looking through telescope with wife and baby at side "Old Salt"/ sailor "Young Tar"/—
Colour: Black with overall red-brown tint

Back Design: Lathework, counters and bank name
Colour: Red

IMPRINT

British American Bank Note Co. Ottawa
British American Bank Note Co. Montreal and Ottawa

SIGNATURES

left	right
none	engr. Wm. Robertson

ISSUE DATING

Engraved

Sept. 1st 1904.

OVERPRINT

"TRINIDAD" at ends and "PAYABLE AT PORT OF SPAIN, TRINIDAD" horizontally across the centre, all in red

Note: A $50 proof is known with a blue tint.

CIRCULATING NOTES

Cat. No.	Denom.	Date	G	VG	F	VF	EF	AU
18-02	$5	1904		No known issued notes				
18-04	$10	1904		No known issued notes				
18-06	$20	1904		No known issued notes				
18-08	$50	1904		No known issued notes				
18-10	$100	1904		No known issued notes				

PROOF NOTES

Cat. No.	Denom.	Date		Unc
18-02P	$5	1904	FACE PROOF	850.
18-04P	$10	1904	FACE PROOF	850.
18-06P	$20	1904	FACE PROOF	850.
18-08P	$50	1904	FACE PROOF	850.
18-10P	$100	1904	FACE PROOF	850.

THE UNION BANK OF LOWER CANADA

1865-1886

QUEBEC (CANADA EAST)

BANK NUMBER 740 ***REDEEMABLE***

This bank commenced operations under a provincial charter in 1865. In 1872 it purchased the Quebec Provident and Savings Bank, and its name was changed to the Union Bank of Canada in 1886.

ISSUES OF 1866

DESIGNS AND COLOURS

740-10-02

$1 Face Design: Andrew Thomson/Crest flanked by man with flag and Indian "Canadian Arms"/shipbuilder
Colour: See subheadings

Back Design: Lathework and bank name
Colour: Green

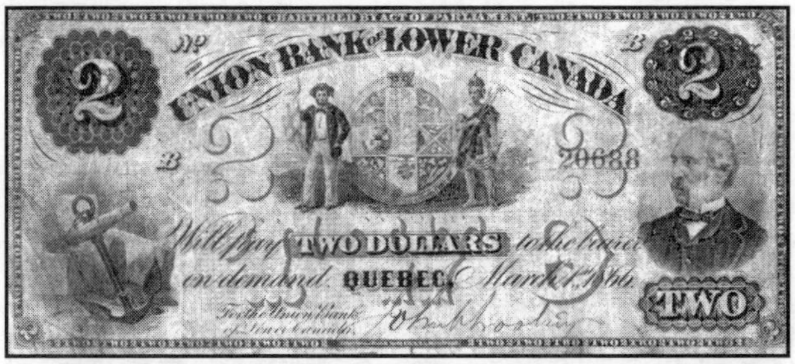

740-10-04

$2 Face Design: Anchor/Crest flanked by man with flag and Indian "Canadian Arms"/Andrew Thomson
Colour: See subheadings

Back Design: Lathework and bank name
Colour: Green

740-10-06

$4 Face Design: Sailors on dock/Crest flanked by man with flag and Indian "Canadian Arms"/ Andrew Thomson
Colour: See subheadings

Back Design: Lathework and bank name
Colour: Green

740-10-08

$5 Face Design: Andrew Thomson/Crest flanked by man with flag and Indian "Canadian Arms"/ sailors on shore with telescope "Looking Out"
Colour: See subheadings

Back Design: Lathework and bank name
Colour: Green

IMPRINT

American Bank Note Co. N.Y. & Montreal
American Bank Note Co. Montreal and N.Y. on some backs

SIGNATURES

left	**right**
none	mss. various

ISSUE DATING

Engraved

March 1st 1866

740-10 **ISSUES WITH GREEN " WORD AND NUMERAL" FACE TINT**

OVERPRINT

Large "S" twice in red
"OTTAWA" twice in blue
"MONTREAL" twice in blue

Cat. No.	Denom.	Date	Variety	G	VG	F	VF	EF	AU
10-02	$1	1866		500.	1,000.	1,400.	2,000.	—	—
10-02a	$1	1866	town o/p	550.	1,100.	1,500.	2,200.	—	—
10-04	$2	1866		1,100.	2,200.	2,700.	—	—	—
10-04a	$2	1866	town o/p	1,150.	2,300.	2,850.	—	—	—
10-06	$4	1866		1,250.	2,500.	3,000.	—	—	—
10-06a	$4	1866	town o/p	1,300.	2,600.	3,200.	—	—	—
10-08	$5	1866		1,250.	2,500.	3,000.	—	—	—
10-08a	$5	1866	town o/p	1,300.	2,600.	3,200.	—	—	—

740-12 ISSUES WITH GREEN "WORD" PROTECTOR NO FACE TINT

740-12-02a

$1 Face Design: Andrew Thomson/Crest flanked by man with flag and Indian "Canadian Arms"/shipbuilder
Colour: Black with no tint

Back Design: Lathework and bank name
Colour: Green

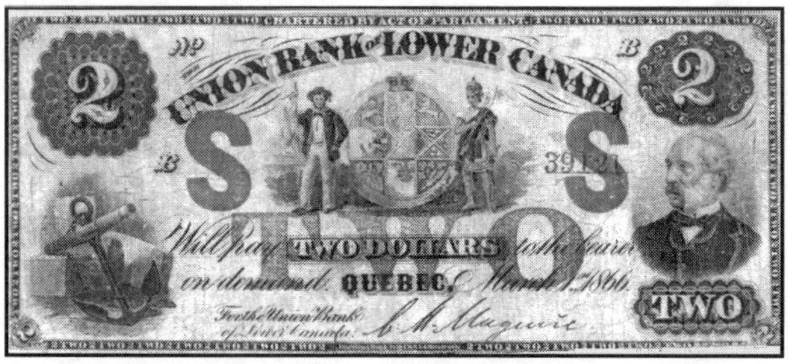

740-12-04

$2 Face Design: Anchor/Crest flanked by man with flag and Indian "Canadian Arms"/Andrew Thomson
Colour: Black with no tint

Back Design: Lathework and bank name
Colour: Green

PROTECTOR

Green "word" on face only

OVERPRINT

Large "S S" in red
Large "S S" in red and "THREE RIVERS" twice in blue

Cat. No.	Denom.	Date	Variety	G	VG	F	VF	EF	AU
12-02	$1	1866		600.	1,200.	1,700.	—	—	—
12-02a	$1	1866	town o/p	650.	1,300.	1,800.	—	—	—
12-04	$2	1866		1,100.	2,200.	2,700.	—	—	—

740-14 ISSUES OF 1870 AND 1871

DESIGNS AND COLOURS

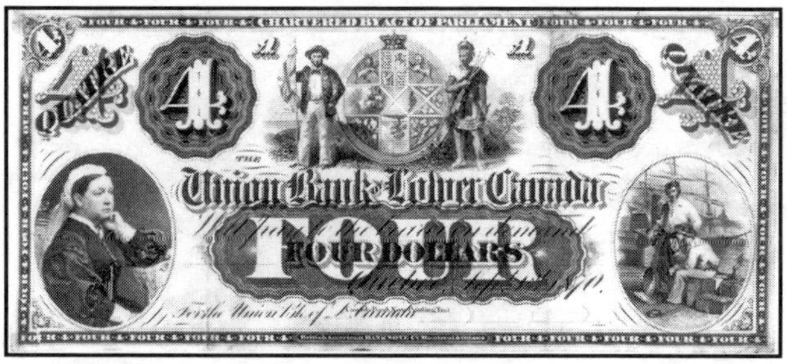

740-14-02P

$4 Face Design: Queen Victoria in widow's weeds/Bank Crest/ sailors at dockside "Mech's & Commerce"
Colour: Black with green tint

Back Design: Lathework, counters and bank name
Colour: Green

740-14-04P

$5 Face Design: Sailors by broken mast with telescope "Coast Scene"/Bank Crest/female at sea being borne aloft by two porpoises
Colour: Black with green tint

Back Design: Lathework, counters and bank name
Colour: Green

740-14-06P
$10 Face Design: Ships and female with flag "Exports"/ Crest/sailor climbing rigging "Going Aloft"
Colour: Black with green tint

Back Design: Lathework, counters and bank name
Colour: Green

740-14-08P
$20 Face Design: —/Crest/—
Colour: Black with green tint

Back Design: Lathework, counters and bank name
Colour: Green

740-14-10P
$50 Face Design: —/Crest/—
Colour: Black wit green tint

Back Design: Lathework, counters and bank name
Colour: Green

740-14-12P
$100 Face Design: —/Crest/—
Colour: Black with green tint

Back Design: Lathework, counters and bank name
Colour: Green

IMPRINT
British American Bank Note Co. Montreal & Ottawa

SIGNATURES

left	right
none	mss. various

ISSUE DATING
Engraved
$4 and $20: Sept. 1st 1870
$5: August 1st 1871
$10: 1st Dec. 1871
$50 and $100: Sept. 1 1870

OVERPRINT
"MONTREAL" twice in red

CIRCULATING NOTES

Cat. No.	Denom.	Date	Variety	G	VG	F	VF	EF	AU
14-02	$4	1870		1,250.	2,500.	3,000.	—	—	—
14-04	$5	1871		1,250.	2,500.	3,000.	—	—	—
14-06	$10	1871		No known issued notes					
14-08	$20	1870		Insitutional collection only					
14-10	$50	1870		No known issued notes					
14-12	$100	1870		No known issued notes					

PROOF NOTES

Cat. No.	Denom.	Date		Unc
14-02P	$4	1870	FACE PROOF	600.
14-04P	$5	1871	FACE PROOF	600.
14-06P	$10	1871	FACE PROOF	600.
14-08P	$20	1870	FACE PROOF	600.
14-10P	$50	1870	FACE PROOF	750.
14-12P	$100	1870	FACE PROOF	800.

THE UNION BANK OF MONTREAL

CA. 1840

MONTREAL, LOWER CANADA

BANK NUMBER 745 ***NONREDEEMABLE***

Originally established in Montreal as the Union Bank, this bank operated for only a short period of time.

745-10 ISSUE OF 1840

DESIGNS AND COLOURS

745-10-02P
$50 Face Design: Kneeling woman with sickle/ ships near harbour, flanked by medallion portraits; small crest below/ farm boy reclining under sheaves
Colour: Black with no tint

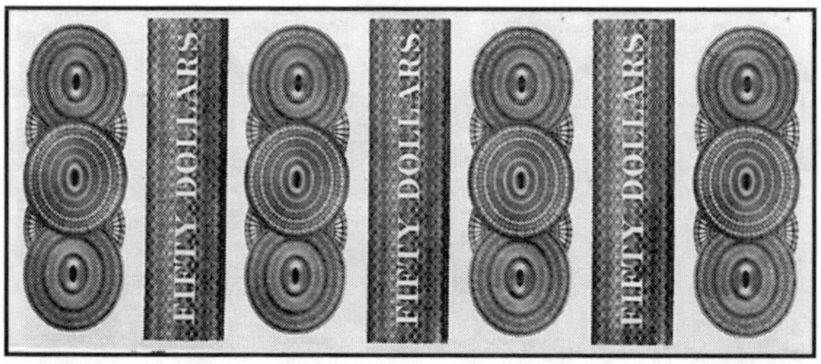

Back Design: Four lathework panels and three panels with "Fifty dollars" outlined in white
Colour: Blue

745-10-04
$100 (£25) Face Design: Seated woman with book/Indians watching steamboat, flanked by medallion portraits; small crest below/man with flag "Lord Byron"
Colour: Black with no tint

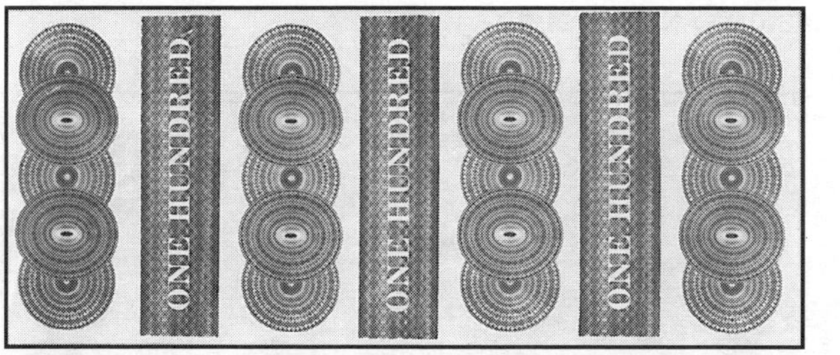

Back Design: Four lathework panels and three panels with "One hundred" outlined in white
Colour: Blue

IMPRINT
Danforth, Underwood & Co. New York
Underwood, Bald, Spencer & Hufty, Philada.

SIGNATURES

left	**right**
ms. Dudley Blinc	Monny Gray

ISSUE DATING
Partially engraved ___ 184__:
1840: January. 1

OVERPRINT
"G" in red at left

Cat. No.	Denom.	Date	Variety	G	VG	F	VF	EF	Unc
10-02	$50	1840		225.	450.	600.	900.	1,500.	—
10-02R	$50	18_	Remainder*	60.	125.	175.	300.	450.	850.
10-04	$100 (£25)	1840		225.	450.	600.	900.	1,500.	—
10-04R	$100 (£25)	184_	Remainder*	60.	125.	175.	300.	450.	850.

* Unsigned, undated and unnumbered.

UNION BANK OF NEWFOUNDLAND

1854-1894

ST. JOHN'S, NEWFOUNDLAND

BANK NUMBER 750 ***REDEEMABLE***

Established in St. John's, Newfoundland, in 1854, this bank failed in 1894 due to disastrous economic conditions and a run on the bank caused by the failure of the Commercial Bank of Newfoundland in the same year. The Newfoundland government assumed the responsibility for redeeming the notes of the failed banks, and the notes of the Union Bank continue to be redeemable for 80 cents on the dollar.

750-10 LARGE-SIZE POUND NOTES 1850s-EARLY 1860s

DESIGNS AND COLOURS

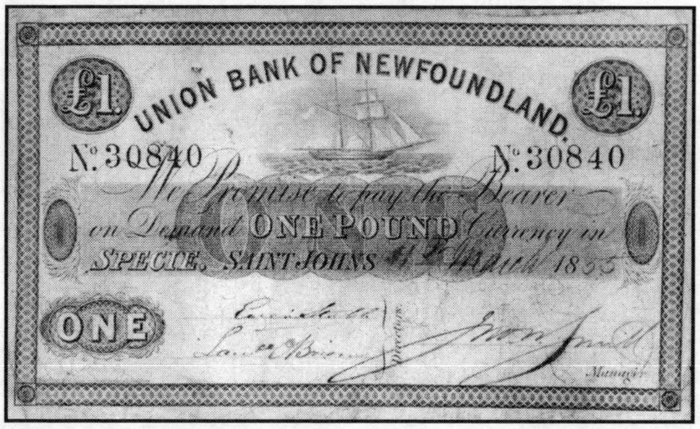

750-10-02
£1 Face Design: —/sailing ship/—
Colour: Black with no tint
Back Design: Plain

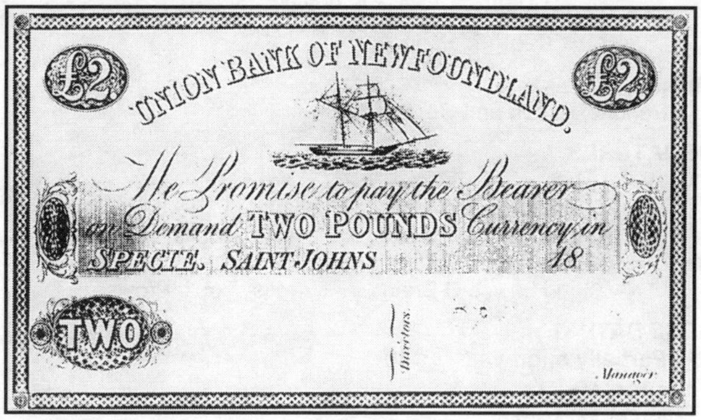

750-10-20
£2 Face Design: —/sailing ship/—
Colour: Black with no tint
Back Design: Plain

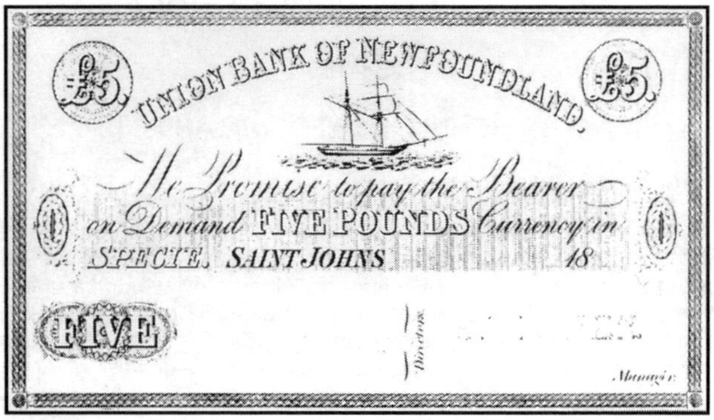

750-10-40

$5 Face Design: —/sailing ship/—
Colour: Black with no tint

Back Design: Plain

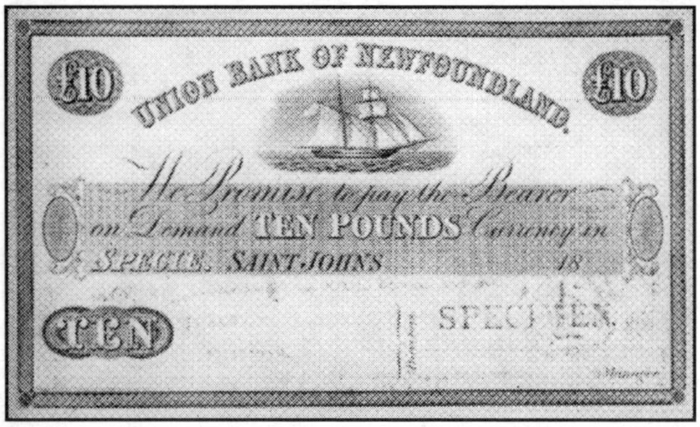

750-10-60

$10 Face Design: —/sailing ship/—
Colour: Black with no tint

Back Design: Plain

IMPRINT

Perkins, Bacon and Co. London

SIGNATURES

left	right
unknown and mss. Jno. W. Smith	mss. Rob't. Prowse
mss. Ewen Stable and Lawce O'Brein	mss. Rob't. Prowse

ISSUE DATING

Partially engraved ___ 18___:

1854: May 18
1855: 1st March

PROTECTOR

1854: Red "word" and mock coins on face and back
1855: Green "word" and mock coins on face and back

CIRCULATING NOTES

Cat. No.	Denom.	Date	G	VG	F	VF	EF	AU
10-02	£1	1854-1855	2,500.	4,500.	6,000.	—	—	—
10-20	£2	18__	No known issued notes					
10-40	£5	18__	No known issued notes					
10-60	£10	18__	No known issued notes					

PROOF NOTES

Cat. No.	Denom.	Date		Unc
10-02P	£1	18__	PROOF	500.
10-20P	£2	18__	PROOF	750.
10-40P	£5	18__	PROOF	750.
10-60P	£10	18__	PROOF	750.

SMALL-SIZE POUND NOTES, 1865-1883

DESIGNS AND COLOURS

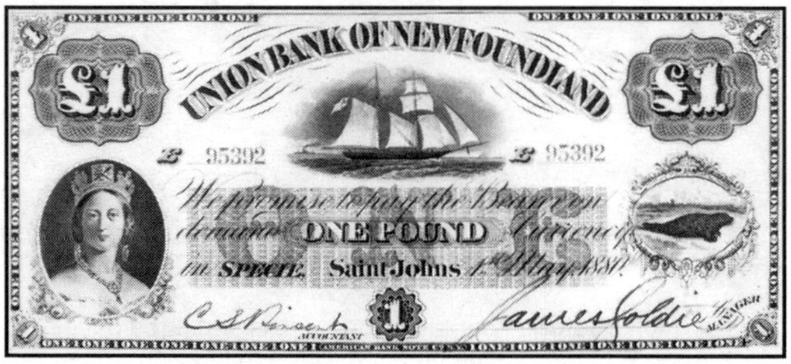

750-14-06

£1 Face Design: Queen Victoria (Winterhalter portrait)/sailing ship "Fishing Smack"/seal in oval
Colour: Black with no tint

Back Design: Plain

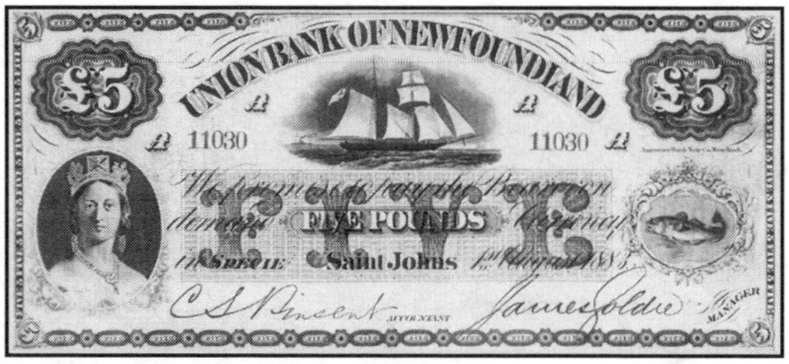

750-14-08

£5 Face Design: Queen Victoria (Winterhalter portrait)/sailing ship "Fishing Smack"/codfish in oval
Colour: Brown

Back Design: Plain

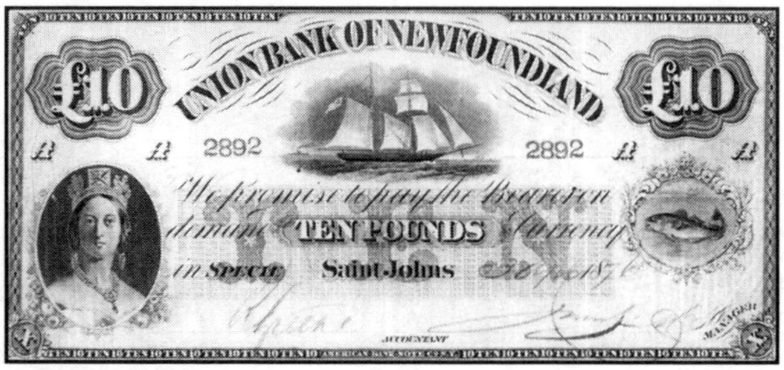

750-12-12

£10 Face Design: Queen Victoria (Winterhalter portrait)/sailing ship "Fishing Smack"/codfish in oval
Colour: Blue

Back Design: Plain

IMPRINT

American Bank Note Co. N.Y.
American Bank Note Co. New York

Note: Some £5 notes have a stamped guarantee of $16 and some £10 notes have $32 on the face.

750-12 ISSUES OF 1865-1881 PARTIALLY ENGRAVED DATE

SIGNATURES

	left	right
1865-1876:	mss. R. Greene	mss. John Smith
1881:	mss. C.S. Pinsent	mss. James Goldie

ISSUE DATING

Partially engraved ___ 18___:

£1, 1865: May 1, 4 Oct.
£5, 1875: 3 Oct.
£5 and £10, 1865: 2 Oct.
£5 and £10, 1876: 3 Apr.
£5 and £10, 1881: 1 Oct.

PROTECTOR

£1: Green "word" on face and on back in mirror image
£5: Blue "word" on face and on back in mirror image
£10: Red "word" on face and on back in mirror image.

CIRCULATING NOTES

Cat. No.	Denom.	Date	G	VG	F	VF	EF	AU
12-02	£1	1865	1,500.	2,400.	—	—	—	—
12-04	£5	1865	Institutional collection only					
12-05	£5	1875	Institutional collection only					
12-06	£5	1876	Institutional collection only					
12-08	£5	1881	1,200.	2,000.	2,600.	3,500.	—	—
12-10	£10	1865	1,500.	2,500.	—	—	—	—
12-12	£10	1876	Institutional collection only					
12-14	£10	1881	1,500.	2,500.	3,250.	4,500.	—	—

SPECIMEN NOTES

Cat. No.	Denom.	Date		Unc
12-10S	£10	18__	SPECIMEN	1,000.

750-14 ISSUES OF 1867-1883 FULLY ENGRAVED DATE

SIGNATURES

	left	right
1867-1880:	mss. C.S. Pinsent	mss. James Goldie
1867:	mss. R. Greene	mss. John Smith
1883:	engr. C.S. Pinsent	engr. James Goldie

ISSUE DATING

Engraved

1st March 1867
1st Septr 1877
1st May 1880
1st August 1883

PROTECTOR

£1: Green "word" on face and back
£5: Blue "word" on face and back

CIRCULATING NOTES

Cat. No.	Denom.	Date	G	VG	F	VF	EF	AU
14-02	£1	1867	900.	1,500.	2,000.	—	—	—
14-04	£1	1877	Institutional collection only					
14-06	£1	1880	300.	600.	850.	1,200.	1,800.	3,600.
14-08	£5	1883	1,200.	2,000.	2,600.	—	—	—

SPECIMEN NOTES

Cat. No.	Denom.	Date		Unc
14-06S	£1	1880	SPECIMEN	1,000.

Note: An uncut sheet of four specimen £1 1877, one and one-half sheets of £1 1880, and an uncut pair of £5 1883, were sold at Christie's ABN Archives Sale in 1990.

750-16 DOLLAR ISSUES OF 1882 AND 1889

DESIGNS AND COLOURS

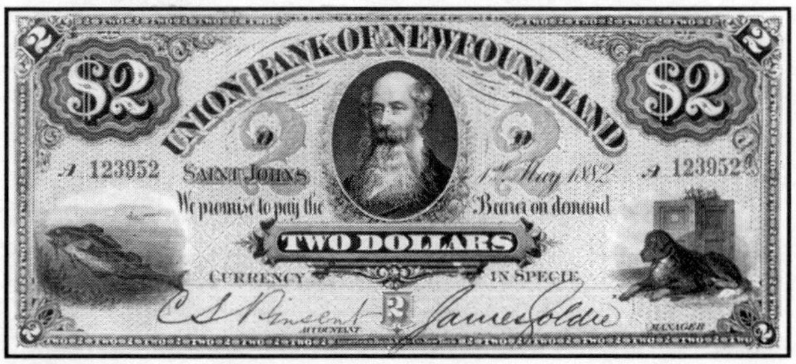

750-16-02

$2 Face Design: Codfish/John W. Smith/dog and safe
Colour: Black with overall green tint

Back Design: Lathework, counters and bank name
Colour: Green

750-16-04

$5 Face Design: Sailing ship "Fishing Smack"/cherub/ steamships and sailboats
Colour: Black with green and yellow tint

Back Design: —/cattle at pond/—
Colour: Green

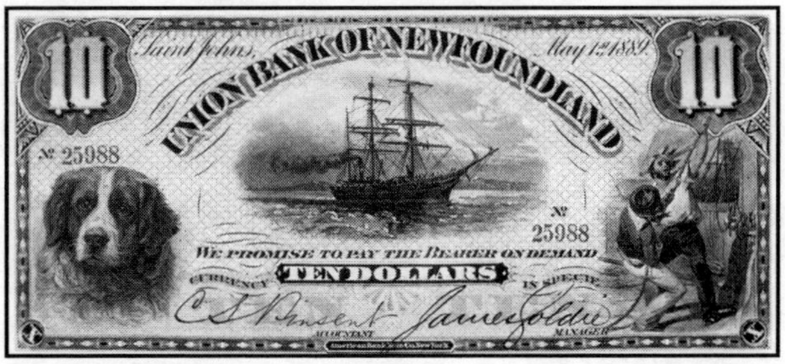

750-16-06

$10 Face Design: Newfoundland dog/sailing ship "Sealing"/ sailors hoisting sails "Show your colours"
Colour: Black with orange and yellow tint

Back Design: —/woman and strongbox/—
Colour: Orange

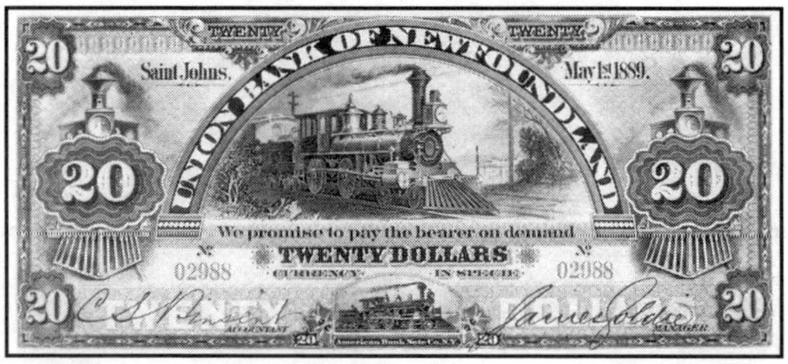

750-16-08
$20 Face Design: 20 counter over front of locomotive /locomotive; small locomotive below/ 20 counter over front of locomotive
Colour: Black with blue and yellow tint

Back Design: —/locomotive/—
Colour: Blue

750-16-10
$50 Face Design: "Justice" figure/bank building/woman, "Rebecca", pouring water for sheep
Colour: Black with brown and yellow tint

Back Design: —/dog by safe (after Landseer)/—
Colour: Brown

IMPRINT

American Bank Note Co. New York

SIGNATURES

left	right
engr. C.S. Pincent	engr. James Goldie

ISSUE DATING

Engraved

1st May 1882
May 1st 1889

CIRCULATING NOTES

Cat. No.	Denom.	Date	G	VG	F	VF	EF	AU
16-02	$2	1882	150.	300.	400.	650.	1,050.	2,100.
16-04	$5	1889	450.	900.	1,200.	2,000.	—	—
16-06	$10	1889	300.	600.	850.	1,300.	2,200.	4,000.
16-08	$20	1889	—	—	1,500.	2,500.	4,000.	6,000.
16-10	$50	1889	—	3,500.	4,500.	7,500.	—	—

Note: Notes which have been stamped with the guarantee the Newfoundland Government, revaluing them at 80% of their former face values, should be considered desirable and unimpaired. Although all known examples have additional cancellation markings, they may command a premium of about 10% above listed prices.

PROOF NOTES

Cat. No.	Denom.	Date		Unc
16-02P	$2	1882	FACE PROOF	500.
16-04P	$5	1889	FACE PROOF	500.
16-06P	$10	1889	FACE PROOF	500.
16-08P	$20	1889	FACE PROOF	500.
16-10P	$50	1889	FACE PROOF	500.

SPECIMEN NOTES

Cat. No.	Denom.	Date		Unc
16-02S	$2	1882	SPECIMEN	750.
16-04S	$5	1889	SPECIMEN	750.
16-06S	$10	1889	SPECIMEN	750.
16-08S	$20	1889	SPECIMEN	750.
16-10S	$50	1889	SPECIMEN	750.

Note: Uncut sheets and part sheets of specimen notes of this issue were sold at Christie's ABN Archives Sale in 1990.

THE UNION BANK OF PRINCE EDWARD ISLAND

1860-1883

CHARLOTTETOWN (PRINCE EDWARD ISLAND)

BANK NUMBER 755 ***REDEEMABLE***

Established in Charlottetown, Prince Edward Island, in 1860, this prosperous bank played an important role in bringing the island into Confederation. However, industrial depression and slow liquidation of lumber and shipping forced it to merge with a stronger institution, and on May 25, 1883, an act providing for the absorption of the bank by the Bank of Nova Scotia received royal assent. This enabled the Bank of Nova Scotia to issue, until July 1, 1891, notes in excess of the paid-up capital to the extent of twice the paid-up capital of the Union Bank. The amalgamation became final on October 1, 1883, and that year $130,000 was written off the reserve fund of the Bank of Nova Scotia to cover the losses.

ISSUES OF 1864-1872

DESIGNS AND COLOURS

755-10-02P

$1 (4s 2d) Face Design: Sailors on dock/lion and shield/ woman, sheep and sheaves "Agriculture"
See subheadings

Colour: Black with no tint

Back Design: Plain

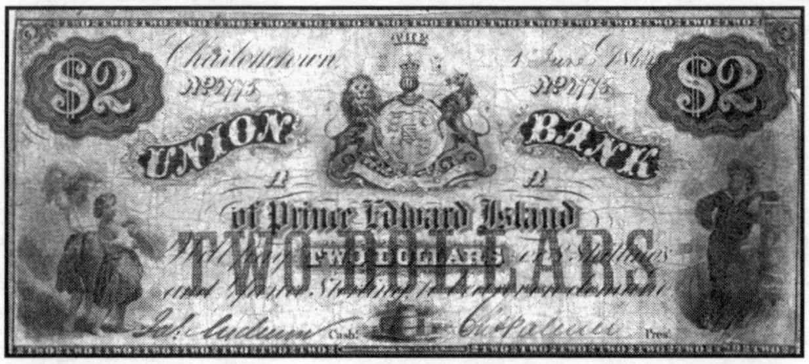

755-10-04P

$2 (8s 4d) Face Design: Two children with sheaves/Royal Arms, cask and bales below/sailor by capstan "On Deck"
See subheadings

Colour: Black with no tint

Back Design: Plain

755-10-06

$5 (20s 10d) Face Design: St. George slaying the dragon/ milkmaid seated in pasture with two cows/steamship and tugboat
See subheadings

Colour: Black with no tint

Back Design: Plain

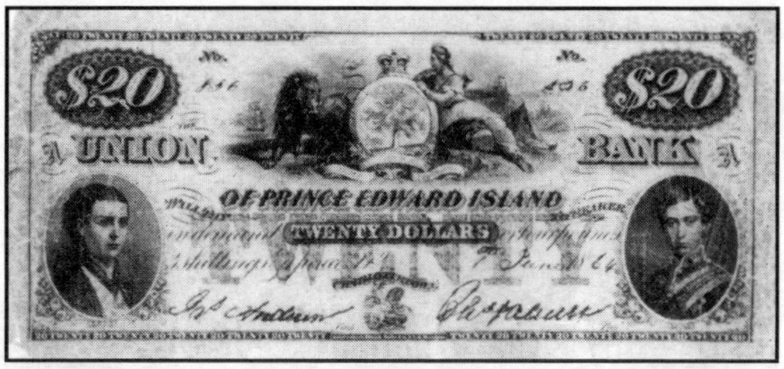

755-10-08

$20 (£4.3.4) Face Design: Princess of Wales/modified P.E.I. Crest, St. George slaying the dragon below/Prince of Wales
See subheadings

Colour: Black with no tint

Back Design: Plain

IMPRINT

American Bank Note Co. N.Y. & Boston

755-10

ISSUE OF 1864-1865
DOLLARS AND STERLING

SIGNATURES

left	**right**
mss. Jas. Anderson	mss. Chs. Palmer

ISSUE DATING

Partially engraved ___ 18___:

1864: 1 June
1865: Jan. 2

PROTECTOR

Green "word" on face and back
Green "two dollars" on face and back in mirror image
Green "5 FIVE 5" on face and back
Green "TWENTY" on face and back

CIRCULATING NOTES

Cat. No.	Denom.	Date	G	VG	F	VF	EF	AU
10-02	$1 (4s 2d)	18__		No known issued notes				
10-04	$2 (8s 4d)	1864		Institutional collection only				
10-06	$5 (20s 10d)	1865		Institutional collection only				
10-08R	$20 (£4.3.4))	18__ Remainder	4,500.	—	—	—	—	—

* The only known remainder note has forged signatures.

PROOF NOTES

Cat. No.	Denom.	Date		Unc
10-02P	$1 (4s2d)	18__	PROOF	600.
10-04P	$2 (8s4d)	18__	PROOF	600.
10-08P	$20 (£4.3.4)	18__	PROOF	600.

755-12

ISSUE OF 1872
DOLLAR ONLY

755-12-02a

$1 Face Design: Sailors on dock/lion and shield/ woman, sheep and sheaves "Agriculture"
See subheadings

Colour: Black with no tint

Back Design: Plain

755-12-04

$2 Face Design: Two children with sheaves/Royal Arms/ sailor by capstan "On Deck"
See subheadings

Colour: Black with no tint

Back Design: Plain

Photo Not Available

755-12-06P

$5 Face Design: St. George slaying the dragon/milkmaid seated in pasture with two cows/steamship and tugboat
See subheadings

Colour: Black with no tint

Back Design: Plain

755-12-08P

$20 Face Design: Princess of Wales/modified P.E.I. Crest, St. George slaying the dragon below/ Prince of Wales
See subheadings

Colour: Black with no tint

Back Design: Plain

IMPRINT

American Bank Note Co. N.Y. and Boston

SIGNATURES

left	right
mss. Jas. Anderson	mss. Chs. Palmer
mss. Wm. Heard	mss. Chs. Palmer
mss. John H. Yeo (p)	mss. Chs. Palmer
mss. Geo. MacLeod	mss. John Ings (v)

ISSUE DATING

Engraved

1st January 1872

PROTECTOR

Green "word" on face and in mirror image on the back

OVERPRINT

$1, $2: "CANADA CURRENCY" twice vertically in red near the ends

CIRCULATING NOTES

Cat. No.	Denom.	Date	Variety	G	VG	F	VF	EF	AU
12-02	$1	1872	No o/p	Institutional collection only					
12-02a	$1	1872	Red o/p	2,000.	3,500.	—	—	—	—
12-04	$2	1872	No o/p	2,000.	3,500.	—	—	—	—
12-04a	$2	1872	Red o/p	Institutional collection only					
12-04C	$2	1872	Counterfeit	50.	100.	125.	175.	225.	—
12-06	$5	1872		No known issued notes					
12-08	$20	1872		Institutional collection only					

Note: Beware of $2 counterfeit notes.

PROOF NOTES

Cat. No.	Denom.	Date		Unc
12-06P	$5	1872	FACE PROOF	600.
12-08P	$20	1872	FACE PROOF	600.

755-14 BABN PRINTINGS 1875 AND 1877

DESIGNS AND COLOURS

755-14-02

$1 Face Design: Two codfish in oval/locomotive/ two seals in oval
Colour: Black with green tint

Back Design: Lathework, counters and bank name
Colour: Green

755-14-04P

$2 Face Design: River pilot at wheel "Lachine Pilot"/ Landseer's Newfoundland on strongbox "Dog Trusty"/woman with sheaf of wheat
Colour: Black with green tint

Back Design: Lathework, counters and bank name
Colour: Green

755-14-08P

$5 Face Design: St. George slaying the dragon/ farm implements and produce "Implements of Agriculture"/ woman with telescope over ornate 5
Colour: Black with green tint

Back Design: Lathework, counters and bank name
Colour: Green

Note: The face tint includes "Canada Currency" twice vertically in green on each note.

IMPRINT

British American Bank Note Co. Montreal

SIGNATURES

left	right
mss. John H. Yeo (p)	mss. John Ings (v)
mss. Geo. MacLeod	mss. Chs. Palmer
mss. John H. Yeo (p)	mss. Chs. Palmer

ISSUE DATING

Engraved

March 1st 1875
Unknown 1877

OVERPRINT

"U" near upper left corner, and "B" at the upper right corner

CIRCULATING NOTES

Cat. No.	Denom.	Date	Variety	G	VG	F	VF	EF	AU
14-02	$1	1875		1,200.	2,000.	3,000.	—	—	—
14-02A	$1	1875	Red UB o/p	1,300.	2,200.	—	—	—	—
14-04	$2	1875		1,650.	2,750.	—	—	—	—
14-04C	$2	1875	Counterfeit	50.	100.	125.	—	—	—
14-06	$2	1877		Institutional collection only					
14-08	$5	1875		Institutional collection only					
14-10	$5	1877		No known issued notes					

Note: Beware of counterfeit $2 notes.

PROOF NOTES

Cat. No.	Denom.	Date		Unc
14-02	$1	1875	FACE PROOF	600.
14-04	$2	1875	FACE PROOF	600.
14-08	$5	1875	FACE PROOF	600.
14-10	$5	1877	FACE PROOF	600.

UNION BANK OF VICTORIA

1865

VANCOUVER'S ISLAND, BRITISH COLUMBIA

BANK NUMBER 758

This bank was unknown until a reference to it was discovered in the American Bank Note Company order book. The bank requested the engraving of "two bills of exchange with margin", and the order was dated 12 July, 1865. No further information concerning this bank is available and notes are unknown.

UNITED EMPIRE BANK OF CANADA

1906-1911

TORONTO, ONTARIO

BANK NUMBER 760 ***REDEEMABLE***

Established in Toronto in 1906 under the name of the Pacific Bank of Canada, it changed its name to the United Empire Bank of Canada later that year and merged with the Union Bank of Canada in 1911. It was a small bank, its growth had been slow and the institution had not held its own with its competitors.

760-10 **ISSUE OF 1906**

DESIGNS AND COLOURS

760-10-02
$5 Face Design: —/seated Britannia flanked by two world globes/—
Colour: Black with green tint

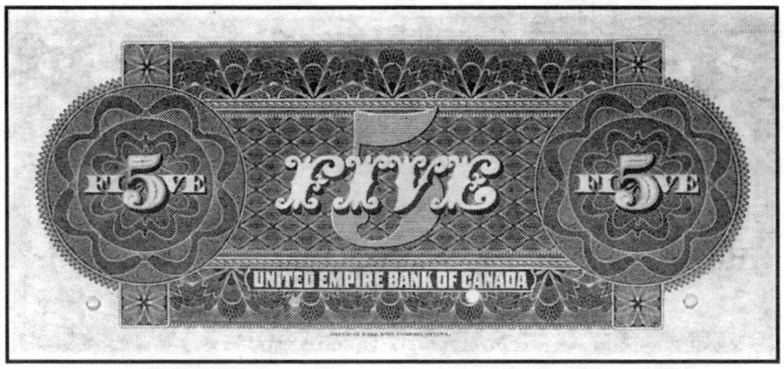

Back Design: Lathework, counters and bank name
Colour: Green

760-10-04
$10 Face Design: Seated "Justice" figure/—/—
Colour: Black with yellow-green tint

Back Design: Lathework, counters, bank name and beavers
Colour: Blue

IMPRINT

American Bank Note Company, Ottawa

SIGNATURES

left	**right**
mss. various	typed Saml. Barker

ISSUE DATING

Engraved

1st August, 1906

CIRCULATING NOTES

Cat. No.	Denom.	Date	G	VG	F	VF	EF	AU
10-02	$5	1906	—	5,500.	—	—	—	—
10-04	$10	1906	—	5,500.	7,500.	—	—	—

PROOF NOTES

Cat. No.	Denom.	Date	Variety		Unc
10-02P	$5	1906	1 Aug.	FACE PROOF	750.
10-02Pa	$5	1906	25 June	FACE PROOF	750.
10-04P	$10	1906	1 Aug.	FACE PROOF	750.
10-04Pa	$10	1906	25 June	FACE PROOF	750.

BANK OF UPPER CANADA

1819 - 1822

KINGSTON, UPPER CANADA

BANK NUMBER 765 ***NONREDEEMABLE***

The residents of Kingston, Upper Canada, were the first to apply to the legislature for a charter in the name of the Bank of Upper Canada. Impatient at the delay in receiving royal assent, they began operations without a charter on April 16, 1819. The private bank had a paid-up capital of £12,000 and issued almost £19,000 in notes. It was intended that it be merged with the Bank of Kingston, which received the substitute charter for the Kingston petition; however, bad times followed. The Bank of Kingston never came into existence, and the private Bank of Upper Canada failed on September 23, 1822.

REGULAR NOTE ISSUES, 1819-1822

DESIGNS AND COLOURS

765-10-02

$1 Face Design: —/steamboat, sheaf and plough, ONE vertically; coin below/—
Colour: Black with no tint

Back Design: Plain

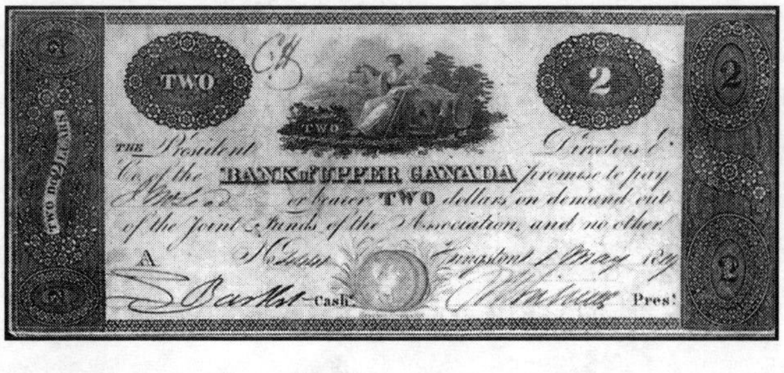

765-10-04

$2 Face Design: —/TWO, seated "Justice" figure and barrels; two coins below/—
Colour: Black with no tint

Back Design: Plain

765-10-14

$5 Face Design: —/fort, harbour area; five coins below/—
Colour: Black with no tint

Back Design: Plain

765-10-16

$10 Face Design: —/fort and Kingston harbour; X over flowers below/—
Colour: Black with no tint

Back Design: Plain

IMPRINT

Graphic company

765-10 REGULAR NOTE ISSUE PARTIALLY ENGRAVED DATE 1819 - 1822

SIGNATURES

left	right
mss. S. Bartlett	mss. B. Whitney
mss. S. Bartlett	mss. Henry Murney (v)

ISSUE DATING

Partially engraved ___ 18___:

$1 and $2, 1819: May 1, 1 May
$1 and $5, 1819: 29 March, 1 May
1822: Apr. 4, May 1, June 3
$10, 1819: 4 Apr., 1 May
1822: June 3

OVERPRINT

"Payable at the Bank of Canada in Montreal" in black on some notes.

Cat. No.	Denom.	Date		G	VG	F	VF	EF	AU
10-02	$1	1819		55.	110.	150.	225.	—	—
10-02R	$1	18__	Remainder	—	—	—	100.	150.	—
10-04	$2	1819		55.	110.	150.	225.	—	—
10-04R	$2	18__	Remainder	—	—	—	100.	150.	—
10-06	$5	1819		50.	100.	125.	200.	300.	—
10-06R	$5	18__	Remainder	—	—	—	100.	150.	—
10-14	$5	1822		50.	100.	125.	200.	300.	—
10-16	$10	1819		50.	100.	125.	200.	300.	—
10-16R	$10	18__	Remainder	—	—	—	100.	150.	—
10-22	$10	1822		50.	100.	125.	200.	300.	—

765-12 REGULAR NOTE ISSUE FULLY ENGRAVED DATE 1820

DESIGNS AND COLOURS

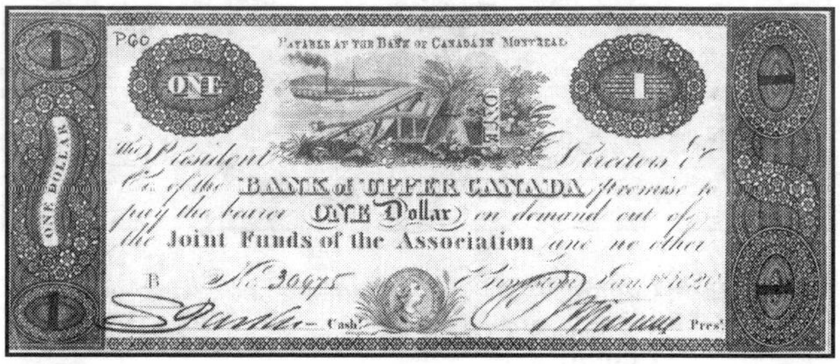

765-12-02

$1 Face Design: —/steamboat, sheaf and plough and ONE vertically; coin below/—
Colour: Black with no tint

Back Design: Plain

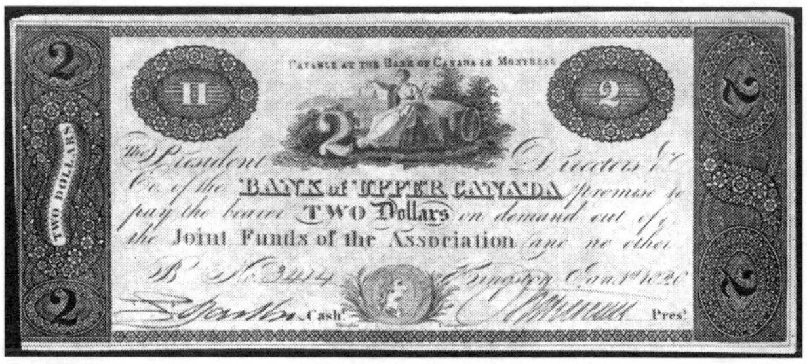

765-12-04

$2 Face Design: —/Numeral 2, seated "Justice" figure and barrels;
two coins below/-
Colour: Black with no tint

Back Design: Plain

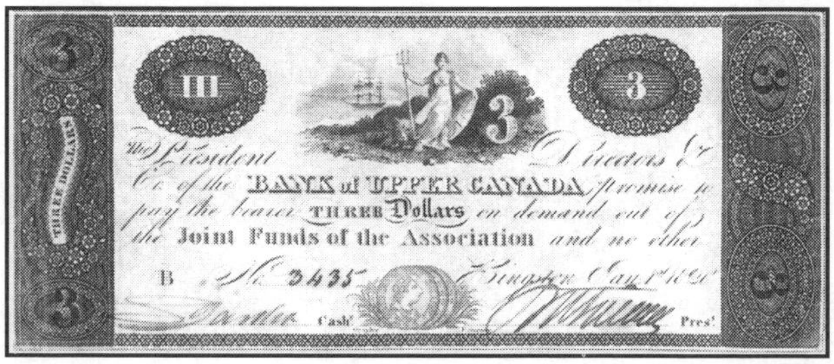

765-12-06

$3 Face Design: —/sailing ship, lion, Britannia, numeral 3, three coins below/—
Colour: Black with no tint

Back Design: Plain

IMPRINT

Graphic Company

Note: The vignettes and counters are slightly different from the 765-10 issue.

SIGNATURES

left	right
mss. S. Bartlett	mss. Henry Murney (v)
mss. S. Bartlett	mss. B. Whitney

ISSUE DATING
Engraved
Jan. 1 1820

OVERPRINT
"Payable at the Bank of Canada in Montreal" in black on some notes

Note: Counterfeits (photocopies) of $1, $2 and $3 notes have been seen.

Cat. No.	Denom.	Date	VG	F	VF	EF	Unc
12-02	$1	1820	50.	70.	105.	180.	350.
12-04	$2	1820	50.	70.	105.	180.	350.
12-06	$3	1820	75.	100.	125.	200.	375.

765-14 SCRIP ISSUE OF 1820

DESIGNS AND COLOURS

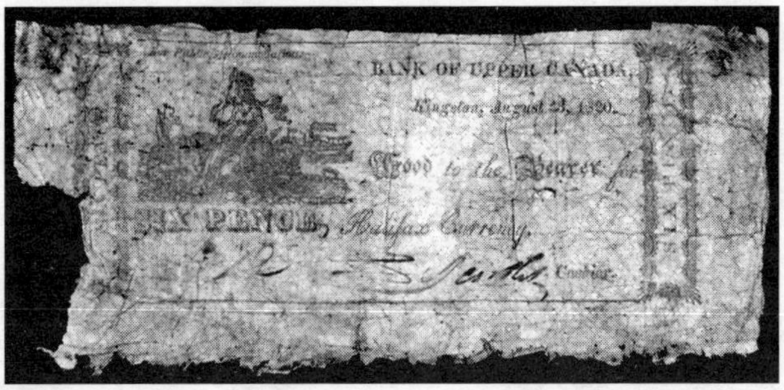

765-14-02

6d Face Design: Seated Britannia/—/—
Marked "For Public Accommodation"
Colour: Black with no tint
Back Design: Plain

IMPRINT
None

SIGNATURES
right only
illegible

ISSUE DATING
Letterpress
August 23, 1820

Cat. No.	Denom.	Date	G	VG	F	VF	EF	AU
14-02	6d	1820	630.	1,260.	1,600.	—	—	—

THE BANK OF UPPER CANADA

1821-1866

YORK, UPPER CANADA

BANK NUMBER 770 ***NONREDEEMABLE***

This bank was established in York, Upper Canada (now Toronto, Ontario), its charter granted by the Province of Upper Canada in 1819, becoming law on April 21, 1821. The charter was to remain in force until June 1, 1848.

The charter of this bank was different from those of other banks in operation in a few essential respects:

1. The Government of Upper Canada was authorized to subscribe for 2,000 out of 16,000 (later 8,000) shares, which were £12.10 each;
2. The bank was given express authority to establish branches;
3. No limit was placed on the value of real estate that the bank could hold to carry on its business;
4. If the bank refused payment of its notes in specie, it was obliged to cease operations until specie payment was resumed, or forfeit its charter;
5. An annual return, properly sworn, was to be made to the provincial legislature.

Soon after its establishment, the bank was accused of using its power in politics; nonetheless, it had grown steadily and was held in high esteem. It was banker to the government for a number of years. However, it made too many loans secured by real estate, and as a consequence, found itself in difficulties for several years, despite efforts to rehabilitate its affairs.

It failed in 1866 and was the first important bank failure in Canadian history. The insolvency was mainly a result of the land boom in Upper Canada between 1857 and 1858 and the depression that followed. Bank management did not observe sound banking principles, particularly with respect to real-estate loans. When real-estate values declined, the bank was left with many unrealizable assets. The shareholders lost all their capital, which at one time amounted to about $3.3 million. The government lost about $1 million, and the depositors and note holders also suffered heavily.

770-10 GRAPHIC PRINTINGS 1822-1832

DESIGNS AND COLOURS

770-10-05

$1 (5s) Face Design: —/seated Britannia, facing left, with arm outstretched over beehive, ship left, one dollar over numeral 1 below/—
Colour: Black with no tint
Back Design: Plain

IMPRINT
Graphic Company

SIGNATURES

Left	right
Mss. Thos. G. Ridout	mss. W. Allan

ISSUE DATING
Add, $1 (5s) 1822: July 24

Cat. No.	Denom.	Date	G	VG	F	VF	EF	AU
10-05	$1 (5S)	1822	One known, damaged G, sold for $572 in Jeffrey Hoare sale #74 May 2002					

770-10-10

$1 (5s) Face Design: —/seated Britannia with beehive and ship; one dollar over numeral 1 below/—

Colour: Black with no tint

Back Design: Plain

770-10-20

$2 (10s) Face Design: —/harbour scene and 2 outlined in white; two coins below/—

Colour: Black with no tint

Back Design: Plain

770-10-32

$4 (20s) Face Design: —/St. George slaying the dragon; four coins below/—

Colour: Black with no tint

Back Design: Plain

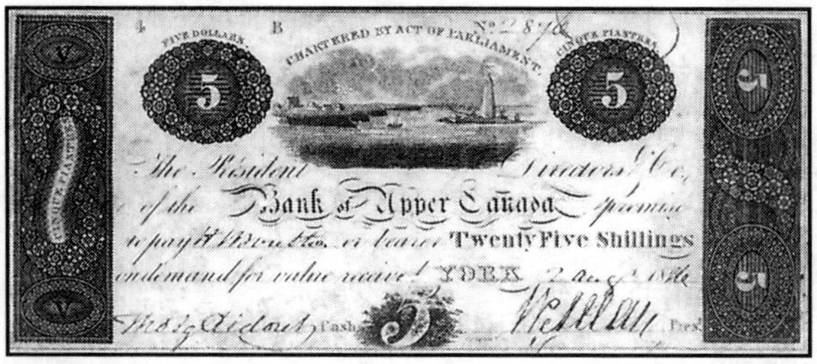

770-10-40

$5 (25s) Face Design: —/view of York; 5 outlined in bushes below/—

Colour: Black with no tint

Back Design: Plain

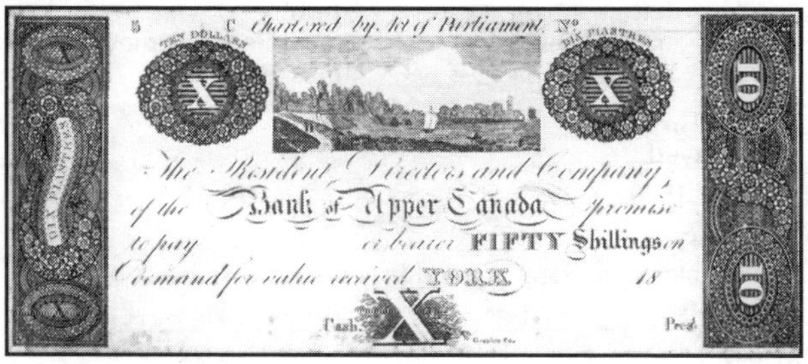

770-10-76

$10 (50s) Face Design: —/harbour scene; X outlined in bushes below/—

Colour: Black with no tint

Back Design: Plain

IMPRINT

Graphic Co.

SIGNATURES

left	right
mss. Thos. G. Ridout	mss. W. Allan

ISSUE DATING

Partially engraved ___ 18___:

$1 (5s), 1829: Mar. 7
1831: 19 March
$2 (10s), 1827: Aug. 3
$4 (20s), 1830: 3 Novr.
1832: 2 Novr.
$5 (25s), 1826: 2 Augt.
1827: 3 Jan.
1830: 1 Jan., 2d Jan.
1832: 19 Sept.
$10 (50s), 1830: 1 Nov.

VARIETIES

$5 (25s): Five Dollars - cinq piastres above counters at top
Five Dollars - cinq piastres below counters at top

Cat. No.	Denom.	Date	Variety	G	VG	F	VF	EF	AU
10-10	$1 (5s)	1829-1831		250.	500.	—	—	—	—
10-20	$2 (10s)	1827		250.	500.	—	—	—	—
10-32	$4 (20s)	1830-1832		300.	600.	—	—	—	—
10-40	$5 (25s)	1826-1832	$5 above	225.	450.	600.	—	—	—
10-64	$5 (25s)	1832	$5 below	300.	600.	—	—	—	—
10-76	$10 (50s)	1830		300.	600.	—	—	—	—

770-12 ISSUE OF THE 1830s PAYABLE AT TORONTO

DESIGNS AND COLOURS

770-12-02P

$1 Face Design: Seated "Justice" figure/ Neptune, flying female and horses; bust of Indian in oval below/—

Colour: Black with no tint

Back Design: Plain

770-12-08

$2 Face Design: Allegorical female and anchor/ Indian shooting arrow; buffalo below/ allegorical female in clouds

Colour: Black with no tint

Back Design: Plain

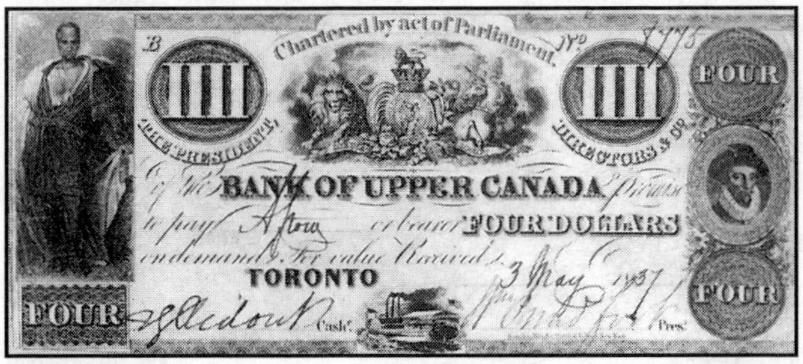

770-12-14

$4 Face Design: Indian "Red Jacket"/Royal Crest; steamboat below/Sir Walter Raleigh

Colour: Black with no tint

Back Design: Plain

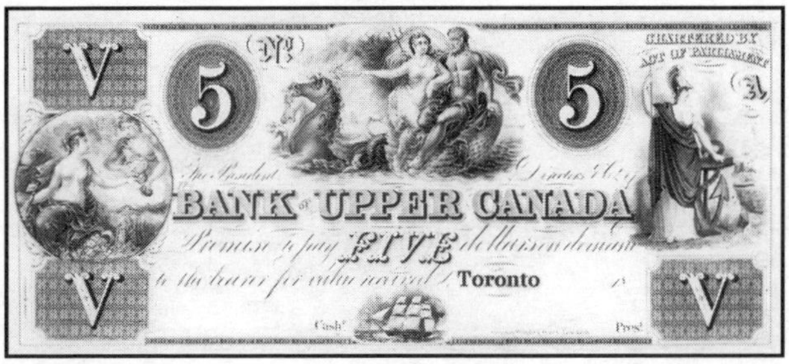

770-12-18P

$5 Face Design: Three allegorical figures/Neptune and woman (Commerce) on shell drawn by seahorses; sailing ships below/ Britannia, anchor and ship

Colour: Black with no tint

Back Design: Plain

770-12-30

$10 Face Design: Two allegorical females/Neptune and woman (Commerce) on shell drawn by seahorses; sailing ships below/cherub with fruit basket on head in oval

Colour: Black with no tint

Back Design: Plain

770-12-32P

$20 Face Design: —/griffin and three allegorical figures; griffin with key below/obelisk

Colour: Black with no tint

Back Design: Plain

770-12-34P

$20 Face Design: —/griffin and three allegorical figures; griffin with key below/Toronto at right

Colour: Black with no tint

Back Design: Plain

770-12-38P

$50 Face Design: Cherub with fruit basket on head in oval/ train and wagons at wharf; griffin with key below/obelisk

Colour: Black with no tint

Back Design: Plain

770-12-46P

$100 Face Design: —/Royal Crest; griffin with key below/obelisk

Colour: Black with no tint

Back Design: Plain

IMPRINT

Rawdon, Wright & Hatch New York or Rawdon, Wright, Hatch & Edson, New York

SIGNATURES

left	right
mss. T.G. Ridout	mss. Wm. Proudfoot

ISSUE DATING

Partially engraved _ 18_:

1836: 6 Nov.
1837: May 3
1838: 1 Jany., 10 Jan'y, 5 June

CIRCULATING NOTES

Cat. No.	Denmo.	Date	G	VG	F	VF	EF	AU
12-02	$1	18--		No known issued notes				
12-08	$2	1836-1838	325.	650.	850.	—	—	—
12-14	$4	1837		Institutional collection only				
12-18	$5	18__		No known issued notes				
12-30	$10	1838	—	650.	850.	1,200.	—	—
12-32	$20	18__ Toronto 1.		No known issued notes				
12-34	$20	18__ Toronto r.		No known issued notes				
12-38	$50	18__ Toronto 1.		No known issued notes				
12-40	$50	18__ Toronto r.		No known issued notes				
12-46	$100	18__		No known issued notes				

PROOF NOTES

Cat. No.	Denom.	Date		Unc
12-02P	$1	18__	PROOF	400.
12-08P	$2	18__	PROOF	400.
12-14P	$4	18__	PROOF	400.
12-18P	$5	18__	PROOF	400.
12-30P	$10	18__	PROOF	400.
12-32P	$20	18__ Toronto l.	PROOF	400.
12-34P	$20	18__ Toronto r.	PROOF	400.
12-38P	$50	18__ Toronto l.	PROOF	450.
12-40P	$50	18__ Toronto r	PROOF	450.
12-46P	$100	18__	PROOF	500.

770-14 ISSUES OF 1849-1856 TORONTO RED PROTECTOR

These issues are engraved "TORONTO" at the bottom centre.

DESIGNS AND COLOURS

All notes have a small image of St. George slaying the dragon at the bottom centre, encircled by "BANK OF U CANADA."

770-14-02P

$1 (5s) Face Design: Reclining lion in oval (part of Royal Crest)/ seated "Commerce" figure with hand on ornate 1/woman, dog and 1 in oval

Colour: Black with no tint

Back Design: Plain

770-14-20P

$2 (10s) Face Design: "Agriculture" figure/two flying griffins flanking 2/portrait of woman
Colour: Black with no tint
Back Design: Plain

770-14-34

$4 (£1) Face Design: Queen Victoria (Chalon portrait) in oval/seated Britannia, lion, cannon and flags/seated "Agricultural Commerce" figure in oval
Colour: Black with no tint
Back Design: Plain

770-14-46

$5 (£1.5) Face Design: Queen Victoria (Chalon portrait) in oval/lion and shield/Prince Consort in oval
Colour: Black with no tint
Back Design: Plain

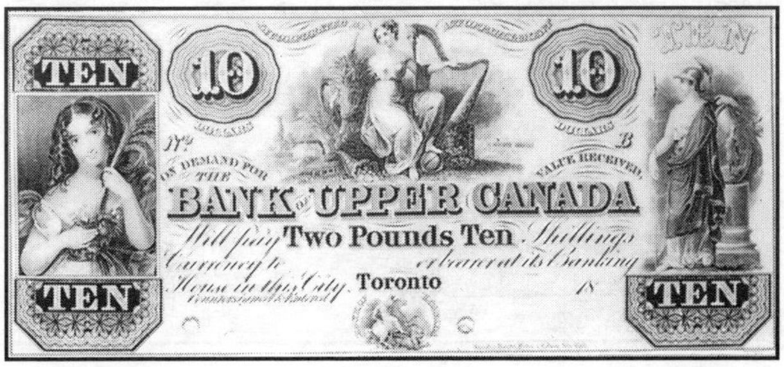

770-14-62P

$10 (£2.10) Face Design: Young woman with wheat stalks/seated woman with sheaf and harp/Britannia
Colour: Black with no tint
Back Design: Plain

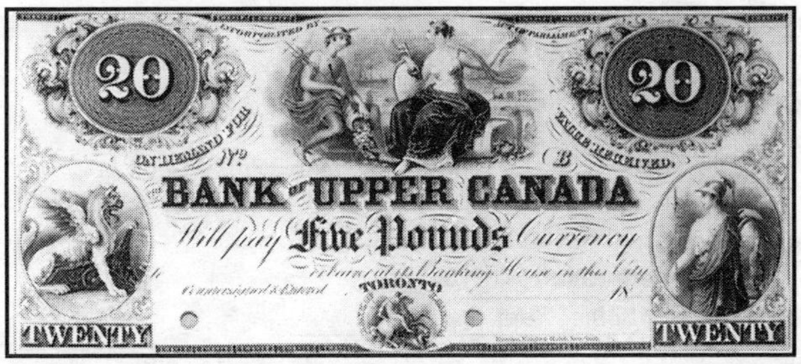

770-14-78P

$20 (£5) Face Design: Griffin in oval/seated Mercury and woman with caduceus, coins key and sheaf/
Britannia in oval
Colour: Black with no tint
Back Design: Plain

770-14-96P

$50 (£12.10) Face Design: Seated "Agriculture" figure/seated woman with cornucopia and coins on Royal Crest/seated Britannia
Colour: Black with no tint
Back Design: Plain

770-14-104P

$100 (£25) Face Design: Queen Victoria (Chalon portrait) in oval/Queen Victoria (Chalon portrait) in oval on Royal Crest/medallion portrait of helmeted man in oval

Colour: Black with no tint

Back Design: Plain

IMPRINT

Rawdon, Wright & Hatch, New-York

SIGNATURES

left	right
mss. Thos. G. Ridout	mss. Wm. Proudfoot
mss. C.S. Murray	mss. Wm. Proudfoot

ISSUE DATING

Partially engraved ___ 18___:

$1 (5s) 1849: Sept. 1
$1 (5s) 1855: 4 Sept.
$4 (£1) 1851: 1 Nov.
1852: 5 Aug.
1856: 7 Nov.; 17 Apr.
$5 (£1.5) 1849: 9 Oct.

PROTECTOR

Issued notes have red "word" on face and back

CIRCULATING NOTES

Cat. No.	Denom.	Date	G	VG	F	VF	EF	AU
14-02	$1 (5s)	1849-1855	350.	700.	950.	—	—	—
14-20	$2 (10s)	18__		No known issued notes				
14-34	$4 (£1)	1851-1856	300.	600.	850.	—	—	—
14-46	$5 (£1.5)	1849	350.	700.	950.	—	—	—
14-62	$10 (£2.10)	18__		Institutional collection only				
14-78	$20 (£5)	18__		No known issued notes				
14-96	$50 (£12.10)	18__		No known issued notes				
14-104	$100 (£25)	18__		No known issued notes				

PROOF NOTES

Cat. No.	Denom.	Date		Unc
14-02P	$1 (5s)	18__	PROOF	400.
14-20P	$2 (10s)	18__	PROOF	400.
14-34P	$4 (£1)	18__	PROOF	400.
14-46P	$5 (£1.5)	18__	PROOF	400.
14-62P	$10 (£2.10)	18__	PROOF	400.
14-78P	$20 (£5)	18__	PROOF	400.
14-96P	$50 (£12.10)	18__	PROOF	450.
14-104P	$100 (£25)	18__	PROOF	500.

770-16 ISSUES OF 1857 RED PROTECTOR

2. MONTREAL ISSUE, 1857

"Montreal" is engraved at the lower right of these issues, and "OFFICE OF THE BANK OF UPPER CANADA IN MONTREAL" is engraved across the top.

DESIGNS AND COLOURS

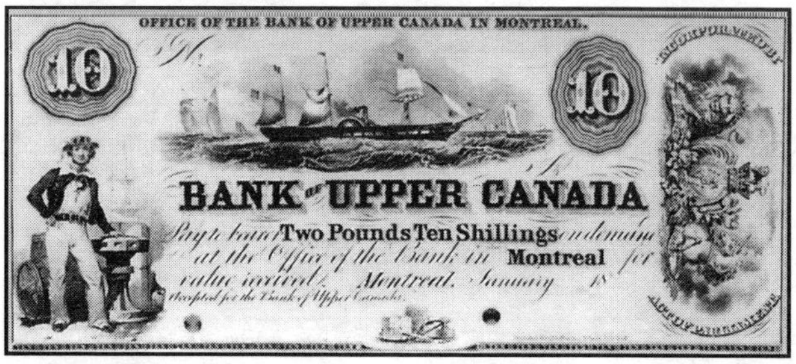

770-16-02-02P

$10 (£2.10) Face Design: Sailor with capstan, kegs and bale/paddlewheel steamship; kegs, bale and anchor below/Royal Crest (sideways) (check letter A notes)

Colour: Black with no tint

Back Design: Plain

Photo Not Available

770-16-02-04P

$10 (£2.10) Face Design: Sailing ships/seated sailor with bale and kegs; bale and kegs below/Royal Crest (sideways) (check letter B notes)

Colour: Black with no tint

Back Design: Plain

IMPRINT

Rawdon, Wright, Hatch & Edson, New York

SIGNATURES

left	right
none	none

ISSUE DATING

Partially engraved January ___ 18___:

PROOF NOTES

Cat. No.	Den.	Date	Variety		Unc
16-02-02P	$10 (£2.10)	18_	Steamship	PROOF	450.
16-02-04P	$10 (£2.10)	18_	Seated sailor	PROOF	450.

4. QUEBEC ISSUE, 1857

"Quebec" is engraved at the lower right of these notes, and "OFFICE OF THE BANK OF UPPER CANADA IN QUEBEC" is across the top.

DESIGNS AND COLOURS

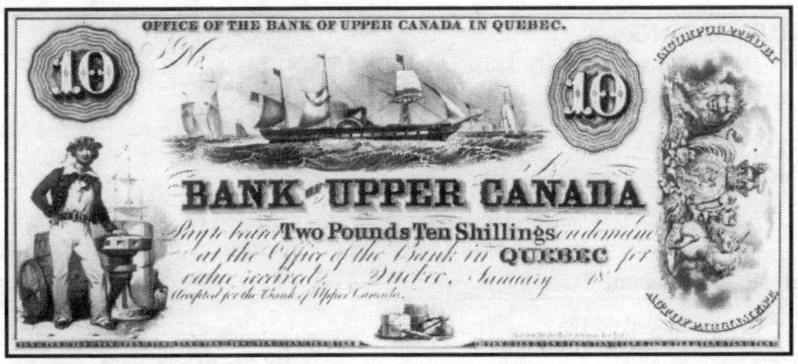

770-16-04-02P

$10 (£2.10) Face Design: Sailor with capstan, kegs and bale/ paddlewheel steamship; kegs, bale and anchor below/Royal Crest (sideways) (check letter A notes)

Colour: Black with no tint

Back Design: Plain

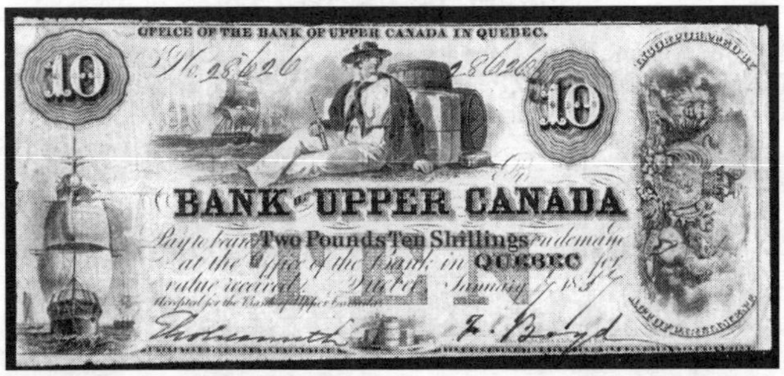

770-16-04-04

$10 (£2.10) Face Design: Sailing ships/seated sailor with bale and kegs; bale and kegs below/Royal Crest (sideways) (check letter B notes)

Colour: Black with no tint

Back Design: Plain

IMPRINT

Rawdon, Wright, Hatch & Edson, New York

SIGNATURES

left	right
mss. illegible	mss. F. Boyd
none	none

ISSUE DATING

Partially engraved January ___18___: January ___ 185___:

1857: January 7

CIRCULATING NOTES

Cat. No.	Den.	Date	Variety	G	VG	F	VF	EF	AU
16-04-02	$10 (£2.10)	185_	Steamship	No known issued notes					
16-04-04	$10 (£2.10)	1857	Seated sailor	350.	700.	900.	1,300.	—	—

PROOF NOTES

Cat. No.	Den.	Date	Variety		Unc
16-04-02P	$10 (£2.10)	185_	Steamship	PROOF	450.
16-04-04P	$10 (£2.10)	185_	Seated sailor	PROOF	450.

770-18 ISSUES OF 1851-1857 BLUE PROTECTOR

DESIGNS AND COLOURS

All notes have a small image of St. George slaying the dragon at the bottom centre, without the encircling bank name.

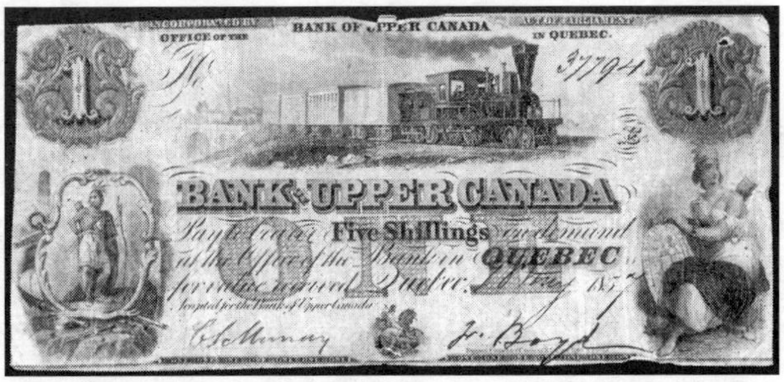

770-18-08-06

$1 (5s) Face Design: Crest and Indian/train/ seated Indian woman and shield

Colour: Black with no tint

Back Design: Plain

770-18-06-04P

$2 (10s) Face Design: Train/men on horseback herding livestock/cows being milked

Colour: Black with no tint

Back Design: Plain

770-18-06-06P

$5 (£1.5) Face Design: Running horse/Queen Victoria (Chalon portrait) in oval on Royal Crest/ dog and strongbox

Colour: Black with no tint

Back Design: Plain

IMPRINT

Toppan, Carpenter, Casilear & Co. New York and Phila

2. BROCKVILLE ISSUE, 1851

"BROCKVILLE" is engraved at the lower right of this issue.

SIGNATURES

left	right
mss. R.J. Church	mss. Wm. Proudfoot

ISSUE DATING

Partially engraved January ___ 185___:

1851: January 9

PROTECTOR

Blue "word" on face only

Cat. No.	Denom.	Date	G	VG	F	VF	EF	AU
18-02-02	$2 (10s)	1851	350.	700.	1,000.	—	—	—

4. KINGSTON ISSUE, 1851

This issue has "KINGSTON, C.W." engraved at the lower right.

SIGNATURES

left	right
mss. various	mss. J.G. Chewett

ISSUE DATING

Partially engraved January ___ 185___:

1851: January. 6

PROTECTOR

Blue "word" on face only

Cat. No.	Denom.	Date	G	VG	F	VF	EF	AU
18-04-02	$1 (5s)	1851	350.	700.	1,000.	—	—	—

5. LONDON ISSUE, 1851

"LONDON C.W." is engraved at the lower right of this newly-dlscovered issue.

SIGNATURES

Left	right
J. Hamilton	J.G. Chewett

ISSUE DATING

Partially engraved January ____185__:

1851: January 6

PROTECTOR

Blue "word" on face only

Cat. No.	Denom.	Date	G	VG	F	VF	EF	AU
18-05-02	$1 (5S)	1851	Only one known, about GOOD; sold for approx. $1,500 in Sept. 2001 Jeffrey Hoare auction.					

6. MONTREAL ISSUE, 1851

"MONTREAL" is engraved at the lower right of these notes.

SIGNATURES

left	right
mss. various	mss. J.G. Chewett

ISSUE DATING

Partially engraved January ___ 185___:

1851: January. 2

PROTECTOR

Blue "word" on face only

CIRCULATING NOTES

Cat. No.	Denom.	Date	G	VG	F	VF	EF	AU
18-06-02	$1 (5s)	1851	Institutional collection only					
18-06-04	$2 (10s)	185_	No known issued notes					
18-06-06	$5 (£1.5)	185_	No known issued notes					

PROOF NOTES

Cat. No.	Denom.	Date		Unc
18-06-02P	$1 (5s)	185_	PROOF	400.
18-06-04P	$2 (10s)	185_	PROOF	400.
18-06-06P	$5 (£1.5)	185_	PROOF	400.

8. QUEBEC ISSUE, 1852-1857

"QUEBEC" is engraved at the lower right of this issue, and "OFFICE OF THE BANK OF UPPER CANADA IN QUEBEC" or "OFFICE IN QUEBEC" is across the top.

SIGNATURES

left	right
mss. C.S. Murray	mss. F. Boyd
mss. various	mss. J.G. Chewett

ISSUE DATING

Partially engraved _ 185_:

$1 (5s) 1853: 1 Jany.
$1 (5s) 1854: May 2, 3 May, 4 May
1856: Augt., 12 Augt.
1857: 18 May
$2 (10s) 1852: 5 May
1853: June 9, 9 Aout.
1854: May 5
1856: Nov. 7
$5 (£1.5) 1857: 9 May

PROTECTOR

Blue "word" on face only

Cat. No.	Denom.	Date	G	VG	F	VF	EF	AU
18-08-04	$1 (5s)	1853-1857	300.	600.	850.	—	—	—
18-08-14	$2 (10s)	1852-1856	300.	600.	850.	—	—	—
18-08-36	$5 (£1.5)	1857	350.	700.	1,000.	—	—	—

Note: The $2 occurs with a fancy blue TWO protector or a slate-blue protector.

770-20 $10 TORONTO BRANCH ISSUE LATE 1850s

DESIGNS AND COLOURS

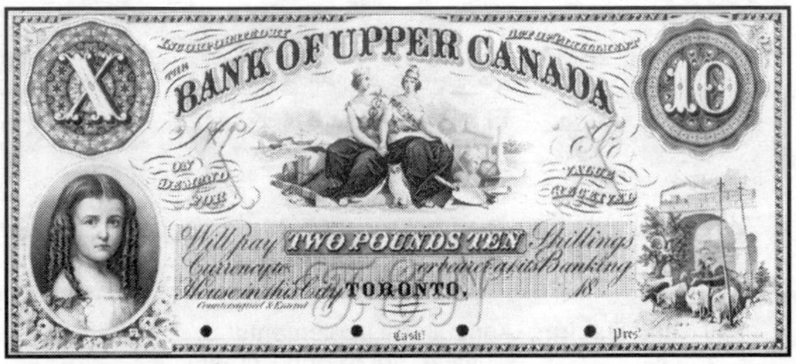

770-20-02P

$10 (£2.10) Face Design: Portrait of young girl with ringlets "Jessie"/ seated "Commerce" figure and Britannia/ cattle being driven under bridge
Colour: See varieties

Back Design: Unknown

IMPRINT
Rawdon, Wright, Hatch & Edson, New York

SIGNATURES

left	**right**
none	none

ISSUE DATING
Partially engraved ___ 18___:

VARIETIES
Face Colour: Black with overall brown-orange tint
Face Colour: Black with overall green tint

PROOF NOTES

Cat. No.	Denom.	Date	Variety		Unc
20-02P	$10 (£2.10)	18__	Overall brown-orange tint	PROOF	500.
20-04P	$10 (£2.10)	18__	Overall green tint	PROOF	500.

770-22 GREEN ISSUES OF 1859 AND 1861

DESIGNS AND COLOURS

770-22-02-02

$1 Face Design: Seated "Justice" figure/ St. George slaying the dragon/ seated Britannia with Crest of Upper Canada
Colour: Black with overall green tint

Back Design: Lathework and counters
Colour: Green

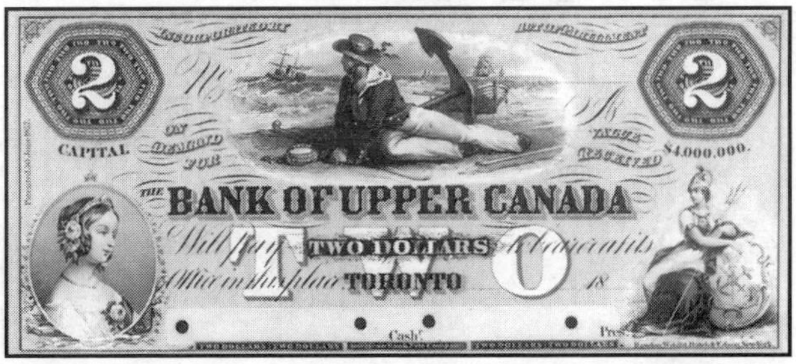

770-22-02-04P

$2 Face Design: Portrait of Queen Victoria as a young girl/ sailor reclining on shore by anchor/ seated Britannia with Crest of Upper Canada
Colour: Black with overall green tint

Back Design: Lathework and counters
Colour: Green

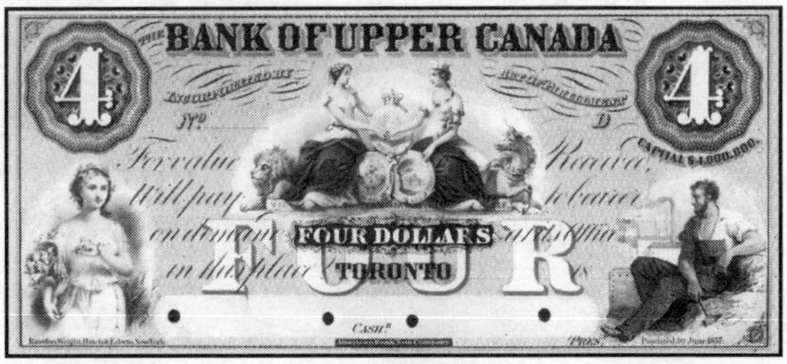

770-22-02-06P

$4 Face Design: Young woman with cornucopia "Autumn" /two women and Crest/seated blacksmith
Colour: Black with overall green tint

Back Design: Lathework and counters
Colour: Green

770-22-06-08a

$5 Face Design: Sailor leaning on capstan, bale and barrel/two women and Crest/ Albert, Prince of Wales in oval
Colour: Black with overall green tint

Back Design: Lathework and counters
Colour: Green

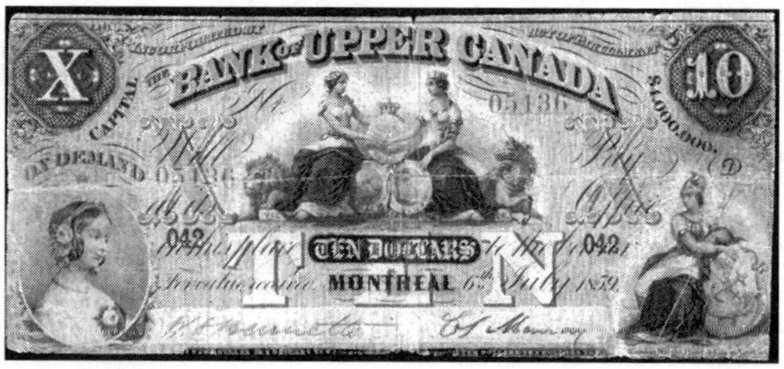

770-22-08-10

$10 Face Design: Portrait of Queen Victoria as a young girl/ two women and crest/seated Britannia with crest of Upper Canada
Colour: Black with overall green tint

770-22-10-10

Back Design: Lathework and counters
Colour: Green

770-22-02-10

$20 Face Design: —/"Justice" figure and Britannia flanking Crest of Upper Canada/ stonemason at work
Colour: Black with overall green tint

Back Design: Lathework and counters
Colour: Green

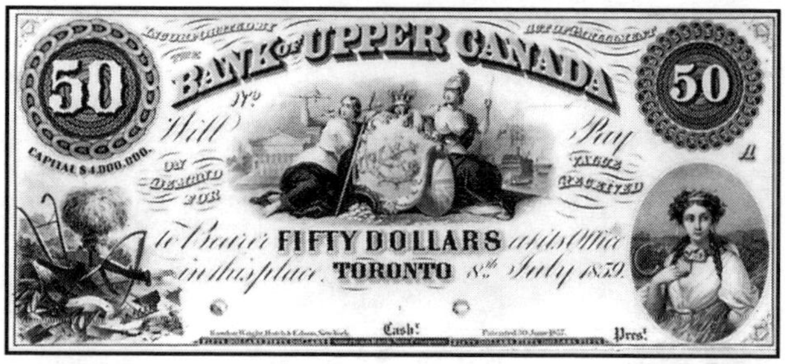

770-22-04-14P

$50 Face Design: Agricultural implements/ "Justice" figure and Britannia flanking Crest of Upper Canada/ woman with sickle and sheaf in oval
Colour: Black with overall green tint

Back Design: Lathework and counters
Colour: Green

770-22-04-16P

$100 Face Design: —/"Justice" figure and Britannia flanking Crest of Upper Canada/seated woman leaning on bale
Colour: Black with overall green tint

Back Design: Lathework and counters
Colour: Green

IMPRINT

Rawdon, Wright, Hatch & Edson. New York
American Bank Note Company

2. TORONTO ISSUE OVERPRINTED DATE 1859-1861

"TORONTO" is engraved at the bottom centre of this issue. Date as black overprint on ___ 18___ plates 1859

770-22-02-10P

SIGNATURES

left	right
mss. W.J. Bennetts	mss. M. Scollard
none	none

ISSUE DATING

Partially engraved ___ 18___ and overprinted:

$1: 1st July 1859
$5: 5th July 1859

OVERPRINT

Various numbers
"5 5" in blue
"64 64" in black

CIRCULATING NOTES

Cat. No.	Denom.	Date	Variety	G	VG	F	VF	EF	AU
22-02-02	$1	1859	Overprinted date	300.	600.	950.	—	—	—
22-02-04	$2	18__			No known issued notes				
22-02-06	$4	18__			No known issued notes				
22-02-08	$5	1859	Overprinted date	300.	600.	950.	—	—	—
22-02-10	$10	18__			No known issued notes				
22-02-12	$20	18__			No known issued notes				
22-02-14	$50	18__			No known issued notes				
22-02-16	$100	18__			No known issued notes				

PROOF NOTES

Cat. No.	Denom.	Date	Variety		Unc
22-02-02P	$1	18__	Green tint	FACE PROOF	400.
22-02-02Pa	$1	18__	B & W	FACE PROOF	275.
22-02-04P	$2	18__	Green tint	FACE PROOF	400.
22-02-04Pa	$2	18__	B & W	FACE PROOF	275.
22-02-06P	$4	18__	Green tint	FACE PROOF	400.
22-02-06Pa	$4	18__	B & W	FACE PROOF	275.
22-02-08P	$5	18__	Green tint	FACE PROOF	400.
22-02-08Pa	$5	18__	B & W	FACE PROOF	275.
22-02-10P	$10	18__	Green tint	FACE PROOF	450.
22-02-10Pa	$10	18__	B & W	FACE PROOF	300.
22-02-12P	$20	18__	Green tint	FACE PROOF	450.
22-02-12Pa	$20	18__	B & W	FACE PROOF	300.
22-02-14P	$50	18__	Green tint	FACE PROOF	500.
22-02-14Pa	$50	18__	B & W	FACE PROOF	350.
22-02-16P	$100	18__	Green tint	FACE PROOF	500.
22-02-16Pa	$100	18__	B & W	FACE PROOF	350.

4. TORONTO ISSUE, ENGRAVED DATE TWO SIGNATURES, 1859

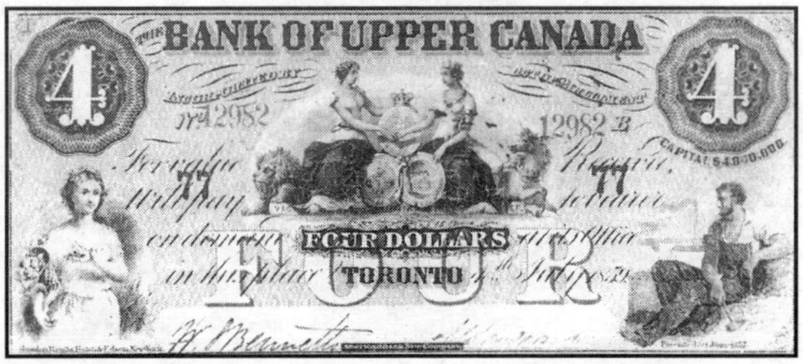

770-22-04-06

SIGNATURES

left	right
mss. W.J. Bennetts	mss. M. Scollard
mss. W.J. Bennetts	mss. C.S. Murray
mss. M. Scollard	mss. C.S. Murray

ISSUE DATING

Engraved

$1: 1st July 1859
$2: 2nd July 1859
$4: 4th July 1859
$5: 5th July 1859
$10: 6th July 1859
$20: 7th July 1859
$50: 8th July 1859
$100: 9th July 1859

OVERPRINT

Numbers in black
Numbers in black and branch names in red
Numbers in red and branch names in red
Branch names in red include:
"52 BROCKVILLE 52"
"49 BROCKVILLE 49"
"GODERICH" twice
"86 KINGSTON 86"
"100 KINGSTON 100"
"08 ST. CATHARINES 08"
"31 ST. CATHARINES 31"
Numbers in black:
"12 12"
"40 40"
"77 77"
"0115 0115"
"0116 0116"

CIRCULATING NOTES

Cat. No.	Denom.	Date	Variety	G	VG	F	VF
22-04-02	$1	1859	no o/p or numerals only	275.	550.	700.	—
22-04-02a	$1	1859	town o/p	350.	700.	900.	—
22-04-04	$2	1859	no o/p or numerals only	300.	600.	800.	—
22-04-04a	$2	1859	town o/p	375.	750.	1,000.	—
22-04-06	$4	1859	no o/p or numerals only	300.	600.	800.	—
22-04-06a	$4	1859	town o/p	375.	750.	1,000.	—
22-04-08	$5	1859		400.	800.	1,075.	—
22-04-10	$10	1859		400.	800.	1,075.	—
22-04-12	$20	1859		No known issued notes			
22-04-14	$50	1859		No known issued notes			
22-04-16	$100	1859		No known issued notes			

PROOF NOTES

Cat. No.	Denom.	Date		Unc
22-04-02P	$1	1859	FACE PROOF	350.
22-04-04P	$2	1859	FACE PROOF	350.
22-04-06P	$4	1859	FACE PROOF	350.
22-04-08P	$5	1859	FACE PROOF	350.
22-04-10P	$10	1859	FACE PROOF	350.
22-04-12P	$20	1859	FACE PROOF	350.
22-04-14P	$50	1859	FACE PROOF	400.
22-04-16P	$100	1859	FACE PROOF	450.

6. TORONTO ISSUE ENGRAVED DATE ONE SIGNATURE, 1861

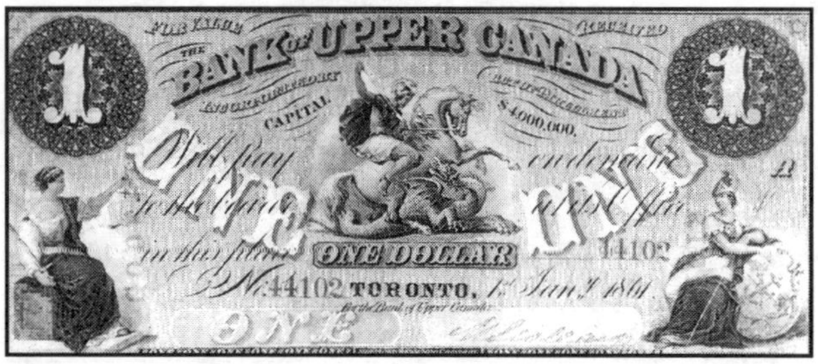

770-22-06-02a

SIGNATURES

right only
mss. C.S. Murray
mss. M. Scollard

ISSUE DATING

Engraved

1st Jany 1861

OVERPRINT

Branch names in black, with or without numbers
Branch names in red, with or without numbers
Branch names in red include:
BARRIE
BELLEVILLE
GODERICH
HAMILTON
KINGS TON
LONDON
OTTAWA
SARNIA
ST. CATHARINES
STRATFORD
WINDSOR C
Branch names and numbers in red:
"B013 LONDON B013"
"B017 ST. CATHARINES B017"
"B023 ST. CATHARINES B023"
KINGSON
"91 KINGSTON 91"

Cat. No.	Denom.	Date	Variety	G	VG	F	VF
22-06-02	$1	1859	no o/p or numerals only	200.	400.	600.	—
22-06-02a	$1	1859	town o/p	250.	475.	700.	—
22-06-04a	$2	1859	town o/p	300.	600.	950.	—
22-06-06a	$4	1859	town o/p	300.	600.	950.	—
22-06-08	$5	1859	no o/p or numerals only	225.	450.	675.	—
22-06-08a	$5	1859	town o/p	275.	550.	775.	1,200.
22-06-10	$10	1859	town o/p	Institutional collection only			

8. MONTREAL ISSUE, 1859

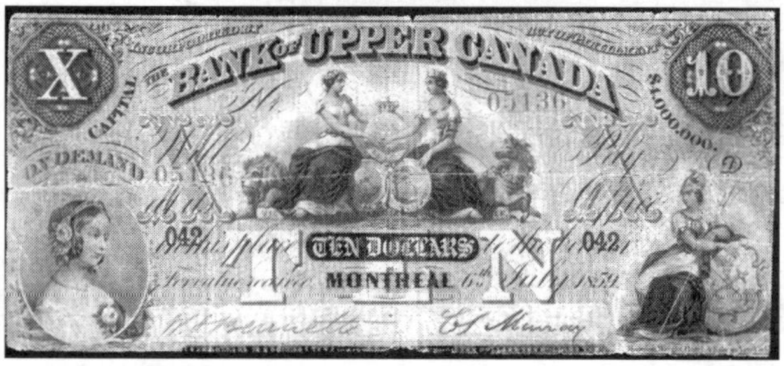

770-22-08-10
"MONTREAL" is engraved at the bottom centre.

SIGNATURES

left	**right**
mss. W.J. Bennetts	mss. C.S. Murray

ISSUE DATING

Engraved

$1: 1st July 1859
$2: 2nd July 1859
$5: 5th July 1859
$10: 6th July 1859

OVERPRINT

"042 042" in blue

Cat. No.	Denom.	Date	G	VG	F	VF
22-08-02	$1	1859	300.	600.	—	—
22-08-04	$2	1859	Institutional collection only			
22-08-06	$4	1859	NOT YET CONFIRMED			
22-08-08	$5	1859	Institutional collection only			
22-08-10	$10	1859	350.	700.	1,050.	—

10. QUEBEC ISSUE, 1859

"QUEBEC" is engraved at the bottom centre of this issue.

770-22-10-08

770-22-10-10

SIGNATURES

left	right
mss. W.J. Bennetts	mss. C.S. Murray

ISSUE DATING

Engraved

$1: 1st July 1859
$2: 2nd July 1859
$5: 5th July 1859
$10: 6th July 1859

OVERPRINT

Various numbers twice in red, ie. 3,6, 8, 10, 11, 36, 42, 48, 53, 084, 087

Cat. No.	Denom.	Date	G	VG	F	VF
22-10-02	$1	1859	300.	600.	—	—
22-10-04	$2	1859	300.	600.	—	—
22-10-06	$4	1859	NOT YET CONFIRMED			
22-10-08	$5	1859	300.	600.	950.	—
22-10-10	$10	1859	Institutional collection only			

12. QUEBEC ISSUE ENGRAVED DATE ONE SIGNATURE 1861

"QUEBEC" is engraved across the bottom centre of this issue.

770-22-12-02

SIGNATURE

Left	right
None	M. Scollard

ISSUE DATING

Engraved

1st Jan'y 1861

Cat. No.	Denom.	Date	G	VG	F	VF
22-12-02	$1	1861	One known. V.G. Est. $1,000.			
22-12-04	$2	1861	NOT YET CONFIRMED			
22-12-06	$4	1861	NOT YET CONFIRMED			
22-12-08	$5	1861	NOT YET CONFIRMED			
22-12-10	$10	1861	NOT YET CONFIRMED			

770-24 NOTES ALTERED FROM THE COLONIAL BANK OF CANADA

Photo Not Available

770-24-02

$1 Face Design: Bust of young woman/woodsman/-
Colour: Black with orange-brown tint
Back Design: Plain

770-24-08

$4 Face Design: Helmeted "Justice" figure/Queen Victoria (Winterhalter portrait)/-
Colour: Black with orange-brown tint
Back Design: Plain

IMPRINT

Jocelyn, Draper & Welch

SIGNATURES (SPURIOUS)

left	right
mss. T.C. Ridout	mss. W. Proudfoot

STAMP

Blue E on face

ISSUE DATING

Partially engraved ___ 18___:

$1, 1859: July 8
$4, 1860: Nov. 15

Cat. No.	Denom.	Date	G	VG	F	VF
24-02	$1	1859	125.	250.	450.	—
24-08	$4	1860	125.	250.	450.	—

770-26 **NOTES ALTERED FROM THE BANK OF WESTERN CANADA**

DESIGNS AND COLOURS

770-26-08

$5 Face Design: Prince Consort in oval/St. George slaying the dragon/seated Britannia with Crest of Upper Canada
Colour: Black with no tint
Back Design: Plain

IMPRINT

American Bank Note Co.

SIGNATURES

left	right
mss. E.J. Butler	engr. E.J. Richardson

ISSUE DATING

Engraved

Sept. 20th, 1859

PROTECTOR

Red "word" on face and back

Cat. No.	Denom.	Date	G	VG	F	VF
26-08	$5	1859	125.	250.	450.	—

THE BANK OF VANCOUVER

1910-1914

VANCOUVER, BRITISH COLUMBIA

BANK NUMBER 775 ***REDEEMABLE***

Organized in 1908, this bank opened for business on July 30, 1910. Its authorized capital was $2 million, and the sum of $1,174,700 was subscribed, of which over $850,000 was paid-up. The bank was riding on the real-estate and industrial boom in British Columbia, which unfortunately did not last. By 1913 the bank was in a weakened condition. There was talk in banking circles of assisting in a peaceful liquidation of this company. This rapidly accelerated the loss of confidence in the Bank of Vancouver, and deposits shrank drastically. On December 14, 1914, it suspended payment. Following this, Mr. Ewing Buchanan was appointed curator and later liquidator. Up until his death in 1918, he collected only $118,911.84, plus $20,940.27 in interest. Mr. R. Kerr Houlgate succeeded as liquidator until the final winding up in 1935. His job was made very difficult in that many debtors simply refused to pay. Their assets shrunk to unmarketable properties. In addition, the War Relief Act meant that some debts could not be collected. The double liability on shareholders amounted to about $150,000. The notes are redeemable at $1.0265 per dollar.

775-10 **ISSUE OF 1910**

DESIGNS AND COLOURS

775-10-02P

$5 Face Design: —/ships in Vancouver harbour/—
Colour: Black with yellow-green and green tint

Back Design: lathework, counters, bank name and Parliament Buildings in Victoria
Colour: Green

775-10-04P
$10 Face Design: Two men cutting down fir tree/—/—
Colour: Black with green and red-brown tint

Back Design: Lathework, counters, bank name and Parliament Buildings in Victoria
Colour: Brown

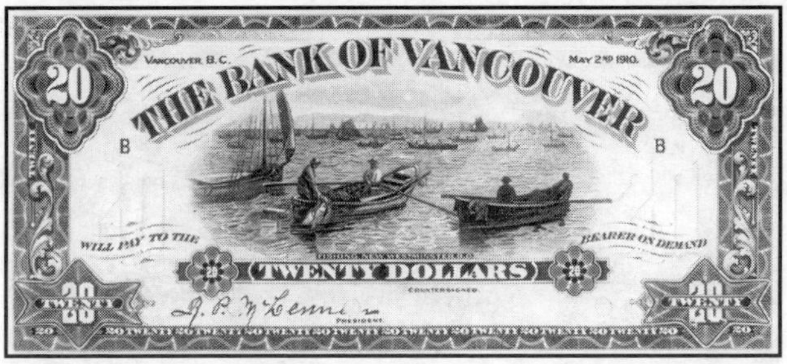

775-10-06P
$20 Face Design: —/fishing at New Westminster/—
Colour: Black with yellow-orange and red tint

Back Design: Lathework, counters, bank name and Parliament Buildings in Victoria
Colour: Red-brown

775-10-08P
$50 Face Design: —/miners at work/—
Colour: Black with blue tint

Back Design: Lathework, counters, bank name and Parliament Buildings in Victoria
Colour: Blue

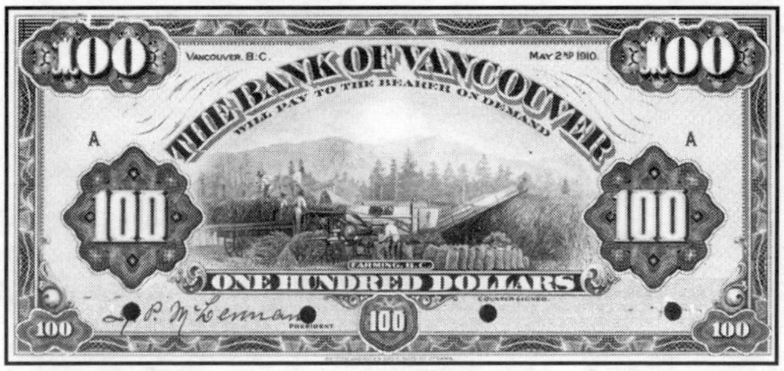

775-10-10P
$100 Face Design: —/farming B.C./—
Colour: Black with olive green tint

Back Design: Lathework, counters, bank name and Parliament Buildings in Victoria
Colour: Olive green

IMPRINT
British American Bank Note Co. Ottawa

SIGNATURES

left	right
engr. R.P. McLennan	mss. various

ISSUE DATING
Engraved
May 2nd 1910

CIRCULATING NOTES

Cat. No.	Denom.	Date		G	VG	F	VF	EF	AU
10-02	$5	1910	uncancelled	—	7,000.	8,500.	10,000.	—	—
10-02	$5	1910	cancelled	—	5,500.	7,000.	—	—	—
10-04	$10	1910	cancelled	—	8,000.	9,500.	—	—	—
10-06	$20	1910		Institutional collection only					
10-08	$50	1910		No known issued notes					
10-10	$100	1910		No known issued notes					

PROOF NOTES

Cat. No.	Denom.	Date	Unc
10-02P	$5	1910	FACE PROOF 3,500.
10-04P	$10	1910	FACE PROOF 3,500.
10-06P	$20	1910	FACE PROOF 3,500.
10-08P	$50	1910	FACE PROOF 3,500.
10-10P	$100	1910	FACE PROOF 3,500.

THE BANK OF VICTORIA

1836

VICTORIA, UPPER CANADA

BANK NUMBER 780 ***NONREDEEMABLE***

Bank notes were ordered in July 1836; however, there is no record of any notes or proofs having survived.

LA BANQUE VILLE-MARIE

1872-1899

MONTREAL, QUEBEC

BANK NUMBER 785 ***REDEEMABLE***

Established in Montreal in 1872, La Banque Ville-Marie suspended payment on June 25, 1899, when it was discovered that there was fraudulent over-circulation of notes that had not been shown on the government return. In addition, a substantial number of bad debts arising from fraudulent transactions had not been reported. Some of the officers and directors had been dissipating assets of the bank through heavy speculation many years prior to bankruptcy. Criminal prosecution was taken against several of them for theft, fraud and the filing of false returns, and the president and chief accountant were sentenced to jail.

785-10 BABN PRINTINGS, 1873 - 1890

DESIGNS AND COLOURS

785-10-02
$4 Face Design: —/Montreal harbour/"John Baptist"
Colour: Black with green tint

Back Design: Lathework, counters and bank name
Colour: Green

785-10-06

$5 Face Design: Samuel de Champlain/Montreal harbour/—
Colour: Black with green tint

Back Design: Lathework, counters and bank name
Colour: Green

785-10-12

$10 Face Design: Jacques Cartier approaching land/ Montreal harbour/—
Colour: Black with green tint

Back Design: Lathework, counters and bank name
Colour: Green

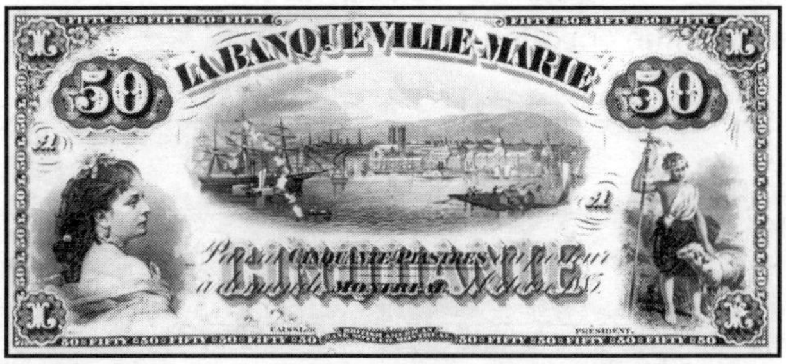

785-10-16

$50 Face Design: Portrait of woman "Lucy"/ Montreal harbour/"John Baptist"
Colour: Black with green tint

Back Design: Lathework, counters and bank name
Colour: Green

IMPRINT

British American Bank Note Co. Montreal & Ottawa

SIGNATURES

	left	right
1873:	mss. P.A. Fauteux	engr. D.E. Papineau
	engr. A. Fourteur	unknown
	mss. U. Garand	mss. W. Weir

ISSUE DATING

Engraved

2. Janvier 1873
2 Jan. 1873
1er Aout. 1879
1 Octobre 1885
1er Sept. 1890

OVERPRINT

"TROIS-RIVIERES" twice in red
"F" in red
"N N" in blue
"SOREL" in red

CIRCULATING NOTES

Cat. No.	Denom.	Date	G	VG	F	VF	EF	AU
10-02	$4	1873	1,100.	1,800.	2,400.	—	—	—
10-04	$4	1879	No known issued notes					
10-06	$5	1873	1,150.	1,900.	2,600.	—	—	—
10-08	$5	1879	No known issued notes					
10-10	$5	1885	1,150.	1,900.	2,600.	—	—	—
10-12	$10	1873	1,150.	1,900.	—	—	—	—
10-14	$10	1885	No known issued notes					
10-16	$50	1885	1,800.	3,000.	4,000.	—	—	—
10-18	$50	1890	No known issued notes					

PROOF NOTES

Cat. No.	Denom.	Date		Unc
10-02P	$4	1873	FACE PROOF	600.
10-04P	$4	1879	FACE PROOF	600.
10-06P	$5	1873	FACE PROOF	600.
10-08P	$5	1879	FACE PROOF	600.
10-14P	$10	1885	FACE PROOF	600.
10-16P	$50	1885	FACE PROOF	600.
10-18P	$50	1890	FACE PROOF	600.

785-12 CANADA BNCo PRINTINGS, 1889

DESIGNS AND COLOURS

785-12-02P
$5 Face Design: Montreal harbour/—/D. Maisonneuve
Colour: Black with overall green tint

Back Design: Lathework, counters and bank name
Colour: Green

785-12-04P
$10 Face Design: Steamship/—/D. Maisonneuve
Colour: Black with overall green tint

Back Design: Lathework, counters and bank name
Colour: Green

785-12-06
$20 Face Design: D. Maisonneuve/griffins surrounding counter/—
Colour: Black with overall green tint

Back Design: Lathework, counters and bank name
Colour: Green

IMPRINT

Canada Bank Note Co. Montreal

SIGNATURES

left	right
mss. U. Garand	mss. W. Weir

ISSUE DATING

Engraved

2me Janvier 1889
2me Jan. 1889
2me Janr 1889

OVERPRINT

"W W" in blue

CIRCULATING NOTES

Cat. No.	Denom.	Date	Variety	G	VG	F	VF	EF	AU
12-02	$5	1889	Red numbers	850.	1,700.	2,300.	3,200.	—	—
12-04	$10	1889	Red numbers	950.	1,900.	2,600.	3,700.	—	—
12-06	$20	1889	Red numbers	950.	1,900.	2,600.	3,700.	—	—

PROOF NOTES

Canada Bank Note company imprint at bottom centre.

Cat. No.	Denom.	Date		Unc
12-02P	$5	1889	FACE PROOF	700.
12-04P	$10	1889	FACE PROOF	700.
12-06P	$20	1889	FACE PROOF	700.

785-14 **BABN PRINTINGS, 1889**

DESIGNS AND COLOURS

They are the same as the Canada BNCo issue apart from the imprint.

785-14-02

785-14-04

IMPRINT

British American Bank Note Co. Montreal

SIGNATURES

	left	right
$5 and $10:	mss. various	engr. W. Weir
$20:	unknown	unknown

ISSUE DATING

Engraved

2me Jan. 1889

2me Janvier 1889

CIRCULATING NOTES

Cat. No.	Denom.	Date	Variety	G	VG	F	VF	EF	Unc
14-02	$5	1889	Blue numbers	850.	1,700.	2,300.	3,200.	—	—
14-04	$10	1889	Blue numbers	950.	1,900.	2,600.	3,700.	—	—
14-06	$20	1889	Blue numbers	950.	1,900.	2,600.	3,700.	—	—

PROOF NOTES

Cat. No.	Denom.	Date		Unc
14-02P	$5	1889	FACE PROOF	600.
14-04P	$10	1889	FACE PROOF	600.
14-06P	$20	1889	FACE PROOF	600.

THE WESTERN BANK OF CANADA

1882-1909

OSHAWA, ONTARIO

BANK NUMBER 790 ***REDEEMABLE***

Chartered on May 17, 1882, this bank operated exclusively in Ontario to promote the manufacturing and exporting interests of the towns along the shores of Lake Ontario. It was a satellite institution of the Ontario Loan and Savings Company, and a number of the directors of the bank sat on the boards of both institutions.

By 1907 the Western Bank of Canada had 26 branches, but the year was characterized by a world-wide stringency in various money markets, from which Canada was not exempt. On November 16, 1908, the Standard Bank of Canada made an offer to purchase the assets of the bank, and a merger took place in 1909.

790-10 **ISSUES OF 1882 AND 1890**

DESIGNS AND COLOURS

790-10-02P

$5 Face Design: R.S. Hamlin/farm implements and produce/ John Cowan

Colour: Black with green tint

Back Design: Lathework, counters and bank name

Colour: Green

790-10-04P

$10 Face Design: R.S. Hamlin/shepherdess with lamb and ewe/ John Cowan

Colour: Black with green tint

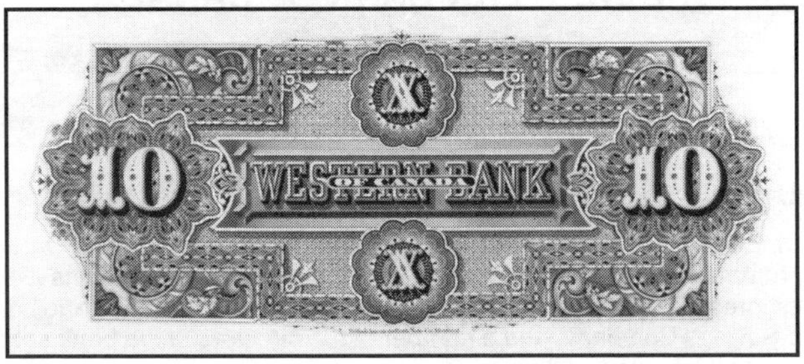

Back Design: Lathework, counters and bank name
Colour: Green

790-10-06P
$20 Face Design: R.S. Hamlin/Ceres seated with cornucopia/John Cowan
Colour: Black with green tint

Back Design: Lathework, counters and bank name
Colour: Green

IMPRINT

British American Bank Note Co. Montreal

SIGNATURES

left	right
mss. various	engr. John Cowan

ISSUE DATING

Engraved

Oct. 2nd, 1882
2nd July 1890

CIRCULATING NOTES

Cat. No.	Denom.	Date	G	VG	F	VF	EF	AU
10-02	$5	1882	1,000.	2,000.	2,750.	4,000.	—	—
10-04	$10	1882	1,250.	2,500.	3,300.	4,800.	—	—
10-06	$20	1890	Institutional collection only					

PROOF NOTES

Cat. No.	Denom.	Date	Variety		Unc
10-02P	$5	1882		FACE PROOF	600.
10-04P	$10	1882		FACE PROOF	600.
10-06P	$20	1890	Green tint	FACE PROOF	650.
10-06Pa	$20	1890	Yellow-orange tint	FACE PROOF	650.

Note: $20 face proof exists with yellow-orange tint. $10 back proof exists in blue.

THE BANK OF WESTERN CANADA

1859-1863

CLIFTON, CANADA WEST

BANK NUMBER 795 ***NONREDEEMABLE***

Established in Clifton, Canada West, on March 31,1859, the act incorporating the bank received royal assent on May 4, 1859. The Bank of Western Canada was controlled by a New York tavern keeper by the name of Paddock, who convinced a respectable old gentleman in Clifton to act as president of the bank by paying for his stock. However, the president had no control over the issue of notes, none of which were redeemed. The government reported that it was discreditable to allow the charter to remain in existence, and it was repealed on August 31, 1863.

795-10 **ISSUE OF 1859**

DESIGNS AND COLOURS

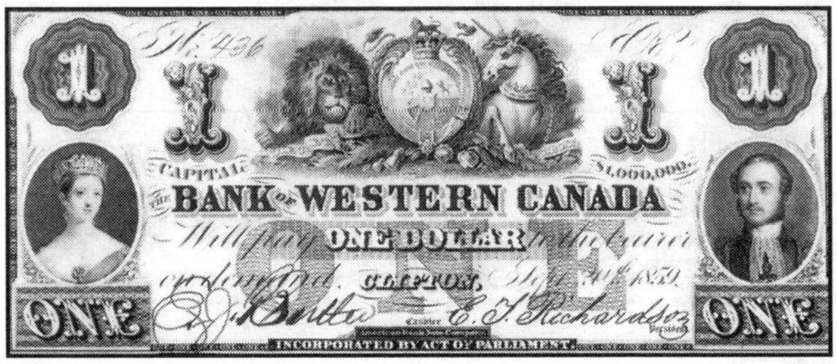

795-10-04
$1 Face Design: Queen Victoria/Royal Crest/Prince Consort
Colour: Black with no tint

Back Design: Plain

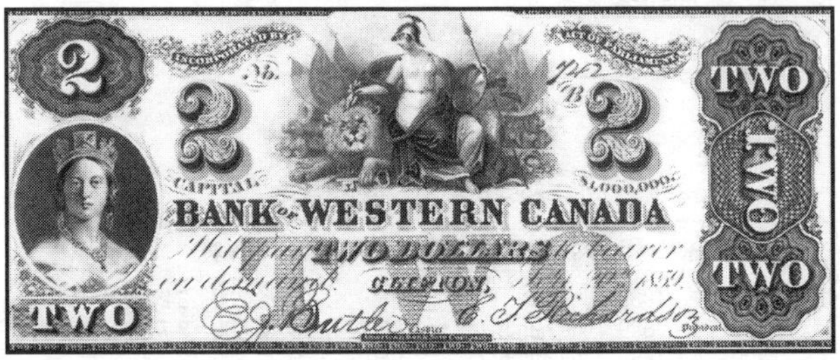

795-10-08
$2 Face Design: Queen Victoria (Winterhalter portrait)/Britannia, lion and flags/—
Colour: Black with no tint

Back Design: Plain

795-10-12
$4 Face Design: Prince Consort/lion/ Queen Victoria (Winterhalter portrait)
Colour: Black with no tint

Back Design: Plain

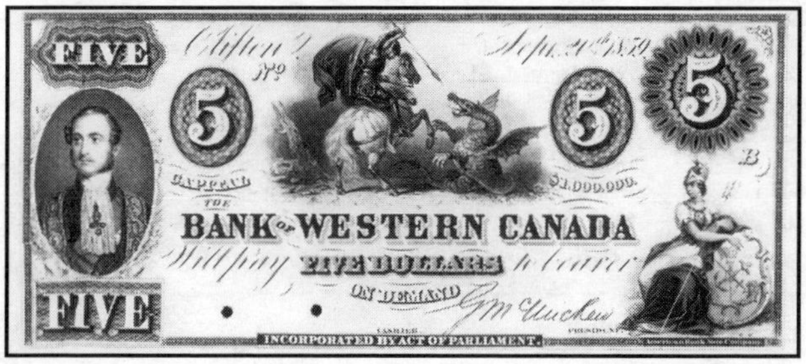

795-10-14P

$5 Face Design: Prince Consort/St. George slaying the dragon/Britannia seated with Crest of Upper Canada

Colour: Black with no tint

Back Design: Plain

IMPRINT

American Bank Note Company

SIGNATURES

left	right
mss. E.J. Butler	engr. G. McMicken
mss. E.J. Butler	engr. E.J. Richardson

ISSUE DATING

Engraved

Sept. 20th, 1859

PROTECTOR

Red "word" on face and on the back in a mirror image.

STAMPS

Small "X" in black, small C-W in black
Small "S-W" in black, small K in black
Large "O" in black, N;Y in black
"BANK NOTE REPORTER OFFICE," etc., in black

CIRCULATING NOTES

Cat. No.	Denom.	Date	Variety	VG	F	VF	EF	AU	Unc
10-02	$1	1859	McMicken, r.	325.	450.	700.	1,150	—	—
10-04	$1	1859	Richardson, r.	50.	70.	100.	190.	220.	275.
10-06	$2	1859	McMicken, r.	325.	450.	700.	1,150.	—	—
10-08	$2	1859	Richardson, r.	50.	70.	100.	190.	220.	275.
10-10	$4	1859	McMicken, r.	375.	500.	750.	1,200.	—	—
10-12	$4	1859	Richardson, r.	75.	100.	140.	240.	275.	350.
10-14	$5	1859	McMicken, r.	325.	450.	700.	1,150.	—	—
10-16	$5	1859	Richardson, r.	50.	70.	100.	190.	220.	275.

* Beware of modern reproductions of $1 1859 (795-10-04). They lack the red protector on face and back, and the imprint is missing. The printing is coarsely done on brown paper, and all examples have sheet number 245.

PROOF NOTES

Cat. No.	Denom.	Date		Unc
10-02P	$1	1859	PROOF	500.
10-06P	$2	1859	PROOF	500.
10-10P	$4	1859	PROOF	500.
10-14P	$5	1859	PROOF	500.

THE WESTMORELAND BANK OF NEW BRUNSWICK

1854-1867

BEND OF THE PETTICODIAC, NEW BRUNSWICK

BANK NUMBER 800 ***NONREDEEMABLE***

Chartered in 1854 with a capital of $60,000, this bank operated in Bend of the Petticodiac, subsequently renamed Moncton. The bank operated agencies at Sackville, N.B., and at Charlottetown, P.E.I. In 1859 a major shipbuilding firm failed and depression struck the area. Debts due to the bank, secured by mortgages on land that could be sold for only a fraction of its former worth, had to be covered from the reserve fund. The position of the bank steadily weakened until its failure on March 13, 1867. The whole capital of the bank was lost, together with an almost equal amount to be covered by the shareholders under the double liability provision in the charter.

800-10 BEND OF PETTICODIAC (sic) ISSUE 1854-1859

DESIGNS AND COLOURS

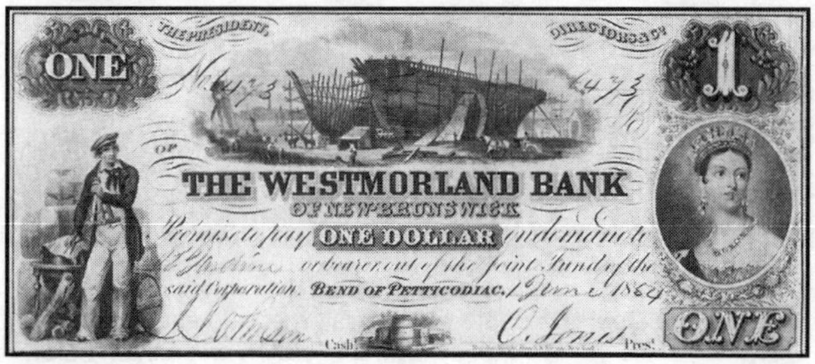

800-10-02

$1 Face Design: Sailor/shipbuilding scene; casks and bale below/Queen Victoria (Chalon portrait) in oval

Colour: Black with no tint

Back Design: Plain

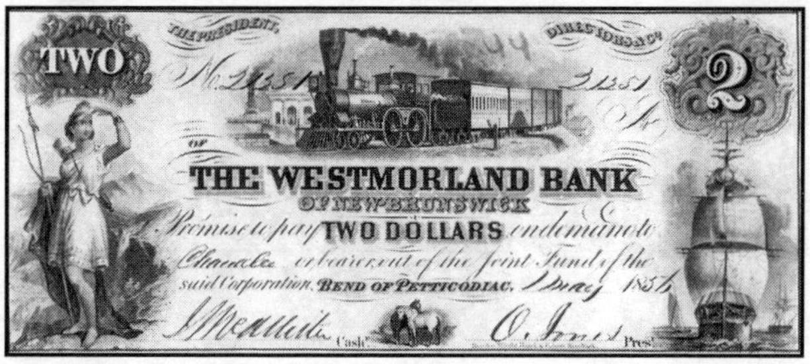

800-10-22

$2 Face Design: Indian maiden/train; two horses below/ sailing ships

Colour: Black with no tint

Back Design: Plain

800-10-36

$4 Face Design: Seated Britannia/farm family with picnic basket; shipbuilding below/ Prince Consort in oval
Colour: Black with no tint

Back Design: Plain

800-10-50

$20 Face Design: Seated Britannia/ornate 20 and woman with rake; swords with crown on cushion below/ seated "Justice" figure and chest
Colour: Black with no tint

Back Design: Plain

800-10-60P

$40 Face Design: Oval portrait of young woman/seated "Justice" figure and Britannia flanking Royal badge; shipbuilding below/two women
Colour: Black with no tint

Back Design: Plain

IMPRINT

Rawdon, Wright, Hatch & Edson, New York
Rawdon, Wright, Hatch & Edson, New York and American Bank Note Co. Boston

SIGNATURES

	left	right
1854:	mss. J. Johnson	mss. O. Jones
1856-1859:	mss. J. McAllister	mss. O. Jones

ISSUE DATING

Partially engraved ___ 18___:

1854: 1 June
1855: 2 Apr.
1856: 1 May
1859: 1 November

CIRCULATING NOTES

Cat. No.	Denom.	Date	Variety	G	VG	F	VF	EF	AU
10-02	$1	1854	Johnson, I.	200.	400.	—	—	—	—
10-06	$1	1855	McAllister, I.	200.	400.	550.	—	—	—
10-08	$1	1856	McAllister, I.	175.	350.	500.	750.	—	—
10-10	$1	1859	McAllister, I.	150.	300.	450.	—	—	—
10-16	$2	1854	Johnson, I.	275.	550.	—	—	—	—
10-20	$2	1855	McAllister, I.	275.	550.	—	—	—	—
10-22	$2	1856	McAllister, I.	250.	500.	675.	—	—	—
10-28	$2	1859	McAllister, I.	225.	450.	—	—	—	—
10-30	$4	1854	Johnson, I.	175.	350.	500.	750.	—	—
10-34	$4	1855	McAllister, I.	225.	450.	600.	—	—	—
10-36	$4	1856	McAllister, I.	200.	400.	550.	800.	—	—
10-42	$4	1859	McAllister, I.	185.	375.	525.	—	—	—
10-44	$20	1854	Johnson, I.	3,750.	7,500.	—	—	—	—
10-50	$20	1856	Johnson, I.	Institutional collection only					
10-60	$40	18__		No known issued notes					

PROOF NOTES

Cat. No.	Denom.	Date	Unc
10-60P	$40	18__	1,500.

Note: Notes occur with their backs stamped with various endorsements from local and foreign businesses, These stamps enhance the historical interest of the notes and in no way detract from them.
A $20 (Moncton) and $40 (Petticodiac) uncut proof pair were in ABN archive sale 1990.

800-12 MONCTON ISSUE, 1861

DESIGNS AND COLOURS

800-12-02b

$1 Face Design: Sailor/shipbuilding scene; casks and bale below/Queen Victoria (Chalon portrait) in oval
Colour: Black with green tint

Back Design: Lathework
Colour: Blue

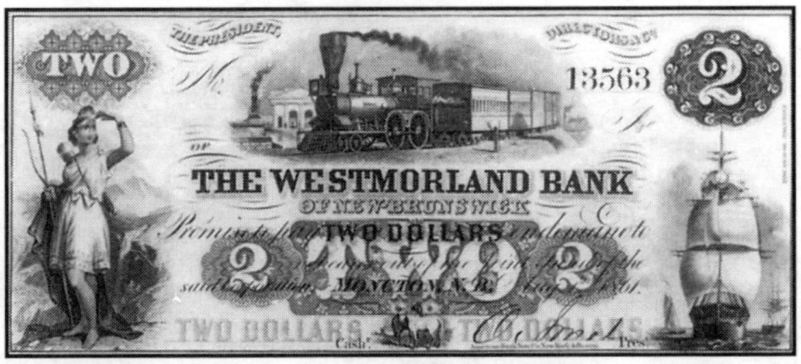

800-12-04R

$2 Face Design: Indian maiden/train; two horses below/ sailing ships

Colour: Black with green tint

Back Design: Lathework

Colour: Blue

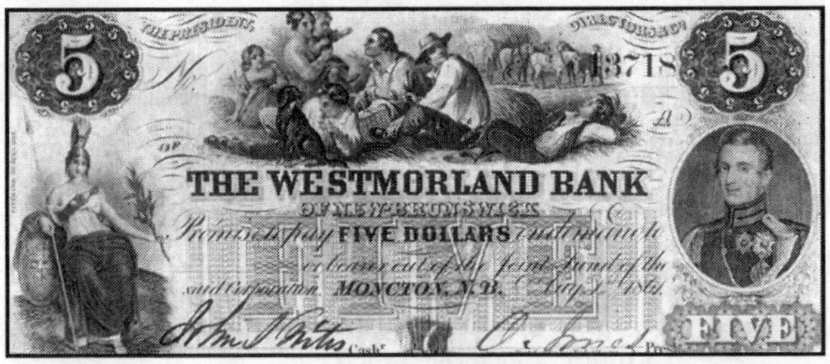

800-12-06b

$5 Face Design: Seated Britannia/farm family with picnic basket; shipbuilding below/ Prince Consort in oval

Colour: Black with green tint

Back Design: Lathework

Colour: Blue

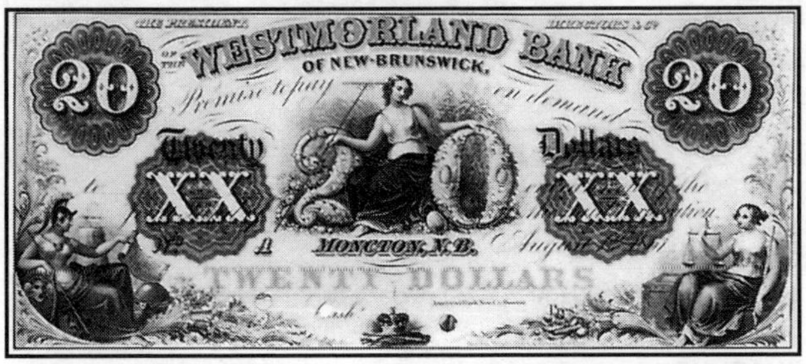

800-12-08

$20 Face Design: Seated Britannia/ornate 20 and woman with rake; swords with crown on cushion below/ seated "Justice" figure

Colour: Black with green tint

Back Design: Lathework

Colour: Blue

IMPRINT

Rawdon, Wright, Hatch & Edson New York and American Bank Note Co. Boston American Bank Note Co. New York & Boston

SIGNATURES

left	right
mss. J. McAllister	mss. O. Jones
mss. Wm. C. Jones	mss. O. Jones
mss. John S. Trites	mss. O. Jones

ISSUE DATING

Engraved

August 1, 1861
Aug. 1st 1861

Cat. No.	Denom.	Date	Variety	G	VG	F	VF	EF	Unc
12-02	$1	1861	McAllister, l.	30.	60.	75.	100.	200.	—
12-02a	$1	1861	Jones, l.	35.	70.	85.	115.	225.	—
12-02b	$1	1861	Trites, l.	200.	400.	650.	—	—	—
12-02R	$1	1861	Remainder*	—	—	—	—	125.	250.
12-04	$2	1861	McAllister, l.	30.	60.	75.	100.	325.	—
12-04a	$2	1861	Jones, l.	35.	70.	85.	115.	350.	—
12-04b	$2	1861	Trites, l.	250.	500.	800.	—	—	—
12-04R	$2	1861	Remainder*	—	—	—	—	125.	250.
12-06	$5	1861	McAllister, l.	30.	60.	75.	100.	250.	—
12-06a	$5	1861	Jones, l.	35.	70.	85.	115.	275.	—
12-06b	$5	1861	Trites, l.	250.	500.	800.	—	—	—
12-06R	$5	1861	Remainder*	—	—	—	—	125.	250.
12-08	$20	1861	McAllister, l.	Institutional collection only					

* These notes may be unsigned, or have "defunct" in the left signature space, or have spurious signatures. All unlisted signatures are spurious.

THE WEYBURN SECURITY BANK

1910-1931

WEYBURN, SASKATCHEWAN

BANK NUMBER 805 ***REDEEMABLE***

Established in 1910 in Weyburn, Saskatchewan, this bank was the successor to the Weyburn Security Company, which found competition with the chartered banks very difficult. The new bank decided to take out a charter under the Bank Act and had a successful business until 1931, when it merged with the Imperial Bank of Canada.

805-10 **ISSUE OF 1911**

DESIGNS AND COLOURS

805-10-02
$5 Face Design: —/train in city/—
Colour: Black with green tint

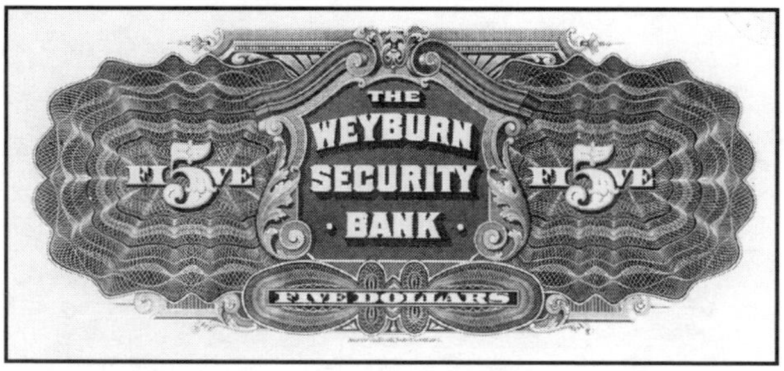

Back Design: Lathework, counters and bank name
Colour: Green

805-10-04
$10 Face Design: —/allegorical women and children/—
Colour: Black with yellow-green tint

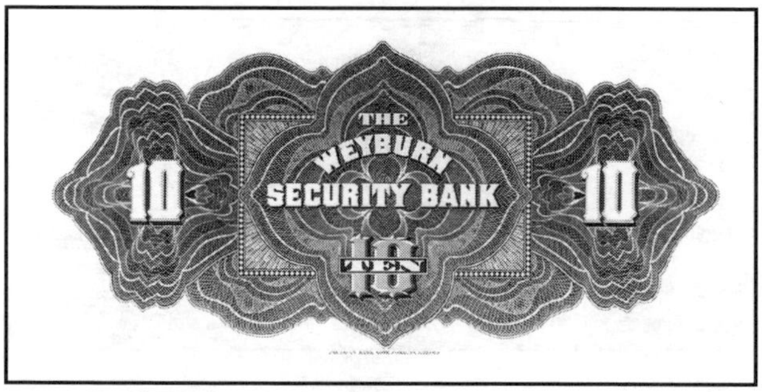

Back Design: Lathework, counters and bank name
Colour: Green

805-10-06
$20 Face Design: —/portrait of woman in oval frame supported by two cherubs/—
Colour: Black with orange tint

Back Design: Lathework, counters and bank name
Colour: Orange

IMPRINT

American Bank Note Co. Ottawa
Canadian Bank Note Company, Limited

SIGNATURES

left	**right**
mss. various	typed Alex Simpson

ISSUE DATING

Engraved

January 3rd 1911.
Jan. 3rd 1911.

Cat. No.	Denom.	Date	G	VG	F	VF	EF	Unc
10-02	$5	1911	600.	1,200.	1,500.	2,000.	2,600.	4,000.
10-04	$10	1911	700.	1,400.	1,800.	2,400.	3,200.	4,500.
10-06	$20	1911	1,500.	3,000.	3,750.	4,500.	5,500.	8,000.

THE BANK OF YARMOUTH

1859-1905

YARMOUTH, NOVA SCOTIA

BANK NUMBER 810 ***REDEEMABLE***

The charter for this bank was given in 1859, and it started business in 1865. It failed, however, in 1905, when it was discovered that dividends had continued for years, despite a severe depletion of capital owing to false and deceptive statements filed with the government. The cashier, president and vice-president were charged, and the cashier was convicted. The president and vice-president pleaded ignorance and the charges against them were dismissed. The directors of the bank were held liable for the dividends paid out.

810-10 $20 ISSUE OF 1860

DESIGNS AND COLOURS

810-10-02

$20 Face Design: Farmer planting seeds/Princess of Wales in oval flanked by lion and unicorn/—ship in drydock
Colour: Black with green tint

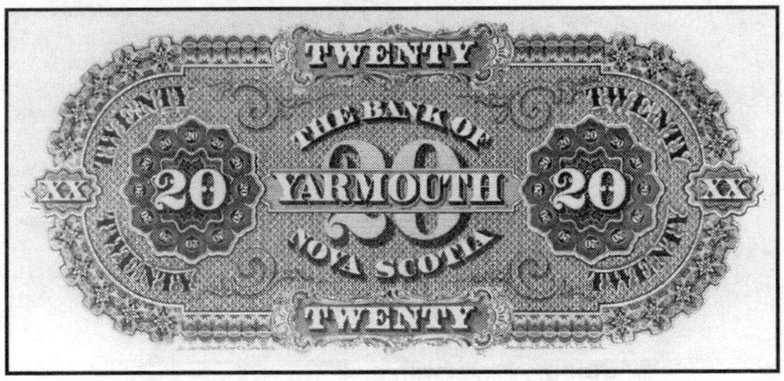

Back Design: Lathework, counters and bank name
Colour: Orange

IMPRINT

American Bank Note Co. N.Y.

SIGNATURES

left	right
mss. J.W.H. Rowley	mss. Wm. Hammond

ISSUE DATING

Partially engraved Dec. 1st 186___:

Dec. 1st 186_

OVERPRINT

"CANADIAN CURRENCY" twice in red

CIRCULATING NOTES

Cat. No.	Denom.	Date	Variety	G	VG	F	VF	EF	AU
10-02	$20	186_	Red o/p		Institutional collection only				

PROOF NOTES

Cat. No.	Denom.	Date		Unc
10-02P	$20	186_	FACE PROOF	800.

810-12 ISSUES OF 1870 AND 1891

DESIGNS AND COLOURS

810-12-02P

$4 Face Design: Allegorical female at sea, borne by two porpoises/—/Indian maiden
Colour: Black with green tint

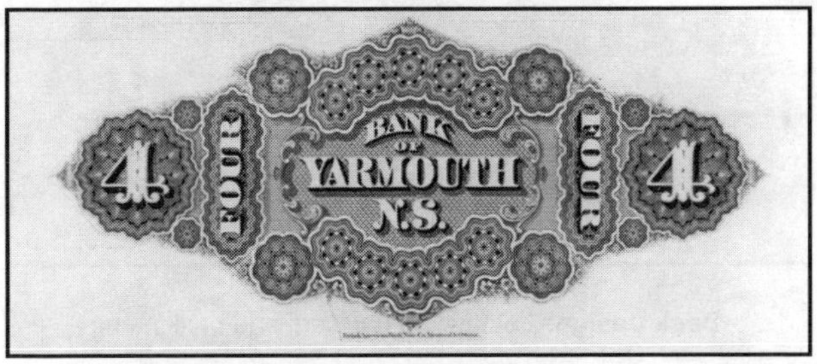

Back Design: Lathework, counters and bank name
Colour: Green

810-12-06

$5 Face Design: Anchor/ships and sea "Great Eastern"/ ships and allegorical female with flag, "Exports"
Colour: Black with green tint

Back Design: Lathework, counters and bank name
Colour: Green

810-12-10

$10 Face Design: —/Queen Victoria in widow's weeds flanked by lion and unicorn/—

Colour: Black with green tint

Back Design: Lathework, counters and bank name

Colour: Green

IMPRINT

British American Bank Note Co. Montreal & Ottawa

SIGNATURES

	left	right
1870:	unknown	unknown
1891:	mss. T.W. Johns	mss. L.E. Baker
	mss. T.W. Johns	mss. John Lovitt

ISSUE DATING

Engraved

July 1st 1870
July 1st 1891

OVERPRINT

1870: "CANADIAN CURRENCY" in red

CIRCULATING NOTES

Cat. No.	Denom.	Date	Variety	G	VG	F	VF	EF	AU
12-02	$4	1870	No o/p	No known issued notes					
12-02a	$4	1870	Red o/p	Institutional collection only					
12-04	$5	1870	No o/p	Institutional collection only					
12-04a	$5	1870	Red o/p	Institutional collection only					
12-06	$5	1891		Institutional collection only					
12-08	$10	1870	No o/p	Institutional collection only					
12-08a	$10	1870	Red o/p	Institutional collection only					
12-10	$10	1891		Institutional collection only					

PROOF NOTES

Cat. No.	Denom.	Date	Unc
12-02P	$4	1870	FACE PROOF 1,000.
12-04P	$5	1870	FACE PROOF 1,000.
12-08P	$10	1870	FACE PROOF 1,000.

THE ZIMMERMAN BANK

1854-1859

ELGIN, CANADA WEST, PROVINCE OF CANADA

BANK NUMBER 815 ***NONREDEEMABLE***

The Zimmerman Bank began operations in October 1854, under the Free Banking Act of 1850, when debentures totaling $100,000 were deposited with the provincial government on October 11, 1854. The founders were Samuel Zimmerman, the Honourable John Hilyard Cameron, Luther H. Holden, James A. Woodruff, James Oswald, John L. Ranney and Richard Woodruff.

In 1855 the bank obtained a charter with authorized capital of $1 million. Actual business as a chartered bank did not begin until June of the following year.

With the death of the major shareholder, Samuel Zimmerman, on March 12, 1857, operations changed overnight with the decision to wind up the affairs of the bank as quickly as possible. From a peak note circulation of $440,000 in December 1856 (both chartered and registered), the final published return in October 1857 showed only $34,000 in circulation.

In early 1858 the Zimmerman Bank made arrangements with the Bank of Upper Canada to take over its note redemption. In 1859 it changed its name to the Bank of Clifton.

815-10 FREE BANKING ISSUE, 1854-1855

These notes have "ELGIN" engraved at the bottom left and "SECURED BY DEPOSIT OF PROVINCIAL SECURITIES" at the bottom centre. Manuscript numbers.

DESIGNS AND COLOURS

815-10-02

$1 Face Design: Clifton House Hotel/ Roebling Suspension Bridge/ seated allegorical female

Colour: Black with no tint

Back Design: Plain

Photo Not Available

815-10-06P

$3 Face Design: Clifton House Hotel/ Roebling Suspension Bridge/ Queen Victoria (Chalon portrait)

Colour: Black with no tint

Back Design: Plain

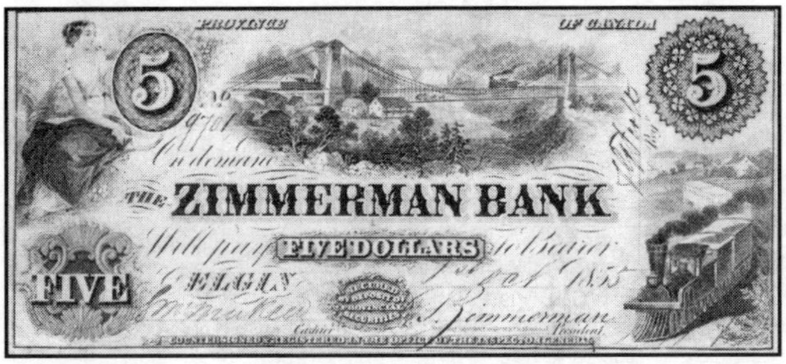

815-10-10

$5 Face Design: Seated allegorical female/ Roebling Suspension Bridge/train
Colour: Black with no tint

Back Design: Plain

Photo Not Available

815-10-12P

$10 Face Design: Roebling Suspension Bridge/ Prince Consort/female with sheaf of grain
Colour: Black with no tint

Back Design: Plain

Photo Not Available

815-10-16P

$20 Face Design: Clifton House Hotel/ Roebling Suspension Bridge/ seated woman with telescope
Colour: Black with no tint

Back Design: Plain

IMPRINT

Toppan, Carpenter, Casilear & Co. Montreal

SIGNATURES

left	**right**
mss. G. McMicken	engr. S. Zimmerman

ISSUE DATING

Partially engraved ___ 185___:

1854: 2 Nov.
1855: 1st Oct.

CIRCULATING NOTES

Cat. No.	Denom.	Date	G	VG	F	VF	EF	AU
10-02	$1	1854	210.	425.	650.	800.	—	—
10-06	$3	185_	No known issued notes					
10-10	$5	1855	210.	425	650.	800.	—	—
10-12	$10	185_	No known issued notes					
10-16	$20	185_	No known issued notes					

PROOF NOTES

Cat. No.	Denom.	Date		Unc
10-06P	$3	185_	PROOF	400.
10-12P	$10	185_	PROOF	400.
10-16P	$20	185_	PROOF	400.

815-12 "CHARTERED BANK" ISSUE FROM ELGIN, 1856

"ELGIN" and "CAPITAL ONE MILLION DOLLARS" are engraved at the bottom centre. Manuscript numbers.

DESIGNS AND COLOURS

815-12-02-04

$1 Face Design: Clifton House Hotel/Roebling Suspension Bridge/seated allegorical female
Colour: Black with no tint

Back Design: Plain, type 2 protector

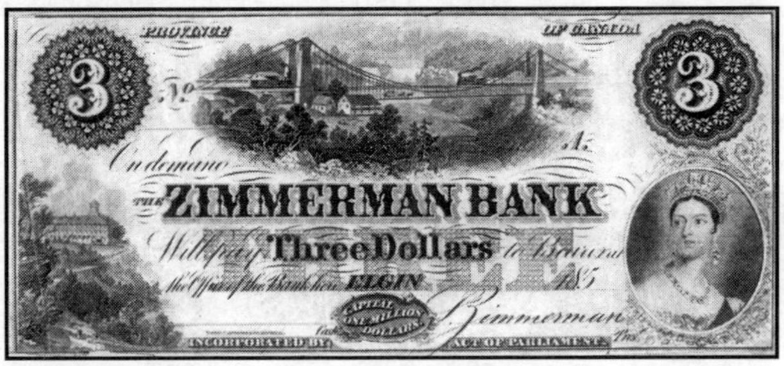

815-12-02-08R

$3 Face Design: Clifton House Hotel/ Roebling Suspension Bridge/ Queen Victoria (Chalon portrait)
Colour: Black with no tint

Back Design: Plain, type 2 protector

815-12-02-12R

$5 Face Design: Seated allegorical female/ Roebling Suspension Bridge/train
Colour: Black with no tint

Back Design: Plain, type 2 protector

Photo Not Available

815-12-02-14

$10 Face Design: Roebling Suspension Bridge/ Prince Consort/female with sheaf of grain
Colour: Black with no tint

Back Design: Plain, Type 1 protector

IMPRINT

Toppan Carpenter & Co. Montreal

SIGNATURES

left	**right**
mss. G. McMicken	engr. S. Zimmerman
mss. J.W. Dunklee	engr. S. Zimmerman

ISSUE DATING

Partially engraved _ 185_:

$1, 1856: June 7, Augt 7, Dec. 1
$5, 1856: July 7, Augt 7
$10, 1856: July 7

2. RED "WORD" PROTECTOR ON FACE AND BACK

VARIETIES

Type 1: Face protector normal, back protector reversed (mirror image)
Type 2: Face protector normal, back protector normal

Note: Many remainders have spurious signatures and dates.

Cat. No.	Den.	Date	Variety	G	VG	F	VF	EF	AU
12-02-02	$1	1856	ONE type 1	125.	250.	325.	500.	—	—
12-02-02R	$1	185_	ONE type 1	60.	125.	175.	250.	400.	600.
12-02-04	$1	1856	ONE type 2	125.	250.	325.	500.	—	—
12-02-04R	$1	185_	ONE type 2	60.	125.	175.	250.	400.	600.
12-02-06	$3	1856	THREE type 1	150.	300.	450.	700.	—	—
12-02-06R	$3	185_	THREE type 1	85.	175.	250.	325.	500.	750.
12-02-08	$3	1856	THREE type 2	150.	300.	450.	700.	—	—
12-02-08R	$3	185_	THREE type 2	85.	175.	250.	325.	500.	750.
12-02-10	$5	1856	FIVE type 1	110.	225.	325.	500.	—	—
12-02-10R	$5	185_	FIVE type 1	60.	125.	175.	250.	400.	600.
12-02-12	$5	1856	FIVE type 2	110.	225.	325.	500.	—	—
12-02-12R	$5	185_	FIVE type 2	60.	125.	175.	250.	400.	600.
12-02-14	$10	1856	TEN type 1	250.	500.	650.	850.	1,000.	—
12-02-14R	$10	185_	TEN type 1	NOT CONFIRMED					
12-02-16	$10	1856	TEN type 2	NOT CONFIRMED					
12-02-16R	$10	185_	TEN type 2	NOT CONFIRMED					

4. BLUE "WORD" PROTECTOR ON FACE AND BACK

Cat. No.	Den.	Date	Variety	G	VG	F	VF	EF	AU
12-04-02R	$1	185_	Blue ONE ptr.*	60.	120.	170.	225.	400.	—
12-04-04R	$3	185_	Blue THREE ptr.*	60.	120.	170.	225.	400.	—
12-04-06R	$5	185_	Blue FIVE ptr.*	60.	120.	170.	225.	400.	—

* Remainder notes. Many notes have spurious signatures and dates.

6. RED "NUMERAL" PROTECTOR ON FACE AND BACK

815-12-08-02

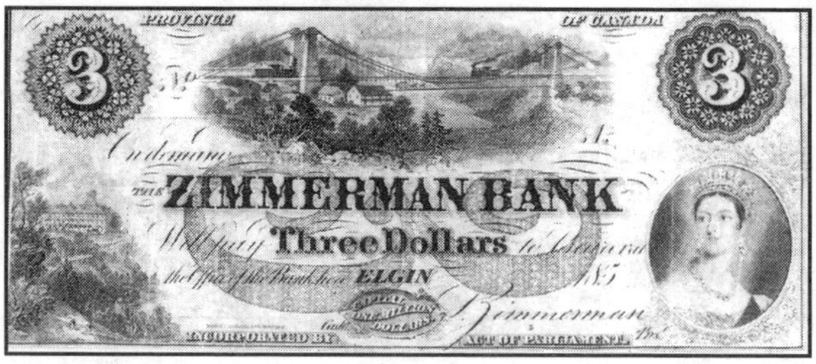

815-12-06-04R

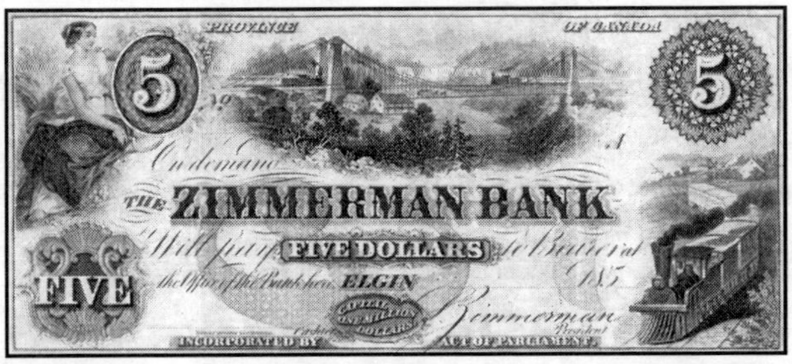

815-12-06-06R

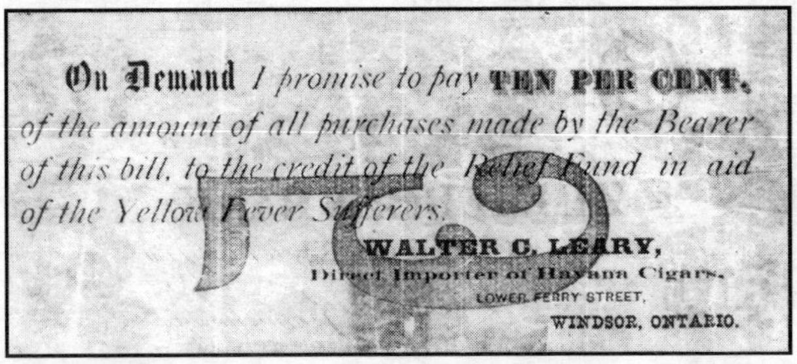

815-12-08-06Ra

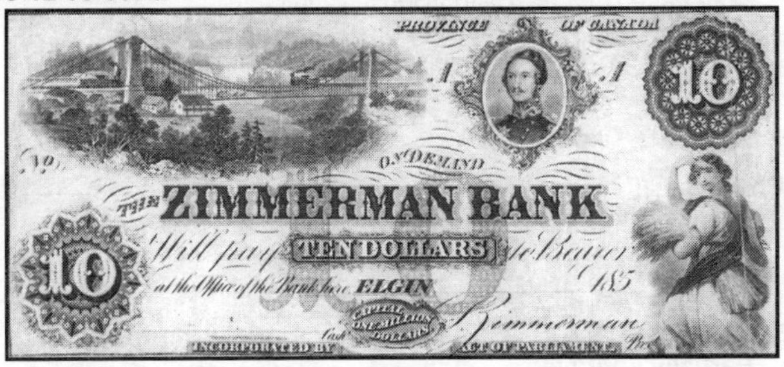

815-12-06-08R

815-12-06-10R

$20 Face Design: Clifton House Hotel/
Roebling Suspension Bridge/
seated woman with telescope
Colour: Black with no tint

Back Design: Plain

Note: Numerals on backs are mirror images.

Cat. No.	Denom.	Date	Variety	G	VG	F	VF	EF	AU
12-06-02R	$1	185_	Red 1 ptr.*	75.	150.	200.	275.	450.	—
12-06-04R	$3	185_	Red 3 ptr.*	90.	180.	250.	350.	550.	—
12-06-06R	$5	185_	Red 5 ptr.*	75.	150.	200.	275.	450.	—
12-06-06	$5	1856	Red 5 ptr.**	125.	250.	325.	500.	—	—
12-06-08R	$10	185_	Red 10 ptr.*	110.	225.	300.	425.	—	—
12-06-10R	$20	185_	Red 20 ptr.*	110.	225.	300.	425.	700.	—

* Remainder - many notes have spurious signatures and dates.
** Issued note.

8. BLUE "NUMERAL" PROTECTOR ON FACE AND BACK

Overprint (on back): "On demand I promise to pay TEN PER CENT of the amount of all purchases made by the Bearer of this Bill, to the credit of the Relief Fund in aid of the Yellow Fever Sufferers. WALTER C. LEARY Direct Importer of Havana Cigars. Lower Ferry Street, WINDSOR, ONTARIO.", in red

Cat. No.	Den.	Date	Variety	G	VG	F	VF	EF	AU
12-08-02	$1	1856	Blue 1 ptr	125.	250.	325.	500.	—	—
12-08-02R	$1	185_	Blue 1 ptr*	40.	80.	110.	150.	250.	—
12-08-04	$3	1856	Blue 3 ptr	175.	350.	—	—	—	—
12-08-04R	$3	185_	Blue 3 ptr.*	70.	140.	200.	275.	400.	—
12-08-06R	$5	185_	Blue 5 ptr*	40.	80.	110.	150.	250.	—
12-08-06Ra	$5	185_	Walter Leary o/p	100.	200.	275.	450.	600.	—
12-08-08R	$10	185_	Blue 10 ptr.*	50.	100.	140.	200.	350.	—
12-08-08Ra	$10	185_	Walter Leary o/p	125.	250.	325.	500.	750.	—
12-08-10R	$20	185_	Blue 20 ptr.*	50.	100.	140.	200.	350.	—
12-08-10Ra	$20	185_	Walter Leary o/p	125.	250.	325.	500.	750.	—
Sheet of 1,1,3,5 dated Dec. 1, 1856 unsigned				—	—	—	1,500.	2,000.	2,500.

* These are remainder notes. Many have spurious signatures and dates.

815-14 "CHARTERED BANK" ISSUE FROM CLIFTON

"CLIFTON" and "CAPITAL ONE MILLION DOLLARS" are engraved at the bottom centre. There are red printed numbers and faces printed in blue, instead of black. All notes of this type are remainders.

DESIGNS AND COLOURS

185-14-02R

$1 Face Design: Clifton House Hotel/
Roebling Suspension Bridge/
seated allegorical female
Colour: Blue

Back Design: Plain

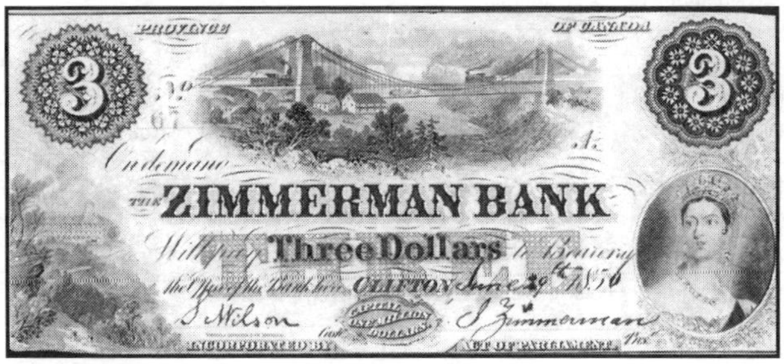

815-14-04R

$3 Face Design: Clifton House Hotel/
Roebling Suspension Bridge/Queen Victoria

Colour: Blue

Back Design: Plain

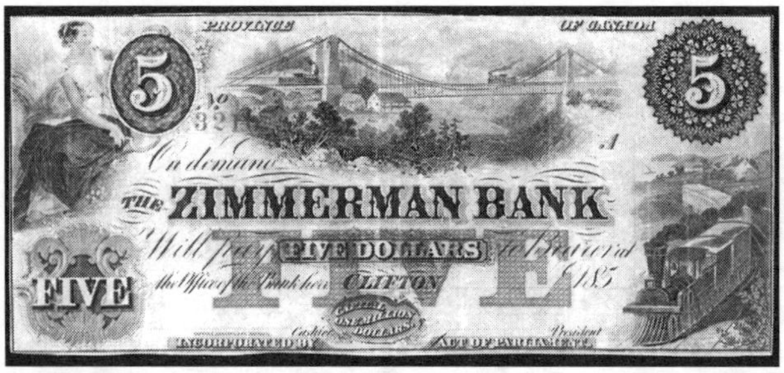

815-14-06R

$5 Face Design: Seated allegorical female/
Roebling Suspension Bridge/train

Colour: Blue

Back Design: Plain

Photo Not Available

815-14-08R

$10 Face Design: Roebling Suspension Bridge/
Prince Consort/female with sheaf of grain

Colour: Blue

Back Design: Plain

815-14-10R

$20 Face Design: Clifton House Hotel/
Roebling Suspension Bridge/
seated woman with telescope

Colour: Blue

Back Design: Plain

IMPRINT

Toppan Carpenter & Co. Montreal

left	**right**
none	none

ISSUE DATING

Partially engraved ___ 185___:

PROTECTOR

Red "word" on face and mirror image on back

Cat. No.	Denom.	Date	Variety	G	VG	F	VF	EF	Unc
14-02R	$1	185_	Remainder*	40.	80.	100.	140.	200.	350.
14-04R	$3	185_	Remainder*	60.	125.	150.	225.	350.	500.
14-06R	$5	185_	Remainder*	40.	80.	100.	140.	200.	350.
14-08R	$10	185_	Remainder*	85.	175.	250.	350.	500.	—
14-10R	$20	185_	Remainder*	85.	175.	250.	350.	500.	—
Full sheet	$1,1,3,5	185_		—	—	—	750.	1,100.	1,800.

* Many notes have spurious signatures and dates.

PRIVATE BANKS AND BANKERS IN CANADA

Information recently compiled would suggest that private bankers in Canada played a much more significant role in the economic development of Canada than previously realized. There were over five hundred of these bankers (over 425 in Ontario), some with several branches, operating in Canada mainly between 1880 and 1900. It is generally assumed that the majority of financial transactions were carried on through the chartered banks and their branches, and this was probably true in the larger towns and cities. In smaller towns and in rural areas, however, many people preferred to deal with the local banker, often a well-known and respected member of the community.

Competition for capital and customers in the cities often forced the private banker to pay higher interest rates and accept loans of greater risk, resulting in a high failure rate. In rural areas this was not the case, and the chartered banks often resorted to buying out the small banker in order to open and operate a successful branch. As a result, private banks slowly disappeared over the years.

Since private bankers could not issue bank notes, a record of their existence is found in local newspapers, street directories, pass books, cheques, deposit slips and other bank stationery. In addition, lists of these bankers were often included in various bankers' directories, both in Canada and in the United States. These various sources have formed the basis of this preliminary listing, and it is hoped it will stimulate further research into this rewarding, yet neglected, aspect of Canadian banking.

ALBERTA

Name of Bank	Manager or Agent	Paid-up Capital	Town	County
Armstrong & Co., J. G.			Ponoka	
Cowdry Bros.			Fort MacLeod	
McDougall & Secord			Edmonton	
Snow & Co., C.E.			Cardston	
White, R.B.			Youngstown	

BRITISH COLUMBIA

Name of Bank	Manager or Agent	Paid-up Capital	Town	County
Bealey & Co. R. J.			Rossland	
Burke, John M.			Kaslo	
Garesche, Green & Co.	A.A. Green		Victoria	
Green, Worlock & Co.			Victoria	
Lafferty & Moore	Wm. Green		Vancouver	
Retallack J.L.			Sandon	Slocan
Wulffsohn & Bewicke, Ltd	G. Alers Hankey	$300,000	Vancouver	New Westminster
Yorkshire Guar. & Secur. Corp (Banking Department)	L. Neville Smith		Chilliwack	Chilliwack

MANITOBA

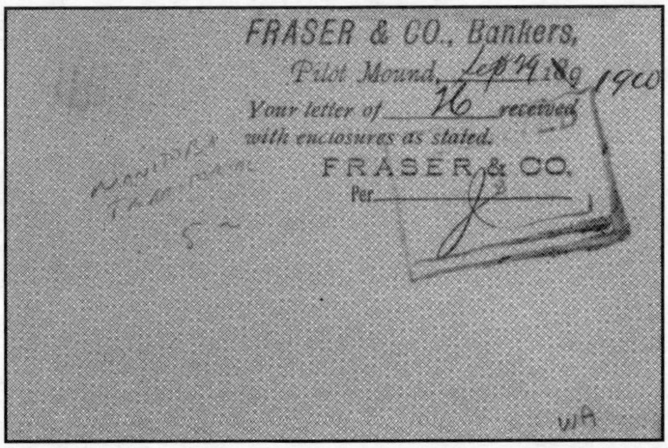
FRASER & CO., Bankers,
Pilot Mound,
Your letter of received
with enclosures as stated.
FRASER & CO.
Per.

Name of Bank	Manager or Agent	Paid-up Capital	Town	County
Alexander & Co., R.S.			Treherne	Macdonald
Alloway & Champion			Winnipeg	Selkirk
Alloway & Champion			Portage la Prairie	Marquette
Andrew & Company			Oak Lake	Brandon
Arnold & Co., C.E.	Charles E. Arnold		Rapid City	Minnedosa
Bailey & Co., W.L.			Gladstone	Westbourne
Bailey & Co., W.S.	W.S. Bailey	$25,000	Gladstone	Westbourne
Beattie & Company			Swan River	Marquette
Bell & Co., F.N.			Morris	Provencher
Canada Perm. Mort. Company			Winnipeg	Selkirk
Comber, E.F.			Selkirk West	Selkirk
Comber, E.F.			Selkirk	Selkirk
Cowdry Bros.			Birtle	
Cruthers & Company	S. Cruthers		Manitou	Selkirk
Denison, E. O.			Minnedosa	
Dickie & Company			Gretna	Lisgar
Dudley, J.C.			Birtle	Marquette

MANITOBA

Name of Bank	Manager or Agent	Paid-up Capital	Town	County
Dudley, Leese & Scarth			Russell	
Dunsford & Company	C.R. Dunsford		Morden	Dufferin
Evans, E.			Brandon	Brandon
Fanning, A.R.			Newdale	Marquette
Fanning & McGill			Newdale	Marquette
Fraser & Company	J.M. Fraser	$5,000	Pilot Mound	Rock Lake
Gibson, R.W.	R.J. Gomley, Cashier	$50,000	Birtle	Shoal Lake
Haley & Sutton			Morden	Selkirk
Hall Co. Ltd.			Winnipeg	Selkirk
Harrison's Bank	W.R. Weare, Cashier	$30,000	Neepawa	Beautiful Pl's
Hopper, D.A.			Brandon	Brandon
Harvey & Company			Dauphin	
Hopper's Banking House	D.A. Hopper		Rapid City	Minnedosa
Ingram, Blain & Co.	D.A. McVicar		Wawanesa	Brandon
Inman & Co., H.	H. Inman		Hamiota	Marquette
Irwin, G.L.			Dauphin	
Laughlin, A.			Cartwright	Lisgar
Laughlin, A.			Neelin	
Laughlin & Co., A.			Neelin	
Ledez, Ch		$25,000	St. Pierre	
Leese & Scarth			Russell	Marquette
Leslie, Ronald			Stonewall	Lisgar
Little, Nathan			Cypress Riv	Marquette
Logan & Co., R.	J.A. Smith		Glenboro	Marquette
Logan & Co., Wm.	Wm. Logan, Cashier		Carberry	Norfolk
Long, M.	N.T. Lee, Cashier	$46,000	Gretna	Manchester
Longan & company	W.M. Logan		McGregor	Macdonald
McArthur, D.			Emerson	Manchester
McLenaghen & Co., James			Portage la Prairie	Marquette
McMicken, A.				Fort Gary
McTavish, E.			Lowe Farm	Provencher
Mortlock, Ernest			Dominion City	Provencher
Mortlock, Ernest			Winnipeg	Selkirk
National Trust Co.,			Winnipeg	Selkirk
Nelson Banking Office	Sutton, Haley & Lafferty		Nelson	Marquette
Newton, F. Y.				Roblin
Nicholls & Co., W.G.			Selkirk	Lisgar
Olser, Hammond & Nanton			Winnipeg	Selkirk
Packard, Gundy & Company			Winnipeg	Selkirk
Pickering, Vere H.		$15,000	Minnedosa	Minnedosa
Pickering's Bank				Minnedosa
Randall & Greenshaw			Shoal Lake	Marquette
Reid & Co., J.T.			Swan Lake	Lisgar
Ritz, H.			Gretna	Lisgar
Ritz & Widmeyer		$320,000	Gretna	Manchester
Robbins & Gill			Miami	Selkirk
Russell, William		$320,000	Winkler	Lisgar
Schimnowski's Bank, A.				Salter
Schimnowski's Bank, A				Selkirk
Schultz' Bank, Frank				Baldur
Stevens, Henry				Bowsman
Strathy & Co., E.K.			Hartney	Selkirk
Stuart, A.P. & F.T.			Deloraine	Turtle Mt'n
Winnipeg Financial Corp.			Winnipeg	Selkirk
Young, A.L.			Souris	Brandon
Young & Co., A. L.			Souris	Brandon
Young & Van Someren			Souris	Brandon

NEW BRUNSWICK

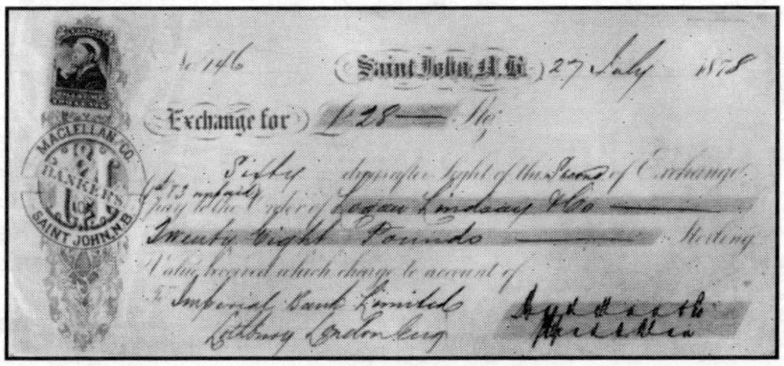

Name of Bank	Manager or Agent	Paid-up Capital	Town	County
Allan, John T.			Woodstock	Carleton
Armstrong, John R.			Saint John	Saint John
Blair & Company			St. John	St. John
Clinch, D.C.			St. John	St. John
Fisher & A. B. Connell			Woodstock	Carleton
Fraser, Wetmore & Winslow			Fredericton	York
Halifax Clearing House Ass'n	R.M. Cotton, President		Halifax	Halifax
Jack, Andrew			Saint John	Saint John
Jack & Bell			Halifax	Halifax
Jones, Oliver			Moncton	Westmoreland
Jones, Simeon			Saint John	Saint John
Jones & Co., Simeon			Saint John	Saint John
Jones & Co., S.			St. John	
Jones, Thomas			Saint John	Saint John
Kaye, Edmund			Saint John	Saint John
Mackintosh, James C.			Halifax	Halifax
Mackintosh & Co., J. C.			Saint John	Saint John
Maclellan & company			Saint John	Saint John
Mahon & Co., W.F.			Saint John	Saint John
McCurdy & Co., F. B.			Saint John	Saint John
McDougall & Cowans			Saint John	Saint John
McLellan, Thomas			Saint John	Saint John
Peck, John Lewis			Hillsboro	Albert
Philps, George			Saint John	Saint John
Powell, H.A.			Sackville	Westmoreland
Robinson & Sons, J.M.			Saint John	Saint John
Robinson & Sons, J.M.			Fredericton	York
Robinson & Sons, J.M.			Moncton	Westmoreland
Robinson, J.M.			Saint John	Saint John
Royal Securities			Saint John	Saint John
Steeves, C. A.			Moncton	Westmoreland
Stevens & Mitchell			St. Stephen	Charlotte
Stone, Joseph			Saint John	Saint John
Stone, Oliver			Saint John	Saint John
Thomson, S.R.			Saint John	Saint John
Van Wart, Gilbert			Woodstock	Carleton
Wilkinson, William			Chatham	Northumberland
Wood, M. & Son			Sackville	Westmoreland

NEWFOUNDLAND

Name of Bank	Manager or Agent	Paid-up Capital	Town	County
Newfoundland Savings Bank	Edward Morris, Cashier		St. John's	

NORTH WEST TERRITORY

Name of Bank	Manager or Agent	Paid-up Capital	Town	County
Behrends, B.M.			Dawson	
Brine, McDonald & Co.,			Qu'Appelle	
Caswell & Co., S.H.			Qu'Appelle	Assiniboia
Cowdry Bros. J. Cowdry			Macleod	Alberta
Flood, E.			Prince Albert	
Gibson, R.W.			Wolseley	
Hepburn, Irwin & Smith			Regina	
Hitchcocke & McCulloch	Harold Jagger	$40,000	Moose Jaw	Assiniboia
Lafferty & Moore	P. G. Gray		Calgary	
Lafferty & Moore	C. F. Strang		Edmonton	
Lafferty & Moore	F. K. Gibson		Moosomin	
Lafferty & Moore	W. R. Robertson		Regina	
Lafferty & Smith	F. G. Smith		Calgary	
Lafferty & Smith	P. G. Gray		Edmonton	
Lafferty & Smith	T. N. Christie		Moosomin	
Lafferty & Smith	Hy. LeJeune		Regina	
LeJeune, Smith & Co.	F. G. Smith		Calgary	
LeJeune, Smith & Co.	A. E. Christie		Moosomin	
LeJeune, Smith & Co.	Hy. LeJeune		Regina	
MacArthur & Knowles			Prince Albert	
MacDonald, Alexander			Battleford	
McDonald & Co., D.H.			Qu'Appelle	Assiniboia
Morrison & company		$3,000	Whitewood	Assiniboia
Pease, R.A. & Co.			Wapella	
Pickering, Vere H.			Yorkton	Assiniboia
Skillister & Co., T.A.			Indian Head	Assiniboia
Skilliter & Co., T.A.	T.N. Christie		Indian Head	Assiniboia
Snow, C.E.			Cardston	
Tryon & Co., C.R. Percy Bell		$25,000	Grenfell	Assiniboia

NOVA SCOTIA

Name of Bank	Manager or Agent	Paid-up Capital	Town	County
Ennis & Stoppani			Halifax	Halifax
Farquhar, Forrest & Co.			Halifax	Halifax
Huse & Lowell			Halifax	Halifax
Jack & Bell			Hollis	Halifax
Jack & Bell			Halifax	Halifax
Jack & Son, Andrew M.			Halifax	Halifax
Lowell & Co., W.L.			Halifax	Halifax
Mackintosh, J.C.			Hollis	Halifax
McCurdy & Co., F.B.			Halifax	Halifax
Pauicy, E.J.H.			Hollis	Halifax
Royal Securities			Halifax	Halifax

ONTARIO

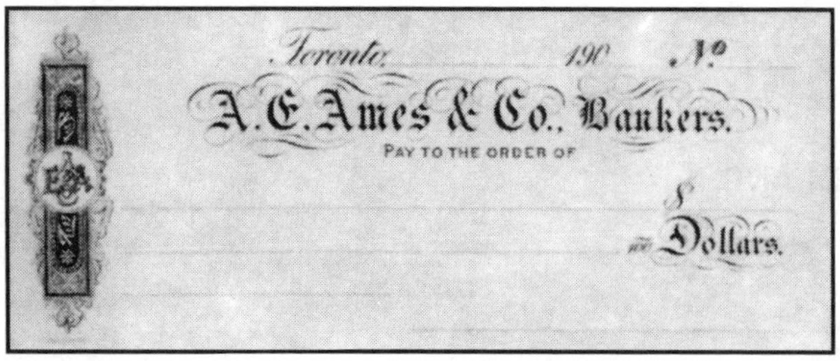

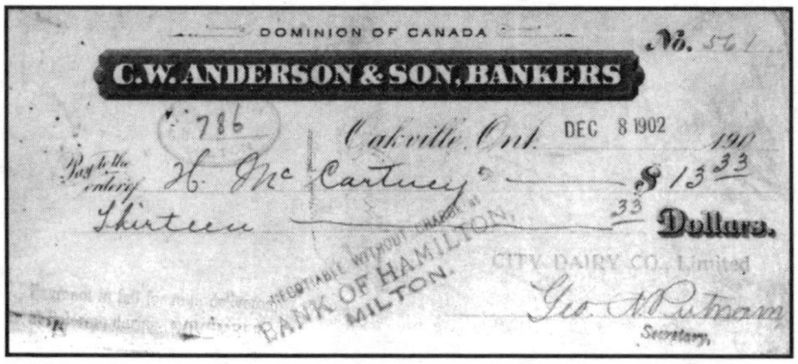

Name of Bank	Manager or Agent	Paid-up Capital	Town	County
Acton Banking Co.	Storey, Christie & Co.		Acton	Halton
Adams, D.J.		$50,000	Port Perry	Ontario
Adams & Duglas			Port Perry	Ontario
Adams & Hutcheson			Port Perry	Ontario
Agur, Robert			Ingersoll	Oxford
Ainslie & Ainslie		$15,000	Comber	Essex
Aiken, H.C.			Tottenham	Simcoe
Allan, H.W.			Harrow	Essex
Allen & McMahon			Port Elgin	Bruce
Allen, G.L.			Mt. Forest	Wellington

ONTARIO

Name of Bank	Manager or Agent	Paid-up Capital	Town	County
Allen, H.A.	A. Miller		Port Elgin	Bruce
Allison, Adam	A. Allison		Belmont	Middlesex
Alloway & Champion			Rat Portage	Rainy River
American Express Co.,			Toronto	York
Ames & Co., A.E.			Toronto	York
Ames & Co., G.W.	G.W. Ames		Wiarton	Bruce
Ames, A.W.			Wiarton	Bruce
Anderson & Co., J.D.		$45,000	Essex	Essex
Anderson & Scott	E.K. Scott		Palmerston	Wellington
Anderson & Son, C.W.			Oakville	Halton
Anderson, C.W.			Oakville	Halton
Anderson, C.W.			Palmerston	Wellington
Anderson, J.D.			Essex	Essex
Andrew & Howarth	Thomas Howarth, Cashier		Oakville	Halton
Annis, David			Woodville	Victoria
Archibald, C. Douglas			Alvinston	Lambton
Armour, Robert			Bowmanville	Durham
Baby & Donelly			Sarnia	Lambton
Baby's Banking House			Sarnia	Lambton
Baby, R.A.			Sarnia	Lambton
Baird, John			Lynden	Wentworth
Baird, Wm. H.			Lynden	Wentworth
Baker, H.C.			Hamilton	Wentworth
Baker, John			Harrington	West
Bancroft, James			Hamilton	Wentworth
Bangs, J.A.			Carleton Place	Lanark
Barfoot's Banking Office, S.			Chatham	Kent
Barfoots Bank	A.F. Falls, H.I.I. Campbell		Chatham	Kent
Barker, Joseph			Brechin	Ontario
Barnes, S.			Collingwood	Simcoe
Bartlett, G.R.			Cooksville	Peel
Baxter, R.G.			Bridgeburg	Welland
Baxter, R.G.			Burlington	Halton
Bazin Company, The P.I.			Ottawa	Carleton
Bearer, J.			Uxbridge	Ontario
Beattie's Banking House	John Beattie		Fergus	Wellington
Beattie, John			Fergus	Wellington
Beaty & Co., K.			Toronto	York
Beaty & Co., Robert			Toronto	York
Beaver Valley Banking Co.	Walter Hunter		Clarksburg	Grey
Bebbington Co., Dean	F. Bebbington		Ottawa	Carleton
Becker & Co., L.	L.H. Slaght		Waterford	Norfolk
Beddome, F.B.			London	Middlesex
Beecroft & Co., T.			Barrie	Simcoe
Belcher & Company	A.E. Belcher		Southhampton	Bruce
Berman, Kenen & Company			Toronto	York
Black & company	Benjamin Madill		Beaverton	Ontario
Black & Co., W.S.	W.C. Smith		Uxbridge	Ontario
Black, A.N.C.			Dutton	Elgin
Bloomer, E.			Collingwood	Simcoe
Box & Son, R.			St. Mary's	Perth
Box, R.S.			St. Mary's	Perth
Boyer, John			Kincardine	Bruce
Bredin, R.S.			Mt. Forest	Wellington
Breese, William			Chatsworth	Grey
Breese, Wm.			Garafraxa	
Breese, Wm. Jr.			Chatsworth	Grey

ONTARIO

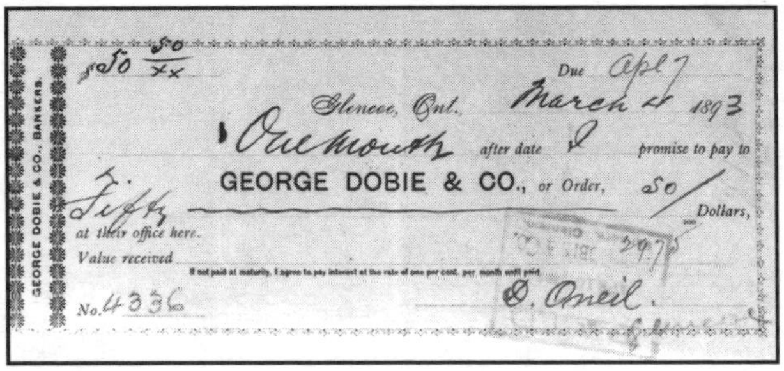

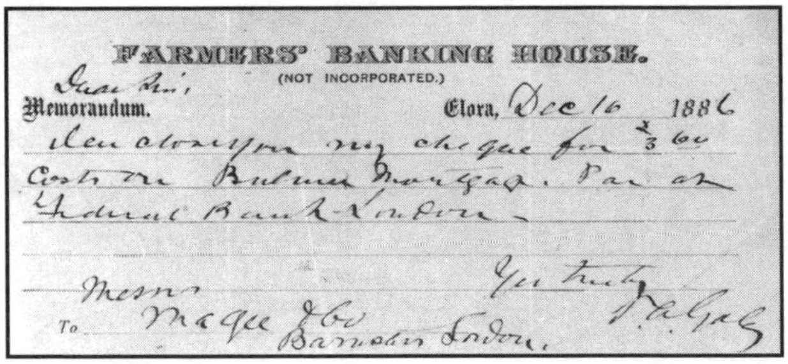

Name of Bank	Manager or Agent	Paid-up Capital	Town	County
Bretts Banking House			Toronto	York
Brigden Banking Co.	W.J. Ward		Brigden	Lambton
British Canadian Securities Co.,			Toronto	York
Brown & Co., G.N.			Alliston	Simcoe
Brown & Co., G.N.			Arkona	Lambton
Brown & Co., W.R.			Toronto	York
Brown's Banking House	Garrett Brown, Cashier		Schomberg	York N.R.
Brown, G.			Schomberg	York, N.R.
Browne & Co., Philip			Toronto	York
Browne, Jas. & Philip			Toronto	York
Bruce Banking House	S.T. Jackson	$26,000	Ripley	Bruce
Bruce, Wm. Jr.			Chatsworth	Grey
Bryden, J.			Collingwood	Simcoe
Bull & Co., W. H.			Toronto	York
Burk & Co., A.A.			Thessalon	Algoma
Burk & Graham			Alliston	Simcoe
Burk & Graham			Creemore	Simcoe
Burk & Graham	J.A. Graham	$100,000	Toronto	York
Butler, W.			Walkerton	Bruce
Byers, N.			Enniskillen	Durham
Cameron & Campbell			Lucknow	Bruce
Cameron & Curry	John Curry, Cashier		Windsor	Essex
Cameron, John			Toronto	York
Campbell & Cassels			Toronto	York
Campbell's Banking Office	M.S. Campbell		Watford	Lambton
Campbell Bros.			Watford	Lambton
Campbell, J.W.			Glencoe	Middlesex
Campbell, M.S.			Watford	Lambton
Carrick Banking Co.	George Curle, President; Charles Schurter		Mildmay	Bruce
Carrick Finance Co.			Mildmay	Bruce
Carruthers, J.B.			Kingston	Frontenac
Carscallen & Co., A.W.			Marmora	Hastings
Carscallen, A.W.		$50,000	Marmora	Hastings
Carson, A.S.	Fred Slaven		Picton	Prince Edward
Cassels Son & Co.			Toronto	York
Castles Bros.			Stirling	Hastings
Chantry, P.O.			Harlem	Leeds
Chatham Savings & Loan Co.			Chatham	Kent
Checkley & Co., E.J.	H.C. Edgar, Cashier; C.R. Hanning, Manager	$10,000	Preston	Waterloo
Checkley, E.J.			Preston	Waterloo
Christopher, A.N.			Ingersoll	Oxford
Claris' Banking House	George T. Claris		St. Thomas	Elgin
Claris, George T.		$50,000	St. Thomas	Elgin
Clark, J.C.			Kingston	Frontenac
Clarke & Co., T.			Mt. Forest	Wellington
Clarke & Sons	Thomas E. Clarke		Bothwell	Kent
Clarke, Thos.			Mount Forest	Wellington
Clay, Sharpe & Co.			Burks Falls	Parry Sound
Collard, Leonard H.			St. Catharines	Lincoln
Collins & Co., T.B.	T.B. Collins		Millbrook	Durham
Collins, T.B.			Millbrook	Durham
Collins, W.B.			Wyoming	Lambton
Conn & Co., J.	M. & J. Conn		Alvinston	Lambton
Conn's Banking House	M. & J. Conn		Alvinston	Lambton
Conn's Banking House	R. & J. Conn		Alvinston	Lambton
Cook, B.S.			Fordwich	Huron
Cook, Christopher			Brantford	Brant
Cook, Thos. H.			Sarnia	Lambton
Cook & Son, Thos. H.			Sarnia	Lambton

ONTARIO

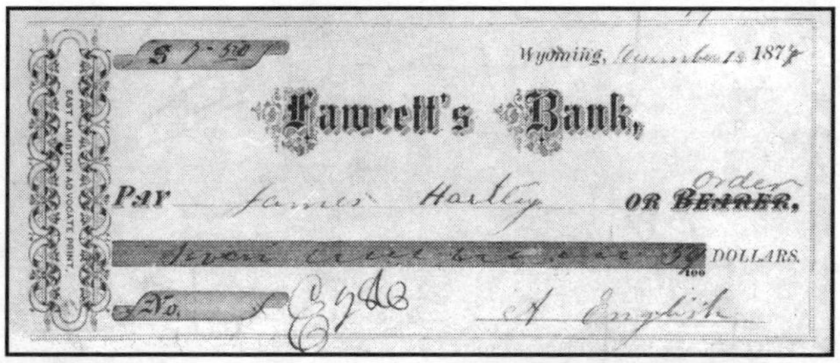

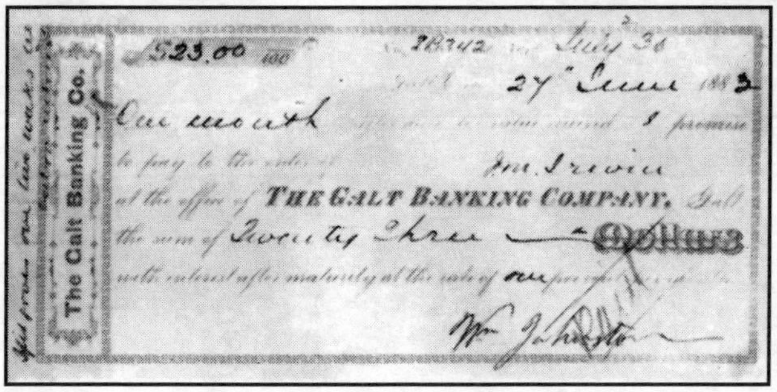

Name of Bank	Manager or Agent	Paid-up Capital	Town	County
Cook & Son, Thos.			Toronto	York
Corbould, W.			Wingham	Huron
Counsell, C.M.			Hamilton	Wentworth
Counsell, Glassco & Co.			Hamilton	Wentworth
Cowdry, N.H.			Waterford	Norfolk
Crombie, D.B.			St. Catharines	Lincoln
Cuddy company			Bothwell	Kent
Cuddy Falls Company			Amherstburg	Essex
Cuddy, Loftus			Amherstburg	Essex
Curtis, C.L.			Kingston	Frontenac
Cutten, Walter			Guelph	Wellington
Dale & Co., J.C.		$30,000	Madoc	Hastings
Dale, J.C.			Madoc	Hastings
Dardis, Thomas			Morrisburg	Dundas
Dempsey, S.			Albury	Prince Edward
Denison & Crease			New Hamburg	Waterloo
Denison, E.R.			Niagara-on-the-Lake	Lincoln
Dobie & Co., George			Glencoe	Middlesex
Doble & company			Sunderland	Ontario
Doble & company	J.B. Vallentyne		Sunderland	Ontario
Dresden Banking Co.			Dresden	Kent
Dube & Co., J.H.			Ottawa	Carleton
Durval, P.			Collingwood	Simcoe
Edwards & Co., R.			Cannington	Ontario
Edwards & Co., R.	O.E. Weens, Cashier	$50,000	Woodville	Victoria
Edwards, Richard			Woodville	Victoria
Elliot & Co.'s Banking House	J.H. Elliot & Co.		Chesley	Bruce
Elliot & Co., J.H.	J.H. Elliot		Chesley	Bruce
Elliot & Company	J.A. Elliot		Ridgetown	Kent
Elliot & Westland	J.A. Elliot		Ridgetown	Kent
Elmira Banking Co.			Elmira	Waterloo
Emmerton, J.			Clinton	Huron
Essex County Bank	Cameron & Curry, John Curry		Windsor	Essex
Essex County Banking House			Windsor	Essex
Falls Bros			Amherstburg	Essex
Farmer, L.N. & Dep C	Telford & Co.		Owen Sound	Grey
Farmers Bank	Logan & Co.		Seaforth	Huron
Farmers' Banking House	T.A. Gale Gale & Archib		Elora	Wellington
Farran & Archibald			Elora	Wellington
Farran & Tisdall	J.P. Tisdall	$75,000	Clinton	Huron
Farran, W.W.			Clinton	Huron
Farran, W.W.			Elora	Wellington
Faulkner's Banking House	G.W. Faulkner		Stirling	Hastings
Fawcett & Livingston & Co.			Dresden	Kent
Fawcett & Livingston			Wallaceburg	Kent
Fawcett & Livingston			Wardsville	Middlesex
Fawcett, Thomas			Listowel	Perth
Fawcett, Thomas			Mitchell	Perth

ONTARIO

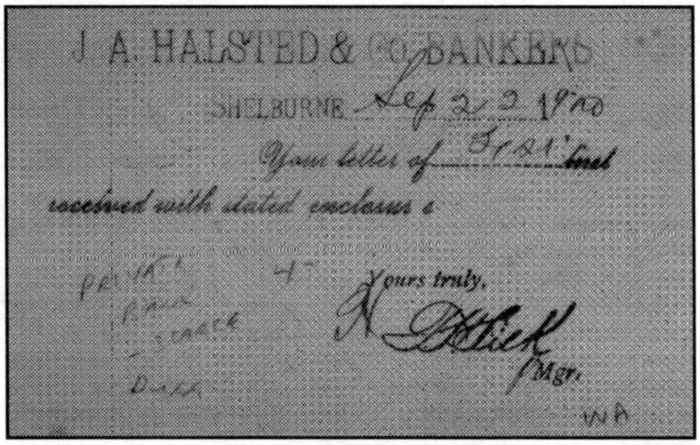

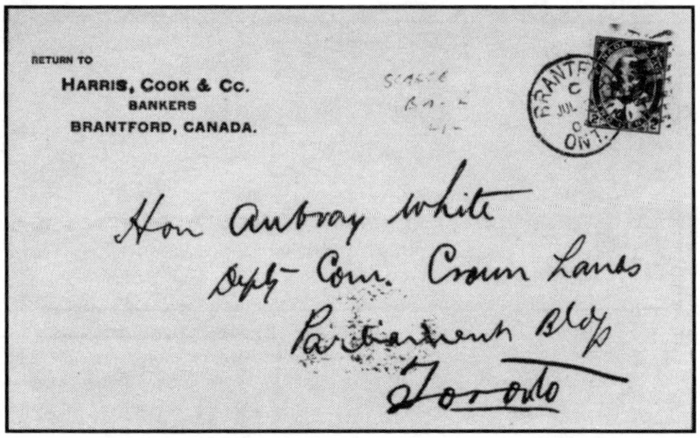

Name of Bank	Manager or Agent	Paid-up Capital	Town	County
Fawcett, Thomas			Stratford	Perth
Fawcett, Thomas			Watford	Lambton
Fawcett's Bank			Alvinston	Lambton
Fawcett's Bank			Arkona	Lambton
Fawcett's Bank			Wyoming	Lambton
Fead, J.S.			Orangeville	Dufferin
Finnie			Arnprior	Renfrew
Fish & Son, Wm. T.	Elbert L. Fish		Cobourg	Northumberland
Fisher, David			Bowmanville	Durham
Fitzgibbon, J.G.			Norwood	Peterboro
Fleming, M.	Henry Barron		Forest	Lambton
Fleming, M.			Sarnia	Lambton
Folger, B.W.			Kingston	Frontenac
Folger Brothers			Kingston	Frontenac
Forbes & company			Toronto	York
Fox, R. & J.	John Fo	$50,000	Lucan	Middlesex
Fraser, Donald			Kingston	Frontenac
Fulford & Co., G.T.			Brockville	Leeds
Fuller & Co., W.S.			Mitchell	Perth
Fuller's Bank	Jacob Fulle	$15,000	Thedford	Lambton
Fuller's Banking Office	P. Phillips, Cashier		Leamington	Essex
Fuller, C.D.			Toronto	York
Fuller, Jacob			Thedford	Lambton
Fuller, T.	Maclaughlin		Blenheim	Kent
Fuller, Thomas	P. Phillips		Leamington	Essex
Fuller, W.S.			Alliston	Simcoe
Galt Banking Company, The			Galt	Waterloo
Gamble & White			Palmerston	Wellington
Gamey, R.R.			Toronto	York
Ganor & Co.,			Sarnia	Lambton
Gardener, Jas.			Meaford	Grey
Gardiner, Samuel			Chatham	Kent
Gardiner, William E.			Chatham	Kent
Garrett, James			Aylmer	Elgin
Gatto, Guiseppe			Toronto	York
Geiser & Willings			Bancroft	Hastings
Gibson, R.C.			Terra Cotta	Peel
Gibson & Co.,			Toronto	York
Gilberts Bank			St. Thomas	Elgin
Gillard, T. B. & Riddell			Wallaceburg	Kent
Gillies & company			Teeswater	Bruce
Gillies & Smith			Brussels	Huron
Gillies & Smith			Teeswater	Bruce
Gillis & Co., John D.			Highgate	Elgin
Gillis & Reycraft	John D. Gillis		Highgate	Kent
Gordon Bros.			Dryden	
Gordon Bros.			Sioux Lookout	
Gordon & Douglas	J.E.W. Branan		Alviston	Lambton
Gordon, A.W.			Orillia	Simcoe
Gould & Bros. I.J.	Isaac J. Gould		Uxbridge	Ontario
Graft, H.H.			Simcoe	Norfolk
Graham & Knight	C.R. Knight	$50,000	Alliston	Simcoe
Graham & Knight	D. McArthur		Creemore	Simcoe
Graham, I.			Uxbridge	Ontario
Graham, J.A.			Toronto	York
Graham, John A.			Toronto	York

ONTARIO

Name of Bank	Manager or Agent	Paid-up Capital	Town	County
Graham, Joseph C.			Tiverton	Bruce
Graydon, W.J.			Streetsville	Peel
Groff, H.H.			Simcoe	Norfolk
Guelph Banking Co.	W.H. Cutten		Guelph	Wellington
Gzowski & Buchan			Toronto	York
Gzowski, C.S., Jr., Broker			Toronto	York
Hale, Horatio			Clinton	Huron
Hallett & Co., J.G.			Woodbridge	York
Halliday, Wm.			Pakenham	Lanark
Halstead & Company			Walkerton	Bruce
Halstead & Co., J.A.			Orangeville	Dufferin
Halstead, J.A.			Mount Forest	Wellington
Halstead, J.A.			Toronto	York
Halstead & Scott			Wingham	Huron
Halstead & Co., J.A.	J.A. Halstead		Mt. Forest	Wellington
Halstead & Co., J.A.	E.A. Smith, F.H. Silk, J.F. Miller		Shelburne	Dufferin
Halton & Co., F.J.		$17,000.	Windsor	Essex
Hamer & Co., W.T.			Gravenhurst	Simcoe
Hamilton & Company	Wm. Lonsdale		Grand Valley	Dufferin
Hamilton Clearing House Asso'n	John Pottenger, Chairman		Hamilton	Wentworth
Hamilton, Davis & Co.			Hamilton	Wentworth
Hamilton Prov. & Loan Soc.	Geo. H. Gillespie, Pr	$1,100,000.	Hamilton	Wentworth
Hamilton, R.E.			Grand Valley	Dufferin
Hanns & Co.,	J.H. Hanns		Arthur	Wellington
Harris, George, F.R.			Emerson	
Harris, Cook & Co.			Brantford	Brant
Harrison & Rathburn			Alvinsto	Lambton
Harrison & Rathburn			Glencoe	Middlesex
Hartman & Company	C.W. Hartman		Clarksburg	Grey
Hartman & Company	C.W. Hartman		Thornbury	Grey
Hartman & Wilgress			Clarksburg	Grey
Haskins & Co., W.F.	Geo. Wilson	$51,000	Dunnville	Haldimand
Haven & Co., W.C.			Kingston	Frontenac
Hay Bros.			Listowell	Perth
Hay Bros.	A. Miller		Tara	Bruce
Hayes, M.P.			Seaforth	Huron
Hayes, N.			Ingersoll	Oxford
Haynes, D. Curtis			St. Catharines	Lincoln
Hey & company			Ailsa Craig	Middlesex
Hey & Jones			Ailsa Craig	Middlesex
Hillhouse, Jas.			Clifford	Wellington
Hime, H.L.			Toronto	York
Holtby & Co., F.B.			Mitchell	Perth
Holtby, F.			Mitchell	Perth
Holton & Co., F.J.			Windsor	Essex
Hood, John			Hawkesbury	Prescott
Hornibrook & Co.			Beamsville	Lincoln
Hornibrook & Co., G.H.			Caledonia	Haldimand
House, F.			Cobourg Nort	Humberland
Howard & Co., G.H.			Niagara Falls	Welland
Howard, L.W.			Chesterville	Dundas
Howett & Kerr			Guelph	Wellington
Howitt, Charles E.	A. Bradshaw		Guelph	Wellington
Howitt, Charles E.	Geo. Bradshaw		Guelph	Wellington
Howitt, Charles E.	L.C. Mercer		Guelph	Wellington
Howitt, Chas. E.	Chas. Mercer		Guelph	Wellington
Hughes, G.P.		$20,000	Tottenham	Simcoe
Hughes, Geo. P.			Keenansville	Simcoe
Hunt's Bank			Bracebridge	Muskoka
Hunt's Bank	Alfred Hunt		Bradford	Simcoe
Hunt, Alfred			Bracebridge	Muskoka
Huron & Bruce			Goderich	Huron
Hurst & Burk			Thessalon	Ontario
Hurst & Burk			Bruce Mines	Algoma
Hurst & Burk			Gore Bay	Manitoulin
Huxley, G.			Clinton	Huron
Irwin, J.M.			Arthur	Wellington
Irwin, J.M.			Galt	Waterloo
Irwin, J.M.			Hespeler	Waterloo
Jackson Brothers	S.T. Jackson		Ripley	Bruce
Jackson, Henry			Beeton	Simcoe
Jackson, T.R.	D. MacLachlan		Blenheim	Kent
James F. Macklem			Chippawa	Welland
Jarvis & Co., Aemilius, Brokers			Toronto	York

ONTARIO

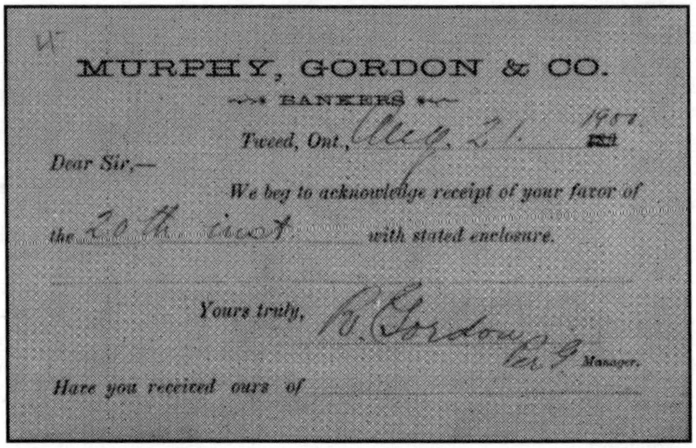
MURPHY, GORDON & CO.
BANKERS
Tweed, Ont., Aug. 21. 1901
Dear Sir,—
We beg to acknowledge receipt of your favor of the 20th inst with stated enclosure.
Yours truly, R. Gordon, Manager.
Have you received ours of

Name of Bank	Manager or Agent	Paid-up Capital	Town	County
Jarvis, S.J.			Wallaceburg	Kent
Jasperson, B.			Kingsville	Essex
Jay & Co., C.H.			Meaford	Grey
Johnson, H.			Springfield	Elgin
Johnston, A.			Sarnia	Ontario
Johnston, Alex			Strathroy	Middlesex
Johnston & Tisdal			Clinton	Huron
Johnston Banking Co.			Amherstburg	Essex
Johnston, G.B.			Goderich	Huron
Johnston, Gale, Tisdal			Clinton	Huron
Jones, Charles T.			Hamilton	Wentworth
Kaine, John			Gorrie	Dufferin
Kemp, D.			Ingersoll	Oxford
Kent Bros.			Kingston	Frontenac
Kerr & McKellar			Guelph	Wellington
Kilbourne & Co., George S.			Owen Sound	Grey
Killmaster, C.S.			Port Rowan	Norfolk
Killmaster & Son, G.S.			Port Rowan	Norfolk
Kippen & Scarff			Tilbury Centre	Kent
Kirby's Banking House	M.J. Kirby, Cashier		Arthur	Wellington
Kirby, Edward D.			Petrolia	Lambton
Kirby, P.M.			Arthur	Wellington
Kirkpatrick, T.W.			Rodney	Elgin
Kittredge Bros.			Teeswater	Bruce
Kittredge Bros.			Walkerton	Bruce
Kittredge, H.H.			Parkhill	Middlesex
Laidlaw & Co.,			Toronto	York
Landed Banking & Loan Co.	C.W. Cartwright	$682,000	Hamilton	Wentworth
Larke, C.			Colborne	Northumberland
Lawrason, J.P.			St. George	Brant
Lemon & Smith			Alvinston	Lampton
Lewis, F.A.			Orangeville	Dufferin
Lillico, Peter	C.H. Smith		Drayton	Wellington
Lillico, Peter	R.L. Lillico		Listowel	Perth
Lillicos Banking House			Drayton	Wellington
Lillicos Banking House	R.E. Lillico		Arthur	Wellington
Linton & Co., J.			Lakefield	Peterboro
Linton & Co., James		$35,000	Orono	Durham
Linton & Co., James	W.H. Benson, Cashier	$35,000	Lakefield	Peterborough
Linton, James			Lakefield	Peterborough
Linton, James			Orono	Durham
Loftus Cuddy			Amherstburg	Essex
Logan			Seaforth	Huron
Logan & Weir			Seaforth	Huron
Long, A.			Uxbridge	Ontario
Lownsbrough & company			Toronto	York
Lucas & Co., William	E.G. Lucas		Dunnville	Haldimand
Lucas & Co., William	E.G. Lucas		Dundalk	Grey
Lucas & Co., William	William Lucas	$30,000	Markdale	Grey
Lucas, Leacock & Co.	H.J. Leacock		Brigden	Lambton
Lucas, Tanner & Co.	Charles E. Tanner		Blyth	Huron
Lucknow Banking Co.	Geo. A. Siddall		Lucknow	Bruce
Lyon, Jr., R.A.			Sault Ste. Marie	Algoma
Macarthur & Company			Zurich	Huron
Macarthur & Company	John Macarthur, Henry Arnold		Hensall	Huron
MacDonald, W.R.			Hamilton	Wentworth
Machray & company	Robert Machray		Ottawa	Carleton

ONTARIO

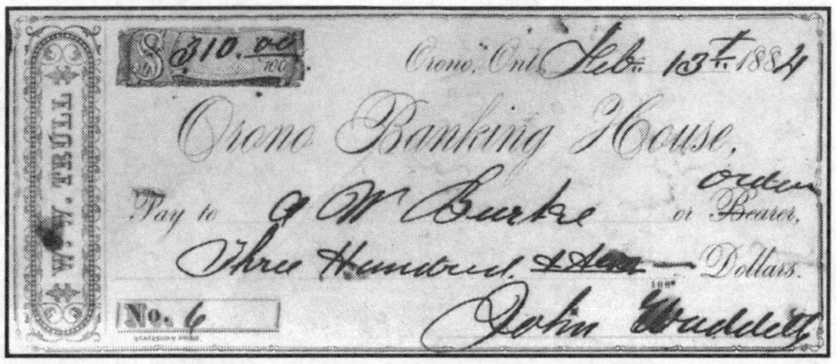

Name of Bank	Manager or Agent	Paid-up Capital	Town	County
Macklem, James F.			Chippawa	Welland
Madill & Co., B.	Benjamin Madill		Beaverton	Ontario
Madoc Banking company			Madoc	Hastings
Mahon, J.A.			London	Middlesex
Mair & Siddall Geo.	A. Siddall	$25,000.	Lucknow	Bruce
Mair & Smith			Teeswater	Bruce
Maitland P. , Ketchum			Brighton	Northumberland
Manson, James			Strathroy	Middlesex
Marten Bros.	C.G. Marten		Leamington	Essex
Martyn, J.P.			St. Thomas	Elgin
Martyn, J.P.			Strathroy	Middlesex
Mason & Co., C.			Shelburne	Dufferin
Mason & Co., C.			Owen Sound	Grey
Matchett, J.			Waterford	Norfolk
Matthews & Co., W.H.			Huntsville	Muskoka
Maxon, G.			Leamington	Essex
Maxon & Maxon			Leamington	Essex
Mayhew & Harmer			Thamesville	Kent
McCall, William			Sarnia	Lambton
McCullough & Young	W.L. Young		Markdale	Grey
McDonald & Co., A.	David Roy		Listowell	Perth
McDonald, H.F.			London	Middlesex
McDonald, J.		$5,000	Chatsworth	Grey
McGee			Walkerton	Bruce
McGregor & Brother			Windsor	Essex
McGregor, D.			Sault Ste. Marie	Algoma
McIntosh & McTaggart	J.M. McIntosh		Brussels	Huron
McIntyre, A.M.			Dutton	Elgin
McIntyre & Son, G.			St. Mary's	Perth
McIntyre's Banking Office	G.H. McIntyre		St. Mary's	Perth
McIntyre, Gilbert H.			St. Mary's	Perth
McKay & Jasperson		$4,000	Kingsville	Essex
McKay, Jos. A.			New Toronto	York
McKeand, Archibald			Hamilton	Wentworth
McKeggie & Co., J.C.			Coldwater	Simcoe
McKeggie & Co., J.C.			Fenelon Falls	Victoria
McKeggie & Co., J.C.	J. McEachern		Creemore	Simcoe
McKeggie & Co., J.C.	J. McEachern		Elmvale	Simcoe
McKeggie & Co., J.C.	J.A. Cameron		Stayner	Simcoe
McKeggie & Co., J.C.	J.H. McKeggie		Barrie	Simcoe
McLelland, R.A.			Brockville	Leeds
McMahon & company			Delhi	Norfolk
McMurchie, J.			Blyth	Huron
McMurchie & Rance			Blyth	Huron
McNally & Adams			Hanover	Bruce
McTaggart Bros.			Clifford	Wellington
McTaggart Bros.			Clinton	Huron
McTaggart & Co.,	D.H. Cameron		Parkhill	Middlesex
McTaggart & Co., A.			Parkhill	Middlesex
McTaggart, Geo. D.			Clinton	Huron
Menzies, Thomas			Peterboro	Peterboro
Merritt, W.E.			Chatham	Kent
Merritt's Banking Office	W.E. Merritt		Chatham	Kent
Messner & Co., F.X.			Formosa	Bruce
Midland Banking Co.	S. Paterson & Bro.	$40,000	Port Hope	Durham
Midland Loan & Savings Co.	Geo. M. Furby		Port Hope	Durham
Midland Trust company	S. Patterson/Co.		Port Hope	Durham
Miers, J.H.			Appin	Middlesex

ONTARIO

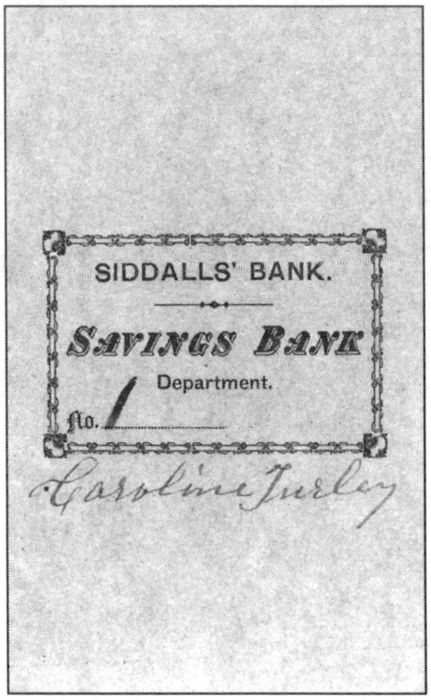

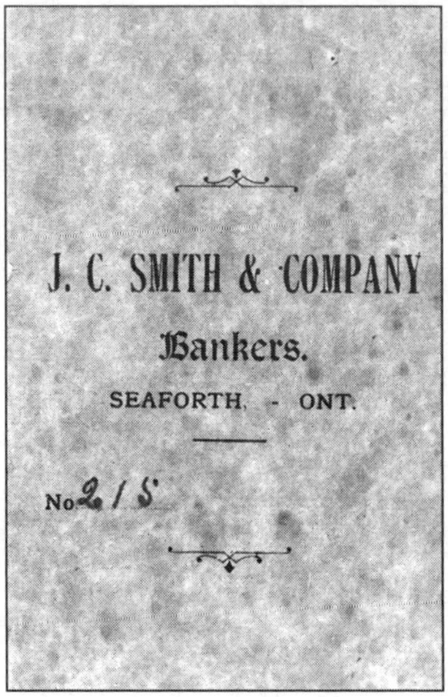

Name of Bank	Manager or Agent	Paid-up Capital	Town	County
Mihell & company			Ailsa Craig	Middlesex
Millbrook Banking Co.			Millbrook	Durham
Miller & company	W.C. Hamilton		Stouffville	York
Miller & company	Walter Miller		Stouffville	York
Miller & Co., J.F.			Shelburne	Dufferin
Mills & Cunningham			Kingston	Frontenac
Mills & Kent			Kingston	Frontenac
Mills, Thos.			Kingston	Frontenac
Milne, John			Essex	Essex
Milner, Wm.			St. Augustine	Huron
Minkler, M.A.			Waterford	Norfolk
Mitchell & Alexander			Ailsa Craig	Middlesex
Mitchell Banking Co.			Mitchell	Perth
Mitchell, George			Flesherton	Grey
Mitchells Banking House	George Mitchell		Flesherton	Grey
Moment, Robert			Orono	Durham
Moore, H.J.			Toronto	York
Morehouse, H.D.			Guelph	Wellington
Morgan, Charles E.			Hamilton	Wentworth
Morison, John			Toronto	York
Morris & Co., S.B.	S.B. Morris		Rodney	Elgin
Morris, R.			Petrolia	Lambton
Morton, Geo. K.		$20,000	St. Thomas	Elgin
Mowat & Son, W. W. Mowat			Stratford	Perth
Mowat, William			Stratford	Perth
Mulholland & Roper	J.H. Roper		Peterboro	Peterboro
Municipal Bankers' Corp.			Toronto	York
Murch, W.H.			St. Thomas	Elgin
Murgatroyd & Sons, R.			Smithville	Wentworth
Munro, James		$20,000	Embro	Oxford
Murphy, Gordon & Co.	R. Gordon		Tweed	Hastings
Murphy, P. & P.			Stoco	Hastings
Murray's Bank	Walter Edgar Murray	$44,000	Aylmer	Elgin
Murray's Bank	W.E. Murray	$44,000	Ayr	Waterloo
Murray, Robert			Embro	Oxford
Murray, W.E.			Aylmer	Elgin
Nelson Mills & Co.,			Hamilton	Wentworth
Newman & Co., W.P.			Elora	Wellington
Nicoletti, F.			Toronto	York
Norsworthy, J.C.			Ingersoll	Oxford
North American Banking Co.	J.C. Smith		Seaforth	Huron
O'Flynn, Frederick, W.			Madoc	Hastings
O'Flynn & Sons, E.D.	E.D. O'Flynn	$150,000	Madoc	Hastings
O'Hara & Co., H., Brokers			Toronto	York
O'Loughlin, B.S.			Yarker	Lennox/Addington
O'Neil, B.S.		$30,000	Exeter	Huron
O'Neil, R.H.			Lucan	Middlesex
O'Neill & Son, R.H.	F.A. O'Neill		Lucan	Middlesex

ONTARIO

Name of Bank	Manager or Agent	Paid up Capital	Town	County
Ontario Bank Co.,			Acton	Halton
Orono Banking House	W.W. Trull		Orono	Durham
Osler & Hammond, Brokers			Toronto	York
Owen & company	J.T. Owen		Ailsa Craig	Middlesex
Oxford Banking Co.			Woodstock	Oxford
Oxnard, G.A.			Guelph	Wellington
Parish & Son, A.	E.S. Clow		Athens	Leeds
Park Hill Banking Co.			Port Arthur	Thunder Bay
Parker Brothers			Stirling	Hastings
Parkhill Banking Co.	Thomas L. Rogers		Parkhill	Middlesex
Parkinson, Thomas			Thedford	Lambton
Parkins(on?), Mrs. T.H.			Thedford	Lambton
Patton, F.			Tamworth	Hastings
Paxton & Co., R.	Robert Paxton	$10,000	Otterville	Oxford
Paxton, Robert			Otterville	Oxford
Pews Banking House			Welland	Welland
Phipps, W.B.			Toronto	York
Pierce, Howard & Co.			Niagara Falls	Welland
Pool, Hockin & Co.			Dutton	Elgin
Pool, James			Dutton	Elgin
Porteous, R.			Paisley	Bruce
Porteous & Saunders	E. Saunders	$100,000	Paisley	Bruce
Porteous Bank of Canada			Paisley	Bruce
Powell, R.J.			Blenheim	Kent
Preston Banking Co.	E.J. Checkley		Preston	Waterloo
Rae, Robert			Thedford	Lambton
Rae, Robert	R.A. Rae		Oil Springs	Lambton
Ranney & Co., R.			Milverton	Perth
Rapley & Co., J.W.			Kincardine	Bruce
Rapley, J.W.			Kincardine	Bruce
Rathburn Co.,	F.S. Rathburn		Deseronto	Hastings
Rathburn Co., The	F.S. Rathburn		Deseronto	Hastings
Rathburn, Isaac			Glencoe	Middlesex
Raven, J.P.			Owen Sound	Grey
Raven, J.R.			Owen Sound	Grey
Ray, Street & company	C.W. Jarvis		Fort William	Thunder Bay
Ray, Street & company	H.A. McKibbin	$75,000	Port Arthur	Algoma
Ray, Street & company	S.W. Ray	$100,000	Port Arthur	Algoma
Reid & Elliot			Essex	Essex
Richardson's Banking Office	Alex. Richardson		Grand Valley	Dufferin
Richardson, A.			Grand Valley	Dufferin
Richardson, Alex			Hillsburgh	Wellington
Riddall & Co., R.T.			Wallaceburg	Kent
Ridley & Bury	Thos. H. Ridley		Duart	Kent
Robertson & Son, Samuel			Harriston	Wellington
Robinson & Roberts			Harriston	Wellington
Robinson & Roberts			Mt. Forest	Wellington
Rogers & company	R.R. Rogers		Stayner	Simcoe
Rogers, T.L.			Parkhill	Middlesex
Rogers, Thomas L.			Parkhill	Middlesex
Ross, Allan J.		$12,000	Iroquois	Dundas
Ross & Co., J.C.			Aurora	York
Rosser, Joseph			Ailsa Craig	Middlesex
Rowland & Co., E.	R.M. Cook, Cas	$66,000	Strathroy	Middlesex
Rowland, E.			Strathroy	Middlesex
Rowley & company			St. Thomas	Elgin
Salter, J.H.			Hagersville	Haldimand
Sarjent, W.J.			Bancroft	Hastings
Scott, C. Tait			Oakville	Halton
Scott, C. Tait			Wingham	Huron
Scott, D.L.			Listowel	Perth
Scott, John			Wallaceburg	Kent
Scott, J.W.	C.R. Knight		Palmerston	Wellington
Scott, J.W.	G.J. Donaldson		Palmerston	Wellington
Scott, J.W.	G.Y. Donaldson		Listowel	Perth
Scott, J.W.	John Hillhouse, F. Walton		Clifford	Wellington
Scott's Banking House	C. Tait Scott		Gorrie	Huron
Scott's Banking House	C. Tait Scott		Oakville	Halton
Scott's Banking House	C. Tait Scott		Wingham	Huron
Scott & Son, J.W.			Listowel	Perth
Scott & Son, J.W.			Palmerston	Wellington
Sealey, W.O.			Waterdown	Wentworth
Seaman, S.M.			Harlem	Leeds
Shaw & Co.'s Bank, John			Wardsville	Middlesex

ONTARIO

Name of Bank	Manager or Agent	Paid-up Capital	Town	County
Shaw, Jr., S.			Toronto	York
Shipley & company			Ailsa Craig	Middlesex
Shipley, James G.			Ailsa Craig	Middlesex
Sharpe, J.W.			Dresden	Kent
Siddall & Mair			Lucknow	Bruce
Siddall's Bank			Lucknow	Bruce
Simcoe Bank			Port Dover	Norfolk
Simpson, Isaac			Kingston	Frontenac
Sinasac, A.E.			Harrow	Essex
Skerritt, J.			Drayton	Wellington
Skerritt, J.			Arthur	Wellington
Skerritt, J. & Company		$18,000	Arthur	Wellington
Smart's Banking House	J.H. Smart	$50,000	Kingsville	Essex
Smart, J.H.			Kingsville	Essex
Smart, William F.P.			Goderich	Huron
Smith, A.M.			Kincardine	Bruce
Smith & Company, J.C.			Seaforth	Huron
Smith & Company			Sombra	Lambton
Smith & Co., L.H.			Strathroy	Middlesex
Smith & Co., L.H.	Montague Smith	$100,000	Forest	Lambton
Smith & Co., L.H.			Fort William	Thunder Bay
Smith & Co., W.O.			Thornbury	Grey
Smith, H.E.			Wingham	Huron
Smith, J.			Terra Cotta	Peel
Smith, J.C.			Orillia	Simcoe
Smith, J.C.			Seaforth	Huron
Smith, R.O.			Chatham	Kent
Smith, R.O.			Windsor	Windsor
Smith, W.O.			Thornbury	Grey
Smith, W.T.			Strathroy	Middlesex
Snell & company	Jos. Snell, Cashier	$10,000	Dashwood	Huron
Snyder, L.P.			North Bay	Nipissing
Somers & Co., G.T.			Cookstown	Simcoe
Somers, Gabriel T.			Beeton	Simcoe
Somers, Gabriel T.			Cookstown	Simcoe
South & company			Pekin	
Squire & Boughner			Bothwell	Waterloo
Stark & Barnes			Stouffville	York
Steinhoff & Lillie	John Lillie		Wallaceburg	Kent
Stephens, James			Dresden	Kent
Stephenson & Co., J.	M. Stephenson	$20,000	Unionville	York
Stewart, Daniel			Aylmer	Elgin
Stewart, J.H.			Trenton	Hastings
Stewart, James	J.W. Hill		Tilbury Centre	Kent
Stewarts Banking House	J.H. Stewart		Trenton	Hastings
Stimson & Co., Geo. A., Brokers			Toronto	York
Stinson, James	Alex H. Moore		Hamilton	Wentworth
Stinsons Bank	James Stinson		Hamilton	Wentworth
Storey, Christie & Co.	D. Henderson		Acton	Halton
Sturtridge, R.			Sutton	York
Struthers Banking House			Elmira	Waterloo
Struthers, R.C.			Essex	Essex
Sutherland, D.F.			Winchester	Dundas
Swaisland & Co., W.	E.O. Swaisland		Glencoe	Middlesex
Swaisland Bros.	E.C. Swaisland		Brantford	Brant
Taillon, A.A.			Ottawa	Carleton
Tanner, J.			Fergus	Wellington
Taylor & Minty			Hamilton	Wentworth
Telford & company			Owen Sound	Grey
Thomas Bros.			Inwood	Lambton
Thomas & Kenward		$16,000	Watford	Lambton
Thompson, H.H.			Penetanguishene	Simcoe
Thompson, U.E.			Belleville	Hastings
Tisdale & Wade			Orillia	Simcoe
Tisdale Private Bank			Orillia	Simcoe
Tisdale, W.B.			Orillia	Simcoe
Tisdale, W.B.			Teeswater	Bruce
Tisdall, J.P.			Clinton	Huron
Tomaluold, Francesco			Toronto	York
Toronto Clearing House	E.Stanger, Secretary		Toronto	York
Townsend, J.			Terra Cotta	Peel
Trow & Sons, J.			Stratford	Perth
Tweed Banking House	Faulknew/McClelland		Tweed	Hastings
Unsworth, Isaac			Florence	Lambton

ONTARIO

Name of Bank	Manager or Agent	Paid-up Capital	Town	County
Unsworth, J.			Florence	Lambton
Vandusen, W.	W.J. Fawcett		Tara	Bruce
Vandusen, Whitford			Tara	Bruce
Vaughn & Fairbank	R. Morris		Petrolia	Lambton
Vaughn & Fairbank	W.J. Savage		Petrolia	Lambton
Wadell, Andrew			Goderich	Huron
Walton, J.M.			Aurora	York
Walton & Co., J.M.			Aurora	York
Ward & Co., W.J.			Brigden	Lambton
Ward & Co., W.J.			New Hamburg	Waterloo
Ward, W.J.			Brigden	Lambton
Warnock, W.			Aylmer	Elgin
Watson, Chas. W.			Dresden	Kent
Watson, F.C.			Sarnia	Lambton
Watson, J.			Leamington	Essex
Waugh & Co., Lewis	W.S. Waugh		Orangeville	Dufferin
Webster, A.F.			Toronto	York
Webster & Son, A.F.			Toronto	York
Webster Bank	W.J. Webster	$20,000	Westport	Leeds
Webster, W.J.			Westport	Leeds
Weir & Co., Wm.			Toronto	York
Westcott, F.			Kingsville	Essex
Westland, Alfred			Wyoming	Lambton
Westland & Co., Alfred		$20,000	Wyoming	Lambton
Westland & Nichol	A.J. Westland		Comber	Essex
Westland, E.A.			Wyoming	Lambton
Whealey & Schwendimann	William Salter		Drayton	Wellington
White's Banking Office	W.H. White		Palmerston	Wellington
White, W.H.	J.M. Watson		Luther	Dufferin
Whitelaw, Charles			Paris	Brant
Whittemore, E.F.			Toronto	York
Whyte, John			Ridgetown	Kent
Whyte, Somerville & McDonald			Ridgetown	Kent
Wilcocks, Joseph			Arkona	Lambton
Wilcox, J.			Arkona	Lambton
Wilgress, A.T.			Clarksburg	Grey
Williams & Co., J.			Wroxeter	Huron
Willis, A.			Toronto	York
Willson & Co., Benj.			Wingham	Huron
Willson & Co., F.M.			Hamilton	Wentworth
Winkler, A.E.			Elmira	Waterloo
Wood & Kells			Millbrook	Durham
Wyatt & Co., Brokers			Toronto	York
Wynne, G.H.			Watford	Lambton
Wynne, J.E.			Watford	Lambton
Wynnes Banking Office	G.H. Wynne		Watford	Lambton
Yarker, G.W.			Toronto	York
Yemen. Thomas F.			Ripley	Bruce

PRINCE EDWARD ISLAND

Name of Bank	Manager or Agent	Paid-up Capital	Town	County
Heartz & Son			Charlottetown	Queens

QUEBEC

Name of Bank	Manager or Agent	Paid-up Capital	Town	County
Alfred & Company				Montreal
Hochelaga				
Archambault & DesJardins			St. Lin	
Beaubien & Cie., L.G.			Montreal	Hochelaga
Beausoleil & Co., Geo.			Montreal	Hochelaga
Brunet, D.W. And A.E.			Montreal	Hochelaga
Bryson, T. Maxwell			Montreal	Hochelaga
Caisse de Depots a Primes			Montreal	Hockelaga
Caisse d'Economie des Cantons de Nord			St. Jerome	
Caisse d'Epargnes des Laurentides			La Laurentides	
Cartier, Laramie & Co.			St. Fran's du Lac	Yam'ka
Cassa, Italia-Candese			Montreal	Hochelaga
Cherrier, A.A.			Montreal	Hochelaga
Cloutier, Jos.			St. Ephrem de Tring	
Commercial Credit Co.,			Montreal	Hochelaga

QUEBEC

Name of Bank	Manager or Agent	Paid-up Capital	Town	County
Comptoire Financier Ltee			Montreal	Hochelaga
Comptoire D'Escompte de Henri de Mascouche			Mascouche	
Cook & Son, Thos.			Montreal	Hochelaga
Dorwin & Co.,			Montreal	Hochelaga
Ethier, H.H.			Laurentides	Assomp'n
Ewing & Fisher			Montreal	Hochelaga
Farrell, Mather & Co.,			Montreal	Hochelaga
Finn, R.			Quebec	
Fisher & Co., D.			Montreal	Hochelaga
Garand, Terroux & Co.		$50,000	Montreal	Hochelaga
Gilmour's Bank		$150,000	Stanbridge East	Missisquoi
Gilmour, A.H.			Stanbridge East	Missisquoi
Greene Co., H.V.			Montreal	Hochelaga
Guilette Co., J.A.			Montreal	Hochelaga
Guimont, Ernest			Montreal	Hochelaga
Harris & Co., N.W.			Montreal	Hochelaga
Huntingdon County Bank	Andrew Somerville		Huntingdon	Huntingdon
Instalment Investment Co.,			Montreal	Hochelaga
Kingstone & Co., H.D.			Montreal	Hochelaga
Laidlaw & Co.,			Montreal	Hochelaga
Lambert, Frigault & Co.,			St. Guillaume d'Upton	
Lazar Bros. & Co.,			Montreal	Hochelaga
LeClerc, Rene T.			Montreal	Hochelaga
LeClerc, Rene T.			Quebec	
Marler, G.R.			Montreal	Hochelaga
McGie & Son, Daniel			Quebec	Quebec
Montreal City & Dist. Sav. Bk.	Sir Wm Hingston	$600,000	Montreal	Hochelaga
Montreal Clearing House Asso'n	W.W.L. Chipman, Manager		Montreal	Hochelaga
National City Co.,			Montreal	Hochelaga
Nutter & Co., J.D.			Montreal	Hochelaga
Panneton, P.E.			Three Rivers	St. Maurice
Panneton et Fils, P.E.			Trois Rivieres	
Picken & Co., J.B.			Montreal	Hochelaga
Rabinovich, Geo.			Montreal	Hochelaga
Rousseau, J.A.			Ste. Anne de la Perade	
St. Mars & Cherrier			Montreal	Hochelaga
Savard Ltee., Ernest			Montreal	Hochelaga
Shearson, Hammill & Co.,			Montreal	Hochelaga
Stanger & Co., J.T.			Montreal	Hochelaga
Stark & Co., N.B.			Montreal	Hochelaga
Stewart, J.P.L.			Montreal	Hochelaga
Strathy Bros., Brokers			Montreal	Hochelaga
Stuart, W.A.			Napierville	Napierville
Sutro Bros. & Co.,			Montreal	Hochelaga
Taillon, A.A.			Sorel	Richelieu
Thompson Co., Frank	Frank Thompson		Sherbrooke	Sherbrooke
Versailles, Vidricaire & Boulais Ltee			Montreal	Hochelaga
Vineberg, Moses			Montreal	Hochelaga
Warner, George W.			Montreal	Hochelaga
Weir & Sons, W.			Montreal	Hochelaga

SASKATCHEWAN

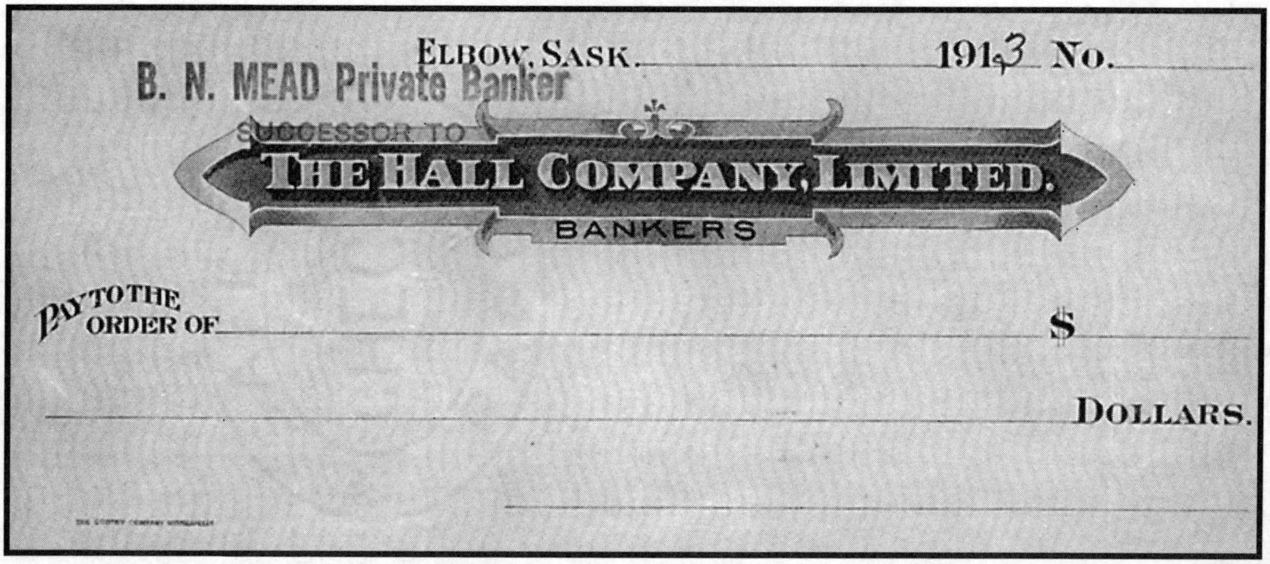

Name of Bank	Manager or Agent	Paid-up Capital	Town	County
Calvert & Co.,			Alameda	
Canada Territories Corp.	A.J. Adamson		Rosthern	
Caswell & Co., S.H.			McLean	
Caswell & Co., S.H.			Qu'Appelle	
Caswell & Co., W.A.			Avonhurst	
Caswell & Co., W.A.			McLean	
Caswell & Co., W.A.			Odessa	
Caswell & Co., W.A.			Qu'Appelle	
Caswell & Co., W.A.			Regina	
Chappel, Son & Co.,	E.O. Chappel		Oxbow	
Chappel, Son & Co.			Frobisher	
Citizen's Security Co.,	J.B. Stoehr	$50,000	Glenside	
Creelman Security Co.,			Creelman	
Cruthers & Co.,			Fort Qu'Appelle	
Estevan Lumber Co. Ltd.			Estevan	
Estevan Security Co.,	Les. Thompson		Tribune	
Farmers' Exchange			Ettington	
Farmers' Exchange			Expanse	
Farmers' Exchange			Limerick	
Farmers' Exchange			Morse	
Frobisher Investment Co.,			Frobisher	
Grenfell Investment Co.,	Jas. Young-Thomson	$200,000.	Grenfell	
Grimmett, Thos.			Arcola	
Hall Co. Ltd.	Orren McElhinney		Hanley	
Hall Co. Ltd.			Outlook	
Hall Company, Limited, The			Elbow	
Hanlon, T.			Swift Current	
Heaslip, J.J.			Alameda	
Hettle Co., J. O.			Saskatoon	
Hettle-Drennan Co.			Saskatoon	
Hitchcock & McCulloch	W. B. Crosbie		Moose Jaw	
Hopper & Co., A. R.			Alameda	
Kirby, Fred D.			Moose Jaw	
Krolick, M.			Grayson	
Lundquist & Sons	Lyn Lundquist		Estevan	
MacDonald & Co., A.			Battleford	
Macoun Security Co.,	A. A. Dahlstrom		Macoun	
March Bros. & Wells	E.F. Kalass		Langenburg	
McDonald & Co., D.H.			Fort Qu'Appelle	
McEchinney, O. K.			Glenside	
McElhinney Co. Ltd.			Glenside	
McGraw, Dan			Lampman	
Mead, B.N.			Elbow	
Mead & Tabler			Elbow	
Morse Farmer's Exchange			Morse	

SASKATCHEWAN

Name of Bank	Manager or Agent	Paid-up Capital	Town	County
Morton-Bartling Co.,		$150,000.	Prince Albert	
Pease, Reade & Co.,	J.H. Croot		Moosomin	
Prudential Exchange Co.,			Glenside	
Prudential Exchange Co.,	A. L. Steidl		Lang	
Prudential Exchange Co.,			Sovereign	
Prudential Exchange Co.,			Weyburn	
Prudential Exchange Co.,			Whitewood	
Prudential Exchange Co.,	C.A. Nelson		Wilcox	
Produce Exchange Bank			Laing	
Stees, Bovee & Co.,			Caron	
Stees, Bovee & Co.,			Ceylon	
Thomson & Parsons			Watson	
Toronto General Trust Co.,			Saskatoon	
Tyvan Security Co.,			Tyvan	
Universal Securities Corp.			Glenside	
Universal Securities Corp.	J.P. Kennedy		Outlook	
Wells Land and Cattle Co.,	E.C. Remick		Davidson	
Weyburn Security Co.,			Halbrite	
Weyburn Security Co.,			McTaggart	
Weyburn Security Co.,			Midale	
Whitelock, F.C.			Davidson	
Wilbur, F.S.			Creelman	
Wilson, David			Fort Qu'Appelle	
Yellow Grass Security Co.,			Yellow Grass	

TABLE I

CANADIAN CHARTERED BANK NOTES OUTSTANDING, FEBRUARY 1989
Redeemable by the Bank of Canada

CANADIAN IMPERIAL BANK OF COMMERCE

The Bank of British Columbia	48,727.00
The Bank of Hamilton	125,737.00
Barclays Bank of Canada	18,590.00
The Canadian Bank of Commerce	1,421,636.00
The Eastern Townships Bank	38,660.00
The Gore Bank	
The Halifax Banking Co.	4,597.18
The Imperial Bank of Canada	450,180.00
The Merchants Bank of P.E.I.	8,764.00
The Niagara Districk Bank	
The St. Lawrence Bank	945.00
The Standard Bank of Canada	121,065.00
The Sterling Bank of Canada	18,825.00
The Western Bank of Canada	7,505.00
The Weyburn Security Bank	15,435.00

THE BANK OF MONTREAL

The Bank of British North America	215,212.00
The Bank of Montreal	1,556,227.00
The Commercial Bank of Canada	9,133.00
The Exchange Bank of Yarmouth	1,099.00
The Merchants Bank of Canada	328,502.00
The Molsons Bank	129,103.00
The Peoples Bank of Halifax	1,123.50
The Peoples Bank of New Brunswick	10,509.00

BANQUE CANADIENNE NATIONALE

Banque Canadienne Nationale	195,850.00
Banque d'Hochelaga	99,052.50
La Banque Nationale	73,064.50

THE BANK OF NOVA SCOTIA

The Bank of New Brunswick	32,180.00
The Bank of Nova Scotia	568,127.42
The Bank of Ottawa	94,645.50
The Metropolitan Bank	10,535.00
The Summerside Bank	43.00
The Union Bank of P.E.I.	8,969.76

Note: The list includes amalgamated and absorbed banks

THE PROVINCIAL BANK OF CANADA

La Banque Jacques Cartier	4,108.00
The Provincial Bank of Canada	129,777.50

THE ROYAL BANK OF CANADA

The Commercial Bank of Windsor	3,324.07
The Crown Bank of Canada	3,325.00
The Merchants Bank of Halifax	10,596.65
The Northern Bank	3,755.00
The Northern Crown Bank	37,207.25
The Quebec Bank	57,394.00
The Royal Bank of Canada	1,310,773.00
The Traders Bank of Canada	39,219.25
The Union Bank of Canada	261,520.50
The Union Bank of Halifax	17,421.52
United Empire Bank of Canada	1,170.00

THE TORONTO-DOMINION BANK

The Bank of Toronto	376,471.00
The Dominion Bank	252,246.50

DEFUNCT BANKS

The Bank of Vancouver	3,376.54
The Bank of Yarmouth	789.82
La Banque de St. Hyacinthe	4,401.00
La Banque du Peuple	7,944.00
Banque Internationale du Canada	1,449.35
La Banque St. Jean	1,847.23
La Banque Ville Marie	5,808.82
The Commercial Bank of Manitoba	5,897.20
The Farmers Bank of Canada	1,883.54
The Home Bank of Canada	35,027.46
The Ontario Bank *	
The St. Stephen's Bank	11,066.67
The Sovereign Bank of Canada	8,664.44

* Redeemable by Royal Trust Co.

Note: The odd cents in the totals are accounted for by some banks having taken over the circulation issued in Halifax currency by earlier institutions. It is also due to the practice of paying only 50 percent of the face value of mutilated notes, of which more than two-fifths of the original was missing, but more than two-fifths remained bearing one signature.

TABLE II

CURRENT CHARTERED BANKS IN CANADA

DOMESTIC BANKS

The Bank of Montreal
The Bank of Nova Scotia
The Canadian Imperial Bank of Commerce
The Canadian Western Bank
The Laurentian Bank of Canada
The National Bank of Canada
The Royal Bank of Canada
The Toronto Dominion Bank

FOREIGN BANK SUBSIDIARIES

ABN Bank Canada
ANZ Bank Canada
Banca Commerciale Italiana of Canada
Banca Nazionale del Lavoro of Canada
Banco Central of Canada
Bank Hapoalim (Canada)
Bank Leumi le-Israel (Canada)
Bank of America Canada
Bank of Boston Canada<R>Bank of Credit and Commerce Canada
Bank of Toyko Canada, The
Banque Nationale de Paris (Canada)
Barclays Bank of Canada
BT Bank of Canada
Chase Manhattan Bank of Canada, The
Chemical Bank of Canada
Citibank Canada
Comerica Bank Canada
Credit Commercial de France (Canada)
Credit Lyonnais Canada
Credit Suisse Canada
Dai-Ichi Kangyo Bank (Canada)
Daiwa Bank Canada
Deutsche Bank (Canada)
Dresdner Bank Canada
First Interstate Bank of Canada
First National Bank of Chicago (Canada), The
Fuji Bank Canada
Hanil Bank Canada
Hongkong Bank of Canada
Industrial Bank of Japan (Canada), The
International Commercial Bank of Cathay (Canada)
Irving Bank Canada
Israel Discount Bank of Canada
Korea Exchange Bank of Canada
Manufacturers Hanover Bank of Canada
Mellon Bank Canada
Mitsubishi Bank of Canada
Mitsui Bank of Canada, The
Morgan Bank of Canada
National Bank of Detroit, Canada
National Bank of Greece (Canada)
National Westminster Bank of Canada
Overseas Union Bank of Singapore (Canada)
Paribas Bank of Canada
Republic National Bank of New York (Canada)
Sanwa Bank Canada
Security Pacific Bank Canada
Societe Generale (Canada)
Standard Chartered Bank of Canada
State Bank of India (Canada)
Sumitomo Bank of Canada, The
Swiss Bank Corporation (Canada)
Taiyo Kobe Bank (Canada)
Tokai Bank Canada
Union Bank of Switzerland (Canada)
United Overseas Bank (Canada)

TABLE III

NON-NOTE ISSUING BANKS

Banks	Established	Remarks
Albert Bank, Saint John, N.B.	1865	Charter not used
Alliance Bank of Canada, Halifax, N.S.	1903	Charter not used
The Anglo-Canadian and Continental Bank, Montreal, Que.	1908	Charter not used
In 1909 name changed to Anglo-Canadian Bank		
The Anglo-Canadian Bank, Toronto, Ontario	1886	Charter not used
Bank of Agriculture, Hamilton, Ontario	1868	Charter not used
Bank of Kingston, Kingston, Ontario	1819	Charter not used
Bank of London, London, Ontario	1865	Charter not used
Bank of Manitoba, Fort Garry, Manitoba	1872	Charter not used
Bank of Northumberland, Cobourg, Ontario	1865	Charter not used
Bank of Simcoe, Simcoe, Ontario	1865	Charter not used
The Bank of the United Provinces, Toronto, Ontario	1874	Charter not used
In 1875 name changed to London and Canada Bank		
Bank of Western Canada, Winnipeg, Manitoba	1966	Charter not used
Bank of Winnipeg, Winnipeg, Manitoba	1884	Charter not used
Bank of Winnipeg, Winnipeg, Manitoba	1903	Charter not used
Bank of Winnipeg, Winnipeg, Manitoba	1908	Charter not used
La Banque des Marchands, Montreal, Quebec	1848	Charter not used
Banque des Trois Rivieres, Trois-Rivieres, Quebec	1841	Charter not used
Bedford District Bank, Waterloo, Ontario	1871	Charter not used
Brant County Bank of Canada, Brantford, Ontario	1883	Charter not used
British Canadian Bank, Winnipeg, Manitoba	1883	Charter not used
In 1883 named changed to North Western Bank		
Canadian Commercial and Industrial Bank, Edmonton, Alberta	1975	Failed
Central Bank of Canada, Montreal, Quebec	1873	Charter not used
The Chartered Bank of British Columbia and Vancouver Island	1862	
Name changed to Bank of British Columbia		
Chartered Bank of London and Canada, Toronto, Ontario	1900	Charter not used
Chartered Bank of London and North America, Montreal, Quebec	1876	Charter not used
In 1882 name changed to Chartered Bank of London and Winnipeg		
Citizens Bank of Canada, Toronto, Ontario	1903	Charter not used
City and County Bank of Canada, Ottawa, Ontario	1903	Charter not used
Colonial Bank (Canada), Montreal, Quebec	1915	Charter not used
Colonial Bank of British Columbia, New Westminster, B.C.	1863	Charter not used
Colonial Bank of Canada, Winnipeg, Manitoba	1906	Charter not used
Continental Bank of Canada, Montreal, Quebec	1886	Charter not used
District Bank of Quebec, Quebec, Quebec	1847	Charter not used
Eastern Bank of New Brunswick, Saint John, N.B.	1865	Charter not used
Great West Bank of Canada, Regina, Saskatchewan	1920	Charter not used
Klondike and Dawson City Bank, Montreal, Quebec	1898	Charter not used
London and Canada Bank, Toronto, Ontario	1874	Charter not used
Manitoba Bank, Winnipeg, Manitoba	1882	Charter not used
Manufacturers' Bank of Canada, Montreal, Quebec	1873	Charter not used
In 1875 named changed to Victoria Bank of Canada		
Mercantile Bank of Canada, Montreal, Quebec	1953	Active
Miramichi Bank, Chatham, N.B.	1857	Charter not used
Monarch Bank of Canada, Toronto, Ontario	1905	Charter not used
Mutual Bank of Nova Scotia, Halifax, N.S.	1864	Charter not used
Niagara Suspension Bridge Bank, Chippewa, Ontario	1835	Failed in 1840
Northern Bank, Chatham, N.B.	1866	Charter not used
Northland Bank, Winnipeg, Manitoba	1976	Active
North-Western Bank, Winnipeg, Manitoba	1882	Charter not used
In 1883 named changed to British Canadian Bank		
The People's Bank, Montreal, Quebec	1969	
Merged in 1970 with the Banque Provinciale du Canada		
Planters' Bank of Canada, Montreal, Quebec	1882	Charter not used
Quebec District Bank, Quebec, Quebec	1847	Charter not used
The Royal Bank of Canada, Toronto, Ontario	1859	Charter not used
Securities Bank of Canada, Toronto, Ontario	1902	Charter not used
Shediac Bank, Shediac, N.B.	1856	Charter not used
Sterling Bank of Canada, London, Ontario	1903	Charter not used
Superior Bank of Canada, Toronto, Ontario	1872	Charter not used
Three Rivers Bank, Trois-Rivieres, Quebec	1873	Charter not used
Union Bank of Canada, Hamilton, Ontario	1856	Charter not used
Unity Bank of Canada, Toronto, Ontario	1972	
Merged in 1977 with La Banque Provinciale du Canada		
Victoria Bank of Canada, Montreal, Quebec	1873	Charter not used
In 1874 name changed to Manufacturers' Bank of Canada		
Western Bank, Yarmouth, N.S.	1871	Charter not used
Woodstock Bank, Woodstock, N.B.	1865	Charter not used
York County Bank, Toronto, Ontario	1890	Charter not used

TABLE IV

BANK MERGERS AND AMALGAMATIONS SINCE JULY 1, 1867

Purchasing Bank	Date	Bank Absorbed
The Bank of Montreal	22/05/1868*	The Commercial Bank of Canada
	13/08/1903	The Exchange Bank of Yarmouth
	27/06/1905	The People's Bank of Halifax
	13/04/1907	The People's Bank of New Brunswick
	12/10/1918	The Bank of British North America
	20/03/1922	The Merchants Bank of Canada
	20/01/1925	The Molsons Bank
The Bank of Nova Scotia	01/10/1883	The Union Bank of Price Edward Island
	12/09/1901*	The Summerside Bank
	15/02/1913	The Bank of New Brunswick
	14/11/1914	The Metropolitan Bank
	30/04/1919	The Bank of Ottawa
The Canadian Imperial Bank of Commerce	19/05/1870*	The Gore Bank
	21/06/1875*	The Niagara District Bank
	31/12/1900*	The Bank of British Columbia
	30/05/1903*	The Halifax Banking Company
	31/05/1906*	The Merchants Bank of Prince Edward Island
	13/02/1909*	The Western Bank of Canada
	29/02/1912*	The Eastern Townships Bank
	31/12/1923*	The Bank of Hamilton
	31/12/1924*	The Sterling Bank of Canada
	03/11/1928*	The Standard Bank of Canada
	01/05/1931*	The Weyburn Security Bank
	01/02/1956*	Barclays Bank (Canada)
	01/06/1961	The Canadian Bank of Commerce
	01/06/1961	The Imperial Bank of Canada
The Consolidated Bank of Canada (since failed)	10/05/1876	The City Bank
	10/05/1876	The Royal Canadian Bank
The Home Bank of Canada (since failed)	15/04/1913	Banque Internationale du Canada
The National Bank of Canada	01/11/1979	La Banque Provinciale du Canada
	01/11/1979	Banque Canadienne Nationale **
	03/08/1970*	The People's Bank
	16/06/1977*	Unity Bank of Canada
	30/04/1924*	La Banque Nationale
The Royal Bank of Canada	31/10/1902*	The Commercial Bank of Windsor
	02/07/1908*	The Crown Bank of Canada
	01/11/1910	The Union Bank of Halifax
	31/03/1911*	United Empire Bank of Canada
	03/09/1912	The Traders Bank of Canada
	02/01/1917	The Quebec Bank
	02/07/1918	The Northern Crown Bank
	31/08/1925	The Union Bank of Canada
The Toronto Dominion Bank	01/02/1955	The Bank of Toronto
	01/02/1955	The Dominion Bank

Note: **1.** Dates since 1900 are those of the authorizing Order in Council.

2. * Previously merged or amalgamated with another bank in this listing.

3. ** Formerly the Bank d'Hochelaga.

INDEX

CANADIAN NOTE-ISSUING BANKS

CANADIAN NOTE-ISSUING BANKS

CANADIAN NOTE-ISSUING BANKS

Bank, Issue, Major Alteration	Bank No.	Issue No.	Major Alteration No.	Page No.
Central Bank of New Brunswick (cont.)				
Blue face and brown lathework back, 1847-1853	95	10	04	75
Blue face and orange lathework back, 1852-1853		10	06	76
Black face and plain back, 1856-1857		10	10	76
Issue of 1860		12	—	76
Charlotte County Bank				
Perkins and Heath Printings, 1852-1859	100	10	—	78
Charlottetown, Bank of				
Pounds, shillings and pence note issue	105	10	—	79
Dollar draft issue, 1852		12	—	80
City Bank, The				
Bilingual issue, 1833-1840s, payable at Montreal, denominations in dollars only	110	10	—	81
Separate branch issues, 1850-1865, dollars/pounds and shillings		12	—	82
Montreal issue, 1851-1853		12	02	82
Toronto issue, 1850-1865		12	04	83
Quebec issue		12	06	85
Common branch issue of 1857, Province of Canada		14	—	85
Orange back		14	02	86
Plain back		14	04	86
Green back		14	06	87
Spurious note issue		16	—	87
City Bank				
New England Bank Note Co. Printings, 1836-1838	115	10	—	87
City Bank of Monteal, The				
Issue of 18(59)	120	10	—	89
Clifton, The Bank of				
Issue of 1859	125	10	—	89
Partially engraved date, two signatures		10	02	90
Fully engraved date, one signature		10	04	90
Issue of 1860-1861		12	—	90
Colonial Bank of Canada, The				
Issue of 1859	130	10	—	91
Two-signature notes, orange-brown tint		10	02	93
One-signature notes, pink tint		10	04	93
Colonial Bank of Chatham, The				
Issue of 1837	135	10	—	94
Commercial Bank (Brockville)				
Draft issue of 1834-1836	140	10	—	95
Commercial Bank (Kingston)				
Draft issue of 1837	145	10	—	96
Manuscript "Commercial" in bank name		10	02	96
Engraved "COMMERCIAL" in bank name		10	04	96
Commercial Bank, The (Montreal)				
Issue of 1837	150	10	—	97
Commercial Bank of Canada, The				
Yellow issue, Canada West branches, 1857	155	10	—	97
Brockville issue		10	02	98
Galt issue		10	04	98
Hamilton issue		10	06	98
Kingston issue, brown back		10	10	98
London issue, plain back		10	12	98
London issue, brown back		10	14	98
Toronto issue		10	16	99
Green issue, Canada West branches, 1857-1861		12	—	99
Belleville issue		12	02	99
Berlin issue				99
Brockville issue		12	04	99
Chatham issue		12	06	99
Hamilton issue		12	08	99
Ingersoll issue		12	10	100
Kingston issue		12	12	100
London issue		12	14	100
Perth issue		12	16	100
Port Hope issue		12	18	100
Prescott issue		12	20	100
Toronto issue		12	22	100
Windsor issue		12	24	9100

CANADIAN NOTE-ISSUING BANKS

CANADIAN NOTE-ISSUING BANKS

CANADIAN NOTE-ISSUING BANKS

CANADIAN NOTE-ISSUING BANKS

CANADIAN NOTE-ISSUING BANKS

CANADIAN NOTE-ISSUING BANKS

CANADIAN NOTE-ISSUING BANKS

CANADIAN NOTE-ISSUING BANKS

CANADIAN NOTE-ISSUING BANKS

CANADIAN NOTE-ISSUING BANKS

CANADIAN NOTE-ISSUING BANKS

SOURCES

Walter D. Allan, Photo and Engraving Archives
Archives of the American Bank Note Co., New York
Archives of the British American Banknote Co., Ottawa
Bradford Rhodes & Co.'s Bankers' Directory and Collection Guide, January 1898
Bank of Canada Numismatic Collection, Ottawa
A History of the Canadian Bank of Commerce, 3 vols., V. Ross, 1922
Canadian Banks and Bank-Notes, A Record, C.S. Howard
Canadian Numismatic Research Society, The Transactions
Centenary of the Bank of Montreal 100 Years, 1817-1917
Charlton Auction Catalogues, various, including the Walter D. Allan sales
The Charlton Standard Catalogue of Canadian Paper Money, 1st edition
The Charlton Press photo archives
The Currency and Medals of Prince Edward Island by the Numismatic Education Society of Canada, 1988
The Essay Proof Society Journals, various
Fiftieth Anniversary of the Royal Bank of Canada 1869-1919
Fifty Years of Banking Service the Dominion Bank, 1871-1921
History of the Bank of Nova Scotia 1832-1900
The House of Joseph in the Life of Quebec, E.C. Woodley, 1946
Journals of the Canadian Paper Money Society, various, 1965-1995
John A. Muscalus, various monographs on the origin of banknote vignettes
The Bank of Nova Scotia 1832-1932
Ontario Private Banks listed by Steven Thorning Town
Rand, McNally & Co.'s Bankers' Directory and List of Bank Attorneys, January 1887
United States Obsolete Bank Notes, James A. Haxby, 1988, 4 vols.
Wrights' 1899 Classified Business Directory

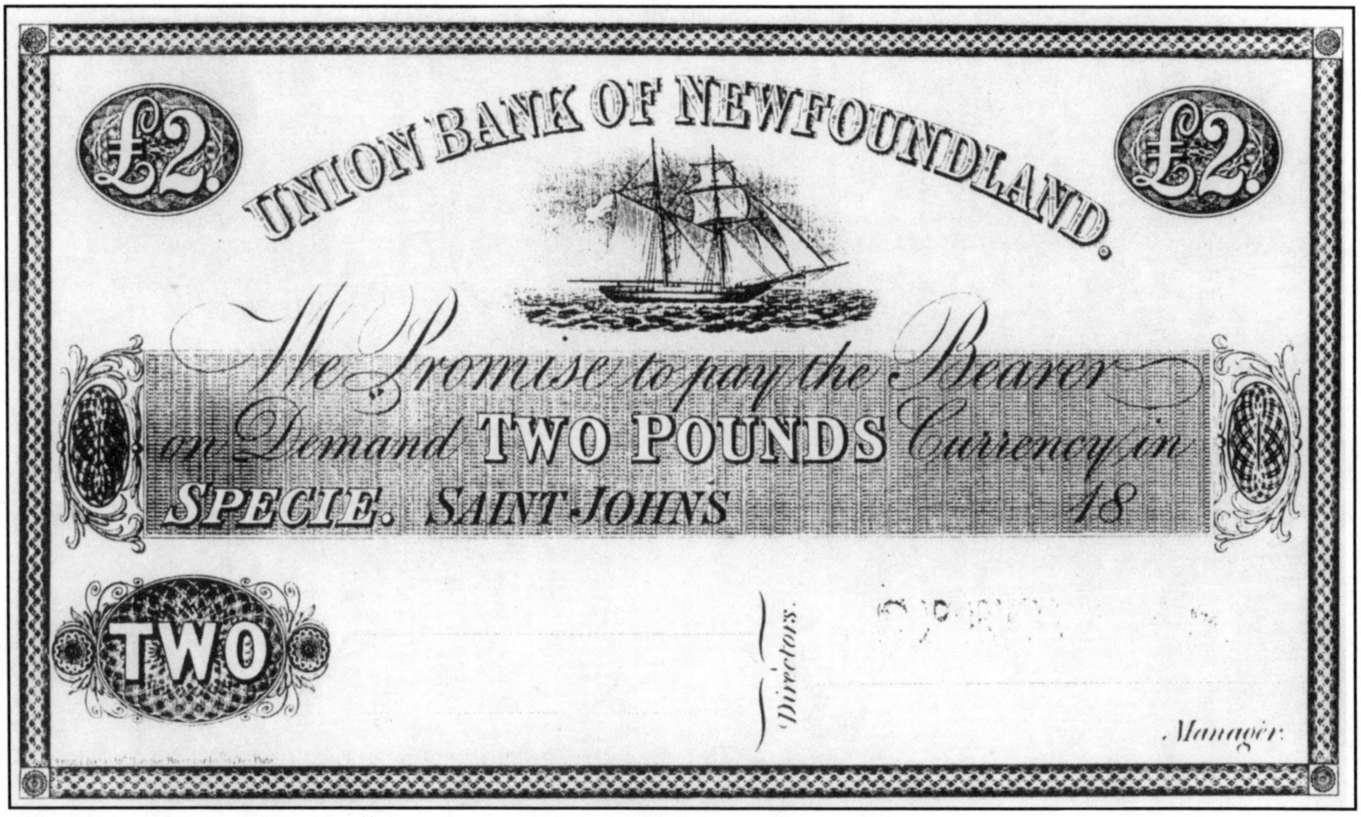
UNION BANK OF NEWFOUNDLAND.
£2.
£2.
We Promise to pay the Bearer
on Demand TWO POUNDS Currency in
SPECIE. SAINT JOHNS 18
TWO
Directors.
Manager.